GENESIS 12–36

CLAUS
WESTERMANN

GENESIS 12–36
A Commentary

Translated by
John J. Scullion S.J.

AUGSBURG PUBLISHING HOUSE
MINNEAPOLIS

GENESIS 12–36
A Commentary

First published 1981 by Neukirchener Verlag, Neukirchen-Vluyn, in the Biblischer Kommentar Series.

First published in English 1985 by Augsburg Publishing House in the USA and in Great Britain by SPCK, Holy Trinity Church, Marylebone Road, London NW1 4DU.

Library of Congress Cataloging in Publication Data

Westermann, Claus.
  GENESIS 12–36.

  Bibliography: p.
  1. Bible. O.T. Genesis XII–XXXVI—Commentaries.
I. Title
BS1235.3.W44313 1985   222'.11077   85-7449
ISBN 0-8066-2172-9

The paper used in this publication meets the minimum requirements of American National Standard for Information Sciences—Permanence of Paper for Printed Library Materials, ANSI Z39.48-1984.

Manufactured in the U.S.A.   APH 10-2542

1   2   3   4   5   6   7   8   9   0   1   2   3   4   5   6   7   8   9   0

To the Society of Biblical Literature
in the United States of America
in Gratitude
for Admission as Honorary Member

Contents

Preface   19
Translator's Preface   21

Introduction to the Patriarchal Story: Genesis 12–50   23

   1. The Significance of the Patriarchal Story   23
      A. The Fathers of the People   24
      B. The Patriarchal Story in the Canon   26
      C. The Composition of the Patriarchal Story   28
   2. The Origin and Growth of the Patriarchal Story   30
      A. The Written Stage of the Patriarchal Traditions—the Literary
          Approach   31
      B. The Oral Stage   35
         I. The Form-Critical Problem   35
         II. Traditions in the Preliterary Stage   41
         III. Narrative and Storytelling   44
         IV. The Types of Narrative: Folk Story (*Sage*), Tale (*Märchen*),
            Legend, Myth   50
   3. The World of the Patriarchal Story and Its Setting:
      The Question of the Time of the Patriarchs   58
      A. The Modern Archaeological Approach   58
      B. Migrations of the People in the Near East and Migrations of the
          Patriarchs   61
      C. Peoples, Territories, and Cities   63
         I. Preliminary Notes: Geographical   63
         II. The Amorites   63
         III. The Aramaeans   66
         IV. Other Peoples and Territories Important for the Patriarchal
            Story   67
         V. Places and Changes of Places in Genesis 12–50   70
      D. The Time of the Patriarchs   73
         I. Life-style (Nomadism)   74
         II. Legal Practices and Customs: Introduction   79
         III. Personal Names in the Patriarchal Story   84

Literature: Genesis 12–50   86
   Introduction   86
   A. The Significance of the Patriarchal Story   87
   B. The Origin and Growth of the Patriarchal Story   89
   C. The World of the Patriarchal Story and the Question of the Time of the Patriarchs   92
  4. The Religion of the Patriarchs   105
   A. Characteristics of the Religion of the Patriarchs   108
     I. The God of Abraham, the ''God of My Father''   108
     II. Was the Religion of the Patriarchs Monotheism?   108
     III. The Personal Relationship to God   109
   B. The Cult   110
   C. The Promises to the Patriarchs   111
   D. The Covenant with the Fathers   112
Literature for Section 4   113
  1. General   113
  2. Religion and the Patriarchs   114
  3. The God of the Patriarchs   116
  4. Names of God   117
  5. Promise   118
  6. Covenant   120

Structure and Growth of Genesis 12–25   123
  1. The Constituent Parts of the Composition   125
  2. The Promises   126
  3. Abraham-Lot Narratives   127
  4. The Composition as a Whole   128
Literature: Genesis 12–25 (Structure and Growth)   130
   A. Abraham   130
   B. Abraham in Later Literature   130

Transition to the Story of Abraham: Genesis 11:27-32   132
  Literature   132
  Text   132
  Form   134
  Setting   136
  Commentary   137
  Purpose and Thrust   140

Promise to Abraham and Migration: Genesis 12:1-9   142
  Literature   142
  Text   144
  Form   145
  Setting   146
  Commentary   146
  Purpose and Thrust   157

The Ancestral Mother in Danger: Genesis 12:10-20   159
  Literature   159
  Text   160

Contents

Form   161
Setting   162
Commentary   163
Purpose and Thrust   167

Abraham and Lot on the Way: Genesis 13:1-18   169

Literature   169
Text   170
Form   171
Setting   173
Commentary   174
Purpose and Thrust   181

Abraham and the Kings: Genesis 14:1-24   182

Literature   182
Text   185
   The History of the Exegesis of Genesis 14   187
Form   190
Setting   192
Commentary   193
Purpose and Thrust   207

The Promise to Abraham: Genesis 15:1-21   209

Literature   209
Text   212
   The History of the Exegesis of Genesis 15   214
Form   216
Setting   216
Commentary   217
Purpose and Thrust   230

Sarah and Hagar: Flight and Promise of a Son: Genesis 16:1-16   232

Literature   232
Text   233
   The History of the Exegesis of Genesis 16   234
Form   236
Setting   237
Commentary   237
   Excursus: The Messenger of God in the Old Testament   242
Purpose and Thrust   249

The Covenant with Abraham: Genesis 17:1-27   251

Literature   251
Text   253
Form   254
   The Structure   255
   Excursus: The Concept of ברית in the Structure of Genesis 17   256
Setting   256
Commentary   256
   Excursus: אל שדי (El Shaddai)   257

Excursus: Circumcision   265
Excursus: The Name Isaac   269
Purpose and Thrust   271

Abraham and the Three Guests: Genesis 18:1-16a   272

Literature   272
Text   273
Form   274
Setting   275
Commentary   276
Purpose and Thrust   282

Abraham Queries the Destruction of Sodom: Genesis 18:16b-33   283

Literature   283
Text   284
Form   285
Setting   286
Commentary   287
Purpose and Thrust   292

The Destruction of Sodom and the Rescue of Lot: Genesis 19:1-29   294

Literature   294
Text   295
Form   297
Setting   299
Commentary   300
Excursus: The Absence of the Portrayal of Nature in the Patriarchal
Stories   305
Purpose and Thrust   308

Lot's Daughters: Genesis 19:30-38   310

Literature   310
Text   310
Form   311
Setting   312
Commentary   313
Purpose and Thrust   314

Abraham and Abimelech: Genesis 20:1-18   316

Literature   316
Text   317
Form   318
Setting   319
Commentary   320
Purpose and Thrust   328

The Birth of Isaac: Genesis 21:1-7   330

Literature   330
Text   330
Form and Setting   331

Contents

Commentary   332
Purpose and Thrust   334

The Expulsion and Rescue of Hagar and Her Child: Genesis 21:8-21   336

Literature   336
Text   336
Form   337
Setting   338
Commentary   338
Purpose and Thrust   343

Dispute over the Wells and Treaty with Abimelech:
Genesis 21:22-24   345

Literature   345
Text   345
Form   346
Setting   347
Commentary   347
Purpose and Thrust   350

Abraham's Sacrifice: Genesis 22:1-19   351

Literature   351
Text   352
    The History of the Exegesis of Genesis 22   353
Form   354
Setting   355
Commentary   356
    Excursus on נסה   356
    Excursus on Human Sacrifice   357
    Excursus: The Fear of God   361
Purpose and Thrust   364

The Descendants of Nahor: Genesis 22:20-24   366

Literature   366
Text   366
Form   366
Setting   367
Commentary   367
Purpose and Thrust   368

Sarah's Death and the Purchase of the Burial Cave:
Genesis 23:1-20   369

Literature   369
Text   370
Form   371
Setting   372
Commentary   372
Purpose and Thrust   376

The Wooing of Rebekah: Genesis 24:1-67   377

    Literature   377
    Text   378
    Form   382
    Setting   383
    Commentary   384
    Purpose and Thrust   391

Conclusion of the Abraham Story: Genesis 25:1-18   393

    Literature   393
    Text   393
    Form   394
    Setting   395
    Commentary   395
    Purpose and Thrust   399

The Abraham Story in Retrospect: Genesis 12–25   401

    Literature   401
    1. On the Transmission of Genesis 12–25   401
    2. The Subsequent History and Significance of Abraham   403

Structure, Origin, and Growth of Genesis 25:19—36:43   405

    Literature   405
    1. History of Research   406
    2. Enumerative Blocks   406
    3. Narrative Blocks   407
    4. Promises and Blessings   408
    5. The Overall Plan   409
    6. The Subsequent History of the Jacob Tradition   409

The Birth of Esau and Jacob: Genesis 25:19-28   410

    Literature   410
    Text   410
    Form   411
    Setting   412
    Commentary   412

The Pot of Lentil Soup: Genesis 25:29-34   416

    Literature   416
    Text   416
    Form and Setting   416
    Commentary   417
    Purpose and Thrust   418

Isaac and Abimelech: Genesis 26:1-35   420

    Literature   420
    Text   421
    Form   423
    Setting   423

Contents

Commentary   424
Purpose and Thrust   429

The Firstborn Cheated of His Blessing: Genesis 27:1-45   431

Literature   431
Text   432
Form   434
Setting   435
Commentary   436
    Excursus: Blessing in the Old Testament   436
Purpose and Thrust   444

Jacob's Departure and Esau's Wives: Genesis 26:34-35; 27:46; 28:1-9   445

Literature   445
Text   445
Form   446
Setting   446
Commentary   447
Purpose and Thrust   448

Jacob's Dream and Vow at Bethel: Genesis 28:10-22   450

Literature   450
Text   451
Form   452
Setting   453
Commentary   453
Purpose and Thrust   460

Jacob and Laban: Marriage with Leah and Rachel: Genesis 29:1-30   461

Literature   461
Text   461
Form   463
Setting   464
Commentary   464
Purpose and Thrust   468

The Birth and Naming of Jacob's Sons: Genesis 29:31—30:24   469

Literature   469
Text   469
Form   471
    1. The Narrative Parts of Chs. 29–30   471
    2. The Genealogical Parts of Chs. 29–30   471
    Conclusion   472
Setting   472
Commentary   473
Purpose and Thrust   477

Jacob Outwits Laban: Genesis 30:25-43   478

Literature   478
Text   478

Form   479
Setting   480
Commentary   480
Purpose and Thrust   484

Jacob's Separation from Laban: Genesis 31:1-54   485

Literature   485
Text   486
Form   489
Setting   490
Commentary   490
Purpose and Thrust   500

Preparation for the Meeting with Esau: Genesis 32:1-22 (Eng., 31:55—32:21)   502

Literature   502
Text   502
Form   504
Setting   504
Commentary   504
Purpose and Thrust   510

The Attack on Jacob at the Jabbok: Genesis 32:23-33 (Eng., 32:22-32)   512

Literature   512
Text   513
Form   514
Setting   515
Commentary   515
Purpose and Thrust   520

The Meeting of the Brothers: Genesis 33:1-20   522

Literature   522
Text   522
Form   523
Setting   524
Commentary   524
Purpose and Thrust   530

Dinah and the Shechemites: Genesis 34:1-31   532

Literature   532
Text   533
Form   535
Setting   537
Commentary   537
Purpose and Thrust   544

Contents

Jacob in Bethel and Hebron, Jacob's Sons, Isaac's Death: Genesis 35:1-29   546

   Literature   546
   Text   547
   Form   548
   Setting   549
   Commentary   549
   Purpose and Thrust   557

Esau's Descendants: Genesis 36:1-43   558

   Literature   558
   Text   559
   Form   561
   Setting   561
   Commentary   562
      The Names   566
      Personal Names Occurring in Other Places   566
      The Formation of the Names   567
   Purpose and Thrust   568

Conclusion to Genesis 12–36   570

   Literature   570
   1. Concluding Remarks on the Origins of the Patriarchal Story   571
      A. The Oral Stage of the Transmission   571
      B. The Written Stage of the Transmission   571
         I. The Yahwist in Genesis 12–36   571
         II. The Question of the Elohist in Genesis 12–36   571
         III. The Priestly Writing in Genesis 12–36   572
         IV. The Redactor in Genesis 12–36   573
   2. Concluding Remarks on the Patriarchal Stories   574
      A. The Patriarchs as Persons   574
      B. The Religion of the Patriarchs: Concluding Remarks   575
      C. The Patriarchal Story in the Pentateuch and in the Old Testament   576
   3. The Later History of the Patriarchal Tradition   577

Abbreviations   579
Index of Hebrew Words   593
Index of Biblical References   594
Index of Names and Subjects   601

Preface

This second volume of the commentary on Genesis comprises fascicules 11–19, which appeared separately in the years 1977–1981, and expounds the patriarchal story. There will be a third and shorter volume on the Joseph story. The primeval story, Genesis 1–11, deals with the beginnings of the world and the human race; the patriarchal story, Genesis 12–36, in the figures of Abraham, Isaac, and Jacob, deals with the beginnings of human society in the family as the prepolitical form of society and God's action in it. The uniqueness and independence of the nomadic patriarchal families, their life-style and social form, their relationship with God, and their significance for the history of human society as well as for theology and the church require still further study. All this can be of great importance for the future of humanity. What is determinative in the patriarchal stories is a basic simplicity in communal life and in the relationship with God.

My thanks are due to the editor, my colleague, Professor H.-W. Wolff. As professor emeritus he accompanied me, also emeritus, with patience and the greatest solicitude along the way from fascicule 11 to 19. My thanks are also due to the Neukirchener Verlag and its staff which, under ever more difficult conditions, made the publication of this volume possible.

I thank everyone who has helped me in the preparation of this second volume: my most recent assistants, Dr. J. Kegler; Andreas Richter, now curate in Würzburg; also Pastor Klemm of Berlin for his contributions to the Corrigenda. Above all, I thank my wife for the many ways in which she has helped; the commentary on Genesis is indeed our common work.

I dedicate *Genesis 12–36* to the Society of Biblical Literature in the United States of America in gratitude for my honorary membership.

St. Leon bei Heidelberg   CLAUS WESTERMANN

Translator's Preface

He who translates a verse verbatim is a liar!
And he who alters it is a villain and a heretic!
(Babylonian Talmud, *Qiddushim* 49a)

The following points should be noted regarding the translation of this volume:

1. The translation of the Hebrew text of Genesis is deliberately rather literal, but attempts in every case to convey Professor Westermann's nuances.

2. Quotations from other parts of the Old Testament, the Apocrypha, and the New Testament are from the Revised Standard Version of the Bible, copyright 1946, 1952, and 1971 by the Division of Christian Education of the National Council of Churches. There is an occasional quotation from the Old Testament of the New English Bible.

3. The spelling of all personal, proper, and place-names in the Bible follows the usage of the Revised Standard Version.

4. Abbreviations of the biblical books are those of the RSV, Common Bible.

Once again I thank Mrs. Leonie Hudson for her excellent typed manuscript, and Shirley Sullivan for her help in reading the galleys.

My colleague, Fr. Brian Moore S.J., and his assistants of Jesuit Theological College made a substantial contribution to the compilation of the indexes. To these, my thanks.

John J. Scullion S.J.
Newman College
(University of Melbourne)
887 Swanston Street
Parkville, Vic. 3052
Australia

Introduction to the Patriarchal Story

1. The Significance of the Patriarchal Story

The primeval story speaks about the basic elements of the world and of humanity, the patriarchal story of the basic elements of human community. It has been said already in the primeval story that man is created for community (Gen. 2), that conflict is part of brotherly existence (Gen. 4), that tension is part of the relationship between children and parents (Gen. 9). These very basic relationships in human community become the object of narrative in the patriarchal story: the relationship of parents to children especially in the Abraham narrative (Gen. 12–25), of brother to brother in the Jacob-Esau narrative (Gen. 25–36), of the several members of the family to each other in the Joseph narrative (Gen. 37–50). The disposition and collation of these three cycles took place at a time when the family had expanded to clans and tribes, and the tribes had passed through tribal unions to become a people and a state. The whole arrangement shows that at the time when a people was coming into being and a state was being formed, the perspective was based on the memory of origin from families and ancestors. Thus is expressed the basic meaning of the family for all further forms of community, and thus is acknowledged that whatever happens in these more developed communities and their spheres of endeavor, be it in politics, economics, civilization, education, art, and religion, goes back to what has happened in the family. No other form of community can ever completely replace the family: "The basis of every human community, from the most primitive to the most complex, is the family" (J. Layard, *Familie und Sippe* [1967] 59; Lit. C.4, "The Time of the Patriarchs"). Elements of family life are encountered in other forms of community; as long as there are people, they cannot die out. Though the basic relationships of human community are the object of the patriarchal story, they are not so in some sort of universal way such as holds good for all mankind; they are there in narratives about their own forefathers, about the ancestors of Israel. The narratives link the generation living in the present with the patriarchs and give it its share in their destiny. The patriarchal story gives those living in the small family circle the sense of a vital link with the ancestors.

The three basic relationships which are the particular object of the patriarchal stories have remained constant in the course of history, even though the shape of the family has altered, and will alter further. They color the patriarchal story, which has been prefaced to the history of the people of Israel, so that the basic elements of community, which are part of every form of human coexistence, are a prelude to, and thereby an insertion into, the story of God's dealings with his people. God's action towards his people, and the words he speaks to them, address an entity, Israel, which could only be the "people of God," "my kingdom of priests, my holy nation" (Ex. 19:6). What happened between Abraham and Sarah, Abraham and Isaac, Jacob and Esau, Joseph and his brothers, continues to happen with countless variations from one generation to the next. These basic elements of community life belong to humankind in general and link God's people with all the peoples of the earth. It is not possible to go into details here as to how the family motifs run through the whole history of Israel, now in the foreground, now in the background, right into the New Testament where the beginning of the gospels, especially of Luke, is again family history. The Yahwist was conscious of this significance of the patriarchal story for the history of Israel, which that story introduces when, in a key passage, Gen. 12:1-3, he sees the basic unity of all forms of community life in the family: "In you [Abraham] will all the families of the earth be blessed [bless themselves]."

The patriarchal story speaks of these basic forms of human community theologically, i.e., they cannot be spoken of without at the same time speaking of God. There is neither a vertical succession of generations down the years nor the horizontal dimension of communal family life without God acting and talking. This does not mean that the religious dimension is something added over and above family events, that relationship to God is an accretion to family relationships; it is rather that the family event as such and the family relationships as such are based on God's action and preserved by it. It follows from the talk about God in the patriarchal story that the foundation of all subsequent religion is the simple, unencumbered relationship to God, just as it is the natural requirement for the small community. The vertical succession of generations is based on blessing; horizontal communal life is based on peace. In crises, salvation is experienced as salvation by God. God's action in the life of the family is simply taken for granted so that normally there is no need to speak of him. The reason for the remarkably secular language of the patriarchal stories is this: one speaks of God only when it is necessary, otherwise not at all. E. Auerbach has recognized this: "The sublime influence of God here reaches so deeply into the everyday that the two realms of the sublime and the everyday are not only actually unseparated, but basically inseparable" (*Mimesis* [1946; Eng. 1953; Anchor Books, 1957] 19).

A. The Fathers of the People

[Translator's Note: the German *Vater* represents the English "patriarch" as well as "father"; the rendering here varies according to context.]

There is no word so characteristic of the patriarchal stories of Gen. 12–50 as *father*. It refers to a type of relationship of occurrences that stretches from the second part of Genesis into the New Testament. Fatherhood is restricted to the genealogies in the primeval story; no one there, not even Adam, is described as the father of generations to come. The fatherhood of Abraham, Isaac, and Jacob stretches across a number of generations and so is something different from that of mere physical begetter. The extension of the idea of father which makes it possible for Jesus' contemporaries to say, "Abraham is our father" (Jn. 8:39), adds to the limited time span that covers a single generation; it adds a span of unlimited length that stretches over whole chains of generations, and so over hundreds of years, through which Abraham remains ''the father.'' What is peculiar to this extended idea of father is that it is irreplaceable: no one in the long series of generations that begins with Abraham can be father as he was. Paradoxically, Abraham remains father from generation to generation. The fatherhood of all the patriarchs who follow him remains limited to their own sons. None of them becomes father even for two generations. The fatherhood of the one, which encompasses generations, excludes any other such fatherhood.

What is happening in this extended idea of fatherhood becomes clear when one sets it over against the earlier forms of speech which a living contemporary uses to express his lineage. He traces the line back beyond his own father to that one's father and then to his father; thus we find the genealogical form of expression. Characteristic of this form is that it can present origin only in a line; it is not possible for an ancestor, however far back, to be father in any other way than in a line of fathers. There are two ways in which the father from whom the race originates can be taken out of the line of fathers so as to become ''the father,'' detached from the line. He can be elevated beyond the human to the realm of the divine. This is extraordinarily widespread and consequently shows many a variation in the history of peoples and religions. The oldest type of this kind of elevation of the first father is the veneration or cult of ancestors.

There has as yet been no study of the relationship of the patriarchal story to the cult of ancestors. It is possible, however, that some expressions of ancestor cult are linked with narratives about the ancestors. Parallels to the patriarchal stories, therefore, should not be excluded. Such a study would be worthwhile.

A variant is the divinization of the ancestor; he becomes God and is venerated as such; the fact that he was the ancestor generally recedes into the background. The third possibility, on the other hand, seems to occur only in the patriarchal stories: the ancestor takes on the character of one who is unique, of the father par excellence; he remains, nevertheless, a man without the slightest trace of divinization or ancestor worship. It is clear from the nature of the traditions in Israel that the father of the people could not in retrospect be divine or semidivine, nor could there be any cult of the ancestors. This is based on the great importance of history in these traditions and on the confession of the one God. It is more difficult, however, to explain why the old, pre-Israelite patriarchal traditions also show no trace at all of ancestor worship or of divinization of the ancestor. We must acknowledge here a parallel between ancestral traditions and the traditions of Israel such as are found in certain aspects of the God of the fathers (Lit. B, Tradition, A. Alt [1929] 95). This is to say that a form of human community was preserved in the traditions of the fathers for which there were neither political nor religious representatives. The only one who could be representative of the whole would be the father who has thereby an importance which he could no longer have in later forms of community.

What is peculiar to the patriarchal stories and characteristic of their permanent meaning for later traditions is that they attribute to the one father at the beginning a significance which surpasses that of his successors. The reason these narratives, which are so limited in their range of vision and which deal with ordinary people, their family experiences, their journeys, and their struggle for survival, have acquired a meaning far surpassing these actual events is this: as stories about the fathers they have validity for the story of all their posterity.

It is still an open question whether the patriarchal stories are really dealing with one or three fathers. The problem admits of no easy answer or solution at one stroke. The way in which Jesus' contemporaries describe Abraham as their father (Jn. 8:39) presumes that he is the real, unique father of the people. This is also the case in Sir. 44:20-26 (Gk and Eng., vv. 19-23) where Abraham is the father of the people and Isaac and Jacob are subordinate to him: vv. 20-23 (Eng., vv. 19-21) speak only of Abraham; vv. 24-25 (Eng., vv. 22-23) continue:

> To Isaac he made the same promise
> for the sake of his father Abraham,
> a blessing for all mankind and a covenant,
> and so he transmitted them to Jacob. . . .

This subordination is strengthened later when the religious significance of Abraham took precedence (Abraham our father in faith) and was increasingly ascribed to him alone and to none other of the patriarchs.

This presupposes a stage in which the fathers were firmly fixed in the traditions as a trio in the formula, "Abraham, Isaac, and Jacob" (Joseph is never mentioned together with them). The construction of the patriarchal stories that have come down to us accords with this formula; the three are brought together in a succession of three generations in which they have the same rank and importance. This is preceded by an even earlier stage in which the traditions each dealt with a single father. The Jacob traditions best illustrate this. The equation of Jacob with Israel (or the naming of Jacob as Israel) is to be understood in the sense that Jacob is regarded as the father of the people Israel. This accords with the tradition of Jacob as the father of twelve sons who bear the names of the twelve tribes of Israel. In both cases Jacob is the father of Israel, and Israel can have no other father besides him. The Isaac tradition is too fragmentary to allow any answer to the question whether he, too, was ever regarded as the father of Israel.

These presuppositions require that the course of the history of the traditions of the patriarchal narratives must have run as follows: all the narratives retained were ascribed to a single father, and the stories about the father of Israel would have grown out of the stories about the fathers. We have to thank those extraordinarily loyal and trustworthy transmitters of the early traditions that the trio of fathers enclosed in the formula "Abraham, Isaac, and Jacob" was preserved, and with it the variety of traditions reflecting the actual state of affairs.

B. The Patriarchal Story in the Canon

The peculiar type of fatherhood attributed to Abraham, Isaac, and Jacob, expounded above as lying somewhere between a mere physical and a divinized ancestor, runs right through the patriarchal traditions of the canon. One must, however, make a distinction. There is, on the one hand, the shaping of the individual patriarchal stories into a whole and its insertion into the traditions of Israel and, on the other hand, the varied presence of the fathers scattered across the traditions from the earliest times through the postcanonical writings into the New Testament.

The theologians and storytellers of the early monarchy thought in specifically historical terms, which explains the insertion of the patriarchal stories into the Pentateuch. Both in Mesopotamia and Egypt the kingship immediately follows primeval time; but the writers of the monarchical period saw the early history of their people as a journey divided into different stages. There was the period from the taking of the land to the rise of the monarchy; before this, the way through the desert to the taking of the land set in motion by the deliverance from

Egypt; and prior to all, the patriarchal story culminating in the migration to Egypt. It is by no means a matter of merely adding the patriarchal story by way of a preface; rather it is part of a historical vision which introduces and prepares in three stages the period of the state, Judah-Israel, and with it the monarchy. This overall plan is particularly clear in the parallel between the beginning of the exodus and the beginning of the patriarchal story (Ex. 1ff., and Gen. 12:1-4a): both Israel and Abraham hear and follow the call to depart with its attendant promise.

One must distinguish from this the presence of the patriarchs through all epochs of the history of Israel and all parts of the canon right into the New Testament. The leading motif throughout is the promise or promises made to them. The recurrence of the promises presupposes that those which appear as the most important, the promises of land and posterity, are not fulfilled in the patriarchal period itself, but only in the course of the history of Israel. Only when the patriarchal stories had become part of the Pentateuch could the promises and their fulfillment be seen in the perspective of the history of Israel. Their significance lies in this: when the gift of the land was in question, the promise of the land was prominent (Deut.); when the existence of the people was in question (the Exile, P), it was the promise of posterity.

A further motif which was part of this process had a religious coloring: the relationship of the patriarchs to God became the exemplar. One must, however, distinguish carefully between the religion of the patriarchs and what made them exemplary, something which can only from time to time be an element of the religion of Israel. Only that could become the exemplar which appeared as such to the later generation from the perspective of its own religious concepts.

Abraham became the father of faith (*Vater des Glaubens*). One must first note that this genitive construction links two ideas which really do not go together; faith does not flow on from father to children. This description relies on Gen. 15:6: Abram "believed the Lord; and he reckoned it to him as righteousness." It will be shown that this verse is not part of an old narrative about Abraham, but represents later reflection. Chapter 22 also, which appears to give a unique presentation of the faith of Abraham, is part of this later reflection.

If Abraham as the father of faith acquires a lofty stature in New Testament exegesis, then it is not the particular exegesis itself that is of prime importance, but the acceptance of the figure of Abraham as such in the New Testament (R. Martin-Achard, *Actualité d'Abraham* [1969] 137-160). The Abraham of Gen. 15:6 is brought into contact with a basic New Testament idea, and so is accepted without reservation. He is not a counter-figure like Moses, who represents the law, or Jacob-Israel, who represents the ancient people of God. "Faith was reckoned to Abraham as righteousness" (Rom. 4:9), and he is forthwith set side by side with those who believe in Christ, of whom the same is said. This verdict on Abraham was the deciding factor that prevented the separation of the New Testament from the Old, or even so much as the possibility of such separation. Abraham is also one of the Christian fathers. Moreover, one cannot overestimate the significance of the fact that Abraham in his religious dimension links the church with the synagogue. The name of Abraham is revered and honored in both the Jewish and Christian religions alike, and this cannot be without its effect. One cannot say this, however, without referring to the importance of Abraham for Islam (R. Martin-Achard, op. cit., 161-174), where he is the most frequently mentioned biblical figure in the Koran. In this context, Islam can be described as the religion of Abraham.

All is not lost, however, when even today the acknowledgment of Abraham has apparently made no difference to the entrenchment and contrariety of the three religions. This much can be said from the present perspective: no single figure of the Old Testament could have such an all-embracing significance as Abraham, for he is not presented in any particular capacity, neither as the founder of a religion, nor a king, nor a prophet.

Jacob in turn became the model of those who strive with God from the narrative of the episode at the Jabbok in Gen. 32. But only rarely is attention drawn to his religious significance for later times. Besides ch. 32, God's revelation in ch. 28 and the prayer of Jacob in 32:9-12 play an occasional role. Jacob, however, never became a truly religious figure such as would become a model for posterity. This is even more so in the case of Isaac; only occasionally is he seen as the suffering one in the context of the narrative of Abraham's sacrifice in Gen. 22.

C. The Composition of the Patriarchal Story

The patriarchal story in the form in which it has come down to us tells of Abraham, Isaac, Jacob, Esau, and Joseph and his brothers, one generation after the other. It begins with the genealogy of Abraham's ancestors and ends with the sons of Jacob. The whole has the form of a family history over three generations.

What is the meaning of this structure? How is the patriarchal story conceived? First of all, it is to be distinguished from biography, the purpose of which is to present the life of an important man or woman. *Important* is the operative word—for a larger community, a city, a people, a religion, a particular civilization. This is not the case with the patriarchal story, even though later times have often understood it in this sense. The traditions about Abraham, Isaac, and Jacob could not have arisen from the importance which these men had for a greater whole, because this whole did not exist at the time when they arose. The modern family novels are closer to the patriarchal story (J. Galsworthy, *The Forsyte Saga* [1922]; T. Gulbranssen, *Und ewig singen die Wälder* [1933]; and *Das Erbe von Björndal* [1935]; Th. Mann, *Die Buddenbrooks* [1901]). These also tell of a family and its fortunes over a number of generations. The difference, however, is so marked that it is not possible to make a detailed comparison here. The narrative in the family novel spans large blocks and shows developments. The patriarchal story has grown out of individual narratives which were first of all told orally and indeed by and among the descendants of those with whom they deal.

This explains the original conception of the patriarchal story. Narratives were told about the fathers because their descendants found their own identity in the storytelling itself; they are what they are only in their derivation from and link with their fathers. Human existence is still experienced in the succession of generations; there was not yet our concept of the individual. At a time when there were neither pictures of parents or grandparents nor letters from nor written records about them, storytelling was virtually the sole link. Remembrance can only be realized in narratives that bridge the gap between the generations and so acquire a vital importance.

This holds only for the very first stage of the history of the patriarchal tradition among the immediate descendants. In any case, the names of the patriarchs and the number three take their origin from this first stage because immediate descendants usually preserve reminiscences only up to three generations. In the next stage the narratives pass on into a wider circle as the descendants branch out and the stories are told among groups that are more and more distant from Abraham,

Isaac, and Jacob. This second stage underscores the typical in the old narratives, i.e., what the father Abraham has in common with other fathers, and what the brothers Jacob and Esau have in common with other brothers. What is told about the fathers must be significant for the many who, generations later, still regard them as their own fathers. This is a stage that is of the utmost importance for the composition of the patriarchal stories. The Abraham narratives, Gen. 12–25, deal mainly with the parent-child relationship; the narratives in Gen. 25–36 mainly concern that of brother to brother. The single narrative of Gen. 37–50 deals with both of these and, in addition, with the relationship of one brother to his other brothers. Thus there are not only differences in theme among the three parts of the patriarchal story; there is a deliberate plan according to which the basic family relationships are dealt with. One can present the realization of the plan in the following way. There were a large number of narratives about the patriarchs in circulation; those were preserved which retained their importance for later generations and they were ordered or collected in such a way as to highlight in the process of transmission what was permanent and typical of the family.

Closer examination shows that the conception of three stages in the patriarchal story is worked out even more carefully than appears at first sight. The Abraham narratives (chs. 12–25), have a strikingly elemental character in that they are often concerned with life and death. They begin with the motif of Sarah's barrenness and Abraham's childlessness, which would mean the end of the line and, in the understanding of that epoch, death. They continue through the narrative of Abraham in Egypt to the birth in ch. 21, and on to the mortal danger that threatens the child in ch. 22 (C. Westermann, ThB 24 [1964] 58f.). They are the proper setting of the motif of the promise. The promise of a son, to which the other promises are attached, is the guarantee to Abraham of the life of his family.

This whole question recedes entirely into the background in the Jacob-Esau narratives, chs. 25–36. Here the main theme is what happens between brother and brother. Institutions that extended far beyond the mere family circle begin to play a major role. It is a matter of regulating ownership, making covenants, legal practices, privileges, and, in the realm of religion, of sacred places and events. All this is at most of marginal interest in the Abraham narratives.

In Gen. 37–50 there enters an additional element which is completely absent from Gen. 12–36, namely, the encounter with the institution of kingship and state. This element is seen not only in the role played by Pharaoh and his court and officials, but also in the confrontation between brothers and the one brother in which the basic phenomenon of kingship, "dominion over brothers," is determinative. The family too is different in Gen. 37–50; it is the family that has grown outwards into the surrounding world and become enmeshed with it.

These three stages in the patriarchal story reveal an overall conception of extraordinary depth which not only sets side by side those relationships which determine family life, but also implies a history: the gradual expansion of the family, contact with broader forms of community and assimilation into them, and contact with the religion and cult of sedentary people. One can recognize in the course of these three stages, even though it be only hinted at, the path from family and clans through tribes to the state and kingship.

To whom do we trace back this conception? Who is at the origin of it? We cannot answer with certainty. It is probable that the first feature, the concentration of the most important family relationships in three cycles, belongs to the stage of oral tradition. The second feature, which betrays a decidedly historical mode of thought, requires the completion of the third stage as outlined and is probably the work of J. It remains to be seen whether the detailed exegesis confirms this. In conclusion, however, we can be certain that the arrangement of the patriarchal story intends not only the succession of three generations, but also the presentation in each of them of particular features of community which color the life of the patriarchs; these features are seen again in a historical succession in which the family form of community is gradually assimilated into the wider forms. Account must also be taken of this three-part plan of the patriarchal story in the question of the historicity of the patriarchs and their period. Taking this basic overall plan as the starting point, the question is not to be considered merely on an individual level; i.e., one does not limit oneself to asking whether Abraham, Isaac, and Jacob really existed or whether what is narrated about them really happened. The three parts are not conceived as a biography. The question must also include the form of community which is presented in its various features in each of the three parts and in the three-fold gradation intended by this succession. It is only in this way that one can set the question of the historicity of the patriarchs on a firm basis and give it a fully positive answer.

A confirmation of this division of content as expounded above can be seen in the following: P, of whom no account has hitherto been taken, likewise shows that he recognizes a division of content in the first two parts of the patriarchal story; he too presents no mere succession of generations, but describes the contents of each stage as he understands them. All this, however, can only be developed from the texts themselves.

2. The Origin and Growth of the Patriarchal Story

Introduction.   I have described the history of research into the patriarchal story in *Erträge der Forschung*: *Genesis 12–50* (1975). The results can be summarized briefly here. When one addresses the task of writing a commentary on the patriarchal story, one must begin by acknowledging a difficulty which, in the present state of scholarship, is well nigh insuperable. Three opposite approaches to the problem are in competition with each other. There have been many attempts to combine two, or even all three of them, but without really overcoming the opposition between them.

The literary-critical approach has lost, or virtually lost, its claim to exclusive right in the field, though few would deny that it still has some part to play. But just what this part is remains a matter of dispute.

The form-critical and traditio-historical approach has won widespread agreement since Gunkel's time in its assumption that the single narrative stands at the beginning of the formation of the tradition and a stage of oral tradition precedes the written stage. This approach, however, has raised a whole host of new problems, foremost among which is that the relationship of the oral stage to the written stage has not yet been explained convincingly.

The significance of the archaeological approach for the history of scholarship is that it believed it had refuted the consequences which Wellhausen had drawn from the source theory, and had aligned itself with the conservative position that preceded the literary-critical aproach. The patriarchal stories by and large were historical accounts of incidents and events in the patriarchal period, which was set between the beginning and middle of the second millennium. Such an understanding of the stories could be combined with an acceptance of the source theory; however, the works of J, E, and P were in this case no mere projections back from the period of the monarchy, but rather different accounts of the same thing, which was demonstrated as historical by the archaeological discoveries.

There was no need for the archaeological approach to confront the form-critical and traditio-historical approach, or even to be concerned with it; the historicity of the patriarchal stories and figures had been demonstrated, and so the question as to how they arose and were handed on had evaporated; with the historicity proven, the reliability of the traditions in the final form was likewise proven, and this was all that mattered.

The opposition among these three different approaches is the reason why studies in the patriarchal stories have, for the most part, proceeded along three parallel paths, and why there has not as yet been a comprehensive meeting and debate among them. There has been a gradual awareness in recent years that such a debate is necessary. An attempt will be made in what follows to present the results of all three approaches in such a way that their mutual relationships, their limits, and their dependence on each other become clear for purposes of exegesis.

A. The Written Stage of the Patriarchal Traditions—the Literary Approach

The literary stage of the origin and growth of Genesis in the Pentateuch has been described in *Genesis 1–11*, ''Formation and Theological Meaning of the Primeval Story'' (see also *Erträge der Forschung* [1975] 14-19).

The literary approach still has the indisputable advantage of having a basis for exegesis in the three (or more) literary sources; each can be explained as the work of one writer with one literary plan and so subject to generally acknowledged literary criteria. The exegesis, therefore, has to do with one text, comprehensible as the original plan of one writer, inasmuch as he belongs to a historical and cultural context. Text and context are here fixed entities, as the new linguistics have shown, where ''text'' has again become a dominating concept. The advantage of dealing with a definite text in a definite context has contributed to the great success of the source theory; this is also the reason why it is still effective in a number of modified forms. The question of the part played by the writers of the large works in the growth of the patriarchal traditions strikes to the heart of the matter. The literary-critical position has maintained its ground even where the form-critical and traditio-critical approach is acknowledged, as scholars of different views have shown in a variety of ways.

O. Eissfeldt acknowledges Gunkel's basic thesis, namely, that the ''smallest unit'' (Gunkel) stands at the beginning of the tradition history; according to his explanation, however, the smallest unit is not the single narrative but the literary source as a whole, that is, the work of the writer (ThBl 6 [1927] 333-337 = KS I [1962] 143-149). One can understand this when one grasps the fact that for Eissfeldt the single narratives are the writer's ''material'' from the oral stage which he uses for his work. One finds a similar understanding among all exegetes who, while not contesting Gunkel's position, do not acknowledge its relevance for exegesis. They consider the old narratives to be the material out of which the writer has fashioned something new. The expression ''material'' or ''raw stuff,'' which is often used in this context, is significant. When the old narratives are recited and heard in a community, they have a vitality of their own. To describe them as material for the writer is to deprive them of this vitality; they have lost their own voice.

Mention must also be made in this context of the important work of A. de

Pury on the Jacob narratives (Lit. B, Tradition [1975]). The way in which the literary position holds its ground is seen in a different way in M. Noth's interpretation of the patriarchal traditions (*A History of Pentateuchal Traditions* [1948; Eng. 1972]). Noth understands the growth of the texts as the result of a process of tradition; however, he limits these traditions which were available to the writers J, E, and P to the period from the time when the tribes became sedentary to the fixation in writing of the basic material (G) by J and E. For Noth, the single narratives have neither their origin nor their literary type with the patriarchs, nor are they passed on by them; Gunkel's decisive stage in the growth of the patriarchal story disappears. It is clear that Noth's methodology and leading idea, "transmission of traditions," bears everywhere the stamp of the written traditions. Nowhere in his treatment of the patriarchal stories does he distinguish the oral stage of the process from the written stage, nor make any attempt to determine more closely the character of the narrative of Gen. 12–50.

Those exegetes who put all the emphasis on what the writer (J, E, or P) wants to say to his own generation by means of the old traditions also show, though in a different way, a one-sided concern with the final literary product. This is particularly the case with those who stress the theological interpretation, like G. von Rad, H. W. Wolff, T. E. Fretheim, and others. The unavoidable consequence is that the theological meaning of the patriarchal stories is seen in what Israel has to say, i.e., in the religion of the patriarchs interpreted from Israel's point of view. The question of the manner in which the religion of the patriarchs differs from that of Israel is not asked. This is further underscored when H. W. Wolff (and with him W. Brueggemann, T. E. Fretheim, and others) speaks of "the kerygma of the Yahwist." Wolff means by this what the Yahwist wants to proclaim to his generation on the basis of the old traditions. He thereby restricts unintentionally the theological meaning of the patriarchal story to the written stage. The idea of kerygma would in any case be inappropriate to the oral stage.

The same is also the case with those who explain the patriarchal story as deriving entirely from the monarchical period and see in it many reflections of that period (A. de Pury, W. Brueggemann, T. L. Thompson, and others), as well as with those who set its origin in late monarchy and/or the exile (J. Hoftijzer, J. Van Seters).

The latest development in the history of the exegesis of the patriarchal story manifests two opposite tendencies with regard to the literary stage. The one moves towards an ever-broadening dissolution of the source theory, even to the extent of radically contesting it. M. Noth, H. Seebass, and others understood the traditio-historical method as complementary to the literary-critical, and the history of the transmission of traditions as closing with the works of J, E, and P. There is now a group of exegetes who want to replace the literary-critical method entirely by the traditio-historical. There remain only traditions and their redaction; writers with an overall plan disappear (e.g., R. Rendtorff).

The other tendency either reverts to the classical source theory, even though with modifications (e.g., R. Kilian, L. Ruppert, A. de Pury), or looks for a literary-critical explanation, linked, however, with a late dating about the time of the exile (e.g., J. Van Seters, J. Hoftijzer).

These opposite tendencies indicate a perplexity which had its origin where the basic presupposition of the source theory collapsed (but which for Wellhausen and his school still remained intact), namely, that the authors of the written sources were writers in the modern sense who created their stories out of their own imagination. The difficulties which arose when one accepted a prehistory of the patriarchal stories, attributing to it an importance for the origins of the text, have not yet been really solved.

There is general agreement as to the limits of the literary-critical position at one point, namely, that even a passage which originated in the written stage cannot be explained by division into sources, but only by traditio-historical reflections. It has become more and more clear that each of the three parts of the patriarchal story had its own history before being brought together as a whole. A series of individual studies have demonstrated this (R. Kilian, D. B. Redford, A. de Pury, J. Van Seters). The differences are obvious: Gen. 12–25 consists essentially of single narratives, chs. 25–36 of larger units, chs. 37–50 are a single, long narrative. This cannot be explained by the literary-critical method of division into sources, but only by positing a different origin and growth for each. There are also important differences in content (see above). It is not possible to explain further these differences in form and content without asking whether there are blocks within each of the three sections out of which the whole has been put together; this requires the transition to the form-critical question.

The observation that the individual parts of Gen. 12–50 had a prehistory before being taken into one of the works has necessitated a change of direction in the literary-critical position. It is certain, at least in this one point, that the authors of J, E, and P were not writers in the modern sense, but bearers of tradition (tradents) who had to pass on something that had come down to them. If the three parts of the patriarchal story already existed before the Yahwist assumed it as a whole into his work, then the possibility remains open that these parts reach far back into the past, possibly to the lifetime of those with whom the stories are concerned.

It is further certain that the meaning of the written works cannot be read simply from the message addressed by the writers to their contemporary listeners or readers with their particular biases. Besides the intention of giving their contemporaries some appropriate advice, exhortations, and admonitions by means of the old stories, there is another intention of equal importance. They intend to pass on to their contemporaries what they themselves have received, something that has no concern with the contemporary situation but which is to be heard and passed on yet again so that it may have a voice in a quite different situation known neither to the listeners nor to the bearer of the tradition. The authors of the literary works as bearers of the traditions have a task which surpasses by far that of a preacher in a particular situation. By passing on what they have received, they have to establish a connection between the patriarchal period and what happened there, and what is happening to the sons of these fathers in the contemporary situation, and what will happen to their grandsons later.

The result of this is that one takes a basically different view of the authors of the written works. If one understands them as bearers of tradition, then one can no longer understand them as writers in the modern sense. The consequence for exegesis is that an individual text in Gen. 12–50—and there are no exceptions—can no longer be regarded without further ado as the creation of one of the authors of the written works. It is possible that a particular text may be such, but one cannot be certain. The exegete must reckon with the possibility of several layers in each case. One can describe the difference from the purely literary view as follows: the literary-critical exegete has done what is decisive for the understanding of a text when he has recognized it as belonging to a particular source. The exegete who regards the author primarily as a bearer of tradition must in each case raise the question whether he (J, E, or P) is speaking for himself alone, or whether there is something underlying the text that someone else has already said before him. The authors of the large works like J and P (and perhaps E), are then less likely to be encountered in the individual narratives than in the overall plan, in the introduction and conclusion, and the transition and link passages. Only those texts in Gen. 12–50 can be attributed in their entirety to J, E, or P alone which contain no demonstrably older traditions, and of which each word is the work of the writer.

The importance of this methodological decision becomes clear in the exegesis of Gen. 12:1-3. G. von Rad recognized the importance of this text as a linchpin which joins the primeval story and the patriarchal story. In this case it could only be the work of the author who joined the two, that is, of the Yahwist. H. W. Wolff accepted and developed this explanation ("The Kerygma of the Yahwist" [1964]; Interp. 20 [1966] 131-158). V. Maag, on the other hand, has discerned a very old tradition in the text, an order to migrate linked with a promise (VT.S 7 [1959/60] 129-153). There is considerable difference between these two explanations. It is enough for the moment to say that, though opposed, they are not necessarily mutually exclusive if the text is seen as composed of several layers, that is, not as a free construction of the Yahwist, but as a construction with an underlying tradition which has been handed down. It is only if one can demonstrate with certainty that any such underlying tradition is excluded from Gen. 12:1-3 that one can say that the passage is a completely new construction of the Yahwist.

As for the narratives, one must from the very start eliminate the possibility that in Gen. 12–50 any of them is a completely new creation of an author. No single narrative in these chapters has been "invented." There is a variety of ways in which an author can work on a narrative; his contribution is greatest in those which are the largest literary units. The Joseph story as a whole is the work of a writer or creative artist even though he has worked over material that has come down to him. In this particular case it is difficult to prove that there were older and shorter individual narratives. The writer's share in the shaping of Gen. 25–36 is more marked than in chs. 12–25. The extent to which the bearer of the tradition shared in each case in the final form of chs. 12–36 and the extent to which he took over material cannot, for the most part, be determined. One must be much more cautious in attributing distinguishing marks of form and content to the author without further ado. Rather one must ask in each case whether it is to be ascribed to the tradition or to the one passing it on. There is one area where this is of special importance, namely, when Gen. 12–50 speaks of the relationship of the patriarchs to God. The view to which Wellhausen gave direction would understand all religious events, expressions, and ideas as reflections of the epoch, thought, and belief of the writer. This view was influential for a long time and still is, even where the thesis of Wellhausen no longer finds acceptance. As the theology of J has been found in Gen. 12:1-3, rightly seen as the introduction to the patriarchal story conceived by J, so also it has been found in all other texts in the patriarchal narrative ascribed to J. It was the new approach of A. Alt ("The God of the Fathers" [1929; Eng. 1966]) that forced scholars to raise the question of the difference between the theology of J and the religion of the patriarchs and to set what was characteristic of the religion of the patriarchs over against what was characteristic of the religion of Israel at the time of J. This has not yet happened. It cannot be denied, however, that in the present state of scholarship the theology of J, as expressed in Gen.

12–50, can only be designated as such if one detaches it from the theology of the old patriarchal narratives, which in any case is separated from it by several centuries. This task remains to be accomplished, and should at least be attempted.

The new approach also radically changes the question of the relationship of the written sources to each other in Gen. 12–50. The task of literary criticism was to assign the individual text to one of these sources. With that done, the text had been adequately situated and one was in a position to explain it on the basis of its epoch and the characteristics of the written source. The chronological allocation of the sources provided the reliable framework which was sufficient to place the individual text in time and content. The new view adds a new dimension: the location of the individual text along the path of the tradition which ended in the particular source. If one surveys the whole path, then an early text can occur in a late source, and a late text in an early source. As for the relationship of the sources to each other, there is the further question of how they receive what came down to them—how they link it together and reshape it. It is here that the distance between P and the older sources becomes obvious. P is not a bearer of tradition in the same sense as the older sources, but a theological writer who composes his own patriarchal story out of the motifs and elements of the older written story which is at his disposal; and it has very little in common with the latter. The work of the writer in shaping the material is such that one can demonstrate without difficulty the same style and the same theological lines throughout. But even with P one can distinguish the shape he gave the work from the traditions available to him.

Over against P, the "older sources" draw closer to each other; together they differ from P in that they are bearers of tradition, and so pass on what has come down to them without molding it into a presentation of their own. The difference is so great that one can see that in Gen. 12–50 an older and a later presentation of the patriarchal story have been joined together which differ from each other in the way already indicated. It is a matter of less importance whether the older presentation (i.e., everything in chs. 12–50 except P) was originally one literary unit, or was worked together out of two (J and E) or three (L, J, and E) originally independent literary works; these latter agree in that their authors want to be bearers of the patriarchal story that has come down to them. This question can no longer be decided by enumerating differences in vocabulary, style, or theology, because these too can have their roots in the texts that preceded them. It can only be decided by demonstrating that there must have been several self-contained conceptions of the patriarchal story as a whole. It can be said in this context that an older source that preceded J (it has different names; Eissfeldt calls it L = lay source) comes to grief here, because one cannot demonstrate for it such an overall conception of Gen. 12–50. Only an exegesis of the individual texts can show whether the Elohist (E) can be regarded as an independent literary work with its own conception of the patriarchal story. We can be certain, however, that the decision whether a text is to be ascribed to J or E can never be so important as the decision whether it is to be ascribed to P or the ancient sources.

B. The Oral Stage

I. The Form-Critical Problem. The basis of the work of the exegetes of the literary-critical school was the firm relationship of the text to the writers. But in the present state of scholarship not even this basis exists any longer. The situation has altered in such a way that the exegete has to ask about the origin and history of texts which have been on the way for hundreds of years before finding their final form as parts of written works. If these texts, or even parts or motifs or traces of them, actually go back to the period of the patriarchs, actually originated with those living persons Abraham, Isaac, Jacob, and Joseph, then the scholar must account for the path of these traditions from that period (2000-1400 B.C.) to the written works in the tenth, eighth, or sixth centuries. And this path is virtually inaccessible because 80% to 90% of it is oral tradition, and all we know of it is the written end product. To bridge the time gap is so difficult a task that no one can expect easy and certain results. A wealth of uncertainties encumbers the explanation of the individual texts of the patriarchal narratives; one can only grope cautiously and, in most cases, not go beyond probability.

A limit of the method of literary criticism emerges in that each of the three parts of the patriarchal story has had its own history of formation (see above). One must raise the question about the history of the Abraham, Isaac, and Jacob tradition, a history that culminates in the literary product that lies before us, and one must affirm that these individual complexes are also put together from single parts. The question about the delimitation and type of the individual parts of the complexes of tradition is the form-critical question. This is an essentially different matter when dealing with the patriarchal texts than when dealing, for example, with the prophetic or psalm texts where the occasion of a lament or a prophetic oracle of judgment is always more or less the same, while a unique occasion lies at the basis of a narrative.

The first thing to note is that the single texts out of which the patriarchal story grew are remarkably varied. This is true both for the form and the content; these are correlative and cannot be separated from each other. The task is to determine exactly the differences among the texts and thereby to find groups that correspond and belong together, or which are of the same type.

Now not all the texts in Gen. 12–50 are narratives; there are enumerative texts as well. In chs. 1–11 the enumerative texts were almost exclusively genealogies; in chs. 12–50 there are in addition itineraries. There is also in chs. 12–50 a group of texts which can be assigned neither to the narrative nor to the enumerative group; they are the promises. It is from here that the form-critical task takes its direction, namely to study the narratives, the genealogies, and itineraries, and the promises each in themselves. The single text finds its context within the group of texts which belong in the same category. This form-critical insight is of particular importance in the case of the promises: the individual promise text in Gen. 12–50 can be explained only from a survey which embraces all the promise texts (C. Westermann, *The Promises to the Fathers* [1976; Eng. 1980]). This holds both for form and content. With regard to content, there is all the difference between the narrow world of chs. 12–36 and the broad world of chs. 37–50. The family narratives form the basic content of chs. 12–36, though they are by no means the only texts. Besides them, the main group consists of those dealing with sanctuaries and encounters with God. Moreover, they differ from the family narratives in that there is always only one person concerned, either Abraham or Jacob. There is another group which has to do with family narratives, but they are colored by a theological interest. This is the case with the promise narratives such as Gen. 15 and 17, as well as with the narrative of the sacrifice of Isaac (Gen. 22), as the very first verse indicates. Yet a further, quite different group of narratives or parts of narratives is concerned with relationships among the tribes, such as Gen. 34; 38; 25:19-23; and the oracles in Gen. 27:27-29, 39-40.

As for the form, there is the greatest contrast between the short, dense narratives of the Abraham cycle and the long, complicated form of the Joseph story. And within the Abraham cycle itself there is a great contrast between Gen. 12:10-20 and 24:1-67 in the length and style of the narration. Again, the detailed narrative can have very different purposes. Gen. 22; 23; and 24 are all detailed; but the interest of the narrator takes a very different direction in each. As to form, one can distinguish clearly between the popular narrative, Gen. 12:12-20, and the artistically developed narrative, Gen. 37–50, as well as Gen. 24. But this is not enough to encompass all differences. The differences in form and content show that the narratives of Gen. 12–50 could not have originated at the same time and in the same place, but point rather to a broad distribution in time and place. The circle in which the narratives had their origin took as much part in their formation as did the narrator; their different interests therefore correspond to the interests of these same circles.

The texts of the patriarchal narratives, therefore, show clear signs of a gradual growth over a long period of time. The first outlines were preserved along the path which they have travelled across the centuries and which extends from the patriarchal period down to the monarchy in Israel. To begin with, no more is proven than that the growth of the patriarchal stories into the form handed down to us required vast intervals, intervals that lay between the emergence of the various individual narratives and groups of narratives and their insertion into the written works in which we find them. But with this proven, and only then, there opens the possibility that narratives which we first meet in J go right back to Abraham.

The possibility of the explanation just outlined renders inadmissible two other explanations. Wellhausen, characteristically, tried to solve the problem by denying utterly the long passage of the patriarchal traditions and setting their origin contemporaneously with the writers in the period of the monarchy: it was they who invented Abraham, Isaac, and Jacob as well as the stories about them. This explanation has been rendered untenable by the discovery of the independent life of the oral tradition which preceded its fixation in writing. It is inconceivable that J would have invented such different types of narrative which obviously belong to different circles and epochs. This holds also for the conclusion of T. L. Thompson (BZAW 133 [1974]; Lit. A). He revives Wellhausen's thesis by and large when he restricts the time of origin of the patriarchal traditions to ''the time when the traditions became part of the literature of Israel, perhaps around the 10th and during the 9th centuries'' (pp. 315ff.). He thereby leaves unexplained the remarkable differences in these traditions which indicate vast intervals of time.

The other and opposite explanation has a variety of distinguishing marks; they all agree, however, in starting from the ''historicity'' of the patriarchal figures and stories and trying to prove it—in contrast to the Wellhausen explanation. What is fundamentally questionable here is a mentality which thinks that all that matters, at least in essence, is to prove the historicity of the patriarchal figures and/or period. It is unnecessary to prove that the tradition extended over several centuries. The traditions would become historical by the very fact that they have historical figures as their object. This represents conservative exegesis of the patriarchal stories both before and after Wellhausen, and it has gathered new strength in the exegesis which takes its orientation from archaeology. One cannot dispute the great importance of archaeological discoveries related to the patriarchal stories; but as long as archaeology is restricted to individual facts and data which are found both in the patriarchal stories and the documents from different places and periods of the ancient near east of the second millennium, it cannot serve as proof for the historicity of the patriarchs and the stories about them. As long as the passage of the traditions from the patriarchs to the written works cannot be explained, then parallels between individual facts and data (e.g., names, legal customs, etc.) prove no more than the possibility that elements of the patriarchal stories go back to this period (J. Van Seters, *Abraham in History.* . ., Lit. B, Tradition [1975]).

Whatever the archaeologically determined exegesis has to say about the passage of the patriarchal traditions, if it says anything at all, it is the same as was said by the pre-Wellhausen conservative exegesis (e.g., by R. Kittel), namely, that it was a historically reliable tradition that spanned these centuries. Here is the decisive error. Is it at all likely that such different narratives originated in the patriarchal period (wherever one sets it), just as we find them in Gen. 12–50, and that they were preserved completely unaltered in all their variety across several centuries? If one explains Gen. 12; 14; 15; 22; and 24 as "historical," without at the same time explaining the profound differences among them, then it is worthless to confirm them as "historical." The archaeological evidence has a further limitation. Archaeologists have discovered names and facts, economic and social conditions from the early and middle of the second millennium in the ancient near east, that correspond to the same in the patriarchal story. But they have not yet discovered parallels in the strict sense. Only whole textual units with corresponding units in the patriarchal story would be real parallels. Gen. 6–9 show that such are possible. It must be conceded that parallels of this sort have not yet been found. However, I have tried to show that this is not impossible, and that in any case parallels are to be found for series of motifs corresponding to the patriarchal stories (in my essay "The Significance of the Ugaritic Texts for the Patriarchal Narratives" in *The Promises to the Fathers* [1976; Eng. 1980]).

Archaeology can only have real meaning for the exegesis of the patriarchal stories when it allows a place for the problem of the shape of the patriarchal tradition and the history of its transmission down the centuries. So far each of these lines of research has gone its own way with virtually no contact, generally standing in opposition to the other. An obvious point of contact, however, is that by asking about the shape of the patriarchal tradition, one is compelled to ask about the forms of community, the life-style and the religion of the circles in which the narratives originated and were handed down (this is missing in M. Noth, *A History of Pentateuchal Traditions* [1948, 1966³; Eng. 1972]). Archaeology too must pursue this question. Moreover, research into the transmission of the patriarchal stories must also pay attention to the alterations which have of necessity taken place as forms of community and economic life have changed, leaving such a variety of traces in the narratives and other texts of Gen. 12–50.

The development of the patriarchal story is to be seen as a long, continuous process which reaches its conclusion in the fixed, written text of Gen. 12–50. This being the case, one can distinguish stages in the process, and one is in a position to raise the question of the earliest stage which goes back to the time of the fathers. The greatest reserve is necessary in assigning individual texts to the stages of development of the patriarchal story; one must be content with but few certain results: (1) It is quite certain that the composition of the patriarchal story as a whole belongs to the latest stage, which we meet in the work of the Yahwist. He is responsible, too, for all those single pieces which are part of the work of composition, such as introductions, transitions, conclusions, link passages. (2) P is evidence that work continued on the patriarchal story right into the exile period. It is also possible that the patriarchal story of J (and E) underwent elaborations and insertions which likewise could extend into the exile period. (3) It is certain too that the long, detailed, and artistically constructed stories of Joseph and the courting of Rebecca (ch. 24) as well as the large complexes, Jacob-Esau and Jacob-Laban, belong to a late stage; it is an open question whether the single narratives in these complexes can go back to the time of the fathers. (4) Narratives with an expressly theological interest, like 15:1-6 and 22:1-19, belong to a relatively late stage, as do also those promise narratives which are directed clearly towards the people of Israel and its land. (5) Texts which are obviously directed towards the life of the tribes belong to a relatively early stage, though not to the period of the fathers themselves. Narratives about a sanctuary in the land of Canaan or a sedentary institution also belong to this stage.

As for the old patriarchal traditions whose point of departure is in the patriarchal period itself, there remain narratives and other texts for which there are no clear criteria for a later stage. However, account must be taken here of the following: (1) With every text in Gen. 12–50 one must reckon with alterations which it has undergone on the long path of tradition. These alterations are the norm; it is quite abnormal for a text to remain completely unaltered through several centuries. Parallel texts like chs. 12; 20; 26 and 16; and 21 demonstrate this very clearly. One should not in any of these cases try to determine what is the original text and what are the secondary variations; one can only ask about their relationship to each other. Which of the forms is likely to belong to an earlier stage; which to a later? All the patriarchal narratives without exception existed in variants (*Genesis 1–11*, 582-583, ''The Criterion of Doublets and Repetitions''); for the most part only one of them has come down to us. (2) Only those narratives and other texts can go back into the patriarchal period which comply with a life-style that precedes the sedentary style or any political organization, or even tribal organization. Moreover, they must not contradict the archaeological evidence available from the area and period in question, and, given the background so far as it is known, must be possible. The archaeological discoveries in this area and period are of the utmost importance. (3) In particular, narratives such as presume a purely family community structure and the life-style of marginal nomads where family situations and events are central and the concern is with living space and provisions for such small nomad groups can belong to the old patriarchal traditions. (4) It is to be noted, however, that narratives and other texts can belong there too, even though they have undergone change in passage and have been adapted to the interests of a later epoch. Three examples can demonstrate this: Gen. 12:1-3 is quite generally regarded as a formation of the Yahwist, belonging therefore to the latest stage of the literary process; it can, however, contain a tradition coming down from the patriarchal period which has been worked over, and can still be recognized as a call to depart and migrate linked with a promise (V. Maag, VT.S 7 [1959-60] 129-153). The second example is Gen. 22: the narrative of the sacrifice of Isaac is transmitted in a late form; it is generally acknowledged that there is an older form behind it. It is possible that in the earliest form the purpose of the narrative was the saving of the child in danger (C. Westermann, ThB 24, 65f., 71f.); in this form, it could have its origin in the patriarchal period. Finally there is Gen. 15:1-6. This is a secondary promise narrative which in v. 6 speaks the language of a much later period; it preserves the motif of the childless father, even in two variants (vv. 2 and 3), which belonged to a lost narrative from the patriarchal period.

The motif of the promises is a typical example of the relationship of the patriarchal story as it has come down to us to the old traditions. The promise of a son to the father or the mother (Gen. 15; 16; 18) in a narrative like Gen. 18 probably goes right back to the patriarchal period. In the course of transmission other promises became attached to it, some of which were certainly intended as links between the patriarchal period and the history of the people (e.g., 50:24); they can only have originated much later. We can perhaps even distinguish three stages: those referring to the patriarchs, the tribes, and the people. The matters at issue here are a typical example inasmuch as, with the motif of the promise, we can trace a few steps along the path of transmission from the patriarchal period to the period when the written works originated.

We will never achieve complete certainty as to which texts in Gen. 12–50 may come from the patriarchal period, and which traces in texts of later origin may go back to it. Even what has been proposed here can make no claim to absolute certainty. We can, however, be quite certain that one cannot contest the possibility that texts, narratives, and motifs in Gen. 12–50 reach back into the patriarchal period.

Granted this possibility, the exegete of the patriarchal story is faced with the difficult task of inquiring into the origin, life, and shape of the patriarchal stories which belong to the preliterary stage. There are new lines of research to follow, but firm, certain results are hardly to be gained. A whole new area must be opened up here, namely, the forms of speech of people who have no writing. In any case, a certain result of inquiry into the forms of speech of the preliterary phase of the growth of the patriarchal stories is that real parallels can only be found in other preliterary phases. We can find them in the forms of speech of peoples of our own day who have no writing. The exegete, therefore, is compelled to inquire of the ethnologist or anthropologist whose area of specialization is the study of the culture of peoples without writing. The application of a field of research so far distant from that of the Old Testament has of course its problems (*Genesis 1–11*, Intro. 3.A); but the possibility of gaining a certain understanding by comparison with the forms of speech of other peoples who have no writing should not be excluded. It has in fact already proved itself. H. Gunkel found the laws formulated by A. Olrik about popular narrative pertinent to the patriarchal stories (Danish [1908]; Eng. ed. A. Dundes, *Studies in Folklore* [1965]; I. F. Wood, working independently of Olrik, reached extensive agreement with him, JBL 28 [1908] 34-41). It is not by chance, then, that Olrik's laws have been applied again in a number of recent works on the patriarchs (e.g., J. Van Seters, *Abraham.* . . [1975]; Lit. B, Tradition).

Reference can be made here to certain points where such a comparison has been fruitful. (1) In an earlier phase, inquiry into the way in which oral tradition functioned was restricted to a comparison with oral tradition among the pre-Islamic Arabs (the early Nordic school, H. S. Nyberg ZAW 52 [1934] 241-254; Lit. B, Tradition). This led to contradictory results and no clear criteria resulted. In a later phase, continuing right up to the present, there has been dialogue with ethnology and anthropology which has led to new results (see below).

(2) H. Gunkel, H. Gressmann, and their successors had restricted the oral forms of speech to the narratives, the "stories" (*Sagen*) (Gressmann ZAW 30 [1910] 1-34; Lit. II; Gunkel, *Kommentar*, "Einleitung" [1910³; 1964⁶]). It has been recognized in the meantime that enumerative forms, like genealogies and

itineraries, are also independent forms of oral tradition. The great importance of genealogies for nonwriting peoples has only been acknowledged as a result of ethnological and anthropological research. A comparison between the treatment of the genealogies by T. L. Thompson (BZAW 133 [1974]; Lit. A) and R. R. Wilson (Lit. B; Genealogy [1972, 1975, 1977]) is a striking example. Thompson, pp. 311-314, by means of a few examples, wants to revive the thesis of Wellhausen, namely, that the genealogies are purely literary constructions. His selection of parallels, however, shows that they are all later formations from writing civilizations. He is clearly not familiar with a history of genealogies. Wilson, on the contrary, has for the first time brought a wealth of parallels for comparison which have been gathered by anthropologists from nonwriting civilizations. Not only has he demonstrated the great importance of genealogies and their setting in life for nonwriting peoples, but he is also able to show that there has been a development in the different types. It is worth remarking that the genealogies of the patriarchal stories bear a closer resemblance to the genealogies of the nonwriting peoples than to those of the ancient near eastern texts.

(3) The remarkable confusion in the terms for the kinds of narrative (folk story, tale, legend, myth), due to the unjustified generalization of types which are chronologically conditioned and geographically restricted, can be clarified if attention is paid to their sociological presuppositions; narratives then are conceived as processes in the community where they have their indispensable functions.

II. Tradition in the Preliterary Stage.   One of the most difficult questions in the explanation of the patriarchal tradition is how to bridge the centuries-long interval between the lifetime of the fathers and the writing down of the patriarchal stories as they lie before us in Genesis. How were the stories passed down over this period? This is the question of tradition.

The ''history of transmission'' or the ''history of tradition'' is pretty generally acknowledged to be a continuation of the literary method; even so, there has been little reflection on tradition and transmission as process. For the most part ''history of transmission'' is understood as the history of what is handed down (*tradita*), not the history of the process of handing down (*tradere*). The starting point must be that ''transmission'' is a two-sided process; to describe it correctly two verbs must be used, ''to pass on'' and ''to receive'' (Hebr. קִבֵּל and מסר). Transmission then always has two sides: the giver and the receiver. The nature of transmission can be explained only when both are included. Oral and written tradition differ first of all in this, that with the former, the giver and the receiver must be within earshot of each other and the giving and receiving take place simultaneously. With the written tradition, the giver and the receiver can be both geographically and chronologically removed from each other; giving and receiving are two distinct and separate processes. R. C. Culley emphasizes this (Lit. II; Tradition [1963 and 1972]): ''Oral tradition depends for its existence upon its acceptance. This interplay between the performer and his audience is the communal element in the creation and preservation of oral literature. The oral artist is always in an immediate relationship to his audience'' (1963, p. 121).

The first question to be asked about oral tradition which has been passed down over a long period is not whether it is to be regarded as reliable or not. It is, rather, whether the process of handing on over so long a time was such as to enable giver and receiver to form a chain which rendered a reliable transmission possible. Without a certain permanence in the form of the community concerned, it is not possible. A glance at the pre-Islamic Arabs shows this (J. R. Porter, JBL 87 [1968] 17-26; Lit. II). Hitherto, scholarship has been dominated by the question of the reliability of the oral tradition. Some defended it with numerous proofs; others contested it just as strongly. This is the case with the Old Testament debate that followed H. S. Nyberg's *Hoseastudien* (1934); (H. Birkeland [1938]; J. van der Ploeg [1947]; J. Laessøe [1953]; E. Nielsen [1954]; G. Widengren [1958]; G. W. Ahlström [1963]; A. Haldar [1973]; Lit. II; Tradition). It could reach no firm conclusion because it was dominated by the question, historical or nonhistorical. The debate about oral tradition among nonwriting peoples in the early stages of civilization and in the study of folklore, brought many new features; it started from the same alternative (described by R. M. Dorson, Fests. K. Ranke [1968] 181-195; Lit. B, Tradition), but then progressed to the real question of the process of oral tradition and its conditions (see W. Caskel [1930]; H. M. and N. K. Chadwick [1932-36]; J. Pedersen [1946]; A. B. Lord [1960]; J. Vansina [1965]; G. I. Jones [1965]; J. R. Porter [1968]; D. P. Henige [1971]; Lit. B, Tradition). R. C. Culley and J. R. Porter show how these results are applied to the Old Testament. Among other things, an important difference between written and oral tradition emerges. One can speak of an "original text" only in the case of written tradition; oral tradition consists essentially of variants because every oral narrative, or recitation of the tradition, is something unique and independent and can diverge in details from what has preceded and what follows (see especially A. B. Lord, and R. C. Culley who refers to him, p. 120).

If one keeps in mind that this is the way in which oral tradition proceeds, then there are of course two very obvious and different possibilities in the process of passing on and receiving: it can be intended or not intended. In every human community there is oral tradition which is not deliberate and not planned, and this is a normal part of life in common. Such would be simple forms like the greeting, conversational pieces and formulas, aphorisms, and also longer forms like songs, rhymes, narratives, games, dances, and the words which accompany them. One must distinguish from these tradition which is deliberately intended and planned, and presumes institutions which serve it, e.g., schools of any sort. Every form of teaching, be it practical or theoretical, is a deliberate transmission of this kind which presumes the consensus of the giver and the receivers. This distinction between preinstitutional and institutional tradition is basic to any understanding of it.

In every case then the question must be asked whether a text has been passed on intentionally or not. While all written tradition is by that very fact intended, oral tradition may or may not be. This distinction gives precision to Gunkel's "setting in life" (*Sitz im Leben*); the setting in life of a tradition can be a process in the life of the community in which the spoken word is transmitted without any express intention. The setting can also be an institution which serves the transmission. M. I. Finley (*History and Theory* 4 [1965] 281-302; Lit. B) introduces a further distinction between individual and group memory. Oral tradition presumes the process of recall, or memory. Individual memory does not usually extend beyond three generations; it is limited to the small circle of personal life. Group memory has to do with events which affect the whole group. Recollections accompany the life of the group; they are carried on because they are also important for the generations to come. There enters here a feature which is of the essence of all oral tradition: it presupposes that the community is interested in this handing on. All is selective; what is passed on is always but a tiny snippet of the life of a group. But this snippet must be motivated. The question must be asked: what was it behind this particular small facet of life that caused it to be passed on?

It is clear then what is decisive: the interest of oral tradition can be very varied, but it is never historical. There is now general agreement that in its earlier stages the object of oral tradition was always the small unit—song, saying, narrative, etc. (R. C. Culley, pp. 118, 120). It is of the very nature of history to be concerned with an overall conception into which the individual event is fitted (e.g., in the succession narrative). When oral tradition deals with narratives, as in the patriarchal stories, then the interest is not in history, but in transmission; there is no sense in which they can have a historical character. M. I. Finley (see above) has shown this convincingly in the case of the origin and growth of the science of history in Greece. The heroic age was described in the mythical-epic tradition; but in the postheroic age, it was not replaced immediately by a historical tradition: "Tradition about the postheroic centuries began with oral tradition" (p. 296). There was a variety of everyday family, short-lived traditions which usually extended over only three generations. It was probably only in distinguished families that there were more extensive and significant traditions which the family was interested in passing on and preserving. The historical writing of Herodotus and Thucydides was, on the other hand, something of an innovation, the sudden appearance of which is not easy to explain: "The new impulse came from the classical πόλις and in particular the Athenian πόλις which for the first time, at least in western history, introduced politics as a human activity" (p. 299).

It is clear that the events of oral tradition are something different from history. R. R. Wilson has demonstrated convincingly that the genealogies did not arise out of historical interest. The consequence is that one cannot apply the idea of history or the historical to the oral stage of transmission. The patriarchal traditions are in no sense history, and the question about the historicity of the patriarchal stories and figures is a question wrongly put. Unfortunately, it has become the ordinary thing to put the question, whether the patriarchs really lived or were mere inventions, as the question about the "historicity" of the patriarchal figures. It would help to clarify matters considerably if all this were left aside. As the patriarchal stories are neither history nor historical writing, one cannot even raise the question about their historicity or that of the figures concerned. The question whether Abraham, Isaac, and Jacob really lived is a different question from that of their historicity. This question can only be put of the traditions in which the patriarchs meet us. The question is what motivated the givers and receivers to pass on these stories. The motive can only have been to tell and hear about the patriarchs so as to preserve in the narrating the link with them. It follows that it is extremely improbable, if not impossible, that all these stories have been invented. Originally only what happened was narrated. To make up a story, to narrate a story that has been made up, is always a secondary cultural phenomenon. Storytelling about the fathers as transmission made sense only if it transmitted something real about real people. It is obvious that the narratives have been adapted considerably in the course of transmission over generations, and that later stories, whose relation to what happened of old was no longer direct, have been added to the older. What is essential, however, is that the patriarchal traditions arose because stories were and had to be told about the patriarchs.

It is likewise an error to understand the patriarchal stories as biography (many writers have done this, as recently as H. Cazelles DBS 7 [1961] 81-156). Oral tradition is usually concerned with the small unit (aphorism, song, narrative, etc.); this is because of the simple person's understanding of time. Such a person does not see the past as a measurable continuum (M. I. Finley, op. cit., 293), but as consisting of a series of individual events which is recalled by way of association, occasioned for the most part by something in the present: ''Do you still know how we. . .?'' When those who lived through such an event pass on their experience of it to the next generation and the one following it, their memory of it is replaced by what has been received by others. This is no longer the actual memory of what happened; it rests, however, on memories out of which it once grew. Inasmuch as tradition derives from memories, there can be memories only of individual events (see above). Consequently, in the process of formation of the patriarchal stories, the individual narratives are primary and the connections among them secondary. The connections are to be regarded neither as ''historical'' nor as ''biographical'' but rather as stages on the way from the individual narratives to the patriarchal story as a whole. They are stages in the history of the tradition of the patriarchal stories.

The history of this tradition can take as its starting point two established facts: (1) at the beginning stands the individual narrative; and (2) the patriarchal story as a whole is neither historical nor biographical, but is to be understood as a process of growth from the individual narrative to the whole.

If we can accept the names of the patriarchs Abraham, Isaac, and Jacob as resting on memory and as names of men who actually lived, then that is due to a peculiarity of oral tradition to which attention has often been drawn in recent times: it preserves with special fidelity the beginnings which link it with the present, while the tradition in between fluctuates a good deal. Referring to African traditions, G. I. Jones writes: ''The real difference between Oral Tradition and History. . . lies in their treatment of time. . .. There is a beginning. . . and an end, but no middle'' (Lit. B, Tradition [1965] 153). R. R. Wilson makes the same observation about the genealogies of nonwriting peoples.

III. Narrative and Storytelling.   The simple fact that the patriarchal stories are narratives has not yet been given sufficient attention. Certainly, since the work of form criticism began, the fact as such has been recognized and subsequently has played a notable role in the study of the patriarchal stories (see J. A. Wilcoxen in J. H. Hayes, ed., *O. T. Form Criticism* [1974] 57-98). For the most part, however, there has not been a sufficiently thorough inquiry as to what a narrative is; one moved quickly on to particulars and specifications which bypassed the essence of storytelling.

H. Gunkel described the stories of Genesis as ''a collection of *Sagen*''; but he did not succeed in defining this term clearly and unequivocally. The basic approach, that Genesis was formed from individual narratives which grew out of oral tradition, has won widespread agreement up to the present; there has not, however, been like agreement about the meaning of the term *Sage* (so also J. A. Wilcoxen 57-69). Consequently, J. Van Seters (*Abraham in History.* . . [1975] 131-138) maintains, without justification, that this lack of clarity about *Sage* renders untenable the basic thesis of Gunkel as a whole. Despite Gunkel's new approach, others have continued to regard the patriarchal stories primarily and essentially as literature, to be explained in strict conformity with the principles of literature. This can also be the case where it is joined to a form-critical method, as for example with O. Eissfeldt (FRLANT 36 [1923] 56-77 = KS I [1962]145-157) and J. Van Seters, or to a traditio-historical method, as with M. Noth (*A History of Pentateuchal Traditions* [1948, 1966³; Eng. 1972]) and A. de Pury (*Promesse divine*. . . [1975]). In this case the voice that is heard is that of the author, the writer. Yet another approach is so preoccupied with the question of historicity that no attention, or as good as none, is paid to the type of presentation; the only interest is the historicity of the text or the historical nucleus. This is particularly so in studies determined by archaeology. The interest of other exegetes was solely in the religion and theology expressed in or derived from the text; this was the only yield that seemed relevant. These studies were concerned either with the theology of the writer in the monarchical period (H. W. Wolff, EvTh 24 [1964] 73-98; Interp. 20 [1966] 131-158; *The Vitality of O.T. Traditions* [with W. Brueggemann] [1976]; T. E. Fretheim, Interp. 26 [1972] 419-436) or with the religion of the patriarchs (A. Alt, ''Der Gott der Väter'' [1929] = KS I [1953] 1-78; Eng. *The God of the Fathers*. . . [1966] 1-66; and the whole ensuing discussion).

What is peculiar to the patriarchal stories is that this part of the Old Testament is narrative. Stories are told about the fathers, ''fathers'' not understood in too narrow a sense, but ''fathers'' in the sense of ancestors, comprising fathers, mothers, and children. The interpreters of the patriarchal stories must therefore take pains to allow these texts to speak as narratives, and above all as narratives that deal with the ancestors. The ultimate goal cannot be to gain some sort of historical or literary or religious result; it is rather to waken the narratives to life so that as narratives they can speak to the present and be effective into the future.

What is a narrative? ''A narrative portrays an event as it moves through climax to resolution'' (C. Westermann ''Arten der Erzählung. . .'' ThB 24 [1964] 40; see further I. Blythin, SJTh 21 [1968] 56-73; W. Richter, BBB 18 [1963]; A. de Pury, *Promesse divine*. . . [1975] II, 451-468). This is not meant to be a comprehensive definition to include all possible types of narrative; it looks rather to what is typical, to what makes a narrative a narrative. This has not changed across place and time. The narrative span, which moves through climax to resolution, gives the spoken product its self-contained unity. It acquires thereby a form which makes the storytelling easier for the narrator and enables the listener to retain it and retell it. Narrator and listener alike have taken an active part in this narrative form.

The definition proposed comprehends all types of narratives. It is appropriate to the tale, but goes beyond it to all narratives of saving, liberating, redeeming. It also fits the folk story (*Sage*) which tells of the deeds of heroes, or the adventure narrative, the love story, the short story. The type of tension can be quite different in its occasion and final resolution. It can range through the most different realms: in the family, on a journey, in struggle; in face of hunger, thirst, catastrophe; in the social area (lord and servant, the youngest, the rivals, the strong one and the weak one, and so on).

An event portrayed as moving to a climax ascends from one level and comes back again to this same level. This is in accord with A. Olrik's first law (Danish [1908, 1921²]; German ZDA 51 [1909] 1-12; Eng. ed. A. Dundes, *Studies in Folklore* [1965] 127-141), ''law of introduction and law of conclusion: one must ascend from the quiet to the eventful''; when speaking of the conclusion, of which the narrative admits no exception, he uses the words *stabilize* and *allay*. The patriarchal narratives can make this law more precise. The ''quiet,'' from which the narrative ascends and to which it descends again, has something of the unvarying about it. This is expressed in its own peculiar way in the patriarchal stories. Language about unvarying occurrences, in which nothing ''special'' happens, is the enumerative language of the genealogies and itineraries (*Genesis 1–11*, Intro. 2). The genealogy, and the itinerary too, often forms the framework for narratives; the narrative grows out of the numerative genealogy or the itinerary. Something like this is found in our own century in the records of an Arabic clan near Bethlehem. B. Couroyer writes: ''The genealogical lists. . . are sometimes interrupted to give a concrete detail or develop into detailed narrative. . .'' (RB 58 [1951] 75f). There is no need to repeat the rest of the epic laws established by Olrik and others; they can be found in the introduction to Gunkel's Genesis commentary, in J. A. Wilcoxen (see above), and in J. Van Seters, op. cit., p. 160. What is essential is that they are valid for all types of narrative which have grown out of oral tradition.

All narrative refers to something that is happening or has happened. One must not impose on the narrative an understanding of reality that is foreign to it. The question whether the event narrated is historical or not is not pertinent to the understanding of reality in these narratives, because they are told among people for whom this alternative did not yet exist. Narrative for them is narration of what happened. W. Benjamin has recognized this: ''The narrator takes what he narrates either from his own or from reported experience and makes it, in turn, the experience of those who listen to his story'' (Lit. II; Tradition [1961] 413). As ''experience'' is something implicitly personal, he thereby distinguishes narrative very clearly from historical report as well as from fiction. Because something has happened and been experienced, it is narrated, and so enters into the experience of others and through them into others yet again.

One must guard the character of narrative against a further misunderstanding. Modern exegesis takes the greatest pains to reduce the patriarchal narratives to an intellectually comprehensible message. One tries to derive this from what the author of the narratives wanted to say to the readers and listeners of his own time. Behind this attitude is the conviction, so deeply embedded in western thought, that every text, and this includes narrative, must have an author. And this author must have something to say to his own contemporaries, even when he is addressing people of times long passed; it is the task of exegesis to extract this message. Many are of this opinion: H. W. Wolff, ''The Kerygma of the Yahwist'' (Lit. B, 1964), T. E. Fretheim, A. de Pury in his two-volume work, and J. Van Seters. All lay great stress on the contemporary message of the text. It is no great surprise then when Wolff, Fretheim, and de Pury understand the message as addressed to Israel of the early monarchy, and van Seters understands the same texts as addressed to Israel in exile. One must say here that the view of van Seters, setting the Yahwist in the exile, is extremely improbable; and for all that, the contemporary message is uncertain because it can rely only on elements in the narratives, not on the narratives as wholes. A narrative is not a text, however it may confront us as a text in its present form. It is something that was narrated and the narration was listened to. Here lies the difference between a narrative and an intellectually conceived text. It would be an example of the latter if the writer intended to offer his contemporaries a word of comfort, admonition, or advice. When Nathan tells the king a story (2 Sam. 12) so as to say to him: ''You are the man,'' this is a completely different matter. But it is not the way narratives arise. Narratives are what they are only in the complete process of narrating and listening; they can never be reduced to the thought content or intention of what is narrated. One can only listen to a narrative; one cannot encapsulate what it has to say in an extract. The possibility that it is addressed to a particular audience at a particular time is by no means to be contested, but only that the address is restricted to one audience and one time. Of its very nature narrative can speak anew to a new era.

W. Benjamin (see above) contrasts narrative and information: "Information is cashiered at the very moment when it is new. Narrative is different; it never exhausts itself. It retains its power within itself and is still capable of releasing it much later" (p. 416). He illustrates this from Herodotus' story about King Psammetichus of Egypt (Hist. II, 4), and says: "He explains nothing. His account is the driest (in contrast with later attempts at explanation). So this story from ancient Egypt is still able, after thousands of years, to arouse amazement and reflection. It is like the grain of seed which has lain shut up for millennia in the air-tight chambers of the pyramids and preserved its vital power up to the present day" (ibid.). One can say the same of the patriarchal stories. This, however, has profound methodological consequences. The exegete, therefore, cannot assume the task of depriving these old narratives of their ongoing dynamism by synthesizing them in a single statement. The exegetical process cannot explain so much in a narrative that there remains nothing more to listen to. The exegete must watch over the boundaries between what can and what cannot be explained. The narrative must remain a narrative even after the explanation. It cannot and must not be allowed to dissolve completely into the explanation. Scarcely any thought has been given to the independent significance of the narrative which sets a limit even to explanation. When this is recognized, the narrative is set in a much broader context. It is a matter of the relevance of narrative for theology and the idea of history broadly conceived. In both of these important fields storytelling and narrative have been misunderstood and devalued all along the line.

The Bible, both Old Testament and New, narrates for the most part something that has happened. When early Christianity came in contact with Greek thought, a theology of logically stringent argument took over: ". . .Christianity did not remain a storytelling community. In contact with the hellenistic world, it lost its narrative innocence" (H. Weinrich, *Concilium* 9 [1973] 331). Christian theology found it necessary to transpose the narrative elements of the Bible into teaching; "the biblical narratives were put into logic" (ibid.). This process has had its effects on exegesis even to the present day. Theological relevance was disallowed to narratives as such; only what could be abstracted from them, be it intellectual, theological or historical, had significance. Today, one can once more set the thesis of "narrative theology" (H. Weinrich) over against the domination of logically stringent theology or, as J. B. Metz puts it: the "inauguration of narrative remembrance and the emphasis on its cognitive precedence in theology" (*Concilium* 9 [1973] 329). This new concern to reinstate storytelling in its hereditary rights makes a special contribution to the exegesis of the patriarchal story, because storytelling about one's ancestors or fathers is one of the sources of all storytelling.

    The relevance of storytelling for the understanding of history.   W. Benjamin (op. cit.) notes that storytelling stands at the beginning of Greek (Herodotus) as well as of modern historical science (the chronicles of the Middle Ages); but it has been more and more excluded. "If not only the exact sciences, but historical science as well, despise storytelling more and more, then the question arises whether it has any rightful place at all in contemporary society" (H. Weinrich, op. cit., p. 333). Historical science has thereby lost an aspect which linked history with experience, both external and internal, on the personal level. The Old Testament was still able to make use of historical narratives in the books of Judges, Samuel, and Kings. The renewed awareness of the importance of storytelling for history as a whole can have a broadening effect; it can extend history's objectified understanding of reality, which is confined within the narrow alternative, true or untrue, to the wider plain of event, experience, and involvement. It can contribute also to overcome the split between objective history and tradition which historical science has created: "The victory of historicism has transformed tradition (even what has been handed down as remembered narrative) into objective history, i.e., into something that historical reason can critically reconstruct. Objective history has taken the place of tradition" (J. B. Metz, op. cit., p. 340).

Once it has been recognized that narrative has its own independent contribution to make to the explanation of the patriarchal story, and that its effects carry over to theology as a whole and to the understanding of history, we can go a step further. We can raise the question of the relationship between the polished narrative passed on as such, and the ordinary unpolished storytelling such as occurs in everyday life.

It is worth noting that this question has not yet been asked, though it is obvious enough. One of the functions of everyday storytelling is to allow others to share in situations and events of which they know nothing, but which it is important that they hear of and "experience," e.g., when two people have been apart for a time and the one who comes back tells of his experiences, or when two friends or lovers tell each other of their lives before they met. In both cases it is a vital interest that motivates the storytelling.

The connection with the patriarchal stories is clear: their intention is to give the listener a share in situations and events of which that person knows nothing, but which it is important for him to hear of and to experience, because the narratives deal with his fathers. The connection remains, though the narratives in the form into which they have been shaped are far removed from everyday storytelling. Communicative storytelling gives rise to narrative which presents what has happened. The listeners are no longer the immediate descendants; the fathers have now become the ancestors. But the motivation has remained. The narratives may well serve the secondary purpose of amusement, religious declaration, or answering current questions; but their primary function remains, namely, to give each new generation a share in the experiences, both external and internal, of the events and dramas which the fathers themselves lived through.

Narrative derives from everyday storytelling; this is the reason why the form-critical explanation, insofar as it is applied to narrative, can cover only one aspect of it and not the whole. The form in itself is not sufficient to distinguish the types of narrative; what is narrated—the content—is indispensable. This, too, is rooted in the derivation of narrative from everyday storytelling whose primary function is to share; hence the experiences and the drama, what actually happened, are the things that are important for the narrator and the listener. The decisive point of divergence is that the arc of tension, which shapes the narrative into a self-contained whole, is not necessary in everyday storytelling; here the narrator lets the memory issue spontaneously into word without any concern for rigid form. It is told as it is received. Where this mutual interest in giving and receiving the experience of others is lacking, there is lacking even the capacity to tell a story; where it is extinct, storytelling too is extinct.

It is because of this peculiar quality that storytelling and reports coalesce here. Typical of everyday storytelling is the formula "and then," which really belongs to the report, not to narrative, and which can be used quite offhandedly to string together very different material after the manner of an enumeration, rather than of a narrative proper. This is consistent with the interest of everyday storytelling because the one wants to tell everything, the other to hear everything. Storytelling, which presupposes a personal relationship between narrator and listener, emerges from the limited perspective of the personal and everyday into the broader perspective of a wider circle of people: storytelling becomes narrative. It becomes a finished work with an arc of tension which throws into relief the event presented as something special, out of the ordinary, worthy of being remembered and narrated. It is here that there first emerges a difference between narrative and report, with different forms and different function. Only now can the narrative be passed on as a finished work; the listeners, in turn, can narrate it. Reporting and the report acquire on the other hand other independent functions. Narrative, as a finished work, retains, however, one essential aspect of everyday storytelling: its content, that which moves up to a climax and down again to a resolution, can be greatly varied; moreover, one can comprehend and specify the event which is narrated—the drama which was formed into a story—only in content, not according to form. The specific content has always to do with the group of people, its way of life, form of community and interests, among whom the narrative was told and heard.

It follows from the relationship of the finished narrative to the as yet unpolished, everyday storytelling, in the first place that narrative is the common property of mankind. Just as storytelling is part of personal community life together, so is narrative, which grows out of it, part of human life. One can understand then why the basic structure of a narrative, as well as the "epic laws" (A. Olrik), are common to all. It follows, further, that both everyday storytelling and narrative are an event in the community. Consequently, when narratives are explained, when they are classified according to types and their function is studied, the first question that must be raised concerns the sort of community in which they arose. It follows, finally, that the function of narrative is not to be found primarily in the sphere of entertainment. This can of course be an additional secondary function; but the primary function derives from everyday storytelling: in storytelling there is sharing, giving, and receiving. New horizons are opened in all storytelling. Every time a story is told, the world of the listeners is broadened. Moreover, storytelling always has a significance that goes beyond mere entertainment; it has the power to open perspectives. If today the vitality of storytelling is restricted almost exclusively to children, the reason is that it retains for them the power to disclose.

It is possible now to set on a new basis the complicated and apparently futile discussion about the types of narrative, tale (*Märchen*), folk story (*Sage*), myth, legend, etc. The confusion is at its worst when a succession of scholars both past and present use these terms so differently in the different European languages. This uncertainty is an indication that generally convincing criteria have not yet been found for the determination of the types of narrative. There can be a fundamental change only when the narrative type is no longer determined by designations of the genres, which have been coined from a group of narratives limited in time and place and then generalized, such as folk story (*Sage*), myth, legend. The point of departure must be individual groups of narratives which belong together in time and place, and these must take their determination, as has not been done in the past, from the total course of the narrative. Side by side with the overlapping criteria of form (the narrative structure as a whole and their application in detail, the "laws of epic") must stand as equally important the criteria of content, which derive from the type of episode narrated—from the group of people among whom and about whom the narrative ranges, their way of life, their forms of community, their interests. Of primary importance is the relationship of the personal circles treated by the narrative to the group to which it is told.

It is neither necessary nor even profitable to classify the patriarchal story under such a distinctive term as *Sage*. We have here narratives which are adequately qualified as "patriarchal stories" or narratives about Israel's ancestors. It is not necessary to enter into a detailed discussion about them in this introduction. I have described the state of the question in *Erträge der Forschung. Genesis 12–50* (1975) 10-20. I refer further to the detailed synthesis of J. A. Wilcoxen (in J. H. Hayes, ed., *O.T. Form Criticism* [1974] 57-98) who gives a very good survey of the history of form criticism from Gunkel and Gressmann to the present.

IV. The Types of Narrative: Folk Story (Sage), Tale (Märchen), Legend, Myth.

The Folk Story (Sage).   The majority of studies on the nature of the patriarchal stories classify them as folk stories (*Sagen*), e.g. H. E. Ryle (1892), H. Gressmann (1910), H. Gunkel (*Komm.*), J. Skinner (*Comm.*), O. Eissfeldt (1923, 1927), O. Procksch (*Komm.*), A. Bentzen (*Intro.* 1948-49), K. Koch (1964, 1974[3]; Eng. 1969); see Lit. B; also the articles by B. D. Eerdmans and E. Jacob in RGG[2]. Any classification under the heading of myth or tale is rejected. They are then classified as folk stories so as to set them apart from historical writing. A. Dillmann writes in his commentary: "Now it is quite obvious that all these narratives about the patriarchal period are not history in the strict sense, but belong to the realm of folk story. . . .. But is this a reason for denying them, one and all, any historical content?" In opposition to the purely literary understanding of the patriarchal story on the part of J. Wellhausen and his school, Gunkel's slogan, "Genesis is a collection of folk stories (*Sagen*)," had the polemical function of pointing out that the single narratives were originally independent and part of oral tradition. The term "folk story" (*Sage*) fulfilled this function and was current at the time. It becomes difficult when one wants to define *Sage* more accurately to specify its relationship to other forms of narrative, and in particular to classify the patriarchal stories under the heading of *Sage*. The essential characteristics of the *Sage* are specified very differently; the terms in the different languages (*saga, Sage, legend, légende*) do not allow reduction to any common denominator, and no agreement has been reached as to which texts are to be classified as *Sagen*. One who has grown up in German-speaking lands and culture tends to identify the word *Sage* with the hero stories (*Heldensagen*) either of classical antiquity or of German tradition (according to E. Petsch the *Sage* is a "particular way of talking about the heroic" DVFLG 10 [1932]; Lit. B). The term is applicable without further ado to the narratives from the period of the judges, Judg. 3:15-19; 4 (cf. L. Alonso-Schökel Bib 42 [1961] 143-166); it is difficult to apply it to the patriarchal stories because they are so different in tone, material, and language.

There has been no basically new approach to a more precise determination of the relationship of the patriarchal stories to the *Sagen* since Gunkel and Gressmann. It is sufficient to refer to some of the syntheses: O. Eissfeldt, *Introduction* [1956[2]; Eng. 1965] §5; A. Bentzen, *Introduction* [1948-49]; E. Jacob, RGG[3] V [1961] 1302-1308; G. Fohrer in *Sagen und ihre Deutung* [1965] 59-80;

K. Koch [1964, 1974[3]; Eng. 1969]; J. A. Wilcoxen, in J. H. Hayes, ed., *O.T. Form Criticism* 58-69; J. Van Seters, *Abraham*. . . [1975] 131-138; H. J. Hermisson, *Enzyklopädie des Märchen*, 1 [1977] 419-441.

It is certainly no accident that students of comparative literature have newly discovered the peculiar nature of the patriarchal stories over against other texts which are listed as *Sagen*. A. Jolles (*Einfache Formen* [1930, 1958[2]], referring to A. Heusler (*Die Anfänge der isländischen Sagen* [1914]), sees the family narrative as a special type. He finds it above all in the Icelandic sagas: "These sagas show how history exists only as family history. . . . They are no longer what we call private events; . . .rather, this area now becomes public." He finds the same type in the biblical patriarchal stories, which he distinguishes sharply from the presentation of "what happens in the house of David. . . . The attitude here is completely different" (p. 87). The special feature is not just that the narratives are played out within the family circle. This is not one circle next to another; rather family and society coincide. E. Auerbach finds the same, but in another way, in his comparison of Gen. 22 with the return of Odysseus: ". . .finally, domestic realism, the representation of daily life, remains in Homer in the peaceful realm of the idyllic, whereas, from the very first, in the Old Testament stories, the sublime, tragic, and problematic take shape precisely in the domestic and commonplace. . . . The sublime influence of God here reaches so deeply into the everyday that the two realms of the sublime and the everyday are not actually unseparated but basically inseparable" (*Mimesis* [1946; Eng. 1953; Anchor Books, 1957], p. 19). Where the family event is what determines reality, where family and society coincide, what happens is no longer trite. The decisive reason for this, according to Auerbach, is that God is involved in the event and determines it. Only when one realizes this can one perceive the peculiar nature of the patriarchal story.

The Etiological Folk Story.   The lively discussion about the etiological sagas or "etiologies" has been synthesized by F. Golka (VT 20 [1970] 90-98; 26 [1976] 410-428; Diss. [1972]) and J. A. Wilcoxen (in J. Hayes, ed., *O.T. Form Criticism* [1974]). The discussion has taken two directions: one is concerned with the question whether or not the etiological narrative as such is historical (A. Alt [1929]; M. Noth [1950], Lit. B; J. Bright [1959], Lit. A); the other with the criteria for determining etiological texts (B. S. Childs [1962 & 1974]; B. O. Long [1968], Lit. B). C. Westermann restricts etiological narratives to those which, taken as a whole, lead to an etiological conclusion (*Arten*. . . [1964]).

The formula "until this day" occurs in the following places in the patriarchal stories: Gen. 19:37-38; 22:14; 26:33; 32:32; 35:20; 47:26; 48:15. There is etiological narrative or motif, without the formula, when a present situation (object) is being explained from an event in the past which caused it, e.g., Gen. 16:14: "that is why men call. . . ." In Gen. 19:37-38 a present-day tribe, and in 16:14 a present-day place-name (or name of a well), is explained by an event in the patriarchal period. The formula "until this day" expresses an interval of time as well as continuity: the situation (object) which originated then is still there today. The continuity factor presupposes a way of life itself stamped by continuity; it is probable that such narratives are best understood in the context of a sedentary way of life. Etiological narratives cease with the advent of historical writing proper, where causal explanation of past events takes the place of the etiological. The conclusion is that they belong to the period before the formation of the state, that is, to the tribal period. The overwhelming number of etiological explanations occurs in texts dealing with the period from the taking of the land to the formation of the state (cf. F. Golka). It is more difficult to determine their *terminus a quo*. F. Golka, following C. Westermann, represents the view that the oldest layer of patriarchal stories (family narratives) is not yet familiar with the etiological explanation. The narratives and motifs in Gen. 12–50 which are obviously etiological would belong, therefore, to later layers which originated in the tribal period (e.g., Gen. 19:37-38: Moab and Ammon). Insofar as they are independent narratives, they can be described as folk stories (*Sagen*), place stories, tribal stories, because they belong to the same period and form of community as the hero stories (*Heldensagen*).

It can be taken as certain that the patriarchal narratives, the oldest layers of which go back to the patriarchal period, have been reshaped and adapted as they have been handed down across the centuries. It is in this process that the etiological motifs were added, which belong to the period of the tribes and their subsequent settlement.

The Tale (Märchen).   It is remarkable that Gunkel and Gressmann, who declared so emphatically that the patriarchal stories are folk stories, could also say that they are really tales (*Märchen*) or originated out of tales. They are following W. Wundt here (1909, II 3), who held that the tale was the oldest form of all narrative, and that the myth and folk story had developed from it. There are, to be sure, some motifs in the patriarchal stories with which we are familiar from the tales, e.g., the youngest son who goes away to make his fortune. However, more recent study of the tale has shown that one cannot draw the conclusion that Gunkel and Gressmann drew. The first reason for this is that the study of the tale (folklore study) has been extended so as to cover the whole world, and the European tale (the fairy tale) is, in so broad a background, but one of many distinct forms of folktale. The motif just mentioned as an example is found all over the world, and in types of folktale which are not at all like ours. The second reason is methodological. The work of V. Propp (*Morphology of the Folk Tale* [Russ. 1928; Eng. 1968², 1975]) and E. Metelinskij (1972, Lit. B) has shown that the tale is to be understood as a whole; the function of each motif is to be explained only from the whole. One can no longer specify and group tales from individual motifs (in general, see K. Ranke, ed., *Enzyklopädie des Märchens* [1977]).

The consequence of the results of the study of folklore is that the study of the patriarchal stories must carry out its comparative work with more discrimination than hitherto. It is no longer enough to demonstrate a folktale motif in a text in Gen. 12–50. One must learn to distinguish between types of tales which have no relationship at all to the patriarchal narratives (e.g., tales of magic), and those folktales which show unmistakable parallels. M. Lüthi states: in the folktale "the family plays a dominant role. . .; it is one of the essential structural elements. The articulation of the family assists the tale in its own articulation" (Fests. K. Ranke [1968] 181-195). One can say something similar about the patriarchal narratives too, whereas the role of the family in the folk story (*Sage*) is notably less. This observation about European tales is confirmed by P. Radin for narratives of the North American Indians where the persons concerned are, without exception, designated according to the families to which they belong (ErJb 17 [1949] 359-419). G. S. Kirk's findings are the same (*Myth. Its Meaning.* . . [1970-71]). Motifs occur here which have parallels in the patriarchal stories: rivalry among brothers, famine as a motif resolving a tension, the person turned to stone.

An essential difference between the patriarchal stories and the ordinary tale is that what is told in the tale remains indefinite as to time and place (cf. G. van der Leeuw, *Phänomenologie*. . . [1933; 1956²] §§ 1, 2); it is distinctive of the patriarchal stories that what happens is fixed in time (genealogies) and place (itineraries). The magical tale draws no definite boundary between human and animal, heaven and earth, time and place; it retains traits of magical thinking. There is not the slightest connection with anything like this in the patriarchal stories; they show practically no magical traits at all.

The Legend.   A. Jolles has specified what is peculiar to the legend as "the imitable." S. Sudhof has described the legend and its history in StGen 11 (1959) 691-699. The very term *legend* indicates its setting in life: legends are the texts to be read at religious gatherings. Monastic communities have retained this practice right up to the present day. The setting in life itself makes it clear that the purpose of the legends is to present something to be imitated in the life, conduct, or suffering of the subject(s) of the narrative. They presuppose a particular religious community, a group assembled for the purpose of religious edification. Accordingly, they occur only in the late Old Testament period, where we know of such groups and circles. Only the narratives of Daniel 1–7 are legends in the strict sense (cf. R. M. Hals, CBQ 34 [1972] 166-176).

Narratives about the founding of a sanctuary, e.g., Gen. 28:10-21, should not be described as "cult legends," as they are by many scholars. The form "legend" is excluded from Gen. 12–50 because its very name indicates a literary origin.

The Myth.   There has been in recent times a broadening of the understanding of myth; the scope of the adjective "mythical" now knows no limits (besides, there is often no clear distinction between "mythical" and "mythological"). Further, the alternative which would describe reality either as myth or history is questionable; it is a mentality whose standpoint is clearly the second possibility. Yet another contribution to the lack of clarity in the question of myth is that the concept has been extended to all kinds and stages of culture, as if the myth were a timeless phenomenon which could appear in any place and at any time. One must distinguish first of all between the myths of the high cultures, characterized by a dramatic happening among several gods with its two main themes of war and love, and the "myths" of early cultures, in which there is usually only one god or supreme being whose other partners in the happening are men. One must distinguish further between primeval myths and those which presuppose the existence of something beyond. The former describe a happening which constitutes the basis of the reality beyond, or part of it. These are the myths of creation, the flood, the founding of civilization, and others. A subdistinction is to be made here between stories about the gods and stories in which the happening takes place between a god and man. The primeval narratives of the Old Testament belong here; they are not myths in the strict sense (cf. *Genesis 1–11*, 22-26, 57-60, and "Myths" in the index).

One can speak of three steps when looking at the function of myth. The first stage regarded myths as literary works. The second was determined by the discovery of the correlation between myth and ritual (S. Mowinckel, I. Engnell, G. Widengren, S. H. Hooke, and others), a phenomenon discovered also in the early civilizations (A. E. Jensen, *Mythos und Kult*. . . [1951], Lit. B). In the third stage it became clear when looking at the early civilizations that the function of myth was not to be limited to ritual; it is now seen to function to determine the whole of existence; so R. Pettazoni, M. Eliade, G. van der Leeuw; also B. Malinowski and H. Baumann; and the structuralists like C. Lévi-Strauss as well as P. Radin, G. S. Kirk, and others. This was accompanied by a gradual broadening of the concept of myth, and showed itself in biblical studies for example, with J. Hempel's definition: ". . .that which we call myth, the direct action of God among humans" (ZAW 65 [1953] 109-167). As a consequence, the patriarchal stories became involved in the question of myth.

Because the primitive "myths" have the character of simple folktales, both were brought together. The title of the first part of G. S. Kirk's book (*Myth. Its Meaning*. . . [1970-71]) is "Myth, Ritual and Folktale"; he says of a group of the myths: "This small group of myths is obviously concerned with family relationship. . . ." P. Radin likewise emphasizes the fluid transition between folktale and myth; he admits that myths developed out of folktales (ErJb 17 [1949] 17ff.). Some scholars understand the establishing of sanctuaries by means of divine appearances as myths; e.g., G. H. Davies: what happens in an epiphany is typical of myth (PEQ 88 [1956] 83ff.).

A quite different point of contact results if my view proves true (see below, on Promise), namely, that many myths are recastings of older nonmythical narratives (similarly, P. Radin) which show similarities to the patriarchal stories. K. Koch has already pointed in this direction (1967, Lit. B). The sequence of motifs—childlessness with the father's complaint, promise of the son, birth of the son—occur in the Keret and Aqhat epic texts from Ugarit, just as in the Abraham narratives. And so a further question arises: behind the myths which describe what happens among gods as predominantly a family event, is there a prehistory in which the same event took place with men as actors? But this is no more than a suggestion.

It follows that the patriarchal stories have no relation to myth in the proper sense of the word. There can only be points of contact either where folk stories are designated as "myths" or where an older form lies behind the myth.

V. Genealogies and Itineraries.   Those people among whom the patriarchal stories arose found their own self-understanding in the regular occurrence of the temporal passing of the generations, that is, in the constantly occurring succession of generations: the birth of a child and its growing up, marriage and begetting a child, old age and death. This came to linguistic expression in the genealogies.

They found as they wandered that the way of the migrant was the constantly happening, regular event across the march of space. This came to linguistic expression in the itineraries.

The genealogy and the itinerary differ from every type of narrative in that they are enumerative in form (*Genesis 1–11*, Intro. 2). The enumerative forms of speech stand in a clearly recognizable relationship to the narrative: what is told begins with a constantly recurring event and comes back to it. If a woman is infertile (Gen. 11:30), the constant course of events is interrupted; something extraordinary happens, which the narrative takes up. If a group is mortally threatened by a famine on its way, the constant course of the journey is interrupted; something extraordinary happens, which the narrative takes up. Now, it follows from this that the forms which describe a constantly recurring event are part of the life of nonwriting groups, just as are the narratives, and hence must go back to the stage of oral tradition. The opinion of the founders of the form-critical explanation of the patriarchal stories, Gunkel and Gressmann, needs revision here; they held that both genealogy and itinerary were literary creations serving to bind the passages together; in this they supported Wellhausen's explanation (cf. *Genesis 1–11*, Intro. 2). The same holds for M. Noth's opinion about the genealogies, namely, that they were secondary formations arising out of the narratives themselves. R. R. Wilson has given a detailed refutation of this view (Lit. B, Genealogy [1972 and 1975]; *Genealogy and History in the Biblical World* [1977]).

Now that it has been demonstrated that the enumerative forms go back to the oral stage of tradition, our view of it is modified very considerably. If one then accepts Gunkel's designation of the patriarchal stories as "poetic narratives," it is now certain that not only these, but also the dry enumeration of a succession of events in time and place, containing no climax at all, belong to the oldest layer of Gen. 12–50. Both "poetry" and "prose" are there together.

This is important for the overall understanding of the patriarchal stories because it reveals a twofold interest on the part of the early oral tradition. The extraordinary events, standing out from the commonplace, which are the object of the narratives are not narrated just because they are extraordinary; rather, they are anchored in a succession of events in time and place which is independent of these narratives and is handed on only because of its factualness. The setting of the narratives in a constant succession of events shows that they, too, intend something that really happened.

Genealogies and itineraries belong together because they present the constantly recurring, that is, they are enumerative; however, apart from this, they have little in common and must be dealt with separately.

Genealogies. (In general, see *Genesis 1–11*, Intro. part 2. For the genealogies in the patriarchal story, see R. R. Wilson, JBL 94 [1975] 169-189; *Genealogy. . .* [1977].) M. Noth had made the distinction between genuine (or "primary") and secondary genealogies (*A History of Pentateuchal Traditions* [1948; Eng. 1972]); he assigned the patriarchal genealogies without exception to the secondary, and explained them as literary constructions, created to link the narratives together (similar to Wellhausen's explanation); the names were taken from the narratives. Wilson, in his study of the Old Testament genealogies, makes use not only of the middle eastern genealogies, but also of the oral genealogies researched by anthropologists; he demonstrates that only these can show the genealogies' real function. Following the results of this research he distinguishes linear genealogies, e.g., Gen. 5, and segmented genealogies, e.g., Gen. 36. The latter present the relationship to each other of the members of a group classified into families by means of their descent. It is the form which originates within the living group; its origins are oral and it is handed down orally. It has a fluidity about it, because it must be adapted to the changes in the group.

Wilson's study has shown that the Old Testament genealogies cannot be understood apart from their oral prehistory; this opens up their vitally important function for forms of community determined by family structures. He has demonstrated by a series of examples that the patriarchal genealogies cannot be mere literary constructions; they must go back to genealogies which had such a function in the community. Contrary to the valuation of the genealogies hitherto, Wilson has rightly rejected as not pertinent the question whether or not they are to be regarded as historical. Their purpose is not to present history; nevertheless, they were held to be in accord with what really happened. Contradictions are to be explained by the necessary fluidity; two contradictory genealogies are to be explained by two different functions in the changing community.

It follows, therefore, that one must raise the question of an oral prehistory for each individual patriarchal genealogy. In any case, it is to be presupposed that the genealogies had a vitally important function in the communities which portray the patriarchal stories. They served to specify the position of the individual in the community to which he belonged; at the same time, by demonstrating descent from one father, they showed the homogeneity of the group and its history. The problems derive from the fact that they are concerned with two stages, that of the tribes and that of the smaller groups with family structures, before the tribes united together. It is generally acknowledged that the twelve sons of Jacob are related to the Israelite tribes (A. Malamat, Lit. A, General [1967]; Lit. B, Genealogy [1973]; R. R. Wilson, *Genealogy*. . . [1977]).

Besides genealogies related to the tribes, Gen.12–50 also contains genealogies related to families or clans, e.g., 23:1-3,18-19, Sarah's death and burial. Only each particular context can show how they are to be distinguished and to which stage of tradition they belong.

Itineraries.   The itineraries are much more restricted in importance than the genealogies. The family and the sense of belonging to a family as expressed in the genealogies is something common to mankind; it remains permanent as the life-styles change. Itineraries are concerned only with a particular life-style, that of the wanderer. They are part of the nomadic way of life, where they determine the whole existence of the wandering group, even when its life-style has two sides, partly nomadic and partly sedentary.

The itinerary is of marginal importance in the completely sedentary life; it belongs to particular undertakings, to journeys, campaigns, business enterprises, and adventures. And so the form of the itinerary changes: it is no longer a simple matter of migrations with stopping places, departures, and settlements; the framework is now departure and return. One can already see clear signs of this distinction in some passages in the patriarchal stories. The difference between genealogies and itineraries is that the genealogy is of importance for mankind in general, whereas the itinerary is restricted to a distinctive life-style of distinctive groups; this is noticeable in Genesis in that the genealogy has an importance which is determinative throughout the primeval history, while the itinerary is first found in the transition from mankind in general to the popular narrative stories of a particular group in process of migration (cf. *Genesis 1–11*, on 11:2). The first itinerary appears at the end of the primeval story and is continued in the verses at the end of Gen. 11, which form the transition to the patriarchal story which tells of the migration of Abraham and his forefathers; this alone shows that those who passed on Genesis considered that the itinerary, as well as the genealogy, was essential and gave structure to the whole, even though preserved in only a relatively few short texts.

The itineraries are of greater importance for the presentation of the wanderings in the desert (Exodus and Numbers). Num. 33:1-49 is the tradition of a comprehensive itinerary that enumerates the stages of journey from the city of Rameses in Egypt to the lowlands of Moab before the crossing of the Jordan. Studies on the itinerary have taken this text as the starting point: G. W. Coats (1972) and G. I. Davies (1974) (Lit. B, Genealogy). Davies' use of the parallel material from the ancient near east and from Greece and Rome is particularly valuable ("Itineraries in the Ancient World," pp. 52-78). The conclusion is: "The itinerary is certainly a literary genre which has its Sitz im Leben in administrative circles" (pp. 80f.). He defines it by noting that in the itinerary "interest is concentrated on the process of movement from place to place"; it is to be distinguished from other reports of journeys "by the repeated use of a stereotyped formula and the continuity of its references to movement" (p. 47). There are many cases where the function of the itineraries is clearly recognizable. One who is responsible gives an account of an expedition, a campaign or some such enterprise. This is the basic reason for the judgment that the itineraries were not invented: "None of the examples studied are obviously fictional" (p. 77). By means of the parallels (beginning from the early Babylonian period), Davies has determined the setting in life and the function of the itineraries; in this he has made an important step beyond M. Noth, who distinguishes between secondary and genuine itineraries (*A History of Pentateuchal Traditions* [1948; 1972], "Itineraries"), but does not ask about their function or their occurrence outside the Old Testament.

The itineraries in the patriarchal stories are of course essentially different from the near eastern and classical parallels, which presuppose a politically structured community, determined for the most part by kingship. They are different, too, from the itineraries in Exodus and Numbers which are concerned with a completely different sort of group on its way from Egypt through the wilderness to Canaan. This is also the reason why the patriarchal itineraries cannot have the same function, namely, to give an account of an enterprise to a higher authority. Nevertheless, they have something in common. The definition given by Davies holds also for the patriarchal itineraries, which make use of the same formula pattern of departure, stop, and arrival. A particularly important point of contact between the wilderness itineraries (p. 50) and the official itineraries of the great empires (pp. 57f., 66) is that the formula pattern can be interrupted by a brief mention of events which happened at particular stopping places. Num. 33:38-39 reports the death of Aaron; Alexander's Σταθμοί contains elaborations consisting of "unfamiliar legends, marvels of natural history, strange local customs. . ." (p. 66). Such sequential agreement constrains one to accept a distinctive form of the same *genre* in the patriarchal itinerary (M. Noth maintains that the patriarchal itineraries are secondary, i.e., constructions).

It is difficult to determine the patriarchal itineraries further; the texts are too few, and none has so far been found that is immediately comparable. So much can be said: the migratory groups of the patriarchal period preserved in the itineraries their stopping places along the route. They did this probably because the routes and the stopping places described the "history" of the group and also because it was important for related nomadic groups as well as for future generations to know these routes. The itineraries could thus form the framework for information or narratives about events which happened on the route or at the stopping places.

The itineraries are by no means uniformly distributed through Gen. 12–50, nor are they constant in their form. The ordinary, simple itinerary is concentrated in Gen. 12–25 and in the short Isaac tradition (ch. 26). Gen. 13:18 is typical of the simple itinerary:

> So Abraham moved his tent
> and went

and settled by the terebinths of Mamre at Hebron
(and there he built an altar).

Or 19:30:

And Lot went up from Zoar
and settled in the hill country. . .
and he lived in a cave. . ..

There is a concentration of this sort at the beginning of Gen. 12–25: Gen 11:31; 12:5; 12:2-7; 12:8; 12:9; 13:18; to which can be added 19:30 and 20:1. All these passages belong to a broader context—the migrations of Abraham and Lot. Gen. 21:22f., and the itineraries of the Isaac tradition (ch. 26) belong to another context.

Itineraries are linked with the motif of the dispute about the well; however, they are missing in the promise narratives (Gen. 15–18) and in the detailed narratives appended at the end of Gen. 22; 23; and 24. One can conclude from this that in an earlier stage of tradition the itinerary formed the frame for a group of Abraham narratives.

Itineraries of the same sort occur also in Gen. 25–36 (33:17-20; 35:8; 35:16-22a; 35:27-29), but they are more on the periphery. It is another form that predominates here: instead of a one-way route with stopping places, there is the journey which starts from a particular point and returns to it; it is structured according to departure and return, not according to a succession of stopping places. It grew out of the sedentary way of life.

There are traces of the itinerary only at the beginning and the end of Gen. 37–50, where they are tied to the Joseph tradition. There are practically no places in the Joseph narrative proper; local fixation, and hence the old itinerary pattern, was no longer of any importance for what is narrated there.

3. The World of the Patriarchal Story and Its Setting: The Question of the Time of the Patriarchs

A. The Modern Archaeological Approach

One of the most radical of the new approaches in the study of the patriarchal stories has been the attempt by means of archaeological discoveries to arrive at direct attestation for the material in the narratives. This new approach was of profound importance. It opened up possibilities never as yet envisaged or tried in the whole course of research, namely, to explain texts, parts of texts, or elements in them by finds which were contemporaneous with facts, names, and events in these texts—a truly fascinating proposal when one considers that thereby a path of tradition extending over thousands of years could be abridged directly by the discovery of contemporaneous material.

Two factors led to this new approach: the one was the result of the history of the study of the patriarchal stories, the other of the rise of archaeology. The critical hypothesis of J. Wellhausen (*Die Composition des Hexateuchs und der historischen Bücher* [1876-1878; 1963[4]]), that the patriarchal stories are to be understood as but a retrojection from the period of the Israelite monarchy, had made a deep impression. The dominance of the literary-critical method facilitated agreement with the hypothesis; the exegete then was certainly dealing with writers from the monarchical period (J and E). Conservative exegesis, which opposed this and wanted to hold on to the historicity of Abraham, Isaac, and Jacob, lacked effective arguments. It was archaeology that supplied them. One can understand, therefore, that the most important goal of all those scholars interested in the new approach was to prove the historicity of the patriarchal figures and period, and this meant victory for them over an outmoded denial of it.

The second factor was the result of the rise and rapid development of archaeology as one of the most promising branches of historical science. Its achievement had been tremendous and its explorations had thrown a great deal of light on the history of the ancient near east. The history of Israel, from the occupation of the land on, had been greatly advanced by archaeological work in the near east and then in Palestine; the next step was obviously to go back into the early period and tackle the question of the results of archaeology and the patriarchs, Abraham, Isaac, and Jacob. The title of L. Woolley's book, *Excavations at Ur: A Record of Twelve Years Work* * [1954], is an impressive example of the way in which Mesopotamian archaeology impinged on the study of the patriarchal stories. In the preface the author recalled the beginning of the excavations in 1854 by the British consul in Basra, J. E. Taylor: "Here he unearthed inscriptions which for the first time revealed that the nameless ruin was none other than Ur, so-called 'of the Chaldees,' the home of Abraham" (p. 9). The new, attractive possibility of laying an archaeological foundation for the patriarchal stories from the finds in places which are mentioned in the narratives is rather forcibly suggested by the subtitle of the book above.

The next inevitable step was that Old Testament scholars take advantage of what was offered here. There is scarcely a trace of this new path of scholarship in H. Gunkel's commentary (1901; 1922[3]), although he belonged to the school of the history of religion and had a very positive appreciation of archaeology. In J. Skinner's commentary (1910; 1951[3]) there is for the first time an expectation that archaeological work at the places mentioned in the patriarchal story can give new information. The change which can be discerned in M. Noth is instructive. In *A History of Pentateuchal Traditions* (1948; 1966[3]; Eng. 1972) the possibility that archaeology might be important for the patriarchal story did not so much as exist; in a later essay, "Der Beitrag der Archäologie zur Geschichte Israels" (VT.S 7 [1960] 262-282), particularly in discussion with American Old Testament scholars, he no longer contested the possibility, even though he retained a reserved attitude.

The consciousness of the archaeological approach is exemplified by W. F. Albright in the introduction to his work, *From the Stone Age to Christianity* (1940; 1957[3]), which he entitles: "The Archaeological Revolution." There is a ring of triumph in his conclusion about the patriarchal stories in *The Biblical Record* (1950): "The archaeological discoveries of the past generations have changed all this [namely, the thesis of Wellhausen]. . . . There is scarcely a single biblical historian who has not been impressed by the rapid accumulation of data supporting the substantial historicity of patriarchal tradition" (p. 3). The practical conclusion resulting from the archaeological approach was that a circle of scholars and a multitude of popular works accepted the historicity of the patri-

---

*Translator's note: The comments in the remainder of this paragraph presuppose the German title of Woolley's book, *Ur in Chaldäa, zwölf Jahre Ausgrabungen in Abrahams Heimat* (1956) [Ur of the Chaldees: Twelve Years of Excavation in the Homeland of Abraham].

archs as definitively proven—a remarkable change from the Wellhausen era. One must emphasize, moreover, that the starting point of a conservative attitude to the patriarchal traditions entailed a grateful acceptance by the conservative wing of interpreters of the arguments offered by archaeology for the historicity of the patriarchs, as is evident in the important article of H. Cazelles (DBS 7 [1961] 81-156). One must acknowledge and admire the achievements of this archaeological investigation, especially by the Americans, but also by the French, English, Israelis, and Dutch. The studies related directly or indirectly to the patriarchal story constitute an extensive and segmented literature which would be difficult to survey comprehensively. It is to be expected that archaeological investigation will yield yet further results in abundance.

A limitation of the archaeological approach is that its "evidence" refers almost without exception to single elements in the patriarchal narratives, not to the narratives as wholes. There is a substantial difference here from the extra-Israelite parallels to Genesis 1–11, where the biblical narratives can be compared with complete extrabiblical narratives, as in the flood story. There is no such parallel in Gen. 12–50. Another limitation is that, because of the absence of direct and integral parallels, it has not yet succeeded in determining the time of the patriarchs with any sort of unanimity. Those studies which reject the archaeological approach point justly to this fact, e.g., T. L. Thompson (BZAW 133 [1974], and J. Van Seters (*Abraham in History*. . .. [1975]), who writes: "There has been little movement in the last fifty years towards agreement in when, within the second millennium, the patriarchs actually lived" (p. 8). This cannot be denied. One should compare also the presentation of R. de Vaux (*The Early History of Israel* [1971; Eng. 1978] 257-266). The period assigned is so different because it is based on single details; but if the period in which the patriarchs are set still fluctuates between 2200 and 1200, then one can speak of a patriarchal period only with the greatest reservation. Further, one can make use of parallels or proofs (evidence) only with caution, all the more so because the points of comparison between the patriarchal stories and the surrounding world deal almost without exception with phenomena which, of their very nature, cannot be fixed within a definite time span. This holds for names of peoples, places, and persons, for practices and customs, for life-styles and forms of community, and for laws. All these phenomena can, under certain circumstances, be set within definite time spans and periods of change, but never, or as good as never, in such a way as to pin them down with historical exactness. One must concede that in the last 50 years the many and extraordinarily different attempts to fix the patriarchal period have, for the most part, not been sufficiently based. It is understandable, then, that in the recent studies mentioned the archaeological approach to the elucidation of the patriarchal stories has been comprehensively contested, and one has gone back to a position close to the thesis of Wellhausen (T. L. Thompson, J. Van Seters, and others).

A weakness of the archaeological approach is that its explanation of the patriarchal stories by means of the discoveries has, for the most part, been too isolated. One has often presupposed that when one has proved that a particular name or custom which occurs in the Old Testament also occurs in documents of the second millennium, one has thereby proved the patriarchal texts had their origin there as well. But such a proof remains uncertain as long as the path of the tradition from the early or middle second millennium down to the present text has not been demonstrated step by step. It is not enough merely to maintain that one can reckon with the reliability of traditions which have remained intact across the centuries, whether this opinion has a basis or not. This does not explain the great variety of these traditions, which presupposes different kinds and periods of origin and passage. Archaeological evidence, e.g., evidence that the same or a similar nomadic way of life with its particular forms of economy is found in Mesopotamia of the second millennium as well as in the patriarchal narratives, is significant for the exegesis of the latter only when one can demonstrate all stages of the tradition which bridges the temporal and spatial interval between the two. Here both form criticism and traditio-historical criticism are indispensable: form criticism, to study the origin and original function of the tradition in a form of community appropriate to it; traditio-historical criticism, to inquire into the path of the tradition in its oral and written stages right down to its final form. Only then is a connection demonstrated between an identical or similar phenomenon which occurs both outside Israel and in the text of Genesis handed down to us. R. de Vaux has made an attempt to combine the archaeological with the form-critical and traditio-critical problem in his section on the patriarchal story (*The Early History of Israel* [1971; Eng. 1978] 153-287).

B. Migrations of Peoples in the Near East and Migrations of the Patriarchs

The thesis that the migrations of Abraham, Isaac, and Jacob belong within the great movements of peoples at the beginning or towards the middle of the second millennium made a deep and lasting impression on the study of the patriarchal stories. If this thesis could be soundly based, it would of itself secure a historical framework in which the patriarchal stories could be anchored in the history of the near east of the second millennium. This is one of the points of contact between the archaeological approach to the patriarchal stories and conservative study of the pre-Wellhausen era. The same thesis is already found in the commentaries of F. Delitzsch (1852; 1887[5]) and A. Dillmann (1875[3]; 1892[6]). Delitzsch writes: "The emigration with which it [the patriarchal story] begins was no mere family event—it was the beginning and perhaps even a motive force of a shift of peoples which has had far-reaching effects on the shape of the Mediterranean lands" (p. 277); similarly Dillmann (p. 216). As a matter of fact, it would be of the greatest significance for the whole understanding of the patriarchal story if the archaeological discoveries could raise this hypothesis to the level of historical certainty. But this has not yet happened, though most archaeologically determined presentations take it as proven with certainty. It is only recently that the connection between the movements of peoples in the near east and the migrations of the patriarchs has been contested.

R. de Vaux presented this connection in an earlier work as follows: ". . .the excavations at Chagar Bazar, Atchana, and chiefly Mari. . . tell us that between the end of the third dynasty at Ur around 2000 B.C. and the Golden Age of Mari in the 18th century there was a great change in population. In the time of the third dynasty of Ur, the basic population was Akkadian in all Upper Mesopotamia, but the kings of Mari in the 19th-18th centuries were West Semites, as were also, in the same period, the princes of Aleppo, Carchemish, and Qatna. West Semites also hold the power in Asshur. This change is only one local aspect of a far-flung movement affecting all the Fertile Crescent. This was the penetration and subsequent settling down of nomadic elements coming from the Syrian desert—those whom the cuneiform texts call the people of the West, 'the men of

Ammurru,' the Amorites'' (ThD 12 [1964] 230). De Vaux then draws the following conclusion: "It is difficult not to see in this situation a historical background which fits admirably with the traditions concerning the patriarchs" (p. 232); similarly J. Bright (*A History of Israel* [1959, 1972 rev. ed.], ch. 2). In his recent history, however, de Vaux writes much more cautiously (*The Early History of Israel* [1971; Eng. 1978]).

A distinction must be made between two factors in assessing this thesis which is supported by the overwhelming majority of recent exegetes. The fact that there were large movements of peoples in the Fertile Crescent in the second millennium is in itself significant, and the discovery of such movements by archaeological excavations is of the greatest importance for the history of the whole area in this period. A relationship to the patriarchal stories, though it be merely background, would only follow if it could be demonstrated from the stories themselves that they belonged to one of these particular movements.

The second factor is the nature of the patriarchal stories themselves: there is nothing in the accounts or memoranda of the migrations of the patriarchs that permits the conclusion that they are part of the great movements of peoples. The decisive criterion is the way in which these migrations are described. They are itineraries. They have two components: (1) information about the route, with the place of departure and the place of arrival; and (2) brief notes about events which happened on the way. Both components presuppose a small migratory group; neither provides any indication that they belong to a large group.

The conclusion must be, therefore, that the thesis that the migrations of the patriarchs belong within the great movements of peoples in the near east in the second millennium finds no support in the text of Genesis. R. de Vaux, after his painstaking study of attempts to fix the patriarchal period (1971; Eng. 1978, pp. 257-266), looks further for a solution (he is more reserved here than in his earlier works, as he notes on p. 263, n. 26); he looks to the broader context of the Amorite movements and sets the migrations to Canaan in the 19th-18th centuries; he expressly rejects the context of the Aramaic movements of the 14th-13th centuries, which M. Noth holds as probable. But to set the patriarchal migrations within the great movements of peoples in the second millennium could only mean either that they were part of these movements or that they took place as a consequence of them. The stories, however, show no trace at all of any connection, direct or indirect. At least such a hypothesis is not necessary to explain the migration of a quite small group such as is described in Gen. 12–50.

More problematic are the attempts to link particular details of the migrations of Gen. 12–50 with particular movements of peoples. The migration of Terah, the father of Abraham, from Ur to Haran is linked with the Amorite movement, in the course of which Ur III was destroyed, and that of Abraham from Haran to Canaan with the Aramaean movement. Both raise considerable difficulties, and even as hypotheses are scarcely tenable (J. Van Seters, *Abraham*. . . [1975], 23-26 and 29-34; T. L. Thompson, *The Historicity*. . . BZAW 133 [1974], ch. 4). Thompson says: "No movement whatever is discernible which resembles a movement from Ur towards the northwest to Harran. If a trend is to be noticed, it is in the opposite direction!" (p. 87). Van Seters makes a similar assertion. The same difficulties impede the attempt to link the migration of Abraham from Haran to Canaan with an Aramaean movement. (H. Cazelles distinguishes a first wave of Amorite movement with Abraham in the 18th century from a second, Aramaean, wave in the Amarna period.)

C. Peoples, Territories, and Cities

I. Preliminary Notes: Geographical. In the first place, names are not invented here. Rather we can presuppose that there is a tradition behind every name that occurs in Gen. 12–50 (individual exceptions are not to be excluded entirely). That is, each of these names has actually functioned as a name; what is designated in it was in fact so called. However, a restriction must be introduced at once: the currency of a name can be very limited both as to time and place. This leads to the second note: in principle, the geographical designations in Gen. 12–50 are not to be evaluated as historical in the modern sense, i.e., historically guaranteed, demonstrable names. The meaning of each of these names is rather to be found and explained in the context of its area of currency. The name does not yet exist as an abstract entity; the action of naming and the person who gives the name (or the group that gives it) belong indissolubly to the name. Consequently, the stability of a geographical name is the exception, the variation the rule. Earlier study, on the whole, was too unreflective and took as its starting point the modern abstract idea of a name; it is only recent study that has realized that we are, in most cases, in error when we expect to encounter something fixed, invariable, and precise in a name.

Further, the geographical designations in the patriarchal stories were used in the earliest stage of the tradition within very small groups; then gradually in larger and larger groups; and finally, in the latest stage, within the people of Israel, they achieved a more extensive stability in time and space. One must from the outset reckon with the fact that in the majority of cases a geographical designation has a meaning that is limited in time and space. Methodologically, therefore, the precise meaning of the name of a people, for example, can be discovered only by unravelling the tradition history of the particular designation; and for the most part there are not enough texts at our disposal to do so. Nevertheless, the most recent studies on the peoples of Israel's world have shown with certainty that in no case is an absolute specification of time, place, extent, etc., satisfactory. We have to do in each individual case with a variety of meanings, that is, with a history of meaning. There are considerable differences here: simple names of territories, rivers, mountains, mountain ranges, steppes, and deserts are more stable than names of places where people are active, that is, settlements, villages, cities, and names of groups—clans, tribes, and peoples. Names are extremely variable among these latter; one must be very careful about the interpretation here. Moreover, the names of groups and persons can be identical.

A necessary consequence for the exegesis of Gen. 12–50 is that one must pay special attention to the context in which each individual geographical designation occurs. It can mean something different from the same name in a text outside Gen. 12–50; it can also have different meanings in different places within these chapters.

II. The Amorites. The Amorite thesis has been of particular importance for the problem of the historicity of the patriarchs. We must, therefore, draw together our current knowledge of them. Only extrabiblical evidence has given access to this knowledge. The designation "Amorites" (Sumerian, MAR.TU; Akkadian, *Amurru*) has been used for more than two millennia, though not always with the same meaning. It covered at various periods the population of the whole area from the Euphrates to the border of Egypt. M. Liverani distinguishes four main meanings (Lit. C, 3, b [1973] 123). Amorites originally designated a people towards the northwest of Mesopotamia in the third to second millennia; they were both sedentary and nomadic, and pushed down into the Mesopotamian area. The second meaning was the western point of the compass (Subartu = north; Elam = east; Sumer = south). These first two meanings of MAR.TU = *Amurru* are very old; inasmuch as the other three points of the compass are likewise names of peoples (or lands), one can presuppose that the primary meaning was that of a people in the west of Mesopotamia. The third meaning is the land, Amurru, in Syria, north of Byblos, both a state and kingdom. The fourth is a general territorial designation covering Syria and Palestine.

However, the mere enumeration of these four meanings does not say much; a historical perspective gives access to a clearer understanding. (1) In the earliest stage the Amurru are immigrants from the west, first individuals or families, later tribes (Liverani, p. 103; the earliest attestation of the name is 2600 B.C.). They are nomads who supply sheep and goats, probably at the time when they are changing pastures. However, it is likely that this Amorite people consists not only of nomads, but also of sedentary groups (M. B. Rowton, BFPLUL 182 [1967] 108, "dimorphic society") such as are settled in villages and cities (A. Haldar, *Who Were the Amorites?* [1971]; J. Van Seters [1975]). Only the nomadic Amorites are important for the Sumerian-Akkadian texts. Their nomadic way of life is vividly described, but from the point of view of sedentary life and so, of course, negatively. However, the descriptions make clear that it is a question of small-cattle nomads (sheep and goats). It becomes clear that the immigrant Amurru are like the sedentary population in varying degrees. (2) Around 2000 Ur came under the domination of Elam; this was the end of Ur III. The Amorites took a notable part in this. Henceforth they were an important constituent of the Mesopotamian population. (3) The Mari texts show a new situation. Mari attests in all respects the two forms of community life witnessed in the previous period; "Amorites" are both citizens and nomads. This designation, however, has now become too general and is used less and less; one has the sense of belonging to a city or to a tribe. There are great differences in the life-styles; over against the city population organized on sedentary lines, there are tribes which are either in the process of becoming sedentary, like the Haneans, or are distinctly independent and nomadic, like the Suteans, and the Benjaminites. (4) A double usage developed in Syria: a defined mountainous region south of Byblos is called the land of Amurru (already in the Mari texts). There is one mention of four kings of the Amurru. Side by side with this, Amurru designates the whole of Syria, including Palestine. The whole area from the Euphrates to the borders of Egypt can now be called Amurru. (5) From the period of the Assyrian Empire on, Amurru becomes more and more a merely archaic designation. The astrological texts and the texts explaining omens show this explicitly: they call Amurru "the west," deliberately leaving vague any specific localization. At the same time the oldest meaning of the word is again in evidence, namely, nomads who come from the west. (6) Consequently, Amurru, as a designation for the whole area from the Euphrates to the Egyptian border, is replaced by Hatti, which has completely displaced Amurru by the middle of the first millennium.

Such being the case, one can understand why there is such great variation among scholars in the precise identification of the name "Amorite" and in the range of its usage. B. Landsberger (1924) describes the broad group (those who have West Semitic names) as East Canaanites, from whom he distinguishes the MAR.TU = Amurru; T. Bauer (1926) follows him; W. von Soden (1947-52) speaks of early Canaanites; D. A. Edzard (1957) of Canaanites (= West Semites); M. Noth of proto-Aramaeans—because the early West Semitic names are close to the Aramaic (all references: Lit. III; 3a-4a). T. L. Thompson (1974) insists that it is not possible to prove the existence of a unified people of MAR.TU with a common historical tradition; it is rather a question of a number of groups which are distinct chronologically, geographically, and culturally, and would be better described as early West Semites (so too A. Haldar, *Who Were the Amorites?* [1971]). One must certainly agree with Thompson's basic reason; nevertheless, the name Amurru has the broad meaning, "westerners," and later it quite deliberately embraces several different units of peoples. The name "Amorites" can designate what Thompson means by "early West Semites." The most important consequence of the history of the name "Amorites" is that, because of the very broad span of its usage and the multiple and considerable changes in its meaning, one may no longer speak of the Amorites as one people with historical continuity. Moreover, it is no longer possible to assign them to a nomadic way of life. In any case, at Mari, and even earlier, there were nomadic and sedentary Amorites = westerners. The earlier opinion that there were great, self-contained movements of Amorites thereby loses its foundation, as does the opinion that the migrations of the patriarchs were related to such migrations.

The positive significance of what the Mesopotamian texts say of the Amorites (MAR.TU = Amurru) lies no longer in a historical context, but rather in the possibility of parallel phenomena. The texts of the Ur III period show that the nomadic immigrants who came into the cultivated land were first of all individuals who hired themselves out for labor and family units (M. Liverani). Later they were tribal units and as such entered the political arena. This is parallel to the sequence of the patriarchal stories and the taking of the land in the Old Testament, where the same stages may be observed.

A further piece of data, important for the patriarchal story, is what M. B. Rowton calls "dimorphic society" (BFPUL 182 [1967] 109-121) and is particularly evident in the Mari texts. The nomadic tribes described there practised agriculture in a limited way. This does not yet involve the transition to sedentary life; the nomadic style was retained. The same is to be observed in the patriarchal narratives. If occasionally there is talk of acquiring or cultivating land, this makes no difference concerning the nomadic way of life of the patriarchs.

The use of the name "Amorites" in the Old Testament.   First, it is important to note that the Old Testament speaks of the Amorites only in the past. Israel knew no Amorites. The description of the country not yet occupied in Josh. 13:2-5 refers to "the boundary of the Amorites" precisely the territory (and later kingdom) in Syria which, from the Mari texts on, and particularly in the 14th and 13th centuries, and even still in the 12th, is called "Amurru"; this corresponds to M. Liverani's third use of the word (see above). It is possible that this same usage is presupposed in Gen. 48:22. The Amorites are mentioned in all lists of the pre-Israelite inhabitants of Palestine. This corresponds to the use of "Amurru" for the whole territory of Syria and Palestine, although it suggests that what is meant is a part of the pre-Israelite population of Palestine that is ethnically and geographically determined. However, the lists do not permit a more exact definition. The same uncertainty is apparent in different literary (or preliterary) layers where "Amorites" and "Canaanites" can have the same function, e.g., when the designation "Amorites" is generally attributed to E and "Canaanite" to J. There is at least a hint of a somewhat more precise determination when the Amorites are linked with a mountainous area as in Num. 13:29; Josh. 11:3; Judg. 1:34; and when the pre-Israelite population of east Jordan is described only as Amorites, never as Canaanites (e.g., Deut. 3:8; Judg. 10:8). The reason for this is that the Egyptian domination over Canaan in the 14th and 13th centuries extended only as far as the Jordan. It is certain that the designation ''Canaanite'' has been in use only since the middle of the second millennium; ''Amorites,'' therefore, is the older designation. Thus it is not possible to distinguish Canaanites and Amorites clearly as two peoples (M. Liverani). It can be stated, therefore, that, on the whole, the undetermined use of the name ''Amorite'' in extrabiblical texts is reflected also in biblical usage.

III. The Aramaeans. Something must be said by way of introduction about the Aramaeans, because the patriarchal stories presuppose a close family relationship between them and the patriarchs, particularly Gen. 11:31; ch. 24; and chs. 29–31. An independent tradition, the finely-honed ''Credo'' formula, says: ''A wandering Aramaean was my father'' (Deut. 26:5). The situation here is very different from that of the Amorites: the Aramaeans are a people whose history is relatively well known, but whose relationship to the patriarchs is problematic. They are first clearly attested as a people under Tiglath-Pileser I (1116-1076 B.C.). They are in alliance with the Ahlamites and the Suteans (who are already there in the Mari period). As the 11th century moved into the 10th, they became a threat to the Assyrian empire after they had gained dominion of the larger part of Syria. There was a long series of campaigns by the Assyrian kings against the Aramaeans until, under Tiglath-Pileser III (747-727 B.C.), they were incorporated into the Assyrian provincial system. The Chaldaeans infiltrating into the south were also subjugated, but remained a dominating factor in the new Babylonian empire.

The history of the Aramaeans as known to us excludes, therefore, any kinship between them and the patriarchs, or any designation of the patriarchs as Aramaeans (Deut. 26:5) before the 12th or 11th century (R. T. O'Callaghan, *Aram-Naharaim* [1948, 1961²] 96ff.). So far as the historical situation is known to us, the settlement of Aramaic kinsmen of Abraham in Haran and Nahor, as presupposed in Gen. 24, can be set only between the 10th and 5th centuries (J. Van Seters [1975] 33). The biblical designations of Aram-Naharaim and Paddan-aram cannot have been in use before the 12th-11th centuries; the area intended is called only ''Naharaim'' from the 15th to the 12th centuries, never Aram-Naharaim (A. Malamat, Lit. III; 3, c [1973] 140). It is somewhat the same with Ur-Kasdim, Ur of the Chaldees. This must be related to the well-known Ur of Mesopotamia which could be qualified as ''of the Chaldees'' only from the 10th to the 6th centuries, in any case, not before the first millennium (H. W. F. Saggs, Iraq 22 [1960] 1-19; T. L. Thompson, BZAW 133 [1974] 313).

These data admit of only two conclusions. The first presupposes the historicity of the Aramaean states, the particulars of the history of the Aramaeans, and their designation in Gen. 12–50; one must in this case hold that the relationship of the patriarchs to the Aramaeans as well as the events narrated about the patriarchs are both unhistorical. For J. Van Seters the consciousness of kinship between the Israelites and the Aramaeans retains a historical nucleus; such a consciousness in the patriarchal stories is possible, he thinks, only after the collapse of the Aramaean states in Syria, that is, after the eighth century. But he gives no reason why this consciousness arose so late and had to be transposed back into the early history of the people. It is important for T. L. Thompson that all these traditions cannot be historical; their purport is purely etiological.

The other possible conclusion from the data is that such names as Aramaeans, Aram-Naharaim, Paddan-aram, and Ur of the Chaldees are anachronisms (e.g., A. Malamat and R. de Vaux). However, it is not enough merely to establish the fact of an anachronism. The bearers of the tradition of the patriarchal story wanted to pass on the idea that the fathers once came to Palestine from the area of Haran. At the time they told it, the Aramaeans lived there; they were so much a part of the area that one could not speak of those who lived there in any other way than Aramaeans. Somewhere along the path of tradition another name was replaced by "Aramaeans," not because bearers of tradition wanted to "modernize" (so Van Seters, p. 33), but so as to make things understandable to the listeners. It is the same when they describe the land with names known to the listeners (Aram-Naharaim, Paddan-aram), though there were no such names in the patriarchal period. It is beyond doubt that Ur-Kasdim (Ur of the Chaldees) means Ur in Mesopotamia. There is an exact parallel to this in the Balaam story (Num. 22–24); it would have had its origin in the tenth or ninth century. At that time, the place which Balaam came from, Pethor on the Euphrates, was in the possession of the Aramaeans (A. Malamat, op. cit., 141). Accordingly, the first oracle of Balaam reads, "From Aram Balak has brought me" (Num. 23:7), though in the period with which the Balaam story is concerned Pethor was not yet Aramaic. R. de Vaux is correct in saying that it was natural to give the place the name with which contemporary readers and listeners were familiar (*Early History. . .* [1971; Eng. 1978] 201, 520).

There is yet another reason. Before the whole territory from the Euphrates to the coast was described as the territory of the Aramaeans, there was only one other comprehensive description of it: the territory of the Amorites. However, it would not have been possible to describe the patriarchs as Amorites or as closely related to them, because the Amorites are mentioned in all lists of the early inhabitants of Palestine, and a part of Israel's Credo is: "It was I who destroyed the Amorite before them" (Amos 2:9). If the destruction of the Amorites was a precondition for the gift of the land, then the patriarchs could not be described as Amorites or as closely related to them. But this is not the case with the Aramaeans.

However, all this gives rise to a serious difficulty for the exegesis of the patriarchal stories: when we use the name Aramaean, when we describe Laban as an Aramaean, when we speak of the relationship of Abraham's family to the Aramaeans, we cannot equate the Aramaeans of history with the Aramaeans mentioned in the patriarchal story. In each case we must substitute earlier inhabitants of what was later Aramaean territory.

IV. Other Peoples and Territories Important for the Patriarchal Story.

It would not be possible with our present state of knowledge to draw a map of the world of the patriarchs even if we could fix the patriarchal period exactly. Only a fluid map would be possible for the various periods of the second millennium in the ancient near east. There would be a few fixed points; the borders and designations of lands and peoples would be in a constant state of flux, apart from many undefined areas. The Amorites and the Aramaeans are important for the patriarchal story as a whole; as for the other peoples and lands which come into consideration, we need no more than summarize their immediate points of contact with the patriarchal stories.

Earlier inhabitants of Palestine: Canaanites.   There is a note added to Abraham's arrival at Shechem: "At that time the Canaanites lived in the land" (Gen. 12:6). It presupposes the later period of the bearers of tradition when the land had become Israelite. The designations "Canaan" and "Canaanite" for the land and its inhabitants are very frequent in the Bible, in fact the most common for the land of which the Israelites took possession. Outside the Bible "Canaan" first occurs in Akkadian texts of the 15th century. In the 14th, the Amarna letters speak of the "province of Canaan"; this corresponds to the designation of the area under Egyptian domination and, since Rameses II, gathered into the one province of Canaan. The latest Egyptian inscription which contains the name distinguishes Philistia from Canaan. The Old Testament equivalent of the official Egyptian terminology is that the eastern border of Canaan is the Jordan, and the northern the land of the Amurru. In Gen. 12:6; 13:7; and 34:30, the Canaanites are the inhabitants of Palestine before the Israelites came into possession of it. This refers to the constituents of the population as a whole, without permitting "Canaanites" to be imposed on a single, distinct people. Consequently, the pre-Israelite population of Palestine can also be described as "Amorites" or "Hittites." Although these three names can appear as synonyms, the name "Canaanite" is distinguished from the other two in being more narrowly restricted, referring to the west side of the Jordan and only as far as Hamath on the Orontes. The Egyptian term "Hurru" can also be a synonym for Canaan (see below).

Consequently, when "Canaanites" are mentioned in the patriarchal stories they are to be understood from the point of view of the bearers of tradition who knew the term as a designation for the early inhabitants of Canaan. The name reveals nothing about the patriarchal period or the names of peoples or groups whom the patriarchs encountered and had dealings with. It is clear that the name functions retrospectively from the fact that in the whole of the Old Testament it is used exclusively for the pre-Israelite inhabitants of the land. There is another important aspect of the appearance of the Canaanites in the patriarchal story to which A. van Selms has drawn particular attention. The severely negative judgment on Canaan and the Canaanites, which runs through the whole of the Old Testament from Exodus on, does not appear in the patriarchal stories. "The relations of the Canaanites to Israel's ancestors are peaceful and indeed very friendly" (OTS 12 [1958] 203). Both intermarriage and the conclusion of contracts are part of this friendly relationship. There is not so much as a single sentence which rejects Canaanite religion or morality. This remarkable contrast to the otherwise harsh condemnation has only one explanation: the bearers of tradition found these peaceful and friendly relationships in the narratives that came down to them—a clear indication that the stories go back to a period before the occupation of the land.

Hittites.   H. A. Hoffner distinguishes four meanings of the name "Ḥatti" which correspond to four different historical stages (TynB 20 [1969] 27-55; *Peoples of OT Times*, ed. D. J. Wiseman [1973], 197-228). (1) The *Ḥatti* were the people whom the immigrant Indo-Europeans found inhabiting the central plateau of Asia Minor, and who were later completely assimilated into the culture of the immigrants. (2) The Indo-European immigrants (ca. 2000 B.C.) won hegemony over the plateau and about 1650 founded the city of Ḥattūsa. The state existed ca. 1700-1200, and reached as far south as Kadesh on the Orontes. (3) After the fall of Ḥattūsa there followed the dissolution of the vassal states; however, the (neo-)Hittite states of Carchemish, Aleppo, and Hamath remained; they are designated in Assyrian inscriptions as *māt ḥatti*, the land of Hatti. (4) These states were absorbed into the Assyrian provincial system and the name was extended to the whole of Syria; from ca. 1100 it was known to the Assyrians under the name of Ḫattu, comprising the whole territory from the Euphrates to the Egyptian border. And so the designation lost its precise ethnic and historical meaning.

The biblical use of the name is limited to the third and fourth meanings. One must abandon the oft repeated opinion that the patriarchs in Palestine had direct dealings with the Hittites of the old Hittite Empire or with that of the neo-Hittite states. The Hittites never advanced farther south than Kadesh on the Orontes. So the first two meanings of the name never occur in the Old Testament. The third meaning is found in a few places (the "kings of the Hittites" in 2 Kings 7:6 can sometimes denote the "land of the Hittites," Syria). All other passages fall under the fourth meaning, which corresponds to the Assyrian designation of the whole population between the Euphrates and Egypt as Ḫatti. H. A. Hoffner is of the opinion that the name in the patriarchal stories has nothing at all to do with the Hittites, but refers to a small group living in the hills with a similar sounding name. They would be natives, because all the Hittites mentioned in the Old Testament carry Semitic personal names. It can remain an open question whether this view is correct; in any case, this meaning too bears no ethnic connection with Hittites.

The fluidity of the names is obvious when the "kings of the Ḫatti" in an inscription of Sargon are almost the same as those designated "kings of the Amurru" in Sennacherib. The same fluidity is obvious in the Old Testament: the Hittite wives of Esau (Gen. 26:34; 27:46; 36:2) are called Canaanites in Gen. 28:1ff.; and the inhabitants of Hebron are called now Hittites (49:29ff.), now Amorites (14:13), now Canaanites (Judg. 1:10).

Consequently, when the name "Hittite" occurs in the patriarchal stories it does not admit of any conclusion to a connection with the older Hittite empire or the later (neo-)Hittite states in Syria. The bearers of tradition make use of the general designation known to them, which corresponds to the Assyrian designation of the whole territory between the Euphrates and Egypt as the "land of the Ḫatti." Hoffner's suggestion can stand, namely, that the Hittites of the patriarchal stories are partly a small native-born group whose name sounds something like that of the classical Hittites.

Hurrians and Hivites. Hurrians (= Horites) already appear in Akkadian inscriptions towards the end of the third millennium B.C.; they are, however, known as minorities among other peoples and cities, e.g., at Nuzi. From about 1500 to 1370 there was a Hurrian Mitanni empire (detailed account in R. T. O'Callaghan, *Aram-Naharaim* [1948; 1961[2]], ch. IV); its official language was Hurrian (non-Semitic). It had reached the high point of its power about 1450, from which time there is evidence of advance towards Syria-Palestine. It was overthrown by the Assyrians in 1436. Nevertheless, a Hurrian cultural influence persisted for a long time. From around 1600 "the land of the Hurru" was an Egyptian designation for Palestine and a part of Syria; it could be used with the same meaning as "Canaan." The biblical use of the name raises difficulties. First, in Gen. 14:6; 36:20-30; and Deut. 2:12,20, the Hurrians are localized in Edom; but there is no proof of this. A possible explanation is that the bearers of tradition knew the general Egyptian designation, "Hurru," and applied it inappropriately to the early inhabitants of Edom (R. de Vaux, J. Van Seters).

The second difficulty comes from the relationship between the Hurrians and the Hivites. There is no extrabiblical attestation for the latter, and the name has not yet been explained. The Hurrians are mentioned in 17 of the 18 lists of the pre-Israelite inhabitants of Palestine, and the Gk. of Gen. 36:2 and Josh. 9:7 has "Hurrians" for the "Hivites" of the MT; hence the conclusion that they are either closely related or identical (I. H. Eybers, OTWSA.P 2 [1959] 6-14). H. A. Hoffner says that in the Old Testament one should seek Hurrians under the name "Hivites" (op. cit. [1973] 225). R. de Vaux, on the contrary, is convinced that the Old Testament intends two different people by the two names (*Early History.* . . [1971; Eng. 1978] 136-137; RB 74 [1967] 481-503). K. J. H. Vriezen supposes that Hivites in the Old Testament refers to a distinct people among the pre-Israelite inhabitants of Palestine which is named in connection with three areas: the Gibeonite Tetrapolis (Josh. 9:7; 11:19), Shechem (Gen. 34:2), and the land of Mizpah at the foot of Hermon (Josh. 11:3; Judg. 3:3; 2 Sam. 24:7) (ZDPV 91 [1975] 135-158). "The men of Hamor, the father of Shechem" (Judg. 9:28; Gen. 33:10; Josh. 24:32) would also refer to the Hivites. In Gen. 34:2 Hamor is called "Hamor the Hivite." The designation of the inhabitants of Edom as Hurrians probably goes back to the Egyptian name for Palestine, "Hurru" (from about 1600).

The study of the names of the peoples (lands)—Amorites, Aramaeans, Canaanites, Hittites, Hurrians, Hivites—insofar as they refer to Palestine or to the pre-Israelite inhabitants of Palestine, leads to the conclusion that none of them supplies accurate historical information about definite peoples and their history. Designations are used throughout with which the bearers of tradition were familiar from their own time; the majority of the names are to be explained from Egyptian and Assyrian usage in which they are applied to large territories without being tied to definite peoples at definite times or in clearly defined areas. Consequently, when these names of peoples or lands occur in the patriarchal stories they provide no adequate foundation for fixing these narratives historically or geographically.

V. Places and Changes of Places in Gen. 12–50. A particularly important and fruitful part of the archaeological achievements consists in the excavations of the remains of settlements in Palestine which include places named in the patriarchal stories. A considerable number of these places have been identified with certainty but some remain uncertain. The excavations at the biblical sites have yielded amazing results. They have enabled us, at a distance of several millennia, to form an accurate, though in many cases limited, idea of the layout of the city, the history of its settlement, the architecture of its houses, the history of its fortifications, of its temples, walls and gates, its watersupply, cisterns, and granaries. As one who has not taken part personally in excavations and who knows the results only from visiting the sites and from reports, I would like to express my gratitude for all that the exegete owes to these achievements. One can scarcely overestimate the importance of the fact that today we have, concerning the place-names which occur in the patriarchal stories, not merely names in extrabiblical sources, but names with which we can associate an accurate and often a very rich fund of knowledge.

It is in this immediate context that there rests the certainty, coming from the texts themselves, that no name occurring in the patriarchal stories has been invented. Each place-name rests on a tradition. When a place is named, it is a real place. However, it must be clearly stated at the very outset that the excavations of the places mentioned in the stories do not admit of any direct connection with the stories themselves. The very texts impose this conclusion; the life-style that they bring to light so clearly and unmistakably is not such as to leave traces behind which the excavator may come across. This is so obvious that it need not be argued any further.

Accordingly, the question about the places which occur in Gen. 12–50 must be put to the texts where they occur. The life-style of the patriarchs is essentially nomadic; hence arises the question about changes of place; this stands in the closest relationship with the question of the itineraries. The situation and significance of individual places and place-names will be dealt with as each occurs; by way of introduction, we will deal with the function of the places and their naming within the framework of the texts.

Places and Place-Names in Gen. 12–25. In general, the city does not play an important role in the texts of Gen. 12–25. Localities are for the most part named as stopping places on the way, and so in itineraries or texts like them. The localities are here no more than sign-posts; they plot the route of a group. They are neither the starting points (even the stopping places named first are not starting points in the strict sense) nor the goals of the journey, and certainly not a place where the action of the narrative happens; no narrative culminates with the founding of a city. Places outside Palestine occur almost exclusively at the beginning, i.e., they mark the route into Palestine from outside (Gen. 11:28, 31, Ur of the Chaldees; 12:4, 5, Haran), not from Palestine to other parts. If on an occasion the route leads out of Palestine, then there is a return, as in 12:10-20 and ch. 24. The conclusion is that the tradition knows of an immigration of Abraham into Palestine, though his subsequent movements remain limited to this territory. It is not of the essence, therefore, whether Abraham's forefathers came from the area of Haran in Syria, or had come previously from Ur in southern Mesopotamia. What is essential for the understanding of the Abraham stories is only that the tradition knows the direction from which he immigrated into Palestine.

All other place-names describe places in Palestine, and relatively few (apart from ch. 14) are mentioned:

Shechem	12:6; 33:18; 35:4; 37:12-14; 48:22
Bethel	12:8; 13:3; 28:19; 31:13; 35:1, 3, 6, 8, 15
Ai	12:8; 13:3
Hebron (Mamre)	13:18; 23:2 (= Kiriath-arba); 23:19; 25:9; 35:27
Shur	16:7; 20:1; (25:18)
Lahai-roi	16:14; 24:62; 25:11
Kadesh	16:14; 20:1
Bered	16:14
Gerar	20:1, 2; 26:1, 6, 17, 26
Beersheba	21:14,21,32,33; 22:19; 26:23-33; 28:10; 46:15
Sodom, Gomorrah	13:10; 18:16b-33; ch. 19
Zoar	13:10; 19:22 (v. 20), 23, 30

Hebron, Lahai-Roi, and Beersheba are mentioned several times; eight other places (apart from Sodom and Gomorrah) are mentioned once or twice. Most place-names occur in itineraries, some in etiological narratives (Lahai-Roi, 16:14; Beersheba, 21:31), and some within the narrative. Most of the narratives are not localized.

Such being the state of the question, one must be very cautious about geographical conclusions. There is not enough evidence to reconstruct Abraham's movements, of which only a fragment is mentioned. An itinerary almost never goes beyond two or three stopping places; no complete itinerary of a longer journey is preserved. One can only say that the three place-names which are mentioned most often, Hebron, Beersheba, and Lahai-roi, probably belong to the oldest part of the Abraham tradition, and these point to the south of Palestine. A city plays an essential role in only one narrative in these chapters: 18:16b-33 and ch. 19 is of itself a narrative about a city, more exactly of its destruction. The scene in front of Lot's house can only take place in a city; it is the only place where there is a "crowd." We will see that the narrative of Sodom and Gomorrah comes from another cycle of tradition and was joined secondarily to the Abraham narratives.

The city plays only a marginal role in Gen. 23; the narrative does not deal with a city, but with the negotiations between Abraham and the citizens of Hebron for the sale of a burial cave. The business is conducted at the city gate where the elders assemble as a body. Mention should also be made of ch. 24 where Abraham's servant has gone to visit Nahor's city, and a picture is presented of the sedentary life of Nahor's family, with the well outside the city and Nahor's large household.

Places and Place-Names in Gen. 25–36. There is a group of place-names of which the function is close to that of the main group of chs. 12–25; they occur mostly in itineraries, and in particular at the end of the Jacob-Esau cycle: 33:12-20 (Succoth and Shechem); 35:8 (the Oak of Weeping at Bethel); 35:16-22a (Bethel, Ephrathah-Bethlehem, Migdal-eder); 35:27-29 (Mamre, Hebron = Kiriath-arba). The place-names in the Isaac tradition also belong to this group (ch. 26, Gerar and Beersheba). The most notable difference from Gen. 12–25 is that in Gen. 27; 29–31; 32:3-21; and 33 the narrative covers an area marked off by departure (or flight) and return. In these passages the account of a journey, with a note about the place of departure (Beersheba) and the goal (Haran) (28:10), takes the place of the itinerary. Haran, the goal, is mentioned again in 27:43; 29:4; and 31:55. Apart from this there are no place-names; only regions are mentioned. Shechem, not Beersheba, is named as the place of return in 33:18. The structure of the travel report belongs usually to the sedentary life-style; it is in that context that one first meets the categories "home" and "abroad."

There is a third group of place-names in Gen. 25–36 in the context of the sanctuary narratives or encounters with God: 28:10-22, Bethel; 32:1-2, Manahaim; 32:22-32, Peniel; 35:1-7, Shechem and Bethel; 35:9-15, Bethel. One notes here a difference from chs. 12–25, in which there is an account of the building of an altar but, as it were, "en route"; chs. 26–36 are concerned with the founding of a sanctuary which is expressed in the naming of the place. The difference points to two stages in tradition. The sanctuary narratives are closer to the sanctuaries of Canaanite civilization and so to the sedentary form of worship than are the narratives of the building of an altar (or something similar) in chs. 12–25. It is to be noted, however, that in chs. 25–36 too there is no narrative of the founding of a city, a certain sign that the transition to a completely sedentary life has not yet taken place. There is also in chs. 25–36, as in chs. 12–25, a text in which a city plays an essential role: the city of Shechem in ch. 34. But this text does not belong strictly to the patriarchal traditions; the narrative takes place in the period of the settlement of the tribes.

Of the places named in Gen. 25–36, one can only say that there is more weight given to the north (especially Shechem and Bethel), and that the Transjordan is mentioned. But we find southern sites also (Hebron and Beersheba). One can conclude no more than that the weight of the movements in

Gen. 25–36 is in the north and the east of Palestine.

Places and Place-Names in Gen. 37–50.   What is most striking about the place-names in Gen. 37–50 is that only places in Palestine are mentioned, and not places in Egypt; i.e., place-names occur only at the beginning and end, but not in the middle of the Joseph narrative. There are a few place-names in the introduction in ch. 37: Hebron (v. 14); Shechem (vv. 12-14); Dothan (v. 17); they recur when the narrative tells of Jacob's journey to Egypt and of his (and Joseph's) death: Beersheba (46:1,5), Ephrathah-Bethlehem (48:7), Shechem (48:22), Machpelah-Mamre (49:30 and 50:13), Goren-Atad = the threshing-floor of Atad (50:10), and Abel-mizraim (50:11).

From the moment when Joseph is sold into Egypt until his death there, we find not a single Egyptian place-name (with the exception that his father-in-law is described as a priest of On in 41:45, 50), but only regions, such as the district of Goshen (45:10; 46:28f., etc.), the district of Rameses (47:11), and the land of Canaan. The Joseph narrative is thereby clearly set apart from chs. 12–25 and chs. 25–36. Gen. 12–36 intends to tell of the movements of the patriarchs in a definite area, while the narrative of Joseph in Egypt is interested only in the "where" in which the story takes place. The places on the map are of no importance for what is happening; the event is detached from places and transferred to the level of humanity in general. In such a literary conception, the locale loses all significance. But this holds only for the central part of the narrative, not for the beginning and the end, ch. 37 and parts of chs. 46–50, where place-names occur as in chs. 12–36, and which really belong to the Jacob traditions (as also in P). One then admits that in the process of formation of the Joseph narrative, an older element from the Jacob traditions has been made the frame for the later narrative of Joseph in Egypt. The place-names at the beginning and end of chs. 37–50 stand in the same situation as those in chs. 25–36: there are places which belong in the north (Shechem) and in the south (Hebron, Beersheba, Machpelah-Mamre); in addition there are some new places (Goren-Attad, Abel-mizraim).

When one compares the naming of places and the function of place-names in the three parts of the patriarchal stories, there are three clear stages. In the first stage, the place-names fulfill their essential function in an itinerary, which is to plot the one-way journey of a small group. This predominates in Gen. 12–25. This function continues in the second stage, but something new is added: the place-names designate the starting point and the goal of the journey, the departure and return echoing the sedentary way of life (so in parts of Gen. 25–36). The founding of sanctuaries with the naming of the place also belongs to this stage (chs. 28; 32; 35); nevertheless, no cities are founded as yet. The third stage sees the complete detachment from localization. The presentation of what is happening no longer needs to be fixed to a geographically determined place; poetic imagination (the short story) transfers the event to the level of humanity in general; localization is satisfied by the mention of lands or regions (so, partly, in chs. 29–31). But just as the second stage, chs. 25–36, retains the function of naming places from the first, so too the third, chs. 37–50, retains on the periphery the function of the first two by means of a frame which belongs to the Jacob traditions.

D. The Time of the Patriarchs

It is a matter of dispute whether one can speak of the time of the patriarchs at all. It is contested because it has been established that the patriarchal stories do not contain historical information in the strict sense, and no historically attested information about persons or events in the stories has been discovered so far in documents from the ancient near east—nor is it to be expected.

The new archaeological approach (see above, par. 3, 1) has given occasion to speak with the greatest energy and certainty of "the time of the patriarchs," because it believed that it had discovered data from the ancient near east which enabled a certain dating of the patriarchal figures and stories. The position seemed so convincing that it won widespread acceptance; especially popular books and articles spoke of the patriarchal period as something taken for granted. The difficulty, however, was that there was nowhere near unanimity about the date, which fluctuated between 2200 and 1200 (see the table in *Erträge der Forschung*, p. 73). The reason for this enormous fluctuation is that different scholars held different data—either from the old Babylonian or the Mari or the Amarna period—to be determinative for the date. This is without doubt a weakness (cf. J. Van Seters [above, 3.A]). The history of the study of the patriarchal period can be outlined as follows. For Wellhausen and his school the question of the patriarchal period was nonexistent; the archaeological approach linked up with the pre-Wellhausen conservative position, which maintained that the patriarchal stories were in essence historical and reliable. What was new was that archaeological finds from the ancient near east were adduced as proof of their historicity. This position won almost universal acceptance over the last 50 years. Only very recently has this position been contested all along the line (T. L. Thompson [1974]; J. Van Seters [1975]), and with it also the possibility of discussing the specific time of the patriarchs at all. The discussion between these utterly opposed positions continues.

Given this situation, we must explain the sense in which the period of the patriarchs is understood in this commentary. I agree with the critical opinions in holding that, in the present state of scholarship, it is not possible to mark off and compute a particular time as "the patriarchal period." None of the attempts to fix a date (assembled in tabular form by C. Westermann, *Erträge der Forschung*, p. 73) can be accepted with certainty; none can with certainty be rejected. Nevertheless, I agree with the archaeological approach in that the study of the world of the patriarchs has shown the possibility of patriarchal life and movement for the period before the Exodus and before the settlement of the tribes in Canaan. The time of the patriarchs in this commentary, therefore, means a real period before the Israelite tribes became sedentary, but a period for which fixed dates cannot be given.

I. Life-style (Nomadism).   The study of the nomadic life-style has made great progress in the last decades due to archaeological discoveries, among which the documents from Mari must take pride of place. This progress is due in part also to general research in the fields of ethnology, sociology, and economic history, and is not confined to the region of the ancient near east. The results so far enable us to determine more accurately the life-style of the patriarchs, and this no longer by referring to texts which offer historically constant parallels, but by showing a conformity with an otherwise proven type of nomadic life, removed in space and time, which renders it credible. The importance of these nomadic life-styles is that they render the patriarchal texts comprehensible and make it the more possible to distinguish different layers of tradition in them. They enable us to see the texts in a social and economic-historical context in which they are the same as, or similar to, other ways of life which have been observed elsewhere. The most remarkable change is that whereas the nomadic life-style of the patriarchs previously could be compared only with that of the bedouin or camel nomads, it is now acknowledged that this is a late form of nomadic life which cannot in any way be compared with that of the patriarchs (R. de Vaux, *Early History*. . . [1971; Eng. 1978] 222ff.). The patriarchs have often been described as ''semi-nomads'' in order to distinguish them from the bedouin; but this demarcation is no longer necessary, because the camel nomads are to be regarded as a later and special form of nomadic life, and no longer as ''complete nomads'' (H.W.F. Saggs, Iraq 22 [1960] 201, n. 8; M.B. Rowton, BFPUL 182 [1967] 109; on terminology, J. Henninger, *Ethnographische Studien*, ed. L. Földes [1967] 53-57).

More accurate study of nomadic life-styles has shown that one argument often used to contest the idea that the life-style of the patriarchs was nomadic is not sound. It was said that the patriarchs are not presented as nomads in Gen. 12–50 because there is often talk of their houses, of buying land, and of agriculture. It has been shown in recent works, however, that these ''varied forms of economy'' are typical of the nomads of the region (M.B. Rowton, op. cit. pp. 114-116, ''Dimorphism and the Dimorphic Society''). It is apparent that the life-style of the patriarchs was really nomadic, because the places mentioned in the stories lie in a climatic zone suitable for the small-cattle breeding so often mentioned (R. de Vaux, ThD 12 [1964] 227-240; *Early History*. . . [1971; Eng. 1978] 222ff.); there is never mention of the founding of a city, and the obvious signs of sedentary life belong to the people whom the patriarchs meet, not to the patriarchs themselves.

I have given an account of the more recent discussion on the nomadic life-style of the patriarchs in *Erträge der Forschung* (1975) pp. 76-81 (cf. also Lit., Intro.). Results achieved so far have caused a thorough revision of the earlier view. In the 19th century the so-called three-stages theory of cultural development, reaching back into ancient times, was dominant; there was everywhere a rectilinear evolution from food gathering through nomadism to agriculture. This theory, which exercised strong influence on the study of antiquity and of the Old Testament, is now generally abandoned. It is generally acknowledged that the mutual relationship of the earliest forms of economy known to us was far more complicated and varied. Above all, it can no longer be maintained that always and everywhere nomadism developed into sedentary farm life. In many places the sedentary life-style preceded the nomadic; nomadism could under certain conditions develop out of farm life (E. Hahn, *Von der Hacke zum Pflug* [1917]; K. Dittmer, *Allgemeine Völkerkunde, Formen und Entwicklung der Kultur* [1954]). When sedentary and nomadic life come in contact, what happens between them is so different as to allow of no formula or uniform, rectilinear scheme of development which would cover all cases. I would refer in particular to the collection of essays, *Das Verhältnis von Bodenbauern und Viehzüchtern in historischer Sicht* (Akademie-Verlag, Berlin, 1968), and L. Vajda, *Untersuchungen zur Geschichte des Hirtenkulturen* (1968).

A characteristic example is the exchange between nomads and sedentaries in the old Babylonian period. Towards the end of the third millennium, nomads began to trickle into the settled area of Mesopotamia at first ''at the level of single individuals and family units'' (M. Liverani, *Peoples of OT Times*, ed. D. J. Wiseman [1973] 103), then gradually in larger groups growing into tribes, at which point they became a military threat. The earlier stage can be compared with the patriarchal stories, the later with the penetration of the Israelite tribes into Canaan. A further example of the varied relationships between nomads and sedentaries comes from the Mari texts—thus far the most instructive evidence. These texts speak about nomadic tribes on the mid-Euphrates about 1830-1760 B.C. who were small-cattle breeders (sheep and goats) with donkeys as beasts of burden. This corresponds to the style of life that we meet in the patriarchal stories, as J. Henninger states: "The economic system of the nomads mentioned in the Mari texts corresponds to that of the biblical patriarchs" (AFLNW 151 [1968] 30). The relationship of the different nomadic tribes mentioned here to the sedentaries is very different. There is by no means the same striving for land and the consequent sedentary life among all nomads (as has often been said when explaining the promise of the land); a variety of possibilities lies open. H. Klengel speaks of nomads who penetrate into the "niches" between the cultivated areas and retain their nomadic life-style there for a long time (*Zwischen Zelt und Palast* [1972]).

Especially, the Mari texts have shown that one and the same tribe can include simultaneously sedentary and nomadic groups (e.g., A. Malamat, JAOS 82 [1962] 143-150). According to more recent works on nomadism, the area in which the nomads of the ancient near east moved in the second millennium is closer to the settled land than was previously thought. Desert nomads first arrived with the camel caravans; previously there were only peripheral nomads who were thrown back on contacts with the inhabitants of the cultivated land. M. B. Rowton describes the contiguous life-styles of nomadic and sedentary groups as "dimorphic society" (op. cit.). J. T. Luke speaks of "village pastoralists" (*Pastoralists and Politics in the Mari Period* [Diss. Michigan, 1965]). Here too one must be careful of generalizations; nevertheless, it can no longer be contested that for the most part the nomadic life-style was not as far removed from the sedentary as was previously thought (R. de Vaux, pp. 222ff.). The impression may have arisen of a sharp contrast and thoroughgoing antagonism between nomads and sedentaries; if so, the reason, at least in part, is that nomadic life has been portrayed by sedentaries who either looked down on or despised them. A series of descriptions of nomadic life is preserved from the Ur III period (M. Liverani, op. cit., pp. 105ff.): they are shepherds who live in the mountains, who have no cities, who know nothing of civilization or agriculture. The most detailed description is found in the "Myth of Martu" where the god Martu says of the nomadic people: "A people who live in tents, exposed to rain and wind, who dig for tuberous plants at the foot of the mountains, who do not bend the knee [i.e., they do not work the land], who consume their food raw, who have no home their whole life long and no grave when they die" (J. Lewy, HUCA 32 [1961] 31-74; R. de Vaux, pp. 63ff.). Despite the obvious prejudice, one can recognize in this description certain essential characteristics of the nomadic life.

When the patriarchal stories speak of large cattle, particularly of oxen and heifers, then this is quite compatible with the life-style of small-cattle nomads. Cattle are mentioned together with sheep when enumerating the possessions of the patriarchs (e.g., Gen. 20:14). In Gen. 18:7 Abraham prepares a calf from the herd for his guests, and a three-year-old heifer is mentioned in the covenant rite in 15:9. The herd plays an important role for Jacob and Laban, but it comprises only small cattle, as do the herds of the various nomads mentioned in the Mari texts. The occasional occurrence of cattle can also at times be conditioned by transitional forms of life, but when the wealth of the patriarchs is described, it is better to see references to cattle as interpolations from a later perspective. In any case, the texts clearly portray the patriarchs as small-cattle breeders; the mention of cattle is a rare exception.

The mention of camels, however, is a problem. It is certain that the patriarchs were not camel nomads. The domestication and breeding of the camel, at any rate on a large scale, cannot be proved before the end of the second millennium (R. Walz, ZDMG 101 [1951] 29-51; 104 [1954] 45-87; W.F. Albright, *Archaeology and the Religion of Israel* [1942; 1953²] 96-102, 132). This terminal point is widely accepted today. Camels are mentioned when details of the wealth of the patriarchs are given (Gen. 12:16; 30:43; 32:8 ["camels" is missing in the LXX of 32:8]). The camel saddle is part of the narrative of the theft of the Teraphim in 31:34, and camels are mentioned 15 times in the narrative of the wooing of Rebecca (ch. 24). Some scholars have tried, by means of an early dating, to explain these passages as corresponding to the patriarchal period; but it is more likely that the mention of camels is an anachronism, and is to be traced to those transmitting the tradition at a later period (R. de Vaux, pp. 222ff.). It is natural for such adaptations to occur in the course of a very long history of tradition. However, the only essential point is that the patriarchs could not have been camel nomads.

W. F. Albright, contrary to the clear statement of the text of Gen. 12–50, has tried to prove from a few passages that the patriarchs were conductors of donkey caravans, and speaks of donkey-nomadism ("Abraham the Hebrew. A New Archaeological Interpretation," BASOR 163 [1961] 36-54, and other essays). This explanation has found very little agreement; R. de Vaux has dealt with it in detail and rejected it (op. cit., 223ff.). C. H. Gordon has proposed a similar explanation ("Abraham and the Merchants of Ura," JNES 17 [1958] 28-31): "It is now clear that Abraham was a merchant prince, a *tamkarūm* from Hittite realm" (p. 31). H. W. F. Saggs has taken up this explanation and given a detailed and convincing refutation of it ("Ur of the Chaldees. A Problem of Identification," Iraq 22 [1960] 200-209). J. Van Seters has contested the nomadic life-style of the patriarchs (*Abraham in History and Tradition* [1975] 310). His view, that the Yahwistic work originated in the exilic period, leads him to explain the life-style of the patriarchs from that period as well. But why an author in the exilic period should have invented the patriarchal figures who, according to his own statements, would have lived about 1000 years earlier, remains obscure. In the chapter, "The Nomadism of the Patriarchs" (pp. 13-38), Van Seters tries to prove that there is no evidence for a nomadic life-style in the texts of Gen. 12–50. In the second part of this chapter (pp. 23-38), he contests any connection between the movements of the patriarchs and the movements of peoples in the second millennium. One must agree with him here (see above). In the first part (pp. 13-22), he lays stress on individual passages which point to a sedentary and agrarian life-style. However, in doing so he does not distinguish between those texts which, according to the general opinion, are either very old or very late. Van Seters argues here just as an ultraconservative exegete who does not acknowledge a literary stratification; e.g., he alleges as proof of a sedentary life-style Gen. 14, among other passages, just as do the exegetes who hold the chapter to be a historical account from the patriarchal period. Contrary arguments are scarcely meaningful in face of such presuppositions. But even Van Seters has to concede: "It is true that he [Abraham] lived in tents and moved his livestock from place to place" (p. 16).

Transhumance and Transmigration. Nomadism is a life-style determined by economic needs. The herds of small cattle are the life support of the nomadic group; migrations are necessary to feed and maintain the herds. Climatic conditions make the change from summer to winter pasture necessary. The movement of the nomads is for the most part identical with the change of pasture. ''From the view point of the nomads the year falls roughly into two parts, geographically and chronologically; the rainy season out in the desert and the dry season in the cultivated land, linked together by periods of wandering of greater or lesser length (L. Rost, ZDPV 66 [1943] 205-216 = *Das kleine Credo und andere Studien zum A.T.* [1965] 102, n. 2, following A. Alt). This semiannual change of pasture took place for the most part in a relatively restricted region; year after year the nomads looked for more or less the same summer and winter feeding places. It was possible that after the winter out in the steppes the group would choose a summer pasture different from the previous year and so gradually move further and further away from the earlier places. But the rhythm of summer and winter remained. It is generally acknowledged today that this change of pasture is a necessity of life for the small-cattle nomads. Recent studies on nomadism lay special emphasis on the contacts made between the nomadic and sedentary groups through the change of pasture (J. Henninger, M. du Buit, H. Klengel, M. B. Rowton, A. Malamat, *et alii*, Lit. III; 4, a-b); these contacts are constant and continually renewed; the result is a variety of exchanges and relationships between the two (cf. esp. M. B. Rowton). On the other hand the nomads preserved their independence and integrity over against the sedentaries by remaining outside the influence of the cities every six months. The texts from Drehem near Nippur show how the nomads, as early as the Ur III period, came into contact with the cities through change of pasture: ''The MAR.TU-people appear in the Drehem texts principally as suppliers of sheep and goats. This fits in with their nomadic life as shepherds; the times for bringing in the supplies seem to point to a seasonal pattern, which could mean that their presence in the area was due to a periodical transhumance'' (M. Liverani, op. cit. [1973] 104ff.). Mari provides many detailed accounts of the change of pasture, and even precise information about the places (cf. M. B. Rowton [1974] 22-30).

One does not expect such precise and detailed information about the change of pasture in the patriarchal stories; they have gone through too long a process of tradition. Nevertheless, certain traits emerge clearly: the patriarchs are portrayed as moving from place to place with their herds; the movements are to be explained for the most part in the context of the necessary change of pasture. During the summer they meet the inhabitants of the land in the cultivated areas. This can occasion strife over the wells, and contracts can be concluded to secure claims to the watering places (Gen. 21:26). All places mentioned in the patriarchal stories lie within the climatic belt that make it possible to maintain herds of small cattle.

The term *transhumance* is generally used to describe the change of pasture. V. Maag has coined the term *transmigration* to describe the movements of a nomad tribe over long distances in times of particular need (VT.S 7 [1959-60] 129-153): ''Transhumance represents. . . a periodical movement across familiar territory; from the standpoint of the history of economy or religion, therefore, it is not to be compared with the phenomenon which I call 'transmigration.' Transmigration takes place under economic pressure. This causes a group to abandon the whole area of its accustomed route to pasture, and to pass through hitherto unknown lands and obstacles to a pasture land which it has never seen before'' (p. 134, n. 2). Maag draws from this far-reaching conclusions for the religion of the patriarchs, and adduces as a modern parallel the Bactrians in the region of the Himalayas. J. Henninger, on the contrary, urges caution here (BiKi 27 [1972] 13-16). He confirms, to be sure, that ''under unusual circumstances a group at times breaks out of the confines of its territory'' (p. 16) and yet asserts that one cannot allow the whole religion of the nomadic group in question to be determined on the basis of one single extrabiblical parallel. The regular change of pasture would in any case be more important. One must concede that Henninger is correct here. Maag's thesis must be restricted: the patriarchal stories speak of extensive movements of the patriarchs which cannot be explained by transhumance (change of pasture). In connection with these special migrations there has been much discussion of route instructions linked with a promise. These are obviously to be distinguished from the movements to change of pasture. There are plenty of parallels to this in Israel's world; but one cannot speak in the same way of ''transmigration'' as a phenomenon familiar to and attested among small-cattle nomads. What is going on in each individual case must remain an open question.

II. Legal Practices and Customs: Introduction.

The patriarchal form of society. The basic presupposition of all that follows, and this is both uncontested and incontestable, is that patriarchal society is prepolitical. It has a family structure, and this too is generally acknowledged. One must add a point, however, to which sufficient attention has too often not been given. The family structure of the prepolitical form of society cannot be understood or judged from the standpoint of the family in politically structured forms of society. ''Family'' is in each case something essentially different. The character of the family is necessarily changed when it becomes a subordinate part of a political society and subject to its structure. Family relationships lose a notable part of their meaning when the status of the individual is no longer solely and essentially dependent on the family system of coordinates (the genealogy), but on the political. One must reckon with another concept of family structure in prepolitical society, different from that current among us which all along conceives the family as a member of a greater whole.

The decisive difference is that the prepolitical family is self-sufficient. That is, it is not part of a larger political, economic, cultural, religious organization; these functions are integrated into it. The family is politically self-sufficient; it is thrown back on its own resources to protect it from without and to order it from within. This is the basic reason why there is no war in the patriarchal stories; war is possible only when several family-structured groups combine together to form a tribe (J. Henninger distinguishes a ''war-like nomadism'' from the nomadism of the small-cattle shepherds, StSem 2 [1959] 69-93). This holds, too, for judicial proceedings: the function of the father is more like that of the judge. Law is identical here with family law which was passed on orally and was never allowed to be separated from custom. Custom and law are still close to each other.

The family is economically self-sufficient. Each wandering clan is an economically independent unit; the means of subsistence are supplied by its own (small cattle) herds and by barter. Prosperity and want are the result of family possessions. There is no possibility of social domination or subordination on the basis of greater or fewer possessions. The family is culturally self-sufficient: all those cultural operations which are differentiated in larger forms of community are here part of the community life of the small family group. This holds for material as well as ''intellectual'' culture of every kind—art, education, tradition, wisdom, knowledge.

The family is religiously self-sufficient: it is not part of any larger religious organization; the small family group itself is identical with the religious community. There is no cult in the sense of large scale cult for which people assemble at a sanctuary; there are no priests; the father exercises the priestly function. Consequently, there is no religious conflict or polemic. But all this does not mean that the patriarchal family is isolated from others. Rather there are constant meetings and contacts, as the patriarchal stories themselves show—contacts with cities and institutions and their kings; with sedentaries and their economy in business and barter; with various aspects of sedentary life; with its sanctuaries and religious institutions. The patriarchal form of community with its family structure is certainly independent, but it is quite open to influences from outside and subject to changes which they bring about.

The new archaeological approach has effectively altered the study of customs and legal practices. Practically all the recent literature on the patriarchal story bases its historicity on parallels between its customs and legal practices and those of the world of the ancient near east of the second millennium. The latter confirm the former. This approach maintains that many customs and practices in Gen. 12–50 can be explained only by means of these documents. In response to this it must be said that these discoveries have broadened in an amazing way our knowledge of all areas of life of the people of the ancient near east of the second millennium: religion, law, economy, forms of society, culture, art, and language. The cooperation between orientalists and Old Testament exegetes has been particularly fruitful and encouraging; a great many studies in this area come from scholars who deal with both fields.

R. de Vaux has collected the extrabiblical sources which have been advanced for comparison with the patriarchal story, and has provided bibliographical references (*Early History*. . ., pp. 233ff.). They are mainly collections of Babylonian, Assyrian, and Hittite laws together with thousands of legal texts, such as contracts and letters, among which the Nuzi texts are particularly fruitful. At the same time, however, de Vaux draws attention to a limitation in the comparison (pp. 237f.); the legal specifications are for the most part directed to a sedentary society, so that they cannot without further ado be applied to the nomadic life-style of the patriarchs. A further limitation in this comparison is that it is a matter both of legal prescriptions and also of narratives (T. L. Thompson [1974] 202, 294). There can be real parallels only when narratives of the same type can be compared, a precondition being that the legal prescriptions and practices are the same. But such parallels are as yet unknown. Even if we admit an agreement between a legal prescription in family law, such as found in the Nuzi texts, for example, and a procedure corresponding to it in one of the patriarchal texts, it is nonetheless questionable from the very outset whether one can conclude that they are contemporaneous. One can never exclude the possibility that the patriarchal narrative intends to tell of the event as a unique case.

Accordingly, there is a growing reserve in more recent works in face of an overreadiness to claim parallels. The synthesis in de Vaux (pp. 241-256) is significant; he holds that the majority of the parallels alleged are questionable or beside the point and prefers now to speak of a common background which is shown by the comparisons. J. Van Seters has shown how problematic is any attempt to date the patriarchal stories by means of parallels, legal customs, and prescriptions from the near east; he refers to a dubious one-sidedness in the use of parallels so far, inasmuch as those adduced are virtually limited to legal texts from the second millennium, while no questions are put to texts of the first. The main reason for this is that it had already been decided that the patriarchal period can be set only in the second millennium. One must grant to Van Seters that the restriction to texts of the second millennium is not justified methodologically. In several cases, however, when there is a close correspondence between texts from the neo-Babylonian period and matters in the patriarchal stories, he draws conclusions about the late dating of the latter (p. 70). In doing so, he is not faithful to his own basic principle, namely, that such parallels do not admit of any conclusions about date.

One should bear in mind with these comparisons that legal specifications and practices which concern the family are by their very nature exceedingly constant. When parallels are found in the form of adoption, though far apart in time and space, that is normal. It would be possible to fix a date of a particular form of adoption, for example, only if the terminus a quo and the terminus ad quem of the form were known in a particular region. But again it is of the nature of the thing that it is impossible to establish this. One should therefore abandon attempts to base a date on coincidence of family customs and family legal practices. It will be shown at the close of this section that the comparison as such does not thereby lose its significance.

The widely dispersed literature can be found in the compilations in R. de Vaux (*Early History*. . . [1971; Eng. 1978] 233-256), T. L. Thompson ([1974] "Nuzi and the Patriarchal Narratives," pp. 196-297), and J. Van Seters ([1975] "The Social Customs of the Patriarchs," pp. 65-103). The comparisons are concerned with family proceedings, almost all of which have to do either directly or indirectly with the three main events in the life of the family: marriage, birth, and death. Because these events form an essential component of the patriarchal stories, there is a considerable bulk of material in Gen. 12–50 for which parallels in ancient near eastern texts have been discovered.

1. Marriage.
Parallels have been found to three special types of marriage.

(a) The marriage of a concubine where there are no children, as with Abraham (Gen. 16 and 21) and, somewhat differently, with Jacob (Gen. 29–31). A distant parallel had been found long ago in the code of Hammurabi, but this is a case of a wife who is a priestess and who is not allowed to have children. There are closer parallels in the marriage contracts from Nuzi and Kültepe. However, there is an Assyrian marriage contract from Nimrod from the seventh century which is more in agreement with Gen. 16 and 21; J. Van Seters has drawn attention to it (p. 70; see also his exegesis of Gen. 16, as well as that of R. de Vaux and T. L. Thompson).

(b) The ancestress: E. A. Speiser thought that he could explain the narratives of Gen. 12; 20; and 26 from a legal practice in the Nuzi texts called *ṭuppi a-ha-tù-ti*, whereby in certain cases the wife acquired the status of the sister of the husband which involved certain privileges (*Biblical and Other Studies* 1, ed. A. Altmann [1963] 15-28). The majority of later interpreters have doubted the validity of the comparative background because the points of agreement are questionable. Here again J. Van Seters has found texts from the first millennium which seem more suitable: Egyptian marriage contracts from the ninth to sixth centuries

describe the wife as sister and at the same time adultery as a "great sin," as in Gen. 39:9 (p. 76). He thinks that these texts can be regarded as "ready material" for Gen. 12; 20; 26. But both E. A. Speiser and J. Van Seters misunderstand the narrative character of the Genesis text. The story is about an exceptional situation which cannot be explained by general legal practices.

(c) Jacob: M. Burrows has advanced a form of marriage called *errēbu*, which appears in cuneiform texts of the second millennium, to explain Jacob's marriages (Gen. 29–31) (JAOS 57 [1937] 259-276; AOS 15 [1938]). A man adopts a son with the intention of marrying him to his daughter. But the text of Gen. 29–31 says nothing about Laban adopting Jacob; moreover, J. Van Seters contests that there was such a form of marriage (p. 79). C. H. Gordon surmises that the same form of *errēbu* marriage lies behind Isaac's marriage (ZA 43 [1936] 146-169; BA 3 [1940] 1-12); but neither does this accord with the text. It may be noted that some (M. Burrows, E. A. Speiser) call on Mesopotamian legal prescriptions in texts of the second millennium as background for the complaint of Laban's daughters about their inheritance (Gen. 31:14-16).

2. Birth.

(a) Rights of the firstborn: The patriarchal texts speak of a prerogative of the firstborn in the cases of Isaac (Gen. 21), Jacob–Esau (Gen. 25; 27), and the sons of Joseph (Gen. 48). It is one of the family rights which is found throughout the whole world and for which there is attestation from all periods of history (for Mesopotamia, J. Henninger, Fests. W. Caskel [1968] 162-183). The Mesopotamian prescriptions are so divergent that one cannot with any certainty base a relationship on individual parallels. A further difficulty is that the statements about the right of the firstborn in Gen. 12–50 are indefinite and often quite obscure. An example: one finds in Assyrian laws and other texts—in the texts of Nuzi and Mari—a prescription that the firstborn receive the double share of the inheritance. But it does not seem that the patriarchs followed this prescription, which occurs so often in the Mesopotamian texts, and is the background of Deut. 21:15-17 (R. de Vaux, p. 250).

(b) Adoption: W. F. Albright maintains that the Nuzi texts have proved that, according to Gen. 15:1-3, Abraham adopted his servant Eliezer (*The Archaeology of Palestine and the Bible* [1932]; *Yahweh and the Gods of Canaan* [1968]). As a basis for this, E. A. Speiser and C. H. Gordon point to a custom attested in a Nuzi text according to which childless people were able to adopt a stranger to assure them maintenance in old age and burial rites. But the Nuzi texts are not concerned with the adoption of a slave, and the text of Gen. 15:1-3 does not require that adoption be linked with inheritance.

The other text advanced for adoption according to Nuzi law, Gen. 29–31, has already been mentioned. It too says nothing of an adoption. On the other hand, Gen. 48 speaks clearly of adoption. Jacob adopts and blesses Ephraim and Manasseh, the sons of Joseph. I. Mendelsohn proposes a Ugaritic parallel (IEJ 9 [1959] 180-183). H. Donner is critical of the parallels (OrAnt 8 [1969] 87-119).

3. Death.

(a) The Last Will of the Dying Father: E. A. Speiser finds a death-bed declaration in the Nuzi texts which is valid in law and compares Gen. 27 with it. J. Van Seters, on the contrary, rightly affirms that one must distinguish between such a death-bed declaration, valid in law, and the blessing of the dying father in

the patriarchal stories (pp. 94ff.). The Nuzi texts do not know of any blessing of the dying father. What is common to both is that the last will of the dying father has particular significance and binding force; but this does not need support, as it is universally attested.

(b) The Purchase of the Burial Place: Gen. 23. M. R. Lehmann has tried to explain this sale on the basis of Hittite laws, without being able to prove that the Hittites were ever in possession of Hebron (BASOR 129 [1953]15-18). This explanation has been accepted by W. F. Albright, J. Bright, C. H. Gordon, and others, but decisively rejected by G. M. Tucker (JBL 85 [1966] 77-84). On the other hand, H. Petschow has referred to contracts of sale from the neo-Babylonian period which agree exactly with Gen. 23 (JCS 19 [1965] 103-120; ZSRG 82 [1965] 24-38). R. de Vaux correctly concludes that the period of this "deed by dialogue" corresponds to the time when P put Gen. 23 into writing.

This example was given in greater detail because it shows how one can come to false judgments when one wants to determine everything in the patriarchal history by apparent parallels from the second millennium. One must reckon with elements entering into the arrangement of the text which can come from the period of the written composition.

The purchase of the cave at Machpelah belongs in one respect to the context of the death of a member of the family, but at the same time to that of patriarchal business and economy. The agreements about the wells and Jacob's service in Laban's household with the enlargement of his herds belong to the same context (cf. the exegesis of the particular passages).

In conclusion, then, the attempt to adduce exact and convincing parallels between patriarchal legal practices and the ancient near east has scarcely succeeded; neither have such parallels been able to date the patriarchal figures more precisely. In a number of cases (as with Gen. 23) the more precise parallels come from a later period. Nevertheless, these comparisons are of the utmost importance for the historical character of the patriarchal stories, but in a way quite different from that of fixed dates. It has been seen that the legal practices which the stories presuppose are concerned for the most part with family matters, and that they center around the main events of the life of the family: marriage, birth, and death. This points clearly to the prepolitical form of society, attested elsewhere in the patriarchal stories, which is completely determined by family structures. Family law plays a dominant role in the legal codes of the ancient near east of the second millennium in contracts and other documents; this corresponds to a stage when the family structures of society still had an important place over against civil and political structures. Moreover, this agrees with what we otherwise know from Mari and Nuzi, and with the role which the nomadic groups played in everything that was going on. In this broader perspective, the center of comparison is the common family structure, so obvious from the documents, and the necessity of regulating it by custom and law; more precise agreement in an individual case is less important and, because of the differences outstanding, not to be expected.

The problems which arise out of the patriarchal narratives are concerned with the family structures, the forms of marriage, the place of the mistress of the home and lesser wives, the division of property, the right of inheritance, the right of the firstborn, etc.; for future progress in the study it will no longer be enough to restrict comparisons to the ancient near east. To be on firmer ground, it will be necessary to introduce the results of ethnological research into the family structures.

III. Personal Names in the Patriarchal Story.   One can detect in the early stages of research in this area a fascination with the discovery of the names of the patriarchs in documents from the ancient near east. How exciting it must have been to discover in the newly found extrabiblical documents names which for two thousand years had been known only from the Bible! One can understand how the first conclusions were colored by emotions of this sort.

In 1905 appeared J. H. Breasted's article, "The Earliest Occurrence of the Name of Abram" (AJSL 21 [1905] 22-36). In a list of 156 cities which Sheshonk I (945-924 B.C.) had taken, he read one detail as "field of Abram" (JAOS 31 [1911] 290-295). In 1909 A. Ungnad discovered a name in a Babylonian document which was understood at the time as having the same meaning as Abram (BASS 6, 5 [1909] 82). H. Gressmann found confirmation in these discoveries that the names of the patriarchs were personal names; this was contrary to earlier attempts to find equivalents of the name Jacob, by means of which E. Meyer and others wanted to explain the names of the patriarchs as names of deities or tribes ("Der Stamm Jakob und die Entstehung der israelitischen Stämme," ZAW 6 [1886] 1-16).

The new archaeological approach was now joined by evidence for the occurrence of patriarchal names in extrabiblical texts; the result was a very strong tendency to prove the historicity of the patriarchal figures and to establish the date of the patriarchal period on the basis of the names discovered. The procedure here was one-sided: the main, or the only, question asked was about the correspondence of names in the period which was regarded as the patriarchal period. Another source of error was that inquiry was limited one-sidedly to an individual name, like Abraham, without paying sufficient attention to the type of name and its components. However, the discoveries at Mari, Chagar Bazar, Ugarit, and elsewhere, have been rich in names, and intensive study of them has been fruitful both philologically and historically.

Only very recently has it been contested that it is possible to determine the patriarchal period by means of patriarchal names in extrabiblical texts (T. L. Thompson; J. Van Seters). The main objection directed against previous study was that the wish to assign an early date to the patriarchs had influenced the question about names and their meaning. "The search for the authenticity of Abraham's name has become, at least for some, a quest for the historical Abraham" (T. L. Thompson, p. 20).

The controversy about the name *A-ba-am-ra-ma* (and several variants), which A. Ungnad discovered in a letter from the old Babylonian period, was representative of both sides of the discussion of extrabiblical names. The question whether the name was the equivalent of the Hebrew אברם was complicated by the question of the meaning: was the verb *r'm*, "to love" (only in East Semitic), or was it *rwm*, "to be exalted" (only in West Semitic)? The question could not be answered as long as the name was considered in isolation. But when the center of the discussion shifted to the type of name to which *Abraham* belonged, and to the occurrence of this type and its constituent parts, then the result was widespread agreement about the identity of *A-ba-am-ra-ma* and Abraham.

The result of the current research into the names of the patriarchs: *Abraham* belongs to the type of name which forms a sentence (the name and the verb in the imperfect); the first part is the designation of a god, the second a statement about the action or nature of this god. This type of name is very widespread in West Semitic and cannot be fixed in any particular period. The same holds for the constituent parts. The term אב, like אח and, less frequently, עם, is a regular designation for God in West Semitic names; the verb *rwm* (רום), "to be exalted," occurs in many formulations in West Semitic names; so the derivation from רום is certain—it is not the East Semitic *r'm*, "to love." The name Abra(ha)m is attested in a number of places from about the middle of the second millennium.

The name *Jacob* is a short form of the type formed from the verb in the imperfect to which is added the name of a god. The root עקב in West Semitic had the meaning, "to protect." The name is to be explained, "may [God] protect." This name is unusually common in the complete form (that is, with *'el*), and is attested a few times in the short form from the old Babylonian period into the first millennium. It is not possible to fix it in any period or place.

Most scholars assign *Isaac* to the same name-type as Jacob. The meaning would be, "May [God] laugh [or laughs]"; "laugh" would be understood as "gracious gift." It would also be possible to understand it as describing a situation, "he laughs" (the father in his joy over the birth of the child, or the newborn child itself). Neither the name *Isaac* nor the root צחק is hitherto proven for West Semitic names.

All other details about the names of the patriarchs and the evidence for their occurrence outside Israel is given in the exegesis on the first occasion that each name occurs.

The present result of research into the names of the patriarchs is that it is not possible to prove the historicity of the patriarchal figures or the patriarchal period from the occurrence of the same or similar names in Mesopotamian or Egyptian texts of the second or first millennium.

The result is positive, in that it shows that the names of the patriarchs belong to a type of name which was common and widespread in the whole West Semitic area. Further, the name *Abraham* occurs many times, *Jacob* is frequent, but *Isaac* is not found. This demonstrates that the names were common personal names, and the possibility that men bearing them stood at the beginning of the tradition that tells of them. In any case, the names are not inventions, but the sort that were used far and wide over a long period. One fact in particular proves that they were names from the ancient past: from the time of the taking of the land, the verb component in the name Jacob (עקב) no longer meant "protect," as it did in the early West Semitic names.

By way of conclusion to the question of the time of the patriarchs, the following may be added to what has already been said. The result of the inquiry is that it is not possible to fix the patriarchal period either by historical data (migrations of peoples), or by the nomadic life-style, or by customs or legal practices from the surrounding world, or by the extrabiblical occurrence of place-names or personal names. The range of hypotheses for a determined period between 2200 and 1200 B.C. has taken these phenomena as points of reference. Consequently, it was possible to revive J. Wellhausen's hypothesis, or even to outdo it, by contesting any talk of a patriarchal period at all.

This being the state of scholarship, it is more important to advance sound arguments in support of the thesis that the patriarchal stories deal with events that happened, and persons who lived, before the exodus and the taking of the land by the tribes. The one really sound argument emerges from the texts themselves. They present the life of small migratory groups whose life together is a family life which shows not the slightest trace of a political structure. These groups are self-sufficient politically, economically, and in religion. They know neither king, nor leader, nor priest. If we compare the form of community which appears in the patriarchal stories with those known to us from the rest of the Old Testament—the tribes at the time they became sedentary, the people politically structured in the monarchy, and finally the religious-cultic community in the province of a great empire—there remains no alternative but to set the group with the form of community presented in the patriarchal stories prior to the period of the tribes.

Accordingly, it is just this historical path that is mirrored so clearly in the conception of the patriarchal story with its three parts: the patriarchal clans gave rise to the tribes (the twelve sons of Jacob); the tribes became sedentary, joined together, encountered kingship and took it over, as indicated in the Joseph story.

A similar process, in which the sequence of stages was in any case the same, took place time and again in the ancient near east. This is particularly clear in the accounts from the old Babylonian period where the nomads advanced from the west to the settled land, first as individuals and in families, then in tribes, and finally acquired a share in the kingship. This is a confirmation of the three successive stages presented in the Old Testament and implied in the patriarchal story. This sequence puts the detailed events about the patriarchs before the period of the tribes and their settlement; it can scarcely be contested, nor has it been seriously contested so far.

The present state of scholarship does not allow anything more definite. One can only be definite that the patriarchal story went through a very long process of growth until it acquired the shape in which it has come down to us. The process, demonstrable in many places in the story, has rendered J. Wellhausen's thesis impossible. It is prudent, therefore, to answer the question of the time of the patriarchs with the caution of A. Malamat: "The patriarchal narratives reflect rather a process of centuries, telescoped into three generations" (CCUL 42 [1967] 131f.).

Literature: Genesis 12–50

Introduction

Surveys of Scholarship. O. Eissfeldt, "Die neueste Phase der Entwicklung der Pentateuchkritik," ThR 18 (1950) 91-112, 179-215, 267-287. H. H. Rowley, ed., *The Old Testament and Modern Study. A Generation of Discovery and Research* (1951). G. E. Wright, "Modern Issues in Biblical Studies. History and the Patriarchs," ET 71 (1959/60) 292-296. J. Bright, *Modern Study of OT Literature*, Fests. W. F. Albright (1961; 1965[2]) 13-31. F. V. Winnett, "Re-Examining the Foundations," JBL 84 (1965) 1-19. N. E. Wagner, "Pentateuchal Criticisms: No Clear Future," CJT 13 (1967) 225-232. W. Weidmann, *Die Patriarchen und ihre Religion im Lichte der Forschung seit Julius Wellhausen*, FRLANT 94 (1968). R. J. Thompson, "Moses and the Law in a Century of Criticism Since Graf," VT.S 19 (1970). P. R. Ackroyd, "Foreign Theological Survey: 1970-71, The OT," ET 83 (1971/72) 36-40. H. Cazelles, "Theological Bulletin on the Pentateuch," BibTB 2 (1972) 3-24. H. S. Nyberg, "Die schwedischen Beiträge zur alttestamentlichen Forschung in diesem Jahrhundert," VT.S 22, VIII (1972). E. Ruprecht, "Die Frage nach den vorliterarischen Überlieferungen in der Genesis-Forschung des angehenden 18. Jh.," ZAW 84 (1972) 293-314. C. Westermann, *Genesis 12–50: Erträge der Forschung Bd. 48* (1975).

Introductory Questions. H. Gunkel, *Ziele und Methoden der Erklärung des AT* (1904) = *Reden u. Aufsätze* (1913). O. Procksch, *Das nordhebräische Sagenbuch: Die Elohimquelle übersetzt und untersucht* (1906). J. Meinhold, "Die jahwistischen Berichte in Genesis 12–50," ZAW 39 (1921) 42-57. J. Pedersen, "Die Auffassung vom Alten Testament," ZAW 49 (1931) 161-181. E. König, *Ist die moderne Pentateuchkritik auf Tatsachen begründet?* (1933). G. von Rad, *Die Priesterschrift im Hexateuch literarisch*

86

untersucht und theologisch gewertet, BWANT 65 (1934). M. Noth, *A History of Pentateuchal Traditions* (1948, 1966³; Eng. 1972). F. M. Cross, *Studies in Ancient Yahwistic Poetry* (1950). C. A. Simpson, "The Growth of the Hexateuch," IB I (1952). C. Sant, *The Literary Structure of the Book of Genesis* (Diss. Malta, 1953). M. S. Seale, "The Glosses in the Book of Genesis and the JE Theory," ET 67 (1955/56) 333-335. M. Fubini, *Genesi e storia dei generi letterari*, "Critica e Poesia" (1956). D. J. Wiseman, *New Discoveries in Babylonia about Genesis* (1953). O. Eissfeldt, *Die Genesis der Genesis. Vom Werdegang des ersten Buches der Bibel* (1958; 1961²). D. N. Freedman, "Pentateuch," IDB III (1962) 711-727. T. R. Henn, "The Bible as Literature," *Peake's Commentary on the Bible* (1962). S. Sandmel, *The Hebrew Scriptures. An Introduction to Their Literature and Religious Ideas* (1963). S. J. de Vries, "The Hexateuchal Criticism of Abraham Kuenen," JBL 82 (1963) 31-57. S. Mowinckel, "Erwägungen zur Pentateuchquellenfrage," NTT 65 (1964). Chr. Brekelmans, "Die sogenannten deuteronomischen Elemente in Genesis bis Numeri. Ein Beitrag zur Vorgeschichte des Deuteronomiums," VT.S 15 (1965) 90-96. J. Muilenburg, "Form Criticism and Beyond," JBL 88 (1969) 1-18. J. G. Vink, "The Date and Origin of the Priestly Code in the OT," OTS 15 (1969) 1-144. D. Greenwood, "Rhetorical Criticism and Formgeschichte: Some Methodological Considerations," JBL 89 (1970) 418-426. J. W. Rogerson, "Structural Anthropology and the OT," BSOAS 33 (1970) 490-500. N. C. Habel, *Literary Criticism of the OT* (1971). G. M. Tucker, *Form Criticism of the OT* (1971). P. Beauchamp, "L'analyse structurale et l'exégèse biblique," VT.S 22 (1972) 113-128. M. Weiss, "Die Methode der 'Total-Interpretation,'" VT.S 22 (1972) 88-112. J. P. Fokkelman, *Vertelkunst in Genesis. Proeven van stilistische en structerele analyse*, Thesis Leiden (1973). T. C. Vriezen–A. S. van der Woude, *De Literatuur van Oud-Israel* (1973⁴). J. H. Hayes, ed., *Old Testament Form Criticism* (1974). A. Schmitt, "Interpretation der Genesis aus hellenistischem Geist," ZAW 86 (1974), 137-163.

A. The Significance of the Patriarchal Story

General. T. Nöldeke, "Die biblischen Erzväter," *Im neuen Reich* 1 (1871) 497-511. E. Renan, *Histoire du peuple d'Israel* 1 (1889¹⁰). H. Winckler *Abraham als Babylonier, Joseph als Ägypter. Der weltgeschichtliche Hintergrund der biblischen Vätergeschichten auf Grund der Keilschriften dargestellt* (1903). H. J. Heyes, *Bibel und Ägypten. Abraham und seine Nachkommen in Ägypten*, I (1904). E. Meyer, *Die Israeliten und ihre Nachbarstämme* (1906). B. D. Eerdmans, *Alttestamentliche Studien*, I-II (1908). R. Kittel, *Geschichte des Volkes Israel* (1909; 1932⁷). M. Maurenbrecher, *Biblische Geschichten. Beiträge zum geschichtlichen Verständnis der Religion*, III. *Erzvätergeschichten* (1909-1910). W. Lotz, "Abraham, Isaak und Jakob," BZfr 5,10 (1910). N. Nikel, "Das AT im Lichte der altorientalischen Forschungen. IV. Die Patriarchengeschichte," BZfr 5, 3 (1912). D. Völter, *Die Patriarchen Israels und die ägyptische Mythologie* (1912; 1921²). A. Eberharter, "Die neueren Hypothesen über die hebräischen Patriarchen Abraham, Isaak und Jakob," ZKTh 38 (1914) 656-704. H. Gressmann, *Die Anfänge Israels*, SAT I, 2 (1914; 1922²). R. Weill, "L'installation des Israélites en Palestine et la légende des Patriarches," RHR 87 (1922) 69-120; 88 (1923) 1-44. J. G. Bellett, *Die Welt vor der Flut und die Patriarchen* (1925). F. M. T. Böhl, *Het tijdperk der Aartsvaders* (1925). J. Kroeker, *Die Patriarchen oder das Prinzip des Glaubens. 1. Mose Kap. 12–50* (1927; 1938²). F. M. T. Böhl, "Das Zeitalter Abrahams. II. Patriarchen," AO 29,1 (1930) = *Opera Minora* (1953) 26-49. A. Lods, *Israël des origines au milieu du VIIIᵉ siècle* (1930; 1949²). D. Devimeux, *La Genèse. II. Les trois poèmes historiques: Abraham, Isaac, Jacob* (o. J.) (1935). O. Eissfeldt, "Altertumskunde und Altes Testament (Sagen der Genesis)," BZAW 66 (1936) 155-161. T. J. Meek, *Hebrew Origins* (1936; 1950²). R. Weill, "La légende des Patriarches et l'histoire," RES (4) (1937) 145-206. W. F. Albright, *From the Stone Age to Christianity. Monotheism and the Historical Process* (1940; 1957³). C. Jakubiec, *Aus der Problematik der Genesis, des Buches der Anfänge Israels, Gen 12–36* (1947). J. J. Dougherty, "The World of the Hebrew Patriarchs," Scrip. 3 (1948) 98-102. H. Junker, "Die Patriarchengeschichte. Ihre literarische Art und ihr geschichtlicher Charakter," TThZ 57 (1948) 38-45. H. S. Nyberg, "Abraham, Isaak, Patriarkena," SBU (1948; 1952²) 658-661. H. H. Rowley, *From Joseph to Joshua. Biblical Traditions in the Light of Archaeology* (1950; 1952²). E. Tisserant, "Notes sur l'histoire des Patriarches," *Miscellanea A. Miller* (1951) 9-14. B. Mariani, "Patriarchi Biblici," EC IX (1952) 953-957. C. H. Gordon, "The Patriarchal

Age,'' JBR 21 (1953) 238-243. M. F. Unger, "The Patriarchs and Contemporary History," BibSacr 110 (1953) 227-233, 289-298. A. Jepsen, "Zur Überlieferungsgeschichte der Vätergestalten," WZ(L) 2/3 (1953/54) 267-281. S. Garofalo, *I Patriachi della Bibbia* (1954). C. H. Gordon, "The Patriarchal Narratives," JNES 13 (1954) 56-59. E. Shochat, "Political Motives in the Stories of the Patriarchs," [in Hebr.] Tarb. 24 (1954/55) 252-267. M. Burrows, "Ancient Israel," in *The Idea of History in the Ancient Near East*, ed. R. C. Dentan (1955) 106-131. N. Glueck, "The Age of Abraham in the Negeb," BA 18 (1955) 1-9. B. Youngman, *Patriarchs, Judges, and Kings: Background of the Bible 1* (1955). J. Bright, *Early Israel in Recent Historical Writing: A Study in Method*, SBT 19 (1956). C. H. Gordon, *The World of the Old Testament* (1954, 1960²). G. Serfatti, "I Patriarchi, la primogenitura e il messia," RasIsr 22 (1956) 99-163. G. von Rad, *Old Testament Theology I* (1957, 1966⁵; Eng. 1962) 179-189. H. Schmökel, *Geschichte des altern Vorderasiens* (1957), esp 154-170. S. W. Baron, *Histoire d'Israël, vie sociale et religieuse* (1958). U. Cassuto, *Abraham, Isaac, Jacob* (1958). G. E. Wright, *Biblical Archaeology*, ch. 3 (1957; 1962²); "Archaeology and Old Testament Studies," JBL 77 (1958) 39-51. J. Bright, *A History of Israel*, ch. 2, "The Patriarchs" (1959; 1974²). R. Dussaud, *La Pénétration des Arabes en Syrie avant l'Islam* (1959) 163-210. J. Gray, "Archaeology and the History of Israel," LQHR (1959) 13-20. P. Montet, *L'Egypte et la Bible*, CAB 11 (1959). F. Michaéli, *Le Livre de la Genèse (Chapitres 12 à 50)* (1960). G. von Rad, "History and the Patriarchs," ET 71 (1960) 292-296; 72 (1961) 213-216. M. A. Beek, *Auf den Wegen und Spuren des Alten Testaments*, B (1961); *Geschichte Israels. Von Abraham bis Bar Kochba* (1971). H. Cazelles, "Patriarches," DBS 7 (1961) 81-156. D. N. Freedman, "The Chronology of Israel and the Ancient Near East," Fests. W. F. Albright (1961; 1965²) 203-214. M. Noth, *Die Ursprünge des alten Israel im Lichte neuer Quellen*, AFLNW 94 (1961). J. A. Soggin, "Alttestamentliche Glaubenszeugnisse und geschichtliche Wirklichkeit," ThZ 17 (1961) 385-398. G. Cornfeld, *Von Adam bis Daniel. Das Alte Testament und sein historisch-archäologischer Hintergrund* (1962). J. C. L. Gibson, "Light From Mari on the Patriarchs," JSSt 7 (1962) 44-62. A. Parrot, *Abraham et son temps*, CAB 14 (1962). J. J. Navone, "The Patriarchs of Faith, Hope, Love," BiTod 1 (1962/63) 379-384. R. de Vaux, "Les patriarches hébreux et l'histoire," SBFLA 13 (1962/63), 287-297. G. Auzou, *Als Gott zu unseren Vätern sprach. Geschichte der Heiligen Schriften des Gottesvolkes* (1963). W. F. Albright, *The Biblical Period From Abraham to Ezra* (1963). F. M. T. Böhl, "Babel und Bibel. II,7: Die Patriarchenzeit," JEOL 17 (1963) 125-140. S. B. Frost, *Patriarchs and Prophets* (1963). C. H. Gordon, "Hebrew Origins in the Light of Recent Discovery," *Biblical and Other Studies*, ed. A. Altmann (1963) 3-14. S. Yeivin, "The Age of the Patriarchs," RSO 38 (1963) 277-302. J. Hempel, *Geschichten und Geschichte im Alten Testament bis zur persischen Zeit* (1964). J. M. Holt, *The Patriarchs of Israel* (1964). A. Malamat, *Sources of Early Biblical History. The Second Millennium B.C.* (1964). J. Scheckenhofer, *Von Abraham bis David. Eine chronologische Beobachtung. I. Einleitung—Die Patriarchenzeit* (1964). F. Vattioni, "Nuovi aspetti del problema dei patriarchi biblici," Aug. 4 (1964) 330-357. C. F. Pfeiffer, *Ancient Israel From Patriarchal to Roman Times. A Study Manual* (1965). R. de Vaux, "Les patriarches hébreux et l'histoire," RB 72 (1965) 5-28; Eng., ThD 12 (1964) 227-240. N. E. Wagner, *A Literary Analysis of Genesis 12–36* (Diss. Toronto, 1965). H. Grushkin, *The World of Abraham* [in Hebr.] (1966). A. S. Kapelrud, *Israel. From the Earliest Times to the Birth of Christ* (1966). L. M. Muntingh, "Die historisiteit van die Hebreeuse aartsvaderverhale in Genesis," SAAWK (1966) 399-406. N. M. Sarna, *Understanding Genesis, The Heritage of Biblical Israel* (1966; 1972²), esp. 81-231. A. Malamat, "Aspects of Tribal Societies in Mari and Israel," CCUL 42 (1967) 129-138. S. Mowinckel, *Israels opphav og eldste historie*, Kap. I-II (1967). R. de Vaux, *Bible et Orient*, ch. 2 (1967). W. F. Albright, *Yahweh and the Gods of Canaan: A Historical Analysis of Two Contrasting Faiths* (1968) 1-95. I. Blythin, "The Patriarchs and the Promise," SJTh 21 (1968) 56-73. G. Fohrer, *Das Alte Testament*, I, 1 (1969). T. H. Gaster, *Myth, Legend, and Custom in the Old Testament* (1969), esp. 139-222. K. Koch, "Die Hebräer vom Auszug aus Ägypten bis zum Grossreich Davids," VT 19 (1969) 37-81. B. Mazar, "The Historical Background of the Book of Genesis," JNES 28 (1969) 73-83. G. Wallis, "Die Tradition von den drei Ahnvätern," ZAW 81 (1969) 18-40. C. F. Whitley, *The Genius of Ancient Israel. The Distinctive Nature of the Basic Concepts of Israel Studied Against the Cultures of the Ancient Near East* (1969). B. Mazar, ed., *The World History of the Jewish People*, II (1971). R. de Vaux, *The Early History of Israel* (1971; Eng. 1978). M. Weippert, "Abraham der Hebräer? Bemerkungen zu W. F. Albright's Deutung der

Väter Israels," Bib 52 (1971) 407-432. W. F. Albright, "From the Patriarchs to Moses: 1. From Abraham to Joseph," BA 35 (1972) 5-33. L. R. Fisher, "The Patriarchal Cycles," AOAT 22, (1973) 59-65. S. Herrmann, *A History of Israel* (1973; Eng. 1976). J. Scharbert, "Patriarchentradition und Patriarchenreligion. Ein Forschungs- und Literaturbericht," VF 19 (1974) 2-22. T. L. Thompson, *The Historicity of the Patriarchal Narratives. The Quest For the Historical Abraham*, BZAW 133 (1974). J. M. Meyers, "The Way of the Fathers," Interp. 29 (1975) 121-140.

B. The Origin and Growth of the Patriarchal Story

Tradition: Narrative, Story, Folktale, Legend, Myth. J. G. Herder, "Über die Legende," *Zerstreute Blätter* (1979) 247-320 = Herder's sämtliche Werke Bd 28 (1884) 172-229; 16 (1887) 387-398. G. L. Bauer, *Hebräische Mythologie des Alten und Neuen Testaments*, I (1802). F. Creuzer, *Symbolik und Mythologie der alten Völker, besonders der Griechen* (1810-1812). I. Goldziher, *Der Mythos bei den Hebräern und seine geschichtliche Entwicklung: Untersuchungen zur Mythologie und Religionswissenschaft* (1876). H. E. Ryle, *The Early Narratives of Genesis*, Cambr. BSC (1892; 1904²). M. Grünbaum, *Neue Beiträge zur semitischen Sagenkunde* (1893). M. Heyne, *Deutsches Wörterbuch* (mit Grimm, 1905²/06). M. J. Lagrange, *Etudes sur les religions sémitiques* (1905²). P. Ehrenreich, "Götter und Heilbringer. Eine ethnologische Kritik," ZE 38 (1906) 536-610. H. Gunkel, *Die israelische Literatur: Die orientalischen Literaturen*, ed. P. Hinneberg (1906; 1925²) = Wissenschaftliche Buchgesellschaft (1963). T. K. Cheyne, *Traditions and Beliefs of Ancient Israel* (1907). A. R. Gordon, *The Early Traditions of Genesis* (1907). W. F. Otto, *Die Manen oder von den Urformen des Totenglaubens. Eine Untersuchung zur Religion der Griechen, Römer und Semiten und zum Volksglauben überhaupt* (1908; 1958²). I. F. Wood, "Folk-Tales in Old Testament Narratives," JBL 28 (1908) 34-41. K. Abraham, *Traum und Mythus. Eine Studie zur Völkerpsychologie* (1909). A. Olrik, "Epische Gesetze der Volksdichtung," ZDA 51 (1909) 1-12 (Danish [1908, 1921²]; Eng. in A. Dundes, ed., *Studies in Folklore* [1965], 127-141). W. Wundt, *Völkerpsychologie*, II, 3 "Märchen" (1909; 1926³). H. Gressmann, "Sage und Geschichte in den Patriarchenerzählungen," ZAW 30 (1910) 1-34. H. Gunkel, *Kommentar*, "Einleitung" (1910³; 1964⁶). T. Kappstein, *Bibel und Sage–Sage, Mythus und Legende* (1913). A. Heusler, *Die Anfänge der isländischen Sage* (1914). H. Gunkel, *Das Märchen im AT* (1917). P. Kahle–H. Schmidt, *Volkserzählungen aus Palästina*, FRLANT 17/18 (1918; 1930²). H. Harari, *Littérature et tradition* (1919). E. Bethe, *Märchen, Sage, Mythus* (1922). E. Cassirer, *Die Begriffsform im mythischen Denken* (1922). P. Saintyves, *Essais de Folklore Biblique* (1922). W. Baumgartner, "Ein Kapitel vom hebräischen Erzählungsstil," FRLANT 36 (1923)145-157. A. T. Clay, *The Origin of Biblical Traditions*, YOS 12 (1923). O. Eissfeldt, *Stammessage und Novelle in den Geschichten von Jakob und von seinen Söhnen*, FRLANT 36 (1923) 56-77 = KS. I (1962) 84-104. A. Lods, "Le rôle de la tradition orale dans la formation des récits de l'Ancien Testament," RHR 88 (1923) 51-64. F. M. T. Böhl, "Volketymologie en woordspeling in de Genesisverhaalen," MAA 59-A (1925) 49-79. F. Ranke, "Grundfragen der Volkssagenforschung," NZV 3 (1925) 12-23 = *Vergleichende Sagenforschung*, ed. L. Petzold (1969) 1-20. B. Malinowski, *Myth in Primitive Psychology* (1926). P. Merker, "Legende," RDL II (1926²-28) 176-200. O. Eissfeldt, "Die kleinste literarische Einheit in den Erzählungsbüchern des Alten Testaments," ThBl 6 (1927) 333-337 = KS I (1962) 143-149. L. Lévy-Bruhl, *Primitive Mentality* (Fr. 1922, 1935³; Eng. 1923). A. Alt, *Der Gott der Väter. Zur Vorgeschichte der israelitischen Religion*, BWANT 3,12 (1929) = KS I (1953; 1963³) 1-78. W. Caskel, "'Aijäm al-'Arab," Isl 3,5 (1930). J. Hempel, "Die althebräische Literatur und ihr hellenistisch-jüdisches Nachleben," HLW (1930-1933) 81-101. A. Jolles, *Einfache Formen* (1930; 1958²). R. Petsch, "Die Lehre von den 'Einfachen Formen,'" DVfLG 10 (1932). H. M. & N. K. Chadwick, *The Growth of Literature* (1932-1936). G. van der Leeuw, *Phänomenologie der Religion* (1933; 1956²), §1 & 2. K. T. Preuss, *Der religiöse Gehalt der Mythen* (1933). H. G. Güterbock, "Die historische Tradition und ihre literarische Gestaltung bei Babyloniern und Hethitern bis 1200," ZA 42 (NF 8, 1934) 1-91; 44 (NF 10, 1938) 45-145. H. S. Nyberg, "Das textkritische Problem des Alten Testaments am Hoseabuch demonstriert," ZAW 52 (1934) 241-254. H. Baumann, Schöpfung und Urzeit des Menschen im Mythus der afrikanischen Völker (1936; 1964) 334-384. H. Birkeland, *Zum hebräischen Traditionswesen* (1938). C. G. Jung–K. Kerényi, *Einführung in das Wesen der Mythologie*

(1941). O. Eissfeldt, "Mythus und Sage in den Ras Schamra–Texten," *Kleine Beiträge zur Orientalistik, Semitistik und Islam–wissenschaft* (1944) 267-283 = KS II (1963) 489-501. E. Auerbach, *Mimesis* (1946, 1971[5]; Eng. 1953-54). E. Jacob, *La tradition historique en Israël* (1946). J. Pedersen, *Den arabiske Bog* (1946). G. von Rad, "Das hermeneutische Problem im Buche Genesis," VF (1946/47) 43-51. J. van der Ploeg, "Le rôle de la tradition orale dans la transmission du texte de l'Ancien Testament," RB 54 (1947) 5-41. H. G. Güterbock, "The Hittite Version of the Hurrian Kumarbi Myths," AJA 52 (1948) 123-134. W. Kayser, *Das sprachliche Kunstwerk* (1948; 1960[6]). A. L. Oppenheim, "Mesopotamian Mythology, II," Or NS 17 (1948). A. E. Jensen, "Die mythische Weltbetrachtung der alten Pflanzer–Völker," ErJb 17 (1949) 421-473. R. Pettazzoni, *Miti e Legende, I* (1948) 301-328. A. Bentzen, *Introduction to the OT*. I, "Narratives" (1948/49; 1952[2]). H. J. Kraus, "Gedanken zum theologischen Problem der alttestamentlichen Sage," EvTh 8 (1948/49) 319-328. G. van der Leeuw, "Urzeit und Endzeit, I," ErJb 17 (1949) 11-52. P. Radin, "The Basic Myth of the North American Indians," ErJb 17 (1949) 359-419. T. H. Gaster, *Thespis: Ritual, Myth, and Drama in the Ancient Near East* (1950; 1966[3]). A. Goetze, "Hittite Myths, Epics, and Legends," ANET (1950; 1955; 1955[3]) 120-128. A. Haldar, "The Notion of the Desert in Sumero-Accadian and West Semitic Religion," UUA 3 (1950). G. van der Leeuw, "Die Bedeutung der Mythen," Festschr. A. Bertholet (1950) 287-293. M. Noth, *History of Israel* (1950, 1960[5]; Eng. 1962). H. Ringgren, "Oral and Written Transmission in the OT," StTh 3 (1950/51) 34-59. A. E. Jensen, *Mythos und Kult bei Naturvölkern. Religionswissenschaftliche Betrachtungen: Studien zur Kulturkunde 10* (1951; 1960[2]). C. Hartlich–W. Sachs, *Der Ursprung des Mythosbegriffes in der modernen Bibelwissenschaft*, SSEA 2 (1952). J. Gray, *Canaanite Mythology and Hebrew Tradition*, OST 14 (1953). J. Hempel, "Glaube, Mythos und Geschichte im AT," ZAW 65 (1953) 109-167. C. A. Keller, " 'Die Gefährdung der Ahnfrau'. Ein Beitrag zur gattungs- und motivgeschichtlichen Erforschung alttestamentlicher Erzählungen," ZAW 66 (1954) 181-191. E. Nielsen, *Oral Tradition. A Modern Problem in OT Introduction*, SBT 11 (1954; 1955[2]). E. Cassirer, *Language and Myth* (1955). E. Lämmert, *Bauformen des Erzählens* (1955). G. H. Davies, "An Approach to the Problem of Old Testament Mythology," PEQ 88 (1956) 83-91. J. Schildenberger, "Mythus—Wunder—Mysterium," BiLi 24 (1956/57). M. Schmaus, ed., *Die mündliche Überlieferung. Beiträge zum Begriff der Tradition* (1957). G. Widengren, *Oral Tradition and Written Literature Among the Hebrews in the Light of Arabic Evidence. With Special Regard to Prose Narratives*, AOK 23 (1958) 201-262. J. Barr, "The Meaning of 'Mythology' in Relation to the OT," VT 9 (1959) 1-10. G. Brillet, *Meditations on the OT. The Narrative* (1959). S. Sudhof, "Die Legende. Ein Versuch zu ihrer Bestimmung," StudGen 11 (1959) 691-699. A. B. Lord, *The Singer of Tales* (1960; 1971[3]). P. G. Rinaldi, *Tradizioni patriarcali e mosaiche, antica letterature Israelitica e storia in Osea* (1960). J. A. Soggin, "Kultätiologische Sagen und Katechese im Hexateuch," VT 10 (1960) 341-347. G. Widengren, "Myth and History in Israelite–Jewish Thought," *Essays in Honour of P. Radin* (1960/61) 467-495. L. Alonso-Schökel, "Erzählkunst im Buche der Richter," Bib 42,2 (1961). W. Benjamin, *Illuminationen*, III, "Der Erzähler" (1961) 409-436. C. M. Edsman, "Sagen und Legenden, I," RGG[3]V (1961) 1300-1302. G. Fohrer, "Tradition und Interpretation im AT," ZAW 73 (1961) 1-30. H. W. Haussig, ed., Wörterbuch der Mythologie, I (1961). E. Jacob, "Sagen und Legenden, II," RGG[3]V (1961) 1302-1308. Y. Kaufmann, "Traditions Concerning Early Israelite History in Canaan," ScrHie 8 (1961) 303-334. S. N. Kramer, ed., *Mythologies of the Ancient World* (1961). G. E. Mendenhall, "Biblical History in Transition," Fests. W. F. Albright (1961; 1965[5]) 32-53. S. Moscati, *Le origini della narrativa storica nell arte del Vicino Oriente antico*, AANL X,2 (1961). I. L. Seeligmann, "Aetiological Elements in Biblical Historiography," Zion 26 (1961) 141-169. J. van der Vries, *Forschungsgeschichte der Mythologie*, OA I,7 (1961). B. S. Childs, *Memory and Tradition in Israel*, SBT 37 (1962) 5-96. C. Lévi-Strauss, *La pensée sauvage* (1962; Eng. 1966). I. L. Seeligmann, "Hebräische Erzählung und biblische Geschichtsschreibung," ThZ 18 (1962) 305-325. G. E. Wright, "Cult and History. A Study of a Current Problem in OT Interpretation," Interp. 16 (1962) 3-20. G. W. Ahlström, "Oral and Written Transmission: Some Considerations," HThR 59 (1963) 69-81. L. Alonso-Schökel, *Estudios de poética hebrea* (1963). P. Barthel, *Interprétation du language mythique et théologie biblique* (1963; 1967[2]). B. S. Childs, "A Study of the Formula 'Until this day,' " JBL 82 (1963) 279-292. R. C. Culley, "An Approach to the Problem of Oral Tradition," VT 13 (1963) 113-125. S. H. Hooke, *Middle Eastern Mythology* (1963). W. Richter,

Traditionsgeschichtliche Untersuchungen zum Richterbuch, BBB 18 (1963). M. Weiss, "Einiges über die Bauformen des Erzählens in der Bibel," VT 13 (1963) 456-475. K. Koch, *The Growth of the Biblical Tradition* (1964; 1974³; Eng. 1969). J. S. Morris, "Biblical Event-Narratives and Historical Truth," USQR 19 (1964) 221-230. C. Westermann, "Arten der Erzählung in der Genesis," ThB 24 (1964) 9-91. H. W. Wolff, "Das Kerygma des Jahwisten," EvTh 24 (1964) 73-98 = ThB 22 (1964) 345-373; "The Kerygma of the Yahwist," Interp. 20 (1966) 131-158. O. Eissfeldt, *Stammessage und Menschheitserzählung in der Genesis*, SSAW 110, 4 (1964/65). M. I. Finley, "Myth, Memory and History," HTh 4 (1965) 281-302. G. Fohrer, "Die Sage in der Bibel," *Sagen und ihre Dichtung* (1965) 59-80. G. I. Jones, "Time and Oral Tradition With Special Reference to Eastern Nigeria," JAfH 6 (1965) 153-160. M. Lüthi, "Gehalt und Erzählweise der Volkssage," *Sagen und ihre Dichtung* (1965) 11-27. J. Vansina, *Oral Tradition: A Study in Historical Methodology* (Fr. 1961; Eng. 1965). M. Weiss, "Weiteres über Bauformen des Erzählens in der Bibel," Bib 46 (1965) 181-206. H. M. Dion, "The Patriarchal Traditions and the Literary Form of the 'Oracle of Salvation,' " CBQ 29 (1967) 198-206. M. Eliade, *Myths, Dreams, and Mysteries* (1967). K. Koch, "Die Sohnesverheissung an den ugaritischen Daniel," ZA 58 (NF 24) (1967) 211-221. H. C. White, *A Form-Critical Analysis of the Patriarchal Cultic Legends* (Diss. Drew 1967). R. M. Dorson, "The Debate Over the Trustworthiness of Oral Traditional History," *Volksüberlieferung: Fests. K. Ranke* (1968), 19-35. W. G. Lambert, "Myth and Ritual as Conceived by the Babylonians," JSSt 13 (1968) 104-112. B. O. Long, *The Problem of Etiological Narrative in the OT*, BZAW 108 (1968). M. Lüthi, "Familie und Natur im Märchen," *Fests. K. Ranke* (1968) 181-195. J. R. Porter, "Pre-Islamic Arabic Historical Traditions and the Early Historical Narratives of the OT," JBL 87 (1968) 17-26. R. Smend, "Elemente alttestamentlichen Geschichtsdenkens," ThSt(B) 95 (1968). J. Gray, *Near Eastern Mythology: Mesopotamia, Canaan, Israel* (1969). E. R. Leach, *Genesis as Myth, and Other Essays* (1969). L. Petzold, ed., *Vergleichende Sagenforschung: Wege der Forschung* 152 (1969). H. Cancik, *Mythische und historische Wahrheit. Interpretation zu Texten der hethitischen, biblischen und griechischen Historiographie*, SBS 48 (1970). F. Golka, "Zur Erforschung der Ätiologien im AT," VT 20 (1970) 90-98; VT 26 (1976) 410-428. B. W. Anderson, "Myth and the Biblical Tradition," ThTo 27 (1970/71) 44-62. G. S. Kirk, *Myth. Its Meaning and Functions in Ancient and Other Cultures* (1970/71). D. P. Henige, "Oral Tradition and Chronology," JAfH 12 (1971) 371-389. S. E. McEvenue, *The Narrative Style of the Priestly Writer*, AnBib (1971). J. Schreiner, "Mythos und Altes Testament," BiLe 12 (1971) 141-153. R. C. Culley, "Oral Tradition and Historicity," *Fests. F. V. Winnett* (1972) 102-116; "Some Comments on Structural Analysis and Biblical Studies," VT.S 22 (1972) 129-142. T. E. Fretheim, "The Jacob Traditions: Theology and Hermeneutic," Interp 26 (1972) 419-436. R. M. Hals, "Legend: A Case Study in OT Form-Critical Terminology," CBQ 34 (1972) 166-176. B. O. Long, "Prophetic Call Traditions and Reports of Visions," ZAW 84 (1972) 494-500. E. Metelinskij, *Zur strukturell-typologischen Erforschung des Volksmärchens* (1969) (in V. Propp 1975). V. Propp, *Morphology of the Folktale* (Russian 1928; Eng. 1968², 1975). W. E. Rast, *Tradition History and the OT* (1972). F. M. Cross, *Canaanite Myth and Hebrew Epic. Essays in the History of the Religion of Israel* (1973). E. Güttgemann, "Einleitende Bemerkungen zur strukturalen Erzählforschung," LingBib 23/24 (1973) 2-47. A. Haldar, "Tradition and History," BibOr 30 (1973) 26-37. D. A. Knight, *Rediscovering the Traditions of Israel. The Development of the Traditio-Historical Research of the OT, with Special Consideration of Scandinavian Contributions*, Diss. Series 9 (1973). B. O. Long, "2 Kings III and Genres of Prophetic Narrative," VT 23 (1973) 337-348. J. B. Metz, "Kleine Apologie des Erzählens," Conc 9 (1973) 334-341. W. Weinrich, "Narrative Theology," Conc 9 (1973) 329-334. M. Weippert, "Fragen des israelitischen Geschichtsbewusstseins," VT 23 (1973) 415-442. B. S. Childs, "The Etiological Tale Re-Examined," VT 24 (1974) 387-397. P. Gibert, "Legende ou Saga?" VT 24 (1974) 411-420. D. Irvin, *Mytharion. The Composition of Tales From the OT and the Ancient Near East*, AOAT (1974). W. G. Lambert, "Der Mythos im alten Mesopotamien, sein Werden und Vergehen," ZRGG 26 (1974) 1-16. J. W. Rogerson, *Myth in Old Testament Interpretation*, BZAW 134 (1974), esp. ch. 8. W. Brueggemann–H. W. Wolff, *The Vitality of Old Testament Traditions* (1975). J. Hermisson, "Allgemeines zu alttestamentlichen Erzählungen," *Enzyklopädie des Märchens*, ed. K. Ranke (1975) 419-441. A. de Pury, *Promesse divine et légende cultuelle dans le cycle de Jacob. Genèse 28 et les traditions patriarcales, I-II* (1975). J. Van Seters, *Abraham in History and Tradition* (1975). B. O. Long, "Recent Field Studies in Oral Literature and their Bearing on O. T. Criticism," VT 26 (1976) 187-198.

Genealogy and Itinerary. F. Wüstenfeld, *Genealogische Tabellen der arabischen Stämme und Familien* (1852; 1853²). A. Elter, *Itinerarstudien* (1908). S. Euringer, "Die Chronologie der biblischen Urgeschichte (Genesis 5 und 11)," BZfr 2 (1909). K. Budde, "Ellä toledōth," ZAW 34 (1914) 241-253. A. Jaussen–J. de Savignac, *Coutumes des Fuqarâ: Mission Archéologique en Arabie*, Vol, III (1914; 1920). E. G. Kraeling, *Aram and Israel* (1918), esp. 18, 41-45. U. Cassuto, "Studi sulla Genesi," GSAI NS 1 (1926) esp. 193-215. B. Moritz, "Edomitische Genealogien, I," ZAW 44 (1926) 81-93. O. Eissfeldt, *Introduction to the Old Testament* (1934, 1964³; Eng. 1964). P. Philippson, *Genealogie als mythische Form: Studien zur Theologie des Hesiod*, SO 7 (1936). H. Charles, *Tribus moutonnières du Moyen-Euphrate: Documents d'Etudes Orientales de l'Institut Français de Damas* 8 (1939). L. Aterman, "Some Repercussions From Late Levitical Genealogical Accretions in P and the Chronicler," AJSL 58 (1941) 49-56. U. Cassuto, "The Ten Generations From Adam to Noah," *L. Ginsberg Jubilee Vol.* (1945) 381-400. R. Montagne, *La Civilisation du Désert* (1947). J. R. Garcia, "Las genealogías y la cronologia genesíacas. Introduccion. Se encuadra el problema," EstB 8 (1949) 327-353. A. Lefèvre, "Note d'exégèse sur les généalogies des Qehatites," RSR 37 (1950) 287-292. B. Couroyer, "Histoire d'une tribu semi-nomade de Palestine," RB 58 (1951) 75-91. A. Goetze, "An Old Babylonian Itinerary," JCS 7 (1953) 51-72. R. A. Bowman, "Genealogy," IDB II (1962) 362-365. J. Koenig, "Itineraires sinaïtiques en Arabi," RHR 166 (1964) 121-141. J. Meysing, "The Biblical Chronologies of the Patriarchs," CNFI 13 (1963) 3-12; 14 (1964) 22-25. L. Ramlot, "Les généalogies bibliques: Un genre littéraire oriental," BVC 60 (1964) 53-70. W. Caskel, *Ğamharat an-Nasab. Das genealogische Werk des Hišām Ibn Muhammad al-Kalbi* (1965). G. Lanczkowski, "Die Sprache von Zūyūa als Initiationsmittel," *Initiation*, ed. C. J. Bleeker (1965) 27-39. J. J. Finkelstein, "The Genealogy of the Hammurapi Dynasty," JCS 20 (1966) 55-118. J. Henninger, "Altarabische Genealogie," Anthr. 61 (1966) 852-870. R. Kilian, *Die vorpriesterlichen Abrahamüberlieferungen*, BBB 24 (1966) esp. 279-283. A. Malamat, "King Lists of the Old Babylonian Period and Biblical Genealogies," JAOS 88 (1968) 163-173. M. D. Johnson, *The Purpose of the Biblical Genealogies with Special Reference to the Setting of the Genealogies of Jesus*, SNTS 8 (1969). J. Scharbert, "Der Sinn der Toledot-Formel in der Priesterschrift," *Fests.* W. Eichrodt (1970) 45-56. G. W. Coats, "The Wilderness Itinerary," CBQ 34 (1972) 135-152. K. Galling, "Der Weg der Phöniker nach Tarsis in literarischer und archäologischer Sicht," ZDPV 88 (1972) 140-181, esp. 162-180. T. C. Hartman, "Some Thoughts on the Sumerian King List and Genesis 5 and 11b," JBL 91 (1972) 25-32. R. R. Wilson, *Genealogy and History in the Biblical World* (Diss. 1972, YNES 7[1977]). A. Malamat, "Tribal Societies: Biblical Genealogies and African Linear Systems," AESoc 14 (1973) 126-136. G. I. Davies, "The Wilderness Itineraries: A Comparative Study," TynB 25 (1974) 46-81. R. R. Wilson, "The Old Testament Genealogies in Recent Research," JBL 94 (1975) 169-189.

C. The World of the Patriarchal Story and the Question of the Time of the Patriarchs

1. The New Archaeological Approach.

a) General: F. Vigouroux, *La Bible et les découvertes modernes en Palestine, en Egypte et en Assyrie* (1881³; 1896⁶). G. A. Barton, *Archaeology and the Bible* (1917). I. Benzinger, *Hebräische Archäologie* (1927). G. Contenau, *Manuel d'Archéologie orientale*, III-IV (1931, 1947). A. G. Barrois, *Manuel d'Archéologie Biblique, I-II* (1939, 1953). M. Burrows, *What Mean These Stones? The Significance of Archaeology For Biblical Studies* (1941). F. G. Kenyon, *The Bible and Archaeology* (1949). H. H. Rowley, "Recent Discovery and the Patriarchal Age," BJRL 32 (1949/50) 44-79 = *The Servant of the Lord and Other Essays* (1952; 1965²) 281-318. M. F. Unger, *Archaeology and the Old Testament* (1951; 1956²). W. F. Albright, "The Old Testament World," IB I (1952) 233-271. J. P. Free, "Archaeology and Bible Criticism, I-VI," BibSac 113 (1956) 123-129, 214-226, 322-338; 114 (1957) 23-29, 123-132, 213-224. J. Pritchard, *Archaeology and the Old Testament* (1958). G. E. Wright, *Biblical Archaeology* (1957, 1962²). M. Noth, "Der Beitrag der Archäologie zur Geschichte Israels," VT.S 7 (1960) 262-282 = GesAufs. I (1971) 34-52. J. A. Soggin, "Ancient Biblical Traditions and Modern Archaeological Discoveries," BA 23 (1960) 95-100. J. Gray, *Archaeology and the Old Testament*

World (1962). J. A. Thompson, *The Bible and Archaeology* (1962; 1972²). D. W. Thomas, ed., *Archaeology and Old Testament Study* (1967). H. Bardtke, *Bibel, Spaten und Geschichte.* Kap. 5, "Palästina"; 6, "Zeitalter der Erzväter" (1969). P. W. Lapp, *Biblical Archaeology and History*, C.IV (1969). A. S. Kapelrud, "Det gamle testamente og arkeologien. Forskningen etter Ras Sjamra," NTT 71 (1970) 65-77. A. Kuschke–E. Kutsch, eds., *Archäologie und Altes Testament*, Fests. K. Galling (1970). B. Hrouda, *Handbuch der Archäologie*, I (1971). R. Harker, *Digging up the Bible Lands* (1972). H. M. Orlinsky, *Understanding the Bible through History and Archaeology: Ancient Israel* (1972). J. E. Huesman, "Archaeology and Early Israel: The Scene Today," CBQ 37 (1975) 1-16.

   b) Ancient East: H. Winckler, *Untersuchungen zur altorientalischen Geschichte* (1889). A. Sanda, "Untersuchungen zur Kunde des alten Orients, I," MVG 7 (1902) 17-96. C. Niebuhr, *Die Amarna-Zeit: Altorientalische Forschungen* I, 2 (1903). A. Jeremias, *Das Alte Testament im Lichte des Alten Orients* (1904; 1930⁴). H. Winckler, *Altorientalische Forschungen* III, 1 (1906). R. Kittel, *Die orientalischen Ausgrabungen und die ältere biblische Geschichte* (1908⁵). P. Dhorme, "Les pays bibliques au temps d'El-Amarna," RB 6 (1909) 50-73. L. Legrain, *Le temps des Rois d'Ur* (1912). B. Luther, *Geschichte des Altertums* III §308 (1913³). B. Meissner, *Babylonien und Assyrien* I-II (1920, 1925). E. Meyer, *GA I-II* (1920; 1953³). E. Chiera–E. A. Speiser, "A New Factor in the History of the Ancient Near East," AASOR 6 (1926) 75-92. S. Smith, *Early History of Assyria to 1000 B.C.: History of Babylonia and Assyria* III (1928). E. A. Speiser, *Mesopotamian Origins* (1930). A. Goetze, *Kulturgeschichte des Alten Orients. Kleinasien*, HdA III, 3, 1 (1933; 1957²). J. A. Montgomery, *Arabia and the Bible*. C.III (1934) 37-53 = The Library of Biblical Studies 35 (1969). F. M. T. Böhl, "Skizze der mesopotamischen Kulturgeschichte 5000–800 v. Chr.," ThSt(U) 19 (1936). W. C. Graham–H. G. May, *Culture and Conscience* (1936). E. W. Andrae, "Vorderasien ohne Phönikien, Palästina und Kypros," *Handbuch der Archäologie* I (1939) 543-796. W. F. Albright, "New Light on the History of Western Asia in the Second Millennium B.C.," BASOR 77 (1940) 20-32; 78 (1940) 23-31. V. Christian, *Altertumskunde des Zweistromlandes. Von der Vorzeit bis zum Ende der Achämenidenherrschaft* (1940). B. Hrozný, *Die älteste Geschichte Vorderasiens* (1940). F. Nötscher, *Biblische Altertumskunde* (1940). W. F. Otto, *Die älteste Geschichte Vorderasiens. Kritische Bemerkungen zu B. Hroznýs gleichnamigen Werk*, SAM II, 3 (1941). A. T. Olmstead, "History, Ancient World and the Bible," JNESt 2 (1943) 1-34. D. G. Hogarth, *The Ancient East* (1945²). P. J. Watson, "The Chronology of North Syria and North Mesopotamia From 10,000 B.C. to 2000 B.C.," *Chronologies in Old World Archaeology*, ed. R. W. Ehrlich (1945). P. van der Meer, *The Chronology of Western Asia and Egypt* (1947; 1963³). C. Rabin, *Ancient West-Arabia* (1951). A. M. van Dijk, "La découverte de la culture littéraire Sumérienne et la signification pour l'histoire de l'Antiquité Orientale," *Journées Bibliques de Louvain* 6 (1954) = *L'Ancien Testament et Orient* (1957) 5-28. J. M. A. Janssen, "L'Ancien Testament et l'Orient," *Etudes présentés aux VIes Journées Bibliques de Louvain 1954* (1957) 31-52. S. Moscati, *Ancient Semitic Civilization* (1957). E. A. Speiser, "The Biblical Idea of History in Its Common Near Eastern Setting," IEJ 7 (1957) 201-217 = *Oriental and Biblical Studies* (1967) 187-210. H. R. Hall, *The Ancient History of the Near East* (1960). G. W. van Beek, "South Arabian History and Archaeology," Fests. W. F. Albright (1961; 1965²) 229-248. W. L. Moran, "The Hebrew Language in Its Northwest Semitic Background," in Fests. W. F. Albright (1961; 1965²). H. Schmökel, ed., *Kulturgeschichte des Alten Orients* (1961). J. J. Finkelstein, "Mesopotamia," JNESt 21 (1962) 73-92. A. Grohmann, "Arabien," *Kulturgeschichte des Alten Orients III*, 4 (1963). J. R. Kupper, "Northern Mesopotamia and Syria," CAH.2, 1 (1963). A. L. Oppenheim, *Ancient Mesopotamia: Portrait of a Dead Civilization* (1964). E. A. Speiser, *The World History of the Jewish People*. II A. *Mesopotamia* (1964). C. H. Gordon, *The Ancient Near East* (1965). K. A. Kitchen, *Ancient Orient and Old Testament* (1966). E. A. Speiser, *Oriental and Biblical Studies* (1967). R. de Vaux, *Bible et Orient* (Collected Essays) (1967). S. S. Ahmed, *Southern Mesopotamia in the Time of Ashurbanipal* (1968). I. M. Diakonoff, ed., *Ancient Mesopotamia. Socio-Economic History. A Collection of Studies of Soviet Scholars* (1969). J. A. Sanders, ed., *Near Eastern Archaeology in the Twentieth Century: Essays in Honor of N. Glueck* (1970). K. Bittel, *Archäologische Forschungsprobleme zur Frühgeschichte Kleinasiens* (1973). J. A. Soggin, *The Old Testament and Oriental Studies*; BibOr 29 (1975).

   c) Palestine-Syria: A. H. Sayce, *Patriarchal Palestine* (1895). R. Hartmann,

Palästina unter den Arabern 632-1516: Das Land der Bibel I, 4 (1915). P. Thomsen, *Palästina und seine Kultur in fünf Jahrtausenden nach den neuesten Ausgrabungen dargestellt*, AO 30 (1917²; 1932³). A. Bertholet, *Kulturgeschichte Israels* (1919, 1920²). W. F. Albright, "Palestine in the Earliest Historical Period," JPOS 2 (1922) 110-138; 15 (1935) 193-234; "The Jordan Valley in the Bronze Age," AASOR 6 (1926) 13-74. R. Dussaud, "Nouveaux renseignements sur la Palestine et la Syrie vers 2000 avant notre erè," Syria 8 (1927) 216-231. A. Musil, *Arabia Deserta* (1927; Eng. 1931); *Northern Neğd* (1928). F. M. Abel, "Exploration du Sud Est de la Vallée de Jourdain," RB 40 (1931) 214-226. A. T. Olmstead, *A History of Palestine and Syria to the Macedonian Conquest* (1931). W. F. Albright, *The Archaeology of Palestine and the Bible* (1932; rev. 1960). N. Glueck, "Explorations in Eastern Palestine, I-III," AASOR (1934-1939). W. F. Albright, "Palestine in the Earliest Historical Period," JPOS 15 (1935) 193-234. A. Bea, *Die Bedeutung der Ausgrabungen von Telēlāt Ghássul für die Frühgeschichte Palästinas*, BZAW 66 (1936). W. F. Albright, "The Present State of Syro-Palestinian Archaeology," *Harvard Symposium on Archaeology and the Bible* (1938) 1-46. N. Glueck, "The Other Side of the Jordan," AASOR 20 (1940). M. Noth, *The Old Testament World* (1940, 1962⁴; Eng. 1962). A. Alt, "Die älteste Schilderung Palästinas im Lichte neuer Funde," PJ 37 (1941) 19-49. N. Glueck, *The River Jordan* (1946; 1954²). P. K. Hitti, *History of Syria Including Lebanon and Palestine* (1951). F. M. Abel, *Histoire de la Palestine* (1952; 1959²). W. F. Albright, "Syrien, Phönizien und Palästina, die Anfänge Israels," *Historia Mundi* 2 (1953) 331-376. A. Jirku, *Die Ausgrabungen in Palästina und Syrien* (1956). P. K. Hitti, *Lebanon in History from the Earliest Times to the Present* (1957). Y. Aharoni, "The Negeb of Judah," IEJ 8 (1958) 26-38. N. Glueck, *Rivers in the Desert. A History of the Negev* (1959); "The Negev," BA 22 (1959) 82-97. K. M. Kenyon, *Archaeology in the Holy Land* (1960) esp.135-161. N. Glueck. "The Archaeological History of the Negev," HUCA 31 (1961) 11-18. G. E. Wright, "The Archaeology of Palestine," Fests. W. F. Albright (1961; 1965²) 73-112. E. Anati, *Palestine Before the Hebrews* (1963). A. Jirku, *Geschichte Palästina-Syriens im orientalischen Altertum* (1963). Y. M. Grintz, "The Land of the Hebrews" [in Hebr.]: OLD Jerusalem (1964) 92-102. H. Klengel, *Geschichte Syriens im 2. Jahrtausend v. n. Z.*, I (1965). M. Liverani, "Il fuoruscitismo in Siria nella tarda et à del bronzo," RSIt 77 (1965) 315-336. W. F. Albright, *Archaeology, Historical Analogy and Early Biblical Tradition*, ch. 2 (1966). K. M. Kenyon, "Palestine in the Middle Bronze Age," CAH 48 (1966²). A. Malamat, *Syrien-Palästina in der zweiten Hälfte des 2. Jahrtausends: Fischer Weltgeschichte* 3 (1966). J. B. Hennessy, *The Foreign Relations of Palestine during the Early Bronze Age* (1967). H. Klengel, *Geschichte und Kultur Altsyriens* (1967). B. Mazar, "The Middle Bronze Age in Palestine," IEJ 18 (1968) 65-97. W. G. Dever, "The 'Middle Bronze I' Period in Syria and Palestine," *Essays in Honor of N. Glueck* (1970) 132-163. P. Lapp, "Palestine in the Early Bronze Age," *Essays in Honor of N. Glueck* (1970) 101-131. H. Klengel, *Syria Antiqua* (1971).

2. Migrations of Peoples in the Near East and Migrations of the Patriarchs.

K. Budde, "Das nomadische Ideal im Alten Testament," PrJ 85 (1896) 57-79. J. W. Flight, "The Nomadic Idea and Ideal in the Old Testament," JBL 42 (1923) 158-226. A. Ungnad, *Die ältesten Völkerwanderungen Vorderasiens* (1923). A. Jirku, "Die Wanderungen der Hebräer im 3. und 2. vorchristlichen Jahrtausend," AO 24, 2 (1924). B. Maisler, *Untersuchungen zur alten Geschichte und Ethnographie Syriens und Palästinas: Arbeiten aus dem orientalischen Seminar der Universität Giessen* 2, 1 (1930). E. A. Speiser, "Ethnic Movements in the Near East in the Second Millennium B.C.," AASOR 13 (1933) 13-54. T. Ashkenazi, "Tribus semi-nomades de la Palestine du Nord," *Etudes d'ethnographie, de sociologie et d'ethnologie* 2 (1938). M. F. von Oppenheim, *Die Beduinen*, I-II (1939, 1943). A. Alt, "Der Rhythmus der Geschichte Syriens und Palästinas im Altertum," *Beiträge zur Arabistik, Semitistik und Islamwissenschaft* (1944) 284-306 = KS III (1954) 1-19. T. H. Robinson, "The History of Israel," IB I (1952) 272-291. J. Starcky, "Abraham und die Geschichte," BiKi 2 (1952) 17-26. S. D. Goitein, *Jews and Arabs. Their Contacts Through the Ages* (1955) esp. 19-32. S. Moscati, *I predecessori d'Israele. Studi sulle più antiche genti semitiche in Siria e Palestina: Studi Orientali* 4 (1956). D. O. Edzard, *Die "zweite Zwischenzeit" Babyloniens* (1957). W. Dostal, "The Evolution of Bedouin Life," SS 2 (1959) 11-34. J. Henninger, "La société bédouine ancienne," SS 2 (1959) 69-93. M. Höfner, *Die Beduinen in den vorislamischen arabischen Inschriften* (1959). J. R. Kupper, "Le rôle des nomades dans l'histoire de la

Mésopotamie," JESHO 2 (1959) 113-127. Y. M. Grintz, "On the Original Home of the Semites," JNES 21 (1962) 186-206. K. Jettmar, *Die frühen Steppenvölker: Reihe "Kunst der Welt. . ."* (1964). W. S. Smith, *Interconnections in the Ancient Near East* (1965). J. Průšek, "Early Nomads and the Book of Karl Jettmar," OLZ 62 (1967) 325-346. W. Helck, "Die Bedrohung Palästinas durch einwandernde Gruppen am Ende der 18. und am Anfang der 19. Dynastie," VT 18 (1968) 472-480. R. Amiram, "The Beginnings of Urbanization in Canaan," *Essays in Honor of N. Glueck* (1970) 83-100. H. Klengel, *Beiträge zur sozialen Struktur des alten Vorderasien: Schriften zur Kultur des alten Orients* 1 (1971). D. O. Edzard, ed., *Gesellschaftsklassen im Alten Zweistromland und in den angrenzenden Gebieten* (1972). H. Klengel, *Zwischen Zelt und Palast. Die Begegnung von Nomaden und Sesshaften im alten Vorderasien* (1972). J. Kaplan, "Further Aspects of the Middle Bronze Age II Fortifications in Palestine" [in Hebr. 1971], ZDPV 91 (1975) 1-17. T. L. Thompson, *The Settlement of Sinai and the Negev in the Bronze Age* (1975).

3. Peoples, Territories, and Cities (plus Geography).

a) Preliminary Notes: C. M. Doughty, *Travels in Arabia Deserta*, I-II (1883 = 1964). O. Glaser, *Skizze der Geschichte und Geographie Arabiens*, I-II (1889). A. Schlatter, *Zur Topographie und Geschichte Palästinas* (1893). F. Buhl, *Geographie des alten Palästina* (1896). F. Hommel, *Grundriss der Geographie und Geschichte des Alten Orients*, I (1904). A. Musil, *Arabia Petraea* (1907-1908). O. Procksch, *Die Völker Altpalästinas* (1914). T. E. Lawrence and C. L. Woolley, *The Wilderness of Zin* (1915). B. Landsberger, "Über die Völker Vorderasiens im dritten Jahrtausend," ZA 35 (1924) 213-238. A. Musil, *Oriental Explorations and Studies: American Geographical Society* (1926). R. Dussaud, *Topographie historique de la Syrie ancienne et médiévale* (1927). A. Musil, *Arabia Deserta* (1927; Eng. 1931). G. A. Smith, *Historical Geography of the Holy Land* (1931; 1936²⁶). F. M. Abel, *Géographie de la Palestine*, I-II (1933 and 1938). G. A. Barton, *Semitic and Hamitic Origins, Social and Religious* (1934; 1943²). A. Alt, "Beiträge zur historischen Geographie und Topographie des Negeb," JPOS 15 (1935) 294-324 = KS III (1959) 409-435; "Völker und Staaten Syriens im frühen Altertum," AO 34 (1936) = KS III (1959) 20-48. A. Ungnad, *Subartu. Beiträge zur Kulturgeschichte und Völkerkunde Vorderasiens* (1936). A. Causse, *Du groupe ethnique à la communauté religieuse. Le problème sociologique de la religion d'Israel*, I-II (1937). J. Simons, *Handbook for the Study of Egyptian Topographical Lists of Western Asia* (1937). M. Noth, "Die syrisch-palästinische Bevölkerung des zweiten Jahrtausends v. Chr. im Lichte neuer Quellen," ZDPV 65 (1942) 9-67. A. Lauha, "Zaphon. Der Norden und die Nordvölker im AT," AAF 8, 49 (1943). M. Noth, "Die Nachbarn der israelitischen Stämme im Ostjordanland. Beiträge zur biblischen Landes- und Altertumskunde," ZDPV 68 (1946-1951) 1-50 = GesAufs. I (1971) 434-475. S. Moscati, *Geschichte und Kultur der semitischen Völker. Eine Einführung* (1953; 1956²). K. Dittmer, *Allgemeine Völkerkunde, Formen und Entwicklung der Kultur* (1954). D. Baly, *The Geography of the Bible* (1957; 1974²). P. Oberholzer, *Geografiese Terme in die Rijtersboek en hulle Vertaling* (1959). J. Simons, *The Geographical and Topographical Texts of the OT: A Concise Commentary* (1959). E. A. Speiser, " 'People' und 'Nation' of Israel," JBL 79 (1960) 157-163. S. Yeivin, *Studien zur Geschichte Israels und seines Landes* [in Hebr.] (1960) esp. 25-61. J. G. Gibson, "Observations on Some Important Ethnic Terms in the Pentateuch," JNES 20 (1961) 217-238. B. Lundman, *Stammeskunde der Völker (Ethnogonie), eine Übersicht* (1961). B. Tadmor and I. J. Gelb, "The Early History of the West-Semitic Peoples," JCS 15 (1961) 27-47. H. Donner, *Israel unter den Völkern*, VT.S 11 (1964). Y. Aharoni, *The Land of the Bible. A Historical Geography* (1967). Y. M. Grintz, *Studies in Early Biblical Ethnology and History* [in Hebr.] (1969). G. Sauer, "Alois Musil's Reisen nach Arabien im ersten Weltkrieg," ArOr 37 (1969) 243-263. W. G. Dever, "The Peoples of Palestine in the Middle-Bronze I Period," HThR 64 (1971) 197-226. H. Donner, "Die Palästinabeschreibung des Epiphanius Monachus Hagiopolita," ZDPV 87 (1971) 42-91. D. J. Wiseman, ed., *Peoples of Old Testament Times* (1973). J. K. Kuntz, *The People of Ancient Israel. An Introduction to O.T. Literature, History and Thought* (1974).

b) Amorites: B. Landsberger, "Die älteste Stammesgeschichte der Semiten, Akkadier und Amoriter," *6. Dtsch. Orientalistentag II* (1924). J. Lewy, "Zur Amoriterfrage," ZA 36 (1925) 139-161; 38 (1929) 243-272. A. Alt, "Amurru in den Ächtungstexten der 11. Dynastie?" ZAW 46 (1928) 77-78. P. Dhorme, "Les Amorrhéens," RB 37 (1928) 63-79, 161-180; 39 (1930) 161-178; 40 (1931) 161-184. T. Bauer, "Eine Prüfung der 'Amoriter' Frage," ZA 38 (1929) 145-170. A. Jirku, "Wer waren die Amoriter?'' ZRK 2 (1935) 225-231. H. Tur-Sinai, ''The Amorite and the Amurru of the Inscriptions,'' JQR 39 (1949) 249-258. J. Lewy, ''Amurritica,'' HUCA 32 (1961) 31-74. E. A. Speiser, ''Amorites and the Civilization of the Amorites,'' BA 24 (1961) 66-86; ''Amorites and Canaanites,'' *The World History of Jewish People*, I (1963) 162-169. G. Buccelati, *The Amorites of the Ur III Period* (1966). K. M. Kenyon, *Amorites and Canaanites* (1966). I. J. Gelb, ''An Old Babylonian List of Amorites,'' JAOS 88 (1968) 39-46. C. Wilcke, ''Zur Geschichte der Amurriter in der Ur III Zeit,'' WO 5 (1969) 1-31. J. R. Bartlett, ''Sihon and Og, Kings of the Amorites,'' VT 20 (1970) 257-277. C. H. J. de Geus, ''The Amorites in the Archaeology of Palestine,'' UF 3 (1971) 41-60. A. Haldar, *Who Were the Amorites?: Monographs on the Ancient Near East 1* (1971). J. Van Seters, ''The Terms 'Amorite' und 'Hittite' in the Old Testament,'' VT 22 (1972) 64-81. M. Liverani, ''The Amorites,'' *Peoples of OT Times*, ed. D. J. Wiseman (1973) 100-133.

c) Aramaeans: A. Sanda, *Die Aramäer* (1902). M. Streck, ''Über die älteste Geschichte der Aramäer mit besonderer Berücksichtigung der Verhältnisse in Babylonien und Assyrien,'' *Klio* 6 (1906) 185-235. S. Schiffer, *Die Aramäer* (1911). R. A. Bowman, ''Aramaeans, Aramaic, and the Bible,'' JNESt 7 (1948) 65-90. A. Dupont-Sommer, *Les Araméens: L'Orient Ancien Illustré* (1949). N. Schneider, ''Aram und Aramäer in der Ur III Zeit,'' Bib 30 (1949) 109-111. S. Moscati, ''Sulle origini degli Aramei,'' RSO 26 (1951)16-22. A. Dupont-Sommer, ''Sur les débuts de l'histoire araméenne,'' VT.S 1 (1953) 40-49. K. Galling, ''Von Nabonid zu Darius,'' ZDPV 69 (1953) 42-64; 70 (1954) 3-5. M. McNamara, ''De populi Aramaeorum primordiis,'' VD 35 (1957) 129-142. M. F. Unger, *Israel and the Aramaeans of Damascus* (1957). B. Maisler, ''The Aramean Empire and its Relation with Israel,'' BA 25 (1962) 98-120. H. Tadmor, ''The Southern Borders of Aram,'' IEJ 12 (1962) 114-122. D. O. Edzard, ''Mari und Aramäer?'' ZA 56 (1964) 142-149 M. Dietrich, *Die Aramäer Südbabyloniens in der Sargonidenzeit*, AOAT 7 (1970). A. Malamat, ''The Aramaeans,'' in *Peoples of OT Times*, ed. D. J. Wiseman (1973) 134-155.

d) Other Peoples and Territories Important for the Patriarchal Story. Canaanites: F. M. T. Böhl, *Kanaanäer und Hebräer. Untersuchungen zur Vorgeschichte des Volkstums und der Religion Israels auf dem Boden Kanaans*, BWAT 9 (1911). T. Bauer, *Die Ostkanaanäer. Eine philologisch-historische Untersuchung über die Wanderschicht der sogenannten ''Amoriter'' in Babylonien* (1926). M. Noth, ''Zum Problem der Ostkanaanäer,'' ZA 39 (1930) 213-222. B. Maisler, ''Canaan and the Canaanites,'' BASOR 102 (1946) 7-12. A. van Selms, ''The Canaanites in the Book of Genesis,'' OTS 12 (1958) 182-213. S. Moscati, ''Sulla Storia del Nome Canaan,'' SBO 3 (= AnBib 12) (1959) 266-269. S. Yeivin, ''Early Contacts Between Canaan and Egypt,'' IEJ 10 (1960) 193-203. W. F. Albright, ''The Role of the Canaanites in the History of Civilization,'' Fests. W. F. Albright (1961; 1965[2]) 328-362. J. Gray, *The Canaanites: Ancient Peoples and Places* 38 (1964). M. Astour, ''The Origin of the Terms 'Canaan,' 'Phoenician,' and 'Purple,' '' JNES 24 (1965) 346-350. A. Malamat, ''Northern Canaan and the Mari Texts,'' *Essays in Honor of N. Glueck* (1970) 164-177.

Hittites: P. Jensen, *Hittiter und Armenier* (1898). J. H. Breasted, ''When Did the Hittites Enter Palestine?'' AJSL 21 (1904/05) 153-158. E. Meyer, *Reich und Kultur der Chetiter* (1914). G. Roeder, ''Ägypter und Hethiter,'' AO 20 (1919). A. E. Cowley, *The Hittites* (1920). E. F. Weidner, *Der Zug Sargons von Akkad nach Kleinasien—die älteste geschichtliche Beziehung zwischen Babylon und Hatti: Boghazköi-Studien 6* (1922). A. Goetze, *Kleinasien zur Hethiterzeit* (1924). D. G. Hogarth, *The Kings of the Hittites: Schweich Lectures 1924* (1926). A. Goetze, *Das Hithiter-Reich*, AO 27, 2 (1928; 1929[2]). F. Schachermeyr, *Hethiter und Achäer* (1935). E. Cavaignac, *Le problème Hittite* (1936). A. Goetze, ''Hethiter, Churriter und Assyrer,'' AASOR 31 (1936). K. Bittel, *Die Ruinen von Boğazköy, der Hauptstadt des Hethiterreiches* (1937). F. F. Bruce, *The Hittites and the Old Testament* (1947). F. Sommer, *Hethiter und Hethitisch* (1948). A. Alt, ''Hethitische und ägyptische Herrschaftsordnung in unterworfenen Gebieten'' (1949) = KlSchr. III (1959) 99-106. O. R. Gurney, *The Hittites* (1952; 1961[3]). A. Dussaud, *Prélydiens, Hittites et Achéens* (1953). H. T. Bossert, ed., *Grosse Kulturen der Frühzeit*, I (1954). M. Riemschneider, *Die Welt der Hethiter: s. bei Bossert*, I (1954). A. Malamat, ''Doctrines of Causality in Hittite and Biblical Historiography: A Parallel,'' VT 5 (1955) 1-12. A. Goetze, ''Hittite and Anatolian Studies,'' Fests. W. F. Albright (1961; 1965[2]) 316-327. H. Otten, *Das Hethiterreich: Kulturgeschichte des Alten Orients*, ed. H. Schmökel (1961). H. G. Güterbock, ''A View of Hittite Literature,'' JAOS 84 (1964) 107-115. G. Walser, ed., *Neuere Hethiterforschung: Historische Einzelschriften* 7 (1964).

H. A. Hoffner, "Some Contributions of Hittitology to Old Testament Study," TynB 20 (1969) 27-55. H. Cancik, *Grundzüge hethitischer und frühisraelitischer Geschichtsschreibung* (Diss. Tübingen 1970). E. & H. Klengel, *Die Hethiter* (1970). F. Cornelius, *Das Hethiterreich als Feudalstaat: Gesellschaftsklassen im alten Zweistromland. . .*, ed. D. O. Edzard (1972); *Geschichte der Hethiter mit besonderer Berücksichtigung der geographischen Verhältnisse und der Rechtsgeschichte* (1973). H. A. Hoffner, "The Hittites and Hurrians," *Peoples of OT Times*, ed. D. J. Wiseman (1973) 197-228. J. Lehmann, *Die Hethiter. Volk der tausend Götter* (1975) = *The Hittites* (1977).

Hurrians and Hivites: H. L. Ginsberg–B. Maisler, "Semitised Hurrians in Syria and Palestine," JPOS 14 (1934) 234-267. W. F. Albright, "The Horites in Palestine. From Pyramids to Paul," *G. L. Robinsen Vol.* (1935) 9-26. R. H. Pfeiffer, "Nuzi and the Hurrians," *Annual Report of the Smithsonian Institution I* (1935) 535-558. I. J. Gelb, *Hurrians and Subarians*, SAOC 22 (1944). J. Paterson, "Abhandlung über die Churriter," *Present Vol. to W. B. Stevenson* (1945) 100ff. G. Contenau, *La civilisation des Hittites et des Hourrites du Mitanni* (1948). E. A. Speiser, "Hurrians and Subarians," JAOS 68 (1948) 1-13; "The Hurrian Participation in the Civilization of Mesopotamia, Syria and Palestine," CHM 1 (1953) 311-327 = *Oriental and Biblical Studies* (1967) 244-269. I. J. Gelb, "New Light on Hurrians and Subarians," *Studi. . .L. della Vida I* (1956) 378-392. I. H. Eybers, "Who were the Hivvites?" OTWSA.P 2 (1959) 6-14. H. Leroy, "Miscellanea Nuziana," Or 28 (1959) 1-25, 113-129. F. Imperati, *I Hurriti* (1964). R. de Vaux, "Les Hurrites de l'histoire et les Horites de la Bible," RB 74 (1967) 481-503. R. Noth, *Hurrians and Hivites*, Bibl 54 (1973) 43-62. K. J. H. Vriezen, "Hirbet Kefire," ZDPV 91 (1975) 135-158.

Edomites and Midianites: F. Buhl, *Geschichte der Edomiter: Leipziger Dekanatsprogramm* (1893). P. Haupt, "Midian and Sinai," ZDMG 63 (1909) 506-530. I. Slabý, *Moab und Edom im Lichte der Forschung von A. Musil* (1909). J. R. Bartlett, "The 'Edomite King List' Genesis XXXVI 31–39 and I. Chronicles I 43–50," JThS NS 16 (1965) 301-314. O. Eissfeldt, "Protektorat der Midianiter über ihre Nachbarn im letzten Viertel des 2. Jahrtausends v. Chr.," JBL 87 (1968) 383-393. J. R. Bartlett, "The Land of Seir and the Brotherhood of Edom," JThS NS 20 (1969) 1-20. M. Weippert, *Edom, Studien und Materialien zur Geschichte der Edomiter auf Grund schriftlicher und archäologischer Quellen* (Habil. Tübingen 1971). J. R. Bartlett, "The Rise and Fall of the Kingdom of Edom," PEQ 104 (1972) 26-37. W. J. Dumbrell, "Midian—A Land or a League?" VT 25 (1975) 323-337.

Hyksos: R. Weill, *La fin du Moyen Empire égyptien*, 2 vols. (1918). A. Mallon, "Les Hébreux en Egypte," Or 3 (1921) esp. 35-39. W. Wolff, "Der Stand der Hyksosfrage," ZDMG 83 (1929) 67-79. K. Galling, "Hyksosherrschaft und Hyksoskultur," ZDPV 62 (1939) 89-115. P. Montet, *Le drame d'Avaris* (1940). A. Alt, "Die Herkunft der Hyksos in neuer Sicht," BAL 101, 6 (1954) 1-39 = KS III (1959) 72-98. Z. Mayani, *Les Hycsos et le monde de la Bible* (1956). J. Van Seters, *The Hyksos* (1966).

Habiru: S. H. Langdon, "The Habiru and the Hebrews. New Material on the Problem," ET 31 (1920) 324-329. A. Jirku, "Mitteilungen. Zur Chabiru-Frage," ZAW 46 (1928) 208-211. H. Parzen, "The Problem of the Ibrim ('Hebrews') in the Bible," AJSL 49 (1933). L. Baeck, "Der Ibri," MGW 83 (NF 47) (1939) 66-80 = (1963). J. Lewy, "Ḥābirū and Hebrews," HUCA 14 (1939) 587-623; "A New Parallel between HABIRU and Hebrews," HUCA 15 (1940) 47-58. A. Parrot, "Les tablettes de Mari et l'Ancien Testament," RHPhR 30 (1950) 1-11. A. Jirku, "Neues über die Ḥabiru–Hebräer," JKAF 2 (1952/53) 213f. J. Bottéro, ed., "Le problème des Habiru à la quatrième Rencontre Assyriologique Internationale," *Cahiers de la Société Asiatique* 12 (1954). E. Dhorme, "Les Habirou et les Hébreux," RH 211 (1954) 256-264. M. Greenberg, *The Hab/piru, American Oriental Series* 39 (1955). A. Alt, "Die habiru = SA. GAZ in Alalach und Ugarit," WO 5, 3 (1956) 237-243. M. G. Kline, "The Ha-BI-ru—Kin or Foe of Israel?," WThJ 19 (1956) 1-24, 170-184; 20 (1957) 46-70. H. Otten, "Zwei althethitische Belege zu den Hapiru (SA. Gaz)," ZA NF 52 (1957) 216-223. R. Borger, "Das Problem der 'apiru ('Ḥabiru')," ZDPV 74 (1958) 121-132. E. Cassin, "Nouveaux documents sur les Habiru," JA 246 (1958) 225-236. H. Cazelles, "Hébreu, Ubru et Hapiru," Syria 35 (1958) 198-217. M. P. Gray, "The Ḥābirū–Hebrew Problem in the Light of the Source Material Available at Present," HUCA 29 (1958) 135-202. M. C. Astour, "Les étrangers à Ugarit et le statut juridique des Ḥabiru," RA 53 (1959) 70-76. J.

Nougayrol, "Documents du Habur," Syria 37 (1960) 205-214. M. B. Rowton, "The Topological Factor in the Hapiru Problem," *Studies in Honour of B. Landsberger* (1965) 375-387. R. de Vaux, "Le problème des Hapiru après quinze années," JNES 27 (1968) 221-228. K. Koch, *Die Hebräer*. . ., VT 19 (1969)37-81. D. O. Edzard, "Kamid el-Loz-Kumidi. Schriftdokumente 5," SBAK 7 (1970) 55-65. R. Hachmann, "Kamid-el-Loz-Kumidi. Schriftdokumente 6," SBAK 7 (1970) 65-94.

   e) Places and Changes of Places in Gen. 12–50: A. Mez, *Geschichte der Stadt Harrân in Mesopotamien* (1892). J. Halévy, *Recherches bibliques* II (1901). C. H. W. Johns, *Assyrian Deeds and Documents Recording the Transfer of Property*, 4 vols. (1898-1923) (cf. AJSL 42 [1926] 170-275); *An Assyrian Doomsday Book or liber censualis of the District Round Harran*, AB 17 (1901). H. Berthoud, "Où fut Charan de Térach et d'Abram?" RThPh 37 (1905) 294-301. H. Vuilleumier, "Quelques réflexions au sujet de l'article de M. Berthoud," RThPh 37 (1905) 302-321. W. Bacher, "Der Jahrmarkt an der Terebinthe bei Hebron," ZAW 29 (1909) 148-152, 221. G. A. Barton, *Documents from the Temple Archives of Tello*, III (1914). E. Sellin, *Wie wurde Sichem eine israelitische Stadt?* (1922). F. M. Abel–L. H. Vincent–E. H. J. Mackay, *Hébron, Le Haram el-Khalil* (1923). C. J. Gadd, *History and Monuments of Ur* (1929). W. Borée, *Die alten Ortsnamen Palästinas* (1930). H. D. Schaedel, "Abrahams Heimatstadt Ur," *Wächterstimmen* 57 (1932) 70-84. W. Zimmerli, "Geschichte und Tradition von Beerseba im AT" (Diss. Göttingen 1932). A. Parrot, " 'Ur en Chaldee,' patrie d'Abraham," EvQ 5 (1933) 89-99. C. L. Woolley, *Abraham. Recent Discoveries and Hebrew Origins* (1936). A. Jirku, "Die ägyptischen Listen palästinensischer und syrischer Ortsnamen," *Klio* 25 (1937). C. L. Woolley, *Ur—Excavations* (1939). J. P. Harland, "Sodom and Gomorrah, I. The Location of the Cities of the Plain," BA 5 (1942) 17-32; II. "The Destruction of the Cities of the Plain," BA 6 (1943) 41-54. K. Galling, "Bethel und Gilgal," ZDPV 66 (1943) 140-155; 67 (1945) 21-43. E. Bilgic, "Die Ortsnamen der kappadokischen Urkunden im Rahmen der alten Sprachen Anatoliens," AfO 15 (1945/51) 1-37. R. T. O'Callaghan, *Aram-Naharaim: A Contribution to the History of Upper Mesopotamia in the Second Millennium B.C.* (1948; 1961[2]). M. Bič, "Bethel, le sanctuaire du roi," *Symbolae Hrozný*, ArOr 17 (1949) 46-63. M. A. Beek, "The History of the Interpretation of Deut XXVI, 5: Das Problem des aramaischen Stammvaters," OTS 8 (1950) 193-212. J. van Beckerath, *Tanis und Theben* (1951) esp. 38-41. S. Lloyd–W. Brice, "Harran," AnSt 1 (1951) 77-112. D. S. Rice, "Medieval Harran," AnSt 2 (1952) 36-84. G. van der Aabeelen, "Cité d'Abraham," RNouv 18 (1953) 95-106. H. H. Figulla–W. J. Martin, *Ur—Excavation Texts* (1953). S. Yeivin, "Beersheba, City of the Patriarchs," Zion 20 (1953) 117-127. S. Mowinckel, "Die Gründung von Hebron," *Fests. H. S. Nyberg* (1954) 185-194 = *Orientalia Suecana 4* (1955) 67-76. C. L. Woolley, *Excavations at Ur. A Record of Twelve Years Work* (1954). J. P. Free, "The Third Season at Dothan," BASOR 139 (1955) 3-9; 152 (1968) 10-18. E. Nielsen, *Shechem, A Traditio-Historical Investigation* (1955; 1959[2]). J. B. Bauer, "Untergang und Auferstehung von Sodom und Gomorrha," BiLi 23 (1955/56) 260-263. M. E. L. Mallowan, *Twenty-five Years of Mesopotamian Discoveries* (1956). B. W. Anderson–W. J. Harrelson–G. E. Wright, "Shechem, 'Navel of the Land,' " BA 20 (1957) 1-32. B. S. J. Isserlin, "Israelite and Pre-Israelite Place-Names in Palestine: A Historical and Geographical Sketch," PEQ 89 (1957) 133-144. A. E. Mader, *Mambre. Die Ergebnisse der Ausgrabungen im heiligen Bezirk Râmet el-Halîl in Südpalästina 1926-1928*, I-II (1957). F. Cornelius, "Geographie des Hethiterreiches," Or 27 (1958) 225-251. C. J. Gadd, "The Harran Inscriptions of Nabonidus," AnSt 8 (1958) 35-92. J. B. E.Garstang–O. R. Gurney, "The Geography of the Hittite Empire," *Bulletin of the British Institute of Archaeology at Ankara* 5 (1959). H. Haag, "Erwägungen über Beer-Seba," BEThL 12 (1959) 335-345. E. Nielsen, *Shechem. A Traditio-Historical Investigation* (1959[2]). S. Lloyd, "Ur—Al Ubaid, Uqair and Eridu. An Interpretation of Some Evidence From the Flood-Pit," *Iraq* 22 (1960) 23-31. A. Malamat, "Hazor 'The Head of All Those Kingdoms,' " JBL 79 (1960) 12-19. M. E. L. Mallowan, "Memories of Ur," *Iraq* 22 (1960) 1-19. H. W. F. Saggs, "Ur of the Chaldees. A Problem of Identification," *Iraq* 22 (1960) 200-209. J. L. Kelso, "The Fourth Campaign at Bethel," BASOR 164 (1961) 5-19. J. R. Ream, *Biblical Correspondences With Nuzi Akkadian* (Diss. Dropsie Coll. 1962). E. F. Campbell–J. F. Ross, "The Excavation of Shechem and the Biblical Tradition," BA 26 (1963) 2-34. C. H. Gordon, "Abraham of Ura," *Hebrew Semitic Studies Presented to G. R. Driver* (1963) 77-84. E. Toombs–G. E. Wright, "The Fourth Campaign at Balâtah (Shechem)," BASOR 169 (1963) 1-61. P. Artzi, "Ur Kasdim," *OLD Jerusalem* (1964) 71-85. L. Ben-Shem, "The

Location of Ur of the Chaldees' [in Hebr.], *OLD Jerusalem* (1964) 86-91. J. A. Brinkman, "Ur: 721-605 B.C.," Or 34 (1965). G. E. Wright, *Shechem* (1965). D. G. Evans, "Rehoboam's Advisors at Shechem, and Political Institutions in Israel and Sumer," JNES 25 (1966) 273-279. G. Buccellati, *Cities and Nations of Ancient Syria: An Essay on Political Institutions, With Special Reference to the Israelite Kingdoms* SS 26 (1967) (reviewed by M. Weippert in ZDPV 89 [1973], 84-96). F. O. Garcia-Treto, *Bethel: The History and Traditions of an Israelite Sanctuary* (Diss. Princeton 1967). J. A. Soggin, "Bemerkungen zur alttestamentlichen Topographie Sichems," ZDPV 83 (1967) 185-187. O. Eissfeldt, "Gilgal or Shechem?," *OT Essays in Honour of G. H. Davies* (1970) 90-101. H. W. Wolff, "Das Ende des Heiligtums in Bethel," Fests. K. Galling (1970) 287-298. D. Baltzer, "Harran nach 610 'medisch'? Kritische Überprüfung einer Hypothese," WO 7 (1973) 86-95. H. N. Richardson, "SKT (Amos 9:11). 'Booth' or 'Succoth'?" JBL 92 (1973) 375-381. D. O. Edzard–G. Faber, *Répertoire Géographique des Textes Cunéiformes. Bd. 2: Die Orts- und Gewässernamen der Zeit der 3. Dynastie von Ur* (1974).

4. The Time of the Patriarchs.

a) General: G. Jacob, *Das Leben der vorislamischen Beduinen* (1895). E. Grosse, *Die Formen der Familie und die Formen der Wirtschaft* (1896). L. W. King, *Legends of Babylon and Egypt in Relation to Hebrew Traditions: Schweich Lectures 1916* (1918). A. Jaussen, *Naplouse et son district* (1927). A. Causse, "La crise de la solidarité de familée et de clan dans l'Ancien Israël," RHPhR 10 (1930) 24-60. C. U. A. Kappers, *Introduction to the Anthropology of the Near East* (1934). E. B. Cross, *The Hebrew Family* (1937). L. Haefeli, *Die Beduinen von Beerseba* (1938). H. Charles, *La sédentarisation entre Euphrate et Balik* (1942). E. A. Speiser, "Some Sources of Intellectual and Social Progress in the Ancient Near East," Fests. W. F. Leland (1942) 51-62 = *Oriental and Biblical Studies* (1967) 517-533. J. Henninger, "Die Familie bei den heutigen Beduinen Arabiens und seiner Randgebiete," IAE 42 (1943) 1-189. S. Nyström, *Beduinentum und Jahwismus. Eine soziologisch-religionsgeschichtliche Untersuchung zum AT. IV* (1946). W. von Soden, *Das altbabylonische Bucharchiv von Mari: Welt des Orients* 1 (1947) esp. 397-403. W. Caskel, "The Beduinization of Arabia," *American Anthropological Memoirs* 76 (1954) 36-46. G. E. Mendenhall, "Mari," BA 11 (1948) 1-19 (cf. BASOR 133 [1954] 26-30). A. Alt, "Zelte und Hütten," Fests. F. Nötscher, BBB1 (1950) 16-25. J. Bottéro–A. Finet, *Archives royales de Mari XV, répertoire analytique des tomes I à V (ARM XV)* (1954). J. R. Kupper, *Les nomades en Mesopotamie au temps des rois de Mari* (1957). R. de Vaux, *Ancient Israel* (1958; Eng. 1962). M. du Buit, "Quelques contacts bibliques dans les Archives de Mari," RB 66 (1959) 576-581. G. Dossin, "Les Bédouines dans les textes de Mari," SS 2 (1959) 35-51. S. Moscati, *The Semites in Ancient History* (1959). V. Maag, "Malkût Jhwh," VT.S 7 (1959/60) 129-153. S. Herrmann, "Das Werden Israels," ThLZ 87 (1962) 561-574. H. Klengel, "Zu einigen Problemen des altvorderasiatischen Nomadentums," ArOr 30 (1962) 585-596. A. Malamat, "Mari and the Bible: Some Patterns of Tribal Organization and Institutions," JAOS 82 (1962) 143-150. D. H. K. Amiram–Y. Ben Arieh, "Sedentarization of Bedouin in Israel," IEJ 13 (1963) 161-181. E. M. Cassin, "Nouvelles données sur les relations familiales à Nuzi," RA 57 (1963) 113-119. J. T. Luke, *Pastoralism and Politics in the Mari Period: A Re-Examination of the Character and Political Significance of the Major West Semitic Tribal Groups on the Middle Euphrates, ca. 1828-1758 B.C.* (Diss. Michigan 1965). A. F. Rainey, "Family Relationship in Ugarit," Or 34 (1965) 10-22. R. de Vaux, "Les patriarches hébreux et l'histoire," RB 72 (1965) 5-28; Eng. (1965) 227-240. H. Klengel, "Sesshafte und Nomaden in der alten Geschichte Mesopotamiens," Saec. 17 (1966) 205-222. H. Cazelles, "Mari et l'Ancien Testament," BFPUL 182 (1967) 73-90. I. Hunt, *The World of the Patriarchs* (1967). J. Layard, "Familie und Sippe," *Institutionen in primitiven Gesellschaften* (1967) 59-76. J. R. Porter, "The Extended Family in the Old Testament," *Occasional Papers in Social and Economic Administration* 6 (1967). M. B. Rowton, "The Physical Environment and the Problem of the Nomads," BFPUL 182 (1967) 109-121. M. Weippert, *The Settlement of the Israelite Tribes in Palestine*, SBT 21, 2nd Series (1967; Eng. 1971). K. H. Bernhardt, "Nomadentum und Ackerbaukultur in der frühstaatlichen Zeit Altisraels," *Akademie Vlg.* Nr 69 (1968) 31-40. J. A. Brinkman, *A Political History of Post-Kassite Babylon, 1158-722 B.C.* (1968). J. Henninger, *Über Lebensraum und Lebensformen der Frühsemiten*, AFLNW 151 (1968). J. L. Kelso, "Life in the Patriarchal Age," ChrTo 12 (1968) 5-8. A. D. Mayes, "The Historical Context of the Battle Against Sisera," VT 19 (1969) 353-360. M. Weippert, "Die Nomadenquelle. Ein

Beitrag zur Topographie der Biqaʻim 2. Jahrtausend v. Chr.,'' Fests. K. Galling (1970). A. Malamat, "Mari," BA 34 (1971) 2-22. L. M. Muntingh, "The Patriarchs as 'Village Pastoralists,' " *Essays in Honour of A. van Selms* (1971). I. M. Diakonoff, "Socio-Economic Classes in Babylonia and the Babylonian Concept of Social Stratification," *Gesellschaftsklassen im Alten Zweistromland. . .,* ed. D. O. Edzard (1972). M. B. Rowton, "Urban Autonomy in a Nomadic Environment," JNES 32 (1973) 201-215. F. Stolz, "Aspekte religiöser und sozialer Ordnung im alten Israel," ZEE 17 (1973) 145-159. M. B. Rowton, "Enclosed Nomadism," JESHO 17 (1974) 1-30. W. H. Stiebing, "When Was the Age of the Patriarchs? Of Amorites, Canaanites and Archaeology," BAR 1 (1975) 17-21.

    b) Life-Style: H. Vogelstein, *Landwirtschaft in Palästina,* I (1894). B. D. Eerdmans, "Der Ackerbau in den Vätersagen," *ATliche Studien II* (1908) 38-48. E. Hahn, *Von der Hacke zum Pflug* (1917). G. Dalman, *Arbeit und Sitte in Palästina,* I (1928); VI (1939) = (1964). H. F. Friedrichs, *Zur Kenntnis der frühgeschichtlichen Tierwelt Südwestasiens,* AO 32 (1933). F. S. Bodenheimer, *Animal Life in Palestine* (1935). E. A. Speiser, "Of Shoes and Shekels," BASOR 77 (1940) 15-20 = *Oriental and Biblical Studies* (1967) 151-159. L. Rost, "Weidewechsel und altisraelitischer Festkalender," ZDPV 66 (1943) 205-216 = *Das kleine Credo und andere Studien im AT* (1965) 101-112. J. P. Free, "Abraham's Camels," JNES 3 (1944) 187-193. H. Lewy, "Assyro-Babylonian and Israelite Measures of Capacity and Rates of Seeding," JAOS 64 (1944) 65-73. O. Eissfeldt, "Gabelhürden im Ostjordanland," FF 25 (1949) 8-10; 28 (1954) 54-56. W. F. Leemans, *The Old-Babylonian Merchant. His Business and His Social Position: Studia et Documenta ad iura orientis antiqui pertinentia* 3 (1950). R. Walz, "Zum Problem des Zeitpunktes der Domestikation der altweltlichen Cameliden," ZDMG 101 (1951) 29-51; "Neue Untersuchungen zum Domestikationsproblem der altweltlichen Cameliden," ZDMG 104 (1954) 45-87. R. J. Forbes, "The Coming and Going of the Camel," *Studies in Ancient Technology* 2 (1955) 187-204. Y. Aharoni–M. Everani, "The Ancient Desert Agriculture of the Negev, III; Early Beginnings," IEJ 8 (1958) 231-268. C. H. Gordon, "Abraham and the Merchants of Ura," JNES 17 (1958) 28-31. J. Lewy, "Some Aspects of Commercial Life in Assyria and Asia Minor in the Nineteenth Pre-Christian Century," JAOS 78 (1958) 89-101. D. O. Edzard, "Altbabylonisch nawûm," ZA 53 (1959) 168-173; 56 (1964) 19-32. R. Walz, "Gab es ein Esel-Nomadentum im Alten Orient?" *Akten des 24. Internationalen Orientalisten-Kongresses, München 1957* (1959). F. S. Bodenheimer, *Animal and Man in Bible Lands* (1960). B. Brentjes, "Das Kamel im Alten Orient," *Klio* 38 (1960) 23-52. O. Eissfeldt, *Der Beutel der Lebendigen. ATliche Erzählungs- und Dichtungsmotive im Lichte neuer Nuzi-Texte* (1960). W. G. Lambert, "The Domesticated Camel in the Second Millennium—Evidence From Alalakh and Ugarit," BASOR 160 (1960). W. F. Leemans, "Foreign Trade in the Old Babylonian Period," SDO 6 (1960). W. F. Albright, "Abram the Hebrew: A New Archaeological Interpretation," BASOR 163 (1961) 36-54. J. Hawkes–C. L. Woolley, *Prehistory and the Beginnings of Civilization: History of Mankind,* I (1963). A. F. Rainey, "Business Agents at Ugarit," IEJ 13 (1963) 313-321. F. E. Zeuner, *A History of Domesticated Animals* (1963). H. Klengel, "Halbnomadischer Bodenbau im Königreich von Mari," VIOF 69 (1968), esp. 75-81. J. Klima, "Soziale und wirtschaftliche Verhältnisse von Mari," VIOF 69 (1968) 83-90. I. Sellnow, "Das Verhältnis von Bodenbauern und Viehzüchtern in historischer Sicht. Vorwort," VIOF 69 (1968) 7-18. J. Henninger, "Zum frühsemitischen Nomadentum: Viehwirtschaft und Hirtenkultur," *Ethnographische Studien,* ed. L. Földes (1969) 33-68. M. Weippert, "Abraham der Hebräer? Bemerkungen zu W. F. Albrights Deutung der Väter Israels," Bib 52 (1971) 407-432. M. C. Astour, "The Merchant Class of Ugarit," *Gesellschaftsklassen im alten Zweistromland. . .,* ed. D. O. Edzard (1972), 1. Beitrag.

    c) Legal Practices and Customs. General: J. Kohler, *Das Recht als Lebenselement der Völker* (1892). B. Meissner, *Beiträge zum altbabylonischen Privatrecht: Assyriologische Bibliothek II* (1893). T. G. Pinches, "Some Early Babylonian Contracts or Legal Documents," JRAS (1897) 489-613. A. Ungnad–J. Kohler, *Assyrische Rechtsurkunden* (1903). G. Wildeboer, *De Patriarchen des ouden verbonds en de wetgeving van Hammoerabi* (1904). A. Jaussen, *Coutumes des Arabes au pays de Moab* (1908; 1948²). C. H. W. Johns, *The Relations Between the Laws of Babylonia and the Laws of the Hebrew Peoples* (1917²). A. Jirku, *Das weltliche Recht im Alten Testament* (1927). V. Korošec, "Über die neuesten sumerischen Gesetzesfragmente aus Ur," BiblOr 25 (1928) 286-289. A. Musil, *The Manners and Customs of the Rwala Bedouins* (1928). S.

Nicolò–H. Petschow, "Babylonische Rechtsurkunden," ZSRG 48-52 (1928-1932). E. Chiera, *Declarations in Court: Joint Expedition With the Iraq Museum at Nuzi* 2 (1930). G. Eisser–J. Lewy, "Die altassyrischen Rechtsurkunden von Kûltepe," MVÄG 35, 1-4 (1930-1935). N. M. Nicolsky, "Das Asylrecht in Israel," ZAW 48 (1930) 146-175. E. A. Speiser, "New Kirkuk Documents Relating to Family Laws," AASOR 10 (1930) 1-73. V. Korošec, *Hethitische Staatsverträge: Ein Beitrag zu ihrer juristischen Wertung* (1931). S. Nicolò, *Beiträge zur Rechtsgeschichte im Bereiche der keilschriftlichen Rechtsquellen* (1931). P. M. Smith, *The Origin and History of Hebrew Law* (1931). R. H. Kennett, *Ancient Hebrew Social Life and Custom as Indicated in Law, Narrative and Metaphor: Schweich Lectures 1931* (1933). G. R. Driver–J. C. Miles, *The Assyrian Laws* (1935). C. H. Gordon, "Parallèles Nouziens aux lois et coutumes de l'Ancien Testament," RB 44 (1935) 34-41. F. Horst, "Der Diebstahl im AT," Fests. P. Kahle (1935). P. Koschaker, "Keilschriftrecht," ZDMG 89 (1935). E. A. Speiser–R. H. Pfeiffer, "One Hundred New Selected Texts," AASOR 16 (1935/36) B. Landsberger, "Die babylonischen Termini für Gesetz und Recht," Fests. P. Koschaker (1939) 219-234. C. H. Gordon, "Biblical Customs and the Nuzu Tablets," BA 3 (1940) 1-12. I. Rapaport, "The Origins of Hebrew Law," PEQ 73 (1941) 158-167. D. N. Lachkarov–E. P. Korovine, *La vie dans les déserts* (1942). H. Liebesny, "The Administration of Justice in Nuzi," JAOS 63 (1943) 128-144. A. Jepsen, "Die 'Hebräer' und ihr Recht," AfO 15 (1945/51) 55-68. D. Daube, *Studies in Biblical Law* (1947) 1-73. A. Adam, "Die Weisungen Gottes in der Rechts- und Sozialgrundlage des Alten Testaments," EvTh 7 (1947/48); 9/10 (1948) 286-303. D. Daube, "Concerning Methods of Bible-Criticism. Late Laws in Early Narratives," ArOr 17 (1949) 88-99. F. Horst, *Das Eigentum nach dem AT*, KiV 2 (1949). R. A. F. MacKenzie, *The Forms of Israelite Law* (Diss. 1949). J. P. M. van der Ploeg, "Studies in Hebrew Law. II. The Style of the Laws," CBQ 12 (1950) 416-427. E. Neufeld, *The Hittite Laws* (1951). S. Nicolò, *Babylonische Rechtsurkunden des ausgehenden 8. und des 7. Jahrhunderts v. Chr.*, AAM 34 (1951). H. Cazelles, "Loi israélite," DBS 5 (1952) 497-530. G. R. Driver–J. C. Miles, *The Babylonian Laws*, I-II (1952, 1955). E. Gräf, *Das Rechtswesen bei den heutigen Beduinen: Beiträge zur Sprach- und Kulturgeschichte des Orients* 5 (1952). J. Pirenne, "Les institutions du peuple hébreu, III. IV. V," RIDA 1 (1952) 33-86; 2 (1953) 109-149; 3 (1954) 195-255. E. A. Speiser, "Early Law and Civilization," *Oriental and Biblical Studies* (1967) 534-555. G. Boyer, "Sur quelques emplois de la fiction dans l'ancien droit oriental," RIDA 3 (1954) 73-100. R. Follet, "De novis legum Babylonicarum investigationibus. II. Familien- u. Strafrecht. In Auseinandersetzung mit Driver–Miles," VAB 32 (1954) esp. 260, 335-344. G. E. Mendenhall, "Law and Covenant in Israel and the Ancient Near East," BA 17 (1954) 26-46, 49-76. J. A. Wilson, ed., *Authority and Law in the Ancient Orient*, AOS 17 (1954). A. Falkenstein, *Die neusumerischen Gerichtsurkunden*, 3 vols.: AAM 39; 40; 44 (1956-1957). F. Horst, *Recht und Religion im Bereich des Alten Testaments* (1956/57). G. Boyer, ed., *Archives royales de Mari. Textes juridiques*, ARM 8 (1958). D. Daube, "Rechtsgedanken in den Erzählungen des Pentateuch," BZAW 77 (1958) 32-41. M. B. Rowton, "The Date of Hammurabi," JNES 17 (1958) 97-111. J. L. Blau, ed., *Essays on Jewish Life and Thought: Presented in Honour of S. W. Baron* (1959). J. Friedrich, *Die hethitischen Gesetze* (1959; 1971²). Z. W. Falk, "Hebrew Legal Terms," JSSt 5 (1960) 350-354. S. Gevirtz, "West-Semitic Curses and the Problem of the Origins of Hebrew Law," VT 11 (1961) 137-158. F. Horst, "Zwei Begriff von Eigentum," Fests. W. Rudolph (1961) 135-152. R. A. F. MacKenzie, *Two Forms of Israelite Law* (1961). E. R. Lacheman, *Family Law Documents: Harvard Semitic Series* 19 (1962). D. J. Wiseman, "The Laws of Hammurabi Again," JSSt 7 (1962) 161-172. R. Tournay, *Family Law Documents: Harvard Semitic Series* 19 (1962). R. Hentschke, *Satzung und Setzender. Ein Beitrag zur israelitischen Rechtsterminologie*, BWANT 5, 3 (1963). H. J. Boecker, *Redeformen des Rechtslebens im Alten Testament* (1964; 1970²). Z. W. Falk, *Hebrew Law in Biblical Times* (1964). R. A. F. MacKenzie, "The Formal Aspect of Ancient Near Eastern Law," *The Seed of Wisdom*, ed. W. S. McCullough (1964) 31-44. E. von Schuler, "Staatsverträge und Dokumente hethitischen Rechts," *Neuere Hethiterforschung*, ed. G. Walser (1964) 34-53. G. Boyer, "Mélanges d'histoire du Droit Oriental: Les tablettes juridiques de Mari," *Recueil de l'Académie de Législation* 92 (1965) 29-43. M. Civil, "New Sumerian Law Fragments," *Studies in Honour of B. Landsberger* (1965) 1-12. Z. W. Falk, *Current Bibliography of Hebrew Law* (1965). R. Haase, *Einführung in das Studium keilschriftlicher Rechtsquellen* (1965). H. Petschow, "Die neubabylonische Zwiegesprächsurkunde und Genesis 23," JCS 19 (1965) 103-120; "Zu den Stilformen antiker Gesetze und Rechtssammlungen," ZSRG 82 (1965) 24-38. J. R. Porter, "The Legal Aspects of the Concept of 'Corporate Personality' in the OT," VT 15 (1965) 361-380. R. Hentschke, "Erwägungen zur israelitischen Rechtsgeschichte," ThViat 10 (1965/66) 108-133. Z. W. Falk, "Legal Archaeology," *Jura* (Naples) 17 (1966) 167-173. J. Morgenstern, *Rites of Birth, Marriage, Death and Kindred Occasions among the Semites* (1966). G. M. Tucker, "The Legal Background of Genesis 23," JBL 85 (1966) 77-84. J. J. Finkelstein, "A Late Old Babylonian Copy of the Laws of Hammurapi," JCS 21 (1967). G. Cardascia, *Les Lois assyriennes* (1969). H. Cazelles, "Le sens religieux de la loi," Populus Dei I: *Communio* 10 (1969) 177-200. H. Schulz, "Das Todesrecht im Alten Testament. Studien zur Rechtsform der Môt-Jûmat-Sätze," BZAW 114 (1969). H. Cazelles, "Shiloh, the Customary Laws and the Return of the Ancient Kings," *OT Essays in Honour of G. H. Davies* (1970) 238-251. S. Paul, "Types of Formulation in Biblical and Mesopotamian Law," *Leshonenu* 34 (1970) 257-266. A. Phillips, *Ancient Israel's Criminal Law: A New Approach to the Decalogue* (1970). D. Skweres, "Das Motiv der Strafgrunderfragung in biblischen und neuassyrischen Texten," BZ 14 (1970) 181-197. G. Liedke, *Gestalt und Bezeichnung alttestamentlicher Rechtssätze: Eine formgeschichtlich-terminologische Studie*, WMANT 39 (1971). A. Marzal, "Mari Clauses in 'Casuistic' and 'Apodictic' Styles," CBQ 33 (1971) 333-364, 492-509. A. Phillips, "Some Aspects of Family Law in Pre-Exilic Israel," VT 23 (1973) 349-361. W. M. Clark, "Law, Custom, Religion," *Old Testament Form Criticism*, ed. J. H. Hayes, (1974) 99-139. A. Phillips, "Nebalah—A Term For Serious Disorderly and Unruly Conduct," VT 25 (1975) 237-242.

Marriage: W. R. Smith, *Kinship and Marriage in Early Arabia* (1885; 1903²) (review by T. Nöldeke, ZDMG 40 [1886] 148-187). L. Freund, *Zur Geschichte des Ehegüterrechtes bei den Semiten* (1909). S. Krauss, "Die Ehe zwischen Onkel und Nichte," Fests. J. Kohler (1913)165-175. A. Eberharter, *Das Ehe- und Familienrecht der Hebräer mit Rücksicht auf die ethnologische Forschung dargestellt*, ATAV 1/2 (1914). J. Neubauer, "Beiträge zur Geschichte des biblisch-talmudischen Eheschliessungsrechts," MVÄG 24 (1919-1920). S. Bialoblocki, *Materialien zum islamischen und jüdischen Eherecht*, AOSG 1 (1928). J. Morgenstern, "Beena Marriage (Matriarchat) in Ancient Israel and its Historical Implications," ZAW 47 (NF 6) (1929) 91-110. H. Granqvist, *Marriage Conditions in a Palestinian Village, I-II: Commentationes Humanorum Litterarum* 3, 8 (1931, 1935). J. Morgenstern, "Additional Notes on 'Beena Marriage (Matriarchat) in Ancient Israel,' " ZAW 49 (1931) 46-58. H. T. Fischer, "Der magische Charakter des Brautpreises," *Weltkreis* 3, 3 (1932). P. Koschaker, "Zum Levirat nach hethitischem Recht," RHAs 2 (1933) 77-89; "Fratriarchat, Hausgemeinschaft und Mutterrecht in Keilschriftrechten," ZA 41 (NF 7) (1933) 1-89. J. J. Rabinowitz, "Marriage Contracts in Ancient Egypt in the Light of Jewish Sources," HThR 46 (1933) 91-97. C. H. Gordon, "The Status of Women as Reflected in the Nuzi Tablets," ZA 43 (1936) 146-169. M. Burrows, "The Complaint of Laban's Daughters," JAOS 57 (1937) 259-276. C. H. Gordon, "The Story of Jacob and Laban in the Light of the Nuzi Tablets," BASOR 66 (1937) 25-27. M. Burrows, "The Basis of Israelite Marriage," AOS 15 (1938); "The Ancient Oriental Background of Hebrew Levirate Marriage," BASOR 77 (1940) 2-15; "Levirate Marriage in Israel," JBL 59 (1940) 23-33. L. M. Epstein, *Marriage Laws in the Bible and the Talmud*, HSS 12 (1942). E. Neufeld, *Ancient Hebrew Marriage Laws* (1944), esp. "Divorce." H. van Praag, *Droit matrimonial assyro-babylonien* (1945). P. Koschaker, "Eheschliessung und Kauf nach alten Rechten, mit besonderer Berücksichtigung der älteren Keilschriftrechte," ArOr 18 (1950) 210-296. D. R. Mace, *Hebrew Marriage* (1953). J. Leipoldt, *Die Frau in der antiken Welt und im Urchristentum* (1954). A. van Selms, *Marriage and Family-Life in Ugaritic Literature* (1954). I. Mendelsohn, "On Marriage in Alalakh," *Essays in Jewish Life and Thought*, ed. J. L. Blau (1959) 351-357. J. J. Rabinowitz, "The 'Great Sin' in Ancient Egyptian Marriage Contracts," JNES 18 (1959). E. Luddekens, *Ägyptische Eheverträge*, ÄgAbh 1 (2960). P. W. Pestman, *Marriage and Matrimonial Property in Ancient Egypt: Papyrologica Lugduno–Batava* 9 (1961). Z. W. Falk, "Endogamy in Israel," Tarb. 31 (1961/62) 19-34. F. C. Fensham, "Widow, Orphan, and the Poor in Ancient Near Eastern Legal and Wisdom Literature," JNES 21 (1962) 129-131. J. H. Chamberlayne, "Kinship Relationship Among the Early Hebrews," *Numen* 10 (1963) 153-164. W. Plautz, "Monogamie und Polygynie im AT," ZAW 75 (1963) 3-26. E. A. Speiser, "The Wife-Sister Motif in the Patriarchal Narratives," *Biblical and Other Studies* I, ed. A. Altmann (1963) 15-28 = *Oriental Studies* (1967). W. Plautz, "Die Form der Eheschliessung im AT," ZAW 76 (1964) 298-318. T. E. McComisky, *The Status of the Secondary Wife; Its Development in Ancient Near East-*

ern Law (Diss. Brandeis 1965), *Diss. Abstr.* 27 (1966/67) 1309A. L. Rost, "Fragen zum Scheidungsrecht in Gen 12,10-20," Fests. H. W. Hertzberg (1965) 186-192. H. Hirsch, "Eine Kleinigkeit zur Heiratsurkunde ICK 1,3," OR 35 (1966) 279-280. N. H. Snaith, "The Daughters of Zelophehad," VT 16 (1966) 124-127. C. J. Mullo Weir, "Nuzi," *Archaeology and OT Studies*, ed. D. W. Thomas (1967) 73-86. D. J. Wiseman, "Alalakh," *Archaeology and OT Studies*, ed. D. W. Thomas (1967) 119-135. J. Van Seters, "The Problem of Childlessness in Near Eastern Law and the Patriarchs of Israel," JBL 87 (1968) 401-408. T. & D. Thompson, "Some Legal Problems in the Book of Ruth," VT 18 (1968) 79-99. S. Greengus, "The Old Babylonian Marriage in Rabbinic and Cognate Literature," JQR 60 (1969/70) 275-329. D. Freedman, "A New Approach to the Nuzi Sistership Contract," JANESCU 2 (1970) 77-85. J. Van Seters, "Jacob's Marriages and Ancient Near Eastern Customs: A Re-Examination," HThR 62 (1970) 377-395. G. W. Coats, "Widow's Rights: A Crux in the Structure of Gen 38," CBQ 34 (1972) 461-466. G. J. Wenham, "Betûlah 'a Girl of Marriageable Age,' " VT 22 (1972) 326-348. H. A. Hoffner, *Incest, Sodomy and Bestiality in the Ancient Near East*, AOAT 22 (1973). L. M. Muntingh, "Amorite Married and Family Life According to the Mari Texts," JNWSL 3 (1974) 50-70.

    Birth: A. Erman, *Zaubersprüche für Mutter und Kind* (1901). E. Chiera, *Inheritance Texts: Joint Expedition with the Iraq Museum at Nuzi* 1 (1927). J. Klima, *Untersuchungen zum altbabylonischen Erbrecht: ArOr Monographien* 8 (1940). H. Granqvist, *Birth and Childhood Among the Arabs* (1947). E. A. E. Jelfuková, "Sale of Inherited Property in the First Century B.C.," JEA 43 (1957) 45-55; 45 (1959) 61-74. I. Mendelsohn, "On the Preferential Status of the Eldest Son," BASOR 156 (1959) 38-40. E. F. Weidner, "Eine Erbteilung in mittelassyrischer Zeit," AfO 20 (1963) 121-24. J. Henninger, "Zum Erstgeborenenrecht bei den Semiten," Fests. W. Caskel (1968) 162-183. H. Cazelles, "Premiers-nés. II. Dans l'Ancien Testament," DBS 8 (1972) 482-491. J. Klima, "La position économique sociale et juridique de l'enfant d'après les sources cunéiformes de Mari (première moitié du IIe millénaire av. n. é)," ArOr 42 (1974) 232-244.

    Adoption: M. David, *Die Adoption im altbabylonischen Recht*, LRSt 23 (1927). S. Feigin, "Some Cases of Adoption in Israel," JBL 50 (1931) 186-200. E. Cassin, *L'adoption à Nuzi* (1938). I. Mendelsohn, "The Family in the Ancient Near East," BA 11 (1948) 24-40. C. B. Welles, "Manumission and Adoption," RIDA 3 (1949) 507-520. M. David, "Adoptie in het oude Israël," MAA 18,4 (1955) 85-103. S. Kardimon, "Adoption as a Remedy for Infertility in the Period of the Patriarchs," JSSt 3 (1958) 123-126. I. Mendelsohn, "A Ugaritic Parallel to the Adoption of Ephraim and Manasseh," IEJ 9 (1959) 180-183. M. H. Prévost, "Remarques sur l'adoption dans la Bible," RIDA 14 (1967) 67-77. E. Szlechter, "Des droits successoraux dérivées de l'adoption en droit babylonien," RIDA 14 (1967) 79-106. H. Donner, "Adoption oder Legitimation? Erwägungen zur Adoption im AT auf dem Hintergrund der altorientalischen Rechte," OrAnt 8 (1969) 87-119. F. Lyall, "Roman Law in the Writings of Paul—Adoption," JBL 88 (1969) 458-466. A. Verger, "Il problema dell' adozione nella Genesi," *Studi in onore di E. Volterra VI* (1969) 483-490. G. Cardascia, "Adoption Matrimoniale et Lévirat dans le droit d'Ugarit," RA 74 (1970) 119-126. E. R. Lacheman, "Real Estate Adoption by Women in the Tablets from URU Nuzi," AOAT 22 (1973). H. J. Boecker, "Anmerkungen zur Adoption im Alten Testament," ZAW 86 (1974) 86-89.

    Death: M. R. Lehmann, "Abraham's Purchase of Machpelah and Hittite Law," BASOR 129 (1953) 15-18. J. J. Rabinowitz, "Neo-Babylonian Legal Documents and Jewish Law," JJP 13 (1961) 131-175. J. A. Callaway, "Burials in Ancient Palestine from the Stone Age to Abraham," BA 26 (1963) 74-91. G. M. Tucker, "The Legal Background of Genesis 23," JBL 85 (1966) 77-84. D. Gilead, "Burial Customs and the Dolmen Problem," PEQ 100 (1968) 16-26. E. M. Meyers, "Secondary Burials in Palestine," BA 33 (1970) 2-29.

    Contracts: A. Jirku, "Neues keilschriftliches Material zum AT. IV. Der Vertrag zwischen Jakob und Laban Genesis 31," ZAW 39 (1921) 144-160. J. Friedrich, "Staatsverträge des Hatti-Reiches in hethitischer Sprache, 1-2," MVÄG 31 (1926); 34(1930) V. Korošec, *Hethitische Staatsverträge* (1931). A. Dupont-Sommer, "Trois stèles Araméennes provenant de Sfiré: Un traïté de vassalité du VIIIe siècle avant J. C.: Les annales Archéologiques de Syrie," RArch 10 (1960) 21-54. J. J. Rabinowitz, "The Susa Tablets, the Bible, and the Aramaic Papyri," VT 11 (1961) 56-76. J. A. Thompson, *The Ancient Near Eastern Treaties and the Old Testament*, TLBA (1963). D. J. McCarthy,

Treaty and Covenant. A Study in Form in the Ancient Oriental Documents and in the Old Testament, AnBib 21 (1963, 1981²). G. M. Tucker, "Covenant Forms and Contract Forms," VT 15 (1965) 487-503; "Witnesses and 'Dates' in Israelite Contracts," CBQ 28 (1966) 42-45.

Legal Procedure: H. Schmökel, "Biblische 'Du-Sollst' Gebote und ihr historischer Ort," ZSRG 36 (1950) 365-390. B. Gemser, "The Importance of the Motive Clause in Old Testament Law," VT.S 1 (1953) 50-66. H. Gese, "Beobachtungen zum Stil alttestamentlicher Rechtssätze," ThLZ 85 (1960) 147-150. I. L. Seeligmann, "Zur Terminologie für das Gerichtsverfahren im Wortschatz des biblischen Hebräisch," VT.S 16 (1967) 251-278. J. Salmon, *Judicial Authority in Early Israel* (Diss. Princeton 1968). H. Gilmer, *The If–You Form in Israelite Law* (Diss. Emory Univ.), *Diss. Abstr.* 31 (1969/70) 821A. H. Mc. Keating, "Justice and Truth in Israel's Legal Practice," CQR 3 (1970) 51-56. S. Segal, *Form and Function of Ancient Israelite, Greek and Roman Sentences*, AOAT 22 (1973). H. Mc. Keating, "The Development of the Law on Homicide in Ancient Israel," VT 25 (1975) 46-68.

d) *Names:* E. Meyer, "Der Stamm Jakob und die Entstehung der israelitischen Stämme," ZAW 6 (1886) 1-16. G. B. Gray, *Studies in Hebrew Proper Names* (1896). F. Schwally, "Über einige palästinische Völkernamen," ZAW 18 (1898). J. H. Breasted, "The Earliest Occurrence of the Name of Abram," AJSL 21 (1905) 22-36. H. Ranke, *Early Babylonian Personal Names* (1905). E. Huber, *Die Personennamen in den Keilschrifturkunden aus der Zeit der Könige von Ur und Nisin*, AB 21 (1907). M. Burchardt, *Die altkanaanäischen Eigennamen in Ägypten*, I-II (1909-1910). A. Ungnad, *Untersuchungen zu den. . . Urkunden aus Dilbat*, BASS 6, 5 (1909). D. D. Luckenbill, "Some Hittite and Mittanian Personal Names," AJSL 26, 2 (1910). J. H. Breasted, "The 'Field of Abram' in the Geographical List of Sheshank I," JAOS 31 (1911) 290-295. K. L. Tallqvist, *Assyrian Personal Names* (1914; 1966). B. Gemser, *De Beteekenis der Persoonsnamen voor onze Kennis van het Leven en Denken der ouden Babyloniërs en Assyriërs* (1924). D. D. Luckenbill, *Ancient Records of Assyria and Babylonia*, I-II (1926-1927). A. Gustavs, "Die Personennamen in den Tontafeln von Tell-'Ta'annek I-II," ZDPV 50 (1927) 1-18; 51 (1928) 169-218. M. Noth, *Die israelitischen Personennamen im Rahmen der gemeinsemitischen Namengebung*, BWANT 46 (1928); "Gemeinsemitische Erscheinungen in der israelitischen Namengebung," ZDMB 81 (1927) 1-45. H. Wuthnow, *Die semitischen Menschennamen in griechischen Inschriften und Papyri* (1930). G. Ryckmans, *Les noms propres sud-sémitiques, Bibliothèque du Muséon II, 1-3* (1934/35). H. Ranke, *Die ägyptischen Personennamen*, I (1935). G. Dossin, "Benjaminites dans les textes de Mari," Mélanges Dussaud, II (1939) 981-996 (cf. RA 52 [1958] 60-62). W. Feiler, "Hurritische Namen im Alten Testament," ZA 45 (1939) 216-219. J. J. Stamm, *Die akkadische Namengebung*, MV (Å) G 44 (1939; 1968²). W. F. Albright, "Mari and Egyptian Excavations of the 20th and 19th Century B.C.: Studies in Personal Names from the Two Sources," BASOR 83 (1941). I. J. Gelb–P. M. Purves–G. MacRae, *Nuzi Personal Names* (1943). C. F. Jean, "Les noms propres de personnes dans les lettres de Mari," *Studia Mariana* (1950) 63-98. N. Schneider, "Patriarchennamen in zeitgenössischen Keilschrifturkunden," Bib 33 (4) (1952) 516-522. M. Noth, "Mari und Israel. Eine Personennamenstudie," Fests. A. Alt (1953) 127-152 = *Ges. Aufs.* II (1971) 213-233. W. F. Albright, "Northwest Semitic Names in a List of Egyptian Slaves from the Eighteenth Century B.C.," JAOS 74 (1954) 222-232. A. Jirku, "Zu einigen Personennamen in Syrien," ZDMG 104 (29) (1954) 352-356. J. Fichtner, "Die etymologische Ätiologie in den Namengebungen der geschichtlichen Bücher des AT," VT 6 (1956) 372-396. A. Goetze, "Remarks on Some Names Occurring in the Execration Texts," BASOR 151 (1958) 28-33; "Amurrite Names in Ur III and Early Isin Texts," JSSt 4 (1959) 193-203. A. Jirku, "Zu einigen Ortsund Eigennamen Palästina-Syriens," ZAW 75 (1963) 86-88. A. F. Key, "The Giving of Proper Names in the OT," JBL 83 (1964) 55-59. H. B. Huffmon, *Amorite Personal Names in the Mari Texts: A Structural and Lexical Study* (1965). J. J. Stamm, "Hebräische Ersatznamen," *Studies in Honour of B. Landsberger* (1965) 413-424. O. Eissfeldt, "Gottesnamen in Personnamen als Symbole menschlicher Qualitäten," Fests. W. Baetke (1966) 110-117. F. Gröndahl, *Die Personennamen der Texte aus Ugarit* (1967). J. Heller, "Namengebung und Namendeutung. Grundzüge der ATlichen Onomatologie und ihre Folgen für die biblische Hermeneutik," EvTh 27 (1967) 255-266. M. Anbar, "Changement des noms des tribus nomades dans la relation d'un meme événement," Bib 49 (1968) 221-232. P. D. Miller, "Animal Names as Designations in Ugarit and Hebrew," UF 2 (1970) 177-186. G. L.

Harding, *An Index and Concordance of Pre-Islamic Arabian Names and Inscriptions* (1971). J. K. Stark, *Personal Names in Palmyrene Inscriptions* (1971). M. Dietrich–O. Loretz–W. Mayer, *Indices zu Personennamen aus Nuzi*, AOAT.

4. The Religion of the Patriarchs

I have described the history of research into the religion of the patriarchs in *Erträge der Forschung: Genesis 12–50* (1975) 94-124. The result can be synthesized briefly here. The history has gone through three stages. In the first stage the conservative understanding was that the God of Abraham, Isaac, and Jacob was identical with the God of Israel, and the religion of the patriarchs was none other than the religion of Israel, modified later in that it saw the religion of the patriarchs as a prelude to the Mosaic religion, emphasizing the close relationship between the two. H. Weidmann has dealt with the representatives of this stage (FRLANT 94 [1968] 36-64). The second stage contested the historicity of the patriarchs, and with it their religion: the patriarchal story arose, it was maintained, as a retrojection from the period of the monarchy; consequently, there was no such thing as a patriarchal religion (J. Wellhausen and his school; J. Hoftijzer has taken up this thesis, *Die Verheissungen. . .* [1956]; also T. L. Thompson, BZAW 133 [1974] and J. Van Seters, *Abraham. . .* [1975]). After some tentative beginnings by H. Gunkel, *Kommentar*, and H. Gressmann (ZAW 30 [1910] 1-34), the third stage began with A. Alt, *Der Gott der Väter* (BWANT 3,12 [1929]). Alt finds in the titles for the divinity, "the God of my father," and "the God of Abraham," elements of a religion which is clearly different from the religion of Israel during the monarchy. This makes inquiry into the religion of the patriarchs possible; the religion corresponds to the form of community and life-style of the patriarchs. Alt refers to identical or similar designations for the divinity in Nabataean and Palmyraean inscriptions.

(Except where indicated, all works mentioned in the following paragraph are to be found in the bibliography at the end of this section, Lit. 4. 2,3,4,5).

As a result of Alt's work attention was once more directed to the religion of the patriarchs as the religion of the patriarchal clans which are to be placed before the exodus from Egypt, and before the taking of the land by the Israelite tribes. One line of the discussion was concerned exclusively with the type of God of the Fathers which Alt had featured. One may mention here the works of J. Lewy (1934), H. G. May (1941), J. P. Hyatt (1955), K. T. Andersen (1962), H. Hirsch (1966); and contributions to the discussion by W. F. Albright (1935), H. Seebass (1966), R. de Vaux (*Early History. . .* 1971; 1978), J. Hoftijzer (1956), F. M. Cross (1962; *Canaanite Myth. . .* 1973), M. Haran (1965), B. Gemser (1958), O. Eissfeldt (1968). For reviews of Alt's work see K. Elliger (1930), J. Hempel (1930), K. Galling (1931).

Both Alt's thesis of 1929 and the discussion that followed—which probably has not yet ended—have their limitations in that they base a religion, or type of religion, exclusively (or almost so) on a designation for God. It is not to be contested that the designation, "the God of my Father" or "the God of Jacob," can express something which is typical of a religion; this is almost certainly the case. However, Alt's thesis and the whole ensuing discussion seem to be stamped unconsciously by the mentality which was dominant in an earlier stage of the history of religion, namely, that a religion is more or less identical with its concept, understanding, or idea of God. It is only with this presupposition as starting point that one can understand how the whole discussion took it for granted that the precise determination of the designation for God also determined precisely the religion of the patriarchs.

The positive contribution of Alt's thesis is that he took as his point of departure a constituent part of the patriarchal texts, and inquired about a really existing religion of really existing people. This claimed the ready agreement of scholars who took their stand on the archaeological approach, in particular W. F. Albright, J. Bright, J. P. Hyatt, and F. M Cross, though Albright and Cross came to very divergent conclusions. Alt's awareness that the religion of the patriarchs is determined by their form of community and life-style, and must correspond to it, is equally important. Alt himself only hinted at this, but did not follow it up; neither did the American scholars, W. F. Albright and F. M. Cross, nor the German scholars, G. von Rad and M. Noth, who agreed with Alt but took no account of this crucial aspect (this is very obvious in the explanation of the promises; see below). Despite far-reaching agreement with Alt, one can understand how neglect of this insight allowed the opposite thesis to gain ground, namely, that the religion of the patriarchs was the El-religion or some form of it. This thesis is understandable: "El" is the only *name* for God which occurs in the patriarchal stories; it need not compete with the designation, "God of my Father," or the like; one can accept without further ado the idea that the god El can be described as "the God of my Father" without causing any difficulty (e.g., O. Eissfeldt, F. M. Cross). This is the reason a number of scholars, even before Alt, held that the religion of the patriarchs was an El-religion (R. Kittel [1920], H. Gunkel *Komm.*, H. Gressmann [1910], W. W. Graf Baudissin [1925 & 1929], R. Dussaud [1957]; cf. Lit 4). Alt himself regarded the *Elim* ["gods"] of Genesis as local Canaanite names; since the discoveries from Ugarit, El has become known as father of the gods and head of the pantheon. Thus, if the religion of the patriarchs has been designated an El-religion, this could only be on the basis of the picture of the father of the Canaanite gods which the Ugaritic texts have painted so clearly and colorfully. When one takes a general survey of the history of scholarship, one understands how the new thesis, that the religion of the patriarchs was an El-religion, established itself: the archaeological approach supported it; it could be explained directly from the new discoveries. W. F. Albright had already found a reference to the El-religion in proper names formed with El; then in 1962, and more extensively in his work of 1973, Cross tried to prove that the divine names in Genesis that include the syllable "El" are to be understood as hymnic predicates of the Canaanite god-king, El. Thus, for Cross, the religion of the patriarchs is a special form of the Canaanite El-religion. Cross, even more than Alt, has concentrated exclusively on the names and designations of God. He advances names from the texts of Gen. 12–50 only; he takes no account of what is said there about the God of the patriarchs, nor of what happens between him and them.

By way of conclusion one can say that this controversy cannot be resolved as long as it remains restricted to names or designations for God. Recent literature offers a whole series of general surveys of the patriarchal religion. Reference may be made to the histories of Israel or of the religion of Israel in the bibliography, Lit. 4.2, 3, as well as to R. de Vaux (*Early History. . .*) and H. Cazelles (DBS 7 [1961] 21-156). They are all syntheses, not real studies; a comprehensive study of the religion of the patriarchs, taking account of all perspectives, remains to be done.

These syntheses agree that one can infer from the patriarchal stories a religion which is to be set in the period before the taking of the land and before the exodus from Egypt, and is comprehensible in this setting in the history of religions; that is, a religion before Israel's meeting with Yahweh. They agree further that the patriarchal religion is not identical with any religion known to us from extrabiblical documents: neither with Canaanite nor Amorite nor any religion known to us from the area of the ancient near east. That is to say, we have no reliable sources for this religion but the texts of the patriarchal story alone.

If one asks more precisely which elements in the texts of Gen. 12–50 can be adduced to show the uniqueness and essential traits of this religion, then problems arise. There is broad agreement that one must adduce the two most frequently recurring groups of designations for God which are the basis of the controversial theses of Alt and Cross; but beyond this almost everything is questionable. Two consequences follow from this. *The first* is that the patriarchal stories received their definitive shape in the period of the early monarchy (one must reckon also with further adaptations and additions in a later period), that is, in the place and in the language of the Yahweh religion. This is clearest in the use of the name Yahweh by J; for him, Yahweh is the God of the fathers. But the language cannot be restricted to the designation for God; the Yahweh religion, or the theology of J, must have affected the final form of the patriarchal stories in many respects. This is confirmed by the interpretations of the stories, which make no distinction at all between the God of Israel and the God of the patriarchal period. An example is the interpretation of G. von Rad. Throughout the whole of his commentary on the patriarchal story he speaks of God's action towards the patriarchs, and of theirs towards him, as if he sees no religious gap between the God of the writer in the period of the monarchy and a God of the patriarchal period, hundreds of years earlier. The modern interpreter follows *de facto* the Yahwist, for whom Yahweh is the God of the fathers.

Here a question of methodology arises. Can the modern interpreter distinguish at all whether a text is dealing with the God of the fathers or with the God of Israel? Often it will not be possible to decide clearly; nevertheless, the question must be put to each text. There are possible criteria for distinguishing. Those traits can be characteristic of the religion of the patriarchs (1) which accord with their life-style and economy, but not with that of the sedentary people of Israel; (2) which do not occur in the religion of Israel as we know it from the time of the Exodus, Sinai, and the taking of the land. But traits (3) which are central to the Yahweh religion, and those which presuppose a rather long development of it and so must be regarded as relatively late, cannot belong to the religion of the patriarchs.

The second consequence: The distinction between the origin of a statement about God from the theology of the Yahwist or from the patriarchal religion is inadequate. If the patriarchal stories have arisen in a very long process of tradition, then one has to reckon with layers and distinctions within the patriarchal religion. This is clear, for example, in the encounter of the patriarchs with the sanctuaries of the land of Canaan. Narratives which can be understood as the foundation of a sanctuary, such as Gen. 28, occur only in chs. 25–36, whereas the building of an altar in chs. 12–25 clearly means something different. A confirmation of this distinction is that institutions play an important role in chs. 25–36, but not in chs. 12–25 (cf. Intro. 1.C). The patriarchal stories reflect different stages of the relationship of the patriarchs to the sanctuaries of the land; and there can be no question that what is reflected in Gen. 25–36 is closer to the taking of the land by the tribes than what is reflected in Gen. 12–25. When one is reckoning with long intervals of time one must not exclude the occasional influence of other religions.

It was a condition of the wandering life-style of the patriarchs that they came to know many areas of religion and different types of sanctuaries and came in contact with a variety of religious practices. This opens up the possibility that the patriarchs took over a great deal, and much else only temporarily. Consequently, it is unwise to accept uncritically every religious trait as characteristic of the patriarchal religion as a whole. An example is the Teraphim of Gen. 31. The occurrence of the Teraphim (images of household gods) in this passage has led all interpreters astray; they state in a quite general way that the Teraphim are a constitutive part of the religion of the patriarchs. But this is extremely questionable. The function of the image of the gods in the narrative of ch. 31 is not religious at all, but completely profane. This allows the much more likely conclusion that from time to time there was something like this, and that it had no real religious significance.

A. Characteristics of the Religion of the Patriarchs

I. The God of Abraham, the "God of my Father."   This designation for God should not be seen and judged in isolation. Alt's discovery that it is a characteristic of talk about God in the patriarchal stories, and occurs in these dimensions only here in the Old Testament, is not to be contested; nor is the fact that this complex acquires a meaning only when one associates a particular type of religion with it, one different from the religion of Israel in all its stages from Exodus and Sinai down to the late period. The bearers of tradition must have been aware of it when in Ex. 3 and 6 they brought this designation for God and the name of Yahweh into a chronological order. These three points which Alt made in his study of 1929 survive the long discussion of his thesis, and are certain. But their significance can become clear only when the question is raised about the importance of their place in the broader context. Firstly a simple statement is to be made. The designations like "the God of my Father" acquire their significance only from the fact that a large part of the narratives in Gen. 12–50 are family narratives, i.e., they take place in a form of community structured on family lines. It is only from this context that the titles acquire their meaning. This means that the designation "the God of my Father" has, in a form of community structured on family lines, precisely the same function as "the God of Israel" in a form of community structured as a people. The title "the God of my Father" says no more about the God so designated than that he is the God who is associated with a community structured on family lines, who deals with it, speaks to it, and is invoked by it. The designation as such does not say what sort of God he is; only the narratives of Gen. 12–50 can say that, insofar as they deal with what he does and says. The syntheses of the patriarchal religion mentioned above described its God as God of a clan, family, or tribe; but this designation still says nothing as long as it is not brought into immediate relationship with the narratives in which this God acts and speaks in this form of society, and in it alone. None of the authors mentioned above does this.

(On this designation of God cf. H. Vorländer, *Mein Gott. Die Vorstellung vom persönlichen Gott im Alten Orient und im Alten Testament*, AOAT 23 [1975], and R. Albertz, *Persönliche Frömmigkeit und offizielle Religion. Religionsinterner Pluralismus in Israel und Babylon*, CThM [1978]. The latter puts the designation for God into the broader context of a personal piety which is to be distinguished from the official religion.)

II. Was the Religion of the Patriarchs Monotheism?   One group of scholars wants to describe the religion of the patriarchs as monotheism, another as monolatry, another as polytheism. But these three concepts with the distinctions based on them are not relative to the religion of the patriarchs; they are inextricably bound up with that outmoded notion of development in the study of the history of religion which saw it as a rectilinear ascent from polytheism through monolatry to monotheism. Only in recent times has it been realized that polytheism is a relatively late formation which occurs above all at the higher levels of civilization. It is no longer to the point to devalue polytheism out of hand when contrasted with monotheism; polytheism by and large appeared relatively late and this gives it a positive significance over against the forms of religion which preceded it. The experience of reality of an articulated society finds its correlative in a veneration of a number of gods, representing in each case an aspect of this reality. The religion of the patriarchs, therefore, is to be regarded as an early form of religion, but not as some sort of victory over a previous polytheistic stage. There is no trace of polytheism in the patriarchal stories; one can only speak of polytheism when something takes place between two or more gods.

The question has been asked whether each of the wandering groups worshiped its own God, that is, whether "the God of Isaac" was different from "the God of Abraham" (so A. Alt, G. Fohrer), or whether the God of the fathers was one and the same for all (B. Gemser, M. Haran). But this is not an appropriate contrast. It would be meaningful to maintain that the God of Abraham and the God of Jacob were different gods only if there were texts in the patriarchal stories in which they appear together and are brought into relationship with each other. But this is not the case. What is decisive is the following. In the individual patriarchal narratives people always stand face to face with only one God; it is always only one God who deals with and speaks to people. Nevertheless, the designation "monotheism" is not appropriate. The first commandment is a clear expression of monotheism: "no other gods besides me." That is, we speak of monotheism when the confession to *one* God is consciously opposed to a possible worship of several gods, or to an apostasy from one god to another. But there is not yet in the patriarchal stories the possibility of such an opposition. They contain no trace of a confrontation with other religions, or any sort of religious polemic. B. Gemser has pointed this out in his study, "God in Genesis" (OTS 12 [1958] 1-21). If, on the other hand, one looks to the relations of the group of people to the God whom they invoke and in whom they put their trust on their wanderings, then he can only be one. V. Maag in particular has shown this.

Not even the term *monolatry* (or *henotheism*) expresses with sufficient clarity this peculiar relationship to God. One can use it, but one must then explain it in the sense just expounded.

III. The Personal Relationship to God. The majority of scholars are unanimous in singling out one trait of the religion of the patriarchs, and many of them regard it as determinative: the personal relationship to God. H. Cazelles begins his presentation with it: "Le rapport personel entre le Patriarche et son dieu." G. Fohrer, too, holds it to be the most outstanding and important trait. It may be noted that this characteristic trait had been seen long before A. Alt. It is independent of the discovery of the type of God of the fathers and the discussion on that.

Many scholars see an attestation of this trait in the group of personal names in which the god is described as a relative of the name-bearer, such as names with *'ab*, *'aḥ*, *'amm* (cf. Intro. 3.C.III). This can well be; but one cannot claim it alone as attestation of the fathers of Israel, because names of this type occur elsewhere.

This personal relationship to God is attested adequately and clearly throughout the patriarchal story. It is a most striking fact that the alternation of sin and punishment, sin and forgiveness, does not occur in Gen. 12–36 (it is different in the Joseph narrative). As far as I know, attention has not been drawn to this in previous presentations of the patriarchal religion. It constitutes a basic difference from the relationship to God which begins with Exodus and Sinai. Insofar as there is fault in chs. 12–36, it is something that happens between people; there is never mention of sin or guilt before God (cf. below on Gen. 13:13; 19). This, in my opinion, is one of the most important traits of the patriarchal religion.

This is confirmed by a further observation: promises play an important role in the patriarchal stories, but their counterpart is missing. The word of judgment or the announcement of judgment is an essential element of the Yahweh-religion; it did not begin with the prophets of judgment. There is nothing corresponding to the pronouncement of judgment or punishment in the patriarchal stories. A further clear distinction between the religion of the patriarchs and the religion of Israel arises out of the life-style of the fathers. It is prepolitical; accordingly, the God of the fathers has no connection with the political scene; he has no connection with the waging of war. He is not a God of war and does not assist in battle.

There is an even sharper division between the presence of God with the fathers, which is exclusively peaceful, and the God of the judges, who conducts the wars of his people. It is important for the later promises that Yahweh puts an end to wars (e.g., Is. 2), that there is a tradition preserved in the Old Testament from the early period in which the God of the fathers had nothing to do with wars. There is, in addition, another essential difference: the patriarchal religion does not yet know of holiness as an attribute of God. The word is found only in connection with a holy place (Gen. 28). Apart from this, God is never described as a holy God; there is not yet a sacred area or a sacred language. This is very intimately linked with the peculiar nature of the cult in the patriarchal stories.

B. The Cult

Our concepts and notions of cult are shaped by the form of the large-scale cult as it has defined itself in the religion of the high cultures. We must distinguish the cult found in the patriarchal stories from this because we are dealing with small, family-structured, wandering groups. Every manifestation of cult in the patriarchal stories is a sign of a way of life corresponding to that of the patriarchs. The decisive difference between the large-scale cult and that of the patriarchs is that the latter does not construct a domain separated from and independent of ordinary life, but is integrated fully into the life-styles of the small wandering group. The three main features of patriarchal cult demonstrate this: sacred place, sacred season, and sacred person, with the resulting sacred observances. The patriarchal stories are familiar with the sacred place, but it is a place along the way, as when Abraham builds an altar at a stopping place, or Jacob discovers a sacred place when fleeing. But the sacred place never has the function that it has in the large-scale cult of sedentary people—the temple in the middle of a settled community to which families come from round about to celebrate a feast in large numbers. Sacred vessels are part of the sacred place; the wandering group is not yet familiar with them, as the sacrifice of Isaac shows dramatically; the vessels used here are the everyday vessels. Sacred stones and trees also belong in this context, though they are never called sacred. It is very likely that they go back to the patriarchal period, because they are characteristic of an early stage of the cult when the sanctuary was not yet an area made by hands, but rather a mountain, a stone, a tree, a spring. Consequently, earlier studies concluded that the religion of the patriarchs was a form of animism. But the natural sanctuary is an early stage in the history of religion all over the world. R. de Vaux points out that stones and trees also play an important role as sacred places among the pre-Islamic Arabs.

There is not much to be said about the sacred season; for all practical purposes there are no feasts in the patriarchal stories. Feasts, however, were certainly a part of pastoral life; a good example is the old pastoral feast of the Passover at the time of the change of pasture, as L. Rost has explained it (ZDVP 66 [1943] 205-216).

The situation is clear in the case of sacred persons. The patriarchal stories know no priest (apart from Gen. 14), and the father of the household carries out the priestly function. He imparts the blessing and offers the sacrifice. Above all, the father receives the word of God directly, in particular the word that shows the group the way. There is no mediator of cult or word. Everything that happens between God and man happens directly, without any mediator.

Cultic action takes place as part of the life of the group, and arises therefrom; it takes place as required, not because of some cultic prescription. If one accepts the idea that the pastoral feast of the Passover (see L. Rost; G. Fohrer and V. Maag accept it) at the time of the change of pasture also belonged to the patriarchal period, then it had the form of a community meal without priest or altar.

A. Alt had described the patriarchs as "bearers of revelation and founders of cult," and many have taken this over (M. Noth, G. von Rad, G. Fohrer). Both descriptions are stamped with the mentality of the high religions, and both are misleading. Alt meant by "bearers of revelation" that the word of God was communicated directly to the patriarchs; the expression, however, has echoes of a sacral status which is certainly not in accord with the patriarchal religion. It is misleading to speak of the patriarchs as "founders of cult," because this introduces the idea of the independent cult of the high religions which was not part of patriarchal life; "cult" was a constitutive part of the life of the community; it was in the community and did not need to be founded.

C. The Promises to the Patriarchs

There are two essential points of difference between the promises to the patriarchs and the announcements of salvation in the rest of the Old Testament. The promises are not communicated through the cult as, for example, the later oracles of salvation, nor through someone who has been commissioned to do so, like the prophets. Everything that happens between God and man is integrated into the life of the people, not through particular persons, nor in a special sort of language, but as a normal part of community life. An example is the instruction linked with the promise, which is carried out when required by the one to whom the communication is made.

Reference has already been made to the second difference: the promises contain nothing like announcements of judgment or proclamations of punishment. The great importance of the promises for the patriarchal story can be understood only in a broader context. One trait runs through all the stories which say something about God and his relationship to the people—he is the protector (the name *Jacob* means "may God protect"), the preserver, the helper, the one who gives success, who accompanies. There is a relationship to God which can only be understood from the life of a wandering group which is constantly in danger, which is not familiar with the possession or exercise of power within or without, which is too small to wage war, but is exposed to the threats of nature, like famine, and has no means of defense. One can understand how in such a life-style God is wholly and exclusively the preserver, the protector, the helper; it is necessarily a different situation with a way of life in which the community itself is in a position to provide various means of security. The patriarchal way of life is in every respect insecure; this is the basic reason why command, admonition, punishment, judgment, and announcement of judgment are completely absent. For a group of people who live in complete insecurity and under constant threat, their God is a God who is with them. The promises are vital in such a way of life. They open up the future in the midst of insecurity and threat.

This explains at the same time the difference between two groups of promises. A distinction is to be made between those which are spoken into a situation of need or anxiety or uncertainty, such as correspond to the way of life of the patriarchs, and those which do not correspond to this situation, and whose fulfillment consequently can take place only much later. To the first group belong the promise of a son, of new pasture lands, and of presence; to the second, the promise of the possession of the land, of an abundant posterity, and blessing in general.

A difference in form corresponds to a difference in content. The promise can be a constituent part of a narrative (as the promise of a son in Gen. 18), in which case it is usually a promise that corresponds to the situation narrated. Or the promise itself can be the object of a narrative (12:1-3; 15; 17), a scene (13:14-17), or an addition (22:15-18), in which case there are generally several promises together which do not correspond to the situation narrated. These differences point to a history of the promises within the patriarchal stories. The oldest layer consists of promises which are a constituent part of a narrative and have belonged to it right from the beginning. Later layers consist of promises which can be detected as insertions into older narratives; here several promises are strung together in a sequence. This is in further agreement with the difference in content: only promises belonging to the older layers correspond to the patriarchal period and life-style; the promises in later layers, the possession of the land and countless posterity, are directed towards the people of Israel. They have been added in the course of the history of the patriarchal traditions.

The promises in the patriarchal story, therefore, have two very different functions: some of them are an important constituent part of the religion of the patriarchs, others consciously want to join the story of the patriarchs with the story of the people in such a way that the promises made to the fathers find their fulfillment in the history of the people of Israel. I have made a study of the individual promises, their relationship to the narratives, their history and posthistory, as well as of their theological meeting, in *The Promises to the Fathers* (1976; Eng. 1980).

D. The Covenant with the Fathers

It is only in Gen. 12–25, and in two places, chs. 15 and 17, and so only with Abraham, that God "concludes a covenant." These passages gained such great importance because the word had acquired a comprehensive theological meaning from the "Sinai covenant"—the covenant with Abraham precedes that of Sinai. But the situation takes on a different aspect when, prescinding from this context, we inquire into the meaning of the word ברית, and what takes place when a covenant is concluded between God and Abraham in chs. 15 and 17 (for details, cf. C.

Westermann, *Genesis 12–50. Erträge der Forschung* Bd. 48 [1975]). Considerable corrections have been made to the uncritical and generalizing talk about a covenant with the patriarchs. The findings can be synthesized in three points.

(1) The studies of A. Jepsen (Fests. W. Rudolf [1961] 161-179) and E. Kutsch (THAT I [1971] 339-352) have shown that the basic meaning of the word is not "covenant." A. Jepsen describes it as a solemn assurance, a self-obligation; the *berit* to Abraham therefore is "a pure assurance, promise." Similarly, E. Kutsch describes it as "obligation" and "assurance." Consequently, Gen. 15:7-21 does not present the concluding of a covenant between God and Abraham which established from that moment on a mutual covenantal relationship, but rather God's assurance or promise to Abraham solemnized by a rite. It can remain an open question as yet whether we are dealing with an early (N. Lohfink) or a late (L. Perlitt, WMANT 36 [1969]) text. In any case, it is no longer possible to base a covenant between God and Abraham on Gen 15:7-21.

(2) The positive result of this correction is that Gen. 15:7-21 belongs in the context of the promises to the patriarchs. If *berit* here does not mean "covenant" but a solemn promise or oath (N. Lohfink), then the text is not dealing with a covenant which God concludes with Abraham, but with the solemn confirmation by oath of the promise of the land. A more precise explanation of the text is possible only in the context of the promises in general and the promise of the land in particular. The text of Gen. 15 ceases to have any relevance for the whole question of a patriarchal covenant or a covenant between God and Abraham.

(3) It is quite different with the text of Gen. 17 (P), both as regards the word ברית and what is described there. It clearly presents a mutual exchange. Abraham's obligation is correlative with God's. The word itself, *berit*, which occurs 13 times, runs through the whole chapter like a leitmotif and obviously establishes a lasting situation which binds God and Abraham in a mutual obligation. The basic meaning of *berit* is deliberately extended here to that of covenant which establishes mutuality. It is not, to be sure, a covenant established between two partners, but the institution founded by God alone and resting on his promise alone. But this new relationship to God, which P designates in 17:7b by the covenant formula, "I will be your God," is really intended for the people of Israel, whom Abraham represents. P is speaking to his people at the time of the exile. Israel is alive because God promised Abraham that he would be his God. The covenant of God with Abraham described by P in Gen. 17 is then an interpretation from the time of the exile, and means in reality the covenant of Yahweh with Israel. This is confirmed by the fact that P has constructed his work with a Noachian covenant and an Abrahamic covenant, but with no Sinai covenant. The covenant with Israel is included in Abraham (C. Westermann, *The Promises. . .* [1980] 159f.).

Literature for Section 4

1. General

N. Söderblom, *Die Religion und die soziale Entwicklung* (1898). H. Zimmern, *Beiträge zur Kenntnis der babylonischen Religion*, AB 12 (1901). A. Jeremias, *Monotheistische Strömungen innerhalb der babylonischen Religion* (1904). K. Breysig, *Die Entstehung des Gottesgedankens und der Heilbringer* (1905). N. Söderblom, *Das Wesen des Gottesglaubens. Untersuchungen über die Anfänge der Religion* (1914; 1926[2]). M. Weber, *Wirtschaft und Gesellschaft*. Kap. V (1921) 245-381. H. Frick, "Über den Ursprung des Gottesglaubens und die Religion der Primitiven," ThR NF 1-2 (1929/30) 241-265. O.

Eissfeldt, "Die Wanderung palästinisch-syrischer Götter nach Osten und Westen im zweiten vorchristlichen Jahrtausend," JPOS 14 (1934) 294-300. E. Dhorme, *Les religions de Babylonie et d'Assyrie* (1945). E. O. James, *The Beginnings of Religion. An Introductory and Scientific Study* (1948). M. Eliade, *Traité des religions* (1949, 1970). H. A. Frankfort, *The Problem of Similarity in Ancient Near Eastern Religions: The Frazer Lecture* (1950). M. Eliade, *Die Religionen und das Heilige* (1954). F. Heiler, *Erscheinungsformen und Wesen der Religion* (1961). S. G. F. Brandon, *Man and his Destiny in the Great Religions* (1962). T. Canaan, "Gott im Glauben der palästinischen Araber," ZDPV 78 (1962) 1-18. J. N. Nougayrol, "Recherches nouvelles sur la religion Babylonienne," Sem. 13 (1963) 5-20. P. Ricoeur, "Guilt, Ethics and Religion," *Talk of God, Lectures II* (1969) 100-117. G. Widengren, *Religionsphänomenologie* (1969). H. Gese–M. Höfner–K. Rudolph, "Die Religionen Altsyriens, Altarabiens und der Mandäer," *Die Religionen der Menschheit 10,2* (1970) 1-231. E. Hornung, *Der Eine und die Vielen. Ägyptische Gottesvorstellungen* (1971). K. Rudolph, "Religionsgeschichte und 'Religionsphänomenologie,' " ThLZ 96 (1971) 241-250. U. Mann, ed., *Theologie und Religionswissenschaft. Der gegenwärtige Stand ihrer Forschungsergebnisse und Aufgaben im Hinblick auf ihr gegenseitiges Verhältnis* (1973). H. Ringgren, *Religions of the Ancient Near East* (1973).

2. Religion of the Patriarchs

K. C. W. F. Bähr, *Symbolik des mosaischen Cultus, I* (1837; 1874[2]). E. Renan, *Histoire générale et système comparé des langues sémitiques, I* (1855); *Nouvelles considérations sur le caractère général des peuples sémitiques et en particulier sur leur tendence au monothéisme,* JA 5 (1859) Sér. 13. A. Dillmann, *Über den Ursprung der alttestamentlichen Religion* (1865). A. Kuenen, *De godsdienst van Israel tot den ondergang van den joodschen staat* (1869-1870). W. W. Graf Baudissin, *Studien zur semitischen Religionsgeschichte I-II* (1876-1879). E. König, *Die Hauptprobleme der altisraelitischen Religionsgeschichte gegenüber den Entwicklungstheoretikern* (1884). F. Baethgen, *Beiträge zur semitischen Religionsgeschichte. Der Gott Israels und die Götter der Heiden* (1888). W. R. Smith, *Lectures on the Religion of the Semites, I* (1889; 1903[2]). E. Sellin, *Jahwes Verhältnis zum israelitischen Volk und Individuum* (1896). A. Lang, *The Making of Religion* (1898; 1909[3]). E. Stucken, *Astralmythen der Hebräer, Babylonier und Ägypter. Religionsgeschichtliche Untersuchungen, I-IV* (1899 & 1901). J. W. Rothstein, *Der Gottesglaube im AT und die religionsgeschichtliche Kritik* (1900). S. I. Curtiss, *Ursemitische Religion im Volksleben des heutigen Orients* (1903). E. König, *Die Gottesfrage und der Ursprung des Alten Testaments* (1903). T. G. Selby, *The God of the Patriarchs. Brief Studies in the Early Scriptures of the OT* (1904). M. Haller, *Religion, Recht und Sitte in den Genesissagen* (1905). O. Meusel, "War die vorjahwistische Religion Israels Ahnenkult? Ein Überblick über die Geschichte des Problems," NKZ 16 (1905) 484-494, 523-545. B. Baentsch, *Altorientalischer und israelitischer Monotheismus. Ein Wort zur Revision in der entwicklungsgeschichtlichen Auffassung der israelitischen Religionsgeschichte* (1906). C. F. Burney, "A Theory of the Development of Israelite Religion in Early Times," JThS 9 (1908) 321-352. E. Zurkellen-Pfleiderer, "Die Religion der Patriarchengeschichten," TARWPV 10 (1908) 29-65. A. Loisy, *The Religion of Israel* (1910). F. M. T. Böhl, *Kanaanäer und Hebräer. . .* BWATq (1911). K. Müller, *Die seit Renan über den israelitischen Urmonotheismus geäusserten Anschauungen* (1911). O. Eissfeldt, *Die Verwertbarkeit der Vätergeschichten in der Genesis für die Rekonstruktion der vormosaischen hebräischen Profan- und Religionsgeschichte,"* PrM 17 (1913) 329-345. H. Gressmann, "Mose und seine Zeit," FRLANT NF 1 (1913) esp. 425-431. J. Hehn, *Die biblische und babylonische Gottesidee* (1913). H. P. Smith, *The Religion of Israel* (1914). C. Steuernagel, *Jahwe, der Gott Israels,* BZAW 27 (1914). W. Wundt, *Völkerpsychologie,* VI, 10 (1915; 1923[2]) 179-194. R. Kittel, *Die Religion des Volkes Israel* (1920; 1929[2]). M. Weber, *Gesammelte Aufsätze zur Religionssoziologie, III, VIII* (1920; 1966[4]). G. Beer, *Steinverehrung bei den Israeliten. Ein Beitrag zur semitischen und allgemeinen Religionsgeschichte, Schr. d. Strasburger Wiss. Ges. in Heidelberg* NF 4 (1921). G. Hölscher, *Geschichte der israelitischen und judischen Religion* (1922). E. König, *Geschichte der alttestamentlichen Religion* (1924[3,4]). C. Steuernagel, *Alttestamentliche Religion und alttestamentliche Religionsgeschichte,* BZAW 41 (1925). W. L. Wardle, "The Origin of Hebrew Monotheism," ZAW 43 (1925) 193-209. G. Beer, *Welches war die älteste Religion Israels?* (1927). E. G. Kraeling, "The

Real Religion of Ancient Israel,'' JBL 47 (1928) 133-159. A. Weiser, *Religion und Sittlichkeit in der Genesis in ihrem Verhältnis zur alttestamentlichen Religionsgeschichte* (1928). I. Rabin, "Studien zur vormosaischen Gottesvorstellung," *Fests. z. 75 jähr. Bestehen des jüd.-theol. Seminars, Breslau* 1 (1929) 237-356. S. A. Cook, *The Religion of Ancient Palestine in the Light of Archaeology, Schweich Lectures 1925* (1930). Y. Kaufmann, "Probleme der israelitische-jüdischen Religionsgeschichte," ZAW 48 (1930) 23-43; 51 (1933) 35-47. W. O. E. Oesterley–T. Robinson, *Hebrew Religion, Its Origin and Development* (1930; 1955³). O. Eissfeldt, "Zwei Leidener Darstellungen der israelitischen Religionsgeschichte," ZDMG 85 (1931) 172-195. C. Toussaint, *Les origines de la religion d'Israël, I* (1931). F. Baumgärtel, *Die Eigenart der alttestamentlichen Frömmigkeit* (1932). S. A. Cook, *Ethical Monotheism in the Light of Comparative Religion* (1932). E. Sellin, *Israelitisch-jüdische Religionsgeschichte* (1933). F. X. Kortleitner, *Religio a patriarchis Israelitarum exercitata* (1936). J. Lindblom, *Israels religion i gamaltestamentlig tid* (1936). W. L. Wardle, *The History and Religion of Israel: The Clarendon Bible OT I* (1936; 1950²). A. Causse, *Du groupe ethnique à la communauté religieuse. Le problème sociologique de la religion d'Israël* (1937). E. Dhorme, *L'évolution religieuse d'Israël, I* (1937). B. Balscheit, *Alter und Aufkommen des Monotheismus in der israelitischen Religion*, BZAW 69 (1938). A. Lods, *The Religion of Israel–Origins: Record and Revelation*, ed. H. W. Robinson (1938) 187-215. H. S. Nyberg, "Studien zum Religionskampf im AT," ARW 35 (1938) 329-382. L. B. Goff, "Syncretism in the Religion of Israel," JBL 58 (1939) 151-161. W. F. Albright, "The Ancient Near East and the Religion of Israel," JBL 59 (1940) 85-112. H. T. Fowler, *The Origin and the Growth of the Hebrew Religion* (1940). J. Pedersen, "Canaanite and Israelite Cultus," AcOrK 18 (1940) 1-14. B. D. Eerdmans, *The Religion of Israel* (1947). H. van der Steinen, "Abraham's Religion," JMES 1 (1947). J. J. Dougherty, *The Religion of the Patriarchs*, (Diss. 1948). H. Schrade, *Der verborgene Gott. Gottesbild und Gottesvorstellung in Israel und im alten Orient* (1949). H. H. Rowley, "The Antiquity of Israelite Monotheism," ET 61 (1949/50) 333-338. J. Gray, "Cultic Affinities between Israel and Ras Shamra," ZAW 62 (1950) 207-220. G. W. Anderson, "Hebrew Religion," *The OT and Modern Study*, ed. H. H. Rowley (1951) 283-309. J. de Fraine, "Individu et Société dans la religion de l'Ancien Testament," Bib 33 (1952) 324-326, 445-448. J. Muilenburg, "The History of the Religion of Israel," IB I (1952) 292-348. W. Eichrodt, "Religionsgeschichte Israels," *Historia Mundi 2* (1953-1969). J. Hempel, "Glaube, Mythos und Geschichte im AT," ZAW 65 (1953) 109-167. S. Mowinckel, *Religion und Kultus* (1953). O. Eissfeldt, "Religionshistorie und Religionspolemik im AT," VT.S 3 (1955) 94-102. I. Lewy, "The Beginnings of the Worship of Yahweh. Conflicting Biblical Views," VT 6 (1956) 429-435. H. H. Rowley, *The Faith of Israel* (1956); "Mose und der Monotheismus," ZAW 69 (1957) 1-21. F. Dumermuth, "Zur deuteronomischen Kulttheologie und ihre Voraussetzungen," ZAW 70 (1958) 59-98. B. Gemser, *Vragen rondom de Patriarchenreligie* (1958). W. Harrelson, "Worship in Early Israel," BiR 3 (1958) 1-14. J. N. Lambert, "Aspects de la civilisation à l'âge du fratriarcat. Etude d'histoire juridique et religieuse comparée," BFDSEUA 28 (1958). V. Hamp, "Monotheismus im Alten Testament," BEThL 12-13 (1959) 516-521. J. Henninger, "La société bédouine ancienne,'' SS 2 (1959) 69-93. Y. Kaufmann, "The Genesis and the Nature of the Religion of Israel" [in Hebr.], *Mōlād* 17 (1959) 331-338. A. Brelich, "Der Polytheismus," *Numen* 7 (1960) 123-136. Y. Kaufmann, *The Religion of Israel. From Its Beginnings to the Babylonian Exile* (1960). L. Rost, "Die Gottesverehrung der Patriarchen im Lichte der Pentateuchquellen," VT.S 7 (1960) 346-359. M. H. Segal, "The Religion of Israel before Sinai," JQR 52 (1961/62) 41-68 = Tarb. 30 (1960/61) 215-230, 301-313. H. Cazelles, "Der Gott der Patriarchen," BiLe 2 (1961) 39-49. J. Muilenburg, *The Way of Israel. Biblical Faith and Ethics*, RPS 5 (1961). R. H. Pfeiffer, *Religion in the OT. The History of a Spiritual Triumph* (1961). L. F. Rivera, "Las invenciones de Dios in el AT," RivBib 23 (1961) 74-81. K. Koch, "Der Tod des Religionsstifters," KuD 8 (1962) 621-649. G. W. Ahlström, *Aspects of Syncretism in Israelite Religion* (1963). J. Lindblom, "Die Vorstellung vom Sprechen Jahwes zu den Menschen im AT," ZAW 75 (1963) 263-288. R. A. F. MacKenzie, *Faith and History in the OT* (1963). R. Rendtorff, "Die Entstehung der israelitischen Religion als religionsgeschichtliches und theologisches Problem," ThLZ 88 (1963) 735-746. H. Ringgren, *Israelitische Religion, I* (1963) 15-25. N. C. Habel, *Yahweh Versus Baal: A Conflict of Religions* (1964). M. Haran, "Descriptive Outline of the Religion of the Patriarchs" [in Hebr.], *OLD Jerusalem* (1964) 40-70. J. P. Hyatt, "The Origin of Mosaic Yahwism," *Studies in Mem. of H. Trantham II* (1964) 85-93. C.

Westermann, "Das Verhältnis des Jahweglaubens zu den ausserisraelitischen Religionen," ThB 24 (1964) 189-218. H. W. Wolff, "Gottesglaube und Selbstverständnis Altisraels," *Jüdischer Geist in Geschichte u. Gegenwart* (1964/65) 5-15 = (1969). M. Haran, "The Religion of the Patriarchs. An Attempt at a Synthesis," ASTI 4 (1965) 30-55. A. S. Kapelrud, "The Role of the Cult in Old Israel," *The Bible and Modern Scholarship*, ed. J. P. Hyatt (1965) 44-56. N. Lohfink, "Welchem Gott brachte Abraham sein Opfer dar? Der Anfang der Offenbarungsreligion im Lichte neuer religionsgeschichtlicher Forschung," ThAk 1 (1965) 9-26. V. Maag, "Jahwäs Begegnung mit der kanaanäischen Kosmologie," AsSt 18/19 (1965) 252-269. J. Maier, "Die Gottesvorstellung Altisraels und die kanaanäische Religion," *Bibel u. zeitgemässer Glaube*, ed. K. Schubert (1965) 135-158. G. W. Anderson, *The History and Religion of Israel* (1966). O. Eissfeldt, "Die israelitisch-jüdische Religion," SWG 2 (1966) 217-260. J. Koenig, "Aux origines des Théophanies jahvistes," RHR 169 (1966) 1-36. H. Seebass, "Der Erzvater Israel und die Einführung der Jahweverehrung in Kanaan," BZAW 98 (1966). V. Maag, "Das Gottesverständnis des Alten Testatments," NedThT 21 (1966/67) 161-207, 459-460. O. Eissfeldt, "Israels Religion und die Religionen seiner Umwelt," NZSTh 9 (1967) 8-27. H. H. Rowley, *Worship in Ancient Israel: Its Form and Meaning* (1967). T. C. Vriezen, *The Religion of Ancient Israel* (1967). P. J. Cools, ed., *Geschichte und Religion des Alten Testaments* (1968). W. Klatt, "Die 'Eigentümlichkeit' der israelitischen Religion in der Sicht von Hermann Gunkel," EvTh 28 (1968) 153-160. B. A. Levine, "On the Presence of God in Biblical Religion," *Essays in Mem. of E. R. Goodenough* (1968; 1970²). W. H. Schmidt, *Alttestamentlicher Glaube und seine Umwelt* (1968; 1975²). H. Weidmann, *Die Patriarchen und ihre Religion im Lichte der Forschung seit Julius Wellhausen*, FRLANT 94 (1968). C. J. Bleeker–G. Widengren, *Historia Religionum: Handbook for the History of Religions, I* (1969). G. Fohrer, *Geschichte der israelitischen Religion* (1969). W. Klatt, *Hermann Gunkel. Zu seiner Theologie der Religionsgeschichte und zur Entstehung der formgeschichtlichen Methode*, FRLANT 100 (1969). T. C. Vriezen, "The Study of the OT and the History of Religion," VT.S 17 (1969) 1-24. K. A. Dickson, *An Introduction to the History and Religion of Israel: From Abraham to the Early Days of Israel in the Promised Land, I* (1970). M. Haran, "The Religion of the Patriarchs: Beliefs and Practices," *The World History of the Jewish People, II* (1970) 219-245. J. J. Stamm, "Zwei Darstellungen der israelitischen Religion," *Fests. W. Eichrodt* (1970) 101-115. F. J. Stendebach, *Theologische Anthropologie des Jahwisten* (Diss. Bonn 1970). R. de Vaux, *Early History of Israel I* (1971; Eng. 1978) ch. 5. J. D. W. Watts, *Basic Patterns in Old Testament Religion* (1971). J. G. González, "La revelácion de Dios en el Antiguo Testamento," *Libro Anual* (1971/72) 11-40. F. M. Cross, *The Religion of Israel: Historical Essays* (1972). J. Henninger, "Der Glaube an den einen Gott. Über religiöse Strukturen nomadischer Gruppen," BiKi 27 (1972) 13-16. E. Nielsen, "Die Religion des alten Israel," *Hdb. d. Religionsgeschichte II*, ed. J. P. Asmussen–J. Lassø (1972) 61-148. S. Herrmann, *Geschichte Israels in alttestamentlicher Zeit* (1973). H. Graf Reventlow, "Die Eigenart des Jahweglaubens als geschichtliches und theologisches Problem," KuD 20 (1974) 199-217. P. R. Ackroyd–C. F. Evans, eds., *The Cambridge History of the Bible, I. From The Beginnings to Jerome* (1975). M. R. Hauge, "The Struggles of the Blessed in Estrangement," StTh 29 (1975) 1-30, 113-146. R. Michaud, *Les Patriarches. Histoire et Théologie* (1975). H. Vorländer, *Mein Gott. Die Vorstellung vom persönlichen Gott im Alten Orient und im Alten Testament*, AOAT 23 (1975). C. Westermann, "Religion und Kult," ZW 46 (1975) 77-86. R. Albertz, *Persönliche Frömmigkeit und offizielle Religion: Religionsinterner Pluralismus in Israel und Babylon* (1977).

3. The God of the Patriarchs

E. Sellin, "Seit welcher Zeit verehrten die nordisraelitischen Stämme Jahwe?" *Fests. P. Haupt* (1926). A. Alt, *Der Gott der Väter. Zur Vorgeschichte der israelitischen Religion*, BWANT 3,12 (1929) = KS I (1953; 1963³) 1-78. K. Elliger, "Zur Frage nach dem Alter des Jahweglaubens bei den Israeliten. Ein Beitrag zur neuesten Erörterung des Problems der ältesten Religion Israels durch A. Alt 'Der Gott der Väter,' " ThBl 9 (1930) 97-103. J. Hempel, "Rezension A. Alt, Der Gott der Väter," ThLZ 55 (1930) 266-273. K. Galling, "Rezension A. Alt, Der Gott der Väter," DLZ 2 (1931) 433-440. W. Vischer, "Der Gott Abrahams und der Gott Isaaks und der Gott Jakobs," ZdZ 9 (1931) 282-297. J. Lewy, "Les textes paléo-assyriens et l'Ancien Testament," RHR 110 (1934) 29-65. G. von Rad, "Der Gott Abrahams, Isaaks und Jakobs," *Neues sächsisches Kirchenbl* 41 (1934)

773-780. C. Steuernagel, "Jahwe und die Vätergötter," *Fests. G. Beer* (1935) 62-71. M. Rist, "The God of Abraham, Isaac, and Jacob: A Liturgical and Magical Formula," JBL 57 (1938) 289-303. A. Alt, "Zum 'Gott der Vater,' " PJ 36 (1940) 53-104. H. G. May, "The God of My Father—A Study of Patriarchal Religion," JBR 9 (1941) 155-158, 199-200; "The Patriarchal Idea of God," JBL 60 (1941) 113-128. J. Bottéro, "Les inventaires de Qatna," RA 43 (1949) 1-40, 137; "Autres textes de Qatna," RA 44 (1950) 105-122. D. Barsotti, *Il Dio di Abramo, L'esperienza di Dio nella Genesi* (1952). D. Sourdel, *Les cultes du Hauran à l'époque romaine* (1952) esp. 54-57, 95-96. H. Donner, "Ein Orthostatenfragment des Königs Barrakab von Sam'al," MIOF 3 (1955) 73-98. J. P. Hyatt, "Yahweh as 'the God of my Father,' " VT 5 (1955) 130-136. B. Gemser, "God in Genesis," OTS 12 (1958) 1-21. V. Maag, "Der Hirte Israels. Eine Skizze von Wesen und Bedeutung der Väterreligion," SThU 28 (1958) 2-28; "Malkût Jhwh," VT.S 7 (1959/60) 129-153. F. M. Cross, "Yahweh and the God of the Fathers in the Light of Recent Epigraphic Discoveries," VT.S 7 (1959/60). H. Hirsch, *Untersuchungen zur altassyrischen Religion* (1961). J. R. Kupper, *L'iconographie du dieu Amurru dans la glyptique de la Ire dynastie Babylonienne* (1961). K. T. Andersen, "Der Gott meines Vaters," StTh 16 (1962) 170-188. F. M. Cross, "Yahweh and the God of the Patriarchs," HThR 55 (1962) 225-259. G. E. Wright, "Cult and History. . ." Interp. 16 (1962) 3-20. O. Eissfeldt, "Jahwe, der Gott der Väter," ThLZ 88 (1963) 481-490 = KS IV (1968) 79-91. R. Aron, "Le Dieu d'Abraham," *La Revue de Paris* 71/72 (1964) 45-57. G. T. Manley, "The God of Abraham," TynB 14 (1964) 3-7. H. Hirsch, "Gott der Väter," AfO 21 (1966) 56-58. V. Maag, "Sichembund und Vätergötter," *Fests. W. Baumgartner* VT.S 16 (1967) 205-218. H. Schmid, "Jhwh, Der Gott der Hebräer," Jud 25 (1969) 257-266. W. H. Schmidt, *Das Erste Gebot. Seine Bedeutung für das AT* (1969). R. de Vaux, "El et Baal, le dieu des pères et Yahweh," Ug 6 (1969) 501-517. P. Artzi–A. Malamat, "The Correspondence of Šibtu, Queen of Mari in ARMX," Or 40 (1971) 75-89. H. Hirsch, "Untersuchungen zur altassyrischen Religion," AfOBeih 13/14 (1972) 35-46. F. M. Cross, *Canaanite Myth. . .* (1973). A. Amassari, *La religione dei Patriarchi* (1976).

4. Names of God

T. Nöldeke, "Über den Gottesnamen El," MPAW (1880/82) 760-762, 1175-1177. P. de Lagarde, *Übersicht über die im Aramäischen und Hebräischen übliche Bildung der Nomina* (1889). G. Kerber, *Die religionsgeschichtliche Bedeutung der hebräischen Eigennamen des AT* (1897). M. J. Lagrange, "El et Yahve," RB 12 (1903) 362-386. J. Dahse, *Textkritische Materialien zur Hexateuchfrage. I. Die Gottesnamen der Genesis* (1912). J. Skinner, *The Divine Names in Genesis*, Exp. 5/6 (1913/14). K. Beth, "El und Neter," ZAW 36 (1916) 129-186. A. Jirku, ZAW 39 (1921) 144-160. W. W. Graf Baudissin, "El Bet-el (Gn 31, 13; 35,7)," BZAW 41 (1925) 1-11. R. Kittel, "Zum Gott Bet'el," JBL 44 (1925) 123-153. F. Zorell, "Der Gottesname Šaddai in den alten Übersetzungen," Bib 8 (1927) 215-219. W. W. Graf Baudissin, *Kyrios als Gottesname im Judentum und seine Stelle in der Religionsgeschichte, II,III* (1929). O. Eissfeldt, "Götternamen und Gottesvorstellungen bei den Semiten," ZDMG 83 (1929) 21-36 = KS I (1962) 194-205; "Der Gott Bethel," ARW 28 (1930) 1-30 = KS I (1962) 206-233. I. Zoller, "Il nomo divino Šadday," RSO 13 (1931/32). O. Grether, "Name und Wort Gottes im AT," BZAW 64 (1934). W. F. Albright, "The Names Shaddai and Abram," JBL 54 (1935) 173-193. E. A. Leslie, *OT Religion in the Light of Its Canaanite Background* (1936; 1947²). A. Vaccari, "Jahve e i nomi divini nelle religioni semitiche," Bib 17 (1936) 1-10. R. Dussaud, *Les découvertes de Ras Shamra (Ugarit) et l'Ancien Testament* (1937; 1941²). A. Vincent, *La religion des judéo-araméens d'Eléphantine* (1937) 562-592. R. Dussaud, "Les combats sanglants de Anat et le pouvoir universel de El," RHR 118 (1938) 133-169. G. Quell, "El und Elohim im AT," ThW II (1938) 79-90; "κύριος" ThW III C (1938) 1038-1095. J. P. Hyatt, "The Deity Beth-el and the Old Testament," JAOS 59 (1939) 81-98. E. Burrows, "The Meaning of El Šaddai," JThS 41 (1940) 152-161. G. Levi della Vida, "'El 'Elyôn in Genesis XIV, 18-20," JBL 63 (1944) 1-9. J. Morgenstern, "The Divine Triad in Biblical Mythology," JBL 64 (1945) 15-37. H. G. Güterbock, *Kumarbi* (1946). E. Vogt, "El nombre de Dios en los nombres biblicos y hebreos," RivBib 9 (1947). A. Heidel, "Special Usage of the Akkadian Term šadû," JNES 8 (1949) 233-235. J. Starcky, "Le nom divin El," ArOr 17 (1949) 383-386. C. Virolleaud, *Légendes de Babylone et de Canaan* (1949). O. Eissfeldt, *El im ugaritischen Pantheon* (1950). V. Maag, "Zum Hieros Logos von Beth-El," AsSt 5

(1951) 122-133. A. Caquot, "Nouvelles Inscriptions Araméennes de Hatra," *Syria* 29 (1952) 102f. E. Dhorme, "Le nom du Dieu d'Israél," RHR 141 (1952) 5-18. E. Jenni, "Das Wort 'ōlām im AT," ZAW 64 (1952) 197-248; 65 (1953) 1-35. A. Murtonen, *A Philological and Literary Treatise on the OT Divine Names* אל, אלוה, אלהים, *and* יהוה *(1952)*. F. Løkkegaard, "A Plea for El, the Bull, and Other Ugaritic Miscellanies," *Fests. J. Pedersen* (1953) 218-235. H. Otten, "Ein kanaanäischer Mythus aus Boğazköy," MIOF 1 (1953) 125-150 (cf. MDOG 85 [1953]). H. M. Pope, *El in the Ugaritic Texts*, VT.S 2 (1955). M. H. Segal, "El, Elohim and YHWH in the Bible," JQR 46 (1955) 89-115. O. Eissfeldt, "El and Yahweh," JSSt 1 (1956) 25-37 = KS III (1966) 386-397. A. E. Draffkorn, "Ilāni/Elohim," JBL 76 (1957) 216-224. R. Dussaud, "Yahveh, fils de El," *Syria* 34 (1957) 233-242. O. Eissfeldt, "Jahwes Verhältnis zu 'Eljon und Schaddaj nach Psalm 91," WO 2 (1957) 343-348 = KS III (1966) 441-447. G. Bertram, "'IKANOΣ in den griechischen Übersetzungen des AT's als Wiedergabe von schaddaj," ZAW 70 (1958) 20-31; "Die Wiedergabe von schadad und schaddaj im Griechischen," DMG (1959) = WO 2 (1957) 502-513. T. Hanlon, "The Most High God of Gen. 14,18sq," Scrip. 11/16 (1959) 110-118. D. N. Freedman, "The Name of the God of Moses," JBL 79 (1960) 151-156. H. Gross, "Biblische Gottesnamen," LThK 4 (1960) 1127-1129. N. Walker, "A New Interpretation of the Divine Name 'Shaddai,' " ZAW 72 (1960) 64-66. N. Krieger, "Der Schrecken Isaaks," Jud 17 (1961) 193-195. S. Mowinckel, "The Name of the God of Moses," HUCA 32 (1961) 121-133. M. Weippert, "Erwägungen zur Etymologie des Gottesnamens 'El šaddaj," ZDMG 111 (1961) 42-62. E. C. B. MacLaurin, "Shaddai," *Abr-Nahrain* 3 (1961/62) 99-118. B. W. Anderson, "The Fear of Isaac," IDB 2 (1962) 260. R. Lack, "Les origines de 'Elyôn, le Très-Haut, dans la tradition cultuelle d'Israël," CBQ 24 (1962) 44-64. F. Zimmermann, "'El and Adonai," VT 12 (1962) 190-195. O. Eissfeldt, "Jakobs Begegnung mit El und Moses Begegnung mit Jahwe," OLZ 58 (1963) 325-331 = KS IV (1968) 92-98. E. O. James, *The Worship of the Sky-God* (1963). E. C. B. MacLaurin, "The Development of the Idea of God in Ancient Canaan," JRH 2 (1963) 277-294. R. Comte du Mesmile du Buisson, "Origine et evolution du Panthéon de Tyr," RHR 164 (1963) 133-136. D. K. Andrews, "Yahweh the God of the Heavens," *Essays in Honour of T. J. Meek* (1964) 45-57. M. Kessler, "The 'Shield' of Abraham?" VT 14 (1964) 494-497. J. Potin, " 'El' d'Ugarit et le Dieu d'Abraham," BTS 69 (1964) 2-3. J. A. Fitzmyer, "The Aramaic Letter of King Adon to the Egyptian Pharao," Bib 46 (1965) 41-44. M. J. Mulder, *Kanaänitische Goden in het Oude Testament* (1965). R. Rendtorff, "El, Ba'al und Jahwe. Erwägungen zum Verhältnis von kanaanäischer und israelitischer Religion," ZAW 78 (1966) 277-292. F. A. Schaeffer, "Nouveaux témoignages du culte de El et de Baal à Ras Shamra-Ugarit et ailleurs en Syrie-Palestine," *Syria* 43 (1966) 1-19. J. P. Hyatt, "Was Yahweh Originally a Creator Deity?" JBL 86 (1967) 369-377. P. D. Miller, "El the Warrior," HThR 60 (1967) 411-431. R. Rendtorff, "The Background of the Title 'El 'Elyon in Gen XIV," 4. *World Congr. of Jew. Studies 1* (1967) 167-170. L. J. Bailey, "Israelite 'El Šadday and Amorite Bêl Šadê," JBL 87 (1968) 434-438. U. Oldenburg, *The Conflict between 'El and Ba'al in Canaanite Religion*: Numen (Suppl) 3 (1969). J. Ouelette, "More on 'El Šadday and Bêl Šadê," JBL 88 (1969) 470-471. J. Lévêque, *Job et son Dieu*, I § 2 (1970). F. Stolz, *Strukturen und Figuren im Kult von Jerusalem. Studien zur altorientalischen vor- und frühisraelitischen Religion*, BZAW 118 (1970). R. de Vaux, "The Revelation of the Divine Name," *OT Essays in Honour of G. H. Davies* (1970) 48-75. N. Avigad, "Excavations in the Jewish Quarter of the Old City of Jerusalem 1971," IEJ 22 (1972) 193-200. J. Blommendaal, *El als fundament en als exponent van het oud-testamentisch universalisme* (Diss. Utrecht 1972). N. C. Habel, " 'Yahweh, Maker of Heaven and Earth': A Study in Tradition Criticism," JBL 91 (1972) 321-337. E. L. Abel, "The Nature of the Patriarchal God 'El Šadday,' " *Numen* 20 (1973) 48-59. J. J. M. Roberts, "The Davidic Origin of the Zion Tradition," JBL 92 (1973) 329-344. A. van der Branden, "Il Dio Eljôn," BibOr 16 (1974) 65-85. K. Koch, "Šaddaj. Zum Verständnis zwischen israelitischer Monolatrie und nord-westsemitischem Polytheismus," VT 26 (1976) 299-332. M. W. Stolper, "A Note on Yahwistic Personal Names in the Murašu Texts," BASOR 222 (1976) 25-28.

5. Promise

W. Eichrodt, *Die Quellen der Genesis, von neuem untersucht*, BZAW 31 (1916) esp. 54-65. J. Pedersen, *Israel: Its Life and Culture, I-II*, "Blessing" (1926; 1946²) 182-212.

K. Galling, *Die Erwählungstraditionen Israels*, BZAW 48 (1928). S. Garofalo, *La nozione profetica del 'Resto d'Israele'* (Diss. Rom 1942). G. von Rad, "Verheissenes Land und Jahwes Land im Hexateuch," ZDPV 66 (1943) 191-204 = GesSt (1958; 1965[3]) 87-100. H. H. Rowley, *The Biblical Doctrine of Election* (1948 = 1950). F. Baumgärtel, *Verheissung. Zur Frage des evangelischen Verständnisses des AT* (1952). W. Zimmerli, "Verheissung und Erfüllung," EvTh 12 (1952/53) 34-59. A. Falkenstein–W. von Soden, *Sumerische und akkadische Hymnen und Gebete* (1953) 89,181f. G. von Rad, "Verheissung" (rev. of Baumgärtel), EvTh 13 (1953). C. Sant, *The Literary Structure of the Book of Genesis* (Diss. Malta 1953) 64-117. T. C. Vriezen, *Die Erwählung Israels nach dem Alten Testament* (1953). P. A. H. de Boer, *Gods beloften over Land en Volk in het OT* (1955). K. Koch, "Zur Geschichte der Erwählungsvorstellung Israels," ZAW 67 (1955) 205-226. J. Hoftijzer, *Die Verheissungen en die drei Erzväter* (1956). J. Barr, "Tradition and Expectation in Ancient Israel," SJTh 10 (1957) 24-34. O. Kaiser, "Traditionsgeschichtliche Untersuchung von Genesis 15," ZAW 70 (1958) 107-126. L. A. Snijders, "Genesis XV. The Covenant with Abram," OTS 12 (1958) 261-279. P. Winter, "The Main Literary Problem of the Lukan Infancy Story," *Vox Theologica* (1958) 117-122. A. Caquot, "Les songes et leur interprétation selon Canaan et Israel," SOr 2 (1959) 99-124. H. Gross, "Zum Problem von Verheissung und Erfüllung," BZ 3 (1959) 3-17. C. Sant, "The Promise Narratives in Genesis," MTh (1959) 1-13. W. Pesch, "Zur Formgeschichte und Exegese von Lk 12,32," Bib 41 (1960) 23-40. S. H. Blank, "Some Observations Concerning Biblical Prayer," HUCA 32 (1961) 75-90. H. Köster, "Die Auslegung der Abraham-Verheissung in Hebräer 6," *Fests. G. von Rad* (1961) 95-109. W. Zimmerli, "The Interpretation of the OT. III. Promise and Fulfilment," Interp. 15 (1961) 310-338. J. Schreiner, "Segen für die Völker in der Verheissung an die Väter," BZ NF 6 (1962) 1-31. R. Rendtorff, "Die Offenbarungsvorstellung im Alten Israel," *Offenbarung als Geschichte* (1963) 21-91. J. Scharbert, "Verheissung," HThG II (1963) 752-759. H. Seebass, "Zu Genesis 15," WuD NF 7 (1963) 132-149. C. Westermann, "The Way of the Promise through the Old Testament," *The OT and Christian Faith*, ed. B. W. Anderson (1963) 200-224. P. Altmann, "Erwählungstheologie und Universalismus im AT," BZAW 92 (1964). W. M. Clark, *The Origin and Development of the Land Promise Theme in the OT* (Diss. Yale 1964). F. W. Marquardt, *Die Bedeutung der biblischen Landverheissung für die Christen* (1964). S. Herrmann, *Die prophetischen Heilserwartungen im AT. Ursprung und Gestaltwandel*, BWANT 5,5 (1965). J. Muilenburg, "Abraham and the Nations. Blessing and World History," Interp. 19 (1965) 387-398. J. Haspekker, "Natur und Heilserfahrung in Altisrael," BiLe 7 (1966) 83-98. R. Kilian, "Der heilsgeschichtliche Aspekt in der elohistischen Geschichtstradition," ThGl 56 (1966) 369-384. R. E. Clements, *Abraham and David. Genesis XV and Its Meaning For Israelite Tradition*, SBT 2,5 (1967). P. Dacquino, "Le promesse di Dio ai Patriarchi secondo le tradizioni della Genesi," RivBib 15 (1967) 449-469. F. C. Fensham, "Covenant, Promise and Expectation in the Bible," ThZ 23 (1967) 305-322. K. Koch, "Die Sohnesverheissung an den ugaritischen Daniel," ZA 58 (NF 24) (1967) 211-221. N. Lohfink, *Die Landverheissung als Eid. Eine Studie zu Genesis 15*, SBS 28 (1967); "Rilievi sulla tradizione dell'alleanze con i Patriarchi," RivBib 15 (1967) 393-406. I. Blythin, "The Patriarchs and the Promise," SJTh 21 (1968) 56-73. O. Eissfeldt, "Der kanaanäische El als Geber der den israelitischen Erzvätern geltenden Nachkommenschaft- und Landbesitzverheissungen," StOr 17 (1968) 45-53 = KS V (1973) 50-62. H. P. Müller, "Imperativ und Verheissung im Alten Testament," EvTh 28 (1968) 557-571. H. D. Preuss, *Jahweglaube und Zukunftserwartung*, BWANT 5,7 (1968); " '. . . .ich will mit dir sein!' " ZAW 80 (1968) 139-173. J. Schreiner, "Berufung und Erwählung Israels zum Heil der Völker," BiLe 9 (1968) 94-114. I. Soisalon-Soininen, "Begreppet funktion i gammaltestamentlig traditionsforskning," SEA 33 (1968) 55-67. J. Guillet, "Le langage spontané de la bénédiction dans l'Ancien Testament," RSR 57 (1969) 163-204. F. Hesse, "Bewährt sich eine 'Theologie der Heilstatsachen' am AT? Zum Verhältnis von Faktum und Deutung," ZAW 81 (1969) 1-17. P. D. Miller, "The Gift of God. The Deuteronomic Theology of the Land," Interp. 23 (1969) 451-465. S. E. McEvenue, "Word and Fulfillment: A Stylistic Feature of the Priestly Writer," *Semitics 1* (1970) 104-110. R. E. Murphy, "History, Eschatology, and the Old Testament," *Continuum* 7 (1970) 583-593. S. E. Loewenstamm, "The Divine Grants of Land to the Patriarchs," JAOS 91 (1971) 509-510. G. W. Coats, "A Structural Transition in Exodus," VT 22 (1972) 129-142; "I Will Be With You," LexTQ 7 (1972) 77-85. B. O. Long, "Prophetic Call Traditions and Reports of Visions," ZAW 84 (1972) 494-500. J. Van Seters, "Confessional Reformulation in the

Exilic Period," VT 22 (1972) 448-495. T. E. Ridenhour, *The OT and the Patriarchal Traditions* (Diss. Duke.), Diss. Abstr. Intern. 33 (1972/73) 6443-A. R. J. Clifford, "The Word of God in the Ugaritic Epics and in the Patriarchal Narratives," *Fests. F. L. Moriarty* (1973) 7-18. H. J. Zobel, "Das Selbstverständnis Israels nach dem AT," ZAW 85 (1973) 281-294. F. J. Helfmeyer, "Segen und Erwählung," BZ 18 (1974) 208-223. W. Beyerlin, ed., *Religionsgeschichtliches Textbuch zum AT: ATD Ergänzungsreihe 1* (1975). C. Westermann, *The Promises to the Fathers. Studies on the Patriarchal Narratives* (1976; Eng. 1980).

6. Covenant

J. J. Valeton, "Bedeutung und Stellung des Wortes brjt im Priestercodex," ZAW 12 (1892) 1-22; "Das Wort brjt in den jehovistischen und deuteronomischen Stücken des Hexateuchs, sowie in den verwandten historischen Büchern," ZAW 12 (1892) 224-260. R. Kraetzschmar, *Die Bundesvorstellung im AT in ihrer geschichtlichen Entwicklung* (1896). P. Karge, *Geschichte des Bundesgedankens im AT* (1910). S. A. B. Mercer, *The Oath in Babylonian and Assyrian Literature* (1912). J. Hempel, "Die altisraelitischen Anschauungen von Segen und Fluch im Lichte altorientalischer Parallelen," ZDMG 79 (NF 4) (1925) 20-110 = *Apoxysmata* (1961) 30-113. W. T. McCree, "The Covenant Meal in the OT," JBL 45 (1926) 120-128. E. Naville, "Le XVII. chapitre de la Genèse," ZAW 44 (1926) 135-145. A. Bertholet, "Zum Verständnis des alttestamentlichen Opfergedankens," JBL 49 (1930) 218-233. E. Crawley, *Oath, Curse and Blessing* (1934). J. Begrich, "Berit. Ein Beitrag zur Erfassung einer alttestamentlichen Denkform," ZAW 60 (1944) 1-11 = GesSt (1964) 55-66. N. H. Snaith, *The Distinctive Ideas of the OT* (1944; 1964⁵), esp. 23-32. S. H. Blank, "The Curse, Blasphemy, the Spell and the Oath," HUCA 23 (1950/51) 73-95. W. F. Albright, "The Hebrew Expression for 'Making a Covenant' in Pre-Israelite Documents," BASOR 121 (1951) 21f. E. Bickermann, *Couper une alliance*, AHDO 5 (1951). J. Henninger, "Was bedeutet die rituelle Teilung eines Tieres in zwei Hälften? Zur Deutung von Gen 15,9ff.," Bib 34 (1953) 344-353. G. E. Mendenhall, "Puppy and Lettuce in North-West Semitic Covenant Making," BASOR 133 (1954) 26-30; "Covenant Forms in Israelite Tradition," BA 17 (1954) 50-76; "Law and Covenant in Israel and the Ancient Near East," BA 17 (1954) 26-46. M. Noth, "Das alttestamentliche Bundschliessen im Lichte eines Mari Textes," *Mélanges I. Levy* (1955) 433-444 = GesSt (1957) 142-154. H. W. Wolff, "Jahwe als Bundesvermittler," VT 6 (1956) 316-320. C. Schedl, "Bund und Erwählung. Das Mysterium Israels in geschichtstheologischer Schau," ZKTh 80 (1958) 493-515. R. de Vaux, *Ancient Israel* (1958; Eng. 1962). K. Baltzer, *Das Bundesformular; sein Ursprung und seine Versendung*, WMANT 4 (1960). A. von Gennep, *Rites of Passage* (1960). S. Grill, "Die religionsgeschichtliche Bedeutung der vormosaischen Bündnisse (Gen 9:9-17; 17:9-14)," *Kairos* (1960) 17-22. D. Piccard, "Réflexions sur l'interprétation chrétienne de trois récits de la Genèse," *Hommage à W. Vischer* (1960) 181-190. W. Zimmerli, "Sinaibund und Abrahambund. Ein Beitrag zum Verständnis der Priesterschrift," ThZ 16 (1960) 268-280 = GesAufs. (1963), 205-216. A. Jepsen, "Berith. Ein Beitrag zur Theologie der Exilszeit," *Fests. W. Rudolph* (1961) 161-179. I. P. Seierstad, "Paktstanken og pakten i Genesis 15," TTK 32 (1961) 10-21. A. Caquot, "L'alliance avec Abram (Genèse 15)," Sem. 12 (1962) 51-66. H. Cazelles, "Connexions et structure de Gen XV," RB 69 (1962) 321-349. F. C. Fensham, "Malediction and Benediction in the Ancient Near Eastern Vassal-Treaties and the OT," ZAW 74 (1962) 1-9. J. L'Hour, "L'alliance de Sichem," RB 69 (1962) 5-36, 161-184, 350-368. L. Bushinski, "Striking a Covenant," BiTod 1 (1962/63) 218-223. S. B. Hoenig, "Circumcision: The Covenant of Abraham," JQR 53 (1962/63) 322-334. J. Coppens, "La nouvelle alliance en Jer 31:31-34," CBQ 25 (1963) 12-21. F. C. Fensham, "Clauses of Protection in Hittite Vassal Treaties and the OT," VT 13 (1963) 133-143. A. Jaubert, *La notion d'alliance dans le Judaisme* (1963). D. J. McCarthy, *Treaty and Covenant. A Study in Form in the Ancient Oriental Documents and in the OT*, AnBib 21 (1963, 1981²). J. Morgenstern, "The 'Bloody Husband' (?) Once Again," HUCA 34 (1963) 35-70. C. F. Whitley, "Covenant and Commandment in Israel," JNES 22 (1963) 37-48. D. N. Freedman, "Divine Commitment and Human Obligation. The Covenant Theme," Interp. 18 (1964) 419-431. G. Jacob, "Der Abrahamsbund," CV 7 (1964) 250-264. N. Lohfink, "Die Wandlung des Bundesbegriffs im Buch Deuteronomium," *Festgabe K. Rahner I* (1964) 423-444. D. J. McCarthy, "Three Covenants in Genesis," CBQ 26 (1964) 179-189. J. A. Thompson, *The Ancient*

Near Eastern Treaties and the Old Testament, TLBA (1964). W. Eichrodt, "Bund und Gesetz," *Fests. H. W. Hertzberg* (1965) 30-49. E. Gerstenberger, "Covenant and Commandment," JBL 84 (1965) 38-51. D. J. McCarthy, "Covenant in the OT: The Present State of Inquiry," CBQ 27 (1965) 217-240. F. Nötscher, "Bundesformular und 'Amtsschimmel,' " BZ NF 9 (1965) 181-214. A. G. Núnez, "El Rito de la Alianza," EstB 24 (1965) 217-238. P. Buis, "Les formulaires d'Alliance," VT 16 (1966) 396-411. M. J. Buss, "The Covenant Theme in Historical Perspective," VT 16 (1966) 502-504. P. J. Calderone, "Dynastic Oracle and Suzerainty Treaty (2 Samuel 7:8-16)," *Logos* 1 (1966). G. Fohrer, "Altes Testament—'Amphiktyonie' und 'Bund'?" ThLZ 91 (1966) 801-816, 893-904 = BZAW 115 (1969) 84-119. J. L'Hour, *La morale de l'Alliance, Cahiers de la RB* 5 (1966). O. Loretz, "Berith—'Band–Bund,' " VT 16 (1966) 239-241. D. J. McCarthy, *Der Gottesbund im AT. Ein Bericht über die Forschung der letzten Jahre*, SBS 13 (1966; 1967[2]). E. Kutsch, "Gesetz und Gnade. Probleme des alttestamentlichen Bundesbegriffs," ZAW 79 (1967) 18-35. M. H. Segal, *The Pentateuch. Its Composition and Its Authorship and Other Biblical Studies*, III,1 (1967). F. Vattioni, "Recenti studi sull'alleanza nella Bibbia e nell'antico Oriente," AION 17 (1967) 181-226. F. R. van Develder, *The Form and History of the Abrahamic Covenant Traditions* (Diss. Drew), Diss. Abstr. 28 (1967/68) 1897f. P. Buis, "La nouvelle alliance," VT 18 (1968) 1-15. S. E. Loewenstamm, "Zur Traditionsgeschichte des Bundes zwischen den Stücken," VT 18 (1968) 500-507. J. A. Soggin, "Akkadisch *Tar beriti* und hebräisch *krt bryt*," VT 18 (1968) 210-215. A. Baruq, "La notion d'alliance dans l'AT et les débuts de judaisme," Populus Dei I, ed. H. Cazelles, *Communio* 10 (1969) 5-110. D. R. Hillers, *Covenant: The History of a Biblical Idea* (1969). C. D. Jathanna, "The Covenant and Covenant-Making in the Pentateuch," *Bangalore Theol. Forum* 3 (1969) 27-54. M. R. Lehmann, "Biblical Oaths," ZAW 81 (1969) 74-92. J. J. Mitchell, "Abram's Understanding of the Lord's Covenant," WThJ 32 (1969) 24-48. A. Ohler, *Mythologische Elemente im AT. Eine motivgeschichtliche Untersuchung* (1969) esp. 13-16. L. Perlitt, *Bundestheologie im Alten Testament*, WMANT 36 (1969). W. Schottroff, *Der altisraelitische Fluchspruch*, WMANT 30 (1969). G. Baena, "La terminologia de la Alianza," EstB 29 (1970) 1-54. P. Beauchamp, "Propositions sur l'alliance de l'Ancien Testament comme structure centrale," RSR 58 (1970) 161-193. G. W. Buchanan, *The Consequences of the Covenant*, NT.S 20 (1970). E. Kutsch, "Sehen und Bestimmen. Die Etymologie von Berith," *Fests. K. Galling* (1970) 165-178. W. Thiel, "Hēfēr Berît. Zum Bundbrechen im AT," VT 20 (1970) 214-229. W. Vogels, *La promesse royale de Yahweh préparatoire à l'alliance. Etude d'une forme littéraire de l'AT* (1970). M. Weinfeld, "The Covenant of Grant in the Old Testament and in the Ancient Near East," JAOS 90 (1970) 184-203. W. Zimmerli, "Erwägungen zum 'Bund.' Die Aussage über die Jahwe-berit in Ex 19–34," *Fests. W. Eichrodt* (1970) 171-190. M. W. Shaw, *Studies in Revelation and the Bible* (1971) esp. 23-32. E. Kutsch, "Verheissung und Gesetz: Untersuchungen zum sogenannten 'Bund' im AT," BZAW 131 (1972). C. van Leeuwen, "Het huidige onderzoek in enkele takken van den oudtestamentische Wetenschap (1965-1971)," NThT 26 (1972) 225-247. D. J. McCarthy, *Old Testament Covenant: A Survey of Current Opinions* (1972). H. C. White, "The Divine Oath in Genesis," JBL 92 (1973) 165-179. E. Kutsch, " 'Ich will euer Gott sein.' Berît in der Priesterschrift," ZThK 71 (1974) 361-388. L. Wachter, "Die Übertragung der Berîtvorstellung auf Jahwe," ThLZ 99 (1974) 801-816. M. Weinfeld, "Berît—Covenant vs. Obligation," Bib 56 (1975) 120-128. C. Westermann, "Genesis 17 und die Bedeutung von berit," ThLZ 101 (1976) 161-170. H. H. Schmid, *Der sogenannte Jahwist. Beobachtungen und Fragen zur Pentateuchforschung* (1976) esp. 119-153.

Structure and Growth
of Genesis 12–25

With the knowledge that the three parts of Gen. 12–50 had each its own independent tradition history before being joined into a continuous story, H. Gunkel
raised the question of the composition of the Abraham stories, which made possible some conclusions about the process of formation. The question had not yet
arisen in the course of literary criticism as such. It is still, therefore, very recent,
and one can understand why the attempts at a solution have hitherto been so divergent and tentative. They scarcely take any account of each other (see H. Gunkel,
Komm. [1922³]; ''Abraham'' RGG² 1 [1927] 65-68; M. Noth, *A History of Pentateuchal Traditions* [1948, 1966³; Eng. 1972]; A. Jepsen, WZ(L) 2/3 [1953/54]
149-151; A. Weiser, ''Abraham'' RGG³ 1 [1957] 68-71; R. Kilian, BBB 24
[1966]; R. de Vaux, *The Early History. . .* [1971; Eng. 1978] 163f.).
    H. Gunkel begins by enumerating eighteen units. When he comes to the
question of composition, he encounters the ''chain of stories'' about Abraham and
Lot to which he attributes in the first place Gen. 12:1-8; 13; 18:1-16a; 19:1-28;
19:30-38. He then goes on to answer the question of the origin of the peoples who
call themselves after Abraham and Lot, and how they came to their place of domicile. The proof that they belong together is that 12:1-8 requires its continuation in
ch. 13, and ch. 13 its continuation in ch. 19; Gen. 18:1-16a and ch. 19 take up the
thread left hanging in ch. 13. The Sodom-Lot story has been inserted into the
Abraham-Lot story. Gunkel sees 18:1-16a; 19:1-28; and 19:30-38 as originally independent stories in this chain. It is scarcely possible to conceive 12:1-6 and ch.
13 as independent units. The chain was then enlarged by 12:10-20; 15; and 16. A
line going through 21:22-34 and ch. 24 is also part of this. Gunkel hesitates before
21:1-7. He sees 18:16b-33 as an ''elaboration'' from a later period. A third hand
has attached the family trees in 22:20-24 and 25:1-6. Finally, Gunkel divided the
process of growth of chs. 12–25 into four stages: (1) the individual stories; (2) the
chain of stories of Abraham and Lot; (3) other stories added; (4) later elaborations,
omissions, and further additions. The result is that a single chain of stories is at the
basis of chs. 12–25; all the rest is a series of additions. This analysis is in many respects unsatisfactory and does not do justice to the variety in these chapters. The
line that leads from Sarah's barrenness (11:30) to the birth and marriage of a son
comes off badly. It is to be noted that scarcely any attention is paid to the motif of
the promises.

The motif of the promise is central for M. Noth. It is the basic element of the whole of the patriarchal stories. When he comes to deal with the Abraham traditions, Noth has already decided that the Isaac and Jacob traditions are older, and that a great deal has been taken over from them. All that remains for Abraham is "the old stock material, common to J and E, coming from G" (= *Grundlage*, "basic material"). But of this, 12:10-20 belongs to Isaac, and likewise 21:22-34; 21:8-21; 16; 21:1-7; 24. All of it was transferred to Abraham secondarily. "So all that remains is Gen. 15." This astonishing supposition, that the original Abraham tradition consists of Gen. 15 alone, is very dubious for the reason that the old literary-critical thesis, that the E source begins in Gen. 15, has been almost universally abandoned. Gen. 15, then, cannot belong to G. Noth sees in Gen. 15 the original introduction to the patriarchal story: "It probably contained as a nucleus a revelation of God to Abraham with the promise of the land and posterity," which described "the really basic element of the tradition of the ancestors." But it is just this that recent studies have put in question. They have shown *(a)* that the oldest texts always contain *one* promise, not several; and *(b)* that the promise of the settled land and countless descendants belongs to a later layer. And so the possibility that Gen. 15 is to be regarded as the only text of the original Abraham tradition collapses.

A. Jepsen (1953/54) comes to the same conclusions as M. Noth in a number of points. He too considers that the Jacob and Isaac tradition is older and that much has been transferred to Abraham secondarily. He also considers Gen. 15 the basis of the Abraham tradition to which the Abraham-Lot tradition has been added (following Gunkel). According to Jepsen, the promises of the land and of posterity dominate the whole Abraham story; nonetheless, he speaks of the promise of a son and, against Noth, correctly sees ch. 18 as being older than ch. 15; he is also correct (against Gunkel) in seeing that the name Lot unites several figures (so too R. Kilian). Like Noth, he sees the original Abraham tradition in the revelation to Abraham of promise and covenant. He does not offer a comprehensive plan of composition of the Abraham story, nor does he raise the question of the types of traditions or of the forms of community in which they arose. A. Weiser's presentation scarcely differs from that of Noth.

R. Kilian's study (1966, pp. 284-340) differs from the preceding ones in that he is concerned only with the written formation of the Abraham story. He understands "history of tradition" as concerned exclusively with the written stage. He presumes a pre-Yahwistic collection of Abraham traditions in Gen. 12f. and Gen. 18f., which J has expanded by other, previously independent, individual traditions, and arranged according to his own plan. There was in addition an Elohistic collection of Abraham traditions (chs. 15; 20; 21; 22) which was joined with the J material in a Yahwistic redaction. Kilian, to be sure, understands Abraham as a "historical individual," but says nothing of the process by which the Abraham traditions came down from him to the form of a written collection. He considers the itineraries and genealogies to be mere, redactional constructions.

R. de Vaux (1971; 1978) shows a basically different understanding of Gen. 12–25. He first simply asks about what these texts deal with, and finds that they are in essence family stories (cf. C. Westermann, ThB 24 [1964] 9-91) in which the interest revolves around the continuance of the family. The promise of a son, therefore, is of central importance (ch. 18). The way is prepared by Abraham's complaint that he has no son (15:2-3) and the remark that Sarah was barren (16:1, to which add 11:30). The theme reaches its goal with the account of the birth of the son (21:1-7). The Hagar narratives (chs. 16 and 21) are joined to the theme by means of the barrenness of Sarah. The marriage of Isaac (ch. 24) forms the natural conclusion. This cycle is linked with the Lot narrative, which is of different origin, and whose nucleus is an old story about the destruction of Sodom (ch. 19). An etiological narrative from the Transjordan about the origin of the Moabites and Ammonites has been attached. De Vaux's outline, though brief, must be supplemented and elaborated; one can, however, agree with the approach.

The attempts hitherto to explain the composition and formation of the Abraham tradition permit of some conclusions. The point of departure must be the text as a whole as it has been handed down to us. Behind it is the plan of a redactor who constructed the final synthesis. It presupposes the literary works (J and P in any case, perhaps also E), but is something of its own over against them. It presupposes beyond these the independent Abraham traditions out of which the literary works were composed. The compositional plan of the redactor is clearly aimed at forming a self-contained Abraham story which is independent of the continuation in chs. 25–50.

1. The Constituent Parts of the Composition

The explanation of the composition of Gen. 12–25 must begin with the question: What did the redactor intend with the Abraham story and how did he understand it? Starting from the text as a whole, the question divides into two parts: what is the text about, and how does it present what it is about? That is to say, there is the question of both content and form. With the question of form, we immediately confront the fact that chs. 12–25 are not a continuous narrative, but have been put together out of a variety of parts, each of which may have had its own individual life before the synthesis, though this question must be raised in each particular case. Enumerative and narrative texts are so obviously distinguishable in Gen. 12–25 that it must have been the redactor's intention to make clear to the reader how very different were the blocks out of which he constructed the Abraham story. Genealogies and itineraries belong to the enumerative texts; the genealogies are in sharper relief than the itineraries. The whole complex of Gen. 12–25 is framed in genealogies: at the beginning 11:27-32; at the end 25:1-18 (also 22:20-24; 23 and 24 insofar as they contain a nucleus of genealogical data). They are of vital importance for the composition; the whole, framed in this way, is concerned with the continuation of the generations. The itineraries are a less striking part of Gen. 12–25, but they run right through it; it is by means of them that the redactor states his intention of presenting Abraham's life-style as nomadic. The itineraries begin with the genealogies in 11:27-32, are continued in chs. 12 and 13, and are linked in particular with the Abraham-Lot cycle.

Then, besides the enumerations, there are the narratives about Abraham. The promises must be distinguished from the narratives proper.

With the question of content, one encounters something which is homogeneous throughout, and which the genealogical framework shows up; but one also encounters something quite different from it. The genealogies in the primeval story have shown how a narrative can grow out of a genealogical elaboration consisting of only one sentence. The remark, "But Sarah was barren; she had no children" (11:30), introduces the line which leads to the birth and marriage of Isaac. The episode of the mother in danger (12:10-20 and the parallel, 20:1-18) belong indirectly to it. Directly belonging to it are the complaint of the childless father (15:2, 3) and the promise of a son (15:4); the stories of the son of the secondary wife (chs. 16 and 21) which are introduced with yet another reference to Sarah's barrenness (16:1); the promise of a son (in 17:15-17[P] and 18:1-16a), and the birth of the son (21:1-7); the child in danger (ch. 22); and the conclusion, the marriage of Isaac (ch. 24). This theme is concerned with the continuation of the life of a family to the next generation (so too R. de Vaux), and what happens between parents and children in the process. The continuation is endangered several times and in different ways, with the resulting tension in the individual narratives. Notice, however, that this is not an original narrative order, but rather the subsequent arrangement by the redactor who is responsible for the present context; the individual narratives can belong to different contexts. Sometimes, as in 15:2-4, it is only one motif which belongs to the line; sometimes, as in ch. 22, only one aspect, but not the narrative as a whole. The redactor has brought together very different individual narratives of different origin into a continuity which itself was the consequence of a sequence of motifs already there before him: the childless father or mother—the complaint of the childless one—promise of a son—(the promise in danger)—birth of the son—the son in danger—the continuation of the generation through the son. This sequence of motifs is in essential agreement with that found in the Ugaritic texts of Aqhat and Keret where it forms *one* self-contained narrative (C. Westermann, *The Promises. . .* 1976; Eng. 1980); this shows that the sequence is prior to the individual narratives in Gen. 12–50 and can go back into the patriarchal period. But nothing is thereby said about the age of the individual narratives which belong to this line.

2. The Promises

The promise of the son is an essential part of the sequence of motifs which lead from Sarah's barrenness to the fulfillment in birth and marriage. It occurs only in the Abraham cycle, where it is of crucial importance for the whole (15:2-4; 17:15-19; 18:1-16a). In 18:1-16a it is an inseparable element of a self-contained narrative.

The promise of the son is the starting point and center of the promise motif in the patriarchal stories (C. Westermann, *The Promises. . .*). It is expanded notably and in the process acquires a new function: it links the patriarchal story with the story of the people. This function is clear in the prolog, Gen. 12:1-3, where it has a deliberately programmatic character. It is equally clear in the two promise narratives, 15:1-6 and 15:7-21 (cf. ch. 17[P]), where the promise, directed towards the people, is pointedly shaped into narratives. They are concentrated in the middle of Gen. 12–25; the promise, both in ch. 15 and ch. 17, takes on the force of a *berit*, an oath, or a self-obligation on God's part, which is to speak out of the story of Abraham to contemporary Israel. The promise made to Abraham expands from this center across the whole complex of Gen. 12–25, and is divided into introduction, (12:1-3) and additions and insertions (12:7; 13:14-17; 16:10; 18:18; 21:12f.,18; 22:15-18).

The difference between these two lines in the composition of Gen. 12–25 points with unusual clarity to a situation which is very instructive. One line corresponds to a coherent process from the complaint about childlessness to the birth of a child, which is typical of the family form of community and well attested. The other line consists of "factitious narratives" (*nachgeahmten Erzählungen*, N. Lohfink, SBS 28 [1967] 33), a literary prolog, and additions to older narratives. One can distinguish thereby the later line of promises of blessing, increase, and possession of the land addressed to the people of Israel in the land from the earlier line of the narrative motif of Abraham's family, and so identify two clearly different stages of the tradition of the Abraham stories. The later line, the promises directed towards the people, is linked with the older line, family narratives, by broadening the promise of the son by the promise of increase (e.g., Gen. 15:1-6). The promise directed to the people could be appended to the promise of a son—which belonged to the old narrative. The decisive criterion for the distinction between the two lines is that properly developed narratives belong only to the older. But neither line is a unity from the standpoint of tradition-history. In the older line, narratives of different kinds from different periods are joined together; in the later, the promise texts, despite their essential likeness in content, are very different from each other. In each individual case the question must be asked about the history of the promises and their combination into texts of promise.

3. Abraham-Lot Narratives

Not all the narratives of Gen. 12–25 are included in the line which leads from Sarah's barrenness to the birth (and marriage) of Isaac. The texts about Abraham and Lot form a line which links several additional narratives. H. Gunkel considered this chain of stories so important as to regard it as the basic framework of all the J material of Gen. 12–25. But this cannot be sustained. References to Lot in Genesis are found in 11:27(P),31(P); 12:4,5(P); 13:1,5-13,14; 14:12-16; 19:1-29, 30-38. P contains a reference to Lot in a genealogy (11:27), two references in an itinerary (11:31; 12:5), but no narrative about him and Abraham. J mentions him in an itinerary (12:4; 13:1,14), in the narrative of 13:5-13, and in the two narratives of 19:1-29 and 19:30-38. What is striking is that all these passages which mention Lot are closely linked with each other: 13:13 introduces 19:1-29 and 19:30-38 is narrated as a direct continuation of 19:1-29. Thus there probably was narrated a connected story about (Abraham and) Lot. However, pieces of very different kinds are gathered together in it. The narrative in ch. 13 differs from the two in ch. 19 in the first place in that ch. 19 deals only with Lot and his family, while 13:5-13 is concerned with a dispute between Abraham and Lot (rather, their shepherds) and its settlement. The references to Lot in 11:27, 31; 12:4-5; and 13:1, 5-13,14 are in accord with the latter. Lot and Abraham are together in all of them. The itineraries (and a genealogical note in P), together with the narrative 13:5-13, belong very closely to the larger circle of Abraham narratives; 19:1-29, 30-38, on the contrary, are clearly traditions of independent origin which first became attached in the course of the growth of the Abraham cycle. The subject matter of both parts of ch. 19 is foreign to that of the Abraham cycle; the destruction of a city by a natural disaster and the rescue of a single individual and his family is close to Gen. 6–9 and so to the primeval event. Gen. 19:30-38 is the narrative of the origin of two of Israel's neighboring tribes. Abraham's role in 18:16-33 also shows this clearly; he does not take part in the event, but is a concerned onlooker who intercedes for the city that God threatens to destroy.

The subject matter of Gen. 13:5-13, on the other hand, is a constituent part of the Abraham narratives which accords with his life-style as a pastoral nomad and deals with an event typical of it. Nevertheless, it differs from the line presented at the beginning, ''the land could not support them both together'' (13:6). It is a story of a dispute about living space and subsistence, which ends with the parties separating in peace (there is a distant parallel here to the Jacob-Esau narrative: two kinsmen, dispute about subsistence, peaceful separation).

There is one certain clue that the redactor, or a predecessor who passed on the tradition, saw the difference between the two narrative lines and indicated it in the composition. The sequence of the narratives of the barren mother and the birth of the child arises out of the genealogy (11:30); the sequence of the narratives of the dispute between Abraham and Lot about living space and subsistence arises out of the itinerary (12:4; 13:1). The one narrative sequence is framed in the genealogy, the other in the itinerary, and this accords with the character of both sequences. This demonstrates at the same time that the genealogies and itineraries in Gen. 12–25 are by no means mere link pieces and supplements, but that they have a clearly discernible function in the composition of the whole. The narrative of 13:5-13, together with the itinerary notes, belongs therefore to the nucleus of the Abraham narratives; both can go back to the patriarchal period. This is not so for the elaboration in ch. 19, which is of another type and origin.

4. The Composition as a Whole

There is the concluding question of the way the three lines discovered so far in the text of Gen. 12–25 joined together or fitted into each other. Ch. 14 can be bracketed out as probably the latest insertion.

The distribution of the promises is such that they accumulate in the middle of chs. 12–25. There one follows the other: 13:14-17; 15:1-6; 15:7-21; (16:1-15, promise in v. 10); 17:1-27 (and 18:1-16a). Of these, 16:1-15 and 18:1-16a belong in another line; but 18:1-16a is, as a whole, a promise narrative, and ch. 16 contains a promise. In any case, it is very easy to recognize the concentration of the promise texts. This block is inserted into the Abraham-Lot sequence, which, considered in itself, is coherent and self-contained: 13:1-13; (18:16b-33); 19:1-29; 19:30-38.

13:1-13		
	13:14-17 15; 17 (18:1-16)	
(18:16b-33) 19:1-29 19:30-38		

When it is recognized that the promises form an independent layer of tradition in chs. 12–25, and a relatively late one at that, then it is immediately evident from the composition of the chapters that the Abraham-Lot narratives originally belonged together. At the same time it becomes clear that the late text of Abraham's intercession for the cities (18:16b-33) serves as a link piece between the two sequences.

The conjunction of the Lot-Abraham narratives in the diagram above, with the insertion of the promise texts, reveals a further step in the process of composition: the "birth of a child" line emerges in its original form as a self-contained piece. It begins with 11:27-30 and 12:10-20, is followed by the composite block of chs. 13–19 (which, however, contains two texts belonging to it, 16:1-15 and 18:1-16a), and is continued in chs. 20–25 without any essential interruption. The result is the following picture of the composition of chs. 12–25:

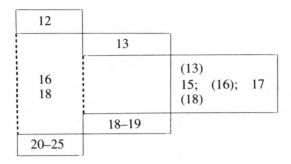

Chs. 16 and 18 most readily drop out of the three-line composition. The reason they were added to the promises block is probably that 16:1-15 contains the promise of the birth of Ishmael and 18:1-16a that of the birth of Isaac. The transmitter of tradition who put them with the promises was so convinced that they belonged there that he took them out of the "birth of the child" line. One can understand this more easily if the tradition history of the promises is relatively late.

So as not to confuse the issue, one can leave out here a series of deviations and exceptions. The question must be asked, however, which texts belong to none of these three lines. If one prescinds from the genealogies and itineraries, there remains but one text which does not fit: 21:22-34, the dispute about the well and the treaty with Abimelech. It would make sense to regard this text as belonging originally to the Isaac tradition (and this is the only such case in Gen. 12–25); in any case, it deals with the same thing as 26:15-23. However, it is also possible that a transmitter of the text interpolated an isolated patriarchal tradition into the Abraham story.

But there is in addition a series of texts that belong to the line of the promise and birth of the child only because of a motif, but not as complete narratives. We note here yet again a situation which is instructive for the composition. The narrative line reaches its natural conclusion with the account of the birth of the child in 21:1-7 (on 27:8-21, see below); the report of Abraham's death would then follow (25:7-8). The redactor has inserted between 21:1-7 and 25:7-10 a further group of Abraham narratives, each of which belongs to the main line only by virtue of a motif, and each of which stands over against it as an independent piece: chs. 22; 23; and 24. They resemble each other in the "detailed narrative style"; moreover, they are literary rather than popular narratives, they stand apart from all preceding narratives in their length, and they all have to do with Abraham's family. In other respects, however, they are very different from each other, and show how the Abraham tradition developed further in quite different directions.

Again, this state of affairs cannot be due to chance. One can recognize here a stage in the tradition: the redactor inserts between the provisional (21:1-7) and definitive (25:7-18) conclusion a group of Abraham narratives which shows the further development of the Abraham tradition beyond the old narratives. It should be especially noted that difficulties have always arisen when one tries to assign these three narratives to particular sources. One can understand this more easily if the interval between these developed narratives and the simple ones is greater than that between the various sources.

It is to be noted further that *all* doublets which appear in Gen. 12–25 are grouped around the provisional conclusion of 21:1-7; 20:1-18 and 12:10-20;

21:8-21 and 16:1-15; 21:27-34 and 26:15-33 (in the Isaac cycle). This too must be intended as part of the composition; how it is to be explained must remain an open question.

Literature: Gen. 12–25 (Structure and Growth)

A. Abraham

S. R. Driver, *Introduction to the Literature of the Old Testament* (1891, 1913[9]). H. A. Ryle, "Abraham," DB(H) I,15 (1900). P. Dornstetter, *Abraham. Studien über die Anfänge des hebräischen Volkes*, BSt 7,1-3 (1902). A. H. Sayce, "The Age of Abraham," *Biblical World* 26 (1906) 248-257. A. Pfeiffer, *Abraham der Prophet Jehovas*, I (1907). F. Wilke, *War Abraham eine geschichtliche Persönlichkeit?* (1907). G. A. Barton, "Abraham and Archaeology," JBL 18,2 (1909). J. Döller, *Abraham und seine Zeit*, BZfr 2,1 (1909). P. Dhorme, "Abraham dans le cadre de l'histoire," RB 37 (1928) 367-385, 481-511; 40 (1931) 364-374, 503-518. F. M. T. Böhl, *Das Zeitalter Abrahams* AO 29 (1930). O. Stockmayer, *Abraham der Vater der Gläubigen: Spener Reihe* 2 (1943; 1953[4]). J. Chaine, "Abraham," *Catholicisme I* (1947) 51-56. U. Cassuto, "Abraham, Beréshit," *Enziklopedia Miqrait I-II* (1950-54). F. Oesterreicher, "Abraham Our Father," *Worship* 25 (1950) 559-573. E. Cardinal Tisserant ed., *Abraham, Père des croyants*, Cahiers Sion 5 (1951). L. H. Vincent, "Abraham à Jérusalem," RB 58 (1951) 360-371. J. Starcky, "Abraham und die Geschichte," BiKi 2 (1952) 17-26. F. Asensio, *Yahweh y su pueblo contenido teológico en la historia biblica de la alección* (1953). N. Schneider, "Die religiöse Umwelt Abrahams in Mesopotamien," *Miscellanea D. B. Ubach* (1953) 49-67. I. Fransen, "Abraham Père des croyants (Gen. 11:27–25:18)," BVC 10 (1955) 73-86. C. H. Gordon, "The Age of Abraham in the Negeb," BA 18,1 (1955). J. Lécuyer, *Abraham, notre père* (1955). C. A. Keller, "Grundsätzliches zur Auslegung der Abraham-Überlieferung in der Genesis," ThZ 12 (1956) 425-445. F. Hesse, "Die Erforschung der Geschichte Israels als theologische Aufgabe," KuD 4 (1958) esp. 11-18. F. J. du Buit–L. Ramlot, "Abraham, père et modèle des croyants," *Evangelie* 38 (1960) 5-95. R. Rendtorff, "Hermeneutik des Alten Testaments als Frage nach der Geschichte," ZThK 57 (1960) 27-40. W. F. Albright, "Abram the Hebrew. . .," BASOR 163 (1961) 36-54. L. Hicks, "Abraham," IDB I (1962) 14-21. E. Jacob, "Abraham et sa signification pour la foi chrétienne," RHPhR 42 (1962) 148-156. F. L. Moriarty, " 'My Father Was a Wandering Aramean,' " BiTod 1 (1962/63) 97-106. M. Buber, "Zur Erzählung von Abraham," MGWJ 83 (1963) 47-65. C. H. Gordon, "Abraham of Ura," *Fests. G. Driver* (1963). A. S. Kapelrud, "Hvem var Abraham?" NTT 64 (1963) 163-174. M. Buber, " 'Abraham der Seher,' " *Werke II* (1964) 881-893. H. Gaubert, *Abraham, l'ami de Dieu* (1964). N. A. von Uchelen, "Abraham de Hebreër. Een literair-historisch-kritische studie naar aanleiding van Genesis 14:13," SSN 5 (1964). J. Muilenburg, "Abraham. . .," Interp. 19 (1965) 387ff. J. L. Kelso, *Archaeology and Our OT Contemporaries* (1966[3]). R. Kilian, *Die vorpriesterlichen Abrahamüberlieferungen. . .*, BBB 24 (1966) 284-320. J. Kelso, "Life in the Patriarchal Age," ChrTo 12 (1968) 5-8. N. Scholl, "Theologische und katechetische Aspekte zur Berufung Abrahams," Katech.Bl 97 (1968) 721-733. N. A. von Uchelen, "Abraham als Felsen (Jes 51:1)," ZAW 80 (1968) 183-191. R. Martin-Achard, *Actualité d'Abraham: Bibliotheque théologique* (1969). M. Weippert, "Abraham der Hebräer?. . .," Bib 52 (1971). G. H. Jones, "Abraham and Cyrus: Type and Anti-Type?" VT 22 (1972) 304-319. N. E. Wagner, "Abraham and David?" *Fests. F. V. Winnett* (1972) 117-140. R. Martin-Achard, "Etudes sur l'Ancien Testament. Essai sur la figure d'Abraham," BCPE 25 (1973) 5-33. T. L. Thompson, *The Historicity. . .*, BZAW 133 (1974). J. Van Seters, *Abraham in History* (1975).

B. Abraham in Later Literature

B. Beer, *Leben Abrahams nach der Auffassung der jüdischen Sage* (1859). J. Freudenthal, *Hellenistische Studien* 1/2 (1874/75) 82-103. O. Schmitz, "Abraham im Spätjudentum und Urchristentum," *Fests. A. Schlatter* (1922) 99-123. W. Völker, "Das Abrahambild bei Philo, Origenes und Ambrosius," ThStKr 103 (1931) 199-207. J. Finkel, "An Arabic Story of Abraham," HUCA 12-13 (1937/38). A. Dupont-Sommer, *Le quatrième livre des Maccabées* (1939). J. Daniélou, "Abraham dans la tradition chrétienne," *Cahiers Sion* 5 (1951) 160-179. S. Sandmel, "Philo's Place in Judaism: A Study of Conceptions of Abraham in Jewish Literature,'' HUCA 25 (1954) 209-237; 26 (1955) 151-232. B. Grill, ''Leitsätze der Kirchenväter für die Erklärung des AT,'' BiLi 23 (1955/56) 43-47, 110-112, 257-259. N. Avigad–Y. Yadin, *Genesis Apocryphon. A Scroll from the Wilderness of Judaea* (1956). M. Dibelius, *Der Brief des Jakobus* (1956[8]) esp. 157-163. E. Y. Kutscher, ''Dating the Language of the Genesis Apocryphon,'' JBL 76 (1957) 288-292. Y. Moubarac, *Abraham dans le Coran* (1958). B. Rothenberg, *Die Wüste Gottes: Entdeckungen auf Sinai* (1961). G. Vermès, *Scripture and Tradition in Judaism: Haggadic Studies* [The Rewritten Bible: The Life of Abraham] (1961). U. Wilckens, ''Die Rechtfertigung Abrahams nach Römer 4,'' *Fests G. von Rad* (1961) 111-127. O. Betz, ed., *Abraham unser Vater. Juden und Christen im Gespräch über die Bibel: Fests. O. Michel* (1963). B. Z. Wacholder, '' 'Pseudo-Eupolemus,' Two Greek Fragments on the Life of Abraham,'' HUCA 34 (1963) 83-113. J. Jomier, ''La figure d'Abraham et le pèlerinage musulman de la Mekka,'' *Mélanges E. Tisserant I* (1964) 229-244. H. Werner, ''Abraham. Der Erstling und Repräsentant Israels,'' ExBib 1 (1965). L. Feldman, ''Abraham the Greek Philosopher in Josephus,'' AmPhAssTr/Pr 99 (1968). J. C. H. Lebram, ''Aspekte der alttestamentlichen Kanonbildung,'' VT 18 (1968) 173-189. J. R. Lord, *Abraham: A Study in Ancient Jewish and Christian Interpretation* (Diss. Duke.), Diss. Abstr. 29 (1968/69), 382-A. E. Käsemann, *Perspectives on Paul* (1969, 1972-74; Eng. 1971) 140-177. M. Delcor, ''La portée chronologique de quelques interprétations du Targoum Néophyti contenues dans le cycle d'Abraham,'' JSJ 1 (1970) 105-119. M. H. Woudstra, ''The Toledot of the Book of Genesis and Their Redemptive-Historical Significance,'' CTJ 5 (1970) 184-189. G. Mayer, ''Aspekte des Abrahambildes in der hellenistisch-jüdischen Literatur,'' EvTh 32 (1972) 118-127. J. Gutmann, '' 'Abraham in the Fire of the Chaldeans.' A Jewish Legend in Jewish, Christian and Islamic Art,'' FMSt 7 (1973) 342-352.

Transition to the Story
of Abraham

Literature

[Cf. Lit. to Gen. 12–50, B., Genealogy and Itinerary, above.] A. H. Sayce, "Ur of the Chaldees," ET 13 (1901/02) 64-66. F. A. Jones, *The Dates of Genesis* (1909). S. H. Langdon, "The Name Abraham in Babylonian," ET 21 (1909/10) 88-90. T. Arldt, "Die Völkertafeln der Genesis und ihre Bedeutung für die Ethnographic Vorderasiens," WZKM 30 (1917/18) 264-317. E. M. Grice, *Records from Ur and Larsa Dated in the Larsa Dynasty*, YOS V (1919), Babylonian Texts. I. Eitan, "Two Onomatological Studies," JAOS 49 (1929) 30-33. W. Borée, *Die alten Ortsnamen Palästinas* (1930). A. Parrot, "Ur en Chaldee," EvQ 5 (1933) 89-99. W. F. Albright, "New Canaanite Historical and Mythological Data," BASOR 63 (1936) 23-36. F. M. Bauer, *Abram, Son of Terah* (1948). G. Ryckmans, "Le nom propre Térah—est-il attesté en safaïtique?" RB 56 (1949) 579-582. M. A. Beek, OTS 8 (1950) 193ff. J. Nougayrol, *Le palais royal d'Ugarit, IV* (1956). F. X. Curley, "Sara, Mother of All Believers," AEcR 135 (1956) 361-369. I. Cunnisen, "History and Genealogies in a Conquest State," AmA 59 (1957). R. K. Harrison, *A History of OT Times*. C.II (1957) 55-65. A. Rasco, "Migratio Abrahae circa annum 1650," VD 35 (1957) 143-154. C. J. Gadd, "The Harran Inscriptions. . .," AnSt 8 (1958) 35ff. S. Kirst, "Sin, Yerah and Jahve. Eine Bemerkung zum vorderasiatischen Mondkult," FF 32 (1958) 213-219. M. E. L. Mallowan–D. J. Wiseman, eds., *Ur in Retrospect: Essays in Mem. of C. L. Wooley, Iraq* 22 (1960). A. Malamat, "Aspects of the Foreign Policies of David and Solomon," JNESt 22 (1963) 1-17. W. W. Hallo, "The Road to Emar," JCS 18 (1964) 57-88. A. F. Key, "Traces of the Worship of the Moon God Sin Among the Early Israelites," JBL 84 (1965) 20-26. Y. Dvir, *Biblical Proper Names and Their Mission* [in Hebr.] (1969). J. Liver, "The Bible and Its Historical Sources," *The World History of the Jewish People II*, ed. B. Mazar (1970) 35-62.

Text

11:27 This[a] is the history of Terah: Terah begot Abram,[b] Nahor[c] and Haran;[d] Haran begot Lot.[e]

28 But Haran died before his father Terah in the land of his kinsmen, Ur[a] of the Chaldees.[b]

29 Abram and Nahor took[a] wives; Abram's wife was called Sarai,[b] and Nahor's Milcah, the daughter of Haran, who was the father[c] of Milcah and Iscah.[d]

30 But Sarai was barren; she had[a] no children.[b]

31 Now Terah took his son[a] Abram, and his grandson Lot, the son of Terah, and his daughter-in-law, Sarai,[b] the wife of his son Abram, and

they set out together[c] from[d] Ur of the Chaldees,[e] to go to the land of Canaan; they came to Haran and settled there.
32 Terah[a] died at Haran at the age of 205 years.[b]

27a Sam reads אלה for ואלה. **b** אבר (from ch. 17 on, אברהם, the change of name in P; so too "Abraham" in the rest of the OT, except in the citations of 1 Chron. 1:27; Neh. 9:4). Both forms of the name are generally understood as dialect variants. The name Abraham is a purely personal name. For a discussion of its origin and meaning, cf. Intro., par. 4,c, and C. Westermann, *Erträge der Forschung* Bd. 48 (1975); detailed discussion with Literature, T. L. Thompson, *The Historicity. . .*, BZAW 133 (1974) 22-36. The name discovered by A. Ungnad (BASS 6, 5 [1909]), *a-ba-am-ra-ma* (and variants), in a letter from the old Babylonian period, does not correspond to the name Abraham, which belongs rather to the context of a number of West Semitic names formed according to the same pattern. This group cannot be set in a definite period, because it occurs over a long time span and in many places. Two questions must be distinguished: (1) the type of name and (2) the individual name. Abraham belongs to the type of name that forms a sentence, consisting of the noun in the nominative and the verb in the perfect. The noun is the name or designation of a god, the verb a statement about this god's action or being. The form is very widespread in West Semitic; in the OT, names of this type are: אביגר, אחירם, אבירם עמרם, יארם (Num. 16:1; 1 Kings 16:34). Both constituent parts are found often. The verb *rwm* (רום) = "to be exalted (high)," in the perfect with the name of a god, e.g., *I-li-ra-ma* (Mari), *I-lu-(An)-ra-ma*, *'ilrm*, *b'lrm* (Ugarit). A designation of a god can take the place of the name of a god, especially when it expresses relationship, as עם, אח, and אב (M. Noth, BWANT 46 [1928] 69f.). The perfect of רום occurs with עם: עמרם (OT), *Ha-mu-ra-ma* (Mari), *Am-rā-mu* (Assyr.); with אח: *Aḥ-ra-am* (Mari), *aḥrm* (Ugarit), *Aḥiramu* (Assyr.), אחירם (OT). With אב, we have the direct parallel to Abraham: it is attested often from about the middle of the second millennium. T. L. Thompson gathers nine different attestations (individual or in groups), including *a-bi-ra-mu* in Akk., *abrm* in the alphabetic texts from Ugarit. Conclusion: Abraham is a West Semitic personal name, belonging to a widely dispersed group of names forming a sentence, often attested outside Israel. Its meaning is, "the father is exalted." **c** Nahor: cf. *Gen. 1–11*, Comm on Gen. 11:23. Gk reads καὶ τὸν Ναχωρ (Vg: *et*). **d** Haran: cf. Comm. Gen. 11:26. **e** Lot: besides Gen. 11:27,31, the name occurs in Gen. 12:4, 5; 13; 14:12-16; 19; Deut. 2:9,19; Ps. 83:9. The origin and etymology of the name is unknown. A connection with the Horite clan of Lotan is possible (Gen. 36:20, 22, 29). Lot as a descendant of Haran does not belong any more to the region around Haran; as ancestor of the Moabites and Ammonites (Gen. 19), he belongs to the later neighbors of Israel on the Transjordan.

28a Instead of באור, Gk reads ἐν τῇ χώρᾳ **b** אור כשדים is ellipse for אור עיר כשדים (Ges-B §125h).

29a ויקח Ges-B §146f.: "The predicate *preceding* two or more subjects may likewise be used in the plural. . .; not infrequently, however, it agrees in gender and number with the first, as being the subject nearest to it"; cf. Brockelmann, *Grundriss* (1966) I 469. Cf. Gen. 7:7; 9:23 **b** שרי together with שרה (change of name in P, ch. 17): an unexplained by-form of שרה; E. A. Speiser takes it as an old genitive ending. **c** אבי hireq *compaginis*. **d** The name יסכה occurs only here; not explained.

30 a Gk reads καὶ οὐκ for אין of MT. **b** Sam reads ילד for ולד. Already in old Canaanite ו has become י; ולד belongs to the rare forms in which initial ו has been retained; cf. Ug. *wld* = *waladu*, "child," Meyer (1966³)I 97.

31a בנו some Gk mss. read καὶ Ναχωρ υἱὸς αὐτοῦ for בנו; obviously a correction. **b** Sam reads after שרי: (כלתו) ואת מלכה, and after אברם: ונחור בניו. **c** ויצאו אתם: Syr reads ויצא; Sam, Gk,L,Vg read ויצאו אתם. **d** for מאור, Gk reads ἐκ τῆς χώρας.

32 a: Gk reads after תרח ימי־: ἐν Χαρραν. **b** Sam: 145 for 205 of MT.

Form

The passage, Gen. 11:27-32, is clearly marked off. V. 27a is a title which introduces the story of Terah (although he has already been mentioned). V. 32 is a conclusion; the story of Terah must end with his death. Vv. 27,31,32 are usually assigned to P, vv. 28-30 to J. However, we must study the structure of the clearly
defined textual unit, 11:27-32, before deciding to which sources the verses belong. The title, v. 27a, describes it as ''toledot''; v. 32 is the conclusion. There
are two parts: vv: 27b-30 is a genealogy, v. 31 a-c is an itinerary. The structure of
the genealogy is: begot—begot—died—wives are taken—was barren. All the
verbs make genealogical statements. The structure of v. 31 a-c is: took—
departed—went—arrived—settled. All the verbs are parts of the account of a migration. The structure of 11:27-32 is thereby clearly defined both in its framework, vv. 27 and 32, and in its two parts, vv. 27b-30 and v. 31a-c. It is impossible
to recognize the structure if one has already separated the passage into literary
sources and tried to determine the structure of each source for itself (I agree here
with U. Cassuto). If one assigns v. 27b to P and has J begin with v. 28, as do most
interpreters, then one cuts through the sequence of the genealogical data beginning in v. 27b; the sequence must begin with the word ''begot.'' But above all,
such separation obscures the arrangement of the whole which sets the genealogy,
vv. 27b-30, and the itinerary, vv. 31a-c, within the frame of vv. 27a and 32. One
must therefore give precedence to a division of the text based on content and form;
and this must be determinative for the exegesis.

Gen. 11:27 is the beginning of the patriarchal story. Terah to be sure is not
one of the patriarchs; he dies in Haran before the entrance into the land of Canaan.
But as the father of Abraham, he belongs to the story that is to be told (R.
Montague, *La Civilization du Desert* [1947]). Gen. 11:27-32 is a preparation for
the patriarchal story. The intention of the bearer of the tradition is clearly discernible: in the first part, vv. 27b-30, he states the transition from what has preceded to
what follows, from the primeval story to the patriarchal story; in the second he
states what is new, what begins only with the patriarchal story: the migrations of
the patriarchs, the goal of which is the promised land and the story of the people of
Israel.

It is only when one realizes the purpose of the arrangement of 11:27-32
that the function of the frame pieces, vv. 27a and 32, becomes clear. They belong
as indisputably to the priestly writing as does 12:1-4a to the Yahwistic. The redactor has provided the patriarchal story with two introductions, each with its own
particular character and function. The P introduction has taken up a block from J,
vv. 27b-30, just as a block from P, 12:4b-5 (which follows 11:31 almost word for
word), has been taken up into the J introduction. The way is prepared for the two
main elements in the patriarchal story by genealogy and itinerary in 11:27-32, and
by the word of God which goes forth and determines it in 12:1-4a.

As for the source division, or the relation of J and P to each other, we are
dealing with a composite text and it is not possible to separate each sentence into
sources.

This has already been recognized in the period when source criticism was dominant. A. Dillmann and J. Skinner were extremely cautious in assigning the verses to
sources; H. Holzinger and H. Gunkel were reserved; recently R. Kilian has proposed that
vv. 29, 31, 32 be understood as a frame built around vv. 28-30, that the information in vv.
28-30 (J) is not complete, and that v. 27b contains elements of the J genealogy (BBB24
[1966]); I agree with him. A Dillmann and J. Skinner hesitate to assign v. 31 to P; this is

because they sensed a tradition proper to v. 31a-c, that is, a text which was not the original work of P.

From the composite character of 11:27-32 there follows an important consequence for the mention of Ur of the Chaldees in v. 28. One can no longer say that it originates from the Yahwist. Ur of the Chaldees is part of a composite text in which one cannot assign with certainty this or that sentence or name to any particular source. J. Skinner remarks that perhaps v. 28a is required by P; J. Van Seters notes likewise that v. 31 presupposes v. 28 (*Abraham. . .* [1975] 225f.). His conclusion, that vv. 26-32 belong to P, goes too far and is not required. It is no longer necessary, then, to regard ''Ur of the Chaldees'' in v. 28 as an addition (so R. Kilian and many others). It is not possible, because of the character of the text, to fix the place-name Ur of the Chaldees in the Yahwistic source, and so in the period of the Yahwist (so too J. C. L. Gibson, JSSt 7 [1962] 44ff. The discussions hitherto had taken it as an established fact that Ur of the Chaldees was already part of the old J source (see comm. on 15:7); this led many scholars to maintain a possible ''historicity'' for the migration of Abraham from Ur to Haran (R. de Vaux, *Early History. . .* [1971; Eng. 1978]). But if this fact is not established, other arguments must decide. One such is that J does not report a migration from Ur to Haran (J. C. L. Gibson), that ''J gives no name at all for the city of origin'' (H. Gunkel), and that J always gives north Mesopotamia, the region around Haran, as the region from which Abraham's family came (H. Gunkel; J. C. L. Gibson; R. T. O'Callaghan, *Aram-Naharaim* [1948, 1961[2]]; F. Vattioni, Aug. 4 [1964] 330ff.; M. Noth, *Die Ursprünge. . .* [1961]; A. Malamat: ''If anything is emphasized, it is that Abraham's forbears and immediate descendants have close racial and regional bonds with Upper Mesopotamia. . .'' BA 34 [1971] 2ff.).

A further difficulty is thereby solved. Vv. 27, 31, 32 speak of Terah:

> 11:27a: This is the family tree of Terah
>   27b: Terah begot. . .
>   31: Terah took. . . and departed. . .
>   32: Terah. . . died.

These verses contain elements of a genealogy which forms the framework; inserted into it is an itinerary whose starting point is Ur of the Chaldees and goal is Canaan. Apart from the genealogical data, all that is said of Terah, the father of Abraham, is that he set out with his family from Ur to go to Canaan. Haran then is only a stopping place on the way (v. 31c). The account of Abraham's further journey from Haran in 12:4b is parallel to v. 31 and ends in v. 5b with the arrival in Canaan. The difference from 12:1-4a (J) is obvious. Terah's departure from Ur and Abraham's from Canaan take place without any call from God or promise. God neither acts nor speaks. P wants thereby to draw a sharp line of separation between the foreign religion of Abraham's ancestors and the new, which begins with the covenant concluded with Abraham in ch. 17. What is said about Terah is restricted to what makes possible the events which are to take place in the promised land (ch. 17), and it is Abraham who brings this to its goal. But according to P, this migration into Canaan has nothing to do with anything like a call of Abraham; it is nothing more than a preparation which is still outside God's revelation. P deliberately departs here from the older presentation by J (12:1-4a). It is here that the place of departure, Ur of the Chaldees, finds its explanation. If it is proper only to P's itinerary and its function in v. 28 is merely to harmonize, then the starting point of Terah's migration corresponds to P's purpose in the introduction to the story of Abraham: Ur of the Chaldees represents the pagan world from which Terah departed for Canaan. The name is not meant primarily to convey geographical information, but to indicate the old capital of the pagan empire. The author of the priestly writing knows that the dominion of the city of Ur is older than that of Babylon; but he designates it by the name which was current for it in his own time and region: Ur of the Chaldees. But he knows too the older tradition, according to which the forefathers of the patriarchs came from north Mesopotamia; he takes it up in such a way as to make Haran a stopping place on the way from Ur to Canaan, which would be a very remarkable route.

The older tradition, which P or a redactor assumed into this framework, had a quite different purpose. It is a purely genealogical introduction to the Abraham story which begins in 12:1-4a with Abraham's departure, following God's command. Most interpreters see here a literary device which prepares for what is to come. R. Kilian develops this in detail (BBB 24 [1966] 279f.): v. 28 is a preparation for 12:1, for the mention of Abraham and Sarah in Gen. 12ff., of Nahor and Milcah (ch. 24), of Haran (chs. 13; 19), and Sarah's barrenness in chs. 15; 18. The passage 11:28-30, therefore, would be a secondary genealogy (following M. Noth), of which the details would be taken from the appropriate narratives. T. L. Thompson proposes something similar (BZAW 133 [1974] 308-311). The genealogy, however, contains the name Iscah, which does not occur in the narratives, and this alone shows that there must be traditions behind vv. 28-30 at least. The genealogy comprises only the three sons of Terah, their wives, and the son of one of Terah's sons. The Abraham narratives, Gen. 12–25, remain within the three generations of this family. Nothing more is said than is necessary. The aim of the genealogy lies in the elaboration in v. 30—Sarah was barren. This motif is the point of departure for several narratives in Gen. 12–25.

Setting

The literary setting of Gen. 11:27-32 is that of an introduction to the patriarchal story; its function is to indicate the place in the sequence of generations where the events to be narrated took place (so in the J-component), and at the same time the geographical origin of the patriarchs (in the P-component), who came from Ur in Chaldea, through Haran, to Canaan. Both parts are so intertwined as to form a self-contained introduction presenting the family of Terah which came to Canaan from foreign parts. It is possible that it originates from P because it has a P-frame (vv. 27a and 32), although the way it is linked with the J-section (vv. 27b-30, 27b being common) speaks more for a redactor.

The origin of each constituent part must be studied separately. Vv. 27b-30 are a genealogy (primary, not secondary) already at hand to J, as the name Iscah indicates, bearing the mark of the genuine genealogy which has undergone development in the narrative motif in v. 30, which forms an elaboration on the succession of generations.

The genealogical frame (vv. 27 and 32) of the P-section (vv. 27a,31-32) belongs to the *toledot*-structure which determines the first part of the priestly work; the details in vv. 27 and 32 follow immediately and without break the *toledot* of the primeval story, forming at the same time a new piece, the introduction to the patriarchal story.

The itinerary of v. 31a-c is inserted into the frame in the language traditional to this form. Its obviously theological intent is to draw a clear line of demarcation between the revelation of God to Abraham in Canaan (ch. 17) and the ancestors who were of foreign origin; consequently, one cannot say whether or not this deliberately constructed itinerary is based on an older tradition.

Commentary

[11:27] The *toledot*-formula introduces the story of Terah. V. 27 repeats in part v. 26; one difference is that v. 26 uses ויהי instead of the *toledot*-formula, P indicating thereby that v. 26 is to be understood in the context of what has preceded (the structure of the sentence is exactly as in v. 24), while v. 27 introduces a new section. A further difference is that v. 26 gives Terah's age, appropriate of course to the begetting of an only son. The genealogy, 11:10-26, concludes with the begetting of three sons, as in Gen. 5:32; here also only one age is given for the begetting of the three. There is a third difference: v. 27 adds, ''Haran begot Lot,'' which would not be appropriate to the conclusion in v. 26, but is necessary to introduce what follows. The comparison between v. 26 and v. 27 shows clearly that v. 26 is a conclusion and v. 27a beginning (against U. Cassuto, T. L. Thompson, and others).

The conclusion is that the purpose of תולדת (*toledot*) is to introduce the story that begins with Terah, and that this does not end with his death in 11:32. It could not, because the function of 11:27-32 is to serve as an introduction. F. Delitzsch's explanation is to the point: ''The heading belongs to the whole subsequent story of Abraham'' (Comm. ad.loc.). Similarly the *toledot* of Isaac in 25:19 introduces the narratives of Jacob and Esau, and the *toledot* of Jacob in 37:2 the story of Joseph (so too F. M. Cross, *Canaanite Myth. . .* [1973] 303f.). A simple explanation is thereby offered for the absence of *toledot* of Abraham, which has concerned the exegetes: it is the absence of a detailed Isaac tradition (only fragments of it are preserved in ch. 26); this would have begun with the heading ''these are the *toledot* of Abraham.'' There is no reason, therefore, to alter the text and substitute Abraham for Terah in 11:27 (so K. Budde, B. D. Eerdmans). Nor is J. Scharbert's explanation necessary, namely, that there could not be a *toledot* of Abraham formula because P had to establish in 16:1 that Sarah was barren (Fests. W. Eichrodt [1970] 45-56). The names are explained in the commentary below.

[11:28] This remark is important for what follows. It is not the normal thing for the father to outlive his son; the purpose of על-פני is to express that the father had to experience the death of his son. The note about the place would not be necessary for this; it takes its meaning only from the text of 11:27-32 as a whole. It is saying that Haran was no longer there at the time of the departure (v. 31, P). ''Haran died in the land of his kith and kin,'' in the land where his kinsmen lived. This is the meaning of the phrase ארץ מולדתו in every place where it occurs (Gen. 11:28; 24:7; 31:13; Ruth 2:11; Jer. 22:10; 46:16; Ezek. 23:15). It can be used as the equivalent of the phrase ''land of birth'' (Jer. 46:16: ''Arise, let us go back to our own people and to the land of our birth. . .''; Ezek. 23:15: ''. . . whose native land was Chaldea''), which makes good sense here too: Haran died in the land of his birth. For Ur of the Chaldees, see below, Comm. on v. 31.

[11:29] The genealogy is expanded after the fashion of a narrative; instead of ''the wife of Abraham was. . .,'' it is narrated that they both ''took wives.'' There is but a mere mention of names; the name of Milcah's father, no longer explicable, is given; that of Sarah's is not. There is no justification for the view that something has fallen out of the text (so H. Ewald and others), or that the name of the father was later struck out because of Gen. 20:12 (so H. Gunkel and others); rather it is a sign that this genealogy is not complete because the names were no longer known. Further, it is striking that Haran is named as the "father of Milcah and Iscah." The latter occurs nowhere else in the patriarchal story and has no significance in the narrative context introduced by 11:27-32. The only explanation of the name is that there was an old tradition which mentioned these two daughters of Haran. They must have occurred as sisters in a narrative of which we no longer know anything, just as Gen. 19:30-38 tells of two sisters. E. A. Speiser explains the marriage of Nahor with the daughter of his deceased brother by a practice known from one of the Nuzi texts: "Juridically, cases of this kind involve adoption (here of an orphaned niece) followed by marriage. The pertinent document in Nuzi would be called *tuppi martūti u kallatūti* = 'document of daughter- and daughter-in-law-ship,' since the husband was also the adoptive father and thereby father-in-law" (Comm. p. 78). T. L. Thompson contests this on the ground that the brotherly adoption contracts from Nuzi are concerned with the transmission of legal conditions of adoption; in the case of a girl, the purpose is to give her in marriage, not to marry her (BZAW 133 [1974] 230-234). I would add as a further reason that it is very questionable whether a contract of this sort, belonging to a sedentary, city-dwelling people, holds also for migratory groups. But in any case, such an explanation is not necessary; marriage between an uncle and a niece is allowed in the Old Testament and is not unusual.

The names Sarah and Milcah form a pair, deriving from their meaning. They are not proper names in the strict sense, but titles: the princess (or lady) and the queen (same meaning as מַלְכָּה). It is striking that the title of lesser rank is that of Sarah: "This difficulty would disappear were one to accept a Babylonian origin, where *šarratu* means queen and *malkâtu* princess" (H. Gunkel ad. loc.). What is more important, however, is that both names, which are really titles, occur in the context of the moon cult which had a special place both in Ur and Haran (cf. P. Dhorme, RB 37 [1928] 367-385, 481-511). *Šarratu* is the name of the wife of the moon god Sin; *Malkâtu* is a name (or title) of Ishtar, daughter of the moon god. This agreement cannot be accidental, inasmuch as it is a question of a pair of names. The two names are connected with the same names belonging to the Mesopotamian moon cult, though we know nothing more about the path which links them. However, there is no trace at all of the moon cult either in this genealogy or in the narratives which follow it: "There is nothing in the stories which suggests any thought of these gods" (H. Gunkel).

[11:30] The genealogy is elaborated by a remark on one of the people already mentioned. Such elaborations always say something particularly worthy of note, such that can be the subject of a narrative, form the nucleus of a narrative, or refer to a narrative already well known (cf. *Genesis 1–11*, 10-12). A narrative can grow out of a genealogy. Gen. 11:30 is the classical example: Sarah's childlessness is the starting point of several narratives (chs. 15; 16; 17; 18); it is a threat, because it breaks the continuity of the generations, a matter of great importance for a community structured on family lines. The verse is a certain proof that vv. 28-30 come from J; only J elaborates the genealogies in this way.

The verse consists of two sentences with virtually the same meaning. B. Jacob contests this and thinks that the purpose of the first sentence is to say that the marriage was childless, and of the second that Sarah as a wife had to go without children (*Komm.* 1934, 1974[2]). But that does not alter the fact that the two sentences are saying almost the same thing. Moreover, there is the rare form of the last word: וֹלֵד instead of יָלַד, "the only word in Hebrew that begins with וֹ" (B. Jacob). It occurs again as *ketib* in 2 Sam. 6:23, and in the same sentence: the narrative tells that Michal remained childless. The occurrence of the same rare form twice in the same context must catch the attention. There is the same parallelism in the same context, but without the rare form, in Judg. 13:2f.: "she was barren and had no children" and in Is. 54:1: "Sing aloud, O barren woman, who did not bear." It is unlikely that the second sentence is meant to explain the first (so M. S. Seale, ET 67 [1955/56] 333-335). One must also reject the explanation that וֹלֵד is a scribal error (H. Gunkel and others). Rather we encounter in 11:30 the lapidary form of a well known and widespread narrative motif which generally functions as an introduction to a narrative. The sentence serves as the *exposition* of a narrative and acquires additional strength from the literary device of parallelism, which is used not only in poetry, but also in narrative so as to emphasize or underscore a statement.

The sentence in 11:30, therefore, together with its parallels in 2 Sam. 6:23; Judg. 13:2f.; Is. 54:1, is an important witness for the significance of the narrative motif of the infertility of a wife in a variety of different contexts. It also makes comprehensible how such a lapidary formula, used as an introduction to a narrative, preserved an old form for child, וֹלֵד, which was not used later.

[11:31]   A presupposition for the understanding of this verse is that it has the form of an itinerary and as such is an originally independent unit (cf. Intro. 2 B IV, "Itineraries"). Its structure accords with old oral tradition: departure, journey, destination, stopping place. P has used this structure to assert that the ancestors of Abraham came from foreign (pagan) parts to Canaan. Several factors show that it is a secondary itinerary: the tremendous distances, the fact that Haran is not normally on the way from Ur in southern Mesopotamia to Canaan, and that the starting point is a city and the destination a country. It is certain that this itinerary did not arise immediately out of or after a journey described here. It is a later construction that originated a very long time after the event it intends to describe. The individual elements, therefore, can have different origins. P knew the tradition of the nomadic life of Israel's ancestors, which he took up, as well as the way in which it was described; he also knew the old tradition that Abraham's ancestors had come to Canaan from northern Mesopotamia, which he took up and used so as to make Haran a stopping place. He then added a new piece of information to what he had received, independent of this tradition, namely, that the ancestors of Abraham came to Canaan from Ur of the Chaldees (cf. remarks on form, above). This explanation presupposes that the name "Ur of the Chaldees" in v. 28b comes from the redactor responsible for putting 11:27-32 together, thereby adapting v. 28b to v. 31, and that consequently it does not belong to J. It is unlikely that "—of the Chaldees" was attached later. Other contexts in the patriarchal story (e.g., Gen. 24:29-31) confirm that upper Mesopotamia in the region of Haran was the place of origin of the patriarchs. There is no trace of any connection with Ur in the south; there is only the name. This too is probably the reason why the Gk has "land of the Chaldees" in every place where the MT has "Ur of the Chaldees," i.e., אֶרֶץ instead of אוּר. The most probable explanation is that the Gk was interpreting a name which no longer meant anything to it.

Ur.   After Leonard Woolley's work at Ur (*Excavations at Ur. A Record of Twelve Years Work [1922-34]* [1954]) the idea that this great and ancient center of civilization must have been "Abraham's homeland" captured the imagination. It did not occur to anybody that the form of community and life-style of the patriarchs, as known to us from the patriarchal narratives, had no relationship at all to life in a southern Mesopotamian "capital city." No scholar who spoke of Ur as the homeland of the patriarchs thought of this.

Ur, on the lower Euphrates, flourished in the third millennium, particularly in the period of the third dynasty. It was destroyed about 1000 with the overthrow of the dynasty, but retained its importance as a religious and commercial center; it flourished again in the neo-Babylonian period (cf. A. Parrot, *Abraham et son temps*, CAB 14 [1962]). Scholars are unanimous that the city of Ur on the lower Euphrates could only be designated "Ur of the Chaldees" from the time of the rise of the neo-Babylonian empire; but the conclusions which are drawn from this are very different. In the 19th century Ur was identified with Urfa, the ancient Edessa; A. Lods also accepts a city of the same name in upper Mesopotamia (*Israel des origines*. . . [1930; 1949²]). But from the time of A. Dillmann's commentary, and thus long before the excavations, Ur on the Euphrates in southern Mesopotamia, already known from the cuneiform inscriptions, was regarded as the likely place. This became generally acknowledged (W. F. Saggs, *Iraq* 22 [1960] 200-209). The difficulties involved here led to a reawakening of the old explanation pointing in the direction of northern Mesopotamia to the city of Ura, which occurs in a cuneiform text of Hattušili III: "The merchants of the Hittite King came from the city of Ura"; "Merchant men, citizens of the city of Ura" (C. H. Gordon, JNES 17 [1958] 28). Many took over Gordon's thesis, but W. F. Saggs has refuted it in detail.

Some scholars still accept Ur on the southern Euphrates as the place named in Gen. 11:28,31; 15:7, and are of the opinion that it attests a southern Mesopotamian origin for Abraham's ancestors (S. N. Kramer, P. Dhorme, A. Parrot, R. J. Ream, N. M. Sarna, F. Schmidtke in BHH, J. Simons, R. de Vaux with reservations); the majority, however, incline to a northern Mesopotamian origin (E. H. Maly, B. W. Anderson, J. Bright, B. Jacob, J. R. Kupper).

"They came to Haran." Haran is an ancient and well-known city on the left bank of the Belikh, a tributary of the Euphrates; in cuneiform it is *Harrānu(m)*, often mentioned in the Mari texts. Some scholars think that the name is Hurrian (F. M. T. Böhl and others); later it was *karrhä*, today once more Harran. The city belonged to the Mitanni empire, then to the Hittite, and afterwards to the Assyrian. The last Assyrian king fled there, and the last Babylonian king, Nabonidus, favored it.

Haran is mentioned in the context of the patriarchal story in Gen. 11:31,32; 12:4,5; 27:43; 28:10; 29:4; in Gen. 24 it is the city of Nahor, Laban, and Rebecca. Such extensive attestation points to the likelihood that it is the place of origin of Abraham's ancestors. In 11:31 Haran appears merely as a stopping place on the way from Ur to Canaan; this is probably due to the secondary linking of the two traditions.

[11:32] The two traditions come together in the genealogical report of the death of Terah. P is relying here on the older tradition according to which Terah was there his whole life long, and died there; according to the MT he was 205 years old, according to the Sam 145; Abraham would have left Haran for Canaan only after the death of Terah.

Purpose and Thrust

The intention of this first introduction to the patriarchal story is to link it in retrospect with the primeval story and at the same time to sketch in anticipation the frame in which the story of Abraham is to play itself out. The stream of generations which flowed from the creation out into the broad expanse of the history of mankind by virtue of the creation blessing, diverges now into that branch which leads from the father, Abraham, through his descendants to Israel, the people of God. But the introduction also presents the "story of Terah"; one must not forget that Abraham is linked with the history of mankind through Terah, his father. Abraham the father is also Abraham the son; as son of Terah he is one with the wide world of the nations (ch. 10), who all derive from the Creator.

The path through the ages which links Abraham with the primeval story and leads through him into the history of Israel is met in the introduction (Gen. 11:27-32) by the path through the territory which determines the life-style of the patriarchs as that of migrants. This life-style also links him with his own fathers; Abraham's departure is not the first; his father too came from afar. The migration continues right through the patriarchal story, and is to reach its ultimate goal in the promised land, the land which is Israel's own. It is no accident that the patriarchal narrative mentions at the beginning the two great empires which are to determine the history of Israel: Mesopotamia and Egypt. In the introduction to the patriarchal story the way leads from Mesopotamia to Canaan; at the beginning of the story of the people, from Egypt to Canaan; after the exile, from Mesopotamia to Canaan.

This introduction, which consists of genealogy and itinerary, contains only one narrative sentence, the remark about Sarah's barrenness; it forms the bridge to the Abraham narratives. The promise of the child begins here and forms in turn the occasion for the promise motif as a whole. The barrenness of the mother, the promise and birth of the child, go through the whole of the subsequent history; the motif appears again at the beginning of the history of the kings (1 Sam. 1:2), and at the beginning of the Gospel of Luke.

Promise to Abraham
and Migration

Literature

Genesis 12:1-4a (cf. Lit. §4: 5, Promise): K. H. Fahlgren, *Ṣedākā nahestehende und entgegengesetzte Begriffe im AT* (1932), esp. pp. 158-208. L. Rost, "Die Bezeichnungen für Land und Volk im AT," *Fests. O. Procksch* (1934) 125-148 = *Das kleine Credo* (1965) 76-101. G. von Rad, *The Form Critical Problem of the Hexateuch. . .* (1938; 1965; Eng. 1964). C. R. North, *The Old Testament Interpretation of History*, "Genesis 12; 20; 26" (1946[rev.]). C. Lattey, "Vicarious Solidarity in the Old Testament," VT 1 (1951) 267-274. S. N. Fisher, ed., *Social Forces in the Middle East* (1955). J. P. Audet, "Esquisse historique du genre littéraire de la 'bénédiction' juive de l' 'eucharistie' chrétienne," RB 65 (1958) 371-399. J. Scharbert, " 'Fluchen' und 'Segnen' im AT," Bib 39 (1958) 1-26. H. Junker, "Segen als heilsgeschichtliches Motivwort im Alten Testament," *Sacra Pagina* (1959) 548-559. A. Murtonen, "The Use and Meaning of the Words lebārēk and berākāh in the OT," VT 9 (1959) 158-177. R. Martin-Achard, "Israël, peuple sacerdotal," VigChr 18 (1964) 11-28. N. C. Habel, "The Form and Significance of the Call Narratives," ZAW 77 (1965) 297-323. H. Langkammer, "Die Verheissung vom Erbe. Ein Beitrag zur biblischen Sprache," BiLe 8 (1967) 157-165. J. Muilenburg, "The Intercession of the Covenant Mediator (Exodus 33:1a,12-13)," *Words and Meanings*, ed. P. R. Ackroyd–B. Lindars (1968) 159-181. C. Westermann, *Der Segen in der Bibel und im Handeln der Kirche* (1968). D. L. Johnson, *The Nature of Nomadism. A Comparative Study of Pastoral Migrations in Southwestern Asia and Northern Africa* (1969). W. H. Schmidt, *Das erste Gebot. Seine Bedeutung für das AT* (1969). H. P. Müller, *Ursprünge und Strukturen alttestamentlicher Eschatologie*, BZAW 109 (1969), esp. pp. 132-171. S. I. Rudenko, *Studien über das Nomadentum*, "Viehwirtschaft und Hirtenkultur," ed. H. Földes (1969) 15-32. L. Diez Merino, "La vocación de Abraham (Gen. 12:1-4a). La vocación de Abraham en el AT, NT y tradición Judia Antigua," CTom 97 (1970) 75-145. W. H. Eckert–N. P. Levinson–M. Stöhr, eds., *Jüdisches Volk—gelobtes Land. Die biblischen Landverheissungen als Problem des jüdischen Selbstverständnisses und der christlichen Theologie* (1970). G. Wehmeier, *Der Segen im AT. Eine semasiologische Untersuchung der Wurzel brk* (Diss. Basel, 1970). O. Steck, "Genesis 12:1-3 und die Urgeschichte des Jahwisten," *Fests. G. von Rad* (1971) 525-554. G. W. Coats, "An Exposition for the Wilderness Traditions," VT 22 (1972) 288-295. W. L. Holladay, "The Covenant With the Patriarchs Overturned: Jeremiah's Intention in 'Terror on Every Side' (Jer. 20:1-6)," JBL 91 (1972) 305-320. B. Spooner, "The Status of Nomadism as a Cultural Phenomenon in the Middle East," *Perspectives on Nomadism*, ed. W. Irons (1972) 122-131. J. Loza, "Exode XXXII et la rédaction JE," VT 23 (1973) 31-55. G. del Olmo Lete, "La vocacion del lider en el Antiguo Israel. Cap. 1: La vocacion de Abrahám (Gen. 12:1-9)," *Bibliotheca Salmanticensis* III,2 (1973) 53-64. J. Scharbert, "Die Geschichte der bārûk-Formel," BZ NF 17 (1973) 1-28. T. C. Vriezen, "Bemerkungen zu Genesis

12:1-7,'' *Fests. F. M. T. Böhl* (1973) 380-392. G. Wehmeier, ''The Theme 'Blessing for the Nations' in the Promise to the Patriarchs and in Prophetical Literature,'' *Bangalore Theol. Forum* 6 (1974) 1-13. E. Ruprecht, ''Der traditionsgeschichtliche Hintergrund der einzelnen Elemente von Genesis xii 2-3,'' VT 29 (1979) 444-464.

Genesis 12:1: L. Rost, *Die Vorstufen von Kirche und Synagoge im AT*, BWANT 4:24 (1938). D. N. Freedman, ''Notes on Genesis,'' ZAW 64 (1952) 190-194. D. F. Rauber, ''Literary Values in the Bible. The Book of Ruth,'' JBL 89 (1970) 27-37. R. Tournay, ''Abraham et le Cantique des Cantiques,'' VT 25 (1975) 544-552.

Genesis 12:2: E. König, *Stilistik, Rhetorik, Poetik in Bezug auf die biblische Literatur komparativisch dargestellt* (1900). W. E. Müller–H. D. Preuss, *Die Vorstellung vom Rest im Alten Testament* (1939; 1973²). W. M. Roth, ''The Anonymity of the Suffering Servant,'' JBL 83 (1964) 171-179. W. H. P. Römer, *Sumerische ''Königshymnen'' der Isinzeit*, (Diss.) OrAnt 13 (1965). C. Westermann, ''Der Weg der Verheissung durch das Alte Testament,'' ThB 55 (1974) 230-249.

Genesis 12:3: J. C. K. von Hofmann, *Weissagung und Erfüllung* (1841-1844). E. W. Hengstenberg, *Geschichte des Reiches Gottes unter dem Alten Bunde*, I (1869). R. Martin-Achard, *Israël et les nations. La perspective missionaire de l'AT*, Cahiers Théol. 42 (1959). H. C. Brichto, *The Problem of ''Curse'' in the Hebrew Bible*, JBL Monogr. Ser. 13 (1963). B. Albrektson, *History and the Gods. An Essay of the Idea of Historical Events as Divine Manifestations in the Ancient Near East and in Israel*, Coniectanea Biblica, OT Ser. I (1967). W. Schottroff, WMANT 30 (1969) 36-44, 141, 170. W. Speyer, ''Fluch,'' RAC VII (1969) 1160-1288. T. C. Vriezen, ''Erwägungen zu Amos 3:2,'' *Fests. K. Galling* (1970) 255-258. S. B. Parker, ''The Marriage Blessing in Israelite and Ugaritic Literature,'' JBL 95 (1976) 23-30.

Genesis 12:5: F. Schmidtke, *Die Einwanderung Israels in Kanaan* (1933). F. A. Munch, ''Verwandtschaft und Lokalität in der Gruppenbildung der israelitischen Hebräer,'' KZS 12 (1960) 438-440.

Genesis 12:6: Lit. §§1, C, III, 3e: F. Stummer, '' 'Convallis Mambre' und Verwandtes. Ein Beitrag zur Erklärung der Vulgata,'' JPOS 12 (1932) 6-21. K. Möhlenbrink, ''Sichem als altpalästinische Königsstadt,'' ChW 10 (1934) 125-134. Z. Mayani, *L'arbre sacré et le rite de l'alliance chez les anciens Sémites* (1935). A. Alt, ''Die Wallfahrt von Sichem nach Bethel,'' *Fests. A. von Bulmerincq* (1938) 218-230 = K Schr I (1953) 79-88. E. Burrows, ''Note on Moreh, Gen XII 6 and Moriah, Gen XXII 2,'' JThS 41 (1940) 152-161. W. J. Harrelson, *The City of Shechem* (Diss. New York, 1953). C. A. Keller, ''Über einige alttestamentliche Heiligtumslegenden I,'' ZAW 67 (1955) 141-168; 68 (1956) 85-97. W. L. Moran, ''Mari, Notes on the Execration Text,'' Or 26 (1957) 339-345; 28 (1959) 213-214. J. Lindblom, ''Theopanies in Holy Places in the Hebrew Religion,'' HUCA 32 (1961) 91-106. W. L. Reed, ''Shechem,'' IDB IV (1962) 313-315. G. E. Wright, *Shechem* (1965). E. F. Campbell–G. E. Wright, ''Tribal League Shrines in Amman and Shechem,'' BA 32 (1969) 104-116. S. Yeivin, ''The Patriarchs in the Land of Canaan,'' *The World History of the Jewish People* II (1960) 201-218. G. R. H. Wright, ''Shechem and League Shrines,'' VT 21 (1971) 572-603. M. Girard, *Louange Cosmique. Bible et animisme* (1973). B. Couroyer, ''Les Aamou-Hyksôs,'' RB 81 (1974) 321-354, 481-523. K. Jaroš, *Die Stellung des Elohisten zur kanaanäischen Religion*, OrBiOr 4 (1974). M. Liverani, ''Le Chêne de Sherdanu,'' VT 27 (1977) 212-216.

Genesis 12:7: W. W. Graf Baudissin, *''Gott schauen'' in der alttestamentlichen Religion*, ARW 18 (1915; 1969²) 173-239. R. M. Dussaud, *Les origines Canaanéennes du sacrifice Israélite* (1921²; 1941³). K. Galling, *Der Altar in den Kulturen des Alten Orients. Eine archäologische Studie* (1925). A. Parrot, ''Autels et installations cultuelles à Mari,'' VT.S 1 (1953) 112-119. G. Fohrer, ''Zum Text von Jes XLI:8-13,'' VT 5 (1955) 239-249. R. de Vaux, *Ancient Israel* (1958; Eng. 1962). J. Barr, ''Theophany and Anthropomorphism in the OT,'' VT.S 7 (1960) 31-38. R. Rendttorff, '' 'Offenbarung' im AT,'' ThLZ 85 (1960) 833-835. F. Schnutenhaus, ''Das Kommen und Erscheinen Gottes im AT,'' ZAW 76 (1964) 1-22. H. Mölle, *Das ''Erscheinen Gottes'' im Pentateuch. Ein literaturwissenschaftlicher Beitrag zur alttestamentlichen Exegese*, Europ. Hochschulschr. XXIII (1973). W. H. Schmidt, ''Ausprägungen des Bilderverbots? Zur Sichtbarkeit und Vorstellbarkeit Gottes im AT,'' *Fests G. Friedrich* (1973) 25-34. P. H. Vaughan, *The Meaning of 'bâmâ' in the OT. A*

Study of Etymological, Textual and Archaeological Evidence, SOTS Mono. Ser. 3 (1974).

Genesis 12:8: J. Marquet-Krause, *Les fouilles de 'Ay (Et-Tell), 1933-1935*, 2 vols. (1949). H. A. Brongers, "Bešēm Jhwh," NThT 11 (1956/57) 401-416; "Die Wendung bešēm jhwh im AT," ZAW 77 (1965) 1-20. J. A. Callaway, "New Evidence on the Conquest of 'Ai," JBL 87 (1968) 312-320. G. E. Wright, "The Significance of Ai in the Third Millennium B.C.," *Fests. K. Galling* (1970) 299-320. R. Amiran, "Reflections on the Identification of the Deity at the EB II and EB III Temples of Ai," BASOR 208 (1972) 9-13.

Text

12:1   Yahweh said to Abram: Go[a] from your land and your kinsmen and your father's house to the land which I will show you.[b]

2   I will make[a] you into a great people and I will bless you and make your name great so that you will be[b] a blessing.[c]

3   I will bless[a] those who bless you and execrate[b] those who curse[c] you. And all the families of the earth are to bless themselves[d] in you.

4   And Abram went[a] as Yahweh told him and Lot went with him. Abraham was seventy-five years[b] old when he left Haran.

5   And Abram[a] took Sarai his wife and Lot his nephew all that they had acquired and the dependents that had become theirs in Haran, and set out for the land of Canaan, and arrived there [in Canaan].

6   And Abram continued on through the land[a] to the sanctuary of Shechem, the terebinth-tree of Moreh.[b,c] At that time the Canaanites were in the land.

7   Yahweh appeared to Abram and said:[a] I give this land to your descendants. So he[b] built an altar there to Yahweh who had appeared[c] to him.

8   He went on from there to the hill country[a] east of Bethel, and pitched[b] his tent,[c] with Bethel on the west and Ai on the east,[d] and built an altar there to Yahweh, and called on[e] the name of Yahweh.

9   So Abram moved by stages[a] towards the Negev.

1a   Ethical dative (Ges-K §119s; Brockelmann, *Grundriss* 242f.).   **b**   A causative with basic transitive stems can take two objects (Ges-K §121c; BrSynt §94a).
2a   וְ with the imperat. or imperf. after verbal sentences serves to indicate consequence (W. Schreiner, *Grammatik des biblischen Hebräisch* [1974], 53, 1.3.2; Joüon, *Gramm.* [1947], 116 b. f. h).   **b**   Gk reads εὐλογητός, Vg *benedictus*, Targ and Syr מְבֹרָךְ; but such a modification fails to appreciate "the power of bold poetic language" (Ges-K §141d).   **c**   Exception (Ges-K §63q). The imper. with *waw copulative* "frequently expresses also a consequence which is to be expected with certainty" (Ges-K §110i).
3a   Sam reads וְאֲבָרֵךְ.   **b**   Some Mss and versions (Gk and Vg) read the plural; so too H. Gunkel.   **c**   The word order Verb/Obj—Obj/Verb is frequent in Hebrew (BrSynt 138 = Brockelmann, *Grundriss*, 317d; cf. also B. Jacob, Comm., 337f.).   **d**   On the perf. consec. as a consequence after sentences in the imperf., cf. Joüon 119c,i,j; H. W. Wolff refers to Gen. 31:44; Amos 1:2; Joel 4:18b.
4a   Syr reads וַיַּעַשׂ.   **b**   "Numerals compounded of tens and units (like 21, 62) take the object numbered either *after* them in the singular or *before* them in the plural" (Ges-K §134h).
5a   Vg omits אברם.
6a   Gk adds לָאָרְכָּהּ; Vg reads *venirent in eam*.   **b**   Targ reads מישרי מורה.   **c**   Gk has τὴν ὑψηλήν, Syr ממרא.
7a   Gk adds αὐτῷ; Sam and Syr לו; Vg *eo*.   **b**   Gk adds Ἀβραμ.   **c**   The participle is sometimes used as a predicate to represent past actions or states in independent noun-clauses (Ges-K §116o).
8a   Old accus. ending expressing direction towards a goal (BrSynt §89; Brockelmann,

Grundriss 197e).   **b** Gk adds ἐκεῖ, Vg *ibi*.   **c** אהלה according to Ges-K §91e, an incorrect form for the suffix of the 3rd pers; Sam reads אהלו.   **d** Brockelmann, *Grundriss* 321b: asyndetic noun clause; Ges-K §156c: circumstantial noun clause.   **e** "בְ is not used instrumentally, but expresses the close relationship be-tween the caller and the one called upon," C.J. Labuchagne THAT II, 673.

9a "The idea of long *continuance* is very frequently expressed by the verb הלך, to go, along with its infinitive absolute," Ges-K §113u.

Form

The story of Abraham has two introductions. The one, 11:27-32, consisting of genealogical material with some itinerary notes, serves as a transition. It is contin-ued in 12:4a, which forms a conclusion to 12:1-3. The genealogical material, 12:4b-5 (P), appears in very much the same way as in 11:27-32; vv. 5c (P and J) and 6-9 (J) report Abraham's movements in Canaan, v. 9 serving as a transition to the narrative in 12:10-20. The other introduction is Gen. 12:1-3 (or 1-4a), and is of a very different kind. It too serves as a transition, but takes its theological orien-tation from the primeval story as a whole, while bracketing the story of the patri-archs and the history of the people (G. von Rad). It consists of a command to de-part joined to a promise; v. 4a reports its execution. The whole emphasis then lies on the promise in vv. 2-3 where J, looking back on Gen. 2–11, shapes the introit to the story of the patriarchs.

These two introductions are joined together in such a way as to form a co-herent account which reaches from 11:27 to 12:9. Gen. 11:27 is a new beginning, the history of Terah. Gen. 12:1, on the contrary, is a sentence in context, presup-posed both by ויאמר and the name, Abraham. The theological introduction, 12:1-3, is built into the itinerary account of which it becomes an (enlarged) con-stituent part by means of the command to depart, 12:1, and its execution in v. 4a. Gen. 12:1-9, which is closely linked with 11:27-32 has two parts: 12:1-4a (with 5c: arrival in Canaan; see Comm. below) and vv. 4b-9.

There is virtual unanimity in attributing only vv. 4b-5 to P; all the rest is from J. The last sentence of v. 5, "and they arrived in Canaan," is common to P and J. The insertion of vv. 4b-5 by P is a continuation of 11:31-32(?), and a pres-entation of Abraham's departure from Haran to Canaan parallel to J. V. 4a (J) is continued in v. 6 (J). The whole of vv. 4a-9 is colored by details about the jour-ney. The only episodes on the way are v. 7 (appearance—promise—building of an altar) and v. 8 (building of an altar—invocation). This succession of journeys and stopping places presents Abraham's life as it really was. The two episodes in vv. 7, 8c indicate that Abraham's relationship with God is intimately linked with this journey and cannot be detached from it.

Hitherto, exegesis has put all the emphasis on 12:1-3, without noticing how, on the one hand, 12:1-4a has been fitted into the broader context of 11:27–12:9, and on the other, 12:1-4a has been marked off by vv. 1 and 4a as a constituent part of Abraham's journey. When vv. 1-3 were detached from their context and overemphasized, vv. 6-9 lost all meaning; they were a small appendix that offered little to start with. The exegesis of the whole of the Abraham story was thereby diverted: what Abraham's life really was, and what really happened between him and God, receded behind a theological explanation detached from this reality. But it is the whole text that requires attention: each part, vv. 1-3 and vv. 6-9, has something important to say on the subject of Abraham.

Setting

It is not possible to determine the setting in which 12:1-9 originated as a unit and was passed on, because the text is not a unity. The determination of the setting of 12:1-3 depends on whether 12:1-4a is a literary construction independent of any available traditional elements, or whether the command together with the promise is an older block (see Comm. below). In the latter case, the basic framework of vv. 1-4a is rooted in traditions from the patriarchal period; 12:1-4a, in the shape in which it lies before us, has its setting in the overall literary plan of J, in which it serves as a link passage. Individual elements in the promise to which J gave shape in vv. 1-3 come from different areas; it can be demonstrated with certainty that a promise originally meant for the king comes from the court protocol.

Nor can any single setting be given for 12:6-9. The dominant element is the itinerary, consisting of sentences loosely tacked together, which can be altered in the course of tradition. The simplest form of itinerary structure is the mere progression from one stopping place to the next with the occasional episode sketched in a few brief sentences; it is characteristic of the nomadic life-style and can go back to the patriarchal period. One must reckon here with alterations in the course of tradition. It is certain that this form had a setting in life required by the nomadic life-style of groups structured on family lines; it was the formula in which the journeys of the group and its stopping places were handed down. The history of the group was preserved on the one side in genealogies, on the other in itineraries.

When the nomadic life-style ceased, the itineraries lived on in accounts of campaigns, expeditions of kings and commercial enterprises. R. C. Culley shows how the original itinerary perseveres right up to the present (VT 13 [1963] 113-125; *Fests. F. V. Winnett* [1972] 102-116).

Commentary

[12:1-4a]   Gen. 12:1-4a is an introit to the story of the patriarchs, shaped by J in such a way as to link the patriarchal with the primeval story (v. 3b "all the families of the earth"), and at the same time to point beyond it to the history of the people of Israel (v. 2b "into a great people"). The language is virtually rhythmic (cf. *Genesis 1–11*, Comm. on 2:23), the structure of the few sentences extremely concentrated and compact.

Vv. 1a and 4a form the frame: Yahweh commands and Abraham carries out the command. Yahweh's introductory address is divided into a command (v. 1b) and the promise which is linked with it (vv. 2-3). The emphasis is on the promise: it is heavily elaborated so as almost to burst the simple structure. (One can experiment by substituting for vv. 2-3 the simple assurance, "I will be with you." The text of vv. 1-4a as a whole has then a different ring, because the individual parts are of equal weight.) The intention of the author is clear from the stress which he puts on the promise. There is a progression: in v. 2 the promise of blessing is made to Abraham; in v. 3a it goes beyond Abraham to those with whom he comes in contact; in v. 3b it affects the whole of mankind.

Though the language of the text is as simple and clear as its division, it has been understood very differently. One reason for this is that the author, J, has compressed such basic and far-reaching material into so few words. Consequently there are ever new attempts to explain it.

Von Rad's interpretation, first proposed in 1938 (*The Form Critical Problem. . .* [1938; Eng. 1964]) and later in further detail in his commentary and theology, remained basic and determinative for a long time. It followed H. Gunkel, who saw in vv. 1-3 a free construction of the Yahwist. The result was a purely literary-theological explanation. The only question raised was what J wanted to express by such a theological construct, what he wanted to say to his generation (so especially,H. W. Wolff [1964]; Interp. 20 [1966] 131-158). This basic understanding yielded important insights into the meaning of the passage; it has its limitations, however, in that it did not pay sufficient attention to the literary and form-critical context.

H. Gunkel, G. von Rad, and their followers did not consider the parallels to 12:1-4a which are to be found in the patriarchal story. Gen. 46:1-5a has a similar structure: an address by God with a command to depart (vv. 2-3), linked with a promise (vv. 3b-4, the same words: "I will make you into a great people") and the execution of the command (v. 5a). In 26:1-3 Isaac receives the command to remain in the land, and so not to depart, linked with a promise; cf. also 31:3; 32:10. These parallels show that there was already, previous to 12:1-4a, a definite structure: it consisted of a command by God to one of the patriarchs to depart, proceed further, or remain, and a promise linked with it or giving the reason for it, followed by the execution of the command. It is in complete accord with the life-style of the patriarchs and their relationship to God for the father of a nomadic group to receive a command from the God of the father together with a promise, and to carry it out (cf. V. Maag, SThU 28 [1958] 2-28; VT.S 7 [1959/60] 129-153). Also, if J strongly interfered with the old form by modifying and broadening the promise, then the possibility cannot be contested that this pattern—which can reach back to the patriarchal period—stands behind 12:1-4.

When the promise was understood independently of its context and as the only important part of 12:1-3, it was easy to identify "Abraham" with Israel (e.g., H. W. Wolff, op. cit.; J. Muilenburg, Interp. 19 [1965] 387-398). But it is very unlikely that Abraham is meant in vv. 1 and 4a, and Israel in vv. 2-3. However, if there are two levels in 12:1-4a, then it becomes possible to understand the text, including the promise in vv. 2-3, from its context between 11:27-32 and 12:4b-9. He who receives the promise is then the same Abraham of whom these two passages speak. What is promised to Abraham points to the *future* Israel. It is the blessing that sheltered and accompanied Abraham, the effects of which are to extend to the Israel of the monarchy and beyond that to all the families of the earth.

[12:1a] The sentence, "Yahweh said to Abraham," follows immediately on 11:30 (J). It is not a beginning, but part of the course of the narrative. The Abraham story begins with the genealogy (11:27-32, J and P); 12:1a shows how an event emerges from a genealogy. Though v. 1a introduces what follows, it is not a real introductory sentence, but a stylization (so H. Gunkel ad. loc.). There is no account of a revelation; the stylization shows that J does not intend to narrate an event, but to pass on a divine oracle whose situation he leaves open, thus enabling it to speak on two levels: he reshapes an oracle once given to Abraham in such a way as to allow it to serve as an introit to the Abraham story.

[12:1b] Yahweh commands Abraham to leave the place where he is and go to a land which he will show him. Abraham is in the region of Haran (11:27-32; so A. Dillmann, Comm., ad loc.); the land which Yahweh will show him is Canaan (Gen. 12:5b,6-9). This half-verse will be misunderstood if considered in isolation. It is part of an action which the structure of 12:1-4a makes clear (see above: Form). One must distinguish, therefore, between the purpose of v. 1b in Abraham's time and the meaning which it acquired from J. In the former it was the instruction of the God of the fathers in a crisis situation, ordering the group to set out for another territory. It was aimed solely at rescuing the group from or preserving it in the crisis. It is a misunderstanding of what is meant here to consider the command to depart as a ''difficult injunction'' (O. Procksch), and to say that Abraham ''had to tear himself away from his homeland with a heavy heart'' (H. Holzinger; likewise many others) is to misunderstand the intent. Some exegetes go even further and speak of a ''test of faith'' (so H. Gunkel, J. Skinner), or of a break with the ancestors and ancestral traditions (B. Jacob; further spun out in the older Jewish exegesis). All these explanations make the serious mistake of understanding Abraham in the context of a sedentary life-style (H. Gunkel: ''he is to cut himself off from homeland, ancestry, family. . ... The ancient lives in his homeland under the security and protection of large and small groups''). But the patriarchs did not have the concept of ''homeland'' in our sense; this became possible only with sedentary life. They could understand the instruction of their God to depart for a land which he would show them only as the offer of a saving hand.

One must distinguish between this and the later meaning which J gave to the verse. Gen. 12:1b cannot be the literal report from the patriarchal period of a divine command to set out, as the formulation shows (this is against V. Maag, who understands the words as an order coming directly from this era). The description of the three circles from which Abraham is summoned is the language of the narrator, not of the divine oracle. It is the language of the sedentary speaking in a triple paraphrase of Abraham's ''homeland'' (''your land and your kinsmen and your father's house''). Neither here nor in the reference to the as yet unnamed and unknown goal does J speak merely of Abraham, but of the history which he now initiates. All this is in accord with the intent of his introit, which echoes the exodus as it reaches out from the patriarchal story to the history of the people, a history also begun with a command from God to depart for an unknown land. J wants to remind the now sedentary people that God's history with them began with a summons, a call into the strange unknown, just as with the patriarchs. One must distinguish carefully between this summons and the call of an individual (e.g., a prophet) which presupposes a larger group among whom and for whom he is called. Gen. 12:1 offers no grounds for speaking of the ''call of Abraham'' (many commentaries give the passage this title).

[12:2-3]   The promise linked with the command to depart is addressed to Abraham, but has a significance reaching far beyond him. J has replaced the promise which corresponds to the situation and accords with the command addressed to the patriarchs in the patriarchal period by one covering both patriarchs and Israel; thus was formed the introit to the patriarchal story. Since the contribution of G. von Rad, the key function of the promise in 12:1-3 has been recognized and studies have proceeded accordingly. R. Kilian goes even further (BBB 24 [1966]); he sees a ''basic layer'' in 12:1-9, namely, vv. 1,4a,6a,7,8, which have been elaborated by J; the promise in vv. 2-3 is part of the elaboration. One must agree with Kilian that vv. 2-3 received their shape from J; but to make a literary separation of them is to misunderstand the structure of 12:1-4a. The parallel passages cited above show that a promise is a necessary concomitant of the command in v. 1, which is carried out in v. 4a. J has reshaped the promise, as well as the command to depart (v. 1).

The promise is partitioned very carefully in accordance with its function as the introit to the patriarchal story, and the partition determines the understanding, as the explanations already given show. It consists of three parts: vv. 2, 3a, and 3b. The root ברך, to bless, blessing, gives the tone; it occurs five times in all, twice in each of the first two parts, and once in the third, and is obviously the key word. There is a gradual progression: v. 2 speaks only of Abraham, v. 3a of the effect of the blessing on those who accept him, v. 3b of the effect of the blessing which accompanies him on all the families of the earth. One can say that "the syntactical progression hastens on to the final sentence"; but it is questionable whether one can conclude, "The kerygma of J can be discerned in its precise form only in 12:3b" (H. W. Wolff). The three parts show a broadening of the circle which the Abraham blessing affects; one can see here a progression; but there is no progression in the promise as such. One could also say that the promise has been fully expressed in the first part, which is also the most elaborately developed, and that the second and third parts are explanatory. However, it is better in so compressed an oracle to allow each individual sentence its meaning for the whole.

[12:2]   V. 2 consists of four sentences. They are arranged on the base of the actual promise of blessing, ואברכך, "I will bless you" (the second sentence); everything else is included in it. The immediate effect of the blessing promised to Abraham is that he will become a great people and his name will be great (the first and third sentences of v. 2). Both as a verb and a noun the root ברך means the power of fertility, growth, success (bestowed). J. Pedersen was the first to show that blessing in the Old Testament, both verb and noun, has an independent theological meaning (*Israel: Its Life and Culture* [1926; 1946[2]] 182-212); C. Westermann referred to this in *Segen in der Bibel. . .* (1968); G. Wehmeier (*Bangalore Theol. Forum* 6 [1974] 1-13) and J. Scharbert (Bib 39 [1958] 1-26) have made comprehensive studies of the root. What is decisive for the meaning of the word in the Old Testament is that God's blessing does not show its effects in individual acts and deeds, but in a continual process.

The reason why the sentence, "I will bless you," does not stand at the beginning is probably due to the overarching function of 12:1-3. The promise is directed to Israel; it is the basis of the people's greatness; and this is to be stated at the beginning. ואברכך: we have here an original construction of J (cf. C. Westermann, ThB 24 [1974] 230-249). Blessing is not of its nature a historical thing. It can be given to anyone, as in Gen. 27. However, it need not, as originally understood, have in view some future point in time; that is, it need not be a promise. In 12:1-3 J links blessing and history, and thereby links the story of the patriarchs with the history of the people. Similarly H. W. Wolff: "If blessing was understood in the old family union as a pronouncement of power immediately effective, it is here a promise directed to the future. 'Blessing' becomes the catchword of the whole of Israel's history" ("The Kerygma. . .").

The effect of the blessing is that Abraham becomes a great people. This sentence expresses in the clearest possible way that J is looking beyond the history of the patriarchs Abraham, Isaac, and Jacob into the future; the promise can apply to the people of Israel only at the height of its prosperity. The word גוי is a political concept; עם really designates kinship (L. Rost, *Das kleine Credo* [1934, 1965] 76-101). This makes it even clearer that J means the politically organized people in the period of the monarchy. The other effect of the blessing, "I will make your name great," must be meant in exactly the same way; it does not mean that Abraham will be renowned some time later, but that the great people which has grown out of the blessing given to him will also be a people of renown. Greatness and name (renown) go together; both will belong to Israel. The formulation of a promise made to Abraham, but reaching fulfillment only in the period of the monarchy, is best thought of in the era of David-Solomon, that is, at the time of the Yahwist. This finds confirmation in the fact that the phrase "great name" is attributed only to the king elsewhere in the Old Testament: ". . .I have destroyed all the enemies in your path. I will make for you a great name like the name of the great ones of the earth" (2 Sam. 7:9: see also 2 Sam. 8:13; 1 Kings 1:47). It follows the court language outside Israel both in Mesopotamia and Egypt, e.g., in a Sumerian hymn to Iddindagan: "Thy exalted name is (renowned) in the land of Sumer, thy name shines forth to the limits of the heavens" (W. H. Ph. Römer [Diss.], OrAnt 13 [1965]); E. Ruprecht cites this example and others (VT 29 [1979] 444-464; cf. C. Westermann, ThB 55 [1974] 291-308). The two effects of the blessing, "I will make you into a great people and I will make your name great," are one of the clearest links between the story of the patriarchs and the history of Israel in Gen. 12–50.

The fourth sentence, "and you are to be a blessing," is very closely linked with the main sentence, "I will bless you." The blessing promised to Abraham has two effects: on Abraham himself, in the history of Israel (great people, great name), and on the people with whom he comes in contact: "and you are to be a blessing." Because Abraham is blessed, he can also become a blessing for others; this is explicated in v. 3a and v. 3b. It has often been proposed that the striking imperative, "and be," should be vocalized as הָיָה (J. Skinner and others); the perfect would then have to refer to the name: "it (the name) is to be a blessing," conforming with v. 3b. This is possible; but the MT is better because it expresses so much more closely the effects of the blessing: on Abraham himself and through him on others (so too G. Wehmeier). J thereby assumes very skillfully into his historical promise of blessing what is characteristic of the nonhistorically conditioned concept of blessing. The story of Jacob and Laban shows how the blessing granted to Jacob also affects Laban; it is a power which is effective on the environment through and beyond the one blessed. J is saying in his promise of blessing: the blessing granted to Abraham is to have its effects on others beyond him, and particularly in the history of Israel.

[12:3] The effects of the blessing beyond Abraham are explicated in the two parts of v. 3. The first is two-sided and has to do with the blessing that is to continue to be effective in the story of Abraham's posterity. In v. 2 the blessing brings about progression (greatness and renown); in v. 3a, security (protection): "I will bless those who bless you, and execrate (bring low) those who curse you." The attitude of others towards Abraham is to determine the attitude of God towards them. Each will receive blessing or curse in accordance with his attitude towards Abraham. J has taken over an already stereotyped phrase; the chiasmus shows the fixed form. One must distinguish here two stages. The older is found in Gen. 27:29 and Num. 24:9; both are exact parallels to Gen. 12:3a because there too the sentences belong to a blessing pronouncement consisting of several parts: "Blessed be every one who blesses you, and cursed be every one who curses you" (Num. 24:9); "A curse upon those who curse you, a blessing on those who

bless you'' (Gen. 27:29). In both places this sentence has the same function as in
12:3a: it is an assurance of protection for the one to whom the blessing is spoken.
The form is different in that it is impersonal, without God as subject; it has its
roots in magical thinking; once the curse or blessing is pronounced it is effective
of itself. This old protection formula is altered in 12:3a so as to make it personal
and accord with the introductory word in v. 2: ''I will bless you.'' J changes the
automatically effective blessing into a promise of blessing (the protection formulas advanced by T. C. Vriezen, *De Literatur van Oude-Israel* [1974[4]]; F. C.
Fensham, VT 13 [1963] 133-143; and W. Schottroff, WMANT 30 [1969] from
the Hittite vassal treaties, ''To the enemy of my Lord I am hostile [and] with the
friends of my Lord [I am] friendly'' [Fensham 136f.], are not real parallels.)
When one considers the two stages of this protection formula, then it is clear, as
Gen. 27:29 and Num. 24:9 show, that only the older can belong to the period before the constitution of the state. It was J who reshaped the formula, made Yahweh the active party and related Yahweh's action to Abraham's posterity in the
history of Israel. Yahweh thus stands on the side of his people and protects them
while intervening against their enemies. There is on the contrary no mention of
any intervention of the God of the fathers against enemies in the promise of presence in the patriarchal period.

[12:3b] ''And all the families of the earth are to bless themselves in you.''

One can only sketch briefly here the long discussion about the translation of נברכו
as it continues to sway now one way, now another. The Gk understood נברכו in the passive
sense and translated it by ἐνευλογηθήσονται. This was taken over by Vg, Targ, Sir.
44:21, the New Testament (Rev. 3:25; Gal. 3:8), and, by and large, by the whole ecclesias-
tical exegesis ''inasmuch as. . . the statement was referred to the communication of salvation which went forth from Abraham's posterity to the nations'' (A. Dillmann, ad. loc.).
Scholarly exegesis since Rashi favored predominantly the reflexive meaning, though E.
W. Hengstenberg (*Geschichte des Reiches Gottes.* . . [1869]) and J. C. K. von Hoffmann
(*Weissagung und Erfüllung* [1841-44]) adhered to the passive. F. Delitzsch, A. Dillmann,
H. Gunkel, H. Holzinger, J. Skinner translate reflexively and give this version a firm base.
Only O. Procksch diverges and translates in a receptive sense, ''are to find blessing in
you.'' G. von Rad goes even further in this direction and comes back to the passive translation. This constant change of direction indicates an uncertainty which has not yet been
overcome. J. Schreiner, moving in the direction of O. Procksch, translates, ''so that in you
they are able to gain blessing'' (BZ 6 [1962] 1-31); similarly H. W. Wolff (''win a blessing''), G. Wehmeier, and A. de Pury. On the other hand J. Muilenburg, J. Scharbert, and
T. C. Vriezen retain the passive.

The uncertainty reveals itself further when G. von Rad thinks that the universal salvific meaning of v. 3 demands the passive, while J. Scharbert thinks that it is quite compatible with the reflexive.

The same uncertainty recurs when assessing the parallels to v. 3b: niph. in Gen.
18:18; 28:14; hitp. in Gen. 22:18; 26:4; outside Genesis, Ps. 72:17 (referring to the king)
and Jer. 4:2 (referring to Israel). The traditio-historical relationship of these passages has
not yet been clarified. H. W. Wolff considers it very important that this sentence, which he
thinks contains the real message of J, occurs here for the first time: ''We have no proof that
this sentence was ever expressed in this way before''; J. Scharbert, on the other hand,
maintains that Gen. 28:14 is older: ''J found the sentence already in the Jacob-Bethel tradition.'' G. Wehmeier holds that the niph. sentences are older and the hitp. are an attenua-
tion; but this is very questionable because in the two late passages there is a niph. (Gen.
18:18) and a hitp. (Gen. 22:18). The parallels in Genesis are so alike (all are linked with the
promise of increase) that once again one must agree with F. Delitzsch that the niph. and
hitp. have the same meaning in this group of passages. The parallel in Ps. 72:17, a royal

psalm, is important: "all the nations of the earth [Gk] are to bless themselves in him [hitp.], all peoples are to praise him with joy." The reflexive meaning is certain here (so too A. Dillmann and G. Wehmeier); it is supported by the parallel sentence. This parallel is important also because it shows how v. 3b, just as v. 2, is in accord with talk about the king; here too (Ps. 72:17a) the prayer for the name of the king precedes. Together with Jer. 4:2 it confirms the reflexive meaning. However, the last word has not yet been spoken.

O. Procksch's middle (receptive) and G. von Rad's passive translation were theologically conditioned; the reflexive translation seemed inadequate for the universal salvific meaning of the sentence. But this opinion is without foundation, as A. Dillmann and F. Delitzsch had already seen. In fact, the reflexive translation is saying no less than the passive or receptive. When "the families of the earth bless" themselves "in Abraham," i.e., call a blessing on themselves under the invocation of his name (as in Ps. 72:17, and even more clearly in Gen. 48:20), then the obvious presupposition is that they receive the blessing. Where one blesses oneself with the name of Abraham, blessing is actually bestowed and received. Where the name of Abraham is spoken in a prayer for blessing, the blessing of Abraham streams forth; it knows no bounds and reaches all the families of the earth. There is then no opposition in content between the passive and reflexive translation (so too G. von Rad, "The Form Critical Problem. . ." n. 99). The reflexive translation is to be preferred because it is philologically more probable (cf. Ps. 72:17) and more concrete (Gen. 48:20); but the niph. in v. 3b is to be understood in the broader sense which includes the concrete fact of being blessed. The controversy then is otiose, and one must agree with T. C. Vriezen ". . . that the plurality of meaning in v. 3b ought to be recognized" (*Fests. F. M. T. Böhl* [1973] 380-392). In any case, what 12:3b is saying is this: God's action proclaimed in the promise to Abraham is not limited to him and his posterity, but reaches its goal only when it includes all the families of the earth.

[12:4a] Abraham follows the command to depart. The introit to the patriarchal story is finished with 12:1-3; it merges into the itinerary which gives the tone to the following verses; v. 4a is no longer concerned with Israel, but only with the man Abraham. The path on which he now sets his feet is that of the nomad shepherd, and one finds there no trace of the future greatness proclaimed for his posterity. If one understands the command to depart as the instruction of the God of the fathers, the guiding God, which is intended to protect Abraham in a crisis situation, then he must follow it; his life is at stake. The commentaries here laud Abraham's obedience, at times in too fulsome a way (F. Delitzsch, H. Gunkel, O. Procksch, A. Dillmann, B. Jacob, G. von Rad, and others); but this is the outlook of a secularized world where obedience or faith has become abnormal. This cannot be the intention of 12:4a. It is the normal and natural thing that Abraham should go as God commanded him; he would be putting himself at risk were he not to go.

"And Lot went with him." Lot is so far mentioned only by P: 11:27b (son of Haran) and 11:31a (he goes with Haran). But 12:4a presupposes that he must have been introduced already. The mention of Lot here is a preparation for the narrative of 13:5-13 which grows out of the itinerary; the words "and Lot went with him" are taken up again in 13:1.

[12:4b-5] There follows in 12:4b-5 an insertion by P. There are other signs that another voice is speaking here, apart from the language characteristic of P: "what

is said in v. 4a is repeated in somewhat greater detail in v. 5 in the Elohistic style''
(F. Delitzsch ad. loc; likewise most exegetes). This insertion is a classical example of the delicate touch of the redactor. It does not disturb the text; vv. 4b-5 give
the impression of filling out rather than repeating, and the sentence immediately
preceding it is identical with the same, or almost the same, sentence in J, which
can therefore be left out. The age given in v. 4b refers to the time of the departure
from Haran; the redactor thereby succeeds in localizing the departure commanded
in 12:1 (J), where it is not yet localized. The departure, therefore, is not that from
Ur, as could appear from 15:7. P uses the old itinerary structure in the sentences
out of which he has constructed v. 5 (cf. 11:31): (1) ''And Abraham took. . .'';
(2) ''they set out (to go to. . .)''; (3) ''they came to. . ..'' P indicates thereby that
he is familiar with the language of the itinerary reaching back into the patriarchal
period and the life-style of Abraham. The itinerary form enables vv. 4b-5 (P) to fit
smoothly into the context of J. The last sentence of v. 5 runs easily on to the continuation in v. 6 (J) because it is common to both.

[12:6-9] Gen. 12:6-9 continues 11:28-30; 12:1-4a (J). It hangs together rather
loosely. It is not narrative but enumerative (or a report) in accordance with the
itinerary style.

The itinerary is different from the departure for a distant land such as is
commanded in 12:1 and carried out in v. 4a; it is concerned with short distances
and is centered only on individual stopping places on the way. The form of the
itinerary depends on the sort of group that is travelling; the patriarchal itinerary,
therefore, must differ from the wilderness itinerary in Exodus and Numbers (cf.
G. Coats, CBQ 34 [1972] 135-152). We are dealing here with the simplest form of
itinerary which mentions only a few individual stopping places as the nomads
move on with their herds. It is this that we meet in 12:6-9. Vv. 6 and 8 go together;
the ''from there'' at the beginning of v. 8 can refer only to the last place mentioned
in v. 6, the terebinth tree at Shechem. V. 7 is not localized; it is originally an independent piece which is to be explained apart from the context. V. 9 is a bridge
verse, belonging as much to 12:10-20 as to 12:6-8.

[12:6] V. 6 consists of three parts, originally independent of each other. ''Abraham continued on through the land'' is both a transition and summary passage due
to the redactor, because J has so far not mentioned any land (cf. Comm. on v. 4a),
and so ''the land'' can refer only to the land of Canaan in v. 5bβ (P). The second
part, the stopping place, is part of a ready-made itinerary. The last sentence is a remark of the narrator for the benefit of his listeners. ''Abraham continued on
through the land''; this sentence describes the nomadic life of Abraham, and
makes clear that the land which God promised to show him (v. 1) is not to become
his own possession where he can settle down; he remains a nomadic shepherd. In
the course of his wandering here and there he comes to a שכם מקום. Later מקום
can mean a cultic site; here it is still the holy place outside the settlement. It is near
the city of Shechem, ''in the heart of the land'' (B. Jacob). שכם means ''shoulder''; it is named after the geographical contour between Ebal and Gerizim, east
of Nablus, the modern Tell Balata, as the excavations have demonstrated. The
city flourished in the 17th century, and the earliest settlement goes back to the
fourth millennium (cf. Lit. to Gen. 12–50, C, 3, e, *Places*. . .; and on 12:6).

''To the terebinth of the oracle.'' מורה can be genitive: tree of the oracle-
giver, ''where the priests who pronounced the oracles sat in ancient times'' (A.

Dillmann); or an attribute: "the tree itself gives the oracle" (O. Procksch); the latter is probable here. The designation can mean a particular type of tree (like *ālāh*), generally explained as a terebinth (cf. IDB,4,574), and by many as an oak (following Gk). Or it is a general sort of designation: "the great tree" (formed with אל?); so H. Holzinger and KBL. The word is a hiph. part. from ירה, and so a tree which gives prophecies or oracles. "Sacred trees which give omens or oracles are widespread among all peoples" (H. Gunkel). It is probably the same tree as that mentioned in Gen. 34:4; Deut. 11:30; Josh 24:24; and Judg. 9:26,37. There is also mention of a holy tree at Mamre and Beersheba.

This single verse at the beginning of the story of Abraham makes clear two facts which are basic to it. The one concerns what happened. Abraham in the course of his wandering comes to a sacred place near the city of Shechem (so E. A. Speiser, E. F. Campbell, A. Malamat, and others). That means, it was already a sacred place before Abraham came across it. There can be no question of the founding of a sacred place. All explanations which see in v. 6 a narrative about the founding of a cult are in error. What we learn here is rather that the patriarchs in the course of their wanderings looked for places that had long since been sacred and lay outside the walls of the settlement.

The other fact concerns the type of sanctuary. It is a tree that makes it a sacred place. The patriarchal story often speaks of particular trees at a particular place. They indicate the early type of sanctuary that is not yet made with hands. This means above all: a sacred place designated by a tree does not need any cultic institution, personnel, or building. It is a sanctuary typical of the life-style of the patriarchs. This can be demonstrated with the utmost clarity. R. de Vaux has drawn attention to it: "These trees have embarrassed later tradition. . ." (*Ancient Israel*, 278-79; *Early History*. . ., 285f.). In Gen. 13:18; 14:13; 18:1, the MT has the plural (contrary to 18:4,8); likewise Deut. 11:30 (contrary to Gen. 12:6). The TargO replaces "terebinth" with "plain"; the Vg follows the same line, *convallis* (Gen. 13:18; 14:13; 18:1). I agree with R. de Vaux that these alterations in the text or versions are to be traced back to the later condemnations of the tree cult which was held to be Canaanite (e.g., Deut. 12:2; 1 Kings 14:23; Hos. 4:13). In a situation which was culturally and cultically completely different, sacred trees endangered the pure worship of Yahweh; one shrank, therefore, from leaving them in the patriarchal stories. The consequence was that later, in the period of the monarchy, these naturally sacred places (a tree, a stone, a spring) became suspect (R. de Vaux, *Ancient Israel*). This cuts away the ground from the theory that the patriarchs were "cult founders" in the sense that the founding of the central sanctuaries at Shechem, Bethel, Beersheba, and elsewhere was traced back to them.

"At that time the Canaanites were in the land." "It goes without saying that only a narrator for whom the Canaanite era is past writes in this way" (H. Holzinger). This note, which earlier was a severe obstacle to the presupposition that Moses was the author of the Pentateuch, has become for us a valuable demonstration of the reliability of the path which the line of tradition followed from the patriarchal period to the monarchy. Only a narrator who wants to indicate the remoteness of the patriarchal period can write in this way. He wants to say to his hearers and readers: this happened in the far distant past, long before the Israelite tribes migrated into Canaan.

[12:7] V. 7 is an independent unit (against H. Gunkel, O. Procksch, G. von

Rad, C. A. Keller, and others). The note in v. 6b closes what has preceded; v. 8a follows on v. 6 in the style of the itinerary; the ''from there'' at the beginning of v. 8 can refer only to the place mentioned in v. 6. This entails the collapse of the widespread opinion that vv. 6-7 (or 6-8) are a cult legend ''to explain the sacredness of the principal centres of cultus by a theophany'' (J. Skinner ad. loc.), as well as the view of R. Rendtorff: ''In the Yahwistic text of Gen. 12:7 and 26:24f. the pattern of the cult etiology is extremely compressed'' (ZThK57 [1960] 27-40). The unit in v. 7 is not in itself localized, but only by being attached to the itinerary in v. 6; it must first be explained apart from this subsequent attachment.

It is an account of a self-contained event in three parts. The central part is the promise: ''I give this land to your descendants.'' The promise is preceded by: ''Yahweh appeared to Abram and said,'' and followed by : ''so he built an altar there to Yahweh who had appeared to him.'' Abraham thereby confirms the promise made to him by, as it were, a silent thanksgiving. The structure of the passage shows that it derives its meaning from the middle piece, the promise; it is introduced in v. 7a and confirmed in v. 7b. The text then can have nothing to do with the founding of a sanctuary; it is rather the promise of the land shaped into a scene, something like Gen. 13:14-17, which has been inserted as such between the two parts of the itinerary (v. 6 and v. 8).

The first part: The expression וירא יהוה אל occurs word for word in Genesis in 17:1 (P), then in 18:1; 26:2; 26:24; 35:9 (in 46:29 it is used of a meeting between two people). It is a demonstrably late arrival in all these places; in 18:1, for example, it is an introduction later prefaced to the narrative (see ad. loc.); in all cases it introduces a speech by God; it stresses the transcendence of the speaker. However, there is no thought of any unusual or supernatural accompanying circumstances. There is no essential difference between this introduction and the simple ויאמר in 12:1 (so too W. H. Schmidt, *Fests. G. Friedrich* [1973] 25-34).

The second part: On the promise of the land, cf. above, Intro. §4, and in detail C. Westermann, *The Promise to the Fathers. . .* (1976; Eng. 1980), where it is demonstrated that the promise of the land serves to link the patriarchal story with the history of the people, and cannot be traced back to the patriarchal period itself. It is particularly the formula ''your descendants'' in 12:9 that shows this: what is promised will come to pass only long after Abraham's death, not even during the lifetime of his sons, and only when Israel has become a people. But later generations will hear this pronouncement saying that the gift of the land, which is now their homeland, had been already promised to their ancestor.

The third part: Abraham built an altar there (i.e., where he received the promise). This sentence has almost universally been understood as follows: by building this altar Abraham founds a cult center; but this is a misunderstanding. The building of the altar is not a general reference to a divine revelation, but to the oracle given to Abraham, the promise. Because the promise refers to the possession of the land, the building of the altar is Abraham's response. B. Jacob has seen this and written appropriately: ''There is a marvellous contradiction here: with the altar, Abraham lays his hand on a land already held fast by other hands. . . . The erection of the altar captures this moment in a memorial'' (Comm., ad. loc.); cf. also O. Procksch: ''For him the altar is more a memorial stone than a stone of sacrifice.'' R. de Vaux shows that there can be no intention of an altar in the later sense, because it is nowhere said that sacrifice is offered on an altar erected by the patriarchs. In the context of the promise of the land, which appears only in a later period, the building of the altar is also meant to be a sign which refers to the later possession of the land.

The last part of the sentence, ''. . . Yahweh who had appeared to him,'' resumes once more the opening words; this forms an inclusion which makes the verse recognizable as a self-contained unit. This concluding stress on God's appearance to Abraham could recall an older narrative behind the present v. 7, in which the promise of new living space was made to Abraham personally as a way out of a crisis. This would introduce a tension into the three-act event of v. 7; there could have been a narrative structured in this way. This is the reason why in my study of 1964 (ThB 24) I called v. 7 the ''report of a narrative.'' But this holds only for the possibility that a still older tradition can be recognized behind v. 7.

[12:8] Gen. 12:8 is a typical itinerary: (1) departure—direction of journey; (2) stopping place (tents) with name; (3) an episode during the stay; (4) continuation (v. 9). What was said about the itinerary in v. 6 holds also for that in v. 8. It can go back into the patriarchal period. The verb ויעתק, with the meaning ''move on,'' occurs only here and in Gen. 26:22 in an itinerary; this accords with a speech form coming from an ancient tradition to which it belongs. The direction is mentioned together with the departure. The first event after the departure is the next rest; departure and rest form the rhythm of nomadic life. The tent, the dwelling of the nomadic shepherd, is pitched. It is worth noting that the wandering group comes to rest in the open between two settlements: ''with Bethel on the west and Ai on the east.''

For the place-names, Bethel and Ai, one should consult the lexicon articles, the archaeological reports, the geographical works (F. M. Abel, J. Simons, and others). Both names raise problems; in any case, it is certain that both were known by other names earlier. This is obvious in the case of hā'ai = heap of ruins; it is not known what this place was called that became a heap of ruins. Gen. 28:19 says that Bethel was earlier called Luz. It does not follow with certainty from 12:8 that the places were known as Bethel and Ai in Abraham's time; in the process of tradition across many generations, places are given names familiar to the listeners, even when their earlier names were different. The words ''with Bethel on the west and Ai on the east'' make it clear to every listener just where Abraham rested at that time.

A necessary part of the relaxation which the rest provides, and this is taken for granted, is the conduct of worship. They stay at any particular place only for a short time; even when it is only a rest place, they erect a marker there which J designates as an altar. It will have been the simplest form of altar (as mentioned in Ex. 20:24) made out of earth or some stones heaped together—not a construction to last for generations, but a temporary arrangement (despite Gen. 13:4).

The second sentence, Abraham ''called on the name of Yahweh,'' occurs also in Gen. 4:26 (cf. *Genesis 1–11*, ad. loc.) and is a ''term for the worship of God'' (H. Gunkel; cf. H. A. Brongers, NThT 11 [1956-57] 401-416, who accepts this general meaning also for Gen. 13:4; 21:33; 26:25). In Gen. 13:4 and 26:25 the sentence is found in conjunction with the building of an altar, in 21:23 with the planting of a tamarisk. One can conclude from this that J wanted to describe worship in the patriarchal period by this two-part event. The expression קרא בשם יהוה stands for the *word* in worship while the building of the altar (or some other action, like the planting of a tamarisk) indicates the *action* in worship. The background of 12:8, so full of meaning for the history of religions, is the awareness that the two basic elements of word and action are already part of worship in its simplest form. The designation of the word element gives notice that the indispensable presupposition for worship is the union of man with God which takes place with the invocation of the name of God. There can be no question of the founding of a sanctuary in either v. 8a or 8b as part of the cult of a sedentary people; what we have here is rather an early form of cult, basically different. The altar, the symbol of God, belongs to the resting place (B. Jacob: "Tent and altars go together"); in this it differs from the temple, which is part of the settlement. Further, there is no priest, no cult mediator (so, e.g., H. Gunkel ad. loc.). We encounter here one of the most important elements of the patriarchal religion: the patriarchs conduct worship themselves; there are no priests (apart from Gen. 14). This is in accord with the family structure of their community (for a Ugaritic parallel, cf. C. Westermann, *The Promise to the Fathers.* . . [1976; Eng. 1980] 167f.).

[12:9] The itinerary is continued: departure follows the rest in v. 8; this time the word is נסע in the hiph. which means to pull up the tent poles (as, e.g., in Gen. 11:2). However, 12:9 is not an itinerary in the strict sense, as no further stopping places are given. This transition verse, which is at the same time a preparation for the narrative in 12:10-20, gathers together a number of stopping places which are not named. Instead, only the territory to which they lead is mentioned, the Negev. The grammatical form הלוך ונסוע indicates once more (cf. 8:3) the gradual movement from place to place. The Negev "is the territory where Abraham really lived out his life" (M. Noth, *A History of Pentateuchal Traditions* [1948; 1966³; Eng. 1972]). R. Rendtorff: "One can perhaps conclude from Gen. 12:9; 13:1; 20:1 that the Negev was the original home of the Abraham tradition" (*Hermeneutik* [1960]). Negev, meaning the "dry land," can designate several areas (H. Cazelles, DBS 7 [1961] 81-156), but for the most part means the territory south of the Judaean hill country as far as Kadesh, where it gradually merges into the wilderness of Sin. The explorations of N. Glueck and others have shown that in earlier times the Negev was more densely populated and cultivated (cf. J. Simons and lexicon articles).

Purpose and Thrust

The starting point of this inquiry into the theological meaning of Gen. 12:1-9 is not the promise in vv. 2-3, but the text as a whole. The patriarchal story begins, after the transition of 11:27-32, with Abraham's journey. It is introduced by God's command to depart, which is linked with a promise; the God of Abraham points the way as Abraham journeys into and through the land of Canaan, moving with his herds from resting place to resting place, pitching and striking his tent, resting, setting up a sign and conducting worship, invoking the name of God with gratitude and hope—it is all part of the journey. This introduction is of great importance for what the Old Testament says about God. The later relationship of Israel to God when it has become a sedentary people in possession of the land, and the form of worship that results therefrom, is not all that the Old Testament has to say about worship, nor is it definitive; the wandering Abraham is also part of it. Neither the sedentary life nor its form of worship is to be Israel's goal and absolute; it can always be otherwise. God does not allow himself to be bound, not even to a particular form of worship or to a particular theology. When Israel's possession reached its high point, the prophets rose up with their cry of judgment over this very possession, and this coheres intimately with the introduction to the patriarchal story. God can command the departure; but he remains with them from resting place to resting place. The Yahwist, the theologian of the monarchical period, has, in the promise of 12:2-3, inserted his own prolog to the patriarchal story into this introduction; it forms at the same time the linchpin reaching backwards to the primeval story and forwards to the history of the people.

The promise given to Abraham, which expands in ever widening circles to the ''families of the earth,'' is not a promise of rescue, but of blessing. J has fitted together the primeval story, the patriarchal story, and the story of the people so as to form a whole, in which the beginning of the story of the people (Ex. 1–15) differs from that of the patriarchal story in that the former is a promise of rescue (Ex. 3) and the latter of blessing (12:1-3). The promise of rescue concerns a people in the making, the promise of blessing concerns a family. The promise of blessing can work itself out directly on mankind, ''the families of the earth,'' the promise of rescue only through the course of the history of a people whose existence is possible not only with, but also in opposition to, other peoples. If one says, as it almost always happens, that salvation history (*Heilsgeschichte*) began with the summoning of Abraham, then one must explain this more clearly. Salvation history as rescue history did not begin with Abraham, but with the exodus. Rescue, insofar as it is rescue vis-à-vis man, has always an effect of separation; with rescue, a particular history begins. By contrast, the promise of blessing to Abraham is aimed at a blessing which embraces mankind. But the story of God's acts of rescue is accompanied by a blessing; this is shown by the universal outlook which appears again and again in this story and comes to the fore more strongly at its end.

In the introduction to the story of Abraham, where God's command to depart is linked with the promise, the Yahwist has succeeded in a striking way in sketching a plan of history: God's universal action, which he presented in the primeval story, continues through the action with Israel's ancestors and then with the people of Israel, towards the goal which God has for ''all the families of the earth.''

The Ancestral Mother in Danger

Literature

Genesis 12:10-20: A. Kuenen, *An Historical-Critical Inquiry into the Origin and Composition of the Hexateuch* (1886). P. E. Kahle–H. Schmidt, *Volkserzählungen.* . ., I "Die verkleidete Frau," FRLANT 17/18 (1918; 1930²) 45-53. H. Schmökel, *Das angewandte Recht im Alten Testament* (1930). E. Haenchen, "Abrahams Lüge und die christliche Wahrheit," (1938) = *Ges. Aufs. II* (1968) 28-49. N. H. Ridderbos, "Zijn de drie stukken Gen 12:10-20; en Gen 26:1-11 te beschouwen als parallele weergaven van eenzelfde verhaal?" GThT 42 (1941). S. H. Hooke, *In the Beginnings* (1947; 1950²). C. A. Keller, "Die Gefährdung der Ahnfrau," ZAW 66 (1954) 181-191. E. H. Maly, "Genesis 12:10-20; 20:1-18; 26:7-11 and the Pentateuchal Question," CBQ 18 (1956) 255-262. E. Osswald, "Beobachtungen zur Erzählung von Abrahams Aufenthalt in Ägypten im 'Genesis Apokryphon,' " ZAW 72 (1960) 7-25. W. Herrmann, "Gedanken zur Geschichte des altorientalischen Beschreibungsliedes," ZAW 75 (1963) 176-197. E. A. Speiser, "The Wife-Sister Motif. . .," *Biblical and Other Studies I*, ed. A. Altmann (1963) 15-28 = *Oriental Studies* (1967). M. A. Klopfenstein, *Die Lüge nach dem AT. Ihr Begriff, ihre Bedeutung und ihre Beurteilung* (1964). B. Z. Wacholder, "How Long Did Abram Stay in Egypt?" HUCA 35 (1964) 43-56. L. Rost, "Fragen zum Scheidungsrecht in Gen 12:10-20," *Fests. H. W. Hertzberg* (1965) 186-192. V. Fritz, "Israel in der Wüste. Traditionsgeschichtliche Untersuchung der Wüstenüberlieferung des Jahwisten," *Marburger Studien* 7 (1970) 107-123. K. Rupprecht, "עלה מן הארץ (Ex 1:10; Hos 2:2): 'sich des Landes bemächtigen'?" ZAW 82 (1970) 442-447. E. A. Speiser, "The Patriarchs and Their Social Background," *The World History of the Jewish People II* (1970) 160-168. P. Grelot, "Un nom égyptien dans l'Apocryphe de la Genèse," RevQ 7 (Nr. 28) (1971) 557-566. O. Keel–M. Küchler, *Synoptische Texte aus der Genesis*, II, BibB 8,2 (1971). G. Schmitt, "Zu Gen 26:1-14," ZAW 85 (1973) 143-156. R. C. Culley, "Structural Analysis: Is it Done with Mirrors?" Interp. 28 (1974) 165-181. W. Brueggemann, "Questions Addressed in Study of the Pentateuch," in *Vitality of the OT Traditions* (1975) 13-28. S. Nomoto, "The Three Wife/Sister Stories in Genesis," *Annual of the Japanese Biblical Institute* 2 (1976) 3-27.

Genesis 12:11-12: J. Muilenburg, "The Linguistic and Rhetorical Usages of the Particle כי in the OT," HUCA 32 (1961) 135-160. J. A. Emerton, "A Consideration of Some Alleged Meanings of ידע in Hebrew," JSSt 15 (1970) 145-180. J. Hoftijzer, "David and the Tekoite Woman," VT 20 (1970) 419-444. D. Marcus, "The Verb 'to live' in Ugaritic," JSSt 17 (1972) 76-82. C. Westermann, "Das Schöne im AT," *Fests. W. Zimmerli* (1977) 479-497.

Genesis 12:13: H. P. Rüger, "1Q Genesis Apocryphon XIX, 19f. im Lichte der Targumim," ZNW 55 (1964) 129-131. B. M. Metzger, "Literary Forgeries and Canonical

Pseudepigrapha,'' JBL 91 (1972) 3-24.

Genesis 12:16: B. S. Isserlin, "On Some Possible Early Occurrences of the Camel in Palestine," PEQ 82 (1950) 50-53. H. J. Stoebe, "Anmerkungen zu 1 Sam VIII 16 und XVI 20," VT 4 (1954) 177-184. A. Jepsen, "Amah und Schiphchah," VT 8 (1958) 293-297. E. A. Speiser, "The Verb *shr* in Genesis and Early Hebrew Movements," BASOR 164 (1961) 23-28. E. Wirth, "Das Problem der Nomaden im heutigen Orient," *Geographische Rundschau* 21 (1969) 41-51.

Genesis 12:17: N. Peters, *Die Leidensfrage im AT* (1923). H. H. Rowley, *Submission in Suffering* (1942). J. A. Sanders, *Suffering as Divine Discipline in the OT and in the Post-Biblical Judaism* (1955). E. F. Sutcliffe, *Providence and Suffering in the OT and NT* (1955). J. Scharbert, "Leid," HThG II (1963) 37-44. E. Kutsch, *Sein Leiden und Tod—unser Heil. Eine Exegese von Jesaja 52,13-53,12*, BSt 52 (1967).

Genesis 12:18: R. Pesch, " 'Kind, warum hast du so an uns getan?' (Lk 2,48)," BZ 12 (1968) 245-248. W. Weinberg, "The Qamās Structures," JBL 87 (1968) 151-165. H. L. Ginsberg, "The Northwest Semitic Languages," *The World History of the Jewish People II*, C.V (1970) 102-124.

Genesis 12:19: C. H. Gordon, "The Accentual Shift in the Perfect with *waw* Consecutive," JBL 57 (1938) 319-325; *Before the Bible. The Common Background of Greek and Hebrew Civilizations* (1963). H. A. Brongers, "Bemerkungen zum Gebrauch des adverbialen we'attāh im AT," VT 15 (1965) 289-299. H. J. Stoebe, *Fests. W. Eichrodt* (1970) 209-225.

Genesis 12:20: L. Kopf, "Arabische Etymologien und Parallelen zum Bibelwörterbuch," VT 8 (1958) 161-215.

Text

12:10 A famine struck the land. So Abram went down to Egypt[a] to live there as an alien, because the famine was so severe in the land.

11 Now[a] when he was approaching[b] the Egyptian border, he said[c] to Sarai his wife: I know well that you[d] are a beautiful woman.

12 When[a] the Egyptians see you, they will say: That is his wife! Then they will kill me, but let you live.[b]

13 Please[a] say you are my sister,[bc] so that it may go well with me on your account, and my life may be spared because of you.

14 Now when[a] Abram arrived in Egypt, the Egyptians saw that the woman was very beautiful indeed.

15 Pharaoh's courtiers saw her and praised her to Pharaoh,[a] and she was taken[b] into Pharaoh's house.

16 But with Abram, all went well because of her,[a] and he acquired sheep and cattle[b] and asses, male and female servants, she-asses and camels.

17 Then Yahweh struck Pharaoh [and his household][a] with severe[b] diseases because of Abram's wife, Sarai.

18 Pharaoh summoned Abram and said:[a] What[b] is this you have done to me! Why[c] did you not tell me she is your wife?

19 Why did you say: she is my sister,[a] so that I took[b] her as a wife? Here is your wife[c] then! Take her[d] and go!

20 And Pharaoh ordered an escort[a] of his men for him, and they sent Abram and his wife on their way with all they had.[b]

10a Old accusative form which indicates goal or direction.

11a ויהי כאשר serves as introduction for narratives or a section of a narrative (Ges-K §111g). **b** The inf. with ל, the direction in which the action is moving (Ges-K §114m). **c** Gk reads Αβραμ after הקריב and ויאמר. **d** Sam reads אתי for את (also v. 13).

12a The כי is here a conjunction introducing a temporal clause. **b** Gk reads περιποιήσονται.

13a Expression of a polite request (Ges-K §110d). **b** Gk reads ἀδελφὴ αὐτοῦ εἰμι, Vg is stronger: *obsecro te, quod soror mea sis.* **c** The word order gives the predicate particular emphasis (Ges-K §1411).

14a ויהי כבוא serves to introduce a new narrative section (Ges-K §111g).

15a Vg: *et nuntiaverint principes.* **b** Gk: εἰσήγαγον αὐτήν.

16a בעבור as preposition (BrSynt 116m). **b** Sam reads after בקר: מקנה כבד מאד; a different order.

17a Probably an addition. **b** Gk: καὶ πονηροῖς.

18a Vg: *et dixit ei.* **b** Questions can acquire special emphasis through demonstratives (Brockelmann, *Grundriss* 116g). **c** Sam reads ולמה.

19a Vg: *esse sororem tuam.* **b** Imperf. consec. expressing a consequence (Ges-K §111m). **c** הנה with noun following can represent a whole sentence (Ges-K §147b; Brockelmann, *Grundriss* 10d). **d** Gk adds: ἐναντίον σου.

20a Gk: περὶ Αβραμ; Vg *super Abram.* **b** Gk: καὶ Λωτ μετ᾽ αὐτοῦ; Sam ולוט עמו.

Form

The relationship of Gen. 12; 20; 26 to each other: Since the time it was realized that these three passages are three different portrayals of the same narrative, discussion has centered about their relationship to each other. Only rarely has there been any attempt to go back to the old view that it is a question of three independent narratives (C.A. Keller, ZAW 66 [1954] 181-191; N.H. Ridderbos, GThT 24 [1941]). Two main theses were held: either 12:10-20 or 26 was regarded as the earliest of the three; ch. 26 by H. Ewald, A. Kuenen, J. Wellhausen, H. Holzinger, O. Eissfeldt, M. Noth, E. H. Maly (commentaries and Lit. above). One reason given was that Gen. 26 is purely secular and v. 8 looks like a particularly ancient touch; another (M. Noth), that the Isaac narratives are older than the Abraham narratives. Ch. 12 is regarded as the earliest variant by A. Dillmann, O. Procksch, H. Gunkel, J. Skinner, G. von Rad (with hesitation) (see commentaries), O. Keel–M. Küchler, G. Schmitt (see Lit. above), and J. Van Seters (*Abraham in History. . .* [1975]). It is the commentary of H. Gunkel that carries greatest weight here, where he has shown that ch. 12, right down to every detail, is the classical example of an early folk narrative. The most important representative of the opposite thesis was M. Noth. He propounded his thesis without coming to terms with Gunkel's explanation and arguments. In the most recent stage of the discussion G. Schmitt, and particularly J. Van Seters, have demonstrated beyond doubt that Gen. 26, as well as Gen. 20, is dependent on Gen. 12, and Gen. 12 is presupposed in Gen. 26. The question can now be considered as settled: Gen. 12 is the earliest of the three variants in Gen. 12; 20; 26.

Other problems arise concerning the relationship of the three variants to each other, above all in what concerns the literary sources; this cannot be gone into here. The relationship among the texts has been studied in detail (with synoptic tables) by K. Koch, *The Growth of the Biblical Tradition* (1964, 1974[3]; Eng. 1969); O. Keel–M. Küchler, BibB 8, 2 (1971); J. Van Seters, *Abraham in History. . .* (1975).

The structure of the narrative is particularly neat and clear; it is determined by the introductory sentence: "A famine struck the land" (v. 10a). What happens during the famine is framed in a to and fro movement: the way from Canaan to Egypt (v. 10b) and from Egypt back to Canaan (v. 20; 13:1). The series of happenings in Egypt is set in motion by a dialog (vv. 11-13), and closed by a dialog (vv. 18-19). What happens between these dialogs is narrated with the utmost brevity. There are only two episodes: the occurrence of what Abraham had foretold and planned (vv. 14-16) and the intervention of Yahweh against Pharaoh (v. 17). What the narrator wants to say is obviously concentrated in the two dialogs; the structure as a whole gives them special emphasis.

Neither K. Koch nor H. Gunkel pay sufficient attention to this structure. Gunkel has not seen that the narrator has put the emphasis on the opening and closing dialogs, and consequently has told the intervening events with the utmost brevity. He thinks that something must have fallen out between vv. 17 and 18; something must have been said about how Pharaoh found out the cause of the disease that struck him, and that Sarah was Abraham's wife. Koch gives this further support when he says that the peripety of the narrative is contained in the lines that have fallen out.* J. Van Seters rightly opposes the view that something has fallen out, basing his opinion on the concentration of the narrative on Abraham which was disturbed by an extended narrative. The listener knows the facts and does not need the detailed narrative. The peripety therefore lies in the words which the Pharaoh addresses to Abraham. J. Van Seters finds the following structure: (1) a crisis situation; (2) a plan to deal with the crisis; (3) the execution of the plan with new complication; (4) an intervention from outside; and (5) consequences. This is possible, but even so it does not state clearly enough that the emphasis is on the opening and closing dialogs. Gunkel's view, however, could indicate that the narrative once had a simpler form in which the emphasis was not yet on the two dialogues; this is presupposed in Pharaoh's accusation of Abraham, as also in chs. 20 and 26. The conclusion of this possible older narrative was not two-sided; rather it told that the powerful Pharaoh yielded to the power that protected the alien.

Setting

The fact that this narrative is preserved in three variants is warranty that its origin lies in oral tradition. It is told twice of Abraham and once of Isaac, an indication that it had a rather long life during the patriarchal period. If one compares the way in which the famine is met here and in ch. 47, then the narratives of chs. 12; 20; and 26 most likely present the older stage, because they are still in complete accord with the nomadic life-style. It is necessary to take into account the life-style when considering the question of the origin, setting, and process of tradition. It is only in this way that the linking of the two leading motifs of famine and foreign power makes sense. Behind the narrative is the experience of small units of nomadic shepherds who had no other way out of a famine crisis but this; Egypt provides a wealth of evidence for it. The narrative makes very clear how the situation arises out of such experiences. It belongs to that large group which deals with preservation in a famine crisis; one of these is selected and linked with the ancestress in danger. It is here, therefore, that those two cycles of motifs come together which determine the narratives of Gen. 12–25: the preservation of the family, living space, and provisions. We see then why the first collector chose precisely this narrative; he already had the Abraham story as a whole in perspective. Gen. 12:10-20 was particularly suited to be the first narrative in chs. 12–25 because it linked together the two leading motifs of the Abraham story.

---

*Translator's note: peripety, Gk περιπέτεια: sudden reversal of fortune in drama or life; the point around which the sudden change revolves.

Commentary

[12:10]   The structure of the verse claims attention because the famine is mentioned twice (v. 10a and c). It is possible that the narrative at one time began with the itinerary (v. 10b), with the reason for it given in v. 10c. But because the narrative was independent, the mention of the famine came to stand at the beginning, sounding the theme.

Famine is a frequent motif in the Old Testament; in Gen. 12–50 in 26:1; 43:1; 47:4 (both places with כבד); Ruth 1:1; 2 Sam. 21:1; 2 Kings 4:38; 8:1. The lamentations also at times have a drought in mind. Famine is one of the basic, critical, human experiences, attested from the earliest records of man right down to the present day. The "severity" of this famine impressed itself deeply on the memory. There are then a variety of stories that tell how a group was saved from a famine; their background is the broader canvas of the struggle between life and death. The Old Testament narratives and the Psalms speak often of God as the one who saves from famine; this is a consequence of what is said about the creation of man in Gen. 1 and 2: human existence depends on the provision of food. God's action, therefore, is often vitally concerned with the alleviation of hunger both in the Old Testament and the New Testament.

A retreat from the south of Palestine as far as Egypt in face of a severe famine is possible. This is also the case in the Joseph story and is frequently attested from Egypt, e.g., in the well-known relief of Ben Hassan (cf. A. Parrot, *Abraham et son temps*, CAB 14 [1962] 73), and in texts such as that on the grave of the general *Her-em-heb*: "Certain of the foreign who know not how they may live have come. . . Their countries are starving, and they live like the beasts of the desert" (J. Van Seters [1975] 16). The two verbs which are constantly used for the journey from the hill country of Palestine to Egypt and back are ירד and עלה (Gen. 13:1). The verb גור "to live as an alien (guest)," is derived from the noun גר, "alien." Behind the word is the outlook of the sedentary.

[12:11-13]   The dialog between Abraham and Sarah at the border (v. 11a) forms an episode. It begins with Abraham's request to his wife that she would pass herself off as his sister in Egypt (v. 13), occasioned by Abraham's fear for his life (vv. 11b-12). The speech shows that it is a matter of dialog even though there is no answer from Sarah. It is part of narrative technique that the answer can be left out where silence suffices; it indicates that Sarah agrees. It is important for the continuation of the narrative that Abraham and Sarah are still a unity at this stage. The address to Sarah consists, after the introduction in v. 11a, of two parts: in vv. 11b-12 Abraham foresees a situation in Egypt which can cost him his life; in v. 13 he proposes to Sarah a way out.

[12:11a]   "When he was approaching the Egyptian border. . . ." The place where the dialog takes place is important for the understanding of what follows. Abraham has set out for Egypt to escape the deadly threat of famine; in the Egyptian power and sphere of influence which he proposes to enter, he sees himself facing yet another deadly danger. Caught between the two, he takes to subterfuge. The exegetes have not for the most part adverted to this situation; when one keeps it in view, one will be more reserved with one's moral condemnation ("a story redounding to God's honor and Abraham's disgrace," F. Delitzsch; H. Holzinger is even more severe).

[12:11b, 12]   As one who has to beg for food, Abraham has no rights. We meet this same feeling, of being delivered to a far superior power without protection, once more in the case of Joseph's brothers on their way down to Egypt. Real experience lies behind this—that of a small group confronted by a superpower. The mighty colossus engenders the feeling of utter powerlessness on the part of the lesser one. It is in this situation in the ancient world that the ruse everywhere has its place. The ruse is the only weapon left for the powerless given over to the mighty.

The ruse that Abraham intends to use is the result of another experience of small groups which have to confront great powers: the potentate, simply because of his power, can appropriate to himself a beautiful woman who takes his fancy. This experience must have made a deep impression on early Israel. The motif occurs three times: in the primeval story, where the sons of the gods take to themselves the daughters of men (Gen. 6:1-4); in the patriarchal story, and at the beginning of the history of the kings in the narrative of David and Bathsheba (2 Sam. 11f.) (cf. *Genesis 1–11*, comm. on 6:1-4). Abraham must reckon with the possibility that the potentates in Egypt may kill him so as to appropriate his beautiful wife. There can be situations then where the beauty of a woman can put a man's life in danger. It is characteristic of this narrative that it speaks of the beauty of a woman as a link in a chain of events. The beauty is not the object of the story, but functional in its consequences for human relations (cf. C. Westermann, *Fests. W. Zimmerli* [1977] 479-497).

[12:13]   Abraham's ruse is that Sarah should pass as his sister. He knows that this subterfuge means the surrender of his wife; he knows he is thereby very culpable. But he sees no other means whereby both he and his wife can remain alive. He does not think of an intervention of God; he does not appear here as a man of faith. Faced with the threat of death, he surrenders what he ought not surrender.

E. A. Speiser is of the opinion that the Hurrian legal form of sister-marriage allows the passage to take on a quite different meaning (*Biblical and Other Studies I*, ed. A. Altmann [1963] 15-28 = *Oriental Studies* [1967]). But this explanation would bypass the sense of the narrative, the intended subterfuge (vv. 11-13), and the successful deception (vv. 18-19). According to Speiser's interpretation, Abraham would only have been explaining the actual legal status of his wife. A number of scholars have shown in detail that the texts alleged by Speiser are not relevant to the situation of Gen. 12:10-20 (T. L. Thompson, *The Historicity. . .* [1974], 234-247; D. N. Freedman, JANESCU 2 [1970] 77-85; H. Donner, OrAnt 8 [1969] 89-119; J. Van Seters, *Abraham in History. . .* [1975] 71-76).

[12:14-16]   The next scene takes place in Egypt, reporting the occurrence of what Abraham had feared: Pharaoh takes the woman for himself. At the same time, however, there is the change in the situation: Abraham, as the alleged brother of Sarah, receives presents. With a deft, unobtrusive increase in tempo the narrative tells how Sarah's beauty arouses the attention of the Egyptians (v. 14b), of the courtiers (v. 15a), and of Pharaoh himself (v. 15b). But the narrator confines himself to the goal and the necessary steps thereto: Abraham's wife is brought into Pharaoh's palace (v. 15b). There is no need to say that she acquiesced in Abraham's request to pass herself off as his sister; but there is need to tell of the consequences for Abraham (v. 16).

[12:15] The little that is said here of Pharaoh (the name means "the large house") and his court is historically correct and well known through Egypt and beyond. The Pharaoh had a large court staff (שׂרים are court officials and court-iers) and a number of wives. The courtiers gain Pharaoh's favor by putting them-selves at his disposal in every possible way. הלל is used here in a secular sense: the praise of the beauty of a woman (cf. 2 Sam. 14:25; Song 6:9; also THAT I, 493-494).

[12:16] The beauty of his wife could have been a deadly threat; the beauty of the alleged sister brings Abraham presents. What is being said here is that the Pharaoh does not merely exercise power. The presents correspond to the custom of the time, and are meant to compensate the brother for the loss of his sister. The first sentence, "But with Abraham, all went well because of her," is to be understood in the context of the beginning of the narrative: the escape from the famine and the new threat of death. The ruse appears to have succeeded; both live and all is well with them; but the marriage and the family are destroyed.

The enumeration of the presents belongs to the theme, "the wealth of the patriarchs," as in Gen. 13:2; 20:14; 24:35; 30:43; 32:15f; cf. Job 1:2; 42:12. It is to be understood functionally, not statistically, and is meant to portray the wealth of the patriarchs for listeners of a later age; the later elaboration and the anachro-nism (camels) are to be explained in the same way. The elaboration is obvious; "male and female servants" has been inserted between "asses" and "she-asses." It is unimportant whether "male and female servants" (H. Gunkel and others) or "she-asses" and "camels" (R. Kilian, B. Brentjes) has been added. In the *Genesis Apocryphon* there is the further addition of "silver and gold" (as in Gen. 13:2). R. Kilian's view, that the whole of v. 16 together with v. 13b is sec-ondary is not necessary. On the *Genesis Apocryphon*, cf. E. Osswald, ZAW 72 (1960) 17-25; on the problem of camels in the patriarchal stories, cf. J. P. Free, JNES 3 (1944) 187-193; B. Brentjes, *Klio* 38 (1960) 23-52; on "male and female servants," cf. A. Jepsen, VT 8 (1958) 293-297.

[12:17-19] The third scene (vv. 17-19) begins where Abraham's ruse comes unstuck; born out of fear of death, it suffices only to preserve his life. The purpose of Yahweh's intervention is the return of the wife and the restoration of the family; however, it is linked with a humiliating reproach to Abraham on the part of Pharaoh.

[12:17] The action in v. 17 follows directly on v. 15; the affliction is a conse-quence of what Pharaoh has done—R. Kilian is correct here. Nevertheless, v. 16 makes good sense: Pharaoh is afflicted even though he has acted in good faith and has given presents to the woman's "brother." One can distinguish two layers in v. 17. There is the old notion: "It was believed. . . that a crime must. . . inexora-bly demand its fated punishment" (E. Renan, *Histoire du peuple Israel I* [1889[10]]; cf. K. Koch, *The Growth of the Biblical Tradition* [1964; 1974[3]; Eng. 1969], par. 10). According to this understanding Pharaoh had violated Abraham's marriage; even though he had done it unwittingly, the fact remains and the conse-quences must follow. The background is the magical notion of the wicked deed that brings about disaster. The later notion is that of the God who is personally at work, who is so powerful that he can protect his charge even against the mighty, and can restore Abraham's wife to him. It is not a question here of a deed and its consequences, but of the vaster context of the history of God with Abraham. However, it would be incorrect to think that the narrator had only the latter in mind: the older notion has its voice too. It is precisely these two notions working together that give the effect intended by the narrator. If the later notion is taken in isolation, then Yahweh's treatment of Pharaoh must seem unjust. It is only the older notion that can be meaningful here: "So holy is the family that even an unwitting violation of marital fidelity brought with it death and the greatest misery" (E. Renan, op.cit.). Nothing is said about the kind of affliction that struck Pharaoh; it may have been illness, but the question remains open. The words ואת ביתו are certainly a gloss, perhaps introduced from Gen. 20:17f.

Is there a point of contact between this verse and the plagues which strike Egypt and Pharaoh in Ex. 5; 7–11? There is certainly no direct link; but it can scarcely be accidental that in both places there is talk of plagues that strike the Pharaoh (and Egypt). There is the same basic motif: in face of the very powerful, the only way in which the small group, as yet incapable of waging war, can be preserved, is the threat of "plague" by the God of the group against the potentate. Something similar also occurs in the Ark narrative, 1 Sam. 5.

[12:18-19]   There are two parts to what Pharaoh has to say to Abraham: the introduction (v. 18a) is followed by the reproachful question (vv. 18b, 19a); the question receives no answer. Abraham remains dumb. The second part consists of the giving back of the wife and the expulsion of Abraham.

[12:18a]   It is essential for the understanding of the narrative that the Pharaoh, with all the power at his disposal, does nothing more to the man who has deceived him and thereby offended his majesty than summon him to his presence and speak to him. The reason Abraham emerges unpunished is solely that the Pharaoh has experienced the power that stands behind him.

[12:18b, 19a]   Pharaoh's reproach is the last word in the narrative and so takes on considerable importance with regard to the whole. It shows at once that the narrator does not approve of Abraham's conduct (so too G. Schmitt, ZAW 85 [1973] 147) and attributes a clear conscience to the Pharaoh. The reproach is justified (so J. Skinner and others) and puts Abraham to shame. There is not a single word that indicates that the speaker is the king; the words are those of a man who has been deceived. The first part, "What is this you have done to me!" is often used in similar situations (e.g., Gen. 20:9; 29:27; Num. 23:11; cf. Luke 2:48). R. Pesch speaks of a "formula of disappointment," BZ 12 (1968) 245-248. This cry of bitter disappointment is unfolded in two questions beginning with "why," which contain the reproach, "Why have you offended me?" The last part, "so that I took her as a wife," gives Abraham's deception as the reason for what was done. Crucial to the reproach are the words, "What is this you have done to me!"; they are the words of the king of Egypt to a stranger who has no rights, of one on the highest level to one on the lowest. This is the high point of the narrative. Abraham is also put to shame by the fact that the speaker too is but a human being; he had forgotten this when he planned to save himself by deception, and in doing so had also forgotten God who can strike Abraham, and the Pharaoh as well.

[12:19b]   It would now be for Abraham to reply. But "Abraham is silent and, shamed and repentent, condemns himself" (F. Delitzsch, Comm.). "The narrator thus shows that it is the Pharaoh who is really in the right'' (H. Gunkel).

Abraham, together with his wife, is dismissed with a brief, brusque word: ''The ignominious dismissal of the couple is a fitting end to a most unheroic episode'' (C. H. Gordon, *Before the Bible.* . . [1963] 133).

[12:20]   The Pharaoh provides an escort to accompany Abraham to the border. He takes care that nothing further can happen to endanger the one party or the other. So Abraham withdraws under security, together with his wife and possessions; but he withdraws as one who has been humiliated (on the use of עַל, cf. L. Kopf, VT 8 [1958] 197f.).

Purpose and Thrust

The narrative from start to finish takes its orientation from the situation at the beginning: Abraham, his family, and his herds are threatened by famine. Then comes the new threat, when the utterly powerless is exposed to the absolute potentate. A man is threatened with death; he is convinced that he can save his life only by the surrender of something which, there being no deadly threat, he must never surrender; how should he conduct himself in these circumstances? This question is still with us today and is becoming more acute. Threatened from both sides, Abraham sees no other way out than to surrender his wife. He has foreseen correctly that the surrender can at least initially save the lives of both of them. Abraham was in fear of death; but the narrative continues to say throughout that there are further options open to God which Abraham does not see. The narrator is quietly pointing out that in such mortal danger a person can decide to surrender nothing by which he might ransom his life, that is, he can decide not to yield to might. But the other possibility is what usually happens: humans are such that in the overwhelming number of cases they do yield to might. Abraham does just this. It always was, and always will be, the extraordinary thing to overcome the fear of death in the confidence that God knows still another way out.

God, however, comes to the aid of the one who does not expect the extraordinary of him, but yields to might. He helps him out of the situation into which his deception had brought him, and does not surrender him. He punishes .him; but the punishment consists only in putting him to shame.

Provided one keeps in mind that there is scarcely a word in the patriarchal stories about the sins of the patriarchs and their consequent punishment by God, then this conclusion of Gen. 12:10-20 is significant for the relationship between them and God. It is like the way parents deal with their children—they shame them only in their watchful care to protect them.

Gunkel's explanation has been taken over by many subsequent commentators right up to the present: ''The narrative glorifies the astuteness of the patriarch, the beauty and self-sacrifice of the mother, and particularly the loyalty of Yahweh. . . . It is characteristic that the qualities of the ancestors and the loyalty of God are praised side by side.'' To this one may say: the narrative does not glorify Abraham's astuteness; neither Pharaoh's words nor the shameful dismissal are appropriate to this. Nor does it glorify the beauty of the mother; this occurs in the *Genesis Apocryphon* (cf. E. Osswald, ZAW 72 [1960] 6-25) and sounds a quite different theme. It is correct to say that the narrative deals with Yahweh's loyalty, but it is a loyalty and help linked with a reprimand. The story is a self-contained whole whose meaning emerges only from the climax and resolution of the whole.

G. von Rad (and W. Brueggemann following him, *The Vitality of O.T.*

Traditions [1975]) sees the sense of the narrative in the meaning that it subsequently acquires by being joined to the promise, Gen. 12:1-3: "When the programmatic significance, which we see in it, is added to the great promise of 12:1-3, then these words have a meaning that goes beyond our story. . . . Yahweh does not allow his work to founder at the very beginning; he saves it and elevates it beyond all human deficiency." This is certainly correct, but this general explanation does not need such a story. The subtleties that emerge only from the narrative as a whole are thereby lost.

Nor is the opposite, purely secular explanation right, which sees the leading motif as the despoiling of the Egyptians, e.g., T. L. Thompson: "The basic motif is that of 'despoiling the Egyptians' (G. W. Coats, VT 18 [1968] 450-457)," *The Historicity.* . ., 246. This too fails to see that the narrator has put the emphasis not on the mere succession of events but on the two speeches.

Abraham and Lot on the Way

Literature

Genesis 13: O. Eissfeldt, *The Old Testament. An Introduction* (1956², 1976⁴; Eng. 1965). B. Gemser, "The rîb- or Controversy-Pattern in Hebrew Mentality," *Fests. H. H. Rowley* VT.S 3 (1955) 120-137. J. Simons, *The Geographical and Topographical Texts. . .* (1959), "The Jordan Pentapolis." R. Kilian, "Zur Überlieferungsgeschichte Lots," BZ NF 14 (1970) 23-37. R. Kessler, *Die Querverweise im Pentateuch. Überlieferungsgeschichtliche Untersuchung der expliziten Querverbindungen innerhalb des vorpriesterlichen Pentateuchs* (Diss. Heidelberg 1972). M. Heltzer, *The Rural Community in Ancient Ugarit* (1976). R. Rendtorff, *Das überlieferungsgeschichtliche Problem des Pentateuch*, BZAW 147 (1976; 1977²), ch. 2. G. Howard, "The Tetragram and the NT," JBL 96 (1977) 63-83.

Genesis 13:1: G. R. Driver, "On עלה 'went up country' and ירד 'went down country,'" ZAW 69 (1957) 74-77. W. Leslau, "An Ethiopian Parallel to Hebrew עלה 'went up country' and ירד 'went down country,'" ZAW 74 (1962) 322-323. W. F. Albright, *Yahweh and the Gods. . .* (1968) II B,59f. V. Fritz, "Erwägungen zur Siedlungsgeschichte des Negeb in der Eisen I-Zeit (1200-1000 v.Chr.) im Lichte der Ausgrabungen auf der Hirtbet el-Mšāš," ZDPV 91 (1975) 30-45.

Genesis 13:6: J. Mouchline, *Yahad and Yahdau in the OT: Transactions of the Glasgow Univ. Or. Society* 102, XIII (1950/51). J. C. de Moor, "Lexical Remarks Concerning Yaḥad and Yaḥdaw," VT 7 (1957) 350-355. E. Koffmann, "Rechtsstellung und hierarchische Struktur des יחד in Qumran," Bib 42 (1961) 433-442.

Genesis 13:7: J. L. Teicher, "A Sixth Century Fragment of the Palestinian Targum?" VT 1 (1951) 125-129.

Genesis 13:8-9: H. J. Boecker, *Redeformen des Rechtlebens im AT* (1970²), esp. pp. 117-121. G. W. Ramsey, "Speech-Forms in Hebrew Law and Prophetic Oracles," JBL 96 (1977) 45-58.

Genesis 13:9: B. Landsberger, *Sam'al* [cuneiform] (1948). A. Rubinstein, "Notes on the Use of the Tenses in the Variant Readings of the Isaiah Scroll," VT 3 (1953) 92-95. M. Fishbane, "The Treaty Background of Amos 1:11 and Related Matters," JBL 89 (1970) 313-318.

Genesis 13:10: V. Aptowitzer, "Schenke und Schenkin. Zu Hammurapi #110," WZKM 30 (1917/18) 359-365. P. Dhorme, "Abraham. . .," RB 40 (1931), esp. pp. 371-373. G. Wagner, "Vom Jordangraben," *Naturwissenschaftliche Monatsschrift* 47, 7/8 (1934). J. Simons, "Two Notes on the Problem of the Pentapolis," OTS 5 (1948) 92-117. B.

169

Gemser, ''Be'ēber hajjardēn: in Jordan's Borderland,'' VT 2 (1952) 349-355. H. Bardtke, *Zu beiden Seiten des Jordan* (1958). P. A. H. de Boer, ''יהוה as Epithet Expressing the Superlative,'' VT 24 (1974) 233-235.

Genesis 13:11: J. Fichtner, ''Der Begriff des 'Nächsten' im AT mit einem Ausblick auf Spätjudentum und Neues Testament,'' WuD NF 4 (1955) 23-52.

Genesis 13:12: H. L. Ginsberg, ''A Preposition of Interest to Historical Geographers,'' BASOR 122 (1951) 12-14. S. R. Isenberg, ''On the Jewish-Palestinian Origins of the Peshitta to the Pentateuch,'' JBL 90 (1971) 69-81.

Genesis 13:14: D. Daube, *Rechtsgedanken*. . . BZAW (1958). M. Noth, ''Das deutsche evangelische Institut für Altertumswissenschaft des Heiligen Landes im Jahre 1965,'' ZDPV 82 (1966) 255-273. T. M. Raitt, ''New Perspectives on the Prophetic Oracle of Salvation'' (paper read at the 105th Meeting of the Society of Biblical Literature, 1969).

Genesis 13:15: J. Schmidt, *Der Ewigkeitsbegriff im Alten Testament* (1940). J. J. Rabinowitz, ''The Suza Tablets,'' VT (1961) 56-76. M. Wilcox, '' 'Upon the Tree'—Deut. 21:22-23 in the NT,'' JBL 96 (1977) 85-99, esp. pp. 94f.

Genesis 13:16: A. Guillaume, ''A Note on Numbers XXIII 10,'' VT 12 (1962) 335-337.

Genesis 13:18: F. M. Abel, ''Mambré,'' *Conférences de Saint-Etienne 1901-1910 (1910)*, 143-218. G. Dalman, ''Von unseren Ausflügen,'' PJ 17 (1921) 75-93. E. F. F. Bishop, ''Hebron, City of Abraham, Friend of God,'' JBR (1948). G. Greif, ''Was war ein 'elōn?'' ZDPV 76 (1960) 161-170.

Text

13:1 And Abram went up from Egypt to the Negeb, he and his wife and all that he had, and Lot with him.

2 And Abram[a] was very rich in cattle and silver and gold.[b]

3 He journeyed by stages from the Negeb as far as Bethel,[a] to the place between Bethel and Ai where[b] he had pitched his tent in the beginning,

4 where he had built the altar the first time. There Abram invoked the name of Yahweh.[a]

5 And Lot, who had journeyed with Abram, also[a] had sheep, cattle, and tents.

6a And the land could not support[a] them both living together,[b] for their possessions were great

6b [and they could not live side by side],

7 so there were quarrels between Abraham's shepherds and Lot's. The Canaanites and Perizzites were living[a] in the land at that time.

8 So Abram said to Lot: Let there be[a] no quarrelling between me and you, between my shepherds and yours, for we are brothers.[b]

9 Look, the whole country is there before you! Let us part company. If you go left,[a] I will go right; if you go right, I will go left.

10 Lot raised his eyes and saw how well watered the whole[a] plain of Jordan was—this was before Yahweh destroyed Sodom and Gomorrah—it was like a garden of the Lord, like the land of Egypt, as far[b] as Zoar,[c]

11a So Lot chose the whole of the Jordan plain and Lot went eastwards.

11b So they parted company.

12a Abram settled in the land of Canaan,

aβ Lot settled in the cities[a] of the plain,

b and pitched his tent in[b] Sodom.[c]

13 Now the men of Sodom were wicked, great sinners against Yahweh.[a]

14 And Yahweh[a] said to Abram, after Lot had parted company from him: Lift up your eyes and look, from the place where you[b] are standing, to

the north, south, east, and west.

15 Yes, the whole land which you see I will give to you and your descendants for ever.

16 I will make your descendants like the dust of the earth; if[a] anyone can count the dust of the earth, he can count your descendants.

17 Up,[a] walk through the length and breadth of the land, for I am giving[b] it to you.

18 So Abram moved his tent and went and settled by the terebinth[a] of Mamre[b] in Hebron, and built an altar to Yahweh[c] there.

2a Vg reads *erat autem,* omitting אברם.   **b** ''The employment of general names as collectives in the singular, to denote the *sum total* of individuals belonging to the class (which may, however, be done just as well by the plural),'' Ges-K §126m (cf. BrSynt §21c). When there are three members to a sentence, often only the last two are linked with the copula *waw,* Ges-K §154a.
3a Gk reads εἰς τὴν ἔρημον ἕως Βαιθηλ.   **b** אשר היה שם (Ges-K §138e).
4a GenApoc reads מרה עלמיא, ''Lord of eternity.''
5a Gk omits גם.
6a Sam reads נשאה for נשה.   **b** Word order, BrSynt §122e.
7a Sam and Gk have the plural; collective sing. for a class, Ges-K §126m.
8a Verbal sentence expressing a wish negatived by אל, BrSynt §8a.   **b** אחים אנשים, nominal apposition, Ges-K §131b.
9a אם־השמאל ellipse in a disjunctive conditional sentence (BrSynt §169b = Brocklemann, *Grundriss* 441b); a verb of four radicals formed on analogy with hiph., denominative from שמאל, Ges-K §56.
10a Sam reads כלו for כלה.   **b** באכה, lit. ''until your coming,'' = until one comes, Ges-K §144h.   **c** Gk reads εἰς Ζογορα for צער; Vg, *in Segor;* Syr צען; Sam צערה.
12a Gk has the sing.   **b** ''The preposition עד often describes not the direction but the place, e.g., Gen. 10:19; 13:12; 25:18,'' H. L. Ginsberg, BASOR 122 (1951) 12-14.   **c** Gk reads ἐν Σοδομοις; in v. 13 οἱ ἐν Σοδομοις.
13a Gk τοῦ θεοῦ (also v. 14).
14a GenApoc reads אלהא.   **b** Gk and Vg add עתה.
16a אשר, conjunction introducing consecutive clause, ''so that,'' Ges-K §166b; אם to introduce unreal conditional clause, Meyer III, 116; BrSynt §165a.
17a The imperative קום is very common as an interjection in asyndeton with verbs of motion, Ges-K §120g.   **b** Some Gk Mss. add καὶ τῷ σπέρματι σου εἰς τὸν αἰῶνα.
18a According to the Gk and Syr, the sing. is to be read.   **b** Syr reads האמרי.   **c** GenApoc reads אל אליון.

Form

The structure of ch. 13 is clear and simple; the main lines of its origin and growth are obvious. It consists of three principal parts: the itinerary (vv. 1-5); the narrative of the separation of Abraham from Lot (vv. 5-13,18); and the promise to Abraham, which is a later insertion (vv. 14-17). The narrative grows out of the itinerary (v. 5 belongs to both), and the promise has been inserted subsequently between the two parts of the narrative conclusion (Lot and Abraham settling in different places).

It is basic to the understanding of this structure that the itinerary and the narrative are different literary forms; the narrative of Abraham and Lot parting company begins only in v. 5. Likewise, the promise in the patriarchal stories is an independent element, so that each promise text in Gen. 12–50 is to be understood in the overall context of the promises.

The itinerary (vv. 1-5): Each individual sentence in vv. 1-5 is to be understood as a constitutive part of the itinerary: Abraham's journey (vv. 1a,3a), who and what accompanied him (v. 1b), details of the goal (vv. 3b,4a); first elaboration; invocation of Yahweh (as in 12:8); second elaboration: wealth (vv. 2,5). The itinerary knows neither a logical nor a narrative context; the movements from stopping place to stopping place form this. The elaborations occur each according to need. The only new element is the elaboration which mentions the wealth of Abraham and Lot; it also forms the beginning of the narrative (vv. 5-18).

This narrative consists of three parts. Its starting point is a quarrel which has arisen (vv. 5,7a). Abraham makes a proposal to settle the quarrel (vv. 8-9) and Lot accepts the proposal (vv. 10-11a). As a consequence, Lot and Abraham part company, going in different directions (vv. 11,12,18). It is a quarrel narrative which is concerned with living space, and so with sustenance. It belongs to the same group as the narratives of quarrels about wells in Gen. 21 and 26.

This group of narratives is typical of the era of the patriarchs and accords with their life-style (B. Gemser, VT.S 3 [1955] 120-137), as does the quarrel which ends with the two parting company. The group of small-cattle nomads cannot grow beyond a certain size and remain viable (R. de Vaux, *Ancient Israel* [1958; Eng. 1962] 7.). Quarrels between herdsmen over pastures and wells are a symptom of the crisis. The only peaceful solution to the problem is for the subordinate group to part company with the main group. "Large families. . . sometimes existed in Ugarit. But the general trend was toward its disintegration, and the large majority of families were small ones. . . .The primary unit inside the rural community was the individual family. . ." (M. Heltzer, *The Rural Community in Ancient Ugarit* [1976]).

What is peculiar to the narrative is that the main thing is missing—the description of the quarrel. Only the reason for the quarrel is given, and the fact that it took place. The conclusion, the settlement of the quarrel, follows immediately on this. It is similar to the quarrels over the wells in chs. 21 and 26. The longer the narrative is passed on, the more the details fade. There is no longer interest in who started it, how it proceeded, and what damage was done. However, it is this very honing down of the narrative that is evidence of a prehistory in which it must have been told more graphically and with further concrete details.

The promise. The narrative closes with both parties setting off in different directions (vv. 11a, 12b,18). This is a well known and typical conclusion; one can recognize with certainty an earlier form in which v. 18 followed immediately on v. 12b. Two passages have been inserted in between: the redactional anticipation of ch. 19 in v. 13 and the promise to Abraham in vv. 14-17. J. Wellhausen had already sensed that the promise was not an original part of the narrative, and this was taken over by H. Gunkel and many others. It can be proved with certainty that vv. 14-17 are a later insertion into an older narrative. First, the promise separates the two parts of the narrative conclusion (vv. 12b and 18), which belong together; second, the promise of numerous descendants, "like the dust of the earth," can scarcely be an original part of a narrative which concludes with Abraham and Lot parting company because their group is only viable if it remains small.

The narrative layer, vv. 6,11b,12 (P), has been worked into the story. The text is a good example of the justification and limits of source division:

13:6   The land could not support them both living together, for their posses-

172

sions were great and they could not live side by side.

11b So they parted company.

12a Abram settled in the land of Canaan, Lot settled in the cities of the plain.

These verses are usually attributed to P; the arguments are, first, that they are superfluous here, and, second, that words such as רכוש point to P (so W. Eichrodt, *Quellen. . .* [1916] 14f.). But these arguments are not sufficient to assign the verses to a particular literary stratum. It is quite different, however, if one regards vv. 6,11b,12a, as a coherent unity. The fact is that these verses are dispensable for the movement of the narrative of vv. 5-13,18, and form a doublet; in content they are a very brief, but quite complete repetition of the same event, that is, they are an abbreviated parallel to vv. 5-13,18, having the same three parts: the reason for the separation (v. 6), the separation (v. 11b), and the consequence of the separation (v. 12a). The parallel, however, shows a different conception of the same event: (1) The quarrel has fallen out, and so what in vv. 5-13,18 was the reason for the quarrel is now the immediate reason for the separation. The two statements in vv. 1b and 5 are brought together in v. 6b, and there follows the consequence of this, which now forms the reason for the separation. This omission of the quarrel occurs again in P in Gen. 36:7, in exactly the same way following that tendency to leave out negative aspects in the presentation of the patriarchs (many commentaries have pointed this out). (2) The consequence of the separation in v. 12a differs from that in vv. 11a,12b,18, in that Abraham and Lot do not, as in the latter, strike tents and go off in different directions, but Abraham remains. . . and settles in. This too indicates P, according to whom the patriarchs were not sedentary from the beginning, but became so. All this is certain proof that the small unit, vv. 6,11b,12a, describes the same event from another point of view. It is a literary parallel which presupposes a different mentality, most probably that of P; the repetition in vv. 6a and 6b also points to P.

Setting

The explanation of ch. 13 given here differs from that of a number of scholars who understand it as an etiological narrative (e.g., H. Gunkel, H. Holzinger, J. Skinner, O. Eissfeldt). This is rejected by B. Jacob: "This (etiological) explanation cannot be maintained. The Israelites never renounced the *kikkar* of the Jordan, nor did Ammon or Moab ever possess it" (Comm. ad.loc.). R. Kilian has taken up the etiological explanation once more (BZ 14 [1970] 23-37). He characterizes the narrative as an acquisition-of-land etiology. Abraham and Lot are not individuals here, but corporate personalities. Abraham represents the inhabitants of the hill country of west Jordan, Lot is the ancestor of a group of tribes in the Jordan area. The etiology originated between 1300 and 1000 B.C. in Israel. The setting of the narrative, therefore, is the question raised by the groups of tribes concerned, namely, how they came to possess the land originally (so too O. Eissfeldt, whom R. Kilian follows). This explanation is questionable because the narrative in ch. 13 has not the form of an etiology (Gen. 19:30-38 on the contrary is clearly an etiological narrative). There is, however, a series of parallels (Gen. 21 and 26, among others) which show clearly that we have here a quarrel narrative, each detail of which accords with the era and life-style of the patriarchs (cf. R. de Vaux, *Ancient Israel* [1962]). The narrative of ch. 13, as the whole cycle of quarrel narratives, has its origin in events of the patriarchal era; conflict about living space and sustenance formed an important part of the coexistence of this small group. The conflicts arose in nomadic groups and were initially handed down, so that the setting in which they took place cannot be determined (against H. Gunkel, M. Noth, and others).

(On the itinerary of 13:1-5, cf. Intro., end of section 2; on the promise of vv. 14-17, cf. Intro., 4, C.)

Commentary

[13:1] It is important for the understanding of v. 1 and its context to decide where it belongs. H. Gunkel, O. Eissfeldt, G. von Rad, and others understand it as the conclusion of the narrative in Gen. 12:10-20. They must, therefore, regard the note, "and Lot with him," as a later gloss, because Lot is not mentioned in 12:10–13:1. R. Kilian also contests that 13:1 is part of the narrative of 12:10-20, and regards both 12:9 and 13:1 as a redactional clamp binding the basic layers of chs. 12 and 13, which he considers pre-Yahwistic; the clamp is secondary, being the work of J, and the note, "and Lot with him," is part of it.

Both explanations agree in maintaining that the itinerary verses are literary formations. But if the itinerary is an independent literary form, then v. 1 is to be regarded neither as the conclusion of the preceding narrative nor as a secondary link to a subsequent narrative, but as a constituent part of the itinerary (vv. 1-5). The one explanation (that of H. Gunkel, O. Eissfeldt, G. von Rad) was correct in perceiving that the new narrative, the separation of Lot and Abraham, begins only in v. 2; the other in seeing that 13:1 is linked not only with 12:10, but also with 12:9, and is not the conclusion of a narrative (Gunkel sensed this when he remarked: "there is no mention at all that the famine was over"). The difficulty is solved when it is realized that the itinerary is an independent form, and that both narratives, 12:10-20 and 13:5-13,18, have grown out of the itinerary. In 12:10 the itinerary merges into the narrative; it is taken up again precisely where the narrative is concluded (12:20 is clearly the conclusion of the narrative); the starting point for the new narrative is in vv. 2 and 5 of the itinerary of 13:1-5.

The journey from Israel down to Egypt is always designated by ירד, and from Egypt up to Israel by עלה (cf. Lit. on 13:1).

[13:2] "A nominal sentence describing a situation with normal word order" (R. Kilian). A sentence of this type is typical as the beginning of a narrative, the prerequisite of which is the situation described in it. H. Gunkel notes: "Vv. 2,5,7a go together." O. Procksch goes further when he says: "V. 2 breaks the continuity of the journey, and would go better after v. 4," and gives as the reason why this verse follows v. 1 the idea that Abraham acquired this wealth in Egypt. Many interpreters accept this. But the narratives, 12:10-20 and 13:5-8,18, originated independently of each other; the latter does not presuppose the former. The opinion that v. 2 breaks the continuity of the journey misunderstands the peculiar nature of the elaborations in the itineraries as well as in the genealogies. The reason the two notes about the wealth of Abraham and Lot do not go together, though they agree in content, is that the itinerary (vv. 1-4) was already in existence before it was joined to the narrative (vv. 5-13,18); v. 5 forms a transition from the itinerary to the narrative. The adjective כבד carries here its basic meaning of "heavy, weighty"; in the context it can only mean "rich" (cf. כבד in THAT I, 794-812; and S. Gevirtz, VT 11 [1961] 141f.; for the details about the wealth, cf. Comm.,

12:16). It is possible that "silver and gold" is a subsequent elaboration because it is of no significance for the narrative. The mention of silver before gold probably points to a time when silver was more valuable.

[13:3,4]   The itinerary of v. 1 is taken up again after the elaboration in v. 2. The verb "he journeyed" at the beginning of v. 3 governs a verbal sentence which only ends with v. 4a, a circumstantial sentence with several elaborations: (1) he journeyed from A to B, with the specification of the place of departure; (2) regarding the destination to the place between A and B with two further specifications, *(a)* where his tent stood in the beginning. . ., *(b)* where he. . . the first time. But the phrase "between A and B," which belongs to the main sentence, separates these. It is only in v. 4a that we have the continuation of the verb "he journeyed" of v. 3: there he invoked the name of Yahweh. Most exegetes say that v. 3f. is redactional (H. Gunkel, J. Skinner, R. Kilian, and others). R. Kilian calls it the "clamp which joins the different layers." The only reason for the verse would be to bring Abraham back to Bethel (so, e.g., J. Skinner). But the way in which vv. 3-4 are arranged would seem to exclude this. Would a redactor have written in this way? Moreover, it is scarcely possible that a redactor would have put the words "between Ai and Bethel" between two further specifications which go together. The whole way in which an itinerary is structured speaks against this; it is put together from small parts and quite brief pieces of information; it is not concerned with anything like a narrative flow. The parallel in Ex. 17:1 is also opposed to the opinion that vv. 3-4 are redactional; it is a similar sentence with the same expression למסעיו, and all interpreters specify it as an itinerary. Gen. 13:3-4, therefore, is not a redactional transition, but the continuation of an itinerary.

This being the case, the meaning of the two sentences at last becomes clear; they refer back to an earlier stopping place: "to the place where he had pitched his tent in the beginning. . ., where he had built the altar the first time." The significance of this reference for the itinerary was to mark out stages in the journeying and thereby preserve them for memory. It was a special experience for the small-cattle nomads to find and see again a "place" where they had once rested and set up a memorial to the God who was guiding them; it impressed itself on their memory and was able to serve to divide up the stages. The conclusions which W. F. Albright draws from 13:1-4 about Abraham's caravan commerce do not accord with the text (*Yahweh and the Gods of Canaan* [1968] 59f.).

[13:5]   The narrative begins with v. 5; it should be noted that the verse is at the same time still part of the itinerary (vv. 1-5): the beginning of the narrative is a piece of information belonging to the itinerary. We understand therefore why the sentence which continues v. 2 does not follow directly on that verse, but is found here where it forms a transition from the itinerary to the narrative. This is a good example of how the narrative arises out of a situation: it is the steady increase of the property of both with the implication that it is the blessing at work that brings the increase. In enumerating the details, a clear distinction is drawn between the property of Lot and that of the wealthier Abraham. The word *tents* and its overtones are important here: the tent is the nomadic living unit and includes those who live in it, that is, the families of the shepherds who are spoken of in v. 7. We learn here that several families belong to each patriarchal group, to Abraham's as well as Lot's, and they go along as shepherds. If we suppose that each had five or six shepherds, then we can count about twenty to thirty for each group.

[13:6] Vv. 6,11,12 form the P-variants of the narrative (see above, "Form"); v. 6 gives the reason why they part company (in vv. 11b,12a) and the quarrel ends. The formulation and the repetition in 6a and 6c seem to underscore that the increase in property (the sentence in the middle), and not a quarrel, rendered the separation necessary.

[13:7a] The narrative begun in v. 5 (J) is continued. While v. 5 forms the exposition, v. 7 is the beginning of the action: a quarrel arises (see above, "Form"). The significance of this narrative becomes comprehensible only when it is realized that small nomadic groups cannot wage war; the quarrel, therefore, takes the place of the war in which the larger unions, from tribes on, engage (C. Westermann, ThB 24 [1964] 66-69). The quarrel is concerned with living space and sustenance, as is war in later times, and is just as serious because it is a question of the very existence of the group. This leads to the conclusion that the quarrel narrative was once a highly developed type; only fragments of it are preserved in the patriarchal stories. A sign that the quarrel type of narrative lies in the distant past is that the narrative of 13:5-13 tells only of the result of the quarrel, and not of the quarrel itself, and the proposal to end the quarrel (vv. 8-9) follows directly on the action (v. 7).

[13:7b] For this aside of the narrator, see the comments on Gen. 12:6b. The Perizzites are added here (cf. Gen. 34:30; Judg. 1:4f.; the name occurs 23 times in the Old Testament, four times along with the Canaanites, and once in the Amarna letters). Scholars have not yet succeeded in determining more precisely who the Perizzites are (so E. A. Speiser, ad.loc.); it has been suggested that the name derives from פרזות = "open villages," hence those who live in open villages as distinct from city dwellers. But in the lists of pre-Israelite inhabitants of Palestine, a group of people is clearly meant (cf. J. Simons, *The Geographical and Topographical Texts*. . . [1959] 71f.). H. Gunkel holds that v. 7b is a gloss which is out of place; one would expect it after v. 5. R. Kilian follows him. But Gunkel's view is not correct. The aside of the narrator can stand only at the beginning of the action, that is, at v. 7; v. 5 is still part of the itinerary.

[13:8-9] Abraham makes a proposal to settle the quarrel. On proposals to end or settle a quarrel, cf. H. J. Boecker, *Redeformen des Rechtslebens im A. T.* (1964; 1970²), 117-121. There are two parts to the proposal which Abraham makes to Lot: in v. 8 he rejects the quarrel on the ground that they are kinsmen; in v. 9 he offers Lot the option of parting company, giving him the open choice of where he will go. Most interpreters speak here of Abraham's nobility and readiness for a peaceful settlement which the narrator emphasizes. But this is not to the point. The quarrel between the shepherds threatens the existence of both groups; it is a question of living space and sustenance. Abraham does not make his proposal as an individual, thereby showing nobility and generosity; rather he is responsible for his family and people and must come to a decision that has in view the life and well-being of his group. In order to avoid at all cost a violent outcome to the quarrel, because this would not accord with Abraham's responsibility for his kinsmen, he makes the proposal that Lot himself choose his pasture. Here too Abraham is the father.

It is essential to this proposal that the increase in property of both subgroups should actually lead to the increase in strength of the group as a whole.

Abraham sees that there can be a peaceful solution to the quarrel only if they separate peacefully; this is a certain indication that the groups of nomadic shepherds
were viable only as small units; looking at it from a later perspective, P says: ''The
land could not support them both living together.'' The narrative then can go right
back to the patriarchal period. The reason that Abraham gives, ''for we are brothers,'' is to be understood from the patriarchal point of view. The outcome of this is
not ''how good it is and how pleasant for brothers to live together'' (Ps. 133:1),
but that they part company in peace. Responsibility for one's brother can express
itself in a solution to a quarrel which results in a peaceful separation. (On אחים
אנשים , cf. B. Jacob, ad.loc.; on אחים, M. Fishbane, JBL 89 [1970] 313-318.)

[13:10,11]   Lot accepts Abraham's proposal and makes his choice. He chooses
the Jordan plain and moves off in that direction. The choice is the result of reflection; but in the manner typical of the patriarchal stories, it is made concrete: ''Lot
raised his eyes. . ..'' What he saw moved him to his decision; there is no need to
narrate the consequence of what he saw. It is Lot's gaze over the well-watered Jordan plain—like a garden of God—that is the climax of the narrative. It is this that
resolves the tension, as it persuades him to accept Abraham's proposal and so end
the quarrel. We meet here once more an example of the fine narrative art of the
storyteller; by means of the comparison, ''like a garden of God,'' he lays an emphasis on what Lot sees that arrests the listener's attention. The Jordan plain that
lies before him becomes something marvellous, arousing desire; it attracts Lot,
and every other consideration recedes into the background. Lot sets out. The artistic touch of the Yahwist is also in evidence in the way in which he reshapes the old
narrative. He preserves with great fidelity its main lines, which are concerned
with the existence of both groups and living space for the nomadic shepherds,
while at the same time allowing people to take the stage, in accordance with his
constant interest in the human element. He contrasts Abraham, who acts with so-
ber responsibility with regard to his people and kinsmen, with Lot, who allows
himself to be drawn by the beauty of the well-watered land—just as J has
portrayed the situation in the story of the garden of God in Gen. 3. But there is just
the merest hint of this; the brief sentences convey it clearly enough. Besides the
human element, this part of the narrative allows us to glimpse the experiences of
the era of the nomadic shepherds; they experience the rich, beautiful, and attractive land which is later, as in ch. 18, to become a danger and a threat.

[13:10]   In detail: V. 10 gives the impression of something put together: ''the
whole verse is somewhat awkward'' (A. Dillmann, ad.loc.). Three additions have
been made: (1) The explanatory addition, ''this was before Yahweh destroyed
Sodom and Gomorrah''; ''it was made necessary by the separation of ch. 13 from
chs. 18–19'' (H. Gunkel). (2) The second comparison, ''like the land of Egypt,''
was added to the first, ''like a garden of the Lord,'' and loses by default; it has no
function in the story. Could it be due to a redactor who had Gen. 12:10-20 in
mind? (3) There follows now, in addition to the temporal, a geographical specification, ''as far as Zoar.'' Its effect after the second comparison is of something
tied on; its proper place would be directly after הירדן where it would not cause any
unevenness; but even that is not absolutely necessary. The question whether it is
an addition can remain open. The narrative would flow much better if v. 10 were
read without the two (or three) additions.

   The precise meaning of ככר הירדן is uncertain. It is usually taken as meaning "the lower part of the *ghōr*" (M. Noth), "the southern part of the *'arābāh* depression" (B. Peucher, BHH II [1964] 884f.; B. Gemser VT 2 [1952] 349-355). R. Kilian translates, "the tortuous stretch of land in the lower Jordan valley," and gives another meaning to הככר in v. 12. Others maintain that it is a description of the whole Jordan valley from Lake Gennesaret to the Dead Sea, but this is unlikely in the context (details in J. Skinner, ad.loc.). The narrative presupposes that there is an extensive view from the place where Abraham and Lot have their tents. "The *būrǧ beitin* SE from the village is described as one of the great viewpoints of Palestine from which the Jordan valley and the north end of the Dead Sea are clearly visible" (J. Skinner, ad.loc.). On the "Garden of God" cf. *Genesis 1–11*, Comm. on Gen. 2:8. The great majority locate Zoar at the southeast end of the Dead Sea; J. Simons puts it at the north end ([1959] 222-229). See Comm. on ch. 18 for further details.

[13:11a]   The narrative merges into the itinerary again in v. 11; that is why the name of Lot is repeated in v. 11a.

[13:12b]   V. 12b, "and he pitched his tent in Sodom," follows directly on this (so H. Holzinger, H. Gunkel, J. Skinner, R. Kilian, and others).

[13:12a]   For the P-variant, vv. 6,11b,12a, see above under "Form." V. 6 gives the reason for the separation, v. 11b the separation, v. 12a its consequence. Short though the variant is, it differs nevertheless from J in that the separation has a different cause and only Lot departs, while Abraham remains. (On ישׁב, J. Skinner writes: "The verb ישׁב is not necessarily inconsistent with nomadic life.")

[13:13]   This verse is not the real continuation of the J narrative; it is rather a new narrative introduction which takes the place-name "Sodom" from the itinerary. The new narrative, however, follows in chs. 18–19, to which v. 13 forms a transition (cf. the general structure as given above, Form); the way is prepared for it by stressing the wickedness of the people of Sodom. The verse still shows signs of two layers; the older form was: "the people of Sodom were very wicked"; this sentence introduced the still independent narrative of ch. 19. With the insertion of the Abraham-Lot cycle, the words וחטאים ליהוה were attached. This is the only way to explain the "unusual juxtaposition" (B. Jacob), namely, that the wickedness of the Sodomites becomes a "sin before Yahweh." The רעים alone occurs also in the flood narrative (Gen. 6:6; 8:21). Both narratives are related (see below on ch. 19); in none of the patriarchal narratives is sin or wickedness a main motif or even an introductory motif; what is meant is the corruption of a whole generation, as in the flood narrative. In both places the corruption is wiped out by a catastrophe, and in both places one person [family] is saved.

[13:14-17]   *Context and structure:*   This passage is the standard example of a promise shaped into a scene. A sign that it is an insertion is that sentences which belong together have been separated, vv. 12bβ,(13),18. A common conclusion to a narrative is that each of the parties concerned in the event goes his separate way: "A" went this way, and "B" went that way. A further sign that the passage is an insertion is that Yahweh's address to Abraham is clamped to what precedes by the sentence, "after Lot had parted company from him." But the main reason is that the content of the promise does not fit the narrative to which it is appended (see above, Form). The address of 13:14-17 differs from the promise of 12:1-3, which is a constituent part of the narrative; however, it is inserted so adeptly that the patriarchal stories must have still been vital for those mediators of tradition who inserted it.

After the introduction and the link verse (v. 14a), the passage contains the promise of the land (v. 15), framed between two imperatives, vv. 14b and 17a; there is a further echo of the promise in v. 17b (inclusio). The promise of posterity in v. 16 lies outside this very tight structure. It is only the promise of the land that has been shaped into an episode in vv. 14-17; the promise of posterity has been appended. One notes here a procedure that recurs often. The main sign that a promise has been shaped into an episode is that the two imperatives of vv. 14a and 17a are not instructions to which a promise has been joined, as in 12:1-4a; they are merely confirmations of the promise. The imperative in 12:1-4a, "Go from your land. . .," is followed by its execution (12:4a); nothing corresponding to this follows the imperative in 13:17a, "Up, walk through. . .." It is only now that the significance of the promise text in the patriarchal tradition becomes evident. First of all, there was a story about Abraham and Lot concerning living space; later there was appended to it the promise that the people of Israel, implied in the mention of Abraham's posterity, would possess the land "for ever"; thus the promise was linked with the patriarch Abraham. Just as the promise of a vast number of descendants was made concrete and given weight by the comparisons, so too was the promise of the land by the solemn action of transfer.

[13:14] The inversion at the beginning underscores the new introduction and its importance. What follows is introduced as an address by God; there is no mention of a revelation. The content of the promise is more important to the mediator of tradition responsible for the appendage than is the process of revelation. The link in the introduction which joins it with what has gone before is a necessary device; it is not to be regarded as a superfluous addition from a later hand (as does R. Kilian).

The injunction is given in solemn language. Abraham, who is addressed here, "Lift up your eyes. . .," is the father of the people, Israel; he is enjoined to cast his gaze over the length and breadth of the land which is later to belong to it. The promise is thus brought to life; it is a picture that will impress itself on many a generation. It can be that there is here a low-keyed but deliberate contrast with the covetous gaze of Lot (v. 10). M. Noth comments on a viewing point northeast of Bethel: "It embraces the coastal plain and the Mediterranean, and on the other side the Jordan valley from Hermon to the Dead Sea, and a great part of the east Jordan mountain range" (ZDPV 82 [1966] 266). It is a different viewing point from that in v. 10.

[13:15] One will misunderstand the relationship of this promise of the land to that in Gen. 12:7 if one regards the connection between them as merely literary. H. Holzinger, for example, saw in 13:15 "in contrast to 12:7 a somewhat impulsive intensification"; O. Procksch on the contrary finds 13:15 "even more effectual than 12:7." Both are very subjective judgments. However, when one concedes to the promise of the land the independence that it has in the history of tradition, then each land-promise text is to be understood from the overall context of the motif in all its various expressions (C. Westermann, *The Promises to the Fathers*. . . [1976; Eng. 1980]). The motif is repeated so often and occurs in such a variety of forms because it presents an independent stage of tradition of the patriarchal stories: it is a link between the old patriarchal narratives which have been handed down and a much later period when the patriarchs, as those to whom the promise of the land was given, have become its guarantors. This derives clearly from the solemn way in which v. 15 is formulated. The word which is used throughout for the promise of the land, נתן, actually comes from a legal act of the transfer of land (so in Gen. 48:22, where Jacob confers a piece of land on Joseph; cf. D. Daube: ''In Oriental law the promise of an estate is already a kind of transfer; yet, as it is not a real, physical transfer, it may well be followed by a second ceremony giving actual effect to it'' *Studies in Biblical Law* [1947] 34f.). The land is not yet given to Abraham, and so the words ''and your descendants'' must be added (cf. M. Wilcox, JBL 96 [1977] 85-99; R. Rendtorff, BZAW 147 [1977²] 42-45). The solemn conclusion, עד־עולם, is particularly expressive, as it is directed to the permanent possession of the land by the people of Israel. E. Jenni writes: ''About forty times the phrase עד־עולם carries characteristic connotations which refer to a succession of generations. The first example is Gen. 13:15'' (ZAW 64 [1952] 213).

[13:16]   A promise of increase is inserted here. One should note the gradually growing tendency throughout the patriarchal story to heap the promises together (cf. C. Westermann, *The Promises. . .* [1980] table, pp. 128-129), so that in the subsequent history (particularly in Deut.) the promises of land and of increase become determinative (e.g., H. H. Schmid, *Der sogenannte Yahwist* [1976] 127-132). The promise of increase probably had its origin in the marriage blessing; the poetic form of the comparisons favors this—''like the dust of the earth'' (see also Gen. 28:14); the descendants are beyond counting (Gen. 15:5; 16:10; 32:13); for a sedentary people, land security and a large population go together.

[13:17]   V. 17 belongs with vv. 14 and 15, the imperative in v. 17 with that in v. 14. The writer is thinking here of a legal custom, like the Roman *ambitus*, according to which one strides out the length and breadth of a piece of land, thereby taking possession of it (D. Daube, *Studies. . .* [1947] 37, and BZAW 77 [1958] 35). B. Jacob: ''According to Rabbi Eliezer, one acquires a piece of land by walking its length and breadth'' (Comm. ad.loc.). Referring to this passage, F. Horst says: ''personal measuring out on foot of the length and breadth of the piece of land is part of the action of taking possession. . .'' (*Fests. W. Rudolf* [1961] 210); (see also Homer, *Iliad* I, 37; Gilgamesh XI, 203). It is possible to present the promise of the land concretely, following private legal usage, only because it is made to Abraham the man. Thus, the symbolic meaning of the injunction emerges more strongly; and to emphasize it further, the passage closes with yet another repetition of the promise of the land.

[13:18]   It has been said already of vv. 11aβ,12bβ that the narrative merges again into the itinerary; this holds too for v. 18 which must be read in immediate conjunction with these verses. The same verb אהל in vv. 12 and 18 is a further sign that they belong together:

> v. 11a   ''So Lot. . . went eastwards. . .
> v. 12b   and pitched his tent in Sodom.
> v. 18   So Abraham moved his tent. . ..''

The narrative of the dispute between Abraham and Lot ends amicably with their parting company and going off in different directions (P is different, v. 12).

It is a typical narrative conclusion, described thus by J. Seeligmann: "The narrative of the short story type is an episode: at the beginning the characters are brought together; at the end they part company and each goes his own way" (ThZ 18 [1962] 308). So, for example, 1 Sam. 24:22b: "Then Saul went home; but David and his men went up to the stronghold"; see too Gen. 18:33; 32:1f.; 33:16f.; Num. 24:25; 1 Sam. 14:46; 15:34; 21:1(Gk); 26:29b; add to these Gen. 13:11,12,18. There is a difference in that Gen. 13:11,12,18 merges into the itinerary, while the narratives from the sedentary period usually end with the parties each returning to his own dwelling, as in the example in 1 Sam. 24:22. The structure of v. 18 is typical of the itinerary; departure—journey—settlement (with place details)—building of an altar. Ch. 13 then closes with a sentence that is in complete accord with Abraham's actual life.

Once more Abraham settles at a sanctuary outside a fixed place; once more it is a natural sanctuary, the terebinth (sing.) of Mamre. This text too is not concerned with the founding of a sanctuary (against H. Gunkel, J. Skinner, and others). Mamre, ממרא, is the name of a person in Gen. 14:13,24, and of a locality in 23:17,19; 25:9; 49:30; 50:13; it is not found outside Genesis. The excavations of A. E. Mader, 1926-28, have identified Mamre as *rāmet el-ḥalil*, three km. north of the ancient Hebron (A. E. Mader, *Mambre*. . . I-II [1957]; G. Dalman, PJ 17 [1921] 75-93; J. Simons; K. Elliger, GHH II [1964] 1135; R. de Vaux, *Ancient Israel* [1962]). Mader's excavations, and the supporting texts which he assembled (e.g., from Josephus and from the fifth-century church historian, Sozomenos), show that Mamre remained a holy place through the centuries, as do the remains of the foundations of the basilica that Constantine built there, which in turn point to older constructions. Mamre is mentioned only in Genesis, but never afterwards; the reason is probably that it was later suspected of being syncretistic (so R. de Vaux).

(Hebron, 36 km. south of Jerusalem, earlier known as *Qiryat-arba*, was built seven years before Zoar in Egypt, Num. 13:22; besides the lexicons, cf. J. Simons, p. 213; A. Parrot, *Abraham et son temps* [1962] 69-72.)

Purpose and Thrust

There is a peculiar tension here between the narrative in the middle and the promise at the end. Abraham is given the promise of a large and spacious land and of a superabundant posterity. The promise reaches fulfillment in the period of the monarchy. But this very fulfillment, a large population in a spacious land, makes war unavoidable. The history of the people of Israel in the monarchy is also a history of the wars of Israel; it ends with utter defeat. The narrative in Gen. 13, on the contrary, tells of a dispute between Abraham and his kinsmen which is settled without violence. Abraham proposes a solution which is not to his advantage, but which settles the dispute peaceably. This tension extends across the history of Israel. The political power of the people which is implied in the promise—and includes making war—is not Israel's ultimate goal.

The promises of the postexilic period, which arose out of the political collapse, speak of a king of peace, a kingdom of peace, and the end of wars. The people of Israel preserved the memory of the patriarchs, who waged no wars, right down into this period. The narrative of Abraham, who brought a dispute to a peaceful solution by personal renunciation, still spoke across the era of Israel's wars; it was a pointer to another way of solving a conflict. The promise of a king of peace had a predecessor.

Abraham and the Kings

Literature

Genesis 14: A. H. Sayce, "The Archaeology of Genesis 14," ET 17 (1905/06) 498-504. J. Meinhold, *1. Mose 14. Eine historisch-kritische Untersuchung*, BZAW 22 (1911); "Abraham und die Könige des Ostens (1. Mose 14)," *Internationale Wochenschrift* 5 (1911) 705-722. E. König, "Genesis 14—der Bericht über Abraham, Kedorlaomer, Melchisedek—von seinem literarkritischen Hauptmomente aufs neue beleuchtet," NKZ 23 (1912) 425-464. J. Morgenstern, "Genesis 14," *Studies in Jewish Literature Issued in Honor of Prof. K. Kohler* (1913) 223-236. P. Asmussen, "Genesis 14, ein politisches Flugblatt," ZAW 34 (1914) 36-41. C. H. Cornill, "Genesis 14," ZAW 34 (1914) 150-154. F. M. T. Böhl, "Die Könige von Genesis 14," ZAW 36 (1916) 65-73. W. F. Albright, "Historical and Mythical Elements in the Story of Joseph," JBL 37 (1918) 111-143; "A Revision of Early Hebrew Chronology," JPOS 1 (1921) 49-70. A. Jirku, "Zum historischen Stil von Gen 14," ZAW 39 (1921) 312-314. F. M. T. Böhl, "Tud'alia I., Zeitgenosse Abrahams, um 1650 v.Chr.," ZAW 42 (1924) 148-153. I. Benzinger, "Zur Quellenscheidung in Genesis 14," BZAW 41 (1925) 21-27. W. F. Albright, "The Historical Background of Genesis XIV," JSOR 10 (1926) 231-269. P. Heinisch, "Abrahams Sieg über die Könige des Ostens und seine Begegnung mit Melchisedek (Gen 14)," StC 2 (1926) 152-178, 217-232. H. G. Güterbock, "Die historische Tradition," ZA 42 (1934) 77-79. P. Jensen, "Alttestamentlich-keilschriftliches, I," ZA 42 (1934) 232-237. J. H. Kroeze, Genesis Veertien, een exegetisch-historische Studië (Diss. Amsterdam 1937). J. Simons, "Topographical Elements in the Story of Abimelech," OTS 2 (1943) 35-78. J. de Fraine, "De chronologia Abrahae secundum documenta nuperrime effossa," VD 26 (1948) 104-109. A. Bruno, *Die Bücher Genesis-Exodus: Eine rhythmische Untersuchung* (1953), esp. pp. 44-46. D. J. Wiseman, *The Alalakh Tablets* (1953). F. Zimmermann, "Some Textual Studies in Genesis," JBL 73 (1954) 97-101. F. Cornelius, "Genesis XIV," ZAW 72 (1960) 1-7; *Geistesgeschichte der Frühzeit*, II,1 (1962); II,2 (1967). J. R. Porter, "The Pentateuch and the Triennial Lectionary Cycle: An Examination of a Recent Theory," *Essays presented to Prof. S. H. Hooke* (1964) 163-174. M. C. Astour, "Political and Cosmic Symbolism in Genesis 14 and in Its Babylonian Sources," *Biblical Motifs, Origin and Transformation*, ed. A. Altmann (1966) 65-112. B. Mazar, "The Book of Genesis in the Light of History," *4th World Congress of Jewish Studies. Papers* 17-22 (1967). J. A. Emerton, "Some False Clues in the Study of Genesis XIV," VT 21 (1971) 24-47; "The Riddle of Genesis XIV," VT 21 (1971) 403-439. W. Schatz, *Genesis 14: Eine Untersuchung* (1972).

Genesis 14:1-9: A. H. Sayce, "The Chedor-Laomer Tablets," PSBA 28 (1906) 193-200, 241-251; 29 (1907) 7-17. J. A. Knudtzon, "Lidt om 1. Mos. 14," NTT 6 (1907) 1-11. C. J. Ball, "Note on the Name Chedor-laomer (Kudur-Lagamar), Gen XIV," ET 19 (1907/08) 41-42. P. Dhorme, "Hammurabi-Amraphel," RB 5 (1908) 205-226. A.

Ungnad, "Keilschrifttexte der Gesetze Hammurapis," ZA 22 (1909) 7-13. J. Hontheim, "Genesis 14 und Hammurapi von Babylon," ZKTh 36 (1912) 48-66. S. Landersdorfer, "Das Land Šin'ar," BZ 11 (1913) 350-363. W. T. Pilter, "Some Amorite Names in Genesis XIV," PSBA 35 (1913) 205-226. F. Hommel, "Zu Genesis 14 und insbesondere zu Ariokh von Ellasar," BZ 15 (1920) 213-218. W. F. Albright, "Shinar-Šangar and Its Monarch Amraphel," AJSL 40 (1924) 125-133. F. W. König, *Die Geschichte Elams* (1931). W. Wreszinski, "Ein neuer Hyksoskönig," OLZ 34 (1931) 1009-1011. G. C. Cameron, *History of Early Iran* (1936), esp. pp. 228-230. I. J. Gelb, "Shanhar," AJSL 53 (1937) 253-255. W. F. Albright, "A Third Revision of the Early Chronology of Western Asia," BASOR 88 (1942) 33-35. M. Gruenthaner, "The Date of Abraham," CBQ 4 (1942) 360-362; 5 (1943) 85-87. J. Lewy, "The Old West Semitic Sun God Hammu," HUCA 18 (1943/44) 429-436. F. M. T. Böhl, "King Hammurabi of Babylon in the Setting of His Time," *Opera Minora* (1953) 339-363. M. Noth, "Arioch—Arriwuk," VT 1 (1951) 136-140. J. C. Craviotti, "La primera expedición biblica," RivBib 65 (1952) 69-73; "La Pentápolis palestinense," RivBib 68 (1953) 37-44. K. Schlesinger, "Zur Wortfolge im hebräischen Verbalsatz," VT 3 (1953) 381-390. K. Jaritz, "Wer ist Amraphel in Genesis 14?" ZAW 70 (1958) 255-256. W. Baumgartner, "Herodots babylonische und assyrische Nachrichten," *Ausgewählte Aufsätze* (1959) 282-331. F. Cornelius, "ERIN-Manda," *Iraq* 25 (1963) 167-170. H. Seebass, "Der Ort Elam in der südlichen Wüste und die Überlieferung von Gen 14," VT 15 (1965) 389-394. G. J. Kuiper, "A Study of the Relationship between a Genesis Apocryphon and the Pentateuchal Targumim in Genesis 14,1-12," BZAW 103 (1968) 149-161. J. A. Thompson, "Samaritan Evidence for 'All of them in the Land of Shinar' (Gen 10:10)," JBL 90 (1971) 99-102. P. Grelot, "Ariōk," VT 25 (1975) 711-719. H. Donner, *Einführung in die biblische Landes- und Altertumskunde* (1976).

Genesis 14:2-3: F. M. Abel, "Histoire d'une controverse," RB 40 (1931) 388-400. E. Sapir, "Hittite siyanta and Gen 14,3," AJSL 55 (1938) 86-88. H. Junker, "Pentapolis," LThK 8 (1963) 257. J. Priest, "The Covenant of Brothers," JBL 84 (1965) 400-406.

Genesis 14:4: E. Wiesenberg, "Chronological Data in the Zadokite Fragments," VT 5 (1955) 284-308, esp. p. 288.

Genesis 14:5: P. Karge, *Die vorgeschichtliche Kultur Palästinas und Phöniziens. Archäologische und religionsgeschichtliche Studien:* "Rephaim" (1917) 609-646. C. Virolleaud, "Les Rephaïms," RES (1940) 77-83; "Les Rephaïms: Fragments du poème de Ras Shamra," *Syria* 22 (1941) 1-30. J. Gray, "The Rephaim," PEQ 81 (1949) 127-139. A. Caquot, "Les Rephaims ougaritiques," *Syria* 37 (1960) 75-77. A. H. van Zyl, *The Moabites* (1960), esp. pp. 31-38, 108-112, 195. A. Jirku, "Rapa'u, der Fürst der Rapa'uma-Rephaim," ZAW 77 (1965) 82f. G. Howard, "Some Notes on the Septuagint of Amos," VT 20 (1970) 108-112. B. Margulis, "A Ugaritic Psalm (RS 24.252)," JBL 89 (1970) 292-304.

Genesis 14:6: H. D. Hummel, "Enclitic *Mem* in Early Northwest Semitic, Especially in Hebrew," JBL 76 (1957) 85-107. J. Blau, "Adverbia als psychologische und grammatische Subjekte/Praedikate im Bibelhebräisch," VT 9 (1959) 130-137. O. Loretz, "Weitere ugaritisch-hebräische Parallelen," BZ 3 (1959) 290-294. A. Robinson, "The Meaning of rî and the Dubiety of the Form *harrê* and its Variants," VT 24 (1974) 500-504.

Genesis 14:7: H. L. Ginsberg, "The Wilderness of Kadesh (Ps 29,8)," JBL 58 (1939) XI. J. Gray, "The Desert Sojourn of the Hebrews and the Sinai-Horeb Tradition," VT 4 (1954) 148-154. M. Tsevat, "The Canaanite God Sälah," VT 4 (1954) 41-49. Y. Aharoni, "Tamar and the Roads to Elath," IEJ 13 (1963) 30-42. M. Rose, " 'Siebzig Könige' aus Ephraim (Jde V 14)," VT 26 (1976) 447-452.

Genesis 14:8: H. Kornfeld, "Eine Konjektur betreffend Gen 14,8 und 19,25: 'Admah und Zwoim,' " BZ 9 (1911) 26.

Genesis 14:10: W. F. Albright, "The Archaeological Results of an Expedition to Moab and the Dead Sea," BASOR 14 (1924) 2-12. E. W. Heaton, "The Root š'r and the Doctrine of the Remnant," JThS.3 (1952) 27-39. A. H. van Zyl, "Die ligging van Sodom en Gomorra volgens Gen 14," HTS 14 (1959) 82-87. G. F. Hasel, "Semantic Values of Derivatives of the Hebrew Root š'r," AUSS 11 (1973) 152-169. M. Delcor, "Quelques cas de survivances du vocabulaire nomade en Hébreu Biblique," VT 25 (1975) 307-322.

Genesis 14:11: E. Nestle, "Genesis 14,11," ZAW 27 (1907) 113-114. F. Willesen, "The *Yālīd* in Hebrew Society," StTh 12 (1958) 192-210.

Genesis 14:13: W. T. Pilter, "The Amorite Personal Names in Genesis XIV," PSBA 36 (1914) 125-142, 212-230. J. Dus, "Das Sesshaftwerden der nachmaligen Israeliten im Land Kanaan," CV 6 (1963) 263-275. G. Schmitt, "El Berit-Mitra," ZAW 76 (1964) 325-327. E. Testa, "De foedere Patriarcharum," SBFLA 15 (1964/65) 5-73. F. F. Bruce, "Tell El-Amarna," *Archaeology and OT Study*, ed. D. W. Thomas (1967) 3-20. M. Greenberg, "Ḥab/Piru and Hebrews," *The World History of the Jewish People II* (1970) 188-200. M. Fishbane, "Additional Remarks on *Rḥmyw* (Amos 1:11)," JBL 91 (1972) 391-393. H. Cazelles, "The Hebrews," *Peoples of OT Times*, ed. D. J. Wiseman (1973) 1-28. E. Lipiński, "'Anaq-Kiryat ʾArbaʿ—Hébron et ses Sanctuaires Tribaux," VT 24 (1974) 41-55.

Genesis 14:14: E. Nestle, "318 = Eliezer," ET 7 (1905/06) 44f; "Gen XIV 14 in the Epistle of Barnabas," ET 7 (1905/06) 139-140. J. C. Matthes, "Bemerkungen zu einigen Stellen aus Genesis und Numeri," ZAW 31 (1911) 128-132. W. R. W. Gardner, "Genesis XIV (עד־דן)," ET 26 (1915/16) 523 f. I. L. Seeligmann, "Indications of Editorial Alteration and Adaptation in the Massoretic Text and the Septuagint," VT 11 (1961) 201-221. S. Gevirtz, "Abram's 318," IEJ 19 (1969) 110-113. S. C. Reif, "Dedicated to חנך," VT 22 (1972) 495-501.

Genesis 14:15: Y. Ben-Shem, "Nocturnal Warfare," BetM 50 (1972) 362-364. D. J. Kamhi, "The Root *ḥlq* in the Bible," VT 23 (1973) 235-239.

Genesis 14:17: J. T. Milik, " 'Saint-Thomas de Phordêsa' et Gen 14,17," Bib 42 (1961) 77-84. A. Wieder, "Ugaritic-Hebrew Lexicographical Notes," JBL 84 (1965) 160-164.

Genesis 14:18-20: E. Sellin, "Melchisedek. Ein Beitrag zur Geschichte Abrahams," NKZ 16 (1905) 929-951. K. Kohler, "Die Malkisedek-Episode in Genesis 14," ZA 28 (1914) 364-370. S. Landersdorfer, "Das Priesterkönigtum von Salem," JSOR 9 (1925) 200-216. V. Aptowitzer, "Malkizedek. Zu den Sagen der Agada," MGWJ 70 (1926) 93-113. G. Bardy, "Melchisédech dans la tradition Patristique," RB 35 (1926) 496-509; 36 (1927) 25-45. G. Wuttke, *Melchisedek der Priesterkönig von Salem*," BZNW 76 (1927). H. W. Hertzberg, "Die Melchisedek-Traditionen," JPOS 8 (1928) 169-179. K. Budde, "Die Herkunft Ṣadok's," ZAW 52 (1934) 42-50. M. Simon, "Melchisédek dans la polémique entre juifs et chrétiens et dans la légende," RHPhR 17 (1937) 58-93. H. H. Rowley, "Zadok and Nehushtan," JBL 58 (1939) 113-141. C. MacKay, "The Order of Melchizedek," CQR 138 (1944) 175-191. B. Piperow, "Melchisedek, Der Prototypus des Christus: Exegetische Forschung über Genesis 14,18-20," JThFUS 22 (1945). B. Holwerda, *De Priesterkoning in het OT* (1946). G. Vajda, "Melchisedec dans la mythologie ismaélienne," JA 234 (1947) 173-183. F. Asensio, "El recuerdo de Melquisedec en Suárez (Gen 14,18-20)," EstEcc 22 (1948) 407-417. H. H. Rowley, "Melchizedek and Zadok (Gen 14 and Ps 110)," *Fests. A. Bertholet* (1950) 461-472. A. J. B. Higgins, "Priest and Messiah," VT 3 (1953) 321-336. A. R. Johnson, *Sacral Kingship in Ancient Israel* (1955; 1967²), esp. pp. 47ff. H. E. Del Medico, "Melchisédech (Gen 14; Ps 110)," ZAW 69 (1957) 160-170. G. W. Ahlström, "Der Prophet Nathan und der Tempelbau," VT 11 (1961) 113-127. S. Abramski, "Melchizedek King of Salem" [in Hebr.], BetM 13 (1962) 105-120. L. R. Fisher, "Abraham and His Priest-King," JBL 81 (1962) 264-270. I. Hunt, "Recent Melkizedek Studies," *The Bible in Current Catholic Thought*, ed. J. L. McKenzie (1962) 20-33. J. A. Fitzmyer, " 'Now this Melchizedek. . .' (Heb 7,1)," CBQ 25 (1963) 305-321; JBL 86 (1967) 25-41. C. E. Hauer, "Who Was Zadok?" JBL 82 (1963) 89-94. J. H. Hayes, "The Tradition of Zion's Inviolability," JBL 82 (1963) 419-426. H. Schmid, "Melchisedek und Abraham, Zadok und David," *Kairos* 7 (1965) 148-151. R. H. Smith, "Abram and Melchizedek (Gen 14:18-20)," ZAW 77 (1965) 129-153. S. van der Woude, "Melchisedek als himmlische Erlösergestalt in den neugefundenen eschatologischen Midraschim aus Qumran-Höhle XI," OTS 14 (1965) 354-373. C. T. Fritsch, "To ʾAntityphon," *Fests. T. C. Vriezen* (1966) 100-107. R. Meyer, "Melchisedek von Jerusalem und Moresedek von Qumran," VT.S 15 (1966) 228-239. J. W. Bowker, "Psalm CX," VT 17 (1967) 31-41, and H. H. Rowley, VT 17 (1967) 485. W. Zimmerli, "Abraham und Melchisedek," *Fests. L. Rost* (1967) 255-264. W. S. Towner, " 'Blessed be YHWH' and 'Blessed art thou YHWH': The Modulation of a Biblical Formula,'' CBQ 30 (1968) 386-399. W. E. Brooks, ''The Perpetuity of Christ's Sacrifice in the Epistle to the Hebrews,'' JBL 89 (1970) 205-214. J. Carmignac, ''Le document de Qumrân sur Melkisédeq,'' RQ 7 (1970) 343-378. M. Delcor, ''Melchizedek From Genesis to the Qumran Texts and the Epistle to the Hebrews,'' JSJ 2 (1971) 115-135. J. G. Gammie, ''Loci of the Melchizedek Tradition of Genesis 14,18-20,'' JBL 90 (1971) 385-396. J. Jeremias, ''Lade und Zion. Zur Entstehung der Ziontradition,'' *Fests. G. von Rad* (1971) 183-198. F. Vattioni, ''Note sul Genesi (Gen 14,17-24; 21,33),'' Aug. 12 (1972) 457-463.

Genesis 14:18: H. Grimme, ''Der Name Jerusalem,'' OLZ 16 (1913) 152-157. A. Vaccari, ''Melchisedec, rex Salem, proferens panem et vinum,'' VD 18 (1938) 208-214, 235-243. R. A. Rosenberg, ''The God Ṣedeq,'' HUCA 36 (1965) 161-177. J. de Fraine, ''La royauté de Yahvé dans textes concernant l'arche,'' VT.S 15 (1966) 134-149. J. F. X. Sheehan, ''Melchisedek in Christian Consciousness,'' ScEcc 18 (1966) 127-138. C. F. Whitley, ''Deutero-Isaiah's Interpretation of ṣedeq,'' VT 22 (1972) 469-475. G. Gerleman, ''Die Wurzel šlm,'' ZAW 85 (1973) 1-14; F. L. Horton, *The Melchizedek Tradition*, SNTS 30 (1976).

Genesis 14:19: P. Humbert, '' 'Qânâ' en hébreu biblique,'' *Festschr. A. Bertholet* (1950) 259-266. H. Schmid, ''Jahwe und die Kulttraditionen von Jerusalem,'' ZAW 67 (1955) 168-197. F. Vattioni, ''Un testo hittita e Gen 14,19,'' RivBib 3 (1955) 165-173. B. J. Alfrink, ''L'expression 'šamaim ou š'mei haš-šamaim' dans l'Ancien Testament,'' *Mélanges E. Tisserant* I (1965) 1-7.

Genesis 14:20: W. von Soden, ''Vedisch magham 'Geschenk'—neuarabisch maǧǧānīja 'Gebührenfreiheit.' Der Web einer Wortsippe,'' JEOL 18 (1965) 339-344.

Genesis 14:22: J. A. Fitzmyer, ''Some Observations on the Genesis Apocryphon,'' CBQ 22 (1960) 277-291. M. Delcor, ''Les attaches littéraires, l'origine et la signification de l'expression biblique 'Prendre à témoin le ciel et la terre,' '' VT 16 (1966) 8-25.

Genesis 14:23: E. Nestle, ''Zum Faden in Gen 14,23,'' ZAW 29 (1909) 230-231. S. Talmon, ''Double Readings in the Massoretic Text,'' *Textus* 1 (1960) 144-184.

Genesis 14:24: S. Speier, ''DS Genesis Apocryphon and Targum Jerushalmi I on Genesis XIV 24,'' VT 8 (1958) 95-97.

Text

14:1 It was in the time of Amraphel[a] king of Shinar,[b] Arioch king of Ellasar,[c] Chedorlaomer[d] king of Elam,[e] and Tidal[f] king of Goiim.[g]

2 They waged war against Bera[a] king of Sodom, Birsha king of Gomorrah, Shinab[b] king of Admah, Shemeber[c] king of Zeboiim,[d] and the king of Bela, that is, Zoar.

3 All these joined together and proceeded to the valley of Siddim,[a] that is, the Salt Sea.

4 They had been subject to Chedorlaomer for twelve years, but in the thirteenth[a] they revolted.[b]

5 Then in the fourteenth year Chedorlaomer and the kings in union with him came and defeated the Rephaim[a] in Ashteroth-karnaim, the Zuzim[b] in Ham,[c] the Emim in Shaveh-kiriathaim,[d]

6 and the Horites in their hill-country[a] of Seir as far as[b] El-paran on the edge of the desert.

7 They came back and went to Enmishpat,[a] that is, Kadesh, and conquered the whole territory[b] of the Amalekites as well as that of the Amorites who lived in Hazazon-tamar.[c]

8 Then the king of Sodom marched out[a] with the king of Gomorrah, the king of Admah, the king of Zeboiim,[b] and the king of Bela, that is, Zoar, and they drew up[c] in battle order against them in the Valley of Siddim,

9 against Chedorlaomer[a] king of Elam,[b] Tidal king of Goiim, Amraphel

185

          king of Shinar, and Arioch king of Ellasar, four kings against five.[c]

10   Now the valley of Siddim was full of bitumen pits;[ab] when the kings of Sodom and Gomorrah[c] fled, they fell into them, but the rest escaped to the mountain range.[d]

11   The four kings took all the possessions[a] of Sodom and Gomorrah and all their provisions and went away.

12   They also took Lot (Abram's nephew, who was living in Sodom at the time) and his possessions and went away.[a]

13   But a[a] fugitive came and informed Abram, the Hebrew,[b] who was dwelling by the terebinth(s)[c] of Mamre, the Amorite, the brother of Eshcol and Aner,[d] who were confederates of Abram.

14   When Abram heard that his kinsman had been taken prisoner, he mustered[a] his retainers, men born in his household, three hundred and eighteen men, and pursued[b] as far as Dan.

15   Abram and his men divided[a] and attacked them by night, defeated them, and pursued them as far as Hobah, north[b] of Damascus.

16   He brought back all the possessions[a] as well as his kinsman Lot and his possessions, together with the women and the captives.

17   On his return[c] from the defeat of Chedolaomer[a] and the kings[b] in union with him, the king of Sodom came out to meet him in the Valley of Shaveh,[d] that is the King's Valley.

18   And Melchizedek,[a] king of Salem, brought out bread and wine; he was priest of[b] El-Elyon.

19   He blessed him[a] and said: "Blessed be Abram by El-Elyon, the creator[b] of heaven and earth.

20   And blessed[a] be El-Elyon, who delivered your enemy into your hand." And he[b] gave him a tithe of all the booty.

21   And the king of Sodom said to Abram: "Give me the people, you take the property."

22   And Abram said to the king of Sodom: "I raise[a] my hand to Yahweh,[b] El Elyon, the creator[c] of heaven and earth;

23   not a thread, not a shoestring, nothing[a] at all of what is[b] yours will I take; you shall not say, I made Abram rich.

24   Nothing for me[a] but what the young men have eaten, and the share of the men who went with me; Aner, Eshcol, and Mamre shall have their share.

1a Gk ἐν τῆ βασιλέια τῆ Αμαρφαλ; Vg *factum est autem in illo tempore*; GenApoc "before these days"; on ויהי בימי as introduction, Ges-K §111,2; E. A. Speiser understands it as a translation from Akk. *enuma*, " 'when,' originally 'in the day, at the time.' "   **b** GenApoc reads בבל for שנער.   **c** for אלסר Vg reads *Ponti*, GenApoc כפתור.   **d** in GenApoc, Chedorlaomer is in first place.   **e** Sym reads Σκυθῶν for עילם.   **f** Gk and Syr read θαργαλ for תדעל.   **g** Gk, Vg, TargO render גוים by "peoples," Sym, Παμφυλιας.
2a Gk[A] Βαλλα; GkMss Βαρα.   **b** Gk reads καὶ Σεννααρ for שנאב.   **c** Sam and GenApoc שמאבד.   **d** Q צבויים.
3a Gk φάραγξ ἡ ἁλυκή, VetLat, *vallis salsa*; Vg *vallis silvestris*; Syr "valley of the Sodomites."
4a Gk, Syr, Vg, Tar, GenApoc read ובשלש.   **b** Vg adds *ab eo*.
5a Sam and Gk have definite article, Gk οἱ γίγαντες.   **b** Sym Ζοιζομμειν (= זמזמים), cf. Deut. 2:20; GenApoc 21:29 indicates זמזמים by the ם written over the central ו; Gk renders by ἔθνη ἰσχυρά.   **c** Instead of בהם some Sam Ms and Jerome read בחם; Gk ἅμα αὐτοῖς; Vg *cum eis*; Gen Apoc בע מון.   **d** Instead of the last two words Gk has ἐν Σαυη τῆ πόλει; GenApoc 21:29 has the place-name קירות.
6a Read בהררי with Gk, Syr, Vg.   **b** Gk ἕως τῆς τερεμίνθου.

7a Gk ἡ πηγὴ τῆς κρίσεως. **b** Gk and Syr presuppose שׂרי instead of שׂדה, probably correctly. **c** TargO and Syr, following 2 Chron. 20:2, read En-gedi.

8a Sing. of verb preceding a plurality of subjects, Ges-K §145o, BrSynt §50a. **b** Q as in v. 2. **c** Syr כל־אלה עשׂו.

9a GenApoc ". . .and the kings with him." **b** The variants in the names as in v. 1, with minor differences. **c** on the article, Ges-K §134k.

10a Sam *plene*. **b** Repetition and the construct state, Ges-K §130e. **c** Gk, Sam, Syr have, more correctly, ומלך עמרה. **d** Sam ההרה.

11a Sam *plene*.

12a Gk tries to correct the awkward arrangement of the sentence by inversion.

13a The article indicates "the one who in such circumstances usually comes" (A. Dillmann, ad.loc.), Ges-K §126g. According to GenApoc the man was one of Lot's shepherds. Gk and Vg alter: *unus qui evaserat*. **b** Gk ὁ περάτης: Jerome, *Transeuphratensis*. **c** with Gk and Syr, read באלון as in 12:6 and 13:18. **d** instead of ענר Gk reads Αὐναν; Syr עניר; Sam ענרם; GenApoc ערנם.

14a Instead of וירק imperf. hiph. from רוק = "empty out," Sam reads וידק (from דוק hiph. "to muster"); so probably Gk ἠρίθμησεν; Vg *numeravit*, TargO וזריז. **b** Gk, Vg, Syr add אחריהם.

15a ἐπέπεσεν, Vg *et divisis sociis inruit super eos*. **b** actually, "to the left of"; northwards (i.e., facing east), KBL.

16a Gk translates by ἡ ἵππος the first time, and τὰ ὑπάρχοντα the second.

17a Written as two words in Lat Mss., including Vg. **b** Gk (variant) reads only והמלכים. **c** שׁוב can mean the return to the starting point, Ges-K §115a, KBL. **d** שׁוה without article, Gk and Sam with article.

18a The name *Melchizedek* is passed on uniformly by the versions. **b** ל indicates the genitive.

19a Sam and Gk ויברך את־אברם. **b** Gk ὅς ἔκτισεν, Vg *qui creavit*.

20a Gk renders the first ברוך by εὐλογημένος, the second by εὐλογητός. **b** "Though Melchizedek is the grammatical subject, logically Abraham must have paid tithes to the priest-king" (W. Schatz, *Genesis 14: Eine Untersuchung* [1972] 72).

22a The Hebr. perfect has a present meaning in direct speech, Ges-K §106; Gk future, Vg present. **b** Missing in Gk, Syr, GenApoc; Sam אל האלהים. **c** Vg renders קנה by *qui creavit* in v. 19, and by *possessorem* in v. 22.

23a Gk and Vg leave out the second אם. **b** On the use of language in oaths, Ges-K §149c.

24a TargO presupposes only בִּלְעָדַי instead of MT בלעדי רק; the meaning is really: "nothing for me."

The History of the Exegesis of Genesis 14

Detailed accounts of the history of research into Gen. 14 may be found in the book of W. Schatz (1972), the articles of J. A. Emerton (1971), the dissertation of J. H. Kroeze (1937) (for all, see Lit. to Gen. 14), as well as in A. Parrot, *Abraham et son temps*, CAB 14 (1962). I will confine myself to an outline of the two main stages. The first stage presupposed the basic unity of the chapter because it did not seem possible to divide it into sources; discussion centered mainly or exclusively around geographical, political, and personal names. It began with the presupposition that the historicity of the event described could be demonstrated by the historical attestation of individual names. The standard example is the equating of Amraphel with Hammurabi, whence the conclusion that Abraham was Hammurabi's contemporary (the equation was first made by E. Schraeder, "Die keilschriftliche babylonische Königsliste," SAB 31 [1887] 579-607; then E. Dhorme [1908], F. Delitzsch, H. Holzinger, et al.; cf. Lit. to Gen. 14:1). No account was taken of the fact that historically attested names can also occur in nonhistorical texts. This explanation received great impetus from the names attested in archaeological finds. W. Schatz synthesizes the texts alleged on behalf of Gen. 14 (pp. 18-30): the Amarna letters, the Chedorlaomer (or Spartoli) texts, the code of Hammurabi and other Babylonian texts, the documents from Boghazköy, Ugarit, Mari, Qumran. There is no limit to the studies on the individual names in Gen. 14 on the basis of such texts.

The second phase began with questions about the unity and nature of the chapter. It was already under way with H. Gunkel, though he remained by and large caught up with the question as it was put in the first phase. It was only very gradually that a few scholars raised the questions of form and tradition criticism which led to results that gave a basis for exegesis, the most important of which was a recognition of the composite character of the chapter and the original independence of each of its three constituent parts (vv. 1-11; 12-17 and 21-24; 18-20; S. Herrmann writes of ". . .Gen. 14 and the traditions which it combines," *A History of Israel* [1973; 1979²; Eng. 1976] 49). There arose at the same time the important question of the relationship of these parts to each other in the history of tradition.

Three main questions have dominated the whole course of the study of Gen. 14:

(1) The question of "historicity."   The two opposed theses, supporting or denying the historicity, have the same questionable basis in method. One maintains that Gen. 14 is an essentially historical report from ancient times (from F. Delitzsch and E. Dhorme to W. F. Albright and N. M. Sarna), the other that it is a later unhistorical midrash, legend, or haggadah (from A. Kuenen, T. Nöldeke, and J. Wellhausen to A. Bentzen, M. Noth, and J. Van Seters). However, this second phase offers no real alternative because of the questionable methodological basis: it is impossible to decide whether Gen. 14 is "historical" or "unhistorical" without further clarification of the question of its unity and character. This also explains why those who defend or contest the "historicity" are constantly changing ground; the question admits of no such obvious answer. One can distinguish here an earlier and a later stage of interpretation. The conservative thesis, which maintains that Gen. 14 is essentially historical, extends in its older stage from the beginnings up to the period before the new archaeological approach; the later stage begins with it. The critical thesis, which understands Gen. 14 as a late midrash (or some such), extends in its older stage from A. Kuenen, T. Nöldeke, and J. Wellhausen to an early essay of W. F. Albright (JBL 37 [1918] 111-143). Albright there took the position that there was no historical basis for Gen. 14; subsequently, in a series of later essays, he defended the historical perspective of the chapter on the basis of new archaeological finds, but with fluctuating reasons, particularly in "The Historical Background. . ." (JSOR 10 [1936] 231-269). The later stage of the critical thesis presupposes the new archaeological approach as well as the perspective introduced by H. Gunkel, and generally distinguishes between old and late elements (so, e.g., O. Eissfeldt and, following him, J. W. Bowker: "Perhaps the best solution. . .is the simplest one that both elements are present: an old tradition survived independently. . .and was incorporated into the Pentateuch at a late stage" [VT 17 (1967) 31-41]).

(2) The question of a document as the basis of Gen. 14.   There is virtual unanimity that Gen. 14 does not belong to any of the known sources, and broad agreement that there is some sort of document as its basis. The majority accept that it is a non-Israelite document; the many names must come from somewhere. But this is as far as agreement goes. H. Ewald had already seen in Gen. 14 the remnant of an ancient work of Babylonian or Canaanite origin (*Geschichte des Volkes Israel* I [1843; 1864²]). This was accepted by R. Kittel, E. Sellin, H. Holzinger, W. Winckler, F. Hommel, C. H. Cornill, A. Jeremias, A. Jirku, P. Jensen, J. Skinner, E. A. Speiser, R. de Vaux, et al. (cf. J. A. Emerton, VT 21 [1971] 30-37). M. C. Astour proposes a new variant of this thesis (in *Biblical Motifs. . .*, ed. A. Altmann [1966] 65ff.): Gen. 14 is directly dependent on an older text which was at the disposal of the Chedorlaomer (Spartoli) texts of the second century, themselves going back to an earlier text of the sixth or seventh century; the author of Gen. 14 belonged to the Deuteronomic school. W. Schatz follows him in this; see J. A. Emerton, pp. 38-46. Others accept only a document of non-Israelite origin (S. Oettli, E. König, P. Heinisch), or speak merely in general terms of an ancient document (E. Dhorme, A. Lods). A very popular view is that the author found the document in the temple archives (from H. Ewald on). E. Meyer (1920) is more reserved and speaks of information gained in Babylon during the exile; similarly A. Lods and J. Van Seters; H. Gunkel says that the narrative contains Babylonian, Canaanite, and Israelite material. An interesting variant is the view that the basis of

Gen. 14 is a poem (so E. Sievers, *Metrische Studien* II, 2 [1905] 267-274; A. Bruno, *Die Bücher Genesis-Exodus: Eine rhythmische Untersuchung* [1953] 44-46; F. M. T. Böhl [1925]); this was taken up again by W. F. Albright (JSOR 10 [1926] 231ff.) and his student D. N. Freedman (ZAW 64 [1952] 190-194), and by N. M. Sarna (*Understanding Genesis* [1966; 1972²]). J. A. Emerton contests this view, as he does the Babylonian origin of a document (VT 21 [1971] 24-27).

In the first phase the question of the character of such a basic document, or whether it was the basis of all constituent parts of the chapter, was scarcely ever raised. The only attitude was that of historicity: if there is such a non-Israelite document, then the historicity of what is reported in Gen. 14 is proved. But once it is recognized that the parts of the chapter have each a different origin, then distinctions must be introduced into the question of a basic document.

(3) The question of the unity and composition of Gen. 14. Scholars soon abandoned earlier attempts to divide the chapter into sources (e.g., H. Winckler, *Abraham als Babylonier.* . . [1893, 1903]; I. Benzinger, BZAW 41 [1925] 21-27), and tried to come to terms with the difficulties by means of traditio-historical methods. Many saw that the Melchizedek episode (vv. 18-20) broke the continuity of vv. 17 and 21-24. Two explanations of this were given. One group of scholars considered vv. 18-20 an original constituent part, and the framework (vv. 17,21-24), the meeting with the king of Sodom, secondary (E. Sellin, O. Procksch, M. C. Astour, et al.). The majority saw vv. 18-20 as a subsequent insertion (J. Morgenstern, H. Gunkel, G. von Rad, E. Kutsch, J. W. Bowker, J. A. Emerton, O. Eissfeldt). This interpolation comes from the postexilic period (B. Duhm, H. Holzinger, O. Procksch, K. Budde, J. Meinhold, J. Van Seters), from the period of the divided kingdom (H. Schmid), or from the time of David (H. H. Rowley, H. S. Nyberg, J. W. Bowker, E. Kutsch, J. A. Emerton). Many maintained that behind the interpolation lies its own tradition (G. von Rad, E. Kutsch, J. A. Emerton), presuming for the most part that the rest of the chapter is a unity. Only at a very late stage was it observed that the two parts of the chapter, vv. 1-11 and 12-24 (without 18-20), are of different types. A. Dillmann had already pointed to this; H. Gunkel had not seen it, nor has J. Van Seters. J. Skinner notes correctly: "The fallacy lies in treating the chapter as a homogeneous and undivisible unity." G. von Rad takes up Gunkel's remark that Abraham (and Lot) do not appear before v. 12, and sees that only vv. 1-11 can have a non-Israelite tradition as background, and not vv. 12-17,21-24; likewise R. de Vaux: "The extrabiblical text cannot have had Abraham intervening in this story." A. Dillmann too had suspected an older narrative behind vv. 11-24.

The question arises then, which of the two parts represents the older and which the later stage of tradition. According to G. von Rad, vv. 1-11 was the older; according to O. Procksch, E. Kutsch, W. Schatz, and J. A. Emerton, who argues the case in detail, it is vv. 12-24 (without vv. 18-20). The decisive argument is the character of the two parts: vv. 12-24 are a hero story about Abraham (so J. A. Emerton), vv. 1-11 are a historical report of a campaign of oriental kings (J. A. Emerton; already noted by J. Skinner). Actual parallels can be found only for this part; there is obviously no possibility of finding parallels to the chapter as a unity. The hero story, therefore, forms the basic material of the tradition; the Melchizedek episode was inserted into it; the composite product was then set in the framework of the account of the campaign (vv. 1-11) with the purpose of introducing Abraham on the stage of world history (J. A. Emerton, p. 437).

Against Emerton's explanation of the origin of Gen. 14, J. Van Seters has revived the old assertion that this chapter as a whole is a literary formation. However, he is able to maintain this only because he has very precisely and accurately determined vv. 1-11 to be a campaign report but then insisted that vv. 12-24 are similarly a campaign report. Thus, just as H. Gunkel, he has not recognized the distinctive character of vv. 12-24.

Scholarship, therefore, finds itself in a completely changed situation. One must first study the constituent parts and the tradition-history of each; only then can one study the chapter as a whole and determine its type and age. Gunkel's remark, which so many have repeated, that "the narrative contains in blatant contrast very credible and quite impossible material,'' is not applicable to each part in the same way. But what is most important is that once it is realized that the passage, vv. 1-11, which does not contain the name of Abraham, is originally independent, then it is no longer possible to draw conclusions about the historicity or period of Abraham from the names and events mentioned in it. Nor is there any further place for scholarly discussion whether Gen. 14 is old or late. The question of age must be put separately for each tradition and be distinguished from the question of the age of the chapter as a whole.

Form

We can use the results of scholarly research as the starting point to determine the form. Gen. 14 is composed of elements of different kinds. Before asking about the form and origin of the whole, one must investigate the form and origin of the individual elements. Three parts are to be distinguished:

    A. The report of the campaign (vv. 1-11 or 12);
    B. The liberation narrative (vv. 12-17, 21-24);
    C. The Melchizedek episode (vv. 18-20).

Part B forms the basic material into which C was later inserted; A was then prefixed to the composite B and C, and consequently determined the whole, with the result that exegesis has for the most part understood the chapter as a report of a campaign of four kings of the east in which Abraham's expedition (B) and the meeting with Melchizedek (C) are two episodes. The report, however, is not continued in vv. 12-24, which are of another type; they are narrative or, more accurately, liberation narrative (for the difference between report and narrative, cf. W. Richter, *Exegese als Literaturwissenschaft* [1970]; C. Westermann, *Genesis 1–11*, Intro.). Only vv. 12-24 are concerned with Abraham and Lot, who are not mentioned in vv. 1-11. Part A is played within the perspective of world history; Part B is restricted to the small territory of Canaan. There is a further difference: the extraordinary enumerative lists (vv. 1b,2,5,8,9) occur only in vv. 1-11 and not in vv. 12-24; within these latter, vv. 18-20 are an originally independent element which breaks the continuity between v. 17 and vv. 21-24. The first question to be raised is that of the structure and nature of each of these three parts; only then can there be discussion of the composite whole. When one recognizes the original independence of each of these parts, many problems solve themselves.

    Part A: 14:1-11. This part consists of a report of a campaign and the lists that have been assumed into it. One can recognize in a number of places, and already in v. 1, that the lists have not been fully integrated into the report. If one reads vv. 1-11 without the lists, one sees a self-contained report of a campaign. We have here something which is frequent and well known from the history of the empires of the ancient near east, particularly from Mesopotamia: a great power makes a campaign against a subject vassal people which has revolted against it by refusing to pay tribute. There are a number of such episodes in the Old Testament in the books of Kings, and a whole series of parallels from outside Israel, particularly in the Babylonian and Assyrian royal inscriptions, where a king reports that he has put down rebellious vassals. They are originally composed in the first person singular, and only secondarily converted into the annalistic style of the third person (J. Van Seters [1975] 300), e.g., the Zakir stele (ANET 555-56). J. Van Seters has analyzed these parts of the royal inscriptions as follows: (1) the reason for the military action, (2) preparations for the campaign, (3) the campaign with route and battles, (4) the results of the campaign: destruction of cities, prisoners and booty, tribute. One can find echoes of this distribution in vv. 1-11. We can be certain then of A's literary type. It is not possible to attach 14:1-11 to a particular campaign of particular kings; however, one can certainly trace the passage back to this type which had its origin in the oriental empires and presupposed domination over vassal peoples and vassal kings.

All this allows two further certain conclusions. First, only Part A falls under this literary type. It is quite impossible that an Assyrian or Babylonian king writing in the first person singular style would have added something like vv. 12ff. to his report of a successful campaign to punish rebellious vassals (so R. de Vaux). Second, the parallels to Gen. 14 from late Jewish writings, in particular the book of Judith, alleged by H. Gunkel and others, are not relevant to the still independent Part A, and they presuppose of necessity the figure of Abraham who is not mentioned in vv. 1-11. The parallelism is relevant only for the composite text of vv. 1-11 and 12-24, that is, for the final stage of tradition when the components B and C were joined with A. So a difficulty is solved which has perplexed a succession of exegetes, namely, how one could advance such very diverse types as Assyrian-Babylonian inscriptions on the one hand, and late Jewish legends on the other.

Part B: 14:12-24 (omitting vv. 18-20). Division: vv. 12, 13 are a link with what precedes (exposition); vv. 14-16, Abraham's campaign of liberation; vv. 17, 21-24, conclusion, meeting with the king of Sodom. Vv. 1-11 are a report, vv. 12-24 a narrative. J. Van Seters has not perceived this, although he has seen that "Lot is not a political figure" (p. 301). The event portrayed here corresponds at every step with the narratives of liberation from the period of the judges (see below, Comm. on vv. 12-17, 21-24; also J. A. Emerton; R. de Vaux). Abraham is the knightly hero who selflessly liberates his kinsmen who have been taken prisoner. Replace Abraham with Gideon and the story could take its place unaltered in the book of Judges. J. A. Emerton has perceived this when he describes vv. 12-24 as a hero narrative, compares the emphasis on the small battalion of 318 warriors with the 300 in the Gideon story, and draws attention to Abraham's courage which is paralleled by the same motif in Judges (Judg. 8:21; 9:54; VT 21 [1971] 431-433). Emerton also mentions narratives from the early monarchical period. In particular one can advance the narrative in 1 Sam. 30 which is a very similar case: the Amalekites have devastated Ziklag and taken prisoners, including David's two wives. David goes after them with 400 men, defeats them, and recovers the booty and the prisoners. Emerton commands agreement when he wants to derive narrative B from the period of the judges on the basis of these parallels; however, he did not ask the meaning of the application of such a narrative to Abraham. One must distinguish between two stages of tradition in answering this question. The application to Abraham represents a second stage in which the patriarchs are exalted by being transformed into hero and savior figures. There are as yet no parallels to this. It would represent the uncovering of the earliest stage in the subsequent history of Gen. 12–25.

Part C: 14:18-20: the Melchizedek episode. Most exegetes acknowledge that vv. 18-20 are a later insertion into the meeting of Abraham with the king of Sodom. One recognizes a further sign that the verses are an insertion in the additional words, "El Elyon, the creator of heaven and earth," which are unsuitable here and form a link with the framework. It should be noted that it is a matter of an insertion into vv. 12-24 before the whole was joined to vv. 1-11; it remains set in the already existing framework of vv. 12-24. The insertion is to be distinguished from the framework; it is an episode, formed and fashioned so as to fit into an already existing narrative. Its function is to legitimate something, namely, what takes place between Abraham and Melchizedek; that is, an event in the patriarchal period is meant to legitimate some existing practice in a later period. It is etiological in character and so is open to a variety of meanings (for details, J. A. Emerton, VT 21 [1971] 407-426). The intention of the author in inserting this episode must be gleaned from its goal and not from the individual elements. The goal is a cultic exchange (blessing and tribute); hence a cult ideology is intended. The insertion, vv. 18-20, is closer in time to the framework in which it is set than to vv. 1-11.

Finally, there is the question of the form and meaning of the chapter as a whole. Gen. 14 in its finished form is determined by the world political perspective into which it is set by vv. 1-11; thus vv. 12-24 and 18-20 become parts of the campaign of the kings. The Abraham of vv. 12-24 thereby becomes victor over the army, or part of it, of the kings of the east, and the Abraham of vv. 18-20 is acknowledged and honored by Melchizedek as such a victor. The purpose of Gen. 14 in its final form is clear and generally recognized: the glorification of Abraham as a great and powerful prince who encounters victoriously the united kings of the great kingdoms of the east.

There are three reasons why the final composition of Gen. 14 can derive only from a late, indeed postexilic, period: (1) The intention of elevating Abraham, precisely as the father of the Israelite people, to a figure of worldwide political significance, is in complete conformity with an attitude that is well known and well attested in the postexilic period. H. Gunkel commands agreement here (see above, under Part A). One can recognize this same tendency in the book of Judith, and already in the book of Daniel. (2) The second reason is that this is the only period in which the setting of vv. 12-24 into the framework of vv. 1-11 is comprehensible. The bizarre synthesis of such diverse elements, stemming from such different periods and areas, into a whole, and the elevation of Abraham to the hero of the resulting story, can be understood only from a period that no longer had any sensitivity to such differentiation (so, rightly, H. Gunkel; also J. Van Seters). (3) The third reason is that vv. 1-11 obviously smack of the scribe's desk; the clumsy way in which the lists have been worked in betrays this, and has given occasion to describe it as "midrash." This academic, antiquarian composition (restricted to vv. 1-11) goes hand in hand with the complete lack of historical perspective. It is only for this late synthesis that Gunkel's remark holds: "The narrative contains in blatant contrast very credible and quite impossible material."

Setting

One can answer the question about the origin and setting of Gen. 14 only by making appropriate distinctions. None of the constituent parts grew out of the patriarchal period itself; only personal names (Abraham, Lot, Sodom and Gomorrah) together with some information about them (the relationship between Abraham and Lot, the destruction of Sodom and Gomorrah), and some individual elements (use of certain words) were taken from the patriarchal story already assembled in the Pentateuch. The narrative 14:12-24 (without the name Abraham) originated in the period of the judges and comes from a cycle of savior narratives. When Abraham becomes the subject of the story, he acquires the importance of a savior hero, analogous to the figures in Judges. The addition (vv. 18-20) very probably arose in the time of David; an experience of Abraham is narrated with the purpose of legitimating cultic innovations in that period. The report of the campaign (vv. 1-11) with its many names is certainly of extra-Israelite origin; it follows in style and structure the royal inscriptions of Assyrian-Babylonian kings. It cannot be traced back to a definite historical event in the form in which it is preserved. The manner of presentation is unhistorical despite the acknowledgment of a historical document which lies behind it; the lists of names are joined to the report of the campaign in a clumsy way. The composite text of vv. 1-11 and 12-24 is the work of a scribe's desk from the late postexilic period, to be compared with other late Jewish writings.

Commentary

[14:1-11] The structure of vv. 1-11: the lists are worked into the report of the campaign. The campaign is introduced: In the time of. . . A and B waged war. The reason for the campaign is given in v. 4, and in v. 5a the departure and the time. The rebel kings drew up in battle order against them, with mention of the place (v. 8). There should follow here a report that the kings of the east defeated the rebels; it is missing, but is presupposed in the continuation in v. 10 which gives an account of the flight of the (defeated) vassal kings. The report concludes in v. 11, noting that after their victory the kings of the east took booty and departed. The report is extremely brief and concise; it says only what is necessary and is completely self-contained. One does not expect any continuation after so clear an ending, except a sentence about the renewal of the vassal status and the return. The report has undergone two elaborations. The first, vv. 5b-7, is the insertion of the report of another campaign which consists almost entirely of an enumeration of conquered peoples. This is a subsequent addition because the reason for the campaign in v. 14 names only the five cities. Further, the geographical sweep scarcely allows one to understand the campaign as a unified enterprise (so, e.g., R. de Vaux). The clumsy transition in v. 5 shows signs of stitching together. The second elaboration consists of the lists in vv. 1, 2, 8, 9. There are two lists which enumerate the opponent kings; the lists of vv. 1, 2 are repeated in vv. 8, 9. This unnecessary repetition in a report which is otherwise so concise, and the very clumsy way in which the lists are worked into vv. 1, 2 as well as vv. 8, 9, clearly betray a secondary hand.

(1) The list of the four great kings in v. 1 and v. 9: in v. 9, as in vv. 4 and 5, Chedorlaomer is the leader and so is mentioned first. In v. 1 Amraphel is taken from his place in the list so as to form the introduction, "It was in the time of Amraphel. . ."; accordingly, Chedorlaomer is moved back into third place. (2) The list of the minor kings of the Pentapolis in v. 2 and v. 8: the names are in the wrong place in v. 2 because v. 3 follows v. 1; "all these" in v. 3 refers to the great kings enumerated in v. 1. The names of the five would be in place at the beginning of v. 4 where the reason for the campaign is given. The reason for the dislocation is that the author wanted to put the lists side by side twice, in vv. 1,2 and vv. 8,9 (where they are not necessary).

[14:1(9)] *Names and countries of the kings of the east.* Amraphel of Shinar: E. Schrader explained the name as Hammurabi ("Die keilschriftliche babylonische Königsliste," SAB 31 [1887] 579-607); many took up this explanation which acquired great importance as proof of the historicity of ch. 14 and of the period of Abraham. But the explanation has been abandoned almost without exception, mainly for philological reasons (particularly because of the final *lamed*). No other explanation has so far prevailed. שנער certainly means the land of Babylon. The first name then is that of a king of Babylon who has not yet been further identified.

אריוך: the name occurs in Dan. 2:14, 15, 24, 25. Earlier it was explained from a Sumerian *Eri-aku* (servant of the moon god), or from *Eri-e-aku* of the Spartoli texts, or derived from Hurrian. F. M. T. Böhl has compared it with the Mari name *A-ri-wu-uk*, the name of a son of Zimri-lim (MNAW, L9,10 [1946] = *Opera Minora* [1953] 339-363); the names correspond, but scarcely the persons.

אלסר: it was equated earlier with Larsa, southeast of Uruk. There are other suggestions, but the name remains uncertain.

כדרלעמר: both parts, *kudur* and *lagamar* occur in Elamite names. The first part *kūdūr* = ''protector'' appears in several proper names, and *lagamar* is the name of a deity. A. Dillmann (1886) had already recognized both. However, the composite name Chedorlaomer is so far not attested.

עילם: the kingdom of Elam is attested elsewhere in the Old Testament, e.g., Gen. 10:22, as well as outside it. The country is attested with certainty only by this kingly name, of which the constituent parts occur in the language.

תדעל (Gr Θαργαλ): F. M. T. Böhl explains it as Hittite *Tudhalia*, a king's name *Du-ad-ha-li-ia* (1946; see under אריוך). The name also occurs in the Chedorlaomer texts. It appears four times as the name of a Hittite king (R. de Vaux, *Early History. . .* I [1971; 1978] 218), as well as of a city prince and a private person.

גוים is puzzling. Gk renders it literally as ''peoples.'' Many interpreters consider it an expression of perplexity, e.g., H. Holzinger (1898): ''it looks like a confused et cetera''; so too H. S. Nyberg (ARW 35 [1938] 358); many hold it to be a translation of *Umman Manda* = ''foreign peoples,'' often designating the Scythians or the Medes (e.g., E. A. Speiser, Comm., ad.loc.). There are a number of other suggestions. What is especially noteworthy is that of the four names of the kings, only Tidal is attested as the name of a historical king, a Hittite; but the author knew only the name, not that he was a Hittite king.

With the exception of Tidal, there is no further documentation to prove that any of the four kings of the east is a historical king. Two of the kingdoms are definite, Elam and Babylon; the third (despite the name Goiim) is very likely the Hittite kingdom. A punitive expedition of a coalition of four empires, Elam, Babylon, Ḥatti, and a fourth, against five city kings is historically improbable, if not inconceivable. This too makes clear that the campaign report and the lists belong originally to different traditions.

[14:2(8)] *The kings of the five cities (Pentapolis).* The list of the four kings of the east is repeated in vv. 1 and 9 (with change of order); the names of the five city kings are given only in v. 2; they are missing in v. 8, where only the names of the cities are listed. The Targums and the Rabbis regard the names of these kings as ''message names'' (Bera = ''in wickedness''; Birsha = ''in evil''). T. Nöldeke and others took this up again (*Untersuchungen zur Kritik des AT* [1869]); there were many other attempts to explain them, but they are all problematic. The names were certainly not made up, for in that case a name would have been made up for the king of Zoar. In any case, there is no evidence for these names elsewhere in the Old Testament or outside it.

The five cities: the designation *Pentapolis* occurs first in Wis. 10:6; it is a late, reflective, and purely literary description which rests on Gen. 14:2,8; it is by no means an assumed geographical designation. The situation, as far as one can follow it, is extremely complicated. The cities appear together only here and no-where else. The first four (without Zoar) are found together in Deut. 29:22 and Gen. 10:19; of these passages, Deut. 29:22 is late exilic, and in Gen. 10:19 "Admah and Zeboiim" are probably an appendage to Sodom and Gomorrah (cf. *Genesis 1–11*, Comm. on Gen. 10:19). Admah and Zeboiim occur only in Hos. 11:8; Sodom and Gomorrah or Sodom alone only in the prophets of Judah (e.g., Is. 1:9ff.) as sinful cities struck by the judgment of God.

     This situation causes one to think of a subsequent combination of a north-ern and a southern tradition (H. Gunkel; W. Zimmerli, Comm. ad.loc.), sug-gested perhaps by the narrative of the neighboring cities of Sodom and Gomorrah in Jer. 49:18; 50:40; Ezek. 16:48, 53, 55; this would explain why Zoar has anoth-er, older name, Bela; the name Zoar takes it origin only from the event of Gen. 19:20-23. The place name Bela is as unclear as the names of the kings in v. 2; it occurs only here as such. Some exegetes understand it as a "message name" = "devouring."

     A further question which is much discussed is whether the cities which are destroyed are thought of as lying at the northern or southern end of the Dead Sea. W. Schatz (*Genesis 14* [1972], pp. 175-181), in opposition to the thesis of J. Si-mons (cf. *Genesis 1–11*, Comm. on Gen. 10:15-19), inclines again to the view that the southern end is more probable. The report of the war and the lists do not cohere, as is shown by the mention of Sodom and Gomorrah only in the account of the battle, vv. 10,11.

[14:3] "All these" can refer only to the kings of the east in v. 1 (so A. Dillmann, S. Driver); they proceed to the place where the rebel vassals are; only in v. 8 do we find the report of the rebels' departure for battle. חבר means "to be joined together" (Ex. 26:3). Only here, with the preposition אל, has it the mean-ing "to proceed joined together. . . ." "The valley of Siddim," עמק השדים, oc-curs only here; J. Skinner writes, "the meaning is unknown." As the name of an area it has been explained in different ways (W. Schatz, 181), e.g., from Akk. *šiddu* = "strip, flat land." The versions did not understand it: Vet Lat gives *vallis salsa*, Vg *vallis silvestris*. The explanatory sentence, "that is, the Salt Sea," is ap-pended (on the Salt Sea, cf. H. Donner, *Einführung in die biblische Landes- und Altertumskunde* [1976] 28). If this is to be understood in the sense that the whole region which was then occupied by the Salt Sea was known by this name (so Tar-gums, Midrash, Josephus; A. Dillmann, H. Gunkel, O. Procksch; for a different view, W. Schatz, et al.), then it cannot be an extensive territory, because it is a ge-ological fact that the Dead Sea did not originate at that time (F. M. Abel, J. Si-mons). At most, it could be the name of a marginal area which would have been applied to the whole region. This being so, and because of the use of the article, the view of T. Nöldeke and J. Wellhausen gains in probability: the text was al-tered; what was originally meant was השדים, "Valley of the demons" (or "spirits of the dead"). So too KBL.

[14:4, 5a] *The reason for the campaign.* The nature of the campaign emerges very clearly here. It is the same sort of thing with the same succession of events as is presented in 2 Kings 18:7ff. (Hezekiah) and 24:1, 20, where it is seen from the point of view of the rebel vassals; it is certainly no accident that the same verb, מרד, is used in both places for the uprising. The succession of events—vassal service, revolt, punitive expedition by the overlord—is well known and frequent-

ly attested. The detailed numbers, in the 12th, 13th, 14th year, are in complete accord with the style of the royal inscriptions that report such undertakings; it goes
back to a historical report of a campaign (so H. Gunkel and many others).

[14:5b-7]   There follows an intermediate passage which is only loosely connected with the report of the campaign in vv. 1-5a,8-11. It consists almost exclusively
of an enumeration of conquered peoples so that it is close to the lists in vv.
1,2,8,9; in contrast to vv. 1-5a,8-11, not one king is named. The passage probably comes from another source; it is difficult to understand it as a detour on the
way to the cities of the rebels mentioned in v. 2. Also, the link between v. 5a and
v. 5b is very clumsy. After what has gone before, the coming of the kings in v. 5a
can only mean their coming to the place of battle with the rebel kings, as is said
again in v. 8; there is no motive for the continuation, "and they defeated the
Rephaim," in 5b.

  The division of the intermediary passage, vv. 5b-7.   One verb, ויכו, "and
they defeated," governs a series of four peoples with their territories (vv. 5b-6); it
is taken up again in v. 7b with two more peoples and their territories. Between
them stands a sentence which describes a movement to and fro (v. 7a). Outside v.
7a nothing happens; there is mere enumeration. If one brackets out v. 7a, one is
left with a series of six peoples which immediately separate into two groups. The
first three, the Rephaim, the Zuzim, the Emim, are legendary peoples, original inhabitants, all described as giants; on the other hand the Horites, the Amalekites
and the Amorites are well-known names of historical peoples. This indicates that
the grouping is a secondary, literary composition.

[14:5b]   The enumeration of the defeated peoples divides itself into three peoples of the east, i.e., of the Transjordan, and three of the south, the Horites
forming the transition from east to south. Three legendary peoples, original inhabitants of the Transjordan, are mentioned, the Rephaim, the Zuzim, and the Emim.
The names are probably taken from the antiquarian notes in Deut. 2:10-12,20,
even though this passage uses a comprehensive name, the original inhabitants of
Moab being the Emim ("the Moabites call them Emim"), and those of Ammon
being the Zamzummim (instead of Zuzim). The Horites as the original inhabitants
of Edom follow (2:12); nevertheless, the dependence on Deut. 2:10-12,20 is
probable.

  רפאים occurs in the Old Testament with the meaning "spirits of the dead"
(e.g., Is. 26:14,19; Ps. 88:11) and as the designation of a group among the giant-
like, pre-Israelite inhabitants (Gen. 15:20), particularly in the Transjordan.
Bashan is described in Deut. 3:13 as the "land of the Rephaim." King Og belongs
to them (Josh 12:4; 13:12), as does Ashtaroth, which accounts for its being mentioned in Gen. 14:5. The designation עשתרות קרנים is to be explained as the
transference of a divine name to a place, "Astarte with two horns" (so, among
others, H. Gunkel).

  זוז: Symmachus has Ζοιζομμειν = זמזמים as in Deut. 2:20; it occurs
only here. The name has not been explained, nor has the place-name Ham (C.
Steuernagel and W. F. Albright have suggested a place of the same name in
Gilead). אימים: according to Deut. 2:12 they are the Rephaim in Moab, and so the
mysterious, original inhabitants of Moab. קריתים is a Moabite city near Hebron,
mentioned in Is. 13:19; Num. 32:37; and elsewhere (cf. H. Donner, *Einführung*. . . [1976] 69).

196

חרי, the Horites; the southern group begins here; they are mentioned in Deut. 2:12 together with the first three peoples as the original inhabitants of Edom: "The Horites lived in Seir at one time" (on Seir, cf. H. Donner, p. 23). On the Horites (Hurrians, Hivites), cf. *Genesis 1–11*, Comm. on 10:16-17; Intro. #3, C, IV, above; also W. Schatz, *Genesis 14* (1972) 110-112. איל פארן: "El-paran on (or before) the edge of the desert." The desert of Paran is south of Judah (Gen. 21:21). The first part of the name corresponds to איל = a huge tree; the place is elsewhere called Elath (Deut. 2:8) or Eloth (1 Kings 9:26). It lies at the northern end of the Gulf of Aqaba. But it is not certain whether this Elath is meant because we do not know whether the desert of Paran extended so far.

[14:7a] It is only the single sentence, v. 7a, that gives the intermediary passage the character of an expedition. Exegetes as a whole cover over this fact by constructing an expedition out of the geographical information in vv. 5b and 6. But these verses are governed only by the single verb ויכו; there is no talk of movement to and fro. This verb is taken up again in v. 7. The sentence, v. 7a, stands within the enumeration but not as part of the organic whole; its purpose is obviously to give this the appearance of a campaign report, or part of such. It says that the conqueror of the desert of El-paran in the south turned back and went to עין משפט, which is equated with קדש. The former name occurs only here, but recalls Ex. 15:25 where there is a report of a spring that was put in order; this stands in the context of the Israelites' stopping place in the desert which in other places is called Kadesh (Num 20:1) and elsewhere Kadesh-barnea (Deut. 1:2), in P Meribah-Kadesh (Ex. 17:7). It is in the Negeb on the southern border.

[14:7b] This region presupposes the Amalekites who are now defeated. M. Noth, referring to this passage, describes them as "the bedouin neighbors who threaten the peasants and small-cattle breeders of southern Palestine" (*A History of Pentateuchal Traditions* [1948, 1963; Eng. 1972]). They are described again in Num. 13:29 as those "who live in the Negeb." The expression, "they conquered the whole territory of the Amalekites," is a rare one even if a territory can under certain circumstances stand for its inhabitants. The reading of the Gk and Syr is better, שׂרי, "they conquered all the princes of the Amalekites," and has been taken up by some exegetes. The last sentence also presents difficulties: ". . .the Amorites who lived in Hazazon-tamar" is scarcely possible. The place where the Amorites lived must have been a region; nowhere else are they described merely as people who lived in a city. If by the city an Amorite enclave were meant, then it should have been expressed in a different way. The place is equated with En-gedi in 2 Chron. 20:2, on the west bank of the Dead Sea. Eusebius understands it as a village, Tamara, on the southern border of Judah. On the Amorites, see Intro. 3, C, II.

[14:8-11] The original report of the campaign is now continued. V. 8 follows directly on v. 5a, which reported the advance of the kings of the east; the Canaanite kings assemble in battle order to confront them. There is no account of the battle itself, but only of the flight of the Canaanite kings and the withdrawal of the kings of the east after they had taken booty.

[14:8-9] The two groups of commanders are enumerated once again, quite unnecessarily. There is a summary conclusion, "four kings against five," in the style of the royal inscriptions of such campaigns.

[14:10]   If one brackets out the lists which are repeated in vv. 8-9, then v. 10a, which gives information about the state of the land in the valley of Siddim, follows directly on v. 8, the marching out and advance of the city kings. The connection is very inept. A sentence like this presupposes an exact report which ought not omit a brief account of the battle; and this all the more so as the whole intermediary passage, vv. 5a-7, is governed by the verb ויכו, "and they defeated." It is very likely that some such sentence before v. 10 has been suppressed by the enumeration (so too H. Holzinger).

The note about the battlefield, "the valley of Siddim was full of bitumen pits," speaks with the voice of the tradition behind vv. 1-5a,8-11; a note of this sort is not invented and it accords with the established geological data (W. F. Albright, BASOR 14 [1924] 9; M. Noth, ZDPV 67 [1945] 66f.; K. Baltzer, "Asphalt," BHH I [1962] 141). This, however, does not in any way alter the clumsy phrasing in v. 10b. What is clear in any case is that a number of fugitives fell into the bitumen pits, "but the rest escaped to the mountain range." The first difficulty is the phrase "the king of Sodom and Gomorrah"; the translations correctly expand this to "the king of Sodom and the king of Gomorrah." The second difficulty: in v. 17 the king of Sodom is still alive; so the reference must be to the followers of the king of Sodom. The third difficulty: only two of the five kings of the Pentapolis are mentioned. This indicates that the lists in vv. 2 and 8 are compositions. The rest escaped into the mountain range; probably the mountains of Moab are meant. We have here once more the basic idea of the "remnant" (cf. W. E. Müller–H. D. Preuss, *Die Vorstellung vom Rest im AT* [1939; 1973²]). Lot also took refuge in the mountains of Moab when he survived the catastrophe of Sodom.

[14:11]   V. 11 is the conclusion of the report. The subject of the sentence is mentioned neither in the preceding sentence nor before it. It can only refer back to the sentence which has dropped out and which reported the victory of the kings of the east. As the whole episode is concerned with a punitive expedition against vassals in revolt, there must have been a report that the vassal relationship was reestablished. V. 11 merely concludes by saying that the kings of the east took booty and went away. But this is not a satisfactory ending (so H. Gunkel, J. Skinner, et alii). The reason the ending was cut off lies obviously in the binding of vv. 1-11 with the narrative beginning in v. 12, for which it was not necessary. Again, as in v. 10, only Sodom and Gomorrah are plundered; the other three cities are not mentioned, for the same reason as in v. 10. To the unsatisfactory ending in v. 11, there corresponds the clumsy transition in v. 12.

[14:12-24]   On the relationship of vv. 12-24 to vv. 1-11, see above, Form. Vv. 12-24 (without vv. 18-20) is structured in two parts: vv. 13-16 narrate Abraham's act of liberation, vv. 17,21-24 the meeting with the king of Sodom.

Abraham hears of what has befallen his kinsmen (vv. 13,14a). He musters a group of 318 of his retainers, sets off in pursuit (v. 14b), and defeats the enemy, superior in numbers, by means of an assault by night; he recovers the booty and frees his kinsmen (vv. 15-16). The second part tells of the meeting with the king of Sodom; it is narrated in detail that Abraham does not wish to enrich himself from the booty, but gives it back to those who had been despoiled.

[14:12]   V. 12 forms a clumsy transition from the report of the campaign to the narrative of Abraham's act of liberation. Captives are not mentioned in v. 11 and so the connection with the statement, "they also took Lot," is not good. What is important is that the naming of Lot takes us into another area: "The mention of Lot, a private person, is rare in a context whose perspective is world wide" (H. Gunkel, ad.loc.). "Lot is not a political figure, he is a story figure" (J. Van Seters). This is confirmed by the appendage, "the son of the brother of Abraham," which transfers us into the area of family events; it is not in place, nor is the closing sentence, "who was living in Sodom." The stylistic clumsiness of the repetition of the verb of v. 11, "and they went away," has often been noted. All these observations show clearly that v. 12 is a patchwork. This explains itself when it is recognized that it is the seam joining two originally independent units of very different styles. Further, it shows just how the author went about the task of joining the two (only this person can have been the one who prefixed vv. 1-11; see above, "Form"). This writer had available the conclusion of the report of the campaign and the exposition of the narrative whose action begins in v. 13. To the latter belonged the name of Lot, his relationship with Abraham, and the place where he lived. The exposition contained in addition the information that Sodom, where Lot lived, was overcome by enemies and Lot was taken away by them as prisoner. This information formed the material of the link with the report of the campaign which itself closed with the same content, except that it did not mention the names of individual prisoners and that the conquerors of the city of Sodom were the four kings of the east. The compositor took from the report the following words: רכוש. . .ויקחו את and וילכו.

[14:13] This verse sets us in a completely different world from vv. 1-11. It is the small world of the Canaanite city states which emerges so clearly from the Amarna letters, with their constant wars among the city princes; over against these are the small seminomadic groups in process of becoming sedentary and forming themselves into tribes who were capable of those individual and astounding military enterprises such as are described in the book of Judges. These groups still retained a strongly marked family structure, as v. 13 shows. The reason for the military intervention is Abraham's bond with his kinsman; though no longer belonging to that group (Gen. 13 and 18-19 are presupposed here), he nevertheless feels himself responsible for it; this is the motive behind his expedition of liberation (cf. Gen. 34). Here, in contrast to vv. 1-11, it is not kings and armies but individuals who are the agents; dialog is in place (not a single word is spoken in vv. 1-11); the story tells of an event in which few people are involved.

It begins with a further passage linking it with the report; v. 10 also mentions escapees. As is often the case in the Old Testament, and in antiquity in general, a messenger comes running from the battle (2 Sam. 18:24ff.). The message was probably delivered in direct speech while the narrative was still independent; it is retained now in indirect speech in v. 14a, and v. 13b is part of the exposition. Abraham is introduced here as העברי. "The appendage, 'the Hebrew,' gives the impression that Abraham is named here for the first time" (H. Holzinger; similarly J. Skinner); "the name of Abraham and the place where he lived are introduced anew" (H. Gunkel). When Abraham is described as a Hebrew (an anachronism in the patriarchal period), this may well be an addition by the compositor, giving his own viewpoint, who wants to introduce Abraham as a member of another people after the many names of peoples in the preceding passage, vv. 1-11, just as Jonah describes himself as a Hebrew to the foreigners in Jon. 1:9 (W. Zimmerli; M.

Greenberg, "Ḫab/Piru and Hebrews," *The World History of the Jewish People*, II [1970] 197; M. Weippert, *The Settlement*. . . SBT 21, 2nd Series [1967; Eng. 1974]). Abraham was living by the terebinth of Mamre, the Amorite; this is an indication that he, in contrast to Lot who had become a city dweller, was still closer to the nomadic life style (on the terebinth of Mamre, cf. Comm. on 13:18; on the Amorites, Intro. 3, C, II).

[14:13b]   Mamre the Amorite is described, somewhat awkwardly, as the brother of Eshcol and Aner, who were obviously allied with Abraham. These three confederates present difficulties in the narrative. They occur again in the last verse where they are to have their share of the booty. The movement of the narrative presupposes that Abraham and his retainers alone carry out the liberation of Lot; only thus does the detail about the small number of retainers make sense. It is probable, therefore, that the confederates of Abraham in vv. 13b and 24b are an addition by the compositor who wanted to have an Abraham alliance corresponding to the two alliances in vv. 1-11 (cf. H. Holzinger; suggested perhaps by Num. 13:22, O. Procksch). The meaning of the names is quite uncertain. It could be a case of the personification of place-names.

אשכל = "cluster"; it is the name of a gorge, probably in the Hebron region; so in Num. 13:23, "They came to the Valley of Eshcol, and cut down from there a branch with a single cluster of grapes. . ..'' As Num. 13:22 mentions three sons of Anak, it is possible that the name was borrowed from here. The two other places where the Valley of Eshcol (bunch of grapes) occurs (Num. 32:9; Deut. 1:24) are parallel to Num. 13:22-23. The other name, ענר, is quite uncertain; the Samaritan reads ענרם, and the only other place where ענר is the name of a locale (1 Chron. 6:55) is textually questionable.

On the phrase בעלי ברית, "who were confederates of Abraham," cf. G. Schmitt (ZAW 76 [1964] 325f.); E. Testa (SBFLA 15 [1964-65] 5-73); T. C. Vriezen ("Eid," BHH I [1962] 374-376); and E. Kutsch (ZAW 79 [1967] 18-35).

[14:14-16]   The narrative of Abraham's act of liberation begins with the action in v. 14 and ends with v. 16. It is very concise and consists of a tightly knit chain of verbs with only the barest modification. V. 14a begins with the messenger motif on which the action follows immediately—"he mustered. . . pursued. . . attacked. . . defeated. . . pursued. . . brought back," this last verb being the goal. He brought back his kinsman (v. 14a) and much more. This "much more" makes the transition to vv. 17,21-24.

[14:14]   The verb שבה "to take away prisoner" is found with this meaning only here and in 34:29 in Genesis; it is frequent elsewhere. Here and in what follows Lot is described as Abraham's brother, in v. 12 as his nephew, indicating a different hand. וירק from ריק, "empty out," is understood by F. Delitzsch in the sense: "he drew them like a sword from its sheath." The Gk however renders by ἠρίθμησεν, presupposing the Sam reading וידק, "he mustered." This reading is to be preferred, as ר and ד are often interchanged. The followers whom he mustered are described in two ways: they are born in his house and so belong to the family, trustworthy slaves (cf. Gen. 15:2; 17:12,13,23,27; 24:2ff.), and they are "dedicated," i.e., proven warriors. S. C. Reif gives a definition: "The word חנך signifies introducing a person or a thing for the first time, to some particular occupation in which it is intended that he should remain," (VT 22 [1972] 499f.).

The Hebrew word occurs in the Egyptian execration texts for followers.* There are 318 of them; it is not necessary to attribute a special significance to this number—the sum total of Eliezer's name in Gen. 15:2, or an astral number. W. Zimmerli comments on the number: ''Abraham therefore must have had a house-hold of at least a thousand men.'' The Abraham of these stories was a small-cattle nomad and such a number is impossible (cf. Gen. 13); it is possible, however, for one of the charismatic leaders of the period of the judges, and in the Gideon story (Judg. 6) a similar number is given. Further, the military undertaking in Gen. 14:14-16 is very like that in Judg. 7:16-22, and is entirely conceivable with 300 men. ''And pursued as far as Dan'': if the narrative comes from the period of the judges, then there is no anachronism in the mention of Dan. In any case the compositor avoided altering the name. Before the Danites conquered it, the city was known as Laish (Judg. 18:29). The distance is great, but not impossible; it could, however, be an exaggeration, as also the phrase, ''as far as Hobah'' (v. 15).

[14:15] ויחלק (the Gk ἐπέπεσεν for ויחלק is not to be followed): literally, ''he divided himself [i.e., his men] by night,'' an abbreviated expression for ''he divided his men into groups and attacked them,'' the same tactic as in Judg. 7:16. ''And defeated them,'' the same word that runs through the account of the campaign in vv. 1-11, where it is the bald account of what happened; here, however, it forms the climax of a narrative in which the defeat of a foe far superior in numbers is meant to arouse in the listeners acknowledgment of the fact and enthusiasm. Part of this climax is the pursuit of the defeated foe far into the north and the recovery of the booty.

[14:16] In v. 16 the narrative descends from its high point. The conqueror comes back from the pursuit of the foe together with his liberated brother and the other captives, laden with the booty recovered. The goal of the undertaking is achieved; but there remains something further to tell: what happens to the booty? Vv. 17,21-24 deal with this.

[14:17a] The second part of the narrative, which begins here, presupposes the personality and excitement of the act of liberation in the first. Not only has Abraham liberated his kinsman Lot, but he has also liberated all the captives and has brought home the booty. And so the problem arises that we know troubled Israel in the period of the judges: should the victorious liberator establish a dynasty for himself out of the spoils of the struggle or not? The question is posed in narrative form and vigorously denied. The hero would no longer be a savior were he to enrich himself on the spoils of the struggle. The king of Sodom, as the representative of Canaanite city kingship, comes out to meet the victorious hero on his return. There is mention now of one king only, and no longer of a coalition of five city kings. While the narrative was still independent, it told only of an attack on Sodom, and the conqueror of Sodom, whom the liberator pursued, was another Canaanite city-king. The old narrative comes through very clearly.

[14:17b] The compositor felt himself all the more obliged to fit an additional parenthesis in here: he adds clumsily that Abraham is on the way back from his victory over Chedorlaomer and the kings in union with him. It is this parenthesis that gives rise to the impossible notion that Abraham conquered four kings of powerful

---

*Translator's note: cf. M. Dahood, *Psalms I*, AncB, 16, p. 7; ANET 328f.

empires with 318 men and chased them through the whole of Palestine.

The description of the place of the meeting is peculiar, "in the Valley of Shaveh, that is the King's Valley." עמק and שׁוה have the same meaning; שׁוה is used in v. 5 in its sense of "Valley, plain." Here it has become a proper name, probably because the name was no longer well known. The explanation, "that is, the King's Valley," could be influenced by vv. 18-20, Salem, because the King's Valley was near Jerusalem; it was there that Absalom had a monument erected for himself (2 Sam. 18:18; cf. J. Simons).

[The explanation of vv. 18-20 is found after v. 24]

[14:21]   ויאמר at the beginning of v. 21 follows directly on ויצא in v. 17. It is no ordinary meeting that is portrayed here; there is no greeting (in contrast to vv. 18-20) and the king in his brief request or demand merely gives the occasion for Abraham's detailed reply. The king of Sodom, as a Canaanite city-king, presupposes thereby that Abraham as victor has the right to the booty, even though it is the property of the citizens of Sodom which the conqueror had seized from them.

[14:22]   But Abraham will not claim his right and confirms his renunciation with a solemn oath. The gesture when taking an oath consists in raising the hand to Yahweh (Deut. 32:40; Dan. 12:7). The name of God, יהוה, is followed by "Elyon, the creator of heaven and earth." This is identical with what is predicated of God in v. 19 and so clamps the insertion, vv. 18-20, neatly in its frame, vv. 17,21-24. The addition of this predicate is neat inasmuch as it is in no way an intrusion into the grammatical structure (otherwise than with v. 12), but suggests a connection between vv. 19 and 22. While the narrative was still independent, there was only יהוה: an oath is taken by the *name* of God; it is not at all possible that the original was merely the divine predicate and that "Yahweh" was added later, as H. Gunkel and J. Skinner have proposed.

[14:23]   The oath of the victor. The אם indicates the conditioned self-cursing: may this and this happen to me if. . .. The oath says quite simply: I take nothing of what belongs to you. The statement is strengthened by the addition: no, not even the smallest thing (not a thread, not a shoestring; a common mode of expression). The first reason Abraham refuses the booty is that "it belongs to you"; there is now a second: the king of Sodom could then boast that he had made Abraham rich. That would offend the honor of the liberator. All commentaries regard Abraham's oath as an expression of nobility and big-hearted generosity: "The pride of a free man is speaking in v. 23b" (O. Procksch). That is true, but it is not a sufficient explanation. If the narrative of vv. 12-17,21-24 originated in the period of the judges, it reflects a basic concern peculiar to the Israel of that time. The king of Sodom is of the opinion that the victorious leader has a claim to the booty, the charismatic leader from an Israelite tribe is of another opinion. The king of Sodom was not the enemy whom Abraham conquered, and so Sodom's property is not his. That is what the second reason suggests: the liberator will not enrich himself on the property of another; some sort of obligation would follow from this, which he rejects. Charismatic leaders do not want power and wealth for themselves; it is this same attitude that leads Gideon to refuse the kingly honor. The saviors of Israel have no need of a dynasty.

[14:24]   The leader claims only what is absolutely necessary for the needs of his troops; he is responsible for them and must take care of them. This holds only for Abraham's own men; the three names of the confederates are probably an appendage (see Comm. on v. 13).

[14:12-17, 21-24]   Closing remarks on 14:12-24 (without vv. 18-20): The exegesis has established that the narrative as a whole and in every detail belongs to the period of the judges and presents Abraham step by step as one of the saviors of Israel, one of its judges. This admits of only one conclusion: a story about the judges narrated orally (so too J. A. Emerton) has been applied to Abraham; practically nothing has been changed apart from the substitution of ''Abraham'' for the original name, and there are a few appendages. If the insertion of vv. 18-20 took place in the period of David–Solomon (see below), then the transfer of the narrative to Abraham must have been completed already, that is, in the period between the judges and the monarchy. This text, therefore, provides us with a valuable witness to the earliest stage of the history of the Abraham tradition. At the time of the occupation of the land a story was told about Abraham as if he were one of the judges, a certain sign that the figure of Abraham had not been forgotten in this period. The text is something like Gen. 34 where a patriarchal figure is transferred into the period of the judges.

[14:18-20]   With the episode in 14:18-20 we are again in another world. The language has a decidedly cultic sound. But this must at once be made more precise: what is presented here is the sedentary cult of which priests, cultic institutions, and tithes are part. None of these belonged to the worship of the patriarchal period. It is as certain that this scene was only later linked with the Abraham of the patriarchal period as it is of 14:12-24 (without 18-20); vv. 18-20 are also a self-contained whole, an originally independent episode, which must first of all be explained as such.

The structure of vv. 18-20: The king of Salem comes out of his city to meet Abraham just as did the king of Sodom in v. 17. The exposition, therefore, is an obvious parallel to v. 17. The scene consists in an exchange. Melchizedek performs an action (v. 18), and speaks (vv. 19,20a); Abraham's reply consists in his silent acceptance of the blessing pronounced and in an action (v. 20b); he acknowledges the priestly dignity of Melchizedek the king by giving him the tithe. The question whether the subject of ויתן־לו is Melchizedek or Abraham (some exegetes maintain that it is Melchizedek) is to be answered from the structure of the whole, which is a cultic exchange.

If vv. 18-20 were inserted as an episode into vv. 17-24, were they already in existence as an independent tradition? J. A. Emerton is cautious: ''There was probably some kind of tradition underlying 14:18-20'' (VT 21 [1971] 426); he rightly rejects the attempts of R. H. Smith (ZAW 77 [1965] 129-153) and L. R. Fisher (JBL 81 [1962] 264-270) to explain it from the Ugaritic texts. The question can be answered as follows: J. A. Emerton rightly points out that vv. 18-20 are an episode and so cannot have existed independently beforehand; nevertheless, he is also right in saying that there was ''some kind of tradition'' underlying them. Vv. 18-20 belong to those narrative texts which have grown out of a permanent event, e.g., a celebration (more about this on Gen. 27). The tradition behind vv. 18-20 is none other than the exchange presented there consisting of the blessing by the priest and the giving of the tithe. This constantly occurring event, known from experience, acquires the character of something special, once and for all, and this by virtue of the introduction formed as a parallel to v. 17 and by the expansion of the blessing on Abraham in v. 19b; it is this that links the constantly occurring event with the once and for all event of Abraham's campaign of liberation.

[14:18]   מלכי־צדק: the name of the king is formed in the same way as אדני־צדק, the name of another Canaanite king of Jerusalem (Josh. 10:1). They both have much the same meaning, "my Lord (king) is צדק" (name of a divinity). But צדק could also be used to mean a quality of the god, "my god is salvation." The priestly name *Zadok* (probably an abbreviation) is also derived from צדק; he too was a priest of the Jerusalem sanctuary and from the time of David (cf. A. Cody, AnBib 35 [1969]); see too the name of king Zedekiah. *Melek* also occurs as the name of a god, frequently as the name of a Canaanite god in the Old Testament, e.g., Jer. 32:35. It occurs also as a Phoenician name, צדקמלך (on Melchizedek, see too W. Schatz, pp. 158-160). מלך שלם: the only other occurrence of שלם is in Ps. 76:3 where it is in parallelism to Zion. The GenApoc 22:13 explains it as "that is, Jerusalem," the TargO renders it "Jerusalem." Eusebius attaches it to Salumias, about 11 km. from Scythopolis; Josephus, however, understands it as Jerusalem and both Jewish and Christian exegesis have for the most part followed him. Jerusalem is attested in the Amarna letters as *uru-salim*. There have been other attempts to explain שלם (e.g., W. F. Albright, BASOR 163 [1961] 52), but none has prevailed (cf. W. Schatz, 187-189).

אל עליון: Melchizedek is described as "priest of El Elyon." The closest parallel to this was already known in the 19th century (see H. Holzinger); Philo of Byblos mentions a god Ἐλιοῦν καλούμενος Ὕψιστος (in Eusebius, *Praep.Ev.* I, 10, 4). It could be either an epithet or the name of a god. Elyon too is attested elsewhere as the name of a god (H. Donner–W. Röllig, *Kanaanäische und Aramäische Inschriften* I,II [1962-64] nr. 222A). El is the older and most widespread Semitic designation for a god.

The designation *El Elyon* occurs elsewhere in the Old Testament only in Ps. 78:35; Elyon is parallel with El in Num. 24:16 and in Ps. 73:11 and elsewhere with Elohim, Shaddai, and Yahweh. "The most high" (ὕψιστος) is a designation of the God of Israel, especially in the later period (e.g., Sirach), as well as in the Fathers of the Church; but it is also an independent divine title or name corresponding to Elyon in non-Israelite texts, as well as in Deut. 32:8; Ps. 82:6. The title *El Elyon* is comprehensible and meaningful in Gen. 14:18-20(22). The purpose is to designate the god of a Canaanite shrine, but at the same time to speak of him in such a way that Abraham can acknowledge him. The title is very suitable for this. El is the Canaanite and general Semitic title for God; it has been taken over so thoroughly in the Old Testament that El could be identified with Yahweh. On the other hand, Elyon, even though it was once an independent divine name, could be understood purely as a divine predicate, "the most high (God)," because it had this meaning too in the secular area (from על, עלה), e.g., Gen. 40:17, "in the highest basket," and because it was natural that the Psalms should praise Yahweh as "the most high," e.g., Ps. 18:14. Moreover, the use of this divine predicate is characteristic of the Jerusalem cult (Pss. 46:5; 48:2; 78:54).

Melchizedek is called priest and king. At the meeting between Abraham and the king of Sodom (vv. 17,21-24) the kingly role alone is to the fore; at the meeting with Melchizedek (vv. 18-20), it is only the kingly function that is stressed. One must bear in mind, however, that both are Canaanite city-kings in exactly the same way and that it is a matter of sacral kingship in both cases (on sacral kingship, cf. C. Westermann, ThB 54 [1974] 291-308; J. de Fraine, VT.S 15 [1966] 134-149). It was this sacral function of the king that the Israelite tribes found strange and novel when they entered the land and that encountered such opposition when the kingship was introduced. The books of Kings testify that David and Solomon exercised the sacral function (see, e.g., 1 Kings 8).

Melchizedek brings out (i.e., as he comes from his city and temple) bread and wine to Abraham who is returning from his campaign of liberation, a picture which in its beauty and dignity has made this brief scene effective over thousands of years and remains so for generations to come. It is an event in which the secular and the sacred are still not separated. Melchizedek brings refreshment to the exhausted liberator and thus as royal host receives him into the peace, the *šalōm*, of his royal domain; but the hands that bring the bread and wine are the hands of the priest, and the food and drink are not to be separated from the blessing which Melchizedek dispenses to Abraham in the name of his God.

[14:19]   There follows the blessing that Abraham receives from Melchizedek. The blessing is pronounced in a poetic rhythm which it takes from the solemn occasion to which it is appropriate (cf. Comm. on 2:23 in *Genesis 1–11*). It is stamped by the ברוך at the beginning of each of the two lines, but with an expressly different sense in each case. In v. 19b, "Blessed be Abraham. . .," the movement is from God, לאל, to the man who receives the blessing of this God; in v. 20a it is the praise that goes up from man to this God. Both are expressed by the same verb, ברך, because its fundamental meaning which goes far back into the distant past, "to endow with power," can be used in both directions. But one cannot use the word in this way in a personal relationship to God; one must distinguish between the two senses of blessing and praise (cf. ברך in THAT 1 [1971] 353-376, and the bibliog. there). The blessing of Melchizedek brings together two elements of worship, blessing and praise of God: the psalm of worship and the blessing dispensed there by a priest. W. Zimmerli in his commentary (and in detail in Fests. L. Rost [1967] 255-264) has expounded the meaning of blessing not only for 14:18-20, but also for the whole of its framework: "The catchword *blessing* is the link with the rest of the Abraham story." One cannot say this, however, without setting out the great gap between what is said in the blessing in 14:18-20 and in those of Gen. 12:1-3 and ch. 27. The priestly blessing does not appear in the religion of the patriarchs, where it is an ordinary man who blesses, one of the patriarchs himself (Gen. 27:49); in 12:1-3 Abraham is not blessed, but blessing is promised to him and his generation. The cultic blessing by the priest in the sanctuary, or from the sanctuary, is foreign to the patriarchal period.

This holds for the predicate of the "most high God," קנה שמים וארץ, which is obviously a fixed cultic formula. It is certain that קנה is used here in the sense of "creator," and the versions render it in this way. It is now also certain that it was a specifically Canaanite cultic formula, cf. in particular F. M. Cross (*Canaanite Myth. . .* [1973] 15f. and n. 20: "In later West Semitic texts we find the liturgical name *'El qōnê 'arṣ*, Hittite *Ilkunis ṣa*, 'El, creator of earth.'" "'El is the creator god of the Canaanites and *qōnê 'arṣ* applies exclusively to him" (pp. 50f. and n. 25). There are further parallels, e.g., Akk. *bāni šamē u erṣiti* = "creator of heaven and earth." See also, M. Pope, *El in the Ugaritic Texts* (VT.S 2[1955]); G. Levi della Vida (JBL 63 [1944] 1-9); and W. Schatz (*Genesis 14* [1972] 207-216). קנה in the Old Testament predominantly means "acquire, possess'' (cf. *Genesis 1–11*, Comm. on 4:1b); in some places it can mean ''create'' (Gen. 14:19,22; Ex. 15:16; Deut. 32:6; Pss. 78:54; 139:13; Prov. 8:22; Is. 11:11). Canaanite influence suggests itself in the cultic formulation in Gen. 14:19,22. But this very formula, ''creator of heaven and earth,'' is certainly foreign to the patriarchal period; the Old Testament would have taken over this formula only after the beginning of the Israelite monarchy, when Israel had become sedentary and borrowed from sedentary Canaan. This is all the clearer because of the acknowledged distinction that is to be made between the creation of the world and the creation of humanity, and the recognition that each has its own tradition; talk about the creator of the world represents a later stage and is characteristic of the cult in the sedentary high cultures (*Genesis 1–11*, 19-47, ''The Creation Narratives''). It is probable then that this cultic formula was taken over into the Jerusalem cult in the early monarchical period.

[14:20a] ''And blessed be El-Elyon who. . ..'' This is very like Ex. 18:10, ''Blessed be Yahweh who has saved you from the power of Egypt. . ..'' It is the same situation; the joy of the occasion gives rise to the same expression of praise of God. It is certainly no accident that in both places it is a matter of salvation, of liberation; it is this that arouses the cry of praise. The verb מגן (piel) in the sense of ''deliver'' occurs only in Hos. 11:8 and Is. 64:6 (subj.; ET v. 7); in the Qal it means ''bestow, show favor.'' In Hos. 11:8 God is also the subject who delivers. Apart from this verb the sentence corresponds to the ''deliverance formula'' of the war of Yahweh. The use of ברוך in two senses, though in a somewhat different context, yet in such a way that now God, now man is the subject, is found in 1 Sam. 25:22ff. when David replies at his meeting with Abigail.

[14:20b] Abraham gives the priest Melchizedek a tenth ''of all''; this can refer only to the booty, even though it stands in contradiction to vv. 22f. And so it is stated expressly that Abraham has accepted the blessing and gifts of the priest-king and the man himself as priest, and acknowledges his sanctuary by presenting the tithe. The meaning of this conclusion to the Melchizedek scene is made quite clear by an inconsistency that is barely perceptible. It is beyond dispute that the tithe is a regular tribute. It is found only in the context of sedentary cult and means the payment of a tenth of the produce at regular intervals, from year to year. The tithe is never spoken of as a tribute paid from something acquired on a particular occasion. The aim of the closing verse (v. 20) is to legitimate the regular payment of the tithe by means of a single event which took place long ago: Abraham presented the tithe from the booty to the priest from Jerusalem. The Melchizedek episode therefore has an etiological character (Intro. 2, B, IV). A current practice, the deliverance by the Israelite farmers of the tenth part of their produce to a former Canaanite sanctuary, is explained and legitimated by an event in former times: the blessing of Abraham by the priest of the sanctuary and Abraham's presentation of the tithe acknowledging the blessing (there is a parallel in Gen. 28:22). It is a classical example of an etiological narrative scene. By means of the narrative the blessing, which the present generation in the monarchical period receives from this sanctuary and its priests, acquires great worth; in it the blessing dispensed to Abraham carries on into the present. It is this cultic exchange that, by means of the narrative, links the present generation with the patriarch of former times.

Purpose and Thrust

Gen. 14, which presented almost insoluble difficulties as long as it was treated as a unity, acquires a plausible explanation when its composite character is recognized and the origin and meaning of the parts are first studied separately.

We can now ask in retrospect about the aim of the chapter as a whole, that is, about the meaning given it by the last stage of tradition which prefixed vv. 1-11. In the late postexilic period, when Judah was a small and insignificant province of a great and powerful empire, Jewish writers endeavored to give figures from their own past a significance that reached out across the boundaries of the great world powers. Particular examples of this are the books of Daniel and Judith. The same tendency appears too in the passage about Abraham in the praise of the fathers in Sir. 44:19-21. The author of Gen. 14 gave Abraham, the father of the people, a significance on the stage of world history by making him victor over four kings of powerful eastern empires. To this end he used a narrative from the period of the judges, and already part of the subsequent history of Abraham, and joined it to a report of a campaign going back to Babylonian tradition. The aim of this late composition was to exalt Abraham; but while conferring on him a reputation reaching out across world history, the author also had in mind Abraham's people with its past greatness and present misery. By presenting his contemporaries with the victorious father, he tried to awaken a glorious past which opened broader horizons to those currently humiliated. He did this not only by means of Abraham as victor in vv. 12-17,21-24, but also through the cultic consecration conferred on Abraham by the priest of the "most high God," a title which acquired new meaning at this period. The goal which determined the author was both comprehensible and meaningful to contemporaries; but the portrayal of Abraham in this form is a very far cry from the Abraham of the old patriarchal stories; it has practically nothing in common with him.

But the figure of Abraham had already undergone change in the narrative from the period of the judges which the compositor used. Here too Abraham is a warrior, but the struggle is of a different kind: a campaign of liberation as in Judges. One can certainly say that Abraham was exalted by being inscribed on the list of liberation heroes from this period, but in a different and rather naive way. By assimilating Abraham to these savior figures who were closer to the contemporary situation, it was possible to preserve the memory of him as father.

The episode of vv. 18-20 has a very different goal. If one takes as one's starting point that the episode is etiological, then it is to be seen in the context of the thinking of circles in the early monarchy which wanted to anchor the new form of worship in the old traditions of ancient Israel. These circles did not shrink from indirectly juxtaposing Yahweh, the God of Israel from Egyptian times, alongside El who was worshiped at a Canaanite sanctuary. Abraham is blessed by the priest in the name of this god, accepts the blessing, and gives the priest the tithe in return. An exchange such as this was possible only in the early monarchy, a period of transition, when David and Solomon were kings of a territory in which Israelites lived peacefully with Canaanites. This is in accord with a characteristic of the patriarchal religion which knew no religious polemic. It accords too with the universal character of blessing in the Old Testament as shown for example in Gen. 1:28. It is in this sense that the typological meaning of the figure of Melchizedek in the New Testament in Heb. 7 retains its significance. When in Heb. 7:9-25 the priesthood of Melchizedek is set over against that of Levi, a priesthood ''not according to a legal requirement concerning bodily descent but by the power of an indestructible life'' (v. 16), then the universal character of the saving work of Christ, described in this way, accords with the universal scope of the blessing of the ''most high God'' which Abraham receives from Melchizedek.

The Promise to Abraham

Literature

Genesis 15: [See also Lit. for Section 4, Intro. §§5-6, Promise and Covenant]. R. Smend, *Die Erzählung des Hexateuch auf ihre Quellen untersucht* (1912). W. Staerk, "Zur alttestamentlichen Literarkritik," ZAW 42 (1924) 34-74. P. Volz, *Grundsätzliches zur elohistischen Frage: Untersuchung von Genesis 15–36: Der Elohist als Erzähler*, BZAW 63 (1933). P. Katz, "Notes on the Septuagint, III: Coincidences Between LXX and TgO in Genesis XV," JThS 47 (1946) 166-168 = *Bibliographica Judaica* 2 (1972). G. Hölscher, *Geschichtsschreibung in Israel. Untersuchungen zum Jahvisten und Elohisten*, SNVAO 50(1952). M. Haran, "Shiloh and Jerusalem: The Origin of the Priestly Tradition in the Pentateuch," JBL 81 (1962) 14-24. C. Brekelmans, "Eléments deuteronomiques dans le Pentateuque," *Recherches Bibliques* 8 (1967) 77-91. P. Beauchamp, *L'un et l'autre Testament, Essai de lecture*, I (1976). J. Bright, *Covenant and Promise* (1976). A. de Pury, "La promesse patriarcale," ETR 51 (1976) 351-366.

Genesis 15:1-6: M. Jastrow, *Die Religionen Babyloniens und Assyriens*, II 1 (1912). H. Gressmann, "Die literarische Analyse Deuterojesajas," ZAW 34 (1914) 234-297, esp. 287-289. L. Koehler, "Die Offenbarungsformel 'Fürchte dich nicht' im AT," SThZ 36 (1919) 33-39. A. Fernández, " 'Ego protector tuus sum. . .," VD 1 (1921) 25-27. J. Begrich, "Das priesterliche Heilsorakel," ZAW 52 (1934) 81-92 = ThB 21 (1964) 217-231. E. L. Ehrlich, *Der Traum im Alten Testament*, BZAW 73 (1953). H. Cazelles, "Ras Schamra und der Pentateuch," ThQ 138 (1958) 26-39. F. Dreyfus, "Le thème de l'héritage dans l'Ancien Testament," RSPhTh 42 (1958) 3-49. W. M. Müller, "Die Bedeutung des Wortes *'sprk* im Genesis-Apokryphon," RQ 2 (1960) 445-447. K. Koch, "Der Spruch 'Sein Blut bleibe auf seinem Haupt' und die israelitische Auffassung vom vergossenen Blut," VT 12 (1962) 396-416, esp. 403-404. S. Plath, "Furcht Gottes. Der Begriff ירא im AT," AzTh II,4 (1963) esp. 114-122. S. Talmon, " 'Wisdom' in the Book of Esther," VT 13 (1963) 419-455, esp. 437f. C. Westermann, "Das Heilswort bei Deuterojesaja," EvTh 24 (1964) 355-373. J. Becker, *Gottesfurcht im AT*, AnBib 25 (1965) esp. 50-55. G. Lanczkowski, "Aufstieg und Untergang des Inka-Reiches," *Universitas* 20 (1965) 847-854, 849. F. N. Jasper, "Early Israelite Traditions in the Psalter," VT 17 (1967) 50-59. K. Koch, "Sohnesverheissung. . .," ZA 58 (1967) 211-221. J. G. Heintz, "Oracles prophétiques et 'guerre sainte' selon les archives royales de Mari et l'Ancien Testament," VT.S 17 (1969) 112-138. L. Derousseaux, *La crainte de Dieu dans l'Ancien Testament, Lectio Divina* 63 (1970) esp. 91, 111f. P. E. Dion, "The 'Fear Not' Formula and Holy War," CBQ 32 (1970) 565-570. R. Labat, A. Caquot, M. Sznycer and M. Vieyra, *Les religions du Proche-Orient asiatique* (1970) esp. 257f. (review ZDPV 87 [1971] 101-106). W. M. Clark, "The Righteousness of Noah," VT 21 (1971) 261-280. F. E. Deist, "Aantekeninge by Gen 15,1.6," NGTT 12 (1971) 100-102. K. Seybold, "Elia am Gottesberg. Vorstellungen prophetischen Wirkens nach 1. Könige 19," EvTh 33 (1973) 3-18. O. Loretz, "*mgn*—'Geschenk' in Gen 15,1," UF 6 (1974) 492. H. A. Kenik, "Code of Conduct For a King: Psalm 101," JBL 95 (1976) 391-403. W. Brueggemann, "A Neglected Sapiental Word Pair," ZAW 89 (1977) 234-258.

Genesis 15:2: A. Schulz, "Eliʿezer?" ZAW 52 (1934) 274-279. M. F. Unger, "Some Comments on the Text of Genesis 15:2-3," JBL 72 (1953) 49-50. R. T. O'Callaghan, "Echoes of Canaanite Literature in the Psalms," VT 4 (1954) 164-176. H. Seebass, "Gen 15,2b," ZAW 75 (1963) 317-319. F. Vattioni, "Ancora su *ben-mešeq* di Gen 15,2," RSO 40 (1965) 9-12. H. L. Ginsberg, "Abram's 'Damascene' Steward," BASOR 200 (1970) 31-32. M. Dandamayer, "The Economic and Legal Character of the Slaves' Peculium in the Neo-Babylonian and Achaemenid Periods," *Gesellschaftsklassen. . .* ed. O. Edzard (1972). F. I. Andersen, *The Sentence in Biblical Hebrew* (1974). H. J. Boecker, *Recht und Gesetz im Alten Testament und im Alten Orient, Neukirchener Studienbücher* 10(1976). H. Tawil, "Hebrew צלח/הצלח, Akkadian *ešēru/šušuru*: A Lexicographical Note," JBL 95(1976)405-413.

Genesis 15:3: U. Cassuto, "The Seven Wives of King Keret," BASOR 119 (1950) 18-20. F. Vattioni, "Due note sull' Ecclesiaste," AION 17 (1967) 157-163.

Genesis 15:6: G. Wildeboer, "Die älteste Bedeutung des Stammes צדק," ZAW 22 (1902) 167-169. A. Weiser, *Glaube und Geschichte im AT*, BWAT (1931). G. H. Davies, "The Yahvistic Tradition in the Eighth-Century Prophets," *Fests. T. R. Robinson* (1950) 37-51. I. C. C. von Dorssen, *De derivata van de stam אמן in het Hebreeuws van het Oude Testament* (1951). G. von Rad, "Die Anrechnung des Glaubens zur Gerechtigkeit," ThLZ 76 (1951) 129-133; *The Problem of the Hexateuch and Other Essays* (1966). P. Wernberg-Møller," צדק, צדיק and צדוק in the Zadokite Fragments (CDC), the Manual of Discipline (DSD) and the Habakkuk-Commentary (DSH)," VT 3 (1953) 310-315. T. C. Vriezen, *Geloven en vertrouwen* (1957). E. Pfeiffer, "Glaube im AT. Eine grammatikalisch-lexikalische Nachprüfung gegenwärtiger Theorien," ZAW 71 (1959) 151-164. M. Gertner, "The Masorah and the Levites. An Essay in the History of a Concept," VT 10 (1960) 241-272. A. Jepsen, "צדק und צדקה im AT," Fests. H. W. Hertzberg (1965) 78-89. R. Smend, "Zur Geschichte von האמין," Fests. W. Baumgartner, VT.S 16 (1967) 284-290. H. Wildberger, " 'Glauben,' Erwägungen zu *h'myn*," VT.S 16 (1967) 372-386. M. G. Kline, "Abraham's Amen," WThJ 31 (1968) 1-11. H. H. Schmid, *Gerechtigkeit und Weltordnung* (1968). H. Wildberger, " 'Glauben' im AT," ZThK 65 (1968) 129-159. H. Gross, "Der Glaube an Mose nach Exodus (4.14.19)," Fests. W. Eichrodt, AThANT 59 (1970) 57-65. F. Hahn, "Genesis 15, 6 im Neuen Testament," Fests. G. von Rad (1971) 90-107. L. Ruppert, "Das Motiv der Versuchung durch Gott in vordeuteronomischen Tradition," VT 22 (1972) 55-63. M. Wilcox, "Upon the Tree. . .," JBL 96 (1977) 85-99.

Genesis 15:7-21: J. Happel, *Der Eid im AT vom Standpunkt der vergleichenden Religionsgeschichte aus betrachtet* (1910). E. M. Good, "Two Notes on Aqhat," JBL 77 (1958) 72-74. J. Muilenburg, "The Form and Structure of the Convenantal Formulations," VT 9 (1959) 347-365. F. Michaéli, "Grammaire Hébraique et Théologie Biblique," *Hommage à W. Vischer* (1960) 145-156, esp. 148. F. Auer, "Das AT in der Sicht des Bundesgedankens," Fests. H. Junker (1961) 1-15. S. J. de Vries, "David's Victory Over the Philistine as Saga and as Legend," JBL 92 (1973) 23-36, esp. 24f. W. Eichrodt, "Darf man heute noch von einem Gottesbund mit Israel reden?" ThZ 30 (1974) 193-206. W. G. Morrice, "New Wine in Old Wineskins. XI: Covenant," ET 86 (1974/75) 132-136. E. Jacob, "Les trois racines d'une théologie de 'Terre' dans l'Ancien Testament," RHPhR 55 (1975) 469-480.

Genesis 15:7: E. Norden, *Agnostos Theos. Untersuchungen zur Formgeschichte religiöser Rede* (1913; 1971[5]) esp. 177-239. A. Poebel, "Das appositionell bestimmte Pronomen der 1. Pers. Sing. in den westsemitischen Inschriften und im AT," AS 3 (1932) 60-72. W. Zimmerli, "Ich bin Jahwe," Fests. A. Alt (1953) 179-209. E. Schild, "On Exodus III 14—'I am that I am,' " VT 4 (1954) 296-302. M. J. Buss, "The Language of the Divine 'I,' " JBR 29 (1961) 102-107. A. Barucq, *Populus Dei, I: Israel* (1966). J. Weingreen, "הוצאתיך in Genesis 15,7," *Essays Pres. to D. W. Thomas* (1968) 209-215. W. Gross, "Die Herausführungsformel—Zum Verhältnis von Formel und Syntax," ZAW 86 (1974) 425-453.

Genesis 15:8: F. Gaboriau, *Le thème biblique de la connaissance* (1969).

Genesis 15:9-18: B. Stade, "Die Dreizahl im AT," ZAW 26 (1906) 124-141. E. Zolli, "L'alleanza sacra nella letteratura antico- e neotestamentaria," RivAnt 30 (1933-1934) 393-402; "Il rito sacrificiale in Genesi XV," *Religio* II (1935) 215-218. W. von Soden, "Ein Opferschaugebet bei Nacht," ZA 43 (1936) 305-308. A. E. Jensen, "Die mythische Vorstellung vom halben Menschen," Paid 5 (1950). O. Masson, "A propos d'un ritual hittite pour la lustration d'une armée: Le rite de purification par le passage entre les deux parties d'une victime," RHR 137 (1950) 5-25. P. von Imschoot, "L'Alliance dans l'Ancien Testament," NRTh 84 (1952) 785-805. F. M. Cross, "A New Qumran Biblical Fragment Related to the Original Hebrew Underlying the Septuagint," BASOR 132 (1953) 15-26. J. Henninger, Bib 34 (1953) 344ff. D. H. Wiseman, "Abban and Alalaḫ," JCS 12 (1958) esp. 126. H. von Sicard, "Zum Verständnis von Genesis 15:9-18," Paid 7 (1959/61) 438-441. A. E. Jensen, "Beziehungen zwischen dem AT und der nilotischen Kultur in Afrika," *Essays in Honor of P. Radin.* (1960) 449-466. R. de Vaux, *Studies in O.T. Sacrifice* (1964). F. Vattioni, "Genesi 15,9-11," *Biblos-Press* 6 (1965) 53-61. J. A. Fitzmyer, *The Aramaic Inscriptions of Sefire,* BibOr 19(1967). S. E. Loewenstamm, "Zur Traditionsgeschichte des Bundes zwischen den Stücken," VT 18 (1968) 500-507. L. Ramlot, "Histoire et mentalité symbolique," *Exégèse et Théologie* (1968). D. J. McCarthy, "The Symbolism of Blood and Sacrifice," JBL 88 (1969) 166-176; 92 (1973) 205-210; "*Berît* in OT History and Theology," Bib 53 (1972) 105-121; "*Berît* and Covenant in the Deuteronomistic History," VT.S 23 (1972) 65-85. E. Kutsch, "Gottes Zuspruch und Anspruch. *Berît* in der alttestamentlichen Theologie," *Questions disputées d'AT,* ed. C. Brekelmans (1974) 71-90. R. Péter, "פר et שׁור, Note de lexicographie hébraique," VT 25 (1975) 486-496.

Genesis 15:10: O. Böcher, *Dämonenfurcht und Dämonenabwehr. Ein Beitrag zur Vorgeschichte der christlichen Taufe,* BWANT 90 (1970); "Der Judeneid," EvTh 30 (1970) 671-681.

Genesis 15:11: F. Delitzsch, *Die Lese- und Schreibfehler im AT* (1920). D. Neiman, "PGR: A Canaanite Cult-Object in the OT," JBL 67 (1948) 55-60. J. H. Ebach, "PGR = (Toten-) Opfer? Ein Vorschlag zum Verständnis von Ez 43,7.9," UF 3 (1971) 365-368.

Genesis 15:12-16: L. Couard, "Gen 15, 12-16 und sein Verhältnis zu Ex 12,40," ZAW 13 (1893) 156-159. V. Chauvin, "Genèse XV, v. 12," *Le Muséon* NS 5 (1905) 104-108. C. Kuhl, "Die 'Wiederaufnahme'—ein literarkritisches Prinzip?" ZAW 64 (1952) 1-11. J. G. Thomson, "Sleep: An Aspect of Jewish Anthropology," VT 5 (1955) 421-433. A. Resch, *Der Traum im Heilsplan Gottes. Deutung und Bedeutung des Traums im AT* (1964).

Genesis 15:13: A. T. Clay, *The Empire of the Amorites* (1919). F. J. Neuberg, "An Unrecognized Meaning of Hebrew Dor," JNESt 9 (1950) 215-217. N. H. Tur-Sinai, "Auf wieviel Jahre berechnet die Bibel den Aufenthalt der Kinder Israels in Ägypten?" BibOr 18 (1961) 16-17. G. W. Coats, "Despoiling the Egyptians," VT 18 (1968) 450-457. J. Heinemann, "210 Years of Egyptian Exile: A Study in Midrashic Chronology (Cf. Ex 12, 40; Gen 15, 13)," JJS 22 (1971) 19-30.

Genesis 15:15: H. S. Gehman, "Some Types of Errors of Transmission in the LXX," VT 3 (1953) 397-400. A. R. Millard, " 'For He Is Good,' " TynB 17 (1966) 115-117. L. Wächter, "Der Tod im AT," AzTh II,8 (1967). C. Westermann, "Der Frieden (Shalom) im Alten Testament," *Studien z. Friedensforschung* 1 (1969) 144-177. J. I. Durham, "שָׁלוֹם and the Presence of God," *OT Essays in Honor of G. H. Davies* (1970) 272-293. C. Barth, *Der Tod im Alten Testament* (1972). J. Milgrom, "The Legal Terms *šlm* and *br'šw* in the Bible," JNESt 35 (1976) 271-273.

Genesis 15:16: S. H. Langdon, "Die neubabylonischen Königsinschriften," VAB 4 (1912) esp. 148. C. F. Jean, "Textes diverses. Transcrites et traduites," ARM 2,37 (1950) 4-14.

Genesis 15:17-18: F. Thureau-Dangin, "Die sumerischen und akkadischen Königsinschriften," VAB I,1 (1907) 89-141. E. F. Weidner, "Der Staatsvertrag Aššurnirâris von Assyrien mit Matti'ilu von Bit-Agusi sowie der Vertrag Samsi-Adads V. mit Bardukzakirsumi I. und der Vertrag Asarhaddons mit Ba'al von Tyrus," AfO 9

(1932/33) 17-34. A. P. Munch, *The Expression hajjôm hāhū'*. Is it an Eschatological Terminus Technicus? (1936). W. Staerk, "Berith—Diatheke—Bund?" ThBl 16 (1937) 281-296. V. Laridon, "De foedere Abrahamitico (Gen 15,18)," CBrug 38 (1938) 49-56. A. G. Barrois, "Sur quelques symboles de Jahvé," *Mélanges Syriens, offerts à M. R. Dussaud*, I (1939) 101-106. R. du Mesmil du Buisson, "Une tablette magique de la région du Moyen Euphrate," *Mélanges. . .M. R. Dussaud*, I (1939) 421-434. J. de Fraine, "Clibanus fumans et lampas ignis (Gn 15,17)," VD 26 (1948) 354-355. A. Lefèvre, "L'expression 'en ce jour-là' dans le livre d'Isaïe," *Mélanges. . .à A. Robert* (1957) 17-60. O. Kaiser, *Die mythische Bedeutung des Meeres in Ägypten, Ugarit und Israel*, BZAW 78 (1959; 1962²) esp. 44-77. S. N. Kramer, *Sumerian Literature and the Bible*, SBO 3 (1959). S. Segert, "Zur Etymologie von lappīd 'Fackel,' " ZAW 74 (1962) 323-324. R. Hillmann, *Wasser und Berg. Kosmische Verbindungslinien zwischen dem kanaanäischen Wettergott und Jahwe* (diss. Halle, 1965). W. Kuhnigk, *De origine Ps 105. Investigationes historiae patriarcharum in psalmo narratae in luce diversarum traditionum theologico-historicarum VT* (diss. Rome, 1965). H. Langkammer, " 'Den er zum Erben von allem eingesetzt hat!' (Hebr 1,2)," BZ 10 (1966) 273-280. M. Haran, "The Rise and Decline of the Empire of Jeroboam Ben Joash," VT 17 (1967) 266-297, esp. 282. M. Weinfeld, "The Period of the Conquest and of the Judges as Seen by the Earlier and Later Sources," VT 17 (1967) 93-113, esp. 101f. J. L. Crenshaw, "Amos and the Theophanic Tradition," ZAW 80 (1968) 203-215. E. Lipiński, "Recherches sur le livre de Zacharie," VT 20 (1970) 25-55, 29. E. Kutsch, " '. . .am Ende des Jahres.' Zur Datierung des israelitischen Herbstfestes in Ex 23,16," ZAW 83 (1971) 15-21. G. S. Ogden, "Time, and the Verb היה in O.T. Prose," VT 21 (1971) 451-469, 462. M. Saebø, "Grenzbeschreibung und Landideal im AT mit besonderer Berücksichtigung der *min—'ad* Formel," ZDPV 90 (1974) 14-37. B. Zuber, *Vier Studien zu den Ursprüngen Israels. Die Sinaifrage und Probleme der Volks- und Traditionsbildung*, Orbis Biblicus et Orientalis 9 (1976) esp. I, 26-31.

Genesis 15:19-21: W. Richter, *Die Bearbeitungen des 'Retterbuches' in der deuteronomischen Epoche*, BBB 21 (1964). J. C. de Moor, "*Rāpi'-ūma*—Rephaim," ZAW 88 (1976) 323-345.

Text

15:1 Now after[a] this the word of Yahweh came to Abram in a vision:[b] Do not be afraid,[c] Abram, I am your shield; your reward will be very great.[de] [OR: I will be your benefactor who will reward you greatly.][f]

2 And Abram said: Lord Yahweh,[a] what can you give me while[b] I pass on childless, and when the son of Meshek[c] (that is Damascus), Eliezer, the son of my house 'will be my heir'!

3 And Abram said: See, you have given me[a] no children, so that a son of my house will be my heir.

4 And the word[a] of Yahweh[b] came to him: No, he shall not be your heir, but[c] the one[d] who comes from your own body,[e] he will be your heir.

5 And he took him outside and said: Look up at the heavens and count the stars—if you can.[a] And he said to him: So[b] will your descendants[c] be.

6 And he believed[a] Yahweh,[b] and he[c] accounted it to him as righteousness.[d]

7 And he said to him: I am Yahweh who led you out from Ur of the Chaldees,[a] to give[b] you this land as your possession.

8 And he said: Lord Yahweh,[a] how am I to know that I shall possess it?

9 And he said to him: Bring me[a] a three-year-old[b] heifer, a three-year-old she-goat, a three-year-old ram, a turtle dove, a young bird.

10 And he brought them all to him. And he cut them down the middle[a] and put each part opposite[b] its counterpart, but he did not cut the birds.

11 Then vultures[a] swooped down on the carcasses,[b] but Abram scared them away.[c]

12 And as the sun was going down[a] a deep sleep[b] fell upon Abram and see, a great terror came upon him.[c]

13 And he said to Abram: You must know[a] that your descendants will be aliens in a land which is not theirs;[b] they will be slaves and they will be oppressed[c] for four hundred years.

14 However, I will pass judgment[a] on the nation which they serve, and after
that they will come out with great possessions.[b]

15 But you,[a] you will go to your fathers in peace, you will be buried in ripe
old age.

16 Only in the fourth generation[a] will they return here, because the wickedness of the Amorites will not have run its course till then.

17 Now when the sun had gone down[a] and it had become quite dark,[b] see,
there was a smoking fire pot and a flaming torch that passed between
the carcasses.

18 On that day[a] Yahweh gave Abram the solemn assurance: I[b] am giving
your descendants this land, from the river[c] of Egypt to the great river,
the Euphrates.[d]

19 The Kenites, the Kenizzites, and the Kadmonites,

20 the Hittites, the Perizzites, and the Rephaim,

21 the Amorites, the Canaanites,[a] the Girgashites, and the Jebusites.

1a אחר originally a substantive, BrSyn §116c.   **b** On the use of the article, Ges-K
§126r, E. König, *Syntax* §299b.   **c** Bergstrasser, II, 10k, explains: "You have no
need to fear!"   **d** Sam reads 1.pers; perhaps to be preferred, as הרבה is unusual as
predicate. On the adverbial use of הרבה, R. Meyer, *Grammatik*, 103,20; Ges-K §131q.,
141e.   **e** On the sentence as a whole, F. I. Andersen, *The Sentence in Biblical
Hebrew* (1974) 43. Parallelism in prose does not necessarily mean a poetic
base.   **f** [Translator's note: reading *mōgēn lak sōkēreka*. . .; Ug. *mgn* = "bestow,"
cf. Gen. 14:20, M. Dahood, *Psalms 1*, AncBib (1966) 17].
2a Sam Gk Mss. read only δέσποτα.   **b** Ges-K §141e: "The noun clause connected by *waw copulative* to a verbal clause. . . always describes a state *contemporaneous* with
the principal action. . .; not infrequently such a *circumstantial* clause indicates at the same
time some contradictory fact: "whereas, while, though" (Gen. 18:27; 20:3; 48:14). On the
participle, Ges-K §116n.; P. Joüon, Gr §159d; R. Meyer, *Grammatik* 119,1.   **c** Gk
"while the son of Mashek, my maidservant"; TargO: "the son of the care of what is in my
house"; Theod. "the son of him who (stands) over my house"; Vg. "the son of the administrator of my house"; Aq. "the son of him who provides drink for my house"; Syr para-
phrases. On the variants, H. Seebass, ZAW 75 (1963) 317-319.
3a On the object at the beginning of a verbal sentence, P. Joüon 155q.
4a Gk φωνή corresponds to קול; deliberate dramatization?   **b** Gk θεοῦ, variants
κυρίου.   **c** כי אם, Ges-K §163a.   **d** אשר without antecedent, P. Joüon §145a,
156k. Syr adds בנך for clarification, but MT is to be retained.   **e** Gk reads ἐκ σοῦ.
5a Indirect question, Ges-K §150i.   **b** כה with reference to preceding as in Num.
22:30; adverb as predicate in nominal sentence, BrSynt §177.   **c** זרע is never used
with גדל.
6a On the perf., Ges-K §112ss; the perf. is used here because the sentence does not carry
the narrative further.   **b** Gk, and following it Rom. 4:3; Gal. 3:6; Jas. 2:23, and versions: באלהים.   **c** Fem. in neuter sense, Ges-K §122q.   **d** Double accus. BrSynt
§94d.
7a ἐκ χώρας Χαλδαίων; cf. Gen. 11:28, 31.   **b** לתת לך, Ges-K §29f, 66i.
8a On the pointing of יהוה, Ges-K §17b.
9a Syr, simplifying, reads 2nd pers.   **b** TargO reads "three"; cf. B. Stade, ZAW
26 (1906) 127f; the plural part. means: "having achieved the third year" (F. Delitzsch
ad.loc.).
10a Sam reads inf. abs. בתור, a scribal error.   **b** Grammatically difficult, Ges-K
§139b, c; cf. Targ Syr Vg.
11a Gk has ὄρνεα = "birds"; the Gk did not know the precise meaning of עיט, as other

passages also indicate.   **b** TargO assimilates to v. 10; Gk expands according to v. 10.   **c** וישב from נשב hiph., "scare away"; Gk derives it from ישב, "to sit"; the versions hesitate.

12a On the construction, Ges-K §114h, i; Bergstrasser II, 110.   **b** Gk renders by ἔκστασις, cf. Gen. 2:21.   **c** On the construction, A. Dillmann ad.loc; P. Joüon §166d.

13a On the construction, P. Joüon §113m; Bergstrasser II 10m,12c.   **b** Asyndetic relative clause, Ges-K §155e; R. Meyer 115, 2a.   **c** Gk adds καὶ κακώσουσιν αὐτούς.

14a The participle can express the future; Ges-K §116p.   **b** On the construction, Ges-K §119n.

15a The *separate* pronoun to emphasize the subject, Ges-K §135a; BrSynt 34b.

16a Ges-K §118 adverbial acc; J. Skinner ad.loc: "as a fourth generation"; cf. Jer. 31:8.

17a Ges-K §111g; pluperf; cf. Gen. 24:15; 27:30; Bergstrasser II 6d: ויהי really belongs to the final clause.   **b** Noun and verb do not agree in gender; this occurs frequently when the predicate precedes the verb, Ges-K §145n,o; Gk presupposes להט.

18a ביום ההוא means "on that day then," ביום הזה "today" Ges-K §136b.   **b** נתתי: the perf. "to express *future* actions, when the speaker intends by an express assurance to represent them as finished. . . in contracts or other express stipulations," Ges-K §106m; BrSynt 41d: "coincidence between statement and fulfillment is expressed by perf."   **c** Many propose מנחל for מנהר (see comm. below).   **d** נהר פרת is probably an explanatory gloss.

19a The grammatical sequence from v. 18 is difficult.

21a Gk and Sam add ואת החוי.

The History of the Exegesis of Gen. 15.

O. Kaiser offers a detailed account of the history of the exegesis beginning with J. Wellhausen (ZAW 70 [1958] 107-126, see 108 n. 4); see also L. A. Snijders (OTS 12 [1958] 261-265); H. Cazelles (RB 69 [1962] 321-325); A. Caquot (Sem. 12 [1962] 51-55); N. Lohfink (SBS 28 [1967] 24-30); and J. Van Seters (*Abraham in History. . .* [1975] 249-253). The following survey is restricted in essence to work since 1958.

1. J. Wellhausen had recognized that in Gen. 15 we are dealing with two independent texts which have been joined together subsequently by means of the modified v. 7, and that the classical division into sources is very difficult here, if not impossible. The majority of scholars have followed Wellhausen in treating vv. 1-6 and vv. 7-21 as independent texts (e.g., G. von Rad: "we are really dealing here with two narratives whose material has had different histories"; E. Ehrlich, BZAW 73 [1953] 37: "A new narrative begins in v. 7"; W. Zimmerli [1976] 53: "One will fully grasp the meaning of vv. 1-6 and vv. 7ff. only when one understands each passage as an originally self-contained account"; so too O. Kaiser [1958]; S. Mowinckel, NTT 65 [1964]; L. Perlitt, WMANT 36 [1969]; H. H. Schmid, *Der sogenannte Jahwist. . .* [1976]). To regard 15:1-21 as a unified text is almost always to divide it into two literary strands: so H. Cazelles (RB 69 [1962] 321ff.); H. Seebass (WuD 7 [1963] 132ff); R. Kilian (BBB 24 [1966]); A. de Pury (*Promesse divine. . .* [1975]). It is clear, therefore, that it is one and the same methodological decision to regard Gen. 15 as a literary unity and again as a composition from literary sources. One need scarcely mention that there is no consensus about the various divisions and assignment to sources. Many critics have remarked on the grave danger of subjectivism here.

There is a group of scholars who take a position of their own in between. They hold that Gen. 15 is a unity, but their exegesis in fact presupposes two texts, vv. 1-6 and vv. 7-21; so N. Lohfink (1967) and J. Van Seters (1975). Methodologically they belong to the former group. The first result of this survey is that there has been progress within the first group, while in the second the hypothetical element is stronger. The old literary-critical view that E begins with ch. 15 has been almost universally abandoned.

2. To what type do 15:1-6 and 7-21 belong? An interim consensus has been reached that these two texts are not patriarchal narratives of the old, simple sort like Gen. 12:10-20;

the only actors are God and Abraham (so, e.g., S. Mowinckel: "These narratives are not of the old patriarchal sort"; they are "theological reflections"). N. Lohfink has described them as "factitious narratives" and has demonstrated their parallel structure.* Later, however, he qualifies them as a "secondary juxtaposition of oracles which have had their own tradition history," which is something different. A. de Pury calls the basic text which he has constructed an "oracle of salvation." J. Van Seters puts a series of detailed questions about the form of Gen. 15, but only comes to the quite correct conclusion that the chapter contains a wealth of elements from different types; he does not say to which type ch. 15 or its two parts belong. C. Westermann (1964) has described Gen. 15:1-6 (Gen. 21–24) and vv. 7-21 (Gen. 29) as promise narratives, i.e., promises which have been secondarily shaped into a narrative (see further, *The Promises to the Fathers. . .* [1976; Eng. 1980]). This means, among other things, that Gen. 15:1-6 and 7-21 can be understood only in the context of the history of the promises as a whole.

3. The question of the time of origin is controversial in the extreme. There is first the negative consensus that it cannot be answered by assigning verses to a literary source; W. Zimmerli's judgment is: "The question is to be put seriously whether Gen. 15 as such has not had its own history of origin and growth." Traditio-historical exegesis has long tended to regard 15:1-6 as late, but vv. 7-21 as early. So H. Gunkel who emphasized the strongly archaic character of the rite in vv. 9-11, 17-18; likewise W. F. Albright, "The covenant between Yahweh and Abraham in Gen. 15 is strikingly archaic" (*Yahweh and the Gods. . .* [1968] 93); G. von Rad, O. Kaiser (vv. 7-21 the ancient kernel, vv. 1-6 the later elaboration), and many others have taken this up; N. Lohfink has tried to underpin it in detail (pre-Yahwistic). But L. Perlitt has demonstrated that the patriarchal oath (ברית), as reinforcement of the old and simple promise to the patriarchs, belongs to the Deuteronomic theology, and has its focal point in Deuteronomy (WMANT 36 [1969]). This oath is always related to the gift of the land in Gen. 12–50; wherever it occurs, the Deuteronomic language is in evidence (Gen. 50:24). "Gen. 15 is an actualization of the promise of the land by means of the theology of the seventh century" (p. 76), at a time when the land was threatened and the simple promise was no longer adequate. The transference of a ritual oath to a god must also be a secondary formation, and so a further sign that it is late. J. Van Seters maintains the unity of ch. 15 and understands it as addressed to the community in exile in the late exilic period. One of his main arguments is that the phrase, "Ur of the Chaldees," makes sense only in the late Babylonian period. In favor of this is the prophetic address in v. 1, which is close to Is. 40:9-10 (here too אַל־תִּירָא and שָׂכָר), and the lament in v. 2, as in Deutero-Isaiah, e.g., 54:1-3, which likens the survivors to a childless woman. Van Seters also sees an argument for late exilic origin in v. 6. He resumes G. von Rad's explanation that the sentence which accounts faith as righteousness has been detached from its original cultic setting and applied to personal faith; but he is of the opinion that this explanation makes sense only from the exilic period on, when the cult was in eclipse and personal faith in the promises took its place.

One may or may not follow L. Perlitt and J. Van Seters regarding the time to which they assign the chapter; in any case they (and others, cf. O. Kaiser ZAW 70 [1958] 107ff.) have provided so many indications of a late origin of both parts that it is scarcely possible any longer to ascribe either vv. 1-6 or vv. 7-21 to the oldest layer of the patriarchal story (see L. Perlitt's statement of position over against N. Lohfink).

4. Covenant and oath: cf. Intro., section 4, "The Cult" and "The Covenant with the Fathers." The theological meaning of the chapter is fundamentally changed with the recognition by modern scholarship that Gen. 15:7-21 is not concerned with a covenant which God concluded with Abraham, but with a solemn oath of promise (covenant is supported by O. Kaiser [1958], H. Cazelles [1962], R. E. Clements [1967]; oath by N. Lohfink [1967], L. Perlitt [1969], A. de Pury [1975], C. Westermann [1976], and H. H. Schmid [1976]).

---

*Translator's note: "factitious narratives," i.e., artificial narratives constructed around, and for the purpose of communicating, the promises.

5. There are three interpretations which relate Gen. 15 closely to David and his court. A. Caquot sees it as the work of a court official who used the Abraham tradition to glorify David (Sem. 12 [1962] 51-66). According to R. E. Clements the Yahwist wanted to present in Gen. 15 the proclamation of the kingship, the possession of the land, and the Davidic kingdom (SBT 2nd series, 5 [1967]). M. Weinfeld argues from Babylonian texts that the conclusion of the covenant with Abraham (and David) is modelled on the pattern of the "royal grant"; that is, royal gifts are bestowed on vassals who have given loyal service (JAOS 90 [1970] 184-203). The difficulty with this explanation is that both parts of ch. 15 probably had a later origin and exhibit a mixture of forms which contain a great variety of different elements of tradition (see O. Kaiser, J. Van Seters).

Form

One can take as one's starting point the existence of a collection of promise texts in the middle of the Abraham story (see Intro., diagram at the end of section 4) and that they are to be understood from the context of the history of the patriarchal promises. This renders comprehensible how two central promise narratives have been juxtaposed, each having as subject matter one of the two important promises which were so decisive in a later period: descendants and land (15:1-6 and 15:7-21). It is obviously the intention to put these two promises, now converted into narratives, in the middle of the Abraham cycle.

These promises have been dressed as narratives; a redactor, by a minimum of alteration, has put them into a narrative setting; by changing the beginning of v. 7, "and Yahweh said to Abraham," to "and he said to him," he made vv. 7-21 a continuation of vv. 1-6. This, however, can in no wise alter the fact that it is a matter of two promise narratives of virtually the same structure (as N. Lohfink), the subject matter of one of which is the multiplication of descendants, of the other the land.

Both are factitious narratives (N. Lohfink; compositions, W. Richter) which shape a promise into a narrative, just as in Gen. 13:14-17 a promise has been shaped into an episode. So both vv. 1-6 and vv. 7-21 each form a self-contained event. Both have this in common that the promise is not accepted at once; in vv. 1-6 it is met with a complaint, in vv. 7-21 with the request for a sign. Hence the far-reaching parallelism between the two to which N. Lohfink has drawn attention. The difference is that in vv. 1-6 a sign is pointed out whereas in vv. 7-21 a confirmation is enacted. In addition the latter is extensively elaborated.

The tradition history qualifies these texts as promise narratives, whence it follows that the promises to the patriarchs were at the disposition of the author of vv. 1-6 and 7-21; they are the structural material at the basis of the narratives. Everything else is decoration serving to shape the promise into a narrative.

Setting

The question of the original setting and time of origin of the two narratives is hotly debated. We can be certain of the new starting point which modern methodology has won for us: from the point of view of tradition history both texts belong to the context of the history of the patriarchal promises. We can be certain further that the texts cannot belong to the earliest stage of this history because they are promises shaped into narratives presupposing that the promises are already at hand. Yet another certain argument is the combination of the promise of a son and the promise of descendants in 15:1-6 (cf. C. Westermann, *The Promises to the Fathers*. . . [1976; Eng. 1980]), and the promise of the land under oath in 15:7-21 which is later than the simple promise. Neither of the two narratives, therefore, can go back to the patriarchal period, though this does not exclude the possibility that individual elements are old.

Whether vv. 1-6 and 7-21 belong to J or E is a matter of contention. Scholarship has almost universally abandoned the attempt to assign vv. 1-6, or a strand of individual verses collated out of 15:1-21, to E; in any case this is extremely questionable. There are still some who would assign vv. 7-21, or a strand unravelled from vv. 1-21 by means of literary criticism, to J (inasmuch as J is reckoned as a work from the 10th to the 9th c.); but the recent studies of L. Perlitt, J. Van Seters, and H. H. Schmid have put this in question. L. Perlitt's judgment on vv. 7-21 is that ''nothing favors a Yahwistic origin'' (p. 76). A pre-Yahwistic origin, therefore (N. Lohfink), is even more dubious.

The present state of scholarship would regard a late stage in the history of the patriarchal promises as the probable period of origin of the texts—a period when the possession of the land (vv. 7-21) and the survival of the people (vv. 1-6) was in danger, and the old patriarchal promises were newly revived so as to give surety to God's promise in a time of national danger (so H. Gunkel, though he did not draw the conclusion).

Commentary

[15:1-6] *Gen. 15:1-6: Structure.* The narrative here is a self-contained episode; it is not really an event, but an exchange, a dialog in three steps. To God's promise (v. 1) Abraham raises an objection in the form of a lament (vv. 2-3). God meets the objection (vv. 4-5) with both a negative (v. 4) and a positive (v. 5) answer. Abraham reacts positively and God acknowledges this (v. 6). There are echoes of the oracle of salvation, which O. Kaiser and others have noted, in that the objection has the form of a lament, while the oracle of salvation is God's answer to the lament. The difficulty that the oracle of salvation precedes the lament is to be explained from the character of 15:1-6 as a ''factitious narrative.''

[15:1a]   אחר הדברים האלה: In Genesis again in 22:1; 22:20; 39:7; 40:1; 48:1. ''An editorial connecting link which looks backwards'' (R. Kilian, BBB 24 [1966] 39). Three of the six attestations of the formula in Genesis occur in chs. 37–50, i.e., in a coherent narrative: what is about to be narrated is made to follow what has just been narrated. It is not, however, a sign of immediate continuation, but always spans an interval back to what has preceded; this is very obvious in 40:1. In the Abraham cycle the formula, 15:1; 22:1; 22:20, presupposes an already coherent Abraham narrative. It can belong, therefore, only to a later, redactional stage when there was no longer any awareness that the Abraham story had grown out of individual narratives. The formula in 15:1 is also to be understood in this sense; it is redactional, linking ch. 15 with what precedes.

היה דבר־יהוה אל־אברם: A. Dillmann notes: ''. . .A very common expression for prophetic revelation; it occurs in Genesis only here and in v. 4''; H. Gunkel comments: ''It points to a relatively late period''; J. Skinner: ''Chiefly in later prophets and superscriptions, specially common in Jer and Ez''; R. Kilian: ''The fact that J and E do not use the formula elsewhere must in any case arouse doubts''; W. Zimmerli: ''Elsewhere God speaks to Abraham directly or by means of a messenger.'' It is important to note the occurrence of the formula in later narrative texts: 1 Sam. 15:10; 2 Sam. 7:4; 1 Kings 12:22; 16:1; 17:2,8; 18:31; 21:17; etc. The formula in Gen. 15:1,4 is close to this group both in content and time.

217

This is confirmed by 1 Kings 18:31 where an oracle concerning Jacob is intro-duced, ''one for each tribe of the sons of Jacob, the man named Israel by the word of the Lord.'' This whole group of passages presupposes prophecy, and the phrase has already become so stereotyped that it can introduce a word to a seer, a man of God, or one of the patriarchs. The occurrence of the formula twice in Gen. 15:1-6, but not elsewhere in the whole of the Pentateuch, is a sign that the passage can have arisen only in the later period of the monarchy.

The phrase which follows immediately, במחזה, confirms the impression of late origin. Many exegetes allege it as an argument for an early date because it occurs in the ancient oracle in Num. 24:4,16 (e.g., R. Kilian). But this is a failure to recognize the fact that the word is used there in its specific sense of the ''trance'' of a seer; Gen. 15:1-6 is not a trance in the real sense (A. Dillmann had already seen this); rather two quite different ways of receiving a divine oracle are secondarily combined; the term is used in a transmuted, modified sense.

[15:1b]   The word of God addressed to Abraham is a stylized oracle of salvation (so the majority of exegetes) consisting of a word of encouragement (so desig-nated in Akkadian, N. Lohfink), ''Do not be afraid,'' with an assurance and the reason in two sentences. Such an introduction would be scarcely comprehensible in a developed narrative. The introduction would have to present Abraham's situ-ation into which the word of encouragement is spoken. In the factitious narrative this introduction serves merely to sound the theme, a promise to Abraham. It is not, therefore, an oracle of salvation directed to a definite situation, but a stylized formula, as every listener knows. In the period of the monarchy this has echoes of a royal oracle which promises a king protection (shield) and booty (שׂכר, similar to Is. 40:10). O. Kaiser has drawn attention to the language of the royal oracle and to Mesopotamian parallels, e.g., an oracle of Ishtar of Arbela to Esarhaddon: ''Esarhaddon, in Arbela I am your gracious shield,'' and many others which be-gin with the word of encouragement: ''Do not be afraid'' (further parallels in A. Labat, *Les religions du Proche-Orient asiatique* [1970]; H. Vorländer, AOAT 23 [1975]; J. G. Heintz, VT.S 17 [1969] 112ff.). There is a similar Egyptian text in W. Beyerlin: ''Amun is behind me, I fear nothing, for Amun is strong'' (ATD, Ergänzungsreihe 1 [1975] 68f.). The same metaphor, ''shield,'' is used for God's protection in the same form of speech, an oracle of salvation, in Deut. 33:29; Pss. 18:3,31; 84:11; 144:2; there is no reason, therefore, to understand מגן as ''gift,'' deriving from the Ugaritic (O. Loretz, UF 6 [1974] 492; E. A. Speiser, comm. ad. loc; M. Dahood, JBL 76 [1957] 38, 62-73), or to alter it in any other way (M. Kessler, VT 14 [1964] 494-497). Again, it would be quite out of character with this type of sentence to conclude from it that Abraham was concerned with a ''war ideology'' or the ideology of the war of Yahweh. The purpose of v. 1 is merely to say in general terms that Abraham is receiving an oracle of salvation from Yah-weh. The call, ''Do not be afraid,'' occurs often in the assurance of salvation in Deutero-Isaiah (41:10,13,14; 43:1,5). A very distant parallel both in time and place can illustrate how general a meaning this assurance can have; it is likewise an address of a god to a king, in this case to a king of the Inca empire: ''Come hith-er, my son, and do not be afraid; for I am your father, the sun god. Know that you are to subject many peoples. . .'' (G. Lanczkowski, *Universitas* 20 [1965] 849). One cannot ask, therefore, what Abraham's ''reward'' consists in, or whether it is a question of protection to be given on the occasion of a particular threat. The vir-tually rhythmic form is a further sign that the sentence is a traditional assurance of salvation. The parallelism of the two sentences which give the reasons for the assurance would be clearer if one were to read the first person in the second sentence, as in the first, following the Sam: "I will make your reward very great."

[15:2-3] Abraham's answer is in two parts: both are introduced by ויאמר אברם, and both say practically the same thing; they are doublets, and the doubling can be explained in different ways. It is very often said that v. 3 has been added so as to elucidate, because v. 2 was not comprehensible. But this explanation does not hold, because v. 2 is comprehensible without 2bβ. One must acknowledge then that two versions of Abraham's lament over his childlessness were before the author and he wanted to preserve both of them. This explanation becomes more comprehensible if in vv. 2 and 3 we have the only part of the factitious narrative that goes back to old narrative traditions.

[15:2] After the introduction, v. 2 consists of Abraham's lament that he has no children, beginning with an address, and is more readily comprehensible when read without v. 2bβ:

אדני יהוה

מה־תתן־לי

ואנכי הולך ערירי

אדני יהוה is not a form of address which occurs in the course of a dialog, but belongs to the realm of prayer; here it is an address to God, part of a lament corresponding to the beginning of a psalm of lament. The address "Lord" (Gk δέσποτα) has its setting in sedentary cult; it is not appropriate to the religion of the patriarchs. According to A. Dillmann, the only other occurrences in the Pentateuch are in Deut. 3:24; 9:26; according to J. Skinner, it occurs only in the vocative in the historical books. "What can you give me?" presupposes v. 1. Abraham counters this general promise (what good is it to me?). His question is like a lament before God and implies a reproach, the reason for which is given in the second part, "while I must go childless!" The whole is in the form of an objection: You have indeed promised me something, but what good is it to me? There is a similar objection in Samson's lament: "Thou hast granted this great deliverance by the hand of thy servant, and shall I now die of thirst and fall into the hands of the uncircumcised?" (Judg. 15:18). Here too the reproach or lament arises out of the objection. This parallel also shows the meaning of v. 2bβ. The three parts of the lament are there: You, O God—I—the others. This is proof that 15:2 is an ancient lament which occurs in like form in other narratives of the early period. It is the lament of the childless one, as impressively attested in the Ugaritic epics (cf. C. Westermann, *The Promises to the Fathers*. . . [1976; Eng. 1980]). U. Cassuto also draws attention to these parallels (BASOR 119 [1950] 157-163); see also S. Talmon (VT 13 [1963] 419-455) and R. T. O'Callaghan (VT 4 [1954] 164-176). ערירי = "childless," attested elsewhere only in Lev. 20:20f. and Jer. 22:30 (Sir. 16:3); it is used only of the husband. For הלך in the sense of "pass on" = "die," see Ps. 39:14.

The conclusion, v. 2bβ, is corrupt and cannot be translated. But as its meaning must accord with the parallel in v. 3b, this is no great loss. Both 2bβ and 3b begin with *waw*; then follows בן־ביתי, which is broken in 2bβ by משק. One can take this firm base as the starting point: "I am childless—and the son of my house. . . .." The sentence can continue only in the following way: "will take the place of the son denied to me"; and this is just what v. 3b says: "the son of my

house will be my heir.'' Inasmuch as this same verb יִרַשׁ occurs twice in God's answer in v. 4, and this verse is the reply to vv. 2 and 3, v. 2bβ can only have had a
similar wording. One can go just a step further to explain how the corruption in v.
2b came about. A well-known trait of the history of the narratives is that minor
characters acquire names in the course of tradition (e.g., in the synoptic gospels);
this is the case here also. The ''son of the house'' has no name in the older form
(v. 3b), the transmitters of the tradition making no alteration despite v. 2bβ; he acquires the name Eleazer in the later form v. 2bβ, and his place of origin is further
added, first as בֶּן־מֶשֶׁק, probably another (older) form of the name, and then as an
elaborated gloss הוּא דַמֶּשֶׂק. These additions are inventions inserted into the narrative, and the result is the present text.

There are plenty of other explanations which cannot be enumerated here.
They have been synthesized by R. J. Ream (*Biblical Correspondences with Nuzi
Akkadian* [Diss. Dropsie College, 1962]); M. Weippert (Bib 52 [1971] 407-432);
A. Caquot (Sem. 12 [1962] 51-66); T. L. Thompson (BZAW 133 [1974]
203-230). ''The son of my house'' means ''one who belongs to my house'' (F.
Delitzsch), ''a member of the household'' (J. Skinner), ''a favorite expression
also in nonbiblical literature from Akkadian to Palmyraean'' (F. Vattioni, AION
17 [1967] 157-163). J. Van Seters compares the Akkadian *mār biti*, ''member of
the household'' (*Abraham in History*. . . [1975], pp. 17ff.). It is possible, though
not certain, that there is the further meaning, ''my administrator'' (H. L.
Ginsberg, BASOR 200 [1970] 31-32, ''my steward''). In recent times it has often
been said that Abraham adopted this ''son of my house.'' This is contested in detail by T. L. Thompson, J. Van Seters, and H. Donner (OrAnt 8 [1969] 87-119).
All three conclude that the text is not speaking of an adoption (so too A. Verger,
Studi in onore E. Volterra VI [1969] 483-490, and R. de Vaux, *The Early History
of Israel* [1971; Eng. 1978]). I agree with J. Van Seters that a slave with the special status given in the text could inherit.

[15:3]   As a doublet, v. 3 has the same function as v. 2; that is, it is to be understood as a counter to v. 1. Both parts of v. 3 are a lament, corresponding more or
less to the two parts of v. 2; the reproachful question, v. 2a, which forms the immediate transition from v. 1, is missing here. V. 3a is a lament directed to God in
the second person, corresponding to the accusation brought against God in the
Psalms; v. 3b states the consequence which follows from this in the third person.
The lament directed to God is concerned solely with the son from his body whom
God has denied to Abraham. The background is the life-style of the small-cattle
nomads who saw the future solely in terms of the succession from parents to children. A life that cannot be continued from father to son, but breaks off with the
childless father, is no integral, prosperous life; it cannot be a life blessed by God.
Abraham, therefore, rejects the general promise made to him by God in v. 1. The
rejection is merely indicated in v. 3 by the twofold הִנֵּה־הֵן. The lament of the
childless father in the form of an accusation against God in v. 3a can go back to the
patriarchal period, just as that in v. 2. But this is questionable for v. 3b, precisely
because of the verb יִרַשׁ. It is only in the sedentary period, when property acquires
a significance that determines life itself, that the son becomes ''the heir'' (2 Sam.
14:7; Jer. 49:1); property cannot have such a meaning in the life-style of the nomad where the son is not the heir, but the one in whom the life of the father as a
whole is carried on. The son continues the life of the father; this is what the genealogy expresses. To have no son does not mean to have no heir, but to have no fu-

ture; there would be no genealogy to trace from Abraham through his son to a coming generation. If 15:1-6 originated as a promise narrative only in the period of the monarchy, then the adaptation of the lament of the childless father can be readily understood. What has remained is childlessness as an affliction which is the matter of complaint before God; but in a long sedentary tradition the emphasis is shifted to the significance of childlessness for family property (J. Skinner: ירש in the sense of inheritance occurs in Gen. 21:10; 2 Sam. 14:7; Jer. 49:1; Prov. 30:23).

[15:4-5] The answer to Abraham's lament and objection follows in vv. 4-5 in two parts. First, God refutes the objection (v. 4) with the promise of a son of Abraham's own body (v. 4b). Second, God confirms the promise with a sign (v. 5). The stars in the heavens, however, and the invitation to count them are not really a confirmation of the promise of a son, but an extension of it through a promise of increase. This beautiful, pregnant episode presupposes that the promises of a son and of descendants have already been joined together: "and it is clear that it is this very increase that is now significant for the current status of Abraham's posterity in the land of promise" (C. Westermann, *The Promises to the Fathers*. . . [1976; Eng. 1980]). A promise has been fashioned into a scene in v. 5, just as in 13:14-17; the promise said: "I will make your descendants like the stars of heaven," and the scene where God shows Abraham the stars culminates in the words: "so will your descendants be."

[15:4] See comments on v. 1 for the opening words. The introductory הנה is to be understood in an adversative sense; the הן—הנה in v. 3, indicating Abraham's objection, is counterbalanced by the הן at the beginning of v. 4, rejecting the objection. It is scarcely possible to translate this; the formulation in v. 4a is found only in Judg. 3:20; 1 Kings 19:9. The dominant theme in God's answer is the repeated ירש. As has been said already, the promise of a son of Abraham's own body is formulated from the standpoint of the author; there is no recognizable trace behind it of a promise of a son from the patriarchal period. The son is described as "one who comes from your own body," an *ad hoc* formulation in opposition to the "son of my house." מעים is regarded as the place whence life originates, as in Gen. 25:23 (cf. G. Fohrer, BHH 1 [1962] 379).

[15:5] This verse shows how even a factitious narrative can achieve the poetic power of a real narrative. Even though what God shows Abraham does not touch directly the point which gave rise to the lamentation, namely, that his wife cannot have children, it is nevertheless a vitalization of the promise of many descendants pronounced in unforgettable language at a time when the people was under threat. The promise to Abraham in this adapted form continues to live in an adapted situation. In Gen. 15:1-6 the promises of a son and of descendants are still clearly juxtaposed; in Deutero-Isaiah there is only the promise of descendants: "Look to Abraham your father and to Sarah who bore you; for when he was but one I called him, and I blessed him and made him many" (Is. 51:2).

It is certainly no accident that the invitation to look up at the stars occurs only once more in the Old Testament, and again in Deutero-Isaiah (40:26). In this case, of course, it refers to the might of the Creator, while in Gen. 15:5 the comparison is between the vast number of the stars and the vast number of Abraham's descendants; nevertheless, in both cases looking at the stars is looking into the broad expanse of the activity of the creator which transports man's gaze from the narrow horizon of human events. It needs only this single sentence: "look up at the stars!" and the imminent threat takes on a different aspect. It is Deuteronomy that compares the vast number of the stars with the people of Israel (Deut. 1:10; 10:22; 28:62); "but now the Lord your God has made you countless as the stars in the sky" (Deut. 10:22). H. Gunkel writes: "a fine and noble picture of the countless number of the people of Israel."

The new introduction, ויאמר לו, effectively separates the promise from the invitation; the כה is retrospective (as in Num. 22:30 and elsewhere). The language of this short sentence is yet another clear sign that in vv. 4-5 two promises have been shaped into a scene, each being adapted to it in a different way (v. 4b "but. . .," v. 5b "so. . .").

[15:6]   The passage ends with Abraham's reaction to the promise in vv. 4-5. It is necessary to narrate this because Abraham had not accepted the promise in vv. 2-3 but countered it; in v. 6 he reacts positively. The verse has an important function in 15:1-6 and is the conclusion of the unit. This then is the definitive rejection of the view that v. 6 is a subsequent addition as well as of the attempt to read 15:1-21 as a textual unit. Vv. 1-6 form a self-contained passage with its conclusion in v. 6.

In all discussions about Abraham and his story v. 6 is the most frequently mentioned. Abraham ultimately became the "father of faith" in later history. That is to say in the first place that 15:1-6 as a whole belongs to the subsequent history of Abraham, and the closing sentence v. 6 represents a theological reflection which pertains to the period of the author of this factitious narrative; there is no trace in the verse of anything which goes back to the patriarchal period. Accordingly the general view of current exegesis is that the verse is a late interpretation resulting from theological reflection. When therefore F. Hahn comments: "One will have to say that Gen. 15:6 anticipates by and large the Pauline interpretation" (Fests. G. von Rad [1971]), he is pointing to a theological reflection on Abraham from the period of the late monarchy which very probably presupposes the idea of faith as formulated in specific terms by Isaiah (so T. C. Vriezen, W. Zimmerli, R. Smend, Fests. W. Baumgartner, VT.S 16 [1967] 284-290). This has profound consequences for exegesis. We are faced here with a "retrojection" (J. Wellhausen): a well-defined attitude towards God which became important in a circle within the later history of Israel has been transferred to Abraham, the father of the people.

In order to explain 15:6 we must firstly inquire into this circle. The most important stage in the history of the idea of faith is its formulation in specific terms by the prophet Isaiah (cf. H. Wildberger, אמן, THAT 1 [1971] 177-209, with bibliog.; also Lit. on v. 6 above). Earlier, before Isaiah, the hiph. of אמן occurred mainly with a negative. It was the normal, natural thing for one to believe God's word; there was no need to state it. What was unusual was not to believe God's word; this merited mention; hence in the early period the word was used rather often with a negative. Isaiah experienced the disbelief of the king, God's anointed, who did not believe the word of God which came to him (Is. 7). The consequence was an awareness of the meaning of faith, and the necessity of explaining the culmination of this problem in Isaiah. This is also the theological-historical background of 15:6. If one takes as starting point that 15:1-6 is a promise which has been subsequently shaped into a narrative, then the faith which is the subject of the story is related to the generation addressed by the author when the promises and the continued existence of the people were in jeopardy. The point at issue then is not the faith of Abraham, but why the author of this promise narrative harks back to him. The promise of descendants (v. 5) presupposes the promise of a son (v. 4); for the author it is one and the same thing. But the promise of a son is most certainly part of the oldest layer of the Abraham narratives. There is therefore a demonstrable traditio-historical connection, even if the actualization of the old Abraham tradition in 15:1-6 is transposed into an era, language, and theological thought-pattern which are no longer the same.

"And he accounted it to him as righteousness": the language and thought of a later period is even more striking in this closing sentence. A theological reflection of this kind is possible neither in the patriarchal period nor in the early monarchy (tenth–ninth century). As G. von Rad has shown, it presupposes cultic language: "The background of 15:6 is the priest's formal acknowledgment of a sacrificial gift as properly offered" (ThLZ 76 [1951] 129-133). One can take an even broader view of the practice inasmuch as a particular attitude to God is declared correct, e.g., Deut. 24:13 (the context is returning a pledge in due time), "and it shall be righteousness to you before the Lord your God." If one takes this broader usage, as does W. M. Clark (VT 21 [1971] 261-280), then J. Van Seters' argument is not compelling: he pursues G. von Rad's explanation ingeniously and says that the substitution of the cultic requirement by faith takes on meaning only in the exilic period when the cult had lost its meaning and trust in the promise had taken its place.

The details: האמין is in the perfect because the sentence does not continue the narrative (H. Holzinger). The verb is usually construed with ב when it is a matter of belief in God. "ב of the person or thing to which faith adheres" (F. Delitzsch). צדקה: the first occurrence of the word in this sense is in Deut. 24:13. Similarly Ps. 106:31: "that has been reckoned to him (Phinehas) as righteousness" (correct comportment in a critical situation); "the attitude of a good, pious, loyal servant of God" (H. Gunkel). This is parallel to the Babylonian prayer: "In my beseeching, in the lifting up of my hands, in all that I do. . . let there be righteousness" (cf. N. Lohfink, SBS 28 [1967] 59).

[15:7-21] *Gen. 15:7-21: Structure.* The text begins with a promise by Yahweh to Abraham to "give you this land as your possession" (v. 7); it ends with the solemn confirmation of this promise (v. 18). Abraham does not accept it immediately but asks for a confirmatory sign (v. 8). Yahweh gives him an assurance which consists in the enactment of a solemn oath (vv. 9-18) divided into preparation (vv. 9-10) and execution (vv. 17-18). The event is a self-contained whole, the end linking up with the beginning. But the whole stands out in relief only when the elaborations are recognized as such. The foretelling in vv. 12-16 cannot be an original part of the solemn action because it is an explanation of history dressed in prophetic garb. The enumeration of the peoples of Canaan is a doublet of the land specification at the end of v. 18, but in another style.

It is not the simple promise of the land that underlies the structure of 15:7-21 (as in 12:7), but the solemn assurance by which it is promised, corresponding to the passages where it is formulated as an oath (Gen. 24:7; 50:24; most passages are in Deut., e.g., 7:8,12,13; 8:1,18; etc.). The text presents in narrative form God's solemn promise of the land, not Yahweh's striking of a covenant with Abraham (so O. Kaiser, W. F. Albright, F. M. Cross, O. Ohler, O. Sant), nor even a sacrificial action (so O. Procksch, W. Zimmerli).

[15:7] The introductory verse of 15:7-21 corresponds to that of 15:1-6 inasmuch as a general sort of promise forms the exposition and is followed by Abraham's objection. A further correspondence is the ''I'' in v. 1 and v. 7, even though formulated differently. Both are signs of a revelatory address or word. If this is clearer in v. 1 than in v. 7, then the reason is probably that a redactor altered the introduction in v. 7 to ויאמר אליו to make vv. 7-21 a continuation of vv. 1-6. This can now be explained more precisely. In the old patriarchal narratives the promises are always addressed directly to one of the patriarchs. Later it was no longer so easy to speak of a divine oracle addressed to an ordinary person; such addresses were now ''revelations'' and had to be qualified as such. This is done in different ways in v. 1 and v. 7. The אני יהוה, ''the formula of self-presentation'' (W. Zimmerli, Fests. A. Alt [1953] 179-209) is therefore a linguistic device of a later period to describe a divine oracle as revelation.

The formula has a broad background in the history of religion (O. Kaiser, ZAW 70 [1958] 107-126); it is the means that the god often uses for self-revelation as the one whom the addressee already knows from previous manifestations (e.g., Gen. 31:13); this is also the case here in the following relative sentence. Many exegetes have noted that the אשר הוצאתיך very strikingly recalls Ex. 20:2; Deut. 5:6; and Lev. 25:38. The parallel in Lev. 25:38 extends to all three parts of 15:7:

אני יהוה אלהיכם
אשר הוצאתי אתכם מארץ מצרים
לתת לכם את־ארץ כנען

It is a fixed formula which actualizes the bringing out from Egypt. In 15:7 it is adapted to the bringing of Abraham out of Ur of the Chaldees.

The third sentence of v. 7 says that the purpose of God in bringing Abraham from Ur was to give him ''this land'' as his possession. There is here the same close link between the bringing out and the promise of the land as in the parallel in Lev. 25:38, which in turn goes back to the promise in Ex. 3:7f. This confirms that the bringing of Israel out of Egypt and the grant of the land is the background to the formula used here. J. Skinner has observed that the words לתת לרשתה are decidedly Deuteronomic. The link between the two verbs is so frequent in Deut. (3:18; 9:16; 12:1; 15:14, and six other places) that the formula in Gen. 15:7 presupposes the same Deuteronomic formula. This also explains the repeated occurrence of ירש in Gen. 15 (vv. 3, 4, 7, 8). The phrase הארץ הזאת likewise occurs in the same context (Deut. 3:12).

J. Van Seters has concluded from the name Ur of the Chaldees that 15:7 can have originated only in the exile, because such a designation makes sense only in the late Babylonian period (on the name, cf. Intro., section 3, C, III, ''the Aramaeans''). One must concede the possibility; but as the language of the text as a whole favors rather the seventh century, according to L. Perlitt's study, one cannot be so certain in assigning it to a later period merely on the basis of the one name. However, it can certainly not have originated in the tenth century.

[15:8] Abraham's question is really a request for a confirmatory sign. ''The question is not an expression of doubt, but a request'' (F. Delitzsch). Recognition because of a sign occurs also in Gen. 24:14: ''in this way I shall know that you. . . .'' The address, אדני יהוה, is the same as in v. 2. It is to be noted that here, as in v. 7, there is no mention of Abraham's posterity (as in 13:15); there is no thought of the chronological gap; Abraham is here the representative of Israel.

[15:9-10] God's answer to Abraham's question consists in an injunction (v. 9) which Abraham carries out (v. 10). The meaning of it is: "so that I can tell it to you, bring me. . .!" The law of saying only what is necessary also holds for the factitious narrative. It is part of the technique too that the execution goes beyond the commission (v. 10b). It is presupposed that the commission itself is enough for Abraham to know what he has to do.

One must attend to several different elements in order to understand the action that now follows: (1) It is almost universally acknowledged that we have here the enactment of a solemn oath. Word and action are part of the oath. There can be the raising of the hand or some other action(s). A standard form which is very common is the conditional self-cursing, as described here. The one who passes between the divided halves of the slain animals invokes death upon himself should he break the word by which he has bound himself in the oath. (2) The oath ritual is here transferred to God. The promise of the land reinforced by the oath weighs on him. It is the promise that is presented as event. The transference of the enactment of the oath to God raises difficulties, because the one who takes the oath invokes a higher power, and the simple assurance on God's part is thereby devalued inasmuch as it is in need of such a confirmation. It is possible to describe the oath taken by God in this way only in a period when the promise of the land and its solemn confirmation by oath had become a fixed formula which gave rise to no further reflection. (3) The cutting of the animals in half in the preparation and execution is conditioned by the secondary transference of the enactment to God, by the representation of God by fire and smoke (oven and torch), and finally by the subsequent assimilation of the enactment to a sacrifice by naming the sacrificial animals (cf. S. E. Loewenstamm, VT 18 [1968] 500-507).

[15:9] This verse contains only the commission to Abraham to bring the different animals: a heifer, a she-goat, and a ram, each three years old, together with a תור and a גוזל, two species of dove. As v. 10 expressly states, the two doves are not divided, i.e., they cannot have been an original part of the ritual of the cutting up of the animals. This is a certain demonstration that the list in v. 9 has been subsequently filled out by naming all sacrificial animals in the sacrificial laws (cf. W. Zimmerli, comm., ad loc.). The cutting up of the animals is thereby interpreted as the offering of the sacrifice. The three times repeated "three year old" is also part of sacrificial practice, but not of the oath ritual; there is no need therefore to look for another meaning in משלשת (R. Péter, VT 25 [1975] 491). In Jer. 34:18f. a calf is killed, and at Mari a donkey, each following the same ritual; the reason for this is that the killing of *an* animal suffices for the rite (M. Noth [1955], GesSt [1957] 142-154; E. A. Speiser, in *The World History of the Jewish People* II [1970] 163f.; the cutting up of a calf is also to be found in H. Donner and W. Röllig, *Kanaanäische u. aramäische Inschriften* I [1962] 222). Both here and in what follows Gen. 15:7-21 is "rather crammed with motifs" (L. Perlitt).

[15:10] The execution goes beyond the commission. Abraham divides the animals down the middle—but not the birds—and lays the parts opposite each other. The verb used for cutting, בתר, occurs only here, the noun בתר here and in Jer. 34:18 where the same rite is described. One can gather from this that the word

בתר, and not כרת, was proper to the original rite; כרת occurs first in v. 18 in connection with God's concluding oracle. The rite itself is only carried out in vv. 17-18.

[15:11]   This is a quite isolated and strange intermezzo: Abraham scares away the vultures that swoop on the carcasses. "There is nothing like this elsewhere in the Old Testament" (W. Zimmerli, ad loc.). One possible explanation is that we have an intermediary scene which delays the action and heightens the tension between the preparation (v. 10) and the execution (v. 17); but then it would not have any ominous significance. Most exegetes understand the swooping vultures as an evil omen which Abraham wards off. A. Dillmann writes: "An evil omen as when harpies want to prey on the sacrificial offering, Vergil, *Aeneid* 3:225ff." In this case v. 11 must be understood as a transition to the insertion vv. 13-16; the style and the evocative language would be suitable.

[15:12]   V. 12 is certainly the introduction to vv. 13-16; it is not part of the oath ritual (vv. 9-10, 17-18) the temporal introduction of which is given in v. 17a. On the contrary, v. 12a is a doublet intended to put the intermediary passage vv. 13-16 into chronological order: Abraham receives the oracle (vv. 13-16) beforehand, as the sun is going down. If v. 12 were the introduction to vv. 17-18 (so W. Zimmerli and others) then the two specifications of time would follow immediately on each other. V. 12 follows the specification of time, "as the sun was going down, a deep sleep fell upon Abraham." As he is aware of nothing in the deep sleep (cf. 2:21), the following sentence is not necessary, whether one deletes one of the nouns or not: "a great terror came upon him" or "the terror of a great darkness came upon him." The two words occur together again in Job 4:12-15 in the description of a vision out of which an oracle is addressed to an individual: deep sleep and terror (there פחד). The two passages have something further in common: the oracle as it is communicated in this divine manifestation has, as in Job, an interpretative meaning; it is to reinforce, to legitimate the explanation. The conclusion from its proximity to Job 4 is that the insertion vv. 12(11)-16 is very late.

[15:13-16]   The oracle communicated to Abraham in v. 12, introduced as revelation, is an explanation of history dressed as a foretelling. The emphatic ידע תדע at the beginning indicates this: "You must with certainty know. . . ." The word "know" connotes "understand" which has special reference to v. 16b, the explanatory sentence (cf. Josh. 23:13, where an explanation of God's action in history likewise forms the introduction). The oracle consists of a prophecy for Abraham's descendants, i.e., for Israel (vv. 13,14,16), with a prophecy for Abraham himself in the middle of it (v. 15), according to which he will die in peace before the harsh period of slavery begins for his descendants. The slavery in Egypt (v. 13) is followed by the return to Canaan (vv. 14b,16a). But the prophecy also includes Israel's enemies: God's intervention against Egypt (v. 14a) and against the Amorites when their wickedness will have run its course (v. 16b). The purpose of this explanation of history now becomes clear: God's righteousness will show itself in his judgment on Israel's oppressors (v. 14a), as well as in his destruction of the inhabitants of Canaan as punishment for their guilt (v. 16b). The God who is active in Israel's history is also the just disposer of the fate of the other peoples—an expressly universal trait.

[15:13]   The slavery in Egypt (without mention of the name) is described from the sedentaries' point of view: aliens—in a land not their own—as slaves—oppressed—for 400 years. All these details about the slavery in Egypt are always but retrojections elsewhere in the Old Testament.

[15:14a]   A reason why Israel is to live through this period of suffering is not stated. But certainly God is to take retribution on Israel's oppressors. Such a reflection on the punishment of Egypt is very striking. It can scarcely be a reference to the plagues, because they occur in the context of the liberation of Israel. The sentence is to be understood in the same sense as v. 16b: it concerns God's just action in the history of the nations.

[15:14b]   What is striking here is that it is not the liberation from slavery that is announced, but the fact of the return, just as in v. 16a. Their departure from Egypt "with great possessions" indicates a compensation, however slight, for their suffering in Egypt. The sentence shows that the old traditions of the exodus are known, but that they have been impressed with a particular outlook.

[15:15]   The prophecy of Abraham's peaceful death would have constituted the conclusion of the prophecy in an earlier form, divided as follows: Your descendants will. . .(13-14); but you will. . .(15); v. 16 is a later appendage. What is announced here is narrated in similar form in 25:8(P). It should be clear that narrative has precedence over prophecy in the patriarchal stories. "This is the first occurrence of the word שלום in the scriptures" (F. Delitzsch). The verse is the classical expression of a "happy death," of which the Old Testament speaks in a number of passages, especially in the patriarchal narratives. When the life span reaches its natural limit, then the old man, with the diminution of his natural powers and the onset of the weaknesses of old age, has led a full life; so he dies a happy death and one can say that he dies "in peace" (opposite in Gen. 42:38). Death does not in this case destroy life's "blessed state" (*Heilsein*), but the blessed state extends right up to death, death in good old age (so too Gen. 25:8; cf. Job 5:26). Part of the happy death is to be buried; the return to the earth unites the deceased with his fathers who have returned to it before him.

[15:16]   It is not v. 15 that is a secondary insertion (as J. Skinner and others have it) but v. 16. The time span shows this: "the fourth generation" is not to be equated with the "400 years" (v. 13b; following Ex. 12:40). The emphasis is on the sentence which gives the reason. The lengthy period rests on God's plan in history which also encompasses the other nations. Other passages also say that God will wipe out the Amorites for their wickedness (Deut. 9:4f.; Lev. 18:24-27; 20:22-24; 1 Kings 14:24). These are very late passages and Gen. 15:16 is chronologically close to them.

The purpose of the insertion of vv. 13-16 is not to be sought in the prophecy but in the interpretation of the event. Its point of leverage must be in the context into which it has been inserted, namely, the promise under oath of the land (between vv. 10 and 17). The solemn promise gives rise to the question, why the long delay? The answer lies in God's plan in history which is revealed to Abraham ("you must know. . ."); the long period of waiting is set at 400 years. One can understand such a reflection on history at a time when the meaning of the promises to the patriarchs has been awakened for the contemporary generation. The long gap between promise and fulfillment must have become strikingly difficult. According to v. 14a the Egyptians could not oppress Israel for so long a time and go unpunished. The subsequent addition of v. 16a is comprehensible from the standpoint of the exile (so J. Van Seters; but he assigns all of vv. 13-16 to the exile). Likewise, the detail about a shorter time (the fourth generation), as well as the explanation of God's nonintervention against Israel's enemies because their guilt has not yet run its course, could reflect the exile and be intended as a word of comfort to the exiles.

[15:17]   The carrying out of the rite follows in v. 17. If vv. 12-16 are a subsequent insertion, then the deep sleep and the great terror are also part of it; the action in vv. 9-10, 17-18 does not contain any visionary traits; it is nothing but an enactment of an oath by God which Abraham experiences in full consciousness (so already A. Dillmann); peculiar to it is merely that it takes place in complete darkness (v. 17a). This is a necessary precondition for the action because no person may see God (Ex. 33:20). Only signs, fire and smoke, which represent God can be seen in the darkness. There are many parallels to the oath ritual of passing between the divided carcass(es); it must have been a very widespread rite practised at quite different periods. The closest biblical parallel is in Jer. 34:18f., where the same rite (with only one animal) has the same meaning, a solemn self-obligation between people. Gen. 15:17 then cannot be merely an archaic rite as H. Gunkel, O. Procksch, G. von Rad, F. Cross, and others think. It appears from Jer. 34:18f. that the most likely meaning is that it represents a conditional self-cursing under the form of the split animals; the one who passes between them calls their fate upon himself should he violate the obligation. This is just the context of Jer. 34:18f.; destruction is announced for those who have broken their pledge.

     There is besides this a variety of other explanations which are derived from the many non-Israelite parallels: A. de Pury (*Promesse divine. . .* [1975] 312-321); T. H. Gaster (*Myth, Legend. . .* [1969]); L. Perlitt (WMANT 30 [1969] 72-74); for Akkadian parallels, E. F. Weidner (AfO 8 [1932-33] 17-34); for Aramaic parallels, A. Dupont-Sommer (*Les inscriptions Araméennes de Sifre* [1958] 17-60); for Mari parallels, M. Noth ([1955] GesSt [1957] 142-154). What is peculiar to Gen. 15:17 in contrast to these parallels and to Jer. 34:18f. is that the oath ritual is transferred to God, inasmuch as the ritual self-cursing is meant to confirm a promise he has made. But if the oath ritual rests on "the parallel fate of animal and the one who takes the oath," then "its application to (a) God is a secondary transference which almost overreaches Israel's image of God" (L. Perlitt, 73f.). Such a transference was possible only because it presupposed the current understanding of the promise of the land as an oath.

[15:18]   The narrative reaches its goal in v. 18; from the very first sentence, "to give you this land" (v. 7), it is concerned with the promise of the land to Abraham. But this verse also has the phrase which has given the narrative the traditional meaning: God concluded a covenant with Abraham. First, one must note the stylistic device of framing which the author uses; the conclusion reverts to the beginning. V. 7 does not say, "in order to make a covenant with you," but "to give you this land as your possession." One deduces from the framing that the real matter of the narrative is the promise of the land. The grammatical arrangement of v. 18 deserves attention. The לאמר means: the כרת ברית consists in (or its content is): "I am giving your descendants this land." The usual translation, "covenant,'' is inappropriate here; ברית must have a broader meaning. Finally, there is a further observation on the narrative structure: v. 18 winds up the procedure in vv. 9,10,17; it completes the solemn oath (v. 18b; cf. Gen. 50:24). The כרת ברית therefore must signify either directly or indirectly this solemn oath or confirmation of a promise in a rather broad sense. More recent studies of the notion of ברית confirm this (see Intro., Lit. on ''Covenant'' at the end of ''Literature for Section 4''; on Gen. 15:18 in particular, N. Lohfink, SBS 28 [1967] 101-113). The difficulty is that the dividing of the animal(s) is part of the rite described in Gen. 15, and apparently explains כרת ברית, words which occur alike in Jer. 34:18f and in the Mari parallel where ''to slay an ass'' can designate to enter into a contract (cf. E. A. Speiser, ad loc.). It is extremely likely then that כרת ברית describes the rite and so the making of a contract or covenant. But the parallel in Jer. 34:18f., where an obligation is undertaken before Yahweh (not with Yahweh), stands opposed to this, as does the striking fact that the rite occurs nowhere in the many Hittite contracts.

The explanation of the difficulty is that when concluding a contract there is often a solemn obligation or an oath. And so the enactment of an oath has in many cases become the way to describe the concluding of a contract (*pars pro toto*); so too with כרת ברית. The phrase, however, means only the undertaking of an obligation. Other matters besides a contract or covenant can fall under an oath; it is the context that shows this in each case. In Gen. 15:17-18 it is clear: God promises the land under oath. כרת ברית designates precisely this. It does not really matter whether or not one agrees with E. Kutsch's translation, ''to set up an obligation'' (BZAW 131 [1972] 121-128); what is decisive is that the Hebrew ברית does not as such mean ''covenant'' but has the broader sense of ''binding obligation,'' so that sometimes it is very close to an oath, sometimes to a promise (often so in Deut.). The translation must express this: ''On that day Yahweh gave Abraham the solemn assurance.'' The perfect נתתי is the form of legal agreement (cf. Gen. 1:29; 9:2,3; 20:6); with the enactment of the oath ''this land'' has become the possession of Israel, Abraham's descendants. Nothing in this agreement can be cancelled.

The establishment of the borders of the area granted is part of the legal aspect: ''from the river of Egypt to the great river, the Euphrates'' (the exact form occurs only in the late passage, Is. 27:12). The almost rhythmic language accords with the solemn agreement; it is very marked in v. 18b—two fours (or a double two), thereby showing that נהר פרת at the end is certainly a later, rather pedantic, explanatory addition. The נהר מצרים can mean only the ''brook of Egypt'' (generally called נחל, e.g., Num. 34:5; Josh. 15:4; J. Simons ''Brook of Egypt,'' so too F. Delitzsch, H. Gunkel, G. von Rad, and others), not the Nile. Jdt. 1:9 also calls it ποταμος Αἰγύπτου; Deut. 11:24 and Josh. 1:4 also name the Euphrates as the border. These details refer to the widest possible extent of the land of the Israelites, not to any particular period of such expansion. M. Saebø deals in detail with the other border limits described in this passage (ZDPV 90 [1974] 20-22).

[15:19-21] Vv. 19-21 are not a smooth grammatical continuation of v. 18; they are heavy prose in contrast to the obvious rhythm of v. 18, and a reduplication of v. 18b; the geographical details (v. 18b) are supplemented by political details. The majority of exegetes consequently judge vv. 19-21 to be an appendage. There are a number of enumerations of the peoples of Canaan (Ex. 3:8,17; 13:5; 23:23,28; 33:2; 34:11; Deut. 7:1; 20:7; Josh. 3:10; etc.); for these lists see W. Richter (BBB 21 [1964]) and N. Lohfink (SBS 28 [1967] 65-75). Most of these lists have five, six, or seven names of peoples; here there are ten. The first three names do not occur in any other list, nor do the Rephaim; on the other hand the Hivites, who occur in most other lists, are missing. It is very likely that the original setting of these lists is in the context of the route from Egypt to Canaan; geographical history shows how important it was to know these people. One concludes that the list has grown gradually, and one must agree with A. Dillmann: "This enumeration, apparently the most complete, seems to be the latest of all." N. Lohfink has tried to demonstrate that the longest list is the oldest; but this is unlikely. For the individual names see *Genesis 1–11*, 498-530 and section 3.C above, as well as the thorough study of the individual names in N. Lohfink (SBS 28 [1967] 65-75).

Purpose and Thrust

Gen. 15 not only stands at the center of the external structure of the Abraham narratives, but also is regarded in the history of exegesis right down to the present as the very heart of the Abraham story. God's covenant with Abraham and Abraham's faith appear as the kernel of what the Bible says about him. The exegesis presented above, which takes its stand on a series of studies that preceded it, changes this perspective somewhat inasmuch as the two parts of the chapter can no longer be regarded as originating from events in the life of the man Abraham. Both arose in the period of the monarchy, and both have as their subject matter promises to Abraham which belong to the later history of his story.

But ch. 15 loses thereby none of its significance. If we maintain that Abraham is not a figure invented in the period of the Israelite monarchy (or even later), but really lived in the ancient history of Israel, and that the patriarchal stories introduced a chain of tradition which extends from this early period right through to the monarchy and further and has never been entirely interrupted, then the carrying on and reshaping of the Abraham traditions acquire a significance which is no less than that of the little we know of Abraham himself.

Ch. 15 is a witness to the continuous life of the genealogical tree of Abraham in a period for which the promises were vital. The promises have undergone change in the course of their transmission; neither the promise of countless descendants nor that of permanent possession of the land was made to Abraham himself, but only the promise of a son and heir (15:4). This is sufficient basis for the development of the promise motif. It was supremely important for the later period that the promises to the patriarchs were unconditional. Later generations, under imminent threat, could reawaken the promises adapted to their situation and dealing with the preservation of the people and the retention of the land, so as to cling to God's assurance when both were in jeopardy.

The statement about Abraham's faith is also to be seen in this perspective. Faith in the promises was the natural thing for Abraham; there was no need to stress this in the ancient narratives. But there came a time when great crises of faith arose, as we know from Isaiah. Paul takes up a statement of faith which arose about that time in Rom. 4. Thus it becomes clearer how the idea of faith acquired in the course of Israel's history the particular meaning which Paul could take as his basis in the presentation of faith in Christ.

The recognition that the two promise narratives of Gen. 15:1-6 and 7-21 belong only to the later history of the Abraham story has the further consequence of arresting any pious idealization of Abraham. Abraham as the "father of faith" and Abraham with whom God struck a covenant became an idealized figure, towering above the simple human being. The old narratives know nothing of this figure, nor do the late promise narratives intend it. The Bible tells the story of the simple people of the ancient history of Israel, of the father with whom God dealt, to whom God showed the way, and promised an averting of trial in the midst of trials. It was taken for granted as a necessary part of his relationship to his God that Abraham believed the promises of God.

Sarah and Hagar:
Flight and Promise of a Son

Literature

Genesis 16: T. André, *L'esclavage chez les anciens Hébreux* (1892). F. Buhl, *Die sozialen Verhältnisse der Israeliten* (1899). H. Gunkel, "Die beiden Hagargeschichten," ChW 15 (1901) 141-145, 164-171. L. G. Levy, *La famille dans l'antiquité israélite* (1904). A. Lods, *La croyance à la vie future et le culte des morts dans l'antiquité israélite* II (1906) esp. 63-70. A. Schulz, *Doppelberichte im Pentateuch* (1908). G. Havelin, *Les doubles récits et la vérité historique de la Genèse* 121 (1909). P. Cruveilhier, "Le droit de la femme dans la Genèse et dans le recueil des lois assyriennes," RB 36 (1927) 350-376. A. Heitzer, "Hagar. Eine kritische und exegetische Untersuchung zu Gen 16 und 21:1-21" (diss. Bonn, 1934). A. Lobina, "Examen de la critica literaria del capitulo XVI del Genesis comparado con el XXI," RevBib 20 (1958) 121-126. G. Cooke, "The Israelite King as Son of God," ZAW 73 (1961) 202-225, esp. 215. O. Eissfeldt, *Stammessage. . .*, SAB 110,4 (1964/65). I. Fransen, "L'hégire d'Agar, fuite ou appel?" BTS 141 (1972) 5-7. A. K. Grayson and J. Van Seters, "The Childless Wife in Assyria and the Stories of Genesis," Or 44 (1975) 485-486. S. E. McEvenue, "A Comparison of Narrative Styles in the Hagar Stories," Semeia 3 (1975) 64-80. H. C. White, "The Initiation Legend of Ishmael," ZAW 87 (1975) 267-306.

Genesis 16:1-6: E. Kutsch, "Die Wurzel עצר im Hebräischen," VT 2 (1952) 57-69. J. Kinal, "Die Stellung der Frau im Alten Orient," Bell 20 (1956) 367-378. B. Halevi, "*Wāt-te'ännäha Saraj* (Gen 16:6)," BetM 11 (1965/66) 111-116. I. Blythin, "A Note on Isaiah XLIX 16-17," VT 16 (1966) 229-230. G. Rinaldi, "Kurze Wort- und Begriffsstudien. bw' *(bó')*," BibOr 9 (1967) 243-244. J. Reich, "Studien zum theologischen Problem der Menschenverachtung im AT" (diss. Leipzig, 1968). J. Van Seters, "The Problem of Childlessness. . .," JBL 87 (1968) 401-408. R. N. Whybray, " 'Their Wrongdoings' in Ps 99,8," ZAW 81 (1969) 237-239. H. W. Wolff, "Herren und Knechte. Anstösse zur Überwindung der Klassengegensätze im Alten Testament," TThZ 81 (1972) 129-139. J. Weingreen, "The Case of the Blasphemer (Leviticus XXIV 10ff.)," VT 22 (1972) 118-123. C. F. Whitley, "Psalm 99,8," ZAW 85 (1973) 227-230. H. C. Waetjens, "The Genealogy as the Key to the Gospel according to Matthew," JBL 95 (1976) 205-230.

Genesis 16:7-14 (15-16): A. Frh. von Gall, *Altisraelitische Kultstätten*, BZAW 3 (1898). M. J. Lagrange, "L'Ange de Jahvé," RB 12 (1903) 212-225. S. Tillinger, *Die flüchtige Hagar. Eine textkritische, philologische Studie*, JSM (1910). A. Lods, "L'ange de Jahvé et l'âme extérieure," *Studien zur semitischen Philologie und Religionsgeschichte*, BZAW 27 (1914) 263-278. O. Rank, *The Myth of the Birth of the Hero* (1914). O. Schroeder, "מלאך = *ma-la-ḫu-um?*" ZAW 34 (1914) 72-73. P. Heinisch, *Personification und*

Hypostasen im AT und im Alten Orient (1921). M. A. Canney, "Skyfolk in the OT," JMUES 10 (1923) 53-58. F. Stier, *Gott und sein Engel im Alten Testament*, ATA 12,2 (1934). P. Humbert, "Der biblische Verkündigungsstil und seine vermutliche Herkunft," AfO 10 (1935/36) 77-80. W. Baumgartner, "Zum Problem des 'Jahwe-Engels,'" SThU 14 (1944) 97-102 = W. Baumgartner, *Zum AT und seiner Umwelt* (1959) 240-246. J. J. Stamm, "Die Immanuel-Weissagung," VT 4 (1954) 20-33. J. Weingreen, "The Construct-Genitive Relation in Hebrew Syntax," VT 4 (1954) 50-59. R. North, *Geographia Exegetica* (1955), esp. 26. A. Lobina, "El conocimiento de Dios en Gén 16,13 interpretado a la luz del Ex 33,21-23," RevBib 19 (1957) 63-68. N. K. Gottwald, "Immanuel as the Prophet's Son," VT 8 (1958) 36-47. L. Dequeker, "Isaie VII 14," VT 12 (1962) 231-335. A. Jeffery, "Arabians," IDB I (1962) 181-184. J. Blenkinsopp, "Structure and Style in Judges 13-16," JBL 82 (1963) 65-76. L. Delekat, "Zum hebräischen Wörterbuch," VT 14 (1964) 7-66, esp. 48. R. Giveon, " 'The Cities of Our God' (II Sam 10,12)," JBL 83 (1964) 415-416. B. S. Childs, "The Birth of Moses," JBL 84 (1965) 104-122. T. Lescow, "Das Geburtsmotiv in den messianischen Weissagungen bei Jesaja und Micha," ZAW 79 (1966) 172-207. F. Zimmermann, "Folk Etymology of Biblical Names," VT.S 15 (1966) 311-326. R. North, "Separated Spiritual Substances in the OT," CBQ 29 (1967) 419-449. M. Dahood, "The Name *Yišmā''el* in Genesis 16,11," Bib 49 (1968) 87-88. G. T. Armstrong, "The Genesis Theophanies of Hilary of Poitiers," StudPatr 10 = TU 107 (1970) 203-207. H. Seebass, "Zum Text von Gen XVI 13b," VT 21 (1971) 254-256. C. Westermann, "Alttestamentliche Elemente in Lukas 2,1-20," Fests. K. G. Kuhn (1971) 317-327. G. I. Davies, "Hagar, *El-Heğra* and the Location of Mount Sinai," VT 22 (1972) 152-163. R. W. Neff, "The Annunciation in the Birth Narrative of Ishmael," BiR 17 (1972) 51-62. H. M. Wolf, "A Solution to the Immanuel Prophecy in Isaiah 7:14—8:22," JBL 91 (1972) 449-456. O. H. Steck, "Beitrage zum Verständnis von Jesaja 7,10-17 und 8,1-4," ThZ 29 (1973) 161-178. A. G. Auld, "Judges I and History: A Reconsideration," VT 25 (1975) 261-285. R. C. Culley, *Studies in the Structure of Hebrew Narratives*, Semeia Supp 2 (1976). I. Eph'al, " 'Ishmael' and 'Arab(s)': A Transformation of Ethnological Terms," JNES 35 (1976) 225-235. H. Schmid, "Ismael im AT und im Koran," Jud. 32 (1976) 76-81, 119-129.

Text

16:1 Now Sarai,[a] Abram's wife, had borne him no children. She had an Egyptian maidservant whose name was Hagar.

2 Sarai said to Abram: See now: Yahweh has not allowed me to bear a child. Go then to my maidservant; perhaps I shall build[a] a family from her. Abram listened to what Sarai said.

3 So Sarai, Abram's wife, took Hagar, her Egyptian maidservant, and gave her to Abram her husband as wife. This was after[a] Abram had been living ten years in the land of Canaan.

4 He went to Hagar and she became pregnant. When she became aware that she was pregnant, her mistress lost cast[a] in her eyes.

5 Then Sarai said to Abram: This outrage to me[a] be upon you![b] It was I who gave my maidservant into your arms! Now that she is aware that she is pregnant, I have lost cast in her eyes. Let Yahweh judge between me and you.[c]

6 Then Abram said to Sarai: Your maidservant is in your power. Do with her what[a] seems best to you. So Sarai ill-treated her and she fled.

7 Now the messenger of Yahweh found her[a] by a spring of water[b] in the desert on the way to Shur.

8 And he said: Hagar, maidservant of Sarai, where have you come from[a] and where are you going? And she said: I am fleeing from Sarai my mistress.

9 And the messenger of Yahweh said to her: Return to your mistress and submit to her ill-treatment.

10 And the messenger of Yahweh said to her: I will multiply your descendants so that[a] they cannot be counted.

11 And the messenger of Yahweh said to her: See, you are pregnant[a] and

will bear a son,[b] and you will call him Ishmael,[c] because Yahweh has heard your cry.[de]

12　He shall be a wild ass[a] of a man, his hand against all and the hand of all against him, and he shall camp in confrontation[b] with all his kinsmen.

13　And she called the name of Yahweh[a] who was speaking to her: You are the God who sees me.[b] She said indeed: Truly I have seen "God"[c] after he saw[d] me.

14　The spring therefore is called[a] Beer-Lahai-roi; it lies between Kadesh and Bered.

15　Then Hagar bore Abram a son. And Abram called his son whom Hagar bore him, Ishmael.

16　Abram was eighty-six years old when Hagar bore him Ishmael.

1a　Precedence of subject in the verbal sentence, Ges-K §142 a,b.

2a　On the form, Ges-K §51g. H. Holzinger: "Gk and Sym suggest a denominative from בֵן"; it is generally understood, however, as niph. of בנה.

3a　On מקץ, H. L. Ginsberg, "The Composition of the Book of Daniel," VT 4 (1954) 272, "after a period of."

4a　On the form, Ges-K §67p.

5a　חמסי Ges-K §135a,m.　　**b** C. F. Whitley, ZAW 85 (1973) 227-230, against R. N. Whybray, ZAW 81 (1969) 237-239, would understand the prep. עַל as "from": "my injury is from you." But this sense is not possible because the same expression חמסי occurs with ירד (cf. THAT I, 583-586).　　**c** Ten times in the Pentateuch. The pointing is excessive, "because בין is elsewhere always pointed as singular with the 2nd pers. suffix" (F. Delitzsch); cf. Ges-K §103o. Sam without *yod*.

6a　Some Mss read כטוב.

7a　וימצאה for אֶהָ. . ., as in 1 Chron. 20:2; Ges-K §60d.　　**b** BrSynt §73a: "Generally definite nouns can leave the *regens* indefinite."

8a　On the perf., Ges-K §106h.

10a　On construction, Ges-K §166a.

11a　On the form, Ges-K §116n; F. Delitzsch: participial adjective as 38:24; 2 Sam. 11:5, etc.　　**b** On the form, Ges-K §80d, 94f. "A mixed Masoretic form which would leave open the choice between perf. cons. and fem. part," O. H. Steck, ThZ 29 (1973) 168f.　　**c** On the name ישמעאל = "God hears," cf. M. Noth, JSSt 1 (1956) 322f. "Ishmael has now turned up in Mari: *Ia-aš-ma-ali-AN* (VI 22,16)," also E. A. Speiser ad loc., E. Unger, RA 54 (1960) 177-185: "The name *Iš-má-i-lūn* occurs in an inscription from Kisik, old Sumerian period."　　**d** עניך "A substantive which has become an infinitive: the situation in which one finds oneself is that of enduring humiliation, cf. 31:42" (L. Delekat, VT 14 [1964] 48).　　**e** Translator's note: Or, "Yahweh has heard you; El has answered you"; cf. M. Dahood, Bib 61 (1980) 89, reading *'anāyākī*.

12a　פרא אדם Ges-K §128k,1.　　**b** Construction, Ges-K §127c, 128b; BrSynt §14cγ.

13a　For יהוה read האל.　　**b** Sam ראה; Gk ὁ θεὸς ὁ ἐπιδών με; Vg *tu deus qui vidisti me* (part. with suff.).　　**c** Instead of the unintelligible הלם, read אלהים.　　**d** Sam ראה; translation uncertain, see Comm.

14a　Syr קראה; for construction, BrSynt §36d.

The History of the Exegesis of Gen. 16

A. Heitzer has synthesized the earlier discussion of ch. 16 (diss. Bonn, 1934). One can distinguish three types of interpretation in recent exegesis.

(1) The tribal history explanation held sway for a long time: "The story tells of Ishmael, the tribal ancestor of the Ishmaelites"; "the story deals with the origin of the tribe of Ishmael" (H. Gunkel, comm.); it is qualified more precisely as an etiological tribal story; it answers the question: "How is it that Ishmael became a bedouin?" H. Gunkel goes even further with the tribal history explanation: the narrative also intends to say that the tribe of Ishmael derives from a primitive people, Hagar, where Hagar is understood as the name of

a people or tribe. A. Bentzen, M. Noth, G. von Rad, and W. Zimmerli also understand the chapter as an etiological tribal story, the latter two seeing in it an additional theological explanation coming from J's overall orientation. J. Skinner diverges, understanding the narrative as explaining "the holiness of the spring and the character of the Ishmaelites." It is striking that O. Eissfeldt, who elsewhere laid such emphasis on the tribal history explanation of the patriarchal stories in opposition to H. Gunkel, sensed in a later study that this was not enough (*Stammessage. . .* SAB, 110, 4 [1964-65]). Certain tribal history elements are reflected there, he says, "but they are almost submerged under the short story form and dressing"; "the tribal history element which lies at the base has been given further depth and extension so as to produce a human story."

R. Kilian differs from this group inasmuch as he sees the older layer in the two etiologies (vv. 11-12 and 13-14) and the later layer in the narrative which precedes them (vv. 1b, 2, 4-7a, 14b; BBB 24 [1966]). The two etiologies stood independently; they were first of all joined together by means of their common subject, the Ishmaelites, and then joined with the narrative to which they first gave rise. Kilian sees the meaning of the narrative in the joining of Abraham and Sarah on the one side with Hagar and Ishmael on the other. He does not think that the individual narrative motifs have any special meaning (and this is the reverse of O. Eissfeldt), not even the messenger of God and his word. R. W. Neff prefers another division of layers (BiR 17 [1972] 449-456). First, he correctly sets out a fixed form for the announcement of a birth which is found in different texts (similarly P. Humbert, AfO 10 [1935-36] 77-80) and sees in Gen. 16 the latest layer; then he considers the promise of descendants (v. 10), which almost all exegetes judge to be a later addition, as part of the original narrative. The structure, therefore, is in three parts: the scene in Abraham's house (vv. 1-6) is followed by the meeting at the spring (vv. 7-10); the third part, Ishmael's birth and settlement in the desert, has dropped out. The goal of the narrative is Ishmael's present state in the desert; the explanation agrees here with the tribal history explanation.

(2) The tribal history explanation is more or less determinative in all those mentioned so far; some more recent explanations, however, regard the narrative about Sarah and Hagar as the basic layer. I myself have designated the main part of ch. 16 a conflict narrative, but joined with other motifs (ThB 24 [1964] 9-91). The motif, "conflict between women," is to be traced back to the patriarchal period and, together with the form, "conflict between men," has a significance which arises out of the forms of community then current.

The two following explanations also proceed from a personal, not a tribal, event as principal motif: J. Van Seters understands Gen. 16 as an anecdotal popular narrative (*Abraham in History. . .* [1975], 192-196): "The focal concentration is on the struggle between the two women." He holds the two expressly etiological verses 13 and 14 to be appendages: "The story has a firm conclusion with v. 12." He sees the following structure: the narrative starts from a crisis situation (v. 1); there is a plan to avert it (v. 2) which is carried out (v. 3). A complication now arises which leads to Hagar's flight (vv. 4-6): "It would seem that Sarah's plan completely failed." A heavenly messenger now intervenes and persuades Hagar to return (there can be no other reason for this intervention). V. 10 is an addition; vv. 11-12, a "prophetic oracle," form the conclusion.

S. E. McEvenue (*Semeia* 3 [1975] 64-80) divides the text into five units: vv. 2-4; 5-6; 7-8; (9-10 redactional addition); 11-12; 13-14. A woman, Sarah, plays the leading role, and the main tension is between the two women. But tension and resolution are presented as interior events: "The place of tension is the mind of Sarai, the place of solution is the mind of God." There are other oral sources behind the narrative which J has concentrated heavily together. What is particularly striking here in relation to the first group is that the etiologies in vv. 13-14 play no role in the explanation of the whole. They are not deleted as an addition, as with J. Van Seters, but are mere echoes of what has preceded; they are an etymological note in which J has taken over older material and E contemporary.

(3) Attempts to explain the narrative theologically, such as those of G. von Rad and W. Zimmerli, form a third group. Both subscribe to the tribal history explanation which, however, recedes well into the background behind the theological or salvation-history ex-

planation. Both want to derive the proper meaning of the narrative from the context of the final written form. The narrative then is concerned with Abraham, the ''bearer of the promise'' (following Gen. 12:1-3 and 15), and speaks negatively about him: ''The Hagar story therefore shows us. . .one of little faith who was not able to leave it to God to go his way but thought that he had to contribute'' (G. von Rad; similarly W. Zimmerli). But the question arises whether one can subscribe to the tribal history explanation on the one hand and then presuppose again from the context as a whole that the text is dealing with an individual who really existed. If one looks for a theological explanation of the narrative, then one must surely take as one's starting point what it says about God.

Form

A survey of the three modern types of interpretation outlined above makes it difficult to understand how so simple a narrative can be interpreted so differently. Firm criteria can emerge only when one begins from the narrative as a whole; it is a family episode, only the announcement in v. 12 extending beyond the family boundaries.

The structure: In the first part (vv. 1-6) Abraham acquires a secondary wife because Sarah is childless. A conflict arises between the two women which leads to Hagar's flight into the desert. In the second part (vv. 7-14) a messenger of God meets Hagar in the desert and promises her a son. The narrative, J, is set within the framework of a genealogical report of P, v. 1a (common to both), v. 3, and vv. 15-16.

The relationship of the two parts, vv. 1-6 and 7-14, to each other is a source of difficulty. It has been noted correctly that a self-contained sequence begins in v. 7 which could form a narrative of its own independent of the conflict between the women: the announcement of the birth of a child with a fixed group of motifs (P. Humbert, AfO 10 [1935-36] 77-80; R. W. Neff, BiR 17 [1972] 449-456). What makes it possible to join the two parts together is that the conflict in the first part is not resolved; Sarah's attempt to acquire children by means of the secondary wife has gone amiss. The narrative, therefore, cannot end with the flight of Hagar; it reaches its goal only with the words which the messenger of God addresses to her. Both parts have been shortened in the process of fusion; but this has been done so skillfully that the whole has the effect of a self-contained narrative. One sees J at work here applying the same narrative technique as in Gen. 2–3. This becomes even clearer when one sees ch. 16 in relationship to ch. 21. Both are very close to each other in the first part, the conflict between the women; both have a different motif sequence in the second. In ch. 16 it is the promise of a son, in ch. 21 it is preservation from dying of thirst. We can assume then an earlier stage in the background where the motif of rivalry between women formed independent narratives. This assumption is strengthened by the intermediary passage, 29:31–30:34, where it is also a matter of rivalry between two women; here too the motif is notably shortened and no longer forms independent narratives.

Here we see a difference between Gen. 12–25 and 25–33. In the Jacob-Esau cycle the main theme is the rivalry between the brothers; in the Abraham cycle it is the rivalry between the women (of which there are echoes in chs. 29–30). The difference is in the subject matter of the conflict: with the men it is living space and food supply, with the women position in the community, hence social rivalry (in Gen. 16 it is more a question of the position of the women; in Gen. 21 of the rights of the sons).

The form-critical context of ch. 16 is thereby indicated; it belongs to the group of narratives about rivalry between women, as do ch. 21 and chs. 29–30. The second part, vv. 7-14, belongs to another cycle of motifs, that of the promise of the birth of a son.

I would like to add a further suggestion: Gen. 29–30 narrates a whole sequence of conflicts between Leah and Rachel; it could be that the first part of chs. 16 and 21 in an older form are likewise part of a sequence of several conflict scenes.

Setting

One must distinguish stages of tradition in the question of the original setting and passage of ch. 16. The narrative in its written form is part of J's patriarchal story, joined by a redactor with P's report in vv. 1a, 3, 15-16. No one contests that it belongs to J; this is clear above all in the technique whereby two older, oral narratives are welded together into one narrative of two scenes.

The narrative of the conflict between the women goes back in oral tradition to the patriarchal period. It presents an important part of community life structured along family lines and constitutes a vital episode therein. Later, its significance receded into the background so that it is retained only in conjunction with other motifs as a narrative part. But the original setting and subject matter of the narrative are in complete harmony with each other.

The same holds for the abbreviated structure of the second part, the announcement of the birth of a son by a divine messenger. Here too it is demonstrable that it is one of a group of narratives, all of which exhibit the same cluster of motifs. The announcement form reaches from the patriarchal period right down to the New Testament, and its accord with the patriarchal religion shows that it has its roots there. An announcement by a *mal'ak yhwh* is mainly concerned with the birth of a child and salvation; both are here in Gen. 16.

The foretelling of the destiny of the child whose birth is announced belongs to the cluster of motifs of this narrative structure. The portrayal of the bedouin life in v. 12 obviously points beyond the patriarchal period; the verse is a tribal proverb. The original setting can only be the coming into being of the tribes in the period of the settlement. The naming of the spring in v. 14 belongs to the same time and place.

Commentary

[16:1-2]   The point of departure of the narrative is Sarah's barrenness. For a married woman to be without children in the patriarchal world is a misfortune of overwhelming proportions. Only the birth of a child can bring relief, and this seems to be excluded. Sarah, therefore, takes means which, though not doing away with the misfortune, can at least alleviate it. The situation is seen through the eyes of the wife (it is different in 15:2-3). It is a question primarily of alleviating the wife's distress; she is going to make a family for herself.

[16:1a]   In v. 1a the narrator resumes the sentence from the genealogy (11:30): "Now Sarah was barren; she had borne no children" (J). This is an elaboration of the genealogy in narrative form, and so it is more understandable that it is common to J and P; P's account of Hagar (16:1a, 3, 15-16; so, e.g., W. Eichrodt, ZAW 31 [1916] 54-65) does not go beyond the genealogy.

[16:1b]   V. 1b is still part of the exposition; it describes the situation out of which the sequence of events arches. Sarah had an Egyptian maidservant named

Hagar. Earlier the designation שפחה was considered almost exclusively from the standpoint of source division (J, שפחה; P, אמה). However, A. Jepsen has shown that there is a recognizable difference between the two (VT 8 [1958] 293-297). Here and in Ps. 123:2; Prov. 30:23; and Is. 24:2 the שפחה is set over against the גבורה, to whom she is in a special way subordinate. It is similar with the maidservants of Leah and Rachel (see also 1 Sam. 25:42). The meaning then is not simply a slave girl, but a personal servant of the wife whose power of disposition over her is restricted to this; the girl stands in a relationship of personal trust to her (it was somewhat similar in the southern states of America before the abolition of slavery). In many cases she was the maidservant whom the parents had given their daughter when she was married. This explains how the special relationship between the two women remained, even if the mistress of the house had given the maid to her husband as a secondary wife. There is no need to explain Hagar the Egyptian by means of Gen. 12:16 ("male and female slaves," as H. Holzinger and others), or by the relationship of the Ishmaelites to the Egyptians (W. Zimmerli and others). There is frequent mention of slaves of other ethnic origin, as well as Egyptian (e.g., 1 Sam. 30:13). The name "Hagar" is meant purely as a personal name; suggestions that it may be a name of a people (H. Gunkel) or an artificial name meaning "the driving out" (M. Noth) are unnecessary and improbable.

[16:2] The action begins with Sarah's address to her husband. The course of events is extremely concentrated. The address, introduced by הנה־נא, has as its central unit a demand to her husband, preceded by the reason for it, and followed by its purpose. Sarah's address is over; Abraham's reaction follows. He agrees and acquiesces in the demand (v. 4a). This tightly packed and laconic exchange in utter frankness catches an excerpt from the shared life of two people which began with betrothal and marriage and led to the express recognition that the union has remained without issue. There is no need to say what suffering, reproach, and bitterness this brought to the couple; it is all compressed into Sarah's opening words, הנה־נא.

Sarah states frankly, "Yahweh has not allowed me to bear a child." On the verb עצר, cf. E. Kutsch (VT 2 [1952] 57-69). It is God who opens the mother's womb (Gen. 29:31; 30:22); he can also close it; and as this affects the very life of the woman she can say: "he has closed my womb." "The great mysteries of begetting, conceiving, bearing were derived from the divinity everywhere in antiquity" (H. Gunkel). But what does that mean in the context of this narrative? What happens now among Sarah, Abraham, and Hagar embraces also their relationship to God; the demand that Sarah directs to Abraham is based on what God has or has not done. Each successive step is now set in this context. If as a consequence Sarah is "built up," then it is God who is active. G. von Rad condemns Sarah's decision: "The narrator sees in it presumably a grave defect" (likewise W. Zimmerli); but this is to introduce into the patriarchal story a theological reflection which is foreign to it. It fails to see that Sarah's decision derives from an awareness of God's action; consequently she must do as she does.

The demand to Abraham is at the same time the expression of a hope which leaves the way open to the solution of the misfortune. The word בא occurs in the same sense in Deut. 21:13; 25:5; cf. G. Rinaldi (BibOr 9 [1967] 243f.). But it would be a misunderstanding to restrict it to sexual intercourse. Sarah's demand "Go then to my maidservant!" means just what it says—Abraham is to turn to

Hagar, spend part of his time with her, so that there arises a mutual understanding between them. The decision means that Sarah must now share her husband with another woman. She can do this because there springs therefrom the hope that "perhaps I shall build a family from her." The verb is read as a denominative from בֵן (Ges-Buhl) or as a niph. from בנה (K-B). The majority of interpreters favor the latter, e.g., E. A. Speiser: "The verb. . .can only mean, 'I shall be built up' "; just as Gen. 30:3 in the same context (there also literally the same demand precedes). It may be a case of a standard formula. J. Blythin advances the same image in Is. 49:16f.: ". . .a woman whose physical integration is built by her children" (VT 16 [1966] 229f.). L. Kopf refers to Arabic parallels (VT 8 [1958] 161-215). This sentence in Gen. 16:2 (with the parallel Gen. 30:3) is a verbalization of patriarchal anthropology which has continued effectively across the centuries: the life of a woman is an integral whole (just as a building or a city is something integral) only when she is a member of a family in which she presents her husband with children. In the patriarchal period there was no other way for a woman to be a member of society.

It is only in this environment that the solution which Sarah adopts is comprehensible. It is a question of the very meaning of her life; she knows no other. The presupposition is that countless women before Sarah have shared her lot and so she has no need to invent a solution; it was there at hand; there is an abundance of examples. The case in #146 of the code of Hammurabi has long been known, even though the situation is somewhat different. A. Heitzer advances a number of parallels (diss. Bonn, 1934). The foremost example is a Nuzi text, translated by E. A. Speiser (AASOR 10 [1930] 1-73), and cited by him in his commentary (AncB 1, 120): "If Gilimninu bears children, Shennima shall not take another wife. But if Gilimninu fails to bear children, Gilimninu shall get for Shennima a woman from the Lullu country (i.e., a slave girl) as concubine. In that case, Gilimninu herself shall have authority over the offspring." Speiser concludes from this: "What Sarah did. . . was in conformance with the family law of the Hurrians." He presupposes that it is a question of adoption. Many have taken over these parallels (e.g., R. H. Ream, diss. Dropsie College, 1962; J. Van Seters, critically, *Abraham in History*. . . [1975]; T. L. Thompson, BZAW 133 [1974], pp. 252-269; H. Donner, OrAnt 8 [1968] 87-119). The results are: (1) Contracts of this kind are so common and so widely distributed in time and space that it seems impossible to show a dependence of the event described in Gen. 16 on any particular document. (2) Private contracts of this kind are on each occasion dealing with an individual, concrete case. (3) The narrative in Gen. 16 is also dealing with an individual, concrete case, not with an example of a legal prescription. The studies mentioned advance many other texts which describe a situation in which a husband, on the occasion of his wife's barrenness, takes the wife's maidservant as his concubine and has children from her; there are many variations of detail. This practice is widely distributed in time and place. There is no question here of adoption in the strict sense (cf. H. Donner, op.cit.; G. Cooke, ZAW 73 [1961] 202-225; T. E. McComisky, diss. Brandeis, 1965; Diss. Abs. 27 [1966/67] 298-318).

The first sentence of v. 4 is also part of the introduction in v. 2: Abraham acquiesces in the demand of his wife.

[16:3] It is generally acknowledged that v. 3 belongs to P. It consists of two verbal sentences: she took—she gave. The first verb, ותקח, follows on 16:1a (P and

J), the second, ותתן, is followed up in v. 15, ותלד. J narrates the event; P merely reports it. The P component of ch. 16 is in relation to the rest of the chapter a standard example of this writer's art. No event is narrated, but facts are ordered one after the other. The Chronicler reduces the whole history of Israel before David to a genealogy. P represents an earlier stage; apart from a very few narratives, this material reduces the patriarchal story to a genealogy.

The facts in v. 3 are the same as in J; P adds the characteristic dating: "after Abraham had been living ten years in the land of Canaan."

[16:4-6] The first sentence of v. 4, which is still part of the introduction, indicates that Sarah's plan will succeed. A child will be born and it will count as Sarah's; but a complication arises immediately. Sarah's complaint (v. 5), to which Abraham yields (v. 6a), leads to Sarah herself driving out the mother of "her" child (v. 6b). Sarah had devised the plan, and she herself causes it to founder. Once again the action is very concentrated. What is peculiar to this passage is that the event has from step to step the character of the once and for all; at every step the slightest nuance would lead to a different outcome (e.g., if Abraham's reply had been somewhat differently expressed). The movement of the narrative gives rise to the impression that an actual event has been transposed into narrative.

[16:4] As soon as Hagar became aware (ראה in this broader sense) that she was pregnant, her attitude to her mistress changed: "her mistress lost cast in her eyes." J. Weingreen correctly notes that the translation "looked with contempt" (J. Skinner, RSV) is too strong: "The writer was referring. . . to Sarah's having lost status, because of the new standing which Hagar had acquired. . . ." (VT 22 [1972] 119). This is just what is expressed by the rendering, "she looked down on her mistress." The wife's esteem grows with her pregnancy (R. de Vaux, *Ancient Israel* [1958, Eng. 1962] 25, 39). The change in Hagar's attitude arises out of the situation: "Natural maternal pride is stronger than the legal status" (O. Procksch, ad loc.). The meaning is not that she behaves insolently towards her barren mistress. (On קלל, see THAT II, 641-647; J. Reich, diss. Leipzig, 1968). This way out of the situation where the wife was barren being so widespread, it is to be presumed that the outcome was often a conflict of this sort. The code of Hammurabi #146 shows that this was the case for Babylonia: "When a seignior married a hierodule and she gave a female slave to her husband and she has then borne children, if later that female slave has claimed equality with her mistress because she bore children, her mistress may not sell her; she may mark her with the slave-mark and count her among the slaves" (ANET). Prov. 30:21-23 shows the same for Israel. The narrator then is not describing a gross violation of law or custom by Hagar, but a conflict which was almost unavoidable, which in any case was the natural outcome of the situation, and which recurred again and again. Sarah's complaint that Hagar's conduct was חמס is but the subjective reaction of the one offended.

[16:5] This is a striking verse, pregnant with meaning and power. Sarah does not confront the offender, but the husband, who is also her husband. He alone has the judicial authority that can effect a change. The verse shows on the one hand that in this form of community the father is also the judge in what concerns the family circle, and on the other that a conflict within the family can take the form of a legal process, as is clear from the formal language.

Sarah's case has three parts: the brief, pregnant accusation חמסי עליך (H.
J. Boecker, *Redeformen des Rechtslebens im AT* [1964, 1970²], see under
"Zeterruf," "appeal for help"), the reason for the accusation, and the demand
for a legal decision. The accusation is saying: I have suffered an injustice and you
are responsible for it! The compressed formula allows for the one addressed being
both party and judge. There are further echoes of the formula in Jer. 51:35. It can
scarcely mean, "the consequences of the injustice done to me be upon you" (A.
Dillmann and others), because, as the reason given states, it is the direct result of
the action of another person. But one can certainly say that Sarah accuses Abraham of allowing their marriage to be attacked. Sarah presents her case in two
parts; the first takes up v. 2b, the second v. 4b, and each is factually relevant. But
what in v. 4b is but an unemotional factual report, becomes here an expression of
revolt and bitterness. As a result (this is the third part of Sarah's accusation) Sarah
demands a legal decision, not in a case between herself and Hagar, but between
herself and Abraham. The demand is again a fixed legal formula: "Let Yahweh
judge between you and me"; cf. Gen. 31:53; Ex. 5:21; 1 Sam. 24:12, 15. The formula does not mean that Sarah appeals to a higher court; Abraham's decision
should give expression to the judgment of God who takes care of the interests of
the disadvantaged. For further discussion of v. 5, see B. Gemser (VT.S 3 [1955]
120).

[16:6] Abraham's decision follows with its effects both direct and indirect. He
yields to Sarah; one cannot understand the decision otherwise. He confirms Hagar's status and consequently allows Sarah freedom of action. The confirmation
reestablishes the former situation (G. von Rad), and the permission allows Sarah a
free hand in her conduct towards Hagar. It is striking that Abraham's decision is
completely in favor of Sarah. H. Gunkel expresses it thus: "Abraham plays a rather unfortunate role between these two stubborn women."

Sarah exercises her freedom of action and "oppresses" (ענה, pi.) Hagar.
It is not said how far this "oppression" goes; however, it is certain that Sarah
makes her maidservant feel that she is once more the mistress. G. Fitzner writes:
"The hand is the instrument of 'beck and call'; might and right originally go together just as ruling and judging (Gen. 16:6)" (BHH 1 [1962] 563f.).

The writer gives expression with amazing skill to something which is part
of life in common as long as people exist. It is described in narrative form in three
acts or steps: (1) "Her mistress lost cast in her eyes"; (2) "Now that she is
aware. . . I have lost cast. . ."; (3) "Sarah ill-treated her. . .." A feels disadvantaged by B; A is liberated from the disadvantage; A disadvantages B. This happens in every area of human life, most notably in the political area; the oppressed
when liberated becomes the oppressor. The narrative of Gen. 16 is saying that this
phenomenon is already present in the basic human community, the family. Such
conflicts are part of human existence; they cannot be abolished. There can only be
a solution when the parties are separated; this is just what the last sentence of v. 6
is saying: "and she fled from her." The story narrates the origin of emancipation.
Abraham had said to Sarah: "your maidservant is in your hand," where "hand"
is the equivalent of power. The word "emancipation" means *e manu capere*,
where *manus* is likewise power. The will to be liberated and the acceptance of
danger to one's life which goes with it is always part of emancipation or the like. It
is precisely this that is reported of Hagar. She cannot and will not endure such
treatment from Sarah; she will be liberated from her, and she sees the only possi-

bility of liberation in flight, even though it endangers her life and that of her un-born child. Hagar's flight into the desert from "legal" oppression by Sarah, exposing herself to all the dangers involved, is a prime example of the human will for freedom.

[16:7-14] The second part of the narrative presents serious difficulties. To begin with, its structure must be determined. After an introductory sentence (v. 7a), vv. 7-13 (v. 14 is an etiological appendage) consist entirely of talking, made up of two exchanges, v. 8 and vv. 9-13. The first (v. 8), with the brief greeting of the mes-senger and Hagar's even briefer reply is equally important for the dialog; the sec-ond (vv. 9-13) is unintelligible without the first. It differs from the first by its length and the three same introductions at the beginning of vv. 9, 10, 11. The con-versation thereby issues into a discourse. This is a clear indication that in the course of the transmission the old narrative was expanded and altered. The second exchange must have corresponded more or less to the first. It is to be assumed that God's messenger did not originally make three different pronouncements, but only one. The two others then would be appendages.

[16:7a] Hagar meets someone on her way through the desert; it is a meeting en route, not a revelation nor a vision nor an epiphany. The beginning of v. 7 makes this very clear. If one strikes out any reference to a meeting, then there is nothing further in the text which gives occasion to think of anything else other than an en-counter between two people at a well in the desert. This is even clearer in v. 8. The messenger greets Hagar with the standard form of inquiry (the inquiry in this con-text is either part of the greeting or the greeting itself). Hagar's reply is possible only if she sees a person in the one who meets her. This is saying something deci-sive for the meaning of מלאך יהוה: it is a messenger of God who in the form of a person meets a person on earth who is en route or about his work (Judg. 13). The initial greeting is a key to the understanding of מלאך יהוה in the Old Testament.

Excursus

The messenger of God (מלאך יהוה) *in the Old Testament.*   The phrase מלאך יהוה (= *m.y.*) occurs 58 times in the O.T., 11 times in the form מלאך אלהים; see further the lexicon arti-cles "Engel" in RGG, EKL, BHH and מלאך, "Bote," in THAT 1, 900-908; the commentaries on Gen. 16:7, and the excursus in H. Gunkel, G. von Rad, and lit. above.

     The narratives about a messenger of God do not usually contain a variety of infor-mation, but only something brief and to the point: the announcement of the birth of a child (Gen. 16; [21]; 18; Judg. 13; Lk. 1) or the announcement of salvation (Gen. 16; 19; 21; 22; 31:11ff.; Lk. 1; 1 Kings 19; cf. EKL 1, 1071-75). Both can be combined as in Gen. 16 and Lk. 1; and the announcement of the birth of a child can also be meant as the good news of salvation. The announcement of a birth follows a fixed formula which has remained from the patriarchal period down to the New Testament. The meeting with a *m.y.* is never con-fined to a particular place or time; it takes place at home, en route, or at work. The use of the formula has been detached from these narrative types, and consequently the meaning of *m.y.* has been altered and extended.

     The defect in most attempts so far to explain the phrase *m.y.* in the O.T. is that one takes as starting point a superimposed concept: either "angel" (such a superimposed con-cept does not occur in the O.T.; so W. Baumgartner; this only arose when the Gk rendered other heavenly beings by ἄγγελος and the Vg introduced the distinction between *nuntius* = a human messenger and *angelos* = a divine messenger, both of which were covered by "angel") or the concept "a manifestation of God" (theophany); e.g., O. Procksch: "the *m.y.* is the theophany of the person of God." It is also quite inappropriate to begin from the nature of *m.y.*, as does H. Gunkel: "It is a divine being. . ." (this is the point of departure for the discussion). But if one begins from the texts and the function which the *m.y.* plays therein, then it is obvious that a clear distinction must be made between *(a)* heavenly beings as, e.g., the seraphs in Is. 6, and *(b)* any other type of theophany or divine manifestation. One must realize that the designation *m.y.* has undergone profound changes from its earliest occurrence in the patriarchal stories down to the postexilic period. It is important that in the early narrative the *m.y.* is the one who meets. He is there only in the meeting. He is not a figure, nor a representative, nor some manifestation of God (so W. Zimmerli and others); he is only the one who meets. This is comprehensible only in the context of the religion of the patriarchs where the figure of a mediator between God and man does not yet appear. One can receive a divine oracle neither through a man of God, nor a seer or prophet, nor through a cultic institution; on each occasion the oracle can proceed only from God by means of a messenger who is a person like anyone else. There is only one way in which he differs from others—he is unknown; he comes from and returns into the unknown. This is a trait common to all narratives about a *m.y.* His coming and going are part of the message of the *m.y.* His coming is often accompanied by a greeting (from Gen. to the "angelic salutation" in Lk. 1); this is to state that he meets a person as a person (16:7 מצא). Only at his departure is he recognized as a messenger of God. The *m.y.* then is not someone like the Greek Hermes. H. Gunkel misses the meaning of *m.y.* when he says, "Like the king or the official, God also has a messenger" (Excursus on Gen. 16:7), and refers to the Babylonian divine messengers. The *m.y.* differs from these in that he is not one and the same who always appears with the same name. These messengers are mythical figures belonging to the history of the gods; the *m.y.* is premythical, the old narratives about him showing no trace of mythical language (against W. H. Schmidt who speaks of a "more or less mythical representation" in Fests. G. Friedrich [1973] 25-34). It is never said for example that the *m.y.* comes from or returns to God, as is always the case with Hermes. It is different in Job 1–2 where the mythical notion of the heavenly court is presupposed.

When the O.T. speaks of the *m.y.*, it is striking that in one and the same narrative Yahweh and the *m.y.* can change places; this is the case in Gen. 16 and 18. The most common explanation is that of H. Gunkel who looks at it from the perspective of the history of religion in his excursus to Gen. 16: an earlier period felt no embarrassment in speaking of a god coming down to earth in the form of a person; one hears his steps and voice, one sees his form. A later period found this a stumbling block and substituted a messenger for God. Likewise, W. Baumgartner says that his study speaks "in favor of the explanation which sees in the *m.y.* an earlier substitute, as Stade, Gunkel, Lods, von Rad, and others" (*Zum A.T. und seiner Umwelt* [1959], 240-246 = SThU 14 [1944] 91-102). Both Gunkel and Baumgartner support their thesis by a number of passages in which what was formerly predicated of God is later predicated of the *m.y.* For example, one said earlier that it was God himself, later that it was the angel of God who led Israel through the desert (Num. 20:16). This is so, but only for a later period. It cannot, however, explain the striking fact that in the old narratives Yahweh and the *m.y.* are interchanged in one and the same story. It is quite irrelevant to say that talk about a *m.y.* arose only from theological reflection (so H. Gunkel, W. Baumgartner, G. von Rad). It is much more a case of narrative transmission of actual and varied experience of an encounter in extreme distress in which the messenger pronounced the oracle that changed the course of events.

W. Baumgartner did not see that his careful study of the usage of the word allows this interpretation. R. Ficker, in his article, מלאך, "Bote," in THAT I, 900-908, presents the various attempts at a solution and continues: "There is no longer any difficulty. . . when one reflects that a *mal'ak* can generally (in profane usage) be identified with the sender" (p. 907), as shown in Judg. 11:13; 2 Sam. 3:12f.; and 1 Kings 20:2ff. The receiver of the message hears the sender in the words of the *m.y.* just as in the case of a human message and can consequently identify the sender with the messenger. R. North rightly rejects the interpretation that with the *m.y.* it is a question of "separated spiritual substance" (so too E. A. Speiser: "a distinct class of supernatural beings is of later date"); the meaning of the word is rather "presence," "a form. . . under which God makes himself present. . ."

(CBQ 29 [1967] 419-449). This is a correct insight, though what is meant is not the divine presence as such, but the fact of a message. God is present not in the messenger, but in the message.

[16:7b]   The general fixing of place and event "by a spring of water in the desert" is sufficient for the narrative. A more precise determination of place is added rather awkwardly, "on the way to Shur." שׁוּר, meaning "wall," refers to the Egyptian border forts. According to E. A. Speiser, "a place near the Egyptian border"; cf. H. Cazelles ("Patriarches," DBS 7 [1961] 105) and J. Simons (*The Geographical and Topographical Texts of the OT* [1959]). G. I. Davies argues against H. Gese (writing on Gal. 4:25 in *Fests. L. Roth* [1967], 81-84) ". . .that the translator used חגרא for שׁוּר in Gen. XVI 7 to bring the geography of the narrative more up to date than it was because he was aware of a legendary association between Hagar and חגרא" (VT 22 [1972] 155). The place is important for the Koran, because there Ishmael was born; it is the hill of Thûr near Mecca. J. Simons proposes, probably correctly, that "by a spring of water on the way to Shur" is an explanatory addition; it would suit v. 14 better.

[16:8]   It is significant that the exegetes do not know how to come to terms with this verse. A. Dillmann, for example, says: "The question of the angel serves merely as a contact point for the dialog." But the greeting, in the form of an inquiry, is essential to the meaning of the narrative. It shows in the first place that it concerns an event taking place on earth; such a greeting would be inconceivable in a theophany. And elsewhere it is part of the encounter with a *m.y.*, e.g., Judg. 6:12. So firm is the connection that it is there too at the meeting with God's messenger in Lk. 1:28ff. The "Ave Maria" has its roots in the meeting with a messenger of God in the patriarchal stories. A greeting occurs only in narratives which are restricted to a small group of people. Today, just as thousands of years ago, the greeting is of vital importance in family and neighborly circles. It is the contact point; it preserves the coherence of the community. Rejection of the greeting means rejection of the community. It is even more important in the desert where its rejection can be a threat to life. By the greeting and inquiry the messenger takes part in Hagar's lot; he accepts her into the realm of *shalom*. He enables her to make a trustful response and show herself ready to accept the word of this stranger. That this unknown one speaks her name indicates that he is an "other," one who knows; his friendly attention to Hagar evokes her trustful reply.

[16:9-12]   These are the words of God's messenger. Vv. 9, 10, 11 each begin with the same formula, ויאמר לה מלאך יהוה. This would not be possible in an ancient narrative. Such mechanical stringing together shows that additional words were added later to the messenger's address by redaction. The question concerns the address that is best suited to the narrative and the reasons for the later additions. If two of the addresses are shown to be additions, the context of vv. 9-13 still retains the form of a real dialog.

[16:9]   The advice to Hagar in v. 9 to return to her mistress and submit to her authority cannot be reconciled with the words in v. 11; v. 9 rejects Hagar's flight; v. 11 approves it. From J. Wellhausen to W. Zimmerli v. 9 is regarded as a compensating addition by the redactor. Ch. 21 presupposes that Hagar and Ishmael are with Abraham and Sarah; so they must have gone back; the messenger's advice in v. 9 brings Hagar back. But a mere redactional explanation is not enough.

The redactor must have had something in mind with this advice. He indicates thereby his own interpretation of the Hagar narrative: he understands God's intervention after Hagar's flight as the fulfillment of Sarah's original plan; if Hagar goes back, Sarah can have a son by means of her.

[16:10] The promise of many descendants stands isolated between the two introductions, vv. 10a and 11a. Most of the exegetes who attribute v. 9 to the redactor explain it by saying that this promise has been appended to the exhortation to go back in v. 9 so as to console Hagar (e.g., R. Kilian, BBB 24 [1966]). But then the new introduction at the beginning of v. 11 would be meaningless. It is much more likely that the promise of descendants has been added to the promise of a son (see comm. on Gen. 15:4-5), even though it precedes it in the present text. When it is acknowledged later that Hagar too, and so Ishmael, will have many descendants, then the author is saying something about the significance of Abraham, the father; he is the father of many peoples, not only of Israel, as is said even more clearly in ch. 17(P).

[16:11-12] In the ancient narrative vv. 11-12 followed immediately on v. 8. The messenger's speech then consisted originally of the inquiry and the promise. Hagar replies to both of these (vv. 8b and 13), so that the second part of the narrative, vv. 7-13, has the form of a dialog in the middle of which stands the messenger's promise of a son. It is here that the narrative reaches its climax and goal.

The promise in vv. 11-12 has a defined structure, attested by a series of parallels, which points to a narrative form which has its base in the oral tradition stage. A comparison between Gen. 16:8 and Lk. 1:28-32 shows this (cf. also Lk. 1:11-17):

Gen. 16:8,11-12	*Lk. 1:28-32*
8: (The greeting of the messenger.)	28: (The greeting of the messenger.)
11: See, you are pregnant and will bear a son, and you will call him Ishmael,	31: You will conceive in your womb and bear a son, and you shall call his name Jesus.
	(30b: For you have found favor with God.)
because Yahweh has heard your cry.	
12: And he will be. . .	32: He will be great and will be called the Son of the Most High.

This is a rare and astounding example of the perseverance of a form over a period of more than a thousand years. A comparison with Lk. 1:11-17 shows that the form is open to variation.

P. Humbert (AfO 10 [1935-36] 77-80) and R. Neff (BiR 17 [1972] 51-62) have studied the form (cf. lit. on ch. 16). P. Humbert ascribes to this form Gen. 16:11-12; Judg. 13:3-5; Is. 7:14-16; Lk. 1:31-32; R. Neff adds Gen. 17:19; 1 Kings 13:2; 1 Chron. 22:9-10; Lk. 1:11-17 belongs here too, and, somewhat at a distance, Gen. 18:1-18 and 1 Sam. 1:20. The form has the following parts: (1) Introduction: a messenger of God is there (greeting); (2) announcement of pregnancy and birth of a son introduced by הנה; (3) specification of the name of the son with the reason explaining the name; (4) announcement of what will become of the child. The constant element, which is never missing, is the announcement of the birth of a son; and this is what the form as a whole is all about; all other parts are directed to or subordinated to this; originally it is probably the announcement of the birth of a son to a childless woman. It is as such the announcement of salvation or of the turning point in a crisis and so coincides with narratives of a messenger of God; he comes to announce the change in lot. But the examples show that the form can also be used in other situations, as in Gen. 16, where the announcement leads to another crisis.

P. Humbert wants to derive the form from oracular inquiry; but it is more likely that there is an earlier stage, where the messenger of God announces the birth of a son, which is to be distinguished from a later cultic stage, where a priest or an oracle answers the inquiry or complaint of the childless wife (Gen. 25:22; 1 Sam. 1). However, the older form, where a messenger of God announces the birth, lived on, as is shown in Is. 7 and Lk. 1.

[16:11]   After the introduction, v. 11 contains a standard succession of three sentences, in the middle of which is the announcement of a son; it moves from the pregnancy to the birth and the giving of the name, the reason for which is found in the last sentence. But the event presented here has a previous history in the woman's cry in distress; God has heard the cry, and the consequence is the announcement by the messenger of the change in lot. The form does not fit exactly here; the pregnancy is not announced by the messenger, but stated. It is adapted to the changed situation in this way: the concluding sentence giving the reason, ''because he has heard your cry,'' which related to the complaint of the childless wife (1 Sam. 1), has acquired the word עָנְיֵךְ, which refers back to the verb וַתְּעַנֶּהָ from the same root, in v. 6b. There is a profound sense of meaning here: Sarah is concerned at the beginning of her plan that she ''build a family'' (from the maidservant); the conclusion narrates that Hagar is heard and ''built'' by God.

The name of the son presupposes that אֵל stood in place of יהוה in a more ancient form. The explanation proposed by M. Dahood, ''for Yahweh has heard you, El has answered you,'' is not necessary (Bib 49 [1968] 87-88).* It is in accordance with more ancient custom that the mother gives the name; with P (e.g., Gen. 17) it is always the father. The giving of the name by the mother need not be a trace of mother's right in the O.T. On the giving of the name by the mother, cf. T. Lescow (ZAW 79 [1966] 172-207, esp. 178).

[16:12]   Part of the announcement of the birth of a son is a preview of his later destiny, as for example: he will be one of renown, a king, a savior. The son in these cases (as Judg. 16; Lk. 1) will be of significance for the people. In Gen. 16:12 a strong, defiant tribe will stem from him. In itself v. 12 belongs to tribal sayings, as Gen. 9:25-27 (cf. *Genesis 1–11*, 490-491) and 27:27-29, 39-40, where the speech in both cases in in poetic prose (cf. H. J. Zobel, ZAW 85 [1973] 289-291). In all these, the future of the tribe stemming from a son is presupposed. These tribal sayings do not belong to the patriarchal period, but to the period when the tribes are coming into being. The fierce, aggressive way of life of the sons of Ishmael, as depicted in such fine poetic manner in Gen. 16:12, is other than the peaceful nomadic life-style of the patriarchs. It presupposes the sedentary and bedouin desert tribes living in Canaan side by side and in confrontation in the period after the settlement. Only at this time can the tribal saying of 16:12 have been shaped. The link is achieved in convincing manner in 16:12 by the figure of Ishmael's mother; the tribal life of the Ishmaelites was in accord with her character: ''This intractable Ishmael is an unruly son of his stubborn mother, who did not want to submit to the yoke'' (H. Gunkel; similarly O. Procksch). It is this saying only, not the narrative as a whole, that is directed to the origin of the tribe of Ishmael. The tribal saying with its jubilant, defiant affirmation of predatory, bedouin life and which, like others of the same kind, was once transmitted independently, points to its origin within this tribe; so too H. Gunkel, W. Zimmerli, R. Kilian; cf. also J. Henniger (SS 2 [1959] 73) and A. Jeffry (IDB I ''Arabians,'' 181-194).

[16:13]   It is not possible to solve the difficulties of v. 13 with the means hitherto

---

*Translator: But see Bib 61 (1980) 89.

at our disposal. There is general agreement only that the text is corrupt and so, as it stands, incomprehensible. None of the attempts at reconstruction has been convincing so far. This being the state of the question, one may be permitted to offer a new proposal. The striking accumulation of motifs at the end of the narrative has always been noted (for a similar accumulation, cf. *Genesis 1–11*, comm. on 3:20-24). One can take it as certain that several lines have converged here. It is not enough to say with H. Gunkel: "It is now that God and the spring get their names." In that case it is merely narrated how a god gets a name (v. 13), while the name of the spring is only affirmed (v. 14). Vv. 13-14 contain two different etiological conclusions, and the question has to do with their relationship to each other. In v. 7 the spring is described only in general terms as עין המים במדבר; in v. 14 it is affirmed that the spring has acquired a name; v. 14 presupposes that Hagar's reaction to the word of God's messenger, narrated in v. 13, has found expression in the naming of the place of the meeting, hence of the spring. Gen. 22 offers a parallel (cf. H. Seebass, VT 21 [1971] 254-256). Here too there is the meeting with a messenger of God whose word means salvation in extreme distress; here too Abraham's reaction to the meeting is the naming of a place, the mountain; and here too the word ראה is used. We can therefore assume an older form of the narrative in which v. 13 narrated the naming of a spring. The naming of the mountain by Abraham is a cry of praise of God, so too the naming of the spring by Hagar. The goal of the narrative of v. 13 in the older form is this cry of praise to God; the name of the spring speaks down the generations to come.

In the form in which it is transmitted to us, v. 13a can be understood as a concluding variant in which at the end the God, not the spring, acquires a name; the goal of the narrative is a cry of praise of God that refers back to the act of salvation: אתה אל ראי.

The verse has the same structure as v. 11b: 13a, naming; 13b, reason for the name. But the first sentence can be understood in only one sense when האל is read for יהוה; and yet the sentence, "You are the God of my seeing (who sees me)" or "the God of seeing," is not a naming but an address, more accurately an address in prayer of the praise of God (cf. Ps. 77:15 [ET, v. 14], "Thou art the God who workest wonders"). This can scarcely be what the original narrative said. One could imagine such a sentence as, "She called the name of the אל who had spoken to her, אל ראי"; also: "She called the name of the אל who had spoken to her, אל ראי, for she said, 'you are the God who sees me!' " In this case it is v. 13a where the naming and the reason for it occur, and v. 13b would be a secondary appendage to it.

Despite these difficulties the meaning of v. 13a is clear: Hagar names the God, whom she identifies with the מלאך יהוה who met her in v. 7, אל ראי. That is not to say that Hagar gives to a hitherto nameless divine being a name that sticks to him everywhere and always; this is never so with a human being in the O.T., but Hagar says: "For me he is, whatever else he may be called, the God who sees me, i.e., the one who came to my aid in my distress" (there is the same use of ראה of God in Ps. 113:6). Thus it is determined that the *yod* in ראי must be a suffix of object, and so not "the God of seeing" (O. Procksch, H. C. White, et alii), but "God who sees me" (F. Delitzsch, R. Kilian, R. de Vaux, et alii); only thus does it make sense in the context.

[16:13b] The giving of the name can be taken as the conclusion of v. 13a, particularly if the כי אמרה is to be read before the last sentence of 13a. V. 13b then is another explanation of the name which has been attached to it later. The הלם in v. 13b is untranslatable. The word can only mean "hither" (not "here," as some exegetes would have it), and that makes no sense here. The simplest emendation is to read אלהים for הלם: "I have seen God after he saw me." So Hagar would be saying: "I have met God" (not, "I have seen him in the sense of a vision") "after he has seen me" (i.e., my plight, or me in my plight). This explanation is possible and makes sense; the only question that remains is why it was attached to v. 13a. J. Wellhausen answers this question with the ingenious and bold suggestion: הגם אלהים ראיתי ואחי אחרי ראי ("Did I really see God, yet remain alive after my seeing him?"). V. 13b then would have been appended so as to explain the other part of the name of the spring (לחי); it is explained in the light of the later concept that one who really sees God must die. Because Wellhausen's textual emendation makes such good sense in the context, it is still worthy of consideration. But there remains together with it the possibility of merely changing הלם to אלהים. H. Seebass has gathered together further attempts to solve the difficulty (VT 21 [1971] 254-256) as have H. C. White (ZAW 87 [1975] 267-306), F. Stier (*Gott und seine Engel im Alten Testament*, ATA 12,2 [1934]), and following him R. Killian.

[16:14] *The concluding etiological note*. The introduction על־כן קרא is, as in Gen. 11:9, the naming of a place. As in most cases one must distinguish between the original meaning of the name and its later significance. On the significance given here, W. Zimmerli says: "It is not likely that the real significance of the name of the place is contained here." "The intricate etymology suggests that there is in the background an old name that was no longer understood." Some, like H. Gunkel, think of the name of an animal; J. Wellhausen, following Judg. 15:18-20, suggests לחי = "jawbone." The significance intended in Gen. 16:14 is also uncertain; most likely, it is that which comes closest to v. 13: "Spring of the living one who sees me"; so many exegetes. Other proposals are: "Spring of the living one whom I saw" (R. Killian), "the well to the living sight" (O. Procksch), "well of the living sight" (E. A. Speiser, H. C. White), "the one who sees me lives" (J. Wellhausen). A. Frh. von Gall sees here a combination of two names (BZAW 3 [1898]).

As regards the locality of the episode, J. Simons says that various writers mention a *ğebel umm ei-barēd* (*The Geographical. . . of the O.T.* [1959]); but so far it has not been possible to demonstrate where the spring lay. The place-name *Bared* occurs only in this passage. One cannot be more precise; it suffices that it was not all that far from Kadesh. A thorough discussion of the geographical setting can be found in F. Delitzsch.

Some exegetes assume that the conclusion is missing: "One expects to hear further how Hagar fared at the spring, how she bore and named Ishmael, how Ishmael grew up and became a people. Perhaps the closing sentence is still preserved in Gen. 25:18" (H. Gunkel). There are two things to say to this assumption. First, the narrative concludes with v. 13 and the etiological note in v. 14; it is complete and needs no further enlargement. Second, it has grown out of a genealogy (cf. comm. on 16:1), and must issue into a genealogy because of the announcement of the birth of a son; this is also the case with vv. 15-16, which, however, come from P. Genealogy and narrative are transmitted in separate lines. One must concede then that H. Gunkel is correct in his suggestion that the genealogy of Ishmael (Gen. 25:12-18) follows directly on the narrative (Gen. 16:1-14). That this is the case is made known to us expressly by the fact that a sentence from the narrative is taken up into the genealogy (16:12b = 25:18b).

[16:15-16]   A genealogy of P follows immediately on a narrative of J, so that the chapter is set within v. 1a and vv. 15-16. The genealogical notes in v. 3 likewise belong to P. The P components of ch. 16 are:

1a:	Sarah was barren
3a:	Sarah took Hagar. . .
3b:	and gave her to Abraham as wife
15a:	Hagar bore Abraham a son
15b:	Abraham called him Ishmael
16a:	Abraham was 86 years old,
16b:	when Hagar bore him Ishmael.

Each individual sentence remains within the genealogical pattern. Only two statements are made: Sarah gives Hagar to Abraham as secondary wife; Hagar bears Abraham Ishmael; only what is absolutely necessary has been appended to this—the reason for the secondary wife (1a) and the name of the son of Hagar (15b). In addition there are two characteristically P datings: the date when Hagar was taken as wife (v. 3a), and the date of Ishmael's birth (v. 16). These two sentences, despite their reduction to sheer fact, contain two variations from Gen. 16(J), both of which are significant for P: according to 16:2 Sarah gives her maidservant to Abraham as secondary wife so that she may acquire a child; according to 16:15-16(P) Hagar bears Abraham a son. The difference is even clearer at the name-giving. In P it is the father, not the mother, who gives the child the name (v. 15b). These alterations are comprehensible only if P is writing in a later period when even family customs have changed.

Purpose and Thrust

When dealing with "Form" surprise was expressed that so simple a narrative as this could undergo such different interpretations. This is somewhat more comprehensible at the conclusion of the exegesis. The narrative contains an abundance of motifs, all of which by no means lie along the same line. It was clearly the narrator's intention to allow many voices to speak which do not echo the main theme. One must be careful then not to force all motifs on to the same line nor to lose sight of the main theme while attending to a secondary motif. One difficulty is that there are really two narratives which have become one: the movement upwards to the climax is a conflict narrative; the movement downwards to the solution is the encounter with the messenger of God. Three different pronouncements of the messenger are transmitted, and the second part issues into the giving of three names: name of the child, name of God, name of the spring.

What the writer wants to say with his narrative must comprehend both parts. The narrative joins the conflict between Abraham's two wives, which arose out of the distressing situation of no children, with a promise narrative. But the promise of a son is not directed to Sarah, but to Hagar, who fled from her. The narrative reaches its goal when God hears; it does not say that God listens to the distress of the barren Sarah, but of Hagar who has had to flee. One confronts this narrative in all its depth only when one listens to both parts. The first part begins with an independent act of one woman, the second with the independent act of the other. Sarah's action was justified; her plan could have succeeded. Hagar's action was of desperation; it had no chance. It is only here that God intervenes and helps Hagar in her distress. "God hears" is the name of the promised son.

There is the social as well as the personal aspect. Sarah is concerned to be "built"; only through a child can she belong to a whole. As she sees it, the only whole to which she can belong is the family. Without this her life has no meaning. But man and wife alone do not constitute this whole. They have no future without a child—as the patriarchal period understood life. But Sarah's attempt to secure the future is put in jeopardy by the conflict between the women in the present. Hagar risks her own life and the child's for the sake of freedom. Only by God giving his approval to this act is Hagar "built," growing into a family.

Finally there is the theological aspect. God has closed Sarah's womb and has announced to Hagar the birth of a son. He grants new life; he denies new life. The one who has suffered injustice in a conflict can appeal to God: "Let Yahweh judge between you and me," because Yahweh intervenes for the one who has suffered injustice. But the one who received justice can also do injustice. The declaration about God that dominates the narrative is that laid down in the name of the son; it is a name of praise: "God hears." The description of God, "You are the God who sees me," is in fact saying the same. In the messenger's greeting Hagar has met God in action, reaching the earth and beholding the human in her distress. It is here that the Hagar narrative reaches into the New Testament where Lk. 1 narrates a similar meeting with a messenger of God which evokes the same reaction: "For he has regarded the low estate of his handmaiden."

There are a number of ways in which God reveals himself in the Old Testament; of all these his revelation through a messenger can be best adopted for the understanding of his self-revelation in the man Jesus. There remain vast differences: Jesus brings a message from God (εὐαγγέλιον); he speaks the words of God and does the deeds of God; this has its analogy in the *mal'ak YHWH* of the Old Testament. So too the *mal'ak YHWH* shows who he really is only in his going away. It would be possible then to understand the confession, "true God and true man," with the Old Testament as point of departure and not primarily from Greek thought patterns. But this would need to be thought through.

The Covenant with Abraham

Literature

Genesis 17 (cf. Intro., "Lit. for Section 4," "Names of God" and "Covenant"): C. Steuernagel, "Bemerkungen zu Genesis 17," ZAWB 34 (1920) 172-179. E. Naville, "Le XVII. chapitre de la Genèse," ZAW 44 (1926) 135-145. R. H. Pfeiffer, *Introduction to the OT. 1.* "God and His Holy Congregation" (1941; 1953²) 191-208. H. W. Robinson, *Redemption and Revelation in the Actuality of History* (1942); *Inspiration and Revelation in the Old Testament* (1946) esp. 153-155. B. Gemser, "Vertraagde openbaringsbewustheid," NedThT 15 (1960/61) 241-263. S. R. Külling, *Zur Datierung der "Genesis–P–Stücke," namentlich des Kapitels Genesis XVII* (1964). L. Legrand, "L'évangile aux bergers. Essai sur le genre littéraire de Luc II,8-20," RB 75 (1968) 161-187. G. C. Macholz, *Israel und das Land. Vorarbeiten zu einem Vergleich zwischen Priesterschrift und deuteronomistischem Geschichtswerk* (1969) esp. 42-44. M. W. Shaw, *Studies in Revelation and the Bible* (1971), esp. 23-35. F. Stolz, "Sabbat, Schöpfungswoche und Herbstfest," WuD NF 11 (1971) 159-175. E. Cortese, *La Terra di Canaan nella storia sacerdotale del Pentateuco: Paideia*, Supp. RivBib 5 (1972). M. Oliva, "Las revelaciones a los patriarcas en la historia sacerdotal," Bib 55 (1974) 1-14. W. H. Schmidt, "Drei Arbeiten zum Pentateuch," VuF 19 (1974) 86-90. C. Westermann, "Genesis 17. . .," ThLZ 101 (1976) 161-170. J. Barr, "Some Semantic Notes on the Covenant," Fests. W. Zimmerli (1977) 23-38.

Genesis 17:1-3: F. Delitzsch, *The Hebrew Language in the Light of Assyrian Research* (1883) 48; *Prolegomena eines neuen hebräisch-aramäischen Wörterbuches zum AT* (1886). P. Haupt, *Florilegium de Vogüé* (1909) esp. 279; also BZAW 27 (1914) 212. F. Nötscher, *"Das Angesicht Gottes schauen" nach biblischer und babylonischer Auffassung* (1924; 1969²). J. Bauer, "Die Gottheiten von Ras Schamra," ZAW 51 (1933) 51-100. G. Duncan, *New Light on Hebrew Origins* (1936) 238. R. Gordis, "The Biblical Root *šdy—šd*," JThSt 41 (1940) 34-43. M. Haller, "Sprache und Kult," Fests. O. Eissfeldt (1947) 141-154. K. Elliger, "Sinn und Ursprung der priesterlichen Geschichtserzählung," ZThK 49 (1952) 121-143 = KS, ThB 32 (1966) 174-198. W. G. Lambert, *Babylonian Wisdom Literature* (1960) 177, 179, 332. J. Bours, " 'Geh einher vor meinem Antlitz! Sei ganz!' Eine Meditation über Gen 17,1-3," BiLe 3 (1962) 57-61. H. R. Moeller, "Four Old Testament Problem Terms," *The Bible Translator* 13 (1962) 219-222. W. Zimmerli, " 'Offenbarung' im AT," EvTh 22 (1962) 15-31. T. C. Vriezen, "Exode XX,2. Introduction au Décalogue: formula de loi ou d'alliance?" *RechBib* 8 (1963) 35-50. N. Lohfink, "Die priesterschriftliche Abwertung der Tradition von der Offenbarung des Jahwenamens an Mose," Bib 49 (1968) 1-8. S. E. McEvenue, "A Source-Critical Problem in Nm 14, 26-38," Bib 50 (1969) 453-465. W. Brueggemann, "The Kerygma of the Priestly Writers," ZAW 84 (1972) 397-414. K. Berger, "Abraham, II. Im Frühjudentum und NT,"

TRE I,3 (1974) 372-382. A. J. Reines, "Birth Dogma and Philosophic Faith: A Philosophic Inquiry," HUCA 46 (1975) 297-329. K. Koch, "Saddaj. . .," VT 26 (1976) 299-332.

Genesis 17:4-8: I. Gelb, "The Double Name of the Hittite Kings," Rocz Or 17 (1953) 146-154. L. G. Rignell, "Isa. LII 13-LIII 12," VT 3 (1953) 87-92. S. Morenz, "Ägyptische und davidische Königsliteratur," ZÄS 79 (1954) 73-74. P. A. H. de Boer, "The Counsellor," VT.S 3 (1955) 42-71. L. Wächter, "Überlegungen zur Umnennung von *Pašḥur* in Māgôr Missābīb in Jeremia 20,3," ZAW 74 (1962) 57-62. J. Morgenstern, "The 'Bloody Husband'. . .," HUCA 34 (1963) 35-70. R. Smend, *Die Bundesformel*, ThSt 68 (1963). N. Lohfink, "Textkritisches zu Gn 17,5.13.16.17," Bib 48 (1967) 439-442. M. Fishbane, "Jeremiah IV 23-26 and Job III 3-13. A Recovered Use of the Creation Pattern," VT 21 (1971) 151-167. M. Tsevat, "The Basic Meaning of the Biblical Sabbath," ZAW 84 (1972) 447-459. B. Kedar-Kopfstein, "Die Wiedergabe des hebräischen Kausativs in der Vulgata," ZAW 85 (1973) 196-219. B. Jongeling, "L'expression *My Ytn* dans l'Ancien Testament," VT 24 (1974) 32-40. I. Rappaport, *The Hebrew Word Shem and its Original Meaning: The Bearing of Akkadian Philology on Biblical Interpretation* (1976).

Genesis 17:9-14: E. Lane, *Arabian Society in the Middle Ages* (1883). J. Wellhausen, *Reste arabischen Heidentums* (1887; 1961³) esp. 175. E. Lane, *The Manners and Customs of the Modern Egyptians* (1890). E. Westermarck, *History of Human Marriage* (1891). F. Schwally, *Das Leben nach dem Tode nach den Vorstellungen des alten Israel und des Judentums* (1892). H. Spencer, *Principles of Sociology, II* (1896/97). S. I. Curtiss, *Primitive Semitic Religion Today* (1902). E. Samter, "Die Bedeutung des Beschneidungsritus und Verwandtes," *Philologus* 62 (1902) 91-94. J. G. Frazer, "The Origin of Circumcision," IR IV (1904) 204-218. J. C. Matthes, "De Besnijdenis," ThT 6 (1907) 163-191; "Bemerkungen und Mitteilungen über die Beschneidung," ZAW 29 (1909) 70-73. C. H. Toy, *Introduction to the History of Religions* (1913) esp. 68-74. W. H. Gispen, "De Besnijdenis (Gen 17)," GThT 54 (1954) 148-182. F. Stummer," אֲמֶלָה (Ez XVI 30A)," VT 4 (1954) 34-40. P. Grelot, "La dernière étage de la rédaction Sacerdotale," VT 6 (1956) 174-189. E. Pfeiffer, "Eine Inversion in Psalm XXIII 1bα," VT 8 (1958) 219-220. C. Weiss, "Ritual Circumcision," *Clinical Practices I* (1962) 65-72; "Worldwide Survey of the Current Practice of *Milah* (Ritual Circumcision)," JSocS 24 (1962) 30-48. J. Hoftijzer, "Deux vases à inscription identique," VT 13 (1963) 337-339. E. Isaac, "Circumcision as a Covenant Rite," Anthr. 59 (1964) 444-456. P. Prigent, "Justin et l'Ancien Testament," IX. *Dialogue* 10-29 (1964) 235-237. H. J. Hermisson, "Sprache und Ritus im Altisraelitischen Kult. Zur 'Spiritualisierung' der Kultbegriffe im AT," WMANT 19 (1965). O. Sander, "Leib—Seele—Dualismus im AT?" ZAW 77 (1965) 329-332. N. P. Bratsiotis, "נֶפֶשׁ—ΨYXH. Ein Beitrag zur Erforschung der Sprache und der Theologie der Septuaginta," VT.S 15 (1966) 58-89. K. Koch, "Sühne und Sündenvergebung um die Wende von der exilischen zur nachexilischen Zeit," EvTh 26 (1966) 217-239. M. G. Kline, *By Oath Consigned. A Reinterpretation of the Covenant Signs of Circumcision and Baptism* (1968). D. Arenhoevel, "Ursprung und Bedeutung der Beschneidung," *Wort und Antwort* 14 (1973) 167-172. E. Kutsch, "Das sogenannte 'Bundesblut' in Ex XXIV 8 und Sach IX 11," VT 23 (1973) 25-30. M. V. Fox, "The Sign of Covenant. Circumcision in the Light of the Priestly *ʾôt* Etiologies," RB 81 (1974) 557-596. W. Beltz, "Religionsgeschichtliche Marginalie zu Ex 4,24-26," ZAW 87 (1975) 209-211. M. Weinfeld, "Jeremiah and the Spiritual Metamorphosis of Israel," ZAW 88 (1976) 17-56.

Genesis 17:15-21: V. Aptowitzer, "Spuren des Matriarchats im jüdischen Schrifttum," HUCA 4 (1927) 207-240; 5 (1928) 261-297. P. Humbert, "Die literarische Zweiheit des Priester-Codex in der Genesis," ZAW 58 (1940/41) 30-57. J. J. Stamm, "Der Name Isaak," Fests. A. Schädelin (1950) 33-38. J. P. Hyatt, "The Translation and Meaning of Amos 5,23-24," ZAW 68 (1956) 17-24. E. A. Speiser, "Background and Function of the Biblical *Nāśīʾ*," CBQ 25 (1963) 111-117. J. J. Scullion, "An Approach to the Understanding of Isaiah 7,10-17," JBL 87 (1968) 288-300. R. W. Neff, "The Birth and Election of Isaac in the Priestly Tradition," BiR 15 (1970) 5-18. K. K. Riemschneider, *Babylonische Geburtsomina in hethitischer Übersetzung* (1970). C. F. Whitley, "Some Remarks on *lû* and *loʾ*," ZAW 87 (1975) 202-204.

Genesis 17:22: A. Schmitt, "Entrückung—Aufnahme—Himmelfahrt. Untersuchungen zu einem Vorstellungsbereich im AT," *Forschung zur Bibel* 10 (1973). K. Koch, "Die Rolle der hymnischen Abschnitte in der Komposition des Amos-Buches," ZAW 86 (1974) 504-537.

Genesis 17:23-24(27): M. Stracmans, "A propos d'un texte relatif à la circoncision égyptienne (Ire période intermédiaire)," *Mélanges I. Lévy* (1955) 631-639; "Encore un texte peu connue relatif à la circoncision des anciens égyptiens," AIEP 2 (1959) 7-15. J. M. Sasson, Circumcision in the Ancient Near East," JBL 85 (1966) 473-476.

Text

17:1 When Abraham was ninety-nine years old, Yahweh appeared to him and said: I am God Almighty[a] [El Shaddai]; live always in my presence and be perfect,

2 so that I may put my covenant between me and you, and I will multiply you in plenty.

3a Then Abraham fell down on his face.

3b And God spoke with him and said:

4 See, this is my covenant that I make with you: You shall be the father of many nations.

5 You[a] will no longer be called by your name Abram; Abraham[b] shall be your name, because I shall make you the father of many nations.

6 I will make[a] you fruitful in plenty; I will make nations out of you, and kings will go forth from you.

7 I am setting up my covenant between me and you and your descendants after you as an eternal[a] covenant, to be[b] your God and the God of your descendants.

8 And I am giving you and your descendants after you the land where you are now aliens, the whole of the land of Canaan[a] as an eternal possession,[b] and I will be God to them.

9 And God spoke to Abraham: Now you, you are to keep my covenant, you and your descendants,[a] generation to generation.

10 This is my covenant between me and you and your descendants that you shall keep: every male among you is to be circumcised.[a]

11 You shall circumcise the flesh of your foreskin,[a] and this shall be the sign of the covenant between me and you.

12 At the age of eight days every male among you shall be circumcised, generation after generation; also those born in your house and any stranger bought with your money, who is not of your blood.

13 Circumcise[a] those born in your house[b] and those bought with your money. And so my covenant shall be on your flesh as an eternal covenant.[c]

14 An uncircumcised male, everyone who has not had the flesh of his foreskin[a] circumcised, his life[b] shall be cut off from his kin. He has broken my covenant.[c]

15 And God spoke to Abraham: Sarai your wife, you shall no longer call[a] her Sarai, but Sarah.

16 I will bless her,[a] and by her too I will give you a son. I will bless her, and she will issue into nations, kings of nations will come forth from her.

17 Then Abraham fell down on his face; he laughed and said to himself: Can a son be born to one who is one hundred years old, and[a] can Sarah bear a son at ninety years?

18 And Abraham said to God: If only[a] Ishmael would live under your care!

19 But God said: No, Sarah your wife shall bear you a son, and you shall call him Isaac.[a] And I will set up my covenant with him and his descendants as an eternal covenant "to be his God."[b]

20 Ishmael too I have heard because of you;[a] See, I bless him and will make him fruitful, and multiply him in plenty. He shall be the father of twelve princes, and I will make him into a great nation.

21 But[a] my covenant I will set up with Isaac whom Sarah will bear to you

at this time next year.
22 And God finished speaking with Abraham and went up and left him.
23 Then Abraham took his son Ishmael and all born in his house and all
    bought with money, all males of his household, and circumcised the
    flesh of their foreskin that very day, as God had told him.
24 Abraham was ninety-nine years old when he circumcised the flesh of
    his foreskin.
25 Ishmael his son was thirteen years old when he was circumcised in the
    flesh of his foreskin.
26 Abraham and Ishmael his son were circumcised on the same day,
27 and all the men of his household, those born there and those bought
    with money from strangers, were circumcised with them.

1a Gk ὁ θεός σου.

5a The את is missing in the Sam and in some Mss; construction, Ges-K
§121b.   **b** Antithesis introduced by simple *waw*, Ges-K §163a.

6a Syr adds והרביתיך; on אתך, B. Kedar-Kosfstein, ZAW 85 (1973).

7a E. Jenni ZAW 65 (1953) 21.   **b** On להיות, E. Weisenberg VT 5 (1955) 291.

8a J. Simons (1959): "Canaan is sometimes used as a short designation of the Promised
Land, e.g., Gen. 17:8."   **b** Construction, Ges-K § 128p, J. M. Allegro, "Use of the
Semitic Demonstrative Element z in Hebrew," VT 5 (1955) 309-312; on "possession," F.
Horst, Fests. W. Rudolf (1961).

9a On וזרעך, M. Wilcox JBL 96 (1977) 85ff.

10a On the verb מול, Ges-K §72ee, B. Jacob comm. ad loc., F. Stummer VT 4 (1954)
34-40.

11a Ges-K §112aa: "In command"; BrSynt §98a; בשר O. Sander ZAW 77 (1965)
329-332; on the acc., Ges-K §121d.

13a BrSynt §93b.   **b** יליד; on the relationship between MT and Sam cf. N. Lohfink
Bib 48 (1967) 439   **c** Construction, E. König, *Stylistik*. . . (1900) I 22.

14a Sam and Gk add "on the eighth day."   **b** Construction, Ges-K §158a, 167b, n.
1; BrSynt §133c; R. Meyer 120, 121; E. Pfeiffer VT 8 (1958) 219. On נפש N. P. Bratsiotis
VT.S 15 (1966) 58-89.   **c** הפר Ges-K §29q, 67v.

15a Construction, Ges-K §143b.

16a Sam and the versions read the masc.; with E. A. Speiser, comm. ad loc., retain MT.
Differently, N. Lohfink Bib 48 (1967) 439.

17a Construction of double question, Ges-K §150g; N. Lohfink, with A. Ehrlich,
(Randglossen 1908) strikes out the ה as a secondary addition; others strike out שרה ה (BH
Appar.).

18a Volition with לו, BrSynt §8b, C. F. Whitely ZAW 87 (1975) 202-204.

19a וקראת Ges-K §49b, J. J. Scullion, JBL 87 (1968) 288-300   **b** To be added with
G.

20a On the use of the perfect, Ges-K §106m; BrSynt §135b.

21a Adversative *waw* at the beginning of a sentence, Ges-K §154a; J. P. Hyatt ZAW 68
(1956) 17- 24

Form

Gen. 17 is not a narrative but a literary construction patterned on a narrative and
presupposing older narratives about Abraham. It differs principally from the older
patriarchal stories in that there is no action in it (apart from vv. 23-27); it is solely a dialog between God and Abraham. God speaks to Abraham (vv.
1b-2,3b-16,19-21). Abraham's reaction is to fall to the ground (v. 3a,17), to
laugh and to argue with himself (v. 17b), and to express a wish (v. 18); in vv.
23-27 he carries out what he has been commanded. The dialog then is very one-
sided; as a whole, it resembles a divine discourse. As God's speech is for the most
part promise, one might call ch. 17 a factitious promise narrative (in this it is like

ch. 15). Since the chapter begins and ends with an appearance of God (vv. 1a and 22), one might also understand it as a narrative of an appearance of God to Abraham; but the two sentences that frame the story have a literary function. The appearance of God simply renders the speech to Abraham possible.

The literary character of Gen. 17 also is seen in the way in which P reworks traditions available to him (from Gen. 12:1-3; 15; 18; traces too from 16; 21). The number of these traditions reveals that the purpose of P's presentation is not to give an account of a single experience, but to concentrate here what he sees to be essential to the whole Abraham story.

The Structure

The division of the chapter is carefully thought out right down to the finest detail; it is an artistic composition. Basic to the understanding of the structure is that God's speech, set between his appearance in v. 1a and his withdrawal in v. 22, is divided into two parts: there is the preamble (vv. 1b-3a) and the divine speech (vv. 3b-21). The preamble contains only a short command with a promise, and Abraham's reply in the manner of the old patriarchal promises, following the structure of Gen. 12:1-4a. The elements of vv. 1b-3a are unfolded in God's speech in vv. 3b-21, showing that they are really a preamble.

God's speech to Abraham is divided into three parts: 3b-8, promise; 9-14, command; 15-21, promise (see my study, ''Genesis 17. . .,'' ThLZ 101 [1976] 161-170). This is meant to tell us that the promise is dominant and all-embracing in what God says; the command is given to the one who has received the promise; the command rests on the promise.

Vv. 3b-8 are colored by the promise of posterity and the divine presence (this designation is abbreviated: it is not the divine presence in itself, but the divine presence for Abraham, as will be explained under v. 7), vv. 15-21 by the promise of a son. The promise is directed to Abraham in 3b-8, to Sarah in 15-21; in both cases it is combined with an alteration of name (Abraham v. 5, Sarah v. 15b). Behind 3b-8 stands Gen. 15; behind 15-21 Gen. 18. In 17:3b-8 and 15-21, P has in fact reworked all the promises of the old patriarchal tradition and brought them into relationship with each other. P is at pains to shape into a whole the variety of promises coming down to him; he is thus on the way to a concept of promise. And so both in the preamble (v. 2) and in the unfolding, the promise of posterity acquires a precedence (vv. 4-6, 16b, 20b); it is joined with the promise of the divine presence in vv. 3b-8 (7b, 8c), and with the promise of a son in vv. 15-21. By contrast, the promise of the land (v. 8) is well in the background; it is mentioned only once and is consciously enclosed by the promise of the divine presence. Further specification is given to the promise in vv. 15-21; the promise of posterity continues in all the children of Abraham; the promise of the divine presence only in Isaac. The command of circumcision (vv. 9-14) stands between these two parts. P is not taking up here a tradition transmitted from the patriarchal story. It is the idea of ברית in the sense of a mutual relationship that binds this part with the two promises: ואתה at the beginning of v. 9 corresponds to the אני הנה at the beginning of v. 4. The meaning is: *I* relate in this way to the ברית; *you* are to do the same. The kernel of vv. 9-14 is the command of circumcision (v. 9f.) and the penalty connected with it in v. 14. This kernel is elaborated with further details (vv. 11a, 12, 13) and an explanation of this meaning as a sign of the covenant (v. 11b). The acceptance of the covenant is confirmed by carrying out the circumcision.

The concluding part (vv. 23-27) gives details of how Abraham carried out God's command (vv. 23, 26, 27); a genealogical ending is added (vv. 1a, 24-25).

Excursus

The concept of ברית *in the structure of Gen. 17.*   ברית serves as the leitmotif of ch. 17, making it a classical example of what a catchword can mean. The methodological consequence is that the sense of a catchword can be understood only from the chapter as a whole. The word occurs 13 times and is distributed throughout with surprising regularity: once in the prologue, 3 times in the command (vv. 9-14). It has been very consciously made into the catchword; the distribution confirms further that P intended the division in this way.

ברית appears in the prolog as part of the theme as a whole; it is there in the first sentence of the first part of the promise speech (vv. 3b-8) where it introduces the promise of prosperity, and in v. 7 (twice) introducing the divine presence. In the second part of the promise speech (vv. 15-21) it describes in v. 17 (twice) and v. 21 the promise to or covenant with Isaac by which he is singled out before Ishmael. It is most heavily concentrated in vv. 9-14, showing a definite interest in the link between circumcision and ברית.

The structure of ch. 17 together with the catchword ברית shows that P intends to present synthetically the promise of God to Abraham, and at the same time to anchor the command of circumcision therein. He does this by framing vv. 9-14 within vv. 3b-8 and vv. 15-21, which on their side correspond to the link between instruction and promise in the prolog (vv. 1b-2), and to the concept ברית which links command and promise. "The covenant between me and you" requires on God's side the fulfillment of the promise, and on Abraham's side the carrying out of the command. The essence of the theology of the priestly writing expresses itself in all its clearness in this chapter (cf. the detailed study of S. E. McEvenue, *The Narrative Style of the Priestly Writer*, AnBib [1971] 145-178).

Setting

This chapter originated as part of the priestly writing; it has its literary setting in the overall composition of this work where it is in turn the center of the priestly presentation of the patriarchal story. Even when there is no doubt about its purely literary origin, that is, that it is the result of theological reflection on the part of the priestly writer, then not all has been said. This priestly theologian was conscious that he was bound to traditions which were not merely at his disposal in literary form, but which he also acknowledged and wanted to preserve as a part of living tradition. Despite thoroughgoing reshaping, Gen. 17 is a stage along the path of the transmission of the patriarchal promises which begins in the patriarchal period itself, experiences modification and interpretation in the old sources of the Pentateuch, and continues on in Deuteronomy. The priestly theologian in turn pursues, with the new shape he has given to the promise to Abraham (which for him is identical with the promise to the patriarchs), his intention of actualizing the promise to the patriarchs for his people in their present situation, as the exegesis will show. His concern is this: he wants to make the promise given to the patriarchs God's binding word for contemporary Israel by means of the link which he has forged with the command of circumcision.

Commentary

[17:1-3a] The preamble is divided thus: V. 1 begins with information about Abraham's age; then there is the further information that Yahweh appeared to Abraham, with the introduction to the following oracle. The oracle consists of three parts: God announces himself by name; a command; and a promise divided into two sentences. Then follows Abraham's prostration.

When one compares vv. 1-3a with God's speech of vv. 3b-21, the difference is striking. Vv. 1-3a are brief and poetic while vv. 3b-21 are very detailed and repetitive. One sees this even more clearly when one compares the single sentence of the command (v. 1b) with the command section (vv. 9-14), and the promise (v. 2) with the two promise sections (vv. 3b-8 and vv. 15-21). The only explanation of this difference is that in vv. 1-3a P passes on a promise to Abraham as he knows it from the tradition, while the divine speeches (vv. 3b-21) differ clearly from this by interpretation and elaboration. P is conscious throughout of the difference between the interpretative speech which he has fashioned and the "real" patriarchal promises; the priestly theologian, writing at the time of the exile, has a distinct historical sense. The difference is confirmed by the close resemblance between the structure of 17:1-3a and 12:1-4a:

12:1-4a	*17:1-3a*
Yahweh said to Abraham	Yahweh appeared to Abraham and said:
Go from your. . .	Live always in my presence and be perfect
I will make you into a great. . .	I will multiply you in plenty. . .
And Abraham went. . .	And Abraham fell down. . .

There are differences of course, but the agreement is so striking that P must have had this or a similar promise before him. One could say with caution that the relationship of vv. 1-3a to 3b-21 is that of text to interpretation.

[17:1] The information that Abraham was ninety-nine years old forms, together with vv. 24-25, the genealogical frame which is so full of meaning for P in such a systematic operation. The preceding genealogical information is in 16:3,16. Abraham will be one hundred years old at Isaac's birth, as Shem was at Arpachshad's. The sentence, "Yahweh appeared to Abram," could just as easily be J's, where it occurs often. P's use of the name Yahweh here has always aroused consternation and given occasion for the most astonishing explanations. It is generally assumed to be a scribal error whereby יהוה has intruded into the place of an original אלהים; so H. Gunkel, O. Eissfeldt, and many others. But it is comprehensible in the explanation given here of vv. 1-3a: P is passing on an ancient patriarchal promise that has come down in which the name of God was given as Yahweh. In the very next sentence, where God introduces himself, he does so by another name; P is thereby putting into perspective the name Yahweh, which has already been in use. At the same time he is indicating the gap between God's revelation to the patriarchs and that made to Israel at the exodus from Egypt, Ex. 6. P uses the designation אל שדי (El Shaddai) only in those places in his patriarchal story where he wants to give emphasis: Gen. 17:1; 28:3; 35:11; 48:3; 43:14(?); Ex. 6:3.

Excursus

אל שדי (El Shaddai): The designation for God, שדי, occurs 48 times in the O.T.: 31 times in the dialogs in Job, 5(6) times in P's patriarchal story, 3 times in ancient blessings (Gen. 49:25; Num. 24:4,16), 2 in Psalms (68:15; 91:1), 2 in Ruth (1:20f.), 2 in the prophetic books (Is. 13:6; Joel 1:15), 2 in Ezekiel (1:24; 10:5). In most places שַׁדַּי stands alone; the juxtaposition of אֵל־שַׁדַּי occurs only in P and Ezek. 10:5, that is 6(7) times.

One can speak of a constant use only in Job (dialogs) and in P; elsewhere the name occurs only once or twice. But in Job too it is but one designation for God side by side with others (especially אֵל and אֱלוֹהַּ). It can be taken for certain that the poet of Job has resumed an old name for God that was not restricted to Israel alone.

P's use manifests a fixed, determined plan which is to be traced back to a theologian who conceived the work as a whole. He uses it as a designation for God only in the patriarchal story (Gen. 17:1; 28:3; 35:11; 48:3; 43:14[?]), and explains its use expressly in Ex. 6:3; Yahweh reveals himself to the patriarchs as El Shaddai. P thereby expressly separates out the revelation to the fathers from Yahweh's revelation to Israel, as well as from the general name for God, *Elohim*, in the primeval story (so, with many others, K. Koch VT 26 [1976] 316: "from 'history of religions' considerations"). P intends to say that primeval event, the patriarchal story, and the story of the people differ in the way in which revelation is given: this shows itself in the name (Elohim—El Shaddai—Yahweh) as well as in the object of the revelation (mankind—patriarchs—the people of Israel). This is one of the most certain signs that there stands behind the P texts of Genesis and Exodus a well thought out plan and so a written theological work, and that P regards the patriarchal story as an independent epoch, even though the text contains little from it.

One must distinguish very carefully between this function which the name אֵל־שַׁדַּי has in P, and its meaning; the function is independent of the meaning.

P takes up in these five places an ancient name for God, well known both in Israel and beyond, just as does the poet in Job (this holds also for most of the other cases; certainly for Ruth 1:20f.; Ezek. 1:24; 10:5; probably for Is. 13:6; Joel 1:15; Ps. 91:1); he joins it to the general name for God, אֵל. One must agree with K. Koch that the etymology, which hitherto has been the center of almost the whole discussion, yields little or nothing for the interpretation of the Shaddai texts. The question is how (El) Shaddai is used in each particular context. It is enough to enumerate the most important attempts to explain it etymologically. According to K. Koch (308 and KBL 950), W. F. Albright derived it from Akk. *šadu*, "mountain" (JBL 54 [1935] 173-193; so previously F. Baethgen [1888]), and understood שַׁדַּי as "the one of the mountain." This word is often used in connection with divinities, and so such a meaning is probable, and has been accepted by many; K. Koch also thinks that it is possible. M. Weippert proposes a root *śdw*, "field" (Hebr. שָׂדֶה), and so "God of the field, God of the steppe" (ZDMB 111 [1967] 42-62; so too R. de Vaux); G. Fohrer derives it from שֵׁד, "my guardian spirit"; M. A. Canney derives it from שַׁד, "mother's breast," and thinks it likely that it was originally a female deity (ET 34 [1922-23] 332). An earlier derivation is from שָׁדַד = "to destroy," "the destroyer"; N. Walker looks to Sum. SA(G).ZU, in Semitic simplification, with the meaning "omniscient" (ZAW 72 [1960] 64-66). And there are still further suggestions.

None of these etymological explanations accords accurately with any group of O.T. passages. It is to be assumed that the appellation was passed on without its original meaning being known. The question then is whether the contexts in which it occurs show anything in common, above all, the P passages: In Ex. 6:3 P assigns and limits the name Shaddai to the patriarchal period. K. Koch notes that in all the four passages in Gen. 17:1f.; 28:3f.; 35:11; 48:3 the name occurs with the promise of posterity. Now this of course is conceived in the language of a later stage of tradition (C. Westermann, *The Promises to the Fathers*. . . [1976: Eng 1980]); it is possible, however, that the memory of the name was bound up with blessing and increase. This is likely also for what are probably the two very early passages, Gen. 49:25 and Num. 24:4,16. K. Koch thinks that there are echoes of it in the use of the name in Job (309-316: "not the Almighty but the one who is close. . ."). It is possible then that the name goes back to the period before Israel was a state and perhaps too shows an affinity to the religion of the patriarchs. Thus one could understand better the function of the name in P. The Gk translation ὁ θεός μου could also favor this (G. Bertram, ZAW 70 [1958] 20-31; H. Vorländer, AOAT 23 [1975]).

There is a long history both within and outside Israel of a God announcing himself by name (cf. W. Zimmerli, Fests. A. Alt [1953] 179-209). It is particularly significant in polytheistic circles where the God who reveals himself announces himself by name so that the one addressed knows with which deity he is dealing. In Gen. 17:1 we have simply the stylistic form of the oracle of revelation; there is no need to ask about a specific meaning from the context.

The oracle addressed to Abraham consists of instruction and promise as in Gen. 12:1-4a and other passages in the patriarchal story. In contrast to these passages, the instruction has been worked over; it is no longer a concrete and specific instruction to a group to move its dwelling place (depart. . . stay in. . .) but to move in a way that determines its whole comportment before God. Once more P has expressed very profoundly a historical gap: for the later period when P is writing God's commands are no longer simple, concrete, and hence limited instructions, but are directed to one's very existence as a whole. P, therefore, does not pass on the old patriarchal instructions by this imperative, but translates it into his own era. By the התהלך לפני God orders Abraham (now representing Israel) to live his life before God in such a way that every single step is made with reference to God and every day experiences him close at hand. This is not meant to be some sort of lofty demand; it is something quite natural, as Ps. 139 prays in reflection and wonder. The second imperative accords with this, והיה תמים. It is not very important whether one translates it as an imperative as such or as a consequence, "then will you be perfect" (so the Zürich Bible and many others). The same imperative occurs also in Gen. 12:1-4a, but in the promise section. This makes it clear that the imperative in Gen. 17:1 is still part of the command; it is better, then, to translate it as an imperative in such a way as it can include a consequence from the first imperative. One might translate תמים with Luther, "and be pious," or with the moderns, "without fault." But neither translation renders the Hebrew word accurately; it has neither moral nor religious echo, but is consciously secular. The nearest approach to the Hebrew would be something like: "and be whole (complete)," even if that sounds strange to us. P wants to say thereby that "belonging to God is in proper order only when it is without reservation and unconditional" (W. H. Schmidt, *Das erste Gebot.* . . [1969] 21; W. Brueggemann, ZAW 89 [1972] 234-258; H. A. Kenik, JBL 95 [1976] 391-403; J. H. Tigay, JBL 89 [1970] 178-186, draw attention to the observation of M. Weinfeld who found in royal covenants of grant the expression "the king's loyalty to his divine patron." Weinfeld refers also to Gen. 17:1, JAOS 90 [1970] 186).

[17:2]   The promise has two parts. The second part is the traditional promise of posterity (on the verb, *Genesis 1–11*, comm. on 1:28); the first is the interpretation of P where he introduces, one may say solemnly introduces, the catchword ברית: he resumes the basic meaning of the word—a solemn, binding assurance which can correspond to an oath, and whose content can be the same as a promise (as in Gen. 15). P introduces the word in such a way that the solemn assurance which God gives (נתן) is something "between me and you." And so he extends the basic meaning of the word, and this is unfolded in the structure of the divine speech which follows.

In v. 2 of the preamble only one of many possible promises is mentioned, that of increase, which thereby acquires precedence, a precedence coming out of the situation into which P is speaking. Israel's existence in the exile takes its stand on the succession of generations; Israel continues to live in its families after the political collapse, from parents to children and to their children. Were no more children to be born, Israel would be cut off. This new situation gives a further nuance to the old promise: it now means not primarily that many derive from one, but that the generations continue into the future.

[17:3a]   Abraham's reaction to the instruction and promise is described in one simple gesture: he falls to the ground on his face. This says so much for P that no further comment is required. The ancient gesture of submission, which had long since become for P an act of cultic reverence before God and a bodily expression of "Amen," accepts the promise, and at the same time gives assent to the command. Inherent in the gesture is that same "between me and you" which determined anew the ברית in God's oracle. It closes the preamble.

[17:3b-8]   The first part of the promise: V. 3b introduces God's speech. It begins with the promise of increase, describing it as in v. 2 as ברית (the succession of 4b on 4a corresponds to that of 2b on 2a and later of 7b on 7a). It is continued in v. 6; in between, the change of name in v. 5 from Abram to Abraham is based on the promise of increase. There follows in vv. 7-8 the promise of the divine presence with that of the land. The emphasis rests on the promise of the divine presence; it is designated and explained in detail as ברית and repeated again in v. 8b. The promise of the land, which occurs only here in the whole chapter, is framed by it in v. 8a.

[17:3b]   The new introduction after Abraham's obeisance in v. 3a confirms that something new begins with v. 3b, namely, God's speech, which unfolds in vv. 1b-3a (on אתו, see L. Rost, *Studien zum AT* [1974] 54f.).

[17:4]   The formula אני הנה, with its echoes of אני אל שדי in v. 1b, solemnly introduces the promise of increase. It is designated as ברית (on ברית, see comments on ch. 15, above). A presupposition for the understanding of the word here is that Hebrew has no specific word for "promise"; it is usually introduced by a verbal sentence: ". . .and God spoke to. . .." ברית with the meaning "binding assurance" is close to the meaning "promise" and can designate God's promise both here and elsewhere. One must attend here to the difference in formulation between vv. 4a and 7a; in v. 4a ברית has this meaning as designating one of the traditional promises. One could just as well translate: "this is my assurance (or promise) which holds for you"; the translation, "covenant," in this passage has its basis in v. 7.
      The promise of increase in v. 4b is already formulated with a view to the change of name in v. 5. It looks back to the stark, direct promise of increase in v. 2b, וארבה אותך, and sets in contrast with it an expansion (see C. Westermann, *The Promises to the Fathers*. . . [1976; Eng. 1980]). This confirms again the relationship of vv. 3bff. to vv. 1-3a. The promise of increase runs like a thread through the whole chapter: vv. 2b,4b,6a,16b,20aβb:

2b,	20aβ	multiplication in plenty
6a,	20aβ	make fruitful in plenty
4b,	5b	father of many nations
6b,	16b	nations and kings, 16b Sarah,
		20bα princes (Ishmael)
16b,	20a	bless and make fruitful (Ishmael, Sarah)
	20bβ	make into a great nation

If one compares this synthesis with promises of increase previous to and apart from P, one finds in it virtually all elements; only here do they occur in such fullness. It is clear then that the promise of increase has a dominating role in ch. 17.

The formulation in v. 4b makes use of the word "father": "you shall be the father of many nations," and "I shall make you the father of many nations" (v. 5b). Abraham is the father. In the old patriarchal narratives he is the father in every aspect of the family realm; he then becomes the father of a people, and P elevates this further to the father of nations including the nation of Ishmael. One can sense from this formulation how Abraham will continue as father in the course and expanse of history.

[17:5]   The word המון is chosen in the formulation of the promise in vv. 4b and 5b with a view to the change in Abraham's name. It contains the syllable הם which is added to the name אברם. המון describes in the first place the roar caused by a throng of people, e.g., Is. 17:12, "the thunder of many peoples," then the multitude, e.g., Is. 5:13. There is no intention at all of explaining the name (on the relationship of the two names to each other, cf. Intro., end of section 3, "Personal Names"). The conferring of a new name marks a new era in life and separates it out from the past; the typical case is that of the king who acquires a new throne name (or several) at his coronation, a practice which shows that the change of name relates in all its essentials to the function of the one whose name is changed. (On the naming of the king, cf. I. J. Gelb, RoczOr 17 [1953] 146-154; S. Morenz, ZÄS 79 [1954] 73-74; A. F. Key, JBL 83 [1964] 55-59). This is presupposed too in Gen. 17 where there is, however, no biographical intention; it is rather that Abraham, by the setting up of the covenant and its sealing by circumcision, is made the father of Israel. The name, therefore, does not describe the period of the man's life which has passed—just as the 99 years are not to be taken strictly biographically, but as an enumeration of the "ancient era" of Abraham—but the simple life of a man in the early period of Israel who belonged to his time, without having to have anything to do with Israel. Behind this change of name one can sense throughout hints that the author of the priestly writing had information of an "Abram" of the patriarchal period who did not stand in this direct relationship to Israel. This would mean that P was conscious of a reshaping of the old Abraham figure. The formulation in v. 5b, נתתיך = "I am giving you," "I am installing you," also favors this. This accords with political language; someone is installed in office by a sovereign. This "installation" of Abraham means his function as father of Israel.

[17:6]   The promise of increase in v. 4 is continued in v. 6. The פרה belongs together with the רבה of v. 2b as in Gen. 1:28, "be fruitful and increase"; this is a further sign that the promise speech unfolds the promise of the preamble. J. Hoftijzer (*Die Verheissungen an die drei Erzväter* [1956] 9-11) comments on the expansion, "nations and kings," and refers to the same word-pair in Is. 41:2; 45:1; 60:3; and Jer. 25:14. These passages, where "nations" and "kings" stand in parallelism, are oracles of salvation to the exilic and postexilic period. The word-pair "nations and kings" has, from the standpoint of tradition history, its primary setting in this late prophecy of salvation. It is here that the language of the promise to the fathers acquires its shape as it grows out of the promise of salvation around the period of the exile; the promise has gone down through the centuries reshaped into the contemporary language of each period.

[17:7a]   It is obvious in v. 7 that P is thinking of the people of Israel when he speaks of Abraham. This is the most detailed of all verses in ch. 17 which have anything to say of the ברית; here lies the strongest emphasis. It is concerned with something more than a promise, as the difference in formulation from v. 4 shows. Here something is "set up," founded, established, and "between me and you"; something between God and Abraham's descendants that is to last through generations; it is to last for ever לברית עולם. This is a really classical description of an institution (J. J. Rabinowitz, VT 11 [1961] 56-76). What becomes an institution here is the relationship to God which rests on the promise. While in v. 4 ברית means the act of promise, in v. 7 it describes a status which is established by this act, something which is to last now and for ever between Abraham's descendants and God. It is agreed that the basic meaning is a binding assurance that will last. But it is deliberately extended. This is made possible by a peculiarity of the Hebrew language which can describe with one word an action and what results from it, e.g., עון, sin and the punishment it entails (cf. *Genesis 1–11*, comm. on 4:13). W. Zimmerli (1970) also understands it in this way. The translation "covenant" is therefore justified (so too W. Eichrodt, ThZ 30 [1974] 205; J. Barr, Fests. W. Zimmerli [1977] 35).

[17:7b]   This extension of the concept ברית is in accord with P's intention for ch. 17 as a whole: God's relationship to Israel grounded in his promise is something established to endure, lasting for ever. Accordingly, the promise which is introduced by להיות לך לאלהים is not something which comes out of the tradition, but the promise corresponding to the "covenant formula," which from the very beginning is directed to the people of Israel. It occurs in Gen. 17:7,8; Ex. 29:45; Lev. 11:45; 22:33; 25:38; 26:45; and Num. 15:41. It is significant that P does not take up the covenant formula with its two parts which was obviously familiar to him ("and you shall be my people"; cf. R. Smend, ThSt 68 [1963] 5f., 28). P expresses clearly in the structure of the chapter that the relationship to God is that of mutual interchange (cf. vv. 9-14 between vv. 3b-8 and vv. 15-23); but the setting up of the covenant is wholly God's action, and this is expressed by the one-way sentence, "I will be your God." In this promise P embraces everything that he has so far said about God's actions and words, not only what is to begin with the institution of the covenant. He will be Israel's God: this embraces the action of the creator, the action of the God who saves, who directs the history of his people, the action of the holy God who acts from the midst of the sanctuary in his כבוד and with his blessing, the action of the God who instructs, who commands and it happens. Ch. 17 is one of the focal points of the priestly work, and v. 7 is its center.

[17:8]   The promise of the land (v. 8a) is enclosed within the promise of the divine presence (vv. 7b,8b). It is not really necessary in the close arrangement of vv. 3b-8 and it would not be surprising if it were missing. It occurs only in this verse. P shows here by the technique in composition that he gives the promise of increase precedence over the promise of the land. The latter could be missing, the former not at all (it is quite different in Deuteronomy). But P does not dispense with the promise of the land; P received it from the tradition and holds on to it but only, one might say, enclosed within the promise of the divine presence. Israel lives only from the action of her God; but God's action in history allows both for the gift of the land and expulsion from it. The promise of the land remains in force—even now; but it does not mean any claim to the land. The only thing that is of vital importance is that God stand by the people, even if it is a people expelled

from the land: "I will be your God." This is the way P spoke to the people of his
age while unfolding God's promise to Abraham.

On the formula נתתי לך, cf. comm. on 15:18; it does not really mean a
promise, but the handing over. The addition "and to your descendants" makes it
clear that he has in mind the land handed over to the people of Israel. P can use as a
conclusion the strongly worded formula "as an eternal possession" because it is
enclosed by the promise of the divine presence. It is only with this explanation that
the description used by P, "the land where you are now aliens," ארץ מגריך, becomes clear; it occurs again in Gen. 28:4; 36:7; 37:1; 47:9; and Ex. 6:4. P's intention is not merely to indicate the contrast between the period when Abraham wandered as an alien in Canaan and the period when Israel lived there as in the land
promised and granted to her; P is speaking at the same time to his own contemporaries to remind them that it is always possible for Israel to be an alien (cf. J. Van
Seters, *Abraham in History. . .* [1975] 16f.).

[17:9-14]   The command of circumcision is divided into the command (vv.
9-13) and the appropriate punishment for rejecting it (v. 14; as in 2:16-17). V. 9a
introduces the second part of God's speech. The command of circumcision in vv.
9b-10b comes to be designated as the confirmation of the covenant; it is this that
binds together vv. 9-14 and vv. 3b-8, especially v. 7. Detailed instructions accompany the command in vv. 11a, 12, 13 together with the explanation of circumcision as the sign of the covenant. The closing verse, v. 13b, underlines this yet
again.

One can synthesize the division as follows: vv. 9-14 consist of the command of circumcision (vv. 10b-11a) and the detailed instructions (vv.
12ab,13a,14a). Everything else in vv. 9-14 brings together the command to
circumcize and the ברית (vv. 9, 10a, 11b, 13b, 14b). Thus:

		9 And God spoke to Abraham: Now you, you are to keep my covenant, you and your descendants, generation to generation.
		10a This is my covenant between me and you and your descendants that you shall keep.
10b	Every male among you is to be circumcised.	
11	You shall circumcise the flesh of your foreskin	
		and this shall be the sign of the covenant between me and you.
12	At the age of eight days every male among you shall be circumcised, generation after generation; also those born in your house and any stranger bought with your money, who is not of your blood.	

263

13   Circumcise those born
in your house and
those bought with
your money.

                                    And so my covenant shall
be on your flesh as an
eternal covenant.

14   An uncircumcised male,
everyone who has not
had the flesh of his
foreskin circumcised,
his life shall be cut
off from his kin.

                                    He has broken my covenant.

      The surprising outcome of this juxtaposition is that vv. 10b, 11a, 12-13, 14a form a coherent, self-contained unit; they are not a command to circumcise, but a legal prescription about circumcision: the prescription that every male is to be circumcised (vv. 10a, 11a), detailed instructions about the time of circumcision (v. 12a), and the group for which this prescription holds (vv. 12b,13a). Then there is the punishment for rejecting it (v. 14a). This is clearly a legal specification making circumcision obligatory for the whole people. Those who reject it are excluded from the community. E. Kutsch had conjectured: ''An originally independent instruction about circumcision was probably at hand for vv. 10-14'' (ZThK 71 [1974] 377). This cannot be so for vv. 9-14 as a whole because of the parts which speak the language of P. But it may well be that a legal specification about circumcision was already at P's disposal. It cannot as such be part of God's speech because of the utterly impersonal legal style. The remaining sentences are additions: attached to the prescription is v. 11b, ''and this shall be the sign of the covenant between me and you''; attached to the detailed instructions is v. 13b, ''he has broken my covenant.'' Each of these additions contains the word ברית.
      Circumcision is really a rite which lies outside the cult. It is found among many peoples in very different contexts, supported by very different reasons. In Israel too circumcision originally had no connection with the worship of God, and that is the reason why there are no prescriptions about it in the older legal codes of the Old Testament. It was a rite, ethnically based, which did not need such prescriptions. But with the political collapse and the exile the situation was changed. Circumcision became a sign of belonging to the people of Yahweh, a confessional sign. It was in this period that the legal prescriptions in vv. 10b, 11a, 12-13, 14a arose; where and how they were transmitted we do not know. P's intention now is to give the prescriptions about circumcision the dignity and status of a divine oracle by inserting them into God's speech and reshaping them into a command in direct speech. By making this intimate link between circumcision and ברית, by drawing circumcision into the covenant, P at the same time extends the concept of ברית in the sense of v. 7: the covenant as a mutual interchange between God and his people resting on God's promise but preserved by the people in its adherence to his command.
      If this explanation is correct, then ch. 17 is an impressive model of the basic theological plan of the priestly writing; the divine presence means for Israel promise (and all that is included in it) and instruction. This is what the preamble says (vv. 1-3a) and this is what God's long speech says (vv. 3b-21), but in such a way that God's promise is primary and comprehensive, embracing the instruc-

tion. This accords with the structure of the priestly writing as a whole, in which the law (Ex. 25 to Num. 19) is enclosed by the promise (Gen. 9; 17; Ex. 6) and God's action towards his people which develops out of it.

Excursus

Circumcision: Circumcision was very widespread in antiquity; it is found in Asia, Africa, America, Australia, but not among the Indo-Germanic people and the Mongols. Circumcision is known among Israel's neighbors in Egypt, Canaan, and among other Semitic groups, but not in Assyria or Babylon, or among the Philistines ("the uncircumcised," 1 Sam. 17:26; 2 Sam. 1:20).

The practice is very old, as the use of stone knives shows (Ex. 4:25; Josh. 5:2f.); ethnological survey, as well as the Old Testament, shows further that circumcision everywhere goes back to the period of the clans and tribes, as indicated by the fact that it was generally the father who carried out the operation.

1. The explanations or bases of the rite are so many and varied that it is impossible to speak of its original meaning. J. Morgenstern gives a good survey (*Rites of Birth, Marriage and Death and Kindred Occasions among the Semites* [1966] 48-80); see too R. de Vaux (*Ancient Israel* [1958; Eng. 1962] 46-48; *The Early History of Israel* 1 [1971; Eng. 1978] 282); J. P. Hyatt (IDB 1, 629-631) (also Lit. above, Intro. #4, 6 "Covenant"). One can gather the most important and common reasons for circumcision under three headings: circumcision was carried out: *(a) For physical, medical, or hygienic reasons* (to preserve cleanliness, to induce fertility, to ward off illness, to facilitate sexual intercourse). *(b) For social reasons:* as an initiation rite at the transition to manhood or the marriageable state (rite of passage). It makes the young man a full member of the tribe with all rights. This is the most common and by far the most widespread explanation. It presupposes that circumcision is performed at the time of puberty, and this is very often attested (between the 6th and the 14th year). One can still discern traces of the link between circumcision and marriage in the Old Testament; in Gen. 34 it is the precondition for marriage with an Israelite girl (cf. also Ex. 4:24-26). This social function of circumcision can also be linked with a physical or religious reason. *(c) For religious reasons:* One must distinguish here an early and a late stage. At an early stage circumcision was, in many places, understood as a kind of sacrifice in which the shedding of blood was important (*pars pro toto*). It can also be thought of as an apotropaic action (Ex. 4:24-26). Many see a connection with the ancestor cult, others with the fertility cult. At a later stage the already existing rite of circumcision was subsequently given a religious meaning; this is the case in Gen. 17. It is here probably that we are to look for the instruction which fixes circumcision on the eighth day after birth; this is further hinted at by the different dates when Ishmael (17:25) and Isaac (21:4) underwent the rite.

2. Circumcision in Israel.   According to Josh. 5:2-9 the Israelites took over the rite of circumcision when they came into the land of Canaan (Gen. 34 too accords with this and in a certain measure also Gen. 17), together with many changes in life-style in the transition to sedentary life. As the rite was prevalent throughout Canaan, it is not necessary to assume that it was taken over from Egypt (where it is many times attested) or from the Midianites, which is scarcely demonstrable. According to Jer. 9:24f., the Egyptians, Edomites, Ammonites, and Moabites were circumcised at that time. This holds too for the pre-Islamic Arabs. Israel did not differ by and large from her Semitic neighbors in the practice of circumcision. When she took it over, it can have had no specifically religious significance. And so there are no instructions about circumcision in the old legal codes; it is mentioned only once, and that as an aside, in Lev. 12:3. The situation changed only with the end of the states of Judah and Israel; only then did circumcision become a sign of belonging to the people of Israel and so to the people of Yahweh (the Babylonians did not practice circumcision then). So it became a "sign of the covenant" and thereby acquired a religious meaning; it is just this that Gen. 17 reflects. On the significance of circumcision during Judaism's later struggles and the early period of the Christian church, see J. P. Hyatt (IDB 1, 629-631).

[17:9,10a]   Vv. 9,10a belong to the P expansion of the covenant prescriptions, and so ברית cannot have a meaning completely different from that in the preceding verses (E. Kutsch); rather, the extended meaning given to "covenant" in v. 7 makes it possible for God to command only the keeping of the covenant. There are echoes there of the late meaning of ברית = "command" or "law"; but P means the mutual interchange of the covenant relationship which was established in v. 7, "between me and you," as v. 10a expressly says. It is this covenant established by God that Israel is ordered to keep in carrying out the command.

[17:10b]   לכם is an addition to the P expansion; it softens the transition from the personal address in vv. 9-10a to the impersonal legal style in vv. 10bff; likewise in v. 11a, the form of address.

[17:11a]   On "foreskin" (ערלה) see B. Jacob, ad.loc.

[17:11b]   The sign of the covenant (P expansion). It has here a different meaning from that in Gen. 9:12-17 (*Genesis 1–11*, comm. ad loc.). In Gen. 9 it is a sign fixed by God in the realm of his creation which, because it cannot be manipulated, stands on its own as the sign of the continuation of God's promise. In ch. 17, on the other hand, circumcision is a sign of a mutual event between God and his people whereby the people is required, in carrying out the command to circumcise from generation to generation, to institute a sign that they belong to their God. This is the basis for understanding circumcision as a confessional sign. The correspondence with Gen. 9:12-17, and what is new with regard to it, is deliberate, showing the carefully thought out structure of the priestly work.

[17:12a]   On the time when circumcision is to be performed, cf. Excursus above; the number eight is a lucky number (cf. F. Heiler, *Erscheinungsformen und Wesen der Religionen* [1961] 168).

[17:12b]   The distinction between those born in the house and those bought as slaves does not come from the period of Abraham, but from a later period when this difference had become important. The extension of the prescription to circumcise to the household can only mean that for P the whole household is a cultic unity, and that the circle of worshippers of Yahweh is expanded by the slaves beyond the members of the Israelite people. This shows a certain openness, conditioned by the strong bond of family unity, which includes the slaves. At the same time the significance of circumcision undergoes adaptation and it becomes explicitly religious. This is to meet a concern that the slaves can take part in family worship.

[17:13]   This verse is but a word for word repetition of v. 12b; it is difficult to understand it correctly; it does not even serve to emphasize. Perhaps the reason for it lies in the working together of the prescriptions with the P expansion.

[17:14a]   ". . .This verse is preserved wholly in the form of a sacral law" (W. Thiel, VT 20 [1970] 138). The background of this penalty is the danger that threatened the Jewish community after the collapse of the state of Israel. Earlier, when circumcision was only a rite, such a penalty could not exist because the rite was not in danger. It becomes necessary when circumcision becomes the sign of belonging to the Jewish community. The punishment fits this—exclusion from the community (on this phrase, cf. K. Koch, EvTh 26 [1966] 231).

[17:14b]   P's final addition is extremely significant: rejection of the sign of the covenant means breach of the covenant.

[17:15-21]   The second part of the promise speech adds the promise of a son immediately to the promise of increase; at the same time Sarah, who also receives a new name, is brought into the promise. This provokes the reaction of doubt on Abraham's part (vv. 17-18), which is joined with his prayer for Ishmael (v. 18). God's response (vv. 19-21) continues the promise (vv. 15-16) and confirms it (vv. 19aβ). The promise continues on in Isaac (vv. 19b-21) and in Ishmael, but in different ways. And so God's speech is ended (v. 22).
    This second part bears on it the deep impress of the tradition at hand to the priestly writer, particularly Gen. 18:1-16. This is evident especially in the way in which God's speech is interrupted in vv. 17-18; the intention is not so much to conduct a dialog as to serve to accentuate God's speech. P takes up the ancient Abraham narrative in all its details, but also modifies it where it seems necessary for what he wants to say to his generation.

[17:15a]   This too is directed to Abraham who also receives the promise destined for Sarah.

[17:15b]   The change of name from Sarai to Sarah is briefly expedited; no particular reason is given. It is probably presupposed that the meaning of the name, "princess," speaks clearly enough (P. Joüon, "Trois noms de personnages bibliques. . .," Bib 19 [1938] 280-285). The change has the same meaning as for Abraham. Sarah is brought into the promise, thus preparing the way for the special place of Isaac over against Ishmael. It is a question of the lawful wife and mother who, with the new significance of the family after the political collapse of 587 B.C., also acquires a new significance.

[17:16]   The verb ברך occurs here for the first time in ch. 17; vv. 16a and 16b begin, "I will bless her"; v. 16a introduces the promise of a son, v. 16b that of increase. Thereby are expressed both the close association of the two as well as what is special to each. But in v. 16a there are echoes of ch. 18, which is colored by the promise of a son. One can discern in 17:15-16 the process of assimilation of the two promises in which, however, the promise of a son is somewhat adapted. In the old narrative of Gen. 18 the promise means salvation before death without children; here it is subordinated to the promise of posterity and separates the posterity of Sarah from the other children of Abraham. The notion that God's blessing issues in increase occurs again, above all in Deuteronomy: "I will bless you and give you increase. . .," e.g., Deut. 7:13. Blessing and increase go together (cf. A. Murtonen, VT 9 [1959] 158-177; G. Wehmeier, *Der Segen im A.T.. . .* [diss. Basel, 1970] 70-96). However, v. 16a, "I will bless her," is meant simply in the sense that she is to have a child.
    The promise speech is interrupted by a reaction of doubt on Abraham's part, a most unusual intermezzo for P. Abraham falls down—but he laughs (v. 17a). He doubts that two people who are so old can have a child (v. 17b). But the falling to the ground which, despite the doubt, signifies reverent acceptance, finds expression in the petition in v. 18 on behalf of Ishmael.

[17:17a]   The gesture of reverence is Abraham's first and, in any case, required reaction. But then he laughs. This is very striking, particularly when seen against 18:10-15 which P presupposes here. There it is Sarah who laughs, and it is a man—one of the three men—a guest of Abraham, who speaks to her, not God himself. Sarah's laughter at the singular announcement is understandable. But Abraham's laughter in 17:17a has something of the bizarre about it in immediate confrontation with God who is making a marvelous promise to him. But that is precisely P's intention; this is shown in v. 19 when God, in responding, does not pursue it. God has promised to act; he continues along his majestic way, which is "above all understanding," beyond Abraham's laughter and doubt. The name of the son, which is a play on Abraham's laughter, will attest this marvelous action of God.

[17:17b]   It is significant that the expression of doubt which thinks of bodily functions in the older tradition (Gen. 18:11) consists correctly but abstractly in P in giving the ages. This is a small but certain proof that Gen. 17(P) must be considerably later than Gen. 18(J). Over and against the genealogical note in 11:30 that Sarah was barren, the information about the very advanced age of the couple is an intensification, following the tendency to intensify miracles in the course of tradition history.

[17:18]   Whereas Abraham was thinking only of himself in v. 17, here he speaks in that same humble attitude expressed in the gesture of v. 17a. But that does not alter the fact that the prayer he utters for Ishmael implies that he does not believe the promise of a son to Sarah. Abraham is expected to follow God's instruction, to be obedient. It is to this that the chapter gives clear expression: faith is not always required in the same measure. P wants to emphasize that God fulfills his promise without being bound to Abraham's faith; what God has promised he does, independently of human attitudes. Abraham, therefore, is not the father in faith for P as he is in Gen. 15:1-6. The figure of Abraham then could have been regarded differently early in its subsequent history.

Abraham's prayer for Ishmael is the expression of fatherly acquiescence in the one son given him by the secondary wife. But P will say more: Abraham can not yet comprehend the extent of the promise: the covenant granted him "between me and you" means the history of the people of God in which the blood line of the first couple is bound with the promise, "I will be your God."

[17:19-21]   God's response has four parts: (1) the promise of a son from Sarah is repeated and extended with the specification of his name (v. 19a); (2) the confirmation and continuation of God's covenant with Abraham are promised to Isaac; (3) Abraham's prayer for Ishmael is to be fulfilled; he receives a promise of blessing, increase, and future greatness; (4) the promise to Isaac is repeated once more, and the time of his birth is announced (v. 21). The division of the response shows that the emphasis lies on the promise destined for Isaac, which is distinguished clearly from that to Ishmael.

[17:19a]   When the promise of a son to Sarah is repeated, a slight qualification is added, אבל, "No" (see KBL). Nothing further is necessary. The specification of the child's name belongs to the very ancient narrative pattern of the promise of a child (see above on Gen. 16:11-12 for parallels). This element is missing in Gen. 18:10-15, whence one concludes that P was familiar with such stories from

268

sources other than Gen. 18. One should note the author's sensitivity in giving no express explanation of the name. He could scarcely connect it directly with Abraham's laughter in v. 17a. Its indirect significance has been explained in the commentary on v. 17.

Excursus

The name Isaac. J. J. Stamm has synthesized the literature (Fests. A. Schädelin [1950] 33-38). Three types or groups of meaning are to be distinguished: (1) An abbreviation of a theophoric name יצחק־אל; according to Stamm this is most probable, "since the Ras Shamra texts have made known to us the laughter of El as a sign of joy and prosperity" (cf. the title of the book by Olav Duun, *Gott Lächelt* [1939]). (2) The name can be explained from the circumstances of the birth: so E. A. Speiser: "X [the father] rejoiced over, smiled on [the child]." This too has a parallel which Speiser quotes: "A Hurro-Hittite tale describes the father (Appu) as placing his newborn son on his knees and rejoicing over him (ZA 49, 220, line 5). Such acts were often the basis for naming the child accordingly" (comm. on Gen. 17:17). One might also think of it as an exclamation in reaction to the child's first laugh: "He is laughing!" (3) The third group covers the four meanings in the narratives of the promise of the birth (Gen. 17:17 and 18:9-15), and at the birth itself (Gen. 21:6a,6b). Explanations (1) and (2) are independent of any narrative and belong in Gen. 17; but chs. 18 and 21 are narratives and the explanation is not to be detached from them. The possibilities then are manifold. In Gen. 17 and 18 the meaning of the name is most intimately connected with the promise of the son; the incredulous laughter indicates unbelief in this promise. In Gen. 21 the name is in the context of the birth; once it is "grateful, joyful laughter" (J. J. Stamm) of the mother at the gift of a son, and once it is the laughter of those who hear of the birth of a son to one so advanced in years.

　　One should note a further difference between these explanations of the name and those of groups (1) and (2). Only explanations (1) and (2) really explain the name, namely, the verb form of the third pers. sing., "he laughs" (whether El, the father, or the child). The four explanations in Gen. 17; 18; 21, however, presuppose only association with laughter; none of them is a direct explanation of the name.

　　What is the outcome of all this? The name יצחק (for which there is no extrabiblical attestation) can just as well have been a theophonic name in abbreviated form: "El smiles," or a name coming from a situation: "He laughs" (the father or the child). Both are indeed possible side by side. On the other hand the "explanations" (Gen. 17; 18; 21) arose only in the context of the narratives; they are really plays on the name יצחק, not explanations, and it is precisely for this reason that they can be different. If we recognize them as puns, each of which arises out of four different narrative situations, then they are a very telling example of the freedom and richness of narrative variants of the same structural type in the oral stage of tradition.

[17:19b] V. 19b takes up v. 7 almost word for word, but with one important difference; the phrase, "between me and you," is missing; in v. 7 this describes the institution of the ברית as something that from that moment persists between God and Abraham. The institution of the covenant took place once only, and that with Abraham. This covenant continues on in Isaac, so that the הקמתי has here more the sense of an act of confirmation.

[17:20] God will also hear Abraham's prayer on behalf of Ishmael (more exactly, his request in the form of a wish). God will bless and increase him; once more the promise of blessing is unfolded in the promise of increase as in v. 16a; here פרה and רבה stand together as in Gen. 1:28. The increase will be "in plenty," just as with Abraham in vv. 2b and 6a; it is likewise promised him that he will become a great nation—a non-Israelite nation, which at times will be Israel's enemy. The reference to history becomes even clearer when the motif "nations and kings" does not appear and mention is made of twelve princes who will be among his descendants. This looks forward to the genealogy in 25:12-18 where these twelve are mentioned in v. 16. With the naming of a number in connection with נָשִׂיא, the promise about Ishmael comes close to the tribal sayings; P probably wants to play on this, and the designation נָשִׂיא is appropriate: "It is the name which is given to the chiefs of the tribes" (R. de Vaux, *Ancient Israel* [1958; Eng. 1962]; see also E. A. Speiser, CBQ 25 [1963] 111-117.)

The promise concerning Ishmael means that the effect of God's blessing extends beyond Israel to other nations as well. That universal trait which appeared in Gen. 1 and 10 continues here. Even though the covenant is carried on only in Isaac, that does not mean that God no longer acts in regard to nations outside Israel; he blesses, increases, and grants greatness to them too. Abraham then is father, not only the father of the people of Israel, but father in a broader sense, so that Ishmael, the tribal ancestor of the Ishmaelite people, remains Abraham's son with not the least diminution. We have here a truly wide-sweeping historical outlook: the God of Israel has to do not only with Israel, but also with other nations; God's blessing is not confined to the borders of Israel (for details, cf. W. Brueggemann, ZAW 84 [1972] 397-414).

[17:21]   The first sentence of v. 21 repeats v. 19b, only more briefly, with a relative sentence taking up v. 19a. This repetition shows again the art of the composition. So God's speech, which has begun with his covenant with Abraham, ends with the covenant going on in Isaac, Abraham's son. The relative sentence (v. 21b) which now follows does not, however, present a genealogical conclusion but replaces it by indicating indirectly the year of Isaac's birth; it agrees almost word for word with Gen. 18:10 and 14. There it gives the sign linked with the announcement, a common motif; here, detached from this function, it is simply information about Isaac's birth. The concluding clause is so close to a report of the birth as to render this no longer necessary. D. Daube writes: "Where a child is promised. . . the birth seems always to take place a year after the promise: Genesis XVII 21; XVIII 10, 14; I Samuel I 20; II Kings IV 16f" (*Studies in Biblical Law* [1947] 148).

[17:22]   God's promise speech was so long that it was necessary to note expressly that it had ended. God now withdraws, balancing his appearance in v. 1. K. Koch writes: "Yahweh's going up on the occasion of a theophany is often expressed by the root עלה (Ps. 47:6; 68:19; Gen. 17:22; 35:13; cf. Judg. 13:20)," (ZAW 86 [1974] 526; cf. A. Schmitt, *Forschung zur Bibel* 10 [1973]).

[17:23-27]   This is an account of the execution of the command. It is encompassed in one sentence: Abraham did (v. 23a) what God had commanded him (last sentence of v. 23). Even though the first sentence is expanded by a wealth of detail, what is essential is said in the first and last parts. The execution of what was commanded is again reported by two verbs: Abraham "took" and "circumcised" (v. 23). This would have sufficed for the report, with the addition of the information in v. 26. Abraham had himself circumcised also.

[17:23a]   The first expansion explains exactly who must be circumcised. Besides Ishmael, the two groups of slaves are mentioned (see v. 12) and this is repeated yet again in v. 27. In other words, ''all males''; this is said a third and fourth time in v. 27. This repetition is not a narrative device, but juristic precision; it concerns the exact carrying out of the instruction.

[17:23b] The second part, ''and he circumcised,'' is also given further precision on juristic grounds: ''on the flesh of their foreskin'' (repeated in vv. 24 and 25), and expanded with specification of the date; it took place on the day that God had commanded it. Abraham obeyed the command without delay.

[17:24, 25] Following P's own way of precise dating, this day must be put into perspective. It was Abraham's 99th year, as had been said in v. 1; this detail serves the genealogical framework of the chapter. Ishmael's age of course is also given: ''Ishmael his son was thirteen years old. . ..''

[17:26, 27] There is here the further information that Abraham himself was circumcised; apart from this, the closing sentence contains only repetitions (a sort of drawing together).

Purpose and Thrust

Ch. 17 forms the center of the patriarchal story in the priestly writing. It is preceded only by Gen. 11:27, 31, 32; 12:4b-5; 13:6, 11b, 12; 16:1a, 3, 15-16. These verses contain genealogical and itinerary information; events are only indicated. The first detailed event of the priestly patriarchal story is ch. 16. Apart from genealogical and itinerary information, only two other events are described in detail: the purchase of the burial plot in ch. 23 and the marriage of the sons of Isaac in chs. 27-28. We can discern in the P text as we have it a plan which gives the patriarchal story, brief though its presentation is, a necessary place and meaning in the P literary work as a whole. P correctly understands the patriarchal story as family history; in the heavily stylized and reduced form that he gives it, he sees in it the foundation of the three precultic rites or customs which assure, in his understanding, the permanence of the family: circumcision, marriage within the confines of one's own people (clan), and burial in one's own land.

Such a function of the patriarchal story is fully comprehensible in the priestly work as a whole, the center of which is the law given on Sinai which binds the people of Israel. Just as the story of the patriarchal families precedes the story of the people, so the basic prescriptions for the family which have grown out of their history precedes the law that binds the people. At the time when the priestly writing took shape, the family once more had a vital function in the continuation of Israel; P therefore deemed it necessary to anchor these basic family prescriptions in the patriarchal story.

It is only from this overall perspective that the meaning and purpose of ch. 17 emerges: it aims to anchor in the family the promise to the fathers, which in fact holds for Israel, by joining it to the command of circumcision, and thereby to base the continued perseverance of Israel after the collapse of the state solely on the promise of God which remains effective even after the defection of Israel in its history as a people and God's judgment upon it. Yahweh will continue to be Israel's God as he promised Abraham before the law was given. The covenant, which God concluded with Abraham, requires on the part of Abraham and his descendants only steadfastness to Yahweh, adherence to their God; the external expression of this is the command of circumcision.

Abraham and the Three Guests

Literature

Genesis 18–19: E. I. Fripp, "Note on Genesis XVIII.XIX," ZAW 12 (1892) 23-29. R. Kraetzschmar, "Der Mythus von Sodoms Ende," ZAW 17 (1897) 81-92. E. Gillischewski, "Zur Literarkritik von Gen 18 und 19," ZAW 41 (1923) 76-83. P. Humbert, "Die neuere Genesis-Forschung," ThR 6 (1934) 207-228. J. P. Harland, "Sodom and Gomorrah," BA 5 (1942) 17-42; BA 6 (1943) 41-54. M. L. Henry, "Das mythische Wort als religiöse Aussage im AT," Fests. D. Müller (1961) 21-31. N. M. Sarna, *Understanding Genesis* (1966; 1972²) 137-151. I. M. Greverus, "Thema, Typus und Motiv. Zur Determination in der Erzählforschung," *Vergleichende Sprachforschung*, ed. L. Petzold (1969) 390-401. I. Lajos, "(Über Gen 18–19)," *Református Szemle* 62 (1969) 83-92.

Genesis 18:1-16a: J. R. Harris, *The Cult of the Heavenly Twins* (1906). R. H. Pfeiffer, "A Non-Israelite Source of the Book of Genesis," ZAW 48 (1930) 66-73. S. N. Kramer, *Sumerian Mythology. A Study of Spiritual Literary Achievement in the Third Millennium B.C.* (1944) esp. 59-62. J. Obermann, *Ugaritic Mythology. A Study of Its Leading Motifs* (1948) esp. 7-8, 27-28. M. Allard, "L'annonce à Marie et les annonces de naissances miraculeuses de l'Ancien Testament," NRTh 88 (1956) 730-733. D. R. Ap-Thomas, "Notes on Some Terms Relating to Prayer," VT 6 (1956) 225-241. W. Baumgartner, *Zum AT und seiner Umwelt* (1959) esp. 154f. W. Herrmann, "Götterspeise und Göttertrank in Ugarit und Israel," ZAW 72 (1960) 205-216. H. Rusche, "Gastfreundschaft. Ein biblischer Grundbegriff," BiLe 6 (1965) 221-223. L. Thunberg, "Early Christian Interpretations of the Three Angels in Gen 18," StPatr 7 (1966) 560-570 = TU 92 (1966). A. Sisti, "L'ospitalità nella prassi e nell'insegnamento della Bibbia," SBFLA 17 (1967) 303-334. A. Jirku, "Zweier-Gottheit und Dreier-Gottheit im altorientalischen Palästina-Syrien," *Mélanges de l'Université Saint-Joseph* 45 (1969) 399-404. V. Hirth, "Gottes Boten im Alten Testament. Die alttestamentliche Mal'ak-Vorstellung unter besonderer Berücksichtigung des Mal'ak-Jahwe-Problems," ThA 32 (1975). B. Vawter, *On Genesis* (1976).

Genesis 18:3: G. F. Moore, *Judaism* I (1950) 535-545. S. Schlechter, *Aspects of Rabbinic Theology* (1961) 170-198. I. Willi-Plein, "חן. Ein Übersetzungsproblem. Gedanken zu Sach XII 10," VT 23 (1973) 90-99.

Genesis 18:9-16a: A. Aarne and S. Thompson, *The Types of the Folk-Tale* (1928) esp. 750-751. E. Peterson, "Le rire de Sara (Gen 18,12)," *Rhythmus du Monde* 4 (1947). D. W. Thomas, "Some Observations on the Hebrew Root חדל," VT.S 4 (1957) 8-16. O. Loretz, "k't hyh—'wie jetzt ums Jahr' Gen 18,10," Bib 43 (1962) 75-78. R. Yaron, "ka'eth hayyah and koh lehay (Gen 18,10.14; II Kg 4,16-17)," VT 12 (1962) 500-501. A.

A. MacIntosh, "A Third Root עדה in Biblical Hebrew?" VT 24 (1974) 454-473. J. H. Otwell, *And Sarah Laughed: The Status of Women in the Old Testament* (1977).

Text

18:1 Now Yahweh[a] appeared to him by the terebinth[b] of Mamre while he was sitting[c] at the entrance of his tent in the heat of the day.[d]

2 He raised his eyes and looked about[a] and behold, there were three men[b] standing before him. When he saw[c] them, he ran from the entrance of his tent to meet them, and bowed low towards the ground.

3 He said: Sir,[a] if I[b] have found favor in your eyes, please[c] do not pass your servant by.

4 Let a little water be brought to wash your feet, and rest under the tree.

5 Let me bring a little food to refresh you,[a] then[b] you can go on, for why else[c] has your journey brought you your servant's way? And they said: Do just as you say.

6 Then Abraham hurried to the tent[a] to Sarah and said: quickly, take three measures of finest flour,[b] knead it and make some cakes.

7 Then Abraham ran to the cattle, took a nice tender calf and gave it to the[a] servant who made haste to prepare[b] it.

8 Then he took curds and milk and the calf which he had prepared, and set it[a] before them; he waited on them[b] himself under the tree while they ate.

9 Then they[a] asked him: Where is Sarah your wife? He replied: Inside the tent.[b]

10 Then he said: I will certainly come back to you this time next year.[a] Sarah then will have[b] a son. But Sarah was listening at the entrance of the tent which was behind him.[c]

11 Now Abraham and Sarah were old, advanced in years,[a] and Sarah no longer experienced the cycle of women.[b]

12 Sarah laughed to herself and said: Now that I am used up, shall I have [sexual] pleasure?[a]—and my husband is old.[b]

13 Then Yahweh said to Abraham: Why[a] did Sarah[b] laugh and say: Am I really[c] to bear a child now that I am old?

14 Is anything too difficult for Yahweh?[a] In due time[a] I will come back to you, this time next year,[b] and Sarah will have a son.

15 But Sarah lied when she said: I did not laugh,[a] because she was afraid. But he said: No,[b] you did laugh.

16a Then the men rose up and left.

1a Gk has ὁ θεὸς; Vg. *Dominus.* **b** Read sing. with Gk and Syr (as in Gen. 12:6). **c** See Ges-K §116o, 141e; BrSynt §139b. **d** BrSynt §109b.
2a On asyndetic narratives, L. Koehler, VT 3 (1953); on הנה, F. I. Andersen, *The Sentence in Biblical Hebrew* (1975) "surprise clauses." **b** איש as Gen. 32:35; Judg. 13:10f. **c** The doubled "then he saw" is a resumption.
3a Read אדֹנָי for אֲדֹנָי, cf. Gen. 19:2. **b** Usual emphasizing of אם; cf. BrSynt §164b. **c** Bergsträsser II 10g: "a mitigated form of request by נא as Gen. 18:4."
5a לבכם elsewhere only Ps. 48:14; Is. 66:14 (H. Holzinger). **b** Some of the versions have ואחר. **c** On כי־על־כן, Ges-K §158b,n.1; R. Meyer III p. 106.
6a Accus. with ending ה, Ges-K §90c,i. **b** Missing in Gk.
7a For the article, Ges-K §126r. **b** Bergsträsser II 11n; E. König 399 p.
8a ויתן without object, Ges-K §117f; R. J. Williams, *Hebrew Syntax* (1967) 178; Bergsträsser II 60. **b** BrSynt §139b, "syndetic circumstantial clause."
9a Gk sing. **b** Ges-K §147b ". . .the simple הנה takes the place of the subject and copula" (cf. Gen. 42:28).

10a Ges-K §118u.   **b** Gk and Syr may have read היה.   **c** Gk fem.; B. Jacob; "The entrance to the tent was behind him"; cf. F. I. Andersen (1975) 87.
11a Ges-K §116d; R. Meyer III 67; E. König 237a.   **b** = כארח נשים; cf. Gen. 31:35.
12a Gk has a variant text. On the sentence, Ges-K §150a. The היתה unreal, (Ges-K §106n and p).   **b** Nominal sentence with adjectival predicate, Ges-K §141e.
13a זה used to emphasize interrogative words, Ges-K §136c. **b** Gk adds ἐν ἑαυτῇ.   **c** F. I. Andersen (1975) 166: "אף as emphasizer"; cf. Gen. 20:12.
14a Gk παρὰ τοῦ θεοῦ. **b** הנה probably to be added.   **c** Cf. note on v. 10; perhaps כעת היה is a gloss here.
15a On the perf., Ges-K §106b.   **b** לא can take the place of the "no"; E. König 352f, 372e; Ges-K §163a; R. J. Williams (1967) 398.

Form

Gen. 18:1-16a, in its present context, is part of a larger narrative complex which covers chs. 18 and 19. It was originally a self-contained narrative consisting of the introduction, the visit of the three men to Abraham (vv. 1-8), and the promise of a son (vv. 9-16a). The goal of the narrative is the announcement of the child (v. 10a), repeated more strongly in vv. 13-14; this meets with Sarah's laughter in vv. 10b-12, which she denies because she is afraid (v. 15a). It is not really a narrative in which a tension moves to a resolution; the only movement to speak of in the course of the story is that the promise of the son encounters not gratitude and joy, but scepticism and doubt. There are in addition two further peculiarities. The introduction is so detailed and carries such weight in itself as to be determinative of the narrative; hence the title that is frequently given it, "the visit of the three men to Abraham." The reader experiences it as an essential part of the story. A further deviation from the simple narrative form is that the point of departure, namely, the childless couple, does not form the exposition at the beginning, but is brought in later by way of parenthesis in v. 11. In addition, the natural goal, the birth and naming of the child, is reported only later (21:1-7). And the promised return of the men is missing. The explanation of these peculiarities is that in Gen. 18:1-16a two narratives have overlapped and been fused into one: *(a)* the promise of a child to a childless couple (or a childless wife), and *(b)* the visit of a divine messenger(s) or a god(s) who rewards the reception and hospitality with a gift, in this case the birth of a child. The structure of *(a)* is: childlessness as an affliction—announcement of the birth of a child as salvation. This structure is presupposed in Gen. 15:2-4; 16 (also 1 Sam. 1), and the Ugaritic parallel, Keret/I K 1-58. Narrative *(b)* is structured thus: visit of the god (messenger)—reception and hospitality—promise of the child (as gift of the guest). The moment of tension is there in that the strangers (or sing.) who as human beings ask to be received as guests, reveal themselves as divine or as coming from God in the course of the visit or on the coming to pass of what was promised.

This overlapping explains why the point of departure of the narrative is brought in only in v. 11, while the visit and the hospitality form the introduction. Moreover, the reason why the birth of the child is not narrated is that in the overall narrative complex of chs. 18–19 its removal was required for the continuation of 18:1-16a in 18:16b-33 and 19. Gen. 18:1b-6 is the introduction not only to 18:1-16a, but to the narrative complex, chs. 18–19, as a whole, where the men play a further role. This broader context would make it easier to understand why Abraham withdraws completely into the background in vv. 9-16a, whereas he alone is the dominating figure in vv. 1b-8 and 16b-33. In an older form the promise of the child could have been directed to the woman as is the case in the majority of parallels (e.g., Judg. 13:8ff.).

The narrative as it lies before us acquires its own unique attraction from the very fact that the visit of the three men to Abraham was prefixed to the promise of the son and told in detailed, slowly moving, narrative style; the effect is that the promise becomes a gift from the mysterious strangers to whom Abraham has shown hospitality.

Setting

The origin of these two once-independent narrative variants and their joining together must be considered as two separate questions.

1. The underlying motif of the promise of a child in the distressing situation of childlessness belongs to the group of narratives about a divine messenger (cf. Excursus to ch. 16). One recognizes it when the messenger of God meets someone person to person in earthly, everyday, utterly secular life without any element of a theophany. There is no way in which one can consider the present event an appearance of God, though the majority of exegetes speak of it in this way. The narrative 18:1-16b does not belong to any of the types of divine appearance in the Old Testament. It follows from this that the title in v. 1a, ''Yahweh appeared to Abraham,'' is redactional; so H. Gunkel and others. A later orientation has smoothed over the difference between the meeting with a divine messenger and an appearance of God.

The characteristic sign of this group of narratives is that the messenger nearly always announces deliverance or the birth of a child (as deliverance from distress). A further sign is that the meeting usually begins with a greeting. Abraham's invitation and its acceptance takes the place of the greeting in 18:1-16a; another narrative motif is added here. The motif of the promise of a son belongs to the patriarchal period (see comm. on 15:2-4), so that it is possible that an older form of the narrative in 18:1-16b goes back to it.

2. The scene in vv. 1b-8 does not necessarily belong to the older form. It is likely that in the course of transmission the narrative of the promise (and birth) of a child as deliverance from distress was joined with a narrative variant in which this same promise was the gift of those whom the childless couple had received as guests (corresponding to the parallel 2 Kings 4:11-17); this is confirmed by the number three, a motif which occurs only here in the Bible, but is common in extrabiblical parallels.

F. Delitzsch had already referred to the strikingly similar parallel in Ovid (Fast. 5, 494ff.), but it was left to H. Gunkel to appreciate its value for explaining our text. He gives the original Greek narrative as follows: ''Zeus, Poseidon, and Hermes. . . are received hospitably by an old Boeotian, Hyrieus; after the meal they ask him to make a wish. As he is childless, he wishes for a son whom he receives from them in a miraculous way. . .. It is Orion'' (Komm. 200). A passage from the Odyssey shows that there were a number of similar stories in Greek mythology:

> Aye, and the gods in the guise of strangers from afar put on all manner of shapes, and visit the cities, beholding the violence and the righteousness of men [Od.XVII, 485-487: Loeb].

H. Gunkel (Komm. ad loc.), W. Baumgartner (*Zum AT und seiner Umwelt* [1959] 154-155), and T. H. Gaster (*Myth, Legend and Custom. . .*

[1969] 156-162) note that this motif is worldwide. The story of the visit of the three gods to Hyrieus is so similar to Gen. 18:1-16a that the question of its explanation imposes itself. H. Gunkel's explanation, which many have accepted, is that the narrative 18:1-16a has its origin in the pre-Yahwistic period when the three messengers were not messengers of Yahweh, but three gods, as in the Greek parallel. There are two reasons which render this explanation difficult and hence in need of modification. First, the story is conceived of as coming from the Yahwist; the question of a possible prehistory which could reach back into the patriarchal period is not raised. But if one has to do with an older form in which the motif of the promise of a son alone shapes the story, then it is just this that is independent of the Greek parallel or its predecessors. The other difficulty is that the Greek parallel comes from a later period and a different culture; the question must be raised of a possible Near Eastern prehistory. From the standpoint of the history of religions, too, the Greek narrative shows signs of being a late form in the development of the motif, because the gods take human form to visit humans in order to test them and so to reward or punish them. Sumerian mythology depicts an early stage in which Enki, for example, is portrayed as visiting the city of Ur and then going on to *Meluḥḥa* where he blesses the inhabitants and their fields and cattle (S. N. Kramer, *Sumerian Mythology* [1944] 59-62). It is not said that Enki assumes human shape; it belongs to his being a god that he visits the people or cities entrusted to him. Coming and visiting is part of the blessing. A further sign that the Greek narratives are late in form is that the hospitality is no longer taken for granted, and that reward and punishment were a necessary part of it. In Gen. 18:1-16a hospitality is still taken for granted. There is a great difference whether the promise of the child is a gift from the guest or a reward for proper behavior.

Narratives of visits by gods to men are so widespread throughout the world that we must assume a long period of development and an abundance of variants. The motif as it appears in Gen. 18:1-16a, therefore, cannot be explained directly as a parallel to the Greek narrative; it is to be traced back through its Near Eastern prehistory; no direct parallel to it has been found so far, though there are traces in Sumerian myths.

3. We can no longer, so far as I see, locate the coming together of these two motifs which once formed independent narratives. One can only conjecture that it is part of the process of the formation of the narrative complex Gen. 18–19 because the first part of 18:1-16a serves it as introduction to the whole. The union of the two variants was possible only because with the addition of the motif of the hospitable reception of the three strangers, these latter were no longer understood as gods in human form, but simply as messengers of God in the sense of מַלְאָךְ יהוה. And this explains the change from singular to plural in 18:1-16a.

Commentary

[18:1-8] *The visit:* This scene portrays in masterly fashion and detail the arrival (vv. 1b-2a), the invitation (vv. 2b-5), and the hospitality (vv. 6-8). We look into the unhurried, intimate, simple life of a small community: the tent, the tree, the old man, the old woman, the strangers. We are a long way here from the later life of the royal court with its justice at the gate and the temple.

The narrative begins with the unexpected arrival of strangers, the invitation to them and the hospitality. Enough has been said of the great importance of hospitality in the life of the nomads and bedouin as well as in the life of sedentary peoples of early cultures. The visit of a stranger could be of vital, decisive importance for the one visited. The stranger comes from another world and has a message from it. This is the starting point of a great number of narratives in which an event is set in motion by one coming from afar. It is no surprise that the motif continues into the New Testament. The admonition in Heb. 13: 2 is based on it: remember to show hospitality, ''for thereby some have entertained angels unawares.'' It is only later reflection that says they are gods in human form or heavenly beings (see also Acts 14:11; 28: 1-6). These narratives preserve the real experience that lies behind them, and this is particularly so in the present story.

[18:1a]   The chapter heading, looking at the story from a later orientation, understands it as an appearance of God, an epiphany (so H. Gunkel, G. von Rad). A similar heading, likewise theologically directed, is Gen. 22:1a. Is the localization, ''by the terebinth of Mamre,'' part of the later heading, or does it belong to the older narrative? If the former, then the narrative would not be localized; however, as v. 4a speaks of ''the tree,'' it is to be assumed that the place is already fixed in the narrative. The heading does not mention Abraham, who is first named in v. 6; this is indicative of the stage of redaction which presupposes a coherent Abraham story. V. 1a, therefore, is probably not presupposed by J, but is a later addition.

One must be clear that the heading, ''Now Yahweh appeared to him,'' which was prefixed later, alters the narrative profoundly. It has a strong power of suggestion so that one reads the subject of the next sentence differently. The subsequent theologizing has all unnoticed won the day in many interpretations.

[18:1b-2a]   Without the heading the narrative must have begun differently, perhaps ואברהם ישב (R. Kilian); the localization then will have followed on האהל. Times of the day are rarely given in the patriarchal narratives; when they are, they have a function: it is the time when the traveller turns aside in search of shade and rest. The sudden arrival of the three strangers is a sign that the visit is unexpected. Both the blazing heat and the unexpected appearance of the strangers are a masterly lead into the scene (similarly Josh. 5:13). The three remain standing in front of Abraham; ''this is the oriental equivalent of knocking'' (F. Delitzsch, ad loc.). So too in Judg. 19:15 the old man stands in the open street waiting for an invitation. The introduction speaks of three men, and so it remains throughout (v. 16a).

The haste is in deliberate contrast to the quiet beginning. It is worth noting that no one is in a hurry elsewhere in the patriarchal stories; here it is haste in the service of others: he saw. . . ran. . . bowed down. . .said. The following picture, the invitation, the acceptance, the entertainment is an element of early civilization whose proper meaning is for the most part misunderstood. We understand civilization primarily in relation to objects (products of civilization); early civilization looks to people; civilization unfolds itself in human relationships. Secondly, hospitality in modern culture is practiced by and large within a chosen circle, whereas it is available in Gen. 18 to whomever needs it. The strangers are invited (see also Lk. 24:29) because they are weary from their journey, hungry and thirsty, and need Abraham's hospitality. So Abraham is completely at their service; hence his availability, haste, and concern. This too is the context in which one is to understand Abraham's bowing down before the three men. Such a mark of honor is something quite outside our understanding of the situation. Abraham does not know who the strangers are, but he cannot and will not exclude the possibility that they are worthy of honor. One who comes as a stranger is honored because a dignity may be his without there being need of any external sign thereof.

[18:3-5] *The invitation:* Abraham's words follow on his comportment in v. 2b: he addresses one of the three men; it is only in vv. 4-5 that he goes over into the plural. One concludes with certainty from the continuation of v. 3 that the address אדני must be understood as singular (so E. A. Speiser ad loc. and others); if one reads the plural with Sam, one must change the verbs into the plural. The consonants אדני can be read as plural "my lords" (Sam), as singular "my lord," or in the form אֲדֹנָי (MT), as an address to God, which would be unique in Genesis. "My lord" is to be read with the majority of exegetes. The אֲדֹנָי of the MT is a deliberate assimilation to the heading, v. 1a (so too W. Zimmerli), and is to be understood in the same theologizing sense.

Abraham addresses one of the men because he regards him as the spokesman for the three; however, this is not a sufficient explanation for the arbitrary variation that follows, the plural in vv. 2, 4, 5, 8, 9, 16, the singular in vv. 3, 10, 13-15. H. Gunkel's solution, "One concludes that the text has been worked over," is unnecessary, as is R. Kilian's recent attempt at source division. The explanation is that two variants have become intertwined, one of which puts the emphasis on the visit of the three, the other on the promise of the child by a messenger of God.

"If I have found favor in your eyes. . . ." C. W. Clark has assembled the passages in Genesis where the expression occurs: 18:3; 19:19; 30:27; 32:6; 33:8,10,15; 34:11; 39:4; 47:25, 29; 50:4 (VT 21 [1971] 261-280), as has I. Willi-Plein who affirms: "One always finds חן in the eyes of the one of higher rank"; "חן is the basis of recourse. . ., something that makes a thing or a person be or appear worthy of regard" (VT 23 [1973] 93, 95); see also H. J. Stoebe (THAT I [1971] 587-597, article "*ḥnn*, to be gracious"). In the present passage the expression aims at giving the one invited the ground for accepting the invitation: "if it is all right with you to accept my invitation." Abraham's prostration allows the three strangers to be addressed as people of higher rank, while avoiding the "I."

[18:4-5a] The following clauses unfold the invitation; they say what the guests are to expect if they accept. "Abraham's hospitality is that of the nomad sheik who entertains an important guest. Even today the custom of nomadic life in the desert recalls the hospitality rites of the patriarchal period" (A. Clamer and L. Pirot, *La Genèse* [1953] ad loc.). Abraham makes an offer to his guests: they can wash their tired, dusty feet, rest in the shade, and receive a meal. It is presupposed that there will be an offer to wash the guests' feet, just as in Lk. 7:44; one travels on foot wearing sandals; see Gen. 19:2; 24:32; 43:24. The understatement "a little water" and then "a little bread" is but the language of politeness; it is meant to minimize the exhausting work of entertainment.

The urging to "rest under the tree" (until the meal is ready) indicates that the tree provides shade. The singular permits the assumption that the plural in v. 1 is a subsequent modification (so R. de Vaux, *Ancient Israel* [1958; Eng. 1962]). נשען "so support you, to refresh you." The offer of "refreshment," as we call it in a like situation, is underplayed. The words: "then you can go on," which occur also in Judg. 19:5, are a clear indication to the guest that he is not being asked to stay on. The following relative clause is meant to confirm the invitation.

[18:5b] The three men accept the invitation. As in v. 2, there are three; this alters nothing. The measured, reserved answer speaks for itself and is appropriate to the situation.

[18:6-8] *The entertainment:* ''A genuine bedouin meal, lavish and generous'' (A. Dillmann). This short scene is a precious example of Old Testament narrative art. It is not a case of enumerating the dishes; rather these become the center of a movement so much alive that one no longer senses any enumeration. Movement is dominant; it begins with Abraham hurrying to be of service; the wife and the servant join in, and it issues in the quiet attention of Abraham as he waits on and stands before his guests, just as they stood before him when he first looked up and saw them when he was sitting under the tree (v. 2 the same words).

[18:6] Sarah is commissioned to hurry and prepare the bread, ''small round ashen cakes baked on hot stones'' (F. Delitzsch). The word עגה occurs with the same meaning in Ex. 12:39; Num. 11:8; 1 Kings 17:13; 19:6; Ezek. 4:12; Hos. 7:8. The measure סאה is for flour and cereals; it is meant to indicate the best; it is not to be measured out exactly. קמח, ordinary flour, is in 1 Kings 5:2 distinguished from סלת, finest flour; here סלת, which is juxtaposed to קמח without any link, is probably added later for effect.

[18:7-8] Abraham himself picks out a ''nice tender calf'' and instructs the boy to kill and prepare it; everything has to be done quickly. The women prepare the bread, the men the meat. Abraham lays two sorts of milk before his guests, fresh milk חלב to quench their thirst, and sour milk חמאה to refresh them. The movement abates as Abraham sets everything before his guests and stands before them to serve them. The entertainment is like that of the divine messenger narrated in the Ugaritic Dan'el epic, 2Aq (II D) V; cf. H. Cazelles (ThQ 138 [1958] 26-39) and W. Herrmann (ZAW 72 [1960] 205-216).

[18:9-16a] It is notable that in the second part, vv. 9-16a, Abraham recedes completely into the background. In v. 9 the men inquire of him about Sarah, and in v. 13 they ask him why Sarah laughed; apart from this he is quite secondary. The promise in v. 10a is meant for Sarah; it is she who reacts to it (vv. 10b-12). The second exchange ends with a direct answer from Sarah (v. 15a), and the messenger addresses himself directly to her (v. 15b). There is an older form behind vv. 9-16a in which the promise was addressed to Sarah. This is the case in the majority of narratives of the promise of a child by a messenger of God (e.g., Judg. 13).

[18:9] The transition in v. 9 thus becomes comprehensible (H. Gunkel explains it differently). After the introduction, vv. 1-8, one expects that the men will address themselves to Abraham and that what follows will center around this group. But the inquiry after Sarah effects the transition to the following scene in which she and the messengers are the center. This is a hint that the coming of the messenger(s) begins as a rule with an inquiry (as a greeting; see comm. on 16:8).

[18:10a] The purpose of the men's visit is the promise that Sarah will have a son (on the promise of a son, cf. C. Westermann, *The Promises to the Fathers. . .* [1976; Eng. 1980]). The promise of a son runs as a leitmotif through the Abraham cycle from Gen. 11:30 through 15:2-4; 16:11; 18:10-14 to 21:1-7 (P: 17:15,16,19,21); it occurs also in Judg. 13:2-5; 1 Sam. 1:17; 2 Kings 4:8-17; Lk.

1–2; there are parallels in the Ugaritic texts of Keret and Aqhat. The detail about the time of the birth occurs word for word in 2 Kings 4:16,17, "this time next year"; this alone is a certain sign that there was a fixed narrative form. Here too it is addressed to a woman (as in 1 Sam. 1 and Judg. 13) and the one who makes the announcement is a human person, "a man of God." Such announcements proceed from human lips in other cases, be it a priest (1 Sam. 1), a man of God (2 Kings 4), or a messenger of God (Gen. 18; Judg. 13) who speaks.

J. Skinner remarks on v. 10: "The definite return to the sing. takes place here." This can now be more readily understood: whereas v. 9, plur., forms the transition from the visit of the three and is resumed in v. 16a, vv. 10-15 belong to the actual promise of the child, the other narrative variant.

B. Jacob treats the phrase כעת חיה in detail (Komm. ad loc.); there are some who contest the usual translation; R. Yaron lists the explanations given so far and then refers to the phrase in W. von Soden (*Akk. Wörterbuch* 99a), *ana balat* ("At this time, next year"), which corresponds exactly (VT 12 [1962] 500-501); O. Loretz adds that the Hittite rendering of *a-na-ba-la-at* in the enumeration of the deeds of Hattušil I (KBO X No. 1, 2, in H. Otten, MDOG 91 [1958] 75) confirms the meaning of the Akkadian and Hebrew phrases as "next year." It occurs only in Gen. 18:10,14; and 2 Kings 4:16,17 in the Old Testament, each time in the same context; this is a certain sign that the phrase, otherwise unknown, was passed on in this particular narrative of the birth of a child (it is there in Gen. 17:21, in the same context, but somewhat altered).

[18:10b]   The narrative in the form in which it lies before us moves very adroitly so as to have the promise addressed to Abraham; Sarah has to hear it because her reaction is to be narrated. The last two words mean "and it [the entrance to the tent where Sarah was standing] was behind him [the speaker]." This detail should be followed immediately by v. 12, Sarah's reaction; the context is interrupted by the parenthesis in v. 11.

[18:11]   The parenthesis interrupts and disturbs the flow of the narrative; one senses very clearly here that different elements have been brought together. The three sentences in v. 11 are circumstantial sentences and as such form a typical narrative introduction:

> Abraham and Sarah were old,
> they were advanced in years;
> Sarah no longer experienced the cycle of women.

The beginning of the action ("one day there came. . .") should follow this introduction which describes the situation. When the two narrative variants were joined together the introduction had to drop out. It is inserted here subsequently as a parenthesis to explain what follows.

There is a second modification. The motif which is the point of departure is Sarah's childlessness in Gen. 11:30; 15:2-3; 16:1, and in all passages outside Genesis. Only in Gen. 18:11 and 17:17 is there mention of the age of the childless couple; according to extrabiblical parallels this belongs to another narrative variant. The visitors come to an old man or married couple (see above, Setting). We may be dealing here with an intensification of the motif or with a variant; both can occur together as in 2 Kings 4:14: "She has no son, and her husband is old." In Gen. 18:11, as in 17:17, the advanced age provokes a reaction of laughter; this explains why in both places, which play on the name Isaac, the motif of the advanced age of the parents is chosen.

[18:12] "Then Sarah laughed. . .." It is obvious that from v. 10 on Sarah is the leading figure: Sarah was listening . . . Sarah laughed . . . Why did Sarah laugh? . . . Sarah is to have a son . . . Sarah lied. It is Sarah's reaction, not Abraham's, that is important for the narrator, although the fem. is not well suited to the name יצחק (on the name, see above, 17:19a, Excursus). Sarah's reaction presupposes that she takes the speaker for a person, a strange man; it is a quite natural reaction. Both for the narrator and the listener the incredulous laughter is yet a further recondite reference to the fulfillment. Sarah laughed to herself, בקרבה; this does not necessarily mean that her laughter could not be heard. B. Jacob comments: "Laughter is not something internal—there is no such laughter." The Hebrew verb יצחק as such describes an external expression.

What makes Sarah laugh finds expression in her words in v. 12b which make it even clearer that her reaction is only that to be expected in the circumstances. It is in fact the same reaction as in 2 Kings 4:16, even though the latter is expressed differently: "No, my lord. . .do not lie to your maidservant" (cf. also Lk. 1:34). The verb בלה, "to be worn out," is used of clothes (Josh. 9:13), of bones that have become dried up (Ps. 32:3), and, only here, of a woman (cf. J. Lévèque, *Job et Dieu* [1970] on Job 14:12). The word עדנה, sexual pleasure, occurs only here. A. A. McIntosh, following Pseudo-Jonathan, proposes the meaning "conception" (VT 24 [1974] 454-473).

[18:13-14] God's messenger rejects Sarah's laughter (v. 13) and sets over against it God's limitless power (v. 14a); he then repeats the promise from v. 10 (v. 14b).

[18:13] "Then Yahweh said to Abraham." A Dillmann explains: "By his knowledge about Sarah God has drawn aside the veil; that is why "Yahweh" is first used here." Likewise G. von Rad: "The guests betray their divine knowledge." The majority of exegetes say something similar; but the narrative itself does not allow this. Such an unveiling without any reaction from the interlocutor is excluded. Judg. 13:20 tells that Manoah and his wife "fell on their faces" in a similar situation. The text cannot intend that Sarah is aware that Yahweh is speaking with her. The explanation of the use of יהוה in this passage is that a messenger (whether of God or of man) represents the one who sends him as he delivers his message; hence the one who gives the commission can be named in place of the one commissioned (cf. Gen. 16:7a, Excursus: *The messenger of God*). The question, "Why did Sarah laugh. . .," has something of an encounter or rejection about it, almost of a rebuke. The reason for Sarah's laughter is repeated yet again, but is deliberately altered and is more reserved than in v. 12. The question is really put to Sarah; v. 15 shows clearly that she considers it addressed to herself.

[18:14] The reason for the question, "Why did. . .," or the rebuke now follows, again in the form of a question. This too is really addressed to Sarah: "Is anything too difficult for Yahweh?" The messenger of God thereby counters the expression of unbelief in Sarah's laughter. פלא is often translated here: ". . .too wonderful for Yahweh"; it is on the basis of this translation that G. von Rad puts the high point of the narrative here. But such a rendering is not suited to the simple language of the narrative. The meaning of the word is precisely that in Deut. 17:8: "When the issue in any lawsuit is beyond your competence. . ." (or Deut. 30:11). The messenger thus counters Sarah by saying that the announcement she has heard comes from God. It is here that the stranger first lets it be known that he is a messenger of God (only at the conclusion of the meeting, as in many מַלְאָךְ יהוה narratives). As such he speaks of Yahweh in the third person and repeats once more the promise of a son to Sarah.

[18:15] Sarah is now afraid because she knows that she is face to face with a messenger of God. Her fear expresses itself in her denial that she laughed. G. von Rad speaks of a "white lie," but this is a misunderstanding. Sarah's denial is rather an attempt to withdraw her laughter (B. Jacob gives a similar explanation); it is only now that she is aware of what she has done.

The messenger of God concludes his commission with his reply to Sarah's denial; he then departs. This last sentence, "No, you did laugh," is a particularly subtle touch on the part of the narrator. Sarah would much prefer to cancel her laughter; but the messenger says: no, the laughter remains a fact. He means: you are to think further on it—thus giving a recondite hint at the name of the child. There are echoes here of something added in other narratives of the promise of a child, namely, the anticipation of the naming: "you will call him. . .."

[18:16] In the present context this verse forms the transition from what precedes to what follows. If vv. 1-16 are regarded as an independent narrative, then v. 16 is its necessary conclusion; the departure of the men in v. 16 balances their arrival in v. 1. The third sentence also belongs to this context; it accords with Abraham's ready hospitality that he accompanies his guests a part of the way. The middle sentence, "and they went in the direction of Sodom," prepares what is to come and was added later when the larger narrative unit chs. 18–19 was being shaped; it joins the visit of the men to Abraham with that to Lot in Sodom.

Purpose and Thrust

The narrative of the promise of a son to Abraham and Sarah belongs to the substance of the Abraham stories which began by saying that Sarah was childless (11:30).

Abraham saw a future only in the continuation of the family in a son; this is what the messenger of God promised him. The history of the promise, which continues right through the Old Testament and links the New with the Old, is continued in a special way in the promise about the "house," the family of the king (2 Sam. 7), which assures future and continuity to the kingdom. It is taken up again at the beginning of the New Testament (Lk. 1–2); but now it is fused with the promise of salvation (Ex. 3); the promised child is the savior.

Abraham Queries
the Destruction of Sodom

Literature

Genesis 18:16b-33: I. Wood, "Folk-Tales in OT Narratives," JBL 28 (1908) 38-39. W. Staerk, *Vorsehung und Vergeltung* (1931). W. L. Knox, "Abraham and the Quest For God," HThR 28 (1935) 55-60. K. Galling, "Vom Richteramt Gottes. Eine Auslegung von Gen 18,17-33," DTh 6 (1939) 86-97. N. Johansson, *Parakletoi. Vorstellungen von Fürsprechern für die Menschen vor Gott in der alttestamentlichen Religion, im Spätjudentum und Urchristentum* (1940). D. Daube, *Studies in Biblical Law*, 1947, pp. 154-189. J. Ruwet, "Misericordia et iustitia Dei in Veteri Testamento," VD 25 (1947) 35-42. H. H. Rowley, *The Biblical Doctrine of Election* (1950; 1964³). K. Koch, "Gibt es ein Vergeltungsdogma im AT?" ZThK 52 (1955) 1-42. J. B. Bauer, "Untergang und Auferstehung von Sodom und Gomorrha," BiLi 23 (1955/56) 260-263. M. L. Henry, *Jahwist und Priesterschrift. Zwei Glaubenszeugnisse des AT*, AzTh II,3 (1960). J. Scharbert, "Die Fürbitte in der Theologie des Alten Testaments," ThGl 50 (1960) 321-338. A. Weiss, "Some Problems of the Biblical 'Doctrine of Retribution,'" Tarb. 31 (1961/62) 236-263. A. Cody, "When Is the Chosen People Called a *Gôy*?" VT 14 (1964) 1-6. J. Scharbert, *Heilmittler im AT und im Alten Orient*, Quaestiones Disputatae 23/24 (1964). J. L. Crenshaw, "Popular Questioning of the Justice of God in Ancient Israel," ZAW 82 (1970) 384-395. K. Heinen, *Das Gebet im AT. Eine exegetisch-theologische Untersuchung der hebräischen Gebetsterminologie* (1971). J. J. Scullion, "*ṣedeq-sedaqah* in Isaiah cc. 40-66 with Special Reference to the Continuity in Meaning between Second and Third Isaiah," UF 3 (1971) 335-348. F. V. Reiterer, *Gerechtigkeit als Heil:* צדק bei Deuterojesaja. Aussage und Vergleich mit der alttestamentlichen Tradition (diss. Salzburg, 1976).

Genesis 18:19: L. Dürr, "Das Erziehungswesen im AT und im antiken Orient," *Handbuch für Erziehungswissenschaft* I (1934) 33-51. J. Hempel, *Das Ethos des Alten Testaments*, BZAW 67 (1938; 1964²). E. Zolli, "Contributo alla semantica di ידע," Sef. 16 (1956) 23-31. J. Muilenburg, *The Intercession of the Covenant Mediator* (1968) 177-179, 180-181.

Genesis 18:20-21: W. R. W. Gardner, "Genesis XVIII 20.21," ET 28 (1917) 384. M. J. Mulder, *Het meisje van Sodom. De targumim op Genesis 18:20-21 tussen bijbeltekst en haggada* (1970). J. Hoftijzer, "The Nominal Clause Reconsidered," VT 23 (1973) 446-510.

Genesis 18:22-32: Z. W. Falk, "Hebrew Legal Terms," JSSt 5 (1960) 350-354. M. Cospisarow, "The Ancient Egyptian, Greek and Hebrew Concept of the Red Sea," VT 12 (1962) 1-13. P. R. Ackroyd, "Hosea and Jacob," VT 13 (1963) 245-259. W. Brueggemann, "From Dust to Kingship," ZAW 84 (1972) 1-18. O. Keel, "Erwägungen zum Sitz im Leben des vormosaischen Pascha und zur Ethymologie von פֶּסַח,'' ZAW 84 (1972) 414-434. C. S. Rodd, ''Shall Not the Judge of All the Earth Do What Is Just? (Gen 18,25),'' ET 83 (1972) 137-139. L. Schmidt, '' 'De Deo'. Studien zur Literarkritik und Theologie des Buches Jona, des Gesprächs zwischen Abraham und Jahwe in Gen 18,22ff. und von Hiob 1,'' BZAW 143 (1976) 131-164. R. Rendtorff, BZAW 147, 1976, 1977².

Text

18:16b But Abraham went with them to see them on their way. And now they were looking down on Sodom.[a]

17 Yahweh reflected: Shall I hide from Abraham[a] what am I to do?

18 Yet Abraham is to become[a] a great and powerful nation, and all the nations of the earth shall find blessing in him.[b]

19 Indeed I have chosen him out,[a] so that[b] he may charge his sons and his house after him to observe the way of Yahweh and to do what is just and right, so that Yahweh may bring upon him what he promised him.

20 And Yahweh said: Great indeed is the outcry[a] over Sodom and Gomorrah;[b] very grave indeed[c] is their[d] sin.

21 I must go down and see if what they have done accords at all[a] with the outcry[b] which has come to me;[c] and if not, I must know.

22 Thereupon the men turned and went in the direction of Sodom, but Abraham[a] remained standing before Yahweh.[a]

23 Abraham approached Yahweh and said: Will you really sweep away the just with the wicked?[a]

24 What if there are fifty just in the city? Will you really sweep them away[a] and not pardon[b] the place[a] for the sake of the fifty just who are in it?[c]

25 Far be it from you to do such a thing, to kill the just with the wicked; to treat the just as[a] the wicked; far be it from you, the judge of all the earth, not to do what is just.

26 Then Yahweh said: If I find fifty just in the city of Sodom, I will pardon the whole place for their sake.

27 Then Abraham replied: May I presume to speak to my Lord though[a] I am but dust and ashes?

28 What if there are fifty less five just?[a] will you destroy the city for want of five? And he said: I will not destroy it if I find forty-five there.

29 And Abraham spoke to him again: What if forty are found there? He said: I will not do it for the sake of forty.[a]

30 And he said: Please do not be angry my Lord if I speak again! What if thirty are found there? He said: I will not do it if I find thirty there.

31 And he said: Please, may I presume to speak to my Lord! What if twenty are found there? He said: I will not destroy it for the sake of twenty.

32 And he said: Please let it not anger my Lord if I speak yet again;[a] what if ten are found there? He said: I will not destroy it for the sake of ten.

33 When Yahweh had finished[a] talking with Abraham he went away, and Abraham returned home.

16a Gk adds καὶ Γομόρρας.

17a Gk adds τοῦ παιδός μου; Philo, τοῦ φιλοῦμου.

18a On orthography of היו Ges-K §75n, the infin. absolute frequently has ׳ for ה׳—.   **b** Perf. after imperf. (BrSynt §41f, 135d).

19a Sam TargOׄ ידעתי; Gk ᾔδειν ὅτι.   **b** Ges-K §1140, 165c: ''equivalent of a final clause.''

20a Sam reads צעקת as v. 21.   **b** H. Gunkel: ''and Gomorrah,'' assimilation to another tradition.   **c**   The כִּי is striking; some assume that בָאָה אֵלַי has fallen out, others that כִּי is corroborative, Ges-K §§148d, 159ee; F. Delitzsch. Gk and Vg pay no attention to the particle כִּי.   **d**   Pronoun of 3 pers. plur. as reference to the inhabitants, BrSynt §22d.

21a   Read כָּלָה.   **b**   Gk, TargO and others read ם.   **c**   Fem. part., Ges-K §138k; perhaps הַבָּאָה is to be read.

22a   According to Tiq Soph the succession of the subjects was originally reversed; cf. F. I. Andersen (1975) 84-85; H. Holzinger.

23a   Gk has a somewhat variant text.

24a   Gk adds αὐτοὺς after תִּסְפֶּה and πάντα after לַמָּקוֹם.   **b**   In common formulae the substantival object is sometimes omitted; (עָוֹן) תִּשָּׂא as Num. 14:19, Ges-K §117g, BrSynt §127b.   **c**   Refers logically to עִיר.

25a   On the construction, Ges-K §116c, BrSynt §126a; R. J. Williams, 1967, 256.

27a   Ges-K §141e: "The noun clause connected by *waw copulativum* to a verbal clause. . . describes a state *contemporaneous* with the principal action. . . [here] with a substantial predicate."

28a   "The numerals from 2 to 10, as being originally abstract substantives, may be connected with their substantives. . . in the absolute state before it," Ges-K §134b; BrSynt §85c.

29a   Gk and Sam read אַשְׁחִית; likewise v. 30.

32a   As Ex. 10:17; E. König 372b; R. J. Williams (1967), 388; F. I. Andersen (1975), 175.

33a   Perf. as expression for pluperfect, Bergsträsser II, 6d.

Form

The text is inserted into the sequence of 18:1-16a and ch. 19 in such a way that a scene is fitted in between the departure of the men from Abraham's tent (18:16a) and their arrival at the gate of Sodom (19:1); it allows a dialog between Yahweh and Abraham: Abraham accompanies the men to a point from which one can look down on Sodom (v. 16b), the city whose fate is the subject of the dialog. When the dialog is ended, Yahweh goes away (v. 33a) and Abraham returns home (v. 33b).

The dialog in vv. 17-32 is self-contained (so too J. Van Seters); Abraham's query (vv. 23-32) presupposes Yahweh's reflection in vv. 17-21. V. 22 seems to divide the text into two scenes; in fact it merely serves to cut out the three men so that Abraham can now converse alone with one. The conversation consists of two parts: the announcement to Abraham of the destruction of Sodom (vv. 17-21) and Abraham's objection or query (vv. 23-32).

One difficulty that arises is that there is no actual announcement of the destruction of Sodom in vv. 17-21; there is only an indication of it in v. 17 while in vv. 20-21 Yahweh decides to inquire whether the situation is such as to warrant the outcry. Because of the contradiction between vv. 17 and 21, L. Schmidt concludes that vv. 20-21 belong to a different author than vv. 17-18 (BZAW 143 [1976] 131-164; so too R. Kilian). But one may ask whether a merely literary-critical solution of the difficulty is adequate. Moreover, L. Schmidt, joining H. Gunkel, regards v. 19 as a late addition to vv. 17-18 (so too G. von Rad, W. Zimmerli, R. Kilian). Here too L. Schmidt uses only literary-critical criteria; he sees in vv. 18 and 19 two mutually exclusive reasons for v. 17; but vv. 17-19 can be explained only from the overall context of the history of the patriarchal promises.

But vv. 17-21 are rather a unit and as such a main part of the dialog of which the other main part, vv. 23-32, can only be understood together with them. The second part, vv. 23-32, is divided into Abraham's query with God's answer,

vv. 23b-26, and the continual and persistent pressing of the same question with the same answer from God in vv. 27-32.

The passage as a whole is a theological inquiry presented in the form of a dialog (so H. Gunkel, L. Schmidt, and others). L. Schmidt, however, does not command assent when he wants to reduce Gen. 18:16-33 to the theoretical treatment of a theological problem. When an inquiry is presented in dialog form in the Old Testament it is never treated in a conceptual, abstract way with the solution at the end. The process remains always a dialog and as such retains a certain suspense which is conditioned by the confrontation of the two speakers.

But H. Gunkel and L. Schmidt are correct when they say that this part did not have its origin in an experience, an event which was narrated and passed on as such, but in inquiry and reflection. Texts like this form a special group within the factitious (constructed) narratives (cf. comm. on ch. 15, "factitious narratives"). In common with such narratives (Gen. 15:1-6,7-21;17), the present text also takes a promise to Abraham as its point of departure; but it differs from them very clearly inasmuch as the promise is no longer the center of the narrative but the introduction to it. The promise forms the presupposition to the communication to Abraham of the decision to destroy and the query to which the decision gives rise, which is then unfolded in vv. 23-32; 18:16-32 arose out of this query. The next question is about the setting, origin, and tradition-history context out of which it grew.

Setting

The concern "that the just meet the same fate as the wicked," this zeal for the justice of God which mounts to ever more intense expression, leads to the question of the setting whence the text originated, its background and insertion into the Abraham story. The point of reference is three quite different groups of texts:

1. The zeal for the justice of God which does not allow "the just to be treated like the wicked" (v. 25b) has its setting in the great complex of proverbs which deal with the just and the wicked. A whole host of sayings insists again and again that the lot of the wicked must be negative, that of the just positive (so too Ps. 1). They belong to the postexilic period (contra L. Schmidt and many others). It is against the background, immediate or somewhat removed, of this great complex that one understands the zeal for the justice of God in ch. 18.

2. The concern, so clearly recognizable in ch. 18, that doubt can be cast on the justice of God, must have a recognizable background. This is clear in the book of Job where, just as in Gen. 18, the discussion turns on God's action in history, especially on his destructive action. In the powerful poem about God's destructive action in history in ch. 12, Job says that it is not true that one can discern the justice of God in his lot: "I am a laughingstock. . ., a just and blameless man," (12:4); "With him are strength and wisdom, the deceived and the deceiver are his" (12:16). Job expresses his objection against his friends in its strongest form in 9:22: ". . .Therefore I say, he destroys both the blameless and the wicked." And in ch. 21 Job alleges experience which shows that his friends are not correct with their doctrine of retribution: "How often is it that the lamp of the wicked is put out?" (21:17). This is the curtain before which the author of Gen. 18 speaks; there were at that time those in Israel who put in question a justice of God which they read in the lot of humans. This is the basis of the concern, the zeal of the present speaker.

3. L. Schmidt has pointed to the third complex. In the period from the exile on, in any case after 587, the quite general question of Yahweh's action in his-

tory, even outside Israel, is raised in a number of passages. Ezek. 14:12-20 is very close to Gen. 18 (cf. W. Zimmerli, *Ezekiel*, ad loc.): if God intends to destroy a land because of its corruption, and the three pious men Noah, Daniel, and Job are living there, they will be saved, though God carries out the destruction. Jer. 18:7-10 (Dtr) speaks in general terms of the criteria on which the destruction or preservation of a people depends. And Jonah chs. 3–4 are concerned with the destruction or preservation of Nineveh (see also Zeph. 2). The question could arise in Israel only after 587; all texts derive from this period. After Israel had ceased to be a state and had become a province of a great empire, the question of Yahweh's disposition of the history of the nations had to assume importance; a particularly urgent aspect was the question how one recognizes God's justice therein. Gen. 18 also belongs to this context and has arisen from reflection of this kind. (By way of appendix reference may also be made to the work of the Chronicler where the zeal to demonstrate the justice of God in his disposition of history appears in a different way; history is reshaped in many places in order that it may be clearly recognizable.) What makes the insertion into the Abraham story possible here is that the author of Gen. 18:17-32 regards the demise of Sodom as a good example which he can use to explain God's justice in the disposition of history. The author was thus able to make a connection with the promise to the fathers and hold up Abraham as the model of the just person of his era; Abraham, the observer of what is just and right, who charged his sons to do the same, is the exemplar of God's just disposition of history. One can also recognize in the late addition, Gen. 15:13-16, the effort to demonstrate the justice of God. The introduction there, "You must know. . .," evokes striking echoes of the introduction here, 18:17; Gen. 15:13-16 may come from about the same time as 18:16b-32.

   There is a further parallel, very distant, but which can serve to increase our understanding of ch. 18. The Gilgamesh epic, Tab. 11, reflects a later stage in tradition inasmuch as the decision to destroy is no longer unanimous. Ea's speech to Enlil expresses the disagreement of some of the gods; playing the part of the accuser he blames Enlil for having brought the flood on mankind rashly (lines 170-178). One passage is important for Gen. 18: "Lay on the sinner his sins, on the wicked his wickedness." This gives voice to a later reflection on God's judgment according to the criterion that the destruction should touch only the wicked, which corresponds more or less to Gen. 18. Here too, in a later stage of reflection, the theologian asks whether total destruction, involving both just and wicked, accords with the justice of God (cf. *Genesis 1–11*, 51-53, 400-401). I correct here the consequence which I drew there for Gen. 18 [51-53]; this too is the source of a later elaboration (Ea's speech) of the disruptive action of the gods started by a decision to destroy.

   R. C. Dentan also explains 18:23-32 as a later insertion: "It is possible that the inclusion in the completed Pentateuch of such a passage as Gen XVIII 22b-33a, concerned as it is with a theological problem rather than with historical tradition, is due to the activity of this final group of redactors" (VT 12 [1962] 50, n.3).

Commentary

[18:17-19] Yahweh's reflection in vv. 17-19 gives the reason for his communication to Abraham in vv. 20-21 which enables Abraham to say something in reply to the decision (vv. 23-32). Vv. 17-19, 20-21, 23-32 belong necessarily together; one should neither cut off vv. 17-19 (as do H. Gunkel and G. von Rad) nor interpret vv. 23-32 in isolation from what has preceded (as do most exegetes).

Yahweh's consideration is a decision to communicate to Abraham what he has in mind, dressed in the form of a question. He bases the decision on the promise that Abraham has received from him, v. 18, and the commission linked with it.

[18:17] As the word order shows, ויהוה אמר (the inversion marks a cutoff point) is a new beginning and does not form a link with what precedes, where there is nothing to give grounds for what Yahweh says or thinks; it is rather a preparation for what follows and as such a conceptual construction. In order to provide the basis for what follows, the communication to Abraham, the whole is dressed as a divine reflection. Why does God want to communicate to Abraham what he proposes to do, namely, destroy Sodom?

[18:18] Vv. 18-19 provide the answer. The fact that the promise made earlier to Abraham is used to argue the divine reflection is a sign that such a pronouncement is not part of a simple promise narrative; it shows rather that the promise to the patriarchs has become part of the traditional material which has travelled a long way and is thought through in its various theological applications. What is before us is this: the promise made long ago raises Abraham to a level of importance and honor such that he is deemed worthy to share in God's plan. This is the late stage in the history of the promises in which they serve to exalt Abraham the father (so too I. F. Wood: "to exalt a national hero"; he understands it, however, as a popular narrative motif; JBL 28 [1908] 34-41). Significant too is that it is not the promise itself that is mentioned in v. 18 but its (secondary) elaboration. It deals with the promise of increase, "I will bless you and multiply you," which is enlarged in many passages by adding, "and I will make you a great nation" (especially Gen. 17). This elaboration is in turn modified from the promise form into a statement in which "great" is further extended by "powerful": "Abraham is to become a great and powerful nation." E. A. Speiser wants to refer עצום to number rather than to strength. L. Schmidt has correctly seen that the use of גוי in v. 18a and b demonstrates with certainty that the sentence belongs to a different period from Gen. 12:3 where משפחה is used (BZAW 143 [1976] 136). If Gen. 12:3 is the Yahwist's, then 18:18 cannot be (on the use of גוי in this context, cf. A. Cody, VT 14 [1964] 1-6).

The second part corresponds to Gen. 12:3, which is resumed in Gen. 22:18; 26:4; 28:14, all passages recognizable as late additions and belonging to a late stage of the promises (cf. comm. on Gen. 12:3, and C. Westermann, *The Promise to the Fathers.* . . [1976; Eng. 1980]).

[18:19] The status of Abraham, which was the reason he was allowed to share God's plan, is now unfolded with a view to his significance for contemporary Israel: him has Yahweh chosen out (the verb ידע occurs only here with this meaning in the patriarchal story) so that the "way of Yahweh" may begin with him and be preserved right down to the present through his instruction (command) to his descendants: the way is that of righteousness and justice. The author expressly adds "and his house after him" to the dative object "his sons"; so P similarly in 17:7. "דרך (way) became a favorite word later for pious observance of the law, and finds expression above all in the Psalms (Ps. 119)" (F. Heiler, *Erscheinungsformen und Wesen der Religion* [1961] 148). Abraham then is the father of משפט and צדקה, "righteousness and justice," and is not seen here as the father of faith (as in Gen. 15:6). The way of Yahweh consists in observing "righteousness and justice" and Abraham is to teach this to his descendants; as Ps. 33:5 says: "He loves righteousness and justice" (see Deut. 33:21); Prov. 21:3: "To do righteousness and justice is more acceptable to the Lord than sacrifice." We are obviously in the postexilic period in those circles where piety consisted in observing "righteousness and justice," and this is now traced back to Abraham.

The last sentence expressly links v. 19 with v. 18. The preservation of the "way of Yahweh" in righteousness and justice is the condition of the fulfillment of the promises to Abraham. The promises to the patriarchs are originally unconditional (Gunkel, ad loc., points this out and bases the late formation on it). From Deuteronomy on they are linked with the condition of obedience. This late, conditioned form of the promise occurs again in Genesis in 22:15-18 and 26:5, which have already been mentioned as later expansions.

M. Noth had regarded v. 19 as a later appendage. L. Schmidt takes this up and argues it in detail, but his argumentation (pp. 134-136) does not take account of the tradition-history of the patriarchal promises. He is of the opinion that the bases of vv. 18 and 19 are mutually exclusive; there is a different conception behind v. 19 from that behind v. 18. But both the promise of blessing for the people in v. 18 and the link between promise and obedience occur together in Gen. 22:15-17 (the noun גוי is also there), even though partly expressed in different words. Gen. 22:15-17, however, is, as a late addition, a self-contained unit; this has never been contested. L. Schmidt has not seen that the promise of increase has been modified and expanded in the course of tradition, and that these late expansions became fixed formulas which were cited and tacked together—often less than in their entirety. It is with such additions that we are concerned here.

The last sentence of v. 19, "so that Yahweh may bring upon him what he promised him," shows expressly that vv. 18 and 19 go together. The context would be destroyed were one to explain v. 19 as a secondary appendage to v. 18. Moreover, it is this very passage that prepares the dialog in vv. 23-32. It is vital for this late piety that the righteousness of God, which is the subject of vv. 23-32, correspond to the righteousness demanded of the pious (v. 19). Any doubt about God's righteousness must cause the piety of the "way of Yahweh" to falter; hence the zeal shown for it in vv. 23-32 (A. Jepsen also stresses this, Fests. H. W. Hertzberg [1965] 78-89).

[18:20-21] God now communicates to Abraham the decision he had made to destroy (vv. 17-19). After the mere hint given in v. 17, "what I am to do," one expects some such statement as, "Because the sin of Sodom is very great I will destroy the city." Abraham's reply in v. 23b is to something of this kind. But here Yahweh simply informs Abraham that he will verify whether the outcry raised over Sodom is justified. The difficulty is not solved by eliminating vv. 20-21 because it contradicts v. 17 (so L. Schmidt). Besides, the execution of Yahweh's intention to inform Abraham of his decision (vv. 17-19) is missing. The elimination of vv. 20-21 renders the context all the more difficult.

Vv. 20-21, read by themselves, show that their primary intent had nothing to do with Abraham. They sound like the prelude to a narrative which deals with the destruction of a sinful city by God (O. Procksch also regards vv. 20-21 as "old building material"). The first sentence could be preserved in Gen. 13:13: "Now the men of Sodom were wicked, great sinners against the Lord." Gen. 18:20-21 could be the immediate continuation of this; the introduction to the narrative would thereby be complete: Yahweh decides to find out for himself. He makes for

Sodom (vv. 22a and 33a) and arrives at the city gate (19:1ff.). The postexilic theologian who inserted vv. 17-32 had before him the old narrative about the coming of God's messengers to Sodom from which he took over vv. 20-21; hence the contradiction to v. 17. This did not trouble the listeners because they knew the old narrative.

The three sentences which comprise vv. 20-21 diverge markedly in style from those surrounding them; this is a sign that the solution of the difficulty is to be sought in the direction indicated. The style is that of narrative with event following event whereas what precedes and follows is determined by theological reflection: loud (or multiple) outcry over Sodom and Gomorrah ("cry murder"; the cries of those subject to violence; F. Delitzsch: "cry for punishment"). Grave guilt has accumulated (the gravity of the guilt has brought about the multiple and loud lamentation). God decides to step in as judge ("I must go down," as in Gen. 11:5 and 7); the intervention begins with a verification, a judicial inquiry, whether the situation is in accord with the cries of lamentation. Again a deliberate interrelation would be destroyed were vv. 20-21 to be eliminated: in v. 25b appeal is made to the judge of all the earth; in vv. 20-21 God is vividly presented in this capacity.

It has become clear that vv. 17-21 are a unity, the first part of the dialog, i.e., the dialog of vv. 17-32. If one eliminates vv. 19-21 in whole or in part, then the first part has not sufficient weight; but the text consists of two equally balanced parts, both of which belong to a dialog which begins and ends with a pronouncement of Yahweh. Yahweh's reflection in vv. 17-19 is therefore to be understood in the following way: because Abraham enjoys such esteem, I will make him privy to my plans. A close parallel is Amos 3:7, also a late appendage (cf. H. W. Wolff, ad loc.). Yahweh's esteem for his servants, the prophets, is such that he does nothing without having revealed his plan to them.

Vv. 17-29 understood in this way acquire a significance for vv. 23-32; it is the one who is deemed worthy of the promise who raises the objection; this gives weight to the answer that Yahweh gives him. It is the exemplary just man who raises his voice (v. 19); this gives great significance to the question about God's righteousness in vv. 23-32 and God's answer. Something similar happens in the apocalypses where God's revelations are made to famous men of old.

[18:22]   In the old narrative, Yahweh now made towards Sodom in accordance with his decision. The author of vv. 27-32 creates here a transition which on the one hand allows the insertion of the dialog, vv. 23-32 (by means of vv. 22b and 23a), while on the other hand he tries to smooth over the difficulty which arises from there being two messengers in 19:1ff., whereas there were three in 18:1-16a. The presentation is such that two men now set out for Sodom but the third remains, while Abraham remains standing before him; he is now described as Yahweh. The separation which the author makes here between Yahweh and his two companions does not follow the narrative in 18:1-16a where the talk about the three and the one is quite deliberately left hanging. A later hand betrays itself in this small detail. This does not really solve the difficulty of the transition from ch. 18 to ch. 19, as is clear from v. 33 which does not square exactly with v. 22. These two verses are really variants.

[18:23-32]   This passage is to be understood as part of a dialog throughout which the first part, vv. 17-21, is to sound constantly. It is a self-contained unity held together by God's consistently repeated answer. The first exchange of question and answer covers vv. 23b-26; in vv. 27-32 the question is gradually sharpened by progressively decreasing numbers. The whole could be summarized in one sentence; but that would not really catch the sense of the text. The progression, with the ever new formulation of the question, is essential. Without this element of tension which makes the listener ask, "How far will Abraham go?" and "How will God react?" the real intent of the text cannot be grasped. But what does this progression, this tension, want to express? What is its goal?

The traditional interpretation is that we have here Abraham's intercession on behalf of Sodom (most exegetes, e.g., H. Gunkel, O. Procksch, G. von Rad, H. W. Wolff, W. Zimmerli; differently B. Jacob, L. Schmidt, R. Rendtorff). But is this really what is meant? Where there is clearly an intercession, especially in the prophetic texts (Amos chs. 7–9; Jer. 11:14f.), then it has a fixed structure and is designated as intercession for. . ., petition for God's mercy concerning. . .. Moreover, at the end comes God's concession or denial. Neither occurs in Gen. 18; its structure is that of question and answer, not of petition and concession. One cannot, therefore, describe vv. 18-23 as a prayer, as many exegetes do; it bears no relation to the prayer formulas. Now if 18:23-32 is neither intercession nor prayer, then what the history of exegesis right down to the present time thought it found there disappears, namely, bargaining, beating down, haggling with God.. . . This cannot be the meaning because Abraham, for all his questioning, is aware from the start that God will go through with his decision to punish Sodom.

[18:23] Abraham approaches Yahweh to put the question which the communication evokes. Is it his business to call in question the decision to destroy? His first question, which determines all that follows, is: "Will you really sweep away the just with the wicked?" This is not to contest God's right to destroy; however, the destruction is just only if it strikes the malefactors alone. God would not be just were he to destroy the just together with the wicked. This is what Abraham's question is concerned with. "The question strikes the keynote of the section" (J. Skinner). The word used here in v. 23, "sweep away" (ספה), occurs also in Gen. 19:15 and 17. It is very likely that the author of 18:16-32 is making a direct link with the older narrative in ch. 19 which was at hand to him.

[18:24] If there are 50 just in the city, then God has to spare it so as not to destroy them with the godless (v. 23); but that would be possible only by his forgiving the wicked their outrage.

[18:25] What follows serves only to corroborate and underscore what has already been said. The corroboration is expressed in the twofold "far be it from you" (A. Dillmann: *profanum tibi sit*) at the beginning and end of the second sentence which vehemently rejects the possibility that God could destroy the just with the wicked, repeating the question with which Abraham approached Yahweh (v. 23b). The second question shows in all clarity the basis of this rejection, "to treat the just as the wicked." This is the heart of what Abraham wants to say here. God's righteousness must really be seen, that is, one must be able to recognize it in the different lot of the pious and the impious. This is underscored all the more forcefully inasmuch as the last sentence of v. 25 puts it into universal perspective: "far be it from you, the judge of all the earth, not to do what is just." The author recalls here the psalms where Yahweh is celebrated as judge of the world, e.g., Ps. 94:2: "Rise up, O judge of the earth. . ."; Elihu likewise asks Job (34:17):

"Shall one who hates justice govern?" Other texts that speak of God's judgment on the pious and the impious are 1 Kings 8:32 (Dtr); Eccles. 3:17; Mal. 3:14.

[18:26]   God assents to Abraham's request. His answer repeats almost word for word one of the alternatives which Abraham had put to him in v. 24. But one must ask more precisely, what is to forgive here? (cf. F. Stolz, נשׂא, THAT II [1976] 109-117). It means nothing more than to annul the decision to destroy. This, therefore, is not a matter of the turning and repenting of a city, the destruction of which has been decided, as in Jer. 18:7-10 and Jon. 3:4. The basis for the annulment of the punishment of Sodom is left aside. It is similar with "for their sake" (also in vv. 24 and 32). The meaning is simply: whether there are 50 just in the city; there is no thought of these 50 exercising an atoning function.

[18:27-32]   The function of the second part is merely to sharpen the question. It should be noted that no further arguments are given; they are all in vv. 23-25. Why this sharpening? Why does Abraham continue to venture further? Behind Abraham's persistence is the persistence of the question about God's righteousness. He is aware how audacious is his unremitting questioning, "May I presume. . ., though I am but dust and ashes" (v. 27). The expression occurs again in Job 30:19; 42:6, and as a description of human nature, as here, only in Sir. 10:9; 17:32. As a comment see v. 32: "Please let it not anger my Lord. . .." Abraham remains throughout the humble questioner but he must know, even to the remotest possibility, whether the decision to destroy is a just decision.

This is the question that lies behind Abraham's progressive appeals which are always followed by God's unvarying, monotonous answer: No, no, no. This repetition has an important function in the dialog: it corroborates God's righteousness from his own very life.

The reason Abraham stops at the number ten is that this represents the smallest group (so B. Jacob and L. Schmidt). If there are fewer than ten in the city, then these are individuals and as such they can be saved from the city as happens in ch. 19. Abraham's query reaches its natural limit with the number ten.

Purpose and Thrust

Surveying the whole, one sees more clearly the three stages which result from the insertion of Gen. 18:17-32:

   I.   God decides to destroy Sodom.
   II. God assures Abraham that he will not destroy Sodom if one condition is fulfilled.
   III. God destroys Sodom.

The theologian who inserted 18:17-32 had before him the old narrative in which God had decided to destroy Sodom, then carried out his decision, but saved Lot. He is bound to the tradition and he knows that his listeners or readers know it. It was taken for granted from the outset that Abraham's intercession could in no way alter the situation. His purpose was to show indisputably that the destruction of Sodom and Gomorrah was a just action. His argumentation is directed at removing any possible doubt about God's righteousness which could arise as a result of the catastrophe. Surely it was obvious to everyone, particularly in the case of a natural disaster, that the pious would perish with the impious! All the reasons given in vv. 23-25 without exception are directed to this question. There is not a sentence that so much as hints that Abraham was imploring God's mercy to avert a disaster from the people (against F. Delitzsch, Komm. ad loc., J. Ruwet and J. Scharbert, lit. to 18:16b-33; J. Schreiner, BZ 6 [1962] 1-31). Such is the concern of Jon. 3:4 where the wording is quite different. One could turn the whole dialog into the form of a hypothetical condition: "Would you destroy Sodom if. . .?"

An earlier explanation was that the passage is concerned with the transition from collectivism to individualism. G. von Rad is of the opinion that a new form of collectivism is here taking the place of an older, but sees that this does not entirely suit the reasoning in v. 23b. However, the concept "collectivism" is too general and as a criterion is inept. The question is rather, what is the relationship between God's action towards the individual, whereby he punishes the impious and rewards the pious, and his action in history, his action towards wholes (collectives)? There was no problem in describing God as judge as long as the reference was to individuals, distinguishing the צדיק from the רשע (v. 23); the problem arose when God was described as judge of the world (v. 25), or of cities, countries, or peoples. There was still no problem while the other cities and peoples were potential enemies of Israel; it arose only when Israel ceased to be a political entity, as was often the case in this period. It was vital to recognize and demonstrate God's righteousness in his action in history in a period when the relationship of people to God was determined by "righteousness and justice" which v. 19 traced back to the patriarch Abraham. God ought not destroy the just with the wicked. Abraham, who charged his children to practice righteousness and justice, approaches God "in the name of righteousness" to receive confirmation that God does not destroy the just with the wicked.

Gen. 18:17-32 understood in this way is part of the subsequent history of the figure of Abraham; it points to the postexilic period when the relationship to God was dominated by the concept of righteousness, and piety, understood as the observance of righteousness and justice, corresponded to the righteousness of God. This period understood Abraham as the father of "righteousness and justice" which he taught his children to observe. He is the one who approaches God in order to receive from God himself confirmation of the divine righteousness against any possible doubt.

The Destruction of Sodom
and the Rescue of Lot

Literature

Genesis 19: M. Blanckenhorn, "Entstehung und Geschichte des Toten Meeres," ZDPV 19 (1896) 1-59; *Naturwissenschaftliche Studien am Toten Meer und im Jordantal* (1912). W. Baumgartner, "Ein Kapitel. . .," FRLANT 36 (1923) 152f. B. K. N. Wyllie, "The Geology of Jobel Usdum, Dead Sea," *The Geological Magazine* 68 (1931) 366-372. R. Köppel, "Uferstudien am Toten Meer," Bib 13 (1932) and ZDPV 55 (1932) 26-42. F. Stummer, *Monumenta historiam et geographiam Terrae Sanctae illustrantia* I (1935). F. G. Clapp, "The Site of Sodom and Gomorrah," AJA 40 (1936) 323-344. N. Glueck, "An Aerial Reconnaissance in Southern Transjordan," BASOR 67 (1937) 19-26. E. F. Sutcliffe, "Sodoma," EB 6 (1965) 778-782. T. H. Gaster, *Myth*. . . (1969) 156-162. M. Haran, "*Zebah hayyamîm*," VT 19 (1969) 11-32. F. Langlamet, "Josué II, et les traditions de l'Hexateuque," RB 78 (1971) 5-17, 161-183, 321-354.

Genesis 19:1-11: J. Reider, "Etymological Studies: ידע or ירע and רעע," JBL 66 (1947) 315-317. L. Koehler, *Der hebräische Mensch* (1953; 1976). W. Rudolph, "Präparierte Jungfrauen? (zu Hosea 1)," ZAW 75 (1963) 65-73. G. Walis, "Die Stadt in den Überlieferungen der Genesis," ZAW 78 (1966) 133-148. G. R. Driver, "Old Problems Re-examined," ZAW 80 (1968) 174-183, esp. 179. A. Ahuvia, "On the Meaning of the Word 'סנורים,' " *Tarbiz* 38 (1968/69) 90-92. F. C. Fensham, "The Obliteration of the Family as Motif in the Near Eastern Literature," AION NS 10 (1969) 191-199.

Genesis 19:12-23: L. W. King, *Babylonian Magic and Sorcery* (1896) esp. 58, 98f. F. J. Spurell, *Notes on the Text of the Book of Genesis* (1896²) esp. 188. J. Friedrich, "Die theologische Bedeutung etymologischer Ätiologien im AT," ThLZ 81 (1956) 333-334. L. Hicks, "Lot," IDB 3 (1962) 162-163. T. C. Mitchell, "The Meaning of the Noun *htn* in the OT," VT 19 (1969) 93-112. J. W. McKay, "*Helel* and the Dawn-Goddess. A Re-examination of the Myth in Isaiah XIV 12-15," VT 20 (1970) 451-464. I. Reindl, *Das Angesicht Gottes im Sprachgebrauch des Alten Testaments*, Erfurter ThSt 25 (1970). Y. Avishur, "*KRKR* in Hebrew and in Ugaritic," VT 26 (1976) 257-261. K. Seybold, "Reverenz und Gebet. Erwägungen zu der Wendung *hillā panîm*," ZAW 88 (1976) 2-16.

Genesis 29:24-29: E. S. Hartland, *The Legend of Perseus III* (1896) esp. 132. I. F. Wood, "Folk-Tales. . .," JBL 28 (1908) esp. 38f. A. H. Krappe, *La genèse des mythes* (1938) esp. 335-337. G. Cocchira, *Genesis dei leggende* (1940³) esp. 41-60. J. Simons, "Two Notes on the Problem of the Pentapolis (Gen 19,24-26)," OTS 5 (1948) 92-117. M. Shalem, "Earthquakes in Jerusalem," [in Hebr.], *Jerusalem* 2 (1949) 22-54. J. B. Bauer, "Uxor Loth repetiitne Sodomam?," VD 38 (1960) 28-33. P. A. H. De Boer, *Gedenken und Gedächtnis in der Welt des Alten Testaments, Franz Delitzsch-Vorlesung* (1962) 5-76. F. C. Fensham, "Salt as Curse in the Old Testament and the Ancient Near East," BA 25

(1962) 48-50. S. Gevirtz, "Jericho and Shechem: A Religio-literary Aspect of City Destruction," VT 13 (1963) 52-62. D. R. Hillers, "Amos 7,4 and Ancient Parallels," CBQ 26 (1964) 221-225. P. D. Miller, "Fire in the Mythology of Canaan and Israel," CBQ 27 (1965) 256-261. M. C. Astour, "Tamar the Hierodule. An Essay in the Method of Vestigial Motifs," JBL 85 (1966) 185-196. H. J. von Dijk, "A Neglected Connotation of Three Hebrew Verbs," VT 18 (1968) 16-30. T. F. McDaniel, "The Alleged Sumerian Influence Upon Lamentations," VT 18 (1968) 198-209. G. E. Weil, "Nouveaux fragments inédits de la Massorah Magna babylonienne (II) MS.TS.DI. no. 5," Texts: *Annual of the Hebrew Univ. Bible Project* 6 (1968) 75-105. G. M. Buccellati, " 'Ma sua moglie guardò indietro e divenne una colonna di sale' (Gen 19,26)," BeO 13 (1971) 226. T. W. Mann, "The Pillar of Cloud in the Reed Sea Narrative," JBL 90 (1971) 15-30. G. F. Hasel, *The Remnant: The History and Theology of the Remnant Idea From Genesis to Isaiah*, AUM 5 (1972).

Text

19:1   When the two messengers[a] arrived at Sodom in the evening, Lot was sitting at the gate of Sodom; when he saw them, he rose to meet them[b] and bowed with his face to the ground

2   And said: Please,[a] my lords, I beg you, turn aside to your servant's house, stay the night and wash your feet; early in the morning you can rise and go your way. But they said: No,[b] we will pass the night in the street.

3   But he pressed[a] them strongly; so they turned aside and went into his house, and he prepared a meal for them and baked bread and they ate.

4   Before they lay down, the men of the city, the men of Sodom, surrounded[a] the house, young and old, the whole people to the last man.

5   And they cried out to Lot: Where are the men who came to you tonight? Bring them out to us so that we may know them.

6   Then Lot went out to them before the door[a] and shut it behind him

7   and said: Please, my brothers, do nothing wicked.

8   Look, I have two daughters who have not known man; let me bring them out to you and you can do with them as you please; only do nothing to these men[a] because they are harbored under the shelter of my roof.

9   But they said: Out of the way! This man has come as an alien, they said,[a] and now he wants to play the judge![b] We will deal worse with him than with them. And they surged forward against the man Lot and moved to break down the door.

10   But the men stretched out their hands and pulled Lot into the house and shut the door.

11   And they struck those at the door with blindness,[a] small and great alike, so that they wearied themselves in vain trying to find the door.

12   Then the men said to Lot: Is there anyone else of yours here? Your. . .[a] sons and daughters and all of yours in the city, lead them away from this[b] place,

13   For we are going to destroy this place because the outcry before Yahweh[a] is great,[b] and he has sent us to destroy it.[c]

14   So Lot went and spoke to his sons-in-law who were to marry[a] his daughters: Up, out of this place, he said, because Yahweh is going to destroy the city; but his sons-in-law thought he was joking.

15   When[a] dawn broke, the messengers hurried Lot saying: Up, take your wife and your two daughters here[b] lest[c] you be swept away in the punishment on the city.

16   But he lingered;[a] so the men seized him and his wife and his two daughters by the hand, because Yahweh wanted to spare him, and led

him away and set him outside the city.

17   Now when they had led them outside he said: Flee for your life; do not look behind;[a] do not stop anywhere in the valley; flee to the mountains lest you be swept away.

18   But Lot said to them: No, no my lords!

19   Look, your servant has found favor in your eyes, you have shown me great favor in saving my life; but I, I cannot flee to the mountains! Disaster may strike me and I may die.

20   But look, that city there is near enough to flee to! Yes, it is only small; let me flee there, small as it is, and save my life.[a]

21   He said to him: Yes, this too I grant you; I will not overthrow the city you speak of.

22   Hurry, flee there, because I can do nothing until you arrive there. And so the city was given the name Zoar.[a]

23   The sun[a] had just risen over the land when Lot arrived at Zoar.

24   Yahweh then rained on Sodom and Gomorrah—brimstone and fire from Yahweh in the heavens;

25   and he destroyed these[a] cities and the whole plain and all the inhabitants of the cities and the produce of the ground.

26   But his wife looked behind her[a] and became a pillar of salt.

27   And Abraham rose early in the morning and went to the place where[a] he had stood in the presence of Yahweh.

28   He gazed down over Sodom and Gomorrah and over the whole of the plain,[a] and look, he saw that the smoke had risen from the land like the smoke of a furnace.[b]

29   And so when God destroyed[a] the cities of the plain he remembered Abraham, and delivered Lot from the midst of the destruction[b] when he destroyed the cities in which Lot lived.

1a Only here and in v. 15; Sam v. 12; Gk v. 16; see comm. v. 1.   **b** ויקם לקראתם is an abbreviation.

2a הִנֶּה pointed thus only here (Ges-K §20d, 100c). **b** לֹא irregular dagesh; F. Delitzsch: emphatic dagesh.

3a פצר elsewhere only in Gen. 19:9; 33:11; Judg. 19:7; 2 Kings 2:17; 5:16.

4a On על used in this sense, G. R. Driver ZAW 80 (1968) 174ff.; E. A. Speiser, comm. ad loc.

6a "Before the door," missing in Gk and Vg.

8a הָאֵל instead of הָאֵלֶּה (so Sam) only in seven other places; orthographic variants.

9a The second ויאמרו is missing in Gk; MT is to be followed.   **b** For the construction, Ges-K §§111m, 113p,r.

11a Or, "a blinding light" (translator); on the plur. BrSynt §19b, 21cγ.

12a חתן has probably slipped in here by error from v. 14. On the meaning of חתן, T. C. Mitchell, VT 19 (1969) 93ff.   **b** Sam and Gk add הזה to מקום.

13a B. Jacob: את פני without the verb always indicates a higher authority.   **b** גדל "does not mean the actual magnitude, but the process of showing itself great" (Mosis: ThW I 938-956).   **c** Vg reads לשחתם.

14a לקחי used here in a futuristic sense, Ges-K §116d; cf. E. A. Speiser and T. C. Mitchell; for different view, BrSynt §99a.

15a כמו A. Dillmann: rare and poetic; used here as a conjunction, BrSynt §163b.   **b** On the syntax, BrSynt §133 a, e.   **c** Gk ἃς ἔχεις; Vg quas habes.

16a Hithpalp. from מהה "to linger"; Gk reads plur., likewise v. 17.

17a תביט for תבֵט, Ges-K §107p; on the sentence, BrSynt §5a.

20a Some Gk mss. add ἕνεκεν σοῦ.

22a Gk Σηγωρ; likewise v. 23.

23a Masc., Sam fem.; cf. Gen. 15:11; שֶׁמֶשׁ in OT masc. and fem. (KBL). On the word order, BrSynt §122n.

25a האל, cf. v. 8; Gk adds אשר ישב בהן לוט, likewise v. 29. Syr has הארץ for הערים.
26a E. A. Speiser and R. Kilian alter to מאחריה.
27a On the relative sentence, E. Schild, VT 4 (1954) 296ff.
28a ארץ הככר occurs nowhere else; the variants in Gk and Syr give grounds for alteration to כל־הככר. **b** The same comparison in Ex. 19:18.
29a For בשחת the Sam reads בהשחית. **b** ההפכה *hapax legomenon* as a noun.

Form

Ch. 19 is one of the finest narratives in Genesis. Destruction and rescue counterbalance each other and maintain the progressive and all-pervading tension, as in the flood story (so too R. de Vaux, *The Early History of Israel I*, 168-169). Both belong to the same type in the history of religions (cf. *Genesis 1–11*, 393-406). Annihilation by water corresponds to annihilation by fire; local features, however, are in evidence in the latter. The inhabitants of a city might well experience its destruction as the destruction of the world. The shock which the survivor or onlooker lives through may be no less severe.

It is such a shock that the story of the catastrophe unleashes. At the beginning of the transmission of the story of the destruction of a city or an area there is always the experience, direct or indirect, of a catastrophe that has left a deep impression.

This means the rejection of the attempt to explain Gen. 19 as a whole as an etiological narrative. H. Gunkel writes: ''The story is concerned with the origin of such a spectacular landscape. . . . Why did Yahweh treat this area thus?'' His answer is that Yahweh executed judgment on a sinful city. The etiological question has certainly contributed to the shaping of the narrative; but it is not of the essence, which is rather the experience of a catastrophe (so too W. Zimmerli). The recollection could live on as a simple item of information; as in the many reports of the judgment upon the two cities in both the Old and New Testaments (see below); but when it became a narrative, the way was open to a profusion of possibilities which could form and fashion it. Two lines of tension simultaneously shape the narrative of Gen. 19—crime and punishment, destruction and rescue. This explains a certain unevenness; the motifs which come together here show signs of their own independent life. A comparison of Gen. 19:1-11 with Judg. 19:15-25 demonstrates this: both narrative parts are very alike. There is much agreement in sentence construction and word usage, and complete agreement in structure:

	Gen.	*Judg.*
arrival and reception	19:1-3	19:15-21
attack and repulse of attack	19:4-11	19:22-25
attack, demand to hand over	19:4-5	19:22
offer by householder	19:6-8	19:23-24
rejection and threat	19:9	19:25a
repulse of attack by guests	19:10-11	19:25b

In order to explain such extensive agreement one must in each case raise the question of the contexts in which the narrative parts occur. The narrative in Judg. 19 continues with the judgment which the tribes pronounce over the city of Gibeah where the crime was committed (Judg. 19:29-30; chs. 20–21). The narrative in Gen. 19 continues with God's judgment over Sodom where Lot is preserved. The basic structure of Judg. 19–21 is: crime (19:1-28)—punishment of the crime

(19:29-21); of Genesis: crime—God's judgment—preservation of the individual. The whole emphasis of Judg. 19–21 lies on the punishment of the crime, the expedition of retribution against the city of Gibeah; of Gen. 19, on the rescue of the individual from the catastrophe which occupies the greater part of the chapter, while the judgment on the city is restricted to vv. 24-25. The motif of the individual who is saved is completely missing from Judg. 19. In Judges it is humans, in the person of the tribes of Israel in the period of the settlement in Canaan, who execute judgment upon the city of the offenders; in Genesis it is God who executes judgment by means of natural disaster, in accordance with narratives about the primeval period (Gen. 6–9). Judges is a historical narrative from the early period of the settlement; Genesis is close to the narratives of the primeval period.

This is confirmed by a large cycle of narratives outside Israel which follow the structure of Gen. 19: crime—divine judgment—preservation of an individual. They agree in content with Gen. 19 that the crime consists in the violation of hospitality and accordingly the one who is saved is the one who received the divinity. H. Gunkel has already drawn attention to such parallels (cf. T. K. Cleyne, *New World* [1892] 239ff.). T. H. Gaster cites further parallels, *Myth, Legend. . .* (1969) 159ff.; he refers to an example from India advanced by E. S. Hartland, *The Legend of Perseus III* (1896): an Indian story relates that once upon a time a holy man was doing penance in the forests of Pettan. One of his disciples went into the city to beg for alms. But the inhabitants maltreated him, with the exception of a shepherd's wife. The holy man therefore decided to punish the city by inundation, but before doing so he ordered the woman to leave the city, and forbade her to turn back. She did not obey him and was turned into stone on the spot. This example is valuable because it contains a number of motifs which are parallel to Gen. 19: (1) hospitable reception and refusal; (2) punishment of a sinful city and saving of an individual; (3) prohibition to look back, disobedience, and changing into stone. More important, however, is the fact that the many widespread examples (to which the story of Philemon and Baukis belongs) present a type of narrative of primeval event. It points beyond Israel, inasmuch as in the whole of the Old Testament it is only in this passage, Gen. 19:26, that a "metamorphosis" occurs (cf. Ovid).

There is a further peculiarity to be noted. There is no event in the whole of Genesis that is mentioned so frequently in the Old Testament as the destruction of Sodom (Sodom and Gomorrah, Admah and Zeboiim): Deut. 29:23; Is. 1:9f.; 13:19; Jer. 49:18; 50:40; Ezek. 16:46-50, 53-55; Amos 4:11; Zeph. 2:9; Lam. 4:6; Ps. 11:6; Admah and Zeboiim: Hos. 11:8; Deut. 29:22 (cf. Gen. 10:19; 14:2, 8). In the New Testament: Mt. 10:15; 11:23f.; Lk. 10:12; 17:29; Rom. 9:29; 2 Pet. 2:6; Jude 7; Rev. 11:8. An example from Deut. 29:23: "the whole land brimstone and salt, and a burnt-out waste. . ., an overthrow like that of Sodom and Gomorrah, Admah and Zeboiim, which the Lord overthrew in his anger and wrath. . .."

The context in which the passages mention Sodom and Gomorrah is always the same: God's judgment on the cities is recalled, generally comparing it with a judgment which has been announced, hence for the most part in prophetic texts of judgment. The name, therefore, points to the well-known proverbial judgment of God in the distant past. Part of this tradition is the fixed expression כְּמַהְפֵּכַת אֱלֹהִים אֶת־סְדֹם וְאֶת־עֲמֹרָה Amos 4:11; Is. 13:19; Jer. 50:40 (this is the only occurrence of אֱלֹהִים in Amos; otherwise it is always יהוה). The presentation of Gen. 19 never indicates "repentance"; this, together with the use of אֱלֹהִים, shows that the prophets rely on a tradition that is independent of Gen. 19. The divine judgment, as in Gen. 6–9, is always passed on a serious crime which has been committed. The tradition of the divine judgment on the cities is the same in all passages whereas the crime, which was the reason for it, is not. W. Zimmerli in particular draws attention to this in his commentary (so too E. A. Speiser): "The sin of Sodom and Gomorrah is portrayed differently elsewhere": Is. 1:10, social oppression; Jer. 23:14, adultery, lying, encouraging the criminal; Ezek. 16:49, presumption, surfeit of food and restless ease. The essence of the tradition consists in the divine judgment on the cities, while the crime that gives rise to it is variable. This tradition itself was not necessarily linked with the motif of a visit by a messenger or messengers of God, reception and a violation of hospitality. It is precisely this that the comparison with Judg. 19 has shown, where the motif appears in a quite different context.

Hence it follows that the frequent references to judgment on Sodom and Gomorrah, above all in the prophetic oracle of judgment, do not necessarily presuppose Gen. 19's understanding of the tradition; it was known in many variants. The different names of the city or cities involved also favor this. The tradition was multiform and for the most part probably not known as part of the Abraham story, of which it is originally independent.

The structure of Gen. 19 shows that it has arisen out of motifs of different origin: vv. 1-3, the arrival of the men and their reception by Lot (parallel, Gen. 18:1-8), and vv. 4-11, the attack and its repulsion, have an exact parallel in Judg. 19:15-25, which then continues quite differently. The second part, vv. 12-17, the command to abandon the city, is concerned only with the rescue of Lot by the men; it is described in great detail and so shifts to the middle of the narrative. The elaboration (vv. 18-22), Lot's request about Zoar as his place of refuge, also belongs here. Only the two verses 24-25 (v. 23 forms the transition) deal with the destruction of the city (or cities), while v. 26 is a separate scene attached to the rescue of Lot. Vv. 27-28 link the whole with Abraham, i.e., with chs. 13; 18–19. V. 29 is a parallel account by P of the destruction of the cities and the saving of Lot.

Summing up: The passage, vv. 24f., is entirely conceivable as an independent account of the destruction of the two cities, not yet linked with the Abraham story. It has been fashioned into a narrative by means of the motif of the rescue of an individual (vv. 12-17, with the expansion, vv. 18-22), which later was linked with the motif of crime and punishment; the one who is saved is the one who has not incurred guilt (vv. 1-11). All this has been shaped into a self-contained, perfectly rounded narrative in which the temporal sequence, evening—dawn—sunrise, serves the structural tension.

Setting

It follows from the study of the form that the core of the tradition, the account of the annihilation of the cities of Sodom and Gomorrah, was autonomous and independent of the Abraham story, which had its origin in the experience of a catastrophe that actually happened. But one runs into grave difficulties when one tries to be more precise in time or place. I refer to the commentary on Gen. 10:9 and 14:2 for details about the names of the cities. The traditions know the name of Sodom standing alone, of Sodom and Gomorrah (never Gomorrah alone), of Admah and Zeboiim (only together); all four cities are found together in some passages. It is not possible to pursue further the relationship of these accounts to each other; one can only say that there was once an account of the city of Sodom and one of Sodom and Gomorrah, but not of Gomorrah alone. Some scholars are of the opinion that the names Admah and Zeboiim are a north-Israelite variant (e.g., W. Zimmerli; cf. H. W. Wolff, *Hosea*, on 11:8). The other difficulty is the geographical locality, about which there has been a long-drawn-out discussion: for the literature, cf. J. Simons (*The Geographical and Topographical Texts of the O.T.* [1959]); J. P. Harland (BA 5-6 [1942-43] 17-32, 41-54); H. Junker ("Pentapolis," LThK 8 [1963] 257); M. Blanckenhorn (ZDPV 19 [1896] 1-59; *Naturwissenschaftliche Studien am Toten Meer. . .* [1912]); J. P. Harland (JDB 4 [1962] 395-97). The question has been raised whether the cities can really have lain on the Dead Sea at all, because no remains have been found as yet, and there is much in the description in Gen. 19 that speaks against the area. On the other hand it has been rightly said that the local coloring of the Dead Sea and its environs is all too clear. It cannot be excluded that there are additional traits which come from other traditions. The question has been raised whether the city (cities) lay at the north or the south end of the Dead Sea. J. Simons has declared himself in favor of the north (§§ 404-414: The Jordan Pentapolis). However, the traditional view (south) has prevailed almost universally (e.g., J. P. Harland, E. A. Speiser, H. Junker). Much in the configuration of Gen. 19 points to the area around the Dead Sea in which the account of the destruction of a city or two cities was handed on. This is also the best explanation of the frequent occurrence of this account in the rest of the Old Testament, which goes back then to a local tradition in the area.

The first part of the narrative, by virtue of comparison with the parallel in Judg. 19, shows itself to be relatively independent: crime against the right to hospitality was a widespread motif and could be shaped into a variety of narratives. H. Gunkel is of the opinion that Judg. 19:15-25 may perhaps be an imitation of Gen. 19:1-11; but this is very questionable because the Judges passage cannot be detached from Judg. 19–20, and the narrative, as a secular historical narrative, gives the impression of an earlier origin, still in the period of the tribes. If one can speak of priority here, and this is questionable, then it falls to Judg. 19 (so too B. Jacob). In any case, however, this part has its origin in the period of the Israelites' transition to city dwelling; the story reflects the experience of crime made possible by city life and which later took on such tremendous significance as the sexual crime of Canaan. This is undoubtedly set in contrast to Gen. 18 which portrays the uncontested and natural hospitality of the nomadic period.

The section vv. 12-17 is tightly knit with the account of the destruction (vv. 24-25) by means of the decision to destroy (v. 13) and the order to flee the catastrophe (v. 12); it is very close to narratives of the great primeval catastrophe; the obvious parallels to Gen. 6–9 illustrate this (cf. *Genesis 1–11*, 47-56, 393-395).

The narrative as a whole is to be attributed to J, whose method is once again discernible—shaping a narrative out of elements of different origin, working them into a self-contained unity.

Commentary

[19:1-3] *Arrival of the men and reception by Lot:* Gen. 19:1-3 is the original continuation of 18:22a(33a) where the detail about the goal of the men "in the direction of Sodom" (cf. 18:16a) serves to link Gen. 18 and 19. The description of the two men as "the two messengers" ("messengers" elsewhere only 19:15) is an explication inserted later (so H. Gunkel; likewise A. Dillmann, J. Skinner, R. Kilian, and others); the original was "the two men." "In the evening" is the first of the details of temporal sequence which runs through the narrative (vv. 15a, 23a). They have a purely narrative function; neither the narrator nor the listeners are concerned that the distance from Hebron to the southern end of the Dead Sea is about 70 km. (some two days journey) and that there is a difference in elevation of 1300 m. This shows that the narratives of chs. 18 and 19 do not belong together. There is no thought of overcoming the gaps by supernatural means.

The invitation and entertainment are similar to 18:1-8, but shorter; a number of details are rather close to Judg. 19:15-25, e.g., in both cases it is a migrant who receives the strangers. Mention of the gate, the place where court hearings and trade and traffic take place, shows the difference from the scene in ch. 18: the stage for what follows is the city (as in Judg. 19); Lot has become a citizen, and the marketplace at the gate (Ruth 4:1ff.; 2 Sam. 18:24; 2 Kings 7:1), where the stranger waits for someone to receive him, represents the city. As in Judg. 19, the host presses the stranger (cf. 1 Kings 13:14-19). The city itself could shelter the travellers, but a house offers more protection. The verb "constrain, press some-one" פצר, qal, occurs only rarely outside vv. 3 and 9 and the parallel, Judg. 19 (Gen. 33:11; 2 Kings 2:17; 5:16); perhaps it belongs to an event such as portrayed here.

[19:4-11] *Attack and its repulsion:* Gen. 18:20-21 (which the author of 18:17-33 took from an older narrative) deals with the crime of Sodom and Gomorrah in general terms; if there is to be an inquiry about the "outcry," then the crime must be portrayed concretely; that is what 19:4-11 does. As in the pri-meval event (Gen. 4:2-16 and the reason for the flood, Gen. 6:5,11) the concern is about wrong which affects the whole of mankind and threatens the worldwide hu-man community. It is this that gives rise to the outcry of the aggrieved and de-spoiled. It is a matter of man threatened by man. The Old Testament takes wrong-doing as a human phenomenon very seriously; in this case it is no mere matter of the judiciary and the state; God is concerned directly with it. The gravity of the sin of Sodom (Gen. 18:20-21) is explicated in 19:4-11 in such a way that the narrative combines two crimes, each of which is serious in itself: unnatural lust (Lev. 18:22) and the violation of the right of guests to protection. Over and above this, and this is typical of the city and determinative of the atmosphere of the event, the crime takes the character of an attack in which the attackers have an absolute supe-riority in numbers by virtue of which they can give free rein to their wickedness. This is portrayed in bold strokes and has been well thought out. It is something that pertains to human existence, to human potentialities, that remains unaltered to the present day.

The words טרם ישכבו, Josh. 2:8, are in the same place in the parallel, Judg. 19:22. The אנשי סדם need not be a gloss, as most of the exegetes think; so correctly B. Jacob, referring to Gen. 13:13 and Judg. 19:22. נסב, niph. "sur-round" where the preposition על indicates the hostile intent. Old and young take part in the attack; the word מקצה, which extends beyond כל־העם, says that all were there, "from one and to the other" (so A. Dillmann, F. Delitzsch, H. Holzinger, J. Skinner, E. A. Speiser) not "even from the furthest limit" (H. Strack). The expression refers to the inquiry (18:20-21) whether the whole city is really corrupt and so must be destroyed.

[19:6-8] Lot had offered the men a roof and so protection. The "shadow of his roof" became thereby the place of security for the guests, the violation of which was a fearful crime with incalculable consequences. The narrative now continues: Lot goes to the extreme in both action (v. 6) and word (vv. 7-8) in his intervention on behalf of his guests. He goes outside the door and exposes himself to the at-tackers without any protection ("and shut it behind him"). He even offers to hand over his daughters to the mob. A warning, in which he addresses them as brothers, precedes the offer. G. von Rad writes "the address. . . rather indicates a situation of legal equality"; it appeals to their responsibility and warns them of the crime. The warning is indeed intended seriously; repentance by the men of Sodom even at this moment would have meant salvation. The offer is aimed at preventing something worse in accordance with that age's way of understanding, and one should neither explain it away (B. Jacob: the Sodomites would certainly have not agreed to it) nor condemn it by our standards (F. Delitzsch: "He commits sin who intends to ward off sin by sin," an example of questionable application of an abstract idea of sin). In any case it is a desperate offer that knows no way out.

[19:9]   The narrative of the attack reaches its climax in v. 9. H. Gunkel takes offense, incorrectly, at the repeated ויאמרו at the beginning of v. 9 and holds that the first three words are an additional amplification. However, the narrator, responding exactly to the situation, deliberately distinguishes the articulated reply to the offer from the mere cry: "Out of the way!" As is often the case in such situations, the reply is saying, with the brutal might of an advancing mob, something correct, or at least apparently correct: "Will a gēr, who must be happy to be tolerated, assume the office of a native born?" (B. Jacob). And so, as usually happens, those who use force not only do what they want, but also want to be in the right. And it has remained so right up to the present day. The threat of those pressing forward renders Lot's offer meaningless, and they want to seize him. The attackers advance; they threaten to break down the door; host and guests are in mortal danger.

[19:10-11]   The strangers intervene in extreme emergency and thus introduce the turning point which consists simply in parrying the immediate danger. It takes place in two scenes. There is nothing of the marvelous in the first; the men seize Lot, pull him inside and shut the door; they do what is routine in the situation. There are now witnesses to the second act. Inside they simply notice that no one breaks down the door and no one comes in; they experience it as a marvel which is expressed thus in their own idiom: the people outside were "struck with blindness." In our idiom too this way of speaking does not mean actual blindness, but a temporary inability to see. This is described here by one word, סנורים, derived by E. A. Speiser from the Akk. šunwurum, by A. Ahuvia, Tarbiz 38 (1968-69) 90-92, from Hebr. סנר; as it occurs only here and in the same context in 2 Kings 6:18, it points to an old narrative way of speaking, the equivalent of our "to strike with blindness," to which the word, later fallen into desuetude, belonged. This narrative trope—threatening foes are struck with blindness at the critical moment—is very common and widespread; it occurs in folktales and in other forms of narrative. For examples and further literature see T. H. Gaster, Myth, Legend. . . (1969) 158f.

[19:12-17]   Order to abandon the city: This introduces the rescue of Lot which continues down to v. 22(23) and to which v. 26 also belongs. No one is miraculously snatched away; human measures are taken within the limits of human potential; the marvellous enters in only where God acts directly (v. 26). What the messengers say stands out against what they do; they take sides with God, vv. 13b, (14b), 15b, (16b), (17b): "We will destroy the place." All these sentences are concerned with the decision to destroy linked in v. 16 with the decision to spare Lot. Two narrative threads, therefore, come together in vv. 12-17; the preservation of Lot and his family from the destruction of the city by the messengers and (following on 19:1-11), giving the reason for it, the decision to destroy the city and to save an individual (following on 18:20-21). The relatively independent narrative, 19:1-11, which has its parallel in Judg. 19:15-25, acquires here the function of an inquiry whether the outcry over Sodom is justified (18:20-21, taken up in 19:13). This is the explanation of the small inconsistencies to which W. Zimmerli refers.

[19:12] The חתן is regarded as a scribal error from v. 14; the singular is not in place and the suffix is missing (both are corrected in translations); the position before "sons and daughters" is unsuitable. As in the flood story, one person and his household (family) is saved. The messengers speak and act as human beings; they say and do what is necessary, they inform themselves and urge haste.

[19:13] There is unevenness (the suffix "their outcry" does not go with "this place") and repetitions in the reason for the destruction which really come from another context; the first sentence of v. 13 does not fit in with the last. R. Kilian sees several literary layers here: according to J, Yahweh destroys (vv. 14, 24); according to the plural layer, the two men (v. 13a); while in between v. 13bβ presupposes the two older layers. But the explanation that two narrative threads come together here is sufficient. It is also possible that the last sentence of v. 13, "and he (Yahweh) has sent us to destroy it," is a later addition with intent to harmonize; in favor of this is, as B. Jacob notes, the fact that "שלח is not used of a messenger elsewhere in Genesis."

[19:14] V. 14 follows immediately on v. 12: Lot does what the men have ordered him, but without effect, because the sons-in-law do not take him seriously (this could be a preparation for vv. 30-38, where Lot's two daughters are without husbands). This minor touch underscores how deadly serious is the divine judgment. The reason Lot gives for his summons to his sons-in-law to abandon the city, "because Yahweh is going to destroy it," is quite in harmony with v. 13a, "for we are going to destroy this place," where the messengers identify themselves with the one who commissioned them.

[19:15,16] "When dawn broke": this statement of time introduces a new section. It implies, "now it is high time!" and is followed by the statement of time at the beginning of v. 23, sunrise, with which the catastrophe starts. An air of pressing tension determines the period between these two (the insertion of vv. 18-22 has a marked retarding effect). What happens here is a perfect reflection of narrative art. A chain of imperatives forms the framework. "Lead them away. . ." (v. 12); "Up, out of this place" (v. 14); "Up, take your wife. . ." (v. 15); "Flee for your life, do not look behind, do not stop anywhere. . ." (v. 17). A special touch is that the imperative in v. 15, "Up, take your wife. . .," is not followed by the necessary imperative, "leave the city"; this is taken for granted, and Lot had already said it in v. 14. This throws into still sharper relief Lot's own dallying, so that the men have to seize him and his wife and daughters and lead them out of the city. The הנמצאת is not an addition (H. Gunkel), but makes good sense in reference to v. 14. Lot's dallying is not so much an indication of his character as a description of the city dwellers' way of life; they feel more secure in the city (v. 14) and only with great difficulty tear themselves from their fixed residence and property. The reason is repeated once more in v. 15b in a formulation which, in accord with the double meaning of עון, describes the catastrophe as a judgment on the crime of the city; this is balanced by the reference to sparing in v. 16.

[19:17] But even now they are not yet safe, though the men could leave them alone. They dismiss him with a directive (vv. 17a,17bβ) and a prohibition (v. 17bα), the prohibition belonging to the directive and refining it. A directive (in the imperative) often serves the purpose of rescue in the Old Testament, because it shows the way out; a prohibition, the purpose of preservation. The cry, "flee for your life," has the same note of urgency about it as the preceding imperatives. The argumentation is the same in content in 17bα and 17bβ, and is merely elaborated in 17bβ by the detail about the goal, "to the mountains." The repetition of almost the same sentence is to be understood from the situation, which is also the reason why the cry "flee for your life" is repeated often. The prohibition to look back or to stop is framed by it. It is primarily an order to greater haste—"your life is at stake"—perfectly understandable in the situation. But the prohibition to look around goes further: no one may observe God's judgment of destruction. Prohibitions like this are common and widespread. For examples and literature, see T. H. Gaster, *Myth, Legend*. . . (1969); G. M. Buccellati (BeO 13 [1971] 226); J. Reindl (Erfurter ThSt 25 [1970]). In an older form of the narrative, vv. 23-25 were attached to this directive which was safeguarded by the prohibition; however, in this case we read, balancing v. 17bβ: "and Lot had now arrived at the mountains."

[19:18-22] *Zoar:* This scene differs markedly in style from those around it. Lot's request (vv. 18-20) is expressed in detailed language which shows no sign of haste. Further, Lot is not in dialog with the men, but with an individual whom he addresses as אדני (the plural in v. 18 is perhaps a correction with intent to harmonize). But it is particularly the concluding etiological remark that is stylistically out of character. Vv. 18-22 then are an etiological scene (cf. comm. Gen. 14:18-20) which has been inserted to explain the name Zoar.

[19:18-20] The scene consists of Lot's request (vv. 18-20) and the granting of it (vv. 21-22). The request consists of a reference back to the previous action of protection (v. 19a), thereby skillfully inserting the elaboration into the context. The request itself has a negative (v. 19b) and a positive part (v. 20). Lot asks that he be allowed to flee to the little city of Zoar because he is afraid that he may not survive the climb into the mountains. Zoar on the contrary is so close and easily accessible. But in that case Zoar must be preserved from destruction. Lot's request makes use of a traditional motif (in Amos 7:3,5 too the motif is linked with the request so as to move God to intervene): "Yes, it is only small." This is deliberately repeated in v. 20 in order to underscore it; hence the name Zoar. The note in v. 22bβ could also stand at the end of v. 20.

[19:21-22] The granting of the request consists in the assurance, literally, "I have lifted up your face" (cf. *Genesis 1–11*, comm. 4:6-7; J. Reindl, Erfurter ThSt 25 [1970]). "This too. . ." does not quite fit the context because Lot has not hitherto made any request. This shows that vv. 18-22 are an insertion. The concession is that the Lord promises not to destroy the city of Zoar. Lot had not explicitly asked for this, but that is what he meant, as the motif, "Yes, it is only small," shows. It is here that the second etiological function comes in, namely, the present situation that Zoar, preserved on the edge of the Dead Sea, escaped destruction. This is traced back to an event in the past, that Lot was granted it as a place of refuge. At the end of vv. 18-22, v. 22a links the etiological insertion with the context just as v. 18a does at the beginning; the cry, "flee for your life" is taken up from v. 17, but here with Zoar as the goal. The reason, "because I can do nothing until. . ." fits into the context and explains the meaning of the time references in vv. 15 and 23. The concluding etiological remark in v. 22 should really run: "For this reason Zoar remained intact when the cities of the plain were destroyed"; but that is not necessary. A note following v. 20 would suffice.

The city of Zoar on the southeastern shore of the Dead Sea (according to Gen. 14:2,8, it was earlier called בלע) is mentioned again in Gen. 13:10; Deut. 34:3; Is. 15:5; Jer. 48:34. There are further mentions of it later. It is generally accepted that it lay at the southeastern end of the Dead Sea (see also the notes on the Pentapolis, comm. on 14:1-11; J. Simons, §404f.). The etiological explanation of the place-name follows the meaning of the word closely here, Hebr. צער, "little, to be slight."

[19:23-25] *The destruction of Sodom.* After a time reference (v. 23) to which the rescue of Lot (vv. 15-17/15-22) has been attached as it were by way of parenthesis, the destruction of Sodom is reported in just two sentences. It has been shown above that they are an account which is independent of the rest of the chapter and can be regarded as a separate tradition. The concise language stands out clearly.

[19:23] The self-contained report of vv. 24-25 is skillfully linked with and inserted into the foregoing narrative by means of the time reference, "the sun was rising (or had just risen) over the land"; it balances that in v. 15a. If one compares v. 23 with v. 15, the action here should also follow immediately on the time reference; the sentence is more effective without the parenthesis that follows (so too J. Skinner). It is possible that the parenthesis was only inserted together with the elaboration vv. 18-22 (so H. Gunkel), and that the goal, "to the mountains" (v. 17b) originally stood in v. 23b.

Excursus

The absence of the portrayal of nature in the patriarchal stories. The first signs of a description of nature in the Old Testament are discernible in the context of the praise of God, e.g., Ps. 104 and in God's speeches in Job 38–41. It is completely absent from the patriarchal stories. This is shown by such verses as Gen. 19:15a, "When dawn broke. . .," and 19:23, "The sun had just risen over the land. . .." These details are purely functional (as in Gen. 15:12,17); they divide the course of events in such a way as to introduce a tension; they are in no way descriptive nor are they to be understood lyrically, whatever effect they may have on later readers. In common with folktales, the early Old Testament narratives know nothing of the portrayal of nature. In other words, the portrayal of nature is not one of the devices of narrative form. Both in folktales and in the early narratives of the Old Testament, humans take their natural environment so much for granted that it does not occur to them to objectify it by description. Echoes of it are but rare: the portrayal of nature begins only when it is no longer taken for granted. When descriptions of nature begin to intrude and to become a device of narrative art, then this is an indication of the loss of that immediacy which has no need for portraying something as an object.

This brings up something well worthy of reflection: oral narrative, to which both the early narratives of the Old Testament and folktales belong, is superior to later narratives both by virtue of expression and tradition; these latter have to be "enriched" and "embellished" by a description of nature. But the listener needs nothing of this because he sees what is happening as he listens. A purely functional detail such as Gen. 19:23, "The sun had just risen over the land. . .," is enough to let him see what is happening together with the whole theater where it is happening; the same holds for vv. 27-28. There is no need of any further description; it would be obtrusive. Listening is brought to such a peak that it needs no description of nature; this would not be a plus but a minus. It is different in the case of the praise of God. In the descriptive praise of God (the hymn) the description of nature has a function; the beauty of creation becomes the object of the praise of God (C. Westermann, *Praise and Lament in the Psalms* [1977⁵, Eng. 1981]). It is understandable that traces of declarative praise are found in the patriarchal stories (in the name ישׁמעאל = "God hears," Gen. 16:17, and in the name "God sees" in Gen. 22:14), but not descriptive praise. But this would require further reflection.

[19:24-25] When an older account is taken up by the narrator, as in vv. 24-25, one ought not try to restore a text that runs smoothly and without inconsistencies. From the very start we have to reckon with variants which are joined together here, but in such a way that each is to speak with its own voice. There is no indication that the cities of the Dead Sea were inundated (that could be the meaning in Gen. 13:10), nor is there any mention at all of the Dead Sea or of water in general.

[19:24] V. 24 says that the two cities were destroyed by a rain of "fire and brimstone"; this is a fixed image for God's judgment in action. The word גפרית = "brimstone" occurs only in this image—besides Job 18:15 (so T. W. Mann, JBL 90 [1971] 15-30):

Ps. 11:6	On the wicked he will rain coals of fire and brimstone.
Ezek. 38:22	I will enter into judgment with him; and I will rain upon him and his hordes. . . fire and brimstone. . . .
Is. 30:33	For a burning place has long been prepared. . .; the breath of the Lord, like a stream of brimstone, kindles it.
Is. 34:9	And her streams shall be turned into pitch, and her soil into brimstone; her land shall become burning pitch.
Deut. 29:22	(ET v. 23) the whole land brimstone and salt, and a burnt-out waste, unsown, and growing nothing, where no grass can sprout, and overthrow like that of Sodom and Gomorrah. . .

Fire and brimstone occur together in these passages, while in others it is fire alone (Ezek. 28:27; 39:6; Lam. 1:13), thus showing that there is a traditional fixed expression in use for God's judgment of destruction (always on a city or a land). It is not meant to describe accurately an individual event, and so one cannot conclude from it to a natural phenomenon whose course can be traced. We can say no more than this: corresponding to the expression is the fact that deposits of asphalt and sulphur are to be found even today on the edge of the Dead Sea and that during earthquakes gases from the earth can catch fire. But it is no longer possible to give an exact explanation of the event (so too H. Donner, *Einführung in die biblische Landes und Altertumskunde* [1976] 27; W. Blanckenhorn, ZDPV 19 [1896] 1-59; J. P. Harland, BA 5-6 [1942-43]).

There follows then the further precision, "from Yahweh in the heavens"; it is there twice, the second perhaps an explanation of the first and earlier sentence (so H. Gunkel and others). More important is that the phrase "from Yahweh in the heavens" does not match well with the beginning, "Yahweh rained (i.e., caused fire and brimstone to rain)." It presupposes rather the *qal*; this follows also from the awkward repetition of Yahweh as the cause in the same sentence. The only explanation of the text is that two different descriptions of God's judgment have merged.

[19:25] V. 25 describes the effects, not the event itself. The traditional verb associated with the story of Sodom and Gomorrah, הפך is used (Gen. 19:21; Deut. 29:23; Is. 1:7; 13:19; Jer. 49:16; 50:40; Amos 4:11; Lam. 4:6). A. Dillmann had already seen that it does not suit v. 24 well: "The verb הפך, which ill matches a rain of brimstone, is used because it had long been a fixed part of the story." It is possible that it is meant to indicate an earthquake (O. Procksch, E. A. Speiser, and others); but as it is a fixed image for a divine judgment it is no more to be attached to a definite event than is our word "catastrophe," which has exactly the same meaning. In any case, it is certain that in vv. 24 and 25 it is a question of two originally different traditions.

The effects of the disaster (v. 25b) range over the cities themselves, their environs (on ככר cf. comm. 13:10), the people, and the vegetation. This imposing sentence brings the turbulent narrative to an awesome conclusion.

[19:26] V. 26 is a self-contained episode, comprising an action and its consequence. It is neither an "appendage" (H. Gunkel) nor an etiological story (e.g., A. Dillmann: "The point of departure of the story is a pillar of salt-stone"; likewise H. Gunkel and G. von Rad). The verse is rather a constituent part of the narrative of the rescue of Lot (vv. 12-17) and presupposes the prohibition in v. 17. The point of departure, therefore, must be a motif within the narrative structure: the prohibition to look back, the transgression, and the changing into salt-stone. It is a very old and widespread motif. H. Gunkel has already referred to examples from Greek literature and "The 1001 Nights"; for further examples cf. G. M. Buccellati (BeO 13 [1971] 226); T. H. Gaster (*Myth, Legend. . .* [1969]). The example cited above under "Form" shows that the motif belongs to the narrative type of the rescue of an individual from the destruction of a city. The narrative motif "taboo on looking back" (T. H. Gaster) goes back to the magical way of thinking; "etiological" is an inadequate description; further, it is inexact just to say that the metamorphosis of a human being in the Old Testament occurs only here (M. C. Astour, JBL 85 [1966] 185-196; B. S. Childs, VT 24 [1974] 389). The point of departure in the case of this widespread motif, which has its roots in magical thinking, is not a pillar of salt or stone resembling a person, but the potency of the taboo or prohibition. This is the case here also. V. 26 is saying that Lot is rescued on the very brink of the abyss. W. Zimmerli's explanation is correct: "In this way the whole horror of the disaster is expressed." The etiological aspect then is secondary and due to local coloring. An illustration of a pillar of salt resembling a person is found in the article of L. Hicks ("Lot," IDB 3 [1962]). That v. 26 has the appearance of an appendage (H. Holzinger: "the suffix of אשתו is left hanging in the air") is due to the construction of the narrative; v. 26 should really follow v. 17; nevertheless it presupposes vv. 24-25 (correctly, R. Kilian).

[19:27-28] There is something majestic about the conclusion of the narrative which the sentence structure brings to the fore: ". . .He rose early. . .; he gazed down. . .; and look. . . ." Each step describes a movement towards a goal; the movement freezes in the awe-inspiring horror of the sight. The man, Abraham, is the subject; and so the narrative of the destruction of Sodom, 19:1-26, which does not mention him, is linked with the figure of Abraham. That is to say, this conclusion was not an original part of the narrative. This suggests that it should be ascribed to the author who attached Gen. 13; 18–19 to a narrative cycle, i.e., to the Yahwist. However, the relative sentence (v. 27b), "where he had stood in the presence of Yahweh,'' seems to be against this, apparently referring back to 18:17-33, or following immediately on it or in any case presupposing it (so the majority of exegetes). But this is very unlikely because 19:27-28 bears a completely different stamp from 18:17-33. It can just as well refer back to 18:16b before vv. 17-33 were added, not excluding that it acquired its present formulation only with the insertion of vv. 17-33. The relative sentence acquires its function by virtue of chs. 13; 18–19 being built into the narrative cycle. It is not enough to look for the meaning simply in the fact that Abraham appears only now in the narrative of the destruction of the cities. The author wanted to say something by having Abraham participate in the event narrated. While Abraham looks down in silence on the scene of the catastrophe he becomes aware that it is God's judgment. The sentence then, taken as a conclusion added by J to the narrative, is to be regarded as a counterpart to 12:1-3: that all the nations of the earth are to find blessing in Abraham does not mean that the human race is the object of blessing alone; humanity lies under the threat of catastrophes and God's judgment; nevertheless, the blessing is still effective. The God who blesses is also the God who judges. Abraham looks down on the scene of the disaster—and is silent.

[19:29] *The destruction of the cities and the rescue of Lot according to P.* This verse is a highly significant example of the adaptation of the old traditions under the changed attitudes of a later era. In the middle of the verse stands the sentence: "Then he (God) remembered Abraham," the precise equivalent of Gen. 8:1: "then God remembered Noah" (on זכר, see *Genesis 1–11*, comm. on 8:1; in addition to the literature given there, see further P. A. H. de Boer, *Gedenken und Gedächtnis in der Welt des AT. Franz Delitzsch Vorlesung* [1962] 5-76). The author is no longer interested in the destination of a city in the distant past, nor even in the fate of Lot as such. The only thing that is important for him is the relationship between God and Abraham which was the object of ch. 17. For Abraham's sake God rescued his relatives from that ancient catastrophe; it is this relationship that the author wants to proclaim to his generation and it is this he wants to resurrect for his contemporaries out of the old stories; even for P they still retain their significance for the present and the future in that they point anew to each generation the meaning of God's promise to Abraham: "I will be your God."

Purpose and Thrust

The motifs indicate that God's judgment on Sodom (and Gomorrah) does not belong directly to the patriarchal period. Nor is Abraham an immediate participator in the judgment. The link with the Abraham story is the figure of Lot. A short notice would have sufficed for this, something like P's in 19:29. Why has the judgment become part of the Abraham story, acquiring such importance in the arrangement of the Abraham-Lot cycle? There is but a hint of J's literary and theological plan there in the background: Abraham becomes a witness of the disaster from which his relative is rescued. This therefore has special significance in the story of Abraham as a whole inasmuch as the story comes in contact with the world at large, the world of the nations, in only a few places; one of these is the prolog, 12:1-3, where the blessing for all peoples is brought into relationship with Abraham. Another place is 19:27-29 where Abraham becomes a witness of the destruction of the cities. It is, as it were, a counterpart to 12:3: the promise of blessing for the peoples has its line of demarcation in God's action as judge; "the peoples of the earth" remain exposed to disasters. J deliberately resumes the primeval motif of Gen. 6–8 into the Abraham story: God's judgments are just as much part of the story that begins with Abraham as is his blessing. Abraham's relative—relatives like Lot and Ishmael are the links with the world of the nations—is rescued on the very brink of disaster, as the fate of his wife shows. The story of Abraham the father reaches its completion in the midst of the story of the nations among whom his God is at work both as one who blesses and one who judges.

Ch. 19 concludes what is to be said about Lot (19:30-38 is in the framework of genealogy and itinerary). The first story about Lot told of his choice of the fertile plain when he separated from Abraham (ch. 13); he became a citizen of Sodom. Both the seriousness of the crime and that of the catastrophe presuppose the gathering of people in a city. The significance of the story of Lot side by side with that of Abraham is this: Abraham remains the nomad shepherd on the barren steppe; Lot, on the contrary, possesses the fertile land, has chosen the city and experiences the dangers and threats that go with it. One of these great disasters caused by outrageous revolt occurs close to Abraham; both are part of the human situation in which Abraham lives and in which his posterity will live. As Abraham gazes in silence over the scene of the disaster (vv. 27-28), he looks beyond himself and his experience into the history of his people and the history of the peoples of the earth.

Lot's Daughters

Literature

A. Lods, ''La caverne de Lot,'' RHR 95 (1927) 204-219. J. J. Stamm, ''Zum Ursprung des Namens der Ammoniter,'' ArOr 18 (1950) 379-382. W. M. W. Roth, ''Hinterhalt und Scheinflucht. Der stammespolemische Hintergrund von Jos 8,'' ZAW 75 (1963) 296-304. S. Luria, ''Tochterschändung in der Bibel,'' ArOr 33 (1965) 207-208. H. R. Stroes, ''Does the Day Begin in the Evening or Morning?'' VT 16 (1966) 460-475. I. O. Lehmann, ''A Forgotten Principle of Biblical Textual Tradition Rediscovered,'' JNES 26 (1967) 93-101. F. W. Basset, ''Noah's Nakedness and the Curse of Canaan. A Case of Incest?'' VT 21 (1971) 232-237. R. J. Clifford, *The Cosmic Mountain in Canaan and the Old Testament. Harvard Semitic Monographs* 4 (1972). A. Baumgarten, ''A Note on the Book of Ruth,'' Fests. T. H. Gaster (1973) 11-15. R. P. Carroll, ''Rebellion and Dissent in Ancient Israelite Society,'' ZAW 89 (1977) 176-204. F. Deist, ''Stilvergleichung als literarkritisches Verfahren,'' ZAW 89 (1977) 325-357.

Text

19:30   Now Lot went up from Zoar and dwelt in the mountain range with his two daughters because he was afraid to dwell in Zoar; he lived in a certain[a] cave together with his two daughters.[b]

31   Then the elder daughter said to the younger: Our father is old, and there is no man in the land to come to us[a] in accordance with the custom of the world.

32   Come,[a] let us make our father drunk with wine and lie with him and so continue the life of our family through[b] him.

33   So they[a] made their father drunk with wine that night;[b] and the elder went and lay with him[c] but he was not aware of her lying and rising.[d]

34   On the following morning the elder said to the younger: I slept last evening[a] with my[b] father. Let us make him drunk with wine again tonight,[c] and you go and lie with him and so continue the life of our family through him.

35   So they made their father drunk with wine that night too and the younger went and lay with him, but he was not aware of her lying and rising.

36   So the two daughters of Lot were pregnant by their father.

37   The elder gave birth to a son and called him Moab;[a] he is the father of the Moabites to this day.

38   The younger too gave birth to a son and called him Ben-Ammi;[a] he is the father of the Ammonites to this day.

30a   Not the art. denoting a class as in Ges-K §126n, but that particular (well known) cave.   **b**   Sam, Gk, Vg add "with him."

31a   על in the sense of אל (so the Gk and Vg read it); cf. Deut. 25:5; 2 Sam. 15:4 (BrSynt §110a).

32a   לכה formula; Sam reads לכי.   **b**   מן as indication of origin (BrSynt §111h); likewise v. 36.

33a   For the verb form (likewise vv. 35,36) Ges-K §47b   **b**   בלילה הוא, I. O. Lehmann points out a textual ambivalence, JNES 26 (1967) 93-101; the ה can refer to the word preceding or following; after BrSynt §23d, to the following.   **c**   Gk adds τὴν νύκτα ἐκείνην.   **d**   The point probably indicates a superfluous letter; cf. v. 35 (J. Skinner).

34a   אמש, according to the Akk. *ina amšat* "(yesterday) evening," only in Gen. 19:34; 31:29,42; Job 30:3 (2 Kings 9:26 doubtful).   **b**   Gk reads אבינו.   **c**   Gk adds ταύτην.

37a   Gk adds λέγουσα ἐκ τοῦ πατρός μου.

38a   Gk adds Ἀμμαν υἱὸς ὁ τοῦ γένους μου. The בן־עמי is in accord with the linguistic usage which always refers to the Ammonites as בן־עמון. On the name, cf. J. J. Stamm, ArOr 18 (1950) 379-382.

Form

Gen. 19:30-38 is not really a narrative but rather a report elaborated by narration consisting of some itinerary information (v. 30) joined with a genealogical note (vv. 36-38). The report is elaborated by means of an episode which tells how Lot's daughters acquired their sons (vv. 31-35). It is in the arrangement of the Abraham-Lot cycle (Gen. 13; 18–19) that 19:30-38 acquires its setting and meaning. The story of Lot, which began with the separation from Abraham in ch. 13, was continued in 19:1-28 and is brought to its conclusion in 19:30-38 in the usual way with a genealogical notice (similarly in the case of Hagar and Ishmael). It is because this concluding report with its itinerary and genealogy corresponds to the Abraham story that it can go back to the patriarchal period, though not in its present form. This would mean that v. 30 is older than its link with the destruction of Sodom, and so is saying nothing more than that Lot withdrew from Sodom (which was still standing) to Zoar whence he went up into the mountain range. The sentence, "because he was afraid to dwell in Zoar," was added only later. The significance of this for vv. 37-38 would be that the names of the two tribes were simple personal names.

    This old account has been developed further in two very different directions. *(a)* As is often the case with genealogies, there has been a transposition: the tribe has replaced the family. The sons of the daughters of Lot have become the progenitors of two tribes (just as in Gen. 9:18-27); there has been a marked abbreviation with the line of succession from the sons to the progenitors omitted. The purpose of the transposition and the abbreviation, which one gathers from the ill-fitting "to this day," is obvious. In the period when Israel was coming into being, her relationship with neighboring peoples was demonstrated in this way. The concluding etiology in vv. 37,38 can have arisen only in the period when the tribes had come together. The judgment of H. Gunkel ("ethnological story"), O. Eissfeldt, R. Kilian ("a tribal etiology"), and a number of others requires correction in this respect; the text is not originally etiological, but has been made so by the conclusion. It is probable that the primal motif was given the form of a narrative at the time of the origins of Moab and Ammon (so H. Gunkel).

(b) The other development comes from the connection with the narrative of the destruction of Sodom. Lot is the one who escapes from the judgment, as did Noah in chs. 6–9. It has been shown that 19:1-28 belongs to the same narrative type as the flood story. The motif of the (partially) new creation of the human race after the disaster belongs to this type (cf. *Genesis 1–11*, 403-404). The remark of one of the daughters, "there is no man in the land" (19:31, anticipated in 19:14) accords with this; it is a matter of preserving the (human) family after the disaster (vv. 32b, 34b). Even though it is only just apparent in the present text, there is nevertheless no doubt that it has its origin in the primeval event (so H. Gunkel, J. Skinner, R. Kilian, and others). There has been a transference here too: the primeval motif has been transferred to a situation in which the disaster is partial and limited; it is no longer a question of the preservation or of the new creation of mankind but of the preservation of a family line. The two developments *(a)* and *(b)* come together here: in the text as it lies before us the goal is the origin of two tribes or peoples.

One must agree with J. Van Seters that it is no longer possible to reconstruct an earlier text (*Abraham in History. . .* [1975]); motifs of different origin are amalgamated into a conclusion to the Abraham-Lot cycle (chs. 13; 18–19) in such a way that a series of characteristics in vv. 30-38, which refer to what has preceded, are comprehensible only in such a literary construction. This is clear too in the structure and style of vv. 30-38. The structure is shaped symmetrically: v. 30, exposition; vv. 31-32, decision; vv. 33-36, execution of decision (v. 33, the elder; vv. 34-35, the younger; v. 36, the result); vv. 37f., birth and naming of sons, etiological conclusion; several sentences are repeated verbatim, or almost so (vv. 32, 34b and vv. 33, 35).

Setting

The constitutive parts of this text originated and developed in three different domains: (1) the motif of new life after an annihilation in the domain of primeval narratives; (2) the etiological explanation of the origin of the neighboring tribes of Moab and Ammon in the domain of tribal story; (3) the construction of 19:30-38 into part of the story about Abraham and Lot, more precisely into the conclusion of what is narrated about Lot, as the patriarchal stories were coming together, and in particular the Abraham-Lot cycle. This is a rejection of the old view that the narratives derive from Israelite polemic or from hate and contempt for the neighboring Moabites and Ammonites (so particularly A. Dillmann, ". . .give expression to Israel's revulsion at the lascivious nature of Moab-Ammon"; H. Holzinger and others).

One cannot exclude that the narrative came to be understood in this way in a later period, but only that it arose out of political polemic of this kind. There is a parallel in 9:18-27 where a primeval and a tribal-historical motif have come together and have been amalgamated in one and the same narrative (there is no discernible connection between the drunkenness of Noah and that of Lot). One can, however, point to a motif which links it with the Abraham cycle, albeit indirectly. A motif that carries the Abraham cycle is that a child is to be born which will assure the continuity of the family; this is also the issue in 19:30-38, though in a very different way: ". . .And so continue the life of our family. . ." (vv. 32, 34).

Commentary

[**19:30**]   Vv. 30 and 36-38 are the report which forms the framework. The sentence, omitting the reason given, is characteristic of the itinerary: "He went up. . .; he dwelt. . . with. . .; he lived. . ." (cf. Intro., "Genealogies and Itineraries," end of section 3). It is a continuation of the itinerary in 13:11-12 which is followed in 13:13 by the introduction to the destruction of Sodom; the sentence in 19:30 giving the reason forms the link with it (it is not to be interpreted psychologically). One sees from this how carefully the story of the destruction of Sodom was fitted into the older itinerary.

It is to be inferred from 19:1-28 that Lot's two daughters are now the only survivors of his family. Vv. 30-38 in their present form are intelligible only as the conclusion of chs. 18–19. It is only from the composition of the Abraham-Lot cycle (chs. 13, 18–19) that there emerges the contrast between Lot's choice, 13:11-12 (the rich land) with the permanent dwelling in the city of Sodom, 19:1ff., and the cave in the mountain range where his flight ended. It is described as "the cave," that is, a particular cave known to the listeners.

[**19:31-32**]   *The decision.* It is obvious that the episode in vv. 31-36 is independent of the framework (v. 30 and vv. 37-38) in that the exposition is not narrative but is transposed into speech (v. 31b). There are two reasons for the proposal that the elder daughter makes to the younger: the first, "our father is old," can only mean in the context that he will not marry again and so could not have any descendants; the second, "there is no man in the land," which H. Gunkel explains: "the story seems to presuppose that everyone was the victim of the catastrophe" (likewise J. Skinner and others). The original primeval context still comes through in v. 31b; this too is the basis of the decision that there must be posterity at any cost. As they saw it, this could be the only reason why their lives had been preserved. The same expression occurs in the same context in the flood narrative (7:3). It is out of place then to make a moral judgment on other life situations, whether one considers the decision reprehensible or heroic (B. Jacob: "Their action is a witness to heroism on a grand scale," agreeing for once with H. Gunkel). In any case one is justified in speaking of a "decision of desperation" (F. Delitzsch, E. A. Speiser, and others). But what is more important here is the point at issue—"and so continue the life of our family." The life which was granted them again in their rescue from the catastrophe is seen in a broader context; only when life reaches beyond the death of the individual does it make sense and achieve its significance, as is also expressed in Abraham's lament (Gen. 15:2-3).

In order to carry out their decision they had to eliminate any resistance on the part of their father. They could do this by making him drunk. This to be sure is a hint that Moab was well known for its wine.

[**19:33-35**]   *Execution of the decision.* What is striking here is the almost literal repetition in both cases (vv. 33 and 35), and that the execution corresponds word for word with the plan which is repeated again in v. 34 in the case of the younger sister. Vv. 33-35 contain virtually nothing new except the remark that Lot noticed nothing; this, also repeated, is simply to say that the plan went without a hitch. Moreover, the daughters are spoken of only as the elder and the younger, giving the episode a somewhat artificial coloring (against H. Gunkel, who sees here a particular narrative art). If it is true that the itinerary and genealogy material (vv. 30, 36-38) was already at hand, then it is possible that the genealogical note was shaped into a narrative by means of the motif of the creation of new life after the catastrophe.

[19:36-38]   In v. 36 the narrative issues into the framework; the verse forms the transition. It reports, without any evaluation, that the plan of the two sisters succeeded (it is not "in order to exonerate Lot," H. Gunkel, J. Skinner). Both became pregnant and gave birth to sons whose names in the underlying genealogy could only be simple personal names. It is a mere fiction that the mothers gave their children, through whom their family was to continue, the tribal names of Moab and Ammon; both the names of the mothers as well as those of the children were unknown to the author.

[19:37-38]   The conclusion in vv. 37 and 38 does not consist in the etiological explanation of names but in the explanation of the origin of Moab and Ammon (so correctly J. Van Seters); "to this day" therefore does not mean, "and these are their names even today," but, "they are still here today as Israel's neighbors." The meanings of the names are not necessary to explain the origins of Moab and Ammon. They simply remind us of them. An etiological explanation of a name had to be introduced: "because they said. . . ." These names are possible only in their well-known meaning as names of tribes or peoples from the period when Moab and Ammon existed as tribes or peoples; hence from the period of the tribes of Israel. The same is true for the interpretation which reads into the name Moab the meaning, "from the father" (מיאב), and into the name *Ben-Ammi*, "son of my kinsman," following the narrative. It is not a case of retrojection. This etiological explanation of the names of these two neighbors of Israel arose only after the immigration of the tribes and with the express purpose of demonstrating the distant relationship of Israel to Moab and Ammon. This relationship through the family of Lot, Abraham's nephew, is the current situation which is explained by an event in the past.

This purpose is further underscored by the awkward addition of the etiological formula, "until this day" (on the formula see B. S. Childs, JBL 82 [1963] 279-292, and literature cited). It refers to "father"; that is, "he is the father. . . to this day," which does not make sense. What is meant is that the Moabites (Ammonites) are our relatives (descendants of the son of Lot) until this day.

It can be demonstrated with certainty that both the names of the sons of Lot's daughters as well as their etiological explanation do not belong originally to the narrative (vv. 31-36). It has been said already that the names of the children must have been originally simple personal names. It is very likely that they were tied up with an interpretation which in turn must have been directed towards the goal of the narrative: not, that is, to trace the lineage from the father of the daughters, but the reason why this desperate act happened, namely, to continue the life of the family. The present interpretation of the names has deflected the action from its goal inasmuch as the formula "until this day" deviates from what actually happened.

Purpose and Thrust

This text is particularly open to misinterpretation. When one makes evaluations such as "incestuous" or "incest" in its title or says at the very beginning, "this revolting story" (A. Dillmann), then one is unable to understand what it intends to say. One can do justice to the text only by taking account of the history of its growth. It goes back into a distant past on which we cannot impose our criteria. Three layers have come together in the long process of growth: the patriarchal story in the form it took in regard to the family of Lot, the primeval story under the aspect of the judgment and annihilation that befell Sodom, and the story of the people in the etiological conclusion whose goal is the peoples of Moab and Ammon, Israel's present-day neighbors.

Central is the primeval motif of the rising again of new life, or of a new generation after an annihilation. This can take a great variety of narrative forms; here it takes the form of the desperate act of two young women whose sole concern is to acquire posterity so that the family may live on. The motif is akin to the Abraham cycle. The framework consists of an itinerary and genealogy containing a report which belongs to the patriarchal story because it is concerned with the nephew of Abraham and is entirely in accord with the itineraries and genealogies of that story. One characteristic of the Abraham cycle is that Abraham is not only the father of Israel but also of the nations; consequently, the lineage of his kinsman Lot is also of significance and it is this that is being brought to an end in 19:30-38. In the conclusion that was added later, Israel's neighbors, Moab and Ammon as descendants of Lot, are described as Israel's kinsmen, distant though the relationship may be. It is viewed positively in Deut. 2:9,19. The later enmity towards the two peoples, which appears in Deut. 23:3-6, can have led to the text being understood in a later period as showing contempt for Moab and Ammon; this, however, is not its purpose as such. The book of Ruth reports the marriage between an Israelite and a Moabite (this has caused some Jewish exegetes to alter the exegesis of Gen. 19:30-38: "Some Jewish exegetes of the birth of Moab chose not to denounce, but rather to praise, that story"; A. Baumgarten, Fests. T. H. Gaster [1973] 11-15). The Moabite Ruth is a member of the family tree of David (Ruth 4:18-22) and Jesus (Mt. 1:5).

The desperate deed of Lot's unnamed daughters stands right in the center of the text. It is striking that the patriarchal story reports a number of acts of rebellion on the part of women—Hagar (ch. 16), Rebekah (ch. 27), Tamar (ch. 38). These acts of revolt against prevailing standards of morality and customs have always the same goal: it is a question of having one's own child and thereby assuring the women their only possible future. These are indications that in all probability we must review the prevailing opinion that in the ancient history of Israel the man alone was the determining party. Gen. 16; 19; 27 indicate that by way of exception and in cases of extreme necessity the woman could take the initiative. In any case women had a greater importance in patriarchal times than is generally acknowledged.

The figure of Lot recedes notably in face of this. G. von Rad tries, at the conclusion of ch. 19, to bring into relief the main lines of this figure as J intended it. However, I think that it is questionable whether that was J's intent and whether one ought not be more cautious with a character portrait of Lot. One can be certain only of one trait, namely, that Lot by choosing the sedentary life of a city dweller exposes himself to the dangers of this life-style. As one rescued from the catastrophe, Lot has of necessity merely a passive role which is continued in vv. 30-38. He has a passive role also in ch. 14. The contrast between his choice at the beginning and his life in the cave at the end is certainly deliberate. One cannot say much more than that.

Abraham and Abimelech

Literature

Genesis 20: W. Eichrodt, *Die Quellen der Genesis*, BZAW 31 (1916) 65-66. I. Lewy, "The Story of the Golden Calf Reanalysed," VT 9 (1959) 318-322. D. Daube, *Sin, Ignorance and Forgiveness in the Bible* (1960). K. Koch, *The Growth of the Biblical Tradition* (1964; 1973[4]; Eng. 1969) § 10. H. W. Wolff, "Zur Thematik der elohistischen Fragmente im Pentateuch," EvTh 27 (1969) 59-72 = ThB 22 (1973[2]) 402-417 = *The Vitality of the OT Traditions*, W. Brueggemann and H. W. Wolff (1975) 67-82. R. A. Carlson, "Elisée—le successeur d'Élie," VT 20 (1970) 385-405. D. L. Petersen, "A Thrice-Told Tale: Genre, Theme, and Motif," BiR 17 (1972) 30-43. J. Schmid, "Bemerkungen zum patriarchalischen Stil," SBFLA 22 (1972) 315-334. R. E. Bee, "The Use of Statistical Methods in Old Testament Studies," VT 23 (1973) 257-272. S. Greengus, "Sisterhood Adoption at Nuzi and the 'Wife-Sister' in Genesis," HUCA 46 (1975) 5-31. R. M. Polzin, "The Ancestress of Israel in Danger," Semeia (1975) 81-97. J. Schüpphaus, "Volk Gottes und Gesetz beim Elohisten," ThZ 31 (1975) 193-210. R. C. Culley, *Semeia*, Supp. 2 (1976). P. Weimar, *Untersuchungen zur Redaktionsgeschichte des Pentateuch*, BZAW 146 (1977) ch. 1.

Genesis 20:1-2: D. A. Lutz, *Early Babylonian Letters From Larsa* (1917) 15, 13. H. J. Stoebe, "Gut und Böse in der jahwistischen Quelle des Pentateuch," ZAW 65 (1953) 188-204. Y. Aharoni, "The Land of Gerar," IEJ 6 (1956) 26-32. W. F. Albright, *Yahweh and the Gods of Canaan* (1968) 51-55. O. Perrot, "Petuhot et Setumot. Étude sur les alinéas de Pentateuque," RB 76 (1969) 50-91. H. Breit, "Überlegungen zur Religionskritik des AT," TEH 170 (1972) 9-29.

Genesis 20:3-8: E. L. Ehrlich, "Der Traum im Alten Testament," BZAW 73 (1953) 125-136. W. Zimmerli, " 'Leben' und 'Tod' im Buche des Propheten Ezechiel," ThZ 13 (1957) 494-508, esp. 497. D. Daube, "Direct and Indirect Causation in Biblical Law," VT 11 (1961) 246-269. N. Walker, "What is a *Nābhî*?" ZAW 73 (1961) 99-100. W. Richter, "Traum und Traumdeutung im AT. Ihre Form und Verwendung," BZ NF 7 (1963) 202-220. R. P. Carrol, "The Elijah–Elisha–Sagas: Some Remarks on Prophetic Succession in Ancient Israel," VT 19 (1969) 400-415. E. C. John, "Forgiveness in the Prophecy of Judgment," IJT 18 (1969) 206-218. E. Jenni, " 'Kommen' im theologischen Sprachgebrauch des Alten Testaments," Fests. W. Eichrodt, ATANT 59 (1970) 251-261. B. Vawter, "Intimations of Immortality and the Old Testament," JBL 91 (1972) 158-171. C. Houtman, "Zu I Samuel 2,25," ZAW 89 (1977) 412-417. J. Milgrom, "The Betrothed Slave-Girl, Lev 19,20-22," ZAW 89 (1977) 43-50.

Genesis 20:9-16: J. H. Hertz, *The Pentateuch* (1929) esp. 175f. E. Zolli, "El 'velo de los ojos' en Gen 20,16," EstB 7 (1948) 327-333. R. North, "Flesh, Covering, and Response,

Ex XXI 10," VT 5 (1955) 204-206. M. Dubarle, "Les textes divers du livre de Judith. A propos d'un ouvrage récent," VT 8 (1958) 344-373. W. L. Moran, "The Scandal of the 'Great Sin' at Ugarit," JNES 18 (1959) 280-281. H. P. Rüger, "1Q Gen. Apoc.," LZNW 55 (1964) 129-131. E. Auerbach, "Das Zehngebot—Allgemeine Gesetzes-Form in der Bibel," VT 16 (1966) 255-276. R. Gordis, "Studies in the Esther Narrative," JBL 95 (1976) 43-58. I. Robinson, "*Běpetaḥ ʿênayim* in Genesis 38:14," JBL 96 (1977) 569. G. Gerleman, "Das übervolle Mass. Ein Versuch mit *ḥaesaed*," VT 28 (1978) 151-164.

Genesis 20:17-18: G. Cooke, *A Text-Book of North-Semitic Inscriptions* (1903) 4-8. E. Nestle, "Genesis 20,17.18 und Herodot I," ZAW 33 (1913) 105. R. Gordis, "Studies in Hebrew Roots of Contrasted Meanings," JQR 27 (1936/37) 55-56. J. Gray, "Canaanite Kingship in Theory and Practice," VT 2 (1952) 193-220, esp. 207f. B. O. Long, "The Effect of Divination Upon Israelite Literature," JBL 92 (1973) 489-497.

Text

20:1 Now Abraham journeyed from there to the territory[a] of the Negeb and settled[b] between Kadesh and Shur. While he was living as an alien in Gerar[c]

2 Abraham said of his wife Sarah, She is my sister.[a] So Abimelech king of Gerar sent and took Sarah.

3 Then God came to Abimelech in a dream by night and said to him: You are a dead man[a] because of the woman[b] you have taken; she is a married woman.[c]

4 Now Abimelech had not approached her, and he said: Lord, will you really kill an innocent one? ( )[a]

5 Did not he himself say to me, She is my sister? And ( )[a] did not she say, He is my brother? In integrity of heart and with innocent[b] hands have I done this.

6 And God said to him in the dream:[a] I too know that you have done this in integrity of heart, and I too have withheld you from sinning against me,[b] and for that reason have not allowed[c] you to touch her.

7 Now[a] give back the man's wife because he is a prophet and will pray on your behalf that you remain alive.[b] But if you do not give her back, know that you and all yours must die.

8 Abimelech rose early in the morning and summoned his servants and told them all these things and they[a] were afraid.

9 Then Abimelech summoned Abraham and said to him: What have you done[a] to us? How have I[b] sinned against you so that you have brought upon me and my kingdom so great a sin? You have done to me what ought not to be done.[c]

10 And Abimelech said to Abraham: What had you in mind that[a] you did such a thing?

11 And Abraham said:[a] Indeed I thought that there was no fear of God at all in this place and they will kill[b] me because of my wife.

12 And in fact[a] she is my sister; she is the daughter of my father but not of my mother, and so she could be my wife.

13 And so when God called me to migrate[b] from my father's house,[a] I said to her: This favor you must do me everywhere we go: say on my behalf that I am your brother.[c]

14 Then Abimelech[a] took sheep and oxen, male and female servants,[b] and presented them[c] to Abraham and returned his wife Sarah to him.

15 And Abimelech said:[a] See, my land is before you, settle where you please.

16 And he said to Sarah: See, I am giving your brother a thousand silver pieces;[a] this is to be a public justification of you before all of yours—you are entirely vindicated.[b]

17   Then Abraham prayed to God for Abimelech and God healed him and his wife and his maidservants and they had children once more.
18   For Yahweh[a] had closed[b] every womb of Abimelech's household because of Sarah, Abraham's wife.

1a ארץ(ה)הנגב as in Gen. 24:62; ה local in construct, Ges-K §90c.   **b** W. F. Albright conjectures an original וישׁר from שׁור from an Arabic verb = "to travel" (*Yahweh and the Gods of Canaan* [1968] 59).   **c** On Gerar in detail, cf. J. Skinner ad loc.
2a Gk adds the reason from Gen. 26:7b.
3a הנך מת as in Deut. 18:20; Is. 38:1; cf. Ges-K §116p.   **b** Sam reads על־אודת as Gen. 21:11,25.   **c** בעלת בעל a married woman, as in Deut. 22:22.
4a גוי to be struck out as dittog. and הגם to be read as in BHS; H. Gunkel, J. Skinner, E. Speiser and others; Gk reads ἔθνος ἀγνοοῦν καὶ δίκαιον.
5a Gk, Syr, Vg read וגם היא.   **b** נקין only here in Pentateuch.
6a Missing in Vg.   **b** חטו unusual spelling for חטא, Ges-K §75qq.   **c** נתן ל "allow" as in Gen. 31:7, Ges-K §157b, note 1.
7a ועתה introduces the final consequence.   **b** On the form וחיה, Ges-K §63q & 110i.
8a Sam, Gk, Vg read כל before האנשים.
9a Syr reads מה עשׂיתי לך, Gk מה־זאת.   **b** Gk plur.   **c** On the relative clause, Ges-K §108n, BrSynt §150c.
10a כי introducing a consecutive clause, Ges-K §166b.
11a Sam adds כי יראתי.   **b** Ges-K §§112x, 153; BrSynt §41f.
12a אמנה as in Josh. 7:20; Sam אמנם as in Gen. 18:13.
13a After "my father's house" the Sam adds ומארץ מולדתי, as in Gen. 12:1.   **b** Plural with אלהים elsewhere only Gen. 31:53; 35:7; Ges-K §§124h, 145; BrSynt §50f.   **c** On the construction, BrSynt §§107i; 152c.
14a Sam and Gk add אלף כסף ו, following v. 16.   **b** "Male and female slaves" is perhaps a gloss following Gen. 12:16.   **c** On the ellipse, BrSynt §137.
15a Gk adds "to Abraham."
16a According to Ges-K §134n שׁקל is omitted.   **b** The last two words are unintelligible. According to H. Gunkel and J. Skinner, who gives a detailed justification (Ges-K §116g and BHS) ואת כלו נכחת is to be read.
18a Sam reads אלהים for יהוה.   **b** On the inf. abs., Ges-K §113n.

Form

[What follows presumes the exegesis of Gen. 12:10-20; some of the literature given there is also relevant.]

Gen. 20:1-18 is not a narrative in the true sense. Neither is it a parallel to chs. 12 and 26 in that the same story is told one way here and in another way in Gen. 12:10-20 and Gen. 26. It is, to be sure, within a narrative framework, but the central part consists in a reflection on what is narrated in ch. 12. According to E. A. Speiser it shows "a marked tendency to explain and justify." Thus ch. 20 presumes a knowledge of ch. 12 (so correctly J. Van Seters, *Abraham in History. . .* [1975] 171-175; B. Jacob, ad loc.). For the author what actually happened is incidental; what is central is how this is to be understood. One cannot say, as does K. Koch (*The Growth of the Biblical Tradition* [1964; 1974[3]; Eng. 1969], §10), that ch. 20 is of the same literary type as 12:10-20; this is clear from the structure of ch. 20. The nucleus of the text, vv. 3-13, consists of dialog; the action is by the way (vv. 1-2 and 14-18). A wrong is committed in vv. 1-2; vv. 3-13 deal with the question of blame; and in vv. 14-18 the wrong is righted.

In detail: Part A (vv. 1-2). The itinerary in v. 1a is followed by the introduction, Abraham in Gerar (v. 1b); in v. 2 there are two brief remarks on the action: Abraham gives out that Sarah is his sister (v. 2a), and Abimelech has her brought to him (v. 2b). No reason is given for any of these three pieces of information nor do they form a coherent context.

There follow in Part B (vv. 3-13), two dialogs—vv. 3-7, 8 between God and Abimelech and vv. 9-13 between Abimelech and Abraham—which together form the main part of the text. An accusation is made in both dialogs (vv. 3-7, God accuses Abimelech and threatens him with punishment; vv. 9-13, Abimelech accuses Abraham), and the accused gives his defense.

In Part C (vv. 14-18), the action is resumed and the wrong is put right in accordance with God's instruction. The further information is added (vv. 17-18) that God had made Abimelech's household infertile.

The whole is scarcely conceivable as a narrative; rather it is a search for answers to questions which the old narrative about Abraham raised. Whereas the action in v. 2 is markedly abbreviated, the dialog in vv. 3-7, 9-13 is very detailed. It is here that the emphasis lies, not on the action. Both dialogs are concerned with accusation and defense; the question is: who is guilty of the wrong that was committed? It takes the form of a dialog of thrust and counterthrust. The discussions demand that elements of the action be rehearsed—certainly not comprehensible from the few details in vv. 1b, 2—but in the form of arguments by defendants countering accusations (Abimelech, vv. 4-5; Abraham, vv. 11-13). The facts as such are not important; they become so only in the context of the disputation.

The story in Gen. 12:10-20 raised many questions for later times, particularly that of guilt, which gave rise to its subsequent rehearsal (R. Smend had already described Gen. 20 as a recasting of the old narrative of 12:10-20; P. Volz agreed with him). It is more exegesis or reflection than narrative. The way of understanding the three passages, so colored by the literary-critical approach, namely, that Gen. 12; 20; 26 are different narratives of the same event, is in need of revision. When one compares Gen. 12 and 20 (see below for ch. 26) only 12:10-20 is a narrative about Abraham which has clearly arisen out of oral tradition. Gen. 20:1-18 is an adaptation which has grown out of reflection on a well-known narrative and shows all the characteristics of a literary origin (thus, and probably correctly, J. Van Seters; see also the remark of R. C. Culley: "Between the two extremes of oral and written there lies a range of possibilities to be considered," *Semeia Supp.* 2 [1976] 65f.) especially in the reduction of the narrative to the dialog form (cf. Gen. 18:23-32).

This is the way then in which the patriarchal stories continued to live. Reflection on questions raised by the old stories takes the shape of adaptations which are no longer concerned with the event but with contemporary questions occasioned by the stories.

Setting

Gen. 20 has been and continues to be attributed to the Elohistic source. Wherever a literary source or layer E is accepted there is virtual unanimity that ch. 20 be attributed to it. The same linguistic and positive criteria are always alleged—אלהים as the designation for God, divine revelation by dream, fear of God, etc. These criteria taken together retain their significance. The language and manner of thinking are obviously different from J. But individual criteria such as word usage and particular ways of thinking are not sufficient to ascribe something to a literary work (cf. *Genesis 1–11*, 588-600). One must be able to recognize an overall plan for this and hitherto in the patriarchal story none such is recognizable for E because ch. 15 can no longer stand as the introduction of the Elohist. Nor is it possible to arrive at conclusions about an Elohistic work from Gen. 20 alone. It must remain an open question whether one can speak of Elohistic fragments (as does H. W. Wolff, see lit. under Gen. 20).

If Gen. 20:1-18 is not a parallel to Gen. 12:10-20 in the sense in which the literary-critical approach understands it, then it is not sufficient to ascribe it to a literary work, or fragments of same, in order to determine its setting. If it is not just another form of the same story given its stamp by the writer E, but an adaptation in response to a question raised by a well-known narrative, then its setting is to be determined by this question. If the question developed in the dialogs in vv. 3-13 is what is most important for the author, then it is this that must be able to give information about the motive for the adaptation. It is a question of the problem of guilt in the theological reflection of a later age; the designation of Abraham as a "prophet" also indicates this.

Commentary

[20:1]   As in Gen. 13:1 (cf. Gen. 12:9) a story about Abraham begins with an itinerary which leads in the direction of the Negev. The itinerary as usual comprises the two elements of departure and stopping place. There is no way of knowing to what מִשָּׁם = "from there" refers; it is a stereotyped phrase and cannot be made more precise when, as here, the itinerary is taken over from an older tradition (B. Jacob tries to locate "from there" at Hebron, Gen. 13:18; G. von Rad and others at Mamre). On the Negev, see comm. on 12:9; 13:1; it is the steppe region in the south contiguous with the Judaean mountain range. Abraham's journey is determined more precisely: he stays "between Kadesh" (Gen. 14:7) and "Shur" (Gen. 16:7), i.e., in the extreme south of the Negev, the limit of the itinerary. The geographical information that follows is a further indication that an originally independent tradition has been taken over here; the last two words (Hebrew) of v. 1 show this: "He was living as an alien in Gerar" do not belong to what precedes (so W. Zimmerli, E. A. Speiser, and others; previously the difficulty was explained on literary-critical grounds by R. Smend, O. Procksch, C. A. Simpson, and others); Gerar is a long way from the line between Kadesh and Shur, near Gaza. K. Koch writes: "Archaeologists are still uncertain whether [Gerar] was on *tell dshemme*, 14 km. south of Gaza (Fl. Petrie) or on *esh-shērīa*, 25 km. southeast of Gaza (Alt), or on *tell abu hurēre*, which is 7 km. from there (*The Growth of the Biblical Tradition* [1964; 1974³; Eng. 1969] 128). The proposal of E. A. Speiser that this detail is the protasis of which v. 2 is the apodosis is correct and is adopted in the translation. This is further supported by the verb וַיָּגָר which does not belong to the itinerary but to the introduction to the narrative taken over from Gen. 12:10 (cf. Gen. 26:3).

[20:2]   The narrative is introduced by two details which would be incomprehensible were not Gen. 12:10-20 presupposed (and perhaps too an earlier form of Gen. 26, because of the names of the place and the king; R. Smend had already noted this). The verb וַיָּגָר requires an explanation, as in Gen. 12 and 26 (famine), but none is given.

The first detail in v. 2, Abraham's statement that Sarah is his sister, hangs completely in the air; thus out of context it would have no meaning at all were it not an abbreviated reference to the well-known story of Abraham and Sarah. The laconic brevity of v. 2a is all the more surprising inasmuch as it is the most important factor in the text, mentioned again in vv. 5a, 9a, 9b, 10, 12, 13, (16). Thus it is clear that it is no narrator who is speaking, but a disputant; one cannot say, as does H. Gunkel, that it is refined narrative style. Above all, no reason is given why Abraham gives out that Sarah is his sister. It reads like an addition that does not really accord with the situation of v. 2. Nor is any reason given why the king of Gerar has Sarah taken (v. 2b). This too makes no sense unless one is familiar with the old story of 12:10-20. The view that the reasons for 2a and 2b were deleted by a redactor (so H. Holzinger, O. Procksch, R. Kilian, K. Koch, and others) is improbable. Why should a redactor have deleted a sentence necessary for the understanding of the text? The Gk has sensed this lack and has inserted 26:7b almost word for word.

V. 2 then is not really the beginning of a narrative but the introduction to a dialog (vv. 3-13). This introductory function of v. 2a-b becomes clearer when it is transposed into a temporal subordinate clause: "While Abraham was living as an alien in Gerar, and Abimelech the king of Gerar sent and took Sarah whom Abraham had given out to be his sister, then God came to him in a dream. . . ."

If v. 3 is seen as the beginning of the action, then the two pieces of information in v. 2 are sufficient; but they are to be understood as a reference to the narrative in 12:10-20.

Abimelech is presented as a Canaanite city-king; the name (theophoric) is genuinely Canaanite (J. Skinner) and occurs as the name of the ruler of Tyre in the Amarna letters. It is to be noted that the attitude to the Canaanites is entirely friendly in the text (A. van Selms, OTS 12 [1958] 182-213) and that the king and his servants are portrayed in a positive light.

[20:3-13] The structure of the dialog (Part B) corresponds to that of v. 2. The dialog between God and Abimelech (vv. 3-7, 8) deals with v. 2b; that between Abimelech and Abraham (vv. 9-13) with v. 2a. This too makes it clear that v. 2 is an introduction to vv. 3-13. Vv. 3-7 raise the question of Abimelech's guilt; vv. 9-13 of Abraham's.

[20:3-8] God's accusation and threat of punishment against Abimelech: This part is introduced and concluded as a revelation in a dream (v. 3a, repeated in v. 6a, and v. 8). Apart from this framework, however, it is a dialog consisting of accusation and threat of punishment by death (v. 3), Abimelech's justification (or defense) (vv. 4-5), and the conditional review of the judgment (vv. 6-7). It is a sort of legal process in which a death penalty is changed into an acquittal.

[20:3] The dialog is introduced as a dream, or more accurately set in the framework of a dream (vv. 3a, 6a, 8). No exegete has seen that what is within the framework does not suit the frame. A legal process with its accusation, sentence, and defense cannot be the matter of a dream. God's address to Abraham in a dream is but a literary vesture just as is the dialog the literary vesture of the discussion of the question of guilt. The frame, the dream, merely enables the dialog between God and the Canaanite king to take place. If this is correct then one must be rather cautious about the criterion for the Elohist which almost all exegetes agree on. One must be more precise and ask whether God's revelation in a dream as mere literary vesture is characteristic of the Elohist. It could be that Gen. 20 does not accord in this point with the other alleged Elohistic passages which speak of a revelation in a dream.

The first sentence, "then God came to. . . in a dream by night and said," occurs word for word in Gen. 31:24 while Num. 22:9, 20 is similar; in both cases God speaks to a non-Israelite or outsider. All three passages are concerned with averting a danger. It is a matter of a fixed form which appears in ancient narratives and has been taken over here.

V. 3b: God's address to Abimelech is the verdict of a judge with the charge on which the verdict is based and in the language of the secular court. The verdict is standard and extremely short: הנך מת (the participle is very common with הנה and suffix to announce a future action or event, cf. Ges-K §116p); see Deut. 18:20 for the announcement of the death penalty or death; Isaiah, in Is. 38:1, announces to king Hezekiah his impending death. The reason (על stands for על דבר as in v. 11) is the objective fact of the abduction of a married woman, primarily an offense against private property. An ancient and widespread attitude saw the wife as the property of the husband: ". . .A married woman is. . . the 'possession' of her *ba'al* Gen. 20:3; Deut. 22:22" (R. de Vaux, *Ancient Israel* [1958; Eng. 1962], p. 26; H. A. Brongers, VT 13 [1963] 267-284, esp. 283). It is precisely this property relationship that the supplementary words, והוא בעלת בעל = "for she is a married woman," underscore. This is to presuppose, and with every justification, that such was generally the case at that time and that the abduction of a married woman was the violation of a divinely sanctioned ordinance. Abimelech's conduct shows that he recognizes this, that is that he is "God-fearing." The Canaanite king hears the voice that speaks as God's voice because it says what he recognizes to be just and valid; the question as to which god it is does not arise: "He speaks to him as if he were his own 'Lord' (*'adonāi*, 20,3f)" (B. Gemser, OTS 12 [1958] 3). The patriarchal story knows neither polemic against strange gods nor discussion on the relationship between different gods.

[20:4-5]   After the verdict of guilt has been passed the defendant responds (likewise in vv. 11-13). This means that vv. 3b-7 are not concerned with a dialog which takes its own course but with an action before a judge which runs its prescribed judicial course. In vv. 4-5 the defendant responds; the accused has his say about the accusation, as in Gen. 3 and 4. This takes place in a question put to the judge after a preliminary in v. 4a; the case for the defense is stated in question form (v. 5a, which contests the accusation), and in an explanation of why there is no guilt.

[20:4]   The introductory sentence, "Now Abimelech had not approached her. . .," does not fit into the process and is not necessary for it; the guilt consists in Abimelech's abduction of a man's wife. The sentence has been added out of excessive caution. The king's answer begins with a question: "Lord, will you really kill the innocent (or an innocent one)?" It is set in the middle of the passage; this is what it is all about. The agitation behind it shows the concern of the one who is speaking. It is a question of the justice of God, as in Abraham's question in 18:23, "Will you really sweep away the just with the wicked?" Abimelech acknowledges the judge, but he can do so only if he judges justly. The theologian who adapts the ancient narrative is concerned with the justice of God, with the question of God's dealing with the figures in the story. The answer to Abimelech's question is implied in vv. 6-7.

[20:5] The accused confronts the judge with the situation: I could not have known that Sarah is married; both of them said that she is Abraham's sister. While Abimelech exonerates himself, he charges Abraham; it is he who is to blame for the outrage. And this is the reproach that he casts at Abraham in vv. 9-10.

In the light of the facts, which are not contested, Abimelech knows that he is innocent. He protests his innocence in a fixed phrase which, with its parallelism, allows us to recognize a solemn formula: "In integrity of heart and with innocent hands." It presupposes the language of a later era; the cultic formula נקי כפים וברדלבב of Ps. 24:4 is almost the same; it too has a similar function as a rejection of guilt in the Liturgy at the Gate (see too Ps. 101:2; 1 Kings 9:4).

[20:6-7] God's answer consists in a withdrawal or revision of his judgment in v. 3b. One ought not presume here some abstract divine attribute such as "omniscience." God shows himself just by acknowledging Abimelech's defense and his asseveration of innocence and acquitting him of guilt. This is expressed in v. 6b and is linked with an explanation of what God has done in regard to Abimelech (v. 6b). But with the acquittal goes the directive to return Sarah (v. 7). If he does not, he is under the threat of death.

[20:6] It is significant that בחלם (missing in the Vg) is repeated once more at the introduction to God's reply (v. 3). It has to be repeated because what is before and after gives no cause to think that it is a dream. It is further significant that בחלם is used as a formula and does not suit the context. It has to mean: "in his dream."

God confirms the integrity of the king's conduct with the words which the latter himself had used in v. 5 and thus acquits him of guilt. The acknowledgment of his innocence is further underscored when God explains to him the purpose of the affliction that had struck him: he wanted thereby to restrain him from committing the sin of adultery. This sentence, v. 6b, together with v. 7, is unintelligible in its place here and becomes meaningful only when subsequently taken up in vv. 17-18: God had struck Abimelech with an illness. It becomes very clear here that the author of ch. 20 presupposes the narrative of 12:10-20 where this is told in v. 17; he deliberately alters a detail. The plague that struck the king (Gen. 12:17; 20:17,18) was not a divine punishment but was meant to prevent the consummation of the sin of adultery. Abimelech's acquittal, therefore, is serious in intent: God shows that he is just towards the innocent; as far as he is concerned, it is not meant to be a punishment.

[20:7] But the acquittal is tied to a condition—ועתה. Abimelech must give the woman back to Abraham. Basically this results from Abimelech's own asseveration of innocence (v. 5); but it must be stated expressly once again because the outrage has taken place: the woman has been abducted from her husband and the consequence is death. This verse throws into sharp relief that ancient way of thinking, the deed/consequence mentality, that an outrage remains an outrage and its effects follow even when committed unintentionally. The other way of thinking presupposed in v. 6, that one who has unintentionally perpetrated something will be acquitted of guilt, stands side by side with neither link nor counterpoint. This is what the author of 20:1-18 represents; nevertheless he allows the old way of thinking its voice. G. von Rad refers to this juxtaposition: "One could almost say that our story has two faces, an ancient and a modern" (comm. p. 228).

The alternative in the last part of v. 7, "But if you do not give her back. . .," follows immediately on the demand to give Abraham's wife back to him. It renews and extends the threat to "all yours." We have an inclusion: God's address to Abraham in vv. 3-7 begins and ends with the threat of death even though it tapers off in an acquittal.

The sentence which gives the reason in the middle of v. 7 does not match the context well; nor is it really the reason for the demand in v. 7a (the reason goes much further: the woman belongs to someone else). By means of the *kî*-clause the author wants to prepare the way for the removal of the harm caused, because Abimelech had just been declared innocent. Its insertion here is contrived. One can understand then why many exegetes have misconstrued the passage seeing Abraham as taboo because he is a נביא (O. Procksch, for example, speaks of the dangerous power of the prophet). But if the *kî*-clause is merely directed to the restoration of the situation in vv. 17-18, then Abraham is described as a נביא (and only here in Gen. 12–25) simply because of his function as intercessor (so A. Dillmann, B. Jacob, and others; also R. P. Carroll, VT 19 [1969] 400-415). The verb התפלל (hith. of פלל) is the term for intercession, cf. H. P. Stähli, פלל hith., "pray" (THAT II [1976] 427-432). The word *prophet* is not used here of Abraham in a technical but rather in a general sense; he is a "man of God," an intercessor, familiar to a later era; to speak or conceive of Abraham in such a way is very far removed from the patriarchal period. Abraham has thereby become a distinguished godly man of that era.

[20:8]   V. 8 is part of the vesture that clothes the dialog as a dream. The author makes skillful use of the dream convention to spread Abimelech's fear of God throughout the court (cf. the Pharaoh in Gen. 41:8) with a view to v. 11 where Abraham's foreboding that there was no fear of God in the place was without foundation. The verse makes a nice transition from vv. 3-7 to vv. 9-13.

[20:9-13]   The second dialog takes place between Abraham and Abimelech. Here too it is a matter of accusation and defense, that is of the question of guilt, but in a quite different way. This is clear from the structure: in vv. 9-10 he lodges his case against Abraham; there is no mention of punishment; in vv. 11-13 Abraham defends (or excuses) himself. However, the third counterpart to vv. 6-7, the equivalent of an acquittal, is missing. Abraham may indeed excuse himself, but he cannot be acquitted of his guilt.

[20:9-10]   *The accusation.* In an address in which one can still experience the emotion, Abimelech accuses Abraham of having deceived him. The first sentence, "What have you done to us?" is common to all three versions (12:18; 20:9; 26:10), and for this reason should not be changed to the first person for the sake of the parallelism with the following sentence, as some have proposed. An old narrative, originally handed down orally, can contain certain characteristic sentences which remain unchanged in the midst of all other adaptations. It is significant for the narrative that such a sentence is the reproach which the pagan king throws at Abraham, the father of the people. The plural "us" refers back to v. 7b. The second sentence, ". . .and what have I done to you?" (really, "have I sinned against you"), is the reproachful question of one unjustly offended which has remained unchanged everywhere to this very day. It is the emotional response of the offended party. What follows is to be understood in this context: emotion tends to magnify the other's guilt. This accounts for the words, ". . .and my kingdom. . .," which are certainly not an addition, as H. Holzinger and C. A. Simpson think, and for "the great sin," an expression which in Egyptian and for the most part elsewhere designates adultery (J. J. Rabinowitz, JNES 18 [1958]; W. L. Moran, JNES 18 [1958] 280-281), even though it did not come to this. The third sentence of the reproach is climactic: Abraham has violated an unwritten ordinance which exists among men. It is a harsh reproach that the king of a Canaanite city directs against Abraham, the patriarch.

[20:10] The new beginning with a new introduction is deliberate and meaningful (against O. Procksch and R. Kilian); B. Jacob has observed correctly that v. 10 puts a real question whereas the preceding ones were rhetorical. Abraham has no reply to make to them whereas he can give some sort of answer to the question why he did it. It is this question in v. 10 that renders possible Abraham's answer in vv. 11-13.

By way of conclusion to vv. 9-10 it is to be said that this part of the dialog, vv. 9-13, comes to a climax in these accusations and reproaches inasmuch as the talk reaches its high point of intensity here. This is important for the understanding of the whole text. Abraham's guilt is neither diminished nor glossed over; the accusations set it in sharp relief. What happens in vv. 14-18 by way of making amends in no wise alters this.

[20:11-13] Abraham's defense consists in a detailed account of the grounds—a reply to the question of v. 10, "What had you in mind that you did such a thing?"—on which he gave out that Sarah was his sister, thus joining v. 13 to v. 11. Between them in v. 12 is a further ground: Sarah is his half-sister. The defense in vv. 11-13 does not contest Abraham's guilt but rather presupposes an acknowledgment of it. It alleges no more than mitigating circumstances.

[20:11] The כי at the beginning shows that Abraham is replying directly to Abimelech's question in v. 10. "The elliptical כי 'indeed' presupposes a ''כֵּן עֲשִׂיתִי (O. Procksch). Like so many excuses this too begins with "I thought. . .." Gen. 12:11-12 is the background of the consideration immediately following (cf. comm. ad loc.) which is scarcely intelligible in itself. The mere facts are not sufficient for Abraham to fear that he will be killed and so, over and above 12:11-12, he adds a theological (intellectual) reason: "There is no fear of God in this place." But even this did not hold true. The concept יראת אלהים is generally regarded as particularly characteristic of E: "It stands in the very center of his theology" (O. Procksch; likewise H. W. Wolff). But one must be rather cautious here. The concept has taken on a very general meaning in the course of time (Prov. 1:7) and is close to our "religion" or "piety." One must then be prepared for its being used quite differently in different contexts, and markedly different uses can point to different origins. The mere use of the phrase is no longer sufficient to demonstrate a universal literary origin (against H. W. Wolff; cf. lit. under Gen. 20).

How is "the fear of God" used in Gen. 20? Only the chapter as a whole can show this. Abraham feared that his life was in danger in Gerar because the people there and its king would have no hesitation in abducting his wife and killing him. The fear of God then means conduct which regards the basic standards of the human community even with respect to aliens. Now vv. 3-8 show emphatically that Abimelech and his household live and act in accordance with such fear of God; Abraham was mistaken in his being afraid. This is significant for the concept

of the fear of God: it does not describe specifically the relationship of a person to
the God of the fathers or to the God of Israel, but a religious or reverential attitude
which one meets even outside Israel, here in the case of a Canaanite king and his
household who are not obliged by the religion of Israel (cf. also v. 9b: ''. . .what
ought not to be done''). The narrative clearly intends to underscore this reverential attitude; Abraham is put to shame for his unjustified fear. One should here put
the further question, whether such talk of the fear of God accords with the writer E
and his use of the concept elsewhere. In any case such usage points to a relatively
late period when non-Israelites were portrayed as pious men.

[20:12]   This verse is to be read as a parenthesis; it is as it were incidental that
Sarah is his half-sister. The circumstantial language belongs to the case for the defense. H. Gunkel says in commenting on the verse that the narrator has taken
scandal at Abraham's lie and is trying to whitewash him; the detail is an ad hoc in-
vention. Though many subsequent writers have accepted this, it does not seem to
me to be an exact understanding of the intention of the text. The explanation
which Abraham gives in vv. 11, 13 is comprehensible and clear; it accords with
what is said in 12:11-12. Does the reason given in v. 12 improve on it in any way?
Does it alter in the least Abraham's explanation in vv. 11 and 13 where he denies
that Sarah is his wife? It is better to see it this way: in the discussion of the question
of guilt which is the basis of the whole passage vv. 3-13, a further question was
considered, namely, that Abraham's guilt may have been diminished because he
had just a little right on his side if Sarah was his half-sister—a practice from the
early period which was not forbidden (2 Sam. 13:13). The author undertook this
attempt to exonerate Abraham so as to show that in fact he does not exonerate
him.

[20:13]   V. 13 is the immediate continuation of v. 11 where we again meet an attempt to exonerate Abraham arising from reflection on his guilt and where again
he is not in fact exonerated. The conversation with Sarah in 12:11-12, which is intelligible from the particular situation on the Egyptian border, is here transposed
to the beginning of Abraham's travels. This generalization, that Abraham told
Sarah once and for all at the very beginning that she was to give it out that she was
his sister, ought have some mitigating effect inasmuch as Abimelech would be the
only one affected. But this lame excuse does not happen to fit 20:11, ''in this
place,'' and moreover does not make sense in such generalization. Gen. 12: 11-12
is only possible in a once and for all situation, and the explanation in 20:13 does
not improve things.

There is a reference to the beginning of Abraham's travels in a sentence
which clearly recalls 12:1, ''And so when God called me to migrate from my father's house. . ..'' Some exegetes have concluded from this that E too had an account of Abraham's departure from the house of his fathers corresponding to
12:1-3 (or 12:1-9). But that is too hazardous a hypothesis because it requires much
the same wording (''father's house'' occurs only in 12:1; 20:13; 24:7 in Gen.
12–50). It is much more likely that the author of Gen. 20 is referring directly to
12:1-3 and that consequently he presupposes 12:10-20 to be the continuation of
12:1-3. This is a further indication that ch. 20 is not a parallel to 12:10-20 but an
adaptation of it. So too 20:13b presupposes Abraham's conversation with Sarah
from 12:11-12 and is altered in accordance with the point of view of the author.
But the unusual plural construction התעו אלהים scarcely belongs to such altera-

tion. Some exegetes (O. Procksch, O. Eissfeldt, and others) are of the opinion that a real plural is intended, "the gods"; it is "an accommodation to pagan ideas" (B. Jacob). But this is most unlikely in the present chapter where the God of Abraham speaks also to Abimelech and gives him instructions. The plural construction therefore is intended in a singular sense (so H. Gunkel and others), something that also occurs elsewhere, as well as in the Amarna letters.

There is nothing corresponding to vv. 6-7 after Abraham's answer to Abimelech's accusation; Abraham is not declared guiltless. He can of course explain how he came to do it, but he cannot deny his guilt. The whole dialog of vv. 3-13 deals with the question of guilt; it is therefore saying clearly that Abimelech is declared guiltless and Abraham is not.

[20:14-18] *Part C: Amends are made.* The conclusion now follows the long dialog of vv. 3-13, including again action and speech. Like vv. 3-13 it is distributed according to the subjects, Abimelech (vv. 14-16) corresponding to vv. 3-7, and Abraham (vv. 17-18) corresponding to vv. 9-13. There is greater detail here than in the introduction (v. 2), because this part not only brings the narrative to a conclusion but also provides the results of the dialog (vv. 3-13), which is the main concern of the author. The significance of this for the exegesis is that vv. 14-18 are to be read closely with vv. 3-13.

[20:14-16] Abimelech makes good the damage; as well as giving Sarah back to her husband (v. 14b) he makes a present to him (v. 14a) and to Sarah (v. 17) and guarantees Abraham freedom of movement throughout the whole of his realm (v. 15).

[20:14] The king gives Abraham's wife back to him as God had commanded. Over and above he gives him generous presents ("male and female servants" is perhaps an addition; cf. comm. 12:16). The presents have a different function from ch. 12 where they were compensation to the brother of the beautiful woman before Pharaoh knew that she was Abraham's wife. Here Abraham receives them in the aftermath; "they are to make amends for the injustice which had occurred" (H. Gunkel). It is to be noted that Abimelech is in no wise obliged to do this; Abraham has certainly not deserved them. They express Abimelech's recognition of the God who spoke to him.

[20:15] The same holds for the guarantee of freedom of movement throughout the land which stands in deliberate contrast to the expulsion in 12:19-20. But even this concession in no wise mitigates Abraham's guilt for the damage incurred; Abimelech thereby honors the God of Abraham.

[20:16] This verse too deals with an action of Abimelech which is accompanied by his words to Sarah. The first sentence הנה נתתי expresses the execution of the presentation (cf. comm. 15:18). He hands the money (a fabulously large sum) to Abraham because by the rules governing such a society the wife cannot acquire it. The kinds of gifts presented in vv. 14 and 16 show that economies based on barter and money still exist side by side; "the real link between a purely natural economy and proper monetary economy is currency in precious metals" (B. Kanael, "Münzen und Gewichte," BHH 11 [1964] 1249-56).

The second sentence explains the meaning of the present to Sarah, introduced by another הנה: "This is to be a covering of eyes. . .." It is clear that the expression is intended in the sense of a justification of her honor, but it is not immediately clear what the image means. It cannot be taken in the sense in which A. Dillmann explains it: ". . .Abimelech thereby confirms the confession of the injustice he did to Sarah" (likewise H. Holzinger: "Penance for the injustice done"); Abimelech's innocence had already been established. Rather "the gift means that the critical eyes of others will be covered so that they will be unable to discover anything shocking in Sarah" (G. von Rad); Sarah's honor is completely restored (J. Skinner); "so that the people will not look disdainfully on her" (B. Jacob). In this case the attached phrase of uncertain meaning, לכל אשר אתך, must refer to the others whose eyes are to be covered: "Before (for) all of yours." On the other hand the last three words are unintelligible. The verb, niph. pret. of יכח, "to be vindicated" (KBL), suggests the conjecture ואת כלו, "you are entirely vindicated" (cf. H. Gunkel, BHK, KBL). The restoration of Sarah's honor is to be understood in the same way as the gift to Abraham: Abimelech does all he can to heal the damage caused though he is in no way to blame. He does it with an awe that Abraham would not have expected from him.

[**20:17-18**] *Abraham (God) reverses the plague.* Abraham appears as an intercessor before God as God had announced to Abimelech (v. 7). God heals Abimelech, i.e., takes away the plague from him and his household so that the women can bear children once more. This is the clumsiest adaptation in v. 20. It is here that we first learn that Abimelech and his household were ill, and this not directly, but only when it is said that God healed them, with the consequence that there was childbearing once more. A hint of something like this is already given in v. 6, but can only be inferred from vv. 17-18. The arrangement shows that the statement in v. 17 is directed only towards the healing. Once again we are confronted with what is of the essence: God accomplishes the healing; Abraham only prays for it. Hence the necessary corollary—the illness too was sent by God.

[**20:18**] Almost all exegetes regard v. 18 as a supplement and the same two arguments are always alleged in favor: (1) God is designated as יהוה; however striking, this is not sufficient to explain the verse as a secondary addition; (2) the other reason is that according to v. 18 only the women are afflicted, but in v. 17 it is Abimelech as well. But this argument does not hold. Would a glossator have made an insertion intended to explain the preceding sentence which does not fit? If one's point of departure is that v. 17 is interested only in the healing, the restoration of order, and so does not advance the reworking still required for the understanding of the verses, then it is only natural to expect that it will follow. By designating childlessness as the affliction that struck Abimelech and his household, the verse is following a tradition which says just that. What is added here has its place in the old narrative between vv. 2b and 3, corresponding to 12:17, a verse which ends with the same words as 20:18. The dialog begins in v. 3 and it presupposes that the affliction strikes Abimelech as well. The explanation of the discrepancy between vv. 17 and 18 is that v. 18 originally had another place in the narrative. The supplement is a corollary from and completion of v. 17, not a gloss.

Purpose and Thrust

Just as the adapted narrative of ch. 20 presupposes the old narrative, so too what is said here with regard to purpose and thrust presupposes the corresponding remarks on 12:10-20. The adaptation is the fruit of reflection on the old narrative and is concerned primarily with the question of guilt. What is amazing is that the Canaanite king is completely exonerated. The theologian who in a later era adapted the Abraham story wants to tell that generation that the fear of God can indeed exist even outside Israel. This author is warning them against a narrow-minded thought pattern of friend versus foe and an attitude inspired by uneasiness about the wickedness of others; without comment Abraham's "excuse" in vv. 11-13 is allowed to speak as a warning. At the same time this adapter wants to tell the contemporary generation that God's action towards his own goes far beyond anything that they with their own planning and behavior can expect from God. Abraham is not acquitted of guilt as is Abimelech; he is guilty of the harm he has caused and this is not glossed over. Abraham's offense cannot hinder God's goodness: "He does not act according to our misdeeds. . .." Abimelech, who is expressly acquitted of guilt, not only gives back Sarah as God had commanded him; he also gives presents, not because of any pressure on him, but out of awe of the alien God.

The adapter thereby hints at something else he wants to tell his generation: Abraham can still be an intercessor despite his guilt; for all his shortcomings and limitations he can invoke God's saving power for others without himself being exalted thereby. This is shown in an impressive way by the contrast between the reproach that Abimelech justly directs against Abraham (vv. 9-10) and the intercession of the patriarch, despite the rebuke, for Abimelech and his household (v. 17). Gen. 20 shows that the patriarchal stories have preserved within them an important characteristic of the patriarchal religion, and this enhances their later effectiveness: they were not aware of any religious polemic. One can discern here a universal note: God speaks and listens to a Canaanite king; the fear of God is with him and his court; in his conduct towards Abraham, who was guilty with regard to him, he gives honor to this God.

The Birth of Isaac

Literature

Genesis 21: N. M. Sarna, *Understanding Genesis* (1966; 1972²), 154-163.

Genesis 21:1-7: W. O. E. Oesterley, *The Sacred Dance. A Study in Comparative Folklore* (1923) ch. 4. A. Hiemer, "Conspectus historiae populi Israel," VD 25 (1947) 80-88. J. J. Stamm, Fests. A. Schädetlin (1950) 33-38. J. Heller, "Der Name Isaak," KrR 22 (1955) 102-104. Z. Souček, "Isaaks Geburt," KrR 22 (1955) 133-134. M. Adinolfi, "(Maria SS.) nelle Postille di Nòcala di Lyre a Gen 21,6; 28,12 e 2 Sam 23,4," RivBib 8 (1960) 337-350. J. Scharbert, "Das Verbum *pqd* in der Theologie des Alten Testaments," Fests. F. Nötscher, BZ NF 4 (1960) 209-226. N. H. Snaith, "Time in the Old Testament," *Essays Presented to S. H. Hooke* (1963) 175-186. R. Gordis, "Job XL 29—an Additional Note," VT 14 (1964) 491-494. H. Fürst, *Die göttliche Heimsuchung* (1965). H. S. Gehmann, ἐπισκέπτομαι. . . in the Septuagint in Relation to פקד and Other Hebrew Roots—A Case of Semantic Development Similar to that of Hebrew," VT 22 (1972) 197-207. C. W. Reines, "Laughter in Biblical and Rabbinic Judaism," *Judaism* 82 (1972) 176-183. W. Speyer, "Genealogie," RAC (1976) 1145-1268. W. Schottroff, "פקד *pqd* heimsuchen," THAT II (1976) 466-486.

Text

21:1 Now Yahweh visited Sarah as he had said, and Yahweh did to Sarah as he had spoken.

2 And Sarah became pregnant and bore Abraham a son in his old age at the time that God[a] had said to him.

3 And Abraham called the son born[a] to him, whom Sarah had borne to him, Isaac.

4 And Abraham circumcised Isaac his son on the eighth day as God commanded him.

5 Now Abraham was one hundred years old when his son Isaac[a] was born to him.

6a And Sarah said: Laughter[a] has God[b] prepared in my regard;

7 And she said: Who would have announced[a] to Abraham: Sarah will suckle a child.[b] Because I have borne "him"[c] a son in his old age,

6b everyone who hears it will laugh (approval) for me.

2a Gk renders κύριος.

3a אשר נולד; as in Gen. 17:21; cf. Gen. 43:12, Ges-K §738k.

5a Pass. with את as in Gen. 4:18; cf. Ges-K §3121b.
6a The root צחק is found only in the Pentateuch (two disputable exceptions), the *Qal* only in the context of the name Isaac.   **b** Syr adds היום.
7a The modal use of the perfect, Ges-K §106p.   **b** Generic plural, Ges-K §124c; cf. Ex. 21:22; 1 Sam. 17:43; Gk has the sing.   **c** Insert לו with Sam.

Form and Setting

Gen. 21:1-7 is an account of the birth of Isaac to which the narrative 21:8-21 is attached. All exegetes who onesidedly take source division as their point of departure for the explanation of 21:1-7 are exposed to a misinterpretation because they do not view the text as a whole. The uncertainty arises from this, that apart from ascribing vv. 3-5 to P, everything remains questionable. A remark of O. Procksch (taken up by W. Zimmerli) could have opened the way to a different understanding of 21:1-7: "In addition, accounts of birth and death always exclude the complete retention of multiple sources because doublets cannot continue standing here."

The structure reveals at first glance a succession of events which determine the whole:

v. 1   Yahweh visits Sarah (does to Sarah)
v. 2   Sarah becomes pregnant and bears a son
v. 3   Abraham names him
v. 4   Abraham circumcises him
v. 5   Abraham's age
v. 6   Sarah gives the reason for the name

The succession of events is independent of source division. It describes the birth of a child; added to it is the flashback that God had foretold or commanded the event. This reference back in vv. 1, 2, and 4 links the genealogy with the preceding narratives: vv. 1 and 2 with the promise of a son in chs. 18 and 17; v. 4 "as God commanded him" with 17:9-14 (P). The conclusion is that 21:1-7 is the work of the redactor who thereby brings the Abraham story to a conclusion. This same author is also responsible for the construction in a similar way of the introduction, 11:27-32, where the motif of Sarah's barrenness is sounded (11:30); the motif is taken up and carried forward in the conclusion, 21:1-7; Sarah has a son. In between stands the promise of a son in chs. 18 and 17 to which 21:1-7 refers. We had already seen in the discussion of ch. 18 that the birth of the child was part of this overarching, self-contained succession of events which runs its course in the link forged with the genealogy that brings the Abraham story to its conclusion (v. 1 in particular shows this).

A further sign that 21:1-7 is the work of the redactor is that, just as in 11:27-32, the conclusion is constructed out of blocks from several sources. The middle part, vv. 3-5, is an untouched piece from P which is really the genealogical conclusion of ch. 17; this is set between two J passages, vv. 1-2 and 6-7, in such a way as to form a self-contained string of events. Vv. 1-2 are common to both J and P because both statements belong equally to the conclusion of ch. 18 (J) and ch. 17 (P); a separation into J and P components is not possible. Vv. 6-7, Sarah's explanation of the name Isaac, belong to J only. One can recognize a suture here: Sarah's explanation presupposes that the mother gave the name (differing from v. 3); vv. 6f. then presumes v. 2 ("to her" instead of "to him") and the missing sentence, "and she named him Isaac."

331

Commentary

[12:1]   V. 1 serves as a complement of the preceding narratives, not only of ch. 18 (so J. Van Seters), but also of ch. 17. Both of its parts speak of an action of Yahweh, as do chs. 17 and 18. This theological conclusion, which is at the same time the transition to the genealogy, stresses the fact of fulfillment: ''And Sarah did in fact get the promised son.'' The parallelism is deliberate and has its own purpose (cf. Num. 23:19). If one does not see this intent and maintains that vv. 1a and b are literary doublets (as do most exegetes), then the deliberate subtlety is lost, for the two verbs taken together combine to say what is meant. They express God's attention and intervention (cf. Lk. 1:68). The redactor thus resumes sentences from the available narratives so that v. 1a would correspond more to J's ch. 18, v. 1b to P's ch. 17; but this is not certain and need not be pressed. In any case it is not necessary to alter יהוה of v. 1b into אלהים. For the verb פקד, cf. Lit. to 20:1-7.

[21:2]   The genealogy begins with v. 2 in which the verbs ותלד ותהר are important (cf. comm. Gen. 4:1). Though next in sequence to v. 1 this sentence remains a consequence of God's action (v. 1); it is therefore part of the conclusion of the narratives of chs. 18 and 17. This is confirmed by two further precisions, ''the son of his old age'' (cf. Gen. 24:36; 37:3; 44:20) and ''at the time. . .''; the latter is intelligible only in the light of what has preceded. Both details belong to the two narratives: 18:11-14 and 17:17, 24 speak of Abraham's age; the promise, 18:10, 14 and 17:21 mentions a point in time, designating it מועד. This makes it clear that 21:1-7 embraces both narratives of the promise of a son and brings them to a conclusion.

From A. Dillmann on, almost without exception, vv. 2a and b have been separated into two sources, 2a being ascribed to J, 2b to P. Two criteria are alleged as decisive: (1) the divine name אלהים speaks for P. But can one be so certain about this criterion when the יהוה of v. 1b is altered into אלהים because 1b must belong to P? (2) למועד in 2b refers to Gen. 17:21, speaking therefore in favor of P. But the same word also occurs with the same meaning in 18:24 (J). It is amazing that though A. Dillmann goes on to remark, ''and of course 18:14,'' later exegetes refer only to 17:21 and pass over 18:14 in silence. Vv. 1-2 then can be described as common material, and this is fully supported by the intent of the redactor to draw chs. 17 and 18 together in one conclusion.

[21:3-5]   It is different with vv. 3-5, every sentence of which can be shown to belong to P. The redactor has taken over a P text as the nucleus of the conclusion (21:1-7) in accordance with the function that the framework serves in P. Gen. 21:3-5 is close to 16:15-16 (P).

[21:3]   A second genealogical detail is now added to the first (pregnancy and birth), the name giving, done by the father (cf. Gen. 16:15) as is always the case with P. This corresponds to the command of 17:16, ''. . .whom you are to call Isaac,'' while the further specification, ''whom Sarah had borne to him,'' corresponds to the announcement ''whom Sarah will bear you'' (17:21). H. Gunkel is of the opinion that הנולד־לו is superfluous and is better placed after v. 4. But neither is it necessary there. In v. 3 it is a deliberate emphasis by means of repetition, a regular stylistic device with P.

[21:4] The third detail is the circumcision in accordance with the command in 17:12 ("eight days old"). This is deliberately underscored in the relative clause in v. 4b, "as God commanded him"; 21:1-7 therefore reflects the correlation of promise and command in ch. 17 in the relative clauses of vv. 1, 2 (promise) and v. 4b (command).

[21:5] The fourth genealogical detail is the age, as is usual with P (cf. 16:16; 17:24), thus drawing the genealogy to a conclusion. What follows in vv. 6-7 belongs directly after vv. 1-2.

[21:6-7] There is an obvious join between vv. 5 and 6. The *waw* at the beginning of v. 6 cannot follow immediately after v. 5 (not even in the adversative, "but Sarah"), but only after v. 3, because it gives the reason for the name. Because it is the father who in v. 3 gives the name, it is not possible for vv. 6-7 to follow directly; it can only be something added afterwards as a detached piece. This is a sign of the precise and careful work of the redactor and of his intention to bring chs. 17 and 18 to a conclusion in 21:1-7. The meaning of the name Isaac is so important a part of the narrative for both J and P that it cannot be missing from the conclusion.

The explanation of the name as an utterance of Sarah presupposes that the mother named the child. The redactor's intention is given clear expression at the beginning of vv. 6 and 7 where both ways of understanding, the earlier and later (P), equal voice. How then is the double introduction, "And Sarah said. . ."—"And she said. . ." at the beginning of vv. 6 and 7, to be understood? Two different explanations of the name Isaac, each of different origin, have been juxtaposed. However, it is questionable to conclude that v. 7 must belong to J and v. 6 (or 6a) to E.

The only criterion by which v. 6 can be ascribed to E is the use of אלהים for God in v. 6a. But it is already clear that this is a dubious criterion in 21:1-7. It looks as if the redactor is deliberately using both designations for God indiscriminately. Most exegetes, however, take as their point of departure that there must be three sources in 21:1-7 because all three must have had an account of the birth of Isaac. This is to beg the question. The basis of this is the hypothesis that E contains an independent Abraham story of which only fragments are extant. It is only by virtue of such a decision already made that one might expect to find an E fragment of this kind in v. 6 (or 6a). But we have discovered so far that the redactor is constructing in 21:1-7 a conclusion only for the two texts which have narrated the promise of a son to Abraham, namely, chs. 17 and 18, to which several allusions are made. It is unlikely, and not in accord with his way of working, that the redactor of 21:1-7 inserted purely mechanically a sentence out of context from another narrative. Only J and P were available to him both for the introduction (11:27-32) and the conclusion (21:1-7).

The two verses raise even further questions. Does v. 6 give one or two explanations of the name Isaac? How does one explain why v. 7 in its present form gives no explanation at all of the name (neither the name nor the verb occur in v. 7)? The function of v. 7 in the context of 21:1-7 can only be, corresponding to v. 6, to explain the name that Sarah gave her child. This difficulty would be met by adopting the proposal of K. Budde (*Die biblische Urgeschichte* [1881] 224 n. 1) to read v. 6b after v. 7 (accepted by H. Gunkel, O. Procksch, J. Skinner). This would answer at the same time the first question: v. 6 contains one explanation of the name Isaac and v. 7 another. With this transposition yet a third difficulty is cleared up, namely, how v. 6b is to be understood. H. Gunkel understands it as contrary to v. 6a: "The old woman is ashamed to have become a mother." On the other hand, F. Delitzsch, A. Dillmann, J. Skinner, and others understand the laughter of v. 6b as joyful surprise. If 6b is read after 7 then the laughter can be meant only in this latter sense (hence לי is not "at me" but "they will laugh in approval"). These reasons suggest agreement with the rearrangement.

A final difficulty still remains. Both explanations of the name Isaac are new with respect to chs. 17 and 18. There is good reason for this, namely, that Gen. 21:1-7 is not to be explained merely by literary-critical separation into sources. The explanation of the name Isaac in chs. 17 and 18 occurs in the context of promise to a childless couple; that in 21:1-7 of the circumstances *following* the birth of the child. The only possible explanation of all this is that the redactor chose from the many explanations of the name available from the tradition those that presupposed the birth of the child. This is a proof that besides the written works at hand to him, the redactor knew a broad oral tradition going side by side with them.

[**21:6**]   The meaning of the name, "Laughter has God prepared in my regard" (v. 6a), corresponds to, or at any rate suggests, a cry of praise (G. von Rad). "Laughter" is here a synonym for joy. The clause in 6b, "everyone who hears. . .," fits with 6a because the hearing has to refer to an event, not to an interpretation. The rearrangement renders the connection smooth, referring the hearing to the birth of the child.

[**21:7**]   ותאמר introduces a statement made by Sarah at the birth of her child which is the basis of the name she gives him. It is a poetic cry of joy in the readily recognizable rhythm of two double-threes (J. Skinner: "the transposition improves the metrical form"). On the rhythmic form of a cry at the climax of a narrative, cf. *Genesis 1–11*, p. 231. What is meant could have been said in this way: "Who would ever have thought that I would have a child after all this!" Instead, Sarah transposes this into an event: the father receives the news that his wife has given birth to a child (cf. Jer. 20:15; Job 3:3). This is what is intended by the words מי מלל לאברהם. The use of the Aramaic verb מלל is striking; it occurs elsewhere only in Ps. 106:2; Job 8:2; 33:3. The announcement consists in the words היניקה בנים שרה. It is to be presumed that this is an ancient traditional form of informing the father: Sarah suckles a child! The plural בנים is a generic plural, as in Ex. 21:22; Is. 37:3, and is better rendered by the singular. In the second part the announcement to the father is confirmed by the cry of joy: I have borne my husband a son in his old age! The final sentence (6b) expresses the joyful surprise of others: "Everyone who hears it will laugh (approval) for me," i.e., will rejoice with me (cf. Ps. 113:9).

The interpretation of the name, understood in this way, goes far beyond any genealogical detail and introduces an ancient oral narrative variant of the birth of Isaac. The fact that vv. 7 and 6b, corresponding to the introductory verse (v. 1), form an inclusion supports the proposal that the conclusion of 21:1-7 is the conscious work of the redactor.

Purpose and Thrust

Gen. 21:1-7 brings to its goal what was introduced in 11:27-32, namely, the story of Abraham and Sarah insofar as it is concerned with the birth of a child. The son is born! Only with the birth of a child is a family really a family and it is on this that the future hangs; so it was with the patriarchs and so it has remained right up to the present. The joy that resonates in the news of the birth of a child (21:6) has remained, despite all changes and crises. Changes in the forms of community life have changed its meaning. During the monarchy the birth of the child acquires a political significance because it makes possible the continuity of the dynasty. It is significant that after the collapse of the monarchy, in the expectation of another, a king of peace, it is this one detail that is preserved: ''For to us a child is born, to us a son is given!'' (Is. 9:6), and this in the ancient form of the birth announcement. It is just this that is revived again in the announcement of the Savior in Lk. 2: ''For to you is born this day a Savior!'' The Savior cannot come unless a child is born.

The Expulsion and Rescue
of Hagar and Her Child

Literature

R. Kittel, "Der scherzende Ismael," ZAW 40 (1923) 155. H. Torczyner, "Zu einigen akkadisch-hebräischen Wortbeziehungen," MGWJ 80 (1936) 13-18. Y. Moubarac, "Ismael chassé au désert," BVC 9 (1955) 22-30. T. Jansma, "Investigation into the Early Syrian Fathers on Genesis," OTS 12 (1958) 69-181, #2. R. B. Y. Scott, "The Hebrew Cubit," JBL 77 (1958) 208-214; "Weights and Measures of the Bible," BA 22 (1959) 22-40. P. Wernberg-Møller, "Observations on the Hebrew Participle," ZAW 71 (1959) 54-67. T. Canaan, "Das Opfer in palästinischen Sitten und Gebräuchen," ZAW 74 (1962) 31-44. H. R. Moeller, "Biblical Research and OT Translation," BiTr 13 (1962) 16-22. A. K. Fenz, *Auf Jahwes Stimme hören*, WBTh 6 (1964). K. W. Neubauer, "Erwägungen zu Amos 5,4-15," ZAW 78 (1966) 292-316. M. Cogan, "A Technical Term for Exposure," JNES 27 (1968) 133-135. O. H. Steck, *Überlieferung und Zeitgeschichte in den Elia-Erzählungen*, WMANT 26 (1968). F. C. Fensham, "The Son of a Handmaid in North-West Semitic," VT 19 (1969) 312-321. A. J. Bjørndalen, " 'Form' und 'Inhalt' des motivierenden Mahnspruches," ZAW 82 (1970) 347-361. D. Vetter, *Jahwes Mitsein: Ein Ausdruck des Segens*, AzTh 1,45 (1971). G. Pfeifer, "Entwöhnung und Entwöhnungsfest im AT: der Schlüssel zu Jes 28,7-13?" ZAW 84 (1972) 341-347. D. Irvin, *Mytharion. The Comparison of Tales from the OT and the Ancient Near East*, AOAT 32 (1974; 1978[2]).

Text

21:8　The child grew and was weaned.[a] Now on the day that Isaac was weaned, Abraham held a great feast.

9　But when Sarah saw the son of Hagar the Egyptian, whom she had borne to Abraham, playing "with her son Isaac,"[a] she said to Abraham:

10　Drive out this servant woman with her son! For the son of this servant woman shall not be heir with my son, with Isaac![a]

11　And this troubled Abraham very much because of his son.[a]

12　Then God said to Abraham: Do not be[a] troubled because of the boy and your maidservant; do whatever Sarah says to you! For your descendants shall be called after Isaac.

13　And moreover I will make the son of the maidservant into a "great"[a] people because he is a descendant of yours.

14　Abraham rose early on the following morning and took bread and a skin of water and gave them to Hagar, and "lifted the child onto her shoulders"[a] and farewelled her. She went and wandered in the desert of Beersheba.

15 Now when the water in the skin[a] was finished, she cast the child under a bush,

16 and went and sat[a] over against him, about a bow shot's distance;[b] and she said: I cannot watch[c] the death of my child. So she sat over against[d] him. But "the child"[e] raised "his" voice and "cried."[e]

17 But God heard the voice of the boy, and the messenger of God called to Hagar from heaven and said to her: What is the matter, Hagar? Do not be afraid, because God has heard the boy's voice "   ".[a]

18 Get up,[a] lift up the boy "from where he is lying"[b] and take his hand; for I will make him into a great people.

19 And God opened her eyes and she saw a well of water.[a] And she went and filled the skin with water[b] and gave the boy a drink.

20 And God was with the boy. And he grew and lived in the desert,[a] and he became a bowman.[b]

21 And he lived in the desert of Paran, and his mother took a wife for him from the land of Egypt.

8a Pausal form meaning "complete, bring to its term"; on the form, Ges-K §51m, on the construction, BrSynt §99b.

9a With Gk, Vg, and the majority of exegetes add: את יצחק בנה; pausal form, Ges-K §52n; construction, BrSynt §103a.

10a "With Isaac" is missing in Sam and TargO.

11a על is strengthened by אודת, etymologically unclear; A. Dillmann: "a rare and outmoded expression." Some Gk Mss. add "Ishmael."

12a Gk adds הדבר; on the clause, BrSynt §35b.

13a Add גדול with Sam, Gk, Vg, Syr, as in v. 18.

14a Rearrange thus with Gk and Syr, cf. BHK.

15a On the form, Ges-K §23f.

16a לה as in Gen. 12:1, Ges-K §119g.   **b** Form, Ges-K §75kk, 113a; P. Wernberg-Møller, ZAW 71 (1959) 54-67.   **c** Ges-K §108b, 119k; BrSynt §§6c, 106a.   **d** BrSynt §111d.   **e** Read with Gk "the child"; cf. BHS.

17a "There where he is lying" is to be read after את־הנער in v. 18. באשר = there where, Ges-K §138e; H. R. Moeller (1962), cf. lit. above, is of the opinion that ב in באשר means "from."

18a On קומי BrSynt §133a.   **b** See note to 17a.

19a Gk adds חיים.   **b** Double accus. with causal conjugations, Ges-K §117cc.

20a Syr adds "Paran."   **b** According to the versions רבה קשת is to be read, BHK, H. Gunkel and others; Ges-K §131b. For details on "bowman," B. Jacob; H. N. Torczyner (1936), cf. lit. above; J. Skinner: "רבה shoot might be a byform of רבב (49,23)."

Form

The first question concerns the structure of 21:8-21. The arch that spans the event rises out of a stable situation (v. 8, part 1) and descends again into a stable situation (vv. 20-21, part 5).

The gradual development of Abraham's two children, peacefully portrayed as they play with each other, is disrupted by Sarah's demand. This sets a process in motion (vv. 9-11, part 2). The execution of the demand follows (vv. 14-16, part 3) and this means misery and distress for Hagar and her child. The narrative reaches its climax here as the child cries. But God brings the change in fortune (vv. 17-19, part 4). The conclusion tapers off into a stable situation once more (vv. 20-21, part 5). It is nothing less than the classical structure of a narrative from the patriarchal period, coherent and self-contained; it is a narrative of particular finesse which can have arisen at that time and which goes back to oral tradition (against J. Van Seters).

Setting

The narrative, without the later elaborations, had its life in the oral tradition of the small migratory groups whose existence was determined by such experiences, particularly by family conflict and the threat of the desert. These are the two events in which God's word and action were experienced first and foremost: God's instruction in a conflict and his help in face of death. What God says here agrees with what we know of the relationship to God elsewhere in the patriarchal period.

When this story was originally told orally, it naturally gave rise to variants. And because the motifs which it treats are so important, it is to be presumed not only that there were many variants, but also that they extended right down to the writing stage. Each of these written narratives can contain traces of several variants (this is particularly clear in the conclusion, vv. 20, 21). A further sign that the narrative had its origin in the patriarchal period is the framing of it with genealogical details in vv. 8 and 20f. One must distinguish between the narrative and the expansions, the setting of which in the history of the patriarchal promises is to be determined. They point to a relatively late stage as the distinction in v. 12f. and the concept גוי גדול in vv. 13,18 show. They are to be understood from the function of the promises to Israel in the period after the settlement.

The literary source of Gen. 21:8-21: In the era when the literary-critical method prevailed the text was without exception ascribed to E. It was sufficient that there was a doublet of ch. 16 (J) which used אלהים throughout while J uses יהוה. Gen. 21:8-21 therefore could be cited as the standard example of an Elohistic parallel to a Yahwistic narrative. One can still concede a relative weight to both criteria. It is improbable that the same writer would have used only יהוה throughout ch. 16 and only אלהים here (this is the reason why J. Van Seters' thesis that ch. 21 belongs to J will scarcely win agreement). One must acknowledge therefore that ch. 21 was added by a hand other than J.

In the previous chapters we found no beginnings of E in ch. 16, no trace in 21:1-7, and we left 20:1-7 an open question. A comparison of possible E texts, 20:1-18 and 21:8-21, shows that they are of such a different kind that it scarcely seems possible that they stem from the same author and the same period. The exegesis of the present passage will show this. If 21:8-21 cannot have come from J then it is to be traced to an interpolator. This is probable for a further reason, namely, that 21:1-7 clearly forms a conclusion. A narrative from the patriarchal period was available to the interpolator.

Commentary

[21:8]   In order to understand v. 8 one must presuppose what has hitherto been said about the genealogies whose regular constituent parts are birth—marriage—death. Further details can be added particularly where, as in the present case, they serve to lead in a narrative. And this is the only way we know that weaning is celebrated with a feast (cf. lit. above and R. de Vaux, *Ancient Israel* [1959; Eng. 1962] 43, 468). A child was usually weaned in its third year; the feast celebrates the close of life's first stage: one could describe it as a ''rite of passage'' (cf. 1 Sam. 1; 1 Kings 11:20). It is a family feast which celebrates what for it is an important event and should be seen against the background of the high mortality rate among less developed peoples, as should also the two verbs ''grew up'' and "was weaned." The child has survived this first and particularly dangerous stage of his life, and it could be expected now that he would continue on. It also enables us to understand v. 10 better. We learn nothing more about the feast except that part of it was a festive meal (משתה, cf. Gen. 19:3).

[21:9] The clause that leads in the action, ותרא שרה, is significant for ancient narratives. Only the action, "she threw a glance," is mentioned, thereby enhancing the compactness; it is expected that the listener will find himself in sympathy with what this glance means. One may compare it with the narrative style of the gospels where, for example, a healing story begins: "And Jesus saw. . . ." H. Gunkel's explanation is correct: "Sarah sees into the future." The intent of her glance is described in the two qualifications about the child's mother: "Hagar the Egyptian" and "whom she had borne to Abraham." This is the source of the conflict. She sees Hagar's son playing; it is probable that with the Gk and Vg the sentence is to be completed with את־יצחק בנה as both the sense and the rhythm require. It is not to be assumed that the verb מצחק is a play on the name Isaac, because Ishmael is its subject, apart from the fact that all previous uses derive from the Qal. It is a peaceful scene that meets Sarah's gaze; but it is precisely there that she senses danger for her own son, as v. 10 expresses it. A biased interpretation understands מצחק negatively (Gal. 4:21-31, ". . .He who was born according to the flesh persecuted him who was born according to the Spirit. . ." v. 29), an interpretation which is found among the reformers and Christian exegetes right down to the 19th century, and among Jewish exegetes to the present (e.g., B. Jacob). Such an interpretation is biased because it is looking for an explanation of Sarah's harshness (v. 10). But this is to misunderstand the text. Even from the purely grammatical point of view מצחק without a preposition cannot mean "to mock" or the like.

[21:10] Sarah's reaction to the sight of her own son playing with "the son of the maidservant" is the harsh demand that Abraham expel the maid and her son. It is not accurate enough to describe her motive as "proud disdain" (F. Delitzsch) or "jealousy" (H. Gunkel). It is rather an uncompromising and relentless intervention on behalf of her son and his future that moves her. We will meet this in another form in the case of Rebekah. This is full of meaning for such an early form of society: the future of a woman lay with her own son and nowhere else. Hagar's son, "whom she had borne to Abraham," threatens both her son's and her own future, even though he is also Abraham's son. And so he must go. The question of "inheritance" is merely symptomatic. What Sarah is providing for is her son's future. To censure Sarah's demand from the point of view of individual ethic or our own religious attitude is to fail to see that Sarah is engaged in a struggle for her own very existence; in later forms of society such struggles are transferred to the social or political sphere, while here they take place within the family circle.

One must note here the difference between chs. 16 and 21. In ch. 15 Hagar is Sarah's maid and serves a physical function; conflict develops primarily between these two; Hagar is portrayed from beginning to end as a proudly self-conscious rival of Sarah. In ch. 21 Hagar is simply Abraham's maidservant (v. 12), and as such his concubine; there is no talk of any previous conflict between Sarah and Hagar. Hagar has no relationship with Sarah here; only Abraham has authority over her. She does not flee as in ch. 16, but is expelled. A real variant of ch. 16 was available to ch. 21; despite the agreements there are two narratives.

[**21:11**]   Sarah's demand troubles Abraham because it concerns a son of his own body. The demand is cruel for all concerned, the father, the mother, and the child. It leads to a bitter conflict and no settlement is in sight.

[**21:12-13**]   A divine oracle now enters the situation, following completely the direction of the old narrative. But one may ask whether the oracle, as it has been passed on, accords with the circumstances. After the introduction it is divided into two parts: the instruction, positive and negative, and the promise which is its basis, likewise in two parts (last clause of v. 12, and v. 13).

[**21:12**]   The divine oracle is introduced in a form corresponding to 12:1, "And Yahweh (God) spoke to Abraham," and is to be understood in a similar way. God's instructions are given directly to the patriarchs without mediation or any special apparatus of revelation. Nothing is said about how it takes place. One cannot conclude with any certainty to a revelation made in a dream in v. 14; when this is meant, it is said.

The opening sentence of God's address takes up Abraham's reaction to Sarah's demand (v. 11) and counters it: "You need not be troubled about your son and your maid!" (this addition is part of the narrative subtlety). Then follows the positive instruction to yield to Sarah's demand. God's instruction is not only accommodated without difficulty to the beginning of the narrative, but it is necessary for the continuation of v. 14 because it explains the process from Abraham's reaction in v. 11 to his action in v. 14. Hence H. Gunkel's view that vv. 12-13 are secondary does not command assent. Both parts of the oracle link instruction and promise, which is so important for the patriarchal story. "Do not be troubled. . ." is an indirect or implicit promise. The execution in v. 14a would be the immediate consequence of the instruction to yield to Sarah's demand.

[**21:12bβ, 13**]   The promise which now follows extends beyond the present situation into the distant future. Both parts look to the history of the descendants of Isaac and Ishmael. The situation is similar to 12:1: the basis there is an instruction to Abraham which has its meaning and function in the patriarchal period; it is expanded by a promise directed to the history of the people who are Abraham's descendants. The conclusion here also suggests that the promises in vv. 12-13, directed to the history of the two peoples, were added only at a later stage of the old narrative. But the proof of this must come from the verses themselves.

[**21:12bβ**]   The sentence, "For your descendants shall be called after Isaac," is not readily comprehensible. F. Delitzsch suggests three possible explanations and decides for the third: "It is to be through Isaac that people are to talk about a seed of Abraham," or more simply: "The people of Israel is to take its beginning from Isaac" (similarly A. Dillmann, O. Procksch, J. Skinner). All attempts at explanation agree that the promise means the people of Israel, that Abraham's seed (Is. 41:8) comes only through Isaac. It belongs, therefore, with those promises which do not reach their fulfillment in the patriarchal period, but only after the occupation of the land. But they cannot be ascribed to any of the promises that frequently occur elsewhere. R. Rendtorff points this out: "Its primary concern is to emphasize the legitimate line of the descendants through Isaac, in contrast to Ishmael, because there is no mention here of numerous progeny" (BZAW 147 [1976] 61). There is a parallel to vv. 12b-13 in 17:19-21 (P) where the concern is precisely with "the legitimate line. . .."

[**21:13**]   Just as in 17:20, so here Ishmael also receives a blessing and the sentence also begins: ''I will make him into a great people'' (גדול is to be supplied following ch. 18 with H. Holzinger, O. Procksch, J. Skinner, and many others; the promise of a great nation is found also in Gen. 18:18; 46:3, all late passages). This parallel between Gen. 21:12b-13 and 17:19-21 can mean only that both have arisen from the common interest in the line of division between the descendants of Isaac and those of Ishmael and that both belong to a late stage of the history of the promises to the patriarchs. This same interest appears in the New Testament in Rom. 9:7 and Heb. 11:18, where Gen. 21:12 is cited.

[**21:14**]   Only what is necessary is said; ''But this silence amidst the bustle is all the more powerful'' (G. von Rad). The narrative preserves the old word for a waterskin, חמת, which occurs elsewhere only in vv. 15 and 19 of this same chapter, a sign that it derives from the early period.

Ishmael is a child in Gen. 21 whereas according to 17:25 he was about sixteen years old. A transmitter has made a rather clumsy attempt at harmonization by changing the object to הילד so as to gloss over Abraham lifting Hagar's child on to her shoulders.

Hagar's departure with her child takes place in the usual way: Abraham rises early (Gen. 19:27; 22:3)—departure must be at daybreak—and prepares the necessary provisions, bread and water in a skin. It can not have been much because Hagar must be able to carry it. The small gesture, Abraham laying the child in the arms of the woman whom he must distressfully dismiss, speaks everything that he cannot now say. The verb וישלחה is not to be translated ''he expelled her''; that has already happened. It is literally ''he dismissed her'' or ''he farewelled her.'' This is the translation I prefer in order to make clear that in Israel and Israel's early period there was no dismissal without a blessing; in the blessing Abraham commends the mother and child to the One who united the command to send Hagar away with the implicit promise, ''Do not be troubled. . ..''

Abraham sends his secondary wife and his child out into the ''desert of Beersheba.'' ''This refers to the rather flat, southern part of the Negev'' (J. Simons).

[**21:15,16**]   Hagar wanders about in the desert—a woman alone with a small child—and the pitiless consequence cannot be delayed; the water runs out and the threat of death by thirst hangs over them, first over the child. Once more the picture is gripping in its brevity and harshness. Only one detail is selected from these hours of gradually increasing torment: Hagar casts the child, now faced with death, under a bush (Job 30:4), her action an expression of her exhaustion; at least he will die in the shade. She sits a bow shot's distance away waiting for the end. The following sentence in the MT is ''and she raised her voice and cried,'' whereas according to the Gk it is the boy who cried. The MT makes good sense and there would be no need to alter it in favor of the Gk did not v. 17 refer the crying to the boy and were it not a question of a standard expression, ''they cried—he heard.'' The text therefore should follow the Gk.

It is certainly a ''moving scene'' (H. Gunkel); ''he. . . intends to grip and move the reader'' (G. von Rad); but is this really the intention? Such would presuppose that the listener (not the reader) were standing at a distance contemplating the narrative objectively as one contemplates a work of art. But in that case what was important would be lost—the participation. This is the goal of the narrator; he does not aim to move. Only one who participates understands what is narrated here.

[21:17-19]   The account of the rescue too can be understood only in this way. The high point and goal of what the narrative intends is that God has heard the voice of the boy. It tells the story of rescue from death, the theme later of so many psalms of praise: "Because he has heard the voice of my weeping." The listeners understand the narrator only when they rejoice with those saved and thank the savior.

The structure of vv. 17-19 presents difficulties because of the two different subjects. "But God heard. . ." (v. 17a) is continued in v. 19a by "And God opened. . ."; in between is the relatively independent address of the "angel of God" (vv. 17b-18). After the introduction the address begins with a question; then follows the call, "Do not be afraid!" which takes up and repeats v. 17a. This promise is followed by the instruction, "Get us. . ." (v. 18a), which in turn takes up and repeats the promise of v. 13. The angel's address with its two repetitions has a cumulative effect.

[21:17aβ-18]   One would expect God's saving intervention to follow "God heard" in 21:17a, as a wealth of parallels shows; but it comes only in v. 19a. One concludes therefrom that 17aβ-18 is a subsequent insertion. The messenger of God who is encountered on earth (cf. Gen. 16:7b) has become an "angel," a heavenly being who calls from heaven. His first words to Hagar are an inquiry (as in Gen. 16:7b) which is more suited to God's earthly messenger. The continuation is another form of speech corresponding to an oracle of salvation: the words of comfort, "do not be afraid," stand on a classical assurance of salvation, "because God has. . .," which repeat v. 17aα. The style of such an oracle requires that a clause in the future follow, like v. 18b. But instead there is an instruction (v. 18a) which would follow better on the inquiry (as in 16:9). The instruction does not fit the context well; the promise that Ishmael is to become a great people is likewise difficult. In addition, it is a repetition of v. 13.

Vv. 17aβ-18 is a later insertion into the narrative which looks to the promise already made to Abraham and is now directed to Hagar as well. It is given the form of an address by God (or an angel) and unites the elements of two different forms of revelation, the oracle of salvation and the message of one sent by God:

A messenger of God. . .	Do not be afraid,
What is the matter Hagar?	because God has heard
	the boy's voice.
Get up, lift up the boy	
from where he is lying	I will make him
and take his hand.	into a great people.

An address of this kind, made up of different forms side by side, is not possible in a narrative that has developed naturally. It is probable that the messenger elements derive from a variant of the Hagar story which is very close to ch. 16. The union with elements of a salvation oracle recalls 15:1. It is striking that these elements, apart from "do not be afraid," consist merely of two repetitions (vv. 17a and 13); the later insertion is here readily palpable. The further qualification, "from where he is lying," does not suit v. 17b and probably belongs to v. 18a, "lift up the boy from where he is lying." (See the lit. on Gen. 15:1; H. M. Dion, CBQ 29 [1967] 198-206; A. de Pury, *Promesse divine*. . . [1975] 229 n. 83; מלאך Excur. to 16:7).

    A sufficient explanation of the insertion of vv. 17aβ-18 is that the promise concerning Ishmael, which only Abraham had heard in v. 13, must also be promulgated to Hagar, because it is she who now takes the place of Ishmael's father, as v. 21 shows. In ch. 17, too, the promise concerning Isaac, which was first promulgated only to Abraham, is further proclaimed to Sarah.

[21:19]   V. 19 follows immediately on v. 17aα. God gives ear and intervenes in accordance with the two-part prayer that he do so. God opens Hagar's eyes and she sees the spring of water hitherto hidden to her. The spring is a "deep hole in the ground (cased with stone) where water gushes below" (H. Gunkel). No further assistance is required; Hagar now does what is necessary to quench the boy's thirst; there is no mention of her own. It could be that a variant of the story concluded with Hagar giving the child the name that commemorates this event ("God hears"); also that the spring receives a name from it, as does the mountain in Gen. 22:14. But neither is necessary.

    The material at hand, therefore, was a patriarchal story without any etiological conclusion. When H. Gunkel comments, "In the original recension this spring is certainly a holy spring; it is there that God appears and listens," this is not a consequence that follows from the narrative; the spring is much rather a place where a single event happened. The narrative span ends satisfactorily with the rescue of the mother and child from the threat of death. The genealogical conclusion needs only to say some more about the course of the life of the child who was saved.

[21:20]   The tension is resolved and the narrative issues once more into a stable situation. There is transition to "God was with the boy" (on God's presence with someone, see the Lit. above to 21:1-7 and 21:8-21; also H. D. Preuss, BWANT 5,7 [1968]). God was with Ishmael as he grew up, as he was with the boy Samuel (1 Sam. 3:19). Both in his saving action and in his blessing the God of Abraham remains with Ishmael, now driven from his family. God's grace is not restricted to Isaac's line. The boy grows by virtue of God's effective blessing. He lives in the desert, which is now no longer a threat; but to sustain life he needs a weapon; Ishmael becomes a bowman. This is the first and virtually the last time that there is mention of a weapon in the patriarchal story.

[21:21]   A further genealogical detail is added which is independent of v. 20. V. 14 spoke of the desert of Beersheba; v. 21 speaks of the desert of Paran west of the Arabah (J. Simons), contiguous with Egypt (B. Jacob); here it means the region where the Ishmaelites pitched their tents. Ishmael is the tribal ancestor of the Ishmaelites who stem from Abraham but who at the same time are related to the Egyptians, because Hagar, herself an Egyptian, gives her son a wife from the land of Egypt. Such is the beginning of a foreign tribe which is at the same time related to Israel.

Purpose and Thrust

As long as human society has existed, so too have outcasts, even as early as the family of Abraham. The outcasts can be guilty or guiltless. Here they are guiltless. In the instruction to Abraham, God gives Sarah her way; but the outcast experiences a miraculous deliverance. Sarah has achieved her purpose, but Hagar's story is told for centuries and centuries. It is narrated that God heard the cry of the child who was dying of thirst; he is only the "son of the maidservant," but God has given ear to him. The old story wants to narrate that there is no doing away with the harshness and cruelty of mankind, whereas the merciful God does not abandon the outcasts but lets them experience God's miraculous deliverance.

It is no mere chance, but basic to the structure of the Old Testament, that the history of the people of Israel also begins with the experience of deliverance (Ex. 1–15). Here it is totally different because it is a different stage in history and a different form of community; but it is the outcasts, the forced laborers exposed to every threat, who have the experience; this is the source of Israel's Credo. Much has changed, but God remains Israel's Savior. It is not only the people who experience God as Savior, but also the individual personally, as Hagar and her child in the desert. A wealth of psalms of praise attests this. At the end of this history Christ comes as *the* Savior. The Bible can speak of God who saves and Christ as Savior only on the basis of the experience of those who have encountered the Savior in the face of death. The story of Hagar and her child in the desert is as vivid today as it was then; everyone understands it.

The narrative has taken on another meaning inasmuch as it has been resumed by and applied to the people of Israel. This was done by inserting the promises about the descendants of Isaac and Ishmael in vv. 12bβ-13 and 17aβ-18, thereby throwing the emphasis in the narrative on the separate destinies of the two children and their descendants. The expulsion of Ishmael limits the people which calls Abraham its father to the single line, the descendants of Isaac. The particular history of this people demands that it be separated from the "son of the maidservant," as God himself had ordered. But God's blessing goes also with Ishmael: he is to be "a great people." Contrary to the friend-foe mentality, a relationship of Israel with other peoples is retained from the early period. Abraham as father, despite the emphasis on the one legitimate line through Isaac, has a significance which bridges the gap to other peoples.

Dispute over the Wells and Treaty with Abimelech

Literature

Genesis 21:22-32: Z. W. Falk, "Forms of Testimony," VT 11 (1961) 88-91. A. Jepsen, "Gnade und Barmherzigkeit im AT," KuD 4 (1961) 261-271. P. Neuenzeit, " 'Als die Fülle der Zeit gekommen war. . .' (Gal 4,4). Gedanken zum biblischen Zeitverständnis," BiLe 4 (1963) 223-239. J. R. Wilch, *Time and Event. An Exegetical Study of the Use of* 'eth *in the OT in Comparison to Other Temporal Expressions in Clarification to the Concept of Time*, diss. Münster (1969). M. O'Rourke-Boyle, "The Covenant Lawsuit of the Prophets, Am III I-IV 13," VT 21 (1971) 338-362.

Genesis 21:33-34: J. Nougayrol, *Ugaritica* V (1968) Text Ugar. Nr. 8; review, H. Cazelles, VT 19 (1969) 504. Y. Aharoni, *Beer-Sheba I: Excavations at Tel Beer-Sheba* (1973); "Nothing Early and Nothing Late: Re-writing Israel's Conquest," BA 39 (1976) 55-76.

Text

21:22 Now at that time Abimelech[a] and Phicol[b] the commander of his army said to Abraham: God is with you in all that you do.

23 Now then swear to me[a] by God[b] that[c] you will not deal falsely with me or with my children or my chilren's children.[d] As I have shown favor to you, so do you to me and my land as long as you live in it as an alien.

24 Then Abraham said: I swear.[a]

25 But Abraham remonstrated[a] with Abimelech about a well of water[b] which the servants of Abimelech had seized.

26 Abimelech replied: I do not know who has done this. You have said nothing about it to me and[a] I, I have heard nothing of it until today.

27 So Abraham took sheep and cattle and gave them to Abimelech, and the two of them made a treaty.

28 And Abraham set seven ewe lambs apart.[a]

29 Then Abimelech asked Abraham: What is the meaning of "these"[a] seven lambs here that you have set apart?[b]

30 He answered: "The"[a] seven lambs you must accept from me so that they may be[b] a witness that I have dug this well.

31 For this reason the place is called Beersheba[a] because there they pledged themselves.

32 So they made a treaty in Beersheba. Then Abimelech and Phicol the

345

commander of his army departed and returned to the land of the Philistines.

33 Now Abraham planted a tamarisk[a] in Beersheba, and he invoked there the name of Yahweh, God eternal.[b]

34 And Abraham lived a long time as an alien in the land of the Philistines.[a]

22a Gk makes an addition following Gen. 26:26; likewise in v. 32.   **b** W. F. Albright, JPOS 4 (1924) 138f: Egyptian = the Lycian.

23a On the form, Ges-K §20f, 51c.   **b** BrSynt §106d.   **c** Ges-K §149c. **d** Only here in the Pentateuch; elsewhere Is. 14:22; Job 18:19; Sir. 41:5; 47:22.

24a On the form, Ges-K §51p.

25a Sam ויוכיח; the perf. "to describe a situation which. . . perseveres up to the present," P. Neuenzeit, lit. above, 226 n. 7; but perhaps the narrative form is to be read, BHK, Ges-K §112tt.   **b** Gk reads plural.

26a וגם־לא וגם־לא "neither/nor" as in Num. 23:25; Ges-K §162b.

28a On the form, Ges-K §91c.

29a Both here and in v. 30 the article is to be added with the Sam.   **b** Pausal form, Ges-K §91f; cf. Gen. 42:46; 30:41.

30a את before numbers, Ges-K § 117d; also G. W. Nebe, ZNW 63 (1972) 283-289.   **b** For the construction, BrSynt §145b, 161a.

31a Gk φρέαρ ὁρκισμοῦ, but in vv. 32,33 φρέαρ τοῦ ὅρκου.

33a The word אשׁל does not seem to have been known to the versions.   **b** Sam reads העולם.

34a V. 34 is missing in Targ[J].

Form

Scholars are so far virtually unanimous that the text of Gen. 21:22-34 consists of two layers: A, vv. 22-24, 27, (31 or)32; and B, vv. 25-26, 28-30, 31 (or 31-32). There is difference only in regard to vv. 31-33. On the other hand there is the greatest uncertainty about the relationship of these layers to each other and whether they are to be ascribed to J or E.

H. Gunkel was the first to determine these two layers clearly; he was certain about ascribing layer A to E (אלהים in vv. 22, 23, and reference to ch. 20, E), but uncertain about ascribing B to J. O. Procksch, J. Skinner, and others followed Gunkel. On the other hand G. von Rad, W. Zimmerli, R. Kilian, and E. A. Speiser ascribe the whole to E, though all insist that it consists of two layers. This then would be the only E text assembled in this way. J. Van Seters sees correctly that neither layer constitutes a complete narrative and comes to the conclusion that layer B (vv. 25-26, 28-31a) is a continuation of ch. 20, and layer A a later supplement to B. If B is a continuation of ch. 20, it must belong to E; A, which is close to ch. 26, must then belong to J. We are on a scholarly merry-go-round: J. Van Seters has gone back to H. Gunkel in that he accepts two literary layers, but ascribes layer A to J and layer B to E.

The peculiar state of research shows that in this case a new approach is needed in order to arrive at more secure ground. The mistake consists in the attempt to determine the strate of 21:22-34 without including the parallel, 26:26-33. Gen. 26:26-33 consists of two units, vv. 26-31 and vv. 32-33. Layer A in 21:22-34 largely corresponds to 26:26-31; 26-32-33, by the same token, is the expansion of the tradition reflected in 21:33-34. But while 26:26-31 is an independent scene, 21:22-34 is not—the arrival of Abimelech and the motive of his request are missing.

The parallel shows that 26:26-31 must be the material of which layer A made use. The latter closes with 21:32, corresponding to 26:31. Both 21:33-34 and 26:32-33 are elaborations. Neither 21:22-24, 27, 31 (A) nor 26:32-33 contain an etiology of the name; on the other hand, the explanation of the name, "well of the oath," is added as a supplement in 21:31b from 26:32-33. As for layer B, 21:25-26, 28-31a, it has no counterpart in ch. 26 and is a self-contained whole which can now be understood as a subsequent addition (the reverse of Van Seters). This scene runs its course with an explanation of the name Beersheba as "seven wells." There is neither oath nor pact.

      Gen. 21:33-34 does not belong to any of the preceding episodes but issues into an itinerary.

Setting

There are peculiarities in the relationship of layers A and B to each other and of these two to ch. 26 which have not hitherto arisen in Gen. 12–21:7. Both in Gen. 26 and Gen. 21 the individual texts are not independent narratives (J. Van Seters has correctly seen this), but scenes in a broader context; they take up motifs from previous texts without which they are incomprehensible. We are then in a stage of tradition which no longer fits individual narratives and reports into a whole, but forms broader complexes out of them. This is shown by formulas such as "at that time" (21:22) or "on the same day" (26:32). This is a fundamentally different way of working from that of J; we are on the way to a coherent history of the patriarchs.

      The anachronism of a visit of a Philistine king to Isaac or Abraham accords with this. Such is possible only in an era which no longer had any clear ideas about the period of the patriarchs. Not only is the name "Philistine" an anachronism but also the very dialog. The idea of the patriarchs as business partners of kings comes from a time when esteem for them was very high. In Gen. 21:22-34 then it is a matter of later narratives which have come together after the conclusion of J's work, which can to be sure contain older traditions, but were attached only in the later period of the monarchy. It must be acknowledged that patriarchal traditions were handed down orally (possibly too in rather small written complexes), side by side with the already existing J work and were later attached to it in the form of supplements like this. The transfer from Isaac to Abraham or the reverse is best understood in this way.

      This provides a new answer to the question of J and E in the patriarchal history. According to the old conception both J and E contained a history of the patriarchs and their relationship was regarded as that of juxtaposition. But such an understanding has not stood the test in the case of the Abraham cycle (chs. 12–25). There was no trace of E in ch. 15; the remaining texts attributed to E are found only in chs. 20 and 21. The very nature of ch. 20 is such as to qualify it as a supplement; 21:22-34 is also a collection of supplements. The texts hitherto attributed to a source E are supplements which were later attached to J's story of Abraham.

Commentary

[**21:22**]   The transition from v. 21 to v. 22 is abrupt and difficult to grasp. V. 22 begins with a formula that forms a link with what has preceded (i.e., with ch. 20, not 21:8-21), "It happened at that time" (cf. 15:1), and that presupposes a coherent Abraham story. The same formula likewise serves as a redactional transition in 38:1. One expects now an account of Abimelech's coming to Abraham corresponding to his departure in v. 32, but it is missing. Instead, an address of

Abimelech to Abraham is introduced (''and Phicol, the commander,'' clumsily brought in from 26:16); no reason is given and it is comprehensible only from 26:26-28. The address consists of a statement (v. 22b) and a request or demand. Abimelech has seen that God is with Abraham; in the parallel (26:28), this statement has a basis (26:12-14), but in 21:22 it has not. The promise of aid, that God will be with the person, does not occur in the Abraham cycle but only in the Jacob cycle (chs. 26–50). This fact confirms that the sentence in 21:22 stems from ch. 26.

[**21:23**]   The ועתה makes the transition from the statement to the demand. Abimelech the king demands that Abraham swear to show him nothing but favor. The effect is grotesque when one reflects on the situation in the patriarchal period itself; the Canaanite king with his commander in chief confronts a nomad shepherd who is utterly powerless, and more, a mere tolerated alien. The demand too is an anachronism; it makes sense only when in the eyes of the author and those addressed Abraham represents Israel. Moreover, it follows from the addition, ''with my children or my children's children,'' that it is a question of the relationship of peoples to each other.

[**21:24**]   Abraham accedes to the request and swears. This brief sentence is missing in the parallel in ch. 26. It is added here because of the insertion of layer B, vv. 25-26; the actual reaction to Abimelech's request follows only in v. 27.

[**21:25-26**]   Abraham's remonstration with Abimelech immediately after his oath of loyalty sounds harsh. But another scene begins with v. 25 which has been subsequently attached to the preceding. It also hangs loosely with ch. 26; in 26:27 Isaac remonstrates with Abimelech, but there it is an organic part of the scene. In both cases it is a matter of a dispute over a well. Both scenes therefore are built on ch. 26. As in 26:15-23 the dispute over the well leads to the giving of a name. However, 21:25-26 diverges from ch. 26 in its bias to see that Abraham emerges superior. It begins already in v. 25 when the alien nomad shepherd remonstrates with the king over a well and continues with the king conceding that he knows nothing of it. The scene is continued in vv. 28-30.

[**21:27a**]   V. 27 continues immediately on v. 24 and so belongs to layer A. Abraham's oath in v. 24 would meet Abimelech's request (vv. 22-23) and the incident would be closed. There is no occasion for gifts of animals from the flock in what has gone before. But when v. 24 is inserted merely because of the interpolated piece, vv. 25-26, then the demand that Abimelech makes of Abraham is met only in v. 27, corresponding to vv. 22-23, as a mutual act. This corresponds to ch. 26 where the ceremony of a pact (vv. 30-31a) consisting of a common meal and a mutual oath follows on Abimelech's words to Isaac (vv. 28-29). One gathers too from ch. 26 that the gift of animals from the flock in 21:27a is the preparation for the ceremony.

[**21:27b**]   The settlement is something like a nonaggression pact (for כרת ברית, see comm. on 15:18); each is to behave in a friendly way towards the other.

[**21:28**]   In vv. 28-30 the scene which was begun in vv. 25-26 is brought to a conclusion. Abimelech's answer in v. 26 was evasive; it was a matter of having him recognize Abraham's rights to the well. Vv. 28-30 narrate how Abraham shrewd-ly brings this about. This has no counterpart in ch. 26. Vv. 25-26 are the necessary presupposition for vv. 28-30: Abimelech's servants had seized a well from Abra-ham (v. 25b); he confronts Abimelech with this in v. 25a, but receives only an evasive answer (v. 26); thereupon he shrewdly maneuvers him to acknowledge his right of possession (vv. 26-28); this event gave the well its name.

Abraham sets seven ewe lambs aside. The theme word "seven" which leads to the giving of the name has been sounded. The article in הצאן presupposes that there has already been talk of the animals; but this is not the case in vv. 25-26. In the present text this can refer only to the "sheep and cattle" of v. 27. The con-clusion is that the interpolator had text A before him.

[21:29, 30] Abimelech asks about the meaning of the seven lambs that have been set aside; he is suspicious. Abraham replies that they are a gift and that he must accept them. He thereby exacts a testimony from Abimelech and confirms his right of possession of the well. The gift has here a binding force; it obliges. Were Abimelech not to accept the gift, it would mean that he did not acknowledge Abraham's right to the well. It is not the gift but the procedure of giving that be-comes the עדה, the witness, because the acceptance takes place before witnesses who can make a statement in case of a future conflict of interests. It is a matter, therefore, neither of an oath nor of a pact nor of concluding a covenant as in v. 32. The acceptance of the gift as such is a public legal act which binds Abimelech with respect to Abraham. Abraham has won the dispute over the well.

[21:31] "As a result of this event the place receives the name of seven wells" (A. Dillmann). There can be no doubt that this is the meaning of v. 31. It is proba-ble that the scene ended with v. 31a and that consequently a clause giving the rea-son is missing because it did not seem necessary. The thrice repeated "seven" and the name "seven wells" (באר שבע) correspond to each other clearly enough. On the other hand it is impossible that the sentence in v. 31b, which gives the rea-son, belonged originally with v. 31a, because in text B (vv. 25-26,28-30) Abra-ham and Abimelech did not swear to each other. There is no reason for a mutual oath here. V. 31b then can be described only as a harmonizing appendage which presupposes that text A (vv. 22-24,27,32) is also geared to an explanation of the name Beersheba. But such is not the case, nor is it in the detailed parallel, 26:26-31; yet the unit vv. 32-33, geared to explain the name Beersheba as "well of the oath," does actually follow ch. 26. It is from here that the appendage 21:31b comes, a further proof that 21:22-24 presupposes ch. 26.

[21:32] V. 32a is a resumption of the same sentence in v. 27b, made necessary by the interpolation of vv. 28-31. "In Beersheba," missing in 26:26-31, has been added in v. 32a.

The parting in v. 32b corresponds to 26:31b. Abimelech and his com-mander Phicol leave and return to the land of the Philistines. All exegetes point out the anachronism. "The anachronism of Philistine dominion over Gerar by Abimelech is introduced from ch. 26" (W. Zimmerli). But in the present context it need not be restricted to mention of the Philistines. It is more in the notion that a dispute over a well takes place between one of the patriarchs and a Philistine city-king. This can have come about only when the story was told to the renown of Abraham a very long time afterwards.

[**21:33**]   V. 33 belongs neither to scene A nor to scene B; it is a constituent of an itinerary like Gen. 12:8; the narrative issues into the itinerary. This is clearly recognizable from the absence of the subject. The versions insert the name "Abraham" after ויטע but this is not necessary. The details of the itinerary follow narratives which deal with Abraham. It is obvious to the listener that Abraham, not Abimelech, is meant (cf. v. 32). This is the only occasion on which he plants a tree at one of the stopping places on his way. This itinerary clause can go back to the patriarchal period. The meaning is not that Abraham "established a cult" as H. Gunkel and a number of exegetes think (cf. comm. 12:7). Abraham is not a cult founder. B. Jacob asks correctly: "Can one plant a holy tree?" and explains, "The tree is meant to be a lasting landmark." When "he invokes the name of Yahweh" there that does not mean that he is practising a cult as understood in the sedentary period, but that he sees that station as the place where he called on his God. On this designation of the tree as אשל = tamarisk, cf. 1 Sam. 22:6; 31:13. The divine name יהוה has here, and only here in the patriarchal story, the additional אל עולם, eternal God or God of eternity (cf. Intro., par. 4. "The Religion of the Patriarchs"). E. Jenni (ZAW 64 [1952] 197-248; 65 [1953] 1-35 and THAT II [1976] 236) writes: "One may conclude from the brief notice in Gen. 21:33 that there existed a pre-Israelite cult of ʾel ʿōlām which the Israelites transferred to Yahweh." F. M. Cross points to the Ugaritic parallel *mlk ʿlm* (*Canaanite Myth and Hebrew Epic* [1973] 13-30). The word does not mean otherworldly eternity opposed to time, but something like time stretching far into the distance (J. Barr, SBT 33 [1962, 1969²]; M. H. Pope, VT.S 2 [1955]).

[**21:34**]   This sentence too is part of the itinerary but it is a late redactional formation to bring vv. 32-33 to a conclusion.

Purpose and Thrust

The text contains two later additions to the Abraham story dealing with wells and rights connected with them. The motif, "dispute over wells," goes back to the patriarchal period; it is vital to the life of the nomad fathers. Even though both texts in 21:22-34 have been subject to later reworking they nevertheless preserve the memory that the existence of the patriarchal families depended on wells along the route. Both additions revere and exalt the father of the people in that a king with his commander in chief is his contracting party in the dispute. The reason a king has to petition Abraham's good pleasure is that God is with him. But Abraham also emerges from the dispute as the superior. This is the way in which it was told in an era when Abraham was regarded and celebrated as the representative of Israel. As God was with him, so may he be with his people Israel so that it may wrest recognition from the kings of the nations and face them as superiors. As Abraham the ancestor planted a tree at the place of the meeting and called on the name of God, so may his seed, the people of Israel, approach their God at the sanctuary and call on his name.

Genesis 22:1-19

Abraham's Sacrifice

Literature

Genesis 22: J. Watson, "Isaac, the Type of Quietness," Exp. 11 (1905) 123-132. E. Nestle, "Wie alt war Isaak bei der Opferung?" ZAW 26 (1906) 281-282. A. E. Mader, *Das Menschenopfer der alten Hebräer und der benachbarten Völker* (1909) esp. 65-69. A. H. Sayce, "What Was the Scene of Abraham's Sacrifice?" ET 21 (1909/10) 86-88. J. Hempel, "Jahwegleichnisse der israelitischen Propheten," ZAW 42 (1924) 74-104, esp. 86-87. K. Fruhstorfer, "Abrahams Kindesopfer (Gn 22)," ThPQ 89 (1936) 18-29. W. O. E. Oesterley, *Sacrifices in Ancient Israel: Their Origin, Purposes and Development* (1937). G. von Rad, "Das hermeneutische Problem. . .," VF (1946/47) esp. 47-48. A. George, "Le sacrifice d'Abraham. Essai sur les diverses intentions de ses narrateurs," *Études de Critique et d'Histoire Religieuses* 2 (1948) 99-110. A. E. Jensen, "Über das Töten als kultgeschichtliche Erscheinung," Paid 4 (1950). D. Lerch, *Isaaks Opferung christlich gedeutet. Eine auslegungsgeschichtliche Untersuchung*, BHTh 12 (1950); ThZ 5 (1949) 321-333. A. Miller, "Zur Typologie des Alten Testaments," BenM 27 (1951) 12-19. M. Buber, "Le sacrifice d'Isaac," DViv 22 (1952) 69-76. P. T. Ros, "El sacrificio de Isaac," CuBi 12 (1955) 20-30, 75-85. H. Gross, "Bedeutet die Opferung Isaaks das Ende der Menschenopfer?" KatBl 82 (1957) 97-99. J. L. McKenzie, "The Sacrifice of Isaac," Scrip. 9 (1957) 79-84. I. Maybaum, "Die Opferung Isaaks," EvTh 17 (1957) 249-264. D. Ben-Shabbetay, "Why Did the Earth Open Its Mouth and the Ram Get Caught in a Thicket by Its Horn?" Tarb. 28 (1958/59) 236. R. A. Rosenberg, "Jesus, Isaac, and the 'Suffering Servant,' " JBL 84 (1965) 381-388. R. Rendtorff, *Studien zur Geschichte des Opfers im alten Israel*, WMANT 24 (1967) esp. 41-42. S. Spiegel, *The Last Trial: On the Legends and Lore of the Command to Abraham to Offer Isaac as a Sacrifice—The Akedah* (1967). H. Graf Reventlow, "Opfere deinen Sohn—Eine Auslegung von Genesis 22," BSt 53 (1968). R. Kilian, *Isaaks Opferung. Zur Überlieferungsgeschichte von Gn 22*, SBS 44 (1970). G. von Rad, *Das Opfer des Abraham*, Kaiser Traktate 6 (1971). L. Ruppert, VT 22 (1972) 55-63. Y. Spiegel, ed., *Psychoanalytische Interpretationen biblischer Texte* (1972). G. W. Coats, "Abraham's Sacrifice of Faith: A Formcritical Study of Genesis 22," Interp. 27 (1973) 389-400. J. Licht, *Testing in the Hebrew Scriptures and in Post-Biblical Judaism* [in Hebr.] (1973). F. Bovon and G. Rouiller, eds., *Exegesis. Problèmes de méthode et exercices de lecture (Genèse 22 et Luc 15)*, BT(N) (1975). A. R. W. Green, *The Role of Human Sacrifice in the Ancient Near East*, diss. Ser 1 (1975). K. Jaroš, "Der Elohist in der Auseinandersetzung mit der Religion seiner Umwelt," *Kairos* NS 17 (1975) 279-283. R. Lack, "Le sacrifice d'Isaac—Analyse structurale de la couche élohiste dans Gn 22," Bib 56 (1975) 1-12. K. Luke, *Studies on the Book of Genesis* (1975). R. L. Wilken, "Melito, the Jewish Community at Sardis, and the Sacrifice of Isaac," TS 37 (1976) 53-69. O. Kaiser, " 'Den Erstgeborenen deiner Söhne sollst du mir geben'. Erwägungen zum Kinderopfer im AT,"

Fests. C. H. Ratschow (1976) 24-48. R. J. Daly, "The Soteriological Significance of the Sacrifice of Isaac," CBQ 39 (1977) 45-75. O. H. Steck, "Ist Gott grausam? Über Isaaks Opferung aus der Sicht des AT," *Ist Gott grausam. . .*, ed. W. Böhme (1977).

Genesis 22:1-19: R. K. Yerkes, "The Location and Etymology of יהוה יראה Gn 22,14," JBL 31 (1912) 136-139. M. J. Bin Gorion, *Sinai und Garizim* (1926) esp. 121-132. G. Dalman, *Jerusalem und sein Gelände* (1930) esp. 125-126. S. Spiegel, "Concerning the Legends of the Akedah. . .," A. Marx Jubil. Vol (1950) 471-547. C. Westermann, "Abraham und Isaak unterwegs," ZdZ 5 (1951) 339-341. S. E. Loewenstamm, "The Climax of Seven Days in the Ugaritic Epos," Tarb. 31 (1961/62) 227-235. P. Humbert, "Étendre la main," VT 12 (1962) 383-395. D. W. Thomas, "A Lost Hebrew Word in Isaiah II 6," JThS. 13 (1962) 323-324. S. McCormick, "Faith as Surrender (Genesis XXII 2)," Interp. 17 (1963) 302-307. G. M. Landes, "The 'Three Days and Three Nights' Motif in Jonah 2,1," JBL 86 (1967) 446-450. P. Zerapa, "The Land of Moriah," Ang. 44 (1967) 84-94. R. Le Déaut, "Lévitique XXII 26-XXIII 44 dans la Targum Palestinien. De l'importance des gloses du Codex Neofiti 1," VT 18 (1968) 458-471. W. L. Holladay, "Isa. III 10-11: An Archaic Wisdom Passage," VT 18 (1968) 481-487. P. Laaf, *Die Pascha-Feier Israels*, BBB 36 (1970). R. North, "Angel-Prophet or Satan-Prophet?" ZAW 82 (1970) 31-67. J. Magonet, "Die Söhne Abrahams," BiLe 14 (1973) 204-210. K. Minkner, *Die Einwirkung des Bürgschaftsrechts auf Leben und Religion Altisraels*, diss. Halle (1974). J. Crenshaw, "Journey Into Oblivion: A Structural Analysis of Gen 22,1-19," Soundings 58 (1975) 243-256. H. Jagersma, ". . .Ten derden dage. . ." (1976). W. J. Peck, "Murder, Timing and the Ram in the Sacrifice of Isaac," AThR 58 (1976) 23-43. H. Donner, "Der Felsen und der Tempel," ZDPV 93 (1977) 1-11. F. W. Golka, "Die theologischen Erzählungen im Abraham-Kreis," ZAW 90 (1978) 186-195.

Genesis 22:15-19: R. Smend, *Jahwekrieg und Stämmebund. Erwägungen zur ältesten Geschichte Israels*, FRLANT 84 (1963). J. C. H. Lebram, "Nachbiblische Weisheitstraditionen," VT 15 (1965) 167-237. D. E. Gowan, "The Use of *ya'an* in Biblical Hebrew," VT 21 (1971) 168-185.

Text

22:1   Now it happened[a] after these events that God tested Abraham. He said to him: Abraham![b] And he answered: Here I am![c]

2   And he said: Take your son, your only[a] son, whom you love,[b] Isaac, and go forth[c] to the land of Moriah,[d] and offer him[e] there as a burnt offering on one of the mountains which I will tell you.

3   So Abraham rose[a] early in the morning, saddled his donkey, and took his two servants and his son Isaac with him. He had split wood for the burnt offering. He set out and went to the place which God had told him.[b]

4   On the third day[a] Abraham raised[b] his eyes and saw[c] the place from a distance.

5   And Abraham said to his servants: Stay[a] here with the donkey; I and the boy want to go there and worship. Then we will come back to you.

6   Then Abraham took the wood for the burnt offering and laid it upon his son Isaac; he himself took the fire-(flint)[a] and the knife. So the two went on together.[b]

7   Then Isaac said to his father Abraham "   ":[a] Father! And he answered: Yes, my son! And he said: Look: the fire and the wood are here, but where is the animal for the sacrifice?

8   And Abraham replied: God[a] will provide an animal for the burnt offering, my son! So the two went on together.

9   And they came to the place which God had told him. And Abraham built the altar there, and arranged the wood on it; then he bound[a] his son Isaac and laid him on the altar on top of the wood.

10   And Abraham stretched out his hand[a] and took the knife to slaughter his son.

11   Then the angel of Yahweh[a] cried to him from heaven and said: Abra-

ham! Abraham! And he answered: Here I am!

12   And he said: Do not raise your hand against the boy,[a] and do him no harm! For now I know that you fear[b] God, because you have not refused[c] me your son, your only son.

13   And Abraham raised his eyes and looked—there was a[a] ram entangled in the bushes by the horns. And Abraham went and took the ram and offered it in sacrifice in place of his son.

14   And Abraham gave this place the[a] name "Yahweh sees," of which one says today:[b] On the mountain[c] Yahweh makes himself seen.

15   And the angel of Yahweh cried out to Abraham a second time from heaven:

16   I swear by myself, an oracle of Yahweh, because you[a] have done this and have not withheld from me[b] your son, your only son,

17   I will bless you and make[a] your seed prosper like the stars in the heavens and the sand on the seashore, and your posterity will possess the gate of your enemies.

18   And all the nations of the earth shall find blessing through your seed, because you have listened to my voice.

19   Then Abraham went back to his servants, and they set out and went together to Beersheba, and Abraham stayed there.

1a   On the form of the sentence, Ges-K §111f-g; BrSynt §42c.   **b**   The name אברהם is not to be repeated, as do some of the versions and some interpreters; here it introduces a call, in v. 11 a cry.   **c**   BrSynt §4: "It stands for a whole sentence."
2a   Gk ἀγαπητόν (Prov. 4:2; Song 6:9).   **b**   BrSynt §41c; Bergsträsser II §6g; E. König §127b.   **c**   On לך־לך see Gen. 12:1; Song 2:10,13: R. Tournay VT 25 (1975) 544ff; T. C. Vriezen, Fests. F. M. T. Böhl (1973) 380ff.   **d**   The versions render it in various ways: Gk τὴν γῆν τὴν ὑψηλήν; see BHK.   **e**   TgO adds לי.
3a   BrSynt §135a.   **b**   BrSynt §152d.
4a   F. I. Andersen: "It's a rare instance, when a new paragraph begins without conjunction," *The Sentence in Biblical Hebrew* (1974) 37.   **b**   Ges-K §111g; BrSynt §123f.   **c**   Ges-K §111b, imperf. consec. after expression of time.
5a   Ges-K §119s; BrSynt §107f.; F. I. Andersen 134.
6a   E. A. Speiser: "Equipment for producing fire"; Akk *išāti*.   **b**   I. C. de Moor, VT 7 (1957) 354: "The local aspect of being united (together) in one point Gen. 13:6;. . .22:6, 8."
7a   Instead of the repeated ויאמר the Gk has here εἶπας.
8a   BrSynt §48. Word order to emphasize the subject.
9a   D. W. Thomas on עקד, JThS 13 (1962) 323f, proposes מְעַקְּדִים.
10a   BHK proposes a transposition of the first two sentences—an improvement, but not absolutely necessary.
11a   Syr reads אלהים, cf. v. 15.
12a   Sam, Gk, Vg read על.   **b**   Ges-K §116g; E. König §241i; BrSynt §27d.   **c**   Ges-K §158a; R. Meyer III §120,1; Bergsträsser II §6b.
13a   Read אחד for אחר; so many mss. and interpreters.
14a   Sam inserts את־.   **b**   On היום, cf. B. S. Childs JBL 82 (1963) 280; R. J. Williams, *Hebrew Syntax* (1967) 492.   **c**   Read with Gk בְּהַר.
16a   On יען אשר R. Meyer III §120, 2a; R. J. Williams 363; D. E. Gowan VT 21 (1971) 177.   **b**   Sam, Gk, Syr, Vg correctly add ממני; cf. v. 12.
17a   Ges-K §75ff.; E. König §219aa.

The History of the Exegesis of Gen. 22

D. Lerch (lit., 1950) has researched the history from the beginning until 1950. G. von Rad has added comments from Luther, Kierkegaard, and Kolakowski, and paintings of Rembrandt (lit., 1971). The history reveals an antithesis, continuing right up to the present, which must be considered. The Jewish and Christian interpretation, which is completely or overwhelmingly positive in its judgment, is confronted by a passionate condemnation by enlightened humanism. Its classical expression comes from Immanuel Kant. In "The Dispute between the Philosophical and Theological Faculties," he remarks: "There are certain cases in which man can be convinced that it cannot be God whose voice he thinks he hears; when the voice commands him to do what is opposed to the moral law, though the phenomenon seem to him ever so majestic and surpassing the whole of nature, he must count it a deception." The note is added: "The myth of the sacrifice of Abraham can serve as an example: Abraham, at God's command, was going to slaughter his own son—the poor child in his ignorance even carried the wood. Abraham should have said to this supposed divine voice: that I am not to kill my beloved son is quite certain; that you who appear to me are God, I am not certain, nor can I ever be, even if the voice thunders from the sky" (Appendix to von de Boor's German translation of S. Kierkegaard's *Furcht und Zittern* [Eng., *Fear and Trembling*] [1949] 160-61). The philosopher of the Enlightenment is convinced that this command can not have come from God because God cannot contradict the moral law; he guarantees it (the same view occurs in the history of exegesis; F. W. J. Schelling speaks of an anti-God principle).

The same condemnation recurs, though in irony, in L. Kolakowski (*Der Himmelschlüssel. Erbauliche Geschichten* [1965]; see example cited by von Rad [1971]).

There is also an important difference of opinion, though nowhere near so great, within the exegesis which takes a positive view of the narrative, that is between Jewish and Christian interpretation. Christian exegesis sees the crucial point of the narrative in what happens between God and Abraham; so Luther, Kierkegaard, and von Rad following them; Jewish exegesis on the contrary sees it in what happens between God, Abraham, and Isaac. This is particularly obvious when the Jewish exegesis speaks of the Akeda (= "binding," עקד, v. 9); what is essential is the concrete event, whereas the Christian interpretation looks to a spiritual happening between God and man.

Since Lerch's study, the discussion of the origin of Gen. 22 has continued without, so far, finding a convincing solution. From the time of J. Wellhausen there has been widespread agreement that the narrative was concerned with the abolition of human sacrifice by substituting an animal, for which there are parallels in the history of religion (H. Gunkel). Some exegetes have gone so far as to understand the chapter as a polemic against human sacrifice. But this thesis has been rejected and not taken up again.

Another explanation of the older narrative begins from the naming of the place in v. 14b; it was understood as a cult story of a sanctuary (H. Gunkel), and related by many to a sanctuary that was still Canaanite (H. Gunkel, M. Noth, R. Kilian). This early form of Gen. 22 then would have arisen, or been taken over, at the time of the taking of the land; it could not go back into the patriarchal period. In 1964 (*Arten der Erzählungen in Genesis* 71) I supported the view that Gen. 22 is to be traced back to an older narrative. While I am of the opinion that it is not possible to reconstruct the older narrative, H. G. Reventlow and R. Kilian (1968 and 1970) have attempted to do so. Reventlow has taken up my suggestion in an adapted form; Kilian accepts three stages in the tradition, the first being an etiological cult narrative. According to J. Van Seters (*Abraham in History. . .* [1975]), who takes a critical stance towards the conclusions of the two exegetes mentioned, we cannot proceed beyond the form that has come down to us. G. W. Coats (Interp. 27 [1973] 389-400) takes as the older form a narrative whose object is child sacrifice; he understands the traditional text as an edifying legend, in which the almost superhuman virtue of the main character is a model of obedience. Neither Van Seters nor Coats regards vv. 15-18 as an appendix, but as an original part of the narrative.

Form

Gen. 22:1-19 differs from all other Abraham narratives in that it begins with a heading or statement of theme (v. 1a) which synthesizes what follows in a pregnant expression: God is testing Abraham. It colors the whole narrative. Testing is to lay a task on the one to be tested; he carries it out, and thus one finds out whether the test has been passed or not. The text of 22:1-19 follows these three elements of a test. J. Van Seters has not seen this, and so his view that the narrative arose out of joining three themes is not necessary. The precise division of G. W. Coats (lit., 1971[3]) too does not make it clear that the text follows the pattern of a test. In the first part (vv. 1b-2) a task is laid on the one being tested; in the second (vv. 3-10) Abraham carries it out, but only as far as the penultimate act; in the third part, the structure of the test is modified in that the last act is taken out of Abraham's hands. The command to kill the child, implied in the command to sacrifice, is revoked (vv. 11-12a), and Abraham is told at the same time that he has passed the test (v. 12b). The verses immediately following are conditioned by the revocation of the command; the return (v. 19) forms the conclusion. This structure shows that vv. 15-18 are an addition; they have no function in it.

It follows from this structure that the narrative is dealing with a test in all three parts; it is not dealing primarily with child sacrifice itself nor child sacrifice forestalled at the last moment. At every stage and with every sentence the narrator has his goal in view: to tell a story about the testing of Abraham. This is the reason why I do not think that it is possible to separate the text into two layers, as R. Kilian and H. G. Reventlow have tried to do (see J. Van Seters' criticism of these attempts at reconstruction). The narrative originated with one object in view; it presupposes, therefore, a single event which it interprets. The idea of "testing" requires further investigation (see comm., v. 1a, Excursus).

It has often been said that Gen. 22 is one of the most beautiful narratives in the Old Testament, and that it also has a special place among the narratives of world literature. Its extraordinary, frightening dimension one can only experience with empathy; a commentary can do no more than hint at it. Here, in particular, exegesis that derives from listening to narrative will lead to listening to this narrative. E. A. Auerbach gives very helpful and sensitive guidance here when he compares Gen. 22 with the scene of the homecoming of Odysseus (*Mimesis* [1946; Eng. 1953, 1974[4]], "The Scar of Odysseus," pp. 1-20). It is the very contrast between the two that brings to light the uniqueness of the biblical narrative. One should also refer to the section on the style of ch. 22 in H. G. Reventlow (lit., 1968, pp. 40-52).

Setting

The determination of the setting presupposes in great part the detailed exegesis itself, to which reference should be made. Gen. 22 is one of those very different types of additions which follow the resolution (in 21:1-7). The statement of theme at the beginning determines it as a theological narrative ("narrated theology" [or "theology through story," transl.]). The question of the theological conception which lies behind the theme is to be raised in terms of the origin of ch. 22. The detailed exegesis will show that it originated relatively late. If the putting to the test of an individual by God presupposes the testing of the people, then the statement of theme points to the theological questioning and concern of a time when the "fear of God" of the individual was acquiring a greater significance for this people. This points to the later period of the monarchy. In 18:17-33, and in a different way, a narrative episode is fashioned out of a theological question; here it is a complete narrative. One might also compare 15:1-6,7-21. The patriarchal stories continued to live on in such a way that in the process of narration, contemporary theological questions were opened up. So it is likely that behind this later interpretation there lay an older narrative which told how Abraham's son (destined to be sacrificed?) was in mortal danger and was rescued from it. This motif, and its linguistic style likewise, correspond to the cycle of Abraham narratives (cf. 21:8-21). The action narrated here takes place among God, a father, and his son; it remains within the family circle. Such an older narrative can go back to the patriarchal period.

Commentary

[22:1a] "It happened after these events." This transition formula occurs again in 22:20; it is typical of the Joseph story (39:7; 40:1; see also Josh. 24:29, and the Elijah stories); similarly Gen. 15:1. Its function is always to insert a single event into a broader context. It presupposes a stage when the Abraham story was already known as a coherent unit, as in the case of the Joseph story.

Excursus

Excursus on נסה: "Then God tested Abraham." On נסה, see G. Gerleman: THAT II (1976) 69-71, with bibliog. The word occurs only here in Gen. with God as subject; see Ex. 15:25; 16:4; Deut. 8:2,hr 16; 13:4; 33:8; Judg. 2:22; 3:1, hr 4; Ps. 26:2; 2 Chron. 32:31. Apart from the late passages, Ps. 26:2; 2 Chron. 32:31, the object of God's testing in every case is Israel; they are concerned with the testing of Israel on the way through the desert and during the process of settling in Canaan. The idea of trial or testing (נסה) was forged in the context of God's action in history or Israel's experiences in history. It developed out of reflection on historical experiences. The testing is concerned with obedience, as here, (Ex. 16:4; Judg. 2:22) or the fear of God (Ex. 20:20). The expression is typical of the Deuteronomic exhortation (particularly Deut. 8:2: "You shall remember. . .these forty years. . .that he might humble you, testing you. . ."). It describes the wandering in the desert, and particularly the harsh experiences on the way, as testing by God. This is presupposed in Gen. 22; the idea that God tries his people by harsh demands is older than that of the trial of an individual person. Gen. 22, in the form in which it has come down, can have arisen only relatively late. Likewise, the closest parallel in content to Gen. 22:1, the prolog to Job, is also a late text. Usage shows that נסה describes the testing by God as a subsequent interpretation of an event, not the event itself.

The narrator who was responsible for the title intended the event to serve as a model: the suffering of a person is presented as a testing by God. In the prolog to Job too, one of the sufferings which tests him is the loss of his children. It is described there as a disaster. When Abraham is required to offer his own son as a sacrifice, there is a gathering climax which suggested itself from the old narrative at hand. It is not a narrative about the sacrifice of a child which was prevented at the last moment; behind Gen. 22 there lies an experience from Abraham's own life, his son in mortal danger, averted at the last moment.

[22:1b] God speaks to Abraham as one person speaks to another. It is a preliterary form of address. The call is the point of contact. The same form occurs again in vv. 7 and 11. The correspondence is deliberate: Abraham and his son belong together so that a simple call is enough for them to listen to and speak with each other; such too is the case with Abraham and God.

[22:2] The command is spoken out of this context of familiar mutual trust. Horrible, inhuman, it is nevertheless the word of his trusted God; the God with whom Abraham belongs must be in this word. This is the reason Kant was unable to understand what is meant here (see above: History of Exegesis); for him, it is possible to abstract the word as "that which is said," from the speaker. He concludes from the content of the word that it cannot be God who spoke it. Abraham cannot abstract from the speaker; God must also be in this word. The command consists of a series of three imperatives: take—go—sacrifice. When the patriarchal stories tell elsewhere of a sacrifice, they never say that one must go to a particular place; this is a later idea, from a time when sacrifice and a pilgrimage to a particular sanctuary are joined (cf. R. Kilian, who speaks here of a pilgrim motif). So the direct command of God—in accord with the patriarchal period—takes the place of the cultic custom, the observance of time and place. The formulation of the order לְךָ־לֶךְ occurs elsewhere only in Gen. 12:1. It may well be that 22:1 alludes to 12:1 (so N. M. Sarna, *Understanding Genesis. . .* [1966, 1972²]; R. Rendtorff, BZAW 147 [1976, 1977²] 59).

To the first command, "Take your son, Isaac," is added, "your only son, whom you love," so as to underscore the difficulty and harshness. However, these words are not really directed to Abraham, but to those who are listening to the narrative (like v. 1a)—a certain sign of a late narrative style. It is to be noted that the addition, "your only son, whom you love," emphasizes the relationship of the father to his child; there is no indication that he is "the son of the promise."

The goal of the journey is the "land of Moriah." There is no land known by this name, which occurs again only in 2 Chron. 3:1 as הַר הַמּוֹרִיָּה, the mountain on which the temple stands in Jerusalem. It is probable that this name is a later intrusion so as to claim the mountain of sacrifice for Jerusalem; it has suppressed the original name. The versions have read something different. The Syr has "the land of the Amorites," a possibility. Of the proposed reconstructions, reference need be made only to H. Gunkel; he suggests "Jeruel." The Samaritans claim Mount Gerizim as the mountain of sacrifice.

The third imperative, the order to sacrifice the son, points back to the fact of child sacrifice in a previous age. This was once the case, so that the narrator can make use of it for the severe testing of Abraham.

Excursus

On human sacrifice (child sacrifice)   (lit. above, bibl. to ch. 22; R. de Vaux, *Ancient Israel* [1958; Eng. 1962] 441-446): The history of religions attests human sacrifice in a number of places, as well as among Israel's neighbors, the Phoenicians, the Ammonites, the Moabites (2 Kings 3:21), in Egypt and Canaan. It should be noted that it scarcely ever occurs in primitive religions, but almost exclusively in the higher and more developed. Apparently it prevailed only for limited periods; one can conclude to this from the fact that in many places it is known that human sacrifice was abolished in favor of animal sacrifice (e.g., Iphigenia). There were two different kinds of human sacrifice; that which was constantly repeated, the sacrifice of the firstborn (Ex. 13:12f.; 34:19f.; Num. 3:44ff.), which was identical with child sacrifice; included here is the Canaanite building sacrifice (1 Kings 16:34). Then there was the individual human sacrifice in a particularly critical situation (2 Kings 3:27; Mic. 6:7); Jephthah's sacrifice of his daughter (Judg. 11) belongs here, as does the sacrifice of prisoners of war. H. Gunkel and others mention as a parallel to Gen. 22 the Phoenician cult story according to which El (Kronos) founded this cult by offering his only son as a burnt offering to his father Ouranos (Philo, in Eusebius, *Praep. Evang.* 1.10.29).

Both kinds of human sacrifice are known in the Old Testament. The sacrifice of the firstborn is commanded in Ex. 22:29 (34:10): "The first-born of your sons you shall give to me," but is simultaneously abolished: "All the first-born of your sons you shall redeem" (Ex. 34:20; 13:13). Child sacrifice to Molech is forbidden under penalty of death (Lev. 18:21; 20:2-5). Whenever it is reported that child sacrifice occurred in Judah, it is always and without exception condemned (Deut. 12:31; 1 Kings 16:34; 2 Kings 16:3; 17:17; see also the prophets, Micah, Jer., and Ezek.).

Gen. 22 is to be understood with this background. Following Ex. 22:29, it is seen as possible that God can demand such a sacrifice. In reality, however, human sacrifice is not possible (Ex. 34:20). It is precisely because of this ambivalence that the command to Abraham is a particularly suitable test. For both the narrator and his listeners, human sacrifice is something in the distant past, as is its abolition and substitution by animal sacrifice. It is probable that the author of Gen. 22 was familiar with stories about the abolition, and allows them to echo in his narrative. But the procedure has already been dealt with in the commands about the sacrifice of the firstborn (Ex. 22:29) and its annullment (Ex. 34:20). One can be certain that this is the material at hand to the narrative of Gen. 22.

והעלהו שם לעלה: the whole burnt offering (holocaust); the whole animal was burnt; Israel probably took over this kind of sacrifice at the time of its coming into Canaan (R. de Vaux); it did not exist in the patriarchal period. However, it is a characteristic of that period that the father offered the sacrifice. Abraham is commanded to offer the sacrifice on a mountain "which I shall name for you." He is told only the land, not the specific place; once more the wording echoes 12:1; every command to Abraham from the very beginning is to have its echo here.

[22:3-10]   The account of the execution of the command follows its commission without more ado (vv. 3-10); this too is parallel to the sequence in 12:1-3 and 12:4a. When God gives a command to one of the patriarchs, it must be carried out without any why or wherefore. The patriarchs live from God's direction; otherwise their existence would scarcely be thinkable. As it was with the direction to depart in 12:1-3, so is it with the incomprehensible and lethal command in 22:1. With these verses begins the characteristically detailed type of narrative which commands not only the attention but also the lively participation of the listener.

[22:3]   The preparations and departure are described in a succession of details: Abraham rose, saddled, took, split the wood, got ready, went. One notes that the splitting of the wood does not stand at the beginning, and that ויקם before וילך seems to be a doublet of וישכם. It is possible that two narrative beginnings have been joined here, one of which merely ran: Abraham split the wood and set out. But this does not impose itself. One notes too in the last sentence, "to the place which God had told him"; in v. 2 he is to be told the place only later. H. Gunkel thinks that between vv. 2 and 3 there has dropped out: "Abraham answered that he was ready, and then God told him the place." But this is unlikely, if only because it would destroy the parallelism with 12:1-4. One must recognize rather an imprecise, vague expression such as, "which God would tell him."

[22:4]   The movement running through the previous vv. 1b-3 halts with the short sentence of v. 4. Abraham sees the mountain, the goal of his journey, in the distance "on the third day"; in Ex. 3:18; 5:3; 8:23, it is a journey of three days to the place where the Israelites want to offer sacrifice in the desert; there is a possible allusion to this. In any case, three days is the period of preparation for more important events in the Old Testament; H. Jagersma refers to Gen. 31:32; 34:25; 40:20; 42:18 (lit., 1976), and G. M. Landes to the three days and three nights of Inanna's journey into the underworld (lit., 1967, and ANET 52ff.). The movement which begins with the commission from God in v. 2 gathers momentum with the preparations for departure, and halts with the sight of the mountain, is the low-keyed means of involving the listener in the tension that shapes Gen. 22. When Abraham looks up at the mountain the tension begins to ease.

[**22:5**]   The two groups in the little caravan separate; Abraham tells the two servants to wait at the foot of the mountain; he explains to them what he and Isaac plan to do, and lets them know that they will be back. One understands now the function of the two servants in the narrative; they represent the house of Abraham. From now on, Abraham and Isaac, father and son, are alone. This is the simple way in which the patriarchal narrative describes the loneliness of so critical an hour. V. 5 prepares the way for the last stage of the journey with its dialog between father and son (vv. 6-8). This is the real reason the servants were left behind; the question, therefore, whether Abraham concealed his purpose (R. Kilian) or just lied is out of place. When he announces, ''we will go there and worship,'' he presupposes a custom which one meets in many early religions, and even today; travelers worship at sanctuaries which lie on their route, whatever they may be. What is peculiar is that this is the only place in the Old Testament where it occurs.

[**22:6-8**]   The last stage of the journey, which Abraham and Isaac cover alone, is a carefully thought out piece of narrative. It is introduced by a new departure, parallel to v. 3 (''he took. . . and they went''), that takes its tone from the way in which the father divides the burdens between himself and his son. Further, it is set into relief by means of the inclusive, ''so the two went on together'' (form: *inclusio*); it is a masterly example of Hebrew narrative art (C. Westermann, lit., 1951; cf. 2 Kings 2:1-8, the last journey of Elijah and Elisha).

[**22:7**]   The dialog is pervaded by the expression ויאמר, which begins v. 7; it occurs five times. This monotonous repetition has the effect of intensifying markedly what is going on: two people are speaking to each other; something happens in dialog. It consists only of a question and an answer. It begins with the contact made by call and reply (cf. v. 1b). The son calls his father, ''My father!'' and he replies, ''Here I am, my son!'' Out of the quiet, where each one is alone, the call creates the contact which makes a dialog possible. The answer responds to the call; it expresses the readiness to listen. This contact occurs elsewhere in Old Testament narratives; it is characteristic of a preliterary stage. It repeats a dialog as it really took place. It has yet a further function: it makes it possible to introduce the dialog with the mutual exchange: ''my father''—''my son'' (v. 7a). ''My son'' is repeated again in v. 8; it is the last phrase of the dialog and, with its inimitable touch, gives it its atmosphere.

The boy's question expects the father to explain to him what he does not understand. The father does not give a direct answer; he conceals the commission he has been given by God and, in the opinion of the narrator, he does right.

[**22:8**]   With the words, ''God will provide an animal for the sacrifice,'' Abraham refers Isaac to God as the one who will answer the question. He does not deceive him, but simply opens up to him as a possibility what for himself (since God gave his command) is a fact. He throws the ball back into God's court, so to speak: ''God will provide.'' At this moment there is still an opening left to God. One must note, however, that the statement has this meaning, and is possible, only in dialog. It is the answer of a father in anguish and love for his son. The name which

Abraham will later give to the mountain confirms this meaning. Rarely does the Bible say so clearly and emphatically that God is a living God.

Isaac can scarcely be satisfied with his father's answer; but he asks no further question. He has sensed that his father can say no more. The dialog had to remain open. This is suggested when the introductory sentence is repeated, ''So the two went on together.'' (E. A. Speiser: ''The short and simple sentence. . . covers what is perhaps the most poignant and eloquent silence in all literature.'')

[22:9-10]   The carrying out of the command (vv. 3-10) ends with vv. 9-10. The arrival in v. 9 corresponds to the departure in v. 3. In the course of the action, v. 9 follows v. 4; v. 5 introduces the quiet interlude which includes vv. 6-8, but which nevertheless is a necessary part of the narrative (against R. Kilian), because the father's answer is taken up again in v. 14. The father carries out what has been commanded him without a word. A Jewish interpretation of this passage has Abraham make a long speech in which he explains to Isaac what is to happen to him, and Isaac joyfully agrees to be sacrificed; this is a misunderstanding. Only the harsh, unrelenting succession of acts right up to the raising of the knife fits the narrative; words can add nothing.

[22:9]   The description of the specific acts in the sacrificial process accords with the practice of the patriarchal period; the father was the one who sacrificed; he had first of all to build the altar of sacrifice (as in 12:8); the instruments or vessels used were not ''holy,'' but were brought from home. Contrary to the opinion of H. Gunkel, O. Procksch, and J. Skinner, the verbs ערך, שחט, and עקד are not sacrificial terms, but are used also for actions outside the cult. In any case, we know nothing about עקד because it occurs only here. Jewish tradition has named Gen. 22 the Akedah (עקדה), after the verb.

[22:10]   The execution of the command has almost reached its conclusion. Abraham has already stretched out his hand (on שלח ידו, see P. Humbert, lit., 1962); the tension reaches the breaking point; release comes at the last second. This, I think, is almost a baroque note, scarcely suited to an ancient narrator. The execution, right to the very end, deviates not a bit from God's command. God has commanded that the son be sacrificed—Abraham stretches out his hand to kill his son. ''The Midrash refers here to Is. 33:7: 'The er'elim cried out and the angels of peace wept bitterly,' '' B. Jacob. (NEB: ''The valiant cry aloud for help, and those sent to sue for peace weep bitterly.'')

[22:11-12]   The turning point comes with an urgent call to Abraham, revoking God's command to kill his son (vv. 11-12a). It is the voice of an angel. V. 12 thereby confirms that Abraham has passed the test (v. 12b). Vv. 11-12 and the heading in v. 1 go together; they determine the narrative of Abraham's testing as a whole.

[22:11a]   The angel of Yahweh calls to him from heaven. Why is God's address not formulated just as in v. 1, by a simple ויאמר אלהים? The address in v. 1 corresponds to that in Gen. 12:1; God speaks a word of command into the course of Abraham's life which introduces something new. In v. 11, on the contrary, the word that comes to Abraham intervenes in the course of an action, a critical situation like 21:11 (see ad loc.). It is in such situations that the patriarchal stories speak of the messenger of God (the early narratives too). When he is mentioned, something has always already taken place. In cases such as these one must distinguish two stages. It is no longer the messenger such as one meets on earth, but a heavenly being (hence the translation ''angel''). The change in the designation for God is important: it is the מלאך יהוה who calls to Abraham, not the מלאך אלהים, as one would expect from the continuous use of אלהים (with or without the article) from v. 1 on. The solution, that the text read originally אלהים and that a redactor altered it (J. Skinner and others), does not seem justified. It is likely that מלאך יהוה was a fixed formula (the combination of מלאך with אלהים is very rare), which the author made use of; i.e., he was not tied down to any particular designation for God, but could use both (just as he varies in the use of the article with אלהים). It follows, moreover, that 22:1 can scarcely be from the same author as 21:17, and this speaks against the same author for 21:1-21 and 22:1-19.

[**22:11b**]   For the third time, following vv. 1b and 7, a call addressed to Abraham is the contact which introduces the dialog. Each of the three steps in the action begins in this way, but each time there is a difference in tone and meaning. The repetition of the name in the call rings loud and clear; it is the turning point in the narrative; it expresses urgency. When it is seen in the context of the composition as a whole, it takes on something further: the call in vv. 1b and 7 introduces words which bowed Abraham down with grief; the repetition in v. 11b resounds with the joy of the good news. It is lofty narrative art!

[**22:12a**]   This is one of the many cases in the Old Testament where a prohibition can be good news. The angel is saying only what was there in God's plan from the beginning: nothing is to happen to the child. V. 12a consists of two sentences in parallelism, both saying the same thing. The repetition echoes the repetition of the name, sounding again the joyful note of deliverance. The relationship of the two parts to each other is thus important: the first sentence forbids Abraham to lift his hand against ''the boy''; this says what has to be said. The angel then adds, ''do nothing to him,'' which takes its meaning from the context. Nothing is to happen to the child, and this was God's intention from the beginning. This half-verse makes clear and confirms that God never intended this cruel fate to befall the child.

The elevated language of the angel's call, the parallelism, and the rhythmic form show further that the language of the narrator often takes on a poetic form at the high point of the narrative.

[**22:12b**]   The reason follows: ''For now I know. . ..'' The original setting and meaning of the phrase עתה ידעתי is that of a cry of joy of a person who has experienced the effects of God's action on his behalf (Pss. 20:7; 56:10; cf. Ex. 18:11; 1 Kings 17:24). It is here transferred to the knowledge that God has gained through the testing of a pious man. The reason consists in a positive and a negative part: now I know that Abraham is God-fearing; this has been shown by the fact that he has not withheld his only son from God. And so he has passed the test.

Excursus

The Fear of God: On the idea of the fear of God (fearing God) see H. P. Stähli, THAT I 765-778, and the bibliog. given there. The three central elements in talk about the fear of God (fearing God) are found in Deuteronomy, Psalms, and the wisdom books. Occurrences are relatively few in the pre-Deuteronomic period and difficult to determine exactly.

The classical source theory regarded the fear of God as a characteristic of E; H. W. Wolff (EvTh 29 [1969] 59-72; Interp 26 [1972] 158-173) describes the fear of God as the most important theme of the Elohist. He brings forward as proof the Elohistic passages in the Pentateuch, Gen. 20:1-18; 22:1-19; 42:18; Ex. 1:(15)17-21; 18:21; 20:18b-21. But the usage is not uniform in these few places. In Gen. 20:11 "the fear of God" is a "lapidary expression for correct moral conduct" (J. Becker, AnBib 25 [1965] 187) such as is found in a Canaanite king and his court. In Gen. 22:12 it is Abraham's perfect obedience, demonstrated in the severest of tests. Gen. 22:12 and Ex. 20:18b-21 seem to be close to each other; in both cases God tests (נסה), and it is a question of proving the fear of God. "God tries his people with harsh tests" (Wolff, referring to both passages). However, God's testing in Ex. 20 is directed towards the people, in Gen. 22 towards the individual. The idea that God tries his people is certainly older than that of trying a individual. Ex. 20:18-21 is not unanimously ascribed to E; L. Perlitt (WMANT 36 [1959] 94, n. 4), with others, sees "rather an interpretation" here.

The reason in v. 12b goes back to v. 2: "your son, your only son." The compliance with the command of v. 2 is described here in retrospect: "you have not withheld him from me"; חשׂך מן is used in the same sense in Gen. 39:9; it is taken up again in Gen. 22:16. Rom. 8:32 uses οὐκ ἐφείσατο in the same way.

[22:13]   Abraham's sacrificial action had been interrupted in vv. 11-12 by the call of the angel; the action of v. 10 is continued in v. 13; Abraham sacrifices a ram, which he now sees, in place of his son. The sacrificial action which had been commanded and begun must be brought to a conclusion; a sacrifice must be offered; only thus is the sacrifice of the child revoked and no longer required. Thereby is made clear what the command to sacrifice meant; the demand remains and the revocation by means of the animal confirms the demand. At the very moment when he heard the angel's voice, Abraham catches sight of a ram (read אחד for אחר) entangled in the bushes (thereby explaining its presence; H. Gunkel: "הנה וירא portrays the surprise"). This is to be understood as a directive from God, like 21:19. No further word is necessary. Abraham now knows that he is doing the will of God by sacrificing the ram instead of his son.

[22:14a]   It is only with v. 13 that the (modified) execution of the command is concluded. Only then is a reaction on Abraham's part possible. (O. Procksch, ad loc: "It is part of the ancient grandeur of the passage that no cry of joy is heard"; G. von Rad accepts the comment). But this is to misunderstand the plain and simple meaning of v. 14a: יהוה יראה sings the praise of God. When Abraham gives this name to the place where the narrative has taken place, he includes in it his reaction to what he hás experienced. H. Gunkel alone among the commentators has understood this: "Abraham remembers with gratitude what he had said to his child in his hour of deepest anguish." The author is not thinking of a place which can be determined geographically. The name is his expression of joy at his release from the depths of anguish; the praise of God in the Old Testament is a cry of joy directed to God. V. 8 confirms that this is the meaning of יהוה יראה: lament is turned about. As a name belonging to the place, it is to continue to say what happened there (the meaning is similar with אל ראי in Gen. 16:13; cf. R. K. Yerkes, JBL 31 [1912] 136-139).

יהוה and not אלהים as the designation for God is a sign that the narrator is taking over a lapidary phrase (as with מלאך יהוה in v. 11). He is not tied down to any fixed word for God; both have the same significance for him.

[22:14b]   The explanation of v. 14a has made it clear that that half-verse has nothing to do with etiology; nor does it contain any etiological motif. The narrative 22:1-19 does not intend to explain a name still existing at the time of the narrator. J. Van Seters too sees no etiology here; he notes that the popularity of the motif of the substitution of human sacrifice by animal sacrifice is sufficient; likewise H. G. Reventlow. V. 14b on the other hand is an etiological addition, a clumsily appended piece of syntax. A discussion of the question, which of the two basic forms of etiological formulas determined by J. Fichtner lies behind the verse, is therefore otiose (VT 6 [1956] 372-396). It can even be that the text is disturbed.

The אשר can refer only to מקום in v. 14a: ''of which one says today'' (or, ''even to this day''). בהר too is not clear; is the sanctuary on the mountain intended? It is clear that the addition (v. 14b) deliberately changes the name to ''Yahweh appears'' (A. Dillmann: ''On the mountain, there is Yahweh seen''); the sanctuary on the mountain is named after the appearance of Yahweh. This could be a deliberate correction of v. 14a, adjusting the name to the commonly accepted view. It may be in that case that there is an allusion to Jerusalem. The addition then would come from the same hand that changed the name of the land to Moriah in v. 2. The many attempts to emend the text of v. 14b or v. 14ab cannot solve the difficulty.

[22:15-18]   There is virtual unanimity that vv. 15-18 are a later addition to the narrative of 22:1-14,19. The most recent commentators alter nothing here (J. Van Seters; G. W. Coats). One needs no deep insight to see the difference in style; vv. 15-18 are not narrative style. There are only a few texts in Gen. 12–50 which are so easily recognizable as an addition.

The exegesis of 12:1-3; 13:14-17; 15:1-6, 7, 21 is presupposed in what follows.

[22:15]   The function of v. 15 is to link the promise that follows to what has preceded. The actual introduction to the promise comes only in v. 16a. This double introduction is further indication of the subsequent insertion. V. 15 repeats v. 11a with the addition of שנית. Here too the interpolator betrays himself: ויקרא is justified in v. 11a, but not in vv. 16-18. This prosaic text is not a call.

[22:16a]   Because of the ויקרא in v. 15, ויאמר is required in v. 16a. The second introduction follows it: the promise is introduced as God's oath; but actually it is the angel of God who pronounces it: ''I swear by myself.'' God swearing by himself occurs elsewhere only in Ex. 32:13 in the same context (cf. Is. 45:23); here too what God swears by himself is posterity. The promise in 15:7-21 is also linked with the taking of an oath. The reinforcement of the promise by an oath points to a late stage in the history of the promises, as does the prophetic form of speech, נאם־יהוה, joined to it; the latter has become a fixed formula, introducing a word of God. The solemn particles of v. 16b belong here.

[22:16b]   The promise, so solemnly introduced, is grounded on Abraham's constancy in the test, ''Because you have done. . ..'' The promises to the fathers are, in essence, free assurances by God. To ground them, as here, on Abraham's achievement is to alter the understanding of them. The Deuteronomic theology with its conditioned promise is presupposed. The ground for the promise is formulated according to v. 12; it acquires further weight by virtue of the repetition in v. 18b which, together with v. 16b, frames it.

[**22:17, 18a**]   The promise itself has three parts. Its core is the blessing and promise of posterity, 17abα; this is linked with a promise of victory, 17bβ, and the effect of the blessing on the nations, 18a. On the blessing and promise of posterity, cf. 12:1-3; 13:16; 15:5; 16:10; 17; 18:18; 21:13-18; see also the syntheses in C. Westermann (*The Promises to the Fathers* [1976; Eng. 1980] 149-155) and R. Rendtorff (BZAW 147 [1976; 1977²] 37-64). The promise of victory over one's enemies, taken over from 24:60, was introduced only in the period of the tribes.

[**22:18**]   See commentary on 12:1-3, as well as 18:18; 26:4; 28:14. The phrase, ''in your seed,'' instead of ''in you,'' as in 12:3, indicates that the concern is more for Israel and her meaning for the nations. It is an open question how one is to understand the juxtaposition of v. 17b (victory over the nations) and v. 18a (blessing for the nations). By way of conclusion, the obedience of Abraham is again underscored in v. 18b; it is understood as meritorious.

[**22:19**]   V. 19 follows originally on v. 14a. The arch of event resolves into stability. After the sacrifice has been offered and Abraham has pronounced the new name over the place, he goes back to the waiting servants. All of them together (יחדו) return to Beersheba. The verse presupposes that the place was mentioned at the beginning. One concludes from this that an older form of the narrative began with an itinerary pattern which contained the name of Beersheba. The introduction to the test-narrative has supplanted it. In v. 19 the narrative flows back again into an itinerary pattern, which could, without any alteration, have concluded the older form.

Purpose and Thrust

The narrative reaches its goal with the naming of the mountain, ''God reveals himself'' or ''God sees.'' There are resonances here of the climax, the call of the angel which restores life to the child and liberates Abraham from his anguish. The name is Abraham's reaction in words. At the same time it takes up the narrative's most poignant moment by resuming literally the answer to the boy's question. The narrative as a whole is to be understood with reference to this goal. The drama takes its beginning from God, and finds its resolution in God. One does not grasp the meaning if one sees the goal merely in the words of the angel: ''because now I know that you are a God-fearing man.'' It would be a one-sided understanding to refer the verse, ''God tested Abraham,'' merely to the result of the test. Rather the words inform the test as a whole, i.e., a father's path of suffering. And this ends only when the substitute victim has been offered and the mountain named.

It is a misunderstanding of the narrative to hear it as the song of praise of a person (F. Delitzsch, J. Skinner; similarly E. Hirsch AfO.B 13/14 [1972] 35-46). The majority of interpreters, even those as different as G. von Rad and R. Kilian, see the narrative holding Abraham up as an exemplar; G. W. Coats speaks very strongly in favor of this. It seems to me, however, that when one refers the praise to Abraham (Kierkegaard), one has not understood the narrative: the addressees are not the onlookers, but the participants, for whom it takes on another meaning. They know what it means to have to give up a child. E. A. Speiser describes their attitude: ''One can only suffer with Abraham in helpless silence.'' The participants therefore do not see in Abraham the one who successfully passes a test of faith, but the anguished father who is under severe trial throughout, from the moment he receives the charge until he can breathe freely with the voice of one liberated, "God reveals himself!" And for Abraham, this does not mean that he has passed the test, but: "My child is saved; thanks be to God!" The narrative looks not to the praise of a creature, but to the praise of God.

Paul says in Rom. 8:32, "He did not spare his own Son, but gave him up for us all." It is probable that he was thinking of Gen. 22 without quoting it. God's saving action in Christ is thereby put into the context of a family event, something that takes place between father and son. For Paul too, the father-son relationship was part of human existence and comprehensible to all. With this statement, then, he put the suffering of Christ into the broader context of the suffering of God; God has suffered because God had to give up his Son for the salvation of mankind. When one listens to Rom. 8:32, one understands better why the patriarchal stories are part of the Bible. The chapter on faith in Heb. 11 says of Gen. 22 that Abraham sacrificed his son out of faith in the resurrection of the dead, and for this reason received him back. It is understandable that it appeared so to the Christian theologian; but such an explanation does not fit the patriarchal period. The resurrection would in no way have altered the fact that Abraham, with the loss of his child, had lost his future. The interval between Gen. 22 and Heb. 11 speaks very loudly. When James (2:21-23) bases the correlation between faith and works on the sacrifice of Abraham, the long interval is likewise evident. However, the differences in these attempts to explain Gen. 22 are not essential; what is, is that the narrative lives on.

The Descendants of Nahor

Literature

M. Noth, *Das System der zwölf Stämme Israels*, BWANT 4,1 (1930; 1966²). B. Maisler, "The Genealogy of the Sons of Nahor and the Historical Background of the Book of Job" [in Hebr.], *Zion* 11 (1946) 1-3. M. Dietrich and O. Loretz, "Zur ugaritischen Lexikographie I," BibOr 23 (1966) 127-133. B. Mazar, "Canaan in the Patriarchal Age," *The World History of the Jewish People II* (1970) ch. 9 169-187. R. B. Coote, "Amos 1:11: *RHMYW*," JBL 90 (1971) 206-208. M. Görg, "Aram und Israel," VT 26 (1976) 499-500.

Text

22:20 Now after[a] these events it happened that Abraham received the news: Milcah also[b] has borne children to your brother Nahor!

21 Uz, his firstborn, and Buz his brother, and Kemuel the father of Aram,[a]

22 Chesed, Haso, Pildash, Jidlaph, and Bethuel.

23 Bethuel begot[a] Rebekah. These eight[b] Milcah bore to Nahor, Abraham's brother.

24 And his[a] secondary wife, whose name was Reumah, bore Tebah, Gaham, Tahash, and Maacah.

20a Sam reads אחר. **b** On the position of גם, F. I. Andersen, *The Sentence in Biblical Hebrew* (1974) 157,166, "focusing *gam*."
21a אבי ארם probably an addition, BHK.
23a Sam הוליד. **b** Ges-K §134k: "The numeral and demonstrative are practically determinate in themselves"; cf. BrSynt §85b.
24a Instead of the suffix perhaps לו is to be read. On the construction, Ges-K §111h and BrSynt §13b.

Form

A genealogy follows, loosely joined to 22:1-19 by v. 20, containing three names which also occur in 11:17-32, Abraham, Milcah, and Nahor. A genealogy of the kinsmen of Abraham opens and closes the Abraham cycle. The link verse (v. 20) reads, "Milcah also. . ."; the "also" refers to what was previously said (21:2f.), namely, that Sarah bore a son to Abraham. Sarah and Milcah are mentioned to-

366

gether in 11:29. One concludes from this that 22:20-24 once followed 21:1-8. This confirms that the history of Abraham in an earlier stage ended with 21:1-7; 22:20-24; 25:1-8, the birth of children to Sarah and Milcah. The cycle of Abraham stories was encompassed by the genealogy 11:27-32 and 21:1-7; 22:20-24. Thus it becomes even clearer that the narratives from 21:8 to the end of ch. 24 (apart from 22:20-24) are supplements: the death of Sarah and Abraham (ch. 23) 25:1-18, with further genealogies, followed after 21:7.

   The structure of 22:20-24: V. 20 is a transitional piece which does not belong to the genealogy. The genealogy consists of two parts which balance each other. The original beginning of the first part can be reconstructed with certainty from v. 20b: "Milcah, Nahor's wife, bore him (eight) sons." The names in vv. 21-22 follow. The beginning of the second part is in v. 24a, "And his secondary wife, whose name was Reumah, bore. . ."; the names of her sons follow. Some additions were then made to the genealogy, clearly recognizable in its original. This is not a tribal list as the majority of exegetes assert (e.g., J. Skinner, E. A. Speiser, and others); rather we have to reckon with a gradual development from the genealogical form of a man's sons, still centered in the family, to the later tribal lists.

   The division of the names of the sons also follows the family pattern: there are eight sons of the principal wife and four of the secondary wife (the same numbers as with Jacob's sons); the names of the wives are not eponyms (against M. Noth), but purely personal. The names of the five sons of Milcah and those of Reumah are also predominantly personal names (against H. Gunkel). The material at hand to 22:20-24 was an old genealogy with a distinct family stamp about it. It follows from this that the number twelve which occurs several times in such genealogies (23:13-16; 36:15-19), originally belonged to the large family or clan and was transferred only as the clans grew into tribes.

Setting

The conclusion is that the genealogy of the sons of Nahor grew out of the history of a family. It was only later that it designated a group of tribes which give expression to their homogeneity by means of their common father and the number twelve. The genealogy was passed on orally and was filled out during the course of the oral transmission. The redactor attached it to the Abraham cycle as a genealogical frame balancing the introduction (11:27-32) and taking it further. Whether J already had it (O. Eissfeldt, R. Kilian, and others) cannot be said with certainty; the transitional v. 20 is the work of the redactor.

Commentary

[22:20]   The redactor has inserted the already existing independent genealogy by introducing it as a narrative. To do this he needs the same formula as in 22:1. The narrative dress makes use of the old form of an announcement to the father that a son has been born to him (cf. 21:7). But the form fits awkwardly with the enumeration of twelve tribes, and is not sustained throughout, as v. 23 shows. It is obvious that it is only a means of transition. The "also" in v. 20b refers back to 21:2f. (on Nahor, cf. *Genesis 1–11*, comm. on 11:22-24; on Milcah, comm. on 11:29).

[22:21]   Only two of the eight names of the sons of Milcah mentioned in vv. 21-22 are certainly place-names as well; they are the names of the two eldest and are set apart from the rest. It is striking that these two, Uz and Buz, are also found together in Jer. 25:20,23 (not side by side, but in the same enumeration). There is a hint that there is some connection between them when Job from the land of Uz (1:1-3) is confronted by Elihu from the land of Buz (32:2). Both of these are attested as regional names, Uz with certainty in northern Edom, Gen. 36:28 (a grandson of Seir), Buz probably near Edom (Jer. 25:33) as *Bâzu* in an inscription of Esarhaddon.

The third name, קמואל, occurs as a personal name in Num. 34:24; 2 Chron. 27:17. The note, "the father of Aram," could be an addition because it interrupts the enumeration. It could well be that the name "Aram" was attached later because it was thought that a reference to the ancestors of the later Aramaeans was meant.

[22:22]   The five names that follow are all personal names and it cannot be proved that any of them are names of places or regions as well. Apart from Bethuel none of them occurs outside this passage. כשׂד, eponym of the Kasdim, "an Aramaean bedouin tribe" (H. Gunkel), is mentioned in Job 1:17 together with the Sabeans (1:15). The singular כשׂד occurs only here. חזו is equated with *Ḥazû* found on an inscription of Esarhaddon, but this is questionable. The next two names are unknown and cannot be explained; KBL suggests that the first may be the name of an animal (spider). Bethuel is a personal name (Gen. 24:15ff.; 25:20; 28:2, 5).

[22:23]   A subsequent elaboration names Rebekah as a daughter of Bethuel, an anticipation of 24:15, 24. V. 23b concludes the first part of the genealogy.

[22:24]   This verse retains unaltered the form of the genealogy. The sons of the secondary wife are listed. פילגשׁ is a non-Semitic word which occurs in several Semitic languages as well as in Greek and Latin. ראומה is "a common name for a girl" (M. Noth), but its meaning is unexplained. R. Coote proposes: "Candidate for *r'm in Hebrew is the name of Nahor's concubine. . ., *Rᵃ'ûmāh*, from something like *ra'ûmat-ili*, 'beloved of El' " (VT 26 [1976] 207).

The names of the first three sons are personal names which occur only here. טבח is perhaps found in 2 Sam. 8:8 (mistake for בטח?—H. Gunkel) as a city of Hadadezer near Kadesh. KBL understands it as a purely personal name identical with טבח = "slaughter" (born at the time of the slaughtering). גחם and תחשׁ are unknown and unexplained. KBL proposes an Arabic word, "bright blaze," for גחם, and for תחשׁ dolphin or seal (Num. 4:6, "a covering of sealskin"). Some compare תחשׁ with *Taḥši* of the Amarna letters. The last name, however, can be determined with certainty as a region on Hermon (E. A. Speiser), 2 Sam. 10:6-8; 1 Chron. 19:6-7; Deut. 3:14; Josh. 12:5.

Purpose and Thrust

Only the first two names, Uz and Buz, and the last, Maacah, certainly refer to geographical regions and these are located in the northern part of Transjordan. But one cannot speak of an Aramaean tribal list. It is a genealogy of Abraham's kinsmen which follows 11:27-32 and takes it further.

Sarah's Death and the Purchase of the Burial Cave

Literature

Genesis 23: A. H. Sayce, "The Purchase of the Cave of Machpelah," ET 18 (1907) 418-422. J. H. Breasted, "The 'Field of Abram'. . .," JAOS 31 (1911) 290-295. M. G. Kyle, "The 'Field of Abram' in the Geographical List of Shoshenq I," JAOS 31 (1911) 86-91. F. M. Abel, L. H. Vincent, and E. H. J. MacKay, *Hébron, le Haran el-Khalil. Sépulture des Patriarches* (1923). F. V. Winnet, "The Founding of Hebron," *Bulletin of the Canadian Society of Bibl-Stud* 3 (1937) 21-29. A. C. Graham, "Hebronite Tradition Behind P in Genesis," JThS 41 (1940) 140-152. E. Z. Melamed, "The Purchase of the Cave of Machpelah" [in Hebr.], Tarb. 14 (1942) 11-18. R. Gyllenberg, "Abraham's gravköp. Gen 23," *Svenska Jerusalems Foreningens Tidskr* 46 (1947) 112-115. C. F. Arden-Close, "The Cave of Machpelah," PEQ 83 (1951) 69-71. M. R. Lehmann, "Abraham's Purchase of Machpelah and Hittite Law," BASOR 129 (1953) 15-18. E. A. Speiser, "A Vivid Sidelight on the Machpelah Episode," *Israel Life and Letters* 1 (1953) 56-59. G. Boyer, "La place des textes d'Ugarit dans l'histoire de l'ancien droit oriental," *Le Palais Royal d'Ugarit III*, ed. J. Nougayrol (1955) 283-308, esp. 297. G. F. Mobbs, "The Eastern Way," ET 68 (1957) 210-212. G. H. Davies, "Judges VIII 22-23," VT 13 (1963) 151-157. B. Perrin, "Trois textes bibliques sur les techniques d'acquisition immobilière," Rev Historique de Droit Français et Étranger 3 (1963) 5-19, 77-95, 387-417. H. Petschow, JCS 19 (1965) 103-120. K. A. Kitchen, "Historical Method and Early Tradition," TynB 17 (1966) 63-96, esp. 71. G. M. Tucker, "The Legal Background of Genesis 23," JBL 85 (1966) 74-84. O. Tufnell, "Palestine: Lachish," *Archaeology and OT Study*, ed. D. W. Thomas (1967) 296-308. H. van der Brink, "Genesis 23: Abrahams Koop," *Rev d'Histoire du Droit* 37 (1969) 469-488. R. Westerbrook, "Purchase of the Cave of Machpelah," *Israel Law Review* 6 (1971) 29-38. H. A. Hoffner, "The Hittites and Hurrians" in *Peoples of OT Times*, ed. D. J. Wiseman (1973) 213-221. M. Dayan, "The Cave of Machpelah—The Cave Beneath the Mosque," *Quadmoniot* 9 (1976) 129-131. Z. Yeivin, "The Cave of Machpela," *Quadmoniot* 9 (1976) 125-129.

Genesis 23:1-4: A. Schulz, "Drei Anmerkungen zur Genesis (8,7-12; 23,3ff.; 50,26)," ZAW 59 (1943) 184-188. K. D. Schunck, "Ophra, Ephron und Ephraim," VT 11 (1961) 188-200. H. Seebass, "Ephraim in 2 Sam XIII 23," VT 14 (1964) 497-500. R. Stadelmann, "Die 400-Jahr-Stele: Chronique d'Egypte," *Bruxelles* 40 (1965) 46-60. F. I. Andersen, "The Socio-Juridical Background of the Naboth Incident," JBL 85 (1966) 46-57. E. Fascher, "Zum Begriff des Fremden," ThLZ 96 (1971) 162-168. R. North, "Ugarit Grid, Strata, and Find-Location," ZDPV 89 (1973) 113-160. G. Gerleman, "Nutzrecht und Wohnrecht. Zur Bedeutung von אחזה und נחלה‎," ZAW 89 (1977) 313-325. U. Kellermann, "Psalm 137," ZAW 90 (1978) 43-58. J. S. Kselman, "The Recovery of Poetic Fragments from the Pentateuchal Priestly Source," JBL 97 (1978) 161-173.

Genesis 23:5-7: E. Gilleschewski, "Der Ausdruk עַם הָאָרֶץ im AT," ZAW 40 (1922) 137-142. C. H. Gordon, "אֱלֹהִים in Its Reputed Meaning of Rulers, Judges," JBL 54,3 (1935). E. Würthwein, "Der *'amm ha'arez* im AT," BWANT 4,17 (1936). H. Grapow, "Wie die alten Ägypter sich anredeten, wie sie sich grüssten und wie sie miteinander sprachen. III," AAB 11 (1943). M. H. Gottstein, "נְשִׂיא אֱלֹהִים (Gen XXIII 6)," VT 3 (1953) 298-299. F. Nötscher, "Zum emphatischen Lamed," VT 3 (1953) 372-380. D. W. Thomas, "A Consideration of Some Unusual Ways of Expressing the Superlative in Hebrew," VT 3 (1953) 209-224. S. Rin, "The מוּת of Grandeur," VT 9 (1959) 324-325. C. Rabin, "*L-* With Imperative (Gen XXIII)," JSSt 13 (1968) 113-124.

Genesis 23:10-11: E. A. Speiser, " 'Coming' and 'Going' at the City Gate," BASOR 144 (1956) 20-23. G. Evans, " 'Coming' and 'Going' at the City Gate: A Discussion of Prof. Speiser's Paper," BASOR 150 (1958) 28-33. H. Graf Reventlow, "Die Völker als Jahwes Zeugen bei Ezechiel," ZAW 71 (1959) 33-43. F. C. Fensham, "Ugaritic and the Translator of the OT," ViTr 18 (1967) 71-74.

Genesis 23:16-20: B. Holwerda, *Historia Revelationis VT* (solum Gen 23,19-35,29) (1954). R. B. Y. Scott, "The Shekel Sign on Stone Weights," BASOR 153 (1959) 32-35. V. Souček, "Die hethitischen Feldertexte," ArOr 27 (1959) 379-395. J. J. Rabinowitz, "Neo-Babylonian Legal Documents. . .," VT 11 (1961) 56-76. M. Delcor, "Le Trésor de la Maison de Yahweh des origines à l'Exil," VT 12 (1962) 352-377, esp. 361.

Text

23:1 Sarah lived[a] one hundred and twenty-seven years;[b]

2 she died at Kiriath-arba,[a] that is, Hebron, in the land of Canaan, and Abraham went in to mourn and weep for her.

3 Then Abraham arose from before his dead[a] and said to the Hittites:

4 I am an alien and sojourner among you; Give me land enough[a] among you so that I may bury my dead properly.

5 The Hittites answered Abraham:

6 Please listen to us[a] my lord; You are a great prince* among us; bury your dead in the best[b] grave we have. None of us will refuse[c] you his grave nor hinder you from burying[d] your dead.

7 Then Abraham arose and bowed low before the people of the land, the Hittites,

8 and he said to them: If you are willing that I bury my dead properly, then listen to me; intercede for me with Ephron, the son of Zohar;

9 ask him to give me the cave of Machpelah[a] which he owns and which is at the end of his field; let him give it to me in your presence at the full current price[b] that I may possess it as a burial place.

10 Now Ephron was sitting among the Hittites; and Ephron the Hittite answered Abraham in the hearing of the Hittites, of all[a] coming in[b] at the city gate; he said:

11 But my lord, please listen to me! The field—I make a present[a] of it to you; the cave which is on it I also present to you; in the presence of my people I present it to you; bury your dead.

12 Then Abraham[a] bowed low before the people of the land;

13 he addressed Ephron in the hearing of the people of the land: But please, if you (will), listen to me![a] I will pay the price of the field; take it from me, that I may bury my dead there.

14 But Ephron answered Abraham:

15 Please listen to me, my lord: a piece of land[a] at four hundred silver shekels—what is that between you and me! Now bury[b] your dead!

16 And Abraham came to an agreement with Ephron. Abraham weighed out for Ephron the four hundred shekels at the current merchants' rate as he had said in the presence of the Hittites.

---

*Or, "the elect of God" (trans.).

17 So Ephron's piece of land at Machpelah, east[a] of Mamre, the field, the cave, and all the trees in the field and in the whole area surrounding it,

18 was made over into Abraham's possession in the presence of all[a] the Hittites coming in at the city gate.

19 After this Abraham buried his wife Sarah in the cave on the field of Machpelah, east of Mamre, that is, Hebron, in the land of Canaan.

20 So the field together with the cave on it[a] were made over by the Hittites into Abraham's possession as a burial place.

1a Read שְׁנֵי חַיֵּי at the beginning with BHK and hence delete the last three words; cf. Gen. 47:9, 28.   **b** On the syntax of numerals, Ges-K §134dh; BrSynt §84c.
2a The name "four-city" suggests four parts of a city, cities, or roads which meet there.
3a מֵת is of both genders, Ges-K §122f.
4a On the juxtaposition, Ges-K §128m.
6a With BHK (vv 5/6) read לֵאמֹר; לוֹ שְׁמָעֵנוּ; likewise vv. 11,13,15, Ges-K §110e.   **b** On בַּמִּבְחַר, Ges-K §128r.   **c** Ges-K §75qq.   **d** Ges-K §119x.
9a Understood by Gk and Vg as "double cave"; occurs elsewhere only in Gen. 25:9; 49:30; 50:13(P); always with the article, and so retaining something of the appellative sense, Ges-K §125e-g.   **b** *Beth* of price, Ges-K §115p.
10a On לְכֹל, cf. Gen. 10:9; Ges-K §143e, BrSynt §31a.   **b** Ges-K §116h.
11a Ges-K §106m.
12a Targ Jon inserts לוֹ.
13a On the construction, BrSynt §170a (anacolouthon).
15a Gk omits אֶרֶץ.   **b** Gk has וְאַתָּה for וְאֶת־.
17a Sam has עַל־פְּנֵי as in v. 19 and Gen. 25:9.
18a Targ Jon has לְכֹל.
20a On the construction, Ges-K §111k.

Form

Gen. 23 is the elaboration of the genealogical account of the death of Sarah, Abraham's wife, which P has made the framework of the chapter. It follows directly on what has preceded in 21:2-5 (P) and is continued in 25:7-8 (P). One has only to read verses 1-2 and 19 together without the elaboration (23:3-18,20) to be convinced that they belong to the priestly framework. Many interpreters have noted that the reference back to ch. 23 on the occasion of the other burials in 25:9, 49:30; and 50:13 confirms the priestly hand.

But one must not separate the elaboration from the framework which enables the deceased (vv. 1-2) to be buried (v. 19); besides, the central part is firmly linked with the framework by the recurrent theme, "Bury your dead!" Ch. 23, therefore, is by origin a unity. There must be a special reason why this report has undergone such an elaboration.

The elaboration (23:3-18,20) gives an account of the purchase of the cave of Machpelah as a burial place for Sarah. It is not a narrative in the strict sense, because it elaborates a report. It could be described as the embellishment of the report of the purchase of a cave by means of the narrative form. The report is divided according to the lines along which the sale proceeds; it is essentially a dialog fashioned entirely after the pattern of the neo-Babylonian "dialog contracts" (H. Petschow, JCS 18 [1965] 103-120), but adapted to Abraham's situation. The dialog proceeds through three stages. First, as an "alien and sojourner" Abraham must petition the council of the city of Hebron to acquire a burial place for his deceased wife (vv. 3-4); his request is granted (vv. 5-6). Second, Abraham specifies the cave that he wants (vv. 7-9) and its owner Ephron offers it to him as gift (vv. 10-11). Third, the sale is clinched (vv. 12-18). After Ephron has named the price (vv. 14-15), Abraham weighs out the amount in the presence of witnesses (v. 16). Finally the transfer of the plot to Abraham is settled (vv. 17-18). What is striking is the emphasis on the theme, "to bury my (your) dead," in vv. 4, 6, 8, 11, 13, 15(19). It is this constant theme that reveals the reason for the elaboration of vv. 3-18, 20. In order to bury "his dead" Abraham must have a piece of property of his own where he can lay them.

Setting

M. R. Lehman (BASOR 129 [1953] 15-18) maintained that Gen. 23 had its origin in Hittite legal practices. He pointed to particular paragraphs in the Hittite legal code, ##46,47,169, and explained the details in Gen. 23 from them, thereby determining the age of the chapter. Many accepted this thesis. However, the Hittite scholar, H. A. Hoffner, contested the connection (in *Peoples of OT Times,* ed. D. J. Wiseman [1973] 197-228), as did H. Petschow (JCS 19 [1965] 103-120) and G. M. Tucker (JBL 85 [1966] 77-84), both referring to the parallels in the neo-Babylonian documents of the seventh to fifth centuries. R. de Vaux presents a detailed discussion in *The Early History. . .1,* 255-256; so too do T. L. Thompson, *The Historicity. . .* 295f., and J. Van Seters, *Abraham in History. . .,* 98-101, both coming to the same conclusion, namely, that the Hittite parallels must be abandoned, but that there are unmistakable points of contact with the neo-Babylonian dialog documents, even though differences remain. H. Petschow, G. M. Tucker, and J. Van Seters have pointed out that a number of further parallels to the portrayal of the sale of a plot of land can be found in other places. E. A. Speiser, for example, points to a similar letter from Qatna (*The World History of the Jewish People*) 11 [1970] 160-168). The parallels reveal that the portrayal of the sale of the plot of land in Gen. 23 follows near eastern custom and style; there is no need to look for particular exemplars even though it is possible that the author was familiar, for example, with the neo-Babylonian dialog documents. One must reject, therefore, the earlier view that Gen. 23 presupposes an older narrative (so O. Procksch; J. Skinner, "some local tradition"; M. Noth, an etiological narrative to explain the "double cave"). Likewise to be rejected is the view of H. Gunkel that P presupposes information that Abraham bought a burial place. Rather P gave the whole chapter its shape; its nucleus is found in the genealogical note, 23:1-2,19, which P himself extended around the portrayal of the purchase of the burial place and, indeed, in language appropriate to such an event. Further, the close parallels to the dialog documents favor the view that P reproduces the sale in a way similar to that in which it was stll taking place in his own day. On the significance of the elaboration see below, "Purpose and Thrust."

Commentary

[**23:1**]   The genealogical information about Sarah's death follows immediately on Gen. 21:3-5 (Isaac's birth) in P. חיי is unusual as subject of יהיו, and the words attached to the end of the verse, שני חיי שרה, are missing in Gk and Vg. One concludes therefore to a scribal dislocation and with the majority of exegetes and BHK reads the words at the beginning as in Gen. 25:7; 47:8, 28.

[**23:2**]   Sarah's death in Hebron: "Here for the first time P mentions a particular place in the land of Canaan" (W. Zimmerli). Its older name was Kiriath-arba, "four city" (so too in Gen. 35:37 and Neh. 11:25; in Josh. 14:15; 15:13 ארבע is understood as a personal name); likewise in Judg. 1:10. Hebron lies 35 km. south of Jerusalem where four ways meet; according to Num. 13:22 it was founded seven years before Zoan = Tanis (on Hebron = Kiriath-arba, cf. F. M. Abel, *Hébron, Le Haran el-Khalil* [1923]; J. Simons, *The Geographical and Topographical Texts in the OT*; S. Mowinckel, Fests. H. Nyberg [1954] 185-194; E. Lipiński, VT 24 [1974] 41-55; A. G. Auld, VT 25 [1975] 261-285). The graves of the patriarchs are localized at the present-day *el-hatil*, east of Hebron, in the caves under the great mosque; on the east side of the deep, narrow valley is the sacred area *el-haram*, which only Muslims may enter. F. Delitzsch reported on the few visitors who could view these caves; cf. J. Simons 213, §351.

Abraham completes the rites of mourning comprehended by the two verbs ספד and בכה, a hendiadys, based on a fixed expression (also in Ezek. 24:23). The further addition of the verb ויבא ("he went in") designates what takes place as a ritual action. A more detailed description of the rite is given in Ezek. 24:15-17, 22-23b. The lament for the dead has its original setting in the family.

[23:3] "Then Abraham arose": he completes the rites of mourning which are carried out sitting or prostrate, cf. Is. 47:1-5; Jer. 6:26. מת (as "corpse") is used for both sexes. The burial must now follow the ritual (v. 19), but to carry it out Abraham has to negotiate with the local inhabitants. They are called בני־חת (v. 10, החתי). "Hittites" is a later term for the pre-Israelite inhabitants of Palestine (in Judg. 1:10 the inhabitants of Hebron are called Canaanites). On the Hittites, cf. R. Hentschke, BHH 1 (1962) 237-240: "The latest layer of the Pentateuch occasionally describes the whole pre-Israelite population of Palestine as Hittites."

[23:4] The first stage of the negotiations is in vv. 4-6, Abraham's request and its guarantee. גר־ותושב is a hendiadys, a more or less fixed phrase: he is a settler come from foreign parts. The phrase belongs to village and city civilization; it occurs in the same sense in Lev. 25:35, 47; Num. 35:15, in a transferred religious sense in Ps. 39:13 which is taken over in 1 Pet. 2:11 as πάροικος καὶ παρεπίδημος; he is a semi-citizen without land ownership which he can acquire only with the agreement of the community. On אחזת־קבר cf. G. Gerleman (ZAW 89 [1977] 313-325); the preposition עם means here "among, in the midst of"; cf. K. D. Schunck (1961), H. Seebass (1964) (both in bibliog. above). The מעלפני is a way of expressing that a dead person is unclean.

[23:5,6] The answer of the citizens of Hebron, conveyed by a courteous dignitary, shows respect and readiness to accommodate. He addresses Abraham by a dignified title meant to overshadow the legal description he had used of himself (a subtlety whereby the בתוכנו strengthens the mere עמכם of v. 4). Neither נשיא (against C. H. Gordon) nor אלהים have any particular significance; both are but respectful acknowledgment; the אלהים can be meant only in an enhancing sense; it is likely, however, that it expresses the divine protection and blessing which covers Abraham. The citizens generously allow Abraham a free choice of their burial places—let him select the best (מבחר): no one will refuse him (H. Gunkel, "a sale is not necessary"). Even though this offer conceals a reluctance to sell (H. Gunkel, J. Skinner) it is nonetheless a very far-reaching accommodation with regard to a stranger. Though there is indeed an urbanity here (the words for "politeness" in the different languages show the different setting in which they arose and were used), nevertheless it is obvious that consideration is paid to the person of

Abraham, as likewise in Gen. 20:1-18. It is no mere chance that the theme, "bury your dead!" occurs twice in v. 6; the citizens show themselves ready to adapt to what the author wants to narrate about Abraham.

[23:7]   The second stage of the negotiation is in vv. 7-11. Abraham replies as he rises and bows to the citizens. The negotiation was conducted sitting, as in Ruth 4. The profound bow is an expression of Abraham's thanks and at the same time a response to the respect shown to him. J. Skinner notes delicately, "The verse has almost the force of a refrain (cf. v. 12)." On עם הארץ, cf. E. Gillischewski (ZAW 40 [1922] 137-142); E. Würthwein (BWANT 4,17 [1936]); R. de Vaux (*Ancient Israel* [1962] 70-72).

[23:8-9]   The citizens had shown themselves willing and left Abraham to choose, as the two sentences of v. 8 indicate, "if you are willing. . .intercede for me with Ephron"; v. 8 then is in full agreement with the offer. It is only when he makes his desired object more specific that it becomes clear that what he wants differs from the offer. This and other subtleties are typical of the way in which the orientals understand a sale as a social event. But the consent prevails and it would now be difficult to reject his request. This is the reason why Ephron agrees without more ado.

The style of the negotiation requires that Abraham first of all submit his request to the citizens of Hebron (שמעוני) and ask for their support before the one from whom he wants to make the purchase (ב פגע does not occur before Jeremiah, 7:16; 27:18 and elsewhere). The names עפרון (also a place-name) and צחר are Semitic. The "cave of Machpelah" is found only in P, here and later in Gen. 25:9; 49:30; 50:13. It could be a derivative of כפל and mean "double cave," but can also be a proper name (place-name). The place is described as that "which is at the end of his field," thus allowing the possibility that it may be detached. Only now at the end of his request does Abraham say how it diverges from the offer made to him: he will buy it at the full current price. He repeats the words, "to possess it as a burial place," which he had used in v. 4; this was his concern right from the beginning. The expression, בכסף מלא = "at the full current price," occurs in 1 Chron. 21:22-24 in the same sense and context where David buys Ornan's threshing floor.

[23:10]   V. 10 introduces Ephron's reply, v. 11. He is presented rather skillfully as one of the citizens of Hebron who are present at the negotiations at the gate so as to emphasize that it is a matter of a public and legal act. Ephron makes his generous offer to Abraham in the presence of the whole citizen assembly which is determined more precisely by the legal term, כל באי שער. The same term is used in Gen. 34:24 with יצא "in the same sense" (H. Holzinger). In both cases it means the local inhabitants who have access to the negotiations at the gate; there is no distinction in their functions in either case (cf. E. A. Speiser [1956]; G. Evans [1958], in bibliog. above). Once again vv. 2 and 4 should be compared. Ephron's answer shows that there was no need to put any pressure on him.

[23:11]   Ephron declares with a broad gesture in the presence of the whole conciliar assembly that he will present Abraham not only with the cave but also with the whole field. Everyone understands this, having heard Abraham's offer in v. 9.

When Ephron's offer ends with the theme, ''Bury your dead!'' this is a sign that Abraham cannot just bury his dead in Machpelah, but that he must lay them to rest in land that has been acquired. The negotiations must therefore enter on a third stage (vv. 12-18).

[23:12,13]   See comment on v. 7. Abraham bows low, not before Ephron, but before the עם הארץ and answers him in their presence. It begins with an anacolouthon, ''But please, if you (will). . .,'' which expresses well the difficulty of his answer. He continues with לי and the phrase used in vv. 5f.,11,14; he does not go into Ephron's offer to make a present of the land but sets his נתתי over against Ephron's נתתי: ''I will pay the price of the field.'' He then presses him, ''Take it!'' and this is the meaning of the final words, ''only that I may bury my dead there!''

[23:14,15] · Ephron replies by naming the price, which is very high, and making it appear but a trifle, ''What is that between you and me!'' One sees how high the sum of 400 shekels is when one compares it with the 17 shekels that Jeremiah pays for a field (Jer. 32:7) and the 6000 that Omri pays for the whole area on which Samaria is to be built (1 Kings 16:24). Ephron concludes by setting the insignificance of the sum over against the importance of what Abraham can now do: ''Now bury your dead!''

[23:16]   Abraham expresses his agreement (וישמע) and carries out the act of payment. He weighs out the silver pieces in the presence of the citizens who thereby become witnesses to the transfer of possession. The amount is mentioned again: 400 shekels at the current merchants' rate. The point of the sale emerges here: Abraham does not say a word; he makes no attempt to beat down the price. The reporter is aware that it is so important for Abraham to gain unimpeachable possession of the burial place that he will pay any amount for it.

[23:17,18]   The deal is clinched; all the details of the transaction are set out again in detail in the manner of a commercial agreement; all is now complete. The very nature of the matter requires that an exact description of the object of sale be given; there are many parallels to this (examples in J. Skinner, G. M. Tucker, and others). For קום with the same meaning and context see Lev. 25:30; 27:14,17,19 (P) (likewise J. J. Rabinowitz, VT 11 [1961] 71). Once again prominence is given to the presence of witnesses; this is necessary because the contract is not set down in writing (as in Jer. 32). This contractlike conclusion does not mention that Abraham bought the plot as a burial place; the purpose is not required in the contract.

[23:19]   Only now (אחרי־כן) can Sarah's burial take place. V. 19 belongs to the genealogy and originally followed v. 2. The different formulation of the place of the grave and the setting (ממרא הוא חברון cf. v. 2) is an indication that v. 19 was once an independent tradition. This piece of information is linked with that on the burial of Abraham (Gen. 25:9), Isaac and Rebekah, Leah (49:30), and Jacob (50:13).

[23:20]   The report in ch. 23 reaches its goal in v. 19, not in vv. 17-18. It is not concerned with the purchase of the cave of Machpelah but with the burial of Sarah in a place belonging to Abraham. V. 20 is not a mere repetition of vv. 17f.; it joins

vv. 17f. and 19 together with the further precision that the plot now belongs to Abraham. Such exactness is characteristic of P. The verse shows yet again that vv. 1-20 as a unified whole come from P.

Purpose and Thrust

There must be a reason for the elaboration of the note about the death and burial of Sarah by means of a detailed account of the purchase of a burial place, all the more so as there are few places in the patriarchal story where P goes into such detail (e.g., Gen. 17; 28). H. Gunkel offers an explanation from the perspective of the history of religion: he thinks that the local population regarded the cave of Machpelah as a sanctuary and believed that "a god or a hero lies buried here." Sarah then took the place of the god/hero; but for P it is merely a profane cave consecrated by the memory of the patriarchs. J. Van Seters has recently resumed this explanation: he thinks it still the best, in contrast to the theological explanation which, he says, has no support in the text. J. Wellhausen proposed a somewhat juristic explanation: by acquiring the plot Abraham acquired a legal claim to the land; there are echoes of this also in O. Procksch. This is rightly rejected by H. Gunkel, G. von Rad, B. Jacob, and others.

G. von Rad gives a theological explanation, and many have followed him. ". . .A fact central to Israel's faith is being described," he writes. Taking as his point of departure the idea of "the land of their sojourning" (Gen. 17:8 and elsewhere), he explains: "In death the patriarchs were heirs and no longer "strangers." A very small part of the promised land—the grave—belonged to them; therefore they did not have to rest in "Hittite earth" or in the grave of a Hittite." At first sight this seems to shed a deal of light. W. Zimmerli has represented a similar thesis, though with reservations, and recently also H. Golka (ZAW 90 [1978] 186-195). But as J. Skinner, J. Van Seters, and others have noted, this explanation has no support in the text. It is the nontheological language of ch. 23 that speaks against a theological explanation.

There is a recurrent theme in Gen. 23 (vv. 4, 6, 8, 11, 13, 19) which must be the starting point for the elaboration and intention of P. It understands the plot that Abraham acquired not as a small portion of the promised land but as a burial place; it is concerned with the procedure of burial, the necessary presupposition for which is the legal acquisition of a piece of land. Such procedure is very unlikely in the patriarchal period as it accords but poorly with the life-style of the small-cattle nomad and is not attested elsewhere. It is, however, completely comprehensible from the period and experience of the exile when those driven from their native land were laying "their dead" to rest and wanted to have a place they could call their own (it is here that the real meaning of the theme comes through).

Gen. 23, therefore, is to be understood in the context of chs. 17; 23; 28, where P enters into greater detail. P makes the patriarchal story the base for what this writer regards as the three most important precultic family rites of birth, marriage, and burial. Along with circumcision (ch. 17) and marriage within one's own people (ch. 28), it also is a case of a procedure that acquired its specific meaning only in a later period. During the exile the family attained a significance which was determinative for the preservation of the people of Israel and its religion; what is basic to the family is for P basic to the people of God (ch. 17 and the code of Sinai).

The Wooing of Rebekah

Literature

Genesis 24: G. Brillet, "Le mariage de Isaac avec Rebecca," *L'anneau d'or* 4 (1945) 15-18. H. van Prag, *Droit matrimonial assyro-babylonien* (1945). N. Tucker, "Gen 24. Der künstlerische Aufbau einer biblischen Erzählung" [in Hebr.], BetM 46 (1971) 326-338. W. M. W. Roth, "The Wooing of Rebekah. A Tradition-Critical Study of Genesis 24," CBQ 34 (1972) 177-187. H. Schulte, *Die Entstehung der Geschichtsschreibung im Alten Israel*, BZAW 128 (1972) esp. 35-43. J. Van Seters, " 'Amorite' and 'Hittite'. . .," VT 22 (1972) 79. G. W. Coats, "Moses in Midian," JBL 92 (1973) 3-10. J. Van Seters, *Abraham in History*. . . (1975) 17, 76-78. S. B. Parker, "The Historical Composition of *KRT* and the Cult of El," ZAW 89 (1977) 161-175.

Genesis 24:1-9: J. Pedersen, *Der Eid bei den Semiten in seinem Verhältnis zu verwandten Erscheinungen, sowie die Stellung des Eides im Islam*, SGKIO 3 (1914). M. Burrows, AOS 15 (1938). R. T. O'Callaghan, *Aram Naharaim*. . . (1948, 1961[2]) 140-145. J. van der Ploeg, "Les chefs du peuple d'Israel et leurs titres," RB 57 (1950) 47-51. F. Horst, "Der Eid im AT," EvTh 17 (1957) 366-384 = ThB 12 (1961) 292-314. E. Dhorme, L'emploi métaphorique des noms des parties de corps en Hébreu et en Accadien (1963[2]) = RB 3-4 (1921-1923). D. K. Andrews, "Yahweh the God of the Heavens," *Essays in Honor of T. J. Meek* (1964) 45-57. J. Wijngaards, "הוציא and העלה. A Twofold Approach to the Exodus," VT 15 (1965) 91-102. H. Cazelles, "Institutions et terminologie en Deut. I,6-17," VT.S 15 (1966) 97-112 esp. 99-100. J. L. Crenshaw, "*YHWH Ṣeba'ôt Semô*: A Form-critical Analysis," ZAW 81 (1969) 156-175. J. Ouellette, "The Solomonic *DeBÎR* According to the Hebrew Text of I Kings 6," JBL 89 (1970) 338-343. F. Vattioni, "Aspetti del culto del signore dei cieli," Aug. 13 (1973) 37-74.

Genesis 24:10-28: T. K. Cheyne, "Notes on Genesis I,1 and XXIV,13," *Hebraica* 2 (1885/86) 49-50. E. Nestle, "Zur traditionellen Etymologie des Namens Rebekka," ZAW 25 (1905) 221-222. F. Heiler, *Das Gebet. Eine religionsgeschichtliche und religionspsychologische Untersuchung* (1909; 1923[5]) 65. N. Glueck, *Das Wort* ḥesed *im alttestamentlichen Sprachgebrauch als menschliche und göttliche gemeinschaftsgemässe Verhaltensweise*, ZAWBeih 47 (1927; Engl. 1967[2]) c.3,I. J. Lewy, "Les textes paléo-assyriens. . .," RHR 110 (1934) 44-46. R. Gordis, "A Note on Gen 24,21," AJSL 51 (1934/35) 191-192. J. Reider, "Etymological Studies in Biblical Hebrew," VT 4 (1954) 276-295. F. Zimmermann, "Some Textual Studies in Genesis (22,14 and 24,16; 35,18; 41,51)," JBL 73 (1954) 97-101. J. Audet, RB 65 (1958) 371-399. R. B. Y. Scott, "Shekel-Fraction Markings on Hebrew Weights," BASOR 173 (1964) 53-64. D. Michel, "'*Ämät*. Untersuchung über 'Wahrheit' im Hebräischen," *Archiv f. Begriffsgeschichte* XII (1968) 50-57 esp. 47-49. L. Wächter, "Salem bei Sichem," ZDPV 84 (1968) 63-72. J. P. Brown, "The Mediterranean Vocabulary of the Vine," VT 19 (1969) 146-170. M.

Mannati, "*Ṭûb-Y.* on Ps XXVII,13: La bonté de Yahvéh, ou les biens de Y.?" VT 19 (1969) 488-493. M. Anbar, "Les bijoux compris dans la dot fiancé à Mari et dans les cadeaux du mariage dans Gn 24," UF 6 (1974) 442-444. W. Speyer, "Baruch," JAC 17 (1974) 177-190.

Genesis 24:29-49: C. H. Gordon, "Fratriarchat in the OT," JBL 54 (1935) 223-231. J. E. Steinmueller, "Etymology and Biblical Usage of *ʿalmāh*," CBQ 2 (1940) 28-43. P. A. H. de Boer, "Psalm CXXXI 2," VT 16 (1966) 287-292.

Genesis 24:50-60: S. Fraenkel, "Labans Scheidegruss an die bräutliche Rebekka und Jizchoks Abschiedsworte an den fliehenden Jakob," JJLG 17 (1926) 95-101. A. Schulz, "Zu Genesis 24,50," ZAW 49 (1931) 323-324. S. Speier, "The Targum Jonathan on Gen 24,56," JQR 28 (1937/38) 301-303. F. S. North, "Four-Month Seasons of the Hebrew Bible," VT 11 (1961) 446-448. H. J. Schilder, " 'Eigenlijk' en 'eneigenlijke' in de Unitdrukking 'Hand Gods,' " GIT 2 (1961) 477-522. D. Lys, "Notes sur le Cantique," VT.S 17 (1968) 170-178.

Genesis 24:61-67: M. H. Gottstein, "A Note on צנח," VT 6 (1956) 99-100. G. R. Driver, "Problems of Interpretation in the Hexateuch," *Mélanges Bibliques. . .A. Robert* (1957) 66-76. P. Wernberg-Møller, "A Note on לָשׂוּחַ בַּשָּׂדֶה in Gen 24,63," VT 7 (1957) 414-416. S. Mowinckel, "Drive and/or Ride in the OT," VT 12 (1962) 278-299. H. P. Müller, "Die hebräische Wurzel שׂיח," VT 19 (1969) 361-371. A. Gibson, "*Ṣnh* in Judges I 14: NEB and AV Translations," VT 26 (1976) 275-283. E. W. Nicholson, "The Problems of צנח," ZAW 89 (1977) 259-266.

Text

24:1   Abraham was now old and advanced in years and Yahweh had blessed[a] Abraham in everything.

  2   So Abraham spoke to his servant, the oldest of his household, who administered all that he had: Now put your hand under my thigh!

  3   I adjure you by Yahweh, God of heaven and[a] God of earth, not to take[b] a wife for my son from the daughters of the Canaanites among whom I live.

  4   Rather[a] you shall go[b] to my own land and my own kinsmen to take a wife for my son Isaac.[c]

  5   And the servant replied: Perhaps the woman will not want[a] to follow me to this land; shall I then bring him back[b] to the land whence you came?

  6   But Abraham said to him: Take care[a] that you do not bring my son back there.[b]

  7   Yahweh, the God of heaven[a] who brought me from the house of my father and the land of my kinsmen, who spoke to me and who swore[b] to me: To your posterity will I give this land—he will send his messenger before you so that you will be able to take a wife for my son from there.

  8   But if the woman is not willing to follow you, then you are free[a] from this oath to me; only do not bring my son back[b] there.

  9   The servant then put his hand under the thigh[a] of Abraham, his master, and swore to him accordingly.

 10   Then the servant took ten of his master's[a] camels and all sorts of gifts[b] from his master and rose and went to Aram Naharaim, to the city of Nahor.

 11   He made the camels kneel down outside the city[a] at[b] the well at evening at the time when the women come out to draw water.

 12   And he said: Yahweh, God of my master Abraham, grant me success here today and show favor to my master Abraham.

 13   Here I am[a] standing at the well and the daughters of the inhabitants of the city are coming out to draw water!

 14   Let it be thus: the girl[a] to whom I say: Please lower your jar that I may drink, and who answers: Drink! and I will water your camels too!—let

her be the one you have destined[b] for your servant Isaac. By this[c] I will know that you have shown favor[d] to my master.

15 Now he had scarcely finished speaking[ab] when Rebekah came out; she was the daughter of Bethuel, son of Milcah, wife of Nahor, Abraham's brother; she was carrying her jug on her shoulder.

16 She was a very beautiful girl, a virgin, whom no man had known. She went down to the well, filled her jug, and came up again.

17 The servant hurried to meet her and said; Please give me a little sip of water from your jug!

18 She said: Drink sir! And she quickly lowered her jug on to her hand and gave him a drink.

19 When she had given[a] him enough to drink, she said: I will also draw water[b] for your camels so that they may have enough to drink.

20 And she quickly emptied[a] her jug into the water trough, hurried again to the well to draw and watered all his camels.

21 But the man stood gazing silently at her[a] to know whether Yahweh had made his journey successful or not.

22 Now when the camels had finished drinking, the man took a golden nose ring weighing half a shekel, "and put it on her face,"[a] and two bracelets for her arms, each weighing ten gold shekels.[b]

23 And he said:[a] Tell me please, whose daughter are you? Is there room in your father's house[b] for us to pass the night?

24 She replied: I am the daughter of Bethuel,[a] son of Milcah, whom she bore to Nahor.

25 And she added: And there is plenty of straw and fodder, and room to stay the night with us.

26 Then the man bowed and prostrated himself before Yahweh

27 and said: Blessed be Yahweh, God of my master Abraham, who has not withdrawn his steadfast love and fidelity from my master. I[a]—he has led me safely along the way to the house of the brother[b] of my master.

28 Then the girl hurried and told her mother's[a] household all that had happened.

29 Now Rebekah had a brother whose name was Laban "   ".[a]

30 When he[a] saw the nose ring and the bracelets on the arms of his sister, and heard what his sister Rebekah had to tell: The man had said this and that to me, he hurried to him at the well[b] and found him still standing there with his camels.

31 He said to him:[a] Come in, blessed of Yahweh![b] Why do you remain standing outside? I have prepared the house and there is room for the camels.

32 So the man came into[a] the house, and Laban unloaded the camels and gave them straw and fodder, and the man and his men water to wash their feet.

33 Then he[a] laid food before him, but he said; I will not eat until I have said what I have to say. He replied:[b] Say it!

34 He said: I am the servant of Abraham.

35 Yahweh has blessed my master so that he has become "very"[a] rich. He has given him sheep and cattle, silver and gold, servants and maidservants, camels and asses.

36 And Sarah, my master's wife, has borne him a son in her old age; it is to him that he has given all that he has.

37 Now my master had made me swear, saying: You are not to take a wife for my son from the daughters of the Canaanites in whose land I live.

38   Rather[a] you shall go to my family and take a wife for my son.

39   I replied: Perhaps the woman will not follow me.

40   He said to me: Yahweh before whose face I have walked will send his messenger with you and will make your journey successful so that you will bring back a wife for my son from my family and the house of my father.

41   Then you will be free from the oath I have laid on you;[a] if you go to my family and they do not give her to you, then you are free from the oath.

42   When I came to the well today, I said: Yahweh, God of my master Abraham, if you are really[a] making the journey I undertake successful—

43   see—I am standing at the well; when a young girl comes out to draw water and I say to her: Please give me a little water to drink from your jug,

44   and she says: Drink! And I will water your camels too![a] Let her be the wife that Yahweh has destined for the son of my master.[b]

45   Now I[a] had scarcely finished my silent prayer when Rebekah came out with her jug on her shoulder, went down to the well to draw water. And I said to her: Please give me a drink.[b]

46   Then she quickly lowered her jug and said: Drink! And I will water your camels too! So I drank and she also watered the camels.

47   And I asked her: Whose daughter are you? And she replied: The daughter of Bethuel, son of Nahor, whom Milcah bore to him. So I put the nose ring on her face and the bracelets on her arms.

48   And I bowed and prostrated myself before Yahweh and blessed Yahweh, God of my master Abraham, who had led me faithfully along the way to take the daughter of the brother of my master for his son.

49   Now,[a] if you are disposed to deal loyally and faithfully with my master, tell me; if not, tell me, so that I may know where I stand.[b]

50   Then Laban and Bethuel[a] answered: This has come from Yahweh; there is nothing we can say one way or the other.

51   Here is Rebekah; take her and go, that she may be the wife of your master's son as Yahweh has destined.

52   Now when Abraham's servant heard these words, he prostrated himself on the ground before Yahweh.

53   The servant then brought out ornaments of silver and gold and garments and gave them to Rebekah, and gave costly gifts[a] to her brother and her mother.

54   Then he and the men with him ate and drank and spent the night there. When they rose in the morning he said: Let me[a] go back to my master.

55   But her brother and her mother said:[a] Let the girl stay with us some days,[b] say ten days, then she can go.

56   But he said to them: Do not detain me. Yahweh has made my journey successful, allow me to go back to[a] my master.

57   So they said: Let us call the girl herself and ask her.

58   Then they called Rebekah and said to her: Will you go with this man? She said: I will go.

59   So they let their sister Rebekah and her nurse go with Abraham's servant and his men.

60   They blessed Rebekah[a] and said to her: You are our sister, may you increase to thousands of thousands,[b] and may your posterity inherit the gate of their enemies.

61   So Rebekah and her maids arose and mounted the camels and followed the man. And the servant took Rebekah and went.

62   Now Isaac had come from. . .[a] as far as Beer-la-hai-roi and was living

in the Negeb.

63 When Isaac went out into the field one evening to take some air,[a] he
    raised his eyes and saw camels coming.

64 When Rebekah raised her eyes and saw Isaac, she dismounted from
    the camel

65 and said to the servant: Who is the man there[a] coming across the field
    to meet us? The servant replied: It is my master. So she took her veil
    and covered herself.

66 Then the servant narrated to Isaac all that he had done.

67 Isaac then led Rebekah to the tent of Sarah, his mother,[a] and took her
    as his wife and loved her. So Isaac was consoled after "the death of
    his father."[b]

1a R. Meyer III §90,1a; 121,2a; E. König §362f.

3a The nomen regens is repeated, Ges-K §128a.   **b** On the final conjunction,
Ges-K §165b; BrSynt §160b; R. Meyer III §114,2b, indications that the language is late.

4a Some 25 Mss, Sam have כי־אם; but כי by itself can have an antithetic meaning, E.
König §372e, F. I. Andersen, *The Sentence in Biblical Hebrew* (1974) 183.   **b** Gk is
somewhat different.   **c** Gk and Vg add משם, as in v. 38.

5a אבה is almost always used negatively.   **b** On the inf. abs. to strengthen a question, Ges-K §113q; E. König §329r.

6a Cf. Gen. 12:1.   **b** Ges-K §152w.

7a Gk adds ואלהי הארץ, v. 3.   **b** Missing in Gk.

8a On נקית, Ges-K §75x.   **b** Ges-K §109d, Sam תשיב; on the construction, E.
König §392f; R. J. Williams, *Hebr. Synt.* (1967) 390; F. I. Andersen 171.

9a On ירך, J. Ouelette, JBL 89 (1970) 339.

10a The first וילך is to be omitted with Gk as a scribal error.   **b** Read מכל with Gk
instead of כל.

11a BrSynt §107a.   **b** Sam reads על for אל.

13a On the sentence, F. I. Andersen 115.

14a נער for both sexes; E. König §247b, Ges-K §17c; cf. παῖς. Sam reads הנערה. On the
sentence BrSynt §152a; Ges-K §167c.   **b** Gk renders by ἡτοίμασας.   **c** Ges-K
§135p, BrSynt §16e.   **d** Syr adds ואמת.   .

15a Ges-K §107c, 152r, proposes יכלה, as v. 45.   **b** Sam, Gk, Vg add אל־לבו as in
v. 45; for the construction, Ges-K §106f, BrSynt §42a.

19a On the construction, Ges-K §164b; R. J. Williams, *Hebr. Synt* (1967)
495.   **b** On the construction, Ges-K §106c; BrSynt §163b; R. J. Williams, 457.

20a Sam reads ותורד.

21a ע probably to be read for א, BHK; according to J. Skinner a derivative form; according to F. Delitzsch a lexical or scribal error; error due to similarity of sound. On the construction, BrSynt §99a; Ges-K §130a.

22a Insert וישם על אפה, as in v. 47. On the construction, BrSynt §148; Ges-K
§156b.   **b** Common specifications of measure; weight can be omitted, BrSynt §148;
Ges-K §134n; R. Meyer III §99,7.

23a Gk inserts καὶ ἐπηρώτησεν αὐτήν before ויאמר, as in v. 47.   **b** Accus. of
place, Ges-K §118g; R. Meyer I §28,1; on the construction, BrSynt §143c.

24a On the nominal sentence, J. Hoftijzer VT 23 (1973) 448.

27a On the emphasizing force of the suffix, Ges-K §135d,e; 143b; E. König §19; R.
Meyer II §92, 4b; retrospective pronoun.   **b** Perhaps with the versions אֲחִי is to be
read, as in v. 48.

28a Syr reads ''her father's.''

29a V. 29b is to be read after v. 30a with A. Dillmann and many interpreters.

30a Sam, probably correctly, reads with the 3rd pers. suff.   **b** See note on v. 29a.

31a Insert לו with Gk, Syr, Vg.   **b** On the construction, Ges-K §116b.

32a Vg reads hiph., cf. J. Skinner, which would avoid a clumsy change of subj.
33a Gk reads καὶ παρέθηκεν = וישם. The explanation is that וישם has been proposed in the margin for ויישם. R. Meyer II §80, 3i; E. König §324d; Ges-K §73f.　　**b** Perhaps the plural is to be read with Gk, Syr.
35a As the verb ברך never occurs with מאד (B. Jacob), ויגדל מאד is to be read with J. C. Ball (comm. 1896), following Syr.
38a Sam כי אם; Gk ἀλλὰ, P. de Boer, VT 16 (1966) 287-292; Ges-K §149c; BrSynt §169b.
41a On the construction, Ges-K §91n, 95n.
42a אם with a nominal sentence and נא, Ges-K §159v, BrSynt §80e, 170a.
44a וגם. . .גם, Ges-K §154a, 162b; F. I. Andersen, 159.　　**b** Gk diverges.
45a On the separated pronoun אני, Ges-K §135a.　　**b** Sam, Syr add מעט מים מכדך, cf. Gk.
49a On the construction, BrSynt §30b, Ges-K §159v.　　**b** On the construction, BrSynt §131; אל is perhaps to be read for על.
50a Addition, or to be replaced by ביתו or אמו.
53a מגדת Ezra 1:6; 1 Chron. 21:3; 32:23; Ar. *magada* = ''be noble'' (J. Skinner); on the construction, BrSynt §122h.
54a Gk, Syr, Vg add ואלך, cf. v. 56.
55a Gk, Syr, Vg מרו אחיה, but cf. Ges-K §146f; R. Meyer III §94,7b.　　**b** Ges-K §139h, ''some days''; but perhaps the text has been disturbed.
56a Perhaps with Sam אל is to be read instead of ל.
60a Some of the Mss of the versions add אחתם.　　**b** Gk reads רבבת; Targ לאלפים ולרבבת; cf. Ges-K §97g, 134g.
62a מבוא not explained; Sam במדבר, Gk διὰ τῆς ἐρήμου.
63a לשוח uncertain; see comm. below.　　**b** On the construction, R. Meyer III §104,3b.
65a Unusual, Ges-K §34f; BrSynt §25b; R. J. Williams, 577.
67a ''Sarah, his mother'' is probably an appendage; Ges-K §127f, ''no doubt only a subsequent insertion.''　　**b** Perhaps מות אביו, translated here, instead of אמו.

Form

Gen. 24:1-67 is the longest narrative in the patriarchal story; there is nothing else like it in Gen. 12–36. Long though it is, its structure is clear and transparent: a commission is given (vv. 1-9); the execution of the commission is told in detail (vv. 10-66); and the result forms the conclusion (v. 67). The purpose of the narrative lies in the last verse—to tell how Isaac acquired his wife. It is a genealogical piece of information whose proper setting is in the genealogy. One could conceive then how the framework outlined above could be shaped into a short report (J. Van Seters). The framework as such has no element of tension; this enters in only with the possibility of the success or failure of the commission that the servant has undertaken. Thus the emphasis is transferred from the principal person (Abraham does not appear after v. 9) to the secondary person, the one commissioned. The tension arises only after the commission has been given; it is expressed in the oath that the servant must take to his master. His whole being is thereby bound to the execution of the commission; success is vital for him. At the same time God's hand takes on an all-embracing importance; the success or failure of the commission depends on whether God grants success or not. Ch. 24 then becomes a ''guidance narrative,'' or a narrative whose purpose is to attest the hand of God in the life of a small community and thus in personal life. Hence one cannot say that the main theme of Gen. 24 is the wise, unselfish servant who is presented as an example (W. M. W. Roth, CBQ 34 [1972] 177-187).

　　　One can conclude from the very arrangement of the whole to a well-conceived literary creation whose basis is a simple genealogical note which becomes the goal of the narrative. The narrative structure—the commission, the journey to a distant land, the negotiations about the marriage, the departure and the marriage—has a parallel in the Ugaritic KRT-epic, as S. B. Parker has shown (ZAW 89 [1977] 161-175).

Setting

One can divide the literary study of this chapter into three stages. The older generation of literary critics (A. Dillmann, J. Wellhausen, H. Holzinger, and others) considered Gen. 24 a unity; the middle group (R. Smend, H. Gunkel, J. Skinner, O. Procksch, O. Eissfeldt, W. Eichrodt) divided it into two sources; the more recent scholars (M. Noth, G. von Rad, W. Zimmerli, E. A. Speiser, J. Van Seters, W. M. W. Roth) once more favor a unity and attribute it to J. But difficulties remain because the style does not correspond to the other J narratives, as H. Gunkel had seen, and Gen. 24 already presupposes the composition of the patriarchal story (so M. Noth, G. von Rad, and others). W. Zimmerli concludes that Gen. 24 must come from a later hand than J, and J. Van Seters attributes it to the late J (about sixth c.). Following what has already been said about chs. 21–23, Gen. 24 is also one of those additions appended to the conclusion, 21:1-7. But this says nothing about its origin.

J. Van Seters is convinced that Gen. 24 can have no preliterary history; it is "a unified literary work of the Yahwist with no indications of any dependence upon a folkloristic tradition. It deals with the theme of divine providence" (*Abraham in History*. . ., 248). But this cannot be maintained when there exist two parallel narratives in Gen. 29:1-14 and Ex. 2:15b-22 which agree point by point with the event narrated in Gen. 24 except for the parts which speak of God's providence (G. W. Coats, JBL 92 [1973] 3-10). A comparison of these three texts is essential to determine the origin and explain the growth of Gen. 24. Broadly speaking, the same event underlies all three—the goal is marriage. The first result of the comparison is that everything that makes Gen. 24 a "guidance narrative" is absent from the two parallels. They are purely family narratives whose basis is a genealogical note. The narrative in an older form may go back to the patriarchal period but it acquired its present shape in all three texts only in the sedentary period (city, house, well before the gate). It arose orally as a family narrative and was first passed on as such, as the variants show. Gen. 24 in the form in which it has come down to us is a reworking of this older narrative from a new point of view, that of divine providence. We have then the rare possibility of being able to distinguish the later reworking from the older narrative, though not by means of source division, which is out of place here because Gen. 24 in its present form is a literary unity. The reworking to make it a guidance narrative shows a different way of conceiving things. This is obvious not only inasmuch as all this is contained in sentences that have no counterpart in Gen. 29 and Ex. 2, but also in the way in which these sentences cohere with each other. At the beginning Abraham assures the servant of God's assistance; at the critical moment the servant asks for guarantee of God's assistance by a sign. The servant's thanks and Laban's utterance confirm the guarantee and Laban becomes a witness of the event by means of the servant's narrative. To present a coherent unity like this as God's providence is rather in line with the simple family narrative as opposed to the self-standing narrative. This further becomes clear inasmuch as the request for a sign in Gen. 29 and Ex. 2

has no counterpart (in 29:4-8 there is an inquiry instead) but only serves to present the meeting as an act of God's providence.

The reworking into a guidance narrative could arise only at a period far removed from the old family narrative. A hint of when this took place may be given at the beginning, where Abraham assures the servant of God's assistance: "Yahweh. . . will send his messenger before you. . .," v. 7. This is a traditional fixed expression for God's assistance and it occurs also in Ps. 91:11, which is an assurance of blessing to an individual at a relatively late period (cf. Ps. 121); the reworking of Gen. 24 into its present form may be temporally close to it. One cannot then ascribe Gen. 24 to J insofar as J is put in the 10th-9th century. A comparison of Gen. 29 and Ex. 2 with Gen. 24 shows that the two former correspond much more to the type of J narrative in the patriarchal story than does the latter, which is unquestionably later.

Commentary

[24:1-9]   Abraham's commission to his servant follows the genealogical introduction (v. 1), and takes the form of a demand for an oath (vv. 2-9). The servant raises an objection (v. 5) to what he is asked to swear (vv. 3-4), and Abraham meets the objection (vv. 6-8). The oath follows (v. 9).

[24:1]   The exposition is a circumstantial clause; as is so often the case, a patriarchal narrative grows out of a genealogical detail, here Abraham's age, as in Gen. 18:11. This could be sufficient; but the second sentence adds something which is a prerequisite for the narrative immediately following; hence the repetition of the name. The blessing continues in 26:12,28.

[24:2]   The threefold qualification of the servant underscores his importance. His office is that of an administrator; his name is not given because the title "servant" or "servant of Abraham" throughout the narrative is intended to point back to Abraham each time. The oath itself is taken in v. 9 only after its details have been settled. The rite of touching the generative organ when taking an oath occurs elsewhere only in Gen. 47:29 where the circumstances are the same, namely, imminent death. The one who is facing death secures his last will by an "oath at the source of life" (O. Procksch; cf. bibliog. above).

[24:3-4]   The hand of the later narrator is seen in the extent, positive and negative, of the commission as well as in the expansion of the basically magical procedure of oath taking (v. 2) by means of an oath which echoes the language of cult. V. 4 could follow directly on v. 2 without anything being lost. The servant is to swear by "Yahweh, God of heaven and God of earth" (cf. v. 7, "Yahweh, the God of heaven"). H. Gunkel writes: "These qualifying names do not occur elsewhere in Genesis, nor even in the whole preexilic literature; but they are frequent in the Persian period, Ezra 1:2; 5:12; 6:2f.. . . ." The qualification of God in Gen. 14:19-22 by קנה is similar, as A. Dillmann had already pointed out. "In the papyri and Elephantine, it is more common in the Aramaic than in the Hebrew texts," D. K. Andrews (*Essays in Honor of T. J. Meek* [1964] 45-57). In any case these divine predicates are "indications of a relatively late origin" (G. von Rad; also W. Zimmerli). The proximity to 14:19-22 indicates the cultic origin and setting of this particular predicate.

The negative formulation of the commission in v. 3b presupposes sedentary life among the Canaanites, and so there is special emphasis on it in

Deuteronomy (e.g., 7:f.): "You shall not. . .take their daughters for your sons!" The positive part of the commission is introduced by כִּי because of v. 3b (in the sense of כִּי־אָם, which some Mss. have). The mention of the goal has echoes of 12:1. Gk and Vg, following the sense and v. 7, correctly expand by adding מִשָּׁם.

[24:5-8] The servant puts a further question for clarification: what is he to do if the woman will not come with him? Abraham replies.

[24:6-9] Abraham's answer comes in v. 8; vv. 6-7 are an expansion of it. He expressly forbids the servant to take Isaac back to where he, Abraham, came from (v. 6); the reason is given in v. 7, thereby setting Gen. 24 within the overall context of the Abraham story and presupposing it already formed. The reason, comprising two (or three) relative sentences with אֲשֶׁר, is at the same time in apposition to the subject of the last sentence of v. 7, that assures the servant of success. It could be that a sentence has fallen out after the second אֲשֶׁר in v. 7 which spoke of God's guiding presence with Abraham. All that remains now of God's all-embracing action with regard to Abraham is the "bringing out" following the wording of 12:1-3, and the promise of the land following the wording of 15:7,18. The juxtaposition of bringing out and the promise of the land (as in Ex. 3) shows that here the promise of the land is *the* promise (R. Rendtorff points out that it holds only for the posterity), as also in 26:3 and 50:24. It was shown in Gen. 15 that the promise of the land by oath is the language of Deuteronomy. This emphasis on the promise of the land is obviously linked with the double command to the servant not to bring Isaac back to Mesopotamia under any circumstances. The assurance to the servant in the last sentence of v. 7, "he will send his messenger before you," is, as in Ex. 23:20; 32:34; 33:2; cf. Num. 20:16, the language of the Deuteronomic divine speeches. These passages, which speak of leading the people through the desert, are presupposed in v. 7; application is made to the individual in late texts such as Ps. 91:11 and Tob. 5:17-22; cf. Gen. 46:4.

[24:9] The servant takes the oath; v. 9 follows on v. 2. The account of Abraham's death probably followed here (H. Gunkel and others) but was dropped with the insertion of the narrative and the anticipation of 25:7-11.

[24:10] The account of the servant's journey is very short; v. 10 deals briefly with the preparations, the departure, and the arrival. The servant takes ten of his master's camels—there are obviously many more. These and the presents he takes with him show that Abraham is thought of as a wealthy cattle owner, something like Boaz in the book of Ruth.

The goal of the journey is Aram-Naharaim, a region on the middle Euphrates in central Mesopotamia; cf. R. T. O'Callaghan (*Aram Naharaim* [1948, 1961²]) and J. Simons (*The Geographical. . .* [1959]). The city itself is not named; cf. L. Wächter (ZDPV 24 [1968] 71); "the city of Nahor" can only be Haran.

[24:11-27] The meeting with Rebekah begins with the stop at the well in front of the city gate (v. 11) and the servant's prayer to God for a sign (vv. 12-14). Immediately a girl comes to the well (vv. 15-16); she complies with the servant's request for a drink and quite unsolicited waters the camels (vv. 17-21). In reply to the servant's question she informs him that she is a relation of Abraham (vv. 22-25), and the servant thanks God (vv. 26-27).

[**24:11**]   The parallel with Gen. 29 and Ex. 2 begins here. Just as the city gate is the place where the men assemble, so too is the well the place where the women and girls gather. The niph. of ברך occurs only here, a certain sign that the word belonged to the old narrative.

[**24:12-14**]   The meeting at the well is framed within the prayer of the servant for a sign and his thanks for the granting of the prayer (vv. 26-27); this is typical of Gen. 24. The servant asks first for a manifestation of favor to his master (v. 12a); קרה niph. = "to allow to happen," as in 27:30. Only then comes the request for a sign (vv. 13-14). From the standpoint of the history of religions it is an interesting amalgam of two basically different phenomena.

The omen is found all over the world as a good, or more often a bad, presage and traces of it remain even today (*Standard Dictionary of Folklore*, 11 [1950], "Omen," 821). It is based on magical thinking and has nothing to do with prayer. In many religions it has given rise to the request for a sign; a prayer for an omen in the context of acquiring a bride is mentioned by F. Heiler (*Das Gebet. . .* [1919] 65): "Thus prays the Batak youth. . .: If I am really to marry the daughter of NN. . . and we are to grow old together, then tell me, great father!"

A prayer for a sign introduced by the same words הנה אנכי is found in Judg. 6:37; it is somewhat different, though without an express request, in 1 Sam. 14:8-10; cf. the request for a sign in the salvation oracles, e.g., Is. 7. In any case the sign confirms a saving action of God, as in Gen. 24.

[**24:13-14**]   V. 13 presents the concrete situation wherein the servant asks that the sign be manifest; v. 14 states in what it is to consist. But the arrangement of the latter shows the request for the sign is a narrative device; it is shaped by the servant's hope. The second part of v. 14 combines two different conclusions of the request: *(a)* The girl. . .is to be the one. . .whom you have destined (so too vv. 43,44). *(b)* If the girl does this. . .and this. . .and this. . .then I will know that you have shown favor to my master.

[**24:15-16**]   The appearance of the girl is portrayed as in the parallel in 29:9. The words, "Now he had scarcely finished speaking. . .," are not well suited to the prayer just uttered, whereas they fit well in 29:9 where a conversation precedes. The difficulty becomes apparent with the clumsy and inept addition of the words, וכדה על־שכמה, at the end of v. 15; they should follow immediately "the girl" (Rebekah), as v. 45 shows. According to 29:5 Laban is the son of Nahor; according to 24:48 Rebekah is the daughter of Nahor. Bethuel plays no part in the story; it is likely that he is a subsequent insertion into 24:15, 24, 44 in anticipation of the P genealogy in 25:20 and 28:2, 5.
On בתולה see A. Strobel (BHH 11 [1964] 914f.). כד, "jug"; Greek κάδος, perhaps an Aegean loanword according to O. Procksch; cf. J. P. Brown (VT 19 [1969] 156).

[**24:16**]   The girl's virginity and beauty are lauded in detail. It is significant for the understanding of beauty in the Old Testament that it be perceived and noted in the ordinary chores of everyday life (cf. 29:17)—here in the descent to the well and in the activity of providing drink.

[24:17-21]   The meeting begins with the request for a drink (cf. 1 Kings 17:10; Jn. 4:7); Rebekah complies, but beyond that also waters the camels (vv. 19-20), while the servant looks on. The request to the girl is polite, "a little water," as in 18:4; the "little" accords with גמא = "sip" (hiph. only here). There follows the girl's polite compliance with the request and the readiness to water the animals (vv. 18-20). The picture of this simple meeting between the man and the young girl at the well, and this is the high point of the narrative, shows that in the patriarchal period civilization was essentially a matter of personal contact between people (see too vv. 31-33, 49, 62-65). The girl's busy activity has as its counterpart the quiet, anxious gaze of the man who looks on, wondering whether God has prospered his journey (v. 21). The arc of tension which began with Abraham's assurance to the servant (v. 7) and led to the servant's prayer (v. 12) reaches its climax here. Everything from now on is a gradual diminuendo with the theme word "successful" sounding yet three more times (vv. 40, 42, 56). The servant waits, tense and silent in his unavowed certainty that the sign is realized.

[24:22-27]   The next passage moves from the inquiry about the girl's family to the welcome they give.

[24:22]   Before the servant asks the questions about which everything revolves, he gives the girl costly presents. This is nothing other than his joyful reaction to the girl's obliging readiness to refresh him and the animals (not some sort of bride price!); his unbounded joy is reflected in the presents: golden jewelry—a nose ring and two bracelets. The nose ring is "a common female ornament from Egypt to India," F. Delitzsch. בקע is a half-shekel (Ex. 38:26); golden bracelets also in 35:4; Ex. 32:2f.; Job 42:11.

[24:23-25]   It is only now that the man inquires about the girl's family and accommodation in her house. She gives him information about both (in v. 24, as in vv. 15 and 50, the name Bethuel is a later insertion).

[24:26-27]   The question of v. 21 is now answered. The thanksgiving, which includes the action in v. 26 and the prayer in v. 27, corresponds to the prayer at the arrival at the city of Nahor (vv. 13-14). The bow and prostration before Yahweh is itself an expression of thanks which is then articulated in words. The prayer follows the basic structure of the *bārūk* sentences in similar situations which also occur in prose, e.g., Ex. 18:10; 1 Sam. 25:32. From this it follows that the simple exclamation of the praise of God consisted solely in the expression ברוך יהוה and the reason for it: "Blessed be Yahweh, for Yahweh has led me safely along the way to the house of the brother of my master." This simple praise of God has been expanded in "hymnic" fashion first by "the God of my master Abraham" in apposition, and the relative sentence, "who has not withdrawn his steadfast love and fidelity from my master," which resembles a verse from the Psalms. There are also signs of cultic or hymnic expansions in 24:3,7. On the *bārūk*-sentences, cf. W. Speyer (JAC 17 [1974] 177-180).

[24:28-32]   Laban hears from Rebekah what has happened (v. 28), hurries outside (vv. 29-30), invites the servant into his house (v. 31); the servant accepts the invitation (v. 32). In v. 28 the scene shifts from the area around the well to the house in the "city of Nahor." Rebekah hurries home and tells of her experience—but "in her mother's house"; the reason for this can only be that her father was dead; this explains the role of her brother Laban who is introduced in the following verse (29). The text of vv. 29-30 runs more smoothly when one acknowledges a copyist's error and reads v. 29b between vv. 30a and 30b. Laban saw. . .heard. . .and hurried. . ... Laban recognizes from what he sees and hears that the man must be a relative and important, so he hastens to invite him in. His friendly and pressing invitation is the act of the master of the household (v. 31). He addresses the stranger as "blessed of Yahweh," the narrator thus resuming the introduction from v. 1. The use of the phrase ברוך יהוה in its two different senses in vv. 27 and 31 is a deliberate subtlety. The invitation is followed by the formal reception into the house with a detailed account of the whole procedure including the washing of the feet (cf. 18:4; 19:2) and the unharnessing of the camels which are lodged in the courtyard.

[24:33-54a]   The second part now follows: the execution of the commission that the servant received from Abraham. According to custom, food and drink (v. 33a) would follow the hospitable reception (v. 32); but the meal comes only in v. 54a, a sentence which could follow immediately on v. 33a. The reason for the long interlude (vv. 33b-53) is that the servant will not touch food before he has carried out his commission (v. 33b). This he does in a long speech (vv. 34-49) which begins with an exposition of the situation (vv. 34-36) followed by a detailed account of the commission from Abraham right up to the meeting with Rebekah (vv. 37-48), and ends with a request for an answer to his quest (v. 49). The brief and favorable reply is followed by thanks to God and presents (vv. 52, 53). Only now do the servant and his retinue sit down to the meal (v. 54a).

[24:34-36]   The servant merely introduces himself without any further personal detail; everything he says concerns his master: "I am the servant of Abraham" (v. 34). Then follows the blessing that Abraham has received from God (v. 35); it should be compared with 12:16; 13:2. On יגדל see 26:13. מאד does not appear anywhere else with ברך, and so is to be read with יגדל, as in the Syr. Property and possessions, be they of an individual or a people, are the effect of God's blessing, according to the Old Testament. It is important to the request the servant has to make that Abraham has already transferred his property to Isaac (v. 36); 25:5 (P) is presupposed here; according to J. Wellhausen this sentence followed 24:1.

[24:37-41]   It is here that the meaning of the detailed repetition is best in evidence: "The facts should speak for themselves and lead to the desired decision" (A. Dillmann). Vv. 37-41 repeat vv. 2-9; vv. 42-48 repeat vv. 11-27. It is natural that there are variations; this is often for the benefit of the listeners, as when in v. 40 Abraham's walking before God (17:1) takes the place of the promise made to him (v. 7).

[24:42-48]   This passage corresponds to vv. 11-14. The servant must repeat his prayer for a sign word for word, because Rebekah's family is to acknowledge that God has spoken by virtue of its being granted (v. 50). The prayer is formulated more precisely here than in vv. 12-14. The passage vv. 45-48 corresponds to vv. 15-27; it is shorter, which makes sense in the address to Rebekah's family. The small modification, that he made his prayer quietly, is significant; cf. comm. on vv. 12-14. In v. 47 the בתואל בן is again an addition; likewise v. 48, in contrast to v. 7.

[24:49] The servant allows his long discourse to issue into the question on which everything hangs, thereby reaching the limit of his responsibility. He goes not a step beyond, neither pressing nor suggesting agreement. His remaining words are but a reference to his master and what the answer means for him: ''Now, if you are disposed to deal loyally and faithfully with my master, tell me!'' He himself withdraws into the background. He has only to know the answer, be it affirmative or negative, so as to be able to act accordingly.

[24:50-59] ובתואל is obviously an addition in v. 50; the father could not be mentioned after the son, and in v. 53 only the mother is mentioned. Either ומלכה or וביתו (BHK) could have stood there. The answer of the family, for whom Laban is spokesman, has three parts: (1) V. 50 is the reaction of the family to the servant's story which has convinced them that God was at work in what he experienced. The finger of God is decisive, and nothing more can be said. For רע או־טוב, meaning ''nothing at all,'' cf. Gen. 31:24, 29; 2 Sam. 13:22. (2) This is the formal consent to the servant's request for Rebekah; it consists in a nominal sentence הנה־רבקה לפניך, a solemn, traditional formula which determines the surrender of the daughter into another family union, and a verbal sentence which gives the surrender a concrete form: take—go—give her as wife. (3) The first part is repeated in other words (v. 51b); the surrender that follows is consequent on the obvious direction of God. דבר in v. 50 is used in the sense of ''event'': ''This has come from Yahweh.'' The verb דבר in v. 51b means: God has spoken in this event.

[24:52-54a] The servant reacts with two gestures: he bows down to the ground before Yahweh (v. 52) and distributes presents (v. 53). There is a particular subtlety here in that the act of thanks consists only in the gesture. He then brings out the presents. Both actions could be designated by the Hebrew ברכה. Rebekah receives the finest presents because it is a real present and not a bride-price. The servant is free at last from his heavy obligation. Now he can relax and recline at table with his retinue.

[24:54b-67] The third and last part of the narrative begins with the servant asking leave to depart (v. 54b). He remains firm despite an invitation to stay longer (vv. 55-56); when the question is put to Rebekah, she consents to go with the servant (vv. 57-58). The sister receives her dismissal with a blessing from her brother (vv. 59-60); the caravan sets out (v. 61). The arrival is narrated as a meeting between Isaac and Rebekah (vv. 62-65). The servant makes his report to Isaac (v. 66), and Isaac takes Rebekah as his wife.

[24:54b-58] The very next morning the servant asks to be allowed to return to his master, but the brother and the mother counter with the request that Rebekah stay with them a short time yet, as was the custom (e.g., Tob. 8:15). The text is uncertain as to how long. In any case it is a question of some days—two periods are given (unlikely are the suggestions of F. S. North, ''for a season or [at least] ten weeks,'' VT 11 (1961) 446-448, and B. Jacob, ''a year or ten months''). The servant, in reply to the family's request, reminds them that God has given success to the commission he undertook on Abraham's behalf and he must communicate this to his master (v. 56). The girl is to make her own decision, and she agrees to go (vv. 57f.). On the expression את־פיה, cf. H. J. Schilder (GIT 2 [1961] 491). The context shows that the agreement concerns the time of the departure. However, the narrator wants to say in vv. 57f. that the family's consent was given, in complete agreement with Rebekah.

[**24:59-60**]   All the travelers now take their farewell together with the nurse (in 35:8 she is called Deborah) who accompanies Rebekah on her journey abroad. Rebekah receives a parting blessing which consists of word and action—embrace and laying on of hands. It is here that we encounter the blessing in its most ancient form, the farewell blessing, which has its setting in the family when a member takes leave of the circle either by death (ch. 27) or, as here, by departure. It is a pronouncement which is to continue to have its effect in the life of the one departing. The blessing is rhythmic in form, as elsewhere in the Old Testament (cf. Gen. 9:25-27). It combines the two wishes of increase and victory. The former probably has its origin in a wedding blessing (a Ugaritic parallel may be found in C. Westermann, *The Promises*. . . [1980] 153ff., 178f.). Here, however, it goes beyond the family and is combined with a political wish. There is a similar blessing, also in rhythmic form, in Ruth 4:14f. and in Tob. 7:12; 10:11, where it is also a farewell blessing. For the literature on blessing, see bibliog. to Gen. 12:1-9.

[**24:61**]   The caravan sets out. The text of v. 61 has not been disturbed (as H. Holzinger and others would have it) nor are vv. 61a and 61b variants (as with J. Skinner and others); after v. 60 there is first the account of the setting out of Rebekah and her attendants, then of the servant's taking over of the group, and finally of the departure of all.

[**24:62-65**]   Rebekah's meeting with the servant reaches its goal in her meeting with Isaac which is portrayed with the greatest reserve. The scene changes; it is the third act in the narrative as a whole; the journey itself is passed over, as was the first journey. In v. 62 Isaac has a new domicile; he had come from . . .to Beer-ha-lai-roi and was living in the Negev (מבוא has not been explained; J. Skinner has synthesized attempts to solve the problem). The meeting begins in v. 63. The meaning of the verb לשׂוח is uncertain, and in KBL left unexplained. Suggestions are "to think" (like שׂיח), "to mediate" (so the versions), or "to pray" (Targum, Kimchi, Luther), "to lament the dead," or "to take a stroll" (like לשׁוט) (Syr, T. Nöldeke, J. Skinner, B. Jacob, and others); this last is the most likely, corresponding as it does to the rendering in v. 65 (on שׂוח cf. bibliog. above). As is often the case in the Old Testament, it is the raising of the eyes that introduces an event; seeing is directed predominantly to something that is actually happening, not to what just is. Rebekah, like Isaac, also raises her eyes (v. 64); just as Isaac sees the camels, so Rebekah sees a man in the distance. These two sentences reduce to a minimum a meeting between two people so as to allow what is unspoken to speak all the more forcefully. Rebekah's query about the man is framed by her two movements (vv. 64b, 65b); all happens at the same time. She wants to show respect for the man who is to be her husband by dismounting from the camel (cf. 1 Sam. 25:23; 1 Kings 5:21; Josh. 15:18) and to comport herself as custom demands. The veil is not worn permanently, though the bride meets the bridegroom veiled (R. de Vaux, *Ancient Israel* [1962] 33-34). This episode presupposes a conception of the relationship between man and woman according to which fixed forms of conduct in the community serve to preserve a certain authenticity.

[24:66]   The servant renders an account of how he fulfilled his commission. It is presupposed that Abraham, to whom the servant was responsible (v. 9), is no longer alive. The wording is peculiar: דברים אשר עשה, ''the words [= events, things] that he had done,'' ''all that he had done in carrying out the commission.'' We meet here an important function of the narrative. In a case like this an account can be rendered only in narrative form. This gives rise to an oral narrative which, as an account rendered of a commission, has an important function in the community. Every oral repetition is a new variant the consequence of which is that at the beginning Rebekah will tell the story a little differently from the servant.

[24:67]   This is one of the few narratives in the Old Testament that ends with a marriage (cf. Ruth 4:13), an ending that is genealogically based. It proceeds in three parts: Isaac conducts Rebekah to his tent (שרה אמו must be an addition as it is grammatically impossible here). This is primarily the welcome of the traveller after the long journey. It should be noted that the narrator wants to point out the difference: Laban had conducted the servant to his ''house.'' The second part is the marriage: Isaac takes Rebekah as his wife and the wedding is celebrated. The third part is the growth in love between husband and wife who had hitherto not known each other. The narrator wants to say that this is what God has designed by granting success to the journey. What began with the first meeting and glance (vv. 63-65) was growing into love.

The narrative ends with a reference back to the beginning, ''And Isaac was consoled after his mother,'' which can only mean ''after the death of his mother.'' It is striking that there has also been an insertion in v. 67a, שרה אמו. Apart from the two additions Sarah does not appear in ch. 24. Looking back over the story, the reference could be only to the father who, at the beginning of the chapter, felt that he was near to death. It is probable therefore that the concluding sentence ran: ''So Isaac was comforted after the death of his father.'' It is likely that 25:11 once followed 24:67 as the conclusion of the chapter.

Purpose and Thrust

The immediate purpose is to narrate how Isaac, Abraham's son, acquired Rebekah as his wife. The episode at the well, which has parallels in Gen. 29 and Ex. 2, stands at the center. All three narratives revolve about a meeting at a well with one who comes from afar which results in marriage. It is a family event which is concerned with the continuation of the line. The same concern is found in other narratives in the Abraham circle, though in a different way. This motif, common to the three variants, does not require any express pronouncement or action on the part of God, as Gen. 29 and Ex. 2 show, any more than does the genealogical statement that Isaac, Abraham's son, took Rebekah as his wife. Ordinary family events in the patriarchal story, birth—marriage—death, are not usually spoken of as an action of God. It was simply taken for granted that God was at work, and there was no need to state it explicitly. The narrative of Gen. 24, like the parallels in Gen. 29 and Ex. 2, is concerned with God's blessing as it effectively continues a family line in such a way as to tell of the extraordinary circumstances that lead to a marriage without any explicit mention of God's providential hand. Narratives of this sort remain the same through the generations right up to the like narrative in the book of Tobit. They always follow the same pattern of birth, marriage, and death.

But the narrative also tells of something which is utterly unique for the participants. In Abraham's family it is the names that attest this. For Abraham to be the point of departure of a history, not only must a child be born (Gen. 15; 16; 18), but also two people must meet, love, and grow in love (v. 67). The story of love is also part of the history of God's dealing with his people; this is so here; love grows after the marriage; it is part of the history of Abraham as it continues in Isaac and Rebekah. The other motif of God's providential action stands out over against this. When this is prefaced to the whole as a leitmotif (somewhat different from 22:1), then God's guiding hand in one's personal life receives a special significance. As counterpart to this is the servant's trustful recourse to God in prayer at every stage; prayer permeates the whole narrative. The narrative is particularly important for the history of prayer in the Old Testament; it is a convincing demonstration that prayer is a response to event and that spontaneous address to God in petition and thanks arising therefrom is the natural expression of life with God. It is not by chance that the servant's spontaneous address to God recalls the prayer of Jesus. Just as the personal relationship of trust in God and his guidance remains the same throughout the Bible, so too does prayer as a response to this guidance when experienced in one's personal life.

Conclusion of the Abraham Story

Literature

Genesis 25:1-11: H. Schmökel, "Jahwe und die Keniter," JBL 52 (1933) 212-229. W. F. Albright, "Dedan," Fests. A. Alt BHTh 16 (1953) 1-12. S. Talmon, "The Sectarian יחד—A Biblical Noun," VT 3 (1953) 133-140. G. Dossin, "L'inscription de *Iaḥdun-Lim*, roi de Mari," Syr. 32 (1955) 1-28. J. Obermann, "Early Islam," in *The Idea of History in the Ancient Near East*, ed. R. C. Dentan (1955) 244-297. H. St. J. Philby, *The Land of Midian* (1957). H. Kosmala, "The 'Bloody Husband,' " VT 12 (1962) 14-28. M. C. Astour, "Sabtah and Sabteca. Ethiopian Pharaoh Names in Genesis 10," JBL 84 (1965) 422-426. O. Eissfeldt, "Protektorat. . .," JBL 87 (1968) 383-390. F. V. Winnett, "The Arabian Genealogies in Genesis," *Essays in Honor of H. G. May* (1970) 171-196. H. von Wissmann, "Madiama," Pauly-W Suppl 12 (1970) 525-552. A. Malamat, "The Period of the Judges," C. VII: *The World History of the Jewish People III* (1971) 129-163. W. J. Dumbrell, "Midian. . .," VT 25 (1975) 327-329. P. D. Miller, "The Blessing of God. An Interpretation of Numbers 6:22-27," Interp. 29 (1975) 240-251. S. Gevirtz, "The Life Spans of Joseph and Enoch and the Parallelism," JBL 96 (1977) 570-571. R. R. Wilson, *Genealogy and History in the Biblical World* (1977).

Genesis 25:12-18: E. Glaser, *Geschichte und Geographie Arabiens II* (1890) esp. 323-325. M. Streck, "Assurbanipal," VAB 7 III (1916ff.) esp. 1-3. W. F. Albright, "The Biblical Tribe of *Massā'* and Some Congeners," Fests. G. Levi Della Vida I StOr (1956) 1-14. R. Borger, *Die Inschriften Asarhaddons, Königs von Assyrien*, AOBeih 9 (1956). A. van der Branden, "'*Umm 'attarsamm*, re di Dûmat," BeO 2 (1960) 41-47. H. P. Rüger, *Das Tyrusorakel Ez 27*, diss. Tübingen (1961) esp. 92-96. A. Malamat, " *'Haṣerîm'* in der Bibel und Mari" [in Hebr.], Yediot 27 (1963) 181-184. B. D. Rathjen, "Philistine and Hebrew Amphictyonies," JNES 24 (1965) 100-104. M. Har-El, " 'And they dwelt from Havilah unto Shur' (Genesis 25,18)" [in Hebr.], BetM 51,4 (1972) 501-502. H. Horn, "Chronique," RB 79 (1972) 425. E. C. Broome, "Nabaiati, Nabaioth and Nabataeans," JSSt 18 (1973) 1-16.

Text

25:1   Abraham took another[a] wife whose name was Keturah.[b]
  2   She bore him Zimran,[a] Jokshan, Medan, Midian, Ishbak, and Shuah.
  3   Jokshan begot Sheba[a] and Dedan. The sons of Dedan[bc] were Asshurim, Letushim, and Leummim.
  4   The sons of Midian were: Ephah,[a] Epher, Hanoch, Abida, and Eldaah. All these are the descendants of Keturah.
  5   Now Abraham gave all his property[a] to Isaac,[b]

6   But he gave presents to the sons of his concubines and while he was still alive sent them away from his son Isaac eastwards, to the eastern country.

7   This is the length of Abraham's life span:[a] he lived one hundred and seventy-five years.

8   Then he breathed his last and died in good old age and full of years[a] and was gathered to his people.

9   His sons Isaac and Ishmael buried him in the cave at Machpelah in the field of Ephron, son of Zohar the Hittite, east of Mamre,

10 the field that Abraham had bought from the Hittites.[a] There Abraham and his wife Sarah were buried.

11 Now after the death of Abraham God blessed Isaac his son, and Isaac lived at[a] Beer-la-hai-roi.

12 These are the descendants of Ishmael, Abraham's son, whom the Egyptian Hagar, Sarah's maid, bore to Abraham.

13 These are the names of the sons of Ishmael in the order of their birth: Nebaioth, the firstborn of Ishmael, then Kedar, Adbeel,[a] Mibsam,

14 Mishma, Dumah, Massa,

15 Hadad, Tema,[a] Jetur, Naphish, and Kedemah.[b]

16 These[a] are the sons of Ishmael and these are their names after which their settlements and encampments were named: twelve princes according to their tribal groupings.[b]

17 This is the length of Ishmael's life span: he lived one hundred and thirty-seven years; then he breathed his last and died and was gathered to his people.

18 They lived[a] from Havilah to Shur, which is east of Egypt as you go to Assyria, settling to the east of his brothers.*

1a   On the construction, Ges-K §120d.   **b**   The name only here (= v. 4 and 1 Chron. 1:32); cf. קטורה "incense burning," Deut. 33:10.

2a   Probably derived from זמר "wild goat."

3a   Gk inserts ותימן.   **b**   These three names are missing in 1 Chron. 1:32f.   **c**   Gk adds Ραγουηλ καὶ Ναβδεηλ.

4a   Gk Γεφαρ.   **b**   Gk Θεργαμα.

5a   Ges-K §16a: four words can be joined by *maq*.   **b**   Sam, Gk, Syr add בנו, probably correctly.

7a   On the form, as in Gen. 5:5, Ges-K §76i.

8a   Read ושבע ימים with Sam, Gk, Syr, and other versions, as in Gen. 35:29.

10a   Syr adds לאחזת קבר.

11a   On the use of עם, BrSynt §113.

13a   Gk Ναβδεηλ.

15a   Gk ותימן.   **b**   Gk וקדמן; 1 Chron. 5:19, Nodab.

16a   On אלה הם, Ges-K §136d.   **b**   אמה elsewhere only in Num 25:15; Ps. 117:1; probably Arabic influence.

18a   Gk, Vg singular; follow MT.

Form

The conclusion of the Abraham story, 25:1-18, is a synthesis of mutually independent texts. The account of Abraham's death, vv. 1-10(11) P, forms the nucleus which would follow immediately on ch. 23 (P), the death and burial of Sarah. The form of the account is a genealogy: details of age (v. 7), death (v. 8), and burial (v. 10). Two genealogies have been prefaced (vv. 1-6) and appended (vv. 12-18); these spell out the secondary lines stemming from Abraham, as is the case

---

*Or, "each made forays against his brothers" (trans.).

elsewhere (e.g., Gen. 36): in vv. 12-18 the genealogy of Ishmael, in vv. 1-6 the genealogy of the sons of Keturah. They differ in that vv. 12-18 are linked with what precedes by v. 12 (chs. 16 and 21) whereas vv. 1-6 are not; the mother as a secondary wife must first be introduced. It is clear from this that vv. 1-6 are a subsequent addition; the link with the Abraham story must first be established.

The form of both these parts, vv. 1-6 and 12-18, is complicated: vv. 1-6 consist of two units, vv. 1-4 and 5-6; vv. 1-4 are a genealogy with four parts and a caption to conclude: (1) the note that Abraham took another wife, but with no indication of when; (2) the list of six sons whom she bore to Abraham; (3) the continuation of the genealogy through one of the six, Jokshan, through two generations; two sons and three grandsons of Jokshan, sons of Dedan, are mentioned; (4) a list of the four sons of Midian which abandons the genealogical form. There is a conclusion—a caption—to the whole (v. 4b), which refers back to v. 1. It is a genealogy in which vv. 3b and 4 are recognizable additions. Vv. 5-6 do not belong there; they are narrative in form and could be a fragment from somewhere or other. It is probably the work of the transmitter who added vv. 1-4 and provided the frame of v. 1 which justified the insertion of the genealogy, vv. 2-4, whereby it is understood that the many additional sons of Abraham do not in any way impair the importance of his one son with his legal rights.

Vv. 12-18 form an immediate continuation of vv. 7-10 and likewise belong to P. The text exhibits a difficulty both at the beginning and the end (O. Eissfeldt, BZAW 31 [1916] 37f.). There are two introductions (vv. 12 and 13a) to the central piece, vv. 13b-16; v. 13a can only be the introduction to vv. 13b, 14; the introduction v. 12 must be followed by "Ishmael begot. . . ." The other difficulty is that the singular in v. 17 is followed by the plural in v. 18; v. 18 is a continuation of v. 16, whereas v. 17 belongs to a *toledot* text. One concludes therefrom that two originally independent units are intertwined in vv. 12-18: the *toledot* of Ishmael, of which only the introduction (v. 12) and the conclusion (v. 17) are preserved, and a list of the Ishmaelite tribes (vv. 13-16,18) which has been inserted into it (so too M. Noth). There is no genealogy in vv. 13b-15 corresponding to the introduction (v. 13a) and the conclusion (v. 16) but a list, i.e., a mere enumeration of names (cf. *Genesis 1–11*, pp. 6-18, esp. p. 10).

Setting

The priestly writing concludes its story of Abraham with 25:7-18—Abraham's death (corresponding to 11:32) and the continuation of a secondary line (corresponding to Gen. 36). Whereas vv. 7-10 (on v. 11 see comm. below) are an independent formation by P, the composite character of vv. 12-18 appears in that P takes over a list of Ishmaelite tribes at hand to him in vv. 13-16, 18a, about whose origin we can say nothing.

Gen. 25:1-6 belongs neither to P's nor J's overall plan and must be a secondary addition (M. Noth: "An addition from an unknown period"). One must distinguish the framework (vv. 1,5-6), probably an ad hoc creation to suit the insertion, from the genealogy, in which there are layers pointing to a tradition which grew gradually. It is not possible to say anything about the original setting and handing down of the genealogy.

Commentary

[**25:1**]   The verb ויסף is to be understood in a literary, not in a biographical sense: its purpose is to associate the names that follow with Abraham (cf. שנית in

22:15); this is done by introducing another wife, a secondary wife. This too is not to be understood biographically; one cannot ask whether she was a principal wife (so here אשה) or a secondary wife (so 25:6 and 1 Chron. 1:32), or whether Abraham took her before or after the death of Sarah. The name קטורה which occurs only here (= 1 Chron. 1:32-33) is an ad hoc formation (perhaps by analogy with Job 42:14 קציעה = perfume) and indicates the land where the tribes live: Arabia is the land of incense or the land whence incense comes (1 Kings 10; Is. 60:6; Jer. 6:20; Ezek. 27:22).

[25:2-4]   It is not possible to say precisely whether the 16 names (6+2+3+5) enumerated here are place-names or personal names. Only some place and tribal names can be identified as well as the region indicated by the name Keturah, the Syro-Arabian desert east of the Jordan.

The six names are personal names (so too KBL), the names of the six sons whom Keturah bore to Abraham. However, Midian occurs elsewhere and often as the name of a people.

זמרן occurs only here and is unknown; reference has been made to "kings of Zimri" (Jer. 25:25; shortly before, "kings of Arabia"; v. 23, Dedan and Tema); Zimri as a personal name, Num. 25:14 (husband of a Midianite); the Zamareni in Pliny VI 158 (already noted by H. Grotius). יקשן, only here and unknown; explained by Arabian genealogies from a tribe Yaqish in the Yemen. P. Tuch, H. Gunkel and others refer to a variant Joktan (Gen. 10:25, 29), the father of Yemenite tribes; a list of Arabian tribal names is attached to him in Gen. 10:26-30 (cf. Genesis 1–11, comm. ad loc). מדן only here and unknown; regarded by many as a doublet of Midian, cf. Gen. 37:36 מדנים for מדינים. מדין Gen. 37:28, 36; Ex. 2; 18; Num. 22; 25; 31; Judg. 6; and elsewhere; an Arabian tribe in the Syro-Arabian desert, probably located on the east side of the gulf of Aqaba. Its frequent occurrence up to the period of the judges indicates its importance. After the judges (with one mention in David's time) it appears no more. ישבק only here and unknown. J. Van Seters, following W. F. Albright: "Ishbak and Shuah appear in Assyrian sources [already H. Holzinger] as Yashbuq and Suhu and are located in the steppe region of Northern Syria" (p. 61). שוח only here and Job 2:11, "Bildad the Shuhite," hence in the east Arabian neighborhood of Palestine, near the land of Uz, in the steppe region of Edom-Midian.

It is striking that four of the six names end in -ān; the long ā in the closed final syllable can be an Arabic element. The only name known with certainty, Midian, points to the Syro-Arabian desert; so too does Jokshan if it is the equivalent of Joktan; Shuah points to the eastern neighborhood of Palestine.

"Jokshan begot. . . ." The names of two sons, Sheba and Dedan, follow. Confirmation is given to the equation of Jokshan with Joktan by the fact that in Gen. 10:28(J) Sheba is one of the Arabian sons of Joktan. In any case in Gen. 10:7(P) Sheba and Dedan are among the descendants of Ham; consequently 25:1-6 cannot come from P. This passage, however, gives support to the correlation of the two names.

שבה: a people in southwest Arabia; דדן Dedan, a people bordering on Edom (cf. Genesis 1–11, comm. 10:7).

The three sons of Dedan—Asshurim, Letushim, Leummim—are missing in 1 Chron. 1:32f., and do not belong to the present context; they are a later, learned addition. These tribes or tribal groups occur only here and are otherwise unknown. The first name has nothing to do with Assyria and can only be an Arabian tribe.

What is peculiar about the names of the five sons of Midian is that they are clearer than all the other personal names. The last two, אבידע and אלדעה, are attested as personal names in Sabaean inscriptions, also as names of kings; the third, חנך, corresponds to Enoch (Gen. 4:17; 5:18-20). The first three names, עפר, עיפה, and חנך, occur as family names in the three Israelite tribes Judah, Manasseh, and Reuben (cf. KBL); J. Skinner writes: "in the tribes most exposed to contact with Midian." This indicates that the five names are related to an earlier stage. עיפה occurs in Is. 60:6 with Midian; this confirms that they are correlatives (J. Simon). כל־אלה occurs here as in Gen. 10:29. For suggestions about the three individual names in vv. 2-4, see W. F. Albright, *Yahweh and the Gods of Canaan* (1968) 34, 74, and the bibliog. above.

[25:5-6] These two verses form a unity. If vv. 5-6 together with v. 1 form the framework into which the genealogy (vv. 2-4) of the Abraham story is inserted (so too W. Zimmerli), the two sentences are necessary in order to say that Isaac was not disadvantaged legally because of Abraham's additional sons. Instead of the inheritance there was a legally secured settlement ("While he was still alive") consisting of gifts. The dismissal of the sons also served to give Isaac security; it follows the pattern of Gen. 21, but is somewhat strange here. All that is intended is "to free Isaac from them" (J. Skinner); it can scarcely be to explain etiologically the places where these tribes dwelt (R. Kilian). The explanation of the apparent repetition in קדמה אל־ארץ קדם is that "eastwards," "the eastern country" is to be understood as a name; cf. J. Simon on Bene-Qedem.

[25:7-11] Here are reported the length of Abraham's life (v. 7), his death (v. 8), and his burial (vv. 9f., P). P reports the death of Isaac in almost the same words (35:28-29). In P, 25:7-11 follows ch. 23. The language of the report makes it clear that death and burial are to be understood as a part of the cycle of life—they are its meaningful conclusion.

[25:7] The several names (days, years, life, years. . .) express the course of a good, long life more eloquently than the mere number. Following 12:4, Abraham died one hundred years after his entry into Canaan. אשר־חי as in Gen. 5:5.

[25:8] The two verbs ויגוע, וימת describe a process, the gradual passing away of one who has grown old and weak. The same two words are used of the death of Ishmael (25:17) and Isaac (35:29). "In good old age," as proclaimed in 15:15; cf. Judg. 8:32, Gideon. The opposite is expressed in Gen. 42:38; 44:29; 31—שיבה ביגון or ברעה. "Old and full of years" describes what we call a "fulfilled life." He "was gathered to his people"; in 15:15 "to his fathers," meaning the same. This does not mean, as most interpreters since B. Stade and H. Gunkel have said, that he was laid to rest in the family grave, nor that "he was put with them in Sheol" (A. Dillmann and others), but that Abraham now "belonged to and was numbered among the dead" (B. Jacob). There is no thought of a state in which the dead find themselves such as could be imagined or represented; the idea is rather what they now mean for the living: they belong to the ancestors who have gone before and whose memory is preserved.

[25:9-10] These verses follow directly on ch. 23; the significance of the purchase of the burial place becomes evident only here. Part of a peaceful death is that Abraham has a place where he can be buried. The two brothers bury him in harmony and peace. P makes no mention of the expulsion of Hagar and Ishmael (cf. 28:1-9).

[25:11]   Most scholars, following A. Dillmann, attribute 11a to P, thus bringing vv. 7-10 to a close, but 11b to J, because of its association with a place (A. Dillmann, R. Kilian, and others as a continuation of v. 6). It is questionable, however, whether 11a belongs to P, because vv. 12-17 are a better immediate continuation of vv. 7-10 whereas 11a would interrupt the style of the *toledot*; P never uses ברך elsewhere in this sense of constituting one in a state: "God blessed the. . .," as in 24:1; 26:2 (neither is P). I agree with J. Van Seters (*Abraham. . .* 248) who is of the opinion that 25:11 belonged to the conclusion of ch. 24 (for 11b, cf. H. Gunkel). As a concluding sentence it would form a nice stylistic balance to 24:1. The mention of Isaac's domicile in 11b would also be better suited to the close of ch. 24.

[25:12-18]   The difficulty inherent in this passage is that the list of Ishmaelite tribes in vv. 13-16,18, is independent of the framework (vv. 12-17). P has inserted them into his framework of the *toledot* of Ishmael in such a way that their original independence is discernible. Only the names of Ishmael's sons in the order of their birth really belong between vv. 12 and 17 (a trace of this is found in v. 13, "the firstborn of Ishmael") and perhaps also details about these sons. V. 17 would be an appropriate continuation of this; it is not in place at the end of the tribal list (vv. 13-16).

[25:12]   אלה תלדת cf. *Genesis 1–11*, comm. 5:1; also 6:9; 10:1; 11:10, 27 (all P). The names and the data of this verse come from chs. 16 and 21. Ch. 17 also shows that P was aware of these older traditions.

[25:13a]   This is another introduction, designating vv. 13-16 as a list of names, as does also the concluding sentence, v. 16 לתולדתם = "according to their families," a meaning of the word different from v. 12.

[25:13b-15]   The list of names comprehends only vv. 13b-15 and, apart from the designation of Nebaioth as the firstborn, is a mere string of names without any articulation, thus differing from vv. 2-4. "The firstborn of Ishmael" has obviously been prefixed so as to strike a balance between vv. 12 and 13a. וקדר is a harsh sequence; originally it followed immediately the preceding name.

נבית: the earlier equation with the Nabataeans (A. Dillmann, F. Delitzsch, and others) has now been abandoned (KBL). The name occurs as a personal name (28:9 P and 36:3 P [?]). Esau marries a daughter of Ishmael, the sister of Nebaioth (both passages probably presuppose 25:13); elsewhere only in Is. 60:7 with Kedar as the name of a region. The name occurs in cuneiform texts as *nabajāti* or *nab'āti*, again together with Qidri, both subjected by Ashurbanipal in the seventh century; it is attested as an Arabian tribe by an inscription from the neighborhood of Tema with the name *nbyt* (E. C. Broome, JSSt 18 [1973] 1-16).
קדר: cf. Nebaioth. Often mentioned in cuneiform texts since the eighth century as an Arabian tribe, *Qidri* or *Qadri*, known as nomads dwelling in tents and as archers; mentioned in the Old Testament only in passages from about the sixth century (Is. 21:16f.; 42:11; 60:7; Jer. 2:10; 49:28; Ezek. 27:21; Ps. 120:5; Song 1:5). Is. 21:16f. is important because several names from Gen. 25:13-16 occur in the oracle against the nations (21:1-17): Dumah, Kedar, and Tema; cf. Gen. 25:2, Dedan; on Kedar, H. P. Rüger, BHH II (1964) 937. אדבאל occurs only here and 1 Chron. 1:29, Akk. *Idiba'il*, Gk Ναβδεηλ. מבשם is likewise unknown; according to 1 Chron. 4:25 a descendant of Simeon, likewise משמע v. 14.

[14]   משמע like מבשם a descendant of Simeon, likewise unknown. דומה, also in Is. 21:11 (cf. on Kedar), situated north of Tema and identified by many with the modern *el Gōt*; but there were several places of this name. According to E. A. Speiser "connected with the oasis *Dūmat al Ghandal* in the Syrian desert," another designation for the same oasis. משא in Prov. 31:1 mentions a king of Massa (also 31:1?); conj. emend. in Ps. 120:5, with Kedar; some scholars, e.g., J. Simons, identify it with Mesha in Gen. 10:30, among the posterity of Joktan; perhaps also mentioned in Akkadian texts with Tema or Kedar.

[15]   חדד occurs only here and is unknown. תימא is identified by many with the present-day Tema in northwest Arabia, known from inscriptions of Tiglath-Pileser. It occurs in Jer. 25:23 with Dedan, in Job 6:19 with Sheba, and in Is. 21:14 with Dumah, Dedan, Kedar. יטור = Ituraeans according to Strabo and Cicero; according to 1 Chron. 5:18-22, neighbors of the Transjordanian Israelites together with נפיש, to be conquered by the Reubenites at the time of Saul. קדמה, only here, unknown; J. Simons wants to link it with the Kadmonites of Gen. 15:19.

[25:16]   V. 16, which is the concluding counterpart to v. 13, unites two conceptions of the list: the one, these are "the names of the sons of Ishmael," that is the names of individuals ("princes and their tribes"); the second deriving from the names themselves which are known as various names of tribes and places, "after which their settlements and encampments were named," together with information about the region where the tribes lived (v. 18). The indecisive meaning given to בגי ישמעאל is deliberate, bearing in mind the promise of twelve princes in Gen. 17:20. The two descriptions of their dwellings refer to the partly nomadic, partly sedentary lifestyle (חצרים: "the Mari term for a nomadic settlement," J. Van Seters, *Abraham. . .*, 18; A. Malamat, BA 34 [1971] 17); טירה is a camp protected by a stone wall (Num. 31:10). The word used for tribe, אמה, is rare in Hebrew, elsewhere only in Num. 25:15; Ps. 117:1; it indicates Arabian influence.

[25:17]   This sentence interrupts the continuity between v. 16 and v. 18; it belongs to the genealogy introduced in v. 12 which has been replaced by the list in vv. 13-16, 18. Both parts of v. 17 correspond to the account of Abraham's death (vv. 7,8).

[25:18]   V. 18 is the continuation of v. 16. There is not sufficient reason to attribute the verse to J, as do R. Holzinger and others; the list, vv. 13-16,18, is a tradition taken over by P. The information about the dwelling places of the tribes previously enumerated belongs to vv. 15-16. The region is designated by two limits, as e.g., in Gen. 10:19, 30 (on Havilah, see *Genesis 1–11*, comm. 2:11); Havilah is here a frontier limit, probably on the Persian gulf. Shur, שור, is "an Egyptian border post" (B. Jacob; cf. 16:7). The second sentence is almost word for word the same as 16:12b; it marks itself out not only by the singular, but also by the style, typical of tribal sayings; it is an addition. The irregular verb נפל, as in Judg. 7:12, shows that it is not just a complementing of 16:12b, but presupposes a variant.

Purpose and Thrust

The two genealogies or lists of tribes, vv. 2-4, 13-16, are two groupings of Arabian tribes; this is certain; they have been brought into relationship with Abraham by means of a son or another wife. They have more in common than first appears, and they cannot be simply distributed into two regions. Vv. 1-6 could be a subsequent expansion of vv. 12-16; cf. the approximation of Midianites and Ishmaelites in Judg. 8:24 and Gen. 37:25ff.; see the suggestion of H. Holzinger that vv. 2-4 is a J variant of vv. 12-18, and of J. Wellhausen that Keturah is a variant of Hagar. What is important is that both texts are determined by the intent to associate the two groups of Arabian tribes or peoples with Abraham. These texts then have a similar function here at the end of the Abraham story to those in ch. 10 at the end of the primeval story: it is more important that the family of Abraham as the progenitor of Israel belongs to a greater whole by means of a bond of relationship than that there are enmities which arose later (e.g., with the Midianites; Judg. 6-8). The family is the dominating form of community in the patriarchal story; hence the emphasis is laid on the family bond far and away beyond political and national divisions, and this in accordance with the programmatic pronouncement in Gen. 12:3. It is of particular significance that the concern is with the large group of Arabian tribes. Human and family bonds have deeper roots than political divisions. Gen. 25 expresses by means of the genealogical form a relationship which is reflected in a singular way in the course of the history of religions, namely, that Abraham is the father in the religion of Israel (as in the Christian religion) just as he is also in Islam.

The Abraham Story in Retrospect

Literature

P. Démann, "Die Bedeutung Abrahams in neutestamentlicher Schau," BiKi 2 (1952) 36-49. H. K. Beebe, *The Old Testament. An Introduction to its Literary, Historical and Religious Traditions* (1970). H. E. Lona, *Abraham in Johannes 8* EHS XXIII 65 (1976). L. Ruppert, *Das Buch Genesis erläutert*. Kap. I Gen. 1-25,18 (1976). W. Brueggemann, *The Land. Place as Gift, Promise, and Challenge in Biblical Faith* (1977). J. F. Craghan, "The Elohist in Recent Literature," BThB 7 (1977) 23-35. G. W. Coats and B. O. Long, *Canon and Authority. Essays in OT Religion and Theology* (1977). J. H. Hayes and J. M. Miller, *Israelite and Judaean History* (1977). J. T. Luke, "Abraham and the Iron Age: Reflections on the New Patriarchal Studies," JSOT 4 (1977) 35-47. L. Schmidt, "Überlegungen zum Jahwisten," EvTh 37 (1977) 230-247. R. N. Whybray, "Response to Professor Rendtorff," JSOT 3 (1977) 11-14. D. J. Wiseman, "Abraham in History and Tradition," NGTT 18 (1977) 158-163. R. Detweiler, *Story, Sign, and Self: Phenomenology and Structuralism as Literary-critical Methods*, Semeia Suppl. (1978). A. Jepsen, "Der Herr ist Gott," *Aufsätze zur Wissenschaft vom AT* (1978) ch. 2. T. L. Thompson, "A New Attempt to Date the Patriarchal Narratives," JAOS 98 (1978) 76-84.

1. On the Transmission of Gen. 12–25

This concluding section presupposes the introduction, in particular the closing pages, "Structure and Growth of Gen. 12–25," on which it follows directly.

A. As regards the written stage, it was left an open question whether there are texts in Gen. 12–25 which are to be attributed to an Elohist (cf. T. F. Craghan [1977] above). The point of departure for an answer is the redactional balance that links the introduction (Gen. 11:27-32) with the provisional conclusion (Gen. 21:1-7): Sarah is barren—Sarah has a child. Both texts are redactional units and unite J and P elements. It follows from this that the texts usually attributed to E in Gen. 20–22 do not belong to the self-contained whole framed by 11:27-32 and 21:1-7, but only to the complements or appendages.

Gen. 20–25 (apart from 21:1-7, which really connects with ch. 19) consists of two complexes: the genealogical texts or the texts related to them, 22:20–25:11, and the group 20:1–22:19 (without 21:1-7). The genealogical texts have their structural position at the conclusion of a section of the patriarchal story. In content they follow immediately on the account of the birth of Isaac, 21:1-7; this sequence is interrupted by the group 20:1–22:19, which have nothing in common internally, though they do outwardly: all of them except Gen. 22 are doublets, Gen. 20:1-18 (par. 12:10-20); 21:8-21 (par. 16:1-16); 21:22-34 A and B (from material in Gen. 26); Gen. 12-19 on the contrary contains no doublets. These texts are usually attributed to E. They do not form a structural part of Gen. 12–25, but are obviously individual additions which do not belong to the corpus of the Abraham story. One could call them Elohistic additions, but a necessary criterion for this would be that they exhibit clearly recognizable and defined characteristics in common. The exegesis, however, shows that this is not the case. Apart from this there is no discernible Elohistic plan of the Abraham story in these five texts.

Surveying the facts of the case, namely, that no text in the synthesis of Abraham stories between 11:27-32 and 21:1-7 can be attributed with certainty to E, that there are no doublets in the complex, and that the texts attributed to E in chs. 20–22 obviously form a collection of additions which show no connection with each other, it makes little sense to view them as part of a literary work E. Similarly F. V. Winnett (JBL 84 [1965] 5-7).

B. The earlier literary-critical view remains intact, namely, that a redactor has worked together already existing written texts of the Abraham story from the J and P traditions, as Gen. 11:27-32 and 21:1-7 in particular show. But the steady march of tradition that led to the written works continued after these became available. Consequently not all texts in Gen. 12–25 belong to J or P or R. The following (with the exception of single verses) are additions: 13:14-17; 14:1-24; 15:1-6; 15:7-21 (with the addition vv. 14-15); 18:16b-33; 20:1-18; 21:8-21; 21:22-34 (A and B); 22:1-19 (addition vv. 15-18); 22:20-24; 24:1-67; 25:1-6. This continued growth presupposes that oral narrative about Abraham continued after the written work received a fixed form. The individual story was the vital element of the patriarchal stories, whether it was first merely narrated orally or conceived at the same time as a written work.

One cannot assign these texts to a definite author or to a literary work; they are rather accretions to the already existing Abraham traditions (I agree with R. Rendtorff here). Just as the Yahwistic Abraham story grew out of individual narratives, so, after it had been put together, further individual narratives (or episodes) were added to it, together with promises and genealogies. The old narratives underwent variations, adaptations, and elaborations and some of this was attached to the already existing written Abraham story. Several written works existed side by side (J, P with substructures) and were accompanied and followed by a process of growth of individual traditions. This process led to the Yahwistic Abraham story as part of a larger work, reached beyond to the amalgamation of the two written works, J and P, and still further right up to the insertion of what is probably the latest text, ch. 14.

Several groups of texts can be distinguished among the additions, the most important being the promises where one can discern a tradition-history independent of J and P. Promises are added to narratives (Gen. 16:10,12; 13:14-17; 22:15-18) or are formed into promise narratives (Gen. 15:1-6; 15:7-21; 17). In other narratives which have been added, Abraham's position of precedence is based on his having received the promises (Gen. 18:18; 24:7). A narrative from the patriarchal period can be adapted from the perspective of a theological question (Gen. 20:1-18); the later problem of the justice of God in his exercise of judgment can be shaped into an episode (Gen. 18:18b-33); Abraham is presented as the one who believes the promise—the pious man who withstands a sore trial

(Gen. 22), as one who trusts in the guidance of God (Gen. 24), but also as the liberator (Gen. 14:13-17, 21-24), as the one who is blessed by the priest-king of Jerusalem (14:18-20), or as a mighty man of war (14:1-11).

C. It follows from this that, for an understanding of the figure of Abraham, one cannot tie oneself down to any one stage of the traditions.

We know only one thing with certainty about the Abraham of the patriarchal period, the point of departure of all these traditions: he was the father. This is what the texts say, and all later traditions agree. It is not possible to be more precise about Abraham's fatherhood. He was neither simply the father of Israel, because other peoples took their origin from him, nor ''the father of faith,'' because that is the interpretation of a later age. The fatherhood can be complemented negatively from two sides: he had a different life-style and a different religion from later Israel. In addition, the Abraham of the Yahwist stands in firm relationship to the history of Israel (Gen. 12:1-3), so firm that Yahweh becomes the God of Israel. This conception is taken up by P in a later stage and adapted out of his situation, a situation that revolved about the threat to the very existence of Israel and her survival; hence the determinative event for P was the making of the covenant; the covenant between God and Abraham (Gen. 17) is concerned with the guarantee of Israel's survival which is anchored in her relationship to God.

Besides these two conceptions there is a whole series of ways of understanding Abraham and his significance for each contemporary situation. Several lines can be distinguished. In one, the promises made to Abraham are determinative. This is represented in the independent history of the transmission of the promises and has its point of departure in the Yahwistic conception (C. Westermann, *The Promises to the Fathers. . .* [1976; 1980]; R. Rendtorff, BZAW 147 [1976]). In the other the person of Abraham and his relationship to God are determinative. This is more in P's line. While the former is more historically oriented (in J's line), the latter is more religious. Abraham is understood here as the believer (15:1-6), the one who walks before God (17:1), the just man who intervenes on behalf of the justice of God (18:16b-33), the one who fears God and has withstood the difficult test (ch. 22), and the one who trusts in the providence of God (ch. 24).

2. The Subsequent History and Significance of Abraham

Only by surveying the whole content of the Abraham traditions can one grasp that the figure of Abraham has a history, unique in breadth and depth, which leads through the Old Testament, the New Testament, and the Koran right into the present life of the three religions. This is set out in the Abraham tradition itself, in which Abraham is not restricted to any one line. Because he is neither the father of *a* people nor the founder of *a* religion, he can be father for Jews, Christians, and Muslims alike.

If one takes account of the fact that the diverse and multiform later history of Abraham is already set out in the traditions, then one will be more cautious about restricting him to any one of the many later interpretations. One cannot then limit him to that interpretation so important for the New Testament: Abraham, father of faith. This is but one interpretation in the text among many others. It is, therefore, in accordance with the diversity of the Abraham traditions when the New Testament interpretations of Paul, the letter to the Hebrews (11:5-22), and James are different. But more important than these differences, even more important than the attempts to give one interpretation precedence over the others, is the fact that the figure of Abraham as presented in the texts is preserved and handed on in the midst of all the diversity.

Consequently, without absolutizing any one interpretation, one will raise the question of common and overlapping material, and of what the texts say independently of later interpretations. What is common to the texts is summed up in the word "Father": a child is born, hence the questions of life, death, and the future. This basic phenomenon of the continuation of human life from one generation to the next is preordained in all other realms of human existence—in political history, the history of religion, economic history, and the history of culture. What Abraham stands for is the nonabsolutizing of these and other areas of life. The second matter common to the texts is linked indissolubly with the first, namely, the future of Abraham, which is decided for him by the birth of a child; it is the effective action of God which reaches him in one word, the promise of a child, the starting point of all other promises. The third matter common to the texts is Abraham's obvious relationship to God. Everything that happens, happens between Abraham and God, God and Abraham. The relationship is simply an element of human existence; it is independent of institutions, of cult in the later sense, of doctrine about God, of laws. It is of the essence of this relationship that there is as yet no religious polemic. The figure of Abraham as presented in the Genesis texts is, in its extension through time and space, an index of what is common and fundamental.

Structure, Origin, and Growth
of Genesis 25:19—36:43

Literature

Genesis 25:19—36:43: E. Meyer, "Der Stamm Jakob und die Entstehung der israelitischen Stämme," ZAW 6 (1886) 1-16. O. Eissfeldt, FRLANT 36 (1923) 145-157. L. Waterman, "Jacob, the Forgotten Supplanter," AJSL 55 (1938) 25-43. H. Eising, *Formgeschichtliche Untersuchung zur Jakoberzählung der Genesis* (diss. Münster, 1940). I. Engnell, "Jakob," SBU (1948). B. D. Napier, *From Faith to Faith* (1955) esp. 85-87. I. Fransen, "Jacob l'avisé," BVC 15 (1956) 66-79. R. L. Hicks, "Jacob (Israel)," IDB 2 (1962) 783. G. Wallis, "Die Geschichte der Jakob-Tradition" (Gemeinschaftsarbeit) W. Z. Halle 13 (1964) 427-440. B. Mariani and A. Cardinali, "Giacobbe patriarca, santo," *Bibliotheca Sanctorum. . .* 6 (1965) 332-343. J. Prado, "Jacob," EB 4 (1965) 282-290. W. Richter, "Das Gelübde als theologische Rahmung der Jakobüberlieferungen," BZ NF 11 (1967) 21-52. W. Gross, "Jakob, der Mann des Segens. Zu Traditionsgeschichte und Theologie der priesterschriftlichen Jakobüberlieferungen," Bib 49 (1968) 321-344. G. Wallis, *Geschichte und Überlieferungen. Gedanken über alttestamentliche Darstellungen der Frühgeschichte Israels und der Anfänge seines Königtums* (1968). B. W. Anderson, "The Contemporaneity of the Bible," *PrincSeminaryBull* 62 (1969) 38-50. J. M. Heuschen, "Jacob of de genadenvolle Uitverkiezing," EThL 45 (1969) 335-358. L. E. Toombs, "The Problematic of Preaching From the OT," Interp. 32 (1969) 306-308. J. G. Michell, "A Study of the Jacob Tradition in the Old Testament," Diss. Abstr 31 (1970/71) 457f-A. P. Weimar, "Aufbau und Struktur der priesterschriftlichen Jakobsgeschichte," ZAW 86 (1974) 174-203. J. Calloud, *Structural Analysis of Narrative*, SemeiaSupp 4 (1975). M. Fishbane, "Composition and Structure in the Jacob Cycle (Gen 25,19-35,33)," JJS 26 (1975) 15-38. R. Rendtorff, BZAW 146 (1976, 1977[2]); *Die Jakobgeschichte* 115-127. W. Thiel, *Die soziale Entwicklung Israels in vorstaatlicher Zeit* (diss. Berlin, 1976). J. F. Craghan, "The Elohist in Recent Literature," BThB 7 (1977) 23-35. P. D. Miscall, "The Jacob and Joseph Stories as Analogies," JSOT 6 (1978) 28-40. F. Diedrich, *Untersuchungen zur Jakoberzählung der Genesis* (diss.). T. L. Thompson, "Conflict of Themes in the Jacob Narratives," Semeia 15 (1979) 5-26. S. Schreiner, "Mischehen—Ehebruch—Ehescheidung. Beobachtungen zu Mal 2,10-16," ZAW 91 (1979) 207-228

Subsequent History of the Jacob Tradition: T. C. Vriezen, "La tradition de Jacob dans Osée XII," OTS 1 (1942) 64-78. E. M. Good, "Hosea and the Jacob Tradition," VT 16 (1966) 137-151. R. B. Coote, "Hosea XII," VT 21 (1971) 389-402. L. Ruppert, "Herkunft und Bedeutung der Jakob-Tradition bei Hosea," Bib 52 (1971) 488-504. F. Diedrich, *Die Anspielungen auf die Jakob-Tradition in Hosea 12,1-13,3. Ein literaturwissenschaftlicher Beitrag zur Exegese früher Prophetentexte, Forschung zur Bibel* 27 (1977).

1. History of Research

A. de Pury, *Promesse Divine.* . . (1975); C. Westermann, *Genesis 12–50. Erträge der Forschung* 48 (1975) 46-56.

As in the case of Gen. 12–25, so too here the history of research into the structure, origin, and growth of Gen. 25–36 is still young because it began only with the realization that each of the parts of the patriarchal story underwent its own independent process of growth. The outlines stand apart from each other and their interrelation has scarcely been discussed. H. Gunkel takes four main blocks as his point of departure: Jacob and Esau, Jacob and Laban, divine manifestations, Jacob's children. R. de Vaux follows him and likewise W. E. Rast, *Tradition History and the Old Testament* (1972). M. Noth, on the other hand, proceeds from geographical location and distinguishes an east and a west Jordan tradition (*A History of Pentateuchal Traditions* [1948; 1966³; Eng 1972]). A. Jepsen (WZ[L] 2/3 [1953-54] 167-281), G. Wallis (see bibliog. above, 1964, 1968), and A. Weiser (RGG³) follow him; O. Eissfeldt, following the principles of literary criticism, starts from the source L, which he says describes the tribal story which subsequently takes on and is overlaid with novelistic features. A de Pury regards the Jacob story in its entirety as a coherent unified narrative which has its center in the divine manifestation of Gen. 28 with its promise and vow; W. Richter understands the vow as the theological frame of the Elohistic narrative. All explanations advanced so far presuppose that the text of Gen. 25–36 as it now lies before us has developed in several stages. There are, however, recent explanations which contest this and oppose to such a "diachronic" explanation a "synchronic" explanation based on linguistic material which does away with all literary, form, and traditio-historical considerations, e.g., J. Fokkelman, *Narrative Art in Genesis* (1973; Eng. 1975) and M. Fishbane (JJS 26 [1975] 15-38). But the question arises whether such one-sided attempts to solve the problem are in accord with the texts. A broader unity rightly understood does not necessarily exclude the working together of originally independent narratives. A purely synchronic explanation certainly brings into focus a point of view to which all too little attention has been given hitherto; but it misjudges the nature of texts whose origin and growth are more than literary.

2. Enumerative Blocks

The distinction between narrative and enumerative texts, between narration and enumeration, is a presupposition for the structure as well as for the origin and growth of the blocks. As in Gen. 12–25 genealogies and itineraries go further, forming the framework as well.

Genealogies frame the whole action, as in Gen. 12–25, with birth, marriage, death, and burial (29:19-26; 35; 36 [partly]); and in between (27:26—28:30; 29:31—30:24). Gen. 26–36 is thereby given its character of a family story. The birth of the two brothers stands at the beginning (25:19-20, 26b [P]) and is expanded by a narrative insertion (vv. 21-26a [J]), thus ensuring that this part of the patriarchal story will deal with both Jacob and Esau and not with Jacob alone. The next piece of genealogical information treats of the marriage of the two brothers (27:46—28:9, P), Jacob's marriages (29:21-30, J), likewise expanded by narrative; this is followed immediately by the account of the eleven sons of Jacob (29:31–30:24) with narrative expansions (P on the contrary is purely enumerative) and the details of the death of Rachel (35:16-20) and Isaac

(35:28-29, P). The death and burial of Jacob come only in Gen. 47–50.

There is a change in the itineraries here over against Gen. 12–25 and 26. In place of the report of the wandering of a group of small cattle nomads there enters a structure well-known and very often used in narrative literature throughout the world, flight—return. The cause is the conflict between the brothers (27:41-45) which colors and gives coherence to the whole field of tension from the flight to the return (this is in agreement with A. de Pury). The structure flight–return makes the transition from the small individual narrative to a broader narrative complex into which various episodes can be assumed. Sedentary life is probably a presupposition for such a narrative structure. Gen. 25–36 is not a single, self-contained short story, as is Gen. 37–50, taking the place of the short individual narrative; it is rather something in between. The broader narrative complex also contains short individual narratives and bears the stamp of this stage of transition (this would require modifications in A. de Pury's presentation, especially in Part V, chs. 2-3).

The arc of tension, flight–return, begins in Gen. 27:41-45 and is conceived as a whole in the perspective of chs. 29–31 as well as of chs. 32–33 (this is against H. Gunkel's view that chs. 32–33 are additional embellishments, as well as against M. Noth and others who are of the view that the stories originated in different places in east and west Jordan). Chs. 35–36 on the other hand do not belong to this complex. This change has impressed itself on the form of the itineraries: here they are no longer independent units, as in Gen. 12–25, but are fitted into the narratives and adapted to the structure, flight–return.

3. Narrative Blocks

The narrative complex, Gen. 27–33, leading from the flight to the return is assembled out of various elements of different origin. The theme is a conflict or rivalry between the brothers Jacob and Esau. The conflict between Jacob and Laban (29–31) is set within it and into this that between Leah and Rachel (29:31–30:24). Gen. 12–25 deals with what happens between parents and children, Gen. 25–36 with what happens between brothers. The vertical dimension of survival from one generation to the next is now replaced by the horizontal dimension of struggle for existence and status. The conflict between Jacob and Esau forms one narrative unity; it is prepared for in the introduction (25:19-34), set in motion by the deception over the blessing (27:1-40), and rises to a climax in the murderous intent of the deceived from which the deceiver escapes by flight (27:41-45). The conflict is resolved when the brother meets his brother on his return after a long absence and in changed circumstances (32–33). There is a unified plan here; the idea of flight (27:41-45) already presupposes a stay abroad as well as a later return. But this unity of plan does not exclude the taking up of blocks of other origin. Deliberate insertion and assimilation of such originally independent units is particularly obvious where chs. 29–31, as well as 29:31—30:24, are taken up into the story and where the encounters with God are fitted as the joins of this complex.

The introduction (25:19-34) stands outside the narrative structure, flight—return, which begins only in 27:41-45. It consists of originally independent units which are only loosely tacked together. The Jacob story begins with the genealogy of Isaac (25:19, 20, 26b[P]) which is brought to a conclusion with 35:28-29(P). This forms the frame for the note about the birth of Jacob and Esau (25:21-25a), elaborated in narrative style, which at the same time introduces the conflict motif. It is taken up in the narrative concluding with the sayings.

The Jacob-Laban narrative, Gen. 29–31, which would require only a brief note in the narrative of the conflict between Jacob and Esau, fills out the period of Jacob's sojourn after his flight. The detailed story, which takes the place of the note, does not presuppose Gen. 27 and 32–33, apart from the flight motif, and Esau does not appear in it. Gen. 29–31 could be narrated as a whole and independently without the framework; in the overall plan it is a variant of the conflict motif, here between uncle and nephew. It too begins with deception and ends with reconciliation. It is a self-contained conflict narrative which has been skillfully worked into Gen. 27–33 as an episode; it too is composite. The introduction, 29:1-14, has independent narrative parallels in Gen. 24 and Ex. 2.

The case of Gen. 29:31—30:24 is rather similar; it is an insertion into an insertion. It consists of genealogical notes tacked together and elaborated in narrative style, all independent of the Jacob-Laban conflict. This is a third form of the conflict motif, a conflict between Jacob's two wives, Leah and Rachel. The many parallels show that these texts which deal with birth and name giving were originally independent.

The encounters with God and the sanctuary narratives are also originally independent (28:10-22; 32:1-2; 32:24-32; 35:1-7; 35:9-15). H. Gunkel recognized this. Jacob alone appears here, never Esau. The parallels show that they belong to a particular genre of narratives. But they have been inserted into and attached to the whole in accordance with a definite plan: the middle passage, 29–31, is separated from the frame, 27 and 32–33, by the two interludes, 28:10-22 and 32:1-2 (together with 32:24-32), which narrate encounters with God. Their content has an important function in the composition in that it brings to the fore the theological aspect of the Jacob-Esau story.

The conclusion, Gen. 35–36, consists mainly of genealogical texts (35:8, 16-20, 23-26, 28-29; the whole of ch. 36 except for vv. 6-8), death notices, and the continuance of genealogical collateral lines (the descendants of Esau). Then there is an appendix on the sanctuary at Bethel, 35:1-7 and 35:9-15(P), which stands quite outside the conflict motif of Jacob and Esau and belongs to sanctuary narratives.

Chs. 26 and 34 are not part of the Jacob-Esau story; both are later additions. Fragments of the Isaac tradition are brought together in ch. 26, while ch. 34 is an episode from the period of the judges attached to Jacob and his sons.

4. Promises and Blessings

The promises formed an essential constitutive part of the texts in Gen. 12–25; they ran right through the whole Abraham story and formed independent narratives (Gen. 15:1-6, 7-21; 17). It is considerably different in Gen. 25–36: the promises appear in only a few texts and their significance is not such as to determine the whole (against M. Noth and A. de Pury). The whole complex of Gen. 25–36 contains only three detailed promise texts corresponding to those in Gen. 12–25, namely, 28:3-4; 28:13-15; and 35:11-12. Two of these belong to P, 28:3-4 and 35:11-12. Both belong to the late stage in the history of the patriarchal promises and both are close to ch. 17. There remains for the older layers only 28:13-14, the promise from the Bethel narrative; but this too, as its language shows, belongs to a relatively late stage. The promise of God's presence or aid, 28:15 (it occurs besides in 31:3), is to be distinguished from this; related to it are Gen. 31:5; 31:42; 32:9, 12; 35:3. It is characteristic of the Jacob-Esau narrative and accords with its function; it is originally and properly a promise for a journey. This promise of aid allows one to assume that it goes back to the oldest layer of the Jacob-Esau text, though it has not such a determinative significance as does the promise of the son in Gen. 12–25.

The blessing, however, does have a dominant significance for the Jacob-Esau narratives. The blessing is central in the rivalry between the brothers both at the beginning in ch. 27 and again at the end when the brothers meet on Jacob's return (ברכה = "gift"). It is central too, though in a different way, in the two insets, the blessing of the cattle, chs. 29–31, and of the womb, 29:31—30:24. A blessing is wrested in the struggle in one of the encounters with God (32:24-32). It plays an essential role in the conflict between Jacob and Laban in that God has blessed Laban for Jacob's sake (30:27, 30). When Jacob and Esau meet, Jacob points to his children whom God has bestowed on him (35:5, 11). The promise of aid is close to the blessing, particularly with its formula, "I will do you good" (32:9, 12).

The survey of Gen. 25–36 shows that it is the blessing, not the promise, that is in the foreground. It shows further that over against Gen. 12–25, Gen. 25–36 has its own history of growth. There is in addition another difference: a characteristic running through Gen. 12–25 is God's direct intervention in the history of people together with his direct address to them. Both are rarer in Gen. 25–36, and in their place human institutions such as legal relationship, contracts, cult places, and traditions acquire increased significance. This further favors the view that in many respects Gen. 25–36 reflects a later stage of development.

5. The Overall Plan

The overall plan is clearly recognizable. The narrative complex of Jacob's flight before his brother Esau and their meeting at Jacob's return forms the central part, chs. 27–33. Jacob's sojourn with Laban, chs. 29–31, is inserted into this, and into the sojourn in its turn the birth and naming of Jacob's sons, 29:31–30:24. Two divine manifestations frame chs. 29–31: Bethel (28:10-22), and later Mahanaim (32:1-3) and Penuel (32:24-32).

The introduction (25:19-34) and the conclusion (chs. 35–36) were subsequently prefixed and appended to the entire complex.

6. The Subsequent History of the Jacob Tradition

The figure of Jacob lived on in a fundamentally different way from that of Abraham. The trio, "Abraham, Isaac, and Jacob," certainly belong together; but what they have in common ends there. Hosea 12 can pronounce negatively on Jacob in the context of an accusation against Israel. Abraham is the father, but Jacob is never spoken of as "the father." On the other hand Jacob *is* Israel; but Abraham is never equated with Israel in the same way; Israel is "seed of Abraham," but not Abraham. Because Jacob-Israel (very often in synonymous parallelism in Second Isaiah) represents Israel across the whole of her history, it too can be the object of Hosea's accusation.

The Birth of Esau and Jacob

Literature

Genesis 25:19-26: E. Nestle, "Genesis XXV 22," ET 22 (1911) 230. R. A. Kraft, "A Note on the Oracle of Rebecca (Gen XXV 23)," JThS 13 (1962) 318-320. I. Kollar, "Gen 25,22-26" [in Hebr.], BetM 50 (1972) 353-357. P. Weimar, *Untersuchungen zur priesterschriftlichen Exodusgeschichte* (1973). G. Krinetzki, " 'Zwei Völker sind in deinem Schoss'. Eine Stilanalyse zu Gen 25,21-26a," Fests. J. Auer (1975) 74-82. D. K. Stuart, *Studies in Early Hebrew Meter*, HSS 13 (1976). P. Hoffken, *Untersuchungen zu den Begründungselementen der Völkerorakel des AT* (diss. Bonn, 1977).

Genesis 25:25-26: F. L. W. Schwartz, *Der Ursprung der Mythologie* (1860) esp. 138-140. R. Andree, *Ethnographische Parallelen und Vergleiche* (1878) esp. 271-273. F. M. T. Böhl, "Wortspiele im Alten Testament," JPOS 6 (1926) 196-212 = *Opera Minora* (1953) 11-25, 475-476. M. Naor, "Ya'aqob and Yiśrā'el," ZAW 49 (1931) 317-321. G. Jacob, "Der Name Jacob," *Litterae Orientales* 54 (1933) 16-19. L. Waterman, "The Authentication of Conjectural Glosses," JBL 56 (1937) 253-255. J. Schmidt, "Das Wortspiel im AT," BZ 24 (1938) 15-16. S. Yeivin, "Ya'qob'El," JEA 45 (1959) 16-18. M. Rutten, "Un lot de tablettes de Manana," RA 54 (1960) esp. 149. D. N. Freedman, "The Original Name of Jacob," IEJ 13 (1963) 125-126. C. Grottanelli, "Il mito origini di Tiro: due 'versioni' duali," OrAnt 11 (1972) 49-63. B. S. Jackson, "The Problem of Exod XXI 22-25 (Ius Talionis)," VT 23 (1973) 273-304 esp. 292. J. Bartlett, "The Brotherhood of Edom," JSOT 4 (1977) 2-27. J. J. Stamm, "Ein ugaritisch-hebräisches Verbum und seine Ableitungen," ThZ 35 (1979) 5-9.

Genesis 25:27-28: D. W. Thomas, "The Root אָהֵב 'Love' in Hebrew," ZAW 57-(1939) 57-64. G. Gerleman, *Contributions to the OT Terminology of the Chase* (1946).

Text

25:19 These are the descendants of Isaac, son of Abraham. Abraham begot Isaac.

20 Now Isaac was forty years old when he took as his wife Rebekah, the daughter of Bethuel the Aramean of Paddan-aram, the sister of Laban the Aramean.

21 And Isaac prayed[a] to Yahweh on behalf of his wife because she was barren, and Yahweh heard his[b] prayer. And Rebekah his wife became pregnant.

22 When the children were crushing[a] each other in her womb she said: If this is so with me, then why[b] do I "live"?[c]

23 So she went to inquire of Yahweh; and Yahweh said to her: Two nations are in your body, Two peoples[a] separating themselves[b] (even)
from your womb. One people is stronger than the other, and the
elder[c] shall serve the younger.[d]

24 When the time came for her to give birth there were indeed twins[a] in
her womb.

25 The first came out red,[a] hairy all over like a cloak of hair, and they
called[b] him Esau.[c]

26 Then his brother came out, his hand grasping Esau's heel,[a] and they
called him Jacob. Now Isaac was sixty years old when they were
born.

27 The boys grew up and Esau became a skilful hunter, a man of the
open field, while Jacob was a quiet man, staying among the tents.

28 Isaac preferred Esau because he supplied him from the hunt, but
Rebekah preferred Jacob.

21a עתר in Arab., "to sacrifice"; J. Wellhausen: "the ideas are close to each
other." **b** The ל expresses the efficient cause, Ges-K §121f.
22a Gk uses the same word as in Lk. 1:41, 44; but there it is a good omen. **b** זה emphasizes the question, Ges-K §136e. **c** Add חיה with Syr; cf. Gen. 27:46; J. Skinner,
comm. ad loc., for other suggestions.
23a לאם, poetic; elsewhere in Pentateuch only in Gen. 27:39, in same context. **b** Probably an addition, so BHK and R. A. Kraft, JThS 13 (1962)
318. **cd** רב צעיר, in the sense of the elder, the younger; E. A. Speiser: "exact parallel in the acc. pair *rabū—seḥrū* in family law."
24a Contraction from תאמים, so Sam, Gen. 38:27; cf. Gk Θωμᾶς.
25a Used in this sense elsewhere only of David (1 Sam. 16:12; 17:42). **b** The plural "one," Ges-K §144a. The change between pl. (v. 25) and sing. (v. 26) can conform
with the manner of the etymologies. **c** The name Esau cannot be explained from the
Hebrew.
26a On עקב, R. B. Coote, VT 21 (1971) 389-402.

Form

Vv. 21-26a (J) are framed by vv. 19-20, 26b (P). V. 26b, "Now Isaac was sixty
years old when they were born," presupposes the account of the birth of the two
sons; אתם presupposes vv. 24-26a grammatically. The introduction to the Jacob-
Esau stories, therefore (vv. 19-26), has been put together by R out of J and P, just
as has the introduction to the Abraham stories. The two introductions are similar
too in other respects. Gen. 25:19-26(28), like 11:17-32, is not a narrative but an
expanded genealogy. As in 11:17-32, so too here R has constructed a coherent,
self-contained succession of events out of elements of P and J: heading, the descendants of Isaac (v. 19); Isaac marries Rebekah (v. 20); cure of her barrenness
and her pregnancy (v. 21); the two infants crushing each other, complaint and oracle (vv. 22f.); birth, individual traits, and naming of the twins (vv. 24-26a); the
note on Isaac's age (v. 26b); the children grow up; their occupations (v. 27); transition to ch. 27 (v. 28).

Every individual event of the genealogy is part of the sequence of happenings. What is peculiar to the genealogical introduction to the Jacob-Esau story is
that twins are born; thus a story is introduced which deals with their coexistence
and their confrontation; consciously and deliberately this differs from the introduction in Gen. 11:27-32. Everything reported here remains within the frame of
the family with the exception of vv. 22f. which are an oracle about the nations.
That this is an independent unit inserted here is clear because v. 24 must follow di-

rectly on v. 21 (the sequence, ". . .became pregnant. When the time came for her to give birth. . .," is frequent in the Old Testament). V. 24b too should properly precede v. 22f. Narratives often grow out of remarks in the genealogy; v. 21 as well as vv. 22ff. are such narrative sentences. Seen thus, they are almost parallel to each other. If vv. 19-28 are read without vv. 22-23, and this latter understood as an originally independent unit inserted here, then both are clearer and more comprehensible.

Setting

Gen. 25:19-28 is the introduction to the Jacob-Esau story constructed by R, corresponding to 11:27-32. R again joins P (vv. 19-20, 26b) with J. There is no basis for separation into sources J and E (following A. Dillmann, H. Gunkel, O. Procksch, and others). R shows by means of this introduction that what follows is dealing with the two brothers and their rivalry. The origin and growth of vv. 22-23 is distinct from this; it is a *vaticinium ex eventu*, the intention of which is to give grounds in antiquity for Israel's victory over Edom. It belongs to the period of David, along with other passages that give an anticipated explanation, e.g., Gen. 27:29; 49:10. R has inserted it from a quite different context in such a way that its content suits the present passage while leaving clear that it is of another origin.

Commentary

[**25:19-20**]   In P, 25:19f. follows the report of the death and burial of Abraham (25:7-10). The story of Isaac now begins, that is, the story of his family which commences with his marriage (v. 20). The sentence which follows the heading, "Abraham begot Isaac," is puzzling here (so too E. A. Speiser and others); perhaps it is meant only to underscore the preceding words, "son of Abraham." Rebekah's origin is reported accurately and in detail; it is just as important for P as it is for the narrative in ch. 24 to which these verses are parallel. (For Bethuel and Laban, cf. comm. 24:15-16, 26-27.) פדן ארם occurs only in P (Gen. 25:20; 28:2, 5-7; 32:18; 33:18; 35:9, 26; 46:15; 48:7); it is the same region as in Hos. 12:13, שדה ארם (R. T. O'Callaghan, *Aram Naharaim* [1948; 1961[2]]).

[**25:21**]   Vv. 21-28 come from J. It is due to the transition from P to J that v. 21 is stylistically clumsy. One would expect a sentence something like 11:30 at the beginning: "But Rebekah was barren. . .." V. 21a would follow better on this: "And Isaac prayed to Yahweh on behalf of his wife. . ."; the addition in v. 21, "and Rebekah his wife," would then be no longer necessary. A comparison with Gen. 30:1-2 (Rachel) shows that v. 21 is concerned with the brief reproduction of an event which has a different ring when narrated. What is simply narrated here is taken out and compassed in the brief reproduction in two forms of the same verb עתר: "Isaac prayed to Yahweh on behalf of his wife—Yahweh heard his prayer." We cannot derive from this what really happened and what was said. It is a term particularly in evidence in the plagues of Egypt (Ex. 8–10; cf. R. Albertz, THAT II [1976] 385f.). The result of Isaac's intercession is that Rebekah becomes pregnant. A narrative from the patriarchal period, now lost to us, lies behind this brief resumption. It is in accord with patriarchal religion in that the father is the intercessor. V. 21 is continued in v. 24.

[**25:22-23**]   The independent unit vv. 22-23 is directed towards the oracle in v. 23 which announces the subjection of an older and greater by a younger and smaller people. It is the pride of the victor speaking who has overcome a larger people (2 Sam. 8:13f.), just as the divine oracle had announced it to the ancestress. The author, whom one can well imagine at the court of David (like the author of Gen. 14:18-20), takes hold of a motif from the patriarchal period, the birth of twin sons to Rebekah, who were later regarded as the progenitors of Israel and Edom. The story told that the two children had tangled in her womb, that the mother regarded this as a bad omen and raised a cry of lament. To this extent the motif can go back to the patriarchal period. There are other examples of enmity between two brothers being traced back to the mother's womb where they confronted each other. Examples may be found in the commentary of J. Chaine (1949), P. Radin, ErJb 17 (1949) 359-419, and among the Indians of North America; H. Gunkel mentions an example from Apollodorus, Acrisius and Proetus, sons of Abas, king of Argos.

The mother's cry of lament can express fear in the face of death or of a miscarriage or the fate of the child as yet unborn. It is the primeval cry of "Why?" about the meaning of life, an expression of anguish across the whole of human history; compare Gen. 27:46 (Rebekah); Jer. 20:18; Tob. 3:15; 1 Macc. 2:7,13; 2 Esd. 5:35 (C. Westermann, ThB 24 [1964] 291).

The sentence, "And she went to inquire of Yahweh," presupposes the institution of consulting an oracle which arose only in the sedentary period. The verb דרשׁ is used about fifty times in the sense of "inquiring of Yahweh"; the texts are predominantly from the period of the monarchy and refer throughout to an institution of the Yahweh oracle (C. Westermann, ThB 55 [1974] 177-183). The sentence then points to the same period of origin as the divine answer.

[**25:23**]   The divine answer is rhythmic, like Gen. 9:25-27; 27:27-29, 39-40, and the tribal sayings. The oracular answer consists of two double-threes (יפרדו is a subsequent addition) in the second pers. sing. directed to the questioner; names are not mentioned but only hinted at. It predicts that two nations (גוים and לאמים are in poetic parallelism) will come forth from the mother's womb (v. 23a) and that the elder will be subjected to the younger (v. 23b). This can be designated a *vaticinium ex eventu*; but what is of the essence of the oracle is the extraordinary poetic craft by which two widely separate historical periods are joined together. The generation of the early period of the monarchy sees in a simple family event of the remote patriarchal period the beginning of what it now experiences. A saying like this can explain why the patriarchal stories continued to live in the period of Israel's monarchy. This is further confirmed by the close parallel in Gen. 27:29, 40: the early period of the monarchy must have had a particular interest in anchoring contemporary happenings in the patriarchal period, and it is this interest which is the background of the Yahwist's overall plan when at the time that the great historical works arose J joined the patriarchal story to the story of the people.

[**25:24-26a**]   The birth of the twins (v. 24) follows on v. 21. A genealogical detail is expanded in narrative form. Only at the birth does it transpire that there are twins. It becomes clear yet again that vv. 22f. have been inserted later. The birth of twins everywhere introduces a special situation (K. K. Reimschneider, *Babylonische Geburtsomina in hethitischer Übersetzung* [1970]: there was an omen in the birth of twin boys). This is clear too from the close parallel in Gen. 38:27-30 where it is also a question of which of the two is the elder. This is understandable because the birth of twins raises the question of so incisive a right as that of the firstborn which is so determinative and important in the area of family rights (in Babylonian family law the eldest inherited a double share). Could not the one born at least on the same day lay claim to the same right?

[25:25] "The first who came out was ruddy." One expects that he be named after this quality and the name could only be "Edom." But a second quality is mentioned, "hairy all over like a cloak of hair" (cf. Zech. 13:4; the "hairy cloak" of the prophet Elijah, 2 Kings 2, and of John the Baptist, Mt. 3:4); one expects him to be named accordingly, שֵׂעָר, Se'ir (Gen. 35:8, 9, the land of Edom, the mountain range Se'ir); but what follows is: "they called him Esau," which follows neither of the qualities mentioned. The only explanation can be that analogy with v. 26 required an explanation of the name of the other twin; but because the narrator at that time could not explain the name Esau, just as we today cannot, he advances instead two allusions which presuppose the equation, well known to his listeners, Esau = Edom and Seir as the land of Edom. These explanations can have been of different origin. The word אַדְמוֹנִי "reddish" or "ruddy," occurs elsewhere only in 1 Sam. 16:12 and 17:42 to portray the handsome youth David. It will have had a meaning like this as well in the etymology at hand to Gen. 25:25. The intention of the other etymology, "hairy all over like a cloak of hair," is "to depict Esau as a sort of Enkidu-figure which is almost the same as 'shaggy with hair was his whole body' applied to Enkidu in Gilg. Tab. I,II,36" (E. A. Speiser). This would obviously correspond to the qualities of Esau in vv. 27 and 29-34. Since F. Delitzsch a link between Esau and Οὐσῶος in Philo of Byblos has been suggested; he too is one of a pair of brothers and has clothes of animal skins (C. Grottanelli, Or Ant 11 [1972] 49-63).

[25:26a] V. 26a differs notably from v. 25, mentioning in three short sentences the birth, the explanation of the name, and the name of the second twin corresponding to it. As is often the case, the child is named after an event which happened at the birth: his hand is grasping his brother's heel; this has nothing to do either with the confrontation in v. 22 or the later meaning, "to deceive" (Gen. 27:36; Hos. 12:4; Jer. 9:3); rather it is a sign observed at the birth which is open to different interpretations (J. Skinner: "to secure the advantage of being born first," like the red thread in Gen. 38:28). The explanation of the name Jacob from the noun עָקֵב = "heel" is no longer aware of the original meaning of the theophoric name: Iaḫkub-ila, "may God protect" (M. Noth, Fests. A. Alt [1953] 142 = Ges. Aufs. II [1971] 213-233); the explanation from עקב = "deceive" (Gen. 27:36), which Hos. 12:4 (Jer. 9:3?) has transferred to Gen. 25:26, is therefore different from the intention of v. 26 (cf. R. B. Coote, VT 21 [1971] 390; also bibliog. above).

[25:26b] The בְּלֶדֶת אֹתָם clamps the double יצא of vv. 25 and 26a together. The account of the birth of the twins in P is not divided; R joins J and P together by framing vv. 21-26a (J) between vv. 19-20 and v. 26b(P). Details about Jacob's age are found at the beginning and at the end of v. 26b.

[25:27-28] Vv. 27-28 stand outside the frame as they form the transition to vv. 29-34 and ch. 27. The development of the boys and their occupations belong to the genealogy, like Gen. 21:20 (Ishmael). A note is attached to the occupation of each that prepares the way for v. 21. Throughout the whole of world literature narratives are often introduced with two brothers embracing different occupations. This motif is a sign that very early in the history of mankind there was serious reflection on the different forms of civilization, and mirrors in its turn historical developments; new forms of civilization arose, older forms disappeared; there was opposition and coexistence between them (see comm. on vv. 29-34 below). Here living in tents (not in houses) claims to be the civilized life-style; different from this is "the man of the open field" (or wilderness) who for the most part spends the night outside in the open.

Different forms of civilization coexist; now one, now the other is preferred; the preference of father and mother (cf. Gen. 37) follows personal lines, the mother loving the son who stays at home, and occupational lines, the father loving Esau because of the products of the chase.

The Pot of Lentil Soup

Literature

Genesis 25:29-34: B. Heller, "Der Erbstreit Esaus und Jakobs im Lichte verwandter Sagen," ZAW 44 (1926) 317-320. P. P. Saydon, "Some Unusual Ways of Expressing the Superlative in Hebrew and Maltese," VT 4 (1954) 432-433. E. Ullendorff, "The Contribution of South Semitics to Hebrew Lexicography," VT 6 (1956) 190-198. B. G. Boschi, "Tradizioni de Pentateuco su Edom," RivBib 15 (1967) 369-383. W. Brueggemann, "Amos' Intercessory Formula," VT 19 (1969) 385-399.

Text

25:29   One day when Jacob was boiling[a] a soup, Esau came in from the field exhausted.

30   And Esau said to Jacob: Let me swallow[a] some of that red soup, that red[b] soup there; I am exhausted. That is why he was called Edom.

31   But Jacob said: Sell me first[a] your right as firstborn.

32   And Esau replied: I am dying of hunger! what use to me is my right as firstborn!

33   And Jacob said: First swear to me! And he swore to him, and sold Jacob his right as firstborn.[a]

34   Jacob then gave Esau bread and the bowl of lentil soup. He ate and drank, rose up and went. He thus disdained[a] his right as firstborn.

29a זוד only here in its basic meaning of "to cook."

30a לעט hiph. hapax.   **b** Gk and Vg appear to differentiate (so too A. Dillmann) with the double אדם; however, the repetition is deliberate.

31a כיום here in the sense of "first of all."

33a C. J. Mullo-Weir, "Nuzi," in *Archaeology and OT Studies*, ed. D. W. Thomas (1967) 73-86; perhaps a Nuzi parallel to Esau's sale of his right as firstborn: "a man sells his brother an orchard or garden for three sheep; this apparently unequal transaction may conceal a birthright exchange" (76f.).

34a בזה, "to express one's disdain by gesture or word" (B. Jacob); elsewhere in the Pentateuch only in Num. 15:31.

Form and Setting

Gen. 25:29-34 is a short, simple, and self-contained narrative inserted here in connection with the genealogical information about the occupations of Esau and Jacob in v. 27; previously it was an independent narrative about the shepherd and the hunter. The same motif runs through it as through vv. 22-23, namely, the younger gains the upper hand over the elder, in vv. 22-23 in the political field, in vv. 29-34 in the economic. It is originally a "civilization myth" (V. Maag, ThZ 13 [1957] 418-429) about the shepherd who gained supremacy over the hunter, and could well have had its origin in the Transjordan where the conditions existed for such a transition. The narrative was then applied to the brothers Esau and Jacob. Esau's attitude towards the loss of his birthright shows that this "Esau" has nothing to do with the Esau of ch. 27. Further, in ch. 33 Esau is portrayed as another person from the Esau of 25:29-34. The "Esau" of the present narrative is neither the tribal ancestor nor the representative of Edom; the etymology in v. 30 is an appendage. What is said about Edom here is in contradiction to what is said in ch. 36 and in the rest of the Old Testament, namely, that it is a people of ancient culture known for its cultivated wisdom.

On the other hand, the caricature makes good sense when the narrative is understood as portraying rivalry between two states; the aspiring shepherd speaks, triumphant and mocking, as he makes fun of the crude, clumsy, and stupid hunter. This is in no wise to be understood as a characterization of the individual Esau. The background is rather that of a self-conscious, waxing civilization: "the shepherd by his planning and regularity has shown himself more capable of coming to terms with life" (V. Maag, op. cit). The older civilization of the hunter and gatherer, which once dominated the whole region, must withdraw into the wilds and lose its significance. When the narrative about the lentil soup is understood in this way, it provides a valuable attestation to the history of civilization, the only one among the patriarchal stories; the civilization of the small-cattle nomads of the patriarchal period looks back on the still older civilization of the hunters and gatherers which is well known throughout the whole world as an early form of civilization, remnants of which remain right up to the present day. The story is applied to Esau and Jacob in order to show that the rivalry between the two brothers extends to civilization and economy and is a determining factor therein. What was really a primeval motif (V. Maag, a civilization myth) has been taken up into the introduction to the Jacob-Esau story (cf. the brothers Cain and Abel) so as to point without comment towards that human dimension in which the Esau-Jacob event is to be played out.

Commentary

[25:29-34]   V. 29 introduces the action; the narrative cannot have begun in this way. The exposition is contained in v. 27. While the narrative was still independent it must have begun with something corresponding to v. 27. The action begins with Esau coming from the hunt ravenously hungry, meeting his brother who is preparing a soup, and demanding to "devour" it. It ends with Jacob acceding to the demand (v. 34) after he has bartered for the birthright, which Esau yields to him and confirms by oath without more ado. The sole purpose of this action, but a few moments in the ordinary course of everyday affairs, is from first to last to set the reflective, clever, farsighted younger one (the shepherd) over against the crude elder (the hunter).

[25:30-31]   Esau's words to Jacob as his eyes fall on the seething pot are a deliberate caricature; הלעיטני = "let me swallow" is not intended to reproduce Esau's actual words but rather to portray his desire (the verb occurs only here; as background a noun "jawbone" is conjectured). The same holds for the object of his desire, "that red soup, that red soup there" (the color includes what we call "brown"), the rough and ready description of the pot twice blurted out; Esau neither knows nor cares what the soup is called. The impression is aroused of a rough man coarse in speech. We meet here a phenomenon both important and well known in the history of civilization: aspiring, climbing status "puts down" the status it has suppressed. In a few strokes it sketches the drama; the one who is growing economically strong despises the one who is waning. This is the root of many social disasters and conflicts. The last sentence of v. 30 is a later etiological appendage which interrupts and disturbs the flow of the narrative. Here "Esau" is not the father of the people of Edom as in vv. 22-23, but the representative of a status.

H. Gunkel: "Jacob is clever and farsighted." Jacob thinks of the future and grasps an opportunity to get on as it presents itself. He demands of his hungry brother as counterpledge (מכר) the בכרה, the right of the firstborn. The word does not occur often in the Old Testament (apart from 25:29-34 only in Gen. 27:36; 43:33; 1 Chron. 5:1, 2; Deut. 21:17), whereas בכר is frequent. Family law was handed down orally in the family; it appears only once in the legal codices (Deut. 21:17). The present text has not in mind particular, established rights, such as the right to a double share of the property, but priority in a general sense—the general prior claim that the elder has.

[25:32]   Esau's answer accords with what he said in v. 30: "I am almost dying of hunger—what use to me is my right as firstborn?" The first part of the answer is not to be understood as, "I must die sometime," but, "I am going to die," i.e., "I am almost dying of hunger. . ." (P. P. Saydon, bibliog. above).

[25:33]   Jacob wants security and makes Esau confirm the transaction by oath; this he does. The second part emphasizes that Esau has thereby lost his birthright for ever.

[25:34]   Esau now receives the pot of soup that he wanted so much, together with bread and drink, a complete meal. עדשים = "lentils," well known from early times in many places in the near east; fragments of lentils have been found in clay jars. The cultivation of vegetables in moderate measure is compatible with the life-style of shepherds.

The second part, "a staccato succession of five verbal forms" (E. A. Speiser), is a further caricature of the rough, obtuse hunter who, after he has devoured everything, gets up and goes away as if nothing had happened. The narrator says by way of conclusion what the listeners sense: thus did Esau disdain his birthright! The remark in 25:5-6 also shows how important this is for later generations.

Purpose and Thrust

On 25:19-34: the introduction to chs. 25–36 that the redactor has inserted shows clearly what this part of the patriarchal story is meant to be about: rivalry, opposition, is part of the coexistence of brothers in a family. The reason for it is that there are privileges which are at the same time vulnerable.

The intention of the redactor in inserting 29:19-34 is to show by way of a prolog that the conflict among brothers living together arises out of the family as the basic form of community (25:19-21[22], 25-26, 27-28), and that it goes on from there into the economic-cultural area (vv. 29-34) and the civil-political (vv. 22-23). Conflicts are part of human coexistence in all areas. This is unfolded in the subsequent narratives about Esau and Jacob. It serves as a corrective to that understanding of brotherhood which one-sidedly idealizes it as something qualified only by mutual love; but this is not truly biblical. In both the Old Testament and the New brotherly existence is characterized by the responsibility which arises out of belonging together, but just as much by the affirmation and prosecution of conflicts.

Isaac and Abimelech

Literature

Genesis 26:1-35: D. A. Lutz, *The Isaac Tradition in the Book of Genesis* (diss. Drew), DissAbstr 29 (1968/69) 2135A.

Genesis 26:1-14: A. Alt, "The Settlement of the Israelites in Palestine," in *Essays on OT History and Religion* (1939, 1966) 135-169 = KS I(1953; 1963³) 126-175. Y. M. Grintz, "The Philistines in Gerar and the Philistines on the Sea Coast" [in Hebr.], in *Studies in Memory of M. Schorr* (1944) 96-112. E. F. Sutcliffe, "A Note on *ʿAl,Lᵉ*, and *From*," VT 5 (1955) 436-439. L. Moraldi, *Espiazione sacrificale e riti espiatori nell'ambiente biblico e nell'Antico Testamento)* AnBib 5 (1956) ch. 4. N. H. Snaith, "The Meaning of the Hebrew אַף," VT 14 (1964) 221-225. S. Levin, "The Traditional Chironomy of the Hebrew Scriptures," JBL 87 (1968) 59-70. V. Wagner, "Umfang und Inhalt der *môt—jūmat*—Reihe," OLZ 63 (1968) 325-328. G. Schmitt, "Zu Gen 26,1-14," ZAW 85 (1973) 143-156.

Genesis 26:15-23: C. J. Labuchagne, "The Crux in Ruth 4,11," ZAW 79 (1967) 364-376 esp. 366. N. Kirst, *Formkritische Untersuchung zum Zuspruch 'Fürchte dich nicht' im AT* (diss. Hamburg, 1968). F. O. Garcia-Treto, "Liturgias de entrada, normas de asilo o exhortaciones preféticas? A propósito de los Salmos 15 y 24," Aug. 9 (1969) 266-298. J. Limburg, "The Root רִיב and the Prophetic Lawsuit Speeches," JBL 88 (1969) 291-304. R. P. Merendino, "Literarkritisches, Gattungskritisches und Exegetisches zu Jes 41,8-16," Bib 53 (1972) 1-42 esp. 26f., 40f. S. Mittmann, "Ri 1,16f. und das Siedlungsgebiet der kenitischen Sippe Hobab," ZDPV 93 (1977) 213-235 esp. 218. N. Wyatt, "The Problem of the 'Gods of the Fathers,' " ZAW 90 (1978) 101-104.

Genesis 26:26-33: C. H. W. Brekelmans, "Exodus XVIII and the Origin of Jahwism in Israel," OTS 10 (1954) 215-224. E. A. Speiser, "Akkadian Documents From Ras Shamra," JAOS 75 (1955) 154-165. A. von Selms, "The Origin of the Title 'the King's Friend,' " JNES 16 (1957) 118-120. H. Donner, "Der 'Freund des Königs,' " ZAW 73 (1961) 269-277. D. W. Thomas, "אַף in Proverbs XXXI 4," VT 12 (1962) 499-500. D. J. McCarthy, "Three Covenants in Genesis," CBQ 26 (1964) 179-189. E. W. Nicholson, "The Interpretation of Exodus XXIV 9-11," VT 24 (1974) 77-97. J. Halbe, "Gibeon und Israel. Art, Veranlassung und Ort der Deutung ihres Verhältnisses in Jos. IX," VT 25 (1975) 613-641.

Genesis 26:34-35: J. Blenkinsopp, "Theme and Motif in the Succession History (2 Sam. XI 2ff.) and the Yahwist Corpus," VT.S 15 (1966) 44-57.

Text

26:1   Now there came a famine in the land, over and above[a] the earlier famine in Abraham's time; so Isaac went to Abimelech, king of the Philistines, in Gerar.

2   And Yahweh appeared to him and said: Do not go down into Egypt;
stay[a] in the land which I will tell you.

3   Sojourn in this land and I will be with you and will bless you, for I will
give all these lands[a] to you and your descendants and so fulfill the oath
which I swore to Abraham your father.

4   And I will multiply your descendants like the stars of the heavens[a] and
will give your descendants all these lands, and all the peoples of the
earth shall bless themselves [b] in your descendants,

5   because Abraham[a] obeyed me and kept my charge,[b] my command-
ments, my statutes, and my laws.

6   So Isaac remained in Gerar.

7   When the men of the place asked about[a] his wife, he said: She is my
sister, because he was afraid to say:[b] She is my wife,[c] (thinking) lest
the men of the place kill me because of Rebekah; for she was
beautiful.

8   Now when they had been there a considerable time Abimelech, king of
the Philistines, looking down through his window,[a] saw Isaac ca-
ressing Rebekah his wife.

9   So Abimelech summoned Isaac and said: Well,[a] she is your wife then!
How could you say: She is my sister! And Isaac said to him: I thought I
would die because of her.[b]

10   And Abimelech replied: What is this you have done to us! One of the
people might easily[a] have lain with your wife and so you would have
brought[b] retribution[c] on us.

11   So Abimelech issued a command to the whole people:[a] Whoever
touches this man or his wife shall be put to death.

12   Now Isaac sowed in that land and in that same year he reaped a hun-
dredfold;[a] and Yahweh blessed him,

13   and the man became wealthier and wealthier[a] until he was very
wealthy indeed.

14   He had flocks and herds and a large household so that the Philistines
were envious of him.

15   Now the Philistines had blocked up[a] and filled with earth all the wells
which his father's servants had dug in the days of his father Abraham.

16   And Abimelech said to Isaac: Depart from among us, for you have become more powerful than we are.

17   So Isaac left the place and encamped[a] in the valley of Gerar and
stayed there.

18   And Isaac dug again the wells which "the servants of his father Abraham"[a] had dug in Abraham's days and which the Philistines had
stopped after the death of Abraham, and gave them the same names
which his father had given them.

19   Now when Isaac's servants dug in the valley[a] they found a spring of
running water.

20   But the shepherds of Gerar contested the claim of Isaac's shepherds
saying: The water is ours. So he named the spring Esek, because they
had disputed the matter with him.

21   Then[a] they dug another well and again they contested the claim; so he
called it Sitnah.

22   He moved on from there and dug another well, but they did not
contest[a] this. So he called it Rehoboth saying: Now Yahweh has made

room for us so that we can be fruitful[b] (spread out) in the land.

23 And he went up[a] from there to Beersheba.

24 And Yahweh appeared to him that night and said; I am the God of Abraham your father; do not fear, for I am with you! I will bless you and increase your descendants for the sake of Abraham[a] my servant.

25 And he built an altar there and called on the name of Yahweh. And Isaac pitched his tent there, and Isaac's servants dug[a] a well there.

26 Now Abimelech came to him from Gerar with his adviser Ahuzzath and Phicol the commander of his army.

27 And Isaac said to them: Why have you come to me? You are my enemies; you have sent[a] me away from you!

28 But they said: We have seen clearly that Yahweh is with you so we thought: We should put each other[a] on oath, we and you, and we should make a treaty with you

29 that you will do us no harm,[a] just as we have not attacked you and done you only good and let you go in peace. You are now indeed[b] blessed by Yahweh.

30 So he prepared them a meal and they ate and drank.

31 Early on the following morning they exchanged oaths; then Isaac farewelled them and they departed from him in peace.

32 The same day[a] Isaac's servants came and told him about the well they had dug. And they said to him:[b] We have found water.

33 He called it[a] Shibah;[b] and so the city is called Beersheba to this day.

34 Now when Esau was forty years old, he took as wife Judith, daughter of Beeri the Hittite, and Basemath, daughter of Elon the "Hittite."[a]

35 They were a source of bitter grief to Isaac and Rebekah.

1a Especially in Deut. and P.

2a The last three words of v. 2 and the first two in v. 3 are missing in the Gk.

3a Gk reads sing.: האל instead of האלה, also in v. 4.

4a The comparison with the stars, Gen. 15:5; 22:17.   **b** Vv. 4b,5 almost word for word as in Gen. 22:18.

5a Gk and Sam add אביך.   **b** שמר משמרת for the priestly service (Deut. 11:1; Lev. 18:30); characteristic of P.

7a On the use of ל, E. F. Sutcliffe, VT 5 (1955) 436-439.   **b** לאמר very seldom used as an actual infinitive.   **c** Sam and Gk read אשתי היא, Ges-K §147a. On the abrupt transition from one person to another, Ges-K §144p.

8a On "window," H. J. Stoebe, BHH I (1962) 470.

9a On אך, N. H. Snaith, VT 14 (1964) 221-225.   **b** On the use of על, BrSynt §110e.

10a כמעט, Ges-K §106p, 112h; perf. for the unrealized.   **b** Sign of emphasis, C. H. Gordon, JBL 57 (1938) 319-325.   **c** אשם, L. Moraldi, AnBib 5 (1956).

11a Sam and Gk read כל־עמו.

12a Some versions and the Gk read שערים = barley; MT is to be retained; cf. T. Jansma, OTS 12 (1958) 69-181, §2.

13a On the construction, Ges-K §113u; BrSynt §93g.

15a Ges-K §60h, 135o; also v. 18.

17a So Gen. 33:18.

18a Insert with Sam and Vg "the servants of his father Abraham."

19a Gk inserts גרר.

21a Gk adds, following vv. 17, 22, ἀπάρας δὲ Ἰσαὰκ ἐκεῖθεν ὤρυξεν.

22a Stress on second syllable because of the following ע.   **b** On the form, Ges-K §112m.

23a On עלה G. R. Driver, ZAW 69 (1957) 74-77; W. Leslau, ZAW 74 (1962) 322-323;

K. Schlesinger, VT 3 (1953) 381-390; F. O. Garcia-Treto, Aug. 9 (1969) 266-298.

24a   Gk adds "your father."

25a   In Num. 21:18 כרה and חפר are used synonymously, both referring to the construction of a well.

27a   For the construction, BrSynt §133d, and K. Schlesinger, see v . 23.

28a   Not to be struck out with the versions; BrSynt §112; Ges-K §103p; cf. 2 Sam. 21:7.

29a   On תַּעֲשֵׂה Ges-K §75hh.   **b**   In Sam and Gk the word order is reversed, perhaps better.

32a   D. J. de Vries, JBL 92 (1973) 23-36.   **b**   Gk reads לֹא; cf. J. L. Seeligmann, VT 11 (1961) 201-221.

33a   Gk and Syr read better שָׁמָּה.   **b**   The versions understood it differently, Vg *abundantiam*. On the three ways of understanding the word, cf. E. A. Speiser, comm. ad loc.; he decides in favor of "oath."

34a   Perhaps read החוי with Sam, Gk, and others.

Form

Ch. 26 is a self-contained piece constructed according to a definite literary plan and clearly recognizable as such, its purpose being to gather together the few Isaac traditions that have been preserved. It is a synthesis of a variety of traditions, but not a "mosaic" (F. Delitzsch and others); not seven units (G. von Rad, R. Kilian; others similarly), but a deliberate composition. The main part consists of a story about Isaac and Abimelech, the king of the Philistines, vv. 12-17 (omitting v. 15) and vv. 26-31. It is something like a narrative in that it begins with an increase in prosperity (vv. 12-14), falls to a low point (v. 16, Isaac is expelled by Abimelech), and finally rises to a high point (v. 31). It has already been demonstrated that the narrative is presupposed in Gen. 21:22-34.

    The narrative (vv. 12-17 and vv. 26-31) frames the nucleus formed out of items of information about the wells (vv. 15, 18, 19-25, 32-33), which were originally part of an itinerary (vv. 17, 22a, 23, 25b) and were clamped to the narrative at the beginning (vv. 15, 18) and end (vv. 32-33); vv. 15, 18 form a link with the Abraham story, and only in them does Abimelech appear. The items of information about the wells are the oldest part of the chapter and they were handed down in the form of the itinerary. There is no problem, therefore, in their not being further elaborated in narrative form, as R. Rendtorff thinks. An old tradition is inserted into a later frame and thereby preserved. The whole is introduced by vv. 1-11. The author takes up the already existing narrative in chs. 12 and 20 and makes use of it to show how Isaac came into Abimelech's realm. The promise, joined with a directive, followed by "the ancestress in danger," puts the beginning of ch. 26 with the beginning of the Abraham story (ch. 12).

Setting

Ch. 26 has been subsequently interpolated into an already existing sequence as a self-contained literary composition; so too H. Gunkel. Ch. 27 follows immediately on 25:19-28, v. 28 forming the transition (vv. 29-34 of ch. 25 being an appendage); ch. 26 was interpolated in between. It cannot then be from J (so too F. V. Winnett, JBL 84 [1965] 1-19). The careful construction indicates a transmitter who preserved an old itinerary ascribed to Isaac which came down to him; he set it within the framework of a later story about Isaac and Abimelech in which Isaac, likened to a Philistine king, represented the people of Israel. Isaac's exaltation is also given expression in the introduction where a motif from the patriarchal period is adapted.

Ch. 26 is theologically very important for the author because Isaac is the heir of the promise to Abraham. He makes use of the introduction to transmit the promise made to Abraham (vv. 2a,3a), and this is repeated in v. 24 as the conclusion of the middle part. On the other hand vv. 2b,3b,4-5 would be a secondary expansion belonging to the late history of the promises to the patriarchs.

Commentary

[**26:1-11**]   The exegesis of Gen. 12:10-20 and 20:1-18 is presupposed here. Gen. 26:1-11 is no more an independent and originally oral narrative than is 20:1-18. It is a literary imitation of 12:10-20 which at the same time takes up motifs from 20:1-18. J. Van Seters demonstrates this (*Abraham in History. . .*, 167-171): "the most colorless and least original form," following the line of H. Gunkel and J. Skinner, who hold that it is the latest of the three parallels (against M. Noth, *A History of Pentateuchal Traditions* [1948, 1966[3]; Eng. 1972]). V. 1, which combines the beginnings of ch. 12 and ch. 20, shows this with special clarity, as does Abimelech's address in vv. 9-10, the first part of which corresponds to 12:19, the second to 20:9a. Several blind motifs and clumsy repetitions like v. 7 or the transition v. 8a show that the narrative is not original but a literary imitation. The adaptation is a unity with the exception of the expansion (vv. 2b, 3b-5). The author has put the narrative at the beginning of his collection of Isaac traditions, first as a parallel to the beginning of the Abraham story, and then in order to bring Isaac to Abimelech.

The exposition is the same as 12:10, and so the author says expressly in v. 1 that it is a different famine from the one in Abraham's time. Isaac evades the famine by going down to Gerar, to Abimelech, the king of the Philistines (S. Mittmann, ZDPV 93 [1977] 218, on Philistines). It is here that the other parallel, 20:1-2, plays its role. The sentence prepares the way for the continuation in 26:12-16 (K. Elliger, BHH 1 [1962] 547-548, Gerar).

[**26:2-5**]   The natural continuation of v. 1 is v. 6, "So Isaac remained in Gerar." This and the fact that there is nothing corresponding in the parallels in chs. 12 and 20 suggests that vv. 2-5 are an addition as elsewhere, e.g., 22:15-18, where promises are subsequently appended to narratives. But the text of vv. 2-5 is not in itself a unity. V. 2a, which introduces what follows as a revelation to Isaac, is followed by two directives (one is omitted in the Gk): in v. 2b Isaac is ordered not to go down into Egypt but to remain in the land God will tell him: "in this land"; this directive is joined with a promise of assistance, "I will be with you," and of blessing (G. W. Coats, LexTQ 7 [1972] 77-85). Vv. 2a, 3a are quite possible between v. 1 and v. 6 and could be from the author of 26:1-11; the following כִּי, however, would follow better on the last sentence of v. 2 than the promise which is the basis of the directive in v. 2a. The promise of the land, v. 3bα, is expanded in what follows. It confirms (cf. the same verb in 17:19) the promise of the land made under oath to Abraham, v. 3bβ (cf. 15:7-21); then follows the promise of increase, v. 4a. The promise of the land is repeated in v. 4bα and is followed by the promise of blessing for the nations, v. 4bβ. This closes the sequence of promises which is based on Abraham's obedience to the laws and statutes. The purpose of this elaboration is obviously to join Isaac to the Abraham tradition by means of a theological clamp. It is Abraham who in fact receives the promise (vv. 3bβ,5) which is aimed at Israel, Abraham's posterity. But Abraham is here the exemplar of obedience to the law in return for which God bestowed the promises on him; this can have been pronounced and written only in a period when Israel's relationship to God was centered on its obedience to the law; that would be the post-Deuteronomic period, as the language of v. 5 clearly shows.

For the individual promises I refer to the comments on 12:1-3; 13:14-17; 15; 17; 22:15-18 and the bibliographies given there. It is peculiar to the present passage that the simple promise of the land has mounted to "all these lands" in vv. 3b,4b (cf. 1 Chron. 13:2; 2 Chron. 11:23). The collation of the terms for command and law in v. 5 presupposes the language of Deuteronomy, e.g., Deut. 11:1.

[26:6-7] V. 6 continues v. 1, perhaps inclusive of vv. 2a, 3a. It is clear that we have a deliberate adaptation when the "men of the place" ask Isaac about Rebekah ("his wife" is clumsy here); but nothing comes of it; it is a blind motif; and again in the patchwork construction: the incoherent sequence of the two כ-sentences and the transition to the first person.

[26:8-11] The last part of the narrative features the discovery by the king (v. 8), his dialog with Isaac (vv. 9-10), and the order that protects him. There is no apparent connection between the question of the men of the place (v. 7) and the discovery by the king (v. 9); nor is there any sign that the king wants to have the beautiful woman for himself. So a link must be created. The king discovers by chance that Rebekah is Isaac's wife; this is not a particularly ancient motif, as M. Noth and others thought. The missing link is supplied by v. 8a; ארך in this sense is found elsewhere only in Ezek. 12:22; 31:5. Next in the old narrative is the question which the king puts, Isaac's excuse, and the king's reproach (vv. 9-10); there is a certain mitigation here when compared with chs. 12 and 20 in that one of the inhabitants of Gerar, and not the king himself, would be guilty of adultery. As in ch. 12 and even more so in ch. 20, the king is portrayed as a God-fearing man: "This must mean that the community would be in a state of guilt before the divinity" (G. Schmitt, ZAW 85 [1973] 143-156). There follows the king's edict concerning anyone who touches Isaac or Rebekah; it is noteworthy that no motive is given for it; it is a case of intensification over against chs. 12 and 20. Isaac and Rebekah are highly honored by the decree of a king granting them protection of this kind. The formulation presupposes the formula of the apodictic laws, but the verse in the present context is not to be explained from current law, because it is a matter of a single occasional edict (against H. Schulz, BZAW 114 [1969]; see criticism of G. Schmitt, op.cit.; on the formula, G. Liedke, WMANT 39 [1971] 120-122).

The concluding sentence, v. 11, has a further function in the structure of ch. 26: it prepares the next part, vv. 12-17, by explaining why Isaac was able to remain and flourish unmolested in the land of the Philistine king.

[26:12-17] Vv. 12-17 belong together with vv. 26-31; vv. 1-11 serve both parts as an introduction. Vv. 12-14a report that Isaac attained great wealth, arousing the envy of the Philistines (v. 14b); for this reason Abimelech banished Isaac (v. 16) and he left (v. 17).

[26:12-14] The portrayal of Isaac's wealth does not accord with the patriarchal period. It is the wealth of a large scale-grazier in the sedentary period, as anachronistic as the king of the Philistines—wealth in grain (v. 12) and in flocks and herds (v. 14). One cannot say that this is a portrayal of the transition to sedentary life, as do some exegetes, nor that it is a description of the occasional enterprise of an individual nomad; the infinitive absolute in v. 13 describes a gradual growth in wealth. Yahweh's blessing, promised to Isaac in v. 3a, is at work here. As in ch. 24, God's blessing is now at work in the life of the patriarch and brings about his state of well-being; on the other hand, the promise of blessing in 12:1-3 works itself out only in the story introduced through Abraham. So by means of God's blessing Isaac becomes an important person in the land of the Philistines (v. 13; this is probably to be read after v. 14). The root גדל is to be found three times in this short sentence (E. Jenni, גדול, THAT 1 402-409, cf. ThW 1 גדל). But this too is a notion transposed into the patriarchal period: "greatness" does not suit the patriarchs either economically or politically. It is only when the life-style of the patriarchs was no longer known that one could speak of them in this way. This greatness arouses the envy of the Philistines with the consequent threat of conflicts (the ו = "so that" refers not to v. 14a but to v. 13).

[26:16-17] The ויאמר at the beginning of v. 16 follows immediately on the last sentence of v. 14; v. 15 goes with v. 18. Abimelech expels Isaac on the grounds that he has become too powerful for the Philistines (different in 12:19). The same is to be said here as on v. 13. Isaac has to yield. The following sentence is the itinerary note which establishes the transition to the next part. It introduces a life-style, characterized by the episodes of the wells, completely different from that of the wealthy grazier of vv. 12-14. It is noteworthy that it has not struck either the author or the commentators that the transition to the nomadic life brought about by the expulsion (v. 17) would in fact have meant the ruin of the "greatness" of Isaac portrayed in vv. 12-14.

[26:15, 18] Vv. 15 and 18 belong together (G. Hoberg, as early as 1899). They form the transition from vv. 12-17 to the accounts of the disputes over the wells in such a way as to link these with the Abimelech-Isaac conflict. The transition is so skillful that one does not notice that vv. 19-25 have nothing to do originally with vv. 12-17 and vv. 26-31. We will find the same kind of join in vv. 32-33. Anticipating the names (why would Abraham have dug wells in the land of the Philistines?), vv. 15,18 contain an ancient account of wells which points to the patriarchal period, first, because it belongs to an itinerary (v. 17), and second, because it describes the sort of dispute over wells that comes from the period of the small-cattle nomads. It is attested only in this passage, and it makes sense only in such an economy and life-style. One group of nomads tries to harm or expel another from its territory by blocking up one of the wells it uses (cf. 2 Kings 3:25). The aggrieved group then shows its vitality by digging out the well again. The function of the name is important here; when the well loses its function it also loses its name; when it can be used again, the name comes to life once more.

[26:19-25] These verses are the centerpiece of ch. 26; they belong, together with the redistributed vv. 15, 18 and vv. 32-33, to the oldest layer of the tradition. The writer who constructed a story about Isaac in ch. 26 out of different traditions had at hand an itinerary with accounts about wells which made sense only in the patriarchal life-style; its function was vital: the very existence of the group of people and their herds depended on the watering places. This is the reason why the itineraries with their information about the wells are handed down; the location of the wells along the route, together with their names, had to be preserved for the next migration; knowledge of this could be a matter of life and death. The information about the wells then is not a matter of abbreviated narratives or fragments thereof, but of constituent parts of itineraries whose function is clearly vital.

The structure of vv. 19-25: the information about the wells (vv. 19-21—two wells, dispute) follows directly on the itinerary (v. 17); the itinerary continues on into v. 22a where there is further reference to a well, its naming, and an explanation of the name. The itinerary proceeds on to v. 23, is continued in v. 25bα with another note on a well v. 25bβ, to which add vv. 32-33.

Itinerary	Wells
26:17	26:19-20
(21a Gk)	21b
22a	22b
23, 25bα	25bβ

In vv. 24, 25a there is the secondary insertion of a divine manifestation with a promise and the building of an altar.

[26:19-21]   V. 19 follows on v. 17. Isaac's household, now expelled from the fertile land, is dependent on water out in the steppe, and so the new well acquires a name. It is called after an event which took place at its discovery (cf. the giving of names to children). The event is a dispute between the herdsmen of two groups over a watering place. The accounts in vv. 15,18 show that a well can change ownership or that different groups can claim the right to use it; this happened often. There is not the slightest hint that it came to armed conflict and killing of opponents; it is a foretaste of war as the names show clearly, עֵשֶׂק and שִׂטְנָה. The verb, hith. עשׂק, and the noun derived from it, occur only here: "to quarrel," "to dispute," "a dispute"; the word has been transmitted in the context of the dispute about the well and is as old as the account itself as well as a specific designation for the dispute. The commonly used רִיב is found in the report, as also in v. 21 (ריב, THAT 1 [1976], 771-777; J. Limburg wants to understand the verb in the sense of "make a complaint against," "complained about," JBL 88 [1969] 291-304). The other name, שִׂטְנָה, which is found only here as a name (as a noun in Ezra 4:6), really means "accusation," contesting the right of another party. What is special to the dispute over the wells is that the names do not express victory, triumph, or superiority, but merely the fact that there was a dispute.

[26:22-23]   There is no mention of the name of a place in the itinerary; all that was still known was that it was the next stopping place along the route. The tradition preserved was that there was no dispute there, a clear indication of the significance of the dispute over the wells. The joy at this is expressed by the name given the well; it is a name of praise: "breadth," רְחֹבֹת, subsequently explained in v. 22b (B. Jacob: "*Wādi Ruḥēbe*, southwest of Elusa, 30 km. from Beersheba"). The כִּי־עַתָּה recalls the earlier experiences (vv. 20,21). The verb רחב = "to create space" is used also in Ps. 4:2 (Eng. v. 1) in a sentence praising God: "Thou hast given me room when I was in distress." The concluding sentence, "so that we can spread out in the land," shows that the explanation was appended later. The next item in the itinerary, v. 23, contains the name Beersheba, which gave occasion for the insertion of a divine manifestation with a promise, corresponding to Gen. 28:10-20. Before the insertion of vv. 24, 25a, the report about the pitching of the tent and the digging of a well in v. 25b followed directly on v. 23.

[26:24, 25a]   Beersheba becomes a sanctuary because of the divine manifestation which Isaac experienced there. The first three words agree with the first three
in v. 2; "that night" is added, recalling Gen. 28:10-20; it is characteristic of the
author of ch. 26 to establish links by means of chronological details. The promise
differs from that in vv. 2-5 by its greater brevity; v. 24bα has the form of an oracle
of salvation (cf. Gen. 15:1) in which Yahweh reveals himself as "the God of
Abraham your father." V. 24bβ joins the promise of blessing with the promise of
increase, like Gen. 12:2; 17:15; Deut. 7:13. Here, as in vv. 2-5, Isaac receives the
blessing for the sake of Abraham; he is the heir of the blessing. Like Abraham,
Isaac's response to the promise is to build an altar and call on the name of Yahweh
(cf. 12:8). The synthetic character of the narrative and the reference to Abraham's
obedience ("my servant," only here in Genesis) demonstrate that the promise is
relatively late, though earlier than vv. 2-5.

[26:26-33]   Vv. 26-31 follow on vv. 12-17. The exegesis of 21:22-34 is presupposed here. Abimelech had expelled Isaac because he had become too wealthy
and powerful and hence there was the threat of conflict with the local inhabitants.
But the situation cannot remain thus: Abimelech and his entourage look for Isaac
at the place where he is presently sojourning (v. 26). Isaac asks why he has come,
referring to his own expulsion (v. 27); Abimelech replies with the request for a
treaty (vv. 28-29); Isaac responds favorably (vv. 30-31a) and then takes leave of
him in peace (v. 31b). A report about a well is appended and linked with vv. 26-31
by means of the name "Oath" which Isaac gives the well.

[26:26-27]   Vv. 26-27 continue the narrative of vv. 12-17; the author cannot
have it end with the expulsion of Isaac. Abimelech comes to Isaac as a petitioner
with Ahuzzath his adviser and Phicol the commander of his army in his entourage.
The name פיכל (Egypt. Lycian?) occurs only here and in Gen. 21:22, 32;
Ahuzzath (= אחזת, "property"?) here only. One is described as confidant or adviser (מרע is found in the same context in Judg. 14:11, 20; 1 Kings 4:5; B. Jacob,
"as in all oriental kingdoms a title and courtly office. . . φίλοι τοῦ βασιλέως";
cf. H. Donner (1961) and A. van Selms (1957) in bibliog. above); the other is
שׂר־צבא (as in 1 Sam. 17:25); the presence of an adviser and an officer gives
weight to the negotiations. Isaac is thereby given status equal to that of a king; the
course of the proceedings that Isaac opens in v. 27 shows the same. He asks re-
proachfully the reason for the embassy; this is an indication that vv. 26-33 belong
with vv. 12-17 (the expulsion).

[26:28-29]   Abimelech's answer has almost a deprecating note. He gives as the
reason for his coming that in the meantime he has realized that God is with Isaac;
this forms the frame of the request, the first and last sentences of vv. 28 and 29 respectively, Yahweh is with you—you are blessed of Yahweh, corresponding to
the promise in v. 3aβ, "I will be with you and will bless you!" The foreign potentate has to acknowledge that Isaac is blessed by Yahweh. The narrative wants to
say to the contemporary generation that the promise given to the patriarchs confers
standing and honor on the people of Israel that the kings of the nations must recognize (1 Kings 10). Because he realizes this, Abimelech asks Isaac to make a treaty
with him, the content of which amounts to a nonaggression pact. Abimelech re-

fers to his conduct towards Isaac in vv. 11,16, understanding the expulsion as ''allowing him to withdraw in peace.'' The request for a pact makes sense only if Isaac represents the people of Israel. The author has in mind the relationship of Israel to neighboring kingdoms made possible by Yahweh's action.

[26:30-31] Isaac seizes the initiative by preparing a meal at the opening of negotiations. The pact is concluded by two acts: the common meal and the mutual oath on the following morning. This type of treaty puts Isaac on the same level as the Philistine king (''covenant'' is not a suitable word for what is meant here); ''the mutual oath is typical of the treaty between equals'' (J. Cahill, CBQ 26 [1964] 186); D. J. McCarthy (*Treaty and Covenant*, AnBib 21 [1963; 1978[2]]) presents Akkadian parallels to such treaties. The practice of sealing treaties like this with a common meal is widespread (for the oath, cf. Gen. 31:46, 52). The mutual oath is to be conceived after the form of invoking a curse upon oneself.

[26:31b] Isaac concludes the negotiations by taking farewell of his guests with the gesture of peace; it is stated expressly, ילכו מאתו בשלום. The ''peace'' concluded does not involve the lifting of the expulsion or the acceptance of Isaac back into Abimelech's territory, but is confined to the mutual pledge to do each other no harm. Peace, therefore, does not mean ''fellowship'' in each and every case. The relationship between people can remain intact when one allows the other ''to withdraw in peace,'' or leaves him in peace.

[26:32-33] Vv. 32-33 are a concluding report about wells which really belong to vv. 19-25; they serve here as a clamp to join vv. 26-31 with vv. 19-25, as also does the word ''oath'' which takes up v. 31. The spelling, שבעה, (Vg renders *abundantia*), can be an indication that the author has adapted the original name of the well to his own situation. Apart from this the report contains nothing peculiar to it; it is merely the discovery of a well as in v. 19 expanded by ''we have found.'' Vv. 32-33 differ from the other well reports by ending up in an etiology; this accords with the function as a clamp; it is the event narrated in vv. 26-31 that is put on record by the name of the well. The etiology belongs in content to the pact between Isaac and Abimelech which gave the place the name.

[26:34-35] These two verses belong to P and are continued in Gen. 27:46–28:9.

Purpose and Thrust

If ch. 26 as it stands is an independent and self-contained Isaac story, it is to be presumed that the author wants to give it an independent meaning within the patriarchal story. The meaning is not to be sought primarily in the narrative in vv. 1-11, which serves as an introduction, but in the linking of the ancient tradition about the digging of wells (apart from 21:30, this is told only of Isaac) with the late narrative about Isaac and Abimelech (vv. 12-16 and 26-31) which frames it. The word שלום acquires particular emphasis here in v. 29, and again in the closing sentence in v. 31. The dispute between Isaac and Abimelech ends with a ''final peace''; Isaac takes leave of him ''in peace.'' B. Jacob points out that a dispute of this kind, ending with a final peace, occurs for the first time in the patriarchal story. But this peace is made possible only by means of Yahweh's blessing which he had promised to Isaac (v. 3) and conferred on him (v. 13), as the king of the Philistines himself has to acknowledge. The transmitter who constructed ch. 26 and in-

serted it in this place in the patriarchal story wanted to point out to later generations that Isaac's "greatness," which grew out of Yahweh's blessing, led not to
the extension of his domain or to victory over his opponents, but to final peace.
The insertion into this narrative of the material about the wells, which belonged to
an ancient tradition, acquires thereby a lasting meaning. The digging of the wells
and the constantly recurring dispute about them is not a matter of greatness but of
brute existence. When the sequence of names given to the wells proceeds from opposition and dispute to "space," it preserves the experience of liberation from oppression which gives the well its name. It is this experience that is later given expression in the Psalms: "Thou hast set my feet in a broad place" (Ps. 31:9; [Eng.
v. 8] cf. Pss. 4:2; 66:12; 118:5).

The introductory narrative that, in contrast to the parallels in chs. 12 and
20, contains a detailed promise, makes Isaac the heir of the promise to Abraham.

The Firstborn Cheated
of His Blessing

Literature

Jakob and Esau, Genesis 27–33: A. Bea, *De Scripturae Sacrae Inspiratione* (1935[2]) esp. 93-114. S. H. Blank, "Studies in Post-Exilic Universalism," HUCA 11 (1936) 159ff. A. Herranz, "Dilexi Jacob, Esau autem odio habui (Malaguias 1,1-5)," EstB 1 (1941) 559-583. G. J. Botterweck, " 'Jakob habe ich lieb—Esau hasse ich.' Auslegung von Malachias 1,2-5," BiLe 1 (1960) 28-38.

Genesis 27: F. Ascensio, "Trayectoria histórico-teológica de la 'Benedición' biblica de Yahweh en habios del hombre," Greb. 48 (1967) 253-283. K. Luke, "Isaac's Blessing: Gen 27," Scrip. 20 (1968) 33-41. J. Goldstain, *Promesses et alliances. Histoire patriarcale Genèse 12–50* (1971) esp. 179-192.

Genesis 27:1-29: H. Junker, "Jakob erschleicht den Erstgeburtssegen," *Pastor bonus* 53 (1942) 149-152. I. Mendelsohn, "On the Preferential Status of the Oldest Son," BASOR 156 (1959) 38-40. A. Levene, "The Blessing of Jacob in Syriac and Rabbinic Exegesis," StPat 7 (1966) 524-530. P. Warmoes, "Jacob ravit la bénédiction d'Isaac (Gen 27,6-40)," *Assemblée du Seigneur* 29 (1966) 16-35.

Genesis 27:1-3: E. A. Speiser, " 'I Know Not the Day of My Death, " JBL 74 (1955) 252-256. C. H. Gordon, "Indo-European and Hebrew Epic," ErIs 5 (1958) 10-15, Fests. B. Mazar. T. C. Vriezen, "The Edomitic Deity Qaus," OTS 14 (1965) 330-353. H. A. Hoffner, "Symbols for Masculinity and Feminity. Their Use in Ancient Near Eastern Sympathetic Magic Rituals," JBL 85 (1966) 326-334. M. Dahood, "Poetry versus a Hapax in Genesis 27,3," Bib 58 (1977) 422-423.

Genesis 27:8: A. Laurentin, *"We'attāh-kai nun.* Formule caractéristique des textes juridiques et liturgiques (à propos de Jean 17,5)," Bib 45 (1964) 168-197, 413-432.

Genesis 27:27-29: F. M. Cross and D. N. Freedman, "The Blessing of Moses," JBL 67 (1948) 191-260. S. Gevirtz, "Patterns of the Early Poetry of Israel. III: Isaac's Blessing over Jacob," *Studies in Ancient Oriental Civilization* 32 (1963) 35-47. K. R. Veenhof, Review: W. Schottroff, *Der israelitische Fluchspruch,* 1969 WMANT 30: VT 22 (1972) 375-382. H. J. Zobel, "Der biblische Gebrauch von *šmn* im Ugaritischen und Hebräischen," ZAW 82 (1970) 209-216. M. Mannati, "Sur le sens de *min* en Ps IV 8," VT 20 (1970) 361-366. D. Vetter, *Seherspruch und Segensschilderung,* CThM A 4 (1974).

Genesis 27:30-40: G. Farmer, "Genesis 27,30," ET 28 (1917) 480. F. Stummer, "Hauptprobleme der alttestamentlichen Vulgata," BZAW 66 (1936) 233-239. G. Rinaldi, "*şl,*" BeO 16 (1974) 212. F. Stolz, "Rausch, Religion und Realität in Israel und seiner

Umwelt,'' VT 26 (1976) 170-186. J. S. Kselman, ''Semantic-Sonant Chiasmus in Biblical Poetry,'' Bib 58 (1977) 219-223.

Genesis 27:41-45: D. W. Thomas, ''A Note on the Meaning of מתנחם in Gen 27,42,'' ET 51 (1939/40) 252. O. Eissfeldt, ''Das AT im Lichte der safatenischen Inschriften,'' ZDMG 104 (1954) 88-118 = KS III (1966) 289-317. P. P. Saydon, ''Meanings and Uses of the Particle את,'' VT 14 (1964) 192-210. T. L. Fenton, ''Ugaritica-Biblica,'' UFen 1 (1969) 65-70. J. G. Heintz, ''Aux origines d'une expression biblique: *ūmūšū qerbū,* in A.R.M., X/6,8'?'' VT 21 (1971) 528-540. E. Jenni, '' 'Fliehen' im akkadischen und im hebräischen Sprachgebrauch,'' Or 47 (1978) 351-359.

Text

27:1 When Isaac had grown old and his eyes were so dim[ab] that he could[c] not see, he called his elder son Esau and said to him: My son! And he answered: Here I am.

2 And he said: Listen now. I have grown old and I do not know when I may die.

3 Now then, take your weapons, your quiver[a] and bow; go out into the fields and hunt me some game,[b]

4 and prepare me a savory dish,[a] such as I like, and bring it to me so that I may eat[b] and give you my blessing before I die.

5 Now Rebekah was listening[a] when Isaac spoke to his son Esau. When Esau had gone into the fields to hunt game for his[b] father,

6 she said to her son Jacob: Listen, I have heard your father speaking to your brother Esau; he said:

7 Bring me some game and prepare me a savory dish so that I may eat and bless you in the presence of Yahweh before I die.

8 Now listen to what I say, my son, and do as I order you.

9 Go to the flock and get me two fine young goats so that I may prepare them as a savory[a] dish for your father, such as he likes.

10 Then bring them to your father so that he may eat and bless you before he dies.

11 But Jacob said to his mother Rebekah: Look! Esau is a hairy man and I, my skin is smooth.

12 My father may touch me and I will seem to be mocking him and will bring a curse upon myself instead of a blessing.

13 But his mother said to him: Upon me be your curse, my son! Now do as I say; go and get me the goats.

14 So he went and got them and brought them to his mother and she made a savory dish, such as his father liked.

15 Then Rebekah took her elder son Esau's best clothes,[a] which she had with her in the house, and put them on Jacob her younger son.

16 And she put the goatskins on his arms and upon the hairless part of his neck.[a]

17 Then she put the savory dish and the bread which she had prepared into the hands of her son Jacob.

18 So he went[a] in to his father and said: My father! And he said: Here I am! Who are you, my son?

19 And Jacob said to his father: I am Esau your firstborn. I have done as you told me. Come, sit up and eat of the game so that you may give me your blessing.

20 Then Isaac said to his son: How is it that you have found it so quickly, my son? And he answered: Yahweh your God has put it in my way.[a]

21 And Isaac said to Jacob: Come close my son that I may touch you and see if you[a] are really my son Esau or not.

22 When Jacob came close to his father Isaac, he touched him and said: The voice is the voice of Jacob, but the hands are the hands of Esau.

23 But he did not recognize him because his arms were hairy, like the arms of his brother Esau. And so he blessed him.

24 And he said to him: Are you[a] my son Esau? And he answered: I am.

25 Then Isaac said: Bring me some of the game my son so that I may eat and give you my blessing. So he brought it to him and he ate; he brought him wine too and he drank.

26 Then Isaac his father said to him: Come close to me, my son, and kiss me.

27 So he came close and he kissed him. When Isaac smelled the smell of his clothes he blessed him and said: See! the smell of my son is like the smell of the field[a] which Yahweh has blessed.

28 May God give you of the dew of the heavens and of the richness of the earth and abundance of grain and wine.

29 Peoples shall serve you, and nations shall bow[a] before you. Be lord[b] over your brothers, and may your mother's sons bow before you. Cursed who curses you, and blessed who blesses you!

30 Just as Isaac had finished blessing Jacob, and Jacob had scarcely left[a] the presence of his father Isaac, his brother Esau came in from the hunt.

31 He too prepared a savory dish and brought it to his father, and said to him: Let my father arise and eat of the game which his son has brought him so that you may give him your blessing.

32 But Isaac his father said to him: Who are you? And he answered: I am your son, your firstborn, Esau.

33 Then Isaac trembled violently all over[a] and said: Who was it then who hunted[b] the game and brought it to me? I have already eaten it (all)[c] before you came; I have blessed him, and[d] he shall remain blessed!

34 When[a] Esau heard his father's words he uttered a loud and bitter cry,[b] and said to his father: Bless me[c] too, my father!

35 But he said: Your brother came deceitfully and took your blessing.

36 And he said: Yes,[a] he is rightly called Jacob. This is the second time he has supplanted me.[b] He took my birthright and now he has taken my blessing. Then he said: Have you not kept[c] a blessing for me?

37 Isaac answered and said to Esau: See, I have made him lord over you and have given him all his brothers as servants, and have bestowed[a] grain and wine on him; What is left for you, my son?

38 Then Esau said to his father: Have you just one blessing, father?[a] Bless me too, my father! And Esau cried out and wept.

39 Then his father Isaac answered and said to him: See, far from the richness of the earth shall be your dwelling, and far from the dew of heaven above.

40 By your sword you shall live, and your brother you shall serve; but the time shall come when you shall tear yourself free,[a] and you shall break his yoke from upon your neck.

41 So Esau bore a grudge[a] against Jacob because of the blessing which his father had bestowed upon him and he reflected: The time[b] of mourning for my father is close, and then I will kill my brother Jacob.

42 When Rebekah was told of what her elder son Esau was saying[a] she sent for her younger son Jacob and said to him: See, your brother Esau will take vengeance[b] on you and will kill you.

43 Now listen to me, my son. Up and flee to my brother Laban in Haran[a]

44 and stay with him a while,[a] until your brother's fury abates,[b]

45 until your brother's anger turns away[a] from you and he forgets what

you have done to him. Then I will send for you and bring you back. Why should I lose[b] both of you in one day?

1:a On the imperf. consec. in a subordinate clause, Ges-K §111q.   **b** כהה on the dimming of the eyes, Deut. 34:7; 1 Sam. 3:2.   **c** On the construction, Ges-K §114d, 119g.

3a תלי here only, from תלה ''to hang up''; really, ''the belt,'' ''the quiver.'' **b** Following Q read ציד.

4a Elsewhere only in Prov. 23:3, 6; ''delicacy''; here ''festive dish,'' E. A. Speiser.   **b** Ges-K §105d, BrSynt §§6d, 176c.

5a As 1 Sam. 17:28; BrSynt §106d.   **b** Read the suffix with Gk.

9a On the double accus., Ges-K §117ii.

15a Abbreviation for בגדי החמדת, actually, objects of value; cf. Judg. 12:14f.

16a Sam reads the sing.

18a The versions read ''he brought''; not necessary.

20a As Gen. 24:12.

21a On זה, Ges-K §136d.

24a Sam reads האתה. Interrogation, Ges-K §150a, BrSynt §54a.

27a Sam, Gk, Vg add מלא; cf. F. Stummer, BZAW 66 (1936) 233-239.

29a Read plural with Q, Gk, and Sam as in v. 29b.   **b** גביר elsewhere only in v. 37; construction, Ges-K §1451.

30a Construction, Ges-K §164b n. 1.

33a עד־מאד, in the Pentateuch only here and in v. 34.   **b** On the form, Ges-K §116b n. 1; on the question, BrSynt §42c, 55b.   **c** Read אכל for מכל, BHK.   **d** Read וגם with Sam and Syr.

34a Perhaps insert ויהי at the beginning with Gk and Sam.   **b** On construction, Ges-K §117pq.   **c** On emphasis given to suffix, Ges-K §135de.

36a Interrogative used to express something well known, Ges-K §150e.   **b** עקב as in Hos. 12:4, ''to outwit,'' different from Gen. 25:26.   **c** On אצל G. Rinaldi BeO 16 (1974) 212.

37a סמך with double accus., Ges-K §117ff.

38a Gk inserts κατανυχθέντος δὲ 'Ισαάκ.

40a The meaning of the verb רוד is uncertain, as the versions and new attempts at translation show. From the certain qal = ''wander'' (cattle), H. Gunkel correctly concludes to the meaning ''to free oneself.''

41a The verb occurs also in Gen. 49:21; 50:15; cf. T. L. Fenton, UF 1 (1969) 65-70.   **b** On the phrase, J. G. Heintz, VT 21 (1971) 528-540.

42a For the use of את, BrSynt §35d and P. P. Saydon, VT 14 (1964) 192-210.   **b** The underlying meaning is ''to take comfort in''; to take the law into one's own hands (by revenge); D. W. Thomas, ET 51 (1939-40) 252.

43a Cf. on Gen. 11:31.

44a ''A while,'' ''some days''; cf. Gen. 11:1; 29:20.   **b** Gk has smoothed over the doubling.

45a On the construction, Ges-K §114d,v.   **b** On the use of שכל, Ges-K §117aa.

Form

This narrative is determinative for the Jacob-Esau cycle as a whole. It is very long, though not diffuse as in ch. 24, but taut, and consists entirely of action without speeches. The length is conditioned by the event narrated. The division is clear: the blessing of Jacob which was intended to be the blessing of Esau, vv. 1-29 (vv. 1-17, preparation, vv. 18-29, execution), and the blessing of Esau, vv. 30-40. Esau's murderous intent and Rebekah's averting of it, vv. 41-45, form the concluding sequence. This narrative stands out as clearly different from those in the Abraham cycle: the tension is not the result of a natural phenomenon (like famine or a wife's barrenness) but of the action of a person who intervenes in an established course of events: the father is facing death and is giving the blessing which confers a prerogative on the firstborn over against the other brothers. It is into this course of events that Rebekah intervenes because she wants to secure the prerogative for the younger son. The intervention gives rise to the drama which leads to the murderous plan of the cheated elder brother. The basic structure of the narrative is the action of blessing culminating in the pronouncement which determines the whole in each of its individual episodes (similarly Gen. 48:8-16):

1. demand of the father and/or the request of the son;
2. identification (or naming) of the one to be blessed;
3. presentation of food and drink, strengthening of the one who blesses;
4. approach and touch (kiss);
5. pronouncement of the blessing on the one to be blessed.

The dramatic tension comes into the narrative through the peculiar nature of the blessing procedure: the blessing can be given to one person only and once given cannot be taken back.

Gen. 27 belongs to that type of narrative of which the basis is a fixed ritual procedure; this then becomes a unique event through the intervention that changes its course. The narrative acquires its particular importance for us because the deathbed blessing is described and passed on to us in full detail; it is a precultic rite which had great significance for the patriarchal life-style. The interruption of this ancient rite by the deception of the father points to a crisis within it which is reflected in the narrative.

It is a typical family narrative. In contrast to the narratives in the Abraham cycle it has to do with the coexistence of brothers; J therefore has set it in a broader context and adapted it along the lines of the rivalry motif. J makes 27:41-45 the exposition of what follows, and so one must take account of the broader context of Gen. 25–33 in the exegesis.

Nevertheless, Gen. 27 is originally a single, oral, independent narrative. One of Olrik's laws is unmistakable here, namely, the law of the single strand; folk narrative is always single-stranded (it does not go back to fill in missing details); and with it goes the law of scenic duality (only two people active in a scene): Isaac and Esau—Rebekah and Jacob—Jacob and Isaac—Esau and Isaac—Rebekah and Isaac (see A. Olrik, [1908-09]; Eng. in A. Dundes, ed., *The Study of Folklore* [1965] 129-141, esp. 135,137). Conversation and dialog are still identical in this kind of narrative. Its effect rests precisely on the fact that though what is happening in the conversation between two is not carried forward, nevertheless, it does as such determine the further course of the event.

Setting

Several stages are to be distinguished in the growth of this narrative. As a family story, first told orally, it can go back into the patriarchal period. The written stage can be recognized when the writer makes it part of a greater whole with the flight–return structure (see A. de Pury, *Promesse divine. . .* [1975] 496-501); it is similar with J in chs. 13–19. This, however, does not answer the question of the growth of ch. 27. Two questions remain: the literary question, whether ch. 27 is a synthesis of J and E, of two literary sources, and the traditio-historical question of the path from the oral to the written form.

(1) The literary-critical question takes on particular significance because many exegetes think that the Elohist makes his appearance in the Jacob-Esau cycle in ch. 27. The problem of source division becomes apparent in the three stages of the history of research into the chapter: first, literary stratification was accepted without it being possible to make a separation (J. Wellhausen). Then the separation was carried through (H. Gunkel and others) without arriving at a convincing result. Finally there was a return to the literary unity of the text (P. Volz, M. Noth). There is real doubling only in vv. 33-34/35-38, but no criteria can be found for source division (J. Skinner); the explanation lies elsewhere (see below). The designations for God are not decisive because the text is a secular one. The exegesis shows that further doublets or contradictions are only apparent.

(2) From the traditio-historical standpoint very different stages of tradition, widely separated from each other, make up the growth of ch. 27, but it is only with the greatest difficulty that they can be determined exactly. The blessing pronouncements, vv. 27b-29 and 39-40, did not have their origin together with the narrative context, but later, because they presuppose the story of the tribes and the people; most exegetes are in agreement here. The narrative text itself reflects so clearly the atmosphere of a later sedentary stage that the earlier form of the narrative must have been changed. This is in accord with the character of chs. 25–36 compared with chs. 12–15. It is scarcely possible to be certain of the individual stages of the adaptation.

Commentary

[**27:1-17**]   The preparation begins after the introduction (v. 1a) and the father's charge to Esau (vv. 1b-4); this is countered by the mother's charge to Jacob (vv. 5-13); Jacob carries out the charge (vv. 14-17).

The short exposition in v. 1a is sufficient; 25:27-28 is part of this: v. 27 is a genealogical note—the old narrative grows out of the genealogy; v. 28 is comprehensible only from ch. 27—it is a clamp binding ch. 25 with ch. 27.

The father, in face of his oncoming death, gives orders to prepare for the deathbed blessing; the passage culminates in this: בעבור תברכך נפשי בטרם אמות.

Excursus

Blessing in the Old Testament: It is characteristic of the older exegetes that they did not raise the question of what a blessing or the act of blessing is. It was the discipline of the history of religions that first tackled the problem. Reference should be made above all to J. Pedersen (*Israel: Its Life and Culture*, 1-11 [1926]); he was the first to direct attention to the independent phenomenon of blessing (1: "The Soul," 99-181, "The Blessing," 182-212); J. Hempel took this up (ZDMB 79 [1925] 20-110 = *Apoxysmata* [1961] 30-113). The exegesis of Gen. 27 by and large ignored these and other works. Only recent works took the matter up again, e.g., G. Weihmer, *Der Segen im A.T.* (diss. Basel, 1970); C. Westermann, *Blessing in the Bible and the Life of the Church* (1968; Eng. 1981); "Segen" (in THAT 1 [1971] 353-375); J. Scharbert (Bib 39 [1958] 1-16).

Reference should be made to these works for further detail and discussion. Talk of blessing in the Old Testament has a clearly recognizable history which compasses a sequence of clearly defined and different stages (cf. Gen. 12:1-3, comm. ad loc.). We meet the earliest stage in ch. 27. Characteristic of the blessing is that its setting in life is the leave-taking or farewell (Gen. 24:60); this is the situation out of which it is to be understood; it is vitality that is passed on by the one who is departing from life to the one who is continuing in life; in this process no distinction is made between the corporal and the spiritual and so both action and word are required. Because the blessing is concerned with vitality as a whole, the blessing cannot return or be subsequently altered. All these characteristics, each of which has many parallels in the history of religions (see J. Pedersen and others; also T. H. Gaster, *Myth, Legend*. . . [1969]), coalesce with amazing clarity and density in the narrative of ch. 27; this is a pretty certain sign that it is colored by the way in which blessing was understood in the oldest layer accessible to us. The blessing pronouncements, which are independent of the narrative, give some insight into the further development of the understanding of the blessing: the significance of the blessing, whose original setting was solely the community form of family life (Gen. 24; 27; 48; etc.), is adapted in the tribes and again when joined with the history of the people; the pronouncements in vv. 27-29, 39-40 reflect both. Finally it acquires its lasting significance in the blessing given in worship.

[27:1-2]   The father is old and his eyes "have faded away" (cf. Gen. 48:10; Deut. 34:7; etc.). The last words of one who is approaching death play an important role in the Old Testament (Gen. 24:1ff.; 48:10-15; 50:24ff.; Deut. 33; Josh. 23; 2 Sam. 23; 1 Kings 2:1-3; 2 Kings 13:14-18; Tob. 14, and the literature of wills and testaments). E. A. Speiser sees in the statement, "Listen now. I have grown old. . .," actual Hurrian legal terminology in the context of a "deathbed declaration"; T. L. Thompson demonstrates that this statement occurs in many regions in the same context and is to be understood in each case from the particular situation (*The Historicity*. . ., BZAW 133 [1974] 285-293 with lit.).

The call with answer at the end of v. 1 has the same function here and in v. 18 as in Gen. 22:1,7; primarily it effects contact between father and son, between son and father. In each case it introduces a dialog which is important for both.

[27:3]   The weapons for the hunt are the point of contact with Gen. 25:27. On the bow and arrow as symbols of masculinity, cf. H. A. Hoffner (JBL 85 [1966] 326-334). The bow became a designation for one of the leading gods in Edom, a land typical of the hunter; cf. T. C. Vriezen (OTS 14 [1965] 330-353).

[27:4]   The word נפש is used here as well as in vv. 19,25,31 for the subject who blesses; the expression goes back to the oldest layer and its understanding of what is meant; נפש too means the whole person, body and soul. It can signify breath or desire or life, and could be translated here: "so that my life may bless you." If it is translated by "soul" then it must be said at the same time that the whole person is meant. The expression, בכל־נפש, corresponding to our "with all (my) heart," is perhaps closest to the sense of נפש in this passage. Isaac wants to bless his son with all his being.

[27:5-13]   The request is followed by its execution which should really be concluded with v. 5b, ". . .Esau went into the fields to hunt game for his father"; vv. 30bβ, 31 continue it. But Rebekah, who had been listening in, intervenes here (v. 5a) and gives Jacob a countercommission. Jacob indeed raises an objection (vv. 11-12), but an objection which implicitly consents to the plan of his mother who parries it (v. 13). The established procedure of the deathbed blessing is thereby interrupted and the commission and countercommission give rise to a drama.

Vv. 5-13 give no occasion for division into sources, as H. Holzinger agrees.

[27:5-7]   Rebekah had been eavesdropping (v. 5a) (as has Sarah in 18:10), and after Esau had gone she lets Jacob know what she had heard; as she repeats it the phrase לפני יהוה is striking: "that I may bless you in the presence of the Lord."

A. Dillmann explains it following 1 Sam. 23:18—to conclude a pact in the presence of Yahweh; B. Stade—in the presence of the image of Yahweh in the house; H. Gunkel—one concludes from this that it is a question of a sacrificial meal; O. Procksch—the invocation of the name of Yahweh; J. Skinner—''in the solemn consciousness of Yahweh's presence''; E. A. Speiser—''with Yahweh's approval''; and there are other explanations. The doubled לפני at the end of v. 7, stylistically extremely harsh, speaks against all these explanations, and such a literary lapse can scarcely be attributed to the narrator of ch. 27. Moreover, the phrase ''bless in the presence of Yahweh'' occurs only in this passage.

I think that the phrase is a subsequent addition and is intended as a balance between the narrative (Isaac blesses) and the pronouncements (Yahweh blesses).

[27:8-10]   Rebekah gives Jacob the commission without further explanation or reason; he is to bring two fine young goats from the flock. It is only the insistent use of maternal authority (v. 8, repeated as an *inclusio* in v. 13) that indicates something questionable about the commission and parries objections. But her intention is expressed unambiguously in the last words of v. 10: ''that he may eat and bless YOU before he dies!'' (the לפני יהוה is missing here). The artistry of the narrator becomes clear in the way in which he has brought in the same sentence as the conclusion of both parts, vv. 5-7 and 8-10.

[27:11-13]   Jacob's objection is directed not against his mother's plan as such but only against its feasibility; rather it implies consent. The narrator thereby perplexes his listeners by saying that Jacob does not object to the deception; he goes along with it. Rebekah does not deal with Jacob's objection but shows him her own firm determination and readiness to incur any risk, even the curse of her husband. The objection is thus met and nothing remains but for Jacob to carry out the commission (vv. 14-17).

[27:14-17]   It is significant that Jacob's part is compressed into three verbs in narrative sequence at the beginning of v. 14, וילך ויקח ויבא, whereas the mother herself takes care of the really important preparations. Dexterous in her deception she makes ready the savory dish so that it tastes like game, takes Esau's festal robe and puts it on Jacob, and makes sure that he will not be recognized. The author's intention is to attribute this deliberately calculated initiative entirely to Rebekah; one cannot therefore entitle the chapter, ''Jacob cheats Esau of the blessing of the firstborn.'' The motive must be sought with Rebekah, not with Jacob; and this is all the more difficult as both Esau and Jacob are the sons of her own womb. It was different with Isaac and Ishmael. The reason given in the exposition (Gen. 25:28), that Jacob was her favorite son, could suffice; but this is part of the transition, not of the ancient narrative.

The old narrative presupposes an understanding of the right of the firstborn which regards it as a privilege which is the exclusive prerogative of the eldest son. In a later era two (Gen. 48) or twelve sons (Gen. 49) could receive a blessing, though on different levels. But in the case of twins the exclusive right of the firstborn is acutely incomprehensible; both are born at virtually the same time. The mother objects to this exclusive prerogative of the one son. Revolt against a ''social'' injustice lies behind her plan. She resists with all means at her disposal a privilege of the ''great'' which excludes the ''small.'' Rebekah is here ahead of her time; the privilege of the eldest which excludes all others did not prevail. As the narrative progresses it shows that this privilege has already lost its effectiveness: the one blessed becomes a slave and must bow before the one who is not blessed.

[27:14] Rebekah prepares a "festal meal" from the flock (v. 14); it is made to taste like game such as the old man liked. A subtle humor, now at the service of the revolt against an injustice, is saying that the substitute must do it also.

[27:15] Rebekah brings out the eldest son's festal robe which is there in the house (v. 15); the verse thus states in the clearest terms that the milieu of the narrative is no longer the life-style of the wandering nomad but of the sedentary. Rebekah clothes Jacob with Esau's festal robe; this presupposes that it is appropriate to the act of blessing and expected by the father, and is an important attestation that specifically defined events in the life of the family are festal celebrations. Esau's festal robe is meant to give Jacob some of Esau's person; its function, however, is not to be a means of recognition; the aroma has another meaning (v. 27).

[27:16] The putting of the goatskins around Jacob's arms and neck is not in conflict with the robe (v. 15); both are quite compatible with each other and are not an indication of two sources.

[27:18-29] This passage forms the center of the narrative. The structure of the event, which consists of the five acts constituent of the blessing ritual (see "Form" above) is basic to its understanding. Four of these acts proceed according to custom. The dramatic moment is centered around the question of identification. The blessing ritual begins with Jacob's entrance and address to his father (vv. 18-19). The sons' request in v. 19 (1) rehearses the father's demand, vv. 2-4, in almost the same words (1). As a preliminary to the identification itself there is the doubt and apprehensive question as to who is standing before him (vv. 20-23). Even though a slight doubt remains, the conversation ends without Isaac recognizing Jacob. He can now proceed to the blessing ritual, as the last sentence of v. 23 says. The ritual procedure actually begins with the formal identification which is part of it, v. 24 (2). Almost all interpreters say that the words of blessing have to follow immediately on "and so he blessed him" (v. 23). But this is a misunderstanding. Blessing consists of action and word; it is the procedure that is introduced with the last part of v. 23. The identification, v. 24, is followed by the presentation of the food and the meal, v. 25 (3), the contact by means of the kiss, vv. 26, 27aα (4), and the words of blessing, vv. 27b-29 (5), to which v. 27aβ is a transition.

[27:18-19] Jacob goes into the place where his father is lying and addresses him (cf. v. 1b). Answering his father's question, "Who are you?" he enters without more ado into the role that Rebekah has assigned to him: "I am Esau." He asks his father to sit up (as in Gen. 48:2) so as to eat the food and then to bless him. The meal is described here as in v. 4 as a constituent part of the blessing ritual (בעבור).

[27:20-23] The course of the rite is halted by Isaac's question concerning who it is who stands before him. Jacob's answer as to how he can have returned so quickly carries within it an unintended but important reference to the religion of the patriarchs, "Yahweh your God." The father's doubt is not laid. Even after he has felt Jacob's arms a lingering doubt remains; the old man, thus deceived, cannot say for certain that Jacob is standing before him. What is he to do? He blesses him there and then. The narrator wants to indicate cautiously how fraught with danger is such a deathbed blessing when the position in life of both the one and the other depends on it.

[27:24]   The blessing ritual begins in v. 24 with the question of identification which here is part of the rite. It can be conferred only after Isaac has assured himself (vv. 18-23). There is no doubling and the ויברכהו at the end of v. 23 is not to be deleted (against P. Volz).

[27:25]   The second act of the rite of blessing is the meal that Jacob lays before his father at the latter's request. It is a complete meal with the bread (v. 17) and the wine (v. 25). The ''magical'' aspect of the blessing is apparent in that the one who blesses, thus passing on to his son his own vital power, must find strength for this by means of a meal. The festal meal is part of the precultic rite, an early form of the later cult meal.

[27:26-27aα]   The third act is the physical contact, an embrace or as here a kiss which is part of the procedure. This too is a sign of the magical mentality; physical contact is a necessary part of the transference of the vital power. These two elements are preserved right through to the liturgical blessing where word and action belong together (the imposition of hands as physical transfer). The blessing is the oldest sacrament.

[27:27b-29]   Whereas the ויברכהו at the end of v. 23 introduces the blessing ritual as a whole, here it introduces the blessing pronouncement, hence ויברכהו ויאמר. The words preceding the verb, ''and he smelled the smell of his clothes,'' form the transition from action to word.

   Vv. 27b-29 is a composite piece and did not originate along with the narrative, as the parallels show (so too M. Noth). The words of blessing divide into three parts: the transition, v. 27b (יהוה), followed by a pronouncement of fertility, v. 28 (אלהים), and a pronouncement of dominion in three parts (no designation for God).

[27:27aβ]   ''And he smelled his clothes.'' The words of the seer in Num. 24:5 begin in a similar manner as he beholds: ''How beautiful are. . .!'' What is perceived through the senses gives reality to what is seen in the future (D. Vetter, CThM a 4 [1976]). The seer's pronouncement is close to the pronouncement of blessing, particularly in the present situation where the one dying looks into the future; it is a widespread motif. It is clear from the parallel that the words have no longer anything to do with the test of identity.

[27:27b]   While v. 27aβ is prose, the pronouncement of blessing as such begins poetically (2:2:2); it is already speaking of the future: the one who is dying smells the aroma of the field which Yahweh has blessed and this blessing will come upon the son. This is a completely self-contained blessing of fertility. It is clearly related to the period after the settlement: ''Field and vineyard are the principal possessions of the Hebrew farmer'' (O. Procksch). The words, ''that Yahweh has blessed,'' also suit the sedentary period, corresponding to the language of Deuteronomy.

[27:28] A second fertility blessing, independent of v. 27 and self-contained, follows with different designations for God. It is a blessing typical of agricultural civilization, though not in the original form of an effective pronouncement. It has been reworked into a wish or prayer, as in the Psalms. The blessing upon Joseph is similar (Gen. 49:25); but here the subsequent reworking is even clearer (v. 25a). The same parallelism in the Ugaritic texts, "the dew of the heavens and the fatness of the earth," show that an ancient blessing formula has been taken over after the settlement in Canaan (S. Gevirtz, *Studies in Ancient Oriental Civilization*, 32 [1963] 35-47; H. J. van Dijk, VT 18 [1968] 16-30; H. Zobel, ZAW 82 [1970] 209-216; cf. Deut. 33:13). It should be noted that the pair, "heavens and earth" (v. 28; cf. Gen. 48:25 and the Ugaritic parallels), does not occur in the context of creation (Gen. 1:11) but of blessing. Heaven and earth are thought of and mentioned together primarily in the experience of those whose existence depends on the gifts of heaven and earth.

". . .Of the dew of the heavens and of the richness of the earth": according to H. J. van Dijk and H. J. Zobel, "the richness of the earth" is to be understood from the Ugaritic parallels as "rain." In any case "dew and rain" would give a better parallelism; but "rain of the earth" is difficult, if not unlikely, and so it is better to understand richness as the equivalent of fertility as in Num. 13:20 and Is. 5:1; 28:4. The fertile land yields its produce, "abundance of grain and wine." The two are often mentioned together (e.g., Deut. 7:13) and occur in a pronouncement blessing (Deut. 33:28).

[27:29] The blessing of fertility is expanded by the blessing of dominion (v. 29). The two are often found together, always in the same order (Gen. 24:60; cf. Gen. 48:15-19; Num. 24:3-9; and others). Their juxtaposition is likewise to be understood from the period when sedentary life was adopted and the tribes were at rivalry with each other. It is obvious that v. 29a and b are not dealing with the brothers Jacob and Esau, and this becomes clearer from the plural "your brothers" in v. 29aα. All three sentences display a well-chiseled parallelism and are independent of each other.

[27:29a] "Peoples and nations" are to serve the recipient of the blessing; this can refer only to Israel after it had become a state. The parallelism עמים—לאמים occurs especially in the later prophets; the parallelism שחה—עבד is characteristic of the Deuteronomic language. The sentence can only be a late addition, but it is in terms too general to allow of any conclusion, such as a reference to the subjection of Edom by Israel, as most interpreters think; the plural is against this. Further, v. 29 originated outside the narrative context. V. 29a is missing in the repetition in v. 37.

[27:29bα] V. 29bα refers to the conflicts between the tribes; the rare imperf. הוה with גביר, occurring only here and in v. 27, points to a fixed formula. It recalls the tribal pronouncements in Gen. 49:8 and Deut. 33:16.

[27:29bβ] The last sentence, v. 29bβ, occurs word for word in Num. 24:9b. It is the older form over against Gen. 12:3: "The countercurse is to render the curse itself ineffective" (W. Speyer, RAC VII, 1160-1288). The three parallels to Num. 24 in vv. 27-29 confirm that they arose at about the same time.

[27:30-40] Isaac blesses Esau. By means of the change of scene the narrator manages always to have only two people in conversation. Both mother and son knew that the deception had to come out. The narrator has the discovery follow immediately and again in the process of identification. Isaac reacts with horror (v. 33), Esau with a loud wail and a pressing request for a blessing (vv. 34-38), which he receives; but it is only a "secondary" blessing (vv. 39-40).

[**27:30-33**] The duplicated introduction in v. 30 (ויהי twice, H. Holzinger) may point to a variant which here serves to underscore the turning point. It is deliberate that vv. 31-32 follow vv. 18-19 almost word for word; but the ritual sequence is shattered by the discovery of the deception. Isaac's horror, v. 33, is set into relief as the climax of the narrative by means of the strong language in which it is clothed, thereby making the deception known to Esau. At the same time we hear the narrator telling his hearers in a later era loudly and clearly that there was an earlier period when it was the blessing of the father that inexorably determined destiny: the father's horror stands powerless before the unalterable. The important sentence anchored in the rite, "so that your soul (life) may bless me" (vv. 4,19,25,31), is here loosed from its moorings and veers into a perplexed entreaty for a blessing (vv. 34,36,38).

[**27:34-38**] The father's profound horror is followed by the brother's loud cry; he too knows that nothing more can be done with a blessing already dispensed. Esau's reaction shows how lament and petition go together: the earnest entreaty grows out of the lament, as later in the psalms used in worship. In both cases the lament is anguish given expression in words (F. Stolz: "*ṣaʿāq* means articulated lament," VT 26 [1976] 170-186). The father's answer in vv. 35 and 37 (the doubling has here the sense of differentiating) expresses most forcefully the ancient understanding of blessing as word that acts: one can deceive someone about it and carry it off like an object of prey (v. 35). Significantly, God is not mentioned as the one who blesses in v. 27 (different in vv. 28-29); Isaac is the one who administers the blessing: ". . .I have made him. . .; I have given him. . ." (v. 37). This confirms that the words of blessing in vv. 28-29 belong to a later stage.

Esau's question in the last sentence of v. 36 follows directly on v. 35; his outburst in between, v. 36a,bβ, is an etiological addition inserted later which explains the name Jacob from עקב, in the sense of "deceive," and presupposes the succession of ch. 27 on ch. 25. It disturbs the context and does not fit the language here. The request for "another," "kept aside" blessing which determines the whole passage (vv. 34-38) sounds quite naive and clumsy; it makes sense only in the context of the whole narrative. It is only here, in Esau's lament and entreaty, that the deception intended and planned by Rebekah is comprehensible. Had all proceeded according to custom, Esau would have had everything and Jacob nothing; and this is just what Esau experiences now, as the father explains (vv. 35-37): he has given the one everything; nothing remains for the other. It is to be noted that the mother's love which prompted Rebekah's action is different from that which we usually understand; there is nothing sentimental about it; she stakes her life against an established right which is clearly unjust, and does not shrink from deception.

Esau's outcry indicates that for him the blessing is more than that which the father has already disposed of and that it is something lost to him beyond recall. The effectiveness of the father's blessing must be more than what custom and right have made of it.

[27:39-40a]   The narrator is saying just this when, despite the father's protesta-
tions that he has no more blessings, he has him nevertheless dispense yet another.
Decisive for the understanding of the sentences immediately following is that they
contain the word תחיה: "you shall live!" Esau is to have a hard life, but he is to
live. The expression is by no means "virtually a curse" (J. Skinner and others); it
is rather a daring intimation of the later and extended meaning of the idea of the
blessing, the blessing as the promise of vital power: "you shall live!"

   The blessing pronouncement in vv. 39-40a has two parts corresponding to
the two parts of the blessing on Jacob and is colored in content by it. The fertile
land, watered by dew and rain, is denied Esau, almost the same words being deliberately used: the מן is partitive in the first case, but privative here. The words,
". . .shall be your dwelling," affirm that one can live in the steppe also. Considerations along the lines that Edom is not just a desert, barren land are unnecessary;
the intention is to present merely the opposite of the blessing on Jacob. The second
part corresponds to Jacob's blessing: Isaac has made Jacob lord of his brothers;
consequently Esau must serve him. The conflict between narrative and oracle is
particularly striking here. In the later narrative about Esau the opposite happens;
the oracles refer not to the two men, but to the later tribes and peoples.

[27:40b]   This addition presupposes application to the history of the peoples of
Israel and Edom and enlarges it by means of a historical *vaticinium ex eventu*:
Edom will later throw off Israel's dominion (2 Kings 8:20, 22). The only sentence
that is not preempted by Jacob's blessing foretells Esau's way of life and that of
his descendants, "by your sword you shall live." The Israelite farmer takes a negative view of a life-style which others regard as particularly noble; but it is never
contested that other tribes can live from rapine and raids, as in the case of Ishmael.

[27:41-45]   This passage is a transition constructed by J as Gen. 25:27-28. The
narrative of Gen. 27 had its natural conclusion in the pronouncement over Esau in
vv. 39-40; Esau's reaction is adequately portrayed in v. 35. But over and above
this are Esau's murderous intent and Rebekah's new plan which serve to lay the
foundation of the whole following section, chs. (28)29–33: Flight and Return.
The introductory words with the preposition על in v. 41, which form an unnecessary link with what has preceded, show that the passage is a transitional
appendage.

[27:41]   Esau becomes his brother's enemy, as did Cain of his brother Abel; like
Cain he resolves to kill him when the period of mourning for the father has passed
(usually seven days, Gen. 50:10). For Jacob, this means that he has achieved
nothing by his deception. His father's blessing is of no help in face of his brother's
hate; blessing can thrive only in a community at peace (Gen. 37–50).

[27:42-45]   Rebekah communicates her counterplan to her son Jacob with the
same authority as she did her previous plan; once more it is she who devises and
decides in parrying the threatening consequences. But there is a difference here.
The exclamation in v. 45 reveals Rebekah's deep emotion; she knows now that
her plan has achieved nothing—perhaps it has lost all. She can now only save
what is to be saved. She is unable to announce a safe way out. Jacob's absence
will not last "a while" but 20 years; there is no calling back, and mother and son
never see each other again. Events go far beyond Rebekah's plan. The narrative

conclusion, vv. 42-45, makes an implicit judgment on the deception; no explicit moralizing condemnation is required.

Purpose and Thrust

Gen. 27 is concerned with the basic phenomenon of ''passing on''; its basis is that man is mortal and wants to transmit beyond death what he has experienced and gained. The determining motif in Gen. 12–25 was survival from one generation to the next; in Gen. 27 it is handing on (tradition, *tradere*), a process which raises the problem, who gets what? The result is conflict. This is the origin of the conflict between Esau and Jacob. The narrative of Gen. 27 presupposes that one of the most important grounds for rivalry or conflict, or even the most important, consists in the handing on from one generation to the next: the father's blessing determines the destiny. This is a very ancient idea, not just the idea of the narrator/Yahwist; he rather preserves the memory that in ancient times the handing on from one generation to the next is a handing on of vital power (= blessing) in which the bodily and the spiritual are still one. Later a distinction was made between the religious ברכה and the profane בכרה concerned with family rights, between blessing (religious) and the right of the firstborn; here in the father's blessing the two are still one. This is a difficult notion because everywhere in the world the handing on of material goods has been detached from what we understand as ''tradition,'' the handing on of spiritual goods and values, one of which is religion. We see here that in a very early stage both could be handed on in the blessing of the dying father, a blessing which is the counterpart of generation; generation finds its fulfillment in the blessing.

When only one son can receive the father's blessing then the others are disadvantaged. The revolt of the disadvantaged youngest son has become a worldwide motif. In Gen. 27 it is the mother who rises up against the exclusive privilege of the elder, as Hagar rises up against Sarah's oppression. J sees this situation in a broader context. The privilege of the firstborn, linked with the father's deathbed blessing, falls apart with the extension of the small, closed family circle into wider areas in which other new factors determine destiny. J portrays the collapse of an old order through changes in the form of the community. However, the catch-phrase, ''so that my soul (life) may bless you,'' points to what is permanent amid the changes; the blessing is permanent amid the changes in the form of the community, though it changes its shape with it as the oracles in Gen. 27:27-29 and 39-40 show. But it remains determinative for the history which leads from the patriarchs to the people.

Mal. 1:2-5 interprets Gen. 27 in such a way that God chooses Jacob but rejects Esau: ''I have loved Jacob but I have hated Esau.'' But this refers to the nations Israel and Edom, as in the oracles, not to the persons, the two brothers, sons of Isaac. The same is true of Rom. 9:13 which cites Malachi. But this interpretation does not hold for the brothers; what is decisive in Gen. 27 is that the ancient right and privilege of the blessing of the firstborn does not prevail in all its rigor: Esau too receives a blessing; he will have a hard life, but he is to live. The blessing extends beyond the circle of ''the elect.''

Jacob's Departure and Esau's Wives

Literature

Genesis 26:34-35: M. Löhr, *Die Stellung des Weibes in Jahwereligion und -kult*, BWAT 4 (1908) esp. 34f. J. Blenkinsopp, "Theme and Motiv in the Succession History (2 Sam XI 2ff.) and the Yahwist Corpus," VT.S 15 (1966) 44-57.

Genesis 28:1-9: L. Rost, "Die Vorstufen. . .," BWANT 4,24 (1938) 18-19. M. Weiss, VT 13 (1963) 469-470. O. Hofius, "Die Sammlung der Heiden zur Herde Israels (Joh 10,16; 11,51f.)," ZNW 58 (1967) 289-291. J. Bright, "The Apodictic Prohibition: Some Observations," JBL 92 (1973) 185-204.

Text

26:34   When Esau was forty years old he took as wives Judith daughter of Be-eri the Hittite and Basemath daughter of Elon the Hittite;

35   and they were a bitter grief to Isaac and Rebekah.

27:46   And Rebekah said to Isaac: I am wearied to death of the Hittite women.[a] If Jacob marries a Hittite woman like those in the land, what's the use of life?

28:1   Then Isaac called Jacob and blessed him and charged him; he said: Do not take a wife from the Canaanite women.

2   Up, go to Paddan-aram[a] to the house of Bethuel your mother's father; take a wife there from the daughters of Laban your mother's brother.

3   May God Almighty bless you and make you fruitful and multiply you so that you become a gathering[a] of nations.

4   May he give you the blessing of Abraham,[a] both you and your descendants, so that you may possess the land where you sojourn which God[b] gave to Abraham.

5   So Isaac dismissed Jacob. He went to[a] Paddan-aram, to Laban, the son of Bethuel the Aramean, the brother of Rebekah, the mother of Jacob and Esau.

6   Now Esau saw that Isaac had blessed Jacob and sent[a] him to Paddan-aram to take a wife there, and that while blessing[b] him he had ordered him: Do not take a wife from the Canaanite women,

7   and that Jacob had obeyed his father and mother[a] and had gone to Paddan-aram.

8   So when Esau saw that his father Isaac did not like the women of
    Canaan,
9   he went to Ishmael and took as wife Mahalath, [a] the daughter of Ish-
    mael, Abraham's son, the sister of Nebaioth,[b] in addition[c] to the wives
    he already had.

27:46a   בנות חת as in Gen. 26:34f., missing in Gk; in Gen. 28:1-9 on the other
hand, בנות כנען.

28:2a   Ges-K §16h, 90i. On Paddan-aram, cf. Gen. 25:20, and J. Van Seters,
Abraham in History (1975) 38.

3a   קהל עמים, Gen. 35:11; 48:4(P); Ezek. 23:24; 32:3; cf. Gen. 17:4f.

4a   Some Mss add אביך. **b**   Sam reads יהוה.

5a   Some Mss add ויקם יעקב.

6a   M. Weiss, lit., pp. 469f., understands the piel as an expression of something
experienced as distinct from something narrated; qal in v . 5.   **b**   On the "concate-
nation of sentences," Ges-K §167c.

7a   Many regard ואל־אמו as a gloss dependent on Gen. 27:43f.; 27:46; this is unlikely because the obedience is referred to father and mother.

9a   Only here.   **b**   Cf. Gen. 25:13; 36:3.   **c**   For the meaning of על, Ges-K
§119a, n. 2.

Form

Gen. 27:46—28:9 is not a narrative in the proper sense. Esau's marrying two Hittite women is a narrative elaboration of the genealogical note, Gen. 26:34f. Just as
Gen. 17 follows directly on an account of a birth and Gen. 23 on the account of a
death, so Gen. 28:1-9 follows directly on a marriage. P makes these three texts the
basis for the three precultic rites which have to do with birth, marriage, and death
and he justifies them from the patriarchal story (cf. comm. on ch. 17 and ch. 23).
It is in accordance with the priestly religion that each of these rites of transition is
linked with a command; circumcision at birth, one's own duly acquired grave at
death, the choice of a wife from one's own people at marriage. The practice in
27:46—28:9 is given its basis in the patriarchal period: the genealogical notes
about the wives of Esau and Jacob which were at hand to P are reworked in such a
way as to express clearly the approval by the parents of Jacob's wives and their rejection of Esau's. P thereby makes use not only of these genealogical reports but
also of the narrative in ch. 27, though only of the motifs of Jacob's journey to
Mesopotamia and the father's blessing which is dispensed to one only, thus
hinting at the rivalry between the brothers. Everything else, particularly the reason for the journey, is completely different. Of all the priestly texts in Genesis,
27:46—28:9 shows most clearly that P is a writer of the exilic period who knows
the old J narratives and can give them a thorough reworking in accordance with his
own genius and outlook. The link between the command and the blessing in vv.
1-4 is determinative for P, just as in the link between the command and the promise in ch. 17. Execution follows command (v. 5) as in ch. 17. The same structure
is reflected in a modified form in the second part, vv. 6-9, where Esau takes his
example from Jacob.

Setting

The text is P's own construction. It is important for its formation that the command that governs the text (vv. 1,6) be explained in the context of the period for

which P is presenting the patriarchal story; so too H. Gunkel and others. It is important too that P is aware of being bound to the genealogical information passed on to him while reworking almost completely the basic narrative.

Commentary

[26:34-35]   These two verses are the proper exposition to 28:1-9. The narrative elaboration grows out of the genealogical detail of v. 34: Esau marries two Hittites, inhabitants of the land of Canaan. This is elaborated in v. 35; the parents are deeply scandalized at Esau's action. Sufficient reason is thereby given for the narrative expansion that follows in 29:1-9; 28:1 could follow immediately on 26:35.

[27:46]   Many interpreters, therefore, maintain that 27:46 is an expansion by R occasioned by the fact that the introduction, 26:34f., necessary for the understanding of 28:2-9, is too far away. If a redactor wanted to ease the transition by means of 27:46, then he could have met P's intention surprisingly well by adapting Rebekah's lament in 25:32 to P's thinking. Here the reason for the lament is that Esau has married women belonging to a foreign people, and to the grief which this has caused is added the concern that Jacob could do the same. The author of 27:46 has turned to account a third motif from ch. 27, the initiative of the mother. It accords further with the intent of a transition that Esau's wives are described as בנות חת in 27:46, as in 26:34-35, whereas בנות כנען is found in 28:1-9.

[28:1-4]   Vv. 1-4 contain Jacob's command to his son Jacob, followed by its execution in v. 5. It is divided in such a way that the whole is described as blessing (farewell blessing) which is preceded by prohibition (v. 1b) and command (v. 2). The blessing follows in the form of a wish.

[28:1-2]   The commission that the father lays on the son in vv. 1-2 recalls Gen. 24:2-4, prohibition and command corresponding to each other in each case. This common disposition favors a relatively late origin for ch. 24; the prohibition in v. 1b had precisely the same form as the prohibition of the decalogue. This passage, together with Gen. 24:3, can show how a general command can arise out of a command enunciated in a particular situation (G. Liedke, WMANT 39 [1971] 187-195). The verb צוה describes "always what a superior says to a subordinate" (ibid., 192); cf. J. Bright (JBL 92 [1973] 185-204).
   The prohibition in this lapidary form against taking a Canaanite wife can have arisen only in a period "when mixed marriages threatened the purity of the community and the religion" (H. Gunkel). The prohibition is followed by the father's command to go to Paddan-aram and take a daughter of Laban as wife (v. 2). The reason is so markedly different from that given in 27:41-45 that the redactor who put 28:1-9 after ch. 27 must have been aware of it. Each motivation had its own actuality both for the writer's understanding and that of the readers.

[28:3-4]   The blessing introduced in v. 1 now follows. But how decisively has the understanding of blessing changed over against ch. 27! All that remains here is that the father blesses the son and that the setting is the farewell blessing (not in face of death, but before a journey, as in 24:60). There remains too an echo of the motif of ch. 27 that only one of the brothers receives the blessing. Every trace of the magical understanding of blessing has disappeared; there is no sign of a rite, not even the act of touching is mentioned. The blessing is no longer the effective word of the father as in 27:37; God is the one who blesses, and the blessing is reworked to a wish or prayer (v. 3a). The most decisive alteration is that the blessing is equated with the promise; v. 3 is the promise of increase, v. 4 the promise of the land, both of which in ch. 17 are God's direct work of promise in the revelation to Abraham (17:1, 22). This leveling of blessing with promise is of very special significance for P. It is no longer of importance for him that they are dealing with basically different procedures. The only thing that is important now is the word from the ancient period of the patriarchs reaching down to the present and addressing the present generation.

For the designation of God as אל שדי, see comm. on 17:1; the promises of blessing and increase, comm. on 17:2, 6, 20; the phrase, קהל עמים, comm. on 17:6, and L. Rost, BWANT 4,24 (1938) II, ''qāhāl im AT''; Gen. 28:3; 35:11; 48:4: ''qāhāl here becomes a notion denoting quantity.'' The promise of increase is linked with the promise of the land, as in 17:8; but here too increase is given precedence. In content the promise to Jacob is the same as that to Abraham; however, the difference both at the beginning and end of 28:4 is clearly indicated: Isaac passes on to Jacob the blessing of Abraham; Abraham is the real recipient of the blessing (in v. 4a ברכה is used directly to describe the blessing); Jacob is its heir. Once again it is clear that blessing and promise have come to mean the same.

[28:5]   The command is followed by its execution, as often with P. The וישלח corresponds to the ויברך (v. 1); Isaac dismisses his son with a blessing. The transition which goes with the farewell is nicely expressed and fully in accord with the style of P by means of the precise and detailed information about the family to which Jacob is now going.

[28:6-9]   V. 5 ends with the two names Jacob and Esau. How strong the tradition is can be seen from the fact that the basic reason for the rivalry is still active even for P, and that also for P the old tradition is concerned not only with Jacob but with Jacob and Esau. At the same time he mitigates the rivalry to such an extent that Esau, who causes his parents grief (26:25) now follows Jacob's example. The passage consists of two reflections of Esau in regard to what was said of Jacob in vv. 1-5, both introduced by וירא עשו (vv. 6-7, 8). The first reflection, vv. 6-7, repeats vv. 1-5; but Esau's thoughts are centered on a blessing that Jacob receives from his father and which Esau sees in the context of Jacob's obedience; thus we find here in v. 7 the וישמע that was required by the account in v. 5. In the second reflection, v. 8, Esau acknowledges the reason: he has caused his parents grief (26:35). He tries now to remedy this by also marrying a relative, a daughter of Ishmael. To do so he undertakes a journey like Jacob. P has now succeeded in presenting Esau in a more friendly light, at the same time indicating why the blessing of Abraham could continue only through Jacob's line.

Purpose and Thrust

One can understand from its historical setting why marriage within one's own people became for P a critical Israelite command. After the dissolution of the Israelite-Judaean state the family became in fact the form of community that preserved the continuity of Israel and its religion. When P bases the prohibition to marry foreigners in the patriarchal period, then it is historically correct that the tradition of the patriarchal stories has preserved the great importance of the family for Israel through all periods, even if he altered the old narrative for his purpose. It is all the more significant, therefore, that the prohibition in v. 1b has never been taken up into the decalogue or any other series of commands. It is a time-conditioned prohibition resulting from a particular historical situation. It is this that gives weight to the fact that P's alteration of the old narrative of ch. 27, which was undertaken out of a particular historical situation, could not change the later effect of this narrative.

Jacob's Dream and Vow at Bethel

Literature

Genesis 28:10-22: F. Bergmann, *Jakobs Traum zu Bethel* (1884). A. Henderson, "On Jacob's Vision at Bethel," ET 4 (1892/93) 151-152. A. Smythe-Palmer, "Jacob at Bethel: The Vision—the Stone—the Anointing. An Essay in Comparative Religion," *Studies on Biblical Subjects* 2 (1899) 133-162. R. Beer-Hofmann, *Jacob's Dream (Gen. 28,12-22): Jewish Publications of America* (1946). J. Aagaard, "Revelation and Religion," StTh 14 (1960) 148-185. C. Sant, MTh (1960) 1-13, 14-27. J. Delorme, "A propos du songe de Jacob," *Mémorial A. Gélin* (1961) 47-54. H. A. Hoffner, "Second Millennium Antecedents to the Hebrew *'ôb*," JBL 86 (1967) 385-401. J. G. Frazer, "Jacob at Bethel," *Myth, Legend, and Custom in the OT*, ed. T. H. Gaster (1969) 182-192. G. Fohrer, *Exegese des Alten Testaments. Einführung in die Methodik* (1973, 1979²) §12, 172-221. M. Oliva, "Visión y voto de Jacob en Bethel," EstB 33 (1974) 117-155. E. G. Clarke, "Jacob's Dream at Bethel as Interpreted in the Targums and the New Testament," RSR = ScR 4 (1974/75) 367-377. F. O. Garcia-Treto, "Jacob's 'Oath-Covenant' in Genesis 28," TUSR 10 (1975) 1-10. J. Hoftijzer and G. van der Kooij, "Aramaic Texts From Deir 'Alla," DMOA 19 (1976). E. Otto, "Jakob in Bethel. Ein Beitrag zur Geschichte der Jakobüberlieferung," ZAW 88 (1976) 165-190. R. Couffignal, "Le songe de Jacob. Approches nouvelles de Genèse 28,10-22," Bib 58 (1977) 342-360. C. Houtman, "What Did Jacob See in His Dream at Bethel? Some Remarks on Genesis XXVIII 10-22," VT 27 (1977) 337-351. B. E. Shafer, "The Root *bḥr* and the Pre-Exilic Concepts of Chosenness in the Hebrew Bible," ZAW 89 (1977) 20-42.

Genesis 28:11-17: R. Otto, *The Idea of the Holy* (1917, 1958³⁰; Eng. 1917; OUP 1923; Pelican 1959). A. M. Blackman, "Oracles," JEA 12 (1926) 176-185. N. H. Ridderbos, "עפר als Staub des Totenreiches," OTS 5 (1948) 174-178. C. A. Patrides, "Renaissance Interpretations of Jacob's Ladder," ThZ 18 (1962) 411-418. J. G. Griffith, "The Celestial Ladder and the Gate of Heaven (Gen. 28, 12 and 17)," ET 76 (1964/65) 229-230; 78 (1966/67) 54-55. A. R. Millard, "The Celestial Ladder and the Gate of Heaven (Gen. 28,12.17)," ET 78 (1966/67) 86-87. E. Lipiński, "Peninna, *Iti'el* et l'Athlète," VT 17 (1967) 68-75. W. G. Dever, "Chronique archéologique: Gezer," RB 76 (1969) 563-567. W. Eisenbeis, *Die Wurzel šlm im AT*, BZAW 113 (1969) esp. 90f. A. Rofé, *Israelite Belief in Angels in the Pre-Exilic Period as Evidenced by Biblical Traditions* [in Hebr.] (diss. Jerusalem, 1969). A. Robert and A. Feuillet, *Introduction to the OT* (1970) esp. 207-214. G. Kretschmar, "Festkalender und Memorialstätten Jerusalems in altkirchlicher Zeit," ZDPV 87 (1971) 167-205. M. Dahood and T. Penar, *Ugaritic-Hebrew Parallel Pairs: Ras Shamra Parallels*, ed. L. R. Fisher (1972) 158 No 137. C. Toll, "Die Wurzel *prṣ* im Hebräischen," OrSuec 21 (1973) 73-86. J. P. Meier, "Two Disputed Questions in Matt 28:16-20," JBL 96 (1977) 407-424, esp. 422. H. Seebass, "Landverheissungen an die

Väter,'' EvTh 37 (1977) 210-229. J. S. Kselman, ''The Recovery of Poetic Fragments from the Pentateuchal Priestly Source,'' JBL 97 (1978) 161-173.

Genesis 28:18-22: G. Westphal, *Jahwes Wohnstätten nach den Anschauungen der alten Hebräer*, BZAW 15 (1908) esp. 231-233. K. Budde, ''Zur Bedeutung der Mazzeben,'' OLZ 15 (1912) 248-252. G. Zuntz, ''Baitylos and Bethel,'' CM 8 (1947) 169-219. H. Cazelles, ''La dîme israélite et les textes de Ras Shamra,'' VT 1 (1951) 131-134. W. H. Gispen, ''De gelofte,'' GThT 61 (1961) 4-13,37-45,65-73. H. Donner, ''Zu Genesis 28,22,'' ZAW 74 (1962) 68-70. E. Kutsch, *Salbung als Rechtsakt im AT und im Alten Orient*, BZAW 87 (1963). G. Ryckmans, ''Sub-arabe *mḏbḥt*—hébreu *mzbḥ* et termes apparentés,'' Fests. W. Caskel (1968) 252-260. M. G. Glenn, ''The Word לוז in Gen. 28,19 in the LXX and in the Midrash,'' JQR 59 (1968/69) 73-76. C. F. Graesser, ''Standing Stones in Ancient Palestine,'' BA 35 (1972) 34-63. E. Stockton, ''Sacred Pillars in the Bible,'' ABR 20 (1972) 16-32. H. Vorländer, ''The Power of Life. The Experience of God in the OT,'' NETR 20 (1973) 7-21. W. J. Dumbrell, ''The Role of Bethel in the Biblical Narratives from Jacob to Jeroboam I,'' AJBA 2.3 (1974/75) 65-75.

Text

28:10 Jacob set out from Beersheba and went on his way to Haran.

11 Now he came to a certain place[a] and he spent the night there because the sun had already gone down. And he took one of the stones of the place and put it at his head and lay down to sleep in that place.

12 And he dreamt[a] that there was a stairway set on the ground and its top reached to heaven; and there were angels of God going up and coming down.

13 And Yahweh stood before him and said: I am Yahweh the God of Abraham your father, and the God of Isaac.[a] The land on which you are lying[b] I give to you and your descendants.

14 And your descendants are to be like the dust of the earth, and you shall expand west and east, north and south, and all the families of the earth shall bless themselves in you (and your descendants).[a]

15 I will be with you and will protect you wherever you go,[a] and I will bring you back to this land; for I will not leave you until[b] I have done all[c] that I told you.

16 When Jacob awoke from his sleep he said: Truly Yahweh is[a] in this place and I did not know it.

17 And he was afraid[a] and said: How awesome[b] is this place; it is none other than the house of God and the gate of heaven.

18 Jacob rose early in the morning and took the stone which he had laid at his head, set it up as a sacred pillar and poured oil on it.

19 And he named that place Bethel; but earlier the name of the city was Luz.

20 Then Jacob made a vow and said: If God is with me and protects me on this journey I am making, and gives me bread to eat and clothes to wear,[a]

21 and I return[a] safely to my father's house, then Yahweh shall be my God,

22 and this stone, which I have set up as a sacred pillar is to be[a] a house of God. And of all that you give me, I will assuredly give a tenth[b] to you.

11a On the article, Ges-K §126r; E. König §296a.
12a On the structure of the report of the dream, F. I. Andersen, *The Sentence in Biblical Hebrew* (1974) 95.
13a After צחק Gk inserts: μὴ φοβοῦ **b** On the construction, BrSynt §123b; 152a.
14a Perhaps an addition; cf. Gen. 12:3; 18:18.

15a After בכל Gk inserts הדרך.   **b** On the construction, BrSynt §163b; Ges-K §106c. **c**   Add כל with Gk.
16a   BrSynt §12.
17a   Syr inserts יראה גדולה.   **b** BrSynt §12; G. Bergsträsser II, §13d.
20a   On the form, R. Meyer II §175.
21a   Gk reads Hiph.
22a   Gk inserts לי.   **b** On the form, BrSynt §93a; E. König §219a.

Form

Gen. 28:10-22 is one of those narratives of encounters with God and of sanctuaries that are inserted between the parts of the Jacob-Esau story (Gen. 32:1-2, 22-32; 35:1-15). It is an accretion of several layers, as almost all interpreters agree. The variety of expansions it underwent are a sign of the great importance it later acquired as a narrative of the origin of the sanctuary of Bethel. The narrative grows out of the itinerary. Though the itinerary note in v. 10 is in itself independent, nevertheless it serves as the exposition of the narrative that follows (G. Fohrer, *Exegese. . .*, UTB 267 [1979²]). The action begins in v. 11; it is divided into the preparation (v. 11) and the dream (v. 12), Jacob's reaction and exclamation (vv. 16-17), Jacob's action after he awakes (v. 18). It reaches its climax in the naming of the place (v. 19). It is a self-contained, close-knit evolvement of an event which happened on a journey. Everything else can be a later addition because it is not essential to the course of events. There is no structured tension; this is replaced by Jacob's surprise expressed in words after he awakes. It is not a narrative in the strict sense, but an account of an experience on a journey (v. 10) expanded to narrative.

This structure is confirmed by the many points of contact with the close parallel, Gen. 32:1-2, which belongs to the same group of narratives. Gen. 32:1-2 is also a story which concerns Jacob only and has the same function in the structure of Gen. 25–36; the texts 28:10-22 and 32:1-2 frame Gen. 29–31. Moreover, their structure is similar; the two texts agree in the following: (1) what is narrated happens in the course of a journey; (2) it is an encounter (the verb פגע in both cases); (3) in both cases occurs the expression מלאכי אלהים, not found elsewhere (except in 2 Chron. 16 in a different sense); (4) the exclamation, "here is. . ."; (5) the naming of the place. These parallels confirm that the narrative, 28:10-12, 16-19, corresponding to this structure, is a self-contained unity. The expansions are due to further growth and are not to be explained on literary-critical grounds.

What is peculiar to this narrative is that it has, so to speak, two faces or aspects; they are not in conflict, however, but rather complement each other. There is the etiological aspect: the goal of the narrative is the origin of a sanctuary or holy place; it concludes with the naming. Then there is the discovery of this holy place as the experience of the discoverer who is in flight. To the first stage corresponds the discovery of a holy place as an independent narrative whose general aim is to explain the origin of the holy place at Bethel which still exists. It is therefore a sanctuary narrative, i.e., a story of the discovery of the holy place which continues to be narrated there. To the second stage corresponds the discovery of the holy place as the experience of a man who comes across it in flight, i.e., as the experience of Jacob in flight before his brother Esau who is intent on murder. The "cult etiology" is attached to the place where it is narrated; this is a story told at Bethel about the founding of this sanctuary. The story acquires its other aspect from its context between ch. 27 and chs. 29–31. It was at hand to J who gave it its second face by means of the context; all he needed to do was to introduce the situation of Jacob who discovered the holy place. It is to this that the promise in v. 15 corresponds. It would seem that J inserted the promise (v. 15) into the old narrative which contained only the dream (v. 12): this promise to be with Jacob, expanded around the motif of flight and return, is determinative for the Jacob-Esau cycle just as is the promise of a son for the Abraham cycle. It was subsequently elaborated around vv. 13 and 14 (and v. 15bβ?) as a comparison with 26:3-5, 24-25 shows, where the promises are heaped up in a similar way. The vow in vv. 20-22 is likewise an expansion; it has long since been noted that it cannot be contemporaneous with the promise in v. 15. The same thing cannot simultaneously be a divine promise and the condition of a vow.

Setting

For a long time the final text of 28:10-22 has been explained as a result of joining together the two literary sources J (for the most part vv. 13-16, 19) and E (for the most part vv. 11, 12, 17-22, omitting v. 19). The main arguments were the different designations for God, doublings, and the argument from content, namely, revelation in a dream. The last named is not relevant here because v. 16 (J) also presupposes a revelation in a dream. For the other arguments, see the exegesis. Each of the different designations for God is to be understood from its own context. The unity of the narrative, vv. 10-12, 16-19 (without the later expansions, vv. 13-15, 20-22), is persuasive against a separation into literary sources, as is the fact that the verses ascribed to J would constitute but a fragment (so too G. Fohrer, W. Richter, O. H. Steck, E. Otto). With regard to the designations for God, יהוה in vv. 13, 16, 21 and אלהים in vv. 12, 17, 20, 21, 22, it is to be stated that אלהים occurs only in the expansion (vv. 20-22) and in two contexts, vv. 12, 17, where its use is conditioned by the material.

The story of the discovery of a sanctuary was narrated and handed on at this sanctuary at Bethel. Excavations have shown that the sanctuary existed long before the immigration of the Israelite tribes; hence the story was already being narrated and handed on long before their arrival. It contains, therefore, only such elements as are known from and widespread in the history of religions. J then takes up a story which arose and was handed on at a sanctuary (F. Delitzsch, P. Volz, F. V. Winnett) and gives it a new meaning in the context of the patriarchal story: it is Jacob who discovered the holy place on his flight from Esau. J's takeover of the pre-Israelite narrative presupposes the takeover of Bethel by the immigrant tribes whereby Jacob became the discoverer of the holy place. Vv. 13b, 14 and vv. 20-22 point to a third stage in the growth of the narrative. It is significant for this stage that the two most important areas of Israel's sedentary life in Canaan have contributed to the process of growth; first, the history of the people in the context of God's dealing with it as reflected in the promise of the land and descendants (vv. 13b, 14); second, the history of worship inasmuch as two cultic practices, the vow and the tithe (vv. 20-22), are anchored in the story of the discovery. The formation of 28:10-22 can be reduced to a few strands in these three stages which correspond to the three stages of the formation of the patriarchal stories in the context of the formation of the people of Israel. Hence there is no place for complicated and hypothetical constructions (e.g., those of A. de Pury and O. H. Steck).

Commentary

[28:10-12]   Vv. 10-12 are a continuation of 27:41-45(J). Jacob's departure from Beersheba for Haran (about 460 km.) is the execution of the commission of his mother (27:43). The statement of the goal indicates that the itinerary note is adapted to the context; there is no mention of individual stopping places on the way, not even between Beersheba and Bethel.

[28:11]   What follows is an experience on the way. The action begins with v. 11. Arrival in the evening after a day's journey is often described in the Old Testament, e.g., Gen. 19:1-3; 24:23-25; Judg. 19:11-21. Here, however, the traveler is overtaken by nightfall and has to pass the night in the open; at sunset he comes to "the place." The article points to the double sense of מקום: for Jacob it is no more than a suitable place to spend the night; but it can also mean the holy place, the discovery of which is now hinted at. When Jacob prepares his camp for the night and lays a stone which is lying there "at his head(s)" (1 Sam. 26:12), the narrator is letting us know that there is nothing to indicate that it is a holy place; Jacob becomes aware of this only through his dream. The narrative is in fact about the discovery of a holy place, not about the chance finding of yet another one already known. Jacob does not use the stone as a "cushion for his head" (H. Gunkel and others) but as a protection behind his head (B. Jacob); other passages also support this (1 Sam. 19:13, 16; 26:7, 11f., 16; 1 Kings 19:6; Jer. 13:18). There is no sign in the text that the stone was "large" and so looked like a giant to Jacob (H. Gunkel, continued by V. Maag).

[28:12]   Jacob has a dream (v. 12). This is the first dream narrative in the Old Testament. The account of the dream consists of only two sentences; it belongs to that group of dreams which consist of but one image. Jacob's reaction on awakening (v. 17) accords with this: the dream has shown him that this is a holy place. The two sentences in v. 12, therefore, are stating something about the place, not something that is happening; it is a vision in the strict sense. It is introduced typically by הנה, and he has the vision of a stairway, not a ladder, which links heaven and earth: "set earthwards, and its top directed towards heaven" (B. Jacob). סלם, an ascent or stairway, occurs only here; it is from the verb סלל, "to heap up," Akk. *simmiltu*. The verb calls to mind a piled-up (stone) construction, a ramp, which reaches from earth to heaven, from heaven to earth. It is not possible to form a precise image of what Jacob saw in his dream (cf. C. Houtmann [1977] bibliog. above).

Similar images surround the Babylonian temple towers (E. A. Speiser; cf. RLA 1 "Babylon" par. 133); in the myth "Nergal and Ereshkigal" the gods ascend "the long stairway (*simmiltu*) of heaven," A. R. Millard (1966/67), see bibliog. above. In the pyramid texts the dead king goes up to his mother Nut on a ladder; here too occurs the expression "the gates of heaven," J. G. Griffiths (1964/65), bibliog. above. Gen. 11:1-9 is also concerned with a link between heaven and earth, cf. *Genesis 1–11* ad loc. But there is no direct influence.

It is essential that the stairway linking heaven and earth in Jacob's dream is set (מצב) in the ground at the place where he is sleeping, thereby making him aware that it is a holy place.

The second part, also beginning with הנה, says nothing new but explains the function of the stairway more clearly by the vision that Jacob has of the מלאכי אלהים going up and down on it. These are heavenly beings, sharply distinct from the singular מלאך יהוה but like the בני אלהים of Job 1:6; 2:1, who by means of their ascent and descent underscore the link between heaven and earth already de-

scribed by the stairway. Heavenly beings are also present in Is. 6 in connection
with God enthroned in his sanctuary. Here too it is essential that the ''angels of
God'' who go up and down link the place where Jacob lies with heaven. Jacob's
reaction in v. 17 corresponds with this second part as well; his two statements
there describe the holy place.

[28:13-15]   The promise: a third הנה introduces a promise to Jacob comprising a
promise of land and descendants, vv. 13-14, such as made to Abraham and
determining chs. 12–25, and a promise of aid directed towards Jacob's present situation (v. 15).

[28:13-14]   The promise is freshly introduced: יהוה נצב עליו (as in Gen. 18:2).
The suffix cannot refer to the stairway, as that would conflict with v. 12b; it refers
to Jacob, ''before him'' or ''opposite him,'' because he is addressed in what follows (see further on v. 15). Then comes the ''self-introduction formula'' whose
function is clearly to put the promise now made to Jacob in line with those made to
Abraham (ch. 15 and elsewhere) and Isaac (26:2-5). This is followed by the promise of the land (v. 13b) and of descendants (v. 14a), and the blessing of the families of the earth through him and his descendants (v. 14b). The introduction itself
indicates that vv. 13-14 are a secondary expansion, and the tradition history of the
promises (the accumulation of them) confirms it. The formulation of v. 13 is
adapted to Jacob's situation by the words, ''the land on which you are lying.'' But
this is a later adaptation, like Gen. 13:14, which does not really correspond to the
context. The place where Jacob is lying is determined otherwise in v. 12. The conclusion which H. Seebass draws from v. 13bα, that all that is promised is the land
in the region of Bethel and that this is the oldest promise of the land, is not legitimate (this is also against A. de Pury who agrees with H. Seebass, BZAW 98
[1966]); ''and your descendants'' always goes with the promise of the land, and is
also a sign that it is destined for Israel.

[28:14]   The peculiar formulation ופרצת occurs also in a promise of increase in
Is. 54:3, ''For you will spread abroad to the right and to the left'' (cf. Ex. 1:12).
Then the four quarters of the heavens are mentioned, though they are really more
suited to the promise of the land as in Gen. 13:14. It is not necessary then to look
for an explanation of the four quarters in the geography of Canaanite mythology
(F. O. Garcia-Treto, TUSR 10 [1975] 1-10). On the extension of the blessing to
all peoples (v. 14b), cf. Gen. 12:3b; 18:18; 22:18; 26:4; the same sequence of land
and increase for the peoples is also found in Gen. 26:3-4. The clumsy ובזרעך at
the end of v. 14 could be a gloss, an assimilation to the last word of v. 13.

[28:15]   The promise in v. 15 differs from that in vv. 13-14 inasmuch as it is not
only adapted to the situation of Jacob in flight but also is fulfilled in his lifetime
and accords with the life-style of the patriarchs. Just as the promise of a son is
characteristic of the Abraham cycle, so is the promise of presence or assistance
characteristic of the Jacob-Esau cycle (Gen. 26:3, 24; 28:15(20); 31:3; 32:10;
46:3[48:15, 21; 50:24]). A promise is not an original part of the old narrative of
the discovery of a holy place. J has inserted the promise of assistance at the beginning of Jacob's flight from his brother—it could be introduced by the first five
words of v. 13—just as he has put the promise at the beginning of the Abraham
story (12:1-3); there too it is set into an itinerary. The words that follow the simple

promise, אנכי עמך, do not add anything to it but merely unfold it. In origin the promise is a promise for the road. Its setting in life is the start of a journey or migration or the like; it belongs above all to nomadic life.

There are obvious examples of a promise of assistance outside Israel; see parallels in H. D. Preuss, ZAW 80 (1968) 139-173. The prayer of Gilgamesh is about the road into a foreign land: "O Utu, I would enter the land; be my ally!" The god answers accordingly (S. N. Kramer, SBO 3 [1959] 155ff.). Later the promise of assistance is given to the king in a royal oracle of the 21st dynasty as he sets out on a campaign (A. M. Blackman, JEA 12 [1926] 176-185).

The awareness that the assurance, "I am with you," belongs properly to a journey has always remained, as Ps. 23 shows, cf. Heb. 13:5. Jacob will experience the assistance assured him as he is protected from the dangers of the road he has to travel, an experience that dominates all personal piety from the Psalms right up to present-day hymn books (cf. G. Sauer, THAT II [1976] 982-987, *šmr*, "protect"). The next sentence, a continuation of Gen. 27:41-45, refers to Jacob's own situation, "I will bring you back. . . ." The last sentence, v. 15bβ, on the other hand, is not part of the promise of assistance but rather collates it ("I will not leave you") with the previous promises, vv. 13-14, "all that I told you," and anticipates its fulfillment, "until I have done"; with the Gk, "all" is to be added. An assurance like this, that God will fulfill what he has promised, belongs to a later style (cf. Is. 40:10f., and the oath in ch. 15 which corroborates the promise).

[28:16-18]   These verses report Jacob's reaction to his dream (v. 12; there is no sign here of any reference to the promise in vv. 13-15): v. 16, he awakes and exclaims in response to the dream; v. 17, his awe and exclamation; v. 18, his response in action—he erects a stone pillar. Both v. 16 וייקץ and v. 17 וירא can follow directly on v. 12. In any case v. 16 presupposes the וישכב in v. 11: Jacob lies down and awakes from sleep. It is not possible, therefore, to separate v. 11 and v. 16 into two sources. The exclamation that follows, in distinction from that in v. 17, refers to Jacob's situation, and "in this place" presupposes v. 11. "In this place," means "where I spent the night as I fled"; "and I did not know it," is to be understood in the same way, the words of one who comes from afar. This is the reason for designating God as יהוה, the God of his father, whose action he had so far known only in the circle of his father's house. It is possible then that v. 16 is an addition by J and belongs more closely with v. 15abβ; this would also make the juxtaposition of vv. 16 and 17 clearer.

[28:17]   V. 17 reproduces Jacob's immediate reaction to the dream. The root ירא occurs twice; Jacob stands in awe of what he has seen. This is the locus classicus for the numinous as an element of the holy (R. Otto, *The Idea of the Holy* [1917, 1958[30]; Eng 1917; 1923; 1959], chs. 4 and 7). It is also the locus classicus in the sense that the numinous proceeds from a place: "How awesome is this place!" What is described here is a phenomenon of religion as a whole; it occurs in many stages in the history of mankind throughout the world (F. Heiler, *Erscheinungsformen und Wesen der Religion* [1961]).

While v. 17a reproduces the immediate impression, the two descriptions of the place which Jacob gives in v. 17b, "house of God" and "gate of heaven," are explanations already there in the tradition. It is possible, therefore, that the two ideas do not complement each other, but rather are in collision. The meaning of בית אלהים hangs loose. In the structure of the sentence it designates not the stone but מקום הזה: this place is the dwelling place of God! Read together with v. 17a it can only mean that this place is forbidden to humans because God dwells here. The holy place was originally and for the most part an area marked out in the open, τέμενος, *templum* (F. Heiler, 128).

The other designation, "the gate of heaven," occurs elsewhere in the Old Testament only in Ps. 78:23, ". . .He. . .opened the doors of heaven, and he rained down upon them. . ." (cf. Gen. 7:11, "windows of heaven," something quite different). "The gate of heaven" is "a place where heaven is open to man" (A. Dillman), i.e., something analogous to the stairway in the dream. But this too is to be understood in the context of v. 17a; the gate does not invite but prohibits entrance; one may not enter the place where God dwells. All these notions center around the locale, the (holy) place, house of God, stairway, door; they are in the context of the dividing line between the divine and the human, the line where awe begins. Both the idea of the locale and the awe connected with it appear here for the first time in the patriarchal stories; both are a general religious phenomenon, not typical of the religion of the patriarchs but indicative of the transition from the patriarchal period to sedentary existence and cult.

[28:18]   Jacob reacts first with an exclamation, now with an action. The first three words indicate that Jacob's reaction of shock to his dream took place during the course of the night; the present action can only have followed in the morning; it too is governed by fear of the holiness of the place. It can mean only that the place is made recognizable as holy, as God's place, by the erection of the stone. Jacob's action in setting up the stone that lay at his head when he had the dream is saying that the stone was near him as he dreamed, that it revealed to him the holiness of the place, that it was the witness to his dream. The stone, therefore, has two functions in Jacob's action: it is a witness (cf. Gen. 31:45-49 for the stone as witness to an agreement), and as an erected stone, a pillar (that is the meaning of מצבה); it is a monument that is later to draw the attention of visitors to the importance of the place (like a stele over a grave). Both these functions are a sufficient explanation of the erection of the stone. It is not necessary to presuppose that the stone itself is the "house" of a god בית־אל; however, the designation בית אל, which occurs in the context of the cult of stones, does point in this direction. A careful distinction must be made between the cult of stones as such and the designation מצבה: the former refers originally to (particular) stones as found in their natural setting, the latter, as the name says, to something set up by man; these have for the most part been dressed, as the archaeological discoveries show.

On the cult of stones cf. F. Heiler, 34-37 and, in detail, A. de Pury, 409-430, with further literature. The designation of a stone as בית־אל belongs to this context. What is meant originally is the power dwelling in the stone, its dynamic energy such as can kill a person. The cult of stones was widespread at one stage, one sign of this being that the Semitic designation בית־אל for a stone pillar has come over into Greek and Latin as a foreign word, βαίτυλος and *baetulus*. A note in Philo of Byblos that steles were described as houses of gods has been confirmed by recent discoveries (A. Dupont-Sommer, RArch 10 [1960] 21-54; H. Donner, ZAW 74 [1962] 68-70). For the *maṣṣebah*, cf. "Mazzebe," BRL (1937; 1977[2]); ZDVP 75 (1959) 1-13, and bibliog. above. C. F. Graesser distinguishes four functions: grave stele, contract stele, memorial stele (to commemorate an event), and cult stele, "to mark the sacred area." It is this last function that is pertinent to

Gen. 28:18. Jacob sets up the stone so as to mark out as holy for others the place he discovered to be such in the dream.

The closing remark, that Jacob anointed the "head" of the stone with oil, presupposes the already existing rite of the anointing of the *maṣṣebah*; it is an addition consequent on this knowledge. A. Bertholet notes correctly that oil as a typical product of agricultural land points to the time of the settlement (JBL 49 [1930] 218-233). Anointing of a *maṣṣebah* with oil is not to be understood as a sacrifice but as "the conveyance of power to the holy object" (A. Bertholet); cf. also E. Kutsch (BZAW 87 [1963]); J. Skinner cites as an example, "on a small stone in a sanctuary of Delphi oil was poured every day. . ." (Pausanias X, 24,6).

[28:19]   The goal of the narrative of the discovery of this holy place is the naming of it. It becomes clear once more in this verse that the בֵּית־אֵל does not designate the stone but the sacred area which is distinguished as such by the stone. A further sign that the interest of the narrative is the naming of the place is the mention of the earlier name which was לוּז = "almond tree," elsewhere in Gen. 35:6; 48:3; Is. 16:2; 18:13; Judg. 1:23. "The later Bethel was situated near the older Luz" (A. Dillmann). Luz is probably the old name of the place which then acquires the name of the sanctuary situated nearby. G. Fohrer supposed that the change of name took place only in the period of the judges or the monarchy. The mention of Bethel in Gen. 12:8 and 13:3 did not worry the transmitters; a place can quite well be called by the later name. This conclusion shows once more how questionable is source division. "V. 19 is not to be separated from vv. 17 and 18. The structure shows that the narrative culminates in the holiness of the place and that its goal is the naming of Bethel" (E. Otto, ZAW 88 [1976] 169,174). It is significant that v. 19, which earlier was almost unanimously attributed to J with vv. 13-16, is once more considered by recent writers to belong to the main part of the narrative which reaches its natural conclusion there (E. Otto, O. H. Steck, A. de Pury). The name achieves continuity; it brings the event in its origin right down into the present.

[28:20-22]   The vow: W. Richter established the following in his study on the vow (BZ 11 [1967] 21-52): Gen. 28:20-22 is the longest of all vows in the Old Testament (Num. 21:2; Judg. 11:30f.; 1 Sam. 1:11; 2 Sam. 15:7-9); a comparison with the other vows shows that Gen. 28:20-22 does not reproduce the vow as it was pronounced but is a literary construction. It is impossible, therefore, for it to be the conclusion of the old narrative. W. Richter (and E. Otto) establish further that vv. 20-22 are without any syntactical or other link with what has preceded; it is therefore an appendage. Two observations on the context confirm this. The sentence in Jacob's exclamation, "it is none other than the house of God!" (v. 17), is not compatible with the sentence in the vow, "this stone is to be a house of God" (v. 22). In addition, the content of a promise (v. 15) could scarcely coincide with the content of a vow (vv. 20, 21a) in one and the same text. One can understand the reason for this subsequent appendage: just as the sanctuary at Bethel is traced back to Jacob, so too are vows and tithes, important cult practices at the present sanctuary, to be legitimated by the father of the people. Vv. 20-22 are to be explained from the growth and development of the old narrative at the sanctuary at Bethel. The structure corresponds to that of the other vows: vv. 20aα, always the same introduction; vv. 20aβb-21b, the conditions; vv. 21b-22, the promises.

[**28:20aα**] The repetition of the same introductory formula together with the same structure indicates a fixed form and custom which can be proved with certainty to be from the early period of the monarchy. It is common to all vows that they are pronounced at a sanctuary (temple). The rite presupposes sedentary cult; it is not to be presumed from this that the practice of the vow already existed in the patriarchal period.

[**28:20aβb, 21a**] The conditions of the promise, introduced by אם in v. 20, are not, as G. von Rad, W. Richter, and others say, three different conditions tacked together, but one expanded condition, as a comparison with v. 15 shows: a promise made to Jacob there is reshaped here into the condition of a vow. There is *one* promise in v. 15, "I will be with you" (cf. v. 20aβ); it is unfolded in two ways: "I will protect you on your journey" (v. 15aβ; cf. v. 20bα), and "I will bring you back" (v. 15bα; cf. v. 21a). The only difference is that in v. 20bβ food and clothing are added to the protection. Two of the other few vow texts in the Old Testament contain the words "return home safely" (Judg. 11:30f., word for word, and 2 Sam. 15:7-9); they allow then the conclusion that this was a typical petition in the vows of the period of the judges and the kings. The author of Gen. 28:20-22 obviously used it to link the vow as it was known to him with the motif of flight–return in the Jacob story. There is no mention of food and clothing in the promise in v. 15; one explanation is that it too was typical of the vow.

[**28:21b-22**] A complete understanding of the promise in vv. 21b-22 depends on the meaning of the difficult first sentence, והיה יהוה לי לאלהים. Another vow, 2 Sam. 15:7-9, helps here: "If the Lord will indeed bring me back to Jerusalem, then I will offer worship (ועבדתי) to the Lord in 'Hebron' " (Gk) (similarly Judg. 11:30f.). The עבדתי is made precise and concrete in an act of cult (sacrifice). The sentence refers to the cultic worship of Yahweh which can begin only with the building of the sanctuary, i.e., with the transition to sedentary life, as presupposed in v. 22b. In vv. 20-22 Jacob represents at the same time the later Israel which is the object of the fulfillment of the vow. This is confirmed by the closeness of v. 21b to Gen. 17:7 (P), "to be God to you [sing.]," also aimed at the cultic worship of God by Israel (in the plural in all other passages). The conclusion from this is that neither v. 21b is to be deleted as a redactional addition (J. Wellhausen and others) nor is יהוה in v. 21b—which presents great difficulties if vv. 20-22 are assigned to E—to be altered to אל (W. Eichrodt and others). V. 21b is necessary because it is the real promise; יהוה is necessary because it is precisely the cult name, the name of God who is worshiped at Bethel. The formulation of v. 21b shows that the author of vv. 20-22 can make use of two designations for God (B. D. Eerdmans). And this writer can surely not be an "Elohist."

[**28:22a**] "This stone. . .is to be a house of God." V. 22a cannot mean that the *maṣṣebah* which has been set up is to be the dwelling of a god. This is impossible not only because of v. 17 but also because of v. 21b. It can only mean: a sanctuary is to arise from this stone, or the stone is to be extended into a sanctuary (or acquire the status of a sanctuary) at which the God, Yahweh (v. 21b), is to be worshiped. It is also certainly intended that a temple is to be built here, though this is not stated explicitly; the hearers know the temple at Bethel. Again it is presupposed that Jacob is the representative of Israel.

[**28:22b**] As the second part of the promise is unfolded the passage takes the form of an address. It is obvious that the author has taken over a fixed expression from the language of the liturgy; it recalls the similar form of address at the presentation of the offering in Deut. 26. It is clear that what is meant is the giving of a tenth part which, after the immigration, is a regular liturgical practice. It consists of the produce of the field, grain, must, oil (Deut. 12:17; 14:22-29; 26:12-15). Whatever it may be, the tithe presupposes sedentary life and regular cult. As in Gen. 14:20, so here the tithe is based on and legitimated by patriarchal institution.

Purpose and Thrust

The narrative in Gen. 28 is of great significance both for the patriarchal story and the religion of Israel. Its appearance first in the Jacob cycle and not in the Abraham cycle corresponds to the facts of the case in Exodus-Numbers where the Sinai tradition is added to the exodus tradition. Gen. 28 is, with reservation, parallel to Ex. 19. In both cases something new for a wandering group is inaugurated with the discovery of a holy place—cult linked with place. Both texts, Gen. 28 no less than Ex. 19, stand on the threshold of sedentary life for which the cult associated with the holy place is determinative. The texts differ in that behind the one, Gen. 28, lies the experience of a migrating individual, and behind the other, Ex. 19, the experience of a migrating group. They agree in that the discovery of the holy place is followed by a series of events associated with it: Gen. 28, vow and tithes (concerned with the individual); Ex. 19, covenant and law (concerned with the people). Both reflect a long development in the matter narrated. Three conceptions of the holy place emerge from Gen. 28: God is in a holy object, the old idea of a holy stone as a "house of God"; God is at a particular place where he has appeared to someone like Jacob, and the place is to be marked out by a monument in the form of an altar or a temple; God's place is in heaven, and there must be a link leading to it like a gate or a stairway.

The narrative preserves a trait characteristic of ancient times that the particular place is awe-inspiring, full of dread. God's place is forbidden to humans. It is here that the idea of the transcendent has its origin, an idea which has travelled the long road from religion to philosophy. It is to be noted that the word "holy" (קדש) does not occur in Gen. 28. It is only by linking the *tremendum* (awe-inspiring) with the *fascinosum* (spell-binding) that, after a long process of development, one arrives at the idea of the holy as met in Is. 6 (again in a vision at a holy place).

In Gen. 28 the promise of v. 15, which concerns the journey and the story of the patriarch Jacob, is added to the experience of the holy; thus there are brought together those two basic religious phenomena which from then on determine between them the history and religion of the people of God: (1) God's assistance and presence on the journey, determining the story of Jacob's life and the history of the people of Israel, and (2) the holiness of God which has appeared at a particular place (v. 12)—history and worship respectively. The same link appears in a different way in the lapidary phrase of the prophet Isaiah, "the Holy One of Israel." These two basic phenomena remain in vital tension with each other. Jacob discovers the holy place at Bethel, but he does not stay there; the Israelites come to Sinai, but they do not settle there; the prophets proclaim destruction to the temple in Jerusalem, but the religion of Israel goes on. Jesus replies to the Samaritan woman's question about the "proper" holy place: ". . .The hour is coming, and now is, when the true worshipers will worship the Father in spirit and truth. . ." (Jn. 4:19-26).

Jacob and Laban:
Marriage with Leah and Rachel

Literature

Genesis 29–31: C. H. Gordon, ''The Story of Jacob and Laban in the Light of the Nuzi Tablets,'' BASOR 66 (1937) 25-27. R. Frankena, ''Some Remarks on the Semitic Background of Chapters XXIX-XXXI of the Book of Genesis,'' OTS 17 (1972) 53-64.

Genesis 29:1-14: D. Daube and R. Yaron, ''Jacob's Reception by Laban,'' JSSt 1 (1956) 60-62. W. Reiser, ''Die Verwandtschaftsformel in Genesis 2,23,'' ThZ 16 (1960) 1-4. J. Scharbert, *''šlm* im AT,'' *Fests. H. Junker* (1961) 209-229. I. L. Seeligmann, ''A Psalm From Pre-regal Times,'' VT 14 (1964) 75-92. W. Brueggemann, ''Of the Same Flesh and Bone (Gen. 2,23a),'' CBQ 32 (1970) 532-542. H. H. Schmid, *šalom ''Frieden'' im Alten Orient und im Alten Testament*, SBS 51 (1971). J. Briend, ''Puits de Jacob,'' DBS 9 (1975) 386-398.

Genesis 29:15-30: B. Stade, ''Lea und Rahel,'' ZAW 1 (1881) 112-116; *Geschichte des Volkes Israel I* (1887; 1899[3]) esp. 378. G. M. Gooden, ''The False Bride,'' *Folklore* 4 (1893) 242-248. P. Arfert, *Das Motiv von der untergeschobenen Braut* (diss. Rostock, 1897). P. Haupt, ''Lea und Rahel,'' ZAW 29 (1909) 281-286. W. Golther, ''Die untergeschobene Braut,'' HDM I (1930/33) 307-319. S. Thompson, *The Folktale* (1951[2]) 117-120. W. Kornfeld, ''Mariage dans l'Ancien Testament,'' DBS 5 (1954) 905-926. R. Yaron, ''The Rejected Bridegroom (LE 25),'' Or 33 (1964) 23-29. O. Eissfeldt, ''Jakob-Lea und Jakob-Rahel (Gen. 29,16-30,24; 35,16-20),'' *Fests. H. W. Hertzberg* (1965) 50-55. N. P. Lemche, ''The 'Hebrew Slave'. Comments on the Slave Law Ex XXI2-11,'' VT 25 (1975) 128-144. M. Lüthi, *So leben sie noch heute* (1976[2]) 117-125. J. Scharbert, ''Ehe und Eheschliessung in der Rechtssprache des Pentateuch und beim Chronisten,'' *Fests. W. Kornfeld* (1977) 213-226.

Text

29:1   Then Jacob continued his journey and came to the land of the peoples of the east.

2   He looked around and saw a well out in the field and three flocks of sheep lying there beside it, because the flocks were watered from it; And there was a[a] large stone over the mouth of the well.

3   When all the flocks[a] had gathered there, they would roll the stone away from the mouth of the well, water the sheep, and then put the stone in its place over the mouth of the well.

4   Jacob said to them: Where are you from, my brothers? They said: We are from Haran.[a]

5   And he said to them: Do you know Laban, the son of Nahor?[a] They
    replied: We know him.
6   And he asked them: Is he well? And they replied: Yes, he is well; and
    look, here is his daughter Rachel coming with the sheep!
7   He said: The sun is still high and it is not yet time to gather the flocks to-
    gether; nevertheless,[a] water the sheep and go and pasture them.
8   But they replied: We cannot until all the flocks[a] are gathered together;
    then the stone is rolled away from the mouth of the well and we water
    the sheep.
9   While he was still speaking with them, Rachel came with her father's
    sheep; she looked after them.
10 When Jacob saw Rachel, the daughter of his mother's brother, and the
    sheep of his mother's brother, he went up and rolled away the stone
    from the mouth of the well and watered the sheep of his mother's
    brother.
11 Then Jacob kissed Rachel[a] and wept aloud.
12 And he told Rachel that he was a relative of her father, a son of
    Rebekah. So she ran and told her father.
13 When Laban heard the news[a] of Jacob his sister's son, he ran to meet
    him, embraced him and kissed him, and brought him to his house.
14 And Laban said to him: Indeed,[a] you are my flesh and blood. And he
    stayed with him a month.[b]
15 Then Laban said to Jacob: Yes, you are indeed[a] my relative! Should
    you therefore work for me for nothing? Tell me what your wage[b] should
    be.
16 Now Laban had two daughters, the elder called Leah, the younger
    Rachel.
17 Leah's eyes were without lustre,[a] but Rachel was beautiful and
    graceful.
18 Jacob loved Rachel and said: I will work for you for seven years for
    your younger daughter Rachel.
19 Laban answered: It is better to give her to you than to anyone else;
    stay with me.
20 So Jacob worked seven years for Rachel, and they seemed but a few
    days—he loved her so much.
21 Then Jacob said to Laban: The time is up! Give me[a] my wife that I may
    go to her.
22 So Laban invited all the men of the place and gave a feast.
23 In the evening, however, he took his daughter Leah and brought her to
    Jacob and he slept with her.
24 Laban also gave his maid Zilpah to "his daughter Leah"[a] to be[b] her
    maid.
25 And in the morning—it is Leah![a] Then "Jacob"[b] said to Laban: What is
    this you have done to me? Did I not work for Rachel? Why have you
    deceived me?
26 Laban replied: It is not the custom[a] among us to give the younger be-
    fore the elder.
27 Complete these seven days of feasting with this one and then we[a] will
    give you the other also in return for a further seven years work.
28 Jacob did so and completed the seven days of feasting. Then Laban
    gave him his daughter Rachel as wife.
29 Laban also gave his maid Bilhah to his daughter Rachel to be her
    maid.
30 Jacob slept with Rachel too; and he loved Rachel[a] more than Leah
    and he worked for Laban for another seven years.

2a   Read without art. as in Sam and elsewhere; construction, BrSynt §41f.

3a   Sam read ''herdsmen''; so E. A. Speiser and others.

4a   For word order, BrSynt §27e.

5a   Another tradition has Laban as the son of Bethuel; cf. ch. 24.

7a   E. A. Speiser: the imper. is not intended as a command, but something like, ''Why don't you. . ..''

8a   Sam and Gk read ''herdsmen.''

11a   On the use of ל, BrSynt §107c; likewise v. 13.

13a   Gk translates τὸ ὄνομα, presupposing שֵׁם.

14a   On אַךְ N. H. Snaith, VT 14 (1964) 373.   **b**   Ges-K §131d.

15a   On הכי, cf. Gen. 27:26; construction Ges-K §150e; BrSynt §54e.   **b**   מֵשְׂכֹּרֶת elsewhere only Gen. 31:7, 41; Ruth 2:12; otherwise שְׂכֹר as in Gen. 30:28.

17a   רַךְ really means ''gentle, soft''; so B. Jacob and E. A. Speiser translate; the present context, however, suggests the meaning ''dull, lustreless''; on the construction, Ges-K §145n; BrSynt §28a; 77f.

21a   TargP expands with לי; on הבה, Ges-K §69o.

24a   MT has, ''And Laban gave to her. . .,'' followed later by ''his daughter Leah''; this could be a sign that the sentence has been taken over from another tradition (P).   **b**   With Sam and others add ל.

25a   On the construction of the sentence, J. Blau VT (1959) 130-137.   **b**   With Gk add ''Jacob.''

26a   ''One does not do that''; likewise Gen. 34:7; 2 Sam. 13:12.

27a   Sam and the versions read first sing.; but the plur. is probably intended; construction, Ges-K §121b; BrSynt §35e.

30a   With the versions delete גם.

Form

The Jacob-Laban episode comprises chs. 29–31. It is divided into the frame, dealing with Jacob and Laban (29:1-30 and 30:25-43; 31:1-54), and the birth of the sons of Jacob (29:31—30:24). The whole is introduced by 29:1-30; this passage itself introduces the frame (Jacob-Laban) in vv. 1-14, and the interlude (29:31–30:24, birth of the sons of Jacob) in vv. 15-30, while the main part, the rivalry between Jacob and Laban, is already beginning in vv. 15-30.

Gen. 29–31 is firmly fitted into the broader context of the Jacob-Esau story by means of the flight–return structure; 29:1-14 presupposes Jacob's flight (27:1-45) and follows directly on 28:10/28:20-22; the return begins with 31:1-21.

Two events are narrated in the introduction, Jacob's arrival (and with it the meeting at the well) in vv. 1-14, and his time in the service of Laban during which he acquires Leah and Rachel as wives, vv. 15-30. Both have been fitted into a single narrative: the girl whom at the beginning (v. 11) Jacob meets at the well becomes at the end (v. 28) his wife. The tension enters in with Laban's plan to deceive (v. 15) and is resolved amicably by Laban's proposal (vv. 21-27). It is demonstrable, however, that both vv. 1-14 and vv. 15-30 go back to independent oral narratives. The meeting at the well is parallel to Gen. 24:11-33 and Ex. 2:15-22. All three parallels are in broad agreement as to the course of the action (see comm. 24:11-27). The basic oral narrative which underlies such a story begins with the meeting at the well and ends with marriage. It becomes still clearer in vv. 15-30 that there is a further independent narrative underlying this; it is the widespread motif known the world over of the substituted bride (see bibliog. above; also T. H. Gaster, *Myth, Legend*. . . [1969] 199-202). The beginning of the second narrative can still be recognized in v. 16: A man by name of X had two daughters. . .. But the two originally independent narratives are so successfully fused as to produce the effect of a self-contained unit (vv. 1-30).

Gen. 29:1-30 is a good example of the way in which the patriarchal stories came into being. The two narratives that lie behind the whole are family narratives that arose and were narrated in a community in which the family was the determining element. Both had their origin in the patriarchal period and both deal with marriage and inheritance. But with the fusion into one narrative and the insertion into the broader context of Gen. 29–31 the span extends beyond the family as indicated in the flight–return structure. It is here that one can discern J's intention to present, from Gen. 27 on, the transition from the small circle of the family to the wider circle of the community. The content makes this evident inasmuch as 29:15-30 links marriage with service and gain, the very thing which is the matter of contention between Jacob and Laban.

Setting

The question of the origin of Gen. 29:1-30 can now be answered clearly: the same narrator who made the seamless join for chs. 29–31 from the flight–return structure to the Jacob-Esau story also shaped 29:1-30 into a unified narrative. J is the composer and the composition emerges as a unity because of the consideration given to form. The attempts to separate 29:1-30 into two sources (usually v. 1, E; vv. 2-14, J; vv. 15-30, E) are very weak here (see A. Dillmann, H. Gunkel). The only point on which there can be certainty is that the new introduction in v. 16, as we have seen, is to be explained otherwise than by literary criticism. Others who hold that 29:1-30 is a unity composed by J are F. Delitzsch, B. D. Eerdmans, P. Volz, M. Noth, E. A. Speiser, who lays particular stress on the unity, F. V. Winnett, and G. von Rad.

Commentary

[**29:1-14**]   The meeting at the well: The itinerary note on Jacob's departure (v. 1) is followed by his arrival at the well (vv. 2-3), his conversation with the herdsmen (vv. 4-8), and the climax of the first scene, the meeting with Rachel (vv. 9-12). The conclusion, which prepares what is coming, consists of Laban's welcome and the reception into his house.

[**29:1-3**]   The itinerary note in v. 1 reports Jacob's departure and his goal; it resumes 28:10 after the interlude (28:11-22). The two sentences, 28:10 and 29:1, are, when carefully examined, a simple itinerary statement which has been divided into two by the interlude (28:11-22). In fact the first three words of v. 1 would fit better immediately after 27:41-45 (on the expression נשׂא see E. A. Speiser and I. L. Seeligmann, VT 14 [1964] 80). The purpose here is merely to indicate the direction (B. Jacob, "to ride eastwards"). On "the sons of the east" cf. Gen. 25:6; Judg. 6:3, 35; Is. 11:14; Jer. 49:38, the tribes of the Syrian-Arabian desert, east or northeast of Canaan.

[**29:2**]   The well is not out "in the open field" (J. Skinner and others) because Laban's house is nearby; in all three variants the well is close to a settlement. Once more the story begins with the raising of the eyes. But Jacob does not just see the well as an object; the well is "the natural meeting point" (O. Procksch). Here he could learn something (והנה. . .והנה). The narrator, by mentioning the three flocks situated at the well, is preparing what is to come. The listeners experience in detail the usual procedure for watering the flocks so as to prepare them for the unusual in what follows. Every day the great stone is lifted from the mouth of the well and then replaced; but this one occasion transformed the everyday into an event that would be narrated for a long time to come.

[**29:4-8**] It should be noted that in the conversation with the herdsmen the question about the early time for watering (vv. 7-8) follows in content directly on the explanation (vv. 2b-3); the narrator has brought the introduction forward so as to highlight Rachel's arrival (v. 9) after she had been sighted (v. 6b). The arrival is not narrated as an instantaneous event but as a progressive movement.

[**29:4-6**] The request for information in a life-style which did not know writing (and that is the setting of the present narrative) is of vital importance. Jacob must rely on the answers that he gets from the meetings. He asks the herdsmen at the well about the place (v. 4), about his relative (v. 5), and his well-being (v. 6). The commentaries draw attention to the lively portrayal of the conversation, especially to the contrast between Jacob's direct and pointed questions and the monosyllabic answers of the herdsmen. However, it is not the narrator's intention to contrast the different characters of Jacob and the herdsmen; he is looking rather to the narrative as a whole and is already indicating the contrast between the greeting of the reserved and somewhat mistrustful foreigners and that of the relatives. It is this that is to determine Jacob's sojourn in a foreign land. The address "my brothers" is, as in Gen. 19:7, nothing more than an endeavor to win good will.

    The series of three questions ends with one about the *šālôm* of his relatives. It is the simple current inquiry as to how they are (cf. Gen. 25:6; 37:14; 41:16; 43:23, 27; Judg. 6:3, 33). But the important word *šālôm* refers to the well-being of the community which is the prerequisite for a peaceful life together. In the greeting that follows, the wanderer in foreign parts is received into the *šālôm* of Laban's house. But will this last?

[**29:7-8**] The question and the answer of the herdsmen in vv. 7-8 follow directly on the explanation in vv. 2b-3 and carry it further. Again the particular is to be set apart from the usual.

[**29:9-10**] While the conversation is going on, Rachel, whose approach had already been announced by the herdsmen in v. 6b, has arrived. Jacob knows who it is that arrives "with the sheep of his mother's brother" and so what he says and does is thereby determined. This nice portrayal of the meeting presupposes that at that period girls helped with the work and were able to move among the men freely and unhindered and without the veil, as attested elsewhere in similar social structures.

[**29:10**] The herdsmen's explanations set Jacob thinking. Happy and excited, he rolls the stone from the well all by himself and waters Rachel's sheep, the sheep of his uncle Laban, his mother's brother. This is a fine example of the narrative art which can portray in wordless action the climax of feeling resulting from a sequence of events. Some interpreters grossly misunderstand the situation with their explanation that Jacob was actually a giant; this would completely destroy the effect that this is the only instance in which Jacob is granted a superhuman power in his service of love.

[29:11-12]   Only after watering the sheep does Jacob tell the girl who he is, greet her with a kiss, as is customary among relatives, and weep "for joy at the success-ful conclusion of his journey" (J. Skinner).

[29:13-14]   After the meeting, Rachel, all excited, had run quickly home—she could leave the flock in Jacob's care. On hearing the news, Laban too runs quickly to meet his nephew (as in Gen. 24:28-30) and greets him with an embrace and a kiss (נשק is in piel here). He brings him to his house. Jacob has now reached his goal. After he has told Laban his story he is acknowledged as a relative (see bibliog.). We meet here an important function of narrative in the patriarchal peri-od ("narration" [v. 13] is distinguished from "information" [v. 12]): it is the pre-requisite to acknowledging as a member of the family one who has hitherto been a stranger (cf. H. Eising, *Formgeschichtliche Untersuchung zur Jacoberzählung der Genesis* [diss. Münster, 1940]). The first part of the narrative concludes in v. 14b with the note that Jacob stayed a month with Laban. E. A. Speiser wants to link v. 14b with what follows: "After Jacob had stayed. . .." But the laws of nar-rative do not allow this. The first part reaches its conclusion in the sentence where movement comes to rest.

[29:15-30]   The oral narrative at hand to vv. 1-14 has marriage as its goal, as do the two parallels in Gen. 24 and Ex. 2. The natural conclusion of vv. 1-14 would be Jacob's marriage to Rachel (v. 28b). The present narrative, however, is ex-panded by Laban's act of deceit whereby Leah becomes Jacob's first wife, thus introducing a new tension which runs beyond 29:1-30—the opposition between Jacob and Laban.

[29:15-20]   There is still peace between Jacob and Laban as the second part be-gins, all in accord with the welcome in vv. 13-14. They come to an agreement of which Jacob himself can determine the conditions. It is based on the fact that Ja-cob has come to Laban with empty hands; otherwise negotiations take place as in the case of Rebekah (ch. 24). Because Jacob can offer no bride-price it is natural that he offers his service (cf. v. 10); his offer is a very considerable part of his work capacity—seven years. It is his love for Rachel that moves him and makes this long period seem short even though it was by no means easy, as Gen. 31:38-40 shows. Laban meets Jacob's offer (v. 19); he stands by the custom that cousins are the privileged suitors (among the Arabs the wife may be addressed as "daughter of my uncle," F. Delitzsch). At each step Laban will hold to custom and practice and use them as security.

The service to which Jacob obliges himself is neither that of a slave nor of a paid worker; it is service in the household of a relative conditioned solely by the circumstances. He remains a free man bound only by the obligation which he has taken upon himself. J wants to show how events in a family (ch. 27) can lead to new living conditions and work relationships in the course of which the family circle can expand with service, achieve-ment, and earnings, thus acquiring an enhanced significance. Because Jacob in foreign parts has not the backing of a father's house he (the one blessed) must serve and put himself at the disposal of his master. The new relationship of master and servant will determine his mode of existence. It would be wrong, therefore, to describe Jacob's service as "freely undertaken temporary slavery" (H. Holzinger) or to think that it is a substitute for a pur-chase price. "A bought marriage has never existed in Israel" (B. Jacob; likewise G. von Rad and others). The מהר is better described as a "compensating sum" (G. von Rad). Jacob's service takes the place of the מהר; it is better understood by analogy with the very widespread motif in tale and story where the suitor (generally one who has come from foreign parts) must produce some worthy achievement to win the bride. The view that Jacob's marriages are to be understood from a practice attested in cuneiform tablets, the *errebu*-marriage, in which the prospective son-in-law is adopted, has been rightly rejected by Van Seters (HThR 62 [1970] 377-395; *Abraham in History.* . ., 78-82, cf. D. W. Thomas, ed., *Archaeology and OT Study* [1967] 50, 73).

[29:21-25a]   But now, in rude contrast to the friendly course of mutual exchange, Laban carries out his plan to deceive Jacob. Only now does his attitude, which had so far been conditioned by family ties, take a turn to that of a man intent on his own advantage. One suspects that Laban is not so much thinking that the agreed time has come; rather he does not want to lose a good worker. Jacob must demand his earnings. Laban arranges a great marriage feast; his self-esteem obliges him to this; the seven-day celebration is attested elsewhere (Judg. 14:12; Tob. 11:20; see M. Haran, VT 19 [1969] 11-32). He conducts Leah to the groom. The custom that requires the bride to be led veiled to the groom makes the deceit possible and the practice of giving the elder daughter in marriage before the younger (also attested elsewhere) serves to conceal Laban's deceit.

If one reads vv. 21-25a attentively from the ויאמר at the beginning of v. 21 to the name Leah at the end of v. 25a, one encounters a classical example of Hebrew narrative art; what is narrated is so close to reality that one experiences what narration intends to be and can in fact be. Only what is absolutely necessary is said; but what is unsaid speaks with such force as to give these few sentences the weight and density proper to noble metal. M. Weiss comments on the last sentence (v. 25a): " 'And in the morning—it is Leah!' There is no trace of direct speech. . .; all is encompassed in three brief words. . .; amazement, indignation that cuts short any utterance" (VT 13 [1963] 464).

[29:24,29]   The attentive reading of vv. 21-25a also makes it evident that the note in v. 24 is a subsequent insertion; v. 25a produces its effect only when it follows immediately on v. 23. V. 24 brings a perceptible disturbance and is comprehensible here only as the addition of a later hand (probably P) who wants to prepare the way for 29:31—30:24. The same holds for v. 29. On marriage, wedding, wedding customs, see lit. Gen. 12–50, pp. 102f., also W. Kornfeld (1954) and J. Scharbart (1977) in bibliog. to ch. 29.

[29:25-31]   The accusation that Jacob directs at Laban ricochets off Laban's self-justification; he had only acted in accordance with the custom of the country (v. 26). At the same time he makes a new proposal to Jacob: if Jacob goes through with the seven days of festivity he can have Rachel after another seven years of service (v. 27). Jacob agrees; he has no option. He now acquires Rachel too as wife (v. 28); he lives in married union with her and serves Laban for a further seven years. There is an additional remark at the conclusion which refers to what follows: Jacob loved her more than Leah. On v. 29, cf. v. 24.

[29:25b]   The two accusations, "What is this you have done to me?" (v. 25b; likewise Gen. 26:10) and "Why have you deceived me?" (end of v. 25; just as the accusations in Josh. 9:22; 1 Sam. 19:17; 28:12), are meant to be in parallelism; the reason for the accusation is inserted between them, "You know that I worked these seven years for Rachel" (v. 25bβ).

[**29:26**]   The accusation of deception slides off Laban. He coldly justifies himself by the custom of the country. It is important that Jacob does not insist: you should have told me! He knows that he can do nothing. He is still the foreigner. The local people (the ''we'' of v. 27) stand behind Laban who has no need to excuse himself.

[**29:27**]   Laban can even be generous, offering Jacob a new work contract and in return Rachel as his second wife. In making the offer he can once more take his stand on custom and practice. ''Complete these seven days of feasting'' (or ''this one's, Leah's, festal week''). It is a local feast and it would have done great harm both to Laban and Jacob to cut it short.

[**29:28**]   Jacob acquiesces: in his humiliating and constrained situation he now acquires Rachel as wife. V. 28b would have meant only joy and fulfillment at the end of v. 22. But everything has changed completely because of the intervening deceit. Laban has destroyed something. He has not only deceived Jacob, but his daughter Rachel as well, who can now only become Jacob's second wife. By his cunning deceit he has infringed crudely on the blossoming love between the two. Jacob's first seven years of service ''seemed but a few days'' (v. 20); the same could not be said of the second seven (v. 30b).

[**29:30**]   This verse sounds the end of the narrative. The love between Jacob and Rachel could not be destroyed by Laban's intervention; it persevered. ''But Jacob loved Rachel more than Leah,'' and so the way is open to conflict, a conflict which is as inculpable as it is unavoidable. It is the subject of the next part (29:31—30:24). But the situation has changed somewhat during these seven years. Jacob is obliged to service; Laban has become his opponent; Gen. 30:25—31:43 narrates the consequences of this.

Purpose and Thrust

Something of J's intention becomes clear from the fusion of two once-independent narratives into one. The first is a simple love story which should end in marriage (cf. parallels); but with the second the harsh demands of external circumstances force their way into the intimate life of two lovers. Poverty and the dependence that comes with it has its effect in the love between husband and wife (Jacob comes empty-handed). This is the first time in the patriarchal story that work in the context of service appears; it is work willingly and joyfully undertaken for a loved one. It can be so, the narrator wants to say; but social and economic interests in the person of Laban lead to a crude intervention in the love between two people. When Jacob arrived he inquired about the ''peace'' (well-being) of Laban and his household; but Laban by his deceit himself threatens in the most extreme way this peace and the well-being of the community. Unavoidable conflicts in the social, economic, and personal areas lie along the way from patriarchs to people; one will prevail at the expense of the other. ''Blessing'' and ''peace'' will undergo profound changes in the process; Jacob must endure what has happened to him. Suffering is part of the way.

The Birth and Naming
of Jacob's Sons

Literature

Gen. 29:31-35: E. Bublitz, "Ruben, Isakar und Sebulon in den israelitischen Genealogien," ZAW 33 (1913) 241-250. S. Mowinckel, " 'Rachelstämme' und 'Leastämme,' " BZAW 77 (1958) 129-150. M. C. Astour, "*Benê-Iamina* et Jéricho," Sem. 9 (1959) 5-20. S. Lehming, "Zur Erzählung von der Geburt der Jakobsöhne," VT 13 (1963) 74-81. B. Halevi, "The Arrangement of the Names of the Twelve Sons in the Jacob Stories," BetM 55 (1973) 494-523. E. Lipiński, "L'étymologie de 'Juda,' " VT 23 (1973) 380-381. H. Weippert, "Das geographische System der Stämme Israels," VT 23 (1973) 76-89. D. N. Freedman, *Early Israelite History in the Light of Early Israelite Poetry* (1974) 3-35. A. R. Millard, "The Meaning of the Name Judah," ZAW 86 (1974) 216-218. J. M. Sasson, "A Genealogical 'Convention' in Biblical Chronology?" ZAW 90 (1978) 171-185. A. Strus, "Etymologies des noms propres dans Gen. 29,32—30,24," Sal. 40 (1978) 57-72.

Genesis 30:1-13: O. Eissfeldt, " 'Gut Glück!' in semitischer Namengebung," JBL 82 (1963) 195-200. W. Janzen, "'*Ašrē* in the OT," HThR 58 (1965) 215-226. Y. Yadin, " 'And Dan, Why did he Remain in Ships' (Jdc 5,17)," AJBA 1 (1968) 9-23. F. I. Andersen, "Note on Genesis 30,8," JBL 88 (1969) 200. A. Globe, "The Muster of the Tribes in Judges 5,11e-18," ZAW 87 (1975) 169-184.

Genesis 30:14-24: C. B. Randolph, "The Mandragora of the Ancient in Folklore and Medicine," PAAAS 12 (1905) 1-3. J. M. Casanowicz, "Note on Some Usages of *lākēn*," JAOS: 30,4 (1910). E. Täubler, "Die Spruch-Verse über Sebulon," MGWJ 83 (1939) 3-37 = (1963) 9-46. M. Eliade, "La mandragore et les mythes de la 'naissance miraculeuse,' " '*Zalmoxis*' III (1942) 1-48. L. Köhler, "Alttestamentliche Wortforschung," ThZ 5 (1949) 395. M. David, "Zabal (Gen XXX 20)," VT 1 (1951) 59-60. J. Hempel, "Ein Vorschlag zu Gen 30,20," ZAW 64 (1952) 286. T. Worden, "The Literary Influence of the Ugaritic Fertility Myth on the OT," VT 3 (1953) 273-297. E. Jacob, *Ras Shamra–Ugarit et l'Ancien Testament*, CAB 12 (1960). O. Haggenmüller, "Erinnern und Vergessen Gottes und der Menschen (*zkr-shk*)," BiLe 3 (1962) 1-15. W. Schottroff, " 'Gedenken' im Alten Orient und im AT," WMANT 15 (1964; 1967²).

Text

29:31   When Yahweh saw that Leah was unloved, he opened her womb, but Rachel remained childless.

32   Then Leah became pregnant and bore a son and named him Reuben because, as she said, Yahweh has looked on my humiliation; my husband will love me.

33 She became pregnant again and bore a son, and she said: Yahweh has heard that I am unloved; and so he has given me this son also. So she named him Simeon.

34 She became pregnant again and bore a son, and she said: Now this time my husband will be united with me because I have borne him three sons. So she named him[a] Levi.[b]

35 She became pregnant again and bore a son, and she said: Now I will praise Yahweh. So she named him Judah. Then she stopped bearing.

30:1 When Rachel found that she bore Jacob no children she became jealous of her sister and said to Jacob: Give me sons or I[a] shall die.

2 Jacob became angry with Rachel and said: Am I in the place of God who has denied you the fruit of the womb?

3 But she said: Here is my maid Bilhah; go to her that she may bear upon my knees and I may build up a family[a] from her.

4 So she gave him her maid Bilhah as wife and Jacob went to her.

5 Bilhah became pregnant and bore Jacob a son,

6 and Rachel said: God has given judgment for me, he has also listened to me and given me a son. So she named him[a] Dan.

7 And Bilhah, Rachel's maid, became pregnant again and bore Jacob a second son.

8 And Rachel said: I have struggled mightily[a] with my sister and have prevailed. So she named him Naphtali.

9 When Leah found that she bore no more children she took her maid Zilpah and gave her to Jacob as wife.

10 Zilpah, Leah's maid, bore[a] Jacob a son.

11 And Leah said: Good fortune is come![a] So she called him Gad.

12 And Zilpah, Leah's maid, bore Jacob a second son.

13 And Leah said: Happy am I, for young women will call me happy![a] So she called him Asher.

14 In the days of the wheat harvest Reuben went out and found some mandrakes in the field and brought them to Leah his mother. And Rachel said to Leah: Give me some of your son's mandrakes!

15 She answered her:[a] Is it a small matter that you have taken my husband?[b] Will you also take my son's mandrakes? Rachel replied: Well then,[c] let him lie with you tonight in exchange for your son's mandrakes.

16 When Jacob came in from the field in the evening Leah went to meet him and said to him: You are to come[a] to me because I have hired you with my son's mandrakes, you are to sleep with me tonight.

17 And God heard Leah and she became pregnant and bore Jacob a fifth son.

18 And Leah said: God has rewarded me because[a] I gave my maid to my husband. So she called him Issachar.[b]

19 Leah became pregnant again and bore Jacob a sixth son.

20 And Leah said: God has endowed me with a fine dowry; now at last my husband will honor me because I have borne him six sons. So she named him Zebulun.[a]

21 After this Leah bore a daughter. She named her Dinah.

22 And God remembered Rachel. God heard her and opened her womb.

23 She became pregnant and bore a son, and she said: God has taken away my humiliation.

24 So she named him Joseph saying: May Yahweh[a] add to me another son!

29:34a With Gk and Sam read קראה (A. Dillmann).   **b**   J. Wellhausen understands לוי as a gentilic to לאה.

30:1a   Cf. Gen. 25:22; 27:46 for the exclamation.

3a   Cf. Gen. 16:2; on the construction, Ges-K §51g.

6a   On the construction, BrSynt §94d,j.

8a   On the form, Ges-K §85n; the verb פתל means "to twist, to plait"; as inf. abs. cf. W. L. Moran, "The Hebrew Language in its Northwest Semitic Background," Fests. W. F. Albright (1961) 54-72.

10a   Gk expands, likewise v. 12; cf. BHK.

11a   Q בא גד; on the prep., B. Hartmann, OTS 14 (1940/65) 115-121; G. Wallis, BHH I 580 derives גד from the root גדד "to cut off," Aram. "to decide"; differently, M. Noth.

13a   On the perf., Ges-K §106n, some propose an imperf.

15a   Gk לאה, Syr לה לאה.   **b**   Syr has perf. which would be better (J. Skinner).   **c**   On לכן, F. Nötscher, VT 3 (1953) 372-380.

16a   Gk and Sam add הלילה.

18a   On the construction, Ges-K §135m.   **b**   The name is composite: איש שכר, see Gen. 45:14f.

20a   According to KBL probably corresponds to the name of a region occurring in the Egyptian proscriptive texts; cf. M. Noth, *Die israelitischen Personennamen. . .* BWANT 46 (1928).

24a   Gk and Syr read אלהים.

Form

The dispute between the wives, Gen. 29:31—30:24, has been inserted into the dispute between Jacob and Laban; in its present form it is not a narrative but rather like a genealogy after which it has been constructed. It is a report of the birth and naming of Jacob's 12 children (11 sons and one daughter) from his two wives and their maids, with some narrative interpolations. What is peculiar to this genealogy is that it is stamped throughout by the rivalry between Jacob's two wives, a narrative motif (cf. Gen. 16; 21) which forms a separate block within chs. 29–30. The problem here is to understand the combination of the genealogy of Jacob's 12 children with the narrative of the rivalry between the women and how it arose. The narrative and genealogical parts have each to be considered separately.

1. The Narrative Parts of Chs. 29–30

Gen. 29:31f. is the beginning of a narrative which resumes v. 30b and so follows on 29:15-30. The broader narrative context is continued with a new episode. The interposed v. 31aβb prepares 30:1-6; vv. 31-32 and 30:1-6 form a self-contained narrative block. The narrative progresses in 30:14-18 with a new episode in the rivalry between Leah and Rachel. The conflict in vv. 14-15 leads to a compromise; but the old narrative is altered in vv. 17-18 by the reviser, as it is in the conclusion (vv. 22-24).

2. The Genealogical Parts of Chs. 29–30

The number 12 and the repetition of the same phrases show that the genealogy of the 12 children of Jacob is an independent element. The names are without exception to be understood as personal names; all explanations of them refer to the family and they are all given by the mother. There is no trace of any reference to the tribes. The reasons given for the names separate into several groups. The prevailing group consists of a sentence in two parts of which the first states an action of God, the second its consequence, always referring to the mother either in its entirety (vv. 32, 33; 30:6, 18, 20), in the first half only (vv. 23, 24, Yahweh is subject; v. 35, Yahweh is object), or in the second half only (v. 34). The synthetic reason is an artificial formation to which no real name giving can correspond. The first part forms a name of praise which carries echoes of the language of the Psalms; the second is far removed from this language and applies the particular action of God to the situation of the mother (each part works for itself). The meanings of the names in this group are characteristic of the reviser who uses quite different reasons for each name. In one group they consist of a verbal sentence in the first person (the mother) reporting an event which explains the birth, and are to be explained solely by the rivalry between the sisters. These reasons, therefore, are most certainly part of the old narrative.

Conclusion

One can distinguish in chs. 29–30 an older from a later layer: the older is a narrative of the rivalry between Leah and Rachel in several acts, the later gives an account of the 12 children of Jacob in the form of a genealogy with the giving of names (S. Lehming, VT 13 [1963] 74-81). The narrative has two parts, 29:31-32 with 30:1-6 and 30:14-16(18) with vv. 22-24 in an earlier form. Both parts together form a self-contained narrative of the rivalry between Leah and Rachel. A later writer, using the system of the 12 that was available, has expanded it to a (secondary) genealogy in the course of which he has taken the reasons for the names from different sources and partly reshaped them. His main concern was to set in relief Yahweh's (God's) action in the birth of Jacob's children. This reviser inserted 29:33-35; 30:4-13, 19-34; and expanded or altered the reason for the names in 29:32b; 30:6b, 17-18, 22-24.

Setting

This conclusion is a rejection of any source division between J and E (some also find sentences from P). Most exegetes since J. Wellhausen accept a separation into J and E in chs. 29–30, though no precise division of the two has so far prevailed (H. Holzinger, ''impossible''). However, the division presented here between an older narrative layer and a later layer expanding into a genealogy shows that the basic narrative is from J (M. Noth, G. von Rad; E. A. Speiser: the basic material is from J). The reviser has altered, probably abbreviated, J's narrative in some places. But all that one can say of the revision is that it is later; the theological thrust too points this way. Finally there is the further question of the origin of the sequence of 12 (11) sons of Jacob. The number 12 referring to sons (tribes) occurs in Gen. 10:26f.; 22:20, 24; 25:1-4; 25:13f.; 35:15-19, 40-43. According to H. Weippert the 12 tribes of Israel are mentioned in 28 places in the Old Testament; the occurrences in Genesis are: 29–30; 35:16-20; 35:22-28; 46:8-25; 49:1-17 (VT 23 [1973] 76-89). M. Noth regards Gen. 49 as the oldest witness with chs. 29–30 in any case later than ch. 49 (*Das System. . .*, BWANT 4,1 [1930; 1966²]). The most striking difference between the two texts is that all explanations of the names in ch. 49 refer to the tribes, their characteristics and history, whereas the explanations in chs. 29–30 are concerned exclusively with the family life of Jacob and remain within the family circle (O. Eissfeldt points this out, Fests. H. W. Hertzberg [1965] 50-55; likewise E. A. Speiser). These facts show that the sequence of 12 as it occurs in ch. 49, that is as the sequence of the 12 tribes of Israel, was at hand to the reviser of chs. 29–30 who nevertheless understands the names without exception as personal names and explains them exclusively from the family circle. It follows from this that no conclusion can be drawn for the 12 tribes of Israel from the 12 names and their explanation in chs. 29–30.

Commentary

[29:31-32] V. 31 is the beginning of a narrative which resumes v. 30b and so continues 29:15-30. "When Yahweh saw. . ." occurs elsewhere as the introduction of a new episode; Yahweh's helping intervention (vv. 31b,32) follows on what Yahweh sees (similarly Ex. 3:7f.); Yahweh "sees. . .opens" (as Gen. 16:2; 21:17); she becomes pregnant and bears a son. A nominal sentence is inserted into the sequence to allow anticipation of the course of the action: "But Rachel (remained) childless"; it prepares 30:1-6. The two motifs of the unloved and childless wife determine what follows. The reviser betrays his authorship of the reason for the name (v. 32b) with his characteristic two-part sentence. The clumsy doubling of כִּי in close succession in v. 32b points to the intervention of the reviser who has suppressed one simple reason for the name (perhaps the correct explanation is רְאוּ בֵן, "see, a son!").

[29:33-35] The reviser, following the system of 12, follows this with three further births and with name giving. Leah has three more sons: Simeon (v. 33), Levi (v. 34), Judah (v. 35).

[29:33] The name שִׁמְעוֹן, probably the name of an animal, a hyena (KBL), is explained by the verb שָׁמַע; the sentence, "Yahweh has heard," is parallel to ". . .has seen" in v. 32; and, as there, the consequence from the mother's point of view is added—Yahweh has presented her with a second son. The sentence: "Yahweh has heard that I am unloved," exhibits the clumsy combination of the language of the Psalms and the situation.

[29:34] The name "Levi" (gentilic: no explanation of meaning) is not explained by means of a two-part sentence because it is not traced back to an action of God but to the consequence of such, namely, that her husband will be united with her. The verb לוה in the niph. means "join oneself to" and occurs only in late passages: Num. 18:2, 4; Is. 14:1; 56:3, 6; Jer. 50:5; Zech. 2:15; Dan. 11:34; Ps. 83:9. What is particularly striking here is that the reasons for the names in Gen. 29–30 do not rely on popular etymology, as is often said, but on literary constructions in which a name already there is artificially adapted to the context by an etymology. The numbering is also typical: Levi is Leah's third son.

[29:35] The name "Judah" (no explanation, originally the name of a region?—J. Hempel, BHH II [1964] 898-900) likewise contains a "cerebrated" meaning; the two sentences in praise of God in vv. 32, 33 are expanded here by a cry of praise which is read into the name Judah. The theologizing intent of the reviser obtrudes here, particularly if one compares the other etymology of the name Judah from the same verb in Gen. 49:8, "Judah, your brothers shall praise you." The sentence stating that Leah stopped bearing with Judah (a cry of praise as a conclusion of a psalm of praise) corresponds to the numbering in vv. 33 and 34.

[30:1-6] The narrative continues in 30:1-6; v. 1a follows immediately on 29:31b. The passage is divided into Rachel's outburst in v. 1b with Jacob's angry retort (v. 2) and the solution which Rachel decides on leading to the birth of Dan from her maid Bilhah (vv. 3-6). Like Leah, Rachel too has a son.

[30:1-2]   This scene, so impressive in its conciseness, achieves its full value only when heard in its original narrative context immediately after 29:31-32: וירא יהוה—ותרא רחל. J has concentrated more into this scene than one can glean at first reading from these tightly packed sentences. To think that after the beautiful, gentle love story of 29:1-20 this angry exchange between the two is our first and only experience of their marriage! It is the suffering of the childless wife, of which we hear so much in the Old Testament (e.g., 1 Sam. 1; Ps. 113), that cries out in Rachel's demand. The suffering is all the more bitter when each day Leah and her son are present: "She became jealous of her sister." It was a pain unto death (cf. Gen. 25:22; 27:16); the childless wife had no future—such is the despair voiced in this outburst. Yet it is understandable that she directs her attack against her husband—someone must listen. Equally understandable is the angry reply; Rachel is demanding the impossible from Jacob: "Am I in the place of God?" (יהוה would not be possible here; even the Yahwist must use אלהים). The king of Israel says the same when he too is faced with an impossible demand (2 Kings 5:7).

[30:3-6]   But in her helpless despair in which not even the husband she loves can help her, Rachel finds a way out, the same that Sarah found (Gen. 16:2). She gives Jacob her maid Bilhah as wife and she bears him a son who is regarded as the son of Rachel the mistress (vv. 5-6). This is expressed in the ritual of bearing on the knees of her mistress (cf. R. de Vaux, *Ancient Israel* [1958; Eng. 1961] 51). The mistress names the child. The clumsy reworking is clearly evident in the reasons given in the naming. In the narrative the name Dan is based on דנני אלהים; this corresponds to a name derived from the verb דין (see A. Globe [1975], who defends the derivation of the "theophoric" name from דין against Y. Yadin [1969]; cf. bibliog. above). It accords with the situation of rivalry between Leah and Rachel: "God has given judgment for me!" To bring it into conformity with his theologizing plan the reviser has inserted: "He has also listened to me and given me a son!"

[30:7-13]   The narrative continues only in v. 14. The glossator, intent on the number 12, inserts vv. 7-13: the birth of Naphtali, a second son of Bilhah (vv. 7-8), and two sons of Zilpah, Leah's maid, Gad (vv. 9-11) and Asher (vv. 12-13). The numbering shows that both go back to the reviser.

[30:7-8]   The reason given for the name of Bilhah's second son (v. 8) presents notable difficulties, first because the noun and the verb occur only here (the name is unexplained), and second because it diverges from the reasons which the glossator otherwise gives. Though נפתלי. . .נפתולי do not occur elsewhere, the meaning, "I have fought a fight" (lit.), is rendered certain by the following גם־יכלתי. Earlier explanations were: "the struggle of prayer against an assault on faith" (F. Delitzsch); "a struggle for God's grace and blessing" (A. Dillmann; similarly H. Gunkel who simply deletes עם־אחתי; "struggles whose outcome God decides," E. W. Hengstenberg, O. Procksch, E. A. Speiser). But the אלהים is to be understood adjectivally with D. W. Thomas (VT 3 [1953] 209-224): "mighty, fearful," because it is obvious that a struggle with her sister is meant. The other difficulty is that it is different from that which the glossator gives elsewhere; it is first person sing., not a two-part sentence, and secular; it is like the reason given in v. 18 which is also first person sing., looking back to an event connected with the birth; v. 18 is part of the original narrative. I suspect that the glossator found the reason already there in the story as part of an independent episode which he omitted; hence we are left with a fragment from a narrative (the reason for the name in v. 8).

[30:9-13] In the underlying narrative it is Bilhah (v. 3), not Zilpah, Leah's maid, who belongs to the narrative movement. Vv. 9-13 are an expansion by the glossator which leans heavily on the narrative; all the phrases and words of vv. 9f. and 12 are taken from it. Only the names Gad and Asher and the explanations of them in vv. 11 and 13 remain as proper to the narrator. Both names are designations for God, or close to it. Twice the reason for the name is an exclamation; it diverges from the reasons elsewhere in its brevity and single component. Vv. 9-13 then (or vv. 9 and 13) prove to be a once independent piece of tradition which the reviser has adapted to the context. גד is a divinity of good fortune mentioned also in Is. 65:11; cf. Josh. 11:17, as well as in several theophoric personal names; בגד originally meant: "with Gad (his help)." On גד as a name for God, cf. M. Noth (*Die israelitischen Personennamen. . .*, BWANT 46 [1928] 126f.) and O. Eissfeldt (JBL 82 [1963] 195-200), who, in opposition to Noth, holds that the explanation given in 30:9-13 is adequate; cf. G. Wallis (BHH I [1963] 580), who derives the divine name גד from *gdd* "to cut off," Aram. "to decide"; M. Noth takes a different view. The word אשר = "happiness" can go with אשרה; others connect it with the god Ashur (M. Noth, op.cit., 131; K. Baltzer, BHH 1, 141).

In v. 13 the exclamation, "happy am I," which gives the reason for the name, is expanded by a second reason loosely and clumsily attached to it, "for daughters [= women, as in Song 6:9] will call me happy." This appendage shows traditions were at hand to the glossator in vv. 11-13 (cf. Lk. 1:48).

[30:14-18] The narrative continues in vv. 14-18: in this new episode in the conflict between Leah and Rachel the love-apples, which Leah's son Reuben finds, become "apples of discord." The conflict ends with a compromise from which both women benefit.

[30:14a] The episode takes place "at the time of the wheat harvest"; in v. 16 Jacob comes in "from the field"; this presupposes an agricultural economy and announces the life-style of that particular civilization. Leah's son Reuben, who was about six years old, finds some "love-apples" out in the field; they are the fruit of the yellow flowering mandragora (mandrake) which in many places is regarded as an aphrodisiac, promoting fertility, mentioned also in Song 7:14 (see M. Eliade [1942], bibliog. to 30:14-24; *Patterns in Comparative Religion* [1958] 314-318; T. G. Gaster, *Myth Legend. . .* [1969] 200).

[30:14b-15a] The rivalry between the two women expresses itself here in an exchange of words. Rachel demands from her sister a share in the love-apples, perhaps because she thinks that as the favored one she has a right to them, or perhaps simply with the hope that she herself will have a child. Leah rejects her request with bitterness: "Is it a small matter that you have taken my husband. . .?" As the first wife, she claims to be Jacob's principal wife. She knows that she has been confirmed in her precedence by the son she has borne to Jacob.

[30:15b] Rachel makes a fair proposal which Leah accepts. She gives Leah her husband for one night (obviously he spent more time with Rachel than with Leah) in exchange for the love-apples.

[30:16]   In the evening Leah goes out to meet Jacob and tells him that he has been the subject of a deal. Jacob plays here a rather lamentable role which is deliberate and speaks for itself. Leah tells him: שָׂכֹר שְׂכַרְתִּיךָ, "I have hired you" ("bought" would be an incorrect translation; "hire" expresses the limitation of time).

[30:17]   The narrative then continued, ". . .And she become pregnant and bore a son and named him Issachar" (שָׂכָר). The reason for the name is an event that preceded the birth. The reviser has intervened here and introduced a reason in two parts: the first is an action of God, "and God heard Leah"; following directly on vv. 14-16 this is most inappropriate and is downright theologizing. Moreover, the reviser adds his numbering, ". . .a fifth son" (in the narrative it was the second).

[30:18]   The second part of the reason for the name imposes on the catchword from the narrative, שָׂכָר, a clearly tendentious meaning with a further theologizing turn: "God has rewarded me. . .," a reason obviously contrived from the narrative setting.

[30:19-20]   The next two births are also additions by the reviser. His hand can be recognized both in the numbering and the two-part reason where he makes use of a different explanation in each; cf. vv. 6 and 13. The first uses the verb זבד = "to bequeath," not otherwise attested, and the noun זבד found only in Sir. 36:24; 40:29. The second uses the verb זבל, piel, "to carry, endure," which is not found elsewhere but whose meaning is to be drawn from the accus. (on name, see bibliog. above).

[30:21]   The glossator adds the birth of Dinah; no reason is given for her name; it is no more than a stopgap to make the number 12, as Benjamin is born only later; or is it a preparation for ch. 34?

[30:22-24]   The narrative was interrupted (altered) in v. 17 so that Leah could have a son. There were two sides, however, to the agreement between Leah and Rachel (v. 15b): Leah had a night with Jacob; Rachel got the love-apples. The effect they had on Rachel is still to be narrated. The narrative traces Joseph's birth back to them. The reviser has left this out and replaced it by v. 22 with conscious theological intent. This verse 22 is put together out of pieces already used with the result that the sequence וַיִּזְכֹּר—וַיִּשְׁמַע is particularly clumsy. V. 23 is equally clumsy and grammatically dubious. The reviser advances two grounds for the name Joseph: in v. 23 it is derived from אסף: "God has taken away my humiliation." The perfect shows that the meaning is contrived inasmuch as it attempts to explain an imperfect; in v. 24 the name is derived from an imperfect (יֹסֵף) as a name expressing a wish. One thus arrives at the original meaning of the name יֹסֵף. It could be complete in this form, but it could also be a short form of the theophoric name יוֹסֵפְאֵל. The meaning or ground for it is attached here by means of לֵאמֹר which is not otherwise used in chs. 29–30 and is possibly a secondary addition (S. Lehming, VT 13 [1963] 74-81). The text gives no indication that "there is allusion to the special place of Joseph" (H. Gunkel). The meaning of the name in no wise sets it in relief, and the same holds for this last name as for all the others, namely, that not one of them is pointed at the son and his future. All have to do with the mothers only.

Purpose and Thrust

A distinction must be made between the intention of J's narrative and the genealogical revision when raising the question of the significance of the chapter. With the rivalry between the women, J has taken up into the Jacob-Esau cycle a motif that always has existed and always will exist in human society—even in modified forms of marriage. His purpose is to show that in the patriarchal period conflict between women was ranked on the same significant level as that between men. Whereas men were basically at strife over living space and means of subsistence, women clashed basically over position and status in the community; here it was still in the simple realm of the family where recognition by the husband and the birth of children were decisive for them. Had the narrative been handed down to us in its original form, without the alterations and probable abbreviations made by the reviser, then J's purpose would be more clearly recognizable. We can still sense that a profound conflict between recognition because of one's function as a mother and recognition because of personal liking had established itself in the society of that era. Chapters 29–30 are among those texts in the patriarchal story where one can recognize a more significant place for women in society. Here, as in a number of other places, it is the woman who is the champion of the interest of the person over against the prevailing interest of the community.

The revision has a theologizing thrust; when a child is named it gives as the reason for the name an action of God in language reminiscent of the Psalms. In the old narrative, however, the few reasons given for the names are secular inasmuch as the narrative as such has a secular character. Several times in the patriarchal stories repetitions and emphatic talk about God belong to later layers; cf. ch. 24, the language of Abraham's servant. This fact demonstrates that the relationship of the patriarchs to God was so natural that the old narratives spoke of God only when the course of events demanded it; otherwise they spoke in secular fashion. In a later era, when the reviser was at work, it had become necessary to set with increasing emphasis what was happening on the human level in its relationship to God. This could well be the situation into which the prophets spoke. This was a time when it made good sense for the reviser to bring the naming of Jacob's sons into the context of God's action within the family of Jacob in this persistent manner (cf. Pss. 31:8; 106:4; 113:5; Lk. 1:46-48). The reviser links the story of the patriarchs immediately with the worship of his day when he gives as the reason for Judah's name his mother's exclamation: ''Now I will praise Yahweh!''

Jacob Outwits Laban

Literature

Genesis 30:25-32: W. Baumgartner, ''Alttestamentliche Einleitung und Literaturgeschichte,'' ThR 8 (1936) 179-222 esp. 200f. F. R. Kraus, ''Staatliche Viehhaltung im babylonischen Lande Larsa,'' MNAW 29/5 (1966). H. N. Richardson, ''A Critical Note on Amos 7,14,'' JBL 85 (1966) 89. F. E. Deist, '''*APPAYIM* (1 Sam I 5) <*PYM*?'' VT 27 (1977) 205-208. E. Otto, *Jakob in Sichem*, BWANT 110 (1979).

Text

30:25   After Rachel had borne Joseph, Jacob said to Laban: Let me go so that I may return to my own house and land!

26   Give me my wives and my children[a] for whom I have served you, and I will go. You know the service that I have given you.

27   Laban said to him: If I have found favor in your eyes—I know (by divination) that Yahweh[a] has blessed me because of you.

28   Name the wages, he continued,[a] which you demand of me[b] and I will give it to you.

29   He answered: You know well how I have served you and what has become of your flocks under me.

30   You had but a few when I came to you; now they have increased abundantly, and Yahweh has blessed you wherever I turned. But it is high time that I took care of my own household.

31   Then he said: What shall I give you? And Jacob said: You shall give me nothing. If you will do for me what I tell you, I will again[a] feed and[b] guard your flocks.

32   I will go through[a] all your flocks today and will pick out[a] all the speckled and spotted[b] animals (and all the black[c] ones among the sheep and the speckled and spotted among the goats),[d] and these shall be my wages.

33   And my own honesty will answer for me later[a] when you come to check my wages. Then everyone that is not speckled and spotted (among the goats and black among the sheep) shall be counted as stolen by me.

34   And Laban said: Agreed, let it be as[a] you have said.

35   Now on the same day he picked out the speckled and spotted he-goats (and the speckled and spotted she-goats, all that had white on

them, and all the black sheep) and gave them to his sons to look after.

36   Then he put three days journey between himself and Jacob, while Jacob tended[a] those flocks of Laban that remained.

37   Then Jacob took fresh rods of poplar (and almond and plane tree) and peeled strips of bark from them[a] (so as to lay bare[b] the white on the rods).

38   Then he stood the rods which he had peeled upright in the troughs (at the watering places[a] where the flocks came to drink) facing[b] the she-goats (and they turned to heat when they came to drink).

39   They went into heat in front of the rods and gave birth to young that were (striped) and speckled and spotted.

40   (And Jacob picked out the sheep and turned their[a] faces in the direction of the striped and all the black in Laban's flocks. And so he bred flocks for himself which he did not add to Laban's.)

41   Whenever[a] the stronger were in heat, Jacob put the rods in the troughs in front of them so that they might breed in front of them.

42   But he did not put them there in front of the weaker.[a] So the weaker fell to Laban's lot, the stronger to Jacob's.

43   So the man[a] became[b] wealthier and wealthier[c] and had large flocks, male and female servants, camels and asses.

26a   Not a gloss.
27a   The translations have אלהים, but MT is to be read.
28a   Gk and Vg omit.   **b**   On the use of על, BrSynt §110b.
31a   As Gen. 26:18; Ges-K §120g,h.   **b**   The asyndetic אשמר may be a gloss, though it can also be deliberate; Gk and Syr add ו.
32aa   Gk and Vg read both verbs as imperfect; construction, Ges-K §112mm.   **b**   J. Skinner: " 'speckled and spotted,' practically synonymous"; טלוא elsewhere only in Ezek. 16:16; Josh. 9:5 (F. Diest [1977] bibliog. above; R. R. Gordon VT 25 [1975] 216-219).   **c**   חום black, "dark brown"; only in this chapter.   **d**   Gk tries to smooth the difficult text.
33a   So too Ex. 13:14.
34a   הן as affirmative answer, BrSynt §4; 56a; on לו , BrSynt §8b; Ges-K §109b; 151e; ל as emphatic particle, F. Nötscher, VT 3 (1953) 372-380; H. N. Richardson, JBL 85 (1966) 89.
36a   There follows in Sam a long expansion corresponding to Gen. 31:11-13. On the construction, BrSynt §59b.
37a   מקל used collectively, Ges-K §123b.   **b**   The sentence structure is scarcely possible; Ges-K §117r; BrSynt §92a.
38a   Sam reads בהשקות; cf. Ges-K §95f.   **b**   This further precision is separated from its context by the expansion.
40a   TargO, J expands כל.
41a   Gk correctly expands according to the sense בכל-עת.
42a   α, Vg, and others paraphrase: the stronger animals conceived in the summer, the weaker in the winter.
43a   האיש as in Gen. 26:13.   **b**   פרץ Gen. 28:14; 30:30.   **c**   מאד מאד elsewhere only in P.

Form

The passage on Jacob outwitting Laban, 30:25-43, has presented exegetes with great difficulties, above all because from Jacob's offer to Laban right up to the very last act it is not clear what is going on. And the explanation is made all the more difficult by the attempt at source division based on doublets.

After several attempts to separate the passage into J and E, M. Noth was convinced that any source division is impossible (so too E. Otto, BWANT 110 [1979] 61-67): it is better to settle for a series of additions without any further precision. The decisive argument against source division is the clear, well thought out structure that would be destroyed by a separation into two strands (so too P. Volz). Vv. 25-43 tell of an agreement between Laban and Jacob (vv. 25b-34) and its execution (vv. 35-42). The agreement is concluded in a conversation in two stages, vv. 25b-30 and 31-34. They are precisely planned and balanced, and it is here that the unity of plan is clearest. Difficulties arise only from vv. 32-33. The agreement introduced by a conversation corresponds in form to the Babylonian dialog contracts, like ch. 23 (see bibliog. to ch. 23). The execution of the agreement follows in vv. 35-42, divided into Laban's action in vv. 35-36 and Jacob's actions in vv. 37-42.

The real difficulties come from vv. 37-42. Jacob's dexterity is a most complicated process and in part incomprehensible. H. Gunkel has perceived correctly that the accumulation of complicated steps with no reason given for any of them would not be possible in an oral narrative. But when ones notes that these accumulations, so inappropriate to the narrative style, occur not only in the execution in vv. 37-42 but already in the agreement in vv. 32-33, then a simple solution presents itself: both the variant words in vv. 32-33 and the variations in the execution in vv. 35-40 belong to one and the same expansion which was handed on in an incomplete state because herdsmen's skills of this sort were no longer understood or of interest.

Setting

If one brackets out the expansions, then the narrative clearly goes back to J. J's hand can be recognized in making the originally independent narrative a constituent part of the Jacob-Laban cycle of Gen. 29–31. Jacob's outwitting of Laban thus balances Laban's outwitting of Jacob in ch. 29. But the narrative which J resumes is one that was concerned solely with the execution of a trick with sheep and goats. It is a "professional" narrative that originated and was handed down among the herdsmen; the expansion too is to be understood from this context.

Commentary

[30:25a]   The first sentence of v. 25 forms a redactional transition joining what follows with Gen. 30:1-24.

[30:25b-30]   The first exchange between Jacob and Laban is formed thus: Jacob (vv. 25b-26), Laban (vv. 27-28), Jacob (vv. 29-30). It begins with Jacob's request to be allowed to go, and ends with the repetition of the same (v. 30b).

[30:25b-26]   To his request to be allowed to go ("to my own place," Gen. 18:33; 29:26; "to my land," Gen. 12:1) Jacob adds the request that his wives and children (who belong to the wives) be handed over to him; he has served Laban 14 years for them and to support his request he refers to the quality of the service which Laban acknowledges and confirms. The request presupposes that Jacob was in a position of dependence in Laban's house. It was by no means to be taken for granted that Jacob at his own wish could make himself independent with regard to his wives and children; this is clear from Gen. 31:43 where Laban lays claim to them; consequently v. 26 cannot be understood as a doublet of v. 25a.

[**30:27-28**]   These two verses portray in lively fashion Laban's embarrassment, perhaps even his surprise. He is very satisfied with the present situation; Jacob's departure from his household can only harm him. His answer is clever, a retort in two parts (the ויאמר at the beginning of v. 28). In the first part he wants only to curry favor with Jacob by means of the standard formula of homage (or request for indulgence, e.g., Gen. 39:21; H. J. Stoebe [BHH I 587-597]: "The person in whose eyes one finds *ḥēn* is always in a superior position"); it is not in place here. Then he hastens to confirm that Jacob's service has in fact brought him many advantages. "I know (by divination) that Yahweh [one would expect אלהים, but Laban deliberately mentions Jacob's God] has blessed me because of you." He stops short of the final sentence after אם־נא (aposiopesis, likewise in Gen. 18:3), as also of the consequence for him arising from the second sentence; but the hidden request is clear enough. It is the presupposition for the second retort in v. 28; alarmed, Laban leaves it to Jacob himself to determine his wages (naturally for the period to come).

[**30:29-30**]   Jacob repeats his request to be allowed to go (v. 30b). As the reason, he refers yet again to what he has accomplished in the service of Laban (v. 39b resumes v. 26b). Jacob knows, and Laban knows it too, that it is he alone who has made something out of Laban's property. There is therefore a clear progression from vv. 25-26 to vv. 29-30; to see a doublet here is to misunderstand the whole transaction, as a glance at ch. 23 shows. Jacob's answer expresses his pride in what he accomplished. Subtly he corrects what Laban has said about the success of his work: ". . .Yahweh has blessed you because of me"; Jacob says: "Yahweh has blessed you wherever I turned," i.e., after I arrived (cf. Is. 41:2). Jacob's response leads to the clarification: "But it is high time that I took care of my own household."

[**30:31-34**]   The second exchange: Laban v. 31aα—Jacob v. 31aβ—Laban v. 34, is determined by the offer that Jacob now makes to Laban. Laban bypasses Jacob's request and repeats his offer for Jacob to choose freely his wages. This is in fact a rejection of Jacob's request to be allowed to leave Laban's house. So far the dialog has achieved nothing. Jacob now reverses his position and freely offers to remain as Laban's herdsman. (The addition of אשמר to ארעה צאנך could be a gloss, as most interpreters think; it could also be a deliberate addition so as to include the liability of the herdsman [Gen. 31:39] within Jacob's commitment.) The first part of Jacob's reply shows he is nonplussed: "You shall give me nothing!" It is to be understood in a way similar to the reply of Ephron the Hittite in the like negotiation in Gen. 23:11: "I give you the land!" In both cases the partner in the dialog knows just where he stands. But the sentence also means that Laban does not yet need to fix the amount of wages. Jacob only lays down a condition; it will emerge only at the end that with this condition he is making careful plans for what he purposed, namely, to provide for his household.

[**30:32**]   The long sentence of v. 32 ends: והיה שכרי, "these shall be my wages," or "my wages shall come from these." This is the second part of Jacob's offer; but the context is not clear at first because the conclusion is such a long way from the beginning. Moreover, the narrative style, which so far has been so taut, is interrupted by a long and complicated enumeration which recurs in vv. 36-42. It is in v. 32 then that the subsequent expansion of the narrative begins. The context is restored if the words from וכל to בעזים are bracketed. The condition that Jacob makes becomes clear only when v. 33 is taken into consideration. Jacob will now pick out the unusually colored animals from the flock so that the flock which he has undertaken to care for contains only the normally colored. After the agreed time has run its course, only the unusually colored are to be his in return for his service. Even this is expressed negatively in v. 33b; what is not unusually colored does not belong to him. This clear and controllable offer, v. 33a, would appeal to the avaricious Laban; only the additions in vv. 32, 33, introducing further refinements, render the offer complicated and difficult. The addition in v. 32, like that in v. 33, distinguishes between sheep and goats: "and all the black ones among the sheep and the speckled and spotted among the goats" (v. 32); ". . .among the goats and black among the sheep" (v. 33). It is the same distinction as added by the glossator in vv. 35 and 40; it is the gloss of a specialist who expands the content correctly, namely, that the unusual coloring among the goats (mainly dark or dark brown) and the sheep (mainly white) must be different.

[30:34]   Laban accepts the offer at once and without hesitation. He must have thought that under such conditions Jacob's wages could only be very meagre.

[30:35-42]   The execution of the agreement is divided into the measures taken by Laban (vv. 35-36) and Jacob (vv. 37-42), respectively.

[30:35-36]   Laban takes precautionary measures. He does not leave it to Jacob to pick out the unusually colored animals (v. 32a), but does it himself and then puts them under the care of his sons (v. 35). He takes further precautions against any possible encroachment by Jacob by putting a distance of three days journey between these flocks and those under Jacob's care (v. 36a).

[30:35]   This is a subsequent addition; as in vv. 32,33 a distinction is made between sheep and goats: "and the speckled and the spotted goats, all that had white on them, and all the black sheep." It is the same expansion of content as in vv. 32,33, but more precise in that the glossator adds: "all that had white on them." His brief addition betrays his intention. He wants to explain that the unusual coloring must necessarily be different in the case of the sheep and the goats. Before this he inserts את־התישים = he-goats, with which he obviously wants to expand עזים = (she-)goats, a further sign of his concern for accuracy. The neutral שׂה would have stood originally in the narrative.

[30:36]   By means of the three days journey Laban wants to secure himself against any possible encroachments by Jacob. V. 36b is a transition piece, linking vv. 35-36 and vv. 37-42 together.

[30:37-42]   The measures that Jacob takes are determined by his original purpose: now, after having worked so long for Jacob, he must take care of his own household (29:31—30:24). Now that Laban has made it clear enough that he will not let him go, there remains no other possibility but cunning. Given Jacob's situation as presented here, "cunning" has the positive meaning that we associate with it; his cunning is the use of ingenuity against the one who has superior power. It cannot be described as deception; Jacob insists that he is to abide by the limits of the agreement (J. Skinner renders צדקת v. 33 by ''fair dealing''). The execution covers only vv. 37-39,41-42 where his dexterity and its result are clearly and simply presented.

[30:37] The verse is colored by both narratives: ''Then he took. . .and peeled. . .." Jacob took switches from the poplar trees which exude a white liquid; there may be a play on לבן here. He peels strips from them (פצלות from פצל only here) ''so as to lay bare the white on the rods,'' a difficult and unnecessary sentence, perhaps the work of the glossator. Two other trees are mentioned with the לבנה, the almond לוז and the plane ערמון, but they have no function in the narrative and may well be part of the expansion.

[30:38, 39] The narrative proceeds on to the end of v. 39. When Jacob had peeled the rods and they appeared multicolored, he put them into the drinking troughs; the effect was to cause the animals to throw multicolored young (v. 39). It should be noted that the narrative up to this point is closely knit, clear, and comprehensible. There are two words for drinking troughs in v. 38, juxtaposed and unconnected; שקתות is probably an explanatory gloss which elucidates the word רהטים from Gen. 24:20 (only in these two passages). What follows is incomprehensible and decked with repetitions as to indicate that the glossator has intervened here as well. He could have been responsible also for v. 38 from בשקתות to לשתות and the three last words of the verse; also for עקדים in v. 39, cf. BHK. The text of the narrative would then be:

> Then he stood the rods which he had peeled in the troughs [   ] facing the goats [   ], and they went into heat in front of the rods, and gave birth to young [   ] that were speckled and spotted.

We have here the artifice of a clever and practised herdsman who by means of visual aids manipulates and brings about a particular breeding effect in the moment of parturition.

Behind this lies the widespread notion that visual impressions at the moment of conception (''he bred flocks for himself'') can affect the progeny of animals. What is peculiar to Jacob's artifice is not the notion behind it, but its deliberate manipulation with the intention of producing a particular breeding effect. There are signs here of an earlier transition from magical to scientific thinking; it is scientific inasmuch as knowledge of animals' habits leads to calculated subjection of such to one's ends. Once more, as in Gen. 8:6-12, a crisis situation leads to a successful discovery.

It was of the greatest importance for small-cattle economy to know how the breeding habits of domesticated animals could be influenced by outside intervention; this is the reason why there was such interest in it as the narrative was handed down; the expansions show this.

[30:40-42] Jacob's artifice whereby he achieves his purpose could have ended with v. 39. Vv. 41-42 present a refinement of the experiment, v. 40 another experiment indicating the hand of the glossator.

[30:40] It is difficult to understand the text. F. Delitzsch could help only by eliminating the middle sentence; B. Jacob concedes that he cannot explain it. When one admits that the glossator in vv. 32-33 differentiates between sheep and goats, then a solution presents itself. The same distinction is made here. The variants over against vv. 37-39 are that in v. 40a Jacob picks out the sheep and makes them face the black (v. 40b), i.e., the goats; they are black only, so that the black and speckled goats exercise the same function as do the rods in vv. 37-39. One must add after the second sentence how the process took place, as had already happened in vv. 38-39. The result in the last sentence of v. 40 shows that this is the intention. Nothing needs to be altered in or deleted from v. 40. The meaning is clear: it is a variant of vv. 37-39, another possible experiment with the same result.

[**30:41-42**]   Vv. 41-42 resume the system of vv. 37-39 and refine it; it is, however, restricted to the stronger animals so that with the increase in progeny the stronger become Jacob's. Vv. 41-42 follow directly on v. 39.

[**30:43**]   The conclusion, v. 43 (not just v. 43b, E. Otto), is strange both in content and language. There is no reason for the designation הָאִישׁ. מְאֹד מְאֹד occurs elsewhere only in P. The details of Jacob's wealth are stylized and out of place here (cf. Gen. 26:13-14). But more, this is not a genuine conclusion to what has been narrated, namely, an event that has taken place between Jacob and Laban. The conclusion must treat of both. Probably the conclusion of vv. 25-42 has fallen out at the expense of ch. 31, and a redactor has substituted the stylized ending.

Purpose and Thrust

The Yahwist has put this herdsmen's narrative into the context of his Jacob-Esau cycle. He has thus handed on a narrative from the cycle of small-cattle nomads which has both an economic and a social aspect. We witness an experiment in breeding that relies as much on ancient magical notions as on observations of the habits of animals. A transition in the occupation of the herdsmen appears here; a rational element of planned experiment to influence breeding enters in. The social aspect: the herdsman in a situation of service is striving for independence (v. 30b); he is alone and powerless; by force of his own ingenuity he devises a new artifice in cattle breeding.

J has given the narrative at hand to him a new look. Jacob comes to Laban as a fugitive; the blessing he has won by deceit has driven him from his father's house and he himself is now deceived in the house of his relatives. But the blessing gives notice of its presence in the service of Laban and Laban acknowledges it (v. 27); it is still only on one who is dependent and is the source of blessing for the overlord. But Laban misuses the blessing by exploiting Jacob's ability for himself alone. It can not be Yahweh's blessing where one gets all, the other nothing. Yahweh, the God of Jacob, is clearly with the weak who is being abused by the strong. He allows Jacob's cunning to succeed and thus free him from dependence. As elsewhere the Yahwist lets the unsaid speak: Laban takes his stand on custom and tradition in his deception; Jacob takes no account of this; he must rely on his own native ingenuity. What he devises therefrom points the way forward.

Jacob's Separation from Laban

Literature

Genesis 31: A. Jirku, "Neues keilschriftliches Material. . .," ZAW 39 (1921) 144-160. M. Noth, "Beiträge zur Geschichte des Ostjordanlandes III," BBLAK 68 (1949) 1-50. J. Simons, *The Geographical. . .Texts. . .* (1959), "The Return of Jacob: Gen. 31–33."

Genesis 31:1-18: P. Kleinert, "Bilderdienst und Bilder im AT," RE[3] III (1896-1913) 217-221. M. Burrows, "The Complaint of Laban's Daughters," JAOS 57 (1937) 259-276. F. C. Fensham, "The Stem *HTL* in Biblical Law," VT 9 (1959) 310-311. R. Weiss, "On Ligatures in the Hebrew Bible (נו = ם)," JBL 82 (1963) 188-194.

Genesis 31:19-21: A. Jeremias, "Urim und Tummim. Ephod, Teraphim," Hilprecht Anniv. Vol. (1909). G. Hofmann, "Teraphim, Masken und Winkorakel in Ägypten und Vorderasien," ZAW 40 (1922) 75-137. C. J. Gadd and S. Smith, "Tablets from Kirkuk," RA 23 (1926) 44-161 esp. 44-46. I. Löw, "Zur Bedeutung der Teraphim," MGWJ 73 (1929) 314-316. S. Smith, "What were the Teraphim?" JThSt 33 (1932) 33-36. E. Sellin, "Ephod und Teraphim," JPOS 14 (1934) 85-93. K. Galling, BRL: HAT I1 (1937) 200-202. R. O'Callaghan, "Historical Parallels to Patriarchal Social Custom," CBQ 6 (1944) 391-405 esp. 399. P. R. Ackroyd, "The Teraphim," ET 62 (1950/51) 378-380. J. Mauchline, "Gilead and Gilgal: Some Reflections on the Israelite Occupation of Palestine," VT 6 (1956) 19-33. M. Noth, "Gilead und Gad," ZDPV 75 (1959) 14-73. L. Wächter, "Gemeinschaft und Einzelner im Judentum," AVTRW 16 (1959) 7-35 esp. 25f. H. M. Gevaryahn, "In Clarification of the Nature of the Terafim in the Bible" [in Hebr.], BetM 15 (1962) 81-86. M. Greenberg, "Another Look at Rachel's Theft of the Teraphim," JBL 81 (1962) 239-248. E. Kutsch, "Beiträge zur Siedlungsgeschichte des *wādi Kuftinği*," ZDPV 81 (1965) 113-131. J. Gray, "Hazor," VT 16 (1966) 26-52 esp. 28. C. J. Labuchagne, "Teraphim—A New Proposal for Its Etymology," VT 16 (1966) 115-117. H. A. Hoffner, "Hittite *TARPIŠ* and Hebrew *TERĀPHÎM*," JNES 27 (1968) 61-68. M. Ottosson, *Gilead. Tradition and History* (1969). H. D. Preuss, *Verspottung fremder Religionen im AT*, BWANT 5 = 92 (1971). B. S. Jackson, *Theft in Early Jewish Law* (1972). E. F. de Ward, "Superstition and Judgment: Archaic Methods of Finding a Verdict," ZAW 89 (1977) 1-19.

Genesis 31:22-42: M. Ginsburger, "Une ancienne crux interpretum," RHPhR 28 (1928) 178-179. H. W. Hertzberg, "Mizpa," ZAW 47 (1929) 161-196. J. Finkel, "Hebrew *Shīr* and *Sūra*," ZAW 50 (1932) 310-312. D. A. McKenzie, "Judicial Procedure at the Town Gate," VT 14 (1964) 100-104. J. J. Finkelstein, "An Old Babylonian Herding Contract and Genesis 31,38f.," JAOS 88 (1968) 30-36. E. Jenni, *Das hebräische Pi`el* (1968). G. W. Coats, "Self-Abasement and Insult Formulas," JBL 89 (1970) 14-26. D. R. Hillers, "Critical Note: *Paḥad Yiṣḥāq*," JBL 91 (1972) 90-92. J. H. Tigay, "Toward the Recovery of *Pohar, 'Company','' JBL 92 (1973) 517-522. O. Loretz, ''Hebräisch ḥwṭ 'bezahlen, erstatten' in Gen 31,39,'' ZAW 87 (1975) 207-208. W. G. E. Watson, ''Reclustering Hebrew l'lyd,'' Bib 58 (1977) 213-215. S. E. Loewenstamm, ''אָנֹכִי אֲחַטֶּנָּה,'' ZAW 90 (1978) 410. A. Lemaire, ''Les benê Jacob,'' RB 85 (1978) 321-337. G. W. Coats, ''Strife without Reconciliation—A Narrative Theme in the Jacob Traditions,'' Fests. C. Westermann (1980) 82-106.

Genesis 31:43-54: J. A. Montgomery, ''Notes on OT: Gen 31, 47. . .m and mā; kī and 'akēn,'' JBL 41 (1922) 140-146. E. F. Weidner, ''Politische Dokumente aus Kleinasien,'' *Boghazköi Studien* 8 (1923) esp. 55ff. N. H. Snaith, ''Genesis XXXI 50,'' VT 14 (1964) 373. F. O. Garcia-Treto,'' Genesis 31,44 and 'Gilead,' '' ZAW 79 (1967) 13-17. H. L. Ginsberg, ''The Northwest Semitic Languages,'' *The World History of the Jewish People II* (1970) ch. 6,102-104. M. B. Barrick, ''The Funerary Character of 'High-Places' in Ancient Palestine: A Reassessment,'' VT 25 (1975) 565-595.

Text

31:2 Now Jacob saw[a] that Laban's attitude toward him was no longer[b] what it had been,

1 and he heard Laban's sons saying: Jacob has taken everything that belonged to our father; all his wealth[a] has come from what belonged to our father.

3 [Then Yahweh said to Jacob: Return to the land of your fathers and to your family; and I will be with you!]

4 Then Jacob sent for Rachel and Leah and called them into the field where his flocks were.

5 He said to them: I see that your father's attitude toward me is no longer what it has been; [but the God of my father[a] has been with me].

6 You yourselves[a] know that I have served your father with all my strength.

7 But your father has cheated me[a] and ten times[b] over has changed[c] my wages; but God[d] has not allowed me to suffer harm.

8 If he said:[a] The spotted ones shall be your wages, the whole flock bore spotted; if he said: The striped ones shall be your wages, the whole flock bore striped.

9 [So God has reclaimed your[a] father's flocks and given them to me.]

10 [At the mating season I lifted up my eyes and saw in a dream that the he-goats mounting the flock were striped and spotted and dappled.]

11 And the angel of God said to me in a dream: Jacob! And I said: Here I am!

12 And he said: [Lift up your eyes and see how all the he-goats mounting the flock are striped and spotted and dappled; for] I have seen all that Laban has done to you.

13 I am the God ''who appeared to you at Bethel,''[a] where you anointed the pillar ''and'' where[b] you made a vow to me. Now rise, go from this land and return to the land of your family.

14 Then Rachel and Leah answered him: Is there any part or inheritance[a] still left for us in our father's house?

15 Are we not regarded by him as[a] foreigners? He has sold us and long since consumed the money paid for us.

16 All the wealth that God[a] has reclaimed from our father belongs to us and our children. And now, do all that God[b] has told you to do!

17 So Jacob prepared himself and put his children and his wives[a] on camels

18 and drove off all his livestock and all the property he had acquired, his livestock and flocks acquired in Paddan-aram, to go to his father Isaac in the land of Canaan.

19   Now when Laban had gone to shear his sheep, Rachel stole her father's teraphim.

20   [But Jacob lulled the heart of Laban the Aramean by concealing[a] from him that he intended to flee.]

21   He fled with all that he had; he set out for and crossed the River and made in the direction of the mountains of Gilead.

22   When on the third day Laban was told that Jacob had fled

23   he took his kinsmen with him, pursued Jacob for seven days, and caught up with him on the mountains of Gilead.

24   [But God came in a dream by night to Laban the Aramean and said to him: Take care to say nothing[a] to Jacob, neither good nor bad!]

25   When Laban overtook Jacob—Jacob had pitched his tent on the mountain. . .,[a] but Laban and his kinsmen had pitched "his tent"[b] on the mountains of Gilead—

26   he said to Jacob: What have "I done to you"[a] that you [have lulled me and][b] abducted[c] my daughters like prisoners of war?

27   Why did you flee secretly and deceive me and say nothing to me? I would have sent you on your way with songs and rejoicing, with tambourine and zither;

28   you did not even allow me to kiss my daughters and their children. You have acted foolishly![a]

29   [Indeed I would have had the power[a] to do you[b] harm, but the God of "your"[c] father spoke to me last night and said: Take care to say nothing to Jacob, neither good nor bad!]

30   But now—you have gone away because you longed so much for your father's house; "but"[a] why have you stolen my god?

31   Jacob replied and said to Laban: [Because I was afraid],[a] because I thought that you would take your daughters from me by force.[b]

32   Whoever you find in possession of your god shall not live; in the presence of my kinsmen point out what they have that is yours[a] and take it.[b] Jacob did not know that Rachel had stolen the god.

33   So Laban[a] went into Jacob's tent and Leah's tent and the tents of the two maids. Then he went from Leah's tent into Rachel's tent.

34   Now Rachel had taken the teraphim and had put it in the camel's saddle[a] and was sitting on it. And Laban searched the whole tent but did not find it.[b]

35   And she said to her father: Do not be angry with me, sir, that I cannot rise in your presence; the lot of women is upon me. So he searched,[a] but did not find the teraphim.

36   Then Jacob became angry and took Laban to task; Jacob retorted to Laban: What wrong have I done? What is my offense that you have come after[a] me?

37   Why have you searched all my possessions? What have you found belonging to your household? Lay it out here between my kinsmen and yours so that they may decide between us!

38   In all the twenty years I have been with you your ewes and she-goats have not miscarried; I have not eaten the rams of your flocks.

39   I have never brought to you a carcass torn by wild beasts; I bore the loss myself;[a] you claimed from me whether the loss was by day or by night.

40   This is how I lived—the heat consumed me by day, the cold by night, and sleep deserted me.[a]

41   Twenty years I have served in your household, fourteen for your two

487

daughters and six for your flocks and you have altered my wages ten times.

42 If the God of my father [the God of Abraham and the Fear of Isaac] had not been with me, you would certainly have sent me away empty-handed. But God saw my affliction and the labor of my hands and rebuked you last night.

43 Laban answered Jacob: The daughters are my daughters, the children are my children, the flocks are my flocks, and all that you see belongs to me. But as for my daughters, what can I do for them now and for the children they have borne?

44 Come now, let us make an agreement you and I, "we will make a cairn"[a] and it shall stand as a witness between us.

45 [Jacob (Laban)[a] took a stone and set it up as a pillar.]

46 And Jacob[a] said to his kinsmen: Gather stones! And they took stones and erected a cairn [and ate there beside the cairn].

47 [Laban called it Jegar-sahadutha, and Jacob called it Galeed.]

48 And Laban said: This cairn is a witness today between you and me [this is why it is called Galeed

49 and Mizpah because it is said[a]]: May Yahweh[b] watch between you and me when we are out of each other's sight.

50 If you ill-treat my daughters or take other wives beside my daughters when no one is there to see,[a] then God is witness between you and me.

51 [Then Laban said to Jacob: See, this cairn and "this"[a] pillar I have erected[b] between you and me;

52 this cairn is a witness and "this" pillar is a witness that I will not pass beyond this cairn to your side, and that you will not pass beyond this cairn and this pillar to my side to do harm;[a]

53a Let the God of Abraham and the God of Nahor "be"[a] judge between us (the God of their fathers)[b].]

53b And Jacob swore by the Fear of Isaac his father.

54 Jacob offered a sacrifice on the mountain, and summoned his kinsmen to the meal. They ate the meal and passed the night on the mountain.

2a וירא. . .והנה F. I. Andersen, "surprise clauses," *The Sentence in Biblical Hebrew* (1974) 95.   **b** On איני (Sam אינם), R. Weiss, JBL 82 (1963) 190f.

1a כבד = wealth as in Is. 10:3; 66:12.

5a Here for the first time, cf. K. T. Andersen, StTh 16 (1962) 173f.

6a ואתנה emphatic form, Ges-K §32f.; elsewhere only 3 times in Ezek.

7a ב in an inimical sense, Ges-K §67n; BrSynt §106h.   **b** מנים only here and v. 41. BrSynt §88; in sense of "several times" as Num. 14:22.   **c** Sam reads imperf; cf. v. 41. Ges-K §112h; for imperf. Bergsträsser II §9b,k.   **d** Sam reads יהוה, likewise vv. 9,16.

8a Structure of sentence, Ges-K §159r,s; BrSynt §164b, 50e.

9a MSS, Sam, אביכן.

13a Expand with Gk, TargO,J.   **b** With some MSS ואשר to be read.

14a Hendiadys, so M. Burrows, JAOS 57 (1937) 259-276; also E. A. Speiser. On נחלה G. Gerlemann, ZAW 89 (1977) 313-325.

15a Sam reads כנכיות.

16a Sam reads יהוה.   **b** Syr reads יהוה.

17a Sam and Gk reverse order.

20a On the construction, BrSynt §52b, 145a; BHK App.

24a מטוב עד missing in Gk, Vg, likewise v. 29.

25a Proposed בהר המצפה; cf. v. 49.   **b** Read אהלו for אחיו.

26a Read with Syr מה אשיתי לך. **b** "Stolen my heart and" is an addition; Gk has in place of it v. 27a. **c** On the construction, Ges-K §111m, 114m, 116k.
28a Instead of עשׂו Sam reads עשׂות; Ges-K §75n; cf. I. L. Seeligmann, VT 11 (1961) 201-221.
29a On the expression (also Mic. 2:1; Prov. 3:27), BrSynt §15g. **b** Sam, Gk sing., so H. Gunkel, BHK App. **c** Read sing. with some MSS.
30a Read ולמה.
31a Addition; missing in Gk. **b** Gk adds some words; BHK.
32a Read מה לך. **b** Gk is more detailed.
33a Gk adds ויחפשׂ and deviates further from MT.
34a כר is understood by many as a sedan chair, a palanquin. **b** The last seven words are missing in the Gk.
35a Gk adds לבן בכל־האהל.
36a As 1 Sam. 27:53.
39a On חטא, cf. S. E. Loewenstamm, ZAW 90 (1978) 410; O. Loretz, ZAW 87 (1975) 207-208.
40a The verb נדד occurs only here in the Pentateuch; on form, Ges-K §67cc, 76a.
44a After ואתה insert נעשׂה גל, BHK.
45a Many exegetes replace Jacob with Laban.
46a VetLat has לבן, accepted by many exegetes (e.g., M. Noth).
49a The first three words of v. 49 are missing in the Vg. **b** Gk reads אלהים.
50a Proposal: read רֹאֶה for רְאֵה (see Gk); N. H. Snaith translates, "when no man of our (father's) kin is watching, God will be witness. . .," VT 14 (1964) 373.
51a TargP and Syr expand correctly here and v. 52 with הזאת. **b** Sam reads ירית for יריתי; on the verb "to erect," F. Stolz, BZAW 118 (1970) 181.
52a Gk has a shorter text, BHK.
53a Sam and Gk have sing. **b** Sam reads אלהי אברהם.

Form

In the Jacob-Esau cycle the return, which leads to the meeting with Esau in chs. 32–33, follows the flight, 27:41-45. In the Jacob-Laban cycle Jacob's arrival in ch. 29 is balanced by the departure which in its turn is a flight. The Jacob-Laban cycle concludes with the treaty between the two; Laban returns home (32:1).

Ch. 31 is an episode within both the broader (Gen. 27–33) and narrower (Gen. 29–31) contexts that is unintelligible without what precedes and follows. The disposition of its parts shows a well-knit, self-contained unit: Jacob's flight—Laban's persecution—Laban's accusation—Jacob's counteraccusation—Laban's treaty with Jacob—Laban's return. The narrative tension rises from Jacob's flight and Laban's persecution to the moment when the two confront each other and Laban demands an account from Jacob. The turning point of the resulting threat to Jacob (the peripeteia) begins with the counteraccusation that Jacob lays against Laban. The narrative reaches its climax in a statement of the praise of God: God has seen my affliction and taken up my cause (v. 42b). The treaty between Jacob and Laban forms the conclusion (vv. 43-54). Jacob can now continue on his way (ch. 32), but he is no longer a fugitive.

The dispute between Laban and Jacob forms the nucleus of this episode (vv. 25-42) and finds its resolution in the treaty (vv. 43-54). What lies behind the chapter and its parts is not an originally independent narrative but a group of well-honed traditions: vv. 25-54 are stamped with legal language and the formulas of legal procedure (H. J. Boecker, *Redeformen des Rechtslebens im A.T.* [1964, 1970²]). Gen. 31 belongs to that group of narratives in which a continual process (as the blessing in Gen. 27) is, in a given situation, shaped so as to give a definite result. The situation in which this takes place is presented in detail in the passage vv. 1-24 which continues what has been narrated beforehand. We have seen that v. 43 is not a satisfactory conclusion to Gen. 30:25-43; the conclusion must be played out between the two partners in the form of an exchange between them. Gen. 31:1-24 is a transition to this and is concluded in vv. 25-43. The conclusion of 30:25-43 is the basis of ch. 31 which has been expanded by the narrator so as to form a conclusion to the whole Jacob-Laban cycle.

The well-knit, self-contained unit of ch. 31 has been subsequently expanded, particularly by the dialog between Jacob and his wives in vv. 4-16 and the treaty in vv. 43-54. It is a matter of two different expansions completely independent of each other.

Setting

The narrator here is the Yahwist; this emerges from the way in which the whole is put together; the exposition will show it in detail. In vv. 25-43 J takes as a base the conventions of the ריב, the confrontation before the court: the prosecution of the delinquent consequent on an offense, the legal process before a tribunal with accusation, defense, inquiry, and instead of a judicial decision the reconciliation of the two parties to the case in an agreement binding on both. There is no Elohistic source to be found in Gen. 31 because the expansions are of different kinds. The expansion in vv. 4-16 has a theologizing thrust such as we have also met in 29:31—30:24; the expansion dealing with the treaty belongs to the context of tribal history and so corresponds to the secondary tribal pronouncements in 27:27-29, 39-40.

Commentary

[31:1-24]   An account of the occasion of Jacob's flight (vv. 1-3) and the conversation with his wives (vv. 4-16) precedes the actual flight (vv. 17-21) and Laban's pursuit (vv. 22-24).

[31:1-3]   There is no subject for the introductory v. 1; v. 2 must have preceded it; this is supported by the frequent use of וירא at the beginning of an episode and the natural sequence of the father (v. 2) and the sons (v. 1). Vv. 1 and 2 are not doublets; rather, v. 1 intensifies v. 2; Laban's dark looks are followed by the hostile remarks of the sons; the danger to Jacob increases.

[31:3]   Jacob therefore decides to flee; he needs the agreement of his wives and gets it in the dialog in vv. 4-16. Yahweh's instruction to flee sounds abrupt between vv. 1-2 and 4; the reason for flight is cogent in vv. 2,1, and the situation requires no divine instruction. J speaks of such an instruction from Yahweh only where it is necessary as part of the action, not where it is one reason among others (R. Rendtorff: "The divine address with the theme of guidance is not a constituent part of the narrative here but serves rather as a theological interpretation," BZAW 147 [1976, 1977²] 58).

[31:4-16]   Jacob's dialog with his wives consists of his address to them (vv. 4-13) and their reply (vv. 14-16). From the outset the broad sweep of what Jacob says is striking; it does not accord with J's style. Moreover, it shows inconsistencies and repetitions; in any case alterations have been introduced later. However, the difficulties are so great that it is no longer possible to reconstruct with certainty the original narrative or to sort out accurately the additions. What I propose can be no more than a suggestion.

[31:4-9] Jacob summons his wives and lets them know that because of the change in attitude of their father (v. 5a, as in v. 2) the situation is dangerous. He is not to blame (v. 6, as 30:26b; v. 6 follows directly on v. 5a; v. 5b could be an addition); rather he blames Laban (v. 7a); Laban's attempts to diminish his wages have been forestalled by God (vv. 7b-9; v. 9 could be an addition). If Jacob presents the conflict with Laban, which ended with such profit to him, differently from 30:25-43, then it is to be explained from the setting and intent of his address to his wives; it does not stand in contradiction to that passage and is no justification for seeing another source (E) here. The listeners at any rate experience no contradiction when in the address to the women God's providence is seen behind the events described in Gen. 30:25-43. The situation is presented adequately in vv. 5-8(9): one awaits now the sequel: it follows in vv. 11,13.

[31:10-13] The present text (vv. 10-13) is preserved only in a corrupt form; one discerns in it two different revelations to Jacob that have been woven together. One refers to the way in which Jacob's flocks increased and which he traces back to a revelation through an angel of God; it has, however, been handed down in a mutilated form. The other contains the instruction to return to his homeland linked with a promise; it is a doublet of v. 3.

[31:10] The ויהי of v. 10 with the indication of time, "and the mating season," indicates a new beginning. One expects something to happen after an introduction like this, but what follows, "I lifted up my eyes. . .," presupposes that something has already happened. Moreover, the imperative (v. 12a), "lift up your eyes. . .," requires that the execution follows; the words of the angel, therefore, must have preceded the execution (v. 10). The text can be reconstructed as follows:

v. 10aα	Now at the mating season,
v. 11	the angel of God said to me in a dream: Jacob! And I said: Here I am!
v. 12a	And he said: Lift up your eyes and see: all the he-goats mounting the flock are striped, spotted, and dappled;
v. 10aβb	and I lifted up my eyes and saw in a dream that the he-goats mounting the flock were striped, spotted, and dappled.

However, the meaning of what was seen in the dream and how it explains Jacob's abundance of flocks is not clear because the corresponding Gen. 30:37-42 is missing. So much is clear: vv. 10aα,11,12a,10aβb are an addition, recalling the additions in Gen. 30:25-43, the purpose of which is to explain the increase in Jacob's flocks by means of a revelation made to him.

[31:11, 13a, 12b, 13b] The second revelation is better preserved in the text. It begins with v. 11. The confusion in the text is caused by the fact that this introduction belongs to both revelations. V. 13a follows on v. 11; ויאמר stands at the be-

491

ginning, and ב הנראת אליך is to be supplied after האל with Gk and TargO,J. V. 12b, which does not make sense after v. 12a, follows on v. 13a, and v. 13b comes after it. The text runs as follows:

v. 11	And the angel of God said to me in a dream: Jacob! And I said: Here I am!
v. 13a	And he said: I am the God who appeared to you at Bethel where you anointed the pillar and where you made a vow to me.
v. 12b	I have seen all that Laban has done to you;
v. 13b	Now rise, go from this land and return to the land of your family.

Vv. 11-13 are in their present form secondary; this is shown by the fact that they are assembled almost completely out of sentences which occur already in other places, and that they presuppose Gen. 28:10-22 in its present form. V. 13b is a doublet of v. 3 and the explanation of it is that the passage vv. 11-13 is an expanded variant of v. 3 which stood in place of vv. 11-13 in the old narrative in accordance with the context. It is not possible to reconstruct the original conclusion of Jacob's address to his wives. In any case it ended with his telling them that God had commanded him to return, and what that meant. And so the unspoken question was addressed to them, would they come with him?

[31:14-16]   The answer of the wives consists of both a negative and a positive part: negative, in that they will leave their father's house (vv. 14b,15a), giving as the reason an accusation that they lay against their father (vv. 15b,16a); positive, in that they agree that Jacob is following the call of God.

[31:14]   Everything now depends on the answer of Jacob's wives. It is of the utmost importance and this is expressed by the solemn, rhythmic form. It is the lapidary renunciation formula that occurs with the same words in 2 Sam. 20:1b (חלק and נחלה are also there) and 1 Kings 12:16 (the separation of the northern tribes from Judah). The latter is also the renunciation of a בית (the house of David); we note here how a formula belonging to family law has passed over into the political domain. While the daughters renounce the house of their father, a new house arises, the house of Jacob. Once again we see the importance of women in patriarchal society.

[31:15]   This appears too in the reason the wives give in v. 15. They blame their father because he has done them harm in the area of family law. It was obviously the custom that the מהר, what the father receives as "compensating sum" when giving in marriage, be passed on at least in part to the daughters. But Laban had given his daughters nothing (i.e., from the fruit of Jacob's work); he had used it all for himself. And so, conclude the wives, he has treated them not as members of the family but as foreigners. When they lay the accusation, "he has sold us," then what they are condemning is a "bought marriage" (cf. 29:15-20, small print).

[31:16]   This verse too is dealing with a legal formulation. The wives lay claim for themselves and their children to a share of the wealth that Jacob has acquired in their father's house (עשׁר = wealth, only here in the Pentateuch; it is part of the legal formula). It stands in opposition to the claim that Laban makes in v. 43. This means separation of the daughters from their father's house; they agree then to flee with Jacob. When the wives designate the God of Jacob as אלהים, it shows that the Yahwist, in the realm of another God of the fathers, had to use אלהים (Syr has יהוה).

[31:17-21]   Jacob's flight: The nucleus of vv. 17-21 is an itinerary note using the language of a report, not of a narrative. It consists of vv. 17, 18aα, 21. The simple style of the itinerary becomes evident when these sentences are read together. It is expressed by an insertion from P in v. 18aβb, and by a parenthesis in v. 19 which is a preparation for vv. 25-30; v. 30 has been added later.

[31:17, 18aα]   With the agreement of the wives (vv. 4-16), the departure (vv. 17,18aα), on which Jacob had already decided (vv. 1-3), is now possible. The departure in Gen. 46:5f. is portrayed in a similar way.

[31:18aβb]   This is an insertion from P (against R. Rendtorff); the language makes it obvious (so W. Eichrodt, BZAW 31 [1916]; against B. D. Eerdmans). P, in contrast to J, takes it that Isaac is still alive.

[31:19]   This is a parenthesis inserted by J in order to prepare vv. 25-30, to which narrative episode it really belongs. V. 19a then is intended as a circumstantial sentence, the inverted perfect being understood as a pluperfect. Shearing is a festal celebration at the place where the flocks are resting. Laban's absence gives Rachel the opportunity to take her father's teraphim. The word teraphim is singular in meaning, as 1 Sam. 19:13,16 shows. H. Gunkel: "Teraphim are images of the gods made in human shape," smaller than life-size and without pedestal. They are household gods such as are found in many religions; in the *Iliad,* Aeneas takes the Penates with him from Troy. As everywhere, the household gods confer protection and blessing (see bibliog. to 31:19-21; also T. H. Gaster, *Myth, Legend. . .* [1919] 200). The reason for the theft emerges from the accusation that Jacob's wives make against their father (vv. 14-16); Rachel thereby secures herself against the injustice done to her.

[31:20]   Jacob lulled the heart of Laban (v. 20); an appendage to the verb גנב, probably following 2 Sam. 15:6 where the image is very appropriate, whereas here it is less clearly defined. Further indication that it is an appendage is the designation of Laban as the Aramean, found elsewhere only in another appendage, v. 24; otherwise only in P.

[31:21]   This verse follows on vv. 17,18aα. J says וכל־אשׁר־לו (which includes persons), whereas P has כל־רכשׁו (v. 18). ויקם, however, is not a doublet of ויקם in v. 17; rather it describes, together with the following verb, an ongoing action. B. Jacob: "The river can be only the Euphrates." "Gilead" is to be understood here in a broad sense.

[31:22-24]   Laban pursues Jacob (vv. 22-24): The narrative describes the action of pursuit in language appropriate to it; Laban gets the news, gathers his followers, sets out in pursuit, catches up. V. 24 belongs neither in language nor in content to this event. The news that Laban gets is cited literally: ברח יעקב. When Laban takes "his brethren" in pursuit with him, the narrator is again drawing attention to Laban's superiority, as happens continually throughout the narrative. It is the superiority in power that has occasioned the addition in v. 24, carried on in v. 29. It is a theologizing addition which uses the opportunity to contrast Laban's superiority with God's protecting hand which is Jacob's guarantee (cf. 1 Sam. 17). Vv. 24 and 29 have no real function in the narrative, which is more tightly knit and clearer without them.

[**31:25-30**]   Laban's pursuit (vv. 21-24) has the purpose of calling Jacob to account; this happens in vv. 25-30. It is a nice narrative touch to interpose v. 25, the peaceful pause into which the busy activity of vv. 22-23 dissipates itself, between the hustling pursuit and the address to Jacob (v. 26). Laban and Jacob camp on two elevations opposite each other. The text of what follows is corrupt; either the words ולבן תקע את־אחיו must be deleted, leaving "and Jacob had pitched his tent on the mountain of Gilead," or the verse mentioned the tents of both, which is more likely; the name of the mountain is then missing in Jacob's camping place, and אהלו is to be read instead of אחיו (so too BHK).

The וישג at the beginning of v. 25 resumes the וידבק of v. 23; Laban has now overtaken Jacob. Many exegetes think that because of v. 49 the name was Mizpah; cf. BHK. This is possible, but not certain.

[**31:26-30**]   The accusation that Laban now makes against Jacob consists of two points: the secret flight (vv. 26-28) and the theft of the teraphim (v. 27a; 30b). The first point is developed in detail and ultimately excused (v. 30a); the serious accusation of theft remains.

[**31:26-28**]   The history of the text shows that the words ותגנב את־לבבי are an addition (as in v. 20). They are missing in the Gk, which has v. 27a instead; Syr has עשׂיתי for עשׂית. Syr has the original text, which was altered by the insertion, because it did not fit properly in front of the latter. It should read therefore: "What have I done to you that you [   ] have abducted my daughters like prisoners of war?" (cf. 2 Kings 6:22). The sentence, "you have stolen my heart [have lulled me]," proves certainly to be an addition because ותגנב־אתי follows immediately in v. 27. Vv. 27, 28 develop the charge made in v. 26, while there is but an indication of the other part of the accusation in v. 17a. The reason given recalls Gen. 29:15-30; once again Laban takes his stand on established custom, on "what is proper." Jacob has deprived Laban of the farewell demanded by custom (cf. 24:60). We learn here, and this only because Laban in his indignation against Jacob gives details of the farewell, that songs and music are part of it ("there must have been a genus of farewell songs," H. Gunkel). With his final accusation, "You have acted foolishly," Laban wants to disparage Jacob in the presence of his wives. The charge of foolishness is very serious (this is the only place where it occurs in the patriarchal story).

[**31:29**]   But Laban's charge, stemming from an apparently righteous anger, is merely covering over the real motive for Jacob's flight, namely, the danger that Laban presents because of his superior power (vv. 2, 1). The narrative very subtly leaves it to the listener to sense the hollowness of Laban's charge. The later reviser, resuming v. 24, takes the opportunity in v. 29 to underscore that while Laban boasts of his superior power, God has warned him not to make use of it.

[31:30] V. 30 is better understood when following immediately on v. 28. Laban is uncertain and senses that he has gone too far with his charge of foolishness. V. 30a sounds like an attempt to excuse Jacob of the first part of the accusation. The whole weight then falls on the second part, the theft, and Laban thinks that here his righteous indignation rests on firm ground. The ועתה at the beginning of v. 30 is part of this concluding question.

[31:31-32] Jacob replies tersely to both charges. The answer to the first uncovers the real situation that Laban wanted to cover with his fair words. Jacob would have feared that Laban would take his wives from him (the explanatory addition כי־יראתי says this expressly). This fear was justified, as v. 1 indicates and Laban confirms in v. 43.

Jacob rejects the second charge and leaves it to Laban to carry out the search which should prove his innocence. Conscious of this innocence he designates the most extreme punishment, the death penalty for the theft. V. 32a is a legal pronouncement in legal style constructed out of the incident and the penalty. "לא יחיה is an expression from sacral law imposing the death penalty (Ex. 19:13) based on holy or royal property. . .," B. Jacob. ". . .In the presence of my kinsmen" shows how the prejuridical accusation passes over into a forensic legal process (cf. H. J. Boecker, *Redeformen*. . . [1964, 1980²] 50-56).

[31:33-35] Laban's fruitless search proceeds in two stages: the first merely enumerates that he goes through the tents of Jacob, Leah, and the two maids. The second narrates an episode in the course of the search. Rachel prevents the discovery of the image of the god by a pretense. This episode, which is narrated with gentle mockery, presupposed that Rachel was conscious that she was in the right when she took her father's teraphim. The injustice that the daughters of Laban were convinced they had suffered forms the background to the theft (vv. 14-16, also 29:15-30). The mockery, however, has a theological aspect which is left unsaid: the almost laughable powerlessness of the wooden image of the god (similarly Is. 46:1-2; cf. H. P. Preuss, BWANT 5-92 [1971]).

[31:36-42] After rejecting Laban's two accusations Jacob lays a countercharge: וירב בלבן. There can be a ריב = "dispute" only where there are opposing charges; an accusation from one side only would not be a ריב. The dispute was of great importance in ancient Israel and in Israel's prehistory firstly as a "prejuridical confrontation" (H. J. Boecker) and then as a "premilitary confrontation." In both cases the dispute can be terminated by an agreement or pact; that is, judicial or military force can be forestalled (cf. B. Gemser, VT.S 3 [1955] 120-137; G. W. Coats, Fests. C. Westermann [1980] 82-106). It is not enough to explain Jacob's counteraccusation psychologically; the ריב-form requires that both parties lay their charges (so too D. A. McKenzie, VT 14 [1964] 100-104).

[31:36-37] Jacob's words are spoken in anger; with irony he rejects Laban's accusation of theft as now proven false. Each sentence comes from judicial language. The innocent accused asks the accuser what his offense consists in (v. 36b); Laban has carried out the search himself; Jacob mockingly pushes it to a conclusion which cannot be realized: the exposition of the corpus delicti to a forum and its decision (v. 37).

[31:38-42]   It is here, in Jacob's countercharge, that the Jacob-Laban narrative reaches its climax. In the first part Jacob gives an account of his stewardship in Laban's service (vv. 38-41a), which is framed within pointed references to its length (vv. 38a,42a). A. Dillmann had already noted, against J. Wellhausen, that this repetition is deliberate and is not to be explained by source division. The countercharge itself follows in the second part: Laban would have cheated him of his wages had God not been with him (vv. 41b-42). God has decided in his favor. In vv. 38f. Jacob expands how carefully he has abided by the strict obligations of his service, and in v. 40 the hardships entailed in it. In v. 41abα he comes back to the long period of service and goes on to the wages involved in it. It is only now that Jacob makes his real countercharge: the wages have not corresponded to this long and difficult service, and without God's intervention on his behalf he would have lost all (vv. 41bβ-42). Commentators as early as F. Delitzsch have remarked on the poetic language of Jacob's speech. It can be that a fixed formula of accountability lies behind vv. 38-41; cf. the report of accountability in another setting in 1 Sam. 12. However, it is also in accord with the enumerative style when at the climax of the conflict between Jacob and Laban Jacob's speech assumes poetic form.

[31:38-39]   The nominal sentence at the beginning of v. 38 could also be translated, ''In these twenty years. . ..'' Jacob has preserved the sheep and goats for his master, the sheep by taking particular care to prevent miscarriage, the goats by not laying any claim to them. V. 39 deals with the obligation to make good the loss. There were early prescriptions in this area, a ''herdsman's law,'' as Ex. 22:10-13 and the Code of Hammurabi (§§261-266) show. It becomes clear that Jacob went far beyond the obligations later codified in his concern for his master's property. As for the history of tradition, a comparison of Gen. 31:38 with Ex. 22:10-13 shows how legal prescriptions for a particular profession were first handed down orally and then became part of a written legal code; cf. J. J. Finkelstein (1968), especially for the verb חטא in this context; also S. E. Loewenstamm (1978); O. Loretz (1975); E. Jenni (1968), who explains the form as an estimative-declarative piel: the necessity of acknowledging that something has gone wrong (p. 267; all references in bibliog. above).

[31:40]   For 20 years Jacob led the hard life of a herdsman exposed to all the inclemencies of the weather. The poetic language is full of meaning here. If one compares this sentence at the end of Gen. 31 with the sentence at the beginning of 29:20, ''and they seemed to him but a few days,'' the apparent contradiction shows something quite characteristic of the narrative art of J. Each sentence reflects genuine experience, but between them are bitter disappointments.

[31:41-42]   Jacob worked 14 of the 20 years for his two wives (v. 41), but of his own free choice only for the first seven. Laban allowed him nothing from the next seven years, and for the following six he tried to cut down his wages in cattle. In v. 42 Jacob goes still further, and this is the real accusation that he makes against Laban: if Laban had had his way, Jacob would have ended up empty-handed after 20 years of hard and loyal service. In the ears of the listeners this was a very serious accusation. From the Book of the Covenant, through the Deuteronomic law to the prophets and into the New Testament, it was a particularly serious crime for the employer not to allow the employee to receive the wages due to him (immediately after the work). It is here that Laban's real culpability lies, and it is most serious.

J speaks here of God's action; it is necessary to do so (in contrast to vv. 24, 29). God is the God who intervenes on behalf of the weaker against the powerful: "If the God of my father had not been with me. . .." It is no accident that this sentence has close echoes of Ps. 124:1 and that v. 42b echoes the language of the Psalms. Jacob speaks of the God who takes the side of the poor and protects them from the powerful. V. 42a requires a sentence rhythm corresponding to Ps. 124:1 and so a simple designation for God, probably just אלהי אבי: "the God of my father" (i.e., of Isaac). אלהי אברהם ופחד יצחק was appended later. This is an understandable step on the way toward the later formulation, "the God of Abraham, Isaac, and Jacob." A further indication that it is an addition is that the God of Isaac is twice formally designated as such. The designation פחד יצחק occurs only here and in v. 53b, which also belongs to a later layer. The conclusion is that it belonged to a special tradition which occurs in this one place only, not that it is an older or later tradition (against A. Alt). The meaning is still contested. פחד is abundantly and certainly attested as "dread (fear)"; moreover, the Old Testament speaks of a dread emanating from God. Of special significance is the refrain verse in Is. 2:10, 19, 21. This would seem to confirm the meaning, "dread of Isaac," in 31:43,53. However, such a designation does not at all suit the God of the Fathers (32:23-33 cannot be alleged in favor); the Isaiah passage shows this.

W. F. Albright, therefore, has proposed another meaning: "Kinsman of Isaac" (*From the Stone Age.* . . [1940, 1957³] 248), invoking another Semitic root, *phd*. Many have accepted this. D. R. Hillers, however, has contested it in a detailed study; "In no Semitic language is there a *phd* = kinsman." On the other hand, however, K. Koch rightly says: "Nowhere can anything like a positive experience of the presence of God be associated with *pahad* (in contrast to *yir'ā*)" (Fests. C. Westermann [1979] 108); consequently this meaning remains unlikely. K. Koch himself proposes to take the second root *phd* in KBL, and suggested by D. R. Hillers, in the sense of loins or penis, so that Jacob swears by the penis of his father in v. 53. This meaning is perhaps possible in v. 53, but I do not see how it can hold for v. 42. L. Kopf now suggests: "perhaps פחד יצחק Gen. 31:42, 53 meant 'the refuge of Isaac,' " VT 8 [1958] 257. In Arabic the substantive means a place of refuge. This meaning is supported by a remark of H. P. Müller (review, ZA 65 [1975] 311): "One should compare *pahad jishaq* Gen. 31:42. . .with the personal name צלפחד = *sel pahad*, LXX Σαλπααδ (protecting) shade of the *pahad*."

With reservation, then, and until new information is forthcoming, one can settle for the meaning "protection of Isaac."

The last sentence of v. 42, ויוכח אמש, "and he rebuked you last night," gives expression to the outcome of the dispute between Laban and Jacob. Jacob was the weaker, the underdog who could not retaliate; but now God has intervened on his behalf and justified him. This sentence too is reminiscent of the language of the Psalms: "Justify me. . .!"

[31:43-54] Laban's contract with Jacob (vv. 43-54): All exegetes agree that this passage is a unity, but contest the way in which it is put together. The text has the form of a dialog. The first question to be asked is which parts give a meaningful dialog:

vv. 43-44	Laban proposes that he and Jacob come to an agreement; a cairn is to be witness to it.
v. 46	Jacob accepts and has his followers erect a cairn.
vv. 48a, 49b, 50	Laban formulates the agreement.
vv. 53b,54	Jacob confirms the agreement with an oath and seals it with a meal.
(32:1	Laban farewells his daughters and grandchildren and returns home.)

This framework can serve as a point of departure; all the rest must await the exegesis.

[31:43-44]   Laban makes a proposal to Jacob. Laban maintains his claim to his daughters and their children and to Jacob's flocks (it is only in v. 43b that Laban gives clear expression to this and so justifies Jacob's fears); but he recognizes defeat. He can no longer give effect to this claim (v. 43b), thereby acknowledging indirectly what Jacob has stated in v. 42. He wraps this admission in his solicitude for the welfare of his daughters and grandchildren which is certainly a matter of concern to him. The agreement that he proposes to Jacob serves to allay this, given the situation presented in v. 43. It is the only thing that he can now do for them (מה־אעשׂה, v. 43). He proposes נכרתה ברית אני ואתה. On כרת ברית see commentary on Gen. 15:18. It is misleading to translate the phrase here by ''make a covenant'' (German, ''*Bund*''). It is not a case of the two being bound together as partners, but rather of an agreement made on a particular occasion, and restricted to a particular matter, and based on a particular situation (v. 43). The last sentence is incomprehensible, והיה לעד ביני ובינך. Grammatically the relationship between היה and ברית (fem.) is impossible; and in fact the ברית cannot be a witness; rather a witness should be required for the ברית. Many exegetes assume therefore that a sentence has dropped out (so too the Gk). A. Dillmann suggested, ''we will make a cairn,'' which is confirmed by the continuation in v. 46.

[31:45]   This sentence has no context either preceding or following. It is part of the expansion and difficult to fit in even there. In any case the text is disturbed.

[31:46-47]   V. 46b follows on v. 44. Jacob follows up Laban's proposal by having his followers erect a cairn. The last sentence of v. 46 and that of v. 47 are part of the expansion. The common meal (a doublet of v. 54) has its place at the end of the rite; it has no meaning before the oath. The naming in two languages may be a scholarly gloss.

[31:48-50]   Laban follows Jacob's action of consent by confirming in v. 48 that the cairn that has just been erected is a witness to the agreement on which they are about to enter. The agreement follows in vv. 49b, 50. In v. 48 an etiology of the name is appended; it is an addition to which the first three words of v. 49 belong; these words can also be an appendix to v. 48. In v. 49b the cairn is a witness that Yahweh watches over the observance of the agreement even when Laban and Jacob are far from each other. In v. 50 the agreement obliges Jacob not to maltreat

Laban's daughters and not to take other wives beside them. Laban had said already, "This cairn is a witness today between you and me" (v. 48); by way of conclusion he now reinforces it, "God is witness between you and me" (v. 59). The text is uncertain here. This last sentence is missing in the Gk. It is possible that the variation in the name of God, יהוה in v. 49b and אלהים in v. 50b, is tied up with the textual uncertainty. The ritual of the oath should follow the agreement, but it comes only in v. 53b; in between is the expansion (vv. 51-53a).

[31:51-53a] There follows in vv. 51-53a an agreement of a completely different kind. In form it is two-sided, the parties concerned promising to do or not to do something. In content it is a sort of nonaggression pact between two groups, Jacob and Laban representing the groups; it is a matter of border disputes between Aram and Israel. Only the pact of vv. 48b, 50 can belong to the Jacob-Laban narrative because its contents deal with family events and it arises out of the preceding narrative. Against the view of the majority of exegetes, the tribal-political pact of vv. 51-53a can only be a later addition (so too H. Gunkel). The juxtaposition of the two pacts is to be explained from the history of tradition, not from literary criticism.

[31:51] The beginning, "Then Laban said to Jacob," does not fit harmoniously into the narrative because Laban has already spoken to Jacob in vv. 48-50. Only the expansion (vv. 51-53) has the combination "cairn" and "pillar" if v. 45 does not belong originally between vv. 44 and 46. A discordance caused by the putting together of the two different pacts is that according to v. 51 Laban erected the *maṣṣebah*, according to v. 45 it was Jacob. In any case the erection of the *maṣṣebah* belongs to the context of vv. 51-53a. It is very likely that the *maṣṣebah* set up by Laban has been added to the cairn set up by Jacob so as to underscore the mutuality of the treaty. It is also determinative for the expansion that the ביני ובינך in v. 51 has a different meaning (purely local) from vv. 48, 49.

[31:52] The agreement now follows; its meaning is clear; both parties undertake not to make hostile incursions into each other's territory. But the text is badly disturbed. The basis of the difficulty is that the cairn, together with the pillar, has two different functions. According to the first sentence it is a witness as in the other agreement (v. 48); in the following sentences it is (together with the pillar) a border sign. Both ideas are mixed in vv. 52f., and this has caused the confusion. If the cairn (with the pillar) is a witness, then the agreement should have the following structure:

> This cairn is a witness:
> if I pass beyond "   " to you,
> and if you pass beyond "   " to me to do harm,
> then let the God of Abraham and the God of
> Nahor judge between us.

But if the cairn (and the pillar) is a border mark then the לא must be there and the object (the את drops out here):

> I will not pass beyond this cairn (and. . .)
> to your side to do harm,
> You will not pass beyond this cairn (and. . .)
> to my side.

One must assume that one of these formulations, probably the first, was at hand from a traditional treaty to the narrator who added his pact; he tried to adapt this to the context of the present situation, but was unsuccessful, and this gave rise to further attempts at correction. This can explain the present state of the text, in particular the juxtaposition of לא and אם and the uncertainty of the object in the two sentences beginning with אם; but it is scarcely possible to give a translation which does justice to the facts of the case.

[**31:53**]   It is clear that both parties must swear to this nonaggression pact. As each party is a tribe or a people, each of the representatives must swear by his own God. The idea is that each binds himself by an oath in the name of his own God. If he breaks the oath, his own God will punish him for it. The designations, ''the God of Abraham and the God of Nahor,'' are adapted to the Jacob-Laban narrative; the later addition, ''the God of their fathers,'' also expresses this (L. Rost, VT.S 7 [1960] 346-359).

[**31:53b-54**]   The sentence, ''. . .and Jacob swore by the Fear (Protection) of Isaac,'' cannot belong to the pact of v. 51 because this requires that both parties take an oath; it follows rather on v. 50. The obligation that Laban lays on Jacob in v. 50 can be the matter for an oath by Jacob only. The common meal follows on the oath; it must be arranged by Jacob because it was he who took the oath (in the sense of a conditioned self-curse). When he summons ''his kinsmen'' to share it, this includes Laban and his followers. The meal seals the conclusion of the dispute (P. Buis, VT 16 [1966] 399).

[**32:1**]   On the following morning Laban can take farewell of his daughters and grandchildren in peace and return home.

Purpose and Thrust

The center of this long chapter is the ''dispute'' between Jacob and Laban caused by the conviction of each that he has suffered an injustice at the hands of the other. The dispute is settled by an agreement; the chapter ends with a meal which unites the two parties. There are two reasons why this settlement is possible. In the foreground are the legal principles which both parties acknowledge. It is a matter of family, property, and work. There are legal prescriptions for all these areas recognized by both sides. Each lays the accusation that the other has violated them. Consequently the chapter is full of legal sayings, legal formulations, and legal procedures. The whole is concluded by a legal act binding both parties. J expresses by means of narrative that harmonious living (brother—brothers) confers on legal norms a meaning that determines coexistence. They enable the injured party to receive justice; but the goal is, as far as possible, a peaceful arrangement. The well-being of a community always includes the possibility of the settlement of a dispute as long as the will for peace remains; this is expressed in Gen. 31 by the common meal.

The peaceful outcome, however, is endangered if there is too strong an imbalance of power between the parties. In this case ''might prevails over right'' even though in many cases justice appears to be done. Faced with this, the narrator speaks of God's action; where right must yield to might—and the addition in vv. 24, 29 underscores this—God's action takes over and he intervenes without exception in favor of the weaker. Where Jacob's claim for just recompense for his work (vv. 38-42) is opposed by Laban's claim to property (v. 43), God intervenes on behalf of the former (v. 42). The narrative reaches its climax in the words of Jacob, ''If the God of my father. . .had not been with me. . .,'' ''. . .and rebuked you last night.'' It is no accident that there are echoes of the language of the Psalms here: ''God has seen my distress and the toil of my hands.'' It should be noted that the accusation that Jacob makes against Laban is concerned with the unjust exploitation of the labor of a subordinate by one in power. This is so important for the narrator that he puts it into the center of the conflict and uses it to show God's intervention on behalf of the weak. The link with two traditions is clear: on the one hand with the laments of the ''poor'' in the Psalms, on the other with the social accusations of the prophets. It is surprising that already in the patriarchal stories the God of the fathers is the one who stands by the weak and the one to whom the weak can have recourse when oppressed by the powerful.

Preparation for the Meeting
with Esau

Literature

Genesis 32:1-2(2-3): I. L. Seeligmann, "Aetiological Elements in Biblical Historiography," Zion 26 (1961) 141-169. K. D. Schunck, "Erwägungen zur Geschichte und Bedeutung von Mahanaim," ZDMG 113 (1963) 34-40. F. C. Fensham, " 'Camps' in the NT and Milhamah," RQ 4 (1963/64) 557-562. M. Balabán, "Fragmentárni aitiologie Machanaim," TPKR 32 (1965) 100-102. C. Houtman, "Jacob at Mahanaim. Some Remarks on Genesis XXXII 2-3," VT 28 (1978) 37-44.

Genesis 32:3-13(4-14): L. Köhler, *Kleine Lichter.* "Der Botenspruch" (1945) 13-17. H. S. Gehman, "Hebraisms of the Old Greek Version of Genesis," VT 3 (1953) 141-148. D. M. Warne, *The Origin, Development and Significance of the Concept of the Remnant in the OT* (unpubl. diss. Edinburgh, 1958) esp. 8-14. A. H. van Zyl, "The Message-Formula in the Book of Judges," OTWSA.P (1959) 61-64. C. Westermann, *Basic Forms of Prophetic Speech* (1960; Eng. 1967, 1980[5]). R. Rendtorff, "Botenformel und Botenspruch," ZAW 74 (1962) 165-177. J. Freund, " 'Thou shalt not abhor an Edomite for he is thy brother. . .' " [in Hebr.], BetM 27 (1966) 117-121. C. M. Carmichael, "A New View of the Origin of the Deuteronomic Credo," VT 19 (1969) 273-289, esp. 279; cf. JBL 96 (1977) 321-336, esp. 326. A. J. Bjørndalen, "Zu den Zeitstufen der Zitatformel. . .כה אמר im Botenverkehr," ZAW 86 (1974) 393-403.

Genesis 32:14-22(15-23): L. Prijs, "Der Ursprung des Reims im Neuhebräischen," BZNF 7 (1963) 33-42. B. Porten-Greenfield, "The Aramaic Papyri from Hermopolis," ZAW 80 (1968) 216-231.

Text

32:1 Laban arose early on the following morning, kissed his grandchildren and daughters and blessed them,[a] and returned home.

2 Jacob too went his way and angels of God met him.

3 When he saw them Jacob said: This is a company of God! And he called that place Mahanaim.

4 Then Jacob sent messengers on ahead to his brother Esau to the region of Seir, to the territory of Edom.

5 He ordered them: You are to say this to my lord Esau: Your servant Jacob[a] says: I have been sojourning with Laban up till now.[b]

6 I have cattle,[a] asses and sheep,[b] male and female servants, and I have sent to tell my lord so as to find favor in your sight.

7 When the messengers returned to Jacob they said to him: We came

upon your brother Esau, but he is already coming to meet you with four hundred men.

8   Then Jacob was very much afraid and distressed[a] [and he divided the people with him, the sheep and the cattle (and the camels)[b] into two companies.

9   He thought: If Esau comes upon one[a] company and destroys it, then the other[b] will survive].[c]

10   And Jacob said: [God of my father Abraham and God of my father Isaac,] Yahweh, [who said to me: Return to your country and to your kinsmen and I will make you prosperous!

11   I am not worthy[a] of all the steadfast love and fidelity that you have shown to your servant. For it was with my staff[b] alone that I crossed the Jordan here, and now I have grown into two companies].[c]

12   Save me, I pray, from the hand of my brother, from the hand of Esau![a] For I am afraid of him lest he come and strike me and mothers and children.[b]

13   [You yourself have said: I will indeed make you prosper and make your descendants like the sand of the sea which cannot be counted for numbers.]

14   And he passed the night there.[a] Then he took from what he had acquired[b] a present for his brother Esau:

15   two hundred she-goats and twenty he-goats, two hundred ewes and twenty rams,

16   thirty milch camels with their young, forty cows and then young bulls, twenty she-asses and ten he-asses.

17   And he put each herd[a] separately into the care of a servant and said to them: Go on before me and put a space[b] between the separate herds.

18   And he gave orders to the first: When Esau my brother approaches[a] you and asks:[b] To whom do you belong? Where are you going? To whom do these belong?

19   then answer him: To your servant Jacob; he sends them as a present to my lord Esau and he himself is coming behind us.

20   He[a] gave the same orders to the second and to the third and to all who went in charge of the herds: Thus are you to speak to Esau when you meet him.[b]

21   You are to say: Your servant Jacob himself is coming[a] behind us. He thought, I will appease him with the gift that goes ahead of me; only then will I see him in person; perhaps he will receive me favorably.

22   So Jacob's present went on ahead of him, while he spent the night in the camp.

1a   Ges-K §122g.

5a   On the messenger formula, cf. bibliog. above; E. A. Speiser, comm. ad loc.   **b**   Syncopated form for וַיֹּאמֶר, Ges-K §64h.

6a   On the collective, Ges-K §123b; שׁוּר R. Peter, VT 25 (1975) 486-496.   **b**   Better וַצֹּאן with Sam and versions.

8a   On the form, Ges-K §67n,p.   **b**   Missing in Gk, addition.

9a   Sam reads masc.   **b**   On שְׁאָר, W. E. Müller and H. D. Preuss, *Die Vorstellung vom Rest im A.T.* (1939, 1973²) 104; G. F. Hasel, AUSS 11 (1973) 152-169.   **c**   Jer. 51:50.

11a   Ges-K §133c; BrSynt §111g.   **b**   Ges-K §119n.   **c**   BrSynt §14bδ.

12a   BrSynt §65b, as Gen. 19:4.   **b**   Proverbially as Hos. 10:14; Ges-K §119aa; 156c; BrSynt §68a; 110g.

14a   On the masc. suffix, Ges-K §135o.   **b**   Art. with part., Ges-K §138k.

17a   Doubling with distributive meaning, Ges-K §123d; BrSynt §129a.   **b**   רוח, ''to be at a distance,'' 1 Sam. 16:23.

18a Form is different in the Mss; Ges-K §60b.   **b** On the form, Ges-K §64f.
20a Gk adds τῷ πρώτῳ.   **b** On the form, Ges-K §74h.
21a With Sam, Gk, Targ add בא.

Form

Jacob's prayer (vv. 10-13) stands in the center of ch. 32; it is framed by the two embassies to Esau (vv. 4-8a, 8b-9, and vv. 14-22). The whole passage between the two encounters with God consists of preparations for the meeting with Esau in which one can sense an increase of tension from the first embassy to the second. However, the text of vv. 4-22 is not a self-contained narrative unity; it is a construction of the narrator who has brought together single episodes so as to form the preparation for the meeting with Esau. The whole is set within the framework of an itinerary (vv. 2, 14, 22); we have to do here with episodes on the way comprising the two encounters with God which are clearly recognizable as originally independent narratives, together with the meeting with Esau.

Setting

The two meetings had their origin as oral narratives at the place where they are localized. The two episodes, vv. 4-8a and 14-22, have been shaped by J, probably without any preexisting material. (The attribution of vv. 4-14a to J and vv. 14b-22 to E is not acceptable because there is an increase of tension from one to the other.) The fragment vv. 8b-9 goes back to an old etiological note. The central part of the prayer (v. 12) originally followed immediately on vv. 4-8a; later it grew to the expanded form (vv. 10-13) and was subsequently inserted between the two episodes, vv. 4-8a (with 8b-9) and vv. 14-22. There are no clear indications for division into literary sources (J. Wellhausen, J. Skinner); the tendency among authors from M. Noth on (and E. A. Speiser) is to attribute the whole text, apart from the expansions, to J.

Commentary

[32:1-3] In 32:1-3 an encounter with God (vv. 2b-3) is joined with the conclusion of the Jacob-Laban narrative (vv. 1-2a). The two contracting parties, who had met in 31:25, part again. Narrative episodes which begin with a meeting regularly end in this way (I. L. Seeligmann, ThZ 18 [1962] 305-325): Gen. 18:33; 33:16f.; Num. 24:25; 1 Sam. 24:23, as one among many in 1-2 Sam. (the giving of a name follows Gen. 33:15f. as in Gen. 32:1-3). This is a fixed and frequently occurring narrative form and so v. 1 is not to be assigned to the preceding unity in ch. 31, thus making ch. 32 begin with v. 2 and destroying the form (H. Gunkel, von Rad). Vv. 1-3 are rather a transition concluding ch. 31 and beginning ch. 32.

[32:1] Laban takes leave of his daughters and grandchildren, kissing and blessing them, just as Rebekah's brothers bless her at the farewell in Gen. 24:60. The farewell blessing, like the meal at evening in 31:54, puts the seal on the agreement that the dispute has ended (31:43-54); blessing and peace go together.

[32:2a] Jacob goes his way, i.e., he can proceed unmolested because he is no longer a fugitive.

[32:2b-3] What is narrated here is an event on the way; it is a journey-note at-

504

tached to the itinerary (C. Westermann, ThB 24 [1964] 34f.). Gen. 32:2b-3 is neither an abbreviated narrative nor a fragment nor a torso, even if there was a narrative of this encounter in the oral stage; it originated as a note attached to the itinerary (H. Gunkel and E. Meyer). In form it has a parallel in Gen. 33:16f., in content
in 28:10-22, which also arose out of an itinerary. Jacob's return from Laban's
house begins with an encounter with God just as did his flight from his family; in
both cases Jacob names the place. The event described is compressed into what is
necessary: Jacob on his way, angels of God meet him, Jacob's reaction in an exclamation (v. 3, כאשר ראם), and the naming of the place of the encounter.

[**32:2b**]   The same verb and subject occur also in Gen. 28:10-22, though in a
somewhat different context. Hence this passage must be advanced to explain the
present text, all the more so as מלאכי אלהים occurs only in these two places (C.
Houtman has stressed this, VT 28 [1978] 37-44). The phrase must have the same
meaning in both cases; it is not מלאך יהוה, which is always in the singular (on the
three men in Gen. 18, see comm. ad loc.), but heavenly beings as in Gen. 28. To
express this it is better to translate by ''angels'' instead of ''messengers.'' For further explanation see comm. on 28:12 (in neither case can אלהים be a sign of E).
The verb פגע can be used in a hostile or friendly sense (cf. C. Houtman); Jacob's
reaction shows that there is no hostile intent. So a further parallel must be advanced to explain v. 2b: in Josh. 5:13-15 Joshua encounters a commander of ''the
army of Yahweh''; this encounter is in a context similar to that of Jacob; both precede a dangerous undertaking. In one case it is a divine commander, in the other a
divine company.

[**32:3a**]   Jacob's reaction, ''this is a company of God,'' points to these parallels
and makes it certain that he must have seen a number of ''angels of God''; otherwise the word מחנה would be meaningless (the sentence is an expression of surprise, as in 28:16f.; in both cases זה is used). We have here a clue to the meaning
of what Jacob saw. Whereas the face in Gen. 28 means the holiness of God, the
מחנה אלהים in 32:2-3 indicates the power of God. H. Gunkel, T. H. Gaster
(*Myth, Legend. . .* [1969]) and others make use of the notion of the ''roving
army'' to explain the passage; but I do not see anything of this in the present short
text; the parallel in Josh. 5:13-15 (cf. Judg. 5:21), however, does point to the idea
of God's army or armies of which there echoes in יהוה צבאת. It should be noted
that 32:2-3; 28:10-22; and 32:22-33 are all originally independent narratives
which J has inserted deliberately at definite points in Gen. 25–36. Vv. 2-3 had
their origin outside the context of the Jacob story and the idea that stamps them is
part of this prehistory. So J's purpose in inserting vv. 2-3 here becomes clear (cf.
the parallel Josh. 5:13-15): Jacob is faced with the threatening meeting with his
brother and is afraid. God's angels confront him in a great host (stressed in 1
Chron. 12:22) which makes him think of a ''company of God.'' J characteristically leaves it open what this means for Jacob in his present situation; it is clear to anyone who listens: the God of the fathers is the powerful One. It is this that Jacob
sees.

[**32:3b**]   Jacob then has fixed upon what he saw when threatened by his brother's
power and has handed it on to later generations in the name of the place,
Mahanaim (v. 3). It is not important whether the name is dual here or not (lit. C.
Houtman, p. 41); in any case it is meant to be singular in the explanation in v. 3b.

The name will remain and in it the experience of the patriarch Jacob in face of a dire threat.

The precise location of Mahanaim is still not certain. A. Dillmann: "One of the most important cities of Gilead, belonging to Gad, on the border with Manasseh;" in detail O. Procksch. According to Josh. 13:26 it is a Levitical city. It is the royal city of Ishbaal (2 Sam. 2:8,12, 29) and David's residence during Absalom's revolt (2 Sam. 17:24-27). Mahanaim is not mentioned in the period of the later monarchy and after the exile. The name has the same origin as many names in many countries formed on the Latin *castrum* (*castra*).

Vv. 2-3, taken with Gen. 28:10-22, show how together with the institutions of community life (economy, judiciary, contracts), cultic institutions also acquire importance in Gen. 25–36, above all sanctuaries at fixed places which serve to link the realm of God and the realm of man. In both cases the traveler discovers a holy place; it is angels, divine beings, that make Jacob recognize it as holy. What he sees in Gen. 28 is the "gate of heaven," in 32:2-3 the "company of God" (God's power). At the same time there is the transition from the God who accompanies to the God who dwells: one can strike a camp; with the naming, a fixed place, associated with sedentary life, takes the place of the movable camp.

[32:4-22]   Between the two encounters with God (32:2-3 and 32:23-33) is the story of Jacob's preparation for his meeting with Esau; Jacob's prayer stands in the middle (vv. 10-13).

[32:4-9]   The sending of the messengers (vv. 4-6); the return and the report of the messengers (v. 7); the effect of the report on Jacob (v. 8a); the division of the company (vv. 8b-9).

[32:4-6]   This passage is a classical example of the sending of a messenger (secular). It was of great importance in antiquity, in an age that was entirely or partly without writing, because it was the only way in which people at a distance could communicate. This is one of the many established practices of community existence that acquires importance in Gen. 25–36. The lapidary language shows that it is an established practice; it is a particularly clear example of the "setting in life" of lapidary forms of speech. That it is so widespread and has lasted so long is an indication of its importance. The speech forms of the sending of a messenger have continued to live in the language of letters. For a detailed discussion of messenger oracles, language, and sending, together with the literature, cf. C. Westermann, *Basic Forms of Prophetic Speech* (1960, 1978[5]; Eng. 1965, 1980[5]).

The sending of the messengers in vv. 4-6 is divided as follows: report of a sending—introduction to the commission—commission given to the messengers—messenger formula—embassy. It is characteristic of the sending of a messenger in an era that is still without writing that the message entrusted to the messenger by the sender is conveyed to the addressee by the messenger in such a way as if the sender stood before him at the moment of its delivery. The words that the messenger speaks are the words of the sender (in the monarchy, the words of the herald). It is this very characteristic that is expressed by the messenger formula, "Thus says X," the meaning of which is to be pinned down neither to the present nor to the perfect (cf. A. J. Bjørndalen [1974]; A. H. van Zyl [1959] in bibliog. to 32:3-13); rather the formula embraces both.

[32:4]   Jacob sends the messengers to the land of Edom. The twofold designation, "region of Seir" (Gen. 36:20) and "territory of Edom" (Judg. 5:4), can well be the result of an additional note, one explaining the other, thus presupposing the tradition that Esau and Edom belong together, cf. Gen. 25:30 (lit. on Edom, see above, p. 97; also ch. 36).

[32:5-6]   As is very often the case, the embassy has two functions, the one to report, vv. 5b,6a, the other to declare its purpose (or an imperative), v. 6b. The goal or intent of the embassy is explained by and (or) based on the former function. The report is brief and reserved, saying only what is absolutely necessary (compare the enumeration with that in vv. 14b-16). The goal is "to find favor in your sight." It is unusual for a brother to speak to his twin in this way. It is the language used when one approaches a person of higher status. When Jacob says that he is concerned to find a favorable reception from his brother, he is silently acknowledging his as yet outstanding guilt; at the same time he indicates by the language of his embassy that he subordinates himself to his brother: "You are to say this to my lord Esau: Your servant. . ." It is only now that the meaning of Jacob's embassy to Esau becomes clear; Jacob makes known to him (להגיד v. 6) that he renounces the privileges deriving from the blessing that he surreptitiously won and concedes them to Esau.

[32:7]   A comparison with Num. 13:28-30 shows that the achievement of the goal and the news of it were part of the form of the report of the messengers. But instead of an answer from Esau the messenger brings news that Esau is already on the way to meet Jacob with 400 men. The listeners can draw their own conclusions. Esau, approaching with 400 men, is presented as the leader of a mercenary army, as the proverb about him in Gen. 27:40 says, "You will live by your sword."

[32:8a]   Jacob reacts anxiously to the report of the messengers. He cannot of course conclude with certainty that Esau is approaching with hostile intent, nor can he reject this possibility; he knows that he is lost in face of such superior force, all the more so because he cannot flee, owing to the problem of the mobility of his caravan with the women, children, and flocks.

V. 8a, together with Jacob's prayer that follows, forms the climax of the narrative of the return (Gen. 31–33). As such it is important for the whole Jacob-Esau narrative. What had begun as a family dispute between brothers now threatens to become war (v. 12, ". . .and strike me, mothers, and children"). J in his overall plan wants to point to the significance of this transition from a dispute to war and show his own generation by an example from the patriarchal period that a last-minute reconciliation is always possible. Jacob's fear (the word צרר describes distress and fear: "he became alarmed") is the natural reaction of one exposed to the threat of a superior power, of one threatened with death. The one who is powerless in face of a mortal threat takes refuge in the only one who can help in such distress: he begs God to save him. This is not all that clear in the present text because the prayer in vv. 10-13 has been separated from v. 8a by vv. 8b-9. It is probable that it followed immediately on v. 8a in an earlier form of the text. Form criticism, because of the succession of two sentences each beginning with ויאמר (vv. 9 and 10), points to a subsequent expansion (vv. 8b-9). The content, with Jacob's anxious reaction and the petition to God to save him, is more appropriate than the half-measures taken in vv. 8b-9; moreover, the division into two companies is an obvious etiological attempt to explain the name Mahanaim ("two companies"). Several explanations of the same name in the one narrative is a frequent occurrence in the patriarchal story. It is very probable then that vv. 8b-9 is originally an independent etiological note (like 32:2-3) of which the concluding sentence, containing the name Mahanaim, has been omitted because of v. 3 when the etiology was fitted into the narrative (J. Wellhausen, H. Gunkel, and others).

[**32:9**] שאר has a positive meaning here; cf. H. Wildberger, THAT 11 (1976) 844-855, with further lit.; G. F. Hasel, AUSS (1973) 152-169.

[**32:10-13**]   Jacob's prayer: the central piece is the cry for help (v. 12); it is preceded by the address in v. 10a which is expanded by a participial sentence (v. 10b) and a survey of God's favors to Jacob (v. 11); it is followed by the remembrance of God's promises (v. 13). It is at once striking that the prayer in the context has a somewhat abrupt effect. The words ויאמר יעקב are not a good introduction for a prayer; one expects a more defined beginning after v. 14a. This is a sign that the original context is not preserved. The prayer itself has the effect of a synthesis rather than of a unity. As it now stands, it cannot have belonged to the old narrative; it has certainly been expanded, and the expansions are clear: the extended address, v. 10 (cf. K. T. Andersen, StTh 16 [1962] 170-188), the survey, v. 11, and likewise the promise attached, v. 13. Jacob's original prayer was a simple cry for help (v. 12a) based on his situation (v. 12b); it followed on v. 8a, which is taken up in the cry for help in v. 12b. This cry alone accords with the style of the narrative in ch. 32, whereas the expansions notably diverge from it. V. 13, which contains a doublet of v. 10, is a further appendage to vv. 10-12. The two expansions in vv. 10 and 13 link Jacob's cry for help with the promises; they belong to the context of the history and tradition of the patriarchal promises; the expansion in v. 11, on the other hand, links Jacob's cry with God's providential dealings with him and establishes a context with the Jacob-Esau story as a whole, including Gen. 29–31. The different expansions arise from different purposes; their significance lies in this that they underscore Jacob's cry for help by interpreting and extending it (v. 11 from the Jacob story as a whole, and vv. 10, 13 from the history of the patriarchal promises). The history of prayer in the Old Testament shows that this is what has also happened with other prayers, e.g., Jer. 32, where the expansions are similar.

A. de Pury's explanation of Jacob's prayer, which follows G. von Rad, K. Elliger, and H. J. Stoebe, does not take account of the history of prayer in the Old Testament and so regards vv. 10-13 as the ipsissima verba of the Yahwist; it bypasses the decisive point, namely, that Jacob in mortal danger cries for help to the God of his fathers. It is only by doing this that he can see in 32:10-13 the theological leitmotiv of the whole Jacob story.

[**32:10**]   The words ויאמר יעקב are a redactional transition; the introduction to the prayer may well have run, "And Jacob cried to the God of his father." The use of יהוה in v. 10a is striking; it is not organic to the whole. It probably contained the original address of the prayer introduced by יהוה הצילני. We know from the Psalms and the prayers that occur in narratives that the address in the prayers in the early period consisted only in the name. The expanded address in v. 10 is to explain that the God invoked is the God of the fathers, the God from whom Jacob receives the promise, as the expansion continues. The statement is fashioned after

Gen. 28:13 (31:5); the promise is put into a general form, "I will make you prosperous." The purpose of this modification is obviously to compass several promises in one statement (similarly Num. 10:26-29); it corresponds, though in a different form, to the later tendency to accumulate the promises. It is only in these
two places (vv. 10 and 13) that the promise occurs in the form איטיב; in Deuteronomy, e.g., 17:4, it is often strengthened by the infin. היטב. It is typical of
Deutero-Isaiah to introduce a divine pronouncement with the participle האמר (Is.
41:13; 44:26, 27, 28).

[32:11]   This fine sentiment is rarely linked with the petition in the individual lament but is frequent in the community lament: "You have. . .done. . ." (surveying God's earlier saving action); here, reflection brings a confession of one's own
unworthiness. The use of חסד in the plural for God's saving acts is a clear sign of
the language of a later period; it occurs in Trito-Isaiah 55:3; 63:7; Lam. 3:22, 32
and late Psalms like Ps. 89:2. The sentence that follows in 32:11b, introduced by
כי, is quite outside the prayer style; it comes from one who looks back on the
Jacob-Esau narrative as a whole and sees in it God's gracious providence toward
Jacob, the father of the people. It is a precious witness how in a later period the Jacob story was seen in the light of the piety of the Psalms. (One can maintain that
these sentences have been composed "in the purest Yahwistic language" [O.
Procksch, A. de Pury] only if one does not take account of the linguistic usage in
the parallels.)

[32:12]   The יהוה from v. 10 is to be supplied as the address at the beginning of
v. 12 which is a cry for help with the reason given in v. 12b, thus likening it to the
lament. A cry of this sort for God's help, arising immediately out of distress or oppression, occurs also in other narratives, e.g., with the verb נצל, Judg. 10:15; 1
Sam. 12:10 (elsewhere only in the Psalms). "From the hand of my brother, from
the hand of Esau," is not a doublet, but an intensification.
        V. 12b gives the reason for the cry for help; it is an open confession of the
fear of one delivered over to superior power. Jacob sees himself helpless and exposed to the possibility of annihilation: ". . .lest he come and strike me. . .." He
is faced with the threat of war in which the opposition is "struck down." The
small patriarchal groups still do not wage war (cf. Gen. 26, "Purpose and
Thrust"). Jacob is afraid that he is no longer able to ward off the destructive attack
of his brother. The vision of war with its horrible effect is before him: "lest he
strike. . .mother with children," literally: "mother over children" (as in Hos.
10:14). It is this that war brings in its train: the helpless and the guiltless and the
noncombatants are slain without mercy. Jacob begs his God to avert this.

[32:13]   This verse has the effect of an anticlimax; it is very obvious that it is part
of the expansion. The ואתה, which is merely a literary link, also shows this. By
way of addition God is reminded of his promises, and v. 10b is repeated with: "I
will indeed make you prosper"; here, however, it is expanded by the stereotyped
promise of increase of prosperity as in Gen. 28:14; 31:3; 22:17 ("each also
secondary"—H. Gunkel).

[32:14-22]   Presents are now sent ahead. This act is portrayed in such detail that
it must be of particular importance to the narrator. Jacob's purpose is clear, the
same as his purpose in sending the messengers, namely, to find favor in Esau's

eyes. There is a progression from the first embassy (vv. 4-7) to the second, particularly in the extent of the gift. The presupposition for the understanding of this
passage is that the Hebrew ברכה = ''blessing'' can also mean gift (Gen. 33:11;
Is. 15:15; Judg. 1:15; etc.). It is this that Jacob offers his brother, using this very
word (Gen. 33:11). It is only thus that 32:14-22 acquires its significance within
the Jacob-Esau narrative as a whole. The ברכה, coming from Jacob, gives back
the blessing that he had once stolen. Jacob had fled because of the consequences
of his trickery; he now restores to his brother what he had taken by trickery. It is an
important characteristic of the Yahwist's narrative style that the writer does not
mention expressly this rather profound aspect; he lets the events speak for themselves; by this act one implicitly confesses one's own guilt; this too need not be
mentioned.

[32:14]   V. 14a, ''and he passed the night there,'' concludes vv. 4-13. Vv.
14b-22 begin without any indication of time; v. 14a is taken up again in vv. 22b.
In v. 14b Jacob selects a part of his possessions as a gift for his brother. מנחה is
neutral and does not determine the particular character of the gift for his brother.
By describing the present as הבא בידו the narrator is referring to the previous part
of the narrative.

[32:15-16]   Almost the same sequence is found in Job 1:3, a sign that it is stereotyped. The enumeration intends to say that the present to Esau constitutes a large
part of Jacob's property (550 animals).

[32:17-20]   Jacob gives careful and precise instructions to the servants. The division into three groups has the effect of a progression and so causes surprise. Esau
receives the same answer to his questions at three distinct intervals; Jacob thereby
expresses with insistence what he intends by the present.

[32:21]   Jacob's intention is expressed yet again in the reflection of v. 21b, this
time quite openly with the verb כפר, ''I will appease him with the present.'' כפר
in the piel is used only here and in Prov. 16:17 for something that happens between people; the meaning in Prov. 16:17 is similar. כפר means ''to cover over'';
''the expression כפר פנים always involves guilt'' (O. Procksch). The consequence of covering the face is that he no longer sees the guilt. Jacob, therefore,
will meet his brother face to face only with the hope that he will then ''lift up his
face,'' i.e., forgive him or show himself gracious to him. Though פנים occurs
four times in v. 21b, it is not to be seen as an anticipation of vv. 23-32; the narrator
wants only to express the transition from rejection to acceptance.

[32:22]   The closing sentence of v. 22a emphasizes once more that Jacob sends
the מנחה ahead, thereby returning the stolen ברכה.

Purpose and Thrust

In the overall context of the Jacob-Esau story, 32:1-22 is the about-face between
the encounters with Laban and that with Esau. It is significant for the Yahwist's
narrative style and more for talk about God in the Old Testament that this about-
face is not ''stated,'' but narrated, and in such a way that the listener can draw
connections to it from the story. Jacob experiences what it is to be exposed to danger, first at Laban's hands, then at Esau's. All he can do is to beg God to save him.

The petition in distress forms the climax of the section of the narrative dealing with Jacob's return. It links the patriarchal narrative with the realities faced by the listeners from generation to generation; petition in distress is perennial, as the Psalms show. The promise, "to be with you," stands in tacit relationship to the petition in distress; Jacob experienced this at Bethel, and the encounter with God's company recalls it albeit by intimation: God is the powerful One.

Tacitly linked with the petition too is Jacob's readiness to restore to his brother the blessing he had stolen and to recognize him as having precedence. It is precisely in these unexpressed and unformulated relationships that the peculiar nature of the relationship to God intended by the narrator is expressed. It is so much taken for granted, so deeply rooted in what has happened, that it has no need to be laid out in theological statements. This relationship to God is always open-ended.

The Attack on Jacob
at the Jabbok

Literature

Genesis 32:23-33(22-32): H. J. Elhorst, "Gen 32:23-33," ZAW 32 (1912) 299-301. J. Rybinski, *Der Mal'akh Jahwe* (1930). P. A. H. de Boer, "Genesis XXXII 23-33: Some Remarks on Composition and Character of the Story," NedThT 1 (1946/47) 149-163. A. Bentzen, "The Weeping of Jacob, Hos. XII 5a," VT 1 (1951) 58-59. K. Elliger, "Der Jakobskampf am Jabbok Gn 32,23ff. als hermeneutisches Problem," ZThK 48 (1951) 1-31 = KS (1966) 141-173. J. Schildenberger, "Jakobs nächtlicher Kampf mit dem Elohim am Jabbok (Gen 32,23-33)," SDM 1 (1954) 69-96. H. J. Stoebe, "Der heilsgeschichtliche Bezug der Jabbok-Perikope," EvTh 14 (1954) 466-474. O. Eissfeldt, "Non dimittam te, nisi benedixeris mihi," *Mélanges Bibl. . .A. Robert* (1957) 77-81 = KS 3 (1966) 412-416. L. Sabourin, "La lutte de Jacob avec Elohim (Gen 32, 23-33)," ScEc 10 (1958) 77-89. F. von Trigt, "La signification de la lutte de Jacob près du Yabboq. Gen XXXII 23-33," OTS 12 (1958) 280-309. J. M. Rézé, "La lutte de Jacob avec l'ange," Christus 9 (1962) 69-77. J. L. McKenzie, "Jacob at Peniel: Gn 32,24-32," CBQ 25 (1963) 71-76. B. W. Anderson, "An Exposition of Genesis XXXII 22-32. The Traveller Unknown," ABR 17 (1969) 21-26. W. Dommershausen, "Gott kämpft. Ein neuer Deutungsversuch zu Gn 32,23-33," TThZ 78 (1969) 321-334. R. Barthès, "La lutte avec l'ange," *Analyse Structurale et Exégèse Bibl.* (1971) 27-39 (Eng. 1974), response by R. Martin-Achard, ibid. 41-62. W. G. Niederland, "Jakobs Kampf am Jabbok, Bemerkungen zur Flusssymbolik," *Psychoanalyt. Interpr. bibl. Texte*, ed. Y. Spiegel (1972). H. J. Hermisson, "Jakobs Kampf am Jabbok (Gen 32, 23-33)," ZThK 71 (1974) 239-261. V. Metelmann, "Der Jakobskampf am Jabbok. Ein Beitrag zum Problem psychoanalytischer Interpretation bibl. Texte," WzM 26 (1974) 69-82. F. E. Deist, "Geskiedenis en eksegese van'n teks: Gen 32,23-33," NGTT 16 (1975) 127-138. S. Gevirtz, "Of Patriarchs and Puns: Joseph at the Fountain, Jacob at the Ford," HUCA 46 (1975) 33-54. A. Cruello, "El relato de Gn 32,23-33," EstFr 78 (1977) 27-92. G. Hentschel, "Jakobs Kampf am Jabbok (Gen 32,23-33)—eine genuin israelitische Tradition?" *Fests. z. 25 jähr. Bestehen des philos.-theol. Studiums im Priesterseminar Erfurt* (1977) 13-37. R. Hermann, "Mal'ak Jahwe—Bote von Gott. Die Vorstellung von Gottes Boten im hebr. AT," *Regensburger St.z. Theol.* 13 (1978). A. de Pury, "Jakob am Jabbok, Gen 32,23-33 im Licht einer alt-iranischen Erzählung," ThZ 35 (1979) 18-34. L. Schmidt, "Der Kampf Jakobs am Jabbok," ThViat 14 (1979) 125-143.

Genesis 32:23-27(22-26): H. Wohlstein, "Zu einigen altisraelitischen Volksvorstellungen von Toten- und Ahnengeistern in biblischer Überlieferung," ZRGG 19 (1967) 348-355.

Genesis 32:28-29(27-28): E. Sachsse, "Der Ursprung des Namens Israel," ZS 4 (1926) 63-69. P. Heinisch, "Der Wechsel der Namen Jakob und Israel in der Genesis," ZThS 6 (1929) 115-117. H. Kruse, "Die 'dialektische Negation' als semitisches Idiom," VT 4

(1954) 385-400. N. Walker, "Israel," VT 4 (1954) 434. B. Z. Dinur, "The Narratives Concerning the Name 'Israel' and the Biblical Tradition Thereon" [in Hebr.], OLD-Jerusalem (1964) 114-141. A. Besters, " 'Israël' et 'fils d'Israël' dans les libres historiques (Genèse-II Rois)," RB 74 (1967) 5-23. R. B. Coote, "The Meaning of the Name Israel," HThR 65 (1972) 137-146. G. Vermeš, "The Impact of the Dead Sea Scrolls on Jewish Studies in the Last Twenty-five Years," JSSt 26 (1975) 1-14, esp. 12-13.

Genesis 32:30-33(29-32): N. Schmidt, "The Numen Penuel," JBL 45 (1926) 260-279. S. A. Cook, "Notes on the Relevance of the Science of Religion," Fests. A. Bertholet (1950) esp. 121-123. R. Meyer, "Probleme der hebräischen Grammatik," ZAW 63 (1951) 221-235. H. Gross, "Penuel," LThK 8 (1963) 266. J. Weingreen, "Oral Torah and Written Records," *Holy Book and Holy Tradition*, ed. F. F. Bruce (1968) 54-67. T. Jansma, "Peshitta Institute Communications X. A Note on Dislocated Extracts from the Book of Genesis in the Syriac Massoretic Manuscripts," VT 21 (1971) 127-129.

Text

32:23 That[a] same night he arose, took his two wives and his two maidservants and his eleven children and crossed the ford of the[b] Jabbok.

24 He took them and sent them across the wadi together with "all"[a] that he had.

25 But Jacob stayed back alone. And a man wrestled[a] with him until daybreak.

26 When he saw that he was unable to overcome him, he touched his thigh [joint so that Jacob's thigh joint was dislocated as he wrestled with him].

27 Then he said: Let me go, dawn is breaking! But he answered: I will not let you go[a] until you bless me.[b]

28 [Then he asked him: What is your name? He answered: Jacob.

29 He said: You are no longer to be called[a] Jacob but Israel,[b] because you have struggled with God and with men and have prevailed.]

30 And Jacob asked him: Now tell me[a] your name! But he said: Why do you ask my name? And he blessed him there.

31 And Jacob named the place [Peniel[a] because (he said) I have seen God face to face[b] and have survived].[c]

32 And the sun rose on him as he passed by Penuel; but he was limping because of his thigh.

33 [This is the reason why the sons of Israel even to this day do not eat the sinew of the nerve along the thigh joint because he had touched[a] the sinew of the nerve along Jacob's thigh joint.]

23a Read ההוא with Sam as in Gen. 14:22; 19:33; 30:16.   **b** Sam has the article.
24a Insert כל־ with the versions.
25a The verb אבק only here and v. 26, echoing יבוק.
27a On the form, Ges-K §60f.   **b** Construction, Ges-K §163c; BrSynt §168, also v. 29.
29a Construction, H. Kruse, bibliog. above.   **b** The name is generally explained (e.g., M. Noth): "God contests" or "may God contest"; the verb שׂרה occurs only here and its meaning is uncertain. Lit. on the name "Israel," see bibliog. above; J. Hempel, BHH II 782-786; H. Seebass, BZAW 98 (1966) 63-97.
30a Add לי with the versions.
31a On the change from *i* to *u* (v. 32) cf. Ges-K §90o; R. Meyer, ZAW 63 (1951) 221-235.   **b** On the phrase, Ges-K §166c.   **c** On the construction, Ges-K §111e; BrSynt §103b; 139b.
33a On the construction, BrSynt §42f.

Form

Only a few exegetes still contest the literary unity of Gen. 32:23-33 and hold to its composition out of two sources; yet there is general agreement that it is not cast from a single mold but that the text has undergone a process of growth (H. J. Hermisson [1974]; R. Martin-Achard [1974]; A. de Pury [1979]; cf. bibliog. above). What is contested is what has been added subsequently and when, and hence the meaning and purpose of the text as a whole. The decisive criterion here is which parts of vv. 23-33 form a self-contained and logical narrative. This question must be pursued first. It is not possible to give more than a passing notice to the very many explanations hitherto given; apart from the commentaries there has been, since 1950, a continuous stream of articles on Gen. 32:23-33 (see bibliog. above). A careful survey of these works would be desirable; there is a brief synthesis in A. de Pury, pp. 19-22.

Most exegetes regard v. 33 as a subsequent addition. An increasing number say the same of vv. 28, 29, the change of Jacob's name, because, like v. 33, these verses presuppose the existence of Israel. Many hold v. 31 also to be secondary because it does not fit in with the preceding narrative. Some recent contributors (E. Otto, BWANT 110 [1979]; G. Hentschel [1977], bibliog. above) maintain that v. 26, or v. 26b, is also secondary; it is a verse that has so far presented exegetes with the greatest difficulties. But there is not as yet a sufficiently firm basis for this.

Reserving the reasons for later, one concludes that the remaining verses, 23-26a, 27, 30, 31a, 32, give a narrative that is self-contained and comprehensible. The introduction is an itinerary note that serves as the exposition; in v. 32 it merges again into the itinerary. The action can be presented schematically:

vv. 23-24	Introduction (itinerary)
25	Attack, a man wrestled with him
26-30	Outcome of the struggle
26a-27a	Opponent's request to let him go
27b-30a	Jacob's counter, condition, request for name
30b	Attacker refuses name, blesses Jacob
31	Conclusion: Jacob names the place
32a	Conclusion: Merging into itinerary

In determining the form one must take into account that, other than in Gen. 28:10-22, no memorial stone is erected at the end to mark the place out as holy; it is therefore not a cult story (against M. Noth and others). It can be described as a local story because what is narrated leads to the naming of the place (W. H. Schmidt, *Alttestamentliche Glaube und seine Umwelt* [1968; 1975²]). More accurately: there is a local story behind what is narrated; an event is narrated that gave the place its name. However, in the framework of the itinerary (vv. 23-24,32a) it is something that happened on Jacob's journey, the experience of a traveler (like vv. 2-3) who is attacked. This is handed down to posterity by means of the name. The description of this experience can be designated as a narrative in the form in which it has been handed down. Without the additions it is closer to a report because the contest is not narrated in detail, e.g., 1 Sam. 17. The text narrates only the beginning and the end of the contest, and all that follows is the naming of the place. The additions bring it closer to narrative. The basis then is a (detailed) narrative, a local story, which explained the name Penuel (or Jabbok), but did not yet contain the name Jacob. It is taken up into an itinerary in the form of an abbreviated report (like vv. 2-3) dealing with Jacob's return.

Setting

All exegetes agree that the basic narrative must be old. It bears distinct animistic traits and is not to be dissociated from the region, the ford, the river. The danger of the ford is personified in the spirit or demon who does not want to let the traveler cross the river (עבר occurs several times) and attacks him so as to prevent him doing so (H. Gunkel, G. Hentschel, against H. J. Hermisson). This accords neither with the religion of Israel nor with that of the patriarchs, but with animistic belief in spirits or demons and has parallels among many peoples (H. Gunkel). It is a markedly typical local story which, because of the wordplay, יבוק—אבק, must have been narrated in the environs of the Jabbok ford. Local stories of this sort usually grow extensively out of experiences. The transference of this narrative to Jacob coincides with its insertion into the itinerary (vv. 22, 24, 32a) which describes Jacob's return after his separation from Laban and before his meeting with Esau. Because the pattern, flight—return, is J's own presentation, then he is the one who shaped the old narrative into an experience of Jacob in his travels. Elements of this itinerary, including an expansion resulting from some corresponding experience, may go back to the patriarchal period. J has inserted the experience in this place as a balance to Gen. 28:10-22 and 32:2-3. Jacob is threatened with annihilation by a more powerful opponent (32:12) but he is not alone; God is with him. The encounter with the "army" of God and its company (32:2-3), in which Jacob is preserved from death and emerges with "power," shows this. All the additions have their origin in a later period, as the exegesis will show. They cannot be claimed for J. Only the exegesis can demonstrate their origin and intent.

Recent exegesis agrees for the most part that the text of Gen. 32:23-33 cannot be separated into two literary sources but has been subsequently expanded into a unity. K. Elliger (1951), pp. 143-148, ascribes it to J, as do J. L. McKenzie (1963), p. 71, R. Martin-Achard (1974), p. 55, H. J. Hermisson; contrary H. Seebass (1974), pp. 242f., L. Schmidt (1979), p. 125 (see bibliog. above for all); also A. de Pury and E. Otto (see above, "Form"); i.e., in the history of the exegesis of the text scholars have been almost entirely preoccupied with solving the problems presented by source division.

It is instructive for the history of the exegesis of 32:23-33 that the prophet Hosea alludes to it (12:4-5); cf. H. W. Wolff, comm. E. M. Good finds five elements from the Jacob-Esau tradition in Hosea: the birth of twins (Gen. 25:24), a struggle with a divine being (Gen. 32:23-33), weeping and lamentation that leads to the naming of a place (Gen. 35:8), the encounter with a divine being at Bethel (Gen. 35), flight to Aram, and servitude (VT 16 [1966] 137-151). But the mention of Gen. 35:8 presupposes a narrative not found in Genesis (weeping and lamentation are not part of 32:23-33) and the judgment on Jacob in the accusation against Israel is entirely negative; hence the allusions in Hosea cannot rest on the written tradition in Gen. 25-36 and so must have their source in oral tradition. If this is the case then the Hosea passages are an important attestation that the patriarchal traditions continued to live side by side with and after the fixed literary form and remained open to different interpretation.

Commentary

[32:23-24] The exposition of the narrative, of which the action begins in v. 25, consists in an itinerary note which corresponds to the character of the narrative as the experience of the traveler. If the exposition is read without v. 24a it appears as a unity and contains the following elements: chronological note; Jacob crosses the ford with his entourage and his possessions (the family and possessions are mentioned only here). This is an itinerary note, originally self-contained and independent of the narrative that follows. V. 23 is apparently repeated in v. 24a; but this is to be understood as a link between the itinerary and the following narrative in which the hiph. of עבר replaces the qal, because Jacob is alone in the narrative, as stated at the beginning of v. 25. V. 24a then is not a real doublet and so cannot be used an an argument for literary sources. The various attempts aimed at explaining v. 23f. as a synthesis of several layers do not see that it is an itinerary note.

[32:23]   The chronological note, "that same night," belongs to the originally self-contained itinerary note and referred to a preceding detail, probably the arrival at the ford. This is the explanation of the difficulty presented in this part by the reference back to 32:33.

[32:24]   V. 24b, "together with 'all' that he had," is an integral continuation of the crossing with his entourage (v. 23). The narrator prepares for v. 25a with v. 24a; Jacob had now sent his entourage across. The text is not clear whether the movement is in a north-to-south direction or the reverse because the itinerary is not preserved intact.

The Jabbok is an eastern tributary of the Jordan and is called "the blue river," *ez-zerqā'*; it flows into the Jordan 40 km. north of the Dead Sea. It is partly (and seasonally) a raging torrent that flows along a deep ravine (G. Sauer, "Jabbok," BHH 11 790; H. J. Hermisson, ZThK 71 [1974] 239-261). This is one of the rare cases in which the specification of the place refers to a region which plays a background role in the narrative.

[32:25]   The first sentence in v. 25 is a transition: it is essential for the struggle that now takes place that Jacob be alone. This transition sentence is saying something important: it is a kind of struggle in which a person can engage only when quite alone; no helper, no rescuer can come from outside. This second point is stated in the next sentence: "And a man (someone) wrestled with him." This means that the struggle is an attack, like the attack by a robber or a murderer, that the victim is defenseless and taken by surprise. Such an attack on one who is defenseless and unsuspecting is a deliberate tactic calculated to make it easy. This rather obvious aspect is for the most part not taken into account. This is not a struggle in which strength is matched with strength and to which the two parties have agreed. The short account exhibits two further features which belong here. Just as the robber must take care not to be arrested, so must the attacker watch out for the break of day. And thirdly, both robber and attacker must conceal their identity; they must not reveal their names. All three features suit the hostile demon or the evil spirit, as attested in many religions throughout the world. A hostile demon, an evil spirit, attacks someone so as to cause harm. This can happen in a variety of ways. In the New Testament it is predominantly the evil spirit that causes illness; here it is the demon of the night or the river, the embodiment of the danger involved in crossing the river. This notion which has its roots in animism is very widespread and is so accurately described in the three features mentioned that one cannot avoid it. The text speaks of a hostile demon or an evil spirit that attacks Jacob; this is a common mark of the fairy tale. Those parallels are not relevant in which two specifically named opponents struggle with each other (examples in F.

Delitzsch, H. Gunkel, and others). The only parallel in the Old Testament, Ex. 4:24-26, names the attacker secondarily as Yahweh, as the textual variants show (BHK); and the manner of the attack is the same. Ex. 4:24-26 also takes place on the way (בדרך v. 24) and at night (במלון v. 24); instead of the ויאבק in Gen. 32:25, which is there because of the etymology of יבק, Ex. 4:24 is more specific: ויפגשהו . . . ויבקש המיתו. There follows also, "So he let him alone" (v. 26), and a naming. The magical counter shows that in Ex. 24-26 also the attacker is a demon. The two texts are very alike. The lethal attack precedes a dangerous meeting in both cases (Ex. 4, a meeting with Pharaoh). The verse ends with a precision of time, "until daybreak." This is a preparation for v. 27. One concludes from this that in an earlier form of the text v. 27 followed directly on v. 25. Referring to the struggle it says clearly that it remained undecided.

[32:26a] And this is just what v. 26aα says: the attacker (who alone can be the subject of וירא) sees that he cannot overpower him (Jacob). One expects him to yield, but this comes only in v. 27. There are two sentences in between which reveal an interference in the text. The first, "and he touched his thigh joint" (or thigh), follows on the preceding v. 26aα without difficulty and is continued in v. 27. The two suffixes of the third pers. sing. (v. 26aα and β) refer to the same person (Jacob), and the subject in each sentence is the attacker. V. 26b falls outside this context and is recognizable as a subsequent addition in that "Jacob" is named as the object. L. Schmidt (ThViat 14 [1979] 126) had noted correctly that Jacob should stand as object in the first sentence and the suffix in the second. V. 26b is part of the same addition as v. 33 and it is only with the exegesis of the latter that the reason can be given that the content of v. 26b argues for a subsequent addition.

    V. 26aβ, "and he touched his thigh," goes with the beginning of ch. 27, "and he said." The difficulty presented by this verse becomes evident from the usual translation: "he struck him on the thigh joint," where H. Gunkel took Jacob as the subject and spoke of a "wrestling trick." But נגע can not mean "strike." If the sentence goes with the first words of v. 27 then the touch on the hip has the effect of a countermove in wrestling (as in v. 32b where only ירך appears; כף is an appendage in v. 26b; ירך is an appropriate object to נגע, but not כף־ירך). One can speak of some sort of magical touch here which has its aftereffect in v. 32b.

[32:26b] Many exegetes want to apply to the whole of v. 26 what holds only for v. 26b, namely, that it is unattached, with no perceptible link either before or after. There is no reason for the attacker's request to let him go in v. 27 if he has already injured his opponent severely. This has long been noted and there has been a variety of attempts to explain it. H. J. Hermisson (ZThK 71 [1974] 249f.) says that v. 26b can be dispensed with because it introduces a lack of clarity; E. Otto (BWANT, 110 [1979], 43) concludes that vv. 26b,32b,33 are additions. The reason for the insertion is found in v. 33. The words, "as he wrestled with him," also support the proposal of an addition; they would be unnecessary in the narrative, but have their meaning in the addition.

[32:27] The attacker's request to let him go is prepared by and follows on v. 26a. It shows that the demon is one who is powerful only by night and loses his strength with the breaking of day. Jupiter says in the Amphitryon of Plautus, 532f.: *Cur me tenes? Tempus est: exire ex urbe priusquam lucescat volo* (Why do you hold me? It is time: I want to leave the city before daybreak). J. Skinner refers to *Hamlet* Act 1,1: "It faded with the crowing of the cock. . ." (the motif in general is very widespread, cf. T. H. Gaster, *Myth, Legend. . .* [1969] 210ff.). One cannot conclude from the request that Jacob is the victor; the struggle remains so far undecided. A struggle that is interrupted prematurely is everywhere regarded as undecided. Because his opponent is hard-pressed, Jacob can make a demand of him. The condition of letting him go is that he bless him. This can mean only that he transfer something of his superhuman power to him. In no other place in the Old Testament can blessing be won through a struggle; it is possible here because to bless = ברך has the derivative meaning of "transfer of strength"; in the old narrative this means the strength belonging to such a spirit that enables him to overpower a person. One can not therefore equate this blessing won by struggle with that received from the father (Gen. 27) or the blessing of Yahweh; one can at most speak of a deliberate allusion.

[**32:28-29**]   Jacob's opponent complies with the condition he sets in v. 30, which is a continuation of v. 27. Vv. 28-29 are clearly recognizable as a subsequent addition, as the majority of exegetes now acknowledge (P. Volz, G. von Rad by way of suggestion, E. Otto, H. J. Hermisson, G. Hentschel). But even the addition can be understood and evaluated differently. In v. 28 the attacker asks Jacob his name and he gives it; he then assigns him a new name, Israel, in v. 29a and gives the reason for it in direct speech: "You have struggled with God(s) and with men and have prevailed" (v. 29b).

The change of Jacob's name presupposes the establishment of Israel. This means that only when Jacob, as the father of the 12 sons who gave rise to the 12 tribes, had become the forefather of the people comprising these 12 tribes, was he given the title "Israel." The addition regards Jacob as the representative of Israel; the title sees in him the people of Israel. The reason given in v. 29b is also to be understood in this way; the old narrative is but the occasion for it. It is an "oracle of praise for Jacob behind which one ought not conjecture some lost Jacob tradition" (H. Seebass, against J. Skinner). "God(s) and men" means a totality expressed by a pair of opposites (L. Schmidt); it is used here as in Judg. 9:9, 13. The rarely used שרה is chosen because of the name Israel.* A further sign of the late origin of v. 28f. lies in the motive for the change of name; it occurs elsewhere only in P in ch. 17 (the change of the names of Abraham and Sarah) and 35:10 (Jacob). Moreover, 32:28f. is a doublet of 35:10 and carries marked echoes of it; it either presupposes the latter or is very close to it. It is only in this addition that Jacob is called the victor in the struggle: ". . .you have prevailed"; but in the narrative the struggle ends indecisively. The later tendency to exalt or idealize the patriarchs appears here; it does not appear in J. This was the motive for the addition. J's aim in the narrative therefore cannot be seen in v. 28f.; further the verses are not an organic part of the narrative.

[**32:30**]   V. 30 follows on v. 27. The attacker's request to let him go brings a momentary respite to the struggle. Jacob can now ask the name of the opponent whom he still holds. Here too there is an animistic notion in the background: if one knows the name of a spirit, one can call it. But the unknown opponent does not give his name; it would be dangerous for him. The same refusal with the same words is found in Judg. 13:18; but there it is the מלאך יהוה who speaks. The un-

---

*Trans: but see G. Vermeš, JJS 26 (1975) 12-13

known one yields to Jacob's first request: "And he blessed him there." He transfers some of his superhuman power to the one he could not overcome (a common feature in narratives of this sort). "There" means at the place where the life-and-death struggle took place. The sequence should be that Jacob lets his opponent go and he withdraws; this is a further sign that we have here only a report.

[32:31] Because the place is significant for Jacob, he names it. The שֵׁם at the end of v. 30 has already prepared this. The namegiving therefore is part of the old narrative, and concludes it (with E. Otto against L. Schmidt). But it is not named a holy place because this would not accord with the narrative, nor does the narrative thereby become a cult etiology. The place is important for the traveler who had the terrifying experience of a hostile attack which nonetheless ended with his wresting a "blessing" from his opponent. Even though it is certain that the naming of the place concludes the narrative, nevertheless the reason presents difficulties; it does not fit in with the preceding narrative because one cannot recognize Jacob's experience in v. 31b. The place is called פְּנִיאֵל here, but פְּנוּאֵל in v. 32a; the latter is the form of the name elsewhere (Judg. 8:8f., 17; 1 Kings 12:25); v. 31 prefers the form with י because it is more like פָּנִים. For the explanation of the vowel change, which perhaps is to be understood from an old case ending, cf. R. Meyer (ZAW 63 [1951] 225f.). The difficulty is patient of solution; the text itself provides a definite clue that the narrative winds up with another naming of the place, i.e., of the river, at the ford where the struggle takes place. The word used for the struggle, אבק, found only in vv. 25, 26 (another word is used in the addition v. 29), is certainly chosen because of the name of the river, יבוק. The naming in v. 31 has suppressed an older one, that of the Jabbok or the ford, probably because the reason, which can no longer be reconstructed, had become offensive. The reason given in v. 31b reproduces an expression current later (Judg. 6:22; 13:22; Ex. 33:20; Deut. 34:10) (cf. F. Nötscher, "*Das Angesicht Gottes zu schauen. . .*" [1924; 1969²], 23, 54ff.; W. H. Schmidt, Fests. G. Friedrich [1973] 28f.); and this too accords with what has been said; but the name Penuel is to be explained otherwise. The geographer Strabo XVI 2,15f. mentions the name of a Phoenician foothill πρόσωπον θεοῦ, "originally the profile of a mountain ridge," H. Gunkel. It is possible that in the course of altering the reason in v. 31b, the similar sentence in Judg. 13:22 was used as a model: "We shall surely die, for we have seen God"; but this is a case of an appearance of God or his messenger. The closing sentence, ותנצל נפשי, "yet my life has been saved," likewise sounds like a formula. But the subsequent alteration of the name giving and the reason cannot help to explain the old narrative. The one who spoke these words ("he said" is to be supplied after כי) is not the one who was attacked here by a powerful and hostile demon. The sentence that supplies the reason is the only one in 32:23-33, apart from the addition in v. 29, that speaks of God. Even if it is presupposed that the present wording of v. 31 belongs to the old narrative, it is not sufficient ground for understanding the narrative as a whole as an encounter between God and Jacob in the strict sense. It is not God but a hostile demon that attacks the traveler, and this does not in any way change right to the end of the narrative. Jacob's question about the name in v. 30 would make no sense if he knew that his opponent was God. All the profound theological consequences drawn from Jacob's supposed encounter with God (the most extensive in K. Elliger) have no basis in the text.

[32:32a] The narrative had begun with an itinerary note in vv. 23-24 and now

merges back into it. Jacob has named the place and now moves on. The chronological note which as such belongs to the itinerary, is characteristically adapted:
"And the sun rose on him as he passed Penuel." The narrator wants thereby to
conclude the narrative and at the same time say something meaningful: Jacob has
held out till dawn in his life-and-death struggle—it is now day. The verse refers
back to v. 27. For Jacob's attacker daybreak means the end of his power; for Jacob, and the לו indicates this, it means that he is free from the horror of the night
and can go on. He has survived the threat of a superhuman power and so can proceed to meet his brother without fear. "But he was limping because of his thigh."
The attacker had touched him on the thigh (v. 26aβ) and this had left its effect
(there is no indication that he was permanently lamed); he limped past Penuel and
the limp reminded him of the mortal danger that he had narrowly escaped. The detail, ". . .by Penuel," would present a difficulty if the new naming of the place
had preceded; this confirms that the name giving in v. 31 is a subsequent
alteration.

[**32:33**]   The touch on the thigh by Jacob's opponent is the basis for a food taboo.
The בני־ישראל shows that this is a later addition; just as in vv. 28, 29, the existence of the people of Israel is presupposed. It is forbidden to eat the גיד הנשה; the
combination occurs only here, but גיד a number of times with the meaning of sinew or tendon; KBL calls it *nervus ischiadicus*, the sinew of the nerve along the
thigh joint. The reason given for the prohibition, which does not occur elsewhere
in the Old Testament, is difficult; the prohibition is concerned with a part of an animal's body whereas the event that gave rise to it was concerned with a person.
The most likely explanation is that this part of the body was subject to taboo because it was regarded as belonging to the reproductive area. J. Weingreen gives a
convincing explanation of the addition in this place: it is due to a particular form of
midrashic approach which flourished in the rabbinic period and "by which
extrapentateuchal regulations are midrashically derived from a scriptural
passage. . .and as having been at some period attached to the biblical text" (in
Holy Book and Holy Tradition, ed. F. F. Bruce [1968] 64). It is certainly a late,
postexilic accretion. The proximity of this addition to Gen. 17(P) also shows this;
the same thing happens there, but in a different way. In ch. 17 circumcision is integrated into the narrative; in 32:33 the food taboo appears as an addition. The expansion in v. 26b shows that there has been an attempt to integrate it into the text,
thus proving that this is part of the addition, v. 33.

Purpose and Thrust

The narrative 32:23-33 has since ancient times given occasion for profound and
extensive theological explanations. Most of these take their stand on vv. 28f.,31b,
or 26b, that is, on the additions, the presupposition being that the narrative as a
whole is to be understood from them. But following the explanation given here
this is no longer possible. V. 26b belongs to the addition, v. 33, which is a late accretion. The addition, vv. 28f., is very close both in time and content to the
changes of name due to P; the change in name of the place, v. 31b, is not integrated. The theological meaning of these additions is to be studied each in itself,
and the theological meaning of the narrative without the additions. The narrative
of Jacob's struggle at the Jabbok that the Yahwist inserted here was the old narrative without vv. 26b,28-29 in their present form, and without v. 33. What J
wanted to say by inserting 32:23-33 here, thus breaking the connection between

Gen. 32 and 33, is to be sought in the meaning that the narrative had without the additions. It was neither Yahweh nor the God of his father who attacked Jacob at the ford, but the river demon who wanted to stop him from crossing. It is not true that Yahweh or the God of the fathers is active only at night and fears the breaking of day. Not for a moment did Jacob believe that he was struggling with the God whom he had called on for help in v. 12. And J was far from saying or hinting at this. Even the broader context gives no ground for such an explanation. It is not possible to explain it as a test (E. A. Speiser; F. van Trigt) nor as an answer to Jacob's prayer in 32:10-13, an explanation that has been taken up again and again since F. Delitzsch. In his prayer Jacob begs God to rescue him from his brother Esau; the answer can only be the rescue itself. What J wants to say by inserting the account of the attack here is simple. The whole return journey in chs. 32–33 is determined by encounters. Here Jacob encounters a lethal danger in the attack of the river demon. Jacob survives, even though limping, and carries from it a power, the "blessing" of the superhuman opponent. "And the sun rose on him" when he continued; he has experienced that God was with him. He can now go on to meet his brother.

The Meeting of the Brothers

Literature

Genesis 33: W. F. Albright, "Some Observations Favoring the Palestinian Origin of the Gospel of John," HThR 17 (1924) 189-195. N. Glueck, "Explorations in Eastern Palestine IV," AASOR 25-28 (1951) 308-310; D. W. Thomas, ed., *Archaeology and Old Testament Study* (1967) 431. P. A. H. de Boer, " 'Vive le roi!' " VT 5 (1955) 225-231 esp. 229. W. Vischer, "La réconciliation de Jacob et d'Esau," VigChr 41 (1957) 41-52. H. J. Franken, "The Excavations at Deir 'Alla in Jordan," VT 10 (1960) 386-394. G. Sauer, "Die Tafeln von Deir 'Allā," ZAW 81 (1969) 145-156. F. O. Garcia-Treto, "The Three-Day Festival Pattern in Ancient Israel," TUSR 9 (1971) 19-30. J. Blenkinsopp, *Gibeon and Israel* (1972). W. Th. InDerSmitten, "Genesis 32—Ausdruck der Volksmeinung?" BiblOr 30 (1973) 7-9. K. Jaroš, *Sichem. Eine archäologische und religionsgeschichtliche Studie mit besonderer Berücksichtigung von Jos 24* (1976). E. W. Nicholson, "The Origin of the Tradition in Exodus XXIV 9-11," VT 26 (1976) 148-160.

Text

33:1 When Jacob lifted up his eyes he saw Esau coming and four hundred men with him.[a] So he divided the children between Leah and Rachel and the two servant maids.

2 Then he put the maids and their children in front, "behind them"[a] Leah and her children, and Rachel and Joseph last.

3 He himself went on before them and bowed to the ground[a] seven times[b] until he came near to his brother.

4 But Esau ran to meet him and embraced him, and fell on his neck and kissed him,[a] and they wept.[b]

5 And when he raised his eyes and saw the women and children he said: Who are these with you? He said: They are the children with whom[a] God has graciously blessed your servant.

6 Then the maids drew near together with their children and bowed down.

7 Leah and her children also drew near and bowed down; and last Joseph and Rachel[a] drew near and bowed down.

8 And he said: What[a] do you intend with all this company I have met? He said: To find favor in the eyes of my lord.

9 But Esau said: I have enough, my brother. Let what is yours be yours!

10 Jacob said: No, I pray you! if I have found[a] favor in your eyes, accept

the present from me! For[b] I have seen your face seeing as it were the face of God, and you have received me favorably.

11 Accept then my gift that "I" have brought you,[a] because God has favored me and I have enough. So he pressed him and he accepted it.

12 Then he said: Let us go on our way and I will go ahead of you.

13 But he said to him: My lord knows that the children are frail and that the sheep and cattle giving suck[a] are a concern to me; if we overdrive them[b] for one day, the whole flock will die.

14 Let my lord go on ahead of his servant and I will push on[a] by easy stages according to the pace of the flocks[b] and the children until I come to my lord in Seir.

15 Then Esau said: Let me leave with you[a] some of the men I have with me to escort you! But he said: Why so? Let me only find favor in the eyes of my lord!

16 So Esau returned that day on his way to Seir.

17 But Jacob set out for Succoth and built himself a house and made sheds[a] for his cattle. And so he called the place Succoth.[b]

18 And Jacob came to Salem[a] the city of Shechem in the land of Canaan, on his return from Paddan-aram; and he camped before the city.

19 And he bought the piece of land where he had pitched his tent from the sons of Hamor, the father of Shechem, for a hundred pieces.[a]

20 And he set up an altar[a] there and called it: El, God of Israel.[b]

1a Order of sentences, BrSynt §27b.

2a With the versions read אחריהם, dittography.

3a "The השתחוה occurred a number of times only by way of suggestion" (A. Dillmann).   **b** BrSynt §93n.

4a Missing in Gk; but the repletion of expression is deliberate, P. Volz. The *puncta extraordinaria* "are as it were a question mark" (F. Delitzsch).   **b** The plural is deliberate; Gk understands it correctly: ἀμφότεροι.

5a חנן with double accus., Ges-K §117ff; BrSynt §90c.

7a Gk and Syr reverse the order, as in v. 2.

8a H. Gunkel would like to read מה for מי; on the other hand, O. Procksch: מי puts the stress on the persons in the company.

10a A conditional sentence can express a request, BrSynt §170c.   **b** כי על־כן means by and large "forasmuch as," Ges-K §158 n. 2; cf. Gen. 18:5.

11a For the form, Ges-K §74g; Sam, Gk, Syr, Vg read better, הבאתי.

13a עלות, root עול, only in the participle.   **b** On the masc. suff., Ges-K §134o; Sam, Gk, Syr ודפקתים. The verb (in qal elsewhere only in Song 5:2) means basically "push too hard." On the form, Ges-K§159e,g.

14a As Ex. 22:7, 10.   **b** Hithp. only here.

15a As Ex. 10:24.

17a Written defectively only here; H. N. Richardson, JBL 92 (1973) 86-95. **b** Succoth also Josh. 13:27; Judg. 8:5,16; 1 Kings 7:46. Probably Deir 'Allā east of the Jordan, so M. Noth and most exegetes (bibliog. above).

18a Gk, Syr, Vg understand Salem as a place-name; Sam reads שלום.

19a Coins or weight of unknown origin and meaning.

20a In an older form of the text מצבה is to be taken with לה.   **b** The versions presuppose another text, BHK.

Form

Gen. 33:1-10 is the conclusion of the Jacob-Esau story of which the underlying scheme is flight (ch. 27) and return (chs. 32–33). The flight had been made necessary by Jacob's offense against Esau; the return is possible only through reconciliation or setting aside the long-standing guilt. The theme of ch. 33 is provided by the scheme flight–return; one can assume then that it has been given its form by J. It is a scene in the large narrative complex which began in ch. 27. Accordingly ch. 33 shows no sign of an older self-contained individual narrative which is the basis of J's presentation; 33:1a clearly introduces not a narrative but a narrative scene (Jacob sees Esau coming). There follow only two episodes: Jacob and Esau greet each other (vv. 1b-11) and separate again (vv. 12-17). Then come only itinerary notes. However, if the whole has the effect of a narrative or part thereof, the reason is that here the tension which determines the whole of ch. 32 is resolved, namely, Jacob's fear: how will my brother meet me? This is due to the fact that the narrator of Gen. 27–33 arranges the conclusion of his narrative so that he gives the meeting its individuality by contrasting the two greetings. Esau greets Jacob as one brother greets the other after a long separation (v. 4); Jacob greets Esau as a vassal greets his patron with a ceremonial which has its origin in the royal court; there is a display of solemnity as becomes rank, the seven-fold obeisance, the submissive address, the presentation of gifts of homage. These two types of greeting are so skillfully worked together that the contrast speaks for itself. The ceremonial greeting of Jacob (vv. 1b-3, 6-7) forms the frame to Esau's warm greeting (vv. 4-5) so as to dominate the whole episode. The listeners are faced with the well-known court ceremonial which, in contrast to Esau's brotherly greeting, speaks a clear message. Narrative technique (like the deathbed blessing in Gen. 27) has thereby shaped a conventional procedure to a once-and-for-all event making use of the particular situation.

Setting

The narrative as a whole is the work of J who does not take up some old narrative but simply makes use of the well-known ceremonial underlying vv. 1b-3,6-7. There have been but few attempts to separate ch. 33 into sources; any contribution from E could be only in the matter of individual sentences or parts of sentences. The appearance of אלהים in vv. 5, 10, 11 can not be alleged as an argument for E: exegetes are virtually unanimous in this (P. Volz 119-123). The origin of the itinerary material in vv. 18-20 will be explained in the exegesis.

Commentary

[33:1-11]   The meeting, divided into the mutual greeting (vv. 1-7) and the gift (vv. 8-11).

[33:1a]   The opening sentence (v. 1a) often introduces a narrative scene (Gen. 18:2; 24:63; 31:10); according to L. Fisher this is also the case in the Ugaritic texts (*Ras Shamra Parallels* [1972]). This is particularly so where an arrival is described, e.g., Gen. 24:63b. Both here and in 24:63b it is a narrative scene which brings to conclusion a rather long narrative. The whole process, set in motion by Jacob's flight after deceitfully getting the blessing, comes to a conclusion here. Esau comes to meet Jacob; Jacob sees him coming and "four hundred men with him." This alarmed Jacob (32:8); it could bring death and destruction to him and his family (32:12).

[33:1b-7]   Jacob's action has nothing to do with protective measures, as in 32:8-9; that would no longer make sense. The text describes an attestation of submission. The whole procedure with all its details is such as could take place be-

tween an overlord and his rebellious or otherwise culpable vassal. The narrator
has in view some such court ritual as, for example, the Amarna letters show, with
the oft-occurring formula, ''I fall prostrate at the feet of my lord, seven and seven
times.'' The division into three groups (vv. 1b-2) corresponds to the order of rank
as in the court ceremonial, even though here it is but the family circle. Jacob,
however, takes precedence to all others in going to meet his brother. The decision,
favor or displeasure, must take place person to person between the brothers. Jacob's gesture of submission is taken up by the three groups of women and children; they are mentioned again each individually and each prostrates before Esau.

[33:4-5]   Esau's greeting stands in sharp contrast to the ceremonial comportment
of Jacob and his wives and children (vv. 4-5). He greets him naturally and warmly
as one who sees his brother again after a long separation. He runs to meet him
(Gen. 18:7; 24:17; 29:13; E. A. Speiser compares v. 4 with Enuma Elish
1,2,53f.), falls on his neck, embraces, and kisses him. What this means, what it
presupposes and says, does not need to be expressed further; the contrast between
the two greetings speaks for itself. The anxious tension with which Jacob faced
this moment is resolved. Further, the warm welcome includes the forgiveness.
Esau has forgiven his brother's guilt, either because he was moved thereto by the
avowal of guilt implied in the gesture and the gifts or because what happened so
long ago is now no longer important to him. The gestures are of great significance
in the world in which this story takes place. They are essential and indispensable
elements of communication. There is silence with regard to the explicit concepts
of confession and forgiveness; but in the silence a modest restraint is at work
which testifies to a deep human awareness. In fact both can be genuine and honest
where they are included in the execution of the action.

[33:5]   The inquiry is part of the greeting. Esau's first interest concerns the people in Jacob's company. He now ''raises his eyes and sees'' (cf. v. 1) the women
and children in three groups and inquires about them. The question means: in what
relationship do they stand to you? Jacob's answer is of great importance; it is his
first address to his brother; so far he has only bowed before him in silence. It is the
word חנן (THAT 1 587-597) that gives it weight. With these children, says Jacob,
God has favored me. It is a statement rich in content. The verb ברך would perhaps
have been more appropriate; but Jacob wants to say that it was the effect of God's
favor that has bestowed these children on him in a long and harsh history. The
verb חנן can include the forgiving grace (as in Ps. 103), the verb ברך could not.
Once again what is said is by way of suggestion; but it is full of meaning. Jacob
speaks of אלהים rather than of יהוה; this is rooted in the situation; Esau comes
from Seir.

[33:8-11]   Esau asks further about the flocks; the relative sentence, אשר פגשתי,
refers to the gifts that were sent on ahead to Esau. Jacob's answer, ''to find favor
in the eyes of my lord,'' accords implicitly with his first answer, חנן (God)—חן
(the brother). But this too is by way of suggestion.

    Such a profound and important parallel between what happens between
brother and brother and what happens between God and humans can speak only to
those who hear the narrative with lively and ready attention.

[33:9]   Esau's brief answer is significant for him. It shows the same contrast as
marked the greeting. The gift has meant so much for Jacob that he has made a

"political event" out of it! Esau brushes it aside lightly: "I don't need anything."
Nothing shows as clearly as this the change that has come about with respect to the
situation in ch. 27. Esau has obviously suffered no disadvantage through the loss
of his prerogative as firstborn. He has even prospered and become powerful without it, and to such an extent that he can do without the substantial gift representing
considerable wealth. The refusal of the gift that means so much to Jacob is another
chapter in the story of the brothers.

[33:10] Jacob, however, does not brook the refusal, but presses his brother to
accept (v. 10). He explains urgently that his own acceptance (חן, v. 8) depends on
the acceptance of the gift. He explains this further by elaborating the
interrelationship between the benevolence of his brother and the benevolence of
God: "As one sees the face of God" (A. Dillmann: יהוה could not stand in place
of אלהים here) in order to find favor with God (cf. Job 33:26), so has he come before the face of his brother in order (על־כן) to find favor, friendly acceptance
(רצה) with him.

[33:11] Jacob repeats his request (v. 11) and calls his gift ברכתי (cf. 1 Sam.
25:27; 30:26), thus stating that he wants to give back the "blessing" to his brother. It is offered to you, he says, because God was favorable to me. He points yet
again to the relationship between "blessing" and "favor": It was only in the
course of the events that took place from the time of my flight that the blessing
turned to favor, and so I give it back to you; as for me, I still have plenty. Esau accepts this explanation, and so can now accept the gift as well.

[33:12-17] The conclusion of the Jacob-Esau story, vv. 12-17, is marked by the
oft-used pattern of each going one's own way after a meeting (I. L. Seeligmann,
ThZ 18 [1962] 305-325, who points out that in the both cases, Gen. 32:1b-2 and
33:16-17, an etiological explanation follows on the twofold departure). It could in
fact be merely the conclusion of chs. 32–33 (that is, the conclusion of the meeting
between the brothers); but the expansion with Esau's invitation to go on together
in v. 12 extends the arc back to ch. 27, the flight of Jacob. The natural consequence of the reconciliation would be that Jacob and Esau go back to the same
place.

[33:12] Esau takes it for granted that they will now go on together. He does not
name the destination; but when he says he will go on ahead, he can mean only (and
this is confirmed by v. 14) that Jacob will live in the place where he is now living.

[33:13-14] But Jacob will not go with him. It is significant that he continues to
address Esau as "my lord" after Esau has addressed him as "my brother" (v. 9)
and impulsively received him as such. His mode of speech indicates that there is
still a distance between them. Jacob explains this by asking for understanding; he
points to the difference between the two caravans. Esau is at the head of a caravan
of 400 men, while Jacob is at the head of a caravan with flocks, women, and children (cf. 32:12b). A caravan like this moves in a different way and Esau can well
understand it. So, vividly and cleverly Jacob makes his brother see that the two of
them now lead different lives, are involved in different forms of community, and
should therefore better not go on together, but remain apart. Jacob's final remark,
"until I come to my lord in Seir," is but a polite way of saying in the circum-

stances that he would not want to contradict his brother. Esau knows quite well that it is not meant to be taken seriously. The decision to separate, veiled though it is, is significant for the narrative as a whole. The narrator wants to say that a reconciliation between brothers need not require that they live side by side; it can also achieve its effect when they separate and each lives his own life in his own way.

[33:15]   Generously and with the best of intentions Esau makes yet another offer (v. 16): he will leave an escort to accompany Jacob. But Jacob refuses this also; a military escort would be a foreign body in his pastoral caravan. However, the offer gives him the opportunity to tell his brother for the third time that his only concern is to be received by him again.

[33:16-17]   There follows now the parting with the separation formula: each goes his way, but it is a peaceful separation. There is no need of a treaty as in the case of Jacob's separation from Laban; Jacob and Esau remain brothers, though each in his separate living space. Esau sets out for Seir; this is his last appearance; his story is brought to a close in the genealogies in ch. 36. Jacob makes for Succoth; this sentence is part of the itinerary and shows that the separation formula serves to allow a narrative that has grown out of the itinerary to merge once more into it. A very striking sentence follows in v. 17b: Jacob builds a house for himself and sheds for his cattle. Nothing of this sort has occurred so far in the patriarchal story. It can be no accident that it appears for the first time in the conclusion of the Jacob-Esau story. This too is one of the fixed itinerary formulas and can have only one meaning in the context: it is the settlement formula (A. de Pury, O. Procksch). It reproduces the original form of the fixed settlement, the house and the stall, and can mean only that the journey described in the preceding itinerary is now at an end. The longtime traveler makes a permanent settlement, providing housing for personnel and animals. The narrator wants to say that the wanderings of the patriarchs came to an end in Canaan and their descendants settled down to sedentary life. This conclusion confirms that the patriarchal story, both Gen. 12–25 and 26–33, understood the patriarchs as wanderers or nomads. The etiology, the naming of the place at the end of v. 17 and so at the end of Gen. 25–33, thus acquires special significance: "And so he called the place Succoth." The narrator thereby presupposes that there was a place with this name (cf. bibliog.), but what is named here at the end of the Jacob-Esau story is more: the name refers to the settlement of the wandering fathers in the land of Canaan at the end of the patriarchal period. The giving of the name then corresponds to the derivation of the 12 tribes of Israel from the 12 sons of Jacob; at the same time it indicates the transition from the patriarchal period to the period of the settling of the tribes in Canaan from which the people of Israel grew.

[33:18-20]   It is immediately evident then that what follows, vv. 18-20, is a subsequent appendage (in fact several). Gen. 33:16-17 is obviously the conclusion of Gen. 25–33; the appendages that follow are to be explained independently of the text complex which they bring to a close; they are to be ascribed neither to E (the majority of exegetes) nor to J (A. de Pury).

Vv. 18-20 belong in form to the itinerary. They can form a coherent piece, but need not. According to H. Gunkel these three verses, together with v. 17, are at the same time the conclusion of ch. 33 and the introduction to ch. 34; but they were previously independent; L. Wächter agrees (ZDPV 84 [1968] 63-72). It is correct that the itinerary statement was originally independent and that with the mention of the place and its inhabitants it introduces ch. 34; but vv. 18-20 are not the conclusion of ch. 33 which ends with v. 17.

[33:18] V. 18aα presents no difficulty if שָׁלֵם is understood as a place-name: "And Jacob came to Salem, the city of Shechem" (so the earlier commentators, and W. F. Albright). The continuation is in v. 18b, "and he camped before the city." Stylistically it is pure itinerary data which has many parallels. It was later expanded by the relative clause, "(which is) in the land of Canaan, on his return from Paddan-aram." This brief sentence contains two typically P phrases which the majority of exegetes rightly trace back to P (a different view in R. Rendtorff, BZAW 147 [1977²] 118). It is not then a complete sentence from the P report (both parts occur in Gen. 35:6, 9, P), but has been taken from P by a redactor and inserted here with the purpose of underscoring the link: Jacob came from Paddam-aram and now enters the land of Canaan.

Recent exegesis for the most part understands שָׁלֵם in v. 18aα as an adverb ("safely") and the two following words, "to the city of Shechem." But this translation presents two difficulties. The adjective שָׁלֵם is never used of people with the meaning "safe, intact"; three times it is said of stones that they are unhewn or intact (Josh. 8:31; 1 Kings 6:7 [uncertain]; Deut. 25:15). Further, when used adverbially the word must stand at the end of the sentence, but that holds equally when it is understood as "peaceable." The second difficulty is that according to the rules of syntax the words עִיר שְׁכֶם cannot mean "the city of Shechem." L. Wächter also stresses this: an epexegetic genitive never occurs after עִיר, whereas a possessive genitive is very common (in v. 19 שְׁכֶם is also a personal name). In addition Gen. 34 speaks only of the "city of Shechem." In any case one must say that the translation of שָׁלֵם by "intact, safely" or "with peaceable intent" (H. Seebass, L. Wächter) is very uncertain. L. Wächter's suggestion is possible; he takes it as a text that has been subsequently expanded: "And Jacob came to Shechem and camped opposite the city," expanded to "And Jacob came peaceably to the city of Shechem and camped opposite the city." If one keeps to the text as it has been handed down, the versions favor a local meaning for שָׁלֵם; Gk, Syr, and Vg understood it as a place-name. "A place of this name in the plain east of Shechem is attested several times in Jewish and Christian literature" (L. Wächter, ZDPV 84 [1968] 70). The attestation goes back to the third cent. B.C. with the Gk. "but the ceramic finds go back centuries earlier" (L. Wächter, after several investigations at the place). The name of the settlement still lives on in the present-day Arab name of the village Salim, corresponding to the Hebrew שָׁלֵם.

The reason the place in v. 18 is called "Salem" can be that at the time of the author Shechem lay in ruins but Salem was still standing.

[33:19] Jacob acquires from the owners the field or piece of land where he pitched his tent. This sentence also belongs to the itinerary data that often specify what the traveler did at a stopping place. V. 19 and v. 18 can have belonged together from the beginning, in which case v. 19aβ would refer back to v. 18b; but this is not certain.

V. 19 shows clearly that we have to do with appendages in vv. 18-20; in v. 19 Jacob is a nomad who lives in tents, which would be impossible so soon after v. 17 where he builds himself a house. V. 19 originated independently of the conclusion, 33:16-17; the purchase of the field recalls ch. 23 (P). This similarity with ch. 23 is probably presupposed when in Josh. 24:32, a later addition, the field now purchased by Jacob is Joseph's burial place. When Jacob acquires the field from the בְּנֵי חֲמוֹר it is presupposed, as in ch. 23, that the sale takes place in the presence of the representatives or men of the place. The dominant family is the בני חמור who is described as the father of Shechem, as in Josh. 24:32 and Judg. 9:28 (חמור need have nothing at all to do with the role of the donkey in concluding treaties; on חמור see J. A. Soggin, BHH 11 692). The name is above all a preparation for Gen. 34 where Shechem is the son of Hamor. The purchase price is given as a hundred *kesita*, an unknown but certainly very old measure which occurs else-where only in Josh. 24:32 and Job 42:11 (J. Lévêque, *Job et son Dieu*, 1, §2 [1970]). There is no indication of the purpose for which the land is to be used; nor is this necessary, because the itinerary data intend to establish only the fact of the purchase and so the right of possession of Jacob and his descendants. It is possible, however, that v. 19, as a transition to Gen. 34, wants to say expressly that Jacob is the owner of a piece of land in the region of Shechem.

[33:20]   The sentence (v. 20) that concludes the chapter is an independent unit despite the שם, which must refer to a place previously named, and has been subsequently added to vv. 18-19 (E. A. Speiser). V. 20 contains two notable difficulties: the verb נצב means ''erect'' and matches מצבה, the same stem, but not מזבח. The setting up of an altar is always described by בנה or עשה (J. L'Hour, RB 69 [1962] 161-184). Elsewhere Jacob is said to have erected a pillar only (Gen. 28:18; 31:45; 35:14-20). One presumes that, because the *masseboth* were later forbidden, a later hand substituted ''altar'' for ''massebah'' in this place (lit. A. de Pury, *Promesse divine*. . . [1975] 442). Further, in contrast to ch. 28, there is no occasion for erecting an altar here; Jacob would have had no need to buy a field to do this (against H. Gunkel). Nor does the text say that the place is destined to become a burial ground. The same holds for the naming of the altar or pillar: ''El, God of Israel'' is not based on an experience; the sentence is appended merely for the sake of the name, and it is the name that presents the second difficulty in v. 20. The majority of exegetes assume that ''Israel'' means the patriarch Jacob (F. M. Cross, *Canaanite Myth*. . . [1973] 49; N. Lohfink, ThAk 1 [1965] 9-26). This would presuppose the change of Jacob's name to Israel in Gen. 32:29 which itself is a later addition. Against this is the fact that in all other places the combination אלהי ישראל means ''the God of Israel'' (the people). W. H. Schmidt points out correctly (THAT 1 145) that there is no comparison for the usage in 33:20; its meaning, therefore, remains questionable. It will not do to compare it with other formations such as ''El Olam'' and the like. It is very probable then that the meaning here is also ''El, the God of Israel (the people)''; a close parallel is Josh. 8:30. It is only the situation that gives meaning to this act of constructing an altar with such a name; it occurs at the moment when Jacob sets foot on the land of Canaan with his own gods. The name thus becomes a confession: ''the name of this altar is a program, indicating that El. . .is also the God of Israel'' (A. S. Kapelrud, ''The Role of Cult in Old Israel,'' *The Bible and Modern Study*, ed. J. P. Hyatt [1965] 44-56; similarly O. Eissfeldt, JSSt 1 [1956] 35f. = KS 111 [1966] 386-397). The confession proclaims: El, the creator God, the supreme God in the Canaanite pantheon, now becomes the God of the people Israel. The setting up of the altar means the beginning of the permanent cult of the God of Israel who now is ''El,'' i.e., God absolutely. V. 20 then reshapes an old itinerary report of the erection of a pillar; as such it was appended to the conclusion of Jacob's journey to Canaan; it sees as the goal of the patriarchs' journeying the cult of the God of Israel which takes the place of the El cult.

Purpose and Thrust

The significance of ch. 33 lies in its being the conclusion of the Jacob-Esau story. Both the social and the religious aspects reach their conclusion here.

The conflict between the brothers is finally resolved by a reconciliation in which the one confesses his guilt and the other forgives, without either act being specifically mentioned as such. Restitution is part of Jacob's confession: in the gifts Jacob restores the stolen blessing to his brother. The reconciliation of the brothers, however, hovers on the edge of the other alternative, war. Both brothers have grown wealthy in the meantime and war or an act of aggression is a possibility. There have already been rumblings of this in the conflict between Jacob and Laban in ch. 31, and Jacob sees himself faced with a deadly threat when the news is brought to him that his brother Esau is advancing as the commander of 400 men. War is now within range of the patriarchs, something which, as nomad herdsmen, they have so far avoided. Jacob is saved (cf. 32:12) from the threat of annihilation which war brings through Esau's magnanimity; he acknowledges the new situation and, though Esau receives him as a brother, submits himself to him as "vassal" following court procedure, i.e., politically. The Yahwist wants to say thereby that conflict between brothers can grow and extend beyond the family limits to confrontation and war. Every war is in essence a war between brothers. At the same time he explains the transition from the prepolitical structure which is introduced with the "sons of Jacob," the tribes. He points out to his contemporary listeners, state dwellers, that they should never forget the other alternative, rising above political conflicts, of coming to a resolution by reconciliation. Reconciliation is also possible when the parties decide to part. And so it is significant for J and an important aspect of his understanding of the Jacob-Esau story that both in ch. 27 and in ch. 33 Esau is portrayed as the more sympathetic of the brothers. His concern is with what happens between the brothers; it is far from J's intention to idealize Jacob as the "father of the people" (for J, this is Abraham).

The theological aspect is hinted at only in v. 5b: ". . .the children with whom God has graciously blessed your servant," and in v. 11: "because God has favored me (with herds) and I have enough" (חנן used twice). By means of the emphasis put on the repeated חנן in his address to his brother, Jacob makes an express confession as he looks back over the history of the conflict: God has shown favor to me in what has happened. He means also what he experienced in his confrontation with Laban (31:42). In his fear in face of Esau's superior power, Jacob begged God for חנן, to show him his favor (32:12); God did this by rescuing him from the danger. The narrator sets this חנן of God over against the ברכה. The ברכה had been the starting point of everything in the contest for the father's blessing; the process then initiated was continued in the contest for property with Laban, and for the blessing of children with the women. But the consequences of the blessing lost their meaning in face of the deadly danger presented by Esau and his soldiers, the background of which was Jacob's guilt before his brother. What determined his course of action was the effect of God's favor with regard to him. The Yahwist uses this theological element further to point to the transition from the patriarchal story to the story of the people (from Jacob of the "sons of Jacob"): the patriarchal story, determined by blessing, passes over into the story of the people determined by God's gracious, saving action.

An entirely different theological point of view which has nothing to do with the patriarchal period emerges from the appendage, v. 20, the name of the altar set up in Canaan: ''El, the God of Israel.'' It is a result of the religious struggle after the settlement to sedentary life in Canaan; the worship of the God of Israel replaces the cult of the Canaanite El. ''El'' is now the God of Israel alone.

Dinah and the Shechemites

Literature

Genesis 34: A. Kuenen, "Dina en Sichem (Gen 34)," *Bijdragen tot de critiek van Penta-teuch en Josua 24* (1880) 257-281. S. Mowinckel, "Levi und Leviten," RGG² III (1929) 1601ff. S. Lehming, "Zur Überlieferungsgeschichte von Genesis 34," ZAW 70 (1958) 228-250. E. Nielsen, "The Levites in Ancient Israel," ASTI 3 (1964) 16-27. H. J. Zobel, *Stammesspruch und Geschichte*, BZAW 95 (1965). M. Kessler, "Genesis 34—An Inter-pretation," RefR(H) 19 (1965/66) 3-8. R. E. Clements, "Baal-Berith of Shechem," JSSt 13 (1968) 21-32. L. Wächter, "Die Bedeutung Sichems bei der Landnahme der Israeliten," W. Z. Rostock 17 (1968) 411-419. A. de Pury, "Genèse XXXIV et l'histoire," RB 76 (1969) 5-49. O. Eissfeldt, "Die levitischen Traditionen in Gen 34 und 49, Dtn 33 sowie Jdc 17-18 und 19-21," in J. Lindblom, *Erwägungen zur Herkunft der josianischen Tempelurkunde* (1971). M. Haran, "Shechem Studies" [in Hebr.], *Zion* 38 (1973) 1-31. A. Lemaire, "Asriel, *šr'l*, Israel et l'origine de la confédération israélite," VT 23 (1973) 239-243. F. C. Fensham, "Genesis XXXIV and Mari," JNWSL 4 (1975) 87-90. C. H. J. de Geus, *The Tribes of Israel. An Investigation into Some of the Presuppo-sitions of Martin Noth's Amphictyony Hypothesis*, SSN 18 (1976). M. Rose, " 'Entmilitarisierung des Krieges'? Erwägungen zu den Patriarchenerzählungen der Gene-sis," BZ NF 20 (1976) 197-211. M. Metzger, "Probleme der Frühgeschichte Israels," VF 22 (1977) 30-43. J. Pitt-Rivers, *The Fate of Shechem, or the Politics of Sex. Essays in An-thropology of the Mediterranean. Cambridge Studies in Social Anthropology* 19 (1977).

Genesis 34:1-24: L. Freund, "Zum semitischen Ehegüterrecht bei Auflösung der Ehe," WZKM 30 (1917/18) 163-176. L. Koehler, *Die hebräische Rechtsgemeinde* (1931). E. J. Bickerman, "Two Legal Interpretations of the LXX (*dos* in Gen 34,12, Ex 22,16; *actio de pastu*: Ex 22,4)," RIDA 3 (1956) 81-105. D. Michel, "Studien zu den sogenannten Thronbesteigungspsalmen," VT 6 (1956) 40-68. E. Hammershaimb, "Some Observa-tions on the Aramaic Elephantine Papyri," VT 7 (1957) 17-34. W. F. Albright, "Some Remarks on the Meaning of the Verb *SHR* in Genesis," BASOR 164 (1961) 28. M. Haran, "The Gibeonites, the Nethinim and the Sons of Solomon's Servants," VT 11 (1961) 159-169. J. Blenkinsopp, "The Prophetic Reproach," JBL 90 (1971) 267-278. G. Gerleman, "Der Nicht-Mensch. Erwägungen zur hebräischen Wurzel *nbl*," VT 24 (1974) 147-158. A. Phillips, "Nebalah. . .," VT 25 (1975) 237-242.

Genesis 34:30-31: P. R. Ackroyd, "The Hebrew Root בָּאַשׁ," JThSt 2 (1951) 31-36. P. Wernberg-Møller, "A Note on זוּר 'to Stink,' " VT 4 (1954) 322-325. H. Weippert, "Jahwekrieg und Bundesfluch in Jer 21,1-7," ZAW 82 (1970) 396-409.

Text

34:1   Now Dinah, the daughter whom Leah had borne to Jacob, went out to visit the women of the land.

2   When Shechem, the son of Hamor the Hivite,[a] chief[b] of the land, saw her, he seized her, lay with her,[c] and dishonored her.

3   But he remained true to Dinah, Jacob's daughter; he loved the girl[a] and spoke feelingly to her.[b]

4   So Shechem said to his father Hamor: Get me this girl[a] for a wife!

5   When Jacob heard that he had violated[a] his daughter Dinah, his sons were with his herds in the field; so he kept silent until they came back.

6   Then Hamor, the father of Shechem, went out to Jacob to speak with him.

7   When the sons of Jacob came in from the field and heard what had happened, the men were indignant and very angry because he had committed an outrage[a] in Israel by lying with[b] Jacob's daughter; such[c] ought not to be done.

8   But Hamor spoke with them; he said: My son Shechem is completely in love[a] with your daughter;[b] give her to him as wife, I beg you!

9   Make a marriage alliance[a] with us,[b] give us your daughters and you take our daughters.[c]

10   Settle with us; the land lies open before you, settle, move about freely[a] in it, and acquire property.[b]

11   And Shechem said to her father and her brothers: Let me find favor in your eyes and I will give what you ask.

12   Fix as high a bride-price and gift as you will, and I will give it; only give me the girl as wife.

13   Jacob's sons gave Shechem and his father Hamor a deceitful reply[a] because he had violated their sister.

14   They said to them:[a] We cannot do such a thing as to give our sister to one who is uncircumcised; that would be a disgrace to us.

15   Only on this condition[a] will we come to terms[b] with you, that all males among you be circumcised like us.

16   Then we will give you our daughters and accept yours, and we will settle with you and become one people.

17   But if you do not listen to us and be circumcised, then we will take our daughter and leave.

18   What they said pleased Hamor and Shechem, the son of Hamor.

19   And so the young man did not hesitate[a] to do what they said because he was taken by Jacob's daughter; he was held in the highest respect in his father's house.

20   So Hamor and his son Shechem went to their city gate and addressed the men of their city:

21   These men are well-disposed[a] toward us. Let them settle in our land and move about in it. The land is broad enough[b] for them. We can take their daughters as wives and give them ours.

22   But only on this condition will the men agree to settle with us and become one people, that every male among us be circumcised as they are.

23   Will not their flocks, their property and their cattle[a] be ours! Let us agree so that they will settle[b] with us.

24   So all who went in and out[a] at the gate of his city agreed with Hamor and his son Shechem, and they were all circumcised, every male,[b] "on the flesh of their foreskin."[c]

25   Now on the third day, when they were still in pain, Jacob's two sons, Simeon and Levi, Dinah's brothers, each took his sword, boldly en-

tered the city[a] and killed every male.

26 And Hamor and his son Shechem too they killed with the blade of the sword,[a] and they took Dinah from Shechem's house and went away.

27 Then Jacob's[a] sons came in over the slain[b] and plundered the city because they had violated their sister;

28 and they took their flocks, their cattle, their donkeys, and all that was in the city and in the field;

29 and they took away[a] all their possessions and all their children and wives and plundered everything that was in the houses.[b]

30 Then Jacob said to Simeon and Levi: You have stirred up trouble[a] for me and made me stink[b] among the inhabitants of the land, the Canaanites and Perizzites; but I, I am few in numbers[c] and if they join forces against me they will strike me down and I shall be destroyed, I and my household.

31 But they answered: Should he treat[a] our sister like a harlot?

35:5 Then they set out and a terrible fear came upon the cities round about, so that they did not pursue the sons of Jacob.

2a Gk החרי.   **b** H. Cazelles, VT.S 15 (1966) 97-112, esp. 99-100.   **c** Point אַתָּה with Gk.

3a נער for both sexes as Gen. 24:14.   **b** As Gen. 50:21; Is. 40:2; Ruth 2:13.

4a The word ילדה is used for a girl elsewhere only in late passages, Zech. 8:5; Joel 4:3; Dan. 11:6.

5a Dishonor, actually desecrate, a cultic notion, common in P; applied in the same sense to a woman only in Ezek. 18:6, 11, 15; 23:17; 33:26.

7a On נבלה, G. Gerleman, 1974, lit. above; A. Phillips, VT 25 (1975) 237-242.   **b** On the form, Ges-K §45g.   **c** Gk reads ויאמרו כן.

8a According to O. Procksch the verb חשק ב occurs only since the time of Deut. 21:12; cf. 7:7; 10:15; Ps. 91:14.   **b** On this compound sentence, Ges-K §140d; D. Michel, 1956, lit. above.

9a T. C. Mitchell, VT 19 (1969) 93-112.   **b** Read אַתָּנוּ.   **c** An almost verbal parallel to this verse in Deut. 7:3.

10a The verb סחר, "to move freely throughout the land," occurs also in Gen. 42:34; Jer. 14:18; the part. then took on the meaning, "merchant" (KBL); on the verb, E. A. Speiser, BASOR 164 (1961) 23-28, against W. F. Albright.   **b** אחז peculiar to P in this sense; cf. 47:27.

13a Read with Syr וידברו במרמה; v. 13b is syntactically difficult and recognizable as a subsequent insertion.

14a Gk has: "But Simeon and Levi, the brothers of Dinah, said to them"; J. Skinner sees here the original reading.

15a ב of price, Ges-K §119p; BrSynt §23e.   **b** Either niph. or intrans. imperf. qal, Ges-K §72h.

19a On the form, Ges-K §64d.

21a Sam and Gk invert, BHK; on construction, BrSynt §30a.   **b** The same expression, Judg. 18:10; Is. 22:18.

23a קנין except for two late passages only P. מקנה and קנין are together in Josh. 14:4 (P), בהמה and מקנה in Num. 32:31 (J). The description of the property, v. 23, in 36:6 (P) has probably been put together out of the two pairs.   **b** Vg adds, "and we shall be one people."

24a As Gen. 23:10,18.   **b** As on v. 15.   **c** Instead of the erroneous repetition, read with Gk, "on the flesh of their foreskin," as in 17:14.

25a Read אל instead of על; בטח refers to Simeon and Levi, not to the city.

26a The expression occurs also in 2 Sam. 15:14; plur. Judg. 1:8 and elsewhere.

27a Sam, Gk, Syr read ובני, likewise at the beginning of v. 28.   **b** Probably read החלים with H. Gunkel, corresponding to כאבים, v. 25.

29a The stylistic difficulties of vv. 28,29 are probably to be traced back to their being shaped or expanded after Num. 31:9-11 (P).   **b** The last sentence probably belongs to v. 26 as an addition.

30a "To make taboo, to render impossible for dealing with others," KBL; also Josh. 6:18; 7:25; Judg. 11:35; 1 Sam. 14:29; 1 Kings 18:17f.   **b** P. R. Ackroyd, 1951, lit. above.   **c** As in Deut. 4:27; 33:6; Jer. 44:28; on construction, Ges-K §141d; BrSynt §§14bδ, 17.

31a On construction, Ges-K §107t.

Form

J. Wellhausen discovered the key to this difficult ch. 34 when he demonstrated from vv. 25-31 a double thread in it which he distinguished not by literary sources but by content and narrative style: there is one thread which remains "firmly within the frame of family history" and another which "is concerned with popular legal relations between the sons of Israel and the sons of Hamor, whose chief city is Shechem" (*Composition des Hexateuchs* [1876-78; 1963[4]] 46). But this insight, though taken up by R. de Vaux and others, did not impress itself sufficiently on the course of scholarship; its point of departure was that the origin of Gen. 34 must be explained in exactly the same way as that of the preceding Jacob story (on the history of scholarship, A. de Pury, lit. above; C. Westermann, *Genesis 12–50: Erträge der Forschung*, Bd. 48 [1975]).

The chapter as handed down has four parts: vv. 1-3, the violation of Dinah by Shechem; vv. 4-24, the negotiations; vv. 25-29, the attack (with the conclusion, 35:5); vv. 30-31, the reaction of Jacob. There is a lack of balance in that the part dealing with the negotiations is disproportionately long; there is too great a space between the deed and its retribution. Furthermore, the names Simeon and Levi appear only very late in the narrative, in v. 25 (S. Lehming [1968], lit. above).

Gen. 34 contains three obvious doublets: the request for Dinah (v. 8, Hamor; vv. 11f., Shechem); the agreement to the conditions set by Jacob's sons (v. 18, Hamor; v. 19, Shechem); the attack (vv. 25-26, 27-29). And the overall structure shows the division into a family narrative (A) and a tribal narrative (B). A forms the frame (vv. 1-3); A and B share in vv. 4-24 and 25-29, those parts belonging to B only being restricted to vv. 4-24. These data allow one to assume that another narrative has been built into the older and shorter one. As is often the case, the later version contains the longer speeches. Beside the doublets the text contains a whole series of inconsistencies; this is clearest in the transition from vv. 25-26 to 27-29, and on several occasions the suffixes do not fit the context. Further, there is the clumsy, uneven style as, for example, in vv. 4-8 where the locale changes from one verse to the other, something that never occurs elsewhere. Finally, one can recognize at every step attempts to make a single narrative out of two different ones; this is particularly obvious when, as often as possible, Hamor and Shechem are at the same time described as negotiator and speaker, even when not suited to the context. The obvious conclusion is that here, as in virtually no other single text of Genesis, there are two different basic narratives which have been subsequently worked into one. The older and shorter is a family narrative (A, called by many the Shechem tradition); into this has been built a tribal narrative (B, called the Hamor tradition); a later narrative has been formed from them uniting the two (C).

A: The narrative tells of an outrage against Dinah, the daughter of Jacob

(vv. 1-3), and its retribution by her brothers Simeon and Levi (vv. 25-26). The tension arises from Shechem wanting to marry the girl he had violated (v. 3). Whereas Jacob's sons are intent on revenge (vv. 5-7), Shechem offers them any sort of reparation they may want and pleads for Dinah (vv. 11-12). The brothers stipulate the condition that Shechem and his household be circumcised (v. 14). Shechem agrees (v. 19). Taking advantage of the period of recuperation, Simeon and Levi kill Shechem in retribution for the outrage and take Dinah away (vv. 25-26). Jacob objects strongly to what they have done, but Simeon and Levi insist that they had to avenge the outrage against their sister.

This is a family narrative (A). It is in some respects close to Gen. 12; 20; 26 (also the threat to the member of a family by a powerful foreigner); but it is to be distinguished from them by its own special trait: it is a narrative of crime and punishment. It cannot be described as an ''anecdote'' (M. Noth, S. Lehming). The narrative is an independent patriarchal narrative, originally told orally, which can go back to the patriarchal period. For the most part it has not been recognized as such because Simeon and Levi have been regarded as personifications of tribes (e.g., H. Holzinger who for this reason rejects J. Wellhausen's distinction). But a purely family narrative excludes this. Simeon and Levi are sons of Jacob and brothers of Dinah in vv. 25, 26, 30, 31 and nothing else. The fact that their names appear only late and that they are not named in vv. 5, 7, 11 (Gk has them in v. 14) is to be explained from the subsequent amalgamation in which the ''sons of Jacob'' are a political entity. It is not to be concluded with S. Lehming and A. de Pury that the names of Simeon and Levi have been inserted later into 34:25-26 from Gen. 49:5-7.

B: The tribal narrative begins in v. 4 with Shechem asking his father to press for Dinah on his behalf. B is thus inserted into A so that Hamor, the chief of the city, now becomes the real negotiator and speaker. But this presupposes vv. 1-3 from A. Hamor negotiates with Jacob (v. 6) and joins a political offer with his suit (vv. 8-10); the sons of Jacob present their condition (vv. 13-17) which he accepts and has confirmed by the city council (vv. 20-24a); consequently all the males of the city have themselves circumcised (v. 24b). This allows the sons of Jacob to attack the city (vv. 27-29); they then slip away under the protection of a ''terrible fear'' (35:5).

This narrative sequence presupposes that of A (in the Odyssey too a similar family event is the occasion for the attack on a city). E. Nielsen (*Shechem: A Traditio-Historical Investigation* [1955; 1959[2]] 252ff.) emphasizes that the narrative that has been inserted cannot stand without the basis having been laid; the circumcision then belongs necessarily to A and B. If one leaves out of B all that also belongs to A, then one is left with Hamor's offer (vv. 9-10), the reply of the sons of Jacob (vv. 15-16), Hamor's agreement (v. 8), and his negotiation with the city council (vv. 21-23) and its consent (v. 24a). This is not a narrative but a report from the period of the occupation of the land. It becomes a narrative only with the addition of the parts taken over from A. This arrangement is to be traced back to C.

C: The author of the present narrative is not therefore just a redactor like R in Gen. 1–11, but an independent writer who forms a new narrative out of two at hand to him. He takes an account of the peaceful settlement of an Israelite group in the region of a Canaanite city and transforms it into a narrative of the plunder of the city and the killing of the male population; at the same time he inserts it into and adapts it to a patriarchal story that tells of the revenge of two brothers for the outrage against their sister. In the background stands the command of Deut. 7:1-5 which forbids intermarriage with the Canaanites and demands their extermination.

Setting

It follows from the study of the form that the origin of ch. 34 is to be sought in three different settings:

(A) The family narrative, which is a self-contained and finished piece, can have originated toward the end of the patriarchal period when contact with sedentary peoples led to problems and caused tensions between fathers and sons (vv. 30-31). This is yet another example that patriarchal stories continued to live on even outside the written works.

(B) An account of the peaceful settlement of an Israelite group in the region of a Canaanite city can come from the period of the occupation of the land precisely because it has been reworked in accordance with Deut. 7; just the same it is in some places already in progress (E. Otto, ZAW 88 [1976] 176). In favor of this too is that "the narrator is clearly concerned to do justice to the Shechemites" (G. von Rad). The account seems to have belonged to a broader context, but nothing more precise can be said.

(C) The author of the narrative as a whole presupposes Deut. 7 and is close to the language of P (O. Procksch, and A. Dillmann regard P as the author). In any case the striking proximity of the language to that of P excludes that "Gen. 34 is to be ascribed to the J source as a literary unity" (E. Otto, op.cit., p. 171). The author works together two available pieces of different kinds and from different periods, like the author of Gen. 14, and this too argues for a late date. One assumes then that the author is speaking into a period when negotiations and intermarriage with non-Israelites had again become a temptation; this points to the exile or thereabouts.

Commentary

[**34:1**] *Exposition:* the situation out of which the episode beginning in v. 2 arose is presupposed in v. 1, not expressed. Jacob's household is camped before the city; the name of the city is not mentioned in ch. 34, but it can only be Shechem (cf. 33:18). Ch. 34 then is closely linked with ch. 33, though separated by a lengthy period of time. The children, who were still frail in 33:13, are now grown up. This makes it clear that ch. 34 does not belong to the sequence of events of chs. 27–33; it is a narrative independent of it that takes place much later, as shown by the way in which the persons are introduced. Dinah is described as the daughter of Leah and Jacob (30:21, elsewhere only in 46:15), Shechem as the son of the local chief Hamor (33:18,19). A striking aspect of the language is that the expression אשר ילדה לו occurs elsewhere only in Gen. 16:15f. and 25:12, both P. Dinah's excursion to visit "the women of the land" (as 27:46, P) indicates a rather long sojourn. The situation here points toward the end of the patriarchal period during the transition to sedentary life which begins by coming into contact with the sedentaries.

[**34:2**] As is often the case, the event begins with the act of seeing, וירא אתה (v.

2). It is presupposed that the girl is able to move about freely and without chaperon even among foreigners. But it is just this contact with city dwellers that gives rise to dangers.

Hamor like his son Shechem is here an individual. He is designated נשׂיא הארץ, ארץ meaning "the region around the city" (B. Jacob). נשׂיא occurs in this sense in the patriarchal story in 17:20; 23:6; 25:16, all P, and is usually translated "prince," better, "chief," head of the tribe.

He is called a "Hivite" (cf. 10:16f.; see lit. above, p. 97, and *Genesis 1–11*, p. 522; Gk reads "Horite," which can indicate the same people; there is no need to alter the text (cf. J. Blenkinsopp [1971], lit. above). The three narratives are not narrating a seduction but a forceful violation, as the word ויענה underscores (also Judg. 15:24; 20:5; 2 Sam. 13:12). However, vv. 3 and 5, and later v. 26, presuppose that Shechem keeps Dinah with him.

[34:3]   The narrative takes a turn in v. 3 as Shechem comes to love Dinah. The accumulation of expressions, "he became attached to her [as in Gen. 2:24] and loved her," therefore, are not a sign of two sources but of intensification, as in 1 Sam. 18:1. The first consequence of this new direction is that "he spoke feelingly to her." He wanted to win her approval so as to make her his wife.

[34:4, 6]   The consent of Dinah's family is necessary for this. Hence the second consequence—Shechem asks his father Hamor to urge his suit with Dinah's family (v. 4, as in Judg. 14:2). Hamor responds and goes to speak with Jacob (v. 6).

[34:5]   In content v. 5 follows on vv. 2f. Jacob hears what has happened to his daughter but will do nothing himself until his sons return from the open country. It is the business of the brothers to do something in such a situation (as in 2 Sam. 13).

[34:7]   V. 7 is an immediate continuation of v. 5; vv. 4 and 6 break the continuity of vv. 1-3, 5, 7. The subsequent joining of two narratives is clear here. The locale changes from one verse to another in vv. 4-8; this does not happen elsewhere in Gen. 12–36 and does not accord with patriarchal narrative style. First, Jacob hears what has happened; then, on their return, the brothers hear. It is said of Jacob merely that he kept silent, but of the brothers that they became indignant.

The first ויתעצבו means in fact "they felt grieved" (the Qal: "to cause grief"); it is found only in Gen. 6:6 as God's reaction to the wickedness of the human race. Just as in Gen. 6:6, an intervention must follow; the brothers feel that their honor has been wounded. The second ויחר להם מאד is the usual expression for an outburst of anger; this verb too demands an action to quench the anger. No reason need be given for the brothers' indignation. The late author (C), however, gives two: "he has committed an outrage in Israel" (Deut. 22:21; Judg. 20:6,10; Josh. 7:15; Judg. 19:23; 2 Sam. 13:12; Jer. 29:23). This is not only an anachronism; the sentence is out of place here because the perpetrator ("he committed") is not an Israelite, as in other passages. The other reason is a grammatically clumsy addition: וכן לא־יעשה. The phrase has the effect of a fixed formula here. In contrast, the two reasons given in 2 Sam. 13:12 are stylistically well-joined; the second runs כי לא יעשה כן בישראל after Tamar has said אל תעני (cf. v. 2); this passage is also an account of a violation; it is probable then that the late author (C) has expanded the old narrative, following 2 Sam. 13.

[**34:8-10**] Next come Hamor's negotiations (Shechem is not mentioned) with Jacob and his sons; this follows on v. 6. The passage is introduced in v. 8a and links the plea to give Dinah to Shechem (v. 8b) with the offer of intermarriage (v. 9) and settlement in the territory (v. 10).

[**34:8**] The introduction (v. 8) continues the singular of v. 6, לדבר אתו, with the plural, וידבר אתם, in v. 8a; this is occasioned by the intervening v. 7 which deals with the sons of Jacob, a certain sign of the intertwining of two threads, just as with "your [plur.] daughter" in v. 8b. Hamor advances his plea to give Dinah to Shechem without mentioning the violation.

[**34:9, 10**] But Hamor, the chief of the city, does not let it rest with his suit for Dinah for his son (vv. 9-10). His offer of intermarriage and settlement in his territory is saying something more important for him in relation to which the quest for Dinah is but merely the occasion; it is the step from family narrative to political event; it is a matter of increasing the extent and wealth of a city by taking into it a nomadic group with large flocks (v. 23 shows this). This is the first instance in the patriarchal story of a clear and often-attested historical event—the incorporation of a nomadic group into a small city-state by peaceful negotiations between the city chief and the "father" of the group (E. Otto, BWANT 110 [1979] 176f.) This is in fact just the way that many small groups of Israelites adopted sedentary life in Canaan. In v. 9 Hamor makes the offer of intermarriage, mutual exchange; the verb התחתן, a denominative from חתן, "son-in-law," is found in the same sense only in Deut. 7:3; Josh. 23:12; Esther 9:14. Deut. 7:3 expressly forbids what Hamor offers Jacob and his household. In addition he makes the offer of settlement in the territory.

[**34:10**] The accumulation of verbs is striking in v. 10. The first expression would suffice, ואתנו תשבו; what follows only explicates it—perhaps to make the offer more attractive or perhaps because the background of v. 10 is the more precise language of a mutual treaty. . . . והארץ תהיה ל as in v. 21; 13:9; 20:15; it too is an offer of free movement. The next two verbs belong to the same context: "settle, move about freely in it"; it is not that a particular tract of land is to be assigned to them, but rather that they are to go through the land and make their own choice. The verb means "to move freely throughout the land" (KBL). The hypothesis that the patriarchs were traders, "caravaneers" (W. F. Albright, C. H. Gordon), cannot lay claim to this passage. The final verb only repeats the invitation to settle in the land; והאחזו בה occurs with the same meaning only in Gen. 47:27; Num. 32:30; Josh. 22:9,19 (all P), the last passage being also an invitation to sedentary life. It is obviously P's term for Israel's conversion to sedentary life in Canaan.

[**34:11-12**] There is a clear break between vv. 10 and 11. The answer of Jacob's household should follow directly on Hamor's offer (vv. 8-10), but it follows only in vv. 13-17. The insertion, vv. 11-12, gives the impression that Shechem addressed the "sons of Jacob" after his father (so F. Delitzsch and B. Jacob explain it); but according to v. 6 Shechem is not present. Shechem's plea (vv. 11-12) stands without any link with that of his father Hamor (v. 8); they are doublets.

This is obvious grammatically inasmuch as there is no antecedent (Dinah) to the suffix to the third pers. fem. at the beginning of v. 11. The antecedent could be בת־יעקב at the end of v. 7; however, it is likely that a sentence with Shechem as subject is now missing. This is clear inasmuch as the content of the pleas of Hamor and Shechem differ significantly. V. 8 does not mention the violation; the same words could have been spoken even if the violation had never taken place and Shechem had simply fallen in love with Dinah. Shechem's plea, on the other hand, is completely colored by the deed that has preceded: consequently he is ready to pay any price the brothers of Dinah demand of him so as to atone for his crime. The gift that Shechem offers is described by two words, מהר and מתן.

מהר is the bridal gift or marriage price, KBL; W. Plautz, ZAW 76 (1964) 298-318; D. J. Wiseman in D. W. Thomas, ed., *Archaeology and OT Study* (1967) 115-135, with a parallel from Alalakh. The word occurs in the Book of the Covenant (Ex. 22:15,16) where מהר has a special function in a seduction; elsewhere only in 1 Sam. 18:25. Whereas the מהר is paid to the family of the bride, the מתן is probably the present to the bride. Gen. 24 clearly distinguishes the present to the bride from the gifts to the family.

[34:13-17] This is the answer to Hamor's offer. It is introduced by v. 13 and the first two words of v. 14. V. 14 is a rejection of the suit of v. 8 with the reason for it. Vv. 15-16 on the other hand refer to the offer of intermarriage and settlement (vv. 9-10). V. 17 combines the two. The answer was shaped by C. The answer of Jacob's sons (Jacob is not mentioned) is intended by the late author to be a reply to Hamor's offer as well as to Shechem's plea (vv. 11-12); it is addressed therefore to Shechem and Hamor even though Shechem had not accompanied him. Hence we can conclude that vv. 13-17 combine two answers.

[34:13] The text of v. 13b is disturbed and one should probably read במרמה וידברו with Syr (BHK); but the disturbance in the text can also be a sign that the last sentence was appended later. The repetition of the introduction at the beginning shows this; במרמה means "with deceitful intent" (likewise, Gen. 27:25); the reason is the outrage to Dinah. The late appendage is from the hand of C.

[34:14] V. 14 contains the answer to Shechem, vv. 11f.; one sees this in the Gk where Simeon and Levi make the reply. Implicit in the reason is the requirement that only this one man be circumcised. Shechem's reply would follow immediately on this: he accepts the condition. The reason, "that would be a disgrace to us," namely, noncircumcision, expresses the notion of circumcision being the mark of belonging to the group; in contrast to Gen. 17 it is given no religious significance here. The author therefore cannot be P.

[34:15, 16] V. 15 is another answer demanding that all כל־זכר be circumcised and serves as the basis for agreeing to Hamor's offer (v. 16). It is a political question (cf. vv. 9-10). The formulation of the condition bears striking resemblance to Gen. 17 (P).

The circumcision command in 17:10 is formulated המול לכם כל־זכר word for word as in 34:15. The niph. of מול is found almost exclusively in P; it is frequent in Gen. 17 and 34; Ex. 12:48 (P), which formulates the prescription presupposed in 34:15; Lev. 12:3 (P, command to circumcise on the eighth day); Josh. 5:8; Jer. 4:4. The phrase כל־זכר is also typical of P (Ex. 12:48; frequent in Lev. 6; 7; Num. 1; 3; 18; 26; S. Lehming, ZAW 70 [1958] 246).

This observation does not allow one to overlook the fact that the formulation of the condition in v. 15 is very close to the priestly language, especially to Gen. 17 and the command in Ex. 12:48. It is the later author (C) who is speaking here. V. 16 merely repeats word for word Hamor's offer in vv. 9-10.

[**34:17**]   The closing part of the answer of Jacob's sons, v. 17, serves as a clamp to join the political offer of vv. 9-10 with the suit of v. 8; what is said clearly presupposes vv. 8-10. V. 17a "has a threatening note" (B. Jacob); Dinah is here with her family (other than in vv. 3, 5, 26). If the other party does not accept the condition of circumcision, Jacob's sons will withdraw with Dinah, thus rejecting the suit. The formulation "our daughter" does not fit v. 17; it is to be understood as corresponding to "your daughter" in v. 8.

[**34:18-19**]   The acceptance of the condition is narrated twice. Vv. 18 and 19 are doublets. V. 18 expresses the agreement of Hamor, the city chief, who alone had made the offer in vv. 8-10 (without Shechem); C strikes a balance by adding Shechem. Shechem's agreement comes only in v. 19 which refers back to v. 14 only. When v. 19a says, "The young man did not hesitate to do what they said...," it means that the condition of circumcision concerns only himself and his house; v. 19aα advances once more his love for Dinah as the motive, and v. 19aβ the regard in which he was held in his father's house as the reason why he can carry it through.

[**34:20-24**]   It is clear once more from the two parallel sentences in vv. 18 and 19 that A is concerned with a family event and B with a political event. V. 18 is continued in v. 20 (the two threads are joined, similar to vv. 5-7; v. 19 breaks the obvious continuity between vv. 18 and 10). Hamor's agreement requires confirmation by the city council whereas in A the regard in which Shechem is held in his family is enough. C has struck a balance in the introduction in v. 20; but in vv. 21-23 the speaker is Hamor alone. The elders have assembled at the city gate so as to hold council publicly in a matter that concerns the general well-being of the community (as in Gen. 23; Ruth 4:11; cf. L. Koehler [1931] and E. Hammnershaimb [1957], lit. above). It is significant that nothing is said in vv. 21-23 about Shechem's personal affair.

[**34:21-23**]   Hamor's speech before the city council in vv. 21-23 is divided into his presentation of the friendly attitude of Jacob's household (v. 21a), his own offer to them (v. 21b), their condition, and an indication of the advantage that this would be to their own general well-being (v. 23). The political character of the offer becomes even clearer from the fact that it is brought before the city council in assembly. It is historically demonstrable that such consultations about whether a nomadic group should be accepted into a particular region did take place in the early stages of the settlement of Israelite tribal groups.

"These men are well disposed towards us" (v. 21): this sentence is an important and unsuspecting proof that Israelite tribal groups migrated peacefully, at least in part, into Palestine, as A. Alt in particular has demonstrated ("The Settlement of the Israelites in Palestine'' in *Essays on OT History and Religion* [1966] 135-169 = PJB 35 [1939] 8-63 = KS 1 [1953, 1963³] 126-175). The sentence and the whole speech show likewise that the scene belongs to the settlement period and not to the patriarchal period. The only difference from vv. 9-10 is that here Hamor wants to win the consent of the council; hence the words, ''the land is broad enough for them.'' The expression רחבת ידים imagines that the arms are stretched out on both sides to indicate the extent of the land. The intermarriage is also formulated as an offer: ''We can . . ..''

[34:22]   Accordingly, the condition in v. 22 is introduced with אך: ''But they require of us only. . ..'' It is here, however, that historical probability ceases. It is most unlikely that at the beginning of the settlement a Canaanite city would have agreed to have its whole male population circumcised in return for increment by a nomadic group. The interest of author C (cf. v. 15) becomes all the clearer here as he speaks from the point of view of a later age.

[34:23]   As the condition laid down is so important, Hamor at the conclusion of his speech (v. 23) wants to make the offer more attractive: the flocks of the newcomers will become the common property of the community. But this is no great thing; what is probably in mind are the claims and shares of the sedentaries. Hamor of course has said nothing about this to Jacob's household, but only to his own. The same nouns are used to describe Esau's property in Gen. 36:6(P), yet another sign of how close the language is to that of P. The speech concludes with a further appeal to receive the nomads.

[34:24]   The citizens agree unanimously with Hamor, and all the males have themselves circumcised. At the end of the sentence the words, ''all who went in and out at the city gate,'' are repeated; this is certainly a scribal error; Gk reads את־בשר ערלתם as in Gen. 17:14, 23, which is probably correct (BHK). It is striking that nothing more is said here of the purpose of Hamor's offer in vv. 9-10. The fulfillment of the condition set by Jacob's sons forms the conclusion. C's interest lies solely in the question of circumcision which makes the annihilation of the men of Shechem possible. Further it is unlikely that all the men underwent circumcision on the same day (cf. v. 22).

[34:25-26]   Vv. 25-26 followed v. 19 in A. Shechem had agreed to the condition without delay, i.e., he had himself and the men of his house circumcised. A's concern is solely that on the third day they were still in pain from the wound and unfit to do battle. This was in accord with the deceitful plan of the brothers Simeon and Levi (v. 13 במרמה). They now had the opportunity to avenge the outrage on their sister. ויהי introduces a new scene. On the third day Simeon and Levi take their swords. This sets into relief their intention to kill. Here, at the very end of the patriarchal story, this is stated for the first time; Jacob opposes it (v. 30). They pass into the city unharmed. The last sentence ויהרגו כל־זכר is a harmonizing addition by C who makes a single event of two acts out of two distinct events. The same is true for the beginning of v. 26 where C again inserts ''Hamor and Shechem'' whereas A had either ''Shechem'' or ''Shechem and the men of his house.'' In the old narrative (A), therefore, Simeon and Levi killed Shechem only to atone for the outrage to their sister. They took her and went away (or escaped).

[34:27-29]   After the departure of Simeon and Levi, v. 27 begins abruptly with

בני ישׂראל as subject (the versions prefix ו). Were "the remaining sons of Jacob" meant, then this should have been said. The beginning of v. 27 is comprehensible only if vv. 27-29 follow on v. 24. The break between vv. 26 and 27 allows the certain conclusion that two different events have been worked together into one. Vv. 25-29 are the starting point for J. Wellhausen's distinction of two individual threads (so also F. Delitzsch). It is content that is the determining criterion: vv. 25-26 deal with a family, vv. 27-29 with a political event. It is Jacob's household, v. 27, a nomadic tribal group, that falls upon the defenseless city, kills all the males who are still indisposed (read החלים, H. Gunkel), and plunder the city. The sentence is uneven; it is difficult to refer אשר טמאו to העיר. It is likely that the harmonizing sentence in v. 25, "and killed every male," is taken from v. 27, so that the reconstruction would be: " 'And' the sons of Jacob came in over the 'disabled,' killed all males because they had dishonored their sister, and plundered the city." The reason given, אשר טמאו אחיתם, is inserted as clumsily here as in v. 13. The harshness of the language is a clear indication that it is a subsequent construction. It reflects the factual difficulty that all the males of the city are held responsible for the violation. The real motive for the violation becomes clearer in vv. 28f.: a raid is described in which the raiders acquire rich booty. The verbose enumeration in vv. 28f. makes it quite clear that the background is a rejoicing over the successful outcome of an attack of an Israelite tribal group on a Canaanite settlement. The repetition eight times of את enumerates the booty in detail. The first pair of words, צאן and בקר, brings the cattle and the sheep together, as Gen. 12:16; 24:35; 47:11 (H. J. Stoebe, VT 54 [1954] 177-184 (cf. 12:16; 47:11). They took whatever they could lay their hands on both inside and outside the city, "in the city and in the field."

V. 29a adds further the household utensils and finally the women and children.

The enumeration is not an organic unity but a tacking together. The author probably had Num. 31:9-10 in mind. This is possible only in a military expedition and is common in tradition. The versions show that the enumeration ended with the verb שבו, "they led them away." The text of the last sentence has been disturbed; according to the versions the ואת is to be put before the verb: "and they plundered all that was in the house." It is striking that the same verb is already at the end of v. 27; it is scarcely possible here. This and the disturbance in the text indicates that we are dealing with a marginal gloss which had been added to v. 26 and then inserted itself incorrectly into the text here; בבית suits only vv. 25, 26, and so is corrected by the versions.

[35:5]   The verses that now follow are the sequel to vv. 25-26 and form the conclusion of the old narrative A. The other narrative B, to which vv. 27-29 belong, has no conclusion; it breaks off in v. 29a with the verb שבו. There should at least be a further note that they depart, corresponding to ויצאו at the end of v. 26. This conclusion is preserved in 35:5 which follows well on v. 29. Most exegetes accept this. The verb ויסעו, therefore, follows immediately on v. 29a. They departed after they had plundered the city. The two sentences that follow this verb explain why they were not pursued, which would only be expected after such a predatory and murderous attack. A "terrible fear" came upon the cities round about and prevented it. The word ("fear of God") occurs only here; but Ex. 23:27 promises such a terrible fear (אימה) to protect Israel when taking the land (Josh. 2:9). This confirms that narrative B belongs to the context of the occupation of the land or the Yahweh wars.

[**34:30, 31**]   The conclusion of narrative A, vv. 30-31, determines the understanding of it. It ends with Jacob severely rebuking his sons Simeon and Levi. The
introduction is followed by the accusation, עכרתם אתי, "you have stirred up
trouble for me." This is made more explicit in the following verb, "you have
made me stink among the inhabitants of the land." It carries the same sense in Ex.
5:21; cf. 1 Sam. 13:4; 2 Sam. 10:6. The further specification of the inhabitants,
"Canaanites and Perizzites," is not necessary in the context and is probably an
addition because they are mentioned in Deut. 7:1. Jacob knows that he is a prey to
them should they undertake to avenge Shechem's death. His group is too small to
offer resistance. The expression, אני מתי מספר, is used of the same situation, the
occupation of Canaan, in Ps. 105:12: "When they were few in number, of little
account. . ."; "when they gather together against me" (also Ex. 32:26; H.
Weippert [1970] lit. above), they will strike him down, as in Gen. 32:12, and he
and his house will be annihilated (Lev. 26:30, often in Deut.). Jacob's rebuke presents an accurate picture of the situation of the nomadic patriarchs whose groups
are so small that they must avoid any military encounters. This has always been
the case, e.g., the strife over wells (ch. 26) and Jacob's prayer (32:12). There can
be no question then that Jacob would have accepted Shechem's offer and regarded
it as adequate satisfaction if Shechem had made Dinah his wife and paid a high
compensation to the family for what he had done.

[**34:31**]   The answer of Simeon and Levi, however, rejecting Jacob's rebuke,
shows a break not only between two generations but between two epochs. For
Dinah's brothers the relationship with the circles of people among whom they live
is determined by honor and disgrace. An outrage perpetrated against them or their
family must be avenged in blood without regard for the consequences. This is in
essence a nationalistic sentiment which demanded killing as necessary in order to
satisfy honor. But they stand here in opposition to Jacob their father who from
now on is no more to be countermanded (in detail, J. Pitt-Rivers [1977], lit.
above; similarly H. McKeating, VT 25 [1975] 46-68).

Purpose and Thrust

The meaning that C has given to the narrative must be the point of departure.
Deut. 7 says of Hamor's offer of intermarriage that even this was forbidden to the
Israelites on entering the land; likewise it is even forbidden to them to make a trea-
ty with the inhabitants of the land; the command runs:

> And when the Lord your God gives them over to you, and you defeat them; then you
> must utterly destroy them; you shall make no covenant with them, and show no mer-
> cy to them. You shall not make marriages with them, giving your daughters to their
> sons or taking their daughters for your sons (Deut. 7:2-3).

There are such clear echoes of this passage in Gen. 34 that it must have been present to the late author C. Only now does his intention in constructing in ch. 34 become clear: he wants to narrate an example of the execution of the law of Deuteronomy. He wants to take a stand in express opposition to the possibility of any
peaceful or contractual agreement with the inhabitants of the land such as was at
hand to him in the tribal account (B). C took this, built it into a patriarchal story
that had come down to him, and so adapted it into a narrative exemplifying the execution of a command of the Torah. Zeal for the law was the motivating drive.

One can call it up to a point a midrash. It would have arisen in a period when intermarriage had again become a particular temptation for the Israelites, that is, at the time of the exile or thereabouts.

If this explanation is correct, we have in B, before its adaptation by C, a precious witness from the early period of the occupation of the land that has preserved an episode of peaceful immigration. A. Alt has laid more emphasis on this peaceful aspect of the occupation over against the purely military conquest of the book of Joshua; B provides a direct proof of it. A has certainly preserved a patriarchal narrative which belongs neither to J nor to P and is retained only here. It is all the more precious in that it is a marginal narrative, on the verge of the transition to the period of the occupation. This is the reason why C was able to join it with a tradition from the period of the occupation. The narrative is colored by the transition; in the middle stands the sentence, "Simeon and Levi, Dinah's brothers, each took his sword."

The trickery to which they have recourse is very different from that used in the Jacob-Esau story; it is a treacherous deception which has killing as its goal. This act of avenging an outrage to which Simeon and Levi felt themselves obliged and which they held to be necessary for their honor, is the beginning of the era of power, wars, and killing for the sake of survival. The narrative finds an echo in the proverb about Simeon and Levi in Gen. 49:5-7 where they are tribes that trace themselves back to the two brothers. The deed of which they are accused in 49:5-7 is only distantly related to that in ch. 34(A). A knowledge of ch. 34 (A) may be presupposed in 49:5-7, but this is not necessary. In any case there is only a loose link between them which cannot be made more specific; part of the link is that in ch. 34 the deed of the brothers is condemned, in 49:5-7 the deed of the tribes. In ch. 34 (A) the emphasis lies on the condemnation of the deed by the father (v. 30). "For all who take the sword will perish by the sword" (Mt. 26:52). When the sons reject their father's rebuke (34:31) this sounds the end of the patriarchal period when war and the killing of enemies were avoided. The sharp contrast between Jacob's complaint (34:30) and the final form of the narrative in which the annihilation of enemies is commanded is an indication of the conflict which later reaches a solution in the prophets of judgment and finally leads to a rejection of war (Is. 9:1-6). The king to come is the king of the kingdom of peace.

The narrative of Gen. 34 is secular in all its three constituent parts; only once, 35:5, is there any indication of the action of God, when the attackers are protected from vengeance by a "terrible fear (fear of God)" as they depart with their booty. But even this mention of God's action, though it is only a hint, is in contradiction to Jacob's words in 34:30 where he fears annihilation because of the violence of his sons.

Jacob in Bethel and Hebron, Jacob's Sons, Isaac's Death

Literature

Genesis 35: H. Hupfeld, *Die Quellen der Genesis und Art ihrer Zusammensetzung von neuem untersucht* (1853).

Genesis 35:1-5: G. Meier, *Die assyrische Beschwörungssammlung Maqlu,* AfO.B 2 (1937) Tf. IV 29f. E. Nielsen, "The Burial of the Foreign Gods," StTh 8 (1954/55) 102-122. G. Posener, "Les empreintes magiques de Gizeh et les morts dangereux," MDAI.K 16 (1958) 252-270. J. A. Soggin, "Zwei umstrittene Stellen aus dem Überlieferungskreis Schechem," ZAW 73 (1961) 78-87. G. Schmitt, *Der Landtag von Sichem,* AzTh 1,15 (1964). J. Jeremias, *Theophanie. Die Geschichte einer alttestamentlichen Gattung,* WMANT 10 (1965; 1977²) esp. 7-16. E. C. Kingsbury, " 'He set Ephraim before Manasseh,' " HUCA 38 (1967) 129-136. B. Porten, "The Religion of the Jews of Elephantine in the Light of the Hermopolis Papyri," JNESt 28 (1969) 116-121. G. R. H. Wright, "The Mythology of Pre-Israelite Shechem," VT 20 (1970) 75-82. J. A. Soggin, " 'La sepoltura della Divinità' nell'iscrizione di Pyrgi (lin. 8-9) e motivi paralleli nell'AT," RSO 45 (1970) 245-252. O. Keel, "Das Vergraben der 'fremden Götter' in Genesis XXXV4b," VT 23 (1973) 305-336.

Genesis 35:6-15: A. Ehrlich, *Randglossen zur hebräischen Bibel* (1908). W. W. Graf Baudissin, "El Bet-el (Gn 31,13; 35,7)," BZAW 41 (1925) 1-11. A. Jirku, "Neues keilschriftliches Material. . .," ZAW 39 (1921); "Der Name El Beth-el Gen 35,7." W. J. Martin, *Stylistic Criteria and the Analysis of the Pentateuch* (1955). Ch. Burchard, "Gen 35,6-10 und 36,5-12 MT aus der Wüste Juda," ZAW 78 (1966) 71-75.

Genesis 35:16-22a: G. Dossin, "Benjaminites dans les textes de Mari," *Mélanges R. Dussaud* II (1939) 981-996. W. F. Albright, "The High Place in Ancient Palestine," VT.S 4 (1956) 242-257. A. M. Haberman, "The Tomb of Rachel and the Term *aphš*" [in Hebr.], *Tarbiz* 25 (1956) 363-368. J. Muilenburg, "The Birth of Benjamin," JBL 75 (1956) 194-201. J. Prado, "Benjamin, lobo rapaz," CuBi 14 (1957) 18f. S. Mowinckel, " 'Rahelstämme' und 'Leastämme,' " BZAW 77 (1958) 129-150. F. Willesen, "The אפרתי of the Shibboleth Incident," VT 8 (1958) 97f. Ch. Rabin, "Etymological Miscellanea," ScrHier 8 (1961) 384-400. J. A. Soggin, "Die Geburt Benjamins, Gen XXXV 16-20(21)," VT 11 (1961) 432-440. M. Tsevat, "Studies in the Book of Samuel," HUCA 33 (1962) II 107-118. J. Blenkinsopp, "Kiriath-Jearim and the Ark," JBL 88 (1969) 143-156. G. Lombardi, "H.Fārāh–W. Fārāh presso 'Anātôt e la questione della Tomba di Rahel (Gen 35, 16-20; 1 Sam 10,2-5; Gen 31,15)," SBFLA 29 (1970) 299-352; *La tomba di Rahel,* SBF 11 (1971). M. Wüst, *Untersuchungen zu den alttestamentlichen Überlieferungen von Landnahme und Landverteilung im Ostjordanland* (diss. Tübingen, 1974). E. Vogt, "Benjamin geboren 'eine Meile' von Ephrata," Bib 56 (1975) 30-36. S.

Garbini, "La tomba di Rachele ed ebr. **bērâ* 'ora doppia di cammino,' " Bi e Or 19 (1977) 45-48. J. M. Grintz, "Some Observations on the 'High-Place' in the History of Israel," VT 27 (1977) 111-113.

Genesis 35:22b-26: T. C. Vriezen, "Exodusstudien Exodus I," VT 17 (1967) 334-353. C. M. Carmichael, "A Ceremonial Crux: Removing a Man's Sandal as a Female Gesture of Contempt," JBL 96 (1977) 321-336.

Text

35:1 Now God said to Jacob: Arise,[a] go up to Bethel[b] and stay there, and build an altar there to the God who appeared to you when you were fleeing[c] from your brother Esau.

2 So Jacob said to his household and to all who were with him: Put away the foreign gods[a] which you have with you, purify[b] yourselves, and change your clothes.

3 Then let us arise and go up to Bethel where I[a] will make an altar to the God who has been with me along the way I have gone.[b]

4 So they handed over to Jacob all the foreign gods that they had with them and the rings they wore on their ears, and Jacob buried them under the terebinth tree near Shechem.[a]

5 [Then they set out and a terrible fear came upon the cities round about, so that they did not pursue the sons of Jacob.]

6 Then Jacob and all the people with him came to Luz[a] [that is, Bethel] in the land of Canaan.

7 He built an altar there and named the place El-bethel[a] because God had revealed himself[b] to him there when he was fleeing from his brother.

8 Rebekah's nurse, Deborah, died and was buried under the oak[a] below Bethel, and he named it the oak of tears.[b]

9 God appeared again to Jacob when he came from Paddan-aram and[a] blessed him;

10 And God said to him: Your name is Jacob;[a] but no longer shall your name be Jacob; Israel shall be your name; so he called him Israel.[b]

11 And God said to him: I am God Almighty;[a] be fruitful and increase! A nation, yes a host of nations shall spring from you, and kings shall come forth from your body.[b]

12 And the land that I gave to Abraham and Isaac I give to you, and to your descendants after you I give the land.

13 Then God went up from him at the place where he had spoken with him.

14 Then Jacob set up a pillar at the place where he had spoken with him, a pillar of stone, and he poured a drink offering over it and poured oil[a] on it.

15 So Jacob called the name of the place where he had spoken to him, Bethel.

16 Then they set out[a] from Bethel, and when there was still some distance to go to Ephrath,[b] Rachel was in labor and her birth pains were severe.[c]

17 And in the midst of her severe pains the midwife[a] said to her: Fear not, you will have yet another son.

18 Then as life left her, for she was dying,[a] she called him Ben-oni [son of my pain]; but his father called him Benjamin [son of fortune].

19 So Rachel died and was buried on the way to Ephrath (that is, Bethlehem).[a]

20 And Jacob set up a pillar over her grave. It is known to this day[a] as the pillar of Rachel's grave.

21   Israel journeyed on and pitched his tent beyond Migdal-Eder.
22a While Israel was living[a] in that region, Reuben went and lay with his father's concubine, Bilhah. When Israel heard of it. . ..[b]
22b Now Jacob had twelve sons:
23   The sons of Leah were: Reuben (Jacob's firstborn), Simeon, Levi, Judah, Issachar, and Zebulun.
24   The sons of Rachel were: Joseph and Benjamin.
25   The sons of Bilhah, Rachel's maid, were: Dan and Naphtali.
26   The sons of Zilpah, Leah's maid, were: Gad and Asher. These are the sons of Jacob who were born to him in Paddan-aram.
27   And Jacob came to his father Isaac at Mamre, Kiriath-arba[a]—(that is, Hebron)[b]—where Abraham and Isaac had sojourned.
28   Now Isaac was one hundred and eighty years old.[a]
29   Isaac breathed his last and died and was gathered to his people,[a] old and fulfilled in life. And his sons Esau and Jacob buried him.

1a On the use of קום, BrSynt §133a.   **b** Gk reads . . . עד מקום ב, cf. 28:11.   **c** Construction, BrSynt §143b.
2a Images of gods are described as "gods"; cf. 31:19; Ex. 20:23.   **b** Hithp. of טהר as in Lev. 14:4, 7, 8, etc.
3a Gk reads plur.   **b** Construction, BrSynt §140.
4a Gk adds: "and he destroyed them even to this day."
6a Cf. 28:19.
7a The El is lacking in Gk, Syr, Vg; Gk τὸ ὄνομα τοῦ τόπου.   **b** Sam, Gk, Syr read sing; on the plur., Ges-K §124b n. 3; 145i.
8a Cf. Gen. 12:6 and the palm of Deborah, Judg. 4:5; on the art., Ges-K §126d.   **b** Cf. Judg. 2:5.
9a Sam and Gk add אלהים.
10a Missing in some Gk mss.   **b** Missing in some Gk mss.
11a As Gen. 17:1.   **b** As 1 Kings 8:19.
14a The noun, 2 Kings 16:13,15 and in Jeremiah (J. Skinner).
16a In Gk v. 21 follows on v. 16a; Gk presupposes Migdal-Eder to be near Jerusalem.   **b** Locative ה.   **c** On the form, J. A. Soggin, VT 11 (1961) 432.
17a As Gen. 38:28; Ex. 1:15.
18a J. A. Soggin op.cit., 433; better, part. as perf.
19a Irrelevant gloss.
20a TargOJ expands הזה; the same, abbreviated עד היום, Gen. 19:37b.
22a On the form, Ges-K §45g.   **b** For the double accentuation, Ges-K §15p; on the gap cf. M. H. Segal, *Tarbiz* 29 (1959/60) 192; v. 22a can be read as a half or as a complete verse. Gk fills out the gap: καὶ πονηρὸν ἐφάνη ἐνάντιον αὐτοῦ.
27a Could also be read as קריתה ארבע.   **b** Gk and Syr add בארץ כנען. On the juxtaposition of Hebron and Kiriath-arba, E. Lipinski, VT 24 (1974) 41-55; A. G. Auld, VT 25 (1975) 261-285.
28a Gk adds אשר חי.
29a S. Talmon, VT 3 (1953) 133-140.

Form

Ch. 35 is a concluding chapter containing pieces of different kind and origin. R combines P's conclusion of the Jacob-Esau cycle (vv. 6, 9-13, 22b-29) with texts from J (vv. 8, 14-15[?], 16-20, 21-22a) and prefixes to it a distinctive account of the construction of an altar at Bethel (vv. 1-7), corresponding to ch. 28; cf. Gen. 11:27-32. Itinerary and genealogy, as always at the beginning and end of sections of the patriarchal history, form the framework. *The itinerary*: vv. (1, 3, 5) 6f.(6P), 8(14f.), 16, 21, 27 (P); *the genealogy*: vv. 8, 16-20, 22b-26(P),

28-29(P); *the journey*: departure from Shechem (1,3)5—arrival in Bethel, 6(P) (8: oak near Bethel)—departure from Bethel, v. 16—stop, Rachel's grave near Ephrath, vv. 16-20—departure, stop at Migdal-Eder—arrival in Mamre, v. 27(P); *birth and death*: the death of Deborah, v. 8—the birth of Benjamin, vv. 16-18—the death of Rachel, vv. 19-20—the sons of Jacob, vv. 22b-26—Isaac's age and death, vv. 28-29. The P passages follow a clearly conceived plan, divided by the two pieces of itinerary data (vv. 6 and 27): Jacob comes to Bethel (v. 6), and this is followed by an appearance of God there (vv. 9-13); he comes to Mamre (v. 27), and there follow the details about Isaac's life span, death, and burial (vv. 28-29). The list of Jacob's sons is prefixed. The non-P passages are part of an itinerary; further, adapted to or inserted into it is the text put together by R, vv. 1-7, which begins with the command to build an altar at Bethel and ends with the execution of the command.

One cannot say with H. Gunkel and others that Gen. 35 is a heap of blocks. Rather it follows a carefully conceived plan.

Setting

It is not possible to determine with certainty the origin of some parts of the texts that R has brought together. Vv. 6, 9-13, 22-29 clearly belong to P; and it is certain that vv. 1-7 with the regular references to past events in vv. 1, 3, 7 is an independent construction of R. It is probable that vv. 14-22a, between the two P complexes, together with v. 8, form a continuous itinerary even though vv. 16-20 (Jacob) and vv. 21-22a (Israel) point to different origins. The abrupt change of name suggests a separation into literary sources (16-20 E, 21-22a J); but it is impossible to ascribe vv. 16-20 and vv. 1-7 to the same source E, as is generally done. Both style and language are too different. Vv. 16-20 are close to J in style and language, and v. 17 refers back to Gen. 30:24(J); it could be a separate tradition close to J. As H. Hupfeld recognized (1853, lit. above; also P. Volz, H. Donner, and others) the difference in the name Jacob-Israel is no certain criterion for distinguishing J from E. It remains an open question how the change from vv. 16-20 to 21-22a is to be explained. L. Perlitt also accepts a late origin for 35:1-7: "It is a question. . .of theological explanations" (WMANT 36 [1969] 257). For the source division in Gen. 35, cf. A. de Pury (*Promesse divine. . .* [1975] 224,531).

Commentary

[35:1-7] One can discern that vv. 1-7 is a construed textual unity from the fact that the two parts of God's commission to Jacob in v. 1 are carried out in vv. 6-7. Jacob passes them on to his household (v. 3) after an introduction in v. 2a. V. 5 reports the departure from Shechem, v. 6 the arrival in Bethel, v. 7 the building of the altar; the naming of the place is added. Another event comprising vv. 2b and 4 is inserted into this self-contained event by making the introduction, v. 2a, which belongs to v. 3, the introduction of a command of Jacob to his household to do away with the foreign gods and to purify themselves. V. 4 reports the execution of the first part of this command; the execution of the second part is missing because Bethel is about 50 km. from Shechem. The text of vv. 1-7 as a whole is not a narrative (it cannot therefore be an etiological narrative as E. Otto and others would have it), but the report of a divine commission to Jacob and its execution joined with Jacob's command to his household to renounce and to purify itself cultically.

[35:1]   There are three parts to the command which God addresses to Jacob: he is
to go up to Bethel, stay there, and built an altar there. The first corresponds to the
travel instructions which are characteristic of the patriarchal story (e.g., 12:1;
26:2; 31:13; and elsewhere); but the verb is a pilgrimage term which is then taken
up in the cohortative in v. 3. The second imperative could mean: "Settle there!"
corresponding to 33:17; but because the execution of this part is missing in v. 7
and Jacob moves from Bethel in v. 16 the second imperative goes with the third:
"stay there so as. . .." What is striking about the third part is that elsewhere the
building of an altar or the erection of a pillar is always narrated as the action of the
patriarch concerned; it needs no divine commission. Moreover, the natural expression in the divine address would be: ". . .and build me an altar there." But
the wording, ". . .to the God who. . .," is an obvious reference back to the appearance of God at Bethel (28:1-22) which is transposed into a divine address.
This reference is important for vv. 1-7; it recurs in vv. 3b and 7b and shows the intention of the author to provide the Jacob story with a conclusion in which what is
still outstanding from 28:10-22 takes place. The author therefore can be only the
redactor who had at hand the texts to which he makes reference.

[35:2a, 3]   Jacob passes on God's commission to his household. This is introduced in v. 2a, but takes place only in v. 3 which follows on v. 2a, "Let us arise
and go up to Bethel. . .." This cohortative corresponds to that in Ps. 122:1, "Let
us go to the house of the Lord!," a call to pilgrimage; the pilgrim term עלה is
found in v. 4. Ps. 122 is a pilgrimage psalm. Joined with this is the announcement
of the building of an altar, again with a reference back as in v. 1, but here corresponding to the call to pilgrimage: "The God who answered me in my day of
trial." This is the language of the Psalms, e.g., the first of the pilgrimage Psalms,
120:1, "In my distress I cry to the Lord, that he may answer me." The pilgrimage
to which Jacob summons his household is thus further defined as a pilgrimage for
the fulfillment of a vow. The author refers to Jacob's vow in 28:20-22, the first
sentence of which follows immediately, "who has been with me along the way I
have gone." Contemporary worship requires that the author balance the vow
made in 28:20-22 with the account of its fulfillment given in vv. 1-7. A. Alt is
justified therefore in speaking of a pilgrimage (Fests. A. von Bulmerincq [1938]
218-230 = KS 1 [1953] 79-88). However, a variety of objections can be raised
against his explanation of the text (C. Westermann, ThB 24 [1964] 85).

[35:2b]   V. 2a introduces at the same time another requirement not commanded
by God in v. 1; neither can it be, as it is generally understood, a preparation for
what God has commanded. Nowhere else does the building of an altar require a
preparation of this sort. Vv. 2b and 4 describe a different situation, the summons
to prepare for cultic involvement, as pronounced by a priest. It presupposes a permanent cult at a holy place; it is not in place here where the command is only concerned with building an altar. This is perfectly clear when the second part of the
requirement falls out in its execution in v. 4. Both parts are closely linked: in order
that the participant may enter purified and ritually unimpeded before God, he
must not only have washed his body and his clothes, but must also have renounced
whatever could hinder or tarnish this meeting with God, namely, any relation to or
link with other gods or.powers. The requirement to wash oneself and purify one's
clothes occurs by itself in Ex. 19:10f., that to renounce false gods in Josh. 24:14.
The two are combined here, but the emphasis lies on the renunciation of the

strange gods because only this is reported in v. 4. There are parallels to both in many religions: there are ritual purifications and change (cleaning) of clothing before a cultic act or entering the house of God (A. de Pury, *Promesse divine. . .* [1975] 573-581); there is likewise the setting aside of the images or symbols of the gods on entering the realm of another god, up to the rite of renunciation in the context of Christian Baptism.

The hand of the late author R can be recognized in the combination of Ex. 19:10f. and Josh. 24:14 as well as in the late language. The command, "Put away!" (חסרו), occurs elsewhere only in the Deuteronomistic context (Josh. 24:14, 23; Judg. 10:16; 1 Sam. 7:3; cf. L. Perlitt, WMANT 36 [1969] 257); the expression, אלהי הנכר, is spoken from the sedentary point of view (also Josh. 24:20), and the hithp. of טהר is exilic or postexilic.

[**35:4**]　With the execution of v. 2b a rite is apparently portrayed that is joined only here to the command to renounce foreign gods and is attested nowhere else. E. Nielsen (1954/55), G. Schmitt (1964), F. O. Garcia-Treto (*Shechem. . .*, diss. Princeton, 1967), and O. Keel (1973), (for all, see lit. above) have tried to explain the action from parallels provided by archaeology; none of these attempts, however, is entirely convincing because 35:2b, 4 describes a once for-all-event. It possibly has a remote connection with a fixed rite, but is too far removed from it because the author of vv. 2b, 4 has obviously no link with it. The tension between the command and the execution to which O. Keel refers (op. cit., p. 321) also shows this. Nor can the meaning of the earrings side by side with the images of the gods be explained with certainty. It is most likely that it is a matter of amulets, as the majority of exegetes think, despite the objection of O. Keel, p. 306, that earrings never have this meaning elsewhere in the Old Testament (cf. Judg. 8:24-27). Burial beneath a holy tree points again to Josh. 24:26; according to M. Noth it could be the same tree.

The reason for the insertion of vv. 2b, 4 becomes clear from the retrospective notes in vv. 1-7. R wants to make clear in his conclusion that images or tokens of foreign gods, which are presumed to belong to the women, servants, and maids from Aram (like Rachel's teraphim), must be laid aside on entering Yahweh's land and his sanctuaries. It is a deliberate insertion by R who in the spirit of his time is concerned with purity of worship. This is the reason why v. 4 reports the execution only of this one part of the command in v. 2.

[**35:5**]　It is certain that v. 5 formed the conclusion of ch. 34. Like ch. 34 it speaks of the בני יעקב, and the threat from the Canaanites is explained only from the acts of the sons of Jacob in Shechem. R had put this verse into his conclusion here so as to join it firmly with what has preceded. The verb ויסעו at the beginning of v. 5 fits nicely between the command in v. 3 and the arrival in v. 6.

[**35:6**]　It is only in v. 6 that we meet an itinerary note which has not been subject to modification; it belongs to P (v. 6a or the whole) in the view of the majority of exegetes. Jacob arrives at Luz (הוא בית־אל is a gloss). R has inserted the itinerary note from P into his conclusion in such a way as to join vv. 6 and 7 indissolubly. The self-contained unity from P, vv. 6, 9-13, 23-29, begins with v. 6; R has used v. 6 to clamp his own construction, vv. 1-7, to the P text. There are still further signs that it is a synthetic text: in v. 1 the place is already called Bethel; in v. 6 it is still Luz (cf. comm. on 28:19); and it acquires the name Bethel only in v. 7. The way in which v. 6 (P) is built into the textual unity vv. 1-7 (R) enables us to recognize clearly that R's construction, vv. 1-7, has been prefixed to the P and J texts at hand to R.

[35:7] Both parts of God's commission are carried out in vv. 6-7: Jacob comes to Bethel (v. 6) and builds an altar there (v. 7). Whereas in v. 1 R formulates the two parts of the commission in his own words, in v. 6f. he uses the P tradition at hand to him (v. 6 or 6a) to describe the execution of the first part. The designation אל בית־אל as the name of the place is striking. It is clear from v. 1 that for R the place is called Bethel; the versions attest this. The name El-bethel can be understood in this way: the place has been equated with the God venerated there by him, as happens often enough elsewhere (E. A. Speiser on 31:13; in an Assyrian-Tyrian treaty *Ilu-Bayti-ilī*). The reference back to Gen. 28:10-22, which is significant for the unit as a whole, forms the conclusion. The dative object in v. 1 ("to the God who. . .") is here the subject of the causative clause ("because God had. . ."), which is a more rounded conclusion. Moreover, there is another word for "to reveal"; אלהים is construed as a plural, but נגלו is singular in meaning, as in Gen. 20:13. Nevertheless it is the same author speaking here as in v. 1 with a variation of expression, thus underscoring yet again that the foundation of the sanctuary rests on the divine revelation at Bethel in Gen. 28. The use of the verb גלה in the niph. is rare for God's revelation; here, as in other places (esp. in the addition in Amos 3:4), it looks back to a divine revelation.

[35:8] V. 8 is difficult because it does not fit the context and it is beyond comprehension what Rebekah's nurse is doing in Jacob's caravan. As far as context goes, v. 8 is an itinerary note like vv. 16-18; it fits in only with the journey. It can be specific only when the stopping place is reached where what is reported took place. The explanation of the other difficulty is that texts from J and P are united in this conclusion that R has constructed. The data about the death of Rebekah's nurse is in the same context as that about Jacob's death in vv. 28-29; the nurse belongs to his generation. Her death therefore can be narrated on reaching the stopping place at Bethel. There was no need to mention her name in 24:59, but it is required in the account of her death. The tree under which Deborah, Rebekah's nurse, was buried (cf. Judg. 4:5, the palm of Deborah) acquires a name; this is characteristic of the patriarchal story. The name, the "oak of tears," preserves the memory in later generations; it recalls the burial of a maidservant who nevertheless belongs to the family as the nurse of the ancestress and is still remembered long after her death.

[35:9-13] The divine address to Jacob (P) that now follows is, as a revelation, introduced (v. 9) and concluded (v. 13) with virtually the same words as those to Abraham in Gen. 17:1, 22. Similarity in content corresponds to similarity in framework: conferring of a new name and promises. The difference in framework consists solely in the local emphasis in the address to Jacob (vv. 9, 13). This extensive parallelism intends to say that the choice of Abraham is continued in Jacob; physical descent is accompanied by the granting of a divine revelation and with it the promise directed toward the people of God. And so for P Abraham represents the patriarchal period, while Jacob with his new name Israel (vv. 9f.) and his 12 sons (vv. 22b-26) represents the people of Israel which takes its beginning from them. The difficulties the passage presents are explained by R's intervention.

[35:9] עוד, "again": this is no gloss in the introduction to the revelatory address; rather R wants to state expressly that the revelation made to Jacob "when he was fleeing from his brother" (vv. 1, 7) has its counterpart at the very place ("when he came from Paddan-aram") where he fulfills the vow then made. The ויברך אתו at the end of the verse goes with the beginning of v. 10: "He blessed him and said to him." The verb ברך has become a designation for the blessing, as in Gen. 48:3 (missing in Gen. 17:6).

[35:10-12] The divine address is itself very uneven; in particular the self-introduction does not appear at the beginning as in 17:2 but only in v. 11. One must agree with H. Gunkel that this divine address of P was a parallel to Gen. 28:10-22 and so took place before the journey to Paddan-aram. It was R who set it in its present place and was responsible for the consequent adaptations.

[35:10] The שמך יעקב in v. 10 (missing in 17:5) is not necessary as the introduction to the change of name, nor is the subsequently added "so he called him Israel" at the end of the verse; both are missing in the Gk. It could be that they are there to offset the embarrassment caused by the absence of any explanation of the new name (as in 17:5b), and with Gen. 32:29 in mind. It is also possible that P had no change of name and that R added it. It could be advanced in support of this that P continues to speak of "Jacob" and not of "Israel."

[35:11-12] The promises of increase and of the land are repeated to Jacob; the promise "to be God to you" (17:7, 8) and of the covenant are missing; these are made only once. The formula, "Be fruitful and increase," recalls Gen. 1:28 as well as 28:3, "May God Almighty bless you and make you fruitful" (cf. the survey in R. Rendtorff, BZAW 147, 45-48). V. 12, "that I gave to Abraham and Isaac," cites the two promise texts 17:8 and 26:3. The language of the promises is in poetic rhythm; this is clear in the two parallel sentences in v. 11b and the two-beat rhythm in v. 12. The promise of the land is emphasized by the הארץ at the beginning and the end of the verse (cf. Gen. 48:3f.).

[35:13] The same sentence as in 17:22 forms the conclusion. Most exegetes hold that the words, "at the place where he had spoken to him," are a dittography from v. 14. J. Skinner gives as the reason the clumsy formulation; E. A. Speiser alleges that the ב is suitable in v. 14 but not in v. 13b. But the passage must remain, despite the repetition and the clumsy expression. R has thereby reshaped the corresponding ויכל לדבר אתו so as to underscore that the revelation at Bethel took place at his return from Paddan-aram. A further reason for retaining v. 13b is that v. 13a would be too short an ending for such an important revelation.

[35:14, 15] V. 14 cannot be from P because P knows neither pillar nor cultic activity before the theophany on Sinai. All exegetes agree on this since A. Dillmann ascribed both verses to P and found himself in difficulties. There is no reason for ascribing v. 15 to P, as is commonly done. Some are of the opinion that vv. 14f. are the natural conclusion of the narrative, vv. 1-15 (e.g., G. von Rad). But this is not possible because vv. 1-7 conclude with the naming of Bethel. Others relate vv. 14f. to v. 8 and understand the monument as a burial monument (C. H. Cornill); this would be possible only if the reason given for setting up the pillar in v. 14 is deleted. The problem of vv. 14f. is that the naming of Bethel is reported three times: 35:7 with the building of an altar, 28:19 and 35:15 with the setting up of a pillar. It is only in 28:19 that it is firmly anchored in a narrative; R intends the setting up of the altar and the naming in 35:7 to be the fulfillment of the vow of ch. 28. In 35:14-15 the reason is given for the setting up of the pillar and the naming in the repeated ''at the place where he had spoken with him.'' Given the context in which R is speaking, this can only refer to the divine revelation in vv. 9, 13(P). R's hand shows itself here in that he further likens the revelation in Gen. 35 to that in Gen. 28 by giving it almost the same conclusion in vv. 14f. (cf. 28:18,19). R comes to terms with the doubling in vv. 7 and 15 because the founding and dedication of the sanctuary at Bethel has great importance for him at the conclusion of the Jacob story. It is likely that this is also the reason he adds the drink offering (J. Gray, ZAW 62 [1950] 211), which suggests the future sacrifice at the sanctuary. It is also possible, however, that R had at hand an independent itinerary report which he took up (O. Procksch) and adapted to his context by the double reference to the preceding revelation.

[35:16-20]   Vv. 16-20 form a self-contained unity. They are itinerary material which nevertheless narrate in detail the event reported, namely, the death of the mother while bearing a child. As in v. 8 the report tells of something that happened during a journey, an obvious pointer to the life-style of the patriarchs. This passage is generally ascribed to E because of the designation ''Jacob.'' Recently, however, one has become more cautious; the use of the names Jacob or Israel can no longer be regarded as a sure criterion for distinguishing between J and E (H. Hupfeld, *Die Quellen der Genesis.* . . [1853]; P. Volz, BZAW 63 [1933]; S. Mowinckel, NTT 65 [1964]; J. A. Soggin, VT 11 [1961] 439, who, like Mowinckel, renounces any source division). Style and language point rather to J, above all the reference back to the birth of Joseph in Gen. 30:24 (J).

[35:16]   The verb ויסעו is typical of the itinerary. The departure takes place from Bethel; this should be followed by: ''and they came to. . .''; but instead the journey is interrupted and the cause is the severe birth pains that have come upon Rachel. There is scarcely a text in the patriarchal stories which shows so clearly the harshness of their life-style. Rachel has accompanied the caravan in an advanced stage of pregnancy; as they journey, the pains come upon her and the birth must take place. Rachel is to die and be buried along the way. The caravan then departs, leaving the grave of the mother behind it, and the newly born child, who has now no mother, is taken along. The report notes that it was a particularly difficult birth (ותקש בלדתה, ''and her birth pains were severe''), and that it took place ''with some distance to go to Ephrath.'' כברה occurs elsewhere only in Gen. 48:7 and 2 Kings 5:19; it is an unknown measure of distance; the Gk understands it as ''as far as a horse can run''; according to E. Vogt (Bib 56 [1975] 30-36), about a mile (league?). The location of the otherwise unknown Ephrath is given precise determination by 1 Sam. 10:2 and Jer. 31:15; it was near Ramah, somewhere along the border between Benjamin and Ephraim (E. Jenni, BHH 1, 421). The equation with Bethlehem in v. 19 is an irrelevant gloss.

[35:17]   A profound insight into the sensitivity of the people concerned in the patriarchal narratives is provided by the midwife who, in the midst of the birth pains, cries out to the woman in labor: ''Fear not!'' (v. 17) (usually a divine pronouncement). She can be comforted in her pain in knowing that she has borne a son. The same cry is found in the same situation in 1 Sam. 4:20; it is a stereotyped phrase for the circumstances. ''You will have yet another son,'' says the midwife, recalling Rachel's wish to have a second son who would be the fulfillment of the name of her first (Gen. 31:24).

[**35:18**]   The mother can accept these words of comfort even in the face of her approaching death, and with her last breath, ''as life left her,'' name her child ''son of my pain,'' derived from אנה, ''to be in sorrow'' (Ch. Rabin [1961]; S. Mowinckel [1968]; cf. lit. above). The name is meant to state that life has gone forth from her mortal sufferings. But the father changes the name, perhaps because he is afraid that it could be an evil omen for the child (J. Skinner). He calls him ''son of the right hand,'' which can also mean ''son of fortune'' (the same double meaning as in the Arabic Yemen = ''southland'' and *Arabia felix*; J. A. Soggin, VT 11 [1961] 433), so as to preserve in the name of the child what the mother intended it to mean. As a tribal name בן־ימין means ''son of the south,'' ''the southern one''; so too in the Mari letters (G. Dossin, *Mélanges Dussaud* 11 [1939] 981-996).

[**35:19**]   Rachel dies and is buried beside the road to Ephrath (as Gen. 47:30). The clarification, ''that is, Bethlehem,'' should have stood in v. 16; it is attached here only as a gloss (as in 48:7; Josh. 15:59, Gk); a grave of Rachel was also pointed out at Bethlehem. The oracle in Jer. 31:15-17, ''A voice is heard in Ramah, lamentation and bitter weeping. . .,'' shows that hundreds of years later Rachel's grave was not only a signpost (cf. 1 Sam. 10:2), but was also linked with a living memory; further Mt. 2:17-18. The ancestress lived on in it and acquired a fresh significance for the present: ''Rachel is weeping for her children.''

[**35:20**]   Jacob sets up a pillar over Rachel's grave (v. 20). The custom has been preserved over the centuries right up to the present: מצבה here means a gravestone. The narrator adds for the benefit of his listeners: ''It is the pillar of Rachel's grave even to this day.'' The etiological formula עד־יום (Targ OJ add הזה) is not the goal to which the text tends; it is not an etiological narrative (J. A. Soggin, op.cit., sees two etiologies in 35:16-20) but an itinerary note joined with a genealogical note. The account of Rachel's death and Benjamin's birth remains independent of the narrator's explanation in v. 20b. It is the explanation alone that has an etiological character, not the text as a whole. J. A. Soggin therefore is correct in maintaining, over against M. Noth, that 35:16-20 is an older tradition than Gen. 29f.

[**35:21-22a**]   Vv. 21, 22a call Jacob ''Israel''; one concludes therefore that vv. 16-20 (Jacob) and v. 21-22a are of different origin. But this does not prove that vv. 16-20 are to be ascribed to E and vv. 21-22a to J. It is only from ch. 37 on that Jacob is regularly referred to as Israel in J; 35:21-22a is the only text in Gen. 25–36 where Jacob is designated as Israel. This does not have its basis in the text of J because J does not report any change of name; it would not be appropriate to J. It can be traced back only to a later transmitter. R saw the continuity preserved by means of the itinerary, despite the harsh transition from vv. 16-20 (Jacob) to vv. 21-22a (Israel).

[**35:21**]   V. 21 is a typical itinerary sentence; it reports departure and arrival. ''He pitched his tent,'' as Gen. 26:25. The locality of מגדל־עדר is unknown.

There were towers in many places to protect flocks from robbers.

[35:22a] A narrative grows out of an itinerary just as it can grow out of a genealogy, as the beginning of v. 22a shows. It reports a misdeed of Reuben, "Jacob's
firstborn" (v. 23), who slept with Jacob's secondary wife. The last two words
(Hebr.), after which the story is broken off, reveal the type of narrative; they are
the same words as follow Shechem's misdeed with Dinah in ch. 34: . . . וישמע.
Both narratives deal with a transgression and its punishment. This is confirmed by
the Reuben oracle in 49:3-4 where the deprivation of the firstborn's privilege follows on the misdeed narrated here. This permits some inference as to what the
missing part of the narrative dealt with. It is no longer possible to know why the
narrative breaks off in midsentence. Reference can be made to the prohibition in
Deut. 22:30 (23:1) (cf. C. M. Carmichael, JBL 96 [1977] 321-336). It is again a
matter of a firstborn and the loss of his right. This "privilege of the eldest" must
have played an important role in the family circle of this society. H. Gunkel draws
attention to a parallel from the *Iliad* IX, 449ff.

[35:22b-29] Vv. 22b-29 (P) have been inserted by R into the conclusion without
alteration. They follow on 35:6, 9-13, the divine revelation to Jacob, and are followed only by Esau's descendants in Gen. 36. The passage consists of a list of the
sons of Jacob (vv. 22b-26), the account of Jacob's return to his father at Mamre
(v. 27), and Isaac's life span, death and burial (vv. 28-29). The genealogical ending is characteristic of the priestly work, and the account of Jacob's return that has
been inserted here brings 28:1-5 to a conclusion.

[35:22b-26] The introduction (v. 22b) gives the number of sons, and the list
with the respective mothers follows: the sons of Leah (v. 23), of Rachel (v. 24), of
Bilhah (v. 25), of Zilpah (v. 26a). The closing remark notes that all 12 sons were
born in Paddan-aram. The enumeration and the ordering of Benjamin among
those born in Paddan-aram is typical of P: the situation that follows from all this,
the permanent state of affairs, is more important for P than the individual events;
there is an appropriate leveling. Typical of P also is the number of sons—12;
Dinah is not mentioned. A further note on this systematic enumeration: it is noted
in v. 26b that all Jacob's sons were born in Paddan-aram; the list at hand to P
therefore was intact before the departure thence (31:17; J. Wellhausen); R was
able to introduce it only after 35:16-20. On the various lists of the sons of Jacob,
cf. H. Weippert (ZAW 82 [1970] 396-409); on Gen. 29f., P. Weimar
(*Untersuchungen zur priesterschriftlichen Exodusgeschichte* [1973]), who is of
the opinion that the list in 35:22b-26 is dependent on Ex. 1:1-5; cf. T. C. Vriezen
(VT 17 [1967] 334-353).

[35:27] Jacob goes back to his father at Mamre (v. 27); cf. 31:18. V. 27 shows
again that J's Jacob-Esau story was at hand to P. P says little about Jacob; the only
event that he reports is Jacob's journey to Paddan-aram (28:1-5) and his return
(31:18; 35:27). This is comprehensible only if P knows the old tradition. The only
significance P saw in the event was that Jacob takes a wife from among his relatives; the social and economic aspects of the rivalry between the brothers are of no
significance to him at a time when the religion of Israel is restricted to formal worship. It is here that the decisive difference between P and J lies; J is concerned with
the relationship to God in all areas of life; but for P, the difference between the no-

madic and the sedentary life-style is scarcely of any significance; the conclusion of v. 27 shows this: "Mamre, where Abraham and Isaac had sojourned as aliens." On גור, see comm. on 12:10 and 32:5. Jacob's return to the place (v. 27a) can mean only that he too settles where Abraham and Isaac had lived and died.

[**35:28-29**]   Jacob's life span and burial are reported in almost the same words as Abraham's. Isaac too is "gathered to his people [= relatives]" and dies "old and fulfilled in life." And just as the sons of Abraham buried their father so too do Esau and Jacob, now peacefully united, bury Isaac. Gen. 49:31 adds the note that Isaac too was buried in the cave of Machpelah. According to v. 28 Isaac lived to 180 years, that is, for a long time after Jacob's return; this stands in contradiction to ch. 27 where he is spoken of as one who is dying. The only explanation is that there are two different conceptions of the patriarchal story.

Purpose and Thrust

The story of Jacob and Esau is brought to an end in ch. 35; it has been a journey through time (genealogies) and space (itineraries). This conclusion unites early and late texts. Jacob achieves the goal of his journey and Isaac the goal of his life. Rebekah's nurse dies on the way as does Jacob's beloved wife Rachel, whom he met at the well and for whom he served years of his life. She dies in the bitter pains of the birth of her second son whose name, changed at his very birth, recalls the death of the mother even in its changed form. But Benjamin is one of the 12 sons of Jacob listed at the end (vv. 22b-26). This chapter with its account of death and birth points back into the history of the patriarchs, from the children to the parents, to Abraham and beyond to the sons of Shem and the patriarchs of the primeval period, following the pattern of being born and dying, as is the lot of the sons of Adam (Gen. 5).

Death is linked more strongly with space than is birth: Deborah is buried under the "oak of tears," and Jacob sets a pillar over the grave of his wife that recalls her death for generations afterwards. Memorials to the dead are part of the journey of the patriarchs. Jacob comes to the goal of his journey in Hebron where Abraham lies buried in the cave of Machpelah. At the beginning of his journey Abraham builds an altar between Bethel and Ai (Gen. 12:8); at the end of his journey Jacob builds an altar in Bethel (35:1-7), and this will remain a sanctuary for Jacob's descendants. It links the goal of Jacob's journey with its beginning (28:10-22); he now fulfills the vow made then. It recalls the distress and rescue on the journey and confirms that God has been with him on the way. The journey through time and space is for the patriarchs a journey with their God, who stayed with them and spoke to them and on whom they called in their distress.

The transition from the patriarchal period to the beginnings of the people of Israel is heralded in ch. 35: Israel is the new name of the 12 tribes of Israel, and the promises made to Jacob in conclusion (vv. 11-12) are the two that are determinative for the people of Israel, namely, increase and the land (so in Deut.).

Esau's Descendants

Literature

Genesis 36: See above, lit., pp. 104f., "Names." B. Moritz, "Edomitische Genealogien," ZAW 44 (1926) 81-93. G. E. Mendenhall, "The Census Lists of Numbers 1 and 26," JBL 77 (1958) 52-66. J. Prado, "Los destinos de Edom," EstEcc 24 (1960) 557-567. M. Weippert, *Edom. . .* (Habil., Tübingen, 1971).

Genesis 36:1-9: O. Eissfeldt, "Biblos geneseōs," Fests. E. Fascher (1958) 31-40; "Toledot," Fests. E. Klostermann (1961) 1-8. W. Helck, "Die Bedrohung Palästinas durch einwandernde Gruppen am Ende der 18. und am Anfang der 19. Dynastie," VT 18 (1968) 472-480.

Genesis 36:10-19: B. Grdseloff, "Edôm, d'après les sources égyptiennes," *Revue de l'Histoire juive en Egypte* 1 (1947) 79-83. M. Weippert, "Semitische Nomaden des 2. Jahrtausends," Bib 55 (1974) 265-280.

Genesis 36:20-30: C. H. Cornill, *Die Bundeslade unter David* (1908). P. Dhorme, "Palmyre dans les textes assyriens," RB 33 (1924) 106-108. D. Yellin, "Recherches bibliques: 1. הַיֵּמִם Génèse XXXVI24," REJ 93 (1932) 93f. O. Glaser, "Der wasserspendende Esel (Gen 36,24)," ZS 9 (1933) 134-136. B. Maisler, "Semitized Hurrians in Palestine and Syria," JPOS 14 (1934) 243-245. F. C. Fensham, "Shamgar ben 'Anath," JNESt 20 (1961) 197f. S. Grill, "Ischodadh von Merw und die hajjemim Gen 36,24," BZ NF 11 (1967) 116f. W. J. Horowitz, "Were There Twelve Horite Tribes?" CBQ 35 (1973) 69-71. A. F. L. Beeston, "What Did Anah See?" VT 24 (1974) 109f. G. R. Driver, "Gen XXXVI 24: Mules or Fishes," VT 25 (1975) 109f.

Genesis 36:31-39: B. Moritz, "Die Könige von Edom," *Le Muséon* 50 (1937) 102-122. J. Morgenstern, "David and Jonathan," JBL 78 (1959) 322-325. J. A. Soggin, *Das Königtum in Israel. Ursprünge, Spannungen, Entwicklung*, BZAW 104 (1967). S. R. Bin-Nun, "Formulas from Royal Records of Israel and of Judah," VT 18 (1968) 414-432. R. de Vaux, "Téman, ville ou région d'Edom?" RB 76 (1969) 379-385. S. Mittmann, "Danaba," ZDPV 87 (1971) 92-94. J. R. Bartlett, "An Adversary against Solomon, Hadad the Edomite," ZAW 88 (1976) 205-226.

Genesis 36:40-43: W. R. Smith, "Animal Worship and Animal Tribes Among the Arabs and in the OT," JP 9 (1880) 75-100. E. Sellin, "Zur Lage von Ezion-geber," ZDPV 59 (1936) 123-125. N. Glueck, "The Topography and History of Ezion-geber and Elath," BASOR 72 (1938) 2-13.

Text

36:1 These are the descendants of Esau (that is, Edom):

2 Esau took his wives from the daughters of the Canaanites: Adah the daughter of Elon the Hittite, Oholibamah the daughter of Anah "the son of"[a] Zibeon the "Horite,"[b]

3 and Basemath,[a] Ishmael's daughter, the sister of Nebaioth.

4 And Adah bore to Esau, Eliphaz; Basemath bore Reuel;

5 and Oholibamah bore Jeush,[a] Jalam, and Korah. These are the sons of Esau who were born to him in the land of Canaan.

6 Then Esau took his wives, his sons, his daughters, and all the members of his household, his cattle, all his beasts, and all his property which he had acquired in the land of Canaan; and he went into the land of "Seir,"[a] away from his brother Jacob.

7 For their possessions were too great for them to dwell together; the land of their sojournings could not support them because of their cattle.

8 So Esau dwelt in the hill country of Seir (Esau is Edom).

9 These are the descendants of Esau, the father of the Edomites in the hill country of Seir.

10 These[a] are the names of Esau's sons: Eliphaz, the son of Adah the wife of Esau, Reuel, the son of Basemath the wife of Esau.

11 The sons of Eliphaz were Teman, Omar, Zepho,[a] Gatam, and Kenaz.

12 Timna was a concubine of Eliphaz, Esau's son; she bore Amalek to Eliphaz. These are the sons of Adah the wife of Esau.

13 These are the sons of Reuel: Nahath, Zerah, Shammah, and Mizzah.[a] These are the sons of Basemath, Esau's wife.

14 These are the sons of Oholibamah the daughter of Anah "the son of" Zibeon, Esau's wife: she bore to Esau Jeush, Jalam, and Korah.

15 These are the chiefs[a] of the sons of Esau. The sons of Eliphaz the firstborn of Esau: the chiefs Teman, Omar, Zepho, Kenaz,

16 Korah,[a] Gatam, and Amalek; these are the chiefs of Eliphaz in the land of Edom; they are the sons of Adah.

17 These are the sons of Reuel, Esau's son: the chiefs Nahath, Zerah, Shammah, and Mizzah; these are the chiefs of Reuel in the land of Edom; they are the sons of Basemath, Esau's wife.

18 These are the sons of Oholibamah, Esau's wife: the chiefs Jeush, Jalam, and Korah; these are the chiefs born of Oholibamah, the daughter of Anah, Esau's wife.[a]

19 These are the sons of Esau, and these are their chiefs (that is, Edom).[a]

20 These are the sons of Seir the Horite, the inhabitants of the land: Lotan, Shobal, Zibeon, Anah,

21 Dishon, Ezer, and Dishan;[a] these are the chiefs of the Horites, the sons of Seir in the land of Edom.

22 The sons of Lotan were Hori and Hemam; and Lotan's sister was Timna.

23 These are the sons of Shobal: Alvan, Manahath, Ebal, Shepho, and Onam.

24 These are the sons of Zibeon: Aiah[a] and Anah; he is the Anah who found the "hot springs"[b] in the wilderness, as he pastured the asses of Zibeon his father.

25 These are the children of Anah: Dishon and Oholibamah the daughter of Anah.

26 These are the sons of Dishon: Hemdan, Eshban, Ithran, and Cheran.

27 These are the sons of Ezer: Bilhan, Zaavan, and Akan.

28 These are the sons of Dishan: Uz and Aran.

29 These are the chiefs of the Horites: the chiefs Lotan, Shobal, Zibeon, Anah,

30 Dishon, Ezer, and Dishan; these are the chiefs of the Horites, according to their clans[a] in the land of Seir.

31 These are the kings who reigned in the land of Edom, before any king ruled in Israel.[a]

32 Bela the son of Beor reigned in Edom, the name of his city being Dinhabah.

33 Bela died, and Jobab[a] the son of Zerah of Bozrah reigned in his stead.

34 Jobab died, and Husham of the land of the Temanites reigned in his stead.

35 Husham died, and Hadad the son of Bedad, who defeated Midian in the country of Moab, reigned in his stead, the name of his city being Avith.[a]

36 Hadad died, and Samlah[a] of Masrekah reigned in his stead.

37 Samlah died, and Shaul of Rehoboth on the Euphrates reigned in his stead.

38 Shaul died, and Baal-hanan the son of Achbor reigned in his stead.

39 Baal-hanan the son of Achbor died, and "Hadad"[a] reigned in his stead, the name of his city being Pau;[b] his wife's name was Mehetabel, the daughter of Matred, daughter of Mezahab.[c]

40 These are the names of the chiefs of Esau according to their families and their dwelling places, by their names: the chief of Timna, the chief of Alvah, the chief of "Jether,"[a]

41 the chief of Oholibamah, the chief of Elah, the chief of Pinon,

42 the chief of Kenaz, the chief of Teman, the chief of Mibzar,

43 the chief of Magdiel, the chief of Iram;[a] these are the chiefs of Edom according to their dwelling places in the land of their possession (that is, Esau, the father of Edom).[b]

2a Read בֶן instead of בַּת־ with Sam, Gk, Syr; likewise v. 14.   **b** Better חרי instead of חוי because of v. 20.

3a Sam reads מחלת because of Gen. 28:9, likewise in vv. 4, 10, 13, 17.

5a With Q, Sam and v. 18 read יעוש.

6a Insert שעיר with Syr (versions different).

10a Sam, Gk, Syr, Vg read ואלה, likewise v. 20.

11a Gk has Σωφαρ, following Job 2:11, also in v. 23.

13a Gk reads Μοζε.

15a Gk ἡγεμών, Vg dux.

16a Missing in Sam.

18a The last four words are missing in Gk.

19a The gloss is more detailed in Gk.

21a Gk ורישן.

24a The ו before איה could indicate that a name has dropped out.   **b** The word is uncertain; the versions vary; most likely is the Vg aquae callidae; cf. Gen. 26:32b; read מים.

30a Perhaps לאלפיהם is to be read with Gk.

31a On the use of ל, Ges-K §129c.

33a Identified with Job by Gk.

35a Gk reads Γεθθαιμ.

36a Gk reads שלמה = Solomon?

39a Read הדד with Sam, Gk, Syr.   **b** Gk Φογορ.   **c** Perhaps ממי is to be read.

40a Read יתר instead of יתת; cf. v. 26.

43a Gk has in addition Ζαφωιν, perhaps correctly.   **b** A gloss.

Form

Two passages, vv. 1-19 and 20-30, each with the same sequence of sons and chiefs, are prefaced to the passage about the kings of Edom: the sons of Esau (vv. 1-14) and the chiefs of Esau (vv. 15-19); the sons of Seir the Horite (vv. 20-28) and the chiefs of the Horites. It is striking that in both cases the names of the chiefs are identical with those of the sons. The sons, however, are presented in the form of a genealogy (vv. 1-14 and 20-28), the chiefs in the form of lists, a mere enumeration of names. This reveals that the older tradition was that of the genealogy. From the point of view of the tribes, the chiefs come from the sons. A new and independent form of transmission appears only with the kings (vv. 31-39); it is like that in the books of Kings. In the history of tradition the tribe appears at that time as a transitional form between the family (clan) and the state.

While the sequence of the parts of vv. 1-19, 20-30, 31-39 forms an organic whole and reveals an overall plan, vv. 40-43 form an appendage, probably inserted under the heading "chiefs of Esau" (11 names) merely to preserve a group of six names which are original over against the names in vv. 1-30. One should note, however, the redactional unity of the whole that reveals a plan in the way in which the parts are put together (R. R. Wilson, JBL 94 [1975] 169-189; *Genealogy and History in the Biblical World*, YNES 7 [1977]).

Setting

As for the setting of the tradition, Gen. 36 makes it possible to arrive at a very clear knowledge of one of the paths of tradition along which Genesis acquired its present form. The starting point is the list of the kings of Edom (vv. 31-39). After David had subdued Edom it was necessary for the purpose of administration to have as exact a knowledge as possible of the land and the people, a knowledge which included the history as well. Consequently, the Edomite king list (from the chancery of the last king of Edom) came into the chancery of the king of Jerusalem (similarly P. Dhorme, Lit. above, and R. Dussaud). A necessary part of this were the catalogs of the territories of the land of Edom; they are found in the lists of chiefs, vv. 15-19, 29-30, 40-43; in Is. 34:12 the chiefs are named side by side with the kings of Edom. The genealogies of the families or clans of the Edomites were able to serve to extend and make more precise the subdivision.

The origin and transmission of Gen. 36 and its three parts is to be understood from its "setting in life," the task of administering a conquered land. The king list aided this task, and the list of the "chiefs" (as catalog of the territories) and the families (structure of the population) was added to it. The fidelity of this tradition is revealed precisely in the fluidity of the family trees. It has its private function in the history of the families, but had lost it with the transition to political structure. The authenticity of these lists was preserved in that no attempt was made to bring their contradictions into agreement. P took over a part of the lists from the royal chancery; vv. 1-5 is P's own formation which P joined with the conclusion to the Esau story (vv. 6-8). One cannot say with certainty whether P or a later redactor appended the following lists, vv. 9-43 (M. Noth, *A History of Pentateuchal Traditions* [1948, 1966²; Eng. 1972] 235); but one cannot say that vv. 15-43 are a succession of supplements (M. Noth, p. 18, n. 52). Rather, vv. 9-43 are an already existing unity from the royal archives. It is not possible therefore to divide these texts into literary sources. The parallel in 1 Chron. 1:35-54 further exhibits the additional leveling off and abbreviation of the genealogy to mere lists.

Commentary

[36:1-5]   The structure of vv. 1-5: v. 1, heading; v. 2, Esau takes two Canaanite wives; their names and the names of their fathers follow; v. 3, Ishmael's daughter, vv. 4-5, the sons whom these women bore to Esau.

P concludes the story of Jacob and Esau with a genealogy of Esau corresponding to that of Ishmael (25:12-18), so as to give expression thereby to the permanent "fraternity of Edom" with Israel (J. R. Bartlett, JThS 20 [1969] 1-20). The genealogy mentions the wives of Esau, following on 26:34; 28:9, and the sons born from them. P takes the names of the wives and sons from the genealogy at hand to him (vv. 9-14) although they do not coincide with the names in 26:34; 28:9 (P) where they are Judith, Basemath, and Mahalath. P does not attempt to harmonize, but does not alter the names of the three wives from the genealogy, vv. 10, 14. P thus reveals that he had different traditions about the names of Esau's wives, probably an Edomite and an Israelite.

[36:1]   The heading: the *toledot*-formula, which articulates the work of P in Genesis, occurs five times in chs. 1–11 and five times in chs. 12–50 (omitting 36:9). The heading here corresponds to 25:19 (Isaac) and 25:12 (Ishmael). The הוא אדום in v. 1 (likewise in vv. 8,14) is an inappropriate gloss intended to give assurance that the person of Esau represents the land of Edom; cf. 25:30 (according to vv. 9, 43, Esau is the father of Edom). J. R. Bartlett, op.cit., gives as the reason for the gloss that in an earlier stage the name of Esau was linked only with Seir.

[36:2]   Esau takes two Canaanite (in the broad sense) women as wives. The first is Adah, the daughter of Elon the Hittite. One of Lamech's wives is also called Adah (Gen. 4:19). In 26:24 Elon is the father of Basemath (a harmonizing tendency). The second wife is Oholibamah (names composed with אהל occur elsewhere), "the daughter of Anah 'the son of' Zibeon 'the Horite.' " The text is dubious; Anah and Zibeon are listed as sons of Seir the Horite in v. 20. The doubled בת then is scarcely possible. If one reads בן instead of the second בת, a better reading, then this does not agree with v. 20. The text remains uncertain. חוי is either another designation for חרי or a scribal error.

[36:3]   The third wife of Esau is Basemath, daughter of Ishmael. P adds "the sister of Nebaioth," another attempt at harmonization; the name comes from 25:13.

[36:4]   The names of the sons follow. It is worthy of note that three of the five names of the sons of Esau occur elsewhere in the Old Testament. Eliphaz is one of Job's friends (Job 2:11); Reuel (in Ex. 2:18; Num. 10:21 and elsewhere); Korah is the name of a Levitical group (Num. 16; 2 Chron. 2:43 and elsewhere).

[36:5b]   The concluding formula, "these are the sons of Esau," is expanded by a relative sentence forming a transition to vv. 6-8.

[36:6-8]   In P's conclusion the genealogy (vv. 1-5) is joined with the itinerary (vv. 6-8), as for example in the introduction, Gen. 11:27-32. This itinerary gives an account of Esau's departure from Canaan (after the Hebron episode, 35:27-29) with his family and possessions for the mountain range of Seir (the name has fallen out of the text), the elevation to the south of the Dead Sea; earlier the name was restricted to a small area, probably to the west of the Arabah. It is significant that the name Seir designates here a person, the tribal ancestor, as well as the territory in which he lives. As is typical of P, there is a detailed account of all that Esau takes with him in the caravan; the same expressions are found in Gen. 12:5; 34:23. The reason for the departure is given, "the land. . .could not support them," as in the case of the separation of Abraham and Lot (13:15f.); in both cases this is given as the reason why their separation was peaceful. But the three last words (Hebr.), "away from his brother Jacob," reveals the concern: Esau cedes the promised land to his brother.

[**36:9-14**]   Vv. 9-14 are neither a repetition nor a mere continuation of vv. 1-5; whereas vv. 1-5 described the family of Esau, the emphasis in vv. 9-14 is on the sons. The text stands halfway between genealogy and list. It has two headings in vv. 9 and 10a (as with the sons of Ishmael in 25:12f.); in v. 10b are the sons of Adah and Basemath, in v. 11 the five sons of Eliphaz, in v. 12a the son of Eliphaz's secondary wife; a formula brings the list of Adah's sons to a conclusion in v. 12b. Likewise the sons of Reuel are designated as sons of Basemath in v. 13b. The three sons of Oholibamah follow in v. 14; they belong to the previous generation. All sons and grandsons are referred to the three wives of Esau, and so to Esau himself. The name Esau therefore embraces the whole of the group designated by the names; the three wives designate three main groups (together with a collateral group through the secondary wife), and the sons and grandsons designate the branching into subsidiary groups. The genealogy does not consist in an enumeration of individual names added one to the other, but in a carefully articulated presentation of a whole, arranged in order. The whole describes the people of Edom who have their origin from Esau; however, it should be noted that each individual name is meant to be a personal name and not the name of a group or a tribe. The people has grown from a family, that of Esau; it is this family aspect alone that is presented here.

The two headings in vv. 9a and 10 show that this genealogy once stood independently and was handed down as such. Its original heading was, "these are the names of Esau's sons" (v. 10a). The heading with the *toledot* formula in v. 9a was prefixed by P. He uses it to insert the genealogy (vv. 10-14) into this work and thus deliberately repeats the *toledot* formula of v. 1 in order to show that the grandsons mentioned in vv. 10-14 also belong to the sons of Esau. P's method itself clearly here. The genealogy contains 12 names, without Amalek, the son of the secondary wife Timna. In vv. 15-19 there are 14 names, and in vv. 40-43 11. The number 12 suggests itself for vv. 9-14; one must delete or add to arrive at it in vv. 15-19 and 40-43. R. R. Wilson (*Genealogy and History in the Biblical World*, YNES 7 [1977] 171, n. 82) rightly advises caution in concluding too quickly to an Edomite 12-tribe confederation. One can say only that the number 12 has at least had an effect on the totality in vv. 9-14, but one cannot put too much weight on it because one has to manipulate Amalek.

[**36:15-19**]   This is a list of the tribal chiefs of Esau which contains traces of a genealogy. The heading in v. 15a is, "these are the chiefs of the sons of Esau," corresponding to the somewhat different closing formula in v. 19; then follow the chiefs (= sons) of Reuel (v. 17a), with the concluding formula, v. 17bβ, followed by yet another formula (the sons of Basemath), and the chiefs (= sons) of Oholibamah, v. 18a, with the concluding formula. The list is closed with v. 19, the formula indicating that it brings vv. 11-14 (which have no concluding formula) and vv. 15-19 to a conclusion.

The list is striking in two ways: without exception it contains the same names as vv. 11-14. In form it relies on vv. 11-14 in that it would be incomprehensible without the family relationships described there. What is new in vv. 15-19 over against vv. 11-14 is merely the use of אלופים which colors the whole list. Vv. 15-19 therefore are clearly a further development of the genealogy in vv. 11-14 showing the transition of the same community from family to political structure. It reflects the transition from clan to tribe in which the ''sons of Esau'' acquire the political function of אלופים, ''the title of a political or military leader.'' The word is probably derived from אלף = ''thousand''; one assumes that at the time when the title arose אלף stood for a lesser number (G. E. Mendenhall, JBL 77 [1958] 52-66, ref. Judg. 6:15). The title is used only by the Edomites and Horites (Ex. 15:15), and so it will be an Edomite term. A related word *ulp* with the meaning ''prince,'' ''local leader,'' is found also in Ugaritic. The list, vv. 15-19, shows at once the transition from family to tribal arrangement; it shows at the same time that it did not develop into a fixed form; rather, family relationships are still determinative here. It is only with the kingship in vv. 31-39 that a corresponding new form develops that gives expression to the succession of kings.

[**36:20-28**]   In vv. 20-28 and 29-30 there is once again a genealogy followed by a list of princes, independent of vv. 9-19. The ''sons of Seir the Horite'' now appear with the ''sons of Esau.'' They are called the ''inhabitants of the land''; in the present context this can mean only the original inhabitants when the sons of Esau arrived there. Two strata of inhabitants therefore are to be distinguished from each other (Deut. 2:12-22 speaks of a subjection of the Horites by the Edomites). The name Seir, elsewhere known only as the name of a region, is here a personal name; the inhabitants of ''Seir'' therefore regard him as their ancestor. The previous inhabitants are described as חרי, Horites. It is quite possible that the term refers to them as cave-dwellers (חר = ''cave,'' so most of the older interpreters). In any case the name is to be distinguished from the ethnic name, the Hurrians; the previous inhabitants of Edom have Semitic names (cf. lit. above, pp. 97, 558).

Seven sons of Seir the Horite are listed in vv. 20b,21a; the sons of these follow in vv. 22-27, eighteen in all; only the sons of Lotan are called ''chiefs of the Horites'' in a sort of concluding formula in v. 21b. But the sons in vv. 20-28 are distinguished from the chiefs in vv. 29-30; v. 21b then would be an addition, probably influenced by vv. 15-19. In v. 22b a daughter is added to the sons, Timna, the secondary wife of Eliphaz. V. 24 mentions Anah as one of the sons of Zibeon and knows a story about him: ''. . .he is the Anah who found the 'hot springs' in the wilderness as he. . . .'' This is a telling example of how a narrative grows out of a genealogy. The text את־הימם (talmudic; Luther, ''mule'') has already been read as המים by Jerome, and certainly correctly, when one compares it with 26:19, and especially with 26:32b, ''we have found water''; it is the same experience in the course of an itinerary. The discovery of a source of water was such a significant event that it was narrated long afterwards. This note in v. 24b proves that a very old genealogy, passed on orally, lay behind vv. 20-28. In v. 25 a daughter of Anah, Oholibamah, is named together with a son: this is probably because she was a wife of Esau; hence a link between an Edomite and a Horite woman; likewise in the case of Timna in v. 22.

[**36:29-39**]   In vv. 29-30 (parallel in 1 Chron. 1:43-50) a list of the chiefs of the Horites follows the genealogy of the sons of Seir the Horite (vv. 20-28). They are the same names as those of the sons in vv. 20b, 21a in the sequence of vv. 15-19 and vv. 9-14, and have the same significance as there: family history is succeeded by tribal history.

The account of the succession of kings in Edom (usually called a king list: but the text has not the form of a list) is a valuable document as it is in fact the only historical document in the strict sense in Genesis. It is an account which reports a succession of events: . . .Reigned in Edom (with the name of his city)—died—. . .reigned in his stead. . .(word for word as in 1 Kings 16:22; 2 Kings 1:17; 8:15; 12:22; 13:24). The sequence is repeated eight times; i.e., the reign of eight kings is reported (on the names, cf. articles in BHH). The scheme describes the new form of political power as contrasted with what had preceded: a man (an adult) becomes king over the whole people and remains so until his death. It is not said how the man became king; the account is purely negative; he is not born to the kingship; it is not a dynastic monarchy. It is clear from the first expansion of the scheme that the father of a new king, when he is named (vv. 32, 33, 35, 38), had never himself been king. The second expansion, the mention of the place of residence, says something further about the type of monarchy. It varies from one king to another; this can mean only that each king resided in his own city like Saul, the first king of Israel. These details lead to the conclusion that it is an early form of kingship in which the king (probably elected) has to rely on the support of his own court, property and people (clan). The simple form of the account pattern is suited to this early form of the monarchy, so like the early form in Israel under Saul.

Besides these two expansions which, with exceptions, run right through the sequence, the report contains only the introduction (v. 31), which consists of the heading borrowed from the headings to the genealogies and suitably adapted, "these are the kings who reigned in the land of Edom," and the chronological note (the only one), "before any king ruled in Israel." This sentence cannot mean, as many exegetes understand it, before a king of Israel ruled (over Edom). First, this is scarcely possible grammatically; and second, an early form of the same simultaneous chronology is at hand which was worked out in the king lists in the comparative chronology between Judah and northern Israel. "Old formulas need time to develop. . .. The formulas reflect the actual development of the recording method at the royal courts. . ." (S. R. Bin-Nun [1968], lit. above). V. 31b can have been added only by Israelite transmitters at the court of David or Solomon. A unique expansion is found in v. 35 which reports the victory of King Hadad of Edom over the Midianites in the land of Moab. Its significance lies in the fact that it shows in a very early stage the path from royal chronicle to history writing (as in the books of Kings): as a king is mentioned in the course of the sequence, an important event from his reign is added. This is an exact analogy to the mention of individual events in a genealogical sequence. An example is v. 24, where the account of the discovery of a spring in the prepolitical form of life-style corresponds to the account of a victory in the political form (vv. 31-39).

The royal annals have no formal conclusion. This accords with the historical fact that during the reign of the last king on the list, Hadad II, the only one whose queen is mentioned, Edom was overcome by David (2 Sam. 8:13b-14). When David "put garrisons in Edom" this made an end of the history of the kingdom of Edom. 1 Kings 11:14 says that an adversary rose up against Solomon, Hadad of the royal house in Edom; this is probably an indication of an attempt to build a dynasty in Edom also. This would be in accord with the mention of the queen of Hadad II.

[36:40-43]   Vv. 40-43 are an appendage in the otherwise organically constructed ch. 36. From the point of view of form, it is the standard example of a list: v. 40a is the heading, vv. 40b-43 the simple enumeration of 11 names with the title אלּוּף, v. 43b the caption. Most of the names have already appeared in one of the preceding parts; the new names are Elah (= Elat ?), Pinon (= Punon, Num. 33:42?), Mizbar (= "fortress"), Magdiel (probably a personal name), Iram. The sequence of the 12 names contains throughout personal, place, and regional names. The type of list, mere enumeration, as well as the mixture of names indicates that the list was first drawn up for the Israelite administration of the Edomite territory. 2 Sam. 8:14 says that David set up garrisons in Edom; the list then would designate the areas where they were stationed.

The Names

Ch. 36 contains more than 200 names, 80 without the repetitions. If one subtracts the four regional and ethnic names and the six names of cities, 70 personal names remain, some of which can also be names of places or regions. Seventy names then are gathered together in these genealogies and lists, five of them being the names of women. About one-half of these are unknown to us and do not occur elsewhere. Most of the unknown names are found in vv. 20-28, among the Horites. But these too are Semitic. It cannot be proved with certainty that there are non-Semitic names in ch. 36, though some are suspected.

Personal Names Occurring in Other Places

(a) From preceding chapters of Gen.: Esau, Edom, Seir, Ishmael (16:11; 28:9); Adah (4:19, 20); Elon, father of Adah (26:34; Judg. 12:11f.); Basemath (26:34; daughter of Solomon, 1 Kings 4:15 = "fragrance"?); Nebaioth (25:13, son of Ishmael, also in cuneiform, 28:9); Uz (10:23, mentioned by P under Aram, 22:21).

(b) Names occurring elsewhere or outside the OT: Anah (old Assyr., Akk.); Eliphaz, friend of Job (2:11); Reuel, father-in-law of Moses (Ex. 2:18; Num. 10:29); Korah, a Levitical group (Num. 16); Kenaz, a Judean tribe (Num. 32:12), father of Othniel (Judg. 13); Amalek, name of a people (Ex. 17:8-16); Zerah, son of Judah and Tamar (Gen. 38:30; 46:10-12; and elsewhere); Shammah, David's brother (1 Sam. 16:9), a warrior of David (2 Sam. 23:11); Jeush, son of Rehoboam (2 Chron. 11:19). Kings: Jobab, king of Madon (Josh. 11:1); Hadad (1 Kings 11:14); Saul (Shaul), king of Israel; Achbor, a priest (2 Kings 22:12,14).

(c) Names which could be related to other names: Oholibamah, Oholiab of the tribe of Dan (Ex. 31:6), Oholibah, Oholah (Ezek. 23); Lotan, Lot (Gen. 19; -an a gentilic ending); Heman, Solomon wiser than Heman (1 Kings 5:11 [Eng. 4:31]); Manahath also 1 Chron. 2:52-54, cf. Manoah, father of Samson (Judg. 13:2). Ebal, cf. Mt. Ebal at Shechem; Onam, Onan (Gen. 38:4, 8); Ithran, Jethro (Ex. 3:6); Bilhan, Bilhah (Gen. 30:4f.); Akan, Jaakan (Deut. 10:6); Bela son of Beor, Balaam (Num. 22:5); Alvah, Alvan (36:23); Jetheth (36:40), Jether. Of these 20 names, 10 can be shown to occur elsewhere in the OT, and about 10 to have some connection (in addition, two which are probably different, occur several times in Gen. 36). The number of names known and unknown is about equal. The personal names reflect an extraordinarily broad connection between Israel and Edom; most striking is the overlapping between Judah and Edom. This points to an extensive connection between the southern tribes and Edomite clans and groups. The connection is clear in the case of קְנַז, according to Josh. 15:17; Judg. 1:13; 3:9,11, the father of Othniel and Caleb, groups in northern Edom who had attached themselves to Judah (R. de Vaux, The Early History. . . 11 [1971; Eng. 1978] 534ff.). Three of the four names of the sons of Reuel are found also among the Israelites: Edom, the brother of Israel (J. R. Bartlett, JThS 20 [1969] 1-20).

(d) Different use of the same names: the fact that the names vary, and this is of the essence of the genealogy, means that the same names are used differently. It is possible that the same name was given to different people; this is certainly the explanation of Hadad in 36:35 and 1 Kings 11:14. The same name can be used as a masculine or feminine: Timna, secondary wife of Eliphaz and chief of Esau; Oholibamah, wife of Esau and chief of Esau. Place and ethnic names are used as personal names: Teman, Seir, Edom, Hori, and perhaps the name of the mountain, Ebal. The genealogical setting of names can often vary; the grandfather of Oholibamah is different in vv. 2,14,25; so too with Anah, Amalek, Korah; Uz, a Horite in v. 28, is mentioned under Aram in 10:23 (P).

Names of women: five women are named. Besides the three wives of Esau, there are Timna, the secondary wife of Eliphaz, mentioned again as sister of Lotan, and Mehetabel, wife of Hadad, a queen of Edom (as name of a male, Neh. 6:10). V. 6 speaks of daughters of Esau, but does not give their names. The reason women are mentioned by name so seldom lies in the function of the genealogies: they describe only the main line of descent which is carried on through the sons.

Names of places and regions: the region of Teman (v. 34) is a territory in Edom (north ?), and is known from Amos 1:2; Jer. 49:7, 20; Ezek. 25:13; Job's friend is Eliphaz the Temanite (2:22); on Teman as a personal name (v. 11), cf. R. de Vaux, RB 76 (1969) 379-385. Edom and Seir are likewise used of places and persons. The name Elah is probably the equivalent of the port Elat, and Pinon of Pinum (Num. 33:42f.). There are copper mines in the area, and there is a place called *Feiman* on the eastern side of the Arabah. Mibzar is the name of an unknown fortress. Further, a number of the unknown names will be place-names. Bozrah, one of the principal places in Edom, is named in the king list, also in Amos 1:12; Is. 34:6; Jer. 49:13, 22; so too the region of Teman. The other places—Dinhabah, Avith, Masrekah, Rehoboth ha-Nahar, Pau—are unknown. Mezahab, מֵי זָהָב, could also be a (unknown) place-name. On Dinhabah, cf. S. Mittmann, ZDPV 87 (1971) 92-94; on other place-names, J. Simons, *The Geographical and Topographical Texts in the OT* (1959).

The Formation of the Names

(a) Names of animals: it is striking how often personal names are identical with the names of animals. Zibeon (hyena), Jalam (chamois), Shobal (lion), Dishon (antelope), Zepho (ram), Aiah (hawk, cf. Job 28:7; 2 Sam. 21:8), Achbor (mouse), Anah (wild ass [?]). The influence of totemism suggests itself (W. R. Smith [1880], lit. above; against this, Th. Nöldeke, rev. ZDMG 40 [1886] 148-187), but this is unlikely. Nevertheless, one can point to the genealogy in 25:1-4 where the names of animals are also frequent. And they are by no means rare in Israelite personal names. One can only say that the names of animals point to an early period; accordingly these names are particularly frequent in vv. 20-30. In general, cf. F. S. Bodenheimer, *Animal and Man in Bible Lands* (1960).

(b) Names with the Ending -ān: these are frequent, as in 25:1-6; e.g., in v. 26 all four sons of Dishon, and in v. 27 the three sons of Ezer bear names of this type.

(c) Theophoric names and names of gods: Hadad is certainly a divine name; Hadad is an old Semitic storm god. J. Lewy (RHR 110 [1934] 43) suggests a divine designation in Anah; this has been considered too for other names in ch. 36, e.g., יְעוּשׁ. It is striking that the theophoric personal names as well as the designations for God and the formation of the names correspond exactly to those in Israel. Regarding El and Baal names, the following are formed with El: Eliphaz = "my God conquers [?]," "is gold"; Reuel = "God is companion"; Magdiel = "God is my gift"; Mehetabel = "God confers benefits"; the abbreviated Zerah = "God shines forth." Formed with Baal is Baal-hanan = "the lord has shown favor." Also belonging indirectly to this group is שָׁאוּל = "the petitioner."

All these names express or suggest the praise of God. Each could also have been uttered in Israel (e.g., El-hanan) without any trace of another religion.

Purpose and Thrust

The importance of ch. 36 is that it attests those same three stages in society, reduced to genealogies and lists, which also determine the course of the history of Israel in the historical books of the Old Testament: from the family (vv. 1-5, 6-8, 20-28) through tribal society (vv. 15-19, 29-30, 40-43) to monarchy (vv. 31-39). This plan in three stages is the basis of the chapter and is found also in the complex from Genesis to the books of Kings. In both cases it reflects the actual course of history. Herein lies the historical importance of ch. 36, in face of which the inconsistencies in the individual names are of no great weight. Gen. 36 is important also for the history of transmission in the Old Testament. Only recently has it been acknowledged in all its comprehensiveness that the genealogy is an independent form of tradition from the oral period of transmission with its own history (R. R. Wilson, *Genealogy and History*. . . [1977] 11-55). And only when it is recognized that the genealogies have a function in the life and changes in the prepolitical forms of history, and that the fluidity of names and relationships is rooted in it, can we arrive at criteria for distinguishing between original and secondary (literary constructions) genealogies or parts thereof; this is particularly important for the exegesis of ch. 36.

Isaac Newton and Ibn Ezra had already recognized that the sentence, "before any king ruled in Israel" (v. 31b) could have been written only after the beginning of the monarchy in Israel. This excludes Mosaic authorship. Beyond that, the telescoping of the three stages which determine the structure of the chapter is possible only for one who overlooks this.

The people of Edom are in ch. 36 Israel's next of kin: "You shall not abhor an Edomite, for he is your brother" (Deut. 23:8[7]; likewise Num. 20:14; Amos 1:11). One must bear in mind that Gen. 36 received its final form only late, after P; at this period Edom had often been Israel's enemy. But this does not alter the fact that Esau was Jacob's brother, and that Esau had married Oholibamah the Horite, and Eliphaz, Esau's son, Timna. The family bond across the generations is stronger here than political enmity: fraternity in the Old Testament is not something which merely grows up; it is already there. The Jacob-Esau story deals realistically with conflicts between brothers; but the conflicts cannot alter the fact that they are and remain brothers. The author lays greater weight on the family relationship than on the political.

Linked immediately with this is something surprising in ch. 36. Because Edom remains Israel's brother, Israel retains a lasting interest in Edom's history: "Our information about Edom rests solely on Israelite sources" (G. von Rad). The documents gathered together here would have perished with the royal chancery in Jerusalem had not the historian of Israel preserved his interest. These documents had lost their economic value; but they retained their importance only because the brothers Jacob and Esau were part of Israel's history. Basic historical facts were thereby preserved (synthesized in five points by J. Skinner): we know that the Horites, also a Semitic people, inhabited the land before the arrival of the nomadic Edomites, that they were subjugated by the Edomites, but that they never united with them. We know that the Edomites already had a monarchy 150–200 years before Israel, and we know a lot about the sort of monarchy. Moreover, we know that there were many contacts and links between the inhabitants of northern Edom and Judean tribal groups.

Finally there are surprising elements in the theophoric personal names. Some also occur in Israel; others could be Israelite. The names expressing praise of God express that praise in the same way as do names and the Psalms in Israel. The name of the Edomite king, Shaul, expresses the experience that prayer for a child has been answered, as does the same name of the Israelite king. And even though this is but a tiny excerpt from the religion of the Edomites, it shows nevertheless something common to both.

Conclusion to Genesis 12–36

Literature

Literary Criticism: H. Ewald, *Die Composition der Genesis* (1823). K. H. Graf, *Die geschichtlichen Bücher des AT* (1866); *Die sogenannte Grundschrift des Pentateuch,* AWEAT 1 (1869) 466-477. A. Kayser, *Das vorexilische Buch der Urgeschichte Israels und seine Erweiterungen* (1874). E. Reuss, *La Bible, Traduction nouvelle avec introduction et Commentaire* (1879). G. Wildeboer, *De letterkunde des Ouden Verbonds naar de tijdoorde van haar ontstaan* (1896²). A. Jirku, "Die Keilschrifttexte von Ras Samra und das AT," ZDMG 89 (1935) 372-386. S. A. Cook, *The OT. A Reinterpretation* (1936); *An Introduction to the Bible* (1945; 1951²). R. de Langhe, *Les Textes de Ras Shamra-Ugarit et leurs rapports avec le milieu Biblique de l'AT* (diss. Lovaniensis, 1945/48). O. Eissfeldt, *Die ältesten Traditionen Israels*, BZAW 71 (1950). G. Braulik ed., *Studien zum Pentateuch. W. Kornfeld zum 60. Geb.* (1977). G. Garbini, "L' 'Apocrifo della Genesi' nella letteratura giudaica," AION 37 (1977) 1-18. E. Otto, "Stehen wir vor einem Umbruch in der Pentateuchkritik?" VF 22 (1977) 82-97. R. M. Polzin, *Biblical Structuralism* (1977). N. Lohfink, "Die Priesterschrift und die Geschichte," VT.S 29 (1977) 189-225.

Tradition: C. U. Wolf, "Terminology of Israel's Tribal Organization," JBL 65 (1946) 45-49. R. C. Culley, *Oral Tradition and OT Studies*, Semeia 5 (1976). D. A. Knight, ed., *Tradition and Theology in the OT* (1977). J. M. Miller, "The Patriarchs and Extra-Biblical Sources. A Response," JSOT 2 (1977) 62-66. S. M. Warner, "The Patriarchs and Extra-Biblical Sources," JSOT 2 (1977) 50-61. J. Licht, *Narrative Art in the Bible* (1978). S. M. Warner, "Primitive Saga Men," VT 29 (1979) 325-335.

History: A. Pohl, "Babylonische Urkönige und biblische Erzväter," StZ 85 (1959/60) 421f. H. Tadmor, "The People and the Kingship in Ancient Israel," *Cahiers de l'Hist. Mondiale* 11 (1968) 46-68. N. K. Gottwald, "Were the Early Israelites Pastoral Nomads?" *Essay in Hon. of J. Muilenburg* (1974) 223-255. N. Weeks, "Mari, Nuzi and the Patriarchs," AbrN 16 (1975/76) 73-82.

Religion: P. Radin, *Gott und Mensch in der primitiven Welt* (1953). L. H. Vincent, "Un sanctuaire dans la région de Jéricho," RB 68 (1961) 161-177. N. K. Gottwald, "Biblical Theology or Biblical Sociology," *Radical Religion* 2 (1975) 46-57. P. Buis, La Notion de l'Alliance dans l'AT," *Lectio Divina* 88 (1976). M. Görg, "Anfänge israelitischen Gottesglaubens," *Kairos* 18 (1976) 256-264. J. W. Rogerson, *Anthropology and the OT* (1978). L. Ruppert, "Erhöhungsvorstellungen im AT," BZ 22 (1978) 199-220. C. Westermann, *The Elements of Old Testament Theology* (1978; Eng. 1982). W. Brueggemann, "Trajectories in OT Literature and the Sociology of Ancient Israel," JBL 98 (1979) 161-185. H. Ringgren, *Die Religionen des Alten Orients im Umkreis Israels* (1979).

1. Concluding Remarks on the Origins of the Patriarchal Story

A. The Oral Stage of the Transmission

The exegesis of Gen. 12–36 has shown that the oral tradition lying behind the written text that has come down to us is richer and more varied than hitherto thought. At times the narratives transmitted are the result of several narratives shaped into one, at times a single motif hints at a more extensive narrative. It has been shown further that the oral reports in the form of genealogy and itinerary are an essential constitutive part of the patriarchal story. Their relationship to the narrative can vary; they can be separated from one another or from a complete unit. A narrative can grow out of an itinerary or genealogy (indicated in but a sentence); the narratives in turn can be reduced to genealogy. P and the Chronicler demonstrate two steps in this process.

B. The Written Stage of the Transmission

The interpretation given here, over against the view of the classical source theory, shows that the patriarchal story as transmitted is considerably more unified than previously thought. There is a synthesis of only two works in Gen. 12–36, J and P. The Yahwistic work has a richly developed and many-faceted prehistory and subsequent history; but there are many more unities in chs. 12–36 than hitherto accepted.

I. The Yahwist in Gen. 12–36.

The purpose of the Yahwist is to give expression in the author's time to the narratives and reports from the patriarchal period by arranging them in a coherent story about the fathers; thereby the history of the ancestors of the people of Israel is presented in the two parts according to those two relationships which are determinative of life and family, parents-children and brother-brother. One line, chs. 12–25, traces itself from the barrenness of Abraham's wife (11:30) to the birth of a son (21:1-7); the other, chs. 25–36, from the deception over the blessing (ch. 27) to the reconciliation (ch. 33). There are in addition a number of other events which happened to Abraham, Isaac, and Jacob. The whole, comprising the two parts, reveals a planned structure with a purpose; it is the work of a writer who is at the same time a transmitter, a storyteller, and a theologian. H. Gunkel's term "collector" describes the author inadequately; even less adequate are the earlier designations of "source" or "document." One can observe J's method from the way in which J arranges the whole out of the available structural elements: individual narratives are characteristic of chs. 12–25, while the overall context (flight—return) is more marked in chs. 25–36. J takes over with little alteration narratives passed on orally; he forges narrative links and shapes into narrative regular, ritual, or institutional events; finally, and quite independently, he forms episodes and transition pieces. But the Yahwist is at the same time a theologian. While giving the account of the patriarchs, he tells of the action and word of God because this is inseparable from their life. Both are so interlocked that J can present only what he wants to say about God as an interchange between God and the patriarchs. It is possible therefore that J is referring to the action of God without expressly mentioning God, e.g., 19:27-28.

II. The question of the Elohist in Gen. 12–36.
a. E in chs. 12–25. The framework that R has provided, 11:27-32 and 21:1-7,

shows that the texts generally attributed to E do not occur within this redactional span, but only in the additions which follow it. The fact that they are additional pieces is of itself sufficient argument against their presenting a tradition parallel to J. Moreover, these texts are too different from each other to be the work of one and the same author, nor do they show any sign of an overall, independent conception of the Abraham story.

b. E in chs. 25–36. The question of E in chs. 25–36 is in essence the question of the overall plan which directs the Jacob-Esau story. J's plan is clearly discernible in the three cycles 27–33; 29–31; 29:31—30:24. One must be able to demonstrate a corresponding plan for E. This has not succeeded so far even in outline. The few fragments to be found in chs. 25–36 do not permit the reconstruction of a whole, and more, E is entirely missing in the two chapters (27 and 33) in which J's blueprint is moored. The source-critical observation that some texts in chs. 25–36 have several layers is relevant. But a better explanation is that each of these is an elaboration that has its own reason and meaning, as has been shown in the exegesis.

III. The priestly writing in Gen. 12–36.

P contains an independent patriarchal story (with divergence in detail, P. Weimar, ZAW 86 [1974] 174-203), differing from J's in that mere genealogical data, to which the story had been broadly reduced, have taken the place of the many detailed narratives and narrative groups. The reason for this is that in J the God-relationship extends to all community forms, whereas in P it is focussed on the cultic community. Despite this, the P texts in chs. 12–36 reveal a whole with a discernible plan consisting of the Abraham and Jacob-Esau stories. The two parts are parallel in structure inasmuch as there is a revelatory address in the middle of each (17; 35:6, 9-13) in which Abraham and Jacob receive a promise and a new name; and there is added to each a narrative elaboration of a piece of genealogical information: 23 (burial); 27:46—28:9 (marriage). A literary plan is also clear in the genealogical and itinerary data.

The genealogical data trace the life of Abraham and the sons of Isaac from birth to death. Abraham's life story falls under the heading of the *toledot* of Terah (11:27). There is no *toledot* heading for Abraham because there is no account of the life story of Isaac (only 25:11ab, 20, 26b; 35:28f.). The life story of Jacob and Esau falls under the heading of the *toledot* of Isaac. The data given under these *toledot* present in full the life stories of Abraham, Jacob, and Esau. Here too one can discern a literary hand at work. The same literary activity, reducing the migrations of the patriarchs to a few journeys, can also be seen in the itineraries. The patriarchal nomadic life-style is here but a distant echo; there are no longer migrations from place to place in accordance with the demands of the life-style of small-cattle nomads, but journeys from a particular starting point to a goal. P thereby gives the traditional itinerary form a theological significance: it now serves to mark off the land of promise as the land of revelation to the patriarchs (17; 35) from foreign parts. Terah and Abraham come from foreign parts, Jacob returns to the land of promise and stays there, while Esau in turn goes to foreign parts.

In addition to the genealogical and itinerary material there are two groups of narrative texts, namely, the two expansions of genealogical data (23; 27:46—28:9) and two divine oracles (17; 35:6, 9-13); the two latter, distributed in parallel fashion through chs. 12–25 and 25–36, are the only self-contained narratives independent of genealogy and itinerary. In J the divine speech is varied and multiform; in P the divine oracle to the patriarchs is virtually identical with the promise. Though in the promises P adheres in essence to previous tradition, nevertheless he contributes something new and unique by linking the promise with the command of circumcision (ch. 17). This has its counterpart in the two narrative expansions of the genealogical data (chs. 23; 27–28). By means of these three texts P is expressing the significance of the patriarchal stories for his own time. They are the basis of the precultic rites which are concerned with the maintenance and continuance of the family. During and after the exile the family is again the most important bearer of the tradition of the people. The precultic rites which grew out of the patriarchal story are thereby firmly linked with the cultic law. P is not only a transmitter, but also a theological writer who reshapes the patriarchal traditions coming down to him so as to make them speak to his time. He thus draws a line of demarcation between the foreign religions of Abraham's forefathers and the revelation made to Abraham, while stressing at the same time that the family of Abraham belongs to a greater whole (especially chs. 25 and 36), thereby pointing back to the primeval story.

IV. The Redactor in Gen. 12–36.

The continuous text of chs. 12–36 as it has come down to us is to be traced to a redactor. It was this person's task to fashion a continuous narrative out of the existing J and P writings, the same task as he had for Gen. 1–11 (see *Genesis 1–11*, p.600). R's hand can be seen above all in the introductions and conclusions which he constructed, in 11:27-32 and 21:1-7 for chs. 12–25, and in 25:19-28 and 35:1-23 for chs. 25–36. R has formed one single patriarchal story out of the two independent patriarchal stories at hand to him, J and P, and R's work can be seen in these introductory and concluding passages where he has in each case constructed a unified text consisting of elements from J and P. These passages at the beginning and the end impress on the whole a unifying stamp. R was able to weave the J and P texts together in such a way as to leave them essentially intact. R could do this because J consisted mainly of narratives and P mainly of genealogies. The work of the redactor consisted, not as classical source criticism understood it earlier, namely, in arranging mechanically a succession of small and tiny fragments out of a number of "sources," but rather in fashioning the two works that lay before him into one, while allowing each to speak for itself. R achieved this with scarcely any alteration of the wording and by leaving the textual unity undisturbed.

But it was not R who created the end product that now lies before us. The process of transmission that led to this stage continued with additions and elaborations of different kinds (cf. those enumerated after comm. on 25:1-18, "The Abraham Story in Retrospect," I, "On the Transmission of Gen. 12–25"; §2). The narrative cohesion in chs. 25–36 is so tight that it was transmitted as a closed unit. Subsequent appendages are but marginal, as Isaac (ch. 26) and Dinah (ch. 34). There are a number of small, individual additions, signs of the path the tradition followed.

The Theological Significance of R's Work.   While making sure to preserve the layers of growth of the patriarchal story, R also preserves the relationship to God manifest in these same layers. R leaves side by side what J and P say about God, preserving beyond that the threefold layer that derives from the preliterary layers (fathers—tribes—peoples). R was aware of the way in which talk about God and relationship to God was sketched in the texts; R affirms this with its contrasts and changes.

2. Concluding Remarks on the Patriarchal Stories

A. The Patriarchs as Persons

Both parts of the patriarchal story are concerned with prehistorical, prepolitical, precultic existence in both their vertical (succession of generations) and horizontal (coexistence) dimensions. Abraham is portrayed as one face to face with those elemental dangers which threaten survival itself: threats from nature, the wife's barrenness, hunger and thirst, threats from humans, and trials sent by God. All is set within the life-style of the small-cattle nomads on the move who go their way in constant danger without economic or political security. The stories about Jacob and Esau portray brothers living a life in common in which the sharing itself must lead to and be endangered by conflicts. However, both the elemental threats on the one hand and the conflicts on the other are experienced vis-à-vis God and have God as their point of reference. The conflicts in the Abraham story are for the most part of a familiar kind. In the Jacob-Esau story they broaden from the family (brothers) into the economic and social domain (institution) and to the very brink of war. Family conflict gives rise to the power struggle where the concern is private interest, gain, and possession. This gradual snowballing leads to the situation in which the prophets later raised their social accusation. There is an obvious bias in the narratives which gives precedence to peaceful coexistence. The conflict between Jacob and Laban, as that between Jacob and Esau, almost ends in war; but on each occasion there emerges a peaceful solution by means of a contract or reconciliation. This bias towards peace J sees as an inheritance from the patriarchal period in an era in which war is the order. J's theological base is that blessing and peace belong together. One can see here an early suggestion that reaches its clearest expression in the promise of a king of peace in the later period of Israel. It is in still clearer contrast to Gen. 34 where war and blood vengeance begin. The same bias is obvious in the relationship to the peoples: the patriarchal clans are prepolitical forms of community and so are still unaware of any enmity towards people with whom they come in contact in the course of life. The relationship to the Canaanites is peaceful throughout (with the exception of ch. 34); Ishmael as a son of Abraham is also an heir of the blessing; Esau remains the brother of Jacob. The genealogies show that the family connection is more important for the tradition than the later enmity. J gathers together these and like indices in the promise of blessing which he formulates for the peoples in 12:3; but this blessing has its limits, as God's judgment shows (19:27-28). The God of Abraham is the God who blesses and saves even the nations. The accounts of birth and death at the end of the patriarchal story, ch. 35, with the steady rhythm of birth and death, bring the succession of the generations of the patriarchs back to the primeval story to which Abraham's ancestors belong.

The patriarchal stories, set between the story of humanity in Gen. 1–11 and the story of a specific people in Exodus–Numbers, are saying that there is no human existence without the vertical and horizontal dimensions, that is, the succession of generations and community belonging within the narrow circle of the commonplace. It is far removed from these stories to glorify the family or to idealize family relationships; the figures of the patriarchal stories are neither heroes nor models. The variety of ways in which these two basic dimensions of human existence unfold points all the more urgently to the significance of their position in the succession from parents to children and to the smallest commonplace community unit, which includes conflicts as well as responsibility.

B. The Religion of the Patriarchs: Concluding Remarks

It has become obvious that the relationship to God that corresponds to the title, ''God of the Fathers,'' is of necessity bound up with the persons who are the subject of the patriarchal stories and their forms of community. The religion of these communities, structured on family lines, is notably different from that of the people of Israel. It is characterized by a personal relationship to God which corresponds in every single detail with the life-style of the patriarchs as they move to and fro and live together as members of a family. God shows them the way, orders them to depart or to stay, is with them on the way just as God has promised. There are altars and memorial stones along the route which recall their worship and encounter with God as they move.

The patriarchal community draws its life from the blessing; it is due to God's blessing that children are born and grow up, that work is crowned with productive growth and expansion, that watering places are found and preserved, that the labor of the herdsmen is fruitful. What is peculiar to the Abraham story is that in the anguish of childlessness the child is promised and the blessing is linked with the promise; what is peculiar to the Jacob-Esau story is that the father's blessing becomes the occasion of the conflict between the brothers, that at the climax of this conflict pardon accompanies God's blessing, a pardon that presupposes the confession of guilt before the brother and the giving back of the ברכה. The blessing is not conditional, as it is in Deut., nor is the promise (except in late passages that presuppose Deut., Gen. 22:15-18; 26:3-5). Blessing is never counterbalanced by curse (as in Deut. 28), promise never by the announcement of judgment; as far as the patriarchs are concerned, God's judgment and punishment are almost entirely absent. There emerges one characteristic which links the patriarchal stories with the later religion of Israel: God intervenes in a special way for the weak, the disadvantaged, the outcast (chs. 12; 16; 21; 32).

All the narratives in chs. 12–36 show that the patriarchs deal always with but one God. Even if one cannot speak of a philosophical monotheism in the case of the religion of the patriarchs, there is yet no trace of the polytheistic influence from the surrounding world in any of these narratives. It is due to this alone that the patriarchal stories became part of the Pentateuch, part of the Bible. What later became the first commandment and confession of the religion of Israel (Deut. 6:4) is present here without command or confessional formula: It is *one* God who deals with and speaks to Abraham, Isaac, and Jacob, their wives and children. It is *one* God whom they invoke and in whom they trust. It is this presupposition alone that renders J's overall plan possible: J presents the history of the people as a coherent story in three stages from the patriarchs, through Moses and the wandering in the desert, up to the settlement of the people.

Prayer and worship. Prayer is taken for granted in the patriarchal stories as a constitutive part of one's relationship to God. There are short, simple cries to God in the form of praise, lament, or petition arising out of those situations in life that make them appropriate, e.g., the lament of Abraham (15:2-3) or Rebekah

(25:22), or Jacob's petition to be saved (32:12). The narrative of the wooing of Rebekah is completely shot through with prayer (ch. 24). After the experience of God's saving action, praise is expressed and preserved in the name given: the child is named "God hears" in ch. 16, the mountain, "God sees [makes himself seen]" in ch. 22, a well, "expansion" in ch. 26. What appears later as the Psalm motif of praise together ("praise with me") and the call to praise is already there in germ in the name giving.

The most significant element in worship in the patriarchal stories is the absence of an institutional cult and the cult mediator; the action or talk between God and the person takes place directly. But over and above this one can glean many traces of a history of worship. There is the gradual but clearly traced path from nature's holy places to those made by humans. There is also the gradual transition from the religious celebrations of the wandering small-cattle nomads (the building of an altar as they stop on route) to the encounter with the shrine of the sedentaries, the one at the beginning, the other at the end. One can detect here a certain parallel between Gen. 28 and Ex. 19. The patriarchal stories are not yet aware of the holiness of God; the idea of קדש is not found. But one perceives how it became possible to come to terms with the idea in the context of the setting apart of the holy place. The narratives reflect different notions of the relationship of the divinity to the shrine. In their broader perspective their purpose is to ground religious institutions of the later, sedentary period in the patriarchal period (14:18-20; 28:20-22).

The simple language in which God is addressed or spoken of corresponds to the immediacy of the relationship to God. There is still no specifically theological language, and in this there is a certain nearness to the synoptic Gospels of the New Testament. What is determinative is what happens between God and the person; theological reflection has scarcely any influence on the language. One must distinguish between the simple narratives from the patriarchal period and the subsequent narratives which are the fruit of theological reflection. It is only on this later level that theological concepts such as trial (ch. 22), faith (15:6), human justice (16:6) and God's justice (18:16-33) receive their significance. These subsequent narratives belong to later adaptations which presuppose the patriarchal period but reshape it by reflection; add to these a number of appendages and supplements.

One can discern a theological bias in a number of narratives. It is no longer enough to speak of God where the context demands; rather must God's intervention be registered and underscored, e.g., ch. 24; 29:31—30:24, and in the supplements of chs. 29–33. A later bias is to exalt the patriarchal figures above the ordinary run of people: P has dropped all negative traits; in ch. 14 Abraham is put on one level with the heroes of the period of the Judges, on another with the vanquishers of kings; in 15:1-6 he is reckoned as just because of his faith, in ch. 17 he becomes the founder of God's covenant with Israel. This exaltation of Abraham continues to grow in later history.

C. The Patriarchal Story in the Pentateuch and in the Old Testament

The Pentateuch is arranged so that its central part, Exodus–Numbers, determined by God's saving act, is framed by God's blessing at work in the human race in Gen. 1–11, in the people now settled in the land in Deut., in the family in Gen. 12–36. Chs. 12–36 form the link between the universal and the historically directed aspect of the blessing. This corresponds to the importance of the family in the period between the story of the human race and the story of the nations. The patriarchal story is linked with the Old Testament as a whole through the promises. The promises made to and fulfilled in the patriarchs themselves are extended in promises which refer to the history of the tribes and then of the people of Israel, particularly those concerned with increase and the possession of the land. The programmatic promise of 12:1-3 extends beyond to the nations of the world. The promises, therefore, make the patriarchal story an indispensable component of the rest of the Old Testament; their fulfillment proceeds step by step through the history of the people of God and, in the promises to the nations, recurring again in Deutero-Isaiah, postexilic prophecy, and apocalyptic, points beyond this history. The promises to the patriarchs become a link between the Old Testament and the New Testament in all three circles of addressees. The same is true for the covenant; the original meaning of ברית is a solemn, binding obligation and it is used in this sense to designate God's promise to Abraham in Gen. 15. In Gen. 17 its meaning is extended to a reciprocal obligation, the "covenant." This is the meaning of the promise of the "new covenant" in Jer. 31:31-34; it is taken up in this sense in the New Testament and used to describe both the old and the new covenant.

3. The Later History of the Patriarchal Tradition

The patriarchal period is followed by the liberation from Egypt, the march through the desert, and the settlement in Canaan with the struggles of the period of the judges. Other forms of community now acquire a determinative significance. The patriarchal traditions, however, continue to live on in the families from generation to generation. This is clear from the passages where they come to life again as occasion demands. At the beginning of the monarchy the family acquires a fresh significance for the people as a whole in the royal dynasty: the royal family shares in the kingship (on the Davidic succession cf. Fests. G. von Rad [1971] 611-619). The patriarchal traditions came to the surface again when the state is under threat and collapses. Deutero-Isaiah speaks of Abraham and Sarah; in exile the family once more becomes the bearer of tradition guaranteeing the continuity of Israel, as the priestly writing and the book of Tobit show.

The book of Ruth is evidence that the genre of patriarchal stories continued to live among the people. It is as a whole a family narrative and deals with the survival of an apparently extinct branch of a family; it concludes with the birth of a child, as does Gen. 21, and begins with a famine, as does Gen. 12. Here too narratives and genealogies are found together. The framework of the book of Job is also a family narrative containing a series of motifs corresponding to the patriarchal stories. The patriarchal figures continue to live on through the Old Testament, and even more strikingly in the New. A difference between Abraham and Jacob attests that the stories about them live on with them: Abraham had an extensive and profound subsequent history, but Jacob not to the same extent; Abraham is the father, Jacob not in the same way. Jacob and Israel were used side by side as a designation for the people of Israel; the prophets can direct accusations against "Jacob," but not against Abraham. Finally, a further survival of an element of the patriarchal stories appears when the New Testament describes the disciples of Jesus as brothers.

Abbreviations

The abbreviations, with very few exceptions, follow S. Schwertner, *Internationales Abkürzungsverzeichnis für Theologie und Grenzgebiete* (Berlin/New York: de Gruyter, 1974).

ÄA	*Äegyptologische Abhandlungen*. Wiesbaden
AAB	*Annuaire de l'Académie r. de Belgique*. Brussels
AAF	*Archives de l'Art Français*. Paris
AAJR or TS.AAJR	*Texts and Studies*. American Academy for Jewish Research. New York
AANL	*Atti dell'Accademia Nazionale dei Lincei*. Rome
AAOJ	*American Antiquarian and Oriental Journal*. Chicago
AASOR	*Annual of the American Schools of Oriental Research*. Philadelphia
AAWW.PH.	*Anzeiger der (k.) Akademie der Wissenschaften in Wien*. Vienna
AB	*Assyriologische Bibliothek*. Leipzig
ABG	*Archiv für Begriffsgeschichte*. Münster
ABR	*Australian Biblical Review*. Melbourne
AbrN	*Abr-Nahrain*. Leiden
AcOrK	*Acta Orientalia*. Copenhagen
ACQ	*American Church Quarterly*. Pelham, N.Y.
ACR	*Australasian Catholic Record*. Manly, N.S.W.
ADAJ	*Annual of the Department of Antiquities of Jordan*. Amman
AEcR	*American Ecclesiastical Review*. Washington
AESoc	*Archives Européennes de Sociologie*.
AFLNW	*(Veröffentlichungen der) Arbeitsgemeinschaft für Forschung des Landes Nordrhein-Westfalen*. Cologne/Opladen
AfO	*Archiv für Orientforschung*. Graz
AHDO	*Archives d'Histoire du Droit Oriental*. Brussels
AION	*Annali del'Istituto Universitario Orientale di Napoli*. Naples
AJA	*American Journal of Archaeology*. Princeton, N.J.
AJBA	*Australian Journal of Biblical Archaeology*. Sydney
AJSL	*American Journal of Semitic Languages and Literatures*. Chicago

AJT	*American Journal of Theology.* Chicago
AKG	*Arbeiten zur Kirchengeschichte.* Berlin
AKM	*Abhandlungen für die Kunde des Morgenlandes.* Leipzig
ALBO	*Analecta Lovaniensia Biblica et Orientalia.* Louvain
ALGM	*Ausführliches Lexicon der griechischen und römischen Mythologie.* Wilhelm Heinrich Roscher, ed. Leipzig
Altertum	*Altertum.* Berlin
ALUOS	*Annual of Leeds University Oriental Society.* Leiden
AmA	*American Anthropologist.* Menasha, Wis.
AmPhAssTr/Pr	*American Philological Association Transactions and Proceedings.* Ithaca N.Y.
AnBib	*Analecta Biblica.* Rome
AncB	*Anchor Bible.* New York
ANET	*Ancient Near Eastern Texts Relating to the Old Testament.* J. B. Pritchard, ed.
Ang.	*Angelicum.* Rome
AnSt	*Anatolian Studies.* London
Antaios	*Antaios*
Anthr.	*Anthropos.* Freibourg (Switz.)
Anton.	*Antonianum.* Rome
ANVAO	*Avhandlinger i Norske Videnskaps-Akademi i Oslo.*
AO	*Der alte Orient.* Leipzig
AOAT	*Alter Orient und Altes Testament.* Kevelaer
AOB	*Altorientalische Bilder zum Alten Testament.* Tübingen
AOH	*Acta Orientalia Academiae Scientiarum Hungaricae.* Budapest
AOS	*American Oriental Series.* New Haven, Conn.
AOT	*Altorientalische Texte zum Alten Testament.* Tübingen 1909, 1926^2
APPP	*Abhandlungen zur Philosophie, Psychologie und Pädagogik.* Bonn
ArOr	*Archiv Orientální.* Prague
ArtAs	*Artibus Asiae.* Ascona
ARW	*Archiv für Religionswissenschaft.* Leipzig
AS	*Assyriological Studies.* Chicago
ASAE	*Annales du Service des Antiquités de l'Égypte.* Cairo
AsR	*Asian Review.* London
AsSt	*Asiatische Studien.* Bern
AStE	*Annuario di Studi Ebraici.* Rome
ASTI	*Annual of the Swedish Theological Institute (in Jerusalem).* Leiden
ATA	*Alttestamentliche Abhandlungen.* Munich
AThANT	*Abhandlungen zur Theologie des Alten u. Neuen Testament.* Zürich
AThR	*Anglican Theological Review.* New York
Aug.	*Augustinianum.* Rome
AUM	*Andrews University Monographs.*
AUSS	*Andrews University Seminary Studies.* Berrien Springs, Mich.
AVTRW	*Aufsätze und Vorträge zur Theologie und Religionswissenschaft.* Berlin
AWEAT	*Archiv für wissenschaftliche Erforschung des Alten Testaments.* Halle
AWR	*Aus der Welt der Religion.* Giessen
AzTh	*Arbeiten zur Theologie.* Stuttgart

Abbreviations

BA	*Biblical Archaeologist*. New Haven, Conn.
Bab.	*Babyloniaca*. Paris
BAR	*Biblical Archaeology Review*.
BASOR	*Bulletin of the American Schools of Oriental Research*. New Haven, Conn.
BASS	*Beiträge zur Assyriologie und semitischen Sprachwissenschaft*. Leipzig
BBB	*Bonner biblische Beiträge*. Bonn
BCPE	*Bulletin du Centre Protestant d'Études*.
BCSBS	*Bulletin of the Canadian Society of Biblical Studies*. Toronto
BEHJ	*Bulletin des Études Historiques Juives*.
Bell	*Belleten*. Ankara
BenM	*Benediktinische Monatsschrift*. Beuron
BeO	*Bibbia e Oriente*. Milan
BetM	*Bet(h) Mikra*. Jerusalem
BEvTh	*Beiträge zur evangelische Theologie*. Munich
BEThL	*Bibliotheca Ephemeridum Theologicarum Loveniensium*. Louvain
BFA	*Bulletin of the Faculty of Arts*. Cairo
BFDSEUA	*Bibliothèque de la Faculté de Droit et de Sciences Économiques de l'Université d'Algier*.
BFPUL	*Bibliothèque de la Faculté de Philosophie et Lettres de l'Université de Liège*.
BHH	*Biblisch-historisches Handwörterbuch*. Göttingen
BHR	*Bibliothèque d'humanisme et Renaissance*. Geneva
BHTh	*Beiträge zur historischen Theologie*. Tübingen
Bib	*Biblica*. Rome
BibB	*Biblische Beiträge*. Einsiedeln
BiblOr	*Bibliothèque orientale*. Paris
BibOr	*Biblica et Orientalia*. Rome
BibSac *or* BSTR	*Bibliotheca Sacra and Theological Review*. Andover, Mass.
Bijdr.	*Bijdragen. Tijdschrift voor Philosophie et Theologie*. Nijmegen
BiKi	*Bibel und Kirche*. Stuttgart
BiLe	*Bibel und Leben*. Düsseldorf
BiLi	*Bibel und Liturgie*. Klosterneuberg b. Wien
BiNot	*Biblische Notizen*. Bamberg
BiR	*Biblical Research*. Chicago
BiTod	*Bible Today*. Collegeville, Minn.
BiTr	*Bible Translator*. London
BJRL	*Bulletin of the John Rylands Library*. Manchester
BLR	*Bodleian Library Record*. Oxford
BRL	*Biblisches Reallexikon*. K. Galling, ed. Tübingen
BrSynt	C. Brockelmann, *Hebräische Syntax* (1956).
BSHT	*Breslauer Studien zur historischen Theologie*. Breslau
BSOAS	*Bulletin of the School of Oriental and African Studies*. London
BSt	*Biblische Studien*. Neukirchen
BThB	*Biblical Theology Bulletin*. Rome
BTS	*Bible et Terre Sainte*. Paris
Burg	*Burgense*. Burgos
BVC	*Bible et Vie Chrétienne*. Paris
BW	*Biblical World*. Chicago
BWANT	*Beiträge zur Wissenschaft vom Alten Testament*. Stuttgart
BZ	*Biblische Zeitschrift*. Paderborn

BZAW	*Beihefte zur Zeitschrift für die alttestamentliche Wissenschaft*. Berlin
BZfr	*Biblische Zeitfragen*. Münster
BZNW	*Beihefte zur Zeitschrift für die neutestamentliche Wissenschaft*. Berlin
CAB	*Cahiers d'Archéologie Biblique*. Neuchatel
CAH	*Cambridge Ancient History*. Cambridge
Cath.	*Catholicisme*. Paris
CBC	*Cambridge Bible Commentary*. Cambridge
CBG	*Collationes Brugenses et Gandavenses*. Ghent
CBQ	*Catholic Biblical Quarterly*. Washington
CBQMS	*Catholic Biblical Quarterly Monograph Series*.
CBrug	*Collationes Brugenses*. Bruges
CCUL	*Congrès et Colloques de l'Université de Liège*. Liège
CD	*Church Dogmatics* I/1—IV/4, Karl Barth (1936-1969).
CEg	*Chronique d'Égypte*. Brussells
CHEg	*Cahiers d'Histoire Égyptienne*. Cairo
CHM	*Cahiers d'Historie Mondiale*. Paris
Christus	*Christus: Cahiers Spirituels*. Paris
ChrTo	*Christianity Today*. Washington
ChW	*Christliche Welt*. Gotha
CiFe	*Ciencia y Fe*. Buenos Aires
CivCatt	*Civiltà Cattolica*. Rome
CJT. (SR)	*Canadian Journal of Theology*. Toronto
CleR	*Clergy Review*. London
CM	*Classica et Mediaevalia*. Copenhagen
CMech	*Collectanea Mechliniensia*. Malines
CNFI	*Christian News from Israel*. Jerusalem
Conc	*Concilium*. London & N.Y.
ConQ	*Congregational Quarterly*. London
CoTh	*Collectanea Theologica*. Warsaw
CPH	*Calwer Predigthilfen*. Stuttgart
CQ	*Classical Quarterly*. London
CQR	*Church Quarterly Review*. London
CRAIBL	*Comptes Rendus de l'Academie des Inscriptions et Belles-Lettres*. Paris
CRB	*Cahiers de la Revue Biblique*. Paris
CThM	*Calwer Theologische Monographien*. Stuttgart
CTJ	*Calvin Theological Journal*. Grand Rapids, Mich.
CTM	*Concordia Theological Monthly*. St. Louis, Mo.
CTom	*Ciencia Tomista*. Salamanca
CuBi	*Cultura Biblica*. Madrid
CuW	*Christentum und Wissenshaft*. Leipzig
CV	*Communio Viatorum*. Prague
CWH	*Calwer Hefte zur Förderung biblischen Glaubens und christlichen Lebens*. Stuttgart
DB(H)	*Dictionary of the Bible*. James Hastings, ed. Edinburgh
DBS	*Dictionnaire de la Bible. Supplément*. Paris
DB(V)	*Dictionnaire de la Bible*. F. Vigouroux, ed. Paris
DLZ	*Deutsche Literaturzeitung*. Berlin
DMOA	*Documenta et Monumenta Orientis Antiqui*. Leiden
DTh or ThR	*Deutsche Theologie*. Stuttgart
DThC	*Dictionnaire de Théologie Catholique*. Paris
DTT	*Dansk Teologisk Tidsskrift*. Copenhagen
DVfLG	*Deutsche Vierteljahrsschrift für Literaturwissenschaft und*

Abbreviations

	Geistesgeschichte. Halle
DViv	*Dieu Vivant*. Paris
EB(B)	*Encyclopaedia Biblica*. Ed. Institutum Bialik et Museum Antiquitatum Iudaicarum. Jerusalem
EBrit	*Encyclopaedia Britannica*. Edinburgh
EC	*Enciclopedia Cattolica*. Vatican City
EHPhr	*Études d'Histoire et de Philosophie Religieuses*. Paris
EHS.T	*Europäische Hochschulschriften. Reihe 23. Theologie.*
EKL	*Evangelisches Kirchenlexicon*. Göttingen
ELKZ	*Evangelisch-lutherische Kirchenzeitung*. Munich
Encounter	*Encounter*. Indianapolis, Ind.
EPAPS	*Early Proceedings of the American Philosophical Society*. Philadelphia
Er	*Eranos*. Uppsala
ERE	*Encyclopaedia of Religion and Ethics*. James Hastings, ed. Edinburgh
ErIs	*Eretz-Israel*. Jerusalem
ErJb	*Eranos-Jahrbuch*. Zürich
EstB	*Estudios Bíblicos*. Madrid
EstEcc	*Estudios eccliásticos*. Madrid
Estfr	*Estudios Franciscanos*. Barcelona-Sarriá
ET	*Expository Times*. Edinburgh
EtCl	*Études Classiques*. Namur
EThL	*Ephemerides Theologicae Lovanienses*. Louvain
ETR	*Études Théologiques et Religieuses*. Montpellier
EvErz	*Evangelische Erziehung*. Frankfurt
EvQ	*Evangelical Quarterly*. London
EvTh	*Evangelische Theologie*. Munich
ExBib	*Exempla Biblica*. Göttingen
Exp.	*Expositor*. London
FF	*Frate Francesco*. Parma
FFC	*Folklore Fellows Communications*. London
FMSt	*Frühmittelalterliche Studien*. Berlin
Folkl.	*Folklore*. London
FRLANT	*Forschungen zur Religion und Literatur des Alten und Neuen Testaments*. Göttingen
FTS	*Frankfurter theologische Studien*. Frankfurt
FuH	*Fuldaer Hefte*. Berlin
GBT	*Ghana Bulletin of Theology*. Accra
Ges-K	*Gesenius' Hebrew Grammar*. E. Kautzsch, ed. (Eng. trans. from 28th German ed. by A. E. Cowley, 1910[2])
GIT	*Gereformeerd Interfacultaer Tijdschrift*. Aalten
GlDei	*Gloria Dei*. Graz
GordR	*Gordon Review*. Boston
Gr.	*Gregorianum*. Rome
GSAI	*Giornale della Società Asiatica Italiana*. Florence
GThT	*Gereformeerd Theologische Tijdschrift*. Aalten
GuW	*Glaube und Wissen*. Munich
HDM	*Handwörterbuch des deutschen Märchens*. Berlin
Hebr.	*Hebraica*. Chicago
HeyJ	*Heythrop Journal*. Oxford
HibJ	*Hibbert Journal*. London
HJ	*Historisches Jahrbuch der Görres-Gesellschaft*. Munich
HK	*Handkommentar zum Alten Testament*. Göttingen
HLa	*Heilig Land*. Nijmegen

HLW	*Handbuch der Literaturwissenschaft*. Potsdam
HO	*Handbuch der Orientalisk*. Leiden
Hokhma(h)	*Revue de Réflexion Théologique*. Lausanne
HomR	*Homiletic Review*. New York
HSM	*Harvard Semitic Monographs*. Cambridge, Mass.
HSS	*Harvard Semitic Series*. Cambridge, Mass.
HT	*History Today*. London
HTh	*History and Theory*. La Haye
HThG	*Handbuch theologischer Grundbegriffe*. Munich
HThR	*Harvard Theological Review*. Cambridge, Mass.
HTS	*Hervormde Teologiese Studies*. Pretoria
HUCA	*Hebrew Union College Annual*. Cincinnati
IAE	*Internationales Archiv für Ethnographie*. Leiden
IB	*Interpreter's Bible*. New York
IDB	*Interpreter's Dictionary of the Bible*. New York
IJT	*Indian Journal of Theology*. Serampore
Interp.	*Interpretation*. Richmond, Va.
Intr.B	*Introduction à la Bible*. A. Robert and A. Feuillet, eds. Paris
Iraq	*Iraq. British School of Archaeology*. London
Isl.	*Islamica*. Leipzig
IThQ	*Irish Theological Quarterly*. Maynooth
JA	*Journal Asiatique*. Paris
JAAR	*Journal of the American Academy of Religion*. Boston
JAC	*Jahrbuch für Antike und Christentum*. Münster
JAfH	*Journal of African History*. London
JANESCU	*Journal of the Ancient Near Eastern Society of Columbia University*. New York
JAOS	*Journal of the American Oriental Society*. Baltimore, Md.
JARCE	*Journal of the American Research Center in Egypt*. Boston
JARG	*Jahrbuch für Anthropologie und Religionsgeschichte*. Saarbrücken
JBL	*Journal of Biblical Literature*. Philadelphia
JBR	*Journal of Bible and Religion*. Boston
JBW	*Jahrbuch der biblischen Wissenschaft*.
JCS	*Journal of Cuneiform Studies*. New Haven, Conn.
JdI	*Jahrbuch des (k.) deutschen archäologischen Instituts*. Berlin
JDTh	*Jahrbücher für deutsche Theologie*. Stuttgart
JEA	*Journal of Egyptian Archaeology*. London
JEOL	*Jaarbericht van het Vooraziatisch-Egyptisch Genootschap 'Ex Oriente Lux.'* Leiden
JESHO	*Journal of the Economic and Social History of the Orient*.
JIAS	*Journal of the Institute of Asiatic Studies*.
JJLG	*Jahrbuch der jüdisch-literarischen Gesellschaft*. Frankfurt
JJP	*Journal of Juristic Papyrology*. New York
JJS	*Journal of Jewish Studies*. London
JKAF (AnaAra)	*Jahrbuch für kleinasiatische Forschung*. Heidelberg
JMES	*Journal of the Middle East Society*. Jerusalem
JMUES	*Journal of the Manchester University Egyptian and Oriental Society*. Manchester
JNES	*Journal of Near Eastern Studies*. Chicago
JNWSL	*Journal of Northwest Semitic Languages*. Leiden
JP	*Journal of Philology*. London
JPOS	*Journal of the Palestine Oriental Society*. Jerusalem
JQR	*Jewish Quarterly Review*. London

Abbreviations

JRAS	*Journal of the Royal Asiatic Society of Great Britain and Ireland.* London
JRH	*Journal of Religious History.* Sydney
JSJ	*Journal for the Study of Judaism.* Leiden
JSM	*Jahresbericht des Staatsgymnasiums in Marburg.*
JSocS	*Jewish Social Studies.* New York
JSOR	*Journal of the Society of Oriental Research.* Toronto
JSOT	*Journal for the Study of the Old Testament.* Sheffield
JSS	*Journal of Semitic Studies.* Manchester
JThFUS	*Jahrbuch der theologischen Fakultät der Universität Sophia.* Tokyo
JThS	*Journal of Theological Studies.* Oxford
JThSB	*Jahrbuch der theologischen Schule Bethel.* Bethel
Jud.	*Judaica.* Zürich
JVI	*Journal of the Victoria Institute.* London
Kairos	*Kairos. Zeitschrift für Religionswissenschaft und Theologie.* Salzburg
KatBl	*Katechetische Blätter.* Munich
Kath.	*Der Katholik.* Strasbourg
KBL	Köhler, Ludwig and Baumgartner, Walter. *Lexicon in Veteris Testamenti Libros.* Leiden
KEH	*Kurzgefasstes Exegetisches Handbuch.* Leipzig
KeTh	*Kerk en Theologie.* Wageningen
KHC	*Kurzer Hand-Commentar zum Alten Testament.* Tübingen
KiV	*Kirche im Volk.* Stuttgart
KKZ	*Katholische Kirchenzeitung.* Salzburg
Klio	*Klio.* Leipzig
KrR	*Křest'anská Revue.* Prague
KuD	*Kerygma und Dogma.* Göttingen
KVR	*Kleine Vandenhoeck-Reihe.* Göttingen
KZS	*Kölner Zeitschrift für Soziologie und Sozialpsychologie.* Cologne
LexTQ	*Lexington Theological Quarterly.* Lexington, Ky.
LingBib	*Linguistica Biblica.* Bonn
LQHR	*London Quarterly and Holborn Review.* London
LR	*Lutherische Rundschau.* Stuttgart
LSSt	*Leipziger semitistische Studien.* Leipzig
LThK	*Lexikon für Theologie und Kirche.* Freiburg
Lum.	*Lumen.* Vitoria
MAB.L	*Mémoires de l'Académie R. de Belgique. Classe des Lettres et des Sciences Morales et Politiques.* Brussels
Man.	*Manuscripta.* St. Louis, Mo.
MAGW	*Mitteilungen der anthropologischen Gesellschaft in Wien.* Vienna
Mar.	*Marianum. Ephemerides Mariologiae.* Rome
MDAI	*Mitteilungen des deutschen archaeologischen Instituts.* Munich
MDOG	*Mitteilungen der deutschen Orient-Gesellschaft.* Berlin
MethR	*Methodist Review.* New York
MGWJ	*Monatsschrift für Geschichte und Wissenschaft des Judentums.* Breslau
MIOF	*Mitteilungen des Instituts für Orientforschung.* Berlin
MNAW	*Mededeling der k. nederlandse akademie van wettenschappen.* Amsterdam
MO	*Monde Orientale.* Uppsala

Mōlād	*Monthly Review of Politics and Letters.* Tel Aviv
MPAW	*Monatsbericht der k. preussischen Akademie der Wissenschaften.* Berlin
MRP	*Magazin für Religionsphilosophie, Exegese und Kirchengeschichte.* Helmstädt
MTh	*Melita Theologica.* La Valetta
MVÄG	*Mitteilungen der vorderasiatisch-ägyptischen Gesellschaft.* Leipzig
MVG	*Mitteilungen zur vaterländischen Geschichte.* St. Gallen
MythBibl.	*Mythologische Bibliothek.* Leipzig
NC	*Nouvelle Clio. Revue Mensuelle de la Découverte Historique.* Brussels
NCent	*Nineteenth Century and After.* London
NedThT	*Nederlands(ch)e theologisch tijdschrift.* Wangeningen
NETR	*The Near East School of Theology Theological Review.* Beirut
NGTT	*Nederduitse gereformeede teologiese Tydskrif.* Capetown
NKZ	*Neue kirchliche Zeitschrift.* Erlangen
NRTh	*Nouvelle Revue Théologique.* Louvain
NThT	*Nieuwe theologische Tijdschrift.* Haarlem
NT.S	*Novum Testamentum. Supplements*
NTT	*Norsk Teologisk Tidsskrift.* Oslo
Numen	*Numen.* Leiden
Numen(Suppl)	*Numen (Supplements).* Leiden
NZSTh	*Neue Zeitschrift für systematische Theologie.* Berlin
NZV	*Niederdeutsche Zeitschrift für Volkeskunde.*
OA	*Orbis Academicus.* Munich
OLZ	*Orientalische Literaturzeitung.* Berlin
Or.	*Orientalia.* Rome
OrAnt	*Oriens Antiquus.* Rome
ORPB	*Oberrheinisches Pastoralblatt.* Freiburg
OrSuec	*Orientalia Suecana.* Uppsala
OSCU	*Oriental Studies of the Columbia University.* New York
OstKSt	*Ostkirchliche Studien.* Würzburg
OTS	*Oudtestamentische Studien.* Leiden
OTSt	*Old Testament Studies.* Edinburgh
OTWSA.P	*Ou Testamentiese Werkgemeenskap in Suid-Afrika.* Papers read. . .Pretoria
PAAAS	*Proceedings of the American Academy of Arts and Sciences (Daedalus).* Boston
Paid.	*Paideuma.* Frankfurt
PAPS	*Proceedings of the American Philosophical Society.* Philadelphia
PBl	*Pastoralblätter für Homelitek, Katechetik und Seelsorge.* Stuttgart
PEFQSt	*Palestine Exploration Fund, Quarterly Statement.* London
PenCath	*Pensée Catholique.* Paris
PEQ	*Palestine Exploration Quarterly.* London
Ph.S	*Philologus. Supp. Bd.* Wiesbaden
PJ	*Palästinajahrbuch des deutschen evangelischen Instituts.* Berlin
PRE	*Paulys Real-Encyclopädie der classischen Altertumswissenschaft.* Stuttgart
PrJ	*Preussische Jahrbücher.* Berlin
PrM	*Protestantische Monatshefte.* Leipzig

Abbreviations

Protest.	*Protestantesimo*. Rome
PSBA	*Proceedings of the Society of Biblical Archaeology*. London
PTh	*Pastoraltheologie*. Göttingen
QDAP	*Quarterly of the Department of Antiquities in Palestine*. London
RA	*Revue d'Assyriologie et d'Archéologie Orientale*. Paris
RAC	*Reallexikon für Antike und Christentum*. Stuttgart
RArch	*Revue d'Archéologie*. Paris
RasIsr	*Rassegna mensile di Israel*. Rome
RB	*Revue Biblique*. Paris
RBL	*Ruch Biblijny i Liturgiczny*. Cracow
RCB	*Revista de Cultura Bíblica*. Rio de Janeiro
RDL	*Reallexikon der deutschen Literaturgeschichte*. Berlin
RE	*Realencyklopädie für protestantische Theologie und Kirche*. Gotha
REB	*Revista Eclesiástica Brasileira*. Petrópolis
RechBib	*Recherches Bibliques*. Bruges
REcL	*Revue Ecclésiastique de Liège*. Liège
Refor.	*Reformation*. Berlin
RefR(H)	*Reformed Review*. Holland, Mich.
RevBib	*Revista Biblica*. Buenos Aires
REJ	*Revue des Études Juives*. Paris
RES	*Revue des Études Sémitiques*. Paris
RevQ	*Revue de Qumrân*. Paris
RGG	*Religion in Geschichte und Gegenwart*. Tübingen
RH	*Revue Historique*. Paris
RHAs	*Revue Hittite et Asiatique*. Paris
RHPhr	*Revue d'Histoire et de Philosophie Religieuses*. Strasbourg
RHR	*Revue de l'Histoire des Religions*. Paris
RIDA	*Revue Internationale des Droits de l'Antiquité*. Brussels
RivAnt	*Rivista di antropologia*. Rome
RivBib	*Rivista Biblica*. Rome
RKZ	*Reformierte Kirchenzeitung*. Freudenberg
RLA	*Reallexikon für Assyriologie*. Berlin
RLV	*Reallexikon der Vorgeschichte*. Berlin
RNouv	*Revue Nouvelle*. Tournai
RoB	*Religion och Bibel*. Stockholm
RoczOr	*Rocznik Orientalistyczny*. Warsaw
RPA	*Revue Practique d'Apologétique*. Paris
RPS	*Religious Perspectives* (series). London
RR	*Review of Religion*. New York
RSIt	*Rivista Storica Italiana*. Naples
RSO	*Rivista degli Studi Orientali*. Rome
RSPhTh	*Revue des Sciences Philosophiques et Théologiques*. Paris
RSR	*Recherches de Science Religieuse*. Paris
RThPh	*Revue de Théologie et de Philosophie*. Lausanne
RThQR	*Revue de Théologie et Questions Religieuses*. Montauban
RTK	*Roczniki Teologiczno-kanoniczne*. Lublin
RVV	*Religionsgeschichtliche Versuche und Vorarbeiten*. Giessen
SAAWK	*Suid-Afrikaanse Akademie vir Wetenskap en Kuns*.
Saec.	*Saeculum*. Munich
Sal.	*Salesianum*. Turin
SAOC	*Studies in Ancient Oriental Civlization*. Chicago
SAT	*Schriften des Alten Testaments in Auswahl*.
SAVK	*Schweizerisches Archiv für Volkskunde*. Basel

SBAK	*Saarbrücker Beiträge zur Altertumskunde.* Saarbrücken
SBFLA	*Studii Biblici Franciscani Liber Annuus.* Jerusalem
SBLASP	*Society of Biblical Literature Abstracts and Seminar Papers.* Chico, Calif.
SBO	*Studia Biblica et Orientalia.* Rome
SBS	*Stuttgarter Bibelstudien.* Stuttgart
SBT	*Studies in Biblical Theology.* London
SBU	*Svenskt Bibliskt Uppslagsverk.* Stockholm
ScC	*Scuola Cattolica.* Milan
ScEcc	*Sciences Ecclésiastiques.* Montreal
Schol.	*Scholastik.* Freiburg
ScrHie	*Scripta Hierosolymitana.* Jerusalem
Scrip.	*Scripture.* Edinburgh
ScrVict	*Scriptorium Victoriense.* Vitoria
SDM	*Scripta et Documenta.* Abadia de Montserrat
SDO	*Studia et Documenta Orientalia.* Cairo
SEÅ	*Svensk Exegetisk Årsbok.* Lund
SEAJT	*South East Asia Journal of Theology.* Singapore
Sef.	*Sefarad.* Madrid
Sem.	*Semitica.* Paris
SGV	*Sammlung gemeinverständlicher Vorträge und Schriften.* Tübingen
Shnaton	*[Shenaton Le-Mikra ule-Heker Ha-Mizrah Ha-Kadum]. An Annual for Biblical and Ancient Near Eastern Studies.* Jerusalem
SJTh	*Scottish Journal of Theology.* Edinburgh
SKG	*Schriften der Königsberger Gelehrten Gesellschaft.* Halle
SKZ	*Schweizerische Kirchenzeitung.* Lucerne
SMSR	*Studi e Materiali di Storia delle Religioni.* Rome
SNVAO	*Skrifter Utgitt av det Norske Videnskaps-Akademi i Oslo.* Oslo
SO	*Symbolae Osloenses.* Oslo
SOr	*Sources Orientales.* Paris
SS	*Studi Semitici.* Rome
SSEA(SESEA)	*Schriften der Studiengemeinschaft der evangelischen Akademien.* Tübingen
SSN	*Studia Semitica Neerlandica.* Assen
SSO	*Studia Semitica et Orientalia.* Glasgow
StANT	*Studia Antoniana.* Rome
StC	*Studia Catholica.* Nijmegen
StGen	*Studium Generale.* Berlin
StHell	*Studia Hellenistica.* Louvain
SThU	*Schweizerische theologische Umschau.* Berne
SThZ or ThZS	*Schweizerische theologische Zeitschrift.* Zürich
StOr	*Studia Orientalia.* Helsinki
StPat	*Studia Patavina.* Padua
StSem	*Studi Semitici*
StTh	*Studia Theologica.* Lund
Studien	*Studiën.* 's-Hertogenbosch
StZ	*Stimmen der Zeit.* Freiburg
SvTK	*Svensk Teologisk Kvartalskrift.* Lund
SWG	*Saeculum Weltgeschichte.* Freiburg
Syr.	*Syria.* Paris
TAPhS	*Transactions of the American Philosophical Society.* Philadelphia

Abbreviations

Tarb.	*Tarbiz.* Jerusalem
TARWPV	*Theologische Arbeiten aus dem rheinischen wissenschaftlichen Prediger-Verein.* Elberfeld
TB	*Theologische Bücherei.* Munich
TBTL	*Tyndale Biblical Theology Lecture.* London
TEH	*Theologische Existenz Heute.* Munich
Textus	*Textus.* Jerusalem
ThA	*Theologische Arbeiten.* Berlin
ThAk	*Theologische Akademie.* Frankfurt
THAT	*Theologisches Handwörterbuch zum Alten Testament.* E. Jenni and C. Westermann, eds. Munich/Zürich
ThBl	*Theologische Blätter.* Leipzig
ThD	*Theology Digest.* St. Mary's, Kan.
ThG	*Theologie der Gegenwart.* Leipzig
ThGl	*Theologie und Glaube.* Paderborn
ThLZ	*Theologische Literaturzeitung.* Leipzig
Thought	*Thought.* New York
ThPh	*Theologie und Philosophie.* Freiburg
ThPM	*Theologisch-praktische Monatsschrift.* Passau
ThPQ	*Theologisch-praktische Quartalschrift.* Linz
ThQ	*Theologische Quartalschrift.* Tübingen
ThR	*Theologische Rundschau.* Tübingen
ThSt(B)	*Theologische Studien.* K. Barth, ed. Zurich
ThSt(U)	*Theologische Studien.* Utrecht
ThStKr	*Theologische Studien und Kritiken.* Hamburg
ThT	*Theologisch Tijdschrift.* Leiden
ThTh	*Themen der Theologie.* Stuttgart
ThTo	*Theology Today.* Princeton, N.J.
ThViat	*Theologia Viatorum.* Berlin
ThW	*Theologische Wissenschaft.* Stuttgart
ThWAT	*Theologisches Wörterbuch zum Alten Testament.* G. J. Botterweck and H. Ringgren, eds. Stuttgart (English: *Theological Dictionary of the Old Testament* 1, 1974ff.)
ThWNT	*Theologisches Wörterbuch zum Neuen Testament.* G. Kittel, ed. Stuttgart (English: *Theological Dictionary of the New Testament*, 10 vols., 1964-1976)
ThZ	*Theologische Zeitschrift.* Basel
TLBA	*Tyndale Lecture in Biblical Archaeology.* London
TOTL	*Tyndale Old Testament Lecture.* London
TPKR	*Theologická Příloha Křesťanská Revue.* Prague
TS	*Theological Studies.* Woodstock, Md.
TS.AAJR	*Texts and Studies. American Academy for Jewish Research.* New York
TRE	*Theologische Realenzyklopädie.* Berlin and New York
TThQ	*Tübinger theologische Quartalschrift.* Stuttgart
TThSt	*Trierer theologische Studien.* Trier
TThZ	*Trierer theologische Zeitschrift.* Trier
TTK	*Tidsskrift for Teologi og Kirke.* Oslo
TUSR	*Trinity University Studies in Religion.* San Antonio, Tex.
TynB	*Tyndale Bulletin.* London
UÄA	*Urkunden des ägyptischen Altertums.* Leipzig
UF	*Ugarit-Forschungen.* Neukirchen
Ug.	*Ugaritica.* Paris
US	*Una Sancta.* Meitingen
USQR	*Union Seminary Quarterly Review.* New York

UTQ	*University of Toronto Quarterly*. Toronto
UUÅ	*Uppsala Universitets Årsskrift*. Uppsala
UVB	*Uruk. Vorläufiger Bericht.*
VAA(EK)	*Veröffentlichungen der Arbeitsgemeinschaft für das Archiv- und Bibliothekswesen in der evangelischen Kirche.* Neustadt
VAB	*Vorderasiatische Bibliothek*. Leipzig
VD	*Verbum Domini*. Rome
VF	*Verkündigung und Forschung*. Munich
VigChr	*Vigiliae Christianae*. Amsterdam
VIOF	*Veröffentlichung. Institut für Orientforschung*. Berlin
VMAW	*Verslagen en Mededeelingen der k. Akademie van Weten- schappen*. Amsterdam
VT	*Vetus Testamentum*. Leiden
VT.S	*Vetus Testamentum Supplements*. Leiden
VuF	*EvTh Beihefte*. Munich
VyV	*Verdad y Vida*. Madrid
WBTh	*Wiener Beiträge zur Theologie*. Vienna
WHJP	*World History of the Jewish People*. London
WiWei	*Wissenschaft und Weisheit*. Freiburg
WO	*Welt des Orients*. Göttingen
WPKG	*Wissenschaft und Praxis in Kirche und Gesellschaft.* Göttingen
WThJ	*Westminster Theological Journal*. Philadelphia
WuD	*Wort und Dienst*. Bielefeld
WUNT	*Wissenschaftliche Untersuchungen zum Neuen Testament.* Tübingen
WVDOG	*Wissenschaftliche Veröffentlichungen der deutschen Orientgesellschaft*. Leipzig
WZKM	*Wiener Zeitschrift für die Kunde des Morgenlandes*. Vienna
WZ(L)	*Wissenschaftliche Zeitschrift der Karl-Marx-Universität Leipzig*. Leipzig
WzM	*Wege zum Menschen. Monatschrift für Arzt und Seelsorge, Erzieher, Psychologen und soziale Berufe*. Göttingen
WZ(R)	*Wissenschaftliche Zeitschrift der Universität Rostock.* Rostock
YNES	*Yale Near Eastern Studies*. New Haven/London
YOS	*Yale Oriental Series*. New Haven, Conn.
ZA n.f.	*Zeitschrift für Assyriologie*. Leipzig
ZÄS	*Zeitschrift für ägyptische Sprache und Altertumskunde.* Berlin
ZAW	*Zeitschrift für die alttestamentliche Wissenschaft*. Berlin
ZBK	*Zürcher Bibelkommentare*. Zurich
ZDA	*Zeitschrift für deutsches Altertum und deutsche Literatur.* Wiesbaden
ZDMG	*Zeitschrift der deutschen morgenländischen Gesellschaft.* Wiesbaden
ZDPV	*Zeitschrift des deutschen Palästina-Vereins*. Wiesbaden
ZdZ	*Zeichen der Zeit*. Berlin
ZE	*Zeitschrift für Ethnologie*. Braunschweig
ZEE	*Zeitschrift für evangelische Ethik*. Gutersloh
ZEvRU	*Zeitschrift für den evangelische Religionsunterricht*. Berlin
ZKG	*Zeitschrift für Kirchengeschichte*. Stuttgart
ZKRU	*Zeitschrift für den katholischen Religionsunterricht an höheren Schulen*. Düsseldorf

Abbreviations

ZKTh	*Zeitschrift für katholische Theologie.* Vienna
ZMR	*Zeitschrift für Missionskunde und Religionswissenschaft.* Berlin
ZNW	*Zeitschrift für die neutestamentliche Wissenschaft.* Berlin
ZRGG	*Zeitschrift für Religions- und Geistesgeschichte.* Cologne
ZRK	*Zeitschrift für Rassenkunde*
ZS	*Zeitschrift für Semitistik und verwandte Gebiete.* Leipzig
ZSRG	*Zeitschrift der Savigny-Stiftung für Rechtsgeschichte.* Weimar
ZThK	*Zeitschrift für Theologie und Kirche.* Tübingen
ZThS	*Zeitschrift für Theologie und Seelsorge.* Freiburg
ZW	*Zeitwende.* Hamburg

Index of Hebrew Words

אדני	278, 304, 322	מהר	540
אל עולם	350	מחנה	505
אל עליון	204	מלאך	242-244, 247, 250, 276,
אל ראי	247		282, 343, 361, 452, 454,
אל שדי	257-258, 260, 448		505, 518
בכר	418	מקום	153, 363, 454, 457
ברך	144, 149, 151, 205, 206, 267,	נביא	324
	386, 388, 409, 436f., 440	נסה	356
	444, 448, 510, 518, 525, 553,	נפש	437
	575	עם־הארץ	374
ברוך יהוה	387-388	פחד יצחק	497
ברית	112f., 228f., 256, 259,	צדיק	288, 293
	262, 264, 266, 269, 348,	קבֵּל	41
	498, 577	קרא בשם יהוה	156
בתולה	386	ריב	427, 495
חנן	525, 530	שאר	508
יצחק	269, 339	שלום	244, 429, 465, 523
יראת אלהים	325, 361f.	שלם	528
כבד	163, 174f.	שפחה	238, 429
מהפכת	298, 307	תולדת	137

Index of Biblical References
(with Apocrypha)

Genesis 1–11

1–11	36, 60, 573, 574, 576
1	163, 270
1:1	441
1:28	207, 261, 269, 553
1:29	229
2–11	145
2–3	236
2	23, 163
2:11	399
2:16-17	263
2:21	213, 226
2:23	146, 205, 334
3; 4	322
3	177, 247
4	23
4:1	332
4:2-16	301
4:6-7	304
4:13	262
4:17	397
4:18	331
4:19-20	566
4:19	562
4:26	156
5	55
5:1	398
5:5	394, 397
5:18-20	397
5:32	131
6–9	38, 127, 298, 300, 312
6–8	309
6:1-4	164
6:5	301
6:6	178, 538
6:9	398
6:11	301
7:3	313
7:7	133
7:11	457
7:21-23	307
8:1	308
8:3	157

8:6-12	483
8:21	178
9	23, 265
9:2	229
9:12-17	266
9:18-27	311, 312
9:23	133
9:25-27	246, 390
10	141, 270, 400
10:1	398
10:7	396
10:9	299, 371
10:16f.	538
10:19	171, 195, 298, 399
10:22	194
10:23	567
10:25	396
10:26-30	396
10:26f.	472
10:28	396
10:29	396
10:30	399
11:1-19	454
11:1	434
11:2	56, 157
11:5, 7	290
11:9	248
11:10-26	137
11:10	257, 398
11:23	133
11:27	398

Genesis 37–50

37–50	36, 58, 73, 217, 443
37	73
37:1	263
37:2	131
37:12-14	71
37:25f.	400
37:28, 36	396
38	36
38:24	234
38:27	411

39:4	278
39:7	356
39:9	82, 362
40:1	217, 356
40:17	204
40:20	358
41:45, 50	73
42:18	358, 362
42:26	346
42:28	273
42:34	534
42:38	227, 397
43:14	257
43:23, 27	465
43:24	278
44:29, 31	397
45:10	73
45:14f.	471
46-50	73
46:1, 5	73
46:3	455
46:4	385
46:8-25	472
46:10-12	566
46:15	60, 71
46:28f.	73
47:4	163
47:9	263, 371
47:11	73, 543
47:25	278
47:26	51
47:27	534, 539
47:28	371
47:29	278
47:30	43, 555
48	82, 437, 438
48:1	217
48:2	439
48:3	257, 458, 553
48:7	73, 554
48:8-16	435
48:10	437
48:14	213

48:15-19	441	12:48	540	20:2-5	357
48:15	51, 455	13:5	229	20:20f.	219
48:20	152	13:12f.	357	20:22-24	227
48:21	455	13:13	357	22:33	262
48:22	65, 71, 73, 180	13:14	479	25:30	374
48:25	441	15:15	564	25:38	224, 262
49	205, 438, 472	15:16	206	25:47	373
49:1-27	472	15:25	197, 356	26:30	544
49:3-4	556	16:4	356	26:45	262
49:5-7	536	17:1	175	27:14, 17, 19	374
49:8	441, 473	17:7	197		
49:21	434	17:8-16	566		
49:25	441	18	396	**Numbers**	
49:29ff.	69	18:10	206, 387	1; 3	541
49:30	73, 371, 374	18:11	362	3:44f.	357
49:31	557	18:21	363	4:6	368
50:4	278	19	460, 576	10:21	562
50:10f.	73	19:6	24	10:26-29	509
50:10	443	19:10f.	550	10:29	566
50:13	73, 371, 374	19:13	495	11:8	279
50:15	434	19:18	297	13:20	441
50:21	534	20	362	13:22	373
50:24	215, 223, 228,	20:2	224	13:22-23	198
	385, 455	20:18-21	362	13:29	66, 200
		20:20	356	14:19	285
		20:23	548	14:22	488
Exodus		20:24	156	15:31	416
1–15	158, 344	21:22	331, 334	15:41	262
1–3	27	22:7, 10	523	16	562, 566
1:1-5	556	22:10-13	496	16:1	133
1:12	455	22:17	495	18	541
1:15, 17-21	362	22:29	357	18:2, 4	437
2	384, 385, 391, 396,	23:20	472	19	265
	408, 466	23:23	229	20:1	197
2:15b-22	383, 463	23:27	543	20:14	568
2:18	562, 566	23:28	229	20:16	243, 385
3	108, 158, 282, 385	25	265	21:2	458
3:1	566	26:3	195	22–24	67
3:7-8	224, 473	29:45	262	22	396
3:8	229	31:6	566	22:5	566
3:17	229	32:2f.	387	22:9, 20	322
3:18	358	32:13	363	22:30	213, 222
4	517	32:26	544	23:7	67
4:24-26	265, 517	32:34	385	23:11	166
4:24	517	33:2	229, 385	23:19	332
4:25	265	33:20	228, 519	23:25	346
5	166	34:10	357	24	218, 441
5:3	358	34:11	229	24:3-9	441
5:21	241, 544	34:19f.	357	24:4	218, 257
6	108, 257, 265	34:20	357	24:5	440
6:3	257-259	38:26	387	24:9	150, 441
6:4	263			24:16	204, 218, 257
7–11	166	**Leviticus**		24:25	181, 504
8–10	412	6; 7	541	25	396
8:23	358	11:45	262	25:14	396
9:25-27	413	12:3	265, 540	25:15	394, 399
10	400	14:4, 7, 8	548	26	541
10:17	285	18:21	357	31	396
10:24	523	18:22	301	31:9-11	535
12:39	279	18:24-27	227	31:9-10	543
12:40	227	18:30	422	31:10	399

32:9	199	17:8	282	9:22	467
32:12	566	18:20	318, 322	10:1	204
32:30	539	19:22	298	11:1	566
32:31	534	20:7	229	11:3	66, 70
32:37	196	21:12	534	11:17	475
33	57	21:13	238	11:19	70
33:1-49	56	21:15-17	82	12:4	196
33:38f.	57	21:17	418	12:5	368
33:42f.	566, 567	22:21	538	13:2-5	65
34:5	229	22:22	318	13:12	196
34:24	368	22:30	556	13:26	506
35:15	373	23:1	556	13:27	523
		23:3-6	315	14:4	534
		23:8	568	14:15	373
		24:13	223	15:4	229
Deuteronomy		25:5	238, 311	15:13	373
1:2	197	25:15	528	15:17	566
1:10, 24	199, 222	26	460	15:18	390
2:8	197	26:5	66	15:59	555
2:9	133, 315	26:12-15	460	22:9, 19	539
2:10-12	196	28:62	222	23	437
2:12-22	564	29:22	195	23:12	539
2:12	69, 196	29:22, 23	298	23:13	226
2:19	133, 315	29:23	307	24:14	550
2:20	69, 182, 196	30:11	282	24:20, 23	551
3:8	66	32:6	206	24:24	154
3:12	224	32:8	204	24:26	551
3:13	196	32:40	202	24:29	356
3:14	368	33	437	24:32	70, 529
3:18	224	33:6	535		
3:24	219	33:8	356		
4:27	535	33:10	394	**Judges**	
5:6	224	33:13	441	1:4f.	176
6:4	109, 575	33:16	441	1:8	534
7	537	33:21	289	1:10	69, 373
7:1	229, 544	33:28	441	1:13	566
7:2-3	544	33:29	218	1:15	510
7:3	534, 539	34:3	305	1:23	458
7:3f.	385	34:7	434, 437	1:34	66
7:7	534	34:10	519	2:5	548
7:8, 12	223			2:22	356
7:13	223, 267, 428, 441			3:1	356
8:1	223	**Joshua**		3:3	70
8:2, 16	356	1:4	229	3:4	356
8:18	223	2:8	301	3:9, 11	566
9:4f.	227	2:9	543	3:15-19	50
9:16	224	3:10	229	3:20	221
9:26	219	5:2-9	265	4	50
10:6	566	5:2f.	265	4:5	548, 552
10:15	534	5:7	542	5:4	507
10:22	222	5:8	540	5:21	505
11:1	422, 425	5:13-15	505	6–8	400
11:24	229	5:13	277	6	396
11:30	154	6:18	535	6:3	464
12:1	224	7:15	538	6:12	244
12:2	154	7:20	318	6:15	564
12:17	460	7:25	535	6:22	519
12:31	357	8:30	529	6:33	465
13:4	356	9:5	479	6:35	464
14:22, 29	460	9:7	70	6:37	386
15:14	224	9:13	281	7:6	507
17:4	509				

7:12	399	**Ruth**		**2 Samuel**	
7:16-22	201	1:1	163	1:20	265
8:5	523	1:20f.	257	2:8, 12, 29	506
8:8f.	519	2:11	137	3:7	567
8:16	523	2:12	463	3:12f.	243
8:17	519	2:13	534	6:23	139
8:21	191	4	374	7	282
8:24-27	551	4:1-3	301	7:4	217
8:24	400	4:14f.	390	7:9	150
8:32	397	4:11	541	8:8	368
9:9, 13	518	4:13	391	8:13	150, 413
9:26	154	4:18-22	315	10:6-8	368
9:28	70, 529			10:6	544
9:37	154	**1 Samuel**		11–12	164
9:54	191	1	162, 246, 274, 280, 338	12	46
10:8	66	1:11	458	13	538
10:15	509	1:17	279	13:12	463, 538
10:16	551	1:20	245	13:13	326
10:23	566	3:2	434	13:22	389
11	357	3:19	343	14:7	221
11:13	243	4:20	554	14:25	165
11:30	458	5	166	15:4	311
11:35	535	7:3	551	15:6	493
12:11f.	500	10:2	554	15:7-9	458
13	242, 280, 566	12	496	15:14	534
13:2-5	279	12:10	509	17:24-27	506
13:2f.	139	13:4	544	18:18	202
13:2, 3-5	243, 245	14:8-10	386	18:24	199, 301
13:8-10	275	14:29	535	20:1b	492
13:10	273	14:46	181	21:1	163
13:18	518	15:10	217	21:8	567
13:20	270, 281	15:34	181	23	437
13:22	519	16:9	566	23:11	566
14:2	538	16:12	411, 414	24:7	70
14:11	428	17	494, 514		
14:12	467	17:26	265		
14:20	428	17:42	411, 414	**1 Kings**	
15:18-20	248	17:43	331	1:47	150
15:18	219	18:1	538	2:1-3	437
15:24	538	18:25	540	3:11	566
P6	246	19:13-16	454, 493	4:15	566
18:10	651	19:17	467	4:31	566
18:29	201	21:1	181	5:2	279
19–21	297	22:6	350	5:21	390
19–20	300	23:18	438	6:7	528
19	297-299, 300	24:12, 15	241	7:46	523
19:1-28	297	24:22	181	8:19	548
19:1-11	300	25:22f.	206	8:32	292
19:5	278	25:23	390	9:4	323
19:7	296, 301	25:27	526	9:26	197
19:11-21	454	25:32	387	10	396, 428
19:15-25	297, 299, 300, 302	25:42	238	11:14	566
19:15	277	26:7, 11f., 16	454	11:20	338
19:22-25	297	26:29b	181	12:16	492
19:22	297, 301	27:53	489	12:22	217
19:23	538	28:12	467	12:25	519
19:29-30	297	30	191	13:2	245
20-21	297	30:13	238	13:14-19	301
20:5	538	30:26	526	14:23	154
20:6, 10	538	31:13	350	14:24	227

16:1	217	5:18-22	399	30:3		311
16:22	565	5:19	394	30:4		341
16:34	133, 357	6:55	200	30:19		292
17:2, 8	217	12:22	505	32:2		368
17:10	387	13:2	518	32:3		281
17:13	279, 318	19:6-7	368	33:3		334
17:24	361	20:2	234	33:26		526
18:31	217-218	21:22-24	374	34:17		291
19	242	22:9-18	245	38–41		305
19:6	279, 454			42:6		292
19:9	221	**2 Chronicles**		42:11		387, 529
20:2-4	243	2:43	562	42:12		192
21:17	217	3:1	357	42:14		396
		11:19	566			
		11:23	425			
2 Kings		20:2	197	**Psalms**		
1:17	565	21:3	382	1		286
2	414	27:17	368	4:2		427, 430
2:1-8	359	32:23	382	11:6		298, 306
2:17	296, 301	32:31	356	18:3		218
3:21, 27	357	36:16	452	18:14		204
3:25	520			18:31		218
3:27	357	**Ezra**		19:1		258
4	280	1:2	384	20:7		361
4:5	428	1:6	382	23		456
4:7	474	4:6	427	24:4		323
4:8-17	279	5:12	384	26:2		356
4:11-17	275	6:2f.	384	31:8		477
4:14	280			31:9		430
4:16	280, 281	**Nehemiah**		32:3		281
4:17	280	6:10	587	33:5		289
4:38	163	9:4	133	39:13		373
5:16	296, 301	11:25	373	39:14		219
5:19	554			46:5		204
6:18	302	**Esther**		47:6		270
6:22	494	9:14	539	48:2		204
7:1	301			48:14		273
7:6	69	**Job**		56:10		361
8:1	163	1–2	243	66:12		430
8:7	195	1:1-3	368	68:15		257
8:15	565	1:2-3	192, 510	68:19		270
8:20-22	443	1:6	454	72:17		151-152
9:26	311	1:17	368	73:11		204
12:22	565	2:1	454	76:3		204
13:14-18	437	2:11	396, 560, 562, 566	78:23		457
13:24	565	3:3	334	78:35		204
16:3	357	4	226	78:54		204, 206
16:13, 15	548	4:12-15	226	82:6		204
17:17	357	5–6	257	83:9		133, 473
22:12, 14	566	5:26	227	84:11		218
24:1, 20	195	6:19	399	88:11		196
		8:2	334	89:2		509
		9:22	286	91:1		257
1 Chronicles		12:4, 16	286	91:11		384, 385
1:27	133	14:12	281	91:14		534
1:29	398	18:15	306	94:2		291
1:32	396	18:19	346	101:2		323
1:33	396	21	286	103		525
1:35-53	561	21:17	286	104		305
2:52-54	566	28:7	567	105:12		544
4:25	398			106:2		334
5:1, 2	418					

106:4	477	14:22	346	20:15	334
106:31	223	15:5	305	20:18	413
113:6	247	15:15	510	22:10	137
113:5	477	16:2	458	22:30	219
113:9	334	17:12	261	23:14	298
117:1	394, 399	18:13	458	25:14	261
118:5	430	21:11	399	25:20	368
119	288	21:14, 16f.	398-399	25:23	368, 399
120:1	550	22:18	534	25:25	396
120:5	399	24:2	238	29:23	538
121	384	26:14, 19	196	31:8	214
122:1	550	27:12	229	31:15-17	555
123:2	238	28:4	441	31:15	554
124:1	497	30:33	306	31:31-34	577
126:2	334	33:7	360	32	375, 508
133:1	177	34:6	567	32:9	375
139	259	34:9	306	32:35	204
139:13	206	34:12	561	34:18f.	225, 228
144:2	258	37:3	334	44:28	535
		38:1	318, 322	46:1-2	495
Proverbs		40:2	534	46:16	137
1:7	325	40:9-10	215	48:34	305
3:27	489	40:26	221	49:1	221
4:2	353	41:2	261, 481	49:7, 13, 22	567
8:22	206	41:8	340	49:16	307
16:17	510	41:10, 14	218	49:18	298
21:3	289	41:13	218, 509	49:20	567
23:3, 6	434	42:11	398	49:28	398
30:21-23	240	43:1, 5	218	49:38	464
30:23	221, 238	44:26-28	509	50:5	473
31:1	399	45:1	261	50:40	195, 298, 307
		45:23	363	51:35	241
Ecclesiastes		47:1-5	373	51:50	503
3:17	292	49:16f.	239		
		54:1-3	215	**Lamentations**	
		54:1	139	1:13	306
Song of Solomon		54:3	455	3:22, 32	620
1:5	398	55:3	509	4:6	298, 307
2:10, 13	353	56:3, 6	473		
5:2	523	56:11	301		
6:9	165, 353	60:3	261	**Ezekiel**	
7:14	475	60:6	396	1:24	258
		60:7	398	4:12	279
		63:7	509	10:5	258
Isaiah		64:6	206	12:22	425
1:7	307	65:11	475	14:12-20	287
1:9f.	195, 298	66:12	488	16:16	479
1:10	298	66:14	273	16:46-50	298
2	110			16:53-55	195, 298
2:10, 19, 21	497			16:48	195
5:1	441			16:49	298
5:13	261	**Jeremiah**		18:6, 11, 15	534
6	243, 455, 460	2:10	398	23	566
7	222, 246, 386	4:2	152	23:15	137
7:14-17	245	4:4	540	23:17	534
9:6	335	6:20	396	23:24	446
10:3	488	6:26	373	24:15-23	373
11:11	206	9:3	414	25:13	567
11:14	464	9:24f.	265	27:21	398
13:6	258	11:14f.	291	27:22	396
13:19	196, 298, 307	13:18	454	28:27	306
14:1	473	18:7-10	287, 292		

31:5	425	**1 Maccabees**		**John**	
32:3	446	2:7, 13	413	4:7	387
33:26	534			4:19-26	460
38:22	306	**Judith**		8:39	24, 26
39:6	306	1:9	229		
				Acts	
Daniel		**Tobit**		14:11	277
1–7	53	3:15	413	28:1-6	277
2:14, 15, 24f.	194	5:17-22	385		
11:6	534	7:12	390	**Romans**	
11:34	473	8:15	389	4	230
12:7	202	10:11	390	4:3	213
		11:20	467	4:9	27
Hosea		14	437	8:32	362, 365
4:13	154			9:7	341
7:8	279	**Sirach (Ecclesiasticus)**		9:13	444
10:14	503, 509	10:9	292	9:29	298
11:8	195, 206, 298, 299	16:3	219		
12	409	17:32	292	**Galatians**	
12:4-5	515	36:24	476	3:6	213
12:4	414, 434	40:29	476	3:8	151
12:13	412	41:5	346	4:21-31	339
		44:19-21	207		
Joel		44:20-26	26	**Hebrews**	
1:15	258	44:21	151	7	207
4:3	534	47:22	346	7:9-25	207
				11	365
Amos		**Wisdom of Solomon**		11:5-22	403
1:11	568	10:6	194	11:18	341
1:12	567			13:2	277
2:9	67	**4 Ezra (2 Esdras)**		13:5	456
3:7	290	5:35	413		
4:11	298, 307			**James**	
7–9	291	**Matthew**		2:21-23	365
7:3, 5	304	1:5	315	2:23	213
		2:17-18	555		
Jonah		3:4	414	**1 Peter**	
1:9	199	10:15	298	2:11	373
3;4	287, 292, 293	11:23f.	298		
				2 Peter	
Micah		**Luke**		2:6	298
2:1	489	1–2	279f., 282		
6:7	357	1	242, 246, 250	**Revelation**	
		1:11-17, 28-32	245	3:25	151
Zephaniah		1:28-32	244	11:8	298
2	287	1:34	281		
2:9	298	1:41, 44	411	**Genesis Apocryphon**	
2:15	473	1:46-48	477	22:13	204
		1:48	475		
Zechariah		1:68	332		
8:5	534	2	335		
13:4	414	2:48	166		
		7:44	278		
Malachi		10:12	298		
1:2-5	444	17:29	298		
3:14	292	24:29	277		

Index of Names and Subjects

Adoption   81-82, 138, 220, 239
Adultery   82, 298, 323, 325, 425
Aetiology (see Etiology)
Ai   71, 156, 557
Altar   58, 72, 107-108, 111, 145, 155-157, 175, 181, 360, 427, 428, 460, 529, 549-550, 552, 553, 557
Amarna Letters   62, 68, 74, 176, 187, 198, 204, 321, 327, 368, 525
Ammon, Ammonites   52, 125, 133, 173, 196, 265, 311-315, 357
Amorites, Amurru   62, 63-70, 198, 226-227, 357
Ancestors, Veneration of   25, 45, 48, 50, 265
Angel (Messenger) of Yahweh   235-237, 242-247, 250, 275-282, 290, 299, 300, 303, 342, 360-361, 384, 455, 499, 505, 506, 519
Animism   111, 515, 516, 518
Apocalypse, Apocalyptic   290, 577
Aram, Arameans   62, 65-70, 368, 515, 551, 553, 556
Aram-naharaim   67, 385
Assur, Assyria   265, 396

Babylon   136, 188, 194, 240
Babylonian Period   74, 84, 133, 215, 243, 413
Barrenness (see Childlessness)
Beersheba   71-73, 154, 341, 343, 349, 364, 427, 453
Bethel   71-73, 151, 154, 156, 175, 179, 408, 452-455, 458-460, 492, 511, 515, 547-554, 557
Blessing   82-83, 111, 147, 149-152, 158, 192, 203, 205-208, 221, 258, 267, 269, 276, 308, 341, 343-344, 384, 388-389, 408-409, 424, 426, 428, 429, 434-449, 455, 466, 484, 489, 493, 504, 507, 509-511, 514, 518-520, 526, 530, 553, 571, 574, 576
Bride Price (Dowry)   466f., 567
Burial   72, 83, 227, 271, 371-376, 394, 397, 407, 412, 446, 529, 549, 552, 554, 556-557, 572

Call   135, 148
Campaign   57, 146, 189, 191, 193-196, 207
Charism, Charismatic   200, 202
Chaldeans   66, 137, 139f.
Childlessness   29, 39, 54, 81, 123, 124-127, 136-138, 219-221, 236, 237, 239-240, 245, 250, 268, 274-275, 280-282, 318, 328, 331, 334, 401, 411-412, 434, 473, 574, 575
Circumcision   256, 261, 263-266, 271, 331, 333, 376, 446, 520, 540-542, 573
Commandment   109, 112, 136, 145-149, 152, 157, 254, 257, 260, 263-266, 270-271, 304, 333, 341, 355-362, 425, 446-449, 540, 544, 549-551, 573, 575
Confession   25, 250, 509, 530, 575
Conflict Narratives   127, 171-181, 235-237, 241, 249-250, 471-477, 495-501, 507, 530, 574
Contract (see Covenant)
Covenant   26, 83, 113, 124, 126, 129, 135-138, 150, 200, 215, 223, 228-231, 239, 256, 259-271, 347-350, 376, 403, 429, 460, 480, 533, 577
Creed, Credo   66, 67, 344
Cult, Cultic   54, 110-111, 156, 203-208, 215, 219, 223, 266, 441, 458-459, 506, 529, 531, 534, 549-551, 553, 576   – Blessing, woe 205, 207   – Establishment of 111, 154, 350   – Formula 323   – Law 573 – Legend 53, 155, 354, 357   – Meal 440 – Places 153f., 155, 409   – of Stones 457
Cuneiform (see Texts)
Curse (see also Punishment)   150, 202, 225, 228, 429, 438, 442

Dan'el, Epic of   279
Daniel   192, 207, 287
Death   29, 163, 165, 321, 323, 338, 343-344, 495, 508, 518-521, 524
Desert, Wilderness   56, 78, 153, 235, 241-247, 278, 338, 341-344, 356, 358, 390, 396, 564
Dothan   73
Dowry (see Bride Price)
Dream   319, 321-323, 340, 452-458, 491

Edom, Edomites   69, 196-197, 265, 368, 396, 412-418, 437, 441, 443, 507, 561-569
El, Elim   106, 269, 357
Elam   64, 194
Elijah-Elisha Stories   359
Etiology   42, 125, 155, 173, 192, 206, 234, 235, 242, 247, 248, 297, 304, 307, 311, 314, 343, 346, 354, 363, 372, 397, 418, 429, 443, 452, 504, 508, 518, 526-527, 549, 555
Euphrates   140, 229, 493

Faith   26, 27, 148, 153, 215, 222-224, 230, 268, 365, 376, 403, 576
Famine   45, 162-167, 174, 424, 434, 574, 577
Fear of God   319, 324, 325-329, 355, 361-364, 403, 425
Festival   111, 338, 439-440, 467
Firstborn   82-83, 357, 398, 413-414, 416-419, 438-439, 444, 526, 556
Flight, Escape   64, 194, 242-250, 300, 406-409, 435, 443, 453, 455, 463-465, 489, 493, 500, 524

Genealogies   25, 28, 36, 40-46, 54-56, 79, 123, 125-129, 134-141, 145-147, 221, 236-238, 240, 248-249, 256, 257, 268, 271, 311, 313-315, 331-334, 338, 343, 366-371, 386, 391, 394-403, 406-408, 411-412, 436, 446, 471-473, 477, 527, 548-549, 556-557, 561-574, 577
Gerar   72, 318, 320-321, 325, 349, 424-425
Gideon   191, 203, 297
Gilgamesh Epic   287, 414, 456
God, Appearance of (see also Theophany)
    55, 72, 156, 226, 242f., 255, 275, 277, 354, 406-409, 426-427, 452, 504, 506, 519, 549, 550, 575
God, Names of (see El)
God, Speech or Word of   134, 148, 222, 224, 243, 250, 257, 264, 267, 340, 356, 361, 363, 413
God of the Fathers   25, 105-108, 110, 148, 152, 326, 521, 575
Guest, Hospitality   274-278, 281-282, 388
Guilt, Culpability   110, 164, 226, 287, 290, 297, 318-329, 425, 497, 507, 510, 524, 530

Hammurabi, Code of   81, 239, 240, 496
Haran, Harran   62, 67, 71, 72, 133-140, 145, 147, 152, 385, 453
Hebron   58, 69, 72-73, 83, 181, 196, 300, 320, 371-376, 459, 557, 562
Heroes   45, 50f., 191-192, 201, 376, 574, 576
Hittites   68-69, 83, 194, 280, 372-373, 446-447, 481, 562
Hivites   69-70, 229, 538
Holy   460   – Mountain 111   – Objects 110-111, 360, 460   – Place 110-111,

153-154, 181, 452-458, 460, 519, 550, 557, 576   – Spring 111, 154, 343   – Stone 110-111, 154, 460   – Time 110-111   – Tree 72, 110-111, 154, 276, 278-279, 349f.
Horites, Hurrians   69-70, 133, 239, 437, 538, 561, 562, 564-569

Inheritance   82, 83, 220, 230, 237, 339, 397, 464
Inscriptions (see also Texts)   190, 193, 196, 198, 368, 397 (Sabaean)
Intercession, Intercessor   111, 128, 157, 291, 324, 328, 329, 576
Ishmaelites   234-235, 238, 246, 343, 395, 397
Itinerary   36, 46, 53, 54-58, 62, 69-73, 125-128, 134-137, 139, 141, 145-146, 152-157, 177-178, 181, 271, 309, 311-313, 315, 320, 349-350, 364, 407, 423-427, 452, 454-456, 493, 514-516, 519, 524, 527-529, 548f., 551, 554-557, 562, 564, 571-573

Job   286, 291f., 356, 368
Judges, Period of   191-192, 207, 396, 408, 459, 576
Judgment   321-323, 444, 490, 545
    – Announcement of 20, 110, 112, 575
    – God's 271, 287, 291, 292, 297-309, 402, 574
Justice (see Righteousness)

Kings, Period of   26, 31, 32, 37, 45, 46, 58, 105, 107, 147, 150, 157f., 181, 191, 206, 207, 218, 221, 222, 230, 347, 355, 413, 458, 506
Kingship, Sacral Kingship   205, 282

Lament   215, 219-221, 290, 362, 413, 442, 447, 509, 515, 575
Law (see also Judgment)   60, 80, 225, 264-266, 271, 288, 354, 372, 416, 424, 425, 460, 544
Laws, Customs   38, 79-86, 164, 180, 239-241, 266-268, 276f., 281, 288, 301f., 321, 348, 371-372, 376, 397, 409, 413-414, 417-419, 424f., 435, 437, 438, 442, 444, 489, 490, 492-493, 495-501
Legend   41, 49, 50, 53, 188, 191, 354
List   – of Kings 561-564, 566, 568   – of Names 190, 193-195, 198, 273, 396, 549, 556, 561, 563-564, 566, 568   – of Peoples 229f.   – of Tribes 367, 368, 395, 398

Machpelah   73, 83, 371, 375-376, 557
Magic   53, 151, 307, 384, 447
Mahanaim   72, 409, 505, 508
Mamre   60, 71-73, 154, 181, 200, 277, 320, 549, 557

Index of Names and Subjects

Mari   61, 64-66, 74, 76, 78, 82, 84, 140, 188, 194, 225, 228, 234, 399, 555
Marriage   81-83, 123, 125-126, 138, 238, 242, 265, 271, 338, 376, 383, 391, 406, 412, 446, 463, 466-468, 492-493, 540, 572   – of Sister 164
Mediator (see Intercessor)
Messenger of God (see Angel of Yahweh)
Midian, Midianites   265, 395-397, 399-400, 565
Migration   39, 77-78, 148   – of Groups 57, 79, 85, 109, 110, 156, 173f.   – of Patriarchs 45, 54, 56-58, 60-63, 65, 71-73, 77-78, 102, 110, 134-135, 140, 168, 175, 289, 320, 326, 349, 406, 527, 572, 575-576
Miracle   247, 267f., 344
Mitanni   69, 140
Moab   52, 56, 125, 133, 173, 196, 198, 265, 312-315, 357, 565
Monotheism, Monolatry   108-109, 575
Mother, Legal Rights of   246
Myth   41, 49, 53-54, 76, 126, 243, 275-276, 280, 354, 358, 417, 454

Nahor   66, 72, 133, 136, 140, 366-368, 385-388, 499-500
Names   – Change of, Renaming 133, 255, 260-261, 267, 458, 514, 518, 520, 549, 555, 557, 572   – Explanation of 63f., 69, 84-85, 137, 248, 269, 314, 331-335, 347, 349, 362, 414, 471f., 476, 508, 526
Naming   26, 63, 71, 72, 220, 237, 245-250, 258, 267-270, 274, 282, 312, 331-333, 343, 348, 354, 364, 408, 409, 411, 414, 458, 472-474, 477, 498, 505, 506, 514-515, 517-521, 527, 549, 553-555, 576
Narrative, Types of (see Legend, Tale)
Nuzi Texts   69, 80-83, 138, 416

Oath   113, 126, 187, 202, 215, 223, 225, 227-229, 259, 347-349, 382-385, 423, 428, 498, 500
Obedience   152, 268, 289, 354, 361-362, 364, 428, 444, 448
Omen   64, 154, 226, 386, 411, 413, 555
Oracle   111, 153-154, 215, 217-218, 235, 246, 342, 386, 411, 413, 428

Paul, Pauline   222, 230, 365, 403
Peace   24, 177, 181, 205, 227, 335, 337, 360, 428-430, 465-466, 468, 500, 527, 537, 541, 545, 574
Peniel (Pniel, Penuel)   72, 409, 514, 520
Polytheism   109, 575
Promise   – of Assistance 110, 111, 151, 343, 347, 409, 424, 428, 453, 455, 459, 460, 511   – of Blessing 29, 112, 126, 146, 149-151, 158, 268, 289, 308, 364, 424, 426, 428, 447, 574-575   – of Increase 124, 126, 151, 179, 216, 221, 235, 244, 255, 259-262, 267-269, 288, 289, 342, 343, 363, 424, 447-449, 455, 552, 557, 577   – of Land 6, 76, 112, 124, 126, 153, 179-181, 215-217, 221, 223-225, 227-231, 255, 260, 262, 376, 385, 448, 453, 455, 553, 557, 577   – of Posterity 112, 124, 172, 179, 181, 216, 221, 223, 226, 230, 267, 340, 344, 453, 455, 509   – of a Son 29, 40, 55, 112, 124-127, 216, 221, 223, 230, 236, 245, 250, 255, 267-269, 274-276, 280, 282, 331, 333, 357, 404, 409, 453-455, 575   – of Victory 364

Revelation (of God)   28, 111, 124, 135, 147, 155, 179, 217, 224, 226, 242, 250, 257, 259, 290, 319, 322, 340, 342, 424, 448, 491, 553-554, 572
Reward   287, 535
Righteousness, Justice   27, 215, 223, 286-293, 322, 403, 537, 576
Rite, Ritual (see also Circumcision)   271, 278, 373, 384, 435, 439, 441, 446, 447, 458, 498, 525, 551, 573

Sacrifice   28, 110, 155, 223, 225, 265, 289, 353-365, 411, 438, 458-459, 554   – Animal 354, 357, 359, 363   – Building 357   – Burnt 357-359   – Firstborn 357   – Human 36, 39, 110, 354-365   – Libation 554
Saga (see Tale)
Salvation   151, 204   – Sal. History 151, 158, 235f.   – Saving Word 111, 218, 261, 386
Sanctuary, Holy Place   36, 39, 73, 80, 107, 111, 154, 181, 204-207, 262, 350, 354, 359, 363, 452-454, 458-460, 551, 553-554, 557, 576   – Founding of 53, 55, 72, 107, 155, 156, 181, 408, 428, 455, 506, 552   – Narrative of 72, 408
Settlement (of Land)   26, 52, 59, 85, 105-108, 203, 340, 354, 537, 541f., 543-544
Shechem   70-73, 154, 528, 535, 537, 542, 549, 551
Sin   82, 110, 167, 178, 287, 289-301, 323, 325
Sinai   107, 110, 112-113, 271, 376, 459-460, 553
Sodom   72, 123, 125, 177, 180, 189, 191-192, 195, 198, 201-204, 206-217, 282, 287, 297-315
Sumerian   234, 276, 358
Swearing (see Oath)

Taboo   307, 520, 535
Tale (Saga)   40-41, 44-45, 49-53, 123, 127, 138, 234-235, 270, 297, 307, 311, 382, 343, 406, 467, 514
Temple   70, 110, 157, 188, 357, 454, 460
Terah   134-138, 140, 145
Teraphim   77, 108, 493-495, 551

Texts (see also Inscriptions)   – Akkadian 64, 68, 69, 228, 280, 302, 311, 399, 429
   – Alalakh 540   – Amarna (see Amarna)
   – Aramean 228, 384   – Babylonian 78, 81, 83, 216, 224, 371   – Cuneiform 82, 398, 467   – Egyptian 85, 201, 471   – Nuzi (see Nuzi)   – Pyramid 454   – Ugaritic 84, 106, 126, 133, 172, 188, 219, 274, 280, 383, 524
Theophany (see also God, Appearance of) 148, 243, 244, 270, 275, 277, 553f.
Transcendence   155, 460
Transhumance   64, 77-79
Treaty (see Covenant)
Tribal History   234-235, 490, 565
Tribal Ancestors   234-235, 269-270, 343

Ugarit (see Texts)
Ur   59, 61, 62, 66, 71, 78, 135-136, 137-141, 153, 215, 276

Vow   223, 406, 453, 458-460, 550, 553, 557

War   79, 110, 112, 176, 181, 190, 193, 195, 206, 218, 357, 427, 507, 509, 530, 543, 544, 545, 574
Wisdom   80, 417
Worship (see also Cult)   157, 203, 205, 266, 440, 442, 453, 459-460, 477, 531, 550, 556, 575